The American Civil War

The American Civil War

A Handbook of
Literature and Research

Steven E. Woodworth, Editor

Robin Higham, Advisory Editor

Foreword by James M. McPherson

Greenwood Press

Westport, Connecticut • London

Library of Congress Cataloging-in-Publication Data

The American Civil War : a handbook of literature and research /
  Steven E. Woodworth, editor ; foreword by James M. McPherson.
      p.   cm.
    Includes bibliographical references and index.
    ISBN 0–313–29019–9 (alk. paper)
      1. United States—History—Civil War, 1861–1865—Bibliography.
    2. United States—History—Civil War, 1861–1865—Audio-visual aids—
  Catalogs.   I. Woodworth, Steven E.
  Z1242.A47   1996
  [E456]
  016.9737—dc20   95–53132

British Library Cataloguing in Publication Data is available.

Library of Congress Catalog Card Number: 95–53132
ISBN: 0–313–29019–9

First published in 1996

Greenwood Press, 88 Post Road West, Westport, CT 06881
An imprint of Greenwood Publishing Group, Inc.

Printed in the United States of America

The paper used in this book complies with the
Permanent Paper Standard issued by the National
Information Standards Organization (Z39.48–1984).

10   9   8   7   6   5   4   3   2   1

Contents

Foreword

James M. McPherson

Nobody knows how many books and articles have been published on the Civil War during the past 130 years. The number approaches six figures and continues to grow at an astonishing rate. In recent years other media have jumped onto the Civil War bandwagon: films, videos, CD-ROMS, and other nonprint materials, including live reenactments of Civil War battles and living history demonstrations. Despite the high-tech entry into the Civil War field, books and articles will undoubtedly remain the best way to learn about this defining event in American history.

The huge number of writings about all aspects of the Civil War is a mixed blessing. No one, not even the most studious of experts, can keep up with the literature in the field. The beginner is overwhelmed and scarcely knows where to start; the seasoned scholar courts a severe case of burn-out trying to stay on top of the subject. But we need lament no more. This splendid collection of bibliographical essays comes to the rescue. It provides a clear and comprehensive guide to every conceivable topic and subtopic in writings about the Civil War—and films, videos, and music as well.

The great virtues of this book are coverage and precision. Several thousand titles are cited and their contents summarized in more than forty essays, each by an expert on the specific subject covered in the essay. No topic is overlooked. Students interested in military campaigns, battles, and leadership can turn to Parts VII and VIII. Those who wish to learn about politics will go to Part IV. Social conditions on the home front are covered in Part IX. There are essays on economic developments, diplomacy, medicine, the Constitution, slavery, emancipation, the causes of the war, and its consequences. The Contents and the indexes make it possible for a searcher to find the writings on any subject in minutes. Every year I receive scores of inquiries from students, colleagues, and laypeople asking for guidance through the maze of Civil War scholarship. I can now point them to *The American Civil War: A Handbook of Literature and Research* as the best place to start, whether they are interested in primary sources or secondary accounts.

The main value of this book is as a reference work, but it is more than that. The chapters can be read as an analysis of evolving and sometimes shifting perspectives on the war during the past generation or two. Race, class, gender, and ethnicity have become important analytical factors in American social history. Because of slavery and emancipation, race has long loomed large in Civil War scholarship, and that theme is reflected here in several essays. Social historians have recently discovered the Civil War, and we therefore now have a growing literature on gender, class, and ethnicity in this era. In many other ways also, these essays chronicle the changing interpretations of America's greatest crisis by historians whose perceptions are shaped by the present in which they live, as well as the past they study. This book can be read as a guide to broader trends in historiography, as well as a guide to sources and writings on specific topics. That is what makes *The American Civil War: A Handbook of Literature and Research* the most important volume for anyone interested in the Civil War to own and consult.

Preface

No other subject in U.S. history, perhaps no other subject in the history of the world, has elicited the tremendous outpouring of writing that has been lavished on the American Civil War. Estimates of the number of books devoted to the topic vary, and although any estimate is little more than an educated guess, some such guesses run as high as 70,000 books—more than a book a day since the war ended over 130 years ago. And interest in the war is not waning. On the contrary, it seems never to have been higher than in recent years. The remarkable response to the 1990 PBS documentary ''The Civil War'' is one indication of this, as is the reception of such films as *Glory* and *Gettysburg*. Dozens of Civil War roundtables nationwide and thousands of reinactments are further evidence of Americans' fascination with the conflict, as is the existence of at least six popular magazines devoted entirely to the war. Trade book publishers offer substantial numbers of Civil War titles geared to popular audiences. Scholarly interest in the Civil War remains intense as well, with a scholarly journal and a tremendous output of scholarly books.

An old midwestern proverb claims that no great ill comes without some small good. In the case of this great bounty of Civil War literature, the reverse may well be true. The excess of fine scholarship and writing (if such work can ever be said to exist in excess) may, by its daunting bulk, begin to obscure almost as much as it enlightens. How is the scholar to find all of the relevant works—and the best ones—on even one small area of Civil War studies. Mastering all the literature of the war would be the work of several lifetimes. Few scholars can hope to do better than gain a working familiarity with the most important works in their own particular subfields of Civil War history. Yet the interrelatedness of history makes a broad grasp of the literature and research necessary in order to begin to understand the significance of any of the isolated events. By bringing together the bibliographical knowledge and insights of over forty Civil War scholars, each an expert in his or her particular subfield, this book seeks to ease some of the constraints of the sheer vastness of Civil War literature. It will guide the reader to works and sources that will be of most value in a particular area of study. It should serve those who are turning to the serious study of the war for the first time—or who have studied it for years and are turning their attention to one of its many facets they have not yet explored—as a guide to the various schools of thought in that area and to the most useful research and literature now available. Using this book should save students of the war—new or experienced—many false starts and much wasted effort and speed them on their way to the productive examination of America's "fiery trial" that consistently yields insights fascinating to both scholars and the lay public.

Directing the production of such a work has been a daunting task. With the exception of my own special subfields, I have had to rely on experts whose knowledge of their own areas of specialization far exceeds my own. These scholars have been the ones best qualified to make individual, case-by-case decisions on which books, articles, and dissertations to include and which, regretfully, to pass over. Several general guidelines have nevertheless shaped our common effort. Emphasis has been placed on works of current usefulness over those of merely historiographical interest. Within this framework, we have also concentrated on works that would be readily available to modern readers without neglecting truly vital items, no matter how obscure. The goal has been to produce a practical guide that will do more than gather dust on reference shelves.

I owe a great debt of gratitude to all of the contributors to this project. It is, after all, their book. They have expended great effort and shown great patience with my hectoring demands for revisions and nagging reminders about deadlines, and they have done so, as far as I can tell, from pure love of scholarship. I would particularly like to thank Robin Higham and Alan C. Aimone for their helpful advice.

Introduction

Steven E. Woodworth

It was about 4:30 A.M., Friday, April 12, 1861, when white-haired old Edmund Ruffin—long an advocate of Southern secession and now, for this occasion, temporarily a private in the Palmetto Guards—jerked the lanyard of Columbiad Number One at the Cummings Point Battery on Morris Island, South Carolina. The huge cannon roared and belched a cloud of dense white smoke. Its projectile sailed out across Charleston Harbor toward Fort Sumter, where the flag of the United States constituted a provocation no longer to be borne by citizens of the self-styled Confederate States of America. In so doing, Ruffin established his claim (in truth, one he probably shared with a number of other gunners around the harbor) to have fired the first shot of America's Civil War. Before it was over, four years and six days later (its end was somewhat delayed west of the Mississippi), it had taken the lives of some 620,000 Americans, far more than all of the country's previous wars put together, and more than any of its wars since. It changed the fabric of American society, altered the American Constitution, rid the land of the curse of slavery, and left scars that remain to this day. It can, without exaggeration, be called the hinge of American history.

Much that came before it in the story of the United States can be seen and explained in terms of events that led up to the war. Historians have long debated—and continue to debate—the issues of the war's causation. Was the war a factor of economic forces, or the result of a generation of politicians who had forgotten how to compromise? Was it, perhaps, the result of social forces, expansion, or any one of dozens of constitutional issues? Was Southern secession engineered by wealthy slaveholders and political leaders, or were the Southern people, as their leaders at the time claimed, actually leading their leaders in the rush to secede? One entire part of this book is devoted to the rich literature that has examined these and other questions of causation.

The leaders themselves have been the subject of considerable research. The literature on Lincoln alone would dwarf that on some entire eras of history. His motivations, inner thoughts, probable actions if not assassinated, and degree of devotion to this or that cherished cause have all stirred debate, besides such mundane matters as his politics or conduct of the war or of wartime Reconstruction. Indeed, an entire book analyzed one of his speeches. Jefferson Davis has received far less scholarship and vastly less adulation. Most scholars have concluded that in some way he failed, but just how and how much remains debated, and even the fact of his failure is not without dispute. The historical debate is by no means closed on these two men, any more than on the various civilian and military leaders who served under them. Scholars are just beginning to sort out the hows and whys of winners and losers alike. While current fashions in history writing may place a premium on attention to the collective masses, the pivotal importance of great leaders in shaping history is unmistakable in the large volume of significant research they continue to attract and the fresh and valuable insights this research yields.

Strategy, tactics, and battles command an even more enormous body of literature, and rightly so. The Civil War was, after all, a war, and, as Lincoln himself pointed out, "War means fighting." One need not like war (and who would?) in order to see the value of its study. Far more than does peacetime, war reveals the human nature as it truly is—at once both noble and fallen. The Civil War offers a rewarding field for study in its vast literature of campaigns and battles. The complexity of its operations guarantees that the exploration of their courses need not become sterile or repetitive in the second century of their study. Even in this area of previous intensive study, new paths remain to be followed and new insights gained. The literature described in this book demonstrates the constant deepening in our understanding of these events—a deepening that continues even now.

The current generation of historians has, over the last twenty years or so, devoted extraordinary attention to social history. The Civil War has received its fair share of this vast outpouring of work. Those who have specialized in the more traditional military and political aspects of the war may be surprised, on reading this book, to discover the vastness of the literature in this area. In this field, as in the others of Civil War history, no abatement appears to be in sight. The field for gathering data is all but limitless, and the ingenuity of scholars in finding new methods of analysis by which to extract insights from that data, little less so.

Most of the chapters in this book point out areas in which further research is needed. Thus, the literature and research on the American Civil War is vital and growing. This book displays its current state of development and the opportunities for study it now offers.

Part I

General Secondary Sources

1

Surveys and Textbooks

Steven E. Woodworth

Some of the finest writing in the vast body of Civil War literature, indeed, some of the finest history writing of any sort, has been devoted to broad overviews of the Civil War. The war's popularity with readers, its continuing fascination for scholars, and the many and intricate insights it affords into the American experience have attracted leading historians to devote years to the production of enormous, highly detailed, and carefully crafted surveys of the war and surrounding events. The best of these rise not only to the level of excellent history but to that of enduring literature as well.

As with all the other literature of the war, works of this genre are numerous—extremely numerous. Addressing even a high proportion of them would become not only excessively lengthy but tedious as well. Thus this chapter assesses only some of the most recent and significant.

MULTIVOLUME WORKS

Among this type of work are some of the towering monuments of Civil War literature. The chief of them are discussed here, though it is doubtful that any will be unfamiliar to students of the war.

Allan Nevins's massive eight-volume *The Crisis of the Union* (1947–1971) remains the standard for completeness. Four volumes deal with events leading up to the war, and the next four, entitled *The War for the Union* (1959–1971), cover the war years themselves. Nevins had planned to produce additional volumes covering Reconstruction but died shortly before the appearance of the final volume of *The War for the Union*. In the volumes on the war years, individually titled *The Improvised War, 1861–1862, War Becomes Revolution, 1862–1863, The Organized War, 1863–1864,* and *The Organized War to Victory, 1864–1865,* Nevins relates the military, political, economic, diplomatic, and social history of the period in remarkable detail. He argues that ''the Civil War accentuated and acted as a catalyst to already developing local tendencies toward organization'' (4:272) and thus changed America. He did not shy from controversy, and he had a negative assessment of the Radical Republicans, a view much out of fashion today. Yet few even now would deny the immense accomplishment of this enormous work.

Bruce Catton's *Centennial History of the Civil War* (1958–1965) sets the standard of eloquence for Civil War writing. The first volume, *The Coming Fury,* goes from the crises of the 1850s through the Battle of Bull Run. The second, *Terrible Swift Sword,* covers the years 1861 and 1862. *Never Call Retreat* brings the story through the close of hostilities. While the ornateness of Catton's prose is not the height of fashion, his remains a very readable retelling of the war. Its usefulness is enhanced by thorough references.

Shelby Foote's three-volume *The Civil War, a Narrative* (1958–1974) currently dominates the landscape of multivolume Civil War surveys. It is enormous, with nearly a thousand pages in each volume, and it is correspondingly thorough and detailed. Like Catton, Foote offers a thoughtful and eloquent retelling of the story of the Civil War. Unlike Catton, Foote's perspective is that of a Southerner. Both works are classics of Civil War literature.

SINGLE-VOLUME WORKS

The previous two decades have seen a remarkable outpouring of this genre, including some pieces that are, in their own sphere, as monumental as the works of Nevins, Catton, and Foote. Such gems run the gamut from excellent scholarly studies to highly popular volumes sometimes a bit cavalier in their interpretations and even in what they present as facts. This discussion treats only the most important single-volume surveys of the past twenty years or so and, since volumes vary considerably in size, notes the approximate lengths of the books discussed.

Peter J. Parrish's *The American Civil War* (1975) provides a solid treatment of the war by a respected British military historian. Parrish ably covers the military, political, and diplomatic aspects of the war. While the past twenty years have brought many new insights into Civil War military history and Parrish's work is less valuable for the lack of them, it remains nevertheless a remarkably comprehensive and perspicacious summary of the war. The book does lack the influence of the ''new military history,'' as well as the heightened interest in social history that has characterized the profession during the last couple of decades. Some readers will no doubt find this a very serious shortcoming. At about 275,000 words, Parrish's length is typical of the large one-volume surveys.

In 1982 appeared the fifth volume of Page Smith's popular narrative history of the United States, begun as a two-volume history of the Revolution and continued through successive volumes. The Civil War tome, entitled *Trial by Fire,* displays all of the engaging storytelling skills and fine writing that made the earlier volumes enjoyable reading. Smith presents his work as ''a people's history,'' and its strongest point is its capturing of the thoughts and feelings of the people who lived through that era. Extensive use of diaries, memoirs, and letters allows Smith to recreate those individuals with great vividness. Some of his insights are excellent, but the work is marred by a larger than usual number of disconcerting errors of fact, as, for example, locating the Ohio River between Illinois and Indiana. Also, some of his interpretations are weak at best. His chapter on the antebellum South makes it a land of planters and plantations, referring only vaguely to certain other whites, even though the planter class made up only a small percentage of the Southern population. Like its predecessors in this series, this volume is not footnoted. It is roughly 230,000 words in length.

Also appearing in 1982 was James McPherson's *Ordeal by Fire.* A comprehensive survey of the social, political, intellectual, and military history of the Civil War and Reconstruction era by an accomplished scholar, *Ordeal by Fire* is characterized by a happy combination of thoroughness, accuracy, and fine writing. About a quarter of the book is devoted to the history of the United States in the nineteenth century prior to the war and to events leading to the war. Another 20 percent is given over to Reconstruction. Its length, about 280,000 words, is comparable to other recent works of this genre, but its quality marks it as a superior academic history.

In 1988 McPherson entered the field again, this time with his Pulitzer Prize– winning *Battle Cry of Freedom,* part of the Oxford History of the United States series, edited by C. Vann Woodward. While it is about 10 percent longer than his earlier work, it does not include coverage of Reconstruction, and thus it can devote half again the space to events leading to the war and nearly one-third again to the previous book's coverage of the war itself. Building on his previous work, McPherson combines a voluminous knowledge of Civil War literature with his own sharp insights to offer as clear and compelling a picture of the nation's pivotal conflict as will likely ever be done in a single volume of comparable length. McPherson makes unmistakably clear that the Civil War was a war about slavery and reflects intelligently on its meaning. He skillfully weaves social, political, and military history into a single flowing narrative and conveys a wealth of information with an accuracy that consistently avoids the small inaccuracies one must overlook in many other works. All of this is conveyed in a clear, crisp writing style that captivates without distracting. In *Battle Cry of Freedom,* McPherson has written the longest of the single-volume Civil War surveys and has also set the standard for the genre.

A brief and well-written overview is provided by Peter Batty and Peter Parish's *The Divided Union* (1987). Aimed at popular audiences and lavishly illustrated, *The Divided Union* includes a sound and lively text by respected historians.

Robert Leckie's *None Died in Vain* (1990) is also aimed at popular audiences. It is not a slim volume, running to over 250,000 words, but it reads well, being the work of an accomplished writer with a long list of popular military history titles to his credit and the added insight that comes of having seen the face of battle himself, as a young marine in World War II. *None Died in Vain* is clearly meant to be colorful, entertaining, and thought provoking, and it is all of these. Leckie weaves extensive biographical sketches into his text. Unfortunately, the book is not footnoted, and the lack is noticeable. I found the urge frequently to check the source of an unusual statement, as, for example, to find out if it really was Clausewitz—and not Lincoln—who first referred to a war of limited violence against civilians as a "rose-water" war. Leckie does not shrink from making some fairly categorical judgments on the characters involved and is engagingly blunt in stating them (engaging, that is, provided one agrees with him). Such idiosyncrasies may limit the book's use in academic settings, but it remains an exciting, fast-paced overview that will no doubt open for many amateur historians the fascinating vistas of Civil War history.

Charles P. Roland's 1991 *An American Iliad,* at about 140,000 words, offers an excellent overview of the war in a volume of moderate length. It begins with a brief discussion of the crises of the 1850s and concludes with the final Confederate surrenders. The work of a very senior and respected Civil War scholar, it offers a thoughtful and intelligent discussion of the war. For a book of modest length, it is amazingly comprehensive, with fine insights into numerous aspects of the conflict. Its value is enhanced by an excellent bibliographic essay.

At only about 55,000 words, Frank E. Vandiver's *Blood Brothers* (1992) is among the shortest of the recent surveys of the Civil War. Though necessarily spare in its coverage, the book has the power of being the mature reflections of another very highly respected Civil War scholar. Vandiver sets the tone with (and devotes nearly one-sixth of this brief book to) an introductory essay on the contrasting nature of rival revolutions wrought by the rival presidents. While that of Lincoln was one of unity and modernity, that of Davis was not against modernity but rather for a different way of approaching the modern world and for a unity of Confederate nationalism. Lincoln's revolution triumphed; Davis's, though it failed, nevertheless carried the South beyond its resources to the point of total exhaustion and at the same time prepared it to become part of the new America to which the war gave birth. Vandiver's is a strikingly eloquent and thoughtful retelling of the story of this conflict.

Allen C. Guelzo's *The Crisis of the American Republic* (1995) displays a truly impressive grasp of the entire body of recent scholarship, not only on the war itself but on the prewar era as well. The decades leading to the war occupy nearly a fourth of the book and set the stage for Guelzo's exuberantly Whiggish interpretation of the conflict. His discussion of military operations, though sound, is influenced by Paddy Griffith's *Battle Tactics of the Civil War* (1989), with its controversial thesis that the war was bloody precisely because the opposing armies were too prone to entrench and not willing enough to charge the enemy boldly. The home front is Guelzo's strongest suit, and he covers it extensively. Minimal space is devoted to Reconstruction, with the author suggesting that Lincoln agreed fully with the Radicals, even to the point of favoring a harsh regime in the conquered South. Guelzo's prose is magnificent, his weaving of the drama and color of the story flawless, and his analysis thought provoking. The result is a work fully up to the high standard set by previous surveys of the war. At about 190,000 words, Guelzo's book fills a niche, shared perhaps with Roland, between the length of Parrish, McPherson, and Leckie, on the one hand, and, Vandiver on the other.

While many of the finest Civil War surveys represent the work of mature scholars reflecting on long careers in the field, Brooks D. Simpson's *America's Civil War* (1996) breaks that pattern. The work of one of the foremost of the rising generation of Civil War scholars, *America's Civil War* offers a well-balanced overview of the war, from secession to the final surrenders, conveying a wealth of information and thoughtful insight in a clear, concise, unlabored form that makes it look easy to recount the rich story of the American Civil War in a scant 60,000 words. No important topic is neglected and no words are wasted, yet the text does not feel dense, and the reader comes away with no impression of having been overwhelmed with facts. Simpson focuses on the interplay of the political and military factors that determined the war's outcome and also shaped events on the home front. The latter area receives brief but adequate coverage in this concise survey.

HISTORIES OF THE CONFEDERACY

Among the best histories of the Confederacy is Frank E. Vandiver's 1970 *Their Tattered Flags*. A thorough, accurate, eloquent, and highly readable survey of the rebellious states and their government, *Their Tattered Flags* also provides a sympathetic but insightful account of Jefferson Davis as Confederate president that remains one of the best such brief accounts available.

Another notable history of the Confederacy is Emory M. Thomas's 1979 *The Confederate Nation, 1861–1865*. This work built on his earlier *The Confederacy as a Revolutionary Experience* (1970). He argues that the antebellum South had by the mid-nineteenth century grown so different from the North as to produce the beginnings of its own separate nationalism. The difference lay in the South's culture, economy, and politics, all tied to the dominant plantation system: slave labor and the production of cotton.

An intriguing and much different approach to Confederate history is provided by Richard E. Beringer, Herman Hattaway, Archer Jones, and William N. Still, Jr., in *Why the South Lost the Civil War* (1986). In a thorough review and analysis of Confederate military history, they argue that none of the previously accepted explanations for Southern defeat (as, for example, the blockade, lack of manpower, or lack of industrial strength) is adequate. Instead they maintain that the Confederacy succumbed to a failure of will created in the Southern populace as a whole when battlefield failure convinced the people that God had decreed their defeat.

The most recent foray into the genre of Confederate history is devoted specifically to Confederate politics. George C. Rable's *The Confederate Republic* (1994) examines the Confederate government as a descendant of eighteenth-century ideas of republican virtue and the ideal of a purified republic, purged of parties, politics, and democratic excesses. Rable provides an account of the political struggles of the Confederacy between nationalists and states'-rights libertarians.

MILITARY HISTORIES

Herman Hattaway and Archer Jones have written a purely military history of the Civil War, *How the North Won* (1983). It provides a solid and comprehensive overview of the war's operations and explains the many technical concepts and terms involved (e.g., What precisely is a "turning maneuver"?). Military history, in this case, does not mean simply the tale of valorous deeds on the battlefield; Hattaway and Jones shed much light on the unromantic but ultimately decisive issue of logistics. Unlike many other surveys, this one does have considerable interpretive bite, as the authors' assessment also represents a significant rehabilitation of much-maligned Union major general Henry Wager Halleck.

THE FUTURE

In a field such as that of general works and surveys of the Civil War, one cannot really speak of a need for further research. The primary purpose of such works is to synthesize and present in concise (and, one would hope, readable) form the findings of the great and constantly growing body of Civil War research. Works such as those of McPherson, Roland, Guelzo, and Simpson ably perform that task for the present state of the art of Civil War history, and do so with admirable grace and eloquence. Yet as ongoing research continues to expand our knowledge and deepen our understanding of the nation's greatest conflict, new syntheses will be needed.

Although surveys of the entire war are numerous and of high quality, the same cannot be said of the available histories of the Confederacy. Existing works that strive to depict the Confederacy as a whole represent fine efforts by first-rate scholars, but much new research has been done since their appearance. Thus the greatest current need is for a new comprehensive history of the Confederacy, incorporating the last decade and a half of research in the areas of social, political, economic, and military history into a single narrative and judiciously weighing the competing arguments of modern scholars. The continuing ability of the Civil War to attract large audiences and fine scholar-writers gives reason to hope that such a work will soon be undertaken. It is a worthy task.

BIBLIOGRAPHY

Batty, Peter, and Peter Parish. *The Divided Union: The Story of the Great American War, 1861–65.* Topsfield, MA: Salem House, 1987.

Beringer, Richard E., Herman Hattaway, Archer Jones, and William N. Still, Jr. *Why the South Lost the Civil War.* Athens: University of Georgia Press, 1986.

Catton, Bruce. *The Coming Fury.* Garden City, NY: Doubleday, 1961.

———. *Terrible Swift Sword.* Garden City, NY: Doubleday, 1963.

———. *Never Call Retreat.* Garden City, NY: Doubleday, 1965.

Foote, Shelby. *The Civil War, a Narrative.* 3 vols. New York: Random House, 1958–1974.

Griffith, Paddy. *Battle Tactics of the Civil War.* New Haven: Yale University Press, 1989.

Guelzo, Allen C. *The Crisis of the American Republic: A History of the Civil War and Reconstruction.* St. Martin's Series in U.S. History. New York: St. Martin's Press, 1995.

Hattaway, Herman, and Archer Jones. *How the North Won: A Military History of the Civil War.* Urbana: University of Illinois Press, 1983.

Leckie, Robert. *None Died in Vain: The Saga of the American Civil War.* New York: HarperCollins, 1990.

McPherson, James M. *Ordeal by Fire: The Civil War and Reconstruction.* New York: Alfred A. Knopf, 1982.

———. *Battle Cry of Freedom: The Civil War Era.* Oxford History of the United States. New York: Oxford University Press, 1988.

Nevins, Alan. *Ordeal of the Union.* Vol. 1: *Fruits of Manifest Destiny, 1847–1852.* New York: Charles Scribner's Sons, 1947.

———. *Ordeal of the Union.* Vol. 2: *A House Dividing, 1852–1857.* New York: Charles Scribner's Sons, 1947.

———. *The Emergence of Lincoln.* Vol. 1: *Douglas, Buchanan, and Party Chaos, 1857–1859.* New York: Charles Scribner's Sons, 1950.

———. *The Emergence of Lincoln.* Vol. 2: *Prologue to Civil War, 1859–1861.* New York: Charles Scribner's Sons, 1950.

———. *The Crisis of the Union.* 4 vols. New York: Charles Scribner's Sons, 1947–1971.

Parrish, Peter J. *The American Civil War.* New York: Holmes & Meier, 1975.

Rable, George C. *The Confederate Republic: A Revolution against Politics.* Chapel Hill: University of North Carolina Press, 1994.

Roland, Charles P. *An American Iliad: The Story of the Civil War.* Lexington: University Press of Kentucky, 1991.

Simpson, Brooks D. *America's Civil War.* New York: Harlan Davidson, 1996.

Smith, Page. *Trial by Fire: A People's History of the Civil War and Reconstruction.* New York: McGraw-Hill, 1982.

Thomas, Emory M. *The Confederacy as a Revolutionary Experience.* Englewood Cliffs, NJ: Prentice-Hall, 1970.

Thomas, Emory M. *The Confederate Nation, 1861–1865.* New York: Harper & Row, 1979.

Vandiver, Frank E. *Blood Brothers: A Short History of the Civil War.* College Station: Texas A&M University Press, 1992.

———. *Their Tattered Flags: The Epic of the Confederacy.* New York: Harper's Magazine Press, 1970.

2

General Reference Works

Daniel E. Sutherland

Several categories of work fall under the rubric of general reference, but this chapter organizes the most important contributions to the literature under five broad headings: biographical directories, dictionaries and encyclopedias, compendiums, almanacs, and battlefield guides. Some of the works assigned to these categories may be discussed under other headings elsewhere in this book, but this chapter will concentrate on their usefulness as general reference tools. Even the most casual researcher will find some of these works indispensable.

BIOGRAPHICAL DIRECTORIES

Most basic are the biographical directories, which are heavily slanted toward the Confederacy. Ezra J. Warner's two volumes on Union and Confederate generals, *Generals in Gray: Lives of the Confederate Commanders* (1959) and *Generals in Blue: Lives of the Union Commanders* (1964), remain the handiest references for their subjects. Each sketch is brief, averaging roughly 250 words in the Confederate volume and 400 words for the Union, but they include all 425 Confederates and all 583 Federals who received appointments as general officers from Jefferson Davis and Abraham Lincoln, respectively. Each entry is accompanied by a photograph of the subject. The sketches are supplemented by excellent introductions that explain the appointment process in both armies and provide composite information about average occupations, age, and wartime casualties. Both books contain bibliographies, although the one for the Confederacy is more detailed, including all known biographies of the subjects.

In some important ways, Warner's Confederate volume, while still useful, has been superseded by William C. Davis, ed., *The Confederate General* (1991). Thirty-three scholars have contributed to these six volumes, with essays that range from 1,000 to 1,500 words. The longer essays allow authors to provide more information and a fuller view of each man's life than does Warner. The contributors have also corrected erroneous dates and incorrect statements made by Warner. While the bulk of each sketch concentrates on the wartime career of its subject, they go beyond basic biographical data to provide more analysis and cast more precise judgments than does Warner. Where Warner offers only a single illustration of each general, the Davis volumes reproduce every known photograph of each man in Confederate uniform. Additionally, besides the recognized 425 Confederate generals, Davis has included in volume 6 sketches of nine "generals" in the trans-Mississippi who received their general officer rank from Edmund Kirby Smith without ever being confirmed by the Confederate government. Finally, Davis includes photographs (though not biographical sketches) of nine bogus brigadier generals who claimed the rank on their own.

Many Confederate officers of lesser rank appear in Robert K. Krick, *Lee's Colonels: A Biographical Register of the Field Officers of the Army of Northern Virginia* (1992). His sketches of 1,968 men average about seventy words each and provide an excellent profile of the majors, lieutenant colonels, and colonels that led the battalions and regiments of Lee's army. An introduction and several tables summarize information and provide a statistical profile of these officers by age, height and weight, education, prewar and postwar occupations, and year of death. Each of the three revised editions corrects errors and adds information. Beginning with the second edition, Krick includes an appendix that lists the names and units (and birth and death dates when known) of 3,510 Confederate field officers who served outside the Army of Northern Virginia and of a few men associated with militia units and irregular organizations.

In 1975, Warner teamed with W. Buck Yearns to produce the *Biographical Register of the Confederate Congress*. Most of the sketches are around 400 words each. An introduction reviews the history of the Confederate Congress and provides a composite statistical view of its members. One appendix lists the dates for each session of the congress, while another lists members by state for the provisional, first, and second congresses. A third appendix lists the members of all standing committees for the three congresses. Not precisely a reference work, Warner and Yearns may be supplemented by Thomas B. Alexander and Richard E. Beringer, *The Anatomy of the Confederate Congress* (1971). This is primarily a quantitative study of voting behavior, but it is based on extensive analysis of individual biographies. Much useful biographical information, including number of slaves owned and financial value in 1860, in addition to how congressmen voted on specific issues, is provided in several tables. Also useful are maps of Confederate electoral districts.

The *Biographical Dictionary of the Confederacy* (1977), by Jon L. Wakelyn, adds another dimension to Confederate sketches by including both military and civilian leaders in a single volume. Wakelyn provides sketches of 651 men and women (six women), of whom only 265 are military and naval officers. Cabinet members, state governors, and congressmen are among the most prominent civilian subjects, and some businessmen and cultural leaders also appear. The sketches are roughly 350 words apiece. Designed to chronicle the career patterns of the most important Confederate leaders, this volume also includes a fifty-five-page introduction and several appendixes. The introduction provides composite information about the antebellum lives, wartime careers, and postwar fates of these leaders. An appendix on geographical mobility organized by place of birth shows where and when each subject was born, residence in 1860, and where and when each died. A second appendix lists, by individual, prewar, wartime, and postwar occupations. A third appendix lists people by religious affiliation, a fourth shows each person's highest level of education, and a fifth indicates prewar and postwar political affiliations. Wakelyn's tabulations are sometimes at odds with those of other authors. For instance, he says 93 congressmen saw military service, while Alexander and Beringer calculate 115. Within the work itself, contradictions exist. The sketches show 67 people being born in Virginia; Wakelyn's analysis says 60. Nevertheless, the sketches are reliable introductions to their subjects.

The Northern counterpart of Wakelyn's work is John T. Hubbell and James W. Geary, eds., *Biographical Dictionary of the Union: Northern Leaders of the Civil War* (1995). The editors present 872 sketches of men and women who "influenced the course of public policy, opinion, and events" (p. ix). Their definition covers a variety of occupations and vocations, including editors, photographers, and reformers, although politicians and soldiers represent the vast majority of their subjects. The entries, which range from slightly over a hundred words to several thousand, provide complete biographical data, but with an emphasis on wartime activities and including an assessment of wartime roles. Subjects range from Abraham Lincoln to "individuals whose obscurity is breathtaking" (p. x), such as Wisconsin congressman Luther Hanchett.

Reacting to the many specialized and sectionally slanted biographical reference works devoted to generals and politicians, Stewart Sifakis has tried to bring all significant personalities of the war together in a single volume. His nearly 2,500 entries in *Who Was Who in the Civil War* (1988) strike a balance between soldiers and civilians, Northerners and Southerners. His definition of people who "most affected the conflict" (p. viii) extends backward in time to the coming of the war. Thus James Buchanan and Stephen A. Douglas join Lincoln and Lee. Sifakis includes most U.S. and Confederate senators and important congressmen, cabinet members, all state governors, and political activists like Frederick Douglass and Clement A. Vallandigham. All Union and Confederate generals have sketches, as do lower-ranking officers "who led forces larger than a regiment for a lengthy period or in major actions" (p. viii). He also recognizes scouts and spies, distinguished junior officers, journalists, surgeons, diplomats, foreign military observers, and others. Some entries include portraits. *Who Was*

Who in the Confederacy (1989), a companion volume, is limited to the Confederate States.

DICTIONARIES AND ENCYCLOPEDIAS

Also containing biographical information but casting a wider net are several important dictionaries and encyclopedias. The classic volume, and a very nearly indispensable research tool, is Mark M. Boatner III, *The Civil War Dictionary* (1988), first published in 1959. Boatner provides definitions of everything from *abatis* to *zouave*, and he describes succinctly all major campaigns and battles, as well as many minor actions. Useful tactical maps and several theater maps are included. In addition, Boatner has entries on such subjects as blockade running, small arms, the principles of war, notable regiments, Lincoln's assassination, and all military theaters and departments. For Boatner's own appraisal of his dictionary, see his article, "How *The Civil War Dictionary* Came into Being," *Civil War History* 34 (September 1988): 188–210.

Similar in scope if not detail is Patricia L. Faust, ed., *Historical Times Illustrated Encyclopedia of the Civil War* (1986), with sixty-two contributors presenting 2,000 entries. Biographical entries are emphasized, but on a broader scale than in Boatner's book. All Confederate generals and most Union generals are profiled, as are major political figures and many people of lesser fame. Excellent entries for all major campaigns and battles are facilitated by sixty-seven maps. In addition, Faust includes entries on political and diplomatic events, the arts, journalism, weapons, technology, and much more. Most of the biographical entries are accompanied by photographs, and the volume boasts nearly a thousand total photographs.

The ultimate Confederate reference work is Richard N. Current, ed., *Encyclopedia of the Confederacy* (1993). Included are the usual biographical sketches and descriptions of campaigns and battles, but its entries also describe Confederate government and political structure, military strategy and tactics, financial system, and social structure, as well as the roles of Indians, African Americans, women, religion, literature, and other neglected topics in Confederate life. Entries by over 300 scholars range between 250 and 17,000 words and are supplemented by over 600 illustrations (both photographs and etchings), 67 maps, and bibliographic citations for each entry. Nine appendixes provide complete texts of key documents in Confederate history, including the Constitution and the parole agreements for the Confederacy's principal armies. For a good review essay, see Joseph G. Dawson, "The Confederacy Revisited: *Encyclopedia of the Confederacy*," in *Civil War History* 40 (December 1994): 308–316.

David C. Roller and Robert W. Twyman, eds., *Encyclopedia of Southern History* (1979), with nearly 3,000 entries by over 1,100 scholars, contains much information related to the war, including biographical sketches, synopses of important battles, and numerous subentries under "Confederate," such as conscription, desertion, diplomacy, economy, flags, judicial system, prisons, strategy, and weapons. By and large, however, these same entries, with more extensive commentary, may be found in the more recent *Encyclopedia of the Confederacy*. A similar work, excellent in its own right but less useful for the war, is Charles Reagan Wilson and William Ferris, eds., *Encyclopedia of Southern Culture* (1989). For an insightful review of this volume and commentary on the recent trend in such encyclopedias see George C. Rable, "Is the Civil War Still Central to the Study of Southern Civilization? Reflections on the *Encyclopedia of Southern Culture*," *Civil War History* 36 (December 1990): 334–342.

COMPENDIUMS

Several military compendiums emphasize command structure and organization. William F. Amann, *Personnel of the Civil War* (1961), largely intended to identify the local designations of Union and Confederate units, represents the republication of several rare works first compiled in the 1870s and 1880s. The first part of volume 1, dealing with Confederate units, lists alphabetically the name of each volunteer Confederate unit, tells when it was raised, and gives the name assigned to the unit in Confederate service (examples, Adams Rifles became 10th Mississippi Rifles; Little Fork Rangers became 4th Virginia Cavalry). Part II identifies alphabetically the Confederacy's military districts, departments, reserve forces, corps, and armies; the dates served by each commander; and, where appropriate, its geographical boundaries. Part III provides an alphabetical listing of general officers and the dates each served in each of his assignments. This last part is incomplete and uneven in detail, but still useful as a supplement to the biographical sketches of these officers found elsewhere.

Amann's second volume covers the Union. It begins with a list of general officers in order of rank, with each category subdivided to show those men who held full and those who held brevet rank. It also indicates whether a man held his commission in the regular army or volunteer service. The date of appointment and resignation is given for each rank held by each man. The second and larger part of volume 2 offers by state an alphabetical listing of "synonyms" for all Federal units, showing their original, or local, designation and their "final or regular" title (for example, in Ohio, the Montgomery Regiment became the 10th Regiment Infantry). The list also has sections for United States Colored Troops, Miscellaneous Units, United States Volunteers (such as Berdan's Regiment Sharpshooters), and Veteran Reserve Corps. There is a comprehensive alphabetical listing of all synonyms that identify the state or category of each unit. Unfortunately, neither volume includes an index.

Even more complete is Frederick H. Dyer, *A Compendium of the War of the Rebellion* (1959), originally published in 1909. Dyer attempts to give a detailed sketch of every regiment, battery, and battalion in the Union army. He states where and when each unit was organized; to which brigades, divisions, and corps it became attached; where it served; military actions in which it engaged;

and where and when it was mustered out of service. In addition, he explains the organization of all Union military divisions, departments, and armies. He also provides mortality statistics and a record of all known combat actions and operations, including Union units engaged in each action.

The most recent and by far most detailed look at the organization of the Union army is Frank J. Welcher's two-volume *The Union Army, 1861–1865* (1989, 1993). Both volumes are identical in the kinds and organization of information provided, and both reach encyclopedic proportions. Welcher's single aim is to provide a "complete and continuous account" of the Union army's organization from military divisions to brigades. Thus Welcher, by omitting the smaller units dealt with by Dyer, is an important supplement to the older work. The first volume explains the organization of the War Department and the army's bureau system. Thereafter, each volume is divided into the same six sections: military divisions, army departments, field armies, army corps, miscellaneous organizations, and battles and campaigns. The first five sections include information on where and when the unit was organized, changes in commanders, composition, and organization, and a brief history of each unit, including all military actions and when each unit was discontinued. The sixth section, proportionately the largest in each volume, describes the roles and movements of Union armies and corps in all major battles and all significant engagements, expeditions, raids, and reconnaissances. A nearly day-by-day itinerary is given for major units during the war's campaigns. An index of battles and campaigns for both volumes is found in volume 2, but, regrettably, neither volume has maps.

The next best thing for the Confederacy is a new series by Stewart Sifakis. Published under the series title *Compendium of the Confederate Armies,* most volumes are devoted to a separate state. Thus far, five volumes have been published, for Alabama, Florida and Arkansas, North Carolina, Tennessee, and Virginia. When completed, one volume will be devoted to the border states of Kentucky, Maryland, and Missouri; another to units organized directly by the Confederacy from state companies; another to units from the Indian nations; and another to tables of organization of the various armies and departments throughout the war. All have the same format. Sifakis devotes separate sections to artillery, cavalry, and infantry and includes as much of the following information about each unit as is known: where and when it was organized, where and when it was disbanded or mustered out, the name of its first commander, the names of its field officers, larger units to which it was assigned, and the battles in which it engaged. While similar works already exist for some Southern states, most notably Louisiana, North Carolina, Tennessee, Texas, and Virginia, this will be the first work providing similar kinds of information for the entire Confederacy.

Two older but still useful works are George W. Cullum, *Biographical Register of the Officers and Graduates of the U.S. Military Academy* (1868), and Francis B. Heitman, *Historical Register and Dictionary of the United States Army* (1903). Cullum's title defines his work, but Heitman's two volumes are more complex. He presents registers of officers in several categories dating as far back as 1789 and extending through the Spanish-American War. The value of his work as a Civil War reference tool comes mainly from two sections. The first, and more detailed, is an alphabetical listing of all officers commissioned in the regular army prior to 1903, including Civil War officers who served on volunteer staffs or attained the rank of brevet general. The lists provide all known details of their military service, including promotions and units served. A second list, which provides only names and units, identifies all field grade officers of militia and volunteer units during the war. Additional lists related to the war present such nuggets of information as the names of regular army officers killed, wounded, or captured in action; captains of light artillery batteries; and officers who left U.S. service to join the Confederacy.

Several of the reference works already noted include wartime casualties, but two standard compendiums provide detailed statistical summaries. The older, and less reliable, study, dealing primarily with Union casualties, is William F. Fox, *Regimental Losses in the American Civil War, 1861–1865* (1889). Fox's work is impressive, and it includes much more than just numbers of dead, wounded, and missing. Fox devotes individual chapters to maximum casualties sustained by individual regiments; comparison of casualties to those of European armies; casualties suffered by generals, surgeons, and chaplains; casualties suffered by black regiments; sketches of army corps, famous divisions and brigades, and 300 selected "fighting" regiments; enlistment figures and aggregate deaths by state; and a brief chapter on Confederate losses. Included, also, are summaries of losses in both the Union and Confederate navies.

Yet Fox's statistics, compiled from regimental muster rolls and records of state adjutant generals' offices before completion of the *Official Records,* have been questioned over the years, and most scholars consider Thomas L. Livermore, *Numbers and Losses in the Civil War in America, 1861–65* (1900), to be more authoritative. Livermore addresses the question of both Union and Confederate statistics and relies primarily on the *Official Records.* While not nearly so detailed as Fox (he makes no attempt to suggest losses for individual units), Livermore does discuss Fox's statistics and tells specifically where and why he disagrees with them. He also reevaluates total numbers of men under arms in the two armies, terms of enlistment, and the number of men engaged in principal battles.

ALMANACS

Another essential tool for the Civil War researcher is a good almanac. Three good ones are available, but E. B. Long and Barbara Long, *The Civil War Day by Day: An Almanac, 1861–1865* (1971) is the most authoritative. Long and Long recapitulate the main military, political, and diplomatic activities for nearly every day of the war years, although military events—everything from major campaigns to scouts and skirmishes—clearly dominate. They begin with Abraham Lincoln's election as president on November 6, 1860, and conclude on August 20, 1866, when the rebellion was declared officially at an end in Texas. They do not try to record every day in 1860, and entries after May 1865 are even more selective. But from January 1861 until the latter date, they omit very few days. An extensive index makes it easy to locate the date of virtually every event. Adding to the volume's usefulness are a number of appendixes that provide handy statistical references for the United States in 1860 (including population and the economy), the size and composition of the armies, casualties (compared to all other American wars), desertion, prisons, navies and the blockade, and the cost of the war. Eight maps are included, although more would be useful. E. B. Long, who served as director of research for Bruce Catton's *Centennial History of the Civil War* (1961–1965), also includes the complete bibliography for that three-volume work.

John S. Bowman, *The Civil War Almanac* (1982), is another worthwhile tool, although not as comprehensive as Long and Long for the war years. Bowman divides his work into four parts. The first, and most valuable, part, accounting for nearly three-fourths of the whole, is a wartime chronology that begins in January 1861 and runs through May 1865. Bowman goes back much further in time than do the Longs in dealing with the causes of the war, specifically, to August 1619 and the arrival of the first African servants at Jamestown. He then gives selected dates and events from that point through 1860. The postwar chronology goes to April 1877 and lists, after the fashion of the prewar years, pivotal dates and events during Reconstruction. Part II offers an essay, with photographs, on the weapons of the war. Pistols and revolvers, rifles and muskets, "machine guns" and artillery, all receive their due. Part III describes the evolution of naval operations during the war, and Part IV offers biographical sketches of some 130 personalities in the war, mostly politicians and military figures.

The most recent entry in this category is Robert E. Denney, *The Civil War Years: A Day by Day Chronicle of the Life of a Nation* (1992). Denney's work is similar to *The Civil War Day by Day* in its chronological scope, which runs from January 1861 through May 1865, with scattered dates through April 1866. However, Denney is not as inclusive in recording events. He lists only the most important military and political events and is not as descriptive as Long for the events he does mention. What sets Denney apart from both Long and from Bowman is his inclusion of excerpts from letters, diaries, and reports for most days of the war. This nice touch provides Denney's almanac with a livelier narrative than the two others. Still, Denney might have improved on this technique by quoting from a wider selection of documents. His prologue provides a concise nine-page overview of the size of the armies, population of the United States in 1860, causes of the war, wartime medical practices, strategy, tactics, logistics, and communications. However, Long's appendixes, covering most of the same topics, are more authoritative. Denney's six maps are all wartime topographical maps that have little practical value in comparison to Long's maps, and he has no bibliography. Denney has also published two similar but more specialized chronicles: *Civil War Prisons and Escapes: A Day-by-Day Chronicle* (1993) and *Civil War Medicine: Care and Comfort of the Wounded* (1994).

One specialized chronology is also worth mentioning. *Civil War Naval Chronology, 1861–1865* (1971), compiled by the Naval History Division of the Navy Department, provides the most complete survey of naval operations. It runs from November 1860 through December 1865, with the same concentration on the period of active military operations as Long and as Bowman. It contains, in addition, a wonderful array of information about the wartime navies. An introductory essay recapitulates the role of the naval operations in the war. A number of appendixes provide essays and statistics on a wide range of subjects, including the U.S. Navy's defense of Washington, D.C., Lincoln's relations with the Navy Department, blockade runners, ships that have been salvaged or memorialized, a description of the major classes and types of ships in the Confederate navy, lists of the privateers commissioned by the Confederate States, the fate of ships in the Confederate river defense fleet, vessels assigned to the Texas Marine Department, and vessels assigned to the Confederate stone fleet. Also of interest are the journal of a marine private kept during David Farragut's operations at and around Mobile (March–August 1864), the memoir of a naval engineer concerning the attack on Mobile Bay, numerous photographs and illustrations, and samples of naval sheet music.

BATTLEFIELD GUIDES

Most scholars and enthusiasts of the Civil War enjoy visiting sites associated with the war, particularly the battlefields. Three guides are particularly useful for this purpose. The oldest and still most complete guide is Alice Cromie, *A Tour Guide to the Civil War* (1990). Cromie lists all known places of interest associated with the war in forty-eight states and the District of Columbia. A street address or highway location accompanies a brief description of the site and its importance for the war. Besides battlefields, Cromie identifies museums, monuments, homes, plantations, cemeteries, parks, forts, arsenals, camps, prisons, legislative and government buildings, historical societies, and similar points.

A handy guide designed exclusively for battlefield visits is Roger W. Hicks and Frances E. Schultz, *Battlefields of the Civil War* (1989). The authors provide brief summaries, maps, and photographs for eighteen key battles and campaigns, from First Manassas to Petersburg. Nine of the sites are in Virginia, four in Tennessee, and none in the trans-Mississippi. Each battlefield chapter discusses the composition and strength of the opposing armies, the terrain, tactical actions, and the strategic role of the battle in the wider war. References to relevant portions of the *Official Records* and *Battles and Leaders of the Civil War* are given, as well as useful U.S. Geological Survey maps. In addition, the battlefield chapters are divided by succinct reviews of such useful subjects as the causes of the war, a chronology of the war, military organization, uniforms, weapons, artillery, signalling, slavery, photography, intelligence, medicine, monuments, naval operations, transportation, rations, atrocities, living history, and the role of women.

Also useful is Frances H. Kennedy, ed., *The Civil War Battlefield Guide* (1990). Forty-two experts on the war provide good strategic and tactical views of sixty-one important military actions in twelve states, from Fort Sumter to Appomattox. Also included are brief chapters on wartime cartography, battlefield preservation, the legacy of the war, the military "staff ride," and the role of slavery in the war. This volume also has a complete list of surviving Civil War battlefields, as well as a list of twenty-two sites that have been all but lost. The battle summaries are more authoritative than those in Hicks and Schultz's book, but the tactical maps are poor.

Finally, stretching the definition of a reference work but nonetheless valuable as a resource for the war's major campaigns and battles is James M. McPherson, ed., *Battle Chronicles of the Civil War* (1989). This six-volume set provides nearly 100 profusely illustrated essays on important military actions by forty authors. All previously published in *Civil War Times, Illustrated,* this anthology is intended for a wide audience. Undergraduate students may find it most useful, but anyone seeking good overviews of the major military actions of the war, complete with excellent maps and helpful illustrations and photographs, will prize this collection. Some of the articles, originally published in the 1960s and 1970s, are dated, but the entire work provides a handy tool for readers desiring more than an encyclopedia sketch. Volumes 1 through 5, each devoted to a separate year of the war, form the meat of the collection, the essays beginning with Fort Sumter and ending with the assassination of Lincoln. Volume 6 provides biographical essays on Abraham Lincoln, Jefferson Davis, Ulysses S. Grant, William T. Sherman, Robert E. Lee, and Thomas J. Jackson. A comprehensive index is included in volume 6.

BIBLIOGRAPHY

Alexander, Thomas B., and Richard E. Beringer. *The Anatomy of the Confederate Congress: A Study of the Influences of Member Characteristics on Legislative Voting Behavior, 1861–1865.* Nashville, TN: Vanderbilt University Press, 1971.

Amann, William F. *Personnel of the Civil War.* 2 vols. New York: Thomas Yoseloff, 1961.

Boatner, Mark Mayo III. *The Civil War Dictionary.* Rev. ed. New York: David M. McKay, 1988.

Bowman, John S. *The Civil War Almanac.* New York: Facts on File, 1982.

Cromie, Alice H. *A Tour Guide to the Civil War.* 3d ed., rev. Nashville, TN: Rutledge Hill Press, 1990.

Cullum, George W. *Biographical Register of the Officers and Graduates of the U.S. Military Academy.* 2 vols. New York: D. Van Nostrand, 1868.

Current, Richard N., et al., eds. *Encyclopedia of the Confederacy*. 4 vols. New York: Simon & Schuster, 1993.

Davis, William C., ed. *The Confederate General*. 6 vols. New York: National Historical Society, 1991.

Denney, Robert E. *Civil War Medicine: Care and Comfort of the Wounded*. New York: Sterling, 1994.

———. *Civil War Prisons and Escapes: A Day by Day Chronicle*. New York: Sterling, 1993.

———. *The Civil War Years: A Day by Day Chronicle of the Life of a Nation*. New York: Sterling, 1992.

Dyer, Frederick H. *A Compendium of the War of the Rebellion*. New ed. 2 vols. New York: Thomas Yoseloff, 1959.

Faust, Patricia L., ed. *Historical Times Illustrated Encyclopedia of the Civil War*. New York: Harper & Row, 1986.

Fox, William F. *Regimental Losses in the American Civil War, 1861–1865*. Albany, NY: Albany Publishing, 1889.

Heitman, Francis B. *Historical Register and Dictionary of the United States Army*. 2 vols. Washington, D.C.: Government Printing Office, 1903.

Hicks, Roger W., and Frances E. Schultz. *Battlefields of the Civil War*. Topsfield, MA: Salem House, 1989.

Hubbell, John T., and James W. Geary, eds. *Biographical Dictionary of the Union: Northern Leaders of the Civil War*. Westport, CT: Greenwood Press, 1995.

Kennedy, Frances H., ed. *The Civil War Battlefield Guide*. Boston: Houghton Mifflin, 1990.

Krick, Robert K. *Lee's Colonels: A Biographical Register of the Field Officers of the Army of Northern Virginia*. 4th ed., rev. Dayton, OH: Morningside Bookstore, 1992.

Livermore, Thomas L. *Numbers and Losses in the Civil War in America, 1861–65*. Boston: Houghton, Mifflin, 1900.

Long, E. B., and Barbara Long. *The Civil War Day by Day: An Almanac, 1861–1865*. Garden City, NY: Doubleday, 1971.

McPherson, James M., ed. *Battle Chronicles of the Civil War*. 6 vols. New York: Macmillan, 1989.

Roller, David C., and Robert W. Twyman, eds. *Encyclopedia of Southern History*. Baton Rouge: Louisiana State University Press, 1979.

Sifakis, Stewart. *Compendium of the Confederate Armies*. 5 vols. New York: Facts on File, 1992.

———. *Who Was Who in the Civil War*. New York: Facts on File, 1988.

———. *Who Was Who in the Confederacy*. New York: Facts on File, 1989.

U.S. Department of the Navy. *Civil War Naval Chronology, 1861–1865*. Washington, D.C.: Government Printing Office, 1971.

Wakelyn, Jon L. *Biographical Dictionary of the Confederacy*. Westport, CT: Greenwood Press, 1977.

Warner, Ezra J. *Generals in Blue: Lives of the Union Commanders*. Baton Rouge: Louisiana State University Press, 1964.

———. *Generals in Gray: Lives of the Confederate Commanders*. Baton Rouge: Louisiana State University Press, 1959.

Warner, Ezra J., and W. Buck Yearns. *Biographical Register of the Confederate Congress.* Baton Rouge: Louisiana State University Press, 1975.
Welcher, Frank J. *The Union Army, 1861–1865: Organization and Operations.* Vol. 1: *The Eastern Theater.* Bloomington: Indiana University Press, 1989.
————. *The Union Army, 1861–1865: Organization and Operations.* Vol. 2: *The Western Theater.* Bloomington: Indiana University Press, 1993.
Wilson, Charles Reagan, and William Ferris, eds. *Encyclopedia of Southern Culture.* Chapel Hill: University of North Carolina Press, 1989.

3

Bibliographies

T. Michael Parrish

At first glance, the universe of Civil War bibliographies of printed works and guides to manuscripts and other sources seems rich and rational, but in many ways it remains incomplete and disjointed. For the general reader and beginning student, several outstanding reference works are available, yet for the serious scholar requiring complete coverage on any given topic, research often proves daunting, tedious, and frustrating. Until the United States Civil War Center at Louisiana State University accomplishes its goal of establishing a comprehensive interdisciplinary bibliographical database describing all printed items, manuscripts, and other relevant sources on the Civil War, the task of locating every relevant item will remain an inexact science. Fortunately for most researchers, as Arthur W. Bergeron, Jr. has observed, ''Discovering that nugget of golden information in some obscure source gives meaning to the phrase *the thrill of the hunt.*''

A first step for asserting order to the confusion can be accomplished by consulting the best general guide to reference books on all aspects of American history, Francis Paul Prucha's *Handbook for Research in American History* (Lincoln: University of Nebraska Press, 1987; rev. ed. 1994). In addition, recently published reference works on American history are evaluated annually in the March issue of *Journal of American History* under the heading ''Research and Reference Tools: Reviews.'' Equally valuable is Carol Bondus Fitzgerald's *American History: A Bibliographical Review* (Westport, CT: Meckler Publishing Co., 1985–1990), an annual publication offering detailed reviews. A comprehensive source for identifying the many reference books published in the United States in all fields of research each year is Bohdan S. Wynar, *American Refer-*

ence Books Annual (Littleton, CO: Libraries Unlimited, 1970–). Also important is *Bibliography Index: A Cumulative Bibliography of Bibliographies* (New York: H. W. Wilson Co., 1945–).

The single most useful bibliography on the Civil War remains *Civil War Books: A Critical Bibliography* (1967, 1969), a two-volume masterpiece by Allan Nevins, James I. Robertson, Jr., and Bell I. Wiley. More than six thousand books, published from the 1860s to the 1960s, are listed in fifteen chapters according to major subjects. Each chapter was compiled by a leading scholar who annotated every entry with a pithy statement briefly evaluating each book's historical worth. Coverage is extremely broad, proof of the editors' intention to include the most prominent books in each subject catagory. There is also a good index.

For the North, the starting point is Eugene C. Murdock's *The Civil War in the North* (1987). Like the Nevins, Robertson, and Wiley bibliography, this book is broadly selective in its coverage, including the most useful books and articles, along with a good index. Divided by subject, it devotes considerable space to military matters as well as to political and social topics.

Part of a series on American presidents, Frank J. Williams's two-volume *Abraham Lincoln: An Annotated Bibliography,* although not yet published, promises pure excellence in selecting and describing the 5,000 most significant books, pamphlets, and articles from the gargantuan, ever-growing field of Lincoln literature.

There is no work for the South comparable to either Murdock's or Williams's. John H. Wright's two-volume *Compendium of the Confederacy* (1989) makes a gallant attempt to be utterly definitive, providing a straight alphabetical list by author of a tremendous mass of books, pamphlets, and articles on all aspects of Confederate history. Although many rare and otherwise unknown titles are evident, a weak index limits the work's convenience and usefulness.

Garold L. Cole's *Civil War Eyewitnesses* (1988) describes almost 1,400 personal accounts by soldiers, civilians, and foreign travelers, divided into Northern and Southern catagories, including books as well as articles, with factual annotations and a useful index. Although restricted to titles published from 1955 to 1986, many of the books listed are reprints and modern scholarly editions of older and enduring works.

Especially effective in accomplishing its purpose is E. Merton Coulter's superb *Travels in the Confederate States* (1948), an annotated bibliography of 492 books by both Southern and Northern soldiers and civilians whom Coulter considered more interesting for their comments on the social and political conditions of the Confederacy than for their discussions of military matters. Although Coulter excluded and overlooked hundreds of worthy titles, this work stands the test of time as a model of bibliographical scholarship, despite a strong tinge of pro-Confederate bias laced throughout his excellent critical annotations.

Less a bibliography than a narrative guide, Douglas Southall Freeman's *The South to Posterity* (1939) is still the best survey for the student interested in discovering some of the classic books on a variety of Confederate topics. Equally readable, but couched more as literary criticism, are Edmund Wilson's *Patriotic Gore* (1962) and Daniel Aaron's *The Unwritten War* (1973). Both Wilson and Aaron evaluated what they considered the best published memoirs and personal accounts of politicians, civilians, and soldiers from the North and South.

Richard Barksdale Harwell's *In Tall Cotton* (1978) is an annotated selective list of two hundred outstanding books on the Confederacy. In a class by itself, *The Confederate Image* (1987), by Mark Neely, Jr., Harold Holzer, and Gabor S. Boritt, is a fine scholarly study of the artistic prints produced from the Civil War period up to the twentieth century, all for the greater glory of the Lost Cause.

Confederate Imprints (1987) by T. Michael Parrish and Robert M. Willingham, Jr., is a bibliography and union list of nearly 9,500 books, pamphlets, broadsides, maps, sheet music, and prints, including government reports and military orders and circulars, as well as commercial and privately produced publications (excluding magazines and newspapers). No comparable bibliography for the North exists. Such a work would involve several times the number of imprints extant for the South.

Strictly military in content, but including coverage of both the North and the South, is the indispensable four-volume *Military Bibliography of the Civil War* (1961–1972, 1987), edited by Charles E. Dornbusch, with assistance in completing the supplement (volume 4) from Robert K. Krick, who also compiled a name index for the entire set. Listing books and articles alike, the volumes are divided into sections by state for unit histories and soldiers' memoirs. Campaign narratives, autobiographical and biographical accounts, and titles on general and specific subjects are listed in corresponding sections. This sophisticated and comprehensive reference work is essential for research on any aspect of Civil War military history.

Devoted to the North's military effort, *The Union Bookshelf* (1982), by Michael A. Mullins and Rowena A. Reed, provides a selective list of the best books, with expert annotations included. Strangely, no comparable work on Confederate military titles exists.

Each of the volumes in an ongoing series titled *A Guide to the Sources of United States Military History* (1975, 1981, 1986, 1993) features a selective list, "The Mexican and Civil War," compiled by Grady McWhiney, whose expertise fits him well for the task of identifying, and highlighting with prefatory commentary, the most significant books published during the preceding several years.

A few special military subjects have received particularly intense treatment. *The Gettysburg Campaign* (1982), by Richard Sauers, is probably as close to a definitive work as a bibliographer, acting alone, can accomplish. Virtually every book, pamphlet, article, and newspaper account published on the great battle from the day it ended in 1863 is listed by author, along with some brief annotations, rounded off with a good index.

Equally impressive in their results are Thomas Moebs's *Confederate States Navy Research Guide* (1991) and his *Black Soldiers, Black Sailors, Black Ink* (1994), both of which reflect the author's tenacity in identifying and describing thousands of books and articles, many of them highly obscure or rare, along with a host of vital facts. Both works boast excellent indexes. A more comprehensive bibliography on African Americans is John David Smith's *Black Slavery in the Americas* (1983), which includes many books and articles on Southern bondsmen and emancipation during the Civil War.

Among several useful works on maps, Richard W. Stephenson's *Civil War Maps* (1989) is by far the most impressive. Handsomely illustrated and rich in technical details and factual annotations, it is based on the extremely large and important collection of maps in the Library of Congress.

Just as with printed materials, holdings of manuscript collections at any library are described most fully by their card catalogs and other finding aids on premises. A fairly good general guide to all categories of manuscript holdings throughout the United States is Lee Ash and William G. Miller's *Subject Collections* (1993). Much more detailed and comprehensive is the *National Union Catalogue of Manuscript Collections,* published annually since 1959 by the Library of Congress. Similarly, the On-line Catalog of the Library of Congress computer database, available for searching at all major libraries, promises to become the quickest and most thorough reference source for manuscripts and books alike.

A large quantity of Civil War manuscripts at dozens of major libraries across the country can be identified conveniently by first consulting two general works: *A Guide to Federal Archives Relating to the Civil War* (1962), by Kenneth W. Munden and Henry P. Beers, and *A Guide to the Archives of the Government of the Confederate States of America* (1968), by Henry P. Beers. Both guides are especially well indexed.

Although limited to brief summary listings of the Library of Congress's numerous collections on the Civil War, several of them massive in size, *Civil War Manuscripts* (1986), by John R. Sellers, is a highly useful guide with a thorough index.

Other guides to outstanding manuscript collections include those by Susan Blosser and Clyde Wilson, Jr. (University of North Carolina); Richard Davis and Linda Miller (Duke University); Waverly Winfrey (Virginia Historical Society); Allen Stokes (University of South Carolina); David Moltke-Hansen and Sallie Doscher (South Carolina Historical Society); Connie Griffth (Tulane University); Chester Kielman (University of Texas); Kermit Pike (Western Reserve Historical Society); Arlene Shy (University of Michigan); William Burton (libraries throughout Illinois); Ann Turner (libraries throughout Indiana); and the Huntington Library guide to American historical manuscripts.

BIBLIOGRAPHY

Aaron, Daniel. *The Unwritten War: American Writers and the Civil War*. 1973. Reprint, Madison: University of Wisconsin Press, 1987.

Aimone, Alan C. *Bibliography of Military History: A Selected and Annotated History of Reference Sources*. West Point, NY: United States Military Academy, 1978.

————. *A User's Guide to the Official Records of the American Civil War*. Shippensburg, PA: White Mane Publishing Company, 1993.

Allard, Dean C., Martha L. Crawley, and Mary W. Edmison. *U.S. Naval History Sources in the United States*. Washington, DC: Department of the Navy, Naval History Division, 1976.

Allen, Albert H. *Arkansas Imprints, 1821–1876*. New York: R. R. Bowker, 1947.

Allen, Ronald R. *Tennessee Imprints, 1791–1875*. Knoxville: Privately printed, 1987.

America: History and Life: A Guide to Periodical Literature. Santa Barbara: ABC-Clio Press, 1965–.

American Antiquarian Society. *Catalogue of the Manuscript Collections of the American Antiquarian Society*. 4 vols. Boston: G. K. Hall, 1979.

American Historical Review. Scholarly journal of the American Historical Association, with a regular section listing "Recently Published Articles" until 1976, when it became a separate publication issued three times a year.

Andrews, J. Cutler. *The North Reports the Civil War*. Pittsburgh: University of Pittsburgh Press, 1955.

————. *The South Reports the Civil War*. Princeton, NJ: Princeton University Press, 1970.

Angle, Paul M. *A Shelf of Lincoln Books: A Critical, Selective Bibliography of Lincolniana*. 1946. Reprint, Westport, CT: Greenwood Press, 1972.

Arnold, Louise. *The Era of the Civil War, 1820–1876. Special Bibliography 11*. Carlisle Barracks, PA: U.S. Army Military History Institute, 1982.

Arskey, Laura, Nancy Pries, and Marcia Reed. *American Diaries: An Annotated Bibliography of Published American Diaries and Journals*. Vol. 2: *Diaries Written from 1845 to 1980*. Detroit: Gale Research Company, 1987.

Ash, Lee, and William G. Miller. *Subject Collections: A Guide to Special Book Collections and Subject Emphases as Reported by University, College, Public, and Special Libraries and Museums in the United States and Canada*. 2 vols. New Providence, NJ: R. R. Bowker, 1993.

Ashby, Charlotte M., and William J. Heymen. *A Guide to Civil War Maps in the National Archives*. Washington, DC: National Archives, 1986.

Atkinson, Edith T., comp. *Louisiana in the Civil War: A Bibliography*. Baton Rouge: Louisiana State Library, 1961.

Baggett, James A. *The Civil War and Reconstruction: A Dissertation Bibliography*. Ann Arbor, MI: University Microfilms, 1979.

Barr, Alwyn. "Texas Civil War Historiography." *Texas Libraries* 26 (Winter 1964): 160–169. Revised, with new title, "An Essay on Texas Civil War Historiography." In *Texas: The Dark Corner of the Confederacy*, 3d ed., Edited by B. P. Gallaway. Lincoln, NE: University of Nebraska Press, 1994.

Barrett, John G. "The Confederate States of America at War on Land and at Sea." In *Writing Southern History: Essays in Historiography in Honor of Fletcher M.*

Green. Edited by Arthur S. Link and Rembert W. Patrick. Baton Rouge: Louisiana State University Press, 1965.

Bartlett, John R. *The Literature of the Rebellion: A Catalogue of the Books and Pamphlets Relating to the Civil War.* 1866. Reprint, Westport, CT: Negro Universities Press, 1970.

Barton, Michael. "A Selected Bibliography of Civil War Soldiers' Diaries." *Bulletin of Bibliography* 35 (January–March 1978): 19–29.

Beers, Henry P. *Guide to the Archives of the Government of the Confederate States of America.* Washington, DC: National Archives, 1968. Reprint, titled *The Confederacy: A Guide to the Archives . . .* Washington, DC: National Archives, 1986.

Bergeron, Arthur W., Jr. *Civil War Records at the Louisiana State Archives.* Baton Rouge: Le Comité des Archives de la Louisiane, n.d.

———. *Guide to Louisiana Confederate Military Units, 1861–1865.* Baton Rouge: Louisiana State University Press, 1989.

Bethel, Elizabeth. *Preliminary Inventory of the War Department Collection of Confederate Records [Record Group 109 in the National Archives].* Washington, DC: National Archives, 1957.

Black, Patti Carr, and Maxyne Madden Grimes. *Guide to Civil War Source Material in the Mississippi Department of Archives and History.* Jackson: Department of Archives and History, 1962.

Blosser, Susan Sokol, and Clyde N. Wilson, Jr. *The Southern Historical Collection: A Guide to Manuscripts.* Chapel Hill: University of North Carolina Press, 1970; Everard H. Smith III, *A Supplementary Guide to Manuscripts, 1970–1975.* Chapel Hill: University of North Carolina Press, 1976.

Bosse, David. *Civil War Newspaper Maps: A Historical Atlas.* Baltimore: Johns Hopkins University Press, 1993.

———. *Civil War Newspaper Maps of the Northern Daily Press: A Cartobibliography.* Westport, CT: Greenwood Press, 1993.

Bradley, Isaac Samuel. *A Bibliography of Wisconsin's Participation in the War between the States, Based upon Material Contained in the Wisconsin Historical Library.* Madison: Wisconsin History Commission, 1911.

Breton, Arthur J. *A Guide to the Manuscript Collections of the New York Historical Society.* 2 vols. Westport, CT: Greenwood Press, 1972.

Broadfoot, Thomas W. *Civil War Books: A Priced Checklist, with Advice.* 3d ed. Wilmington, NC: Broadfoot, 1990.

Brown, Ida C. *Michigan Men in the Civil War: A Descriptive Bibliography of Their Letters and Diaries.* Ann Arbor: University of Michigan, 1977.

Burton, William L. *Descriptive Bibliography of Civil War Manuscripts in Illinois.* Evanston, IL: Northwestern University Press, 1966.

Byne, Richard H. *Confederate States of America Philatelic Subject Index and Bibliography, 1862–1984.* Louisville, KY: Leonard H. Hartmann, 1986.

Cain, Barbara T., Ellen Z. McGrew, and Charles E. Morris. *Guide to Private Manuscript Collections in the North Carolina State Archives.* Raleigh, NC: North Carolina Department of Cultural Resources, Division of Archives and History, 1981.

Civil War History: A Journal of the Middle Period. Quarterly journal first published in 1955 by the State University of Iowa, later by the University of Iowa, and now by the Kent State University Press, including, until 1978, regular lists of articles recently published in periodicals.

Clizbee, Azalea. *Catalogue of the Wymberley Jones De Renne Georgia Library, 1700–1929.* 3 vols. Wormsloe, GA: Privately printed, 1931. [Collection at the University of Georgia]

Cole, Garold L. *Civil War Eyewitnesses: An Annotated Bibliography of Books and Articles, 1955–1986.* Columbia, SC: University of South Carolina Press, 1988.

Coleman, J. Winston, Jr. *A Bibliography of Kentucky History.* Lexington: University of Kentucky Press, 1949.

Coletta, Paolo E. *A Bibliography of American Naval History.* Annapolis, MD: Naval Institute Press, 1981.

Cooling, Benjamin F. *The Era of the Civil War, 1820–1876.* Carlisle Barracks, PA: Army Military History Research Collection, 1974.

Coulter, E. Merton. *Travels in the Confederate States: A Bibliography.* 1948. Reprint, Wendell, NC: Broadfoot Publishing Co., 1981; Baton Rouge: Louisiana State University Press, 1995.

Crozier, Emmet. *Yankee Reporters, 1861–1865.* New York: Oxford University Press, 1956.

Cunliffe, William H., et al. *A Guide to Civil War Maps in the National Archives.* Washington, DC: National Archives, 1986.

Davis, Lenwood G., and George H. Hill. *Blacks in the American Armed Forces, 1776–1983: A Bibliography.* Westport, CT: Greenwood Press, 1985.

Davis, Richard C., and Linda Angle Miller. *Guide to the Catalogued Collections in the Manuscript Department of the William R. Perkins Library, Duke University.* Santa Barbara, CA: Clio Books, 1980.

Decker, Eugene Donald. *A Selected, Annotated Bibliography of Sources in the Kansas State Historical Society Pertaining to Kansas in the Civil War.* Emporia, KS: Kansas State Historical Society, 1961.

Dissertation Abstracts International. Ann Arbor, MI: University Microfilms, 1938–.

Donald, David. *The Nation in Crisis, 1861–1877.* New York: Appleton-Century-Crofts, 1969.

Dornbusch, Charles E., and Robert K. Krick. *Military Bibliography of the Civil War.* 4 vols. New York: New York Public Library, 1961–1972; and Dayton, Ohio: Morningside, 1987.

Dunlap, Lloyd A., and Arthur G. Burton. *Abraham Lincoln: An Exhibition at the Library of Congress in Honor of the 150th Anniversary of His Birth.* Washington, DC: Library of Congress, 1959.

———. *The American Civil War: A Centennial Exhibition.* Washington, DC: Library of Congress, 1961.

Eberstadt, Charles. *Lincoln's Emancipation Proclamation.* New York: Duschnes Crawford, 1950.

Eicher, David. *The Civil War in Books: An Annotated Bibliography.* Urbana: University of Illinois Press, forthcoming.

Emory University. Robert W. Woodruff Library. *Manuscript Sources for Civil War History: A Descriptive List of Holdings in the Special Collections Department.* Atlanta, GA: Robert W. Woodruff Library, 1990.

English, Thomas H. *Roads to Research: Distinguished Library Collections of the Southeast.* Athens: University of Georgia Press, 1968.

Fishwick, Marshall W., and William H. Hollis. *Preliminary Checklist of Writings about*

R. E. Lee. Charlottesville: Bibliographical Society of the University of Virginia, 1951.

Frazier, J. L. "Civil War Bibliography [on Colorado]." *Colorado Magazine* 38 (January 1961): 65–69.

Freidel, Frank, and Richard K. Showman. *Harvard Guide to American History*. Cambridge, MA: Harvard University Press, 1974.

Freeman, Douglas Southall. *A Calendar of Confederate Papers . . . Preliminary Report of the Southern Historical Manuscripts Commission . . .* Richmond, VA: Confederate Museum, 1908.

————. *A Confederate Book Shelf*. Chicago: Abraham Lincoln Bookshop, ca. 1950. Based on Freeman's list in the appendix to *The South to Posterity* (see below), plus a few "Books Added to the Book Shelf."

————. *Lee's Lieutenants: A Study in Command*. 3 vols. New York: Scribner's, 1942–1944.

————. *R. E. Lee*. 4 vols. New York: Scribner's, 1934–1935.

————. *The South to Posterity: An Introduction to the Writing of Confederate History*. 1939. Reprint, Wilmington, NC: Broadfoot, 1983.

Freeman, Frank E. *Microbes and Minie Balls: An Annotated Bibliography of Civil War Medicine*. Cranbury, NJ: Farleigh Dickinson Press, 1993.

Friend, Llerena. "A Tentative Bibliography of Books on Texas and Texans in the Civil War." *Texas Military History* 4 (Fall 1964): 197–211.

Gilbert, Benjamin F. "California and the Civil War: A Bibliographical Essay." *California Historical Society Quarterly* 40 (December 1961): 289–307.

Gottschall, Irwin. *A Bibliography of Maps of Civil War Battlefield Areas*. Washington, D.C.: U.S. Geological Survey, 1962.

Griffith, Connie G. *Inventory of the Louisiana Historical Association [Confederate] Collection on Deposit in the Howard-Tilton Memorial Library, Tulane University, New Orleans*. New Orleans: Tulane University, 1983.

Hamer, Philip M. *A Guide to Archives and Manuscripts in the United States*. New Haven, CT: Yale University Press, 1961.

Harris, Katherine. *Guide to Manuscripts [Iowa State Historical Department]*. Iowa City: State Historical Society Division, 1973.

Hartwig, D. Scott. *The Battle of Antietam and the Maryland Campaign of 1862: A Bibliography*. Westport, CT: Meckler Corporation, 1990.

Harwell, Richard Barksdale. *Confederate Belles-Lettres: A Bibliography and Finding List of Fiction, Poetry, Drama, Songsters, and Miscellaneous Literature Published in the Confederate States of America*. Hattiesburg, MS: Book Farm, 1941.

————. *The Confederate Hundred: A Bibliophilic Selection of Confederate Books*. 1964. Reprint, Wendell, NC: Broadfoot, 1982.

————. *Confederate Music*. Chapel Hill: University of North Carolina Press, 1950.

————. *Cornerstones of Confederate Collecting*. 1953. Reprint, Wendell, NC: Broadfoot, 1982.

————. *In Tall Cotton: The 200 Most Important Confederate Books for the Reader, Researcher, and Collector*. Austin: Jenkins Publishing Co. and Frontier America Corp., 1978.

Hess, James W. *Guide to Manuscripts and Archives in the West Virginia Collection [West Virginia University]*. Morgantown: West Virginia University Library, 1974.

Hill, Gertrude. "The Civil War in the Southwest, 1861–1862: A List of Books, Old and New." *Arizona Quarterly* 18 (Summer 1962): 166–170.

Historic New Orleans Collection, Manuscripts Division. *Papers Relating to the Civil War at the Historic New Orleans Collection.* New Orleans: Historic New Orleans Collection, Manuscripts Division Update, 1985.

Hogan, William Ransom. *Guide to the Manuscript Collections in Louisiana: The Department of Archives, Louisiana State University.* University, LA: Department of Archives, Louisiana State University, 1940.

Hoogerwerf, Frank W. *Confederate Sheet-Music Imprints.* Brooklyn: Institute for Studies in American Music, Conservatory of Music, Brooklyn College of the City University of New York, 1984.

Hummel, Ray O., Jr. *More Virginia Broadsides before 1877.* Richmond: Virginia State Library 1975.

———. *Southeastern Broadsides before 1877.* Richmond: Virginia State Library, 1971.

Huntington Library. *Guide to American Historical Manuscripts in the Huntington Library.* San Marino, CA: Huntington Library, 1979.

Irvine, Dallas D. *Military Operations of the Civil War: A Guide-Index to the Official Records of the Union and Confederate Armies, 1861–1865.* 5 vols. Washington, D.C.: National Archives, 1968–1980.

Jessup, John E., Jr., and Robert W. Coakley. *A Guide to the Study and Use of Military History.* Washington, D.C.: Center of Military History, 1979.

Jones, Lewis P. *Books and Articles on South Carolina History.* 2d ed. Columbia, SC: University of South Carolina Press, 1991.

Jordan, William B., Jr. *Maine in the Civil War: A Bibliographical Guide.* Portland: Maine Historical Society, 1976.

Journal of American History. Quarterly journal published by the Organization of American Historians, each issue including a list of recent articles on American history published in periodicals, as well as recently completed doctoral dissertations.

Journal of Southern History. Quarterly journal published by the Southern Historical Association, the May issue including a list of articles on Southern history published in periodicals during the previous year.

Jumonville, Florence M. *Bibliography of New Orleans Imprints, 1764–1864.* New Orleans: Historic New Orleans Collection, 1989.

Kaplan, Louis. *A Bibliography of American Autobiographies.* Madison: University of Wisconsin Press, 1961.

Kibby, Leo P. *Book Review Reference for a Decade of Civil War Books, 1950–1960.* San Jose, CA: Spartan Bookstore, 1961.

Kielman, Chester V. *The University of Texas Archives: A Guide to the Historical Manuscripts Collections in the University of Texas Library.* Austin: University of Texas Press, 1967.

Kinnell, Susan K. *Military History of the United States: An Annotated Bibliography.* Santa Barbara, CA: ABC-CLIO, 1986. (Abstracts of journal articles published 1974–1985)

Krick, Robert K. *Neale Books: An Annotated Bibliography.* Dayton, OH: Morningside, 1977.

Kuehl, Warren F. *Dissertations in History: An Index to Dissertations Completed in History Departments of United States and Canadian Universities, 1873–1960 [and]*

1961–June 1970 [and] 1970–June 1980. 3 vols. Lexington: University of Kentucky Press, 1965; and Santa Barbara, CA: ABC-CLIO, 1985.

Lambert, William H. *Library of the Late Major William H. Lambert of Philadelphia.* 5 vols. New York: Anderson Galleries, 1914.

Lane, Jack C. *America's Military Past: A Guide to Information Sources.* Detroit: Gale Research Company, 1980.

LeGear, Egli. *The Hotchkiss Map Collection: A List of Manuscript Maps.* Washington, D.C.: Library of Congress, 1951.

Lennon, Donald R. *A Guide to Military Resources in the East Carolina Manuscript Collection.* Greenville, NC: East Carolina University, 1979.

Lentz, Andrea D. *Guide to Manuscripts at the Ohio Historical Society.* Columbus: Ohio Historical Society, 1972.

Library of Congress. *The American Civil War: A Centennial Exhibition.* Washington, D.C.: Library of Congress, 1961.

———. *National Union Catalogue of Manuscript Collections.* Washington, D.C.: Library of Congress, 1959–.

———. *President's Papers Index Series.* 23 vols. Washington, D.C.: Manuscript Division, 1960–1976.

Lincoln Lore. Monthly bulletin containing regular bibliographical listings of books and articles on Abraham Lincoln; published by the Louis A. Warren Lincoln Library and Museum, Fort Wayne, Indiana.

Lively, Robert A. *Fiction Fights the Civil War: An Unfinished Chapter in the Literary History of the American People.* Chapel Hill: University of North Carolina Press, 1957.

Long, E. B., and Barbara Long. *The Civil War Day by Day: An Almanac, 1861–1865.* New York: Doubleday and Co., 1971.

Louisiana Historical Association. *Calendar of the Jefferson Davis Postwar Manuscripts in the Louisiana Historical Collection, Confederate Memorial Hall, New Orleans, Louisiana.* 1943. Reprint, New York: Burt Franklin, 1970. [Collection now at Tulane University]

McCarley, J. Britt. *The Atlanta Campaign: A Civil War Driving Tour of Atlanta-Area Battlefields.* Atlanta: Cherokee Publishing Company, 1989.

McPherson, James M. *Ordeal by Fire: The Civil War and Reconstruction.* 2d ed. New York: McGraw-Hill, 1992.

McWhiney, Grady. "The Mexican War and the Civil War." In *A Guide to the Sources of United States Military History.* 4 vols. Edited by Robin Higham and Donald J. Mrozek. Hamden, CT: Archon Books, 1975, 1981, 1986, 1993.

Massachusetts Historical Society. *Catalogue of Manuscripts of the Massachusetts Historical Society.* 9 vols. Boston: G. K. Hall, 1969, 1980.

Massey, Mary Elizabeth. "The Confederate States of America: The Homefront." In *Writing Southern History: Essays in Historiography in Honor of Fletcher M. Green.* Edited by Arthur S. Link and Rembert W. Patrick. Baton Rouge: Louisiana State University Press, 1965.

Master's Theses in the Arts and Social Sciences. Cedar Falls, IA: Research Publications, 1977–.

Matochik, Michael J. *The Civil War, 1861–1865: The Bibliographical Guide to the Microfiche Collection.* Ann Arbor: University Microfilms, n.d.

Matthews, William. *American Diaries in Manuscript, 1580–1954: A Descriptive Bibliography.* Athens, GA: University of Georgia Press, 1974.

May, George S. *Michigan Civil War History: An Annotated Bibliography.* Detroit: Wayne State University Press, 1961.

Menendez, Albert J. *Civil War Novels: An Annotated Bibliography.* New York: Garland, 1986.

Meneray, Wilbur E. *A Brief Guide to the Manuscripts Section of the Special Collections Division, Tulane University Library.* New Orleans: Tulane University Library, 1977.

Merideth, Lee W. *Civil War Times and Civil War Times, Illustrated 30 Year Comprehensive Index (April 1959–February 1989).* Twentynine Palms, CA: Lee W. Meredith, 1990.

———. *Guide to Civil War Periodicals.* Vol. 1: 1991. Twentynine Palms, CA: Historical Indexes, 1991.

Miami University, Walter Havighurst Special Collections Library. *The Samuel Richey Collection of the Southern Confederacy in the Walter Havighurst Special Collections Library of the Miami University Libraries.* Oxford, OH: Miami University, n.d.

Milhollen, Hirst D., and Donald H. Mugridge. *Civil War Photographs, 1861–1865: A Catalog of Copy Negatives Made from Originals Selected from the Mathew B. Brady Collections.* Washington, D.C.: Library of Congress, 1961.

Moebs, Thomas Truxton. *Black Soldiers, Black Sailors, Black Ink: Research Guide on African-Americans in U.S. Military History, 1526–1900: List of Officers . . . Bibliography . . . Writings of Civilian and Military African-American Authors . . .* 4 vols. Chesapeake Bay and Paris: Moebs Publishing Company, 1994.

———. *Confederate States Navy Research Guide: Confederate Naval Imprints . . . Chronology of Naval Operation and Administration; Marine Corps and Naval Officer Biographies; Description and Service of Vessels' Subject Bibliography.* Williamsburg, VA: Moebs Publishing Company, 1991.

Moltke-Hansen, David, and Sallie Doscher. *South Carolina Historical Society Manuscript Guide.* Charleston: South Carolina Historical Society, 1979.

Monaghan, Jay. *Lincoln Bibliography, 1839–1939.* 2 vols. Springfield: Illinois State Historical Library, 1943–1945.

Moore, C. Moffett. *Nathan Bedford Forrest and the Civil War in Memphis: A Subject Bibliography of Books and Other References.* Memphis: Memphis Public Library, 1961.

Moore, John Hammond. *Research Materials in South Carolina: A Guide.* Columbia: University of South Carolina Press, 1967.

Moss, William. *Confederate Broadside Poems: An Annotated Descriptive Bibliography Based on the Collection of the Z. Smith Reynolds Library of Wake Forest University.* Westport, CT: Meckler, 1988.

Mott, Frank Luther. *A History of American Magazines, 1850–1865.* Cambridge, MA: Harvard University Press, 1938.

Mugridge, Donald H. *The American Civil War: A Selected Reading List.* Washington, DC: Library of Congress, 1960.

———. *The Civil War in Pictures, 1861–1961: A Chronological List of Selected Pictorial Works.* Washington, DC: Library of Congress, 1961.

Mullins, Michael A., and Rowena A. Reed. *The Union Bookshelf: A Selected Civil War Bibliography*. Wendell, NC: Broadfoot, 1982.

Munden, Kenneth W., and Henry Putney Beers. *A Guide to Federal Archives Relating to the Civil War*. 1962. Reprint, *The Union: A Guide to Federal Archives*. Washington, DC: National Archives, 1986.

Murdock, Eugene C. *The Civil War in the North: A Selective Annotated Bibliography*. New York: Garland, 1987.

National Historical Publications and Records Commission. *Directory of Archives and Manuscript Repositories in the United States*. Washington, DC: NHPRC, 1988.

National Inventory of Documentary Sources in the United States. Teaneck, NJ: Chadwyck-Healey, 1983–.

Neagles, James C. *Confederate Research Sources: A Guide to Archive Collections*. Salt Lake City: Ancestry Publishing, 1986.

Neely, Mark E., Jr., Harold Holzer, and Gabor S. Boritt. *The Confederate Image: Prints of the Lost Cause*. Chapel Hill: University of North Carolina Press, 1987.

Nevins, Allan, James I. Robertson, Jr., and Bell I. Wiley. *Civil War Books: A Critical Bibliography*. 2 vols. 1967, 1969. Reprint, Wendell, NC: Broadfoot, 1980, 1984.

New York Public Library. *Dictionary Catalogue [Manuscript Division]*. 2 vols. Boston: G. K. Hall, 1967.

Newman, Ralph G., and E. B. Long. *A Basic Civil War Library: A Bibliographical Essay*. Springfield, IL: Civil War Centennial Commission, 1964.

Nicholson, John P. *Catalogue of the Library of Brevet Lieutenant-Colonel John Page Nicholson . . . Relating to the War of the Rebellion, 1861–1866*. Philadelphia: Privately printed, 1914. [Collection at the Huntington Library, San Marino, CA]

Norona, Delf, and Charles Shetler. *West Virginia Imprints, 1790–1863*. Moundsville: West Virginia Library Association, 1958.

Norton, Mary Beth. *American Historical Association's Guide to Historical Literature*. 2 vols. New York: Oxford University Press, 1995.

Nute, Grace Lee, et al. *Guide to the Personal Papers in the Manuscript Collections of the Minnesota Historical Society [and] Manuscript Collections*. 3 vols. St. Paul: Minnesota Historical Society, 1935, 1955, 1977.

O'Quinlivan, Michael, and Rowland P. Gill. *An Annotated Bibliography of the United States Marines in the Civil War*. Washington, DC: U.S. Department of the Navy, 1968.

O'Reilly, Noel, David Bosse, and Robert W. Karrow. *Civil War Maps: A Graphic Index to the Atlas to Accompany the Official Records of the Union and Confederate Armies*. Chicago: Newberry Library, 1987.

Pamphlets in American History: A Bibliographic Guide to the Microform Collections. Ann Arbor: University Microfilms International Research Collections, forthcoming.

Parish, Peter J. *The American Civil War*. New York: Holmes & Meier, 1975.

Parrish, T. Michael. *Civil War Texana: An Annotated Bibliography for Book Collectors and Researchers*. Austin: Book Club of Texas and Michael D. Heaston, Rare Books and Manuscripts, 1995.

———. "The R. E. Lee 200: An Annotated Bibliography of Essential Books on Lee's Military Career." In *R. E. Lee, the Soldier*. Edited by Gary W. Gallagher. Lincoln: University of Nebraska Press, 1995.

———. *Women of the Civil War Era, 1845–1880: A Comprehensive Bibliography*. An ongoing project sponsored by the U.S. Civil War Center, Louisiana State University.

Parrish, T. Michael, and Robert M. Willingham, Jr. *Confederate Imprints: A Bibliography of Southern Publications from Secession to Surrender, Expanding and Revising the Earlier Works of Marjorie Crandall and Richard Harwell.* Austin, TX, and Katonah, NY: Jenkins Publishing Co. and Gary A. Foster, 1987.

Paul, William G. *Wisconsin's Civil War Archives.* Madison: State Historical Society of Wisconsin, 1965.

Pedley, Avril J. M. *The Manuscript Collections of the Maryland Historical Society.* Baltimore: Maryland Historical Society, 1968.

Pike, Kermit J. *A Guide to the Manuscripts and Archives of the Western Reserve Historical Society.* Cleveland: Western Reserve Historical Society, 1972.

Pressly, Thomas J. *Americans Interpret Their Civil War.* 1954. Reprint, New York: Collier Books, 1962.

Rampp, Lary C., and Donald L. Rampp. *The Civil War in the Indian Territory.* Austin, TX: Presidial Press, 1975.

Randall, James G., and David Donald. *The Civil War and Reconstruction.* 2d. ed., rev., with en. bibliography. Boston: Little, Brown, 1969.

Rittenhouse, Jack D. *New Mexico Civil War Bibliography: An Annotated Checklist of Books and Pamphlets.* Houston: Stagecoach Press, 1961.

Robertson, James I., Jr. *Iowa in the Civil War: A Reference Guide.* Iowa City: State Historical Society of Iowa, 1961.

Rudolph, E. L. *Confederate Broadside Verse: A Bibliography and Finding List of Confederate Broadside Ballads and Songs.* New Braunfels, TX: Book Farm, 1950.

Russell, J. Thomas. *Preliminary Guide to the Manuscript Collection of the U.S. Military Academy Library.* West Point, NY: U.S. Military Academy, 1968.

Ryan, Carmelita S. *Preliminary Inventory of the Treasury Department Collection of Confederate Records (Record Group 365 [in the National Archives]).* Washington, D.C.: National Archives, 1967.

Ryan, Daniel J. *The Civil War Literature of Ohio: A Bibliography with Explanatory and Historical Notes.* Cleveland: Burrows Brothers Co., 1911.

Sacconaghi, Charles D. "A Bibliographical Note on the Civil War in the West." *Arizona and the West* 8 (Winter 1966); 349–364.

Sampson, F. A., and W. C. Breckenridge. "Bibliography of Slavery and Civil War in Missouri." *Missouri Historical Review* 2 (April 1908); 233–248.

Sanders, Doug, and Ronald R. Seagrave. *Civil War Books: Confederate and Union [A Price Guide].* Fredericksburg, VA: Sgt. Kirkland's Museum and Historical Society, 1995.

Sauers, Richard A. *The Gettysburg Campaign, June 3–August 1, 1863: A Comprehensive, Selectively Annotated Bibliography.* Westport, CT: Greenwood Press, 1982.

Schatz, Walter. *Directory of Afro-American Resources.* New York: R. R. Bowker, 1970.

Scott, Kim Allen. *Special Collections of the University of Arkansas Libraries: Manuscript Resources for the Civil War.* Fayetteville, AR: Center for Arkansas and Regional Studies and University of Arkansas Libraries, 1990.

Seagrave, Ronald R. *Civil War Autographs and Manuscripts: Prices Current 1994.* Fredericksburg, VA: Sgt. Kirkland's Musuem and Historical Society, 1994.

Sellers, John R. *Civil War Manuscripts: A Guide to Collections in the Manuscript Division of the Library of Congress.* Washington, D.C.: Library of Congress, 1986.

Sherman, Stuart C. *Guide to the Manuscript Collections in the Brown University Library.* Providence, RI: Brown University Library, 1974.

Shetler, Charles. *West Virginia Civil War Literature: An Annotated Bibliography.* Morgantown: West Virginia University Library, 1963.

Shy, Arlene P. *Guide to the Manuscript Collections of the Clements Library [University of Michigan].* Boston: G. K. Hall, 1978.

Sibley, Judith A. *A Preliminary Guide to Nineteenth Century Manuscripts in the U.S. Military Academy Library.* West Point, NY: United States Military Academy, 1990.

Sinclair, Donald A. *A Bibliography: The Civil War and New Jersey.* New Brunswick: Friends of the Rutgers University Library, 1968.

Skemer, Don C., and Robert C. Morris. *Guide to the Manuscript Collections of the New Jersey Historical Society.* Newark: New Jersey Historical Society, 1979.

Smith, Alice E., et al. *Guide to the Manuscript of the Wisconsin Historical Society.* 3 vols. Madison: State Historical Society of Wisconsin, 1944, 1957, 1966.

Smith, David R. *The Monitor and the Merrimac: A Bibliography.* Los Angeles: University of California at Los Angeles Library, 1968.

Smith, John David. *Black Slavery in the Americas: An Interdisciplinary Bibliography, 1865–1980.* 2 vols. Westport, CT: Greenwood Press, 1982.

Smith, Myron J., Jr. *American Civil War Navies: A Bibliography.* Metuchen, NJ: Scarecrow Press, 1972.

Smith, Sam B. *Tennessee History: A Bibliography.* Knoxville: University of Tennessee Press, 1974.

Smithsonian Institution. *Guide to Manuscript Collections in the National Museum of History and Technology.* Washington, D.C.: Smithsonian Institution Press, 1978.

Sommers, Richard J. *Manuscript Holdings of the Military History Research Collection.* Carlisle Barracks, PA: U.S. Army Military History Research Collection, 1972.

Spehr, Paul C. *The Civil War in Motion Pictures: A Bibliography of Films Produced in the United States since 1897.* Washington, D.C.: Library of Congress, 1961.

Stanford University Library. *Catalogued Manuscripts: Department of Special Collections, Manuscript Division.* Stanford, CA: Department of Special Collections, 1973.

Starr, Louis M. *Bohemian Brigade: Civil War Newsmen in Action.* New York: Alfred A. Knopf, 1954.

Stephenson, Richard W. *Civil War Maps: An Annotated List of Maps and Atlases in the Library of Congress.* Washington, D.C.: Library of Congress, 1989.

Stokes, Allen H., Jr. *A Guide to the Manuscript Collections of the South Caroliniana Library, University of South Carolina.* Columbia, SC: University of South Carolina, 1982.

Taylor, Joe Gray. ''The White South from Secession to Redemption.'' In *Interpreting Southern History: Historiographical Essays in Honor of Sanford W. Higginbotham.* Edited by John B. Boles and Evelyn Thomas Nolen. Baton Rouge: Louisiana State University Press, 1987.

Thomas, Emory M. ''Bibliography and Historiography.'' In *Encyclopedia of the Confederacy.* Edited by Richard N. Current. 4 vols. New York: Simon & Schuster, 1993.

———. *The Confederate Nation, 1861–1865.* New York: Harper & Row, 1979.

Thompson, Lawrence S. *The Southern Black, Slave and Free: A Bibliography of Anti-*

and *Pro-Slavery Books and Pamphlets of Social and Economic Conditions in the Southern States from the Beginnings to 1950. Works Available in Microform.* Troy, NY: Whitston Publishing Co., 1970.

Thompson, W. Fletcher. *The Image of War: Pictorial Reporting in the American Civil War.* 1960. Reprint, Baton Rouge: Louisiana State University Press, 1995.

Thornton, Mary Lindsay. *A Bibliography of North Carolina, 1589–1956.* Chapel Hill: University of North Carolina Press, 1958.

Trelease, Allen W. "The Civil War and Reconstruction, 1861–1876." In *Writing North Carolina History.* Edited by Jeffrey J. Crow and Larry E. Tise. Chapel Hill: University of North Carolina Press, 1979.

Tufts College Library. *A Calendar of the Ryder Collection of Confederate Archives at Tufts College Library.* Boston: W.P.A. Historical Records Survey, Massachusetts, 1940.

Turner, Ann. *Guide to Indiana Civil War Manuscripts.* Indianapolis: Indiana Civil War Centennial Commission, 1965.

U.S. Army Military History Institute. *Civil War Campaign and Battle Bibliographies.* Ongoing series available from the Historical Reference Branch, Carlisle Barracks, Carlisle, Pennsylvania 17013–5008.

U.S. Department of Commerce. National Oceanic and Atmosphere Administration. National Ocean Survey. *National Ocean Survey Cartobibliography: Civil War Collection.* Rockville, MD: National Ocean Survey, Physical Science Services Branch, Map Library, 1980.

U.S. National Gallery of Art. *The Civil War: A Centennial Exhibition of Eyewitness Drawings.* Washington, D.C.: National Gallery of Art, 1961.

U.S. Newspaper Program. *United States Newspaper Program National Union List.* Dublin, OH: Online Computer Library Center, 1989

U.S. Superintendent of Documents. *Checklist of United States Public Documents, 1789–1909.* 3d ed. Washington, D.C.: U.S. Government Printing Office, 1911.

University of California. Santa Barbara. Library. *Author-Title Catalog [and] Subject Catalog of the William Wyles Collection.* 5 vols. Westport, CT: Greenwood, 1970.

———. *A Checklist of Manuscripts.* Santa Barbara: Department of Special Collections, 1970.

Virginia Historical Society. *Confederate Engineers' Maps: Jeremy Francis Gilmer Collection.* Richmond: Virginia Historical Society, 1989.

Weisberger, Bernard. *Reporters for the Union.* Boston: Little, Brown, 1953.

Williams, Frank J. *Abraham Lincoln: An Annotated Bibliography.* 2 vols. Westport, CT: Greenwood Press, forthcoming.

Williams, Herman Warner. *The Civil War: The Artists' Record.* Washington, D.C.: Corcoran Gallery of Art, 1961.

Wilson, Edmund. *Patriotic Gore: Studies in the Literature of the American Civil War.* New York: Oxford University Press, 1962.

Winfrey, Waverly K., et al. *Guide to the Manuscript Collections of the Virginia Historical Society.* Richmond: Virginia Historical Society, 1985.

Winkler, Ernest W., and Llerena B. Friend. *Check List of Texas Imprints, 1861–1876.* Austin, TX: Texas State Historical Association, 1963. Includes many Union military imprints not listed in Parrish and Willingham, *Confederate Imprints.*

Wolf, Edwin, II. *American Song Sheets, Slip Ballads, and Poetical Broadsides, 1850–*

1870: A Catalogue of the Collection of the Library Company of Philadelphia.
     Philadelphia: Library Company of Philadelphia, 1963.
Wright, John H. *Compendium of the Confederacy: An Annotated Bibliography; Books,
     Pamphlets, Serials.* 2 vols. Wendell, NC: Broadfoot, 1989.
Writings on American History. Washington, D.C.: American Historical Association,
     1902–1990.

4

Periodical Indexes

Alan C. Aimone

Continued and growing interest in the Civil War has led the American civilian press to give extensive coverage to various aspects of the conflict. America's long-running military periodical *Army and Navy Journal*, currently named *Armed Forces Journal International*, has also dealt with the war. Other magazines came into being as outlets for the reminiscences of veterans, and interest did not flag after the veterans were gone. The *Journal of Southern History* began publication in the 1930s, and a renewed interest in Lincoln studies during those years gave birth to the *Lincoln Herald*. *Civil War History* began publication in 1955 and was followed by a series of popular magazines with Civil War themes. Many periodical reference indexes assist the researcher in locating articles from all of these magazines and more, plus specific articles identified as of lasting value in subject bibliographies.

OLD INDEXES

Larger public and academic libraries will have many of the following periodical indexes.

Poole's Index to Periodical Literature, 1800–1906 (1971) covers the longest period and indexes 479 American and English periodicals by subject. *Poole's Index* has citations for the following titles that have Civil War articles:

- *American Historical Register and Monthly Gazetteer of the History, Military and Patriotic Hereditary Societies of the United States,* 1894–1896.
- *Godey's Lady's Book, and Ladies' American Magazine,* 1840–1876.

- *Harper's New Monthly Magazine,* 1850–1950.
- *Historical Magazine, and Notes and Queries Concerning the Antiquities, History, and Biography of America,* 1857–1875.
- *Military Service Institute, Journal of Military Science Institution of the United States,* 1879–1906.
- *Land We Love, a Monthly Magazine Devoted to Literature, Military History, and Agriculture,* 1866–1869.
- *Magazine of American History, with Notes and Queries,* 1877–1893.
- *United States Service Magazine,* 1864–1866.

Combined Retrospective Index Set to Journals in History, 1838–1974 is a useful keyword, subject, and author index to 928 periodicals covering U.S. history, as well as genealogy and biography. A chronological subarrangement is a nice user feature, although shortcomings are found in the cross referencing. Volume 6 is the biography/genealogy volume; volume 7 covers secession, military, political, economic, social, and diplomatic topics for both the Union and the Confederacy. State historical society publications are also indexed.

Writings on American History, 1902–1961 and *Writings on American History: A Subject Bibliography of Articles, 1962–1990,* published by the American Historical Association, is a major bibliographic aid. Published annually, it employs a classified indexing arrangement with author, title, and subject indexes. Regional and chronological subdivisions and content and descriptive notes further assist researchers. Many of the listings derive from the "Recently Published Articles" section of *American Historical Review* (1895–1976) and the separately, triannually published *Recently Published Articles* (1976–1990). The section "United States: Civil War and Reconstruction (1861–1877)" covers older scholarly articles from local, state, and regional historical periodicals.

NEW INDEXES

From 1954 on, *Historical Abstracts* has indexed and abstracted historical periodicals (and books). In 1963, *America: History and Life* began providing concise abstracts of articles from over 2,000 scholarly social science periodicals published in the United States and Canada. It employs a classified order arrangement for its annual author and biographical indexes. The five issues are divided into topical sections, with the first four issues containing abstracts, reviews, and dissertation citations. The fifth issue of each year is the cumulative annual index. Regional and chronological divisions are also used to assist researchers. A CD-ROM version of *America: History and Life,* updated three times yearly, is available for current issues, with editorial plans to add retrospective issues. The index is also available through CompuServe and File 38 of the Dialog Information Services.

There are three journals dealing almost exclusively with Civil War and Southern history, which are thoroughly indexed in *America: History and Life: Civil*

War History examines the war, its causes, and the aftermath in scholarly articles written by history professors and doctoral students. It will appeal to Civil War students as well as to historians of this period. A bibliography about the Civil War era in the United States was featured in June issues until 1974, when it was moved to the December issue. *Civil War History* publishes an annual cumulative index with the last issue of each volume.

The *Journal of Southern History* is the distinguished and learned journal for students of the South's rich history. Each number features four documented articles written by history professors from all over the United States. An annual feature is a bibliography of articles about Southern history. This, together with excellent book reviews, is the premier source for historical study of the South.

The third quarterly of note is *Lincoln Herald,* which has many scholarly and book review articles with either an Abraham Lincoln or Civil War theme. Book reviews and news about current events reflecting information about Abraham Lincoln's life and ideals and/or the Civil War are reported. *Lincoln Herald*'s articles and reviews are particularly useful for Lincolniana book and article collectors.

The *Guide to Civil War Periodicals* (more than 30,000 listings) is exceptionally well prepared and well executed. The work includes a subject index and several comprehensive lists: articles listed by author, book reviews listed by book title, and a chronological list of articles in each numbered edition. The *Guide*'s subject headings are set in boldface type followed by categories and subcategories, such as ''Articles,'' ''Book Reviews,'' and ''Illustrations,'' which relate to the major subject entry. Along with this extensive subject index, articles are listed by author and chronologically arranged by magazine title. This *Guide* lists all people, places, military units, naval vessels, Medal of Honor recipients, and preservation efforts.

Merideth's *Guide to Civil War Periodicals* partially indexes seven popular Civil War magazines:

- *America's Civil War Magazine* (May 1988–November 1990), which features well-illustrated articles about soldiers' daily lives, strategy sessions of commanders, and personality sketches.

- *Civil War* (issues 1–26, 1990), which features popular illustrated articles.

- *Blue and Gray Magazine* (August 1983–December 1990), which focuses on battlefield studies and offers travel information for Civil War site visits.

- *Civil War Times, Illustrated* (March 1989–December 1990), which features lively illustrated articles about battles, political issues, weapons and social life.

- *Gettysburg Magazine* (issues 1–3), which is devoted to Gettysburg battle literature and includes detailed maps.

- *Military History Magazine* (August 1984–December 1990), which has illustrated articles covering Civil War battles, weapons, personality profiles, and historic travel.

• *Morningside Notes,* an occasional publication with scholarly footnoted articles on various Civil War topics.

BIBLIOGRAPHIES WITH INDEXES OF SELECTED ARTICLES

A Guide to the Sources of United States Military History edited by Higham, is a guide with supplementary volumes, which evaluate recent literature. The three areas of interest to Civil War researchers are "The Navy in the Nineteenth Century, 1789–1889," "Science and Technology in the Nineteenth Century," and "The Mexican War and the Civil War." An essay describes recent research in each area suggesting topics for further study and lists primary source material and recently published important articles.

Military History of the United States: An Annotated Bibliography, compiled by Kinnell, is an impressive compilation of significant Civil War articles published before 1985 and were indexed in *America: History and Life.*

Murdock's *The Civil War in the North: A Selective Annotated Bibliography,* is a listing of books and articles describing Union Civil War military, social, and political histories. The bibliography is volume 9 of the Wars of the United States series.

Smith's *American Civil War Navies* is the most complete and best bibliography of Civil War naval and marine corps material yet compiled. It does not annotate but includes books, articles, and government documents.

Wright's *Compendium of the Confederacy* identifies over 20,000 Confederate articles from 200 minor serials published through 1988 that are not widely indexed in other reference books. Civilian, fictional, naval, and political titles are included with military monographs. Entries (topically arranged in alphabetical order by author or title) include place and date of publication, number of pages, and content notes.

REPRINTED SERIALS WITH NEW INDEXES

Confederate Veteran (1893–1932) contains the largest collection of Confederate memoirs, anecdotes, incidents, and personal stories. More Confederate enlisted soldier recollections were published in this magazine than in any other single source. The magazine is also notable for its photographs of veterans and for its recently completed in-depth index of the serial's complete run.

The *Papers of the Military Historical Society of Massachusetts* (1896–1918) are published papers originally read before the society by field grade officers, all of whom who had participated in Civil War battles. The sometimes opinionated and often controversial papers discuss all land aspects of the Civil War as well as some naval battles. This series of unofficial accounts and observations supplements the *War of the Rebellion: A Compilation of the Official Records of the Union and Confederate Armies* and stands as one of the most comprehensive and literate anthologies for any military event in history.

The recollections of enlisted soldiers and officers often provide different views of the same actions and personalities. *The Military Order of the Loyal Legion of the United States* (1887–1915) is such a series and provides insights into conditions, scenes, attitudes, impressions, and observations not found in *Official Records*. Its three-volume cumulative index provides citations to the best collection of first-hand Union enlisted and officer accounts of battles, leaders, and campaigns.

Southern Bivouac (1882–1887) originated as the publication of historical papers read before the Kentucky branch of the Southern Historical Society; featured are contemporary sketches of soldiers distinguished in the war and articles related to Southern life during the war. The journal has a thorough name and place index.

The *Southern Historical Society Papers* (*SHSP*) (1876–1959) provide a gateway into the Confederate army. They are second only to the *Official Records* in providing primary sources about the Confederacy. No other single source provides such a wide variety of information on Confederate daily life, battles, leaders, and life in the wartime South. Personal recollections by both soldiers and civilians, as well as official battle reports, were published in *SHSP* and provide information not found in the *Official Records*. Some Confederate reports, particularly the Gettysburg reports and correspondence, were published in the *SHSP* but not in the *Official Records*. Every name in the *SHSP* index has been checked for accurate spelling and unit identification. Entries have been organized by subcategories to facilitate research. The index also provides references to geographical and other subjects not found in the War Department's *Official Records*.

Interest in reading about the American Civil War has continued to grow with each new generation. Periodicals on microfilm and in microfiche format preserve original journals and encourage a wider availability for study. The use of CD-ROM technology, still shots, digital interactive vido, laser video disks, optical disks, and electronic publishing will make still more articles available to more researchers. Modern computer technology has allowed the indexing of sources previously not indexed and facilitated accurate reindexing of poorly indexed sources. Key word, name, place, chronological, and military unit terms are used in modern periodical indexes and save researchers much time and frustration. Electronic mail, faxes, interlibrary loans, and overnight mail delivery will accelerate information delivery into the hands of historical researchers. Expanding online access to full text articles from serial publications will continue to improve information access for Civil War researchers and will expand and improve the quantity and quality of Civil War scholarship, not only in America, but worldwide.

BIBLIOGRAPHY

America: History and Life: Article Abstracts and Citations of Reviews and Dissertations Covering the United States and Canada. Vol. 1, July 1964 to date. Quarterly, with annual and five-year cumulations starting in 1964. Santa Barbara, CA: ABC-CLIO.

America's Civil War Magazine. May 1988, vol. 1, no. 1, to date. Bimonthly. Leesburg, VA: Empire Press.

Army and Navy Journal. August 29, 1863–May 6, 1950; to date, name now changed to *Armed Forces Journal International;* rept. edition, University Microfilm Incorporated. Published a cumulative annual index for each volume.

Blue and Gray Magazine. August–September 1983, vol. 1, no. 1, to date. Bimonthly. Columbus, OH: Blue & Gray Enterprises.

Civil War, the Magazine of the Civil War Society (formerly *Virginia Country's Civil War*). 1983, vol. 1, to date. Bimonthly. Berryville, VA: Cool Springs Associates.

Civil War History: A Journal of the Middle Period. March 1995 to date. Quarterly. Kent OH: Kent State University Press.

Civil War Times, Illustrated; A Magazine for Persons Interested in American History, Particularly in the Civil War Period. April 1959 to date. Bimonthly. Harrisburg, PA: Cowles Magazines. *Civil War Times Illustrated Index,* comp. Gary R. Planck and Robert D. Hoffsommer. Gettysburg, PA: Historical Times. 1959 to date. Annual with five-year cumulations. This has been supplanted by *Civil War Times and Civil War Times Illustrated 30 Year Comprehensive Index* (April 1959–February 1989.) Compiled by Lee W. Merideth. Twentynine Palms, CA: Historical Indexes, 1990.

Confederate Veteran: Published Monthly in the Interest of Confederate Veterans and Kindred Topics. 43 vols. include 3 vols. index, 1893–1932, rept.; Wilmington, NC: Broadfoot Publishing Co., 1990.

C.R.I.S.: Combined Retrospective Index Set to Journals in History, 1838–1974. Edited by Annadel N. Wile. 11 vols. Washington, D.C.: Carrollton Press, 1977–1978.

The Gettysburg Magazine: Historical Articles of Lasting Interest. July 1989, no. 1 to date. Irregular. Dayton, OH: Morningside House.

Guide to Civil War Periodicals. Vol. 1, 1991. Compiled by Lee W. Merideth. Twentynine Palms, CA: Historical Indexes, 1991.

Higham, Robin, ed. *A Guide to the Sources of United States Military History.* Hamden, CT: Archon Books, 1975; Supplement 1, edited by Robin Higham and Donald J. Mrozek, 1981; Supplement 2, 1986; Supplement 3, 1993.

Historical Abstracts. 1955 to date. Quarterly, with annual and five-year cumulative indexes. Santa Barbara, CA: ABC-CLIO.

Kinnell, Susan K., ed. *Military History of the United States: An Annotated Bibliography.* Santa Barbara, CA: ABC-CLIO, 1986.

Lincoln Herald: A Magazine of Lincoln and the Civil War (formerly *Mountain Herald* until 1938). 1901 to date. Quarterly. Harrogate, TN: Lincoln Memorial University Press. *Lincoln Herald Analytical Index, 1937–1949.* Compiled by Helen Hart Metz. Harrogate, TN: Lincoln Memorial University Press, 1954. The issues covered begin with October 1937, vol. 40, no. 1, and close with December 1949, vol. 51, no. 4. *Lincoln Herald Index,* vols. 77–81, Spring 1975–Winter 1979.

Compiled by Daniel Scott Hurley. Harrogate, TN: Lincoln Memorial University, 1981.

Military Historical Society of Massachusetts. *Papers of the Military Historical Society of Massachusetts.* 15 vols., 1896–1918. Reprint, Wilmington, NC: Broadfoot Publishing Co., 1990.

Military History Magazine. August 1984, vol. 1, no. 1, to date. Bimonthly. Leesburg, VA: Empire Press.

Military Order of the Loyal Legion of the United States. 69 vols., 1887–1915. Reprint, Wilmington, NC: Broadfoot Publishing Co., 1992–1995. Originally published by the various state commanderies.

Morningside Notes (from the catalog of the Morningside Bookshop). Spring 1982, "Notes 1," to date. Irregular. Dayton, OH: Morningside House.

Murdock, Eugene Converse, ed. *The Civil War in the North: A Selective Annotated Bibliography.* New York: Garland Publishing, 1987.

Poole's Index to Periodical Literature, 1802–1881. Rev. ed. Boston: Houghton, 1891, 2 vols. rept. with supplements. Edited by William Frederick Poole and William I. Fletcher. Rev. ed. rept., 5 vols. Gloucester, MA: Peter Smith, 1958. *Cumulative Author Index for Poole's Index to Periodical Literature, 1800–1906.* Compiled by C. Edward Wall. Ann Arbor, MI: Pierian Press, 1971.

Smith, Myron J., Jr. *American Civil War Navies: A Bibliography. American Naval Bibliography.* Vol. 3. Metuchen, NJ: Scarecrow Press, 1972.

Southern Bivouac: A Monthly Literary and Historical Magazine. 6 vols., 1882–1887. Reprint, Wilmington, NC: Broadfoot Publishing Co., 1994.

Southern Historical Association. *Journal of Southern History.* February 1935 to date. Quarterly. Houston, TX: Southern Historical Association, Rice University. *Journal of Southern History, Index to Volumes XXXI–XL, 1965–1974.* New Orleans, LA: Southern Historical Association, 1976. Covers February 1965–November 1974. Supplements the index to the first twenty volumes, published in 1962, and the index to volumes 12–30, published in 1968.

Southern Historical Society. *The Southern Historical Society Papers.* 55 vols. incl. 3 vols. index. Reprint, Wilmington, NC: Broadfoot Publishing Co., 1990–1991.

Wright, John H., comp. *Compendium of the Confederacy: An Annotated Bibliography, Books—Pamphlets—Serials.* 2 vols. Wilmington, NC: Broadfoot Publishing Co., 1989.

Writings on American History, 1902–1961. 49 vols. Washington, D.C.: American Historical Association. *Writings on American History; A Subject Bibliography of Articles, 1962–1990.* Compiled and edited by James J. Dougherty. Reprint, Millwood, NY: KTO Press, 1976. *Recently Published Articles* (vol. 1, no., February 1976–vol. 15, no. 3, Autumn 1990).

5

Genealogical Sources

Alan C. Aimone

Tracing almost 3.5 million individuals who served as Civil War regulars, volunteers, and militiamen is possible through a variety of books, microfilm and document collections. A beginning is Everton's *Handy Book for Genealogists,* which lists archives, libraries, and historical societies by state and indexes printed census statistics, mortality schedules, maps, bibliographies, research guides, and histories. The American Association for State and Local History regularly revises its *Directory of Historical Societies,* which provides descriptive listings of over 13,000 historical societies, museums, and private and public historical organizations in the United States. Addresses, telephone numbers, and collection strengths organized alphabetically by state and then location make this a superb general record source.

Tracing Your Civil War Ancestor by Bertram Groene is the best single source to read before beginning serious Civil War genealogy research. Groene identifies research strategy, clarifies primary sources, and lists helpful institutions holding personnel files and rosters of nearly 7,000 Confederate and Union military units. The book is targeted for those who know nothing about Civil War veterans and those whose information is superficial. The author details how and where to unlock the records in archives and libraries, after a researcher has first identified the subject's full name and military unit.

The *Official Records of the Union and Confederate Armies* is the most quoted set of Civil War records. Many officers and lower-rank soldiers are mentioned by name in the *Official Records,* information that often leads to the military organization and the state. Each of the 128 books has a detailed index of both Union and Confederate reports, orders, and memorandums issued, posted, filed, or printed. Alan Aimone and Barbara Aimone's *User's Guide to the Official Records of the American Civil War* details the *Official Records* and offers hints for using them. Ronald Mosocco's *The Chronological Tracking of the Civil War Per the Official Records* presents a daily condensation of every military event, 1861 through 1865, making it easy to track both Union and Confederate army batteries and regiments at significant battles and campaigns.

The best source for identifying unit histories, prisoner of war memoirs, biographies, and reunion literature is Charles Dornbusch's three-volume *Military Bibliography of the Civil War,* updated by a fourth volume, compiled by Robert Krick. Two microfilm versions (University Microfilms Inc., *Regimental Histories of the American Civil War,* and University Publications of America, *Civil War Unit Histories*) have reproduced Dornbusch-listed books, and added works not cited in Dornbusch.

Contemporary published viewpoints of the war are annotated in Ellis Coulter's *Travels in the Confederate States,* continued by Garold Cole's *Civil War Eyewitnesses.* Cole has added nearly 1,400 published diaries, journals, letters, and memoirs. *Military Images,* a bimonthly magazine, features photographs of Civil War–era people and often includes a biographical sketch. Contemporary unpublished accounts of the Civil War are numerous because the war provided many young men an opportunity to leave their homes, and they wrote about their experiences. The *National Union Catalog of Manuscripts,* located in most college libraries, describes such manuscripts, which are collected in institutions throughout the country. The very thorough volume indexes are useful in searching for an individual or a unit, if there is any possibility that manuscripts were saved.

NATIONAL ARCHIVES

The nation's largest Civil War record collection is found in the main building of the National Archives in Washington, D.C., the major depository for Union records. *The Guide to Genealogical Research in the National Archives* has well-written chapters covering regular army records, volunteer service records, naval and marine service records, and pension records. The *Guide* shows how to use the National Archives, what type of records are preserved, and what specific information about individuals is included in each record. Military records, including compiled military service files from the Civil War, are generally structured around the following service branches: Volunteer Union Army, Volunteer Union Navy, Regular Union Army, Regular Union Navy and Marines, Confederate Army, Confederate Navy, and the Confederate Marines.

The Union, compiled by Kenneth Munden and Henry Beers, is a thoroughly written, well-organized, and well-indexed guide to the Northern war effort. Beers also wrote the companion volume, *The Confederacy,* which describes Confederate records held by the National Archives, the Library of Congress, and twenty-nine other institutions.

The Military Service Records: A Select Catalog of National Archives Microfilm Publications indexes microfilm copies of original documents about military units and individuals with Civil War army or naval service. Microfilm copies of service records for Union and Confederate soldiers are found in each of the twelve regional National Archives branches, in larger libraries, and in Latter Day Saints Family History Centers.

Many state militias, originally raised for state border defense, saw Civil War service. Since a state militia was never attached to Federal or Confederate units, its records are available only from individual state archives. State indexes, generally available in each Confederate state library, historical society, or university, are much smaller and more manageable than the National Archives indexes. State archives vary in quality, dependent on funding; they usually answer requests faster than the National Archives and are especially valuable for Confederate state militia and pension records. (Some states accepted pension applications from resident Confederate veterans regardless of their original service state.)

THE CONFEDERACY

Enlisted Soldiers

Many other invaluable resources—county histories, cemetery lists, obituaries, historical society card files, family records—combine to make Confederate record searching an interesting and challenging venture with a high success rate. With few exceptions, an unsuccessful Confederate record search means the researcher failed to look widely enough or in the proper places. J. H. Segars's "In Search of Confederate Ancestors" has helpful addresses and tips for beginning researchers. Another useful source for Confederate unit identification is Stewart Sifakis's *Compendium of the Confederate Armies.* This ten-volume series organizes each state military unit (artillery, cavalry, and infantry) by numerical designation, commander, home region, size, nickname, dates of service, and battles. It recommends additonal sources for Confederate enlisted soldier records.

Several useful photographic sources of Confederate soldier pictures are available, with biographical sketches of over 2,000 soldiers. William Albaugh's *Confederate Faces* and *More Confederate Faces,* William Turner's *Even More Confederate Faces,* and Dominick Serrano's *Still More Confederate Faces* capture a sense of what the Confederate soldier looked like.

For researchers who have the exact name of a Confederate soldier, there are several good sources. Robert Krick's introduction to N. A. Strait's *Roster of Confederate Soldiers* provides guidelines and tables for further identification of Confederate soldiers and units. It is the cumulative index to 1 million Confederate soldiers' names transcribed from National Archives microfilm, entitled *Consolidated Index to All Confederate Soldiers.* Each soldier's listing contains last name, first name, middle name, highest rank, unit of service, and state in which he either enlisted or was commissioned. The United Confederate Veterans' 65,000 members contributed their anecdotes, photographs, reunion pictures, incidents, and personal stories to various issues of the *Confederate Veteran.* A very small number of Confederate soldiers was awarded the exclusive Cross of Honor for exceptional service; they are identified in the *Confederate Roll of Honor.*

Officers

Some information about prominent Confederate officers can be found in individual biographies. However, most Confederate officers did not write biographies and have only a military service sketch found in various publications. *Who Was Who in the Confederacy* has more than a thousand illustrated biographical sketches of principal Confederate officers. Jon Wakelyn's *Biographical Dictionary of the Confederacy* is more selective, with only 651 sketches of political and military leaders. Wakelyn's entries are more analytical than *Who Was Who* or Ezra's Warner's illustrated *Generals in Gray,* and include citations to both biographical articles and books.

To find the service records of Confederate officers, use Francis Heitman's *Historical Register and Dictionary of the United States Army.* Although some entries are incomplete, Heitman provides a list of Confederate general officers who died of wounds or were killed in action and a list of officers who left the U.S. Army beginning November 2, 1860, and joined the Confederate army. James Spencer's *Civil War Generals* has sixteen categories, including generals by rank, college, before and after occupation, and place of death. George Cullum's *Biographical Register* of West Pointers sketches graduates and includes cadets who matriculated but did not graduate.

A few sources identify lower-ranking Confederate officers. Clement Evans's extended edition of *Confederate Military History* contains biographical supplements to 5,925 concise profiles of personnel from all the Confederate states. For many of the lesser-known officers and most of the lower-ranked individuals, these informative sketches provide major biographical data. Robert Krick's *Lee's Colonels'* expands on John Wright's *List of Field Officers, Regiments, and Battalions in the Confederate Army, 1861–1865* and includes information on 1,954 field-grade officers who served in Lee's army as well as many others who held field grades in other Confederate military units. Krick's entries direct researchers to specific archives and burial site records. *The Southern Historical Society Papers* are an excellent source for names of staff officers. The comprehensive index covers Confederate names and includes military units, ships, and battles in which a soldier or sailor participated, the places where he was stationed, and areas through which he passed. Other sources such as county histories and family histories may include additional sketches of Confederate commissioned officers.

THE UNION

Enlisted Soldiers

Union soldiers comprise the largest number of Civil War veterans. The easiest way to find information about them is to identify their military unit and trace the unit's history. William Amann's *Personnel of the Civil War* provides valuable information on local unit designations, general officer assignments, and the organizational structure of geographical commands. All Federal unit histories can be located in Frederick Dyer's *Compendium of the War of the Rebellion,* which is considered the best Union army reference. Dyer compiled and arranged state adjutant general reports, army registers, and other reliable documents. The compendium contains a concise history of every regiment, battery, and other organizations mustered by the states for service in the Union army.

For locating a Union soldier who died in service, the U.S. Army Quartermaster's Department *Roll of Honor* lists over 300,000 Union soldiers buried in national, post, and private cemeteries, more than two-thirds of them having been reinterred from their original battlefield burial sites. Entries are arranged alphabetically by burial site and provide the veteran's name, rank, regiment, company, and date of death.

Two sources are recommended for sketches of Union soldiers, sailors, and officers who were awarded the Congressional Medal of Honor: Walter Beyer and Oscar Keydel's *Deeds of Valor* (extensively illustrated) and *Congressional Medal of Honor,* from Sharp & Dunnigan Publishing.

A reference source that identifies over 12,000 African-American servicemen and information about their military service during the Civil War is Thomas Moebs's *Black Soldiers, Black Sailors, Black Ink.* Medal of Honor winners, regimental service records, and Confederate writings on military use of African Americans are found in this book.

State adjutant general reports provide regimental and company rosters, casualty lists and location, in/out muster dates, promotion information, dismissals, desertions, deaths, missing, and names of enlisted men receiving honors from the secretary of war. These individual state rosters are identified in Charles Dornbusch's *Military Bibliography of the Civil War.*

Officers

Information on local state militia officers can be found in various state adjutant general reports. The U.S. Adjutant General's Office's *Official Army Register* contains biographies of all Federal army regular officers during the war. The eight-volume *Official Army Register of the Volunteer Force of the United States Army* lists only the volunteer army officers mustered into Federal service. Many volunteer officer sketches are expanded in Guy Henry's *Military Record of Civilian Appointments.* John Hubbell and James Geary's *Biographical*

Dictionary of the Union is more comprehensive than Ezra Warner's *Generals in Blue,* with analyses of major figures, career evaluations, and updated sources. Francis Heitman's *Historical Register* and George Cullum's *Biographical Register* of West Pointers are also useful for Civil War officer service records. Roger Hunt and Jack Brown's *Brevet Brigadier Generals in Blue* contains 1,367 illustrated officer sketches. (The brevet rank made an officer eligible for command at that rank; however, the brevet rank has no effect on the officer's pay, emoluments, or seniority.) Hunt includes Civil War service for brevets, places of birth and death, occupation, burial site, photographic credit, and references. Additional listings of Union generals by rank, college, before- and after-war occupation, and place of death including battlefields are found in James Spencer's *Civil War Generals.*

Several sources identify supporters of the North's cause. The *Military Order of the Loyal Legion of the U.S.* published sixty-nine volumes containing over a thousand biographical sketches of contributors. N. A. Strait's *Roster of All Regimental Surgeons* identifies war service and in some cases cited a surgeon's value, from "doubtful" to "unsound mind." Mary Holland's *Our Army Nurses* sketches over one hundred women who also served.

NAVAL AND MARINE CORPS

A significant role was filled by Civil War naval and marine corps personnel on the high seas, on coastal blockades, and in river warfare. Myron Smith's *American Civil War Navies* surveys books and articles, published from the 1850s to 1972, that identify naval biographies and personnel sketches. Both the U.S. Navy's *Register of the Commissioned, Warrant, and Volunteer Officers of the Navy* and Edward Callahan's *List of Officers of the Navy of the U.S. and of the Marine Corps* list service members alphabetically, with dates of appointment, progressive rank, and reason for service termination. Lewis Hamersly's *The Records of Living Officers of the U.S. Navy and Marine Corps* is a series of short biographies of U.S. naval officers still living in 1870. For biographical sketches of Naval Academy graduates or anyone who attended the academy for any length of time since 1845, one can consult the U.S. Naval Academy Alumni Association *Register of Alumni.* Fewer naval officers than army officers joined the Confederate military services.

Three sources best identify Confederate naval and marine corps service records: Thomas Moebs's *Confederate States Navy Research Guide,* which includes "Footnote Biographies" from Scharf's *History of the Confederate States Navy,* "Biographical Data of Confederate Marine Corps and Naval Officers" (a rework of the U.S. Navy Department's 1931 *Register of Officers of the Confederate States Navy*), and Ralph Donnelly's *The Confederate States Marine Corps.* The companion set to the *Official Records* (Army) is the *Official Records of the Union and Confederate Navies in the War of the Rebellion.* The (Navy) *Official*

Records often provide overlooked information about army activities as well as naval actions.

Naval and marine corps personnel can also be traced through ships on which they served. The eight-volume *Dictionary of American Naval Fighting Ships* provides dimensions, illustrations, and service histories of Civil War naval ships. The National Archives has available *A List of Log Books*—a ship's official record—and includes orders, battle actions, and personnel matters. Additional sources identifying naval enlisted men can also be found in state adjutant generals' published annual reports listed in Charles Dornbusch's *Military Bibliography of the Civil War.*

SUMMARY

Future research using Civil War genealogical sources will increasingly benefit from microfilm, microfiche, CD-ROM, and digital copies of ephemeral documents and aging books and magazines. A number of classic Civil War genealogical sources have been reprinted on high-quality paper and indexed using modern standards of cross reference, subject entry, and name entry including variant spelling entries. The National Park Service, in conjunction with the National Archives, the Genealogical Society of Utah, and the Federation of Genealogical Societies, has developed a computerized listing on compact discs (Civil War Soldiers System) of over 3.5 million compiled military service records of Confederate and Union soldiers. One of the goals is to determine whether a soldier or his regiment was present on a particular battleground. Beside each soldier's name, the database will cite his company and regiment, whether Confederate or Union, and his rank upon entering and leaving the service. To this names index will be added other computerized information on the 7,000 wartime regiments and units, the regiments' participation in major battles, and burial records from Civil War cemeteries managed by the National Park Service. An estimated 5.5 million names will be entered in the database because of aliases and alternate name spellings.

Growing interest in the Civil War is not surprising, given the nature of that conflict, undoubtedly the most influential force to shape the contemporary United States. The Civil War divided states, communities, and even families in powerful and often poignant events that even today cannot be matched for drama. One of eight Americans fought in the Civil War's almost 11,000 separate engagements, from Maryland to New Mexico and Minnesota to Florida. As many as one-half of today's American citizens have an ancestor who took up arms between 1861 and 1865. The desire to search for one's Civil War roots will continue as each new American generation discovers the Civil War.

BIBLIOGRAPHY

Aimone, Alan C., and Barbara A. Aimone. *A User's Guide to the Official Records of the American Civil War.* Shippensburg, PA: White Mane Publishing Co., 1993.

Albaugh, William A., III. *Confederate Faces: A Pictorial Review of the Individuals in the Confederate Armed Forces.* 1970. Reprint, Wilmington, NC: Broadfoot Publishing Company, 1993.

―――. *More Confederate Faces: A Pictorial Review.* Washington, D.C.: ABS Printers, 1972.

Amann, William. *Personnel of the Civil War.* 2 vols. New York: Thomas Yoseloff, 1961.

Beers, Henry Putney. *The Confederacy: A Guide to the Archives of the Confederate States of America.* Washington, D.C.: National Archives and Records Administration, 1968.

Beyer, Walter Frederick, and Oscar F. Keydel, comps. *Deeds of Valor: How America's Heroes Won the Medal of Honor.* 2 vols. Detroit: Perrien-Keydel Co., 1900–1902.

Callahan, Edward W., ed. *List of Officers of the Navy of the U.S. and of the Marine Corps, 1775–1900.* 1901. Reprint, Gaithsburg, MD: Olde Soldier Books, 1989.

Cole, Garold L. *Civil War Eyewitnesses: An Annotated Bibliography of Books and Articles, 1955–1986.* Columbia: University of South Carolina Press, 1988.

Confederate Roll of Honor, Minutes of the Confederate Congress General Orders Number 64. Richmond, August 10 1864. Reprint, Mattituck, NY: Carroll and Co., 1985.

Confederate Veteran Magazine. 43 vols. incl. 3 vols. index, 1893–1932. Reprint, Wilmington, NC: Broadfoot Publishing Company, 1986.

Congressional Medal of Honor: The Names, the Deeds. Forest Ranch, CA: Sharp & Dunnigan, 1984.

Coulter, Ellis Meton. *Travels in the Confederate States: A Bibliography.* Reprint, Baton Rouge: Louisiana State University Press, 1994.

Cullum, George Washington. *Biographical Register of Officers and Graduates of the U.S. Military Academy at West Point, N.Y., 1802 to 1950.* 10 vols. New York: Association of Graduates, 1950.

Directory of Historical Societies and Agencies in the United States and Canada. Edited by Mary Bray Wheeler. 14th ed. Nashville, TN: American Association for State and Local History, 1990.

Donnelly, Ralph W. *The Confederate States Marine Corps.* Shippensburg, PA: White Mane Publishing Co., 1990.

Dornbusch, Charles E. *Military Bibliography of the Civil War.* 4 vols. New York: New York Public Library, vols. 1–3 rept. and vol. 4, Dayton, OH: Morningside Press, 1961–1987.

Dyer, Frederick Henry. *A Compendium of the War of the Rebellion.* 3 vols. 1908. Reprint, 2 vols. Wilmington, NC: Broadfoot Publishing Company, 1994.

Evans, Clement A., ed. *Confederate Military History.* Ext. ed. Edited by Robert S. Bridgers. 19 vols. incl. 2 vols. index. 1899. Reprint, Wilmington, NC: Broadfoot Publishing Co., 1987.

Everton Publishing Staff. *Handy Book for Genealogists: United States of America.* 8th ed. Baltimore, MD: Clearfield Co., 1991.

Groene, Bertram Hawthorne. *Tracing Your Civil War Ancestor.* Rev. and updated ed. Winston-Salem, NC: John F. Blair, 1993.

Hamersly, Lewis R. *The Records of Living Officers of the U.S. Navy and Marine Corps.* 1870. Reprint, Mattituck, NY: John M. Carroll, 1983.

Heitman, Francis Benard, comp. *Historical Register and Dictionary of the United States*

Army. 2 vols., 1903. Rev. ed. Reprint, Baltimore, MD: Genealogical Publishing Co., 1994.

Henry, Guy Vernon. *Military Record of Civilian Appointments in the United States Army.* 2 vols. New York: D. Van Nostrand, 1869, 1873.

Hollard, Mary A. Gardner, comp. *Our Army Nurses: Interesting Sketches and Photographs of over One Hundred of the Women . . .* Boston: Lounsbery, Nichols & Worth, 1897.

Hubbell, John T., and James W. Geary, eds. *Biographical Dictionary of the Union.* Westport, CT: Greenwood Press, 1995.

Hunt, Roger D., and Jack R. Brown. *Brevet Brigadier Generals in Blue.* Gaithersburg, MD: Olde Soldier Books, 1990.

Krick, Robert K. *Lee's Colonels: A Biographical Register of the Field Officers of the Army of Northern Virginia.* 3d rev. ed. Dayton, OH: Morningside, 1991.

Military Images (formerly *Military Images Magazine*). Bimonthly, Henryville, PA: 1979–.

Military Order of the Loyal Legion of the U.S., 1887–1915. 69 vols. incl. 3 vols. index. Reprint, Wilmington, NC: Broadfoot Publishing Company, 1994.

Moebs, Thomas Truxton, comp. *Black Soldiers, Black Sailors, Black Ink: Research Guide on African-Americans in U.S. Military History, 1526–1900 . . .* Chesapeake Bay, MD: Moebs Publishing Co., 1994.

———. *Confederate States Navy Research Guide . . .* Williamsburg, VA: Moebs Publishing Co., 1991.

Mosocco, Ronald A., ed. *The Chronological Tracking of the American Civil War per the Official Records of the War of the Rebellion.* Williamsburg, VA: James River Publications, 1994.

Munden, Kenneth W., and Henry Putney Beers. *The Union: A Guide to Federal Archives Relating to the Civil War.* 1962. Reprint, Washington, D.C.: National Archives and Records Administration, 1986.

Roster of Confederate Soldiers, 1861–1865. 10 vols. Wilmington, NC: Broadfoot Publishing Co., 1995–1996.

Scharf, J. Thomas. *History of the Confederate States Navy.* New York: Roger and Sherwood, 1887.

Segars, J. H. "In Search of Confederate Ancestors: The Guide." *Journal of Confederate History Series* 9 (1993).

Serrano, Dominick A. *Still More Confederate Faces: A Photographic Collection of Southern Soldiers from the Civil War.* Bayside, NY: Metropolitan Co., 1992.

Sifakis, Stewart. *Compendium of the Confederate Armies.* 10 vols. New York: Facts on File, 1992–.

———, ed. *Who Was Who in the Civil War.* New York: Facts on File, 1988.

———. *Who Was Who in the Confederacy . . .* New York: Facts on File, 1988.

Smith, Myron J. *American Civil War Navies.* Metuchen, NJ: Scarecrow Press, 1972.

The Southern Historical Society Papers. 55 vols., 1876–1959; rept. incl. 3 vols. index. Wilmington, NC: Broadfoot Publishing Company, 1994.

Spencer, James, comp. *Civil War Generals: Categorical Listings and a Biographical Directory.* Westport, CT: Greenwood Press, 1986.

Strait, N. A., comp. *Roster of All Regimental Surgeons and Assistant Surgeons . . . 1882.* Reprint, Gaithersburg, MD: Olde Soldier Books, 1989.

Turner, William A. *Even More Confederate Faces*. Orange, VA: Moss Publications, 1983.

U.S. Adjutant General's Office. *Official Army Register*. Washington, D.C.: 1861–1865.

———. *Official Army Register of the Volunteer Force of the United States, Army, 1861– 1865*. 8 vols., 1865–1867. Reprint, 9 vols., Gaithersburg, MD: Ron R. Van Sickle Military Books, 1987.

U.S. Library of Congress. *National Union Catalog of Manuscript Collections*. Washington, D.C.: 1959–. *Index to Personal Names in the National Union Catalog of Manuscript Collections, 1959–1984*. 2 vols. Alexandria, VA: Chadwyck-Healey, 1987.

U.S. National Archives and Records Service. *Guide to Genealogical Research in the National Archives*. Rev. ed. Washington, D.C.: 1985.

———. *A List of Log Books of the United States Navy, Stations, and Miscellaneous Units, 1801–1947*. Washington, D.C.: 1986.

———. *Military Service Records: A Select Catalog of National Archives Microfilm Publications*. Washington, D.C.: 1985.

U.S. Naval Academy Alumni Association. *Register of Alumni*. Annapolis, MD: 1886 and annually since 1908.

U.S. Navy. *Register of the Commissioned, Warrant, and Volunteer Officers of the Navy of the United States, Including Officers of the Marine Corps and Others*. Washington, D.C.: Government Printing Office, 1862–1904.

U.S. Navy Department. *Dictionary of American Naval Fighting Ships*. 8 vols. Washington, D.C.: 1959–1981.

———. *Official Records of the Union and Confederate Navies in the War of the Rebellion*. Edited by Richard Bush et al. 31 vols., 1894–1927. Reprint, Dayton, OH: Morningside Bookshop, Broadfoot Publishing Company and Historical Times, 1992.

U.S. Quartermaster's Department. *Roll of Honor: Names of Soldiers Who Died in Defense of the American Union, Interred in the National Cemeteries*. 27 vols., 1865–1871. Reprint, 15 vols., Baltimore: Genealogical Publishing Co., 1994–.

U.S. War Department. *War of the Rebellion: Official Records of the Union and Confederate Armies*. Edited by Robert N. Scott et al. 128 vols. Washington, DC: Government Printing Office, 1881–1901.

Wakelyn, Jon L. *Biographical Dictionary of the Confederacy*. Westport, CT: Greenwood Press, 1977.

Warner, Ezra J. *Generals in Blue: Lives of the Union Commanders*. 1964. Reprint, Baton Rouge: Louisiana State University Press, 1981.

———. *Generals in Gray: Lives of the Confederate Commanders*. 1959. Reprint, Baton Rouge: Louisiana State University Press, 1981.

Wile, Annadel N., ed. *C.R.I.S.: Combined Retrospective Index Set to Journals in History, 1838–1974*. Washington, D.C.: Carrollton Press, 1977–.

Wright, John. *Compendium of the Confederacy: An Annotated Bibliography*. 2 vols. Wilmington, NC: Broadfoot Publishing Company, 1994.

Wright, John. *List of Field Officers, Regiments and Battalions in the Confederate Army, 1861–1865*. Bryan, NC: J. M. Carrol, 1983.

Part II

General Primary Sources

6

Memoirs, Diaries, and Letters

Judith Lee Hallock

Perhaps the most exciting accounts of events during the Civil War are found in primary source materials. The people who lived during this stirring time were remarkably prone to write about their adventures and hardships. Many kept meticulous diaries and journals; loved ones wrote letters back and forth; and after the war was over, many people relived what was often the most exciting time of their lives by writing memoirs. Over the years, thousands of these items have been published, making them accessible to the general public.

The primary focus of this chapter is the more recently published or reprinted works that are readily accessible. For fuller listings of published primary sources there are several bibliographies available: Garold L. Cole's *Civil War Eyewitnesses: An Annotated Bibliography of Books and Articles, 1955–1986* (1988), C. E. Dornbusch's *Regimental Publications and Personal Narratives of the Civil War: A Checklist* (1961–1972), and *Civil War Books: A Critical Bibliography* (1967–1969), edited by Allan Nevins, James I. Robertson, Jr., and Bell I. Wiley. To locate the many thousands of unpublished works, the *Guide to Archives and Manuscripts in the United States,* edited by Philip M. Hamer, and the *National Union Catalog of Manuscript Collections* are useful.

Memoirs and reminiscences were the first primary sources to appear in any number, with a few being published during the war. These must be used with caution. Many of the writers served in the lower ranks of the military, thereby limiting their perspectives. Often the writer had a particular point to make, a criticism to refute, or a reputation to rehabilitate. Actions later regretted tended to be ignored or distorted to fit the image the author wished to present to the public. And these writings were always created for others to read: the general public, the author's own family, or future generations of the family.

Diaries and journals, written primarily for the author's own amusement, may be more candid, but given the nature of changing day-to-day circumstances and the inaccuracy of news and rumors that the diarist may report, one must keep in mind that much of what is recorded may not be what actually happened. The reader can nevertheless enter the lives of the authors and experience their uncertainties, hopes, fears, joys, and sorrows. On occasion a diarist later decided to publish the work, in which case she or he, or an editor or publisher, might have edited the original document, sometimes to such an extent that it became a memoir rather than a true diary or journal.

Letters, like diaries and journals, allow the reader to enter the world of the writer. Wives writing to their husbands detailed their troubles and joys; described the doings of the children, the neighbors, and the community; and expressed their fears for the safety of their families and husbands. Soldiers wrote of their adventures, the battles they fought, their loneliness, and their worries about families back home. Most collections of letters have been published only fairly recently; the writers themselves never dreamed their correspondence would someday be read by strangers generations later. With careful editing, collected letters provide fascinating sources of information about the people and the times of the Civil War.

Ordinary soldiers were perhaps the most prolific writers. They wrote letters to family and friends; they kept journals and diaries of their daily lives; and after the war they enjoyed recalling their days of boredom, discomfort, and occasional glory through writing memoirs. The more noteworthy military officers are covered elsewhere in this book; this chapter includes only soldiers ranging from not-so-noteworthy officers to privates.

Federal officers made many contributions to the literature on the war. Abner Doubleday's *Reminiscences of Forts Sumter and Moultrie in 1860–'61* (1876) is a detailed account of the days leading up to the outbreak of the war, the first shots fired, and the surrender of the fort to the Confederates. John Gibbon's memoir, *Personal Recollections of the Civil War* (1928), is a reliable source by a commander of the Iron Brigade, making his narrative of the Gettysburg campaign of particular interest. Two large collections of letters contribute significantly to our understanding of the Army of the Potomac. *Life and Letters of Alexander Hays* (1919) carries the reader up to the Wilderness, where the writer was killed, and *The Civil War Letters of General Robert McAllister* (1965) covers the entire war, from First Manassas to Appomattox. Joshua Chamberlain's *The Passing of the Armies* (1915) is especially notable for his lyrical and moving description of the ceremony accepting the surrender of the Army of Northern Virginia at Appomattox. The *Reminiscences of General Herman Haupt* (1901) affords a glimpse into the Union's transportation problems from the perspective of the head of the Bureau of Military Railroads.

Staff officers often chronicled the activities and events that occurred at headquarters. Horace Porter tells us much about Ulysses S. Grant's command style in *Campaigning with Grant* (1961). Theodore Lyman's letters, *Meade's Headquarters, 1863–1865* (1922), provide detailed accounts of the Army of the Potomac's activities and politics during the last year and a half of war. Franklin Aretas Haskell, on the staff of John Gibbon, was at the precise section of the Federal line at Gettysburg against which Pickett's men charged. Two weeks later he wrote a letter describing his experience, which was eventually published as *The Battle of Gettysburg* (1898) and has become a classic military eyewitness account.

Confederate officers also left a wealth of material for posterity. Two of the best accounts are by the same man. Edward Porter Alexander's *Military Memoirs of a Confederate* (1962) provides insight into the operations and personalities of the Army of Northern Virginia. A more complete publication of the original manuscript, *Fighting for the Confederacy* (1989), is not as polished as the first volume but includes more of the finely honed comments and fascinating gossip about well-known people that Alexander had been reluctant to reveal to the general public. The *Reminiscences of General Basil W. Duke* (1911) covers not only military affairs in the West but also politics, social life in the South, prison life, and the fleeing of the government from Richmond at war's end. *Liddell's Record* (1985), by St. John Richardson Liddell, gossips about the doings in the upper echelons of the Army of Tennessee, while Arthur M. Manigault's *A Carolinian Goes to War* (1983) provides more on the day-to-day activities, campaigns, and battles of that army. *The Civil War Diary of General Josiah Gorgas* (1947) recounts not only the difficulties faced by the Confederacy's chief of ordnance but also discusses many aspects of the South during the war.

Confederate staff officers, like their Union counterparts, also wrote of headquarters activities. Henry Kyd Douglas had the good fortune to serve on the staff of, or to meet, several of the most colorful Confederate generals. In *I Rode with Stonewall* (1940) he portrays them in all their glory (or lack thereof). Gilbert Moxley Sorrel served on Longstreet's staff and narrated his experiences in *Recollections of a Confederate Staff Officer* (1958). His insight on the higher echelons of the Army of Northern Virginia affords a better understanding of that organization. Another memoir that provides an inside view of that army and its commander is Walter Herron Taylor's *Four Years with General Lee* (1962). On the war in the West, Irving Buck's *Cleburne and His Command* (1908) provides a useful source.

Both the Union and the Confederate armies enjoyed the services of foreign officers who wrote of their experiences. French nobleman and U.S. Major General Philippe Trobriand's *Four Years with the Army of the Potomac* (1889) was written soon after the war from notes and a diary and was limited to the things he personally witnessed of the upper echelons. His counterpart was the observant and spirited Prussian, Heros von Borcke, who recounted his exciting adventures with Jeb Stuart in *Memoirs of the Confederate War for Independence* (1866).

Two British officers visited the Southern armies as observers, and together their accounts cover a full year in the life of the Confederacy. Lieutenant Colonel Arthur James Lyon Fremantle of the Coldstream Guards arrived first. His account, *Three Months in the Southern States: April–June, 1863* (1864), reveals that he saw much of the Confederacy during his brief stay, including the Battle of Gettysburg. The lively story by Captain Fitzgerald Ross of the Imperial Austrian Hussars, *Cities and Camps of the Confederate States* (1958), picks up where Fremantle leaves off. Both writers were strongly pro-Confederate, observed much of the South, and met some of its most powerful leaders.

Primary sources written by the lower echelons of the armies number in the thousands. Union soldiers enthusiastically recounted their adventures. Events that took place in the eastern theater were thoroughly documented by many writers during and after the war. Rufus R. Dawes's memoir, *Service with the Sixth Wisconsin Volunteers* (1890), was based on his wartime journal, letters he had written home, and official records. He chronicled the fortunes of the Iron Brigade with sensitivity and humor, including the minutiae of daily existence and the attitudes of his fellow soldiers. George Thomas Stevens allows the reader to view army life through the eyes of a surgeon. Written from extensive notes, official reports, and letters from army officers, *Three Years in the Sixth Corps* (1870) informs the reader about the organization of the medical department, shortages of medicines and supplies, illnesses, wounds, ravages of disease, and the horrifying work following a battle. One of the best descriptions of army life appears in John Davis Billings's *Hardtack and Coffee* (1960), the memoir of an artillerist from Massachusetts. His narrative details life in camp but includes no accounts of battle.

Two Union diaries are particularly useful on eastern matters. Charles Shiels Wainwright's *A Diary of Battle* (1962) is a comprehensive source on the Army of the Potomac. He was interested in everything and expressed strong opinions on a variety of subjects. Elijah Hunt Rhodes detailed his experiences in his diary, published as *All for the Union* (1985). Rhodes joined as a private in May 1861, and by the time he received his discharge in July 1865 he had risen in rank to lieutenant colonel. His diary includes solid battle accounts, as well as notes on the everyday hardships and delights of army life.

Collections of letters also add to our knowledge of affairs in the Army of the Potomac. *Fallen Leaves* (1991) gives the reader an unadorned glimpse of the horrors of war, the routine of daily life in the army, and camp politics as seen through the eyes of young Henry Livermore Abbott. Another young man, Edward King Wightman, also wrote candidly, describing his experiences in the army, including the terrors of trench warfare. *From Antietam to Fort Fisher* (1985) ends with Wightman's father's account of his own journey to Fort Fisher to recover his son's body for burial back home.

Several memoirs and reminiscences detail the experiences of Union soldiers serving in the western theater. John Beatty, *The Citizen-Soldier* (1879), observed a variety of military matters and personnel. John Hill Brinton, who saw service in both the East and the West, in *Personal Memoirs of John H. Brinton* (1914) describes hospitals and battlefields; provides vignettes on people such as Grant, Halleck, Sheridan, and Rosecrans; and delights in sharing army society and gossip. Michael Hendrick Fitch also left sketches of high commanders. In *Echoes of the Civil War as I Hear Them* (1905), he also details the activities of the 21st Wisconsin Infantry in battles from Perryville to Bentonville. Samuel Calvin Jones's *Reminiscences of the Twenty-second Iowa Volunteer Infantry* (1907) recounts army travels and adventures in the western and trans-Mississippi theaters before being transferred to the East, where he spent five months in captivity. Leander Stillwell's *The Story of a Common Soldier of Army Life in the Civil War, 1861–1865* (1920) is an exciting narrative and particularly useful on Shiloh and the siege of Vicksburg. Wilbur F. Hinman relates his four years of service in the West in his memoir, *The Story of the Sherman Brigade* (1897).

Suzanne Colton Wilson put together a useful volume based primarily on diaries kept by two young brothers, supplemented with diaries from other members of the unit, connecting their stories with her own commentary. *Column South: With the Fifteenth Pennsylvania Cavalry from Antietam to the Capture of Jefferson Davis* (1960) thus became essentially a unit history, detailing day-to-day life in the cavalry and ending with its role in chasing down the Confederate government after it fled Richmond.

With an enthusiasm that matched that of their Union counterparts, Confederates too wrote of their experiences. In the eastern theater, John Overton Casler's *Four Years in the Stonewall Brigade* (1893) provides a humorous view of army life by a less-than-ideal soldier. He stole whiskey and food, straggled, went AWOL and was arrested several times, and spent time in Fort McHenry after his capture by Union troops. John Edward Dooley recounted his adventures in *John Dooley, Confederate Soldier: His War Journal* (1945). Dooley's description of his feelings as he first came under fire at Antietam gives the reader insight into how novices viewed that baptism. An engrossing memoir by a private is the informative *Detailed Minutiae of Soldier Life in the Army of Northern Virginia, 1861–1865* (1882) by Carlton McCarthy. In *Gunner with Stonewall* (1957), William Thomas Poague explains the role of artillery during battle, as well as telling many anecdotes about the daily existence of the enlisted men.

Another artilleryman, Edward Manigault, kept an extremely detailed record of the siege of Charleston, South Carolina, in *Siege Train: The Journal of a Confederate Artilleryman in the Defense of Charleston* (1986).

A Confederate Surgeon's Letters to his Wife (1911) describes battles, marches, rations, army morale and health, scavenging the battlefield, and field medicine as seen by Spenser Glasgow Welch.

In the western theater, too, Confederate soldiers wrote of their experiences. R. M. Collins's witty account, *Chapters from the Unwritten History of the War between the States* (1893), describes his many adventures during his service, including his capture and time spent in Federal prisons. Samuel T. Foster's *One of Cleburne's Command* (1980) provides a detailed look at the Army of Tennessee from Chickamauga to Franklin. William Williston Heartsill's *Fourteen Hundred and 91 Days in the Confederate Army* (1876) narrates his experiences as a soldier and as a prisoner of war. His story of the battle of Chickamauga is gripping. *"Co. Aytch"* (1952) is a rousing account that must be used with extreme caution, as Samuel R. Watkins was much given to exaggeration.

Robert Patrick's diary, *Reluctant Rebel* (1959), provides information on army logistics and home front conditions in the western theater. John S. Jackman's *Diary of a Confederate Soldier* (1990) recounts everyday army life as viewed by an adjutant's clerk at brigade headquarters. Due to his many bouts of illness, Jackman's diary reveals the extent to which civilians were called upon to care for the sick of the Army of Tennessee.

Saddle Bag and Spinning Wheel (1981) contains the letters exchanged between Kate Featherston Peddy and her husband, George W. Peddy. Together, the letters represent both the home front in Georgia and the military affairs of the Army of Tennessee.

Cannon Smoke (1971) provides a first-hand account of soldiering in the trans-Mississippi West, for, as with the Peddy collection, these are letters from both John J. Good and his wife, Susan Anna Floyd Good, providing insight into both the home front and the army.

Three journals describe the Confederate experience in the Southwest. A. B. Peticolas provides detailed descriptions and drawings of the terrain, the people, and army life in *Rebels on the Rio Grande* (c. 1984). Both William Randolph Howell, *Westward the Texans* (1990), and Morgan Wolfe Merrick, *From Desert to Bayou* (1991), describe their adventures during the invasion of New Mexico.

A fine collection that spans the entire war in the trans-Mississippi is *Letters of a Confederate Surgeon, 1861–1865* (1960). Written by Junius Newport Bragg to his wife, Josephine, he describes camp life, battle, commanders, and illness, as well as relating the latest gossip and rumors.

There is little primary material on the experiences of blacks in the army. *On the Altar of Freedom: A Black Soldier's Civil War Letters from the Front* (1991) is therefore a valuable contribution to the war literature. Corporal James Henry Gooding, of the 54th Massachusetts (Colored) Regiment, wrote the letters for newspaper publication. In addition to noting the same concerns as white soldiers, Gooding also described racial discrimination and the 54th's celebration of the first anniversary of the emancipation proclamation. *Blue-Eyed Child of Fortune* (1992), the letters of Robert Gould Shaw, chronicles life in a black regiment from the perspective of a white officer, as does Thomas Wentworth Higginson's *Army Life in a Black Regiment* (1900).

Primary sources on the navy are also scanty. Alvah Folsom Hunter spent a year in the Federal navy and chronicled his adventures in a memoir, *A Year on a Monitor and the Destruction of Fort Sumter* (c. 1987). William Frederick Keeler's letters, *Aboard the USS Monitor* (1964), provide a lively narrative of the duel of the ironclads and recount daily life and activities aboard the *Monitor* and the blockader *Florida*. *The Wounded River* (1993) contains the letters of

John Vance Lauderdale describing his experiences caring for sick and wounded soldiers aboard a hospital ship on the Mississippi, Ohio, and Tennessee rivers in mid-1862. From the Confederate side, *The Journal of George Townley Fullam* (1973), of the *Alabama,* tells how he boarded captured vessels and decided whether the captain and the official papers should be transferred to the Confederate ship for interrogation by Captain Raphael Semmes. He also tells of searching for prizes, sea chases, difficulties with crew, and the routine details of voyages. His account ends with preparations being made for the *Alabama*'s engagement with the Union *Kearsage.*

Some captured soldiers focused their accounts on their experiences as prisoners of war. Bernhard Domschcke reported on the conditions at several Southern prisons in his memoir, *Twenty Months in Captivity* (1987). Amos E. Stearns devoted about half of his slim volume to his imprisonment. *The Civil War Diary of Amos E. Stearns, a Prisoner at Andersonville* (1981) is without rancor, but his matter-of-fact reporting makes all the more striking the great number of deaths that occurred at prison camps. From the Confederate perspective, *Prison Echoes of the Great Rebellion* (1874) by Daniel Robinson Hundley offers an inmate's view of conditions at the Federal prison on Johnson's Island in Ohio.

A few sources include short memoirs or reminiscences on a particular event or topic. *Battles and Leaders of the Civil War* (1887) and *Confederate Veteran* (1893–1932) provided forums for soldiers of both sides to explain their actions, to argue issues with their former enemies or allies, or to reminisce about days gone by.

For those interested in the experiences of a Civil War–era conscientious objector, *The Civil War Diary of Cyrus Pringle* (1962) recounts his imprisonment and the cruel military discipline meted out to him for several months before Lincoln ordered his release.

A tiny number of women disguised themselves as men and served in the ranks of both armies. Emma Sarah Edmundson's account of her adventures in the Union army is titled *Unsexed: or, The Female Soldier* (1865); another version is *Nurse and Spy in the Union Army* (1865). A woman who claimed to have served in the Confederate army, Loreta Janeta Velazquez, recounts her quite incredulous tale in *The Woman in Battle* (1876).

Two female Confederate spies left accounts of their services. Rose O'Neal Greenhow wrote of her arrest and imprisonment early in the war in *My Imprisonment and the First Year of Abolition Rule at Washington* (1863). Belle Boyd's dramatic narrative of her activities as a spy, *Belle Boyd in Camp and Prison* (1865), have proven to be quite reliable.

Women on both sides turned to nursing as a way of contributing to their respective causes, and many of them recorded their experiences. Louisa May Alcott's memoir, *Hospital Sketches* (1960), relates her few months of nursing in a military hospital. Julia Susan Wheelock Freeman's memoir, *The Boys in White* (1870), gives details about visiting field hospitals and searching for wounded men for desperate relatives. Susie King Taylor was a black woman who nursed Union black soldiers in South Carolina and Georgia. She recalled this episode in her life in *Reminiscences of My Life in Camp with the 33rd United States Colored Troops, Late 1st S. C. Volunteers* (1902).

Amanda Akin Stearns combined her letters and diary to produce *The Lady Nurse of Ward E* (1909), a detailed account of her daily activities at a Washington, D.C., military hospital. The letters and diary of Hannah Ropes were also combined to form a narrative of her brief service as a nurse before succumbing to typhoid pneumonia. *Civil War Nurse: The Diary and Letters of Hannah Ropes* (1980) follows her path from homemaker to activist during the Civil War.

Men also served as nurses. Walt Whitman's *Memoranda during the War* (1875–1876) provides a powerful image of the suffering, horror, and grief associated with Civil War hospitals.

On the Confederate side, Phoebe Yates Pember wrote a memoir of her experiences in a Richmond military hospital, *A Southern Woman's Story: Life in Confederate Richmond* (1959). Kate Cumming nursed for the Army of Tennessee. *Kate: The Journal of a Confederate Nurse* (1959) is an excellent source on the state of medicine and on the care of sick and wounded soldiers in the western theater.

Most women, of course, remained at home. Their lot was not an easy one, and many sought comfort through writing. Some produced memoirs, but the vast majority wrote for a restricted audience. Diaries and journals, nonpublic documents intended for personal consumption, became a popular outlet for countless women. Others poured out their hopes and fears in letters to loved ones, often a husband serving in the military forces; this form of writing, too, was confidential, meant for the eyes of only one person. Fortunately, in recent years numerous private chronicles have been published, expanding and enriching our understanding of women's lives during the momentous period of the Civil War.

Northern women experienced the war more from afar. Mary Simmerson Cunningham Logan, wife of Union general John Logan, wrote *Reminiscences of a Soldier's Wife: An Autobiography* (1913). A New York woman, Maria Lydig Daly, recorded her observations on the events of the Civil War as they pertained to her home in *Diary of a Union Lady, 1861–1865* (1962). Perhaps the most valuable source by a Union woman is the recently published *Wartime Washington: The Civil War Letters of Elizabeth Blair Lee* (1991). Lee was the daughter of Francis Preston Blair and married Samuel Phillips Lee, a distant cousin of Robert E. Lee. The collection is taken from her daily letters to her husband in which she discussed politics, war strategy, sketches of public figures, her daily activities, and news of their young son. As a member of the powerful Blair family, Lee was an insider of the highest political and social circles of Washington, D.C. Because the letters were intended for her husband's eyes only, her writing was uninhibited, revealing the true thoughts and opinions of an intelligent, sensitive, and articulate woman.

Southern women had a much closer view of the war—at times within their own communities and, indeed, within their own homes. Many of the best published diaries and journals therefore were written by Confederate women. The most famous of all women's Civil War writings is Mary Boykin Chesnut's diary. Over the years it has undergone many forms. The earliest version, *A Diary from Dixie,* debuted in 1905, and in 1949 a somewhat expanded edition appeared under the same title. In 1981, the publication of *Mary Chesnut's Civil War* revealed that Chesnut had spent years editing and revising her original day-to-day record of the war, and the work was now declared a novel, although meticulously based on the factual daily journals. The latest version is *The Private Mary Chesnut: The Unpublished Civil War Diaries* (1984). It contains the original journals Chesnut kept during the war in which she recorded immediate and frank observations on the people and events touching her life. Comparisons of the original version with those edited and revised by Chesnut reveal that though she did rework her diaries, she did not distort or compromise the authenticity of her first impressions. Her writing remains an important primary source for information on the famous and the influential in the high social, political, and military circles of the Confederacy.

Sallie Brock Putnam's *Richmond During the War* (1867) provides a sober, factual eyewitness account of life in Confederate Richmond. Mary Ann Webster Loughborough wrote of her experiences during the lengthy siege of Vicksburg in *My Cave Life in Vicksburg* (1864). Cornelia Peake McDonald recorded the suffering and despair of a woman left to fend for herself and nine children in an area occupied by the enemy in *A Woman's Civil War* (1992). Catherine A. D. Edmondston's *"Journal of a Secesh Lady"* (1979) recounts the daily life of the residents of a North Carolina plantation during the war. In *The Diary of Miss Emma Holmes: 1861–1866* (1979) the author discusses a host of issues and individuals, and a constant theme throughout is her intense hatred of the North. Eliza Frances Andrews kept *The War-time Journal of a Georgia Girl, 1864–1865* (1908) in which she depicts social life in Georgia following Sherman's march to the sea, vividly describing the destruction, trials, and hardships of the last nine months of the war. Ella Gertrude Clanton Thomas's *The Secret Eye* (1990) illustrates the changes in women's lives brought about by the Civil War. Born into a Georgia family of wealthy slaveholders, Thomas eventually became a wage earner. *The Civil War Diary of Sarah Morgan* (1991) portrays home-front life in Louisiana during the Civil War and also shows the impact of the war on gender roles in the South.

Several diaries and journals kept by civilian men also merit attention. Volume 1 of *The Salmon P. Chase Papers* (1993) records the activities and opinions of Lincoln's secretary of the treasury, including his impressions and observations on the assassination of the president. *Diary* (1960), kept by Gideon Welles, Lincoln's secretary of the navy, is an important source for both official and unofficial life in Washington during the war. A nice complement to this volume is *Confidential Correspondence of Gustavus Vasa Fox, Assistant Secretary of the Navy, 1861–1865* (1918–1919), which reveals much concerning Federal na val operations. *The Diary of George Templeton Strong* (1952) provides insight into the attitudes and activities of a prominent civilian New Yorker on local and national levels.

The inner workings of the Confederate War Department are exposed in the diaries of two men. John Beauchamp Jones recorded his views and passing gossip in *A Rebel War Clerk's Diary* (1935). A more reliable and discerning account kept by the head of the Bureau of War, Robert Garlick Hill Kean, is titled *Inside the Confederate Government* (1957).

The voluminous *Diary of Edmund Ruffin* records the activities of one of the South's most colorful residents. Ruffin was an early secessionist, fired the first shot of the war, and committed suicide at the end of the war, claiming despair at the prospect of living under the domination of the Yankees. Ruffin led a long and busy life and was influential in the course of Southern history.

A final group of people of interest to Civil War students is the war correspondents. Sylvanus Cadwallader's *Three Years with Grant* (1955) narrates his experiences through much of the war, as does Charles A. Dana's *Recollections of the Civil War* (1898). Charles Carleton Coffin reported for the *Boston Journal;* he spent time with both the army and the navy and wrote of his travels in *The Boys of '61; or Four Years of Fighting* (1896). A fine account of the Mississippi region during the war is found in *Camp-fire and Cotton-field: Southern Adventure in Time of War* (1865) by Thomas Wallace Knox.

The published primary sources discussed here are the tip of the iceberg. There are thousands of volumes of diaries, journals, memoirs, reminiscences, and letters, each portraying a distinctive flavor and viewpoint, and surely there are yet more to be found.

BIBLIOGRAPHY

BIBLIOGRAPHIC GUIDES

Published Works

Cole, Garold L. *Civil War Eyewitnesses: An Annotated Bibliography of Books and Articles, 1955–1986.* Columbia: University of South Carolina Press, 1988.

Dornbusch, C. E., comp. *Regimental Publications and Personal Narratives of the Civil War: A Checklist.* 2 vols. New York: New York Public Library, 1961–1972.

Nevins, Alan, James I. Robertson, Jr., and Bell I. Wiley, eds. *Civil War Books: A Critical Bibliography.* 2 vols. Baton Rouge: Louisiana State University Press, 1967–1969.

Unpublished Works

National Historical Publications Commission. *Guide to Archives and Manuscripts in the United States.* Edited by Philip M. Hamer. New Haven, CT: Yale University Press, 1961.

U.S. Library of Congress. *National Union Catalog of Manuscript Collections.* Washington, D.C.: Library of Congress, 1961–.

MEMOIRS

Alcott, Louisa May. *Hospital Sketches.* Edited by Bessie Z. Jones. Cambridge, MA: Belknap Press, 1960.

Alexander, Edward Porter. *Military Memoirs of a Confederate.* New ed. Bloomington: Indiana University Press, 1962.

———. *Fighting for the Confederacy: The Personal Recollections of Edward Porter Alexander.* Edited by Gary W. Gallagher. Chapel Hill: University of North Carolina Press, 1989.

Beatty, John. *The Citizen-Soldier; or, Memoirs of a Volunteer.* Cincinnati: Wilstach, Baldwin, 1879.

Billings, John Davis. *Hardtack and Coffee: The Unwritten Story of Army Life.* Edited by Richard Barksdale Harwell. Chicago: Donnelley, 1960.

Borcke, Heros von. *Memoirs of the Confederate War for Independence, by Heros von Borcke.* Edinburgh and London: W. Blackwood and Sons, 1866.

Boyd, Belle. *Belle Boyd in Camp and Prison, Written by Herself.* 1865. New ed., prepared by Curtis Carroll Davis. New York: Thomas Yoseloff, 1968.

Brinton, John Hill. *Personal Memoirs of John H. Brinton, Major and Surgeon U.S.V., 1861–1865.* New York: Neale Publishing Company, 1914.

Buck, Irving. *Cleburne and his Command.* 1908. New ed., edited by Norman D. Brown. Austin: University of Texas Press, 1980.

Buel, Clarence Clough, and Robert Underwood Johnson, eds. *Battles and Leaders of the Civil War.* 4 vols. 1887. Reprint, New York: Castle Books, 1956.

Cadwallader, Sylvanus. *Three Years with Grant, as recalled by War Correspondent Sylvanus Cadwallader.* Edited by Benjamin P. Thomas. New York: Knopf, 1955.

Casler, John Overton. *Four Years in the Stonewall Brigade. By John O. Casler, Private, Company A, 33rd Regiment Virginia Infantry, Stonewall Brigade, 1st Division, 2d Corps, Army of Northern Virginia, Gen. Robert E. Lee, Commanding.* 1893. Reprint, edited by James I. Robertson, Jr. Dayton, OH: Morningside Bookshop, 1971.

Chamberlain, Joshua Lawrence. *The Passing of the Armies; an Account of the Final Campaign of the Army of the Potomac, Based upon Personal Reminiscences of the Fifth Army Corps.* 1915. Reprint, Dayton, OH: Morningside Bookshop, 1974.

Coffin, Charles Carleton. *The Boys of '61; or, Four Years of Fighting; Personal Observations with the Army and Navy, from the First Battle of Bull Run to the Fall of Richmond.* Boston: Estes and Lauriat, 1896.

Collins, R. M. *Chapters from the Unwritten History of the War between the States; or, The Incidents in the Life of a Confederate Soldier in Camp, on the March, in the Great Battles, and in Prison.* St. Louis: Nixon-Jones Printing Co., 1893.

Confederate Veteran. Nashville, TN, 1893–1932.

Dana, Charles Anderson. *Recollections of the Civil War; with the Leaders at Washington and in the Field in the Sixties.* New York: D. Appleton and Company, 1898.

Dawes, Rufus R. *Service with the Sixth Wisconsin Volunteers.* 1890. Reprint, edited by

Alan T. Nolan. Madison: State Historical Society of Wisconsin for Wisconsin Civil War Centennial Commission, 1962.

Domschcke, Bernhard. *Twenty Months in Captivity: Memoirs of a Union Officer in Confederate Prisons.* Edited and translated by Frederic Trautmann. Rutherford, NJ: Fairleigh Dickinson University Press, 1987.

Dooley, John Edward. *John Dooley, Confederate Soldier: His War Journal.* Edited by Joseph T. Durkin. Washington, D.C.: Georgetown University Press, 1945.

Doubleday, Abner. *Reminiscences of Forts Sumter and Moultrie in 1860–'61 by Abner Doubleday.* New York: Harper & Brothers, 1876.

Douglas, Henry Kyd. *I Rode with Stonewall.* Chapel Hill: University of North Carolina Press, 1940.

Duke, Basil Wilson. *Reminiscences of General Basil W. Duke.* Garden City, NY: Doubleday, Page & Company, 1911.

Edmundson, Sarah Emma. *Unsexed: or, The Female Soldier. The Thrilling Adventures, Experiences and Escapes of a Woman, as Nurse, Spy and Scout, in Hospitals, Camps and Battle-Fields.* Philadelphia: Philadelphia Pub. Co., 1865.

————. *Nurse and Spy in the Union Army, Comprising the Adventures and Experiences of a Woman in Hospitals, Camps, and Battle-Fields.* Hartford, CT: W. S. Williams & Co., 1865.

Fitch, Michael Hendrick. *Echoes of the Civil War as I Hear Them.* New York: R. F. Fenno & Company, 1905.

Foster, Samuel T. *One of Cleburne's Command: The Civil War Reminiscences and Diary of Capt. Samuel T. Foster, Granbury's Texas Brigade, CSA.* Edited by Norman D. Brown. Austin: University of Texas Press, 1980.

Freeman, Julia Susan (Wheelock). *The Boys in White: The Experiences of a Hospital Agent in and around Washington.* New York: Lange & Hillman, 1870.

Gibbon, John. *Personal Recollections of the Civil War by John Gibbon, Brigadier-General, U.S.A.* New York: G. P. Putnam's Sons, 1928.

Greenhow, Rose O'Neal. *My Imprisonment and the First Year of Abolition Rule at Washington.* London: R. Bentley, 1863.

Haskell, Franklin Aretas. *The Battle of Gettysburg.* Madison: Wisconsion History Commission, 1908.

Haupt, Herman. *Reminiscences of General Herman Haupt.* Milwaukee, WI: Wright & Joys Co., Printers, 1901.

Heartsill, William Williston. *Fourteen Hundred and 91 Days in the Confederate Army.* 1876. Reprint, edited by Bell Irvin Wiley. Jackson, TN: McCowat-Mercer Press, 1953.

Higginson, Thomas Wentworth. *Army Life in a Black Regiment.* 1900. Reprint, Lansing, MI: State University Press, 1960.

Hinman, Wilbur F. *The Story of the Sherman Brigade. The Camp, the March, the Bivouac, the Battle; and How "The Boys" Lived and Died during Four Years of Active Field Service.* Alliance, OH: Author, 1897.

Hundley, Daniel Robinson. *Prison Echoes of the Great Rebellion.* New York: S. W. Green, Printer, 1874.

Hunter, Alvah Folsom. *A Year on a Monitor and the Destruction of Fort Sumter.* Edited by Craig L. Symonds. Columbia: University of South Carolina Press, 1987.

Jones, Samuel Calvin. *Reminiscences of the Twenty-second Iowa Volunteer Infantry,*

Giving Its Organization, Marches, Skirmishes, Battles, and Sieges, as Taken from the Diary of Lieutenant S. C. Jones of Company A. Iowa City, 1907.

Knox, Thomas Wallace. *Camp-fire and Cotton-field: Southern Adventure in Time of War. Life with the Union Armies, and Residence on a Louisiana Plantation.* New York: Blelock and Company, 1865.

Liddell, St. John Richardson. *Liddell's Record.* Edited by Nathaniel C. Hughes. Dayton, OH: Morningside House, 1985.

Logan, Mary Simmerson Cunningham. *Reminiscences of a Soldier's Wife: An Autobiography.* New York: C. Scribner's Sons, 1913.

Loughborough, Mary Ann Webster. *My Cave Life in Vicksburg. With Letters of Trial and Travel. By a Lady.* New York: D. Appleton and Company, 1864.

McCarthy, Carlton. *Detailed Minutiae of Soldier Life in the Army of Northern Virginia, 1861–1865.* Richmond: McCarthy, 1882.

Manigault, Arthur M. *A Carolinian Goes to War: The Civil War Narrative of Arthur Middleton Manigault, Brigadier General, C.S.A.* Edited by R. Lockwood Tower. Columbia: University of South Carolina Press, 1983.

Pember, Phoebe Yates. *A Southern Woman's Story: Life in Confederate Richmond.* Edited by Bell I. Wiley. Jackson, Tennessee: McCowat-Mercer Press, 1959.

Poague, William Thomas. *Gunner with Stonewall: Reminiscences of William Thomas Poague, a Memoir, Written for His Children in 1903.* Edited by Monroe F. Cockrell. Jackson, TN: McCowat-Mercer Press, 1957.

Porter, Horace. *Campaigning with Grant.* Edited by Wayne C. Temple. Bloomington: Indiana University Press, 1961.

Putnam, Sallie Brock. *Richmond during the War.* 1867. Reprint, Alexandria, VA: Time-Life Books, 1983.

Ross, Fitzgerald. *Cities and Camps of the Confederate States.* Edited by Richard Barksdale Harwell. Urbana: University of Illinois Press, 1958.

Sorrel, Gilbert Moxley. *Recollections of a Confederate Staff Officer.* Edited by Bell I. Wiley. Jackson, TN: McCowat-Mercer, 1958.

Stevens, George Thomas. *Three Years in the Sixth Corps. A Concise Narrative of Events in the Army of the Potomac from 1861 to the Close of the Rebellion, April 1865.* New York: D. Van Nostrand, 1870.

Stillwell, Leander. *The Story of a Common Soldier of Army Life in the Civil War, 1861–1865.* Erie, KS: Franklin Hudson Publishing Co., 1920.

Taylor, Susie King. *Reminiscences of My Life in Camp with the 33rd United States Colored Troops, Late 1st S. C. Volunteers.* 1902. Reprint, edited by Patricia W. Romero. New York: Markus Wiener Publishing, 1988.

Taylor, Walter Herron. *Four Years with General Lee.* Edited by James I. Robertson, Jr. Bloomington: Indiana University Press, 1962.

Trobriand, Philippe Regis Denis de Kereden, comte de. *Four Years with the Army of the Potomac.* Translated by George K. Dauchy. Boston: Ticknor and Company, 1889.

Velazquez, Loreta Janeta. *The Woman in Battle: A Narrative of the Exploits, Adventures, and Travels of Madame Loreta Janeta Velazquez, Otherwise Known as Lieutenant Harry T. Buford, Confederate States Army.* Edited by C. J. Worthington. Hartford, CT: T. Belknap, 1876.

Watkins, Samuel R. *"Co. Aytch," Maury Grays, First Tennessee Regiment: or, A Side Show of the Big Show.* 1882. Reprint, Jackson, TN: McCowat-Mercer, 1952.

Whitman, Walt. *Memoranda during the War.* Camden, NJ: Author's Publication, 1875–1876.

DIARIES AND JOURNALS

Andrews, Eliza Frances. *The War-Time Journal of a Georgia Girl, 1864–1865.* 1908. Reprint, edited by Bidwell King, Jr. Atlanta: Cherokee Publishing Co., 1976.

Chase, Salmon Portland. *The Salmon P. Chase Papers.* Vol. 1: *Journals, 1829–1872.* Edited by John Niven. Kent, OH: Kent State University Press, 1993.

Chesnut, Mary Boykin. *A Diary from Dixie.* Edited by Isabella D. Martin and Myrta Lockett Avary. New York: Appleton, 1905.

———. *A Diary from Dixie.* Edited by Ben Ames Williams. Boston: Houghton Mifflin, 1949.

———. *Mary Chesnut's Civil War.* Edited by C. Vann Woodward. New Haven, CT: Yale University Press, 1981.

———. *The Private Mary Chesnut: The Unpublished Civil War Diaries.* Edited by C. Vann Woodward and Elisabeth Muhlenfeld. New York: Oxford University Press, 1984.

Cumming, Kate. *Kate: The Journal of a Confederate Nurse.* Edited by Richard Barksdale Harwell. Baton Rouge: Louisiana State University Press, 1959.

Daly, Maria Lydig. *Diary of a Union Lady, 1861–1865.* Edited by Harold Earl Hammond. New York: Funk and Wagnalls Company, 1962.

Edmondston, Catherine A. D. *"Journal of a Secesh Lady": The Diary of Catherine Ann Devereux Edmonston, 1860–1866.* Edited by Beth G. Crabtree and James W. Patton. Raleigh: North Carolina Division of Archives and History, 1979.

Fremantle, Arthur James Lyon. *Three Months in the Southern States: April–June, 1863.* New York: Bradburn, 1864.

Fullam, George Townley. *The Journal of George Townley Fullam: Boarding Officer of the Confederate Sea Raider ALABAMA.* Edited by Charles G. Summersell. University: University of Alabama Press, 1973.

Gorgas, Josiah. *The Civil War Diary of General Josiah Gorgas.* Edited by Frank E. Vandiver. University: University of Alabama Press, 1947.

Holmes, Emma. *The Diary of Miss Emma Holmes: 1861–1866.* Edited by John F. Marszalek. Baton Rouge: Louisiana State University Press, 1979.

Howell, William Randolph. *Westward the Texans: The Civil War Journal of Private William Randolph Howell.* Edited by Jerry D. Thompson. El Paso: Texas Western Press, University of Texas at El Paso, 1990.

Jackman, John S. *Diary of a Confederate Soldier: John S. Jackman of the Orphan Brigade.* Edited by William C. Davis. Columbia: University of South Carolina Press, 1990.

Jones, John Beauchamp. *A Rebel War Clerk's Diary at the Confederate States Capital.* 2 vols. Edited by Howard Swiggett. New York: Old Hickory Bookshop, 1935.

Kean, Robert Garlick Hill. *Inside the Confederate Government: The Diary of Robert Garlick Hill Kean, Head of the Bureau of War.* Edited by Edward Younger. New York: Oxford University Press, 1957.

McDonald, Cornelia Peake. *A Woman's Civil War: A Diary, with Reminiscences of the War, from March 1862.* Edited by Minrose C. Gwin. Madison: University of Wisconsin Press, 1992.

Manigault, Edward. *Siege Train: The Journal of a Confederate Artilleryman in the Defense of Charleston.* Edited by Warren Ripley. Columbia: University of South Carolina Press for the Charleston Library Society, 1986.

Merrick, Morgan Wolfe. *From Desert to Bayou: The Civil War Journal and Sketches of Morgan Wolfe Merrick.* Edited by Jerry D. Thompson. El Paso: Texas Western Press, University of Texas at El Paso, 1991.

Morgan, Sarah. *The Civil War Diary of Sarah Morgan.* Edited by Charles East. Athens: University of Georgia Press, 1991.

Patrick, Robert. *Reluctant Rebel: The Secret Diary of Robert Patrick, 1861–1865.* Edited by F. Jay Taylor. Baton Rouge: Louisiana State University Press, 1959.

Peticolas, A. B. *Rebels on the Rio Grande: The Civil War Journal of A. B. Peticolas.* Edited by Don E. Alberts. Albuquerque: University of New Mexico Press, c. 1984.

Pringle, Cyrus Guernsey. *The Civil War Diary of Cyrus Pringle.* 1918. Reprint, Lebanon, PA: Sowers Printing Company, 1962.

Rhodes, Elijah Hunt. *All for the Union: The Civil War Diary and Letters of Elijah Hunt Rhodes.* Edited by Robert Hunt Rhodes. New York: Orion Books, 1985.

Ropes, Hannah. *Civil War Nurse: The Diary and Letters of Hannah Ropes.* Edited by John R. Brumgardt. Knoxville: University of Tennessee Press, 1980.

Ruffin, Edmund. *The Dairy of Edmund Ruffin.* Edited by William Kauffman Scarborough. 3 vols. Baton Rouge: Louisiana State University Press, 1972, 1976, 1989.

Stearns, Amanda (Akin). *The Lady Nurse of War E.* New York: Baker & Taylor Company, 1909.

Stearns, Amos E. *The Civil War Diary of Amos E. Stearns, a Prisoner at Andersonville.* Edited by Leon Basile. East Brunswick, NJ: Associated University Presses, 1981.

Strong, George Templeton. *The Diary of George Templeton Strong.* Edited by Allan Nevins and Milton Halsey Thomas. 4 vols. New York: Macmillan, 1952.

Thomas, Ella Gertrude Clanton. *The Secret Eye: The Journal of Ella Gertrude Clanton Thomas, 1848–1889.* Edited by Virginia Ingraham Burr. Chapel Hill: University of North Carolina Press, 1990.

Wainwright, Charles Shiels. *A Diary of Battle: The Personal Journals of Colonel Charles S. Wainwright, 1861–1865.* Edited by Allan Nevins. New York: Harcourt, Brace & World, 1962.

Welles, Gideon. *Diary.* 3 vols. Edited by Howard K. Beale. New York: W. W. Norton, 1960.

Wilson, Suzanne (Colton). *Column South: With the Fifteenth Pennsylvania Cavalry from Antietam to the Capture of Jefferson Davis.* Compiled by Suzanne Wilson. Edited by J. Ferrell Colton and Antoinette G. Smith. Flagstaff, AZ: J. F. Colton, 1960.

LETTERS

Abbott, Henry Livermore. *Fallen Leaves: The Civil War Letters of Major Henry Livermore Abbott.* Edited by Robert Garth Scott. Kent, OH: Kent State University Press, 1991.

Bragg, Junius Newport. *Letters of a Confederate Surgeon, 1861–65.* Edited by Mrs. T. J. Gaughan. Camden(?), AR, 1960.

Fox, Gustavus Vasa. *Confidential Correspondence of Gustavus Vasa Fox, Assistant Secretary of the Navy, 1861–1865.* 2 vols. Edited by Robert Means Thompson and

Richard Wainwright. New York: Printed for the Naval History Society by the DeVinne Press, 1918–1919.

Good, John J. *Cannon Smoke: The Letters of Captain John J. Good, Good-Douglas-Texas Battery, CSA.* Compiled and edited by Lester Newton Fitzhugh. Hillsboro, TX: Hill Junior College Press, 1971.

Gooding, James Henry. *On the Altar of Freedom: A Black Soldier's Civil War Letters from the Front. By Corporal James Henry Gooding.* Edited by Virginia M. Adams. Amherst: University of Massachusetts Press, 1991.

Haskell, Franklin Aretas. *The Battle of Gettysburg.* Madison: Wisconsin History Commission, 1908.

Hays, Alexander. *Life and Letters of Alexander Hays, Brevet Colonel United States Army, Brigadier General and Brevet Major General United States Volunteers.* Edited by George Thornton Fleming. Compiled by Gilbert Adams Hays. Pittsburgh, 1919.

Keeler, William Frederick. *Aboard the USS Monitor: 1862; the Letters of Acting Paymaster William Frederick Keeler, U.S. Navy, to his wife, Anna.* Edited by Robert W. Daly. Annapolis: U.S. Naval Institute, 1964.

Lauderdale, John Vance. *The Wounded River: The Civil War Letters of John Vance Lauderdale, M. D.* Edited by Peter Josyph. East Lansing: Michigan State University Press, 1993.

Lee, Elizabeth Blair. *Wartime Washington: The Civil War Letters of Elizabeth Blair Lee.* Edited by Virginia Jean Laas. Chicago: University of Illinois Press, 1991.

Lyman, Theodore. *Meade's Headquarters, 1863–1865: Letters of Colonel Theodore Lyman from the Wilderness to Appomattox.* Edited by George R. Agissiz. Boston: Atlantic, 1922.

McAllister, Robert. *The Civil War Letters of General Robert McAllister.* Edited by James I. Robertson, Jr. New Brunswick, NJ: Published for the New Jersey Civil War Centennial Commission by Rutgers University Press, 1965.

Peddy, George W. *Saddle Bag and Spinning Wheel: Being the Civil War Letters of George Peddy, M.D., Surgeon, 56th Georgia Volunteer Regiment, C.S.A., and His Wife Kate Featherston Peddy.* Edited by George Peddy Cuttino. Macon, GA: Mercer University Press, c. 1981.

Shaw, Robert Gould. *Blue-Eyed Child of Fortune: The Civil War Letters of Robert Gould Shaw.* Edited by Russell Duncan. Athens: University of Georgia Press, 1992.

Welch, Spenser Glasgow. *A Confederate Surgeon's Letters to his Wife, by Spenser Glasgow Welch.* 1911. Reprint, Marietta, GA: Continental Book Co., 1954.

Wightman, Edward King. *From Antietam to Fort Fisher: The Civil War Letters of Edward King Wightman, 1862–1865.* Edited by Edward G. Longacre. Rutherford, NJ: Fairleigh Dickinson University Press, 1985.

7

Published Papers

Michael L. Renshawe

Published papers are collections of original documents that have been edited, reprinted, and published in an orderly sequence. Civil War papers are collections of documents issued during the war by prominent military and political leaders. The documents range from military dispatches and battle reports with maps attached, to personal correspondence written by important figures to family and friends. Great modern events—and the Civil War was the first war to be so thoroughly documented—spawn millions of papers.

Editing and publishing papers is time-consuming and expensive. First, the originals have to be located. Often this means tracking them down in hundreds of scattered locations in government archives and libraries or in privately owned collections. The originals are copied, and the copies analyzed, categorized, and prepared for publication. Many require transposing from nineteenth-century handwritten script into modern text. The final step is to index and publish. The entire process can take years to complete. Not all papers are important. It is the editor's responsibility to determine which are historically worth publishing and which are not. Publication, however, is well worth the effort because it not only makes the papers easily accessible to the public but also protects the originals from wear and tear and from the inevitable self-destruction that is inherent in nineteenth-century acidic paper.

Published papers are the paper trail foundation on which history is written and are considered by historians and other scholars to be primary sources, not yet colored by analysis or interpretation or distorted by the vagueness of memory.

Unlike history books that describe and analyze historical events, papers are not intended to be read from beginning to end. By themselves they do not tell a complete story. Further analysis is needed. Instead, published papers are intended to be used as references that can provide bits and pieces, documentary evidence, from which a coherent story might be drawn.

Official papers cannot be presumed to be accurate or comprehensive. There may be gaps, with papers missing, lost, or destroyed. Many of General Robert E. Lee's military dispatches, for example, were burned during the retreat to Appomattox. The papers may describe what was intended, rather than what happened, or include factual errors based on incomplete or inaccurate information available at the time. Therefore, each paper, each letter, telegram, or general's report must be weighed judiciously with and against other documents and other pieces of historical evidence, and conclusions based on all available evidence must be drawn carefully.

The earlier sets of Civil War papers lack the sophisticated editing found in the more recent collections. Cross referencing—the linking of related documents, events, or people to one another—is rudimentary or lacking. Analytical notes providing background information or clarification of confusing documents are not provided.

The modern trend in publishing papers is to enhance the value of the collection by adding scholarly and extensive indexing, footnoting, cross referencing, and annotations. Modern collections are edited by experienced historians. Calling it a "high point" in his professional career, William W. Freehling, who once considered editing papers a lesser calling than writing history, changed his mind after coediting secession papers (Freehling and Simpson, *Secession Debated: Georgia's Showdown in 1860,* 1992). "I relished making previously obscure documents available, documents that invite readers to be their own historians. . . . May the editorial revolution continue," he wrote in *The Reintegration of American History: Slavery and the Civil War* (p. 4).

The next anticipated development in the editorial revolution will be for the full text of papers to be published on CD-ROM. This will enable users to search the cumulative body of text for words or phrases wherever they occur and will save library shelf space.

There is no question as to the value and importance of Civil War papers. James McPherson, to give but one of many examples, refers to various collected papers repeatedly in his Pulitzer Prize–winning one-volume history of the Civil War, *Battle Cry of Freedom* (1988). Indeed, it is difficult to imagine how history could be written without these key primary sources.

Following is a selection of significant Civil War papers that have been published or are in process of being published.

THE OFFICIAL RECORDS

Three compilations of the *Official Records* (*OR*) of the Civil War have been published by the U.S. government: the *OR-Armies,* the *OR-Atlas,* and the *OR-Navies.*

The *OR-Armies*

The War of the Rebellion (1880–1901) is the oldest, biggest, and best-known set of Civil War papers. This famous collection reproduces thousands of Union and Confederate telegrams, dispatches, orders, battle reports, and other primary military sources. *OR-Armies* was intended for the use of veterans, but historians, social scientists, journalists, genealogists, and a host of others have found it to be a virtual treasure trove documenting American life during the war.

The idea for the creation of the *OR-Armies* was inspired by Union General-in-Chief Henry W. Halleck, who in 1863, frustrated at the difficulty he had had in finding copies of military documents needed for his annual report, urged Congress to provide for their collection and publication. The following year Congress passed, and President Lincoln signed, a joint resolution calling for the printing of all important Union military records.

Although work began almost immediately, it was not until 1881 that the first eighteen volumes under the editorship of Robert N. Scott were published. By that time Confederate documents had been added. It took many years before the project was finished. Finally, in 1901, almost forty years after the original authorization, and at a cost in excess of $3 million dollars, the *OR-Armies* were complete.

The *OR-Armies* is massive and complicated. The set has seventy volumes made up of 127 different books, or parts. The papers are arranged by topic and then chronologically within topic.

The papers are subdivided into four series. Series I, the most complicated, consists of fifty-three volumes of 111 books. It contains army orders, dispatches and reports arranged by campaign and theater of operation, followed by correspondence. Union documents are reprinted first, followed by Confederate documents relating to the same event, and then correspondence.

Series II, eight volumes, with one book per volume, reprints Union and Confederate correspondence, orders, and reports relating to prisoners of war and political prisoners. Documents relating to post–Civil War trials, including the Lincoln assassination conspiracy trial, are included in this series.

Series III contains miscellaneous organizational and logistical papers. It consists of five one-book volumes.

Series IV, three volumes, also contains miscellaneous items, such as Confederate government correspondence, acts passed by the Confederate congress, and documents relating to conscription and blockade running.

The last volume is a revised general index of names, places, and military units. It also lists each volume and part of the full set and provides a summary of each.

All available documents deemed significant and official, and written during the war, are reprinted, with several categorical exceptions: routine correspondence, papers relating to individuals of lower rank, and documents previously published.

The *OR-Atlas*

The *Atlas to Accompany the Official Records of the Union and Confederate Armies* was compiled and published in five volumes (1891–1895). This set reprints 821 maps, 106 engravings, and 209 drawings. The maps are of varying size and scale, and most were originally attached to reports reproduced in *OR-Armies*. Sketches, fortification plans, landscape photographs, and drawings of equipment, weapons, uniforms, buttons, and flags are also included.

The maps are arranged chronologically. There are exceptions, however, because some maps were placed out of order to avoid wasting page space, and others were discovered too late to have been included in their proper chronological order and were tacked into later volumes. Actual battle maps are rare, although Sheridan's map of Perryville and Sherman's of Shiloh are reprinted. Military maps are reproduced with colors added—blue indicating Union lines and red for Confederate lines. Sketches of uniforms and flags are also illustrated in colors.

Less than a third of the maps are Confederate. Confederate maps were difficult to find after the war, in part because of the scarcity in general of Confederate documents due to the ravages of the war, and partly because the Confederacy lacked the resources needed to produce enough maps, especially toward the end.

There are cross references between documents in the *OR-Armies* and their accompanying maps in the *OR-Atlas*. However, because of the publishing sequence, many *OR-Armies* volumes were published before the *OR-Atlas* work began, so these references can be confusing. Early *OR-Armies* volumes contain some references to maps that "will appear in the Atlas" but lack a page number. Others refer to maps not available at publication but were found in time to be reprinted in the *OR-Atlas*. In the latter case, the references are one way only—from the *OR-Atlas* back to the *OR-Armies*.

The *OR-Navies*

The *Official Records of the Union and Confederate Navies in the War of the Rebellion* is a naval counterpart to the *OR-Armies,* not a supplement. The *OR-Navies* was published in a thirty-one-volume set, the first of which appeared in 1894. New volumes were published thereafter on a regular basis until printing was temporarily halted during World War I. The last three volumes were published in 1921 and 1922.

The naval records are divided into two series. Series I, twenty-seven volumes, contains official reports and documents relating to Union and Confederate naval operations. The papers in Series I are grouped according to where the action took place—on the high seas, on rivers, or on the Atlantic or Gulf coasts. They are further subdivided by geographic region—the "South Atlantic," the "Potomac and Rappahannock Rivers," and so on. Within subcategories the arrangement is chronological.

Series II, the last three volumes published after World War I, contains a variety of statistics, muster rolls, Navy Department correspondence, and the "Pickett Papers." Named after Colonel John T. Pickett, a Confederate diplomat and soldier from whom they were purchased in 1872, the "Pickett Papers" are historically very valuable because they comprise the Confederate State Department's foreign relations' archive.

Although there is no map supplement, the *OR-Navies* reproduces many maps, as well as sketches of ships, tables, and photographs.

Using the *OR*s

Together, the *OR*s provide a wonderful, rich, and unique source of primary materials; 147,668 pages of text and 1,136 maps and sketches. Copies were freely distributed by Congress to individuals and libraries. The *OR*s were also published as part of the Congressional Serial Set found in U.S. government depository libraries around the country. Today those original volumes may be in poor physical condition, with dry, split bindings and brittle pages. Reprint editions in paper and in microform have been published and can be found in many libraries. Individual original volumes can be acquired from antiquarian book dealers. The Broadfoot Publishing Company in Wilmington, North Carolina, has embarked on the ambitious task of reprinting the *OR*s on CD-ROM.

The *OR*s are difficult to use, by beginner and expert alike. Their huge mass can be intimidating. But it is their complexity of arrangement (especially the *OR-Armies*), generally poor indexing and cross referencing, and the lack of notes that can quickly lead users astray. Finding aids or guides can make the task much easier.

OR Finding Aids and User Guides

Military Operations of the Civil War: A Guide-Index to the Official Records of the Union and Confederate Armies, 1861–1865 (1966–1980), was created by the National Archives and Records Service (now the National Archives Records Administration) to counter these problems. This extensive *Guide-Index,* in five volumes with nine parts, cross references items found in the three *OR* sets. Thus, researchers can bypass the poor original indexing and referencing. The *Guide-Index* is essential for the serious researcher but in itself requires considerable effort to master.

Alan Aimone and Barbara Aimone's *A User's Guide to the Official Records of the American Civil War* (1993) is easier to use and should be consulted by anyone with even a passing interest in the *OR*s. The slim, 125-page paperback provides a quick and useful insight into the quirks found in the *OR*s. It does not provide better indexing, but it does provide historical background and alerts users to many shortcomings and limitations. The *User's Guide* also provides bibliographies of other finding aids, *OR* reprint editions, Union and Confederate documents and sources not found in the *OR*s, congressional documents relating to the war, map sources not found in the *OR*s, and correlation charts showing where *OR* volumes can be located in the Congressional Serial Set.

PAPERS OF IMPORTANT CIVIL WAR FIGURES

Abraham Lincoln (1809–1865)

The definitive edition of Lincoln's papers is *The Collected Works of Abraham Lincoln* (1953–1955), edited by Roy P. Basler and others. The basic set has nine volumes, volume 9 being the index. Two supplemental volumes, 1974 and 1990, reproduce documents discovered after the basic set had been completed.

All of Lincoln's writings and speeches that could be found are included, with the exception of his legal papers. The legal papers are being collected by the Lincoln Legal Papers Project, and it is anticipated that they will eventually be published on CD-ROM (Benner 1994).

For speeches where the original text was not available, newspaper accounts are used. Papers that Lincoln wrote and documents he signed but did not write are included. Papers not reprinted in full are noted chronologically (calendared). Updated papers, known writings for which no text has been found, papers that are known to be forgeries, and spurious or dubious papers are chronologically listed in volume 8.

The Collected Works of Abraham Lincoln is well indexed, provides extensive and useful footnoting, and contains many interesting facsimiles and illustrations. The arrangement is chronological for both the main work and supplements, making updating easy.

Andrew Johnson (1808–1875)

The Papers of Andrew Johnson (1967–), published in eleven volumes to date, cover his full life and political career. The first volumes contain a wide array of items, including his marriage license and property deeds. The last four volumes emphasize political papers and documents, with a large selection of personal and official letters written by him and to him. The arrangement is chronological.

The war years are covered in volumes 4 through 8, followed by papers relating to his presidency during Reconstruction and the aftermath of the war. Modern editing techniques add considerable value; for example, people referred to are identified, and text is clarified with square bracketed inserts whenever necessary.

Jefferson Davis (1808–1889)

Eight volumes of *The Papers of Jefferson Davis* (1971–), edited by Haskell M. Monroe and others, have been published. When finished, this edition will be the definitive collection of Davis papers, superseding *Jefferson Davis, Constitutionalist, His Letters, Papers, and Speeches* (1923), collected and edited by Dunbar Rowland in ten volumes. The first eight volumes cover Davis's career through 1862.

The bulk of Davis papers is massive and increases dramatically through the war years. Monroe is comprehensive in his coverage through 1853 and thereafter becomes, by necessity, more selective. From 1853 on, the emphasis is on personal and political correspondence, speeches, letters of recommendation, foreign affairs, military matters, annual reports, and budgets. The arrangement is chronological.

The papers are calendared when not reprinted in full. All are cross referenced, extensively footnoted, and annotated. Brief biographies of people referred to are given. Each volume is indexed and has a bibliography of sources cited. When complete, it is expected that the set will have twenty to twenty-five volumes. The last volume will contain a cumulative bibliography and index and genealogical charts.

The Messages and Papers of Jefferson Davis and the Confederacy, Including Diplomatic Correspondence 1861–1865 (1905), edited by James D. Richardson, begins with the provisional Constitution of the Confederacy. Richardson reprints messages, proclamations, inaugural addresses, and other official papers without comment or notes. Brief biographical sketches of Jefferson and other leaders, and brief accounts of more than 100 battles fought by the rebels, are included. The arrangement is chronological by Confederate session of congress. A reprint edition, with an introduction by Allan Nevins, was published by Chelsea House in 1966.

Ulysses Simpson Grant (1822–1885)

The Papers of Ulysses S. Grant (1967–), twenty volumes of which are available to date, will cover his entire military and political careers when finished. The volumes covering the Civil War (volumes 2–14) have been published.

The Grant papers are an excellent example of the benefits of modern scholarly editing. The collection includes all known papers. Significant papers are published in full; other are calendared without reproducing their full text.

The arrangement is chronological, and editorial insertion has been kept to a minimum. Grant's misspellings, grammatical errors, and errors in punctuation have been reproduced exactly as in the originals. Extensive notes provide additional information about persons, places, or events. Sentences or words crossed out by Grant appear as ~~cancelled text~~.

Each volume is carefully indexed by person, place, or event and includes a preface and a chronology of major events covered in that volume. Location symbols are used to indicate where the original documents were found.

George Brinton McClellan (1826–1885)

McClellan's papers are found in *The Civil War Papers of George B. McClellan* (1992), edited by Stephen Sears. This one-volume compilation reprints 813 selected papers, many related to military matters. One-third had never been published, and another 192, letters to his wife, are published for the first time in uncensored form. Sears drew heavily on these papers in writing his excellent biography of the general, and they serve as an interesting companion volume to the biography.

Robert E. Lee (1807–1870)

General Lee's papers are found in three sources. The *OR-Armies* reprint many of his strictly military papers.

Lee's Dispatches: Unpublished Letters of General Robert E. Lee, C.S.A. to Jefferson Davis and the War Department of the Confederate States of America, 1862–65 (1915) were reprinted from the manuscripts privately owned by Wymberley Jones De Renne, a Georgia bibliophile. Douglas Southall Freeman, later the author of the Pulitzer Prize–winning four-volume biography *R. E. Lee* (1934–1935), worked for five years editing and compiling these important papers that document the special relationship between Lee and Davis, and the Confederate government. A new edition, with additional dispatches, and a foreword by Grady McWhiney, was published in 1957. A paperback reprint of the McWhiney edition was published in 1994.

The Wartime Papers of Robert E. Lee (1961), edited by Clifford Dowdey and Louis Manarin, compiles Lee's most significant wartime papers. About one-sixth of the more than 6,000 known papers are reproduced. Dowdey concentrates on personal letters to Mrs. Lee and the children and messages concerning the general's major military operations. Administrative documents have been excluded.

Lee's battle reports are reprinted, except for the years 1864 and 1865. These, and much correspondence, were burned on the road to Appomattox. General Order No. 9 (April 10, 1965), his "affectionate farewell" to his soldiers, is reprinted in full.

Lee's spelling and grammar have been preserved. There are few inserts or notes in the body of the text. Notes, cross references to the *OR-Armies,* original document locations, and an index are given separately.

Frederick Douglass (1817–1895)

The Frederick Douglass Papers (1979–) are edited by John W. Blassingame and others. The five volumes of series 1, "Speeches, Debates, and Interviews," have been published. When complete, series 2 and 3 will reprint his published writings and letters.

The war years are covered in volumes 3 and 4 of series 1. Douglass, a former slave, the son of a slave and a white man, became a major antislavery speaker and writer. In addition to slavery, he pronounced on foreign affairs, women's rights, and a host of other political and social issues. His speeches and debates are chronologically arranged. Useful and full footnotes are provided, and each volume is carefully indexed.

BIBLIOGRAPHY

Aimone, Alan C., and Barbara A. Aimone. *A User's Guide to the Official Records of the American Civil War.* Shippensburg, PA: White Mane Publishing Company, 1993.

Benner, Martha L. "The Abraham Lincoln Legal Papers: The Development of the Complete Facsimile Edition on CD-ROM." *Documentary Editing* 16 (December 1994).

Davis, Jefferson. *Jefferson Davis, Constitutionalist, His Letters, Papers and Speeches.* 10 vols. Edited by Dunbar Rowland. Jackson, MS: Printed for the Mississippi Department of Archives and History, 1923.

———. *The Messages and Papers of Jefferson Davis and the Confederacy, Including Diplomatic Correspondence 1861–1865.* 2 vols. Edited by James D. Richardson. New York: Chelsea House, 1966.

———. *The Papers of Jefferson Davis.* 8 vols. Edited by Haskell M. Monroe, Jr., et al. Baton Rouge: Louisiana State University Press, 1971–.

Douglass, Frederick. *The Frederick Douglass Papers.* Series 1. 5 vols. Edited by John W. Blassingame et al. New Haven: Yale University Press, 1979–.

Freehling, William W. *The Reintegration of American History: Slavery and the Civil War.* New York: Oxford University Press, 1994.

Freehling, William W., and Craig M. Simpson, eds. *Secession Debated; Georgia's Showdown in 1860.* New York: Oxford University Press, 1992.

Freeman, Douglas Southall. *R. E. Lee: A Biography.* 4 vols. New York: S. Scribner's Sons, 1934–1935.

Grant, Ulysses Simpson. *The Papers of Ulysses S. Grant.* 20 vols. Edited by John Y. Simon. Carbondale: Southern Illinois University Press, 1967–.

Johnson, Andrew. *The Papers of Andrew Johnson.* 11 vols. Edited by LeRoy P. Graf et al. Knoxville: University of Tennessee Press, 1967–.

Lee, Robert Edward. *Lee's Dispatches: Unpublished Letters of General Robert E. Lee, C.S.A. to Jefferson Davis and the War Department of the Confederate States of America, 1862–65, from the Private Collection of Wymberley Jones De Renne, of Wormsloe, Georgia.* 1915. Reprint, edited by Douglas Southall Freeman. Baton Rouge: Louisiana State University Press, 1994.

———. *The Wartime Papers of Robert E. Lee.* Virginia Civil War Centennial, 1961–1965. Edited by Clifford Dowdey and Louis H. Manarin. Boston: Little, Brown, 1961.

Lincoln, Abraham. *The Collected Works of Abraham Lincoln.* 9 vols. Edited by Roy P. Basler, Marion Dolores Pratt, and Lloyd A. Dunlap. New Brunswick, NJ: Rutgers University Press, 1953–1955.

———. *The Collected Works of Abraham Lincoln. Second Supplement, 1848–1865.* Edited by Roy P. Basler and Christian O. Basler. New Brunswick, NJ: Rutgers University Press, 1990.

————. *The Collected Works of Abraham Lincoln. Supplement, 1832–1865.* Edited by Roy P. Basler. Westport, CT: Greenwood Press, 1974.

Mahan, Harold E. "The Arsenal of History: The Official Records of the War of the Rebellion." *Civil War History* 29 (1983): 5–27.

McClellan, George Brinton. *The Civil War Papers of George B. McClellan: Selected Correspondence, 1860–1865.* Edited by Stephen W. Sears. New York: Da Capo Press, 1992.

McPherson, James M. *Battle Cry of Freedom: The Civil War Era.* New York: Ballantine Books, 1989.

National Archives and Records Service. *Military Operations of the Civil War: A Guide-Index to the Official Records of the Union and Confederate Armies, 1861–1865.* 9 parts, 5 vols. Washington, D.C.: Government Printing Office, 1966–1980.

United States. Navy Department. *Official Records of the Union and Confederate Navies in the War of the Rebellion.* 31 vols. Washington, D.C.: Government Printing Office, 1894–1927.

United States. War Department. *Atlas to Accompany the Official Records of the Union and Confederate Armies.* 5 vols. Washington, D.C.: Government Printing Office, 1891–1895.

————. *The War of the Rebellion: A Compilation of the Official Records of the Union and Confederate Armies/Prepared Under the Direction of the Secretary of War . . .* 128 books in 80 vols. Washington, D.C.: Government Printing Office, 1880–1901.

8

Unpublished Manuscript Collections

Steven Fisher

In the introduction to their classic *Civil War Books, A Critical Bibliography* (1969), editors Allan Nevins, James I. Robertson Jr., and Bell I. Wiley discuss their criteria for selection of the materials covered. Regarding unpublished manuscripts they note that these "were excluded because . . . in many instances the manuscripts are so widely scattered that compilers would have been unreasonably burdened if they attempted to include them and . . . for the most part, users of manuscripts are professional historians who already know where and how to gain access to these sources" (p. vii). Not only were manuscripts excluded, but most published guides to manuscript collections were as well.

One can sympathize with the desire not to burden compilers. However, while it is true that in most cases the users of these documents are professional historians, it is doubtful that even they always have a clear idea about where the manuscripts they seek are located and how to access them.

In 1967, when *Civil War Books* was published, the primary method of communication between scholars about the location of primary sources was word of mouth. Thankfully this is no longer true. In the years since its publication, a number of useful tools have emerged to aid the researcher in search of unpublished manuscript collections relating to the Civil War.

Manuscript collections are the raw material on which scholarly research is built. To state that the Civil War was well documented is, of course, an understatement. In fact, perhaps no other single event in our history was so well documented; it is the subject of over 50,000 published works. This is not surprising. Individuals involved in the conflict sensed that what they were involved in was monumental. Many, like President Rutherford B. Hayes, would look back upon it as the high point in their lives. Virtually every regiment to see action on both sides produced elaborate histories. Governmental agencies on both sides were well aware of the future significance of the war and preserved thousands of feet of records.

It has been estimated that over 80 percent of the combatants could read and write, and it was quite common for them to send frequent letters and keep detailed diaries of their daily activities. A surprising number of these documents survived, passed down in families North and South from generation to generation. Many have found their way into libraries, archives, and museums.

While the sheer weight of primary source material attracts researchers, there is a downside. Unlike many other countries where the majority of documents are housed in one or two large central libraries, U.S. records are scattered throughout the land, often in places one would never think of looking. For example, at my own institution, the Special Collections Department of the University of Denver library houses a proclamation naming Jefferson Davis the U.S. secretary of war. The document is signed by President Franklin Pierce. Scrawled in one corner is a note stating that the document was seized by Union troops from Davis's home near the end of the war. How it ended up in Colorado is a mystery. Though we know it has been in our possession for decades, we have been unable to find any history of its ownership or record of its donation.

Researchers seeking to explore the papers of the more familiar war leaders face a daunting challenge. Letters and papers of such luminaries as U. S. Grant and Robert E. Lee are preserved in over twenty different repositories. Logically, much material is preserved near the center of conflict, in such places as Washington D.C., Virginia, Maryland, and Pennsylvania, but significant collections are found as far away as California, where little fighting occured. Fortunately, there now exist a number of research tools that tell us what is available and where, and most institutions housing Civil War documents are more than happy to assist researchers.

The majority of manuscript repositories compile detailed finding aids to their individual collections. These may be referred to as guides, registers, indexes, inventories, or calendars. Occasionally these guides are published, depending on the significance of the material. If so, it is probably possible to obtain them through interlibrary loan. If unpublished, most institutions will supply a copy of internal finding aids for a small copying fee. One has only to scan the acknowledgments in most published Civil War monographs to recognize the essential bond that has been established between researchers and archivists, curators, and librarians.

Because of the wide dispersal of manuscript material it is likely that in many cases the researcher will have to travel some distance, and so consulting finding aids first is essential. Donald L. DeWitt, in his *Guides to Archives and Manuscript Collections in the United States,* observes that "consulting them before visiting the repository holding the collection could save researchers time and money. For those attempting research by mail, these finding aids could be of immeasurable help in formulating appropriate and specific research questions'' (p. ix).

Many manuscript repositories have small staffs and limited hours, and the researcher should be prepared to describe the nature of his or her interest. Many collections are restricted to use by qualified researchers, and for good reason. Most original documents from the Civil War era are fragile in nature, and repeated use may shorten the life of the material. Repository staff therefore want to ensure that the researcher's needs are such that they could not possibly be met with secondary sources. Still, in most cases the term ''qualified researcher'' is interpreted loosely. The researcher should also inquire of the repository staff if anyone else is currently pursuing a similar topic, as this may save much wasted time.

Security is a major concern in manuscript repositories. Thefts do happen. For this reason, researchers are usually asked to fill out detailed user forms and to surrender coats and briefcases, which are placed in a separate area. Pens are discouraged, and pencils encouraged, for obvious reasons.

Copyright is an issue that should not be ignored by the researcher, despite the age of Civil War records. The staff at the institution where the research is being conducted can advise the researcher as to any restrictions regarding use of material. This is best done at the beginning, to prevent a waste of the researcher's time.

The computer has dramatically changed the way in which researchers can and will access information about Civil War resources. Most libraries have replaced the traditional card catalog with PACS (public access catalogs) online. Many belong to consortia with shared catalogs, allowing the researcher to search other libraries in the region at the same time. The two largest electronic databases for library materials, the On-line Catalog of the Library of Congress and the Research Libraries Information Network, are now available to the public in many academic libraries. Indexes once produced only on paper are now becoming available as CD-ROM products.

Researchers now have at their fingertips collection data from hundreds of institutions by ''Gopher'' systems, an Internet information retrieval system that makes available the holdings of a number of institutions online. Subject interest groups known as lists abound on the Internet, an international e-mail source. One in particular, titled ''H-net Civil War,'' is dedicated to discussion of Civil War topics and is subscribed to by prominent scholars, archivists, librarians, and students. This is an excellent means by which to locate fugitive material. No matter how small the collection or seemingly trivial the topic, chances are that someone on the list has seen or worked with it at one time or another.

Many academic institutions are now connected to the Internet and make it available to faculty and students. A growing number of public libraries have access. Many commercial services offer Internet connections, known as ''gateways,'' for home computer use. Three of the larger vendors are America Online, CompuServe, and Prodigy.

GENERAL SOURCES FOR MANUSCRIPT COLLECTIONS

A number of sources give broad information about unpublished Civil War manuscripts. By far the best source is *the Library of Congress's National Union Catalog of Manuscript Collections* (NUCMC), a multivolume compilation of individual manuscript collection records of all types, issued annually by the Special Materials Cataloging Division of the library from 1959 to 1993. Manuscript repositories fill out special collection record forms issued by the Library of Congress and return them for inclusion in the catalog. In 1994 it was decided to eliminate paper volumes. A decision is forthcoming concerning publication in alternative electronic format, such as a CD-ROM product.

Currently, NUCMC contains over 70,000 collections, taken from records submitted by over 1,400 repositories. Typical NUCMC entries provide a great deal of information about the individual collections described. This includes a summary statement about the contents of the collection, the size of the collection, any access restrictions, how the collection was acquired, and whether a finding aid exists.

NUCMC has always been considered difficult to use because it is arranged not by subject or collection name but by collection numbers referring to the year the record form was sent to the Library of Congress. Each volume must be used with a separately published index. Eight separate cumulative indexes match collection name to number, and the researcher had to search all eight compilations to find collections of interest. The only merged catalog is at the Library of Congress. That problem was partially solved with the publication of Harriet Ostroff's *Index to Personal Names in the National Union Catalog of Manuscript Collections, 1959–1984* (1988), which merges the eight compiled indexes into two volumes.

Most other general guides to manuscript collections are arranged by either broad subject headings or geographic location. Lee Ash's *Subject Collections* (1993) lists manuscript repositories and libraries by subject and contains a substantial Civil War section. It is not as detailed or comprehensive as the NUCMC but is much easier to access and provides such useful information as repository address, telephone number, and hours of operation. However, like any other compilation based on responses to a questionnaire, it should be used with caution. Many large collections are not represented.

Several guides organize manuscript material by geographic locale. Though published more than thirty years ago, the best of these is still Philip M. Hamer's *A Guide to Archives and Manuscripts in the United States* (1961). A handy single-volume work, it describes the manuscript holdings of some 1,300 repositories and contains a detailed subject index. *The Directory of Archives and Manuscript Repositories in the United States* (1988), a project of the National Historical Publications and Records Commission, is a geographical compilation that provides collection information for over 4,000 repositories by state. A repository and subject index is also provided.

The Subject Directory of Special Libraries and Information Centers, edited by Brigitte Darney and John Nimchuk (1985), is a five-volume compilation arranged geographically by broad subject areas. Civil War material is found in the History section. Nearly 2,000 "history libraries" are cited. Major collections in each repository are listed, along with the address and telephone number of each. Especially helpful are the names of the key repository personnel. A subject index is provided.

Donald DeWitt's *Guides to Archives and Manuscript Collections in the United States: An Annotated Bibliography* (1994) is the first one-volume general listing of guides to collections of all types. While not exhaustive, it is a long-awaited resource and includes a section describing a number of federal, state, and local guides to Civil War collections, with accompanying commentary.

Special Collections in Libraries of the Southeast, edited by J. B. Howell, is a valuable regional guide with descriptions of a number of Civil War collections, primarily Confederate, arranged by state. This compilation was the result of a survey conducted in 1977 by a special committee of the Southeast Library Association. For this reason the amount of detail about individual collections varies. A subject index is included.

GOVERNMENTAL RECORDS AND PRESIDENTIAL PAPERS

It is not surprising that war records of the U.S. government are both more voluminous and complete than those of the Confederate States of America. Henry Putney Beers comments in his *Guide to the Archives of the Government of the Confederate States of America* (1968) that "even had the Government of the Confederate States of America been in a position to protect, evaluate, and organize its own archives at the end of the Civil War there probably would not have survived as intact and complete a collection of the general records of government as exists for the Government of the United States for the war period. Indeed, differing concepts within the Confederacy of the political character of national government, the greater autonomy of State government and a wartime situation all mitigated against the creation of complete documentation of a general character" (p. 1). The federal government, of course, survived the war and continued to produce war-related records for decades after the fighting ended. The vast majority of fighting took place in the South, with the usual destruction that accompanies war. Beers also observed that "many of the Confederate archives have been lost or destroyed" (p. v).

The National Archives in Washington, D.C., contain the largest amount of Civil War governmental records, both Federal and Confederate. Anyone considering pursuing research at the National Archives should consult *Regulations for Public Use of Records in the National Archives* (1991), a booklet that describes access restrictions, fee structures for searching and copying, and hours of operation.

Twenty-five years after publication, the standard source for information about Civil War governmental records continues to be Kenneth W. Munden and Henry Putney Beers's *The Union: A Guide to Federal Archives Relating to the Civil War* (1962) and Beers's companion volume, *Guide to the Archives of the Confederate States of America* (1968). Meticulous in detail, these volumes describe Civil War records from the various branches of the Federal and Confederate governments, including Congress, the judiciary, the presidency, Departments of State and Treasury, War Department, Attorney General, Post Office, Navy, Interior, Agriculture, and miscellaneous departments.

Federal and Confederate governmental records are also housed in other federal records centers and various state and private institutions. Munden and Beers detail these holdings. Both volumes include a substantial subject and name index.

Since George Washington, presidents have considered papers created in the White House as personal property. After his death, Abraham Lincoln's papers passed through several hands, until many were deposited in the Library of Congress. Other important Lincoln collections are housed at the Chicago Historical Society, the University of Chicago, the Illinois State Historical Library, Brown University, the Huntington Library, Harvard University, and the New York Public Library. Each of these institutions has produced detailed finding aids to its holdings—for example, *The Lincoln Collection of the Illinois State Historical Library* by Paul M. Angle (1940).

The Munden and Beers volumes relate the interesting history of both Lincoln and Jefferson Davis papers. Many of Davis's papers were destroyed as the government fled south from Richmond, but some were seized by the Union army and turned over to the War Department in Washington in 1865. Outside of the Library of Congress, the most important Davis collections are found at the Louisiana Historical Association, the Mississippi Department of Archives and History, and Duke University. One published guide to Davis papers is *The Calendar of the Jefferson Davis Postwar Manuscripts in the Louisiana Historical Association Collection* (1970).

We associate Lincoln with the war, but several later American presidents played active roles, including James A. Garfield, Ulysses S. Grant, and Rutherford B. Hayes, and much Civil War material is contained in their papers. Garfield rose to the rank of major general in the war, after serving as chief of staff in the Army of the Cumberland. His military correspondence is housed in the Library of Congress, along with his presidential papers.

Grant was a notoriously poor record keeper. In his *Records of the Presidency* (1989) Frank L. Schick quotes a close associate of Grant, noting that when he first met him in 1861 his "office was substantially in his hat or his pockets" (p. 86). Despite this reputation, the Library of Congress contains over one hundred volumes of significant Civil War papers generated by the future president. Other major Grant collections are housed at the Huntington Library and the New-York Historical Society.

Hayes's Civil War career, while perhaps not as distinguished as that of his fellow presidents, is of interest. He commanded an Ohio regiment and was brevetted major general of volunteers in 1865. Unlike Grant, he was a meticulous record keeper all of his life, and his wartime letters served as the basis for T. Harry Williams's *Hayes of the Twenty-third* (1965). Hayes's Civil War papers are preserved at the Hayes Library, Fremont, Ohio, where more than 1 million manuscript pieces and 70,000 books are kept.

A number of recent works dealing with presidential manuscript collections have been produced. Unfortunately, they deal primarily with the presidential library system that has evolved since the Hoover administration. One notable exception is *Records of the Presidency* by Frank L. Schick et al. (1989), which offers a detailed description of the papers of each president. *Presidential Libraries and Collections* by Fritz Veit (1987) traces the efforts to collect and describe presidential papers throughout our history and describes how the various collections came to be located where they are.

MISCELLANEOUS FINDING AIDS

A large number of finding aids have been produced that describe Civil War manuscript collections in a general way, statewide or in individual institutions. These include descriptions of holdings in miscellaneous governmental archives, historical societies, and public and private libraries. They range from booklets of several pages giving broad descriptions to large, detailed compilations of several hundred pages. Many were produced during or just after the Civil War centennial. Several are worthy of note as strong examples of the various types.

Confederate Guides

Among the best Confederate institutional guides is the *Guide to Civil War Records in the North Carolina State Archives,* produced by the North Carolina State Department of Archives and History (1966). This work includes detailed content notes to each collection. Another of note is Patti Carr Black and Maxyne Madden Grimes's *Guide to Civil War Source Material in the Department of Archives and History, State of Mississippi* (1962). Among the more extensive state guides is Allen D. Candler's *The Confederate Records of the State of Georgia* (1972), a five-volume set. *Confederate Research Sources: A Guide to Archive Collections,* by James C. Neagles (1986), is geared primarily toward genealogical research.

Union Guides

There are a number of excellent resources for Northern collections. An excellent institutional compilation of state archival records is *Wisconsin's Civil War Archives,* compiled by William G. Paul (1965) and published by the State Historical Society of Wisconsin. Among the better state guides are the comprehensive *Descriptive Bibliography of Civil War Manuscripts in Illinois* by William L. Burton (1966). Ann Turner's *Guide to Indiana Civil War Manuscripts* (1965) is a fine work arranged by military units. Individual collections are described in detail.

DIARIES

Diaries constitute a unique primary resource. A large percentage of the hundreds of known Civil War diaries have been transcribed and printed in whole or in part, but many remain unpublished. Some useful bibliographies have been created to assist the researcher in finding out what diaries have been published. William Matthews, considered the greatest American bibliographer of diaries, confessed that "so numerous are the diaries of Americans who took part in the Civil War that when I was making my bibliography of American diaries, my courage failed me and I called a halt at 1860." The Matthews bibliography, *American Diaries in Manuscript,* would later be expanded through the year 1954 and is an excellent source for locating Civil War diaries. It describes over 5,000 diaries from 400 institutions, with an index to names.

Diaries offer a first-hand, unedited view of the war. Consider the role of women and African Americans in the war. Our understanding of the role of women in the war is enhanced through diaries because in general they had no official role in the conflict and so are absent from the institutional record. The same is true of African Americans. While only a small percentage were able to read and write, quite a few left diaries for us to study.

Several institutions contain large diary collections, but few have produced separate guides to their diary holdings. A notable exception is *A Guide to Manuscript Diaries and Journals in the Special Collections Department, Rutgers University,* compiled by Donald A. Sinclair. Over three hundred separate items are described, including biographical information about the diarist. Reid Mitchell's *Civil War Soldiers* (1988) was based largely on diaries and letters of the common soldier and contains an excellent bibliography listing over forty diaries he consulted at over twenty institutions. Not suprisingly, Mitchell found the largest number of diaries at the National Archives, but he found other significant collections at Tulane University, the University of Michigan, the New-York Historical Society, and the University of Texas at Austin.

MAJOR REPOSITORIES

A few repositories are worthy of note for depth and quality of material. Institutions that house Civil War manuscripts naturally differ in quality, quality of the physical structures housing materials, and quality of collections. They also differ in size, size of budget, and size of staff. These differences are the result not only of luck, location, and historical accident but also the commitment of interested and dedicated people and organizations.

Chicago Public Library, Chicago

The Special Collections department houses the Civil War and American History Research Collection, which includes manuscripts of Ulysses S. Grant, William Tecumseh Sherman, and John C. Breckinridge, as well as records of the Army of the Potomac. These and other collections are described in *Treasures of the Chicago Public Library,* compiled by Thomas A. Orliando and Marie Gecik (1977).

Duke University, Durham, North Carolina

The Special Collections department of the William R. Perkins Library contains a number of collections of prominent Confederate military leaders, including Robert E. Lee, P.T.G. Beauregard, Braxton Bragg, James Longstreet, Joseph E. Johnston, and George E. Pickett. Researchers may refer to the *Guide to the Cataloged Collections in the Manuscript Department of the William R. Perkins Library, Duke University,* edited by Richard C. Davis and Linda Angle Miller (1980), which lists nearly 6,000 collections.

Henry E. Huntington Library, San Marino, California

The Huntington Library contains a vast array of Civil War manuscripts, including letters of Braxton Bragg, Jubal Early, U. S. Grant, Henry W. Halleck, Joseph Hooker, Joseph E. Johnston, George B. McClellan, William T. Sherman, J.E.B. Sherman, J.E.B. Stuart, Charles Sumner, and Gideon Welles. For more information consult Richard C. Davis's *Guide to American Historical Manuscripts in the Huntington Library* (1979).

Library of Congress, Washington, D.C.

The library holds the largest single repository of Civil War–related manuscripts. In addition to governmental records, it contains collections of papers of Benjamin F. Butler, James A. Garfield, U. S. Grant, Horace Greeley, Robert E. Lee, George B. McClellan, John Nicolay, George E. Pickett, Edmund Ruffin, William H. Seward, Philip H. Sheridan, William T. Sherman, Edwin M. Stanton, and Gideon Welles, among others. Consult the *National Union Catalog of Manuscript Collections* for descriptions of the individual collections.

New-York Historical Society, New York City

The society's holdings include letters and papers of Salmon P. Chase, Jefferson Davis, U. S. Grant, Abraham Lincoln, George B. McClellan, and Robert E. Lee.

University of North Carolina, Chapel Hill

The Southern Historical Collection contains over 7 million items, in nearly 4,000 separate collections. Included are papers of Robert E. Lee, T. J. Jackson, E. Kirby Smith, and John C. Pemberton. For more information see *The Southern Historical Collection: A Guide to Manuscripts,* by Susan Sokol Blosser and Clyde Norman Wilson, Jr. (1970), and *The Southern Historical Collection: Supplementary Guide to Manuscripts, 1970–1975* by Everard H. Smith (1976).

University of Virginia, Charlottesville

Though probably better known for its Jefferson collection, the Manuscripts Department of the Alderman Library houses a number of Civil War diaries, as well as papers of Jubal Early, Robert E. Lee, John S. Mosby, and J.E.B. Stuart.

BIBLIOGRAPHY

Angle, Paul M. *The Lincoln Collection of the Illinois State Historical Library.* Springfield: The Library, 1940.

Ash, Lee. *Subject Collections: A Guide to Special Book Collections and Subject Emphases as Reported by University, College, Public, and Special Libraries in the United States, the Territories, and Canada.* 7th ed. New York: Bowker, 1993.

Beers, Henry P. *Bibliographies in American History.* Rev. ed. New York: H. W. Wilson, 1982.

———. *Guide to the Archives of the Confederate States of America.* Washington, D.C.: National Archives and Records Service, 1986.

Bergerson, Arthur W. Jr. *Civil War Records at the Louisiana State Archives.* Baton Rouge: Le Comité des Archives de la Louisiane, 1981.

Berthrong, Donald J. *The Civil War Collection of the Illinois State Historical Society.* Springfield: The Society, 1949.

Bethel, Elizabeth., comp. *Preliminary Inventory of the War Department Collection of Confederate Records (Record Group 109).* Washington, D.C.: National Archives, 1957.

Billington, Ray A. "Guides to American History Manuscript Collections in Libraries of the United States." *Mississippi Valley Historical Review* 38 (December 1951): 467–496.

Black, Patti C., and Maxyne M. Grimes. *Guide to Civil War Source Material in the Department of Archives and History, State of Mississippi.* Jackson: Mississippi Department of Archives and History, 1962.

Blosser, Susan S., and Clyde N. Wilson Jr. *The Southern Historical Collection: A Guide to Manuscripts.* Chapel Hill: University of North Carolina Library, 1970.

Burton, William L. *Descriptive Bibliography of Civil War Manuscripts in Illinois.* Evanston: Northwestern University Press, 1966.

Candler, Allen D. *The Confederate Records of the State of Georgia . . .* Atlanta: C. P. Byrd, 1972.

Columbia University Libraries. *The Townsend Library of National, State, and Individual Civil War Records at Columbia University, New York City.* New York, 1899.

Confederate Memorial Literary Society. *A Calendar of Confederate Papers*... Richmond: Southern Historical Manuscripts Commission, 1908.

Darney, Brigitte T. and John Nimehuk, eds. *Subject Directory of Special Libraries and Information Centers*. 5 vols. Detroit: Gale Research Company, 1985.

Davis, Richard C. *Guide to American Historical Manuscripts in the Huntington Library*. San Marino, CA: H. E. Huntington Library and Art Gallery, 1979.

Davis, Richard C., and Linda Angle Miller. *Guide to the Catalogued Collections in the Manuscript Department of the William R. Perkins Library, Duke University*. Santa Barbara, CA: Clio Books, 1980.

Decker, Eugene D. *A Selected Annotated Bibliography of Sources in the Kansas State Historical Society Pertaining to Kansas in the Civil War*. Emporia: Kansas State Teachers College, 1961.

DeWitt, Donald L. *Guides to Archives and Manuscript Collections in the United States: An Annotated Bibliography*. Westport, CT: Greenwood, 1994.

Dornbusch, Charles E. *Regimental Publications and Personal Narratives of the Civil War: A Checklist*. New York: New York Public Library, 1961.

Evans, Frank B. *Modern Archives and Manuscripts: A Select Bibliography*. Chicago: Society of American Archivists, 1975.

Freeman, Douglas S. *A Calendar of Confederate Papers, with a Bibliography of Some Confederate Publications*. Richmond, VA: Confederate Museum, 1908.

Hamer, Phil. *A Guide to Archives and Manuscripts in the United States*. New Haven: Yale University Press, 1961.

Howell, J. B., ed. *Special Collections in Libraries of the Southeast*. Jackson, MS: Howick House, 1978.

Irvine, Dallas D., et al. *Military Operations of the Civil War: A Guide-Index to the Official Records of the Union and Confederate Armies, 1861–1865*. Washington, D.C.: National Archives, 1968–1977.

Katz, Laura H., comp. *Manuscript Sources for Civil War Research in the Virginia Tech Libraries*. Blacksburg, VA: University Libraries, 1991.

Louisiana Historical Association. *Calendar of the Jefferson Davis Postwar Manuscripts in the Louisiana Historical Association Collection*. New York: Burt Franklin, 1970.

Maine State Archives. *Records Relating to the Civil War Career of Joshua Lawrence Chamberlain*. Augusta: The archives, 1977.

Matthews, William. *American Diaries in Manuscript. A Descriptive Bibliography, 1580–1954*. Athens: University of Georgia Press,

Mitchell, Reid. *Civil War Soldiers: Their Expectations and Their Experiences*. New York: Viking, 1988.

Munden, Kenneth, and Henry P. Beers, comps. *The Union: A Guide to Federal Archives Relating to the Civil War*. Washington, D.C.: National Archives, 1986.

Neagles, James C. *Confederate Research Sources: A Guide to Archive Collections*. Salt Lake City: Ancestry Publications, 1986.

Nevins, Alan, James I. Robertson, Jr., and Bell Wiley, eds. *Civil War Books: A Critical Bibliography*. Wendell, NC: Broadfoot, 1970.

New York State Education Department. State Archives. *Civil War Records in the New York State Archives*. Albany: State Education Department, 1985.

North Carolina State Department of Archives and History. *Guide to Civil War Records in the North Carolina State Archives.* Raleigh: State Department of Archives and History, 1966.

Orliando, Thomas A., and Marie Gecik, comps. *Treasures of the Chicago Public Library.* Chicago: The library, 1977.

Ostroff, Harriett, ed. *Index to Personal Names in the National Union Catalog of Manuscript Collections, 1959–1984.* 2 vols. Alexandria, VA: Chadwyck-Healey, 1988.

Paul, William G., comp. *Wisconsin's Civil War Archives.* Madison: State Historical Society of Wisconsin, 1965.

Pease, Marguerite J. *Guide to Manuscript Materials of American Origin in the Illinois Historical Society.* Urbana: Illinois Historical Survey, 1965.

Schick, Frank L., et al. *Records of the Presidency: Presidential Papers and Libraries from Washington to Reagan.* Phoenix: Oryx Press, 1989.

Schieber, Philip, et al. *A Guide to Special Collections in the OCLC Database.* Dublin, OH, 1988.

Scott, Kim Allen, comp. *Special Collections of the University of Arkansas Libraries, Manuscript Resources for the Civil War.* Fayetteville: Center for Arkansas and Regional Studies, 1990.

Sellers, John R., comp. *Civil War Manuscripts: A Guide to Collections in the Manuscript Division of the Library of Congress.* Washington, D.C.: Library of Congress, 1986.

Smith, Everard H. *The Southern Historical Collection: Supplementary Guide to Manuscripts, 1970–1975.* Chapel Hill: University of North Carolina Library, 1976.

Turner, Ann. *Guide to Indiana Civil War Manuscripts.* Indianapolis: Indiana Civil War Centennial Commission, 1965.

Sinclair, Donald A., comp. *A Guide to Manuscript Diaries and Journals in the Special Collections Department, Rutgers University.* New Brunswick, NJ: Archibald Stevens Alexander Library, Rutgers University, 1980.

United States. Library of Congress. *National Union Catalog of Manuscript Collections.* 27 vols. Washington, D.C., 1957–.

United States National Historical Publications and Records Commission. *Directory of Archives and Manuscript Repositories in the United States.* 2d ed. Phoenix: Oryx Press, 1988.

United States. National Archives and Records Administration. *Military Service Records: A Select Catalog of National Archives Microfilm Publications.* Washington, D.C., 1965.

Veit, Fritz. *Presidential Libraries and Collections.* Westport, CT: Greenwood Press, 1987.

Williams, T. Harry. *Hayes of the Twenty-third.* New York: Alfred A. Knopf, 1965.

Part III

Illustrative Materials

9

Maps, Charts, and Atlases

David Bosse

The planning and prosecution of military operations depend to a large degree on a knowledge of geography and topography. In the case of the American Civil War, which ranged over a vast expanse of territory, cartography played a significant role in the formulation of strategy and tactics. Evidence of this appears in the wartime and postwar writings of the war's participants, and more concretely in the enormous corpus of maps created in direct response to military needs. Not only did maps provide essential intelligence, they also recorded victories and defeats. Official mapping agencies, military personnel in the field, commercial cartographic firms, and newspapers and periodicals all contributed to the war's cartography. As a result of their efforts, the numbers of maps produced far exceeded those of all previous American wars combined.

At the beginning of the war, neither Union nor Confederate commanders had detailed maps of the interior South available to them. Although less apparent in 1861, the Federal government held a decided advantage in maps, along with most other types of war materiel. Since early in the nineteenth century, the Corps of Topographical Engineers and the civilian U.S. Coast Survey had been mapping westward expansion and internal improvements. They now devoted themselves to supplying Union armies and by war's end had generated thousands of maps. In contrast, the Confederate government had no mapping agency. Not until June 1862 did the Department of Northern Virginia's Engineering Bureau establish a map reproduction office in Richmond. Eventually Confederate map production increased, but throughout the war, the burden of mapping fell to topographers attached to armies in the field.

The study of Civil War cartography serves two primary purposes: maps unquestionably augment narrative description by elucidating warfare's spatial dimension and help us understand why events occurred as they did. This chapter will act as an introduction to the variety of period and historical maps awaiting the researcher. The discussion is limited to assemblages of maps that are deemed the most valuable and readily available sources.

PERIOD MAPS

Undoubtedly the best compendium of wartime cartography is the U.S. War Department's *Atlas to Accompany the Official Records of the Union and Confederate Armies* (1891–1895) The *Atlas* contains over 800 maps and plans, most of which relate to military operations in the field. Campaign maps, battlefield maps of troop positions and movements, and reconnaissance sketches together depict many of the war's actions. Despite their contemporaneousness, relatively few maps reproduced in the *Atlas* actually saw use by commanders in the field. The majority are redrawings of the maps that originally accompanied the reports of Union and, to a far lesser extent, Confederate officers. Charts of naval operations can also be found in the *Atlas,* with outstanding coverage for campaigns such as Charleston, Mobile Bay, and Fort Fisher, North Carolina. Postwar surveys of battlefields conducted between 1867 and 1890 and items from various War Department files account for other categories of maps represented in the *Atlas.* A note on each map indicates its source (e.g., "original in possession of Gen. Meade") or identifies the letter or report it relates to in the *Official Records.*

Readers seeking another source of official cartography can find it in *Atlas to Accompany Confederate Military History* (1962). As part of a reprint edition of *Confederate Military History,* edited by Clement A. Evans, the maps originally found in the set's twelve volumes have been brought together into a single atlas. Confederate maps from the official atlas comprise most of the contents of the *Atlas to Accompany Confederate Military History.*

While neither as numerous nor as conveniently gathered as the maps in the official atlas, researchers should not overlook the maps published in the U.S. War Department's *The War of the Rebellion: A Compilation of the Official Records of the Union and Confederate Armies* (1880–1901). Produced to illustrate official reports, these maps embody an important supplement to the official atlas and often supply particulars not found elsewhere. In certain cases, such as the Vicksburg campaign, they add especially valuable coverage of engagements and movements. An index to the over 400 maps scattered throughout the fifty-three volumes of Series 1 of the *Official Records* appears in the frontmatter of the official atlas. The general index to the *Official Records* alerts readers to the few maps found in Series 2 and 3 but indicates their location by volume number only.

Similarly, the thirty-one volumes of the U.S. Navy Department's *Official Records of the Union and Confederate Navies* (1894–1922) contain reproductions of maps and charts done during the war. Reproductions of these maps, numbering just under one hundred, mostly occur in the earlier volumes. A few folding color maps stand out among the black and white plans of forts and battles and the charts of coastlines. Diagrams of gunboat positions and river reconnaissance will interest researchers working on combined infantry-naval operations. Also noteworthy are maps of the engagements at Port Royal, South Carolina, and Sabine Pass, Texas, depicted here but not in the official atlas. Because the cumulative index volume does not indicate maps, users must consult the list of maps and other illustrations at the beginning of each volume of the naval *Official Records.*

Civil War Naval Chronology, 1861–1865, published by the Naval History Division of the Navy Department (1971), also offers a small number of charts of inland and coastal operations. The charts are greatly outnumbered by other types of illustrations, but among the thirty reproduced are several manuscript items of considerable interest. Most of the charts date from the time of the war.

The U.S. Coast Survey formed a vital branch of the Federal mapping effort. Many Coast Survey technicians served as cartographers with military units, and the survey's plant in Washington, D.C., printed the majority of maps issued to Union troops. In observance of the war's centennial, the U.S. Geodetic and Coast Survey published *Selected Civil War Maps, Reproduced from Originals Made by the U.S. Coast Survey* (1961). This folio of twenty black and white reproductions includes manuscript and printed charts, battle plans, reconnaissance maps, and general topographical maps, several of which had never before been reproduced before. While most relate to coastal or river operations, also present are maps of Manassas, Chickamauga, Chattanooga, and the Atlanta campaign. A note on each reproduction briefly explains the military situation and gives information on who created the map or chart and when.

Many of the extant maps created by the Department of Northern Virginia's Engineer Bureau now reside in the Virginia Historical Society. The society's publication, *Confederate Engineers' Maps: Jeremy Francis Gilmer Collection* (1989), reproduces sixty-seven wartime maps done under the supervision of Gilmer. The publication of the maps permits greater access to one of the most extensive collections of official Confederate military cartography. These full-size, black and white facsimiles primarily depict Virginia counties. A few maps of cities, fortifications, regions (e.g., the lower Shenandoah Valley), and portions of North Carolina constitute the exceptions. Surveyed, compiled, and drawn in the field, these maps were later reproduced in Richmond for distribution to field commanders.

Recently a portfolio of color reproductions of ten manuscript and printed maps has been published as *A Limited Edition Set of Civil War Maps* (1993). Chosen by Christopher Nelson, these items from the Library of Congress include topographical campaign maps, battle maps, and sketches of military positions. Two maps drawn by nonprofessionals make this a representational cross section of Civil War cartography. A pamphlet discussing the varieties of Civil War maps briefly describes the contents of the portfolio. Reduced versions of these maps also appear in Nelson's *Mapping the Civil War.*

One of the most prolific forms of map production during the war appeared in newspapers. David Bosse has examined journalistic cartography in *Civil War Newspaper Maps: A Historical Atlas* (1993). This atlas of forty-five maps and interpretive text follows an illustrated essay discussing the cartographic methods practiced by daily newspapers. A selection of maps from papers in Chicago, St. Louis, New York, Philadelphia, and Cincinnati shows the manner in which newspapers depicted both celebrated and obscure battles for an eager audience. In a related project, Bosse compiled *Civil War Newspaper Maps: A Cartobibliography of the Northern Daily Press* (1993). This finding aid allows researchers to locate over 2,000 maps, many drawn by reporters who observed military operations in the field.

American Heritage Battle Maps of the Civil War (1992) by Richard O'Shea also features period maps. Several wartime manuscript maps from the collections of the U.S. Military Academy at West Point stand out among this odd assemblage of cartographic examples. The book includes a series of perspective drawings by David Greenspan, selections from a 1986 West Point atlas, National Park Service maps, details from maps printed in the official atlas and postwar government battlefield atlases, and modern aerial photos. Some readers will enjoy the eclectic nature of the selection; others may find the contents of this miscellany lacking cohesion.

Those who wish to make a serious study of maps and mapmaking during the war should consult original maps. The abundance of Civil War maps in public institutions has not, however, inspired the publication of numerous collection guides. Happily, the National Archives and the Geography and Map Division of the Library of Congress, together housing the greatest riches of wartime cartography, have issued highly useful guides to their holdings. In each case, illustrations of representative maps add to the value of these books.

A Guide to Civil War Maps in the National Archives (1986) provides an overview of the more than 8,000 war-related maps, charts, and plans in the Cartographic and Architectural Branch. Federal agencies and Union military personnel produced nearly all of these maps for use in the field or to illustrate official reports. Those interested in Confederate cartography will find little here, as the archives possesses only a handful of captured maps. The first part of the *Guide* surveys the entire collection; particularly notable maps, of which there are many, receive more detailed descriptions in the book's second part. Map entries in this "Special List" indicate the presence of important military or topographical information and original annotations on the maps. Of particular interest to naval historians are the 160 charts described under the Records of the Geodetic and Coast Survey.

Unlike the National Archives, whose collections include little commercial cartography, the Library of Congress holdings comprise all varieties of maps. *Civil War Maps: An Annotated List of Maps and Atlases in the Library of*

Congress (1989), compiled by Richard W. Stephenson, describes over 2,000 maps and seventy-six atlases and sketch books dating from the time of the war until the twentieth century. Among these are numerous battle and theater of war maps issued separately or printed in books, atlases, newspapers, and periodicals by commercial publishers. Manuscript and printed Union and Confederate maps and sketches, created by individuals and military mapping organizations, account for over half of the maps listed. Beyond providing a complete cartobibliographical citation, each entry notes important military, cultural, or terrain features portrayed on the map.

The National Ocean Survey Cartobibliography: Civil War Collection (1980), by the U.S. Department of Commerce, National Oceanic and Atmospheric Administration, lists over 200 maps housed in its Rockville, Maryland, library. Many of the maps represent the work of the U.S. Coast Survey, precursor to the National Ocean Survey. The Civil War Collection consists of both manuscript and printed maps used by Union forces and postwar battlefield surveys. A small number of historical maps and atlases are also listed. The library's map holdings encompass the entire South, with the greatest emphasis on Virginia campaigns.

In addition to the institutions already noted, many public and academic libraries and archives own Civil War maps. The Illinois State Historical Library in Springfield, U.S. Military Academy Library at West Point, New York, University of Georgia Library, Museum of the Confederacy in Richmond, Harvard University Map Collection, Western Reserve Historical Society in Cleveland, Virginia Historical Society in Richmond, New York Public Library Map Division, Rucker Agee Collection at the Birmingham (Alabama) Public Library, Historical Society of Pennsylvania in Philadelphia, and Virginia Polytechnic Institute and State University Library in Blacksburg are among the noteworthy map collections open to researchers.

HISTORICAL MAPS

An atlas designed for teaching U.S. Military Academy cadets remains one of the most useful collections of historical maps of the war. In 138 maps, many in two or more parts, *The West Point Atlas of the Civil War* (1962) clearly and concisely depicts military operations. The atlas follows a formula adopted by most other Civil War atlases. Small-scale campaign maps establish the context of operations by showing the armies' prior positions and movements, while large-scale maps, often in a sequence, illustrate battles. By printing military information in color on gray base maps and pairing each map with a page of text describing events, the atlas effectively informs the reader. Unfortunately, several important western actions, such as Wilson's Creek, Pea Ridge, and Perryville, receive no coverage.

Readers unable to locate a copy of the West Point atlas can find a revised version, under the title *Atlas for the American Civil War* (1986). This atlas, part of the West Point Military History Series, reputedly emphasizes the "totality of the war to a greater extent" than the earlier West Point atlas, but it numbers fewer than half as many maps. Apart from the addition of color and occasional notes on the maps themselves (the atlas lacks any other text), much of the contents essentially duplicate the *West Point Atlas of the Civil War*. General theater of war maps account for the greatest difference between them, as the *Atlas for the American Civil War* furnishes new contributions of that variety.

Like the West Point atlas, Craig L. Symonds's *A Battlefield Atlas of the Civil War* (1973) originated out of a need for reference maps to illustrate lectures, in this case at the U.S. Naval Academy. Symonds demonstrates his nautical bent by furnishing maps of the engagements at Port Royal, New Orleans, and Fort Fisher in addition to the expected land battles. In all, Symonds portrays twenty-six campaigns in forty-three maps. Most afford a good overview of military actions, but some, like the Shiloh map, give only a vague impression of operations. A page of text keyed to each map furnishes a synopsis of the events shown, mitigating the few instances of insufficient military information.

Noncartographic depictions play a dominant role in Time-Life Books' *Echoes of Glory: Illustrated Atlas of the Civil War* (1991). Paintings, photographs, and drawings outnumber maps nearly three to one, creating a product calculated to appeal to a wide audience. The numerous illustrations of battles greatly enhance the text while adding a visual adjunct to the maps. While the 138 full-color campaign maps are quite legible, color and shading used to highlight troop movements inexplicably vary over the course of the atlas. Major operations such as Gettysburg and Antietam receive as many as 11 maps each, allowing for considerable detail.

The 200 specially commissioned full-color maps of *The Atlas of the Civil War* (1994), edited by James M. McPherson, make it the most extensive historical atlas of the war. Excellent text and numerous illustrations complement the maps, many of which represent smaller engagements overlooked by most historical atlases. By employing a relatively complex scheme of symbolization and color, the maps comprise a great deal of information. They succeed in conveying their message, but some maps may initially appear confusing. Several suffer from a want of generalization, so that every known road and stream needlessly crowd the map. Explanations keyed to each map aid readers in deciphering highly detailed troop movements.

In the past few years, battlefield guides have become a popular publication genre. With regard to maps, *The Civil War Battlefield Guide* (1990), edited by Frances Kennedy, takes a novel approach. The *Guide* encourages readers to visit battlefields, and for that reason black and white reproductions of large-scale U.S. Geological Survey (USGS) maps serve as the canvas on which historical events are portrayed. With troop positions and movements printed in color, readers can easily follow the broad strokes of the battle over the current landscape as seen on modern topographical maps. Important locations or features existing at the time of the battle have also been added to the USGS base maps.

Insightful essays by authorities on each battle add greatly to the value of the book.

Those seeking a battlefield guide with more detailed maps should consult *National Geographic Guide to the Civil War National Battlefield Parks* (1992), by A. Wilson Greene and Gary W. Gallagher. The authors' knowledgeable essays are matched by the exemplary cartography of the thirty-one battlefield maps. Unfortunately the *Guide's* pocket-size format necessitates small maps, and maps that spread across two pages suffer some loss in the book's gutter. Despite these drawbacks, the *Guide* makes an excellent reference source.

Over the years certain campaigns have received notable cartographic coverage. One of the earliest examples treats the Second Battle of Manassas, or Bull Run. As part of the published court-martial proceedings against Union general Fitz-John Porter, an atlas of twenty-two maps accompanies the *Proceedings and Report of the Board of Army Officers . . . in the Case of Fitz-John Porter* (1879). The maps attempt to demonstrate the conduct of Porter's command during the battle. Therefore, a single base map, surveyed by G. K. Warren of Gettysburg fame, appears throughout the atlas to ensure uniformity. On it are recorded troop positions and movements, topographical details, and timing of events as witnessed by individuals present at the battle. Henry Kyd Douglas, Thomas Rosser, James Longstreet, and others contributed information to the atlas.

Two other Civil War battles have generated official atlases, both in large format. The Chickamauga and Chattanooga National Park Commission issued the *Atlas of the Battlefields of Chickamauga, Chattanooga and Vicinity* (1901) consisting of fourteen plates (seven in the 1896–1897 edition). Along with maps of the park and the general theater of operations, seven maps represent the field at Chickamauga during the two days of battle, and individual maps show movements from Chickamauga to Chattanooga, and actions at Wauhatchie, Orchard Knob, Lookout Mountain, and Missionary Ridge. A page of legends narrates each map, and a two-page list details the organization of the opposing armies.

Not to be outdone, the Antietam Battlefield Board produced the *Atlas of the Battlefield of Antietam* (1904). This atlas tracks military operations from daybreak to 5:30 P.M. on September 17, 1862. Fourteen highly detailed maps, drawn at a scale of 1:10,000, show the situation at a particular moment or encompass a brief span of time, such as noon to 12:15 P.M. In addition to troop positions and movements, terrain and cultural features are meticulously plotted.

Of all the battles fought during the war, Gettysburg has most often been mapped. *Gettysburg: A Battlefield Atlas* (1992), by Craig L. Symonds, continues the cartographic representation of this pivotal battle. In twenty-four maps the atlas follows the campaign from the Union defeat at Chancellorsville to Lee's withdrawal across the Potomac. Cartographically, Symonds's treatment of the battle surpasses the detail of his previous atlas. Preceding the sixteen maps of the infantry battle of July 1–3 are maps of the famous cavalry action at Brandy Station, Virginia, and J.E.B. Stuart's Pennsylvania raid of June 20–25. The fight between Stuart and David Gregg's cavalry east of Gettysburg on July 3 and a map of the modern battlefield park complete the atlas. Period photographs and drawings add to the textual analysis of the campaign's various facets.

Nearly all of the many histories of military units feature maps. Quite appropriately, Thomas Van Horne's *History of the Army of the Cumberland* (1875) particularly emphasizes cartography, for that army went to great lengths to furnish its officers with maps. Edward Ruger, superintendent of the Topographical Engineer's Office of the Department of the Cumberland, compiled an atlas forming volume 3 of the *History* (subsumed in volume 2 of the reprint edition). Immediately after the war, Ruger supervised surveys of all the Union and Confederate works pertaining to the Atlanta campaign, along with many of the Army of the Cumberland's battlefields. Ruger availed himself of these surveys, official records of the department, and General George Thomas's personal military papers while preparing the atlas. The resulting twenty-two maps record the army's operations from Logan's Cross Roads (January 1862) to Bentonville (March 1865). Most maps indicate the sources Ruger consulted, including captured Confederate documents.

Perhaps more than any other publication, *Battles and Leaders of the Civil War* (1887–1888), edited by Robert U. Johnson and Clarence Buel, brought historical war maps to the attention of a vast audience. The four-volume set quickly became a standard source for maps and illustrations, so much so that other publications frequently pirated them. To secure accurate cartographic information, the editors drew upon what were then considered authoritative works and sought the help of qualified individuals like Jedediah Hotchkiss. Official and personal documents supplied by the officers who contributed articles may have also assisted in the compilation of maps. Many of the 198 maps in *Battles and Leaders* are still considered valuable sources, and authors and publishers continue to reproduce them.

THE LITERATURE OF CIVIL WAR CARTOGRAPHY

While the maps themselves serve as silent witnesses to the war's prosecution, researchers may benefit from an understanding of the practice of Civil War cartography. Sources are somewhat limited, but an examination of period and modern accounts reveals information on mapmaking, map availability, map accuracy, and, to a lesser extent, map use. One of the best records of mapmaking during the war appears in the journal of Jedediah Hotchkiss, General "Stonewall" Jackson's renowned topographer. A published version of Hotchkiss's journal, *Make Me a Map of the Valley* (1973), describes his service with Jackson, Richard Ewell, and Jubal Early. Hotchkiss frequently mentions his cartographic duties, thereby contributing to our knowledge of how maps were made and under what circumstances.

Two recent books focus on Hotchkiss. Peter W. Roper's *Jedediah Hotchkiss: Rebel Mapmaker and Virginia Businessman* (1992) offers the most complete biography of its subject. Roper discusses Hotchkiss's mapmaking, with particular regard to the compilation of Hotchkiss's famous map of the Shenandoah Valley. Much of the book deals with Hotchkiss's postwar occupations, including his involvement with the official atlas and several battlefield histories.

Like Roper, William J. Miller, author of *Mapping for Stonewall* (1993), relies on Hotchkiss's journal and letters for facts. Miller, however, supplies more details on military mapmaking and writes at greater length on Hotchkiss's participation in the campaigns of the Army of Northern Virginia. The book features excellent reproductions of sixteen of Hotchkiss's wartime manuscript maps, some never before published.

Reproductions constitute the centerpiece of Christopher Nelson's *Mapping the Civil War* (1992). Readers expecting a thorough treatment of Civil War cartography will not find it here but will discover an exceptional array of period maps. Nelson's text largely restricts itself to narrating military campaigns, with little space devoted to the role of maps or mapmaking. Illustration captions and "map influence statements" offer some insight into the war's cartography, and Richard W. Stephenson's foreword provides an overview of map production during the war.

Stephenson's introduction to his *Civil War Maps* (1989) and Henry Steele Commager's introduction to *The Official Atlas of the Civil War* (1956 reprint) are particularly valuable essays on the war's cartography. Stephenson concentrates on cartographic techniques and the variety of maps engendered by the war. Color reproductions accompany many of his examples chosen from the Library of Congress. Commager summarizes the state of military cartography at the start of the war and its subsequent advances, and notes incidents where maps, or the lack thereof, affected campaigns. He also discusses the work of several cartographers and mapping agencies before concluding with an account of the creation of the official atlas.

Cartography is one of the subjects of James L. Nichols's *Confederate Engineers* (1957). A history of the origin and organization of the engineering administration serves as a prelude to the chapter "Confederate Map Supply." Here Nichols documents the initial attempts to map the Virginia theater of war. The obstacles faced by topographers and the consequent dearth of maps that plagued the Confederate command, especially early in the war, form twin themes. Despite his careful research, Nichols says little about the mechanics of map production in Richmond, and virtually nothing about the situation outside Virginia.

Albert Campbell, the officer in charge of map reproduction in Richmond, defends the accomplishments of his bureau in "The Lost War Maps of the Confederates" (1888). This brief memoir recounts the state of Confederate mapping prior to the Seven Days' battles, the limited utility of maps during those battles, and the redoubled efforts of the engineering department afterward. Campbell gives an insider's view of mapping operations in Virginia while offering details on the fate of the maps transported out of Richmond in April 1865.

Accusations of ineffective maps were not solely confined to Confederate creations. Theodore Lyman, a volunteer aide on General George Meade's staff, left one of the few analyses of maps written by a participant in the war. As the title suggests, "Uselessness of the Maps Furnished to Staff of the Army of the Potomac" (1905) decries the inaccuracy of Union maps prior to 1864. Lyman, who mapped the positions of Union corps during the Wilderness campaign, argues that the quality of maps made by engineers in the field far surpassed those issued from Washington.

Few other writers have critically examined Civil War cartography. Articles by H. V. Canan ("Maps for the Civil War," 1956), James B. Rhoads ("Civil War Maps and Mapping," 1957), and A. Philip Muntz ("Union Mapping in the American Civil War," 1963) describe mapping organizations or individual maps, with little attempt to explore the larger role of cartography in the war. Brief discussions of the relationship of maps to military decisions appear in "Mapping the Atlanta Campaign" (1982), by Richard W. Stephenson, and "Lost in Battle" (1986), by Harold Gulley and Louis DeVorsey. Their work suggests a direction future studies could take. While the history of Civil War cartography has shown recent signs of vitality, it offers ample opportunities for further research.

BIBLIOGRAPHY

Aimone, Allan C., and Barbara A. Aimone. *A User's Guide to the Official Records of the American Civil War.* Shippensburg, PA: White Mane Publishing, 1993.

Antietam Battlefield Board. *Atlas of the Battlefield of Antietam, Prepared under the Direction of the Antietam Battlefield Board.* Washington, D.C.: Government Printing Office, 1904.

Atlas for the American Civil War. Wayne, NJ: Avery Publishing, 1986.

Atlas to Accompany Confederate Military History. New York: Thomas Yoseloff, 1962.

Bechler, Gustavus. *Atlas Showing Battles, Engagements, and Important Localities Connected with the Campaigns in Virginia.* Philadelphia: G. R. Bechler, 1864.

Bosse, David. *Civil War Newspaper Maps: A Cartobibliography of the Northern Daily Press.* Westport, CT: Greenwood Press, 1993.

———. *Civil War Newspaper Maps: A Historical Atlas.* Baltimore: Johns Hopkins University Press, 1993.

Campbell, Albert H. "The Lost War Maps of the Confederates." *Century Magazine* 35 (1888): 479–481.

Canan, H. V. "Maps for the Civil War." *Armor* 65 (1956): 34–42.

Chickamauga and Chattanooga National Park Commission. *Atlas of the Battlefields of Chickamauga, Chattanooga, and Vicinity.* Washington, D.C.: Government Printing Office, 1901.

Greene, A. Wilson, and Gary W. Gallagher. *National Geographic Guide to the Civil War National Battlefield Parks.* Washington, D.C.: National Geographic Society, 1992.

Gulley, Harold, and Louis DeVorsey. "Lost in Battle." *Geographical Magazine* 28 (1986): 1–18.

Hotchkiss, Jedediah. *Make Me a Map of the Valley: The Civil War Journal of Stonewall*

Jackson's Topographer. Edited by Archie P. McDonald. Dallas: Southern Methodist University Press, 1973.

Johnson, Robert U., and Clarence Buel, eds. *Battles and Leaders of the Civil War.* 4 vols. 1887–1888. Reprint, New York: Thomas Yoseloff, 1974; Secaucus, NJ: Castle Books, 1974, 1983, 1991.

Kennedy, Frances, ed. *The Civil War Battlefield Guide.* Boston: Houghton Mifflin, 1990.

Lilley, David A. "Anticipating the Atlas to Accompany the Official Records: Post War Mapping of Civil War Battlefields." *Lincoln Herald* 82 (1980): 37–42.

Lyman, Theodore. "Uselessness of the Maps Furnished to Staff of the Army of the Potomac Previous to the Campaign of May 1864." *Papers of the Military Historical Society of Massachusetts.* Vol. 4. 1905. Reprinted, Wilmington, NC: Broadfoot Publishing, 1989–1990.

McPherson, James M., ed. *The Atlas of the Civil War.* New York: Macmillan, 1994.

Miller, William J. *Mapping for Stonewall: The Civil War Service of Jed Hotchkiss.* Washington, D.C.: Elliott & Clark Publishing, 1993.

Muntz, A. Philip. "Union Mapping in the American Civil War." *Imago Mundi* 17 (1963): 90–94.

Nelson, Christopher. *Mapping the Civil War.* Washington, D.C.: Starwood Publishing, 1992.

———. *A Limited Edition Set of Civil War Maps.* Golden, CO: Fulcrum Publishing, 1993.

Nichols, James L. *Confederate Engineers.* 1957. Reprint, Gaithersburg, MD: Olde Soldier Books, 1987.

O'Riley, Noel, David Bosse, and Robert W. Karrow, Jr. *Civil War Maps: A Graphic Index to the Atlas to Accompany the Official Records of the Union and Confederate Armies.* Chicago: Newberry Library, 1987.

O'Shea, Richard. *American Heritage Battle Maps of the Civil War.* Tulsa, OK: Council Oak Books, 1992.

Paris, Louis Philippe Albert d'Orleans, comte de. *Histoire de la Guerre Civile en Amerique, Atlas.* Paris: Librarie Nouvelle, 1874–1883.

Proceedings and Report of the Board of Army Officers, Convened by Special Orders No. 78, Headquarters of the Army, Adjutant General's Office, Washington, April 12, 1878, in the Case of Fitz-John Porter. Washington, D.C.: Government Printing Office, 1879.

Rhoads, James B. "Civil War Maps and Mapping." *Military Engineer* 49 (1957): 38–43.

Roper, Peter W. *Jedediah Hotchkiss: Rebel Mapmaker and Virginia Businessman.* Shippensburg, PA: White Mane Publishing, 1992.

Stephenson, Richard W. *Civil War Maps: An Annotated List of Maps and Atlases in the Library of Congress.* Washington, D.C.: Library of Congress, 1989.

———. "Mapping the Atlanta Campaign." *Bulletin, Special Libraries Association Geography and Map Division* 127 (1982): 7–17.

Symonds, Craig L. *A Battlefield Atlas of the Civil War.* Annapolis, MD: Nautical & Aviation Publishing Co., 1973.

———. *Gettysburg: A Battlefield Atlas.* Annapolis, MD: Nautical & Aviation Publishing Co., 1992.

Time-Life Books, ed. *Echoes of Glory: Illustrated Atlas of the Civil War.* Alexandria, VA: Time-Life Books, 1991.

U.S. Department of Commerce. National Oceanic and Atmospheric Administration. *National Ocean Survey Cartobibliography: Civil War Collection.* Rockville, MD: NOAA, 1980.

U.S. Geodetic and Coast Survey. *Selected Civil War Maps, Reproduced from the Originals Made by the U.S. Coast Survey, 1861–1865.* Washington, D.C.: U.S. Geodetic and Coast Survey, 1961.

U.S. Military Academy. *The West Point Atlas of the Civil War.* New York: Frederick A. Praeger, 1962.

U.S. National Archives. *A Guide to Civil War Maps in the National Archives.* Washington, D.C.: National Archives Trust Fund Board, 1986.

U.S. Navy Department. *Civil War Naval Chronology, 1861–1865.* Washington, D.C.: Government Printing Office, 1971.

U.S. Navy Department. *Official Records of the Union and Confederate Navies in the War of the Rebellion.* 1894–1922. Reprint, New York: Antiquarian Press, 1961; Harrisburg, PA: National Historical Society, 1987.

U.S. War Department. *Atlas to Accompany the Official Records of the Union and Confederate Armies.* 1891–1895. Reprint, New York: Yoseloff, 1958; New York: Arno Press, 1978; New York: Fairfax Press, 1983.

————. *The War of the Rebellion: A Compilation of the Official Records of the Union and Confederate Armies.* 1880–1901: Reprint, Harrisburg, PA: National Historical Society, 1971–1972; Wilmington, NC: Publishing, 1985; Dayton, OH: Morningside Bookshop, 1994.

————. Office of the Chief of Engineers. *Military Maps Illustrating the Operations of the Armies of the Potomac and James, May 4th 1864 to April 9th 1865.* Washington, D.C.: Government Printing Office, 1867.

Van Horne, Thomas. *History of the Army of the Cumberland, Its Organization, Campaigns, and Battles.* 2 vols. with atlas volume by Edward Ruger. 1875: Reprinted, Wilmington, NC: Broadfoot Publishing, 1992.

Virginia Historical Society. *Confederate Engineers' Maps: Jeremy Francis Gilmer Collection.* Richmond: Virginia Historical Society, 1989.

10

Photographs and Drawings

Charles Edmund Vetter and Gary Dillard Joiner

The Civil War left behind a visual legacy that continues to fascinate both scholars and casual students. Traditional methods of depicting activities were used—drawings, etchings, paintings, and maps—and photography, a revolutionary means of recording war, was employed as well. Although still in its infancy, photography brought to its viewer not simply an artist's impression of a battle but the battle itself and, more dramatically, the aftermath of battle.

The visual record of the war can be cataloged by type of medium: photographs; sketches, etched plates, and paintings; maps; and modern illustrated histories and paintings. With the exception of modern illustrated histories and paintings, these materials can be grouped into two broad areas: publicly owned and privately owned collections. Publicly owned materials consist of collections and individual documents in federal, state, or municipal agencies and are available through libraries, archives, and museums across the United States. Privately owned collections are also available to the researcher and are easily accessible. The Bettmann Archives is an example of an excellent privately owned collection.

PUBLIC DOCUMENTS

The largest number of Civil War images are owned by the U.S. government. The great repositories are the National Archives and the Library of Congress (both in Washington, D.C.), the United States Army Military Institute at Carlisle Barracks, Pennsylvania, and the Naval Historical Center at the Washington

(D.C.) Navy Yard. Other extensive collections are found at the various national military parks operated by the National Park Service, Department of Interior.

Both the National Archives and the Library of Congress publish catalogs of their holdings. Every photograph, map, and sketch is indexed by subject and often by location. Individual items are identified by content and item catalog number. These collections are among the finest in existence, and catalogs can be purchased from the National Archives and the Library of Congress.

The Library of Congress has separate divisions that hold broad interest for the Civil War researcher. Although most of the material in narrative form is located in the Manuscript Division, the Library of Congress has a wealth of holdings in other departments.

The Geography and Map Division contains both manuscripts and published maps related to the war. Most of these were done by Union field cartographers and engineers, and many others were printed in the North by commercial publishers. This division is also the repository for many Confederate maps. The most famous of these holdings are the maps created by Jedediah Hotchkiss, General Thomas J. "Stonewall" Jackson's cartographer in the Shenandoah Valley campaign. These maps are noted not only for their accurate portrayal of the valley but also for their beauty and their large size.

The Rare Book Division is mainly dedicated to preserving thousands of out-of-print volumes; however, this division should not be overlooked by students interested in a visual history of the war. The division holds an extensive number of Union and Confederate recruiting posters and other broadsides.

The Prints and Photographic Division contains an impressive collection of glass photographic negatives and prints by Matthew Brady and other period photographers. This division also contains field sketches and drawings—battle scenes as well as scenes of life in the armies—made by artists on both sides of the conflict. The most notable artists represented here are Edwin Forbes and Alfred R. Waud, who provided on-site realistic drawings and sketches of various aspects of the war. Forbes and Waud are important sources for any serious student of the visual aspect of the Civil War. Lithographic collections are also based here. The best known are the Currier and Ives lithographs. Although they were very popular in their time, they tended to romanticize the war and were highly inaccurate historically. Among other lithographic holdings are those of Private Alfred E. Mathews of the 31st Ohio Infantry Regiment. Mathews's work is considered to be some the most exquisite of contemporary Civil War lithographs.

The United States Army Military Institute at Carlisle Barracks (USAMI) is the repository for the largest collections of photographs from the Civil War era. Of particular interest are the photographs from the Military Order of the Loyal Legion of the United States, an organization of Union army officers. These include several hundred Matthew Brady and T. C. Roche negatives and photographic portraits of almost every Union and Confederate officer and enlisted man who participated in the war. USAMI is continuing its quest to obtain a copy of every existing photographic image of all participants and related subjects in the Civil War. This is an outstanding collection and an absolute necessity for the Civil War researcher.

For scholars and students interested in the naval aspects of the war, the Naval Historical Center at the Washington Navy Yard has a particularly well-rounded series of photographs of both Union and Confederate naval vessels and crews. When supplemented by materials from USAMI, the National Archives, and the Library of Congress, the student of Civil War naval history will have a fine collection to view and study.

Many universities and state historical society archives have collections of manuscripts and illustrations, some of them extensive in size and well known— for example, the Archives of the University of Notre Dame, the University of Virginia, and Duke University. Some of the better-known state historical societies with photographic materials are the Ohio Historical Society, the New-York Historical Society, and the Texas Historical Society. Other materials can be found in the national military parks and state commemorative areas of battlefields not in the federal system. Most of these sites contain archives.

MULTIVOLUME SETS

Multivolume sets of photographic histories began to appear for the general public in 1911 with the fiftieth anniversary of the beginning of the war. The first to be published was the *Photographic History of the Civil War* by Francis T. Miller. It was originally published in ten volumes and contains hundreds of photographs of battle sites and participants. A narrative accompanies the photographs. Although extremely popular, it was out of print for many years until the Blue and Grey Press produced another printing in 1987. The reprint has been compressed into five volumes, but no images or plates have been deleted. It is still in print and remains a classic. The quality of the reprint is not as well defined as the original; however, it still makes an eloquent statement in its thoroughness.

A more recent photographic presentation is *The Image of War, 1861–1865,* a six-volume set by William C. Davis. This work is grouped by subject matter and is well documented in the location of its sources. Davis corrects some of the errors made by the Miller work. This work is a standard source for Civil War historians. Davis has also published the three-volume *Rebels and Yankees,* which includes not only photographs but illustrations of flags, uniforms, and army equipment. This is an excellent work and should be consulted for its detail.

William A. Frassanito has published three volumes—*Gettysburg: A Journey in Time* (1974), *Antietam* (1978), and *Grant and Lee* (1983)—that are valuable for Civil War students; they combine photos and narratives to cover their individual subjects. These volumes are not as thorough or complete as the Davis works but are nevertheless important sources.

Perhaps the best multivolume illustrated series ever produced for both the novice and the serious researcher of the Civil War is Time-Life's *The Civil War* (1983–1987). The series treats its subjects thoroughly, has excellent maps and text, and is a good starting point for more detailed research. At the end of each volume, picture credits are listed by the page on which they appear. A full bibliography and index are also included.

Finally, an outstanding and unique series still in progress is *Portraits of Conflict* (1990) by Carl Moneyhon and Bobby Roberts. It will eventually cover each Confederate state. Only three volumes are now available, for Arkansas, Louisiana, and Texas, but work continues on this fine project, and soon volumes on Mississippi, Alabama, and South Carolina will be available. Exhaustive research to obtain the photographic material from specific Confederate states makes this series unique. The common soldier and uncommon battlefield scenes are their hallmark. The photos and the stories behind them provide the basis for the volumes and take the reader to a level of the Civil War often neglected. As of this writing, there is no similar project planned for the Northern states.

SINGLE-VOLUME WORKS

Among the single-volume photographic histories, two are worthy of mention. Perhaps the more successful is *The American Heritage Picture History of the Civil War* (1960), with narrative by the great Civil War historian Bruce Catton. It has never been out of print and has been printed in several different formats. When the Public Broadcasting Service aired the epochal eleven and a half hour *Civil War* by Ken Burns in 1990, Alfred Knopf published a companion volume by the same name with the series. It was written by Geoffrey C. Ward, Ric Burns, and Ken Burns. This excellent work utilizes many of the photographs, maps, and other images seen in the series. If it has a shortcoming, it is that each photograph is not credited separately for the serious researcher.

Two important works that researchers must consult are *Gardner's Photographic Sketch Book of the Civil War* (1959), by Alexander Gardner, and *Russell's Civil War Photographs* (1982), by Andrew J. Russell. Gardner's works originally appeared in 1866 and were the first published collection of Civil War photographs. They can be purchased in a reprint by Dover Publications. Andrew J. Russell was a photographer who served with the 141st New York Volunteers and was attached on special assignment to General Herman Haupt, who commanded the U.S. Military Railroad Construction Corps. Russell's responsibility was to create a photographic history of the corps. His works include railroad construction, battlefields, camp sites, gunboats, and combat scenes. Many of his works were attributed to Matthew Brady, but recent research has led to Russell's receiving the credit he deserves.

In recent years, a number of high-quality photographic essay books have been published, generally depicting modern views of the great battlefields of the war. Some show monuments, reenactors, and beautiful photographic scenes of battlefields. Some have aerial views, and most are of a uniformly fine design.

However, they are more art than history and do not provide a major source of material for the serious historian. One outstanding example of this genre is *The Blue and the Gray* (1992), by Thomas B. Allen with photography by Sam Abell, which combines contemporary images with modern photographs and an excellent narrative. The color photos of present-day sites are stunning. Sam Abell also collaborated with Brian C. Pohanka in two other fine works: *Distant Thunder: A Photographic Essay on the American Civil War* (1988) and *The Civil War: An Aerial Portrait* (1990).

There is an abundance of drawings, etchings, and paintings from the period of the Civil War; most can be found in the Prints and Photographic Division of the Library of Congress and at the Smithsonian Institution, Washington, D.C. Among the Civil War artists who later became famous for other works, Winslow Homer stands above and apart from the others. By the time the war had begun, Homer had developed a keen eye for observing his surroundings and had an enormous talent for translating what he saw onto paper and other media. His work is primarily housed in the Cooper-Hewitt Museum of Decorative Arts and Design, Smithsonian Institution, Washington, D.C. Fortunately for researchers who are unable to examine this collection at length, there is a recently published reprint volume of these works, *The Civil War: Battle Fields and Camp Grounds in the Art of Winslow Homer* (originally published as *Echo of a Distant Drum: Winslow and the Civil War* by Julian Grossman. The art in this volume consists of pencil, charcoal, crayon, pen and ink, wash, watercolor, wood engravings, lithographs, and oil paintings. It is a superb representation of Homer's work.

PERIODICALS

The two most popular magazines of the Civil War were *Harper's Weekly* and *Frank Leslie's Illustrated Journal.* The *Life* and *Time* magazines of their day, they chronicled the war and gave readers not only a written narrative of the battles and campaigns but were luxuriously illustrated with engravings from on-the-scene sketches and sometimes of photographs. Sometimes their accounts were distorted due to the preferences of their reporters and the need to sell copies. In addition, they were both Northern publications. Both of these periodicals have been reprinted and are available. Some images were created from photographic plates, but most were sketches sent back to the magazines, where they were redrawn on hardwood blocks and printed as line cuts. The quality is excellent, and readers will feel the full impact of the intentions of the original publisher in reading and viewing the illustrations in the same manner as readers of the Civil War era. Some of the artists who drew for *Harper's Weekly* were Alfred and William Waud, Thomas Nast (later a nationally recognized political cartoonist), Winslow Homer, and Theodore R. Davis. Artists working for *Frank Leslie's Journal* included Edwin Forbes, Henri Lovie, Frank H. Schell, William T. Crane, and J.F.E. Hillen. Of these artists the most famous was Edwin Forbes. Although he did few sketches of actual fighting, his works on camp life, battle line formation, artillery, and cavalry are renowned. An excellent reprint of Forbes's work is *Thirty Years After: An Artist's Story of the Great War* (1993). The only major artist to draw for the Confederacy was an Englishman, Frank Vizetelly, who was dispatched by the *Illustrated London News* to cover the war, and most of his works appeared in this periodical.

Several soldiers and sailors created their own art, and some became quite well known. James Walker was best known for *Gettysburg: The First Day;* Conrad W. Chapman executed the most famous painting of the Confederate submarine, *C.S.S. Hunley* (painting by the same title); and Gilbert W. Gaul was best known for his paintings *The Skirmish Line* and *Exchange of Prisoners.* Henry W. Walke, Allan C. Redwood, and William L. Sheppard were all published in the four-volume *Battle and Leaders of the Civil War,* edited by Robert U. Johnson and Clarence C. Buel. Some of these works are housed in the library at the United States Military Academy.

The best single-volume collection of color plates of fine oil paintings is in the 1993 edition of *Mine Eyes Have Seen the Glory: The Civil War in Art,* by Harold Holzer and Mark E. Neely, Jr. The authors not only display the art as color plates but provide information on the work by size and location and offer a precise narrative concerning the subject, placing the art in the context of the action it depicts. This is an excellent volume for those interested in the art of the Civil War.

Finally, the works of modern Civil War artists cannot be overlooked. Don Troiani, Keith Rocco, Mort Kunstler, Jeremy L. Scott, and Clyde Heron have combined their artistic talents with historical accuracy to produce some of the best of the modern paintings and drawings of the Civil War. Prints of their work can be purchased from the artists, galleries, or, if the limited edition prints are sold out, other collectors.

Although this chapter focuses on photographs and drawings of the Civil War, maps too are a visual record of the conflict and provide excellent insight into the battles and campaigns. The bible of atlases covering the Civil War is the U.S. War Department's *Atlas to Accompany the Official Records of the Union and Confederate Armies.* It includes intricate and detailed maps, excellent engineering sketches of fortifications, and a number of photographs that will be of interest to the Civil War scholar. The atlas was originally published in 1895 and has seen periodic reprints. The best reprint on the market today is by Fairfax Press. The maps retain their original colors, and all of the original material is in the volume. The atlas contains 821 maps, 106 engravings, and 209 drawings. It is indispensable for the Civil War historian.

NEW TECHNOLOGIES

Changing technology has allowed for new avenues of research in recent years. Photographic images are available on compact disks for use with computers, and a number of videocassette tapes of high quality are on the market. The PBS series *The Civil War* is available, and the Smithsonian Institution has released the series *Battles of the Civil War*. Also, the Arts and Entertainment Network's *Civil War Journal* is available on tape. These are excellent studies using reenactments and compelling narrative.

The Civil War is perhaps the pivotal period in U.S. history; it changed the nation's life forever. The war occurred at the dawn of the age of photography. The Industrial Revolution and the technology it created made mass communication possible. These advancements have bestowed on later generations an amazing account of this great upheaval. We are the benefactors of this plethora of material. From glass plate photographic processes to artists' sketches, explicit maps, and fine art paintings, the Civil War has provided a window on the past as no previous period could or has done.

BIBLIOGRAPHY

A Guide to Civil War Maps in the National Archives. Washington, D.C.: National Archives Trust Fund Board, 1990.

Abell, Sam, and Brian C. Pohanka. *Distant Thunder: A Photographic Essay on the American Civil War.* Charlottesville, VA: Thomasson-Grant, 1988.

———. *The Civil War: An Aerial Portrait.* Charlottesville, VA: Thomasson-Grant, 1990.

Allen, Thomas B., and Sam Abell. *The Blue and the Gray.* Washington, D.C.: National Geographic Society, 1992.

Barnard, George N. *Photographic Views of Sherman's Campaign.* New York: Dover Publications, 1977.

Catton, Bruce. *The American Heritage Picture History of the Civil War.* New York: American Heritage, 1960.

Davis, William C. *Rebels and Yankees.* 3 vols. New York: Smithmark Publishers, 1991.

———. *The Image of War, 1861–1865.* 6 vols. Garden City, NY: Doubleday, 1983.

Donald, David, et al. *Divided We Fought: A Pictorial History of the War, 1861–1865.* New York: Macmillan, 1952.

Forbes, Edwin. *Thirty Years After: An Artist's Story of the Great War.* Baton Rouge: LSU Press, 1993.

Frassanito, William A. *Gettysburg: A Journey in Time.* New York: Charles Scribner's Sons, 1974.

———. *Antietam.* New York: Charles Scribner's Sons, 1978.

———. *Grant and Lee.* New York: Charles Scribner's Sons, 1983.

Gardner, Alexander. *Gardner's Photographic Sketch Book of the Civil War.* New York: Dover Publications, 1959.

Grossman, Julian. *The Civil War: Battlefields and Campgrounds in the Art of Winslow Homer.* New York: Abradale Press/Harry N. Abrams, 1991.

Guernsey, Alfred H., and Henry Mills Alden, eds. *Harper's Pictorial History of the Civil War.* New York: Fairfax Press, 1993.

Holzer, Harold, and Mark E. Neely, Jr. *Mine Eyes Have Seen the Glory: The Civil War in Art.* New York: Orion Books, 1993.

Hunt, O. E., ed. *Photographic History of the Civil War.* 5 vols. Secaucus, NJ: Blue and Grey Press, 1987.

Johnson, Neil. *The Battle of Gettysburg.* New York: Four Winds Press, 1989.

Johnson, Robert U., and Clarence C. Buel, eds. *Battles and Leaders of the Civil War.* 4 vols. Secaucus, NJ: Castle, 1987.

Miller, Francis T. *The Photographic History of the Civil War,* 10 vols. New York: Review of the Reviews, 1911.

Moat, Louis Shephard, ed. *Frank Leslie's Illustrated History of the Civil War.* New York: Fairfax Press, 1977.

Moneyhon, Carl, and Bobby Roberts. *Portraits of Conflict.* 3 vols. Fayetteville: University of Arkansas Press, 1990.

Russell, Andrew J. *Russell's Civil War Photographs.* New York: Dover Publications, 1982.

Stephenson, Richard W., ed. *Civil War Maps: An Annotated List of Maps and Atlases in the Library of Congress.* Washington, D.C.: Library of Congress, 1989.

Time-Life Books. *The Civil War.* 28 vols. Alexandria, VA: Time-Life Books, 1983–1987.

United States War Department. *The Official Military Atlas of the Civil War.* New York: Fairfax Press, 1983.

Ward, Geoffrey C., Ric Burns, and Ken Burns. *The Civil War: An Illustrated History.* New York: Alfred A. Knopf, 1991.

VIDEOTAPE SETS

Public Broadcasting Service. *The Civil War.* 9 vols. 1990.

Smithsonian Institution. *Battles of the Civil War.* 7 vols. 1993.

Arts and Entertainment Network. *Civil War Journal.* 6 vols. 1993.

Part IV

Causation—Events Leading to the War

11

Slavery, Race, and Culture

Eric H. Walther

Of all the factors that contributed to secession and Civil War, the role of slavery and race in motivating both Southerners and Northerners usually draws the most attention and the hottest debate. Certainly political and economic concerns played their part, yet these hinged invariably on issues and competing interests that arose from slavery and the institutions and ideals built upon that institution. Many "unreconstructed Southerners" continue to insist that the sectional conflict originated over states' rights, not slavery, although these people seldom complete the thought by specifying which "rights" they mean. This reasoning usually entails the arguments that few white Southerners owned slaves and therefore had no interest in preserving the institution, and that most white Northerners were racist and did not initially invade Dixie for any desire to free African Americans. Although truth exists in both of these assumptions, an enormous amount of scholarship on these very issues points to the centrality of slavery and race in the coming of the war.

The following works rank among the most influential for understanding the development of African slavery and its role in shaping antebellum white society and thought. Winthrop Jordon, in *White over Black: American Attitudes toward the Negro, 1550–1812* (1968), established that white people's belief in the inferiority of African peoples and the development of chattel slavery reinforced each other and grew stronger over time. George Frederickson introduced the concept of *herrenvolk* democracy in *The Black Image in the White Mind: The Debate on Afro-American Character and Destiny, 1817–1914* (1971) to explain how a bond of interests among white people developed through their shared set of assumptions about the racial inferiority of slaves. Edmund Morgan's *Amer-*

ican Slavery, American Freedom: The Ordeal of Colonial Virginia (1975) applies these ideas to the very beginnings of the peculiar institution in colonial America and demonstrates how they became incorporated into Virginians' version of republican ideology. A system of forced labor racially defined, Morgan explained, helped define liberty, underscore the value of independence, and unite all white people—whether or not they personally owned slaves—by providing stark, living examples of dependence, inferiority, and the loss of freedom. As white colonists perceived a growing menace of arbitrary and tyrannical power, their special appreciation of liberty compelled them to rebel against the British.

This heightened sensitivity to independence and equality continued and increased in the United States, with Northerners replacing the British in Southern eyes as a potential source of danger. William J. Cooper, Jr., has demonstrated how Southern politicians and voters alike worked to protect the institution of slavery as a mark of their own independence from outside interference and control. In *The South and the Politics of Slavery, 1828–1856* (1978), Cooper shows that Whigs and Democrats alike vied for support among the electorate by striving to convince them of their ability to defend slavery more ably, while casting their opponents as weak on slave questions. Cooper expands chronologically his paradigm in *Liberty and Slavery: Southern Politics to 1860* (1983) to argue that Southern politics from the colonial era through secession hinged on the political defense of slavery as a hallmark of white independence. Combining many of the central themes of Cooper and Morgan, Kenneth Greenberg, in *Masters and Statesmen: The Political Culture of American Slavery* (1985), found the dread fear of enslavement at the core of Southern political culture. Living in a world where slavery was tangible and drawing from an ideological heritage that emphasized independence, these Southerners, Greenberg insists, simultaneously resisted anything that smacked of subjugation to the will of another while insisting on their own right to possess slave property. Again concurring with Cooper and Morgan, Greenberg concludes that despite the irony involved, it made sense that those white Americans who most eloquently defended their own liberty could also own slaves. Like Cooper, Greenberg, and others, Bertram Wyatt-Brown, in his chapter "Honor and Secession," in *Yankee Saints and Southern Sinners* (1985), shows that honor and secession were linked because the reality of slavery gave substance to core Southern fears of inequality, humiliation, and dishonor in the face of mounting Northern attacks on the morality of slaveholders and on the freedom of white men to do as they pleased.

A growing body of literature demonstrates that the *herrenvolk* ideal among whites extended upward from the ranks of ordinary white Southerners just as much as it radiated outward from politicians, that the political characteristics of the region had a firm grounding among the masses. As Southern historians begin to pay serious attention to the plain folk of the region, many find that the peculiar institution profoundly shaped class structure and consciousness. Bruce Collins's *White Society in the Antebellum South* (1985) found that a sense of racial solidarity helped transcend the tension and inequality that did exist among economic classes of white people. By assigning dependence and degradation (at least in theory) to a racially defined and distinct group, a common defense of African slavery forged unity for whites in a culture that assigned tremendous value to personal independence. For different portions of Georgia, Steven Hahn, *The Roots of Southern Populism* (1983), and J. William Harris, *Plain Folk and Gentry in a Slave Society: White Liberty and Black Slavery in Augusta's Hinterlands* (1985), both demonstrate how common interests in slavery and fear of its demise intertwined social strata in their mutual concerns for racial hegemony. Bill Cecil-Fronsman, *Common Whites: Class and Culture in Antebellum North Carolina* (1992), found the same situation to have existed in North Carolina, with racial interests and unity limiting class conflict between ordinary white folk and the gentry.

Of course, the region's commitment to slavery was not total. William Freehling, in *The Road to Disunion: Secessionists at Bay* (1990), provides the most sensitive treatment of the diversity among Southerners and their varied interests in relation to slavery. And yet an overpowering slaveholding ethos reveals itself in places that few have traditionally expected. In *Mountain Masters, Slavery, and the Sectional Crisis in Western North Carolina* (1989), John C. Inscoe has overturned the conventional wisdom that mountaineers in the South uniformly stood apart from slaveholders by demonstrating a commitment to slavery and to slaveholding among western North Carolinians that came closer to the Deep South than to the other mountain regions or border states. Michael P. Johnson and James L. Roark demonstrate in *Black Masters: A Free Family of Color in the Old South* (1984) that slave ownership and slave abuse formed part of a desperate (and futile) attempt by the Ellison family of South Carolina to gain acceptance from their white neighbors. Similarly, Gary B. Mills describes, in *The Forgotten People: Cane River's Creoles of Color* (1977), the dedication to both slaveholding and, later, the Confederacy among a family of creoles of color in northwestern Louisiana.

As antislavery and abolitionist agitation gathered momentum in the North in the 1830s, Southern whites reacted by defending slavery as a positive good rather than a necessary evil. Drew Gilpin Faust provides the best explanation of the rise and development of this doctrine in her introduction to *The Ideology of Slavery: Proslavery Thought in the Antebellum South, 1830–1869* (1981). The emerging, comprehensive proslavery ideology depicted Southern society and culture as unique and superior to the North in every way. Leaders of this intellectual counterattack held that the Bible sanctioned human bondage, that slavery had historically formed the foundation of great civilizations like Greece and Rome, that scientific "truths" proved that Thomas Jefferson's declaration of universal and natural equality was wrong. The proslavery argument came to serve the dual purpose of defending Southern society as it attacked the North. By asserting that slave societies gave rise to organic communities with reciprocal obligations between masters and slaves, slavery's apologists argued that white Southerners provided blacks with advantages and a fundamental humanity that

Northern free workers lacked. The proslave critique of Northern society condemned "so-called free labor" as wage slavery and considered the North's growing materialism an affront to Christian precepts. The "mud-sill" theory presented as an argument what many historians would later recognize as reality: by assigning drudgery and degradation to a single, racially identifiable group, all white Southerners achieved a unique sense of unity, common interests, and destiny.

Proslave ideology manifested itself everywhere in the Old South. One of the striking examples comes from religion. In *The South and the North in American Religion* (1980), Samuel S. Hill, Jr., argued that antebellum Southern churches vigorously supported slavery, so much so that as war approached, religious leaders became convinced that their section was the more virtuous and more Christian of the two. Hill concluded that "the South disdained social activism because of its theology, which was linked to a hands-off policy concerning slavery" (p. 70). The individualistic and otherworldly character of evangelical religion blended with general social and political values in the South to support sectionalism and, eventually, sanctify secession. And although Anne Loveland, in *Southern Evangelicals and the Social Order, 1800–1860* (1980), argues that most evangelicals were at odds with Southerners who pronounced slavery a positive good, she notes that, nevertheless, starting in the 1830s, all major denominations backtracked drastically from emphatically antislavery positions taken earlier in the century. Mitchell Snay's *Gospel of Disunion: Religion and Separatism in the Antebellum South* (1993) provides the most thorough discussion of the link between proslave religion and secession.

Several studies explore the breadth of intellectual and cultural manifestations of slavery in the antebellum South. John McCardell's *The Idea of a Southern Nation: Southern Nationalists and Southern Nationalism, 1830–1860* (1979) shows that for many Southerners, the impact of slavery and proslavery ideology on diverse realms such as education, religion, literature, the economy, and territorial expansion produced the perception that they and Northerners constituted different peoples. Eric H. Walther argued, in *The Fire-Eaters* (1992), that neither wealth, status, personal background nor experience necessarily linked leaders of secession; what did was a commitment to the ideal of an independent, slaveholding society. The only thing that separated fire-eaters from the bulk of other white Southerners was their belief that this society was possible only in a separate republic. In *The Slaveholders' Dilemma: Freedom and Progress in Southern Conservative Thought, 1820–1869* (1992), Eugene Genovese demonstrates that long before 1861, white Southerners came to see African slavery as the foundation for freedom and progress, not an obstacle to either, yet more and more saw their values under attack from world opinion. Finally, he explains, these men found themselves confronted with the choice of remaining within the Union as a section besieged (and hoping the Constitution would protect them) or seceding and risking an effort to perfect a slaveholders' republic.

In a variety of state studies on secession, the protection of slavery presents itself as the central issue, although scholars have developed this theme with significant variations. Steven Channing's *Crisis of Fear: Secession in South Carolina* (1970) explains how white Carolinians' fear of losing control over their slave majority prompted them to secede with such haste. Channing's work supports the conclusions of William Freehling's *Prelude to Civil War: The Nullification Controversy in South Carolina, 1816–1836* (1965): that decades before secession, the nullification crisis signaled Carolinians' fear that if they could not stop federal action on a particular issue they considered unconstitutional (protective tariffs), then they would be doomed if the Northern majority ever decided to act. William L. Barney, in *The Secessionist Impulse: Alabama and Mississippi in 1860* (1974), agreed with Channing and Freehling that fear motivated men in those states to secede but found that the most frightened were younger planters, those most vulnerable to geographical confinement of slave territory and corresponding declines in slave prices and farm profits. Michael Johnson's account of disunion in Georgia, *Toward a Patriarchal Republic: The Secession of Georgia* (1977), maintains that a twofold revolution occurred there: a revolt against the external threat to slavery posed by Republicans and a second one, embodied in the new state constitution of 1861, to secure the hegemony of planters against an internal challenge of white yeomen.

Slavery and race obviously also affected society, culture, and politics in the North. Few scholars argue that a majority of white Northerners chose to attack the South in 1861 for their concern for the plight of slaves and a determination to bring about racial equality; quite the contrary. The essential monograph for those seeking an understanding of the ubiquitous racism in antebellum Northern society is Leon Litwack, *North of Slavery: The Negro in the Free States, 1790–1860* (1961). Nevertheless, for a variety of reasons, race and slavery drove Northern society toward a collision with the South.

Race and racism provoked a variety of critical responses to both slavery and to slaveholders among the people in the antebellum North. In *The Frontier against Slavery: Western Anti-Negro Prejudice and the Slavery Extension Controversy* (1967), Eugene H. Berwanger contends that white racism and fear that the West would be overrun by slaves or free blacks—and thereby lost to exclusive white expansion—formed the core of the free-soil movement and the fundamental appeal of the Republican party among westerners. Frederick J. Blue's *The Free Soilers: Third Party Politics, 1848–1854* (1973) describes members of this small group as variously idealistic humanitarians and as white supremacists, sometimes involved in politics to help African Americans, sometimes simply for their own ambitious purposes. Eric Foner insisted, in *Free Soil, Free Labor, Free Men: The Ideology of the Republican Party Before the Civil War* (1970), that unity prevailed among Republicans because of their view that slavery was incompatible with free labor and would sooner or later have to go. Republicans believed that the persistence of slavery, especially in the territories, thwarted possibilities for free men to prosper and rise in an open, mobile society that rewarded work. As white Southerners ever more identified slavery as the basis of civilization and rejected the materialism and lack of cohesion they believed characterized Northern society, Foner explains, "Northerners came to view slavery as the very antithesis of the good society, as well as a threat to their own fundamental values and interests" (p. 9). Even the Northern Know-Nothings, according to Tyler Anbinder, in *Nativism and Slavery: The Northern Know Nothings and the Politics of the 1850s* (1992), owed their brief surge of popularity to their stand against the extension of slavery, a policy quickly subsumed by Republicans. William E. Gienapp, in *The Origins of the Republican Party, 1852–1856* (1987), stresses the importance of ethnocultural issues (like temperance, immigration, and anti-Catholicism) in tearing down the second-party system in the North but concurs that Northern opposition to slavery expansion provided the galvanizing force for the new Republican party.

The question remains, How could a society grow so upset about slavery that its people became willing to go to war, even though these very people most likely did not care about the slaves themselves? A wide range of literature provides a solid answer to the apparent paradox. Citing examples such as the gag rule of 1836–1844, a proslavery mob attack on an abolitionist in Alton, Illinois, in 1837, and the fugitive slave law of 1850, Russell B. Nye, in *Fettered Freedom: Civil Liberties and the Slavery Controversy, 1830–1860* (1949), argued that the institution of slavery and the vitriolic, zealous defense that it created caused many Northerners to fear for their own civil liberties, thereby provoking opposition from people who opposed the slave power whether or not they cared about the slave. A growing number of Northerners came to believe genuinely that Southern politicians and their Northern harpies aimed to dominate the country and to use Federal power to promote African servitude, as described vividly by David Brion Davis in *The Slave Power Conspiracy and the Paranoid Style* (1969).

While the overwhelming majority of Northerners' antipathy toward slavery stemmed largely from selfish concerns, racism, and resentment of a "slave power," it is critical to remember that a small core of Northerners believed slavery both sinful and un-American and that all Americans shared a duty to destroy it. George Frederickson, in *The Inner Civil War: Northern Intellectuals and the Crisis of the Union* (1965), pointed out that the tide of egalitarianism and democracy that defined Jacksonian America convinced many that African Americans (and women, among others) belonged to the human race and were due equality. Among the most radical of these, Wendell Phillips called for laws that would protect the equal rights of all races, religions, and ideas. Ronald Walters, in both *The Antislavery Appeal: American Abolitionism after 1830* (1976) and *American Reformers, 1815–1860* (1978), places abolitionists solidly within the mainstream of antebellum reformers, who combined evangelical Protestantism "with a leavening of rhetoric from the American Revolution and a dash of economic and scientific thought" (*American Reformers,* p. 214). Although no modern scholars deny that racism persisted even within the ranks of those most devoted to abolition, Hans Trefousse's *The Radical Republicans:*

Lincoln's Vanguard for Racial Justice (1969) demonstrated that many Radical Republicans had a genuine commitment to emancipation and civil rights for blacks before the war and, once war came, helped influence a willing president to act on both.

Antislavery sentiment and the variety of its manifestations in the North resembled Southern proslavery in its variety and breadth. Edward Magdol, in *The Antislavery Rank and File: A Social Profile of the Abolitionist Constituency* (1986), meticulously reconstructed the working-class support for abolition in selected cities in Massachusetts and New York. He discovered that the grassroots supporters, many of them women, were both racially disinterested and steadfastly opposed to aristocracy and monopoly on land that they associated with slaveholders. Benjamin Quarles, in *Black Abolitionists* (1969), emphasized the role that African Americans played in the war against slavery, arguing that "the black abolitionist phalanx was not just another group of camp followers" (p. vii). Among more recent scholarship that concurs with Quarles about the important contribution of blacks to abolition but points out that no racial "phalanx" existed is Shirley Yee's *Black Women Abolitionists: A Study in Activism, 1828–1860* (1992). Yee examines the activities of black women born in free families as well as those who had escaped slavery, and reminds us that regardless of gender, black abolitionists were not of a single mind anymore than were black and white abolitionists.

The social and cultural conflict over slavery and race reached critical proportions during the 1850s and the general election of 1860. Kenneth M. Stampp concluded, in *And the War Came: The North and the Secession Crisis, 1860–1861* (1950), that "this conflict was the product of deep and fundamental causes and that most of the compromise proposals were essentially superficial. There was no basis for sectional harmony as long as Negro slavery survived and as long as Northerners used their overwhelming political power in Congress to advance their special interests at the expense of the South." Stampp argues that preventing war by 1860 would have "required of the North, in fact . . . not a compromise but a complete surrender" (p. 151) and that for the North, "the real purpose behind the conciliatory gestures of many [Republicans] was not to save the Union by compromise but to gain some strategic advantage over the secessionists" (p. 153). Similarly, Allan Nevins's *The Emergence of Lincoln* (1950) took the position that "the main root of the conflict (and there were minor roots) was the problem of slavery *with its complementary problem of race-adjustment.* . . . It was a war over slavery *and* the future position of the Negro race in North America" (2:468).

In what remains the best single volume on the coming of the war, David Potter, in *The Impending Crisis, 1848–1861* (1976), concluded that in culture, values, and economic structure, slavery uniquely isolated the South from the North. As this isolation increased, each section began reacting against the other not based on reality but on ever more distorted images of each other. As this tendency increased, the people in each section saw fewer similarities in values and culture, with slavery issues offering each side a false sense of clarity to the many and diffuse problems of the 1850s. Potter said that the South had reason to fear Lincoln's election, not because he threatened to interfere with slavery where it existed but because the Republican victory promised disruption of the "closed system of social and intellectual arrangements upon which the South relied for perpetuation of slavery" (p. 477).

Other scholars have also emphasized the centrality of race and slavery to Civil War causation. Secession and war, according to Richard J. Carwardine, in *Evangelicals and Politics in Antebellum America* (1993), provided confirmation for the millennialist expectations in both pro- and antislavery camps. James M. McPherson devoted a third of *Battle Cry of Freedom: The Civil War Era* (1988) to the mounting sectional conflict over slavery and slave expansion. McPherson never minimized the racist component of the free-soil or Republican movements, but he agreed with William H. Seward that conflicting sectional views of the morality of slavery and its place in American society and politics led to an irrepressible conflict. In his subsequent essay on the causes of the Civil War for Richard Current, ed., *The Encyclopedia of the Confederacy* (1993), McPherson addressed those causal explanations that assert slavery had nothing to do with the conflict and tersely dismissed them as the "virgin birth theory of secession" (1:317). Roger L. Ransom, in *Conflict and Compromise: The Political Economy of Slavery, Emancipation, and the American Civil War* (1989), dedicates over half of his book to an analysis of the coming of war, emphasizing the Southern determination to preserve its institution intact, the growing Northern determination to intrude upon it, and the resulting inability of the political system to resolve the conflict. The title of Bruce Levine's *Half Slave and Half Free: The Roots of the Civil War* (1992) once again reveals the importance of race and slavery to both North and South in bringing secession and war. "The distinctive ways in which North and South organized their labor systems," Levine argued, "left their mark on all aspects of regional life—including family, gender, and leisure patterns and both religious and secular ideologies." These cultural changes, Levine demonstrates, directly influenced the politics of both sections. Like McPherson, Levine leaves the last word on the causes of the Civil War to William H. Seward: "Thus, these antagonistic systems are continually coming into closer contact, and collision results" (pp. 14–15).

BIBLIOGRAPHY

Anbinder, Tyler. *Nativism and Slavery: The Northern Know Nothings and the Politics of the 1850s.* New York: Oxford University Press, 1992.

Barney, William L. *The Secessionist Impulse: Alabama and Mississippi in 1860.* Princeton: Princeton University Press, 1974.

Berwanger, Eugene H. *The Frontier against Slavery: Western Anti-Negro Prejudice and the Slavery Extension Controversy.* Urbana: University of Illinois Press, 1967.

Blue, Frederick J. *The Free Soilers: Third Party Politics, 1848–1854.* Urbana: University of Illinois Press, 1973.

Carwardine, Richard J. *Evangelicals and Politics in Antebellum America*. New Haven: Yale University Press, 1993.

Cecil-Fronsman, Bill. *Common Whites: Class and Culture in Antebellum North Carolina*. Lexington: University of Kentucky Press, 1992

Channing, Steven A. *Crisis of Fear: Secession in South Carolina*. New York: W. W. Norton, 1970.

Collins, Bruce. *White Society in the Antebellum South*. London: Longman, 1985.

Cooper, William J., Jr. *The South and the Politics of Slavery, 1828–1856*. Baton Rouge: Louisiana State University Press, 1978.

———. *Liberty and Slavery: Southern Politics to 1860*. New York: 1983.

Current, Richard N., ed., *The Encyclopedia of the Confederacy*. 4 vols. New York: Simon & Schuster, 1993.

Davis, David Brion. *The Slave Power Conspiracy and the Paranoid Style*. Baton Rouge: Louisiana State University Press, 1969.

Faust, Drew Gilpin. *The Ideology of Slavery: Proslavery Thought in the Antebellum South, 1830–1860*. Baton Rouge: Louisiana State University Press, 1981.

Foner, Eric. *Free Soil, Free Labor, Free Men: The Ideology of the Republican Party before the Civil War*. New York: Oxford University Press, 1970.

Frederickson, George M. *The Black Image in the White Mind: The Debate on Afro-American Character and Destiny, 1817–1914*. New York: Harper & Row, 1971.

———. *The Inner Civil War: Northern Intellectuals and the Crisis of the Union*. New York: Harper & Row, 1965.

Freehling, William W. *Prelude to Civil War: The Nullification Controversy in South Carolina, 1816–1836*. New York: Harper & Row, 1965.

———. *The Road to Disunion: Secessionists at Bay*. New York: Oxford University Press, 1990.

Genovese, Eugene D. *The Slaveholders' Dilemma: Freedom and Progress in Southern Conservative Thought, 1820–1860*. Columbia: University of South Carolina Press, 1992.

Gienapp, William E. *The Origins of the Republican Party, 1852–1856*. New York: Oxford University Press, 1987.

Greenberg, Kenneth S. *Masters and Statesmen: The Political Culture of American Slavery*. Baltimore: Johns Hopkins University Press, 1985.

Hahn, Steven. *The Roots of Southern Populism: Yeoman Farmers and the Transformation of the Georgia Upcountry, 1850–1890*. New York: Oxford University Press, 1983.

Harris, J. William. *Plain Folk and Gentry in a Slave Society: White Liberty and Black Slavery in Augusta's Hinterlands*. Middletown, CT: Wesleyan University Press, 1985.

Hill, Samuel S., Jr. *The South and the North in American Religion*. Athens: University of Georgia Press, 1980.

Inscoe, John C. *Mountain Masters, Slavery, and the Sectional Crisis in Western North Carolina*. Knoxville: University of Tennessee Press, 1989.

Johnson, Michael P. *Toward a Patriarchal Republic: The Secession of Georgia*. Baton Rouge: Louisiana State University Press, 1977.

———, and James L. Roark. *Black Masters: A Free Family of Color in the Old South*. New York: W. W. Norton, 1984.

Jordon, Winthrop. *White over Black: American Attitudes toward the Negro, 1550–1812*. Chapel Hill: University of North Carolina Press, 1968.

Levine, Bruce. *Half Slave and Half Free: The Roots of the Civil War.* New York: Hill and Wang, 1992.

Litwack, Leon F. *North of Slavery: The Negro in the Free States, 1790–1860.* Chicago: University of Chicago Press, 1961.

Loveland, Anne C. *Southern Evangelicals and the Social Order, 1800–1860.* Baton Rouge: Louisiana State University Press, 1980.

McCardell, John. *The Idea of a Southern Nation: Southern Nationalists and Southern Nationalism, 1830–1860.* New York: W. W. Norton, 1979.

McPherson, James M. *Battle Cry of Freedom: The Civil War Era.* New York: Oxford University Press, 1988

Magdol, Edward. *The Antislavery Rank and File: A Social Profile of the Abolitionists' Constituency.* Westport, CT: Greenwood Press, 1986.

Mills, Gary B. *The Forgotten People: Cane River's Creoles of Color.* Baton Rouge: Louisiana State University Press, 1977.

Morgan, Edmund S. *American Slavery, American Freedom: The Ordeal of Colonial Virginia.* New York: Norton, 1975.

Nevins, Allan. *The Emergence of Lincoln.* 2 vols. New York: Charles Scribner's Sons, 1950.

Nye, Russell B. *Fettered Freedom: Civil Liberties and the Slavery Controversy, 1830–1860.* East Lansing, MI: Michigan State College Press, 1949.

Potter, David M. *The Impending Crisis, 1848–1861.* New York: Harper & Row, 1976.

Quarles, Benjamin. *Black Abolitionists.* New York: Oxford University Press, 1969.

Ransom, Roger L. *Conflict and Compromise: The Political Economy of Slavery, Emancipation, and the American Civil War.* Cambridge: Cambridge University Press, 1989.

Snay, Mitchell. *Gospel of Disunion: Religion and Separatism in the Antebellum South.* Cambridge: Cambridge University Press, 1993.

Stampp, Kenneth M. *And the War Came: The North and the Secession Crisis, 1860–1861.* Baton Rouge: Louisiana State University Press, 1950.

Trefousse, Hans L. *The Radical Republicans: Lincoln's Vanguard for Racial Justice.* New York: Knopf, 1969.

Walters, Ronald G. *American Reformers, 1815–1860.* New York: Hill and Wang, 1978.

———. *The Antislavery Appeal: American Abolitionism after 1830.* Baltimore: Johns Hopkins University Press, 1976.

Walther, Eric H. *The Fire-Eaters.* Baton Rouge: Louisiana State University Press, 1992.

Wyatt-Brown, Bertram. *Yankee Saints and Southern Sinners.* Baton Rouge: Louisiana State University Press, 1985.

Yee, Shirley J. *Black Women Abolitionists: A Study in Activism, 1828–1860.* Knoxville: University of Tennessee Press, 1992.

12

Constitutional and Political Factors

Frederick J. Blue

The sheer number of historical works dealing with the constitutional and political factors contributing to the causes of the Civil War makes a bibliographic study of the most important secondary sources a difficult task at best. The problem is made more complex because the two areas are often approached by historians as separate and distinct fields, though they are closely related. As a result, few of the interpretations integrate the two topics. Thus, while judicial decisions dealing with sectional issues directly affected the political situation and in fact seriously altered the two-party structure of the antebellum years, historians have logically emphasized only one of the fields even as they recognized the impact of the other.

CONSTITUTIONAL ISSUES

Constitutional studies dealing with the years leading to the Civil War have emphasized issues relating to slavery and the resulting jurisdictional disputes between central and state governments. While many accounts focus narrowly on limited aspects of the constitutional issues relating to slavery, that of Harold Hyman and William M. Wiecek, *Equal Justice under Law: Constitutional Development, 1835–1875* (1982), fuses political narrative with constitutional development. In fact, the authors show that constitutional issues in these years were often closer to politics than they were to jurisprudence. Although they treat all aspects of constitutional history, their emphasis is on the familiar but frequently misunderstood slavery controversy and how it evolved during the tenures of chief justices Roger B. Taney and Salmon P. Chase. Sympathetic to the antislavery movement, the authors are especially critical of the Taney Court's *Dred Scott* opinion, which, because of its lack of objectivity, guaranteed that there could be no judicial solution to the issue of slavery.

Such a conclusion is to be expected in the light of Wiecek's earlier study, *The Sources of Antislavery Constitutionalism in America, 1760–1848* (1977), which surveys the legal arguments of those opposed to slavery. Wiecek traces how the early consensus that slavery was subject only to state jurisdiction ended in a barrage of abolitionist attack by the 1830s. Most antislavery proponents agreed with William Lloyd Garrison that the Constitution was a proslavery document, while moderate free-soil elements went further in arguing that the containment of slavery by the Federal government was the most they could hope for. But Wiecek also develops the little-known position of a few radical abolitionists who insisted that the Constitution could and should be interpreted as an antislavery document obligating the Federal government to oppose the peculiar institution wherever it existed. Thus the author brings together the diverse strands of antislavery legal theory as it evolved through the end of the Mexican War.

Two interpretations emphasize the role of the fugitive slave in the framework of constitutional law. Robert M. Cover's *Justice Accused: Antislavery and Judicial Process* (1975) looks at how four antislavery justices were forced to place traditionalism over their humanitarian ideals in regard to the law of slavery. Included in his account are four who abhorred slavery morally but could see no way around the constitutional requirement to aid Southerners in the return of fugitives. The four Cover selected are John McLean and Joseph Story of the Supreme Court and Lemuel Shaw and Joseph Swan of state supreme courts. Paul Finkelman's *An Imperfect Union: Slavery, Federalism, and Comity* (1981) focuses on whether states would enforce the laws of another state with regard to slaves in transit. The issue frequently raised was the degree to which Northern states were obligated to recognize the property rights of owners traveling with their slaves. Cover suggests that before 1830, comity was usually granted, but in later years Northerners increasingly endorsed the argument that slaves became free in free states.

Two studies published in the early 1970s deal with state and federal law relating to fugitives and the extent to which escaped slaves were accorded protection. Thomas D. Morris's *Free Men All: The Personal Liberty Laws of the North, 1780–1861* (1974) treats the contrast between law in Northern states, which presumed a person free until proven otherwise, with Southern states, which assumed that all African Americans were by definition slaves. Morris concentrates on five key Northern states and shows how jurists and legislators initially cooperated with slaveholders in their efforts to recapture alleged fugitives. By the mid-1830s many of the free states responded to the federal fugitive slave acts of 1793 and 1850 with personal liberty laws designed to protect the rights of the accused. Morris traces the Federal response to these laws in key cases from *Prigg v. Pennsylvania* (1842) through *Ableman v. Booth* (1859). Stanley Campbell's *The Slave Catchers: Enforcement of the Fugitive Slave Law, 1850–1860* (1970) suggests that the act of 1850 was more generally enforced than is usually recognized. Campbell notes that despite protests by abolitionists, most suits brought to trial under the law resulted in the slaves' being reclaimed by their owners.

Several studies trace the degree to which slaves and opponents of slavery could expect any satisfaction from Federal law. Phillip S. Paludan's *A Covenant with Death: The Constitution, Law and Equality in the Civil War Era* (1975) looks at five leading Northern constitutional authorities whose writings failed to produce significant legal protection for African Americans before, during, or after the war. Paludan's title reflects Garrison's emphasis on a proslavery constitution that is confirmed in the thinking of Francis Lieber, Joel Parker, Sidney George Fisher, John Norton Pomeroy, and Thomas M. Cooley. They concluded, collectively and individually, that the constitutional tradition of federalism prohibited the central government from intervening in behalf of the slave community. Three articles reach similar conclusions in describing Supreme Court decisions of the antebellum years. Arthur Bestor's "The American Civil War as a Constitutional Crisis" (1964) traces the various arguments in relation to territorial slavery, which climaxed when "four irreconcilable constitutional doctrines were presented to the American people in 1860" (p. 351). Robert Russel's "Constitutional Doctrines with Regard to Slavery in the Territories" (1966) examines the views of those advocating the variety of positions on territorial slavery, including the Wilmot Proviso, popular sovereignty, and the Calhoun doctrine of guaranteed territorial slavery, climaxing in the *Dred Scott* decision of 1857. William Wiecek's "Slavery and Abolition before the United States Supreme Court, 1820–1860" (1978) considers the cases chronologically and concludes that the *Scott* decision was not an aberration but rather "a natural result of judge-made doctrines and tendencies that had been developing for two decades" (p. 35). Inevitably, all constitutional interpretations point to the momentous ruling of the Taney Court in 1857, *Dred Scott v. Sandford.* The case has received exhaustive treatment by Don Fehrenbacher in *The Dred Scott Case: Its Significance in American Law and Politics* (1978), which was also published in an abridged version, *Slavery, Law, and Politics: The Dred Scott Case in Historical Perspective* (1981). Fehrenbacher describes how Taney and the majority resolved the critical territorial issue in favor of the South. The author traces the background and the many immediate and sweeping ramifications of the case, devoting less than one-third of his study to the actual litigation. Fehrenbacher makes no effort to hide his own bias as he concludes that the Court's ruling was "egregiously wrong" (p. 336). Taney in fact sought to destroy the antislavery argument and "to reinforce the bastions of slavery" (p. 341) but instead succeeded only in further polarizing North and South and hastening the fast-approaching sectional confrontation.

POLITICAL ISSUES

Traditional Studies

The task of reviewing the literature that addresses the political factors contributing to the Civil War is even more difficult than that dealing with constitutional issues because the contributing elements are more complex and controversial. Included are traditional histories that emphasize slavery as the basic cause of party realignment and eventual war. Within this approach are studies with a national perspective, as well as those with either a Northern or Southern emphasis, some of them dealing with an individual state and others taking a regional approach. In addition, recent years have seen the emergence of a new political history arguing that ethnocultural issues must share the spotlight with slavery in explaining the evolution of the party system in the 1850s, especially in the North.

The complexity of approaches and emphases is best introduced by the synthesis of David Potter, *The Impending Crisis, 1848–1861* (1976). With Potter's death in 1971, the final two chapters and editing were completed by Don E. Fehrenbacher. The volume is a comprehensive overview of the period between the Mexican War and secession. Potter and Fehrenbacher describe and analyze four presidential elections and evaluate such critical issues as the Compromise of 1850, the transcontinental railroad, Kansas and popular sovereignty, and party changes. The authors emphasize slavery over all other issues as central to the sectional crisis and succeed in presenting a traditional view in an evenhanded manner. A less extensive but highly effective overview of the economic, social, and political history of the years between the Revolution and the Civil War is Bruce Levine's *Half Slave and Half Free: The Roots of the Civil War* (1992). Its greatest contribution is in describing and evaluating the economic and social differences between Northern and Southern cultures. In outlining political changes, Levine stresses the centrality of slavery rather than the religious and ethnic issues underlined by the new political historians.

Levine's emphasis on the competing labor systems of North and South establishes him as a supporter of Eric Foner, who set forth the free labor argument in *Free Soil, Free Labor, Free Men: The Ideology of the Republican Party before the Civil War* (1970). Foner's pathbreaking study stresses the irreconcilable ideologies that competed in the 1850s, with Republicans believing in the superiority of their dynamic, expanding, capitalistic society with the dignity of labor as a central tenet over the backward, degraded slave labor system. Foner goes on to describe the various factions that came under the new Republican umbrella in the mid-1850s, including antislavery radicals led by Chase and Charles Sumner, Democrats angered by the proslave policies of the Pierce and Buchanan administrations, Whigs of the Clay-Webster tradition, and nativists fearful of foreign influence. The last group, says Foner, found its position quickly submerged by the party's emphasis on the containment of slavery.

While Foner described the ideology of the early Republican party, other historians have dealt with the political system preceding that party's formation. As the second-party system dominated by the Jacksonians and their opponents began to founder with the North-South polarization in the 1840s, Democrats and Whigs struggled to keep their fragile coalitions together. The Wilmot Proviso controversy of the Mexican War years was the catalyst that accelerated the process of party change and is the subject of Chaplain Morrison's *Democratic Politics and Sectionalism: The Wilmot Proviso Controversy* (1967). Morrison describes the sectional issues that destroyed Democratic party unity during the Polk administration. It was the Van Buren wing of antislavery Northerners that pushed the proviso and eventually bolted the party when it did not get its way. A similar split developed among Northern Whigs centered in Massachusetts and emerged during the same years. It is faithfully described by Kinley Brauer in *Cotton Versus Conscience: Massachusetts Whig Politics and Southwestern Expansion, 1843–1848* (1967). In the Bay State, a group of young Whigs led by Summer and Charles Francis Adams challenged the old guard Webster faction and its alliance with Southern producers of cotton. When denied party control, the rebels walked out. A third faction of Liberty party abolitionists also sought a broader-based antislavery party as the issue of slavery in Mexican War territories began to dominate sectional politics. The western element of Liberty men led by Chase and Gamaliel Bailey is the subject of Vernon Volpe's *Forlorn Hope of Freedom: The Liberty Party in the Old Northwest, 1838–1848* (1990). Volpe emphasizes the religious motivation that dominated much of the Liberty group's approach to antislavery in the Great Lakes states.

In 1848, Liberty members and antislavery factions of Democrats and Whigs united to form the Free Soil party, the more inclusive third party that Chase and Bailey had sought. These events provide a central part of Richard Sewell's *Ballots for Freedom: Antislavery Politics in the United States, 1837–1860* (1976). Sewell describes the formation of both the Liberty and Free Soil parties and concludes his study with the Republican party of the 1850s. The free-soil movement is also the subject of Frederick J. Blue's *The Free Soilers: Third-Party Politics, 1848–54* (1973). Blue stresses both the practical politics and the antislavery idealism that dominated free-soil thinking. All of these authors are quick to point out the racism of most antislavery politicians who were typically more concerned with protecting the interests of their white constituents than they were with economic, social, and political equality for African Americans.

Those who remained Whigs or Democrats throughout these tumultuous years are the subject of several recent accounts. Merrill D. Peterson's *The Great Triumvirate: Webster, Clay, and Calhoun* (1987) brings together the three central Whig figures whose political careers began during the era of the War of 1812 and who worked together in the 1830s and after primarily out of common opposition to Andrew Jackson. Their coalition was tenuous, a union that Peterson details through the deaths of the party patriarchs in the early 1850s. The Whig party itself is the subject of two studies. Daniel Howe, in *The Political Culture of the American Whigs* (1979), examines the lives and values of a dozen Whig leaders, including such opposites as John Quincy Adams, Lyman Beecher, and Alexander H. Stephens. Howe, an admirer of the Whigs and their approach, evaluates various aspects of their rhetoric, including endorsements of social improvement and morality. Thomas Brown's *Politics and Statesmanship: Essays on the American Whig Party* (1985) covers some of the same ground but puts more emphasis on the Whig ideal of statesmanship. The party's failure came in part, says Brown, because its statesmanship proved incompatible with the partisan politics of the late 1840s and early 1850s. Jean Baker's *Affairs of Party: The Political Culture of Northern Democrats in the Mid-Nineteenth Century* (1983) has a similar goal in describing the opposition party in the Civil War era. In rehabilitating the sagging reputation of Northern Democrats, she effectively describes the dilemma they found themselves in before the war in a party dominated by Southerners. Their belief in republican government and economic liberalism was tempered by racism and acceptance of the proslavery ideology.

Three works by well-known scholars in the field of antebellum politics add significantly to our knowledge of some of the critical events of the 1850s. Holman Hamilton's *Prologue to Conflict: The Crisis and Compromise of 1850* (1964) remains the standard account of the complex package of bills that Henry Clay and Stephen A. Douglas guided through Congress and that established a temporary truce in the sectional struggle. James A. Rawley's *Race and Politics: Bleeding Kansas and the Coming of the Civil War* (1969) shows how the crisis created by Douglas's Kansas-Nebraska Act of 1854 dominated sectional politics for the next five years and ended any hope that the settlement of 1850 would hold. Rawley expertly traces the complexities of the struggle between pro- and antislavery forces that made Kansas Territory a battleground. Kenneth Stampp's *America in 1857: A Nation on the Brink* (1990) argues that by 1857, the Kansas controversy and the *Dred Scott* ruling meant that North and South had reached ''a political point of no return'' (p. viii), in large part brought on by the political ineptitude of President James Buchanan.

The Slave States

Political developments in the slave states have received substantial attention from scholars. Included are four recent overviews of the years before the Civil War and several that look at the secession crisis as it affected the entire South or specific states and regions.

William W. Freehling has undertaken a two-volume study of the period between the Revolution and the Civil War. In *The Road to Disunion,* volume 1, *Secessionists at Bay, 1776–1854* (1990), he emphasizes that despite the determination of some to destroy the Union, disunionists were held in check from the time of the Revolution through the mid-1850s by the overwhelming majority who were dedicated to the Union's survival. Freehling emphasizes the extremists' efforts during the nullification crisis and the gag rule and Texas annexation confrontations. In volume 2 *Secessionists Triumphant, 1854–1861* (forthcoming), he will describe how and why they finally got their way.

Two studies by William J. Cooper also look at the South in broad perspective. The first, *The South and the Politics of Slavery, 1828–1856* (1978), is a detailed account of Southern politics on both the state and national levels from the formation of the second two-party system through the decline of the Whigs in the 1850s. Cooper maintains that Southern politicians throughout these years were fully dedicated to the preservation of slavery and subordinated all other issues. In *Liberty and Slavery: Southern Politics to 1860* (1983), he presents a broader view of the South's role in national politics from colonial times to the Civil War, a study designed for the general reader more than the specialist. Cooper defines liberty as the efforts and determination of Southern whites to defend themselves from outside interference with slavery. This was necessary, he maintains, because their way of life was dependent on the survival of the peculiar institution. Finally, a study by William Barney, *The Road to Secession: A New Perspective on the Old South* (1972), emphasizes the frustrations of Southern politicians and planters as they concluded by 1860 that slavery was to be excluded from further territorial expansion. They believed that slavery had to expand to survive; yet the events of the 1850s convinced them that the Republican policy of containment had triumphed, leaving them no choice but disunion through secession.

Several studies of the secession crisis itself provide additional detail on the crisis brought on by Lincoln's victory in 1860. Eric Walther's *The Fire-Eaters* (1992) examines the lives of nine slave state political leaders who pushed hardest for disunion. Among those studied in this collective biography are Robert B. Rhett, William Yancey, Edmund Ruffin, and James B. DeBow, all of whom viewed secession as the only means by which Southern liberty and honor could be preserved. They were, says Walther, radicals but not outsiders. They believed that slavery was threatened by centralized power and that only local government could check the threat that the Federal government under a Republican administration represented in 1860. Several state studies shed additional light on disunionist thinking. Steven A. Channing's *Crisis of Fear: Secession in South Carolina* (1970) argues that Lincoln's victory convinced South Carolinians that abolition was now inevitable and with it would come racial rebellion, economic, social, and political disaster, and the destruction of the white supremacy on which slavery rested. Secession was thus the only way to prevent such a catastrophe. William Barney's *The Secessionist Impulse: Alabama and Mississippi in 1860* (1974) challenges the image of a monolithic Old South driven in unity to form the Confederacy. While Breckenridge secessionist Democrats quickly triumphed in Mississippi, in Alabama a much more divided electorate gave only a narrow victory to the secessionists. Those who resisted were the genteel patriarchs and cavaliers; younger men on the make were more racist and determined to protect their future through secession.

Among the best of the state studies of secession is Walter L. Buenger's *Se-

cession and Union in Texas (1984), which again reveals the deep division within the white population as it moved from staunch unionism in 1859 to a solid secessionist majority by 1861. Buenger treats the various parts of the state, showing how regional differences and self-interest determined the degree of loyalty to growing Southern nationalism. Finally, Daniel Crofts provides a much-needed view of those who resisted secession in Virginia, North Carolina, and Tennessee in *Reluctant Confederates: Upper South Unionists in the Secession Crisis* (1989). A long-neglected group, Southern Unionists were outside the mainstream of Southern life. Yet a vigorous two-party system allowed them to defend their position despite their minority position. In fact, the Unionists won the first round of votes in early 1861, until Lincoln's call for troops in April forced these three critical states to join the Confederacy and submerge the Unionist movement. In total, these studies collectively demonstrate the diversity of Southern approaches to the crisis of 1860–1861 rather than the single-mindedness that many have assumed.

The New Political History

For the most part, the emphasis in studies of Southern politics has remained on slavery and race. Interpretations of Northern politics, on the other hand, have at times focused on the controversy created by the new political history. This approach first emerged with Lee Benson's *The Concept of Jacksonian Democracy: New York as a Test Case* (1961), an interpretation of an era just prior to that which stresses Civil War causation but one that looks at politics from a broad range of social variables, including ethnic and religious differences. As they have applied it to the 1840s and 1850s, new political historians have sometimes employed quantification techniques in studying voting behavior of the electorate and of Congress. This in turn has led to an ethnocultural interpretation of voter motivation. In essence, historians using this approach conclude that religion and ethnic identity, along with the resulting social attitudes, were significant determinants of voter preference. At the same time, some have de-emphasized slavery and sectional conflict as major factors in voting behavior. Much of the controversy has centered around the disappearance of the Whig party in the 1850s in the transition from the second- to the third-party system. To the new political historians, issues such as temperance and nativism and questions of ethnic and religious conflict were as central to this transition as North-South divisions over slavery, which traditionalists have always emphasized. Thus to those stressing ethnocultural questions, the American or Know Nothing party was much more than a brief interlude for some on their route to an inevitable joining of the Republican party. It was, rather, a viable alternative, and the Know Nothings had a legitimate chance of becoming a member of the two-party system.

One of the first historians to apply the new approach to the antebellum period was Joel Silbey in his *The Shrine of Party: Congressional Voting Behavior,*

1841–1852 (1967), which uses quantification to argue that partisanship was more important than sectionalism in determining voting patterns on most issues in Congress in the 1840s. But it was Michael Holt's article, "The Politics of Impatience: The Origins of Know-Nothingism" (1973), which set the stage for a major controversy within the historical profession. Holt argues that the Know Nothing appeal to anti-Catholic sentiments helped cause the decline of the Whig party rather than simply benefiting from Whig disintegration caused by its failures on sectional issues. Whigs, Holt suggests, had been too passive on religious and ethnic issues, and a more militant approach was needed. He develops this theme more fully in *The Political Crisis of the 1850s* (1978), where he argues that Northern voters were more interested in local ethnocultural issues, especially anti-Catholicism and temperance, than in slavery. In the 1850s, he continues, voters lost faith in the ability of Democrats and Whigs to address their concerns. For the most part, Holt and other new political historians have been most concerned with party realignment in the 1850s and only indirectly with Civil War causation.

The ethnocultural approach to the politics of the 1850s found an important disciple in William E. Gienapp, who has studied the formation of the Republican party in detail unmatched by any other historian. Gienapp's views first became apparent in "Nativism and the Creation of a Republican Majority in the North before the Civil War" (1985), in which he contends that the party had a substantial nativist component in virtually every Northern state, and in those states where Republicans refused cooperation, the Know Nothings won control. While Eric Foner argues that nativism declined dramatically after 1857, Gienapp suggests that the Republicans kept the issue in the forefront through Lincoln's election. In his long and intricate *The Origins of the Republican Party, 1852–1856* (1987) Gienapp shows that the party realignment of the 1850s was a two-step process, first to the American and then to the Republican. Although Gienapp recognizes that slave-related issues were a primary focus of the Republican appeal, party leaders appealed to ethnocultural fears as well. In the contest between the two new parties, the Know Nothings had the initial advantage, but their inexperience allowed Republicans to outmaneuver and undermine their appeal and finally appropriate their electoral base.

While Holt and Gienapp have focused on the broad ethnocultural themes of the 1850s, others of the same school have either looked to earlier years for its roots or developed more limited aspects of the appeal itself. Ronald Formisano, in *The Transformation of Political Culture, Massachusetts Parties, 1790s–1840s* (1983), extends the principles of ethnocultural analysis to the Massachusetts political environment of the Jacksonian era. Reliance on quantification leads him to the conclusion that organized parties in the modern sense in the Bay State did not fully develop until the 1830s and that the two-party system of the 1840s was based on a complex interaction of cultural and social as well as political factors. A series of essays edited by Stephen E. Maizlish and John J. Kushma, *Essays on American Antebellum Politics, 1840–1860* (1982), brings together the works of Gienapp, Thomas Alexander, Holt, Maizlish, and Silbey and represents the views of the new political history in their emphasis on the ethnocultural appeal of antebellum parties.

Holt has also collected his many essays in a single volume, *Political Parties and American Political Development from the Age of Jackson to the Age of Lincoln* (1992), which recognizes that while the ethnocultural interpretation is an essential element in the political appeal, we must look at sectional and economic aspects as well. Yet he concludes that antislavery efforts that stress the impact of the Kansas-Nebraska Act must share the spotlight with nativism, religious trends such as evangelicalism, and temperance for a fuller understanding of antebellum politics. The theme of religion in politics is developed by Richard J. Carwardine in *Evangelicals and Politics in Antebellum America* (1993). The author shows how Protestant evangelicals helped to shape political development and the important role they and the issues they raised played in sectional tensions.

The differences between traditional and ethnocultural views have been outlined further in several studies emphasizing both state and sectional histories. Dale Baum's *The Civil War Party System: The Case of Massachusetts, 1848–1876* (1984) argues that the Republican party created its majorities in the 1850s by stressing economic rather than nativist themes. In fact, he suggests that few Know Nothings joined the Republican party in Massachusetts. In contrast, John R. Mulkern's *The Know-Nothing Party in Massachusetts: The Rise and Fall of a People's Movement* (1990) adopts the Holt-Formisano approach in emphasizing the ethnocultural populist theme that led to significant reform legislation and eventually contributed to the Republican appeal in the Bay State. Tyler Anbinder's *Nativism and Slavery: The Northern Know Nothings and the Politics of the 1850s* (1992) returns to the traditional emphasis on slavery to explain voter attitudes in the 1850s. He argues that antislavery sentiment, not nativism, undermined the Whigs and that Republicans made few concessions to nativist principles in gaining the votes of American party members later in the decade. In essence, says Anbinder, slave-related issues caused both the origins and the demise of the Know Nothing movement.

Thus the issues raised by traditional and new political historians remain unresolved and continue to create controversy. Most recently, Ronald Formisano has argued in "The Invention of the Ethnocultural Interpretation" (1994) that it was the critics of the new political history who in fact created the ethnocultural interpretation. Its actual practitioners, Formisano suggests, instead have emphasized a multicausation approach in which religion and ethnicity are only two of many aspects of import. One of the leading critics, Don Fehrenbacher, provides an overview of the different emphases in "The New Political History and the Coming of the Civil War" (1985). Although Fehrenbacher rejects the ethnocultural approach, his conclusions accurately confirm that slavery will continue to vie with ethnicity and religion in any consideration of the political factors leading to the Civil War.

BIBLIOGRAPHY

Anbinder, Tyler. *Nativism and Slavery: The Northern Know Nothings and the Politics of the 1850s.* New York: Oxford University Press, 1992.

Baker, Jean H. *Affairs of Party: The Political Culture of Northern Democrats in the Mid-Nineteenth Century.* Ithaca: Cornell University Press, 1983.

Barney, William L. *The Road to Secession: A New Perspective on the Old South.* New York: Praeger, 1972.

———. *The Secessionist Impulse: Alabama and Mississippi in 1860.* Princeton: Princeton University Press, 1974.

Baum, Dale. *The Civil War Party System: The Case of Massachusetts, 1848–1876.* Chapel Hill: University of North Carolina Press, 1984.

Benson, Lee. *The Concept of Jacksonian Democracy: New York as a Test Case.* Princeton: Princeton University Press, 1961.

Bestor, Arthur. "The Civil War as a Constitutional Crisis." *American Historical Review* 69 (1964): 327–354.

Blue, Frederick J. *The Free Soilers: Third Party Politics, 1848–54.* Urbana: University of Illinois Press, 1973.

Brauer, Kinley. *Cotton Versus Conscience: Massachusetts Whig Politics and Southwestern Expansion, 1843–1848.* Lexington: University of Kentucky Press, 1967.

Brown, Thomas. *Politics and Statesmanship: Essays on the American Whig Party.* New York: Columbia University Press, 1985.

Buenger, Walter L. *Secession and Union in Texas.* Austin: University of Texas Press, 1984.

Campbell, Stanley. *The Slave Catchers: Enforcement of the Fugitive Slave Law, 1850–1860.* Chapel Hill: University of North Carolina Press, 1970.

Carwardine, Richard J. *Evangelicals and Politics in Antebellum America.* New Haven: Yale University Press, 1993.

Channing, Steven A. *Crisis of Fear: Secession in South Carolina.* New York: Norton, 1970.

Cooper, William J. *Liberty and Slavery: Southern Politics to 1860.* New York: Knopf, 1983.

———. *The South and the Politics of Slavery, 1828–1856.* Baton Rouge: Louisiana State University Press, 1978.

Cover, Robert M. *Justice Accused: Antislavery and the Judicial Process.* New Haven: Yale University Press, 1975.

Crofts, Daniel. *Reluctant Confederates: Upper South Unionists in the Secession Crisis.* Chapel Hill: University of North Carolina Press, 1989.

Fehrenbacher, Don. *The Dred Scott Case: Its Significance in American Law and Politics.* New York: Oxford University Press, 1978.

———. "The New Political History and the Coming of the Civil War." *Pacific Historical Review* 54 (1985): 117–142.

————. *Slavery, Law and Politics: The Dred Scott Case in Historical Perspective.* New York: Oxford University Press, 1981.

Finkelman, Paul. *An Imperfect Union: Slavery, Federalism and Comity.* Chapel Hill: University of North Carolina Press, 1981.

Foner, Eric. *Free Soil, Free Labor, Free Men: The Ideology of the Republican Party before the Civil War.* New York: Oxford University Press, 1970.

Formisano, Ronald P. "The Invention of the Ethnocultural Interpretation." *American Historical Review* 99 (1994): 453–477.

————. *The Transformation of Political Culture: Massachusetts Parties, 1790s–1840s.* New York: Oxford University Press, 1983.

Freehling, William W. *The Road to Disunion: Secessionists at Bay, 1776–1854.* New York: Oxford University Press, 1990.

————. *Secessionists Triumphant, 1854–1861.* New York: Oxford University Press, forthcoming.

Gienapp, William E. "Nativism and the Creation of the Republican Majority before the Civil War." *Journal of American History* 72 (1985): 529–559.

————. *The Origins of the Republican Party, 1852–1856.* New York: Oxford University Press, 1987.

Hamilton, Holman. *Prelude to Conflict: The Crisis and Compromise of 1850.* Lexington: University of Kentucky Press, 1964.

Holt, Michael. *The Political Crisis of the 1850s.* New York: John Wiley and Sons, 1978.

————. *Political Parties and American Political Development from the Age of Jackson to the Age of Lincoln.* Baton Rouge: Louisiana State University Press, 1992.

————. "The Politics of Impatience: The Origins of Know Nothingism." *Journal of American History* 60 (1973): 309–331.

Howe, Daniel W. *The Political Culture of American Whigs.* Chicago: University of Chicago Press, 1979.

Hyman, Harold, and William M. Wiecek. *Equal Justice under Law: Constitutional Development, 1835–1875.* New York: Harper & Row, 1982.

Levine, Bruce. *Half Slave and Half Free: The Roots of the Civil War.* New York: Hill and Wang, 1992.

Maizlish, Stephen E., and John J. Kushma, eds. *Essays on American Antebellum Politics, 1840–1860.* College Station: Texas A&M University Press, 1982.

Morris, Thomas D. *Free Men All: The Personal Liberty Laws of the North, 1780–1861.* Baltimore: Johns Hopkins University Press, 1974.

Morrison, Chaplain. *Democratic Politics and Sectionalism: The Wilmot Proviso Controversy.* Chapel Hill: University of North Carolina Press, 1967.

Mulkern, John R. *The Know-Nothing Party in Massachusetts: The Rise and Fall of a People's Movement.* Boston: Northeastern University Press, 1990.

Paludan, Philip S. *A Covenant with Death: The Constitution, Law and Equality in the Civil War Era.* Urbana: University of Illinois Press, 1975.

Peterson, Merrill D. *The Great Triumvirate: Webster, Clay, and Calhoun.* New York: Oxford University Press, 1987.

Potter, David. *The Impending Crisis, 1848–1861.* New York: Harper & Row, 1976.

Rawley, James A. *Race and Politics: Bleeding Kansas and the Coming of the Civil War.* Philadelphia: J. B. Lippincott, 1969.

Russel, Robert. "Constitutional Doctrines with Regard to Slavery in the Territories." *Journal of Southern History* 32 (1966): 466–485.

Sewell, Richard. *Ballots for Freedom: Antislavery Politics in the United States, 1837–1860.* New York: Oxford University Press, 1976.

Silbey, Joel. *The Shrine of Party: Congressional Voting Behavior, 1841–1852.* Pittsburgh: University of Pittsburgh Press, 1967.

Stampp, Kenneth. *America in 1857: A Nation on the Brink.* New York: Oxford University Press, 1990.

Volpe, Vernon. *Forlorn Hope of Freedom: The Liberty Party in the Old Northwest, 1838–1848.* Kent: Kent State University Press, 1990.

Walther, Eric. *The Fire-Eaters.* Baton Rouge: Louisiana State University Press, 1992.

Wiecek, William. "Slavery and Abolition before the United States Supreme Court, 1820–1860." *Journal of American History* 65 (1978): 34–59.

———. *The Sources of Antislavery Constitutionalism in America, 1760–1848.* Ithaca: Cornell University Press, 1977.

13

Economic Factors

James M. Russell

Two questions are important to an understanding of the causes of the American Civil War. Why did eleven states risk war by seceding from the Union, beginning with South Carolina on December 20, 1860? And why did the North choose to fight to preserve the Union? The bulk of the historiography on Civil War causation attempts to answer only one of these questions at a time, with far more work addressing the topic of Southern secession. It is fair to add that most studies on the causes of the Civil War have downplayed economic factors.

In an historiographical survey, "The Irrepressible Conflict," included in his *The Imperiled Union: Essays on the Background of the Civil War* (1980), Kenneth Stampp divides most twentieth-century work on Civil War causation into three categories: those that argue for economic determinism; those that embrace a "slavery/cultural concept," which minimizes economic factors; and those that adhere to James G. Randall's "blundering generation hypothesis," which rejects the importance of both economic and cultural factors and emphasizes instead the significance of irresponsible, fanatical agitators and incompetent politicians.

MARXIST PERSPECTIVES

Not surprisingly, those who fit into Stampp's first category—economic determinism—have been Marxist historians, who tend to follow Marx's tenet that economic factors are the prime moving forces in history. One of the first to apply Marxist thinking to the causes of the Civil War was A. M. Simons. In his *Social Forces in American History* (1920), Simons began by dismissing the idea that Northern concern over the plight of the slaves had anything to do with the North's decision to make war on the South. Slaves, he wrote, "were as well, if not better treated in 1860 than at any time in their history," while "it is certain that the general moral conscience of the North had seldom been lower than in the years when competitive capitalism was gaining the mastery in American industrial life." The cause of the Civil War, Simons stated in classic Marxist rhetoric, was the clash between Northern, bourgeois, industrial capitalists and Southern "chattel slave owners," whom Simons equates with the "feudal" aristocracy that capitalism had already overrun in Europe. Given Marxist assumptions about the evolution of economic systems, the victory of the North in the struggle was inevitable in Simons's opinion.

In *The Rise of American Civilization* (1937), Charles and Mary Beard offered an interpretation of the outbreak of the war that is better grounded in historical facts but is still essentially Marxist. The South, they argue, was a static, agrarian, staple-producing region, while the North was expanding, commercialized, and rapidly industrializing. The North's victory—the triumph of Northern industrial capitalism over Southern plantation agriculture—constituted a "Second American Revolution." The South was fighting "the census returns" and could not hope to prevail.

More recent Marxist interpretations include those of Eugene Genovese and Raimondo Luraghi. Genovese's *The Political Economy of Slavery* (1965) argued that Southerners lived in a "pre-bourgeois" world whose essential character was formed by "paternalism," a special relationship between master and slave. Southern secession was the only hope for the threat posed by a Northern bourgeois, industrial capitalistic society whose values threatened to overwhelm those of the South. Genovese's *The World the Slaveholders Made* (1969) elaborated some of these themes. Luraghi's *The Rise and Fall of the Plantation South* (1978) focused on the idea of planter hegemony, employed also by Genovese and borrowed from the Italian Marxist Antonio Gramsci. The "southern seigneurial class" had hegemony (rule) over its world (the plantation), which was the center of its civilization. This "tropical civilization" had remained static while that of the capitalistic North was ever changing and expanding into an industrial and commercial giant. The North had gained and the South had lost political and economic power rapidly as the Civil War approached. This kind of fight (industrial powers against "backward" agrarian neighbors) is called "colonialism," Luraghi concluded bitingly.

SOUTHERN ECONOMIC SECTIONALISM

An older work, which fits best into Stampp's "slavery/cultural concept," is Robert R. Russel's *Economic Aspects of Southern Sectionalism, 1840–1861* (1923), still perhaps the most complete inventory of economic issues that caused antebellum Southerners to think about disunion. Federal subsidies to improve harbors in the Northern states, the exclusion of foreign vessels from the coastal trade to benefit Northern shipping interests, Northern control of the export trade (of which Southern cotton provided more than half the value between 1815 and 1860), the reliance of Southern planters upon Northern banks for the redemption of foreign bills of exchange, and especially protective tariffs were all economic irritants to the South. Russel concluded, however, that even the cumulative effect of all these problems was not enough to cause the South to secede. According to Russel, the root cause of Southern secession was "the need to preserve slavery and maintain southern honor." On the other hand, the economic burdens of remaining in the Union caused some in the South to believe throwing off the bonds of Northern oppression would at least not result in serious economic disadvantages. Russel's conclusions are similar to those reached in most of the older general surveys of the period. In Allan Nevins's *The Emergence of Lincoln: Prologue to Civil War, 1859–1861* (vol. 2, 1950) economic factors were only a few of many "wedges of separation." The classic textbook originally written by James G. Randall and revised later by David Donald—*The Civil War and Reconstruction* (1969)—adopts the same phraseology to describe the importance of economic conflicts as a cause of disunion.

An early test of the divisive power of the most crucial economic issue, the tariff, came in 1832 when South Carolina attempted to nullify the tariff of that year. Two good books on this topic are Richard E. Ellis's *The Union at Risk: Jacksonian Democracy, States' Rights, and the Nullification Crisis* (1987) and William W. Freehling, *Prelude to Civil War: The Nullification Controversy in South Carolina, 1816–1836* (1966). The crisis was defused when Congress passed the compromise tariff of 1833, which lowered tariff duties just enough to satisfy South Carolina hotheads. Freehling emphasizes, however, that only the legislatures of Georgia and Virginia even considered South Carolina's invitation to pass their own nullification ordinances. James M. McPherson in *Ordeal by Fire: The Civil War and Reconstruction* (1992) suggests that what South Carolina nullifiers really feared was not so much high tariffs but centralization of Federal government power, which might eventually threaten slavery itself.

THE ECONOMICS OF SLAVERY EXPANSION

The extent to which the crises of the 1850s involved economic issues depends mainly on how one views the issue of slavery expansion. A classic essay by Charles W. Ramsdell, "The Natural Limits of Slavery Expansion" (1929), argued two points in reference to the crises of the decade: (1) slavery could never have been exported to the West of the 1850s because there was insufficient rainfall in that area for cotton cultivation; (2) cotton plantation agriculture had so thoroughly exhausted much of the soil of the antebellum South by 1860 that it was fast becoming economically inefficient. Ramsdell's essay became an important cog in the argument of those who favored the blundering-generation hypothesis. For them it was ultimate proof that the Civil War was a needless one that accomplished an end to slavery, but that would have happened anyway in perhaps one generation without the terrible bloodshed of the war. David

Potter's *Lincoln and His Party in the Secession Crisis* (1962) implied support for this viewpoint by pointing out that the war cost the life of one soldier for every six slaves who were freed.

Scholars have challenged both of Ramsdell's arguments. While it is certainly true that it would have been difficult, if not impossible, to export cotton plantation slavery to the West of the 1850s, it might have been possible—as Jefferson Davis himself insisted on the floor of the U.S. Senate in the 1850s—to use slave labor in mining or industrial ventures outside the South. Both Charles R. Dew in *Ironmaker to the Confederacy: Joseph R. Anderson and the Tredegar Iron Works* (1966) and Robert S. Starobin in *Industrial Slavery in the Old South* (1970) offer convincing evidence that slave labor could be profitably employed in factory settings. On the other hand, the question of whether it was possible for slavery to exist in urban settings—which as the nineteenth century went on became the typical locale for factories—is more debatable. Richard Wade in *Slavery in the Cities* (1964) held that slavery could not survive in the city mainly because of control problems, while Claudia Goldin in *Urban Slavery in the American South, 1820–1860: A Quantitative History* (1976) contradicted Wade's conclusions.

Scholars have vigorously debated the issue of whether slavery within the South was a dying institution in 1860. In *Time on the Cross* (1974), Robert W. Fogel and Stanley Engerman attacked long-held assumptions about the profitability of slave labor. Fogel and Engerman stated, for example, that agricultural slave labor was 30 percent *more* profitable than free labor on farms in the Northwest. Paul A. David et al. in *Reckoning with Slavery* (1976) and Herbert G. Gutman in *Slavery and the Numbers Game* (1975) flatly rejected the conclusions of Fogel and Engerman about the profitability of slave labor. Although most historians currently do not agree with Fogel and Engerman about the profitability of slavery, they do agree with the conclusion of William J. Cooper, Jr., in his *Liberty and Slavery* (1983) that there was still vast territory within the South in 1860 into which slave agricultural labor could have been extended. This point alone is enough to convince many historians that Ramsdell's thesis that slavery was dying within the South by 1860 is untenable.

ECONOMIC INTERPRETATIONS OF SOUTHERN SECESSION

The many studies of Southern secession in 1860–1861 make it clear that the motives underlying the movement were usually only tangentially related to economic considerations. Among the general studies of Southern secession are Dwight L. Dumond's *The Secession Movement, 1860–1861* (1931), Ulrich Bonnell Phillips's *The Course of the South to Secession* (1939), and William L. Barney's *The Road to Secession: A New Perspective on the Old South* (1972). While still valuable, the studies of Dumond and Phillips cover only marginally the movement for Southern economic independence, which reached its rhetorical heights in the Southern commercial conventions of the 1850s. For both Dumond and Phillips, the most important motive behind secession was Southerners' fears that Lincoln's election was a threat to the survival of slavery. Phillips specifically tied Southern anxieties about the abolition of slavery to white racial supremacy rather than economic concerns.

Barney's work presents a more complex thesis than the studies of Dumond and Phillips, and it does involve economic issues that have not been mentioned earlier. Barney argued that secession was centrally related to land and slave prices in the South—an argument echoed in his later local study, *The Secessionist Impulse: Alabama and Mississippi in 1860* (1974). Barney maintained that the control of the presidency by the Republican party, dedicated to preventing the expansion of slavery to the territories, was a threat to the economic survival of the South, because it meant that there was nowhere to go to replace land exhausted by cotton cultivation. He thus implied that slaveholders were, in fact, interested in exporting cotton plantation slavery to the territories, even if rainfall was inadequate for that purpose. Without more land for cotton cultivation, he added, slaveholders could not earn a profit, and prices for slaves would rise beyond their means. Rising prices for slaves thus was one reason that some slaveholders supported reopening the African slave trade in the late 1850s— which Lincoln and the Republican party firmly opposed. Barney conceded, however, that the South was far from united on the desirability of reopening the slave trade; slaveholders in Virginia and other states in the upper South actually favored a scarce supply of slaves, because they were making money by selling them to planters in the southwestern states.

There are now studies that analyze the secession movement in all eleven Confederate and the border states as well. Almost all of these works, especially the older ones, interpret secession primarily as a movement to preserve slavery. In some of these monographs, specific economic motives, which apply to one state but not necessarily another, are also described as playing significant roles in the movement toward disunion. Walter L. Buenger's *Secession and the Union in Texas* (1984) maintained that most Texans remained Unionist until very near the time that the state legislature passed its ordinance of secession on February 28, 1861. Congress's unwillingness to provide sufficient funds to guard against Indian attacks as cotton plantation slavery spread across the state was a key factor that tipped the balance against the Unionists. Virginia, according to Henry T. Shanks in *The Secession Movement in Virginia, 1847–1861* (1934), was torn apart by conflicting economic allegiances. The state sent livestock, and reexported wheat and corn from the West, to the North, but the bulk of its most important cash crop, tobacco, was shipped South. Arkansas, according to James M. Wood's *Rebellion and Realignment: Arkansas's Road to Secession* (1987), had the "economic doldrums" throughout most of the antebellum era; however, the state became a major slaveholding and cotton-producing state late in the period. The election of Lincoln in 1860 was especially galling in Arkansas because it threatened this newfound prosperity. North Carolina, wrote Joseph

Carlyle Sitterson in *The Secession Movement in North Carolina* (1939), did not identify as much with slavery and the plantation system as did states in the lower South, but it had influential Southern rights proponents who stirred up support for secession with complaints about high tariffs, Federal support for what became the Union Pacific Railroad, and the refusal of Congress to use income generated from the sales of public lands in the West to reduce tariff duties. A more recent study of secession politics in North Carolina, Marc W. Kruman's *Parties and Politics in North Carolina, 1836–1865* (1983), contradicts Sitterson's conclusions about the importance of slavery in the politics of that state. Kruman points out that about 25 percent of the free families in North Carolina owned slaves on the eve of the Civil War, which is a slightly higher percentage of slaveholders than among free families in the whole region.

Two additional excellent local studies offer provocative explanations of secession that have economic components. J. Mills Thornton's *Politics and Power in a Slave Society: Alabama, 1800–1860* (1978) related early nineteenth-century Republican ideology and Jacksonian politics to the secession movement. For Thornton, the secession movement in Alabama was the culmination of the revolt of the common man against established power—first identified with the Whig party because of its support of "oppressive" banks and railroads but later including Lincoln's Republican party, which the state's common folk perceived as intent on telling them what to do with their slave property. Even if they had no slaves, ordinary Alabamians were so imbued with Jeffersonian Republicanism that they resented any attempt to infringe upon their individual rights to hold such property someday in the future. Lacy Ford's *Origins of Southern Radicalism: The South Carolina Upcountry, 1800–1860* (1988) offers a sophisticated argument about how Republican ideology and the spread of the cotton kingdom into the state's upcountry caused plain folk to unite with planters in defense of any threat to the preservation of slavery. Common evangelical values also brought together plain folk and planters, but cotton agriculture was an essential bond between the two.

Perhaps underemphasized as a cause of secession was the financial disaster that emancipation of the slaves would cause. Although Lincoln at the time of his election publicly stated that he had no intention of ending slavery in the South, many antebellum Southern planters did not believe him. A sampling of their fears, economic and otherwise, is well represented in *Secession Debated: Georgia's Showdown in 1860* (1992), edited by William W. Freehling and Craig W. Simpson. Donald E. Reynolds analyzed what Southern newspaper editors had to say about the same topic in *Editors Make War: Southern Newspapers in the Sectional Crisis* (1970). Estimates of the actual cost of emancipation vary, but the economic impact on the South was obviously immense. Using the figure of $865 for the value of an average slave in 1859 given by Roger L. Ransom and Richard Sutch in *One Kind of Freedom* (1977), the capital loss alone caused by emancipation of the more than 3.5 million slaves in the eleven Confederate states in 1860 was more than $3 billion.

Several other studies on various topics are relevant to an understanding of economic motives behind secession. Ralph A. Wooster in *The Secession Conventions of the South* (1962) provides a detailed analysis, state by state, of slaveholding patterns among the men who served in the legislatures and special conventions that voted on secession. David R. Goldfield's *Urban Growth in the Age of Sectionalism: Virginia, 1847–1861* (1977) argues on thin evidence that the attempts of urban Virginians to build cities and railroads expressed sectionalist animosities. Vicki Vaughn Johnson's *The Men and Vision of the Southern Commercial Conventions, 1845–1871* (1992) is a thorough analysis of those who were most active in arguing the need for Southern economic independence from the North, which in some states became an important element in the secession movement. Eric H. Walther's *The Fire-Eaters* (1992) deals with extremist Southern nationalists, of whom only two—James D. B. DeBow and Edmund Ruffin—are described as economic sectionalists. Otto Clark Skipper's *J. D. B. DeBow: Magazinist of the Old South* (1958) describes DeBow's career in more detail. The most balanced biography of Ruffin is still Avery O. Craven's *Edmund Ruffin, Southerner* (1932). David F. Allmendinger's *Ruffin: Family and Reform in the Old South* (1990) relates Ruffin's thinking to his family and personal life.

ECONOMIC INTERPRETATIONS OF NORTHERN UNIONISM

On the general topic of why the North fought the Civil War to preserve the Union, several excellent studies touch upon economic factors. One of the best is Eric Foner's *Free Soil, Free Labor, Free Men* (1970). Foner shows how well Republican party ideology fitted into the growing nationalistic movement in the North and West. According to Foner, antebellum Southern planters, whose numbers were always overestimated by Republican party spokesmen, more and more were perceived as "un-American." The South was led by a feudal aristocracy living off the sweat of other men's (slaves) brows; the North stood for opportunity for free men and American democracy (government of the people, by the people, and for the people). Kenneth M. Stampp's *And the War Came: The North and the Secession Crisis, 1860–61* (1950) has a broader focus, which includes discussion of "the clash of material interests." "The South was exploited," wrote Stampp, "and the North was the exploiter." Stampp's *America in 1857: A Nation on the Brink* (1990) pays special attention to both the impact of the 1857 depression and that year's political events on sectional tensions. For contemporary Northern newspaper editors' views on the economic conflicts between North and South, see the excellent well-chosen selections in Howard Cecil Perkins's *Northern Editorials on Secession* (1942).

The most recent effort (and one of the best) to pull together much of the earlier historiography on the outbreak of the Civil War may be found in the first two chapters of McPherson's *Ordeal by Fire*. Much of the same material (but without the tabular data) is also in McPherson's Pulitzer Prize–winning *Battle Cry of Freedom: The Civil War Era* (1988). McPherson gives ample coverage to the economic and social bases underlying sectional hostilities. His account resembles Nevins's description of the "wedges of separation" in *Ordeal of the Union,* except McPherson uses modernization theory to contrast North and South. In McPherson's analysis, the North by 1860 fit all the criteria to qualify as a developed nation: its industry was capital rather than labor intensive; its agriculture, with a decreasing number of farmworkers due to technological advances, produced surpluses to feed urban populations; its society possessed a high level of mass education and literacy; and its cultural values encouraged a work ethic and, above all, a willingness to change. The South was the almost complete antithesis of the North: it had little industry, a labor-intensive, staple-producing agriculture, a free population far more illiterate than that of the North, and a value system that emphasized tradition and stability at the expense of change and progress. The South was static because it equated change with attacks upon slavery, the linchpin of its entire social system. "Arrested development" best described the region's society and economy. McPherson's summary of the basic social and economic differences between the regions will likely be the starting point in the near future for other studies of the outbreak of the Civil War.

BIBLIOGRAPHY

Allmendinger, David F., Jr. *Ruffin: Family and Reform.* New York: Oxford University Press, 1990.

Barney, William L. *The Road to Secession: A New Perspective on the Old South.* New York: Praeger, 1972.

———. *The Secessionist Impulse: Alabama and Mississippi in 1860.* Princeton: Princeton University Press, 1974.

Beard, Charles A., and Mary R. Beard. *The Rise of American Civilization.* 2d rev. ed. New York: Macmillan, 1937.

Buenger, Walter L. *Secession and the Union in Texas.* Austin: University of Texas Press, 1984.

Cooper, William J., Jr. *Liberty and Slavery: Southern Politics to 1860.* New York: Alfred A. Knopf, 1983.

Coulter, E. Merton, ed. *The Course of the South to Secession: An Interpretation by Ulrich Bonnell Phillips.* 1939. Reprint, New York: Hill and Wang, 1964.

Craven, Avery. *Edmund Ruffin, Southerner.* New York: D. Appleton & Co., 1932.

David, Paul A., et al. *Reckoning with Slavery: A Critical Study in the Quantitative History of American Negro Slavery.* New York: Oxford University Press, 1976.

Dew, Charles B. *Ironmaker to the Confederacy: Joseph R. Anderson and the Tredegar Iron Works.* New Haven: Yale University Press, 1966.

Dumond, Dwight Lowell. *The Secession Movement, 1860–1861.* New York: Macmillan, 1931.

Ellis, Richard E. *The Union at Risk: Jacksonian Democracy, States' Rights, and the Nullification Crisis.* New York: Oxford University Press, 1987.

Fogel, Robert William, and Engerman, Stanley L. *Time on the Cross: The Economics of American Negro Slavery.* Boston: Little, Brown, 1974.

Foner, Eric. *Free Soil, Free Labor, and Free Men: The Ideology of the Republican Party before the Civil War.* New York: Oxford University Press, 1970.

Ford, Lacy K. *Origins of Southern Radicalism: The South Carolina Upcountry, 1800–1860.* New York: Oxford University Press, 1988.

Freehling, William W. *Prelude to Civil War: The Nullification Crisis in South Carolina, 1816–1836.* New York: D. Appleton & Co., 1966.

Freehling, William W., and Craig Simpson, eds. *Secession Debated: Georgia's Showdown in 1860.* New York: Oxford University Press, 1992.

Genovese, Eugene D. *The Political Economy of Slavery; Studies in the Economy and Society of the Slave South.* New York: Pantheon Books, 1965.

———. *The World the Slaveholders Made: Two Essays in Interpretation.* New York: Pantheon Books, 1969.

Goldfield, David R. *Urban Growth in the Age of Sectionalism: Virginia, 1847–1861.* Baton Rouge: Louisiana State University Press, 1977.

Goldin, Claudia Dale. *Urban Slavery in the American South.* Chicago: University of Chicago Press, 1976.

Gutman, Herbert G. *Slavery and the Numbers Game: A Critique of Time on the Cross.* Urbana: University of Illinois Press, 1975.

Johnson, Vicki Vaughn. *The Men and Vision of the Southern Commercial Conventions, 1845–1871.* Columbia: University of Missouri Press, 1992.

Kruman, Marc W. *Parties and Politics in North Carolina, 1836–1865.* Baton Rouge: Louisiana State University Press, 1983.

Luraghi, Raimondo. *The Rise and Fall of the Plantation South.* New York: New Viewpoints, 1978.

McPherson, James M. *Battle Cry of Freedom: The Civil War Era.* New York: Oxford University Press, 1988.

McPherson, James M. *Ordeal by Fire: The Civil War and Reconstruction.* 2d rev. ed. New York: McGraw-Hill, 1992.

Nevins, Allan. *The Emergence of Lincoln: Prologue to Civil War, 1859–1861.* 2 vols. New York: Charles Scribner's Sons, 1950.

Perkins, Howard Cecil. *Northern Editorials on Secession.* 2 vols. 1942. Reprint, Gloucester, MA.: Peter Smith, 1964.

Phillips, Ulrich Bonnell. *The Course of the South to Secession: An Interpretation.* New York: Appleton-Century, 1939.

Potter, David M. *Lincoln and His Party in the Secession Crisis.* 2d rev. ed. New Haven: Yale University Press, 1962.

Ramsdell, Charles W. "The Natural Limits of Slavery Expansion." *Mississippi Valley Historical Review* 16 (1929): 151–171.

Randall, James G., and David Donald. *The Civil War and Reconstruction.* 2d rev. ed. Lexington, MA.: D. C. Heath, 1969.

Ransom, Roger L., and Richard Sutch. *One Kind of Freedom: The Economic Consequences of Emancipation.* Cambridge: Cambridge University Press, 1977.

Reynolds, Donald E. *Editors Make War: Southern Newspapers in the Sectional Crisis.* Nashville: Vanderbilt University Press, 1970.

Russel, Robert Royal. *Economic Aspects of Southern Sectionalism, 1840–1861.* Urbana: University of Illinois Press, 1923.

Shanks, Henry T. *The Secession Movement in Virginia, 1847–1861.* Richmond: Gannett & Massie, 1934.

Simons, Algie M. *Social Forces in American History.* New York: Macmillan, 1920.

Sitterson, Joseph Carlyle. *The Secession Movement in North Carolina.* Chapel Hill: University of North Carolina Press, 1939.

Skipper, Otis Clark. *J. D. B. DeBow: Magazinist of the Old South.* Athens: University of Georgia Press, 1958.

Stampp, Kenneth M. *America in 1857: A Nation on the Brink.* New York: Oxford University Press, 1990.

————. *And the War Came: The North and the Secession Crisis, 1860–61.* Baton Rouge: Louisiana State University Press, 1950.

————. *The Imperiled Union: Essays on the Background of the Civil War.* New York: Oxford University Press, 1980.

Starobin, Robert S. *Industrial Slavery in the Old South.* New York: Oxford University Press, 1970.

Thornton, J. Mills, III. *Politics and Power in a Slave Society: Alabama, 1800–1860.* Baton Rouge: Louisiana State University Press, 1978.

Wade, Richard. *Slavery in the Cities: The South, 1820–1860.* New York: Oxford University Press, 1964.

Walther, Eric H. *The Fire-Eaters.* Baton Rouge: Louisiana State University Press, 1992.

Wood, James M. *Rebellion and Realignment: Arkansas's Road to Secession.* Fayetteville: University of Arkansas Press, 1987.

Wooster, Ralph A. *The Secession Conventions of the South.* Princeton: Princeton University Press, 1962.

Part V

International Relations

14

Union International Relations

Daniel K. Blewett

The objective of Union diplomacy during the Civil War was to support the federal government's goal of defeating the rebellion of the Southern states. The Union diplomats operated from a position of strength, since the North held most of the money and industrial capacity that interested other powers, as well as having an established diplomatic organization up and running when the war started. The fledgling Confederate foreign service lacked these advantages. The State Department's aim was to keep other countries from helping the South, either by purchasing its cotton, lending it money, sending it arms or other supplies, recognizing the Confederate government, or, in the worst possible case, sending in troops to enforce an armed truce and division of the United States. Because some European countries saw the United States as becoming too powerful and potentially threatening to their own colonial empires, as well as harboring dangerous ideas of equality and the freeing of slaves, there was some danger that other powers would forcibly intervene. Northern diplomats skillfully had to play the countries and their selfish interests off one another, since the balance of power in Europe was in constant need of attention at this time. Luck also played a big part, as timely Union victories, an increasingly effective naval blockade, and other distractions kept the great powers restrained in their attempts to influence the course of the Civil War. The items below are only some of the titles available for research in this subject area; the bibliographies in the first section should be consulted as well for further bibliographic citations. Researchers should also read Chapter 15 on Confederate diplomacy.

REFERENCE BOOKS

Bibliographies and Research Guides

In addition to those general bibliographies and research guides on the American Civil War mentioned elsewhere in this book, one should also consult items that focus specifically on diplomatic history. The *Guide to American Foreign Relations since 1700* (1983), by Richard Dean Burns, is a huge annotated volume that is useful. It includes dissertations, books, and articles, all arranged by subject category. Chapter 11 covers the Civil War in nineteen pages. The sources are primarily in English and are annotated. The Burns book complements the old standard *Guide to the Diplomatic History of the United States, 1775–1921* (1935), compiled for the Library of Congress by Samuel Flagg Bemis, one of the great historians of American diplomatic history. Chapter 13 is the relevant chapter and is forty-three pages long. It has many more titles than the Burns compilation, particularly of foreign-language items needed for extensive research. However, it lacks complete bibliographic citations or lengthy annotations.

Gerald K. Haines and J. Samuel Walker presented a historiographical review of this subject in their *American Foreign Relations* (1981). Elmer Plischke's bibliography, *U.S. Foreign Relations* (1980), tends to focus more on the procedural aspects of foreign relations. See also *The Department of State and American Diplomacy* (1986), by Robert Goehlert and Elizabeth Hoffmeister, which has listings for guides to U.S. government publications. One of the more general Civil War bibliographies to look at is Eugene C. Murdock's *The Civil War in the North: A Selective Annotated Bibliography* (1987). Chapter 2 has 153 items listed for foreign affairs. Norman Ferris compiled a 38-page section of annotated bibliographic citations on diplomacy for *Civil War Books* (1967), which was edited by Allan Nevins et al. *Records of the Presidency* (1989), by Frank Schick, will aid one in deciding how to access some of the primary research material for Abraham Lincoln's administration. Researchers should also review *The Presidency: A Research Guide* (1985), by Robert Goehlert and Fenton Martin, both political science librarians. The U.S. National Archives compiled three inventories of U.S. State Department records that will be of interest to students of this period: *Preliminary Inventory of Records Relating to Civil War Claims: United States and Great Britain* (1962), *List of Foreign Service Post Records* (1967), and *Preliminary Inventory of the General Records of the Department of State* (1963). There is a chapter on the State Department in *The Union: A Guide to Federal Archives Relating to the Civil War* (1986), by Kenneth W. Munden and Henry P. Beers, which includes a historical sketch of the State Department, descriptions of documents and record groups, with references to other books and articles on related information. The primary method to find records for manuscript collections around the country is by using the *National Union Catalog of Manuscript Collections* (1962–), from the U.S. Library of Congress.

Since Union diplomacy did not operate in a vacuum, it cannot be studied from just the American viewpoint. The efficient researcher will examine sources dealing with other countries as well. A good bibliography of over 4,100 entries on French diplomatic history is William Echard's *Foreign Policy of the French Second Empire* (1988); chapter 18 has 9 entries on the slavery question and 184 entries on the Civil War. Extremely valuable for researching British policies and hard-to-find documents is Robert Jones's "The American Civil War in British Sessional Papers" (1963). One will also want to check *The Anglo-American Relationship* (1988), by David A. Lincove and Gary R. Treadway. The *Bibliography of United States–Latin American Relations since 1810* (1968), by David Trask et al., along with its 1979 supplement, has thousands of entries for English- and foreign-language materials on this subject. James Cortada put together *A Bibliographical Guide to Spanish Diplomatic History* (1977). Louise Atherton has compiled *Never Complain, Never Explain: Records of the Foreign Office and State Paper Office* (1994), to help researchers find their way through the maze of British official documentation. One should also consult bibliographies that focus on individual countries for further items dealing specifically with American relations with that particular country.

Chronologies

The main reference title in this field is the *Chronological History of United States Foreign Relations, 1776 to January 20, 1981* (1985), by Lester Brune. The first volume of this two-volume work covers the period from 1776 to 1920. There are twenty-two pages for the Civil War period. The entries lack helpful references to writings on the subjects included in the chronology, but there is usually a paragraph of narrative and analysis that the general Civil War chronologies lack. See also the chronologies in the appendixes of the two dictionaries listed next.

Dictionaries and Encyclopedias

The *Dictionary of American Foreign Affairs* (1993), by Stephen A. Flanders and Carl N. Flanders, covers people, concepts, places, and events, with four pages on the Civil War. The appendixes include a time line of U.S. foreign affairs, a glossary, maps, lists of the important members of the executive branch, the American ambassadors, congressional committees, conferences and summits, and a guide to further sources of information. With a similar format is *Dictionary of American Diplomatic History* (1989), by John E. Findling. It contains lengthy entries, with bibliographic references. The appendixes are very helpful, with a chronology, a list of key diplomatic personnel arranged by presidential administration, a description of the initiation, suspension, and termination of diplomatic relations, and locations of manuscript and oral history collections. Alexander DeConde's *Encyclopedia of American Foreign Policy* (1978) contains essays on "Public Opinion," "Blockades and Quarantines," "Freedom of the Seas,'' and "The King Cotton Theory,'' among other topics. For a detailed listing of who was stationed at which foreign diplomatic post, consult Walter B. Smith's *America's Diplomats and Consuls of 1776–1865* (1986) and the State Department's *United States Chiefs of Mission, 1778–1988* (1988).

Directories

Two books are guides to collections: the *Directory of Archives and Manuscript Repositories in the United States* (1988), by the U.S. National Historical Publications and Records Commission, and *Subject Collections* (1993), by Lee Ash and William Miller. The latter is a guide to the special subject collections at public, special, and academic libraries, as well as museums. Both works provide addresses, telephone numbers, and indications of the collection strengths of the reporting libraries.

Indexes and Abstracts

The periodical literature can provide many details and viewpoints unavailable in books. For contemporary writings, one should consult *The New York Times Index* (1851–), *Palmer's Index to the Times Newspaper, 1859–1866,* and *Poole's Index to Periodical Literature* (1893). Other applicable reference tools for historical articles in scholarly journals include *America: History and Life* (1960–), the *Combined Retrospective Index to Journals in History* (CRIS) (1977), and *Writings on American History* (1904–).

GENERAL HISTORIES OF AMERICAN DIPLOMACY

For those new to research in this field, it might help to read a general survey of U.S. diplomatic history to establish a framework to work from. Robert H. Ferrell's *American Diplomacy: A History* (1975) is certainly one place to start, along with *A History of United States Foreign Policy* (1980), by Julius Pratt, Vincent DeSantis, and Joseph Siracusa. Thomas A. Bailey, in his *The Man in the Street* (1948), discusses how the power of public opinion has influenced American foreign policy makers. Public opinion, frequently based on emotion rather than education or logic, has for the most part restrained the government, perhaps reflecting America's isolationist streak. During the Civil War there were emotional calls in the North for action against Britain, France, Canada, and Mexico that would have led to a diversion of the war effort and possible defeat for the Union.

For general accounts of Civil War diplomacy, one can start with David Crook's *The North, the South, and the Powers, 1861–1865* (1974), which was issued as an abridged edition of *Diplomacy during the American Civil War* (1975). The effect of the American Civil War in other countries is described in Harold Hyman's *Heard 'Round the World: The Impact Abroad of the Civil War*

(1969), and *Europe and the American Civil War* (1931), by Donaldson Jordan and Edwin J. Pratt. Philip Stern's *When the Guns Roared* (1965) also discusses how the Union and Confederacy maneuvered against each other in foreign lands, particularly Europe. *The Union, the Confederacy, and the Atlantic Rim* (1995), edited by Robert E. May, contains essays on Lincoln's involvement in diplomacy, the significance of blacks, possible British intervention, and how the Caribbean basin looked at the war. Norman Graebner is a noted expert in American foreign affairs, and his "Northern Diplomacy and European Neutrality" (1960) should not be missed by any student of this field. See also his "European Interventionism and the Crisis of 1862" (1976). The rest of the world interacted with a divided nation.

SECONDARY WORKS

Readers using these secondary works should always check the notes and bibliography for further sources.

Abraham Lincoln

How Lincoln dealt with the events in Europe—when Germany, Russia, and Austria-Hungary collaborated to impose their rule in eastern Europe—is described in *Lincoln and the Emperors,* by A. R. Tyrner-Tyrnauer (1962). Jay Monaghan dealt with Lincoln's approach to foreign relations in *Diplomat in Carpet Slippers* (1962). The president's efforts to stop the Southern trade in cotton is discussed by Thomas O'Connor in "Lincoln and the Cotton Trade" (1961). For further items on the president, see chapter 16 in this book.

William Seward

Frederick Bancroft wrote a standard biography of the complicated American secretary of state in 1900, *The Life of William H. Seward,* but Glyndon G. Van Deusen's *William Henry Seward* (1967) and John Taylor's *William Henry Seward* (1991) are important too. Henry Temple wrote a chapter on Seward for *The American Secretaries of State and Their Diplomacy* (1958), and Gordon H. Warren did the same for *Makers of American Diplomacy* (1974). Norman B. Ferris wrote about Seward's 1861 policies designed to distract Southern interest in revolt and keep the other countries out of American affairs, in *Desperate Diplomacy* (1976). Kinley J. Brauer also interpreted the secretary's motives in "Seward's 'Foreign War Panacea' " (1974). Ferris then elaborated on the Lincoln-Seward relationship in "Lincoln and Seward in Civil War Diplomacy" (1991). *The Foundations of the American Empire: William Henry Seward and United States Foreign Policy* (1973), by Ernest Paolino, is a well-documented text. Mary O'Rouke's dissertation is "The Diplomacy of William H. Seward during the Civil War" (1963).

Relations with Great Britain

The British Empire was the number one concern of Union diplomats, and therefore has a corresponding amount of relevant published material available to the researcher. Whitehall had a tradition of extensively documenting decisions, and this vast quantity of records available in English makes it a primary area of research in foreign relations. The fact that many of these documents have been published or microfilmed and are available in the United States is a great benefit to the researcher who cannot travel abroad.

England at this time had the naval and economic power that could have brought victory to the South if placed at the rebels' disposal. The American government had to play a cautious game of resisting British pressures to a point short of war. Fortunately, Her Majesty's government was worried about the moral issue of slavery, seccessionist movements at home, as well as political developments in other parts of the world and so left the United States alone to solve its own problems. Paul Kennedy, in "The Tradition of Appeasement in British Foreign Policy, 1865–1939" (1976), argues that an overextended British Empire, greatly concerned with events on the Continent, was bound to compromise with the United States unless its strategic interests (e.g., Canada) were threatened. Kennedy shows how England was turning its attention to continental affairs, particularly the disturbing increase in German power, in his *The Rise of the Anglo-German Antagonism* (1980). Britain's foreign policy problems with the United States are summarized in A. P. Newton's chapter, "Anglo-American Relations during the Civil War," in *The Cambridge History of British Foreign Policy, 1783–1919* (1923). This is a more thorough account than the thirteen pages allotted to the subject by Bradford Perkins in *The Cambridge History of American Foreign Relations* (1993). One can complement this with Brian Jenkins's *Britain and the War for the Union* (1974) and Kenneth Bourne's *The Foreign Policy of Victorian England* (1970). Howard Jones's *Union in Peril* (1992) focuses specifically on the possibility of British intervention during 1862, when the Confederacy looked strongest. Jones examines the humanitarian and economic factors influencing British intervention and concludes that the secretary for war, George Cornewall Lewis, was the primary cabinet opponent to such a policy.

Researchers should read Ephraim Adams's *Great Britain and the American Civil War* (1957); his documented sources provide many leads to pursue. Martin Crawford reported his research into British misconceptions about the United States that led to diplomatic frictions in "The Anglo-American Crisis of the Early 1860's" (1983). Charles Francis Adams, the son of John Quincy Adams and the American ambassador to England (1861–1868), wrote *Studies Military and Diplomatic, 1775–1865* (1911), which contains chapters on Anglo-American relations. His son wrote a biography on the diplomat *Charles Francis Adams* (1909), as did Martin Duberman, *Charles Francis Adams* (1961). Norman Ferris focused on Adams in London in "Tempestuous Mission, 1861–

1862'' (1962). Stanley Gallas, in his study of ''Lord Lyons and the Civil War'' (1982), presents a view of the new British ambassador in Washington containing Seward's impulses and eventually working well with the emotional Secretary of State.

The *Annual Register of World Events* for the Civil War years contains summaries of parliamentary debates, which can provide leads to British documents. Robert Jones took another look at the interaction between Washington and London in ''Anglo-American Relations, 1861–1865: Reconsidered'' (1963). Kinley Brauer has investigated the sensitive issue of British diplomatic intervention in ''British Mediation and the American Civil War'' (1972). Noted diplomatic historian Max Belof reassessed the British-American relationship in ''Historical Revision No. CXVIII: Great Britain and the American Civil War'' (1952). One specialized study of the venerable British foreign relations establishment is Eugene H. Berwanger's *The British Foreign Service and the American Civil War* (1994).

Relations with Canada

The nation to the north of the United States provided a convenient area for Confederates to make contact with foreign governments, as well as conduct espionage and other subversive operations against the Union. This naturally angered the government in Washington a great deal, but American leaders had to tread carefully. Since Canada was still under the rule of the Her Majesty's government, American relations with it were directly tied to relations with Great Britain.

One general work on American-Canadian relations to consult is Hugh Keenleyside's *Canada and the United States* (1929). *Canada and the United States: The Civil War Years,* by Robin W. Winks (1971), is a standard work on this topic and is more focused than Lester Shippee's earlier *Canadian-American Relations, 1848–1874* (1939); researchers will not want to miss Winks's informative ''A Note on Sources.'' Kenneth Bourne, in his *Britain and the Balance of Power in North America* (1967), emphasizes that a full and effective defense of Canada was virtually impossible given the geography of the continent, American power, and British interests elsewhere. Whitehall had to please its firebrands in London and Ottawa while at the same time soothing Washington. See also James Barry's ''U.S.-Canadian Frictions along the Great Lakes–St. Lawrence Border'' (1989), Helen Grace Macdonald's *Canadian Public Opinion and the American Civil War* (1926), and Allen Stouffer's ''Canadian-American Relations in the Shadow of the Civil War'' (1977).

Relations with France

France was the second-most important country in Europe, and a long-time rival of Great Britain. Through careful manipulation, it could be used to distract the British. The State Department could appeal to the history of French-

American relations, when Paris had helped the American colonies break away from London. Diplomatic relations were complicated by France's takeover of Mexico, which Washington saw as a direct challenge to the Monroe Doctrine. But the United States put off any serious confrontation over this intrusion into its sphere of influence until after the war.

An important work is Lynn Case and Warren Spencer's *The United States and France: Civil War Diplomacy* (1970). Elliot Evans focused on the French emperor in his "Napoleon III and the American Civil War" (1941). For a general background to U.S.-French relations, one can read Henry Blumenthal's two works: *France and the United States: Their Diplomatic Relations, 1789– 1914* (1970) and *A Reappraisal of Franco-American Relations, 1830–1871* (1959). The activities of the French ambassador, who favored European inter- vention for economic reasons, is covered by Daniel B. Carroll in *Henri Mercier and the American Civil War* (1971). Warren West surveyed how French public opinion affected that country's foreign policy in his *Contemporary French Opin- ion on the American Civil War* (1924). See also Lynn M. Case's *French Opinion on the United States and Mexico* (1936), which is a collection of extracts (in French) from the reports of the Procureurs Généraux. "Paris Newspapers and the American Civil War" (1991), by George M. Blackburn, analyzes how the political divisions of the country were reflected in the coverage of the war, with pro-Napoleon papers favoring the South. American opinion about France is re- ported by Elizabeth White in her *American Opinion of France from Lafayette to Poincaré* (1927). Allan Nevins summarized French and British concerns about the Civil War in "Britain, France and the War Issues" (1960).

Relations with Mexico

America had long considered its immediate southern neighbor as falling within its sphere of influence, and so resented any expansion of European in- fluence in the area. This policy was expressed as the Monroe Doctrine, and noted historian Dexter Perkins wrote about the early period of this policy in *The Monroe Doctrine, 1826–1867* (1965). But until the war was over, there was little that the United States could do except file diplomatic protests about the French expedition to Mexico. The French takeover of the Mexican government due to financial difficulties of the latter is discussed in *Napoleon III and Mexico* (1971), by Alfred Jackson Hanna and Kathryn Abbey Hanna. A general account of relations is Karl Michael Schmidt's *Mexico and the United States, 1821– 1973* (1974). The efforts of Senator James A. McDougall from California to have the United States pressure the French on the Mexican situation are re- counted in Marvin Goldwert's "McDougall vs. Maximilian" (1981).

The Rio Grande port of Matamoros became a primary point where supplies from foreign countries would arrive for smuggling to the Confederacy. James Daddysman wrote about this in his "British Neutrality and the Matamoros Trade" (1985), an outgrowth of his *The Matamoros Trade* (1984). For a longer view of the matter of cross-border trade, read Samuel E. Bell and James Small-wood's "Zona Libre: Trade and Diplomacy on the Mexican Border, 1858–1905" (1982). Benjamin Gilbert wrote about American worries of French control in "French Warships on the Mexican West Coast, 1861–1866" (1955). See also Paul Reuter's "United States–French Relations Regarding French Intervention in Mexico" (1968).

Relations with Russia

One popular assumption has been that the visit of the Russian fleet to New York in 1863 was to show Russian support to Washington in the face of a possible European intervention for the South. A popular account of the visit of the Russian ships can be found in Ernest Schell's "Our Good Friends, the Russians" (1981). Other items on this topic include "The Russian Fleet on the Eastern Seaboard, 1863–1864: A Maritime Chronology" (1960), by Robin Higham, as well as his "When the Russians Conquered New York" (1972); "The Visit of the Russian Fleet to the United States: Were Americans Deceived?" (1949), by William Nagengast; Earl Pomery's "The Myth of the Russian Fleet, 1863" (1950); and "Abraham Lincoln and the Russian Fleet Myth" (1970), by Charles Stevenson. One can also review *Russo-American Relations, 1815–1867* (1930), by Benjamin Thomas, for further information.

The American minister to Russia at this time was Cassius Clay, and his mission to St. Petersburg is covered by James R. Robertson in *A Kentuckian at the Court of the Tsars* (1935), and "Cassius M. Clay's Mission to Russia" (1969), by Florence Pattock. One survey of U.S.-Russian relations is *Distant Friends* (1991), by Norman Saul.

Relations with Spain

Spain was perhaps the third-most important country for the United States at this crucial time, due to its colonies and influence in Latin America. *Spain and the American Civil War,* by James W. Cortada (1980), is a good account of Spanish-American relations. For an account of the activities of the Spanish minister in Washington at that time, read Kinley Brauer's "Gabriel Garcia y Tassara and the American Civil War" (1975). See also LeRoy Fisher, "United States–Spanish Relations during the American Civil War" (1973), and "Cuba, Spain, and the American Civil War" (1968), by Clifford Egan.

Relations with Poland

Far-off Poland was undergoing a division by the Great Powers of the European continent during the 1860s, and this served to distract European attention from the American conflict. For information on this topic, see Dennis Reinhartz's "A Convergence of Eagles: Poland and the Cold War Diplomacy of the American Civil War Era, 1856–1867" (1987); "A Favorable Interval: The Polish Insurrection in Civil War Diplomacy" (1978), by Laurence Orzell; and *A Polish Chapter in Civil War America* (1967), by Joseph W. Wieczerzsk.

Relations with Japan

Japan at this time was given only scant attention by America. The American aim in the 1860s was to prevent Confederate commerce raiders from using Japanese ports, as well as gaining ports for American fishing vessels to use. For reviews on U.S.-Japanese relations, see Wada Teijun's *American Foreign Policy towards Japan during the Nineteenth Century* (1928), *The First Japanese Embassy to the United States of America* (1920), and William Griffis' *Townsend Harris, the First American Envoy in Japan* (1895). See also Payson Treat's *The Early Diplomatic Relations between the United States and Japan, 1853–1865* (1917).

Maritime Affairs and Trade with Other Countries

One cannot overemphasize the importance of maritime trade at this time. One of the reasons that America had fought England in the War of 1812 was due to the British quarantine of a Europe ruled by Napoleon. During the Civil War, the United States found itself in an uncomfortable position of establishing a similar blockade to cut off trade by neutrals with the rebels. The federal government argued that because this was an internal insurrection, neutrals did not have any trading rights with the rebels. Consult Chapters 23 and 24 in this book for further relevant works about their operations in foreign countries.

Robert Albion and Jennie Pope discuss Washington's view of international law with regard to naval operations, neutral rights, and the importance of overseas trade in *Sea Lanes in Wartime* (1942). For an examination of Southern smuggling from the Caribbean area, see Kenneth Blume's dissertation, "The Mid-Atlantic Arena: The United States, the Confederacy, and the British West Indies" (1984). Frank L. Owsley, in "America and the Freedom of the Seas, 1861–1865" (1935), blames the ignorance of the American government and navy with respect to history and international law that allowed lawyers to direct the Union blockade efforts that led to problems with the European powers.

The biggest crisis that had the potential to bring about British recognition of the Confederate government, if not actually bring about an English-Union armed confrontation, was in 1861 when a Union ship seized two Confederate envoys traveling on the British ship *Trent* to London from Havana. Gordon Warren described the crisis over the *Trent* seizure in *Fountain of Discontent* (1981). See also Edward Chalfant's "A War So Near: Imagined Steamers in the Trent Affair" (1990) and Norman Ferris and David Pletcher's *The Trent Affair* (1977).

After the *Trent* affair, the most troublesome issue between Washington and London was the fact that Confederate raiders were built in British ports. Frank J. Merli, in *Great Britain and the Confederate Navy* (1970), wrote that a pragmatic British government was hampered by old laws in dealing with the delicate situation. The dispute over what to do with Union ships captured by the rebels and brought into foreign ports as prizes of war is reviewed in Stuart Bernath's *Squall across the Atlantic* (1970). Warren F. Spencer, in *The Confederate Navy in Europe* (1983), was broader in his coverage of how the South was able to use neutrality laws to acquire ships and supplies and how the North tried to counter it.

Miscellaneous

Kinley Brauer discussed the vexing moral issue of slavery in "The Slavery Problem in the Diplomacy of the American Civil War" (1977), as did James Duram in "A Study of Frustration" (1965). The diplomatic activities of U.S. naval officers, who frequently had to operate independently of control from Washington, is related in chapter 15 of David F. Long's *Gold Braid and Foreign Relations* (1988). David J. Alvarez argues in "The Papacy in the Diplomacy of the American Civil War" (1983) that the Vatican was pragmatic in its view of the terrible conflict in America. The role of the chairman of the U.S. Senate Foreign Relations Committee is analyzed by Thomas Peyton, Jr., in "Charles Sumner and United States Foreign Relations during the American Civil War" (1972), and in Victor H. Cohen's earlier "Charles Sumner and Foreign Relations" (1951). Before that, Moorfield Storey had written *Charles Sumner* (1900) as part of the American Statesmen series.

PRIMARY SOURCE MATERIAL

Autobiographies, Journals, Diaries, Letters, and Correspondence

John Hay was a secretary for Lincoln, so *Lincoln and the Civil War in the Diaries and Letters of John Hay* (1939) can be very useful for an insider's view of the president at work. Matias Romero describes his perceptions of America during the Civil War in *A Mexican View of America in the 1860's* (1991). Not necessarily as useful, despite its promising title, is Albert Woldman's *Lincoln and the Russians* (1952), which contains many extracts from the letters of the Russian ambassador to the United States. The *Memoir and Letters of Charles Sumner* (1877–1878) is necessary for research into the activities of this powerful U.S. senator. Seward's son and secretary, Frederick W. Seward, wrote *Reminiscences of a War-Time Statesman and Diplomat, 1830–1915* (1916).

For items relating to England, one can review *Private and Confidential: Letters from British Ministers in Washington to the Foreign Secretaries in London, 1844–67* (1993), by James J. Barnes and Patience P. Barnes. Benjamin Morse was the secretary to the American legation in London (1855–1873), and his *Journal* (1948–1949) provides many interesting comments on the diplomatic dance in the British capital at this time. This can be complemented by two collections of the writings of Henry Adams, the private secretary to the American ambassador to the Court of St. James: *Henry Adams and His Friends: A Collection of His Unpublished Letters* (1947) and *Letters of Henry Adams* (1930–1938). American ambassador Charles Adams wrote *Charles Francis Adams* (1900), for his view of affairs in London.

Document Collections and Papers

Ruhl J. Bartlett's *The Record of American Diplomacy* (1947) has a chapter on Civil War diplomacy that includes reprints of the "Foreign Policy of William H. Seward" and a rejected French proposal of mediation. The primary documents collection for any research into U.S. foreign affairs is the U.S. State Department's *Foreign Relations of the United States* series (FRUS), which consists of a multitude of reports, letters, and official statements. Charles Bevans collected texts of treaties for his *Treaties and Other International Agreements of the United States of America, 1776–1949* (1968). *Correspondence Concerning Claims against Great Britain* (1869–1871), also from the State Department, reprints the official documents relating to the *Alabama* raider claims. The *British Documents on Foreign Affairs* series, from the Foreign Office, has official British reports and statements. The State Department published a collection of official documents with a narrative, *Policy of the United States toward Maritime Commerce in War* (1934), that is useful for this field. Published during the war by the State Department was *Papers Relating to Foreign Affairs* . . . (1861–1864).

For the papers of individuals, see *The Collected Works of Abraham Lincoln* (1953), for primary material from the Union leader. The Library of Congress has the major collection of items from and about Lincoln. LeRoy P. Graf and Ralph W. Haskins have been editing *The Papers of Andrew Johnson* (1967–). The papers of Secretary of State Seward are deposited at the University of Rochester Library and are described in the *University of Rochester Library Bulletin* for Autumn 1951. Research Publications has released *The Papers of William H. Seward* on 198 reels of microfilm, and Janice Budeit edited a guide and index to the set (1983). The fifth volume of the *Works of William H. Seward* (1884) covers the diplomatic history of the war. *The Papers of Charles Sumner* (1988), edited by Beverly Wilson Palmer, are available on microfilm from Chadwyck-Healey.

The National Archives has released several compilations of State Department records on microfilm, such as *Despatches from Special Agents of the Department of State* (1955–1965), *Despatches from U.S. Consuls, Despatches from U.S. Ministers* . . . [to various countries], *Diplomatic and Consular Instructions,* and diplomatic notes from various foreign legations to the State Department (such as *Notes from the British Legation in the U.S. to the Department of State, 1791–1906,* (1943). These are grouped by country and time period. Scholarly Resources has for several years been the vendor for National Archives microfilm; it produces a catalog of its items for sale. One can also view these sets at the

National Archives or its regional branches, or obtain them through interlibrary loan.

BIBLIOGRAPHY

Adams, Charles Frances. *Studies Military and Diplomatic, 1775–1865.* New York: Macmillan, 1911.

Adams, Charles Francis, Jr. *Charles Francis Adams.* Boston: Houghton Mifflin, 1909.

Adams, Ephraim Douglass. *Great Britain and the American Civil War.* Gloucester, MA: P. Smith, 1957.

Adams, Henry. *Henry Adams and His Friends: A Collection of His Unpublished Letters.* Compiled by Harold Dean Carter. Boston: Houghton Mifflin, 1947.

———. *Letters of Henry Adams.* 2 vols. Edited by Worthington Chauncey Ford. Boston: Houghton Mifflin, 1930–1938.

Albion, Robert Greenhalgh, and Jennie Barnes Pope. *Sea Lanes in Wartime: The American Experience, 1775–1942.* New York: W. W. Norton, 1942.

Alvarez, David J. "The Papacy in the Diplomacy of the American Civil War." *Catholic Historical Review* 69 (2) (1983): 227–248.

America: History and Life. Santa Barbara, CA: ABC-CLIO, 1964–.

The Annual Register of World Events: A Review of the Year . . . London, New York: Longmans, Green, 1758–.

Ash, Lee, and William G. Miller. *Subject Collections.* 2 vols. New Providence, NJ: R. R. Bowker, 1993.

Atherton, Louise. *Never Complain, Never Explain: Records of the Foreign Office and State Paper Office.* London: Public Record Office Publications, 1994.

Bailey, Thomas A. *The Man in the Street.* New York: Macmillan, 1948.

Bancroft, Frederick. *The Life of William H. Seward.* 2 vols. New York: Harper and Brothers, 1900.

Barnes, James J., and Patience P. Barnes. *Private and Confidential: Letters from British Ministers in Washington to the Foreign Secretaries in London, 1844–67.* Selinsgrove, PA: Susquehanna University Press; London: Associated University Presses, 1993.

Barry, James P. "U.S.-Canadian Frictions along the Great Lakes–St. Lawrence Border." *Inland Seas* 45 (2) (1989): 75–89; 45 (3) (1989): 183–191.

Bartlett, Ruhl J., ed. *The Record of American Diplomacy: Documents and Readings in the History of American Foreign Relations.* New York: Knopf, 1947.

Bell, Samuel E., and James M. Smallwood. "Zona Libre: Trade and Diplomacy on the Mexican Border, 1858–1905." *Arizona and the West* 24 (1982): 119–152.

Belof, Max. "Historical Revisionism No. CXVIII: Great Britain and the American Civil War." *History* 37 (1952): 40–48.

Bemis, Samuel Flagg, and Grace Gardner Griffin. *Guide to the Diplomatic History of the United States, 1775–1921.* 1935. Reprint, Gloucester, MA: Peter Smith, 1963.

Bernath, Stuart L. *Squall across the Atlantic: American Civil War Prize Cases and Diplomacy.* Los Angeles: University of California Press, 1970.

Berwanger, Eugene H. *The British Foreign Service and the American Civil War.* Lexington, KY: University Press of Kentucky, 1994.

Bevans, Charles I., ed. *Treaties and Other International Agreements of the United States of America, 1776–1949.* Washington, D.C.: Government Printing Office, 1968.

Blackburn, George M. "Paris Newspapers and the American Civil War." *Illinois Historical Journal* 84 (3) (1991): 177–193.

Blume, Kenneth John. "The Mid-Atlantic Arena: The United States, the Confederacy, and the British West Indies." Ph.D. diss., State University of New York, 1984.

Blumenthal, Henry. *France and the United States: Their Diplomatic Relations, 1789–1914.* Chapel Hill, NC: University of North Carolina Press, 1970.

———. *A Reappraisal of Franco-American Relations, 1830–1871.* Chapel Hill, NC: University of North Carolina Press, 1959.

Bourne, Kenneth. *Britain and the Balance of Power in North America, 1815–1908.* Berkeley: University of California Press, 1967.

———. *The Foreign Policy of Victorian England, 1830–1902.* Oxford: Clarendon Press, 1970.

Brauer, Kinley J. "British Mediation and the American Civil War." *Journal of Southern History* 38 (1) (1972): 49–64.

———. "Gabriel Garcia y Tassara and the American Civil War: A Spanish Perspective." *Civil War History* 21 (1) (1975): 5–27.

———. "Seward's 'Foreign War Panacea': An Interpretation." *New York History* 55 (April 1974): 133–157.

———. "The Slavery Problem in the Diplomacy of the American Civil War." *Pacific Historical Review* 46 (3) (1977): 439–469.

Brune, Lester. *Chronological History of United States Foreign Relations, 1776 to January 20, 1981.* New York: Garland, 1985.

Budeit, Janice L., ed. *The Papers of William H. Seward: Guide and Index to the Microfilm Collection.* Woodbridge, CT: Research Publications, 1983.

Burns, Richard Dean. *Guide to American Foreign Relations since 1700.* Santa Barbara, CA: ABC-CLIO, 1983.

Carroll, Daniel B. *Henri Mercier and the American Civil War.* Princeton: Princeton University Press, 1971.

Case, Lynn Marshall. *French Opinion on the United States and Mexico.* New York: Appleton-Century, 1936.

Case, Lynn Marshall, and Warren F. Spencer. *The United States and France: Civil War Diplomacy.* Philadelphia: University of Pennsylvania Press, 1970.

Chalfant, Edward. "A War So Near: Imagined Steamers in the Trent Affair." *Journal of Confederate History* 6 (1990): 139–159.

Cohen, Victor H. "Charles Sumner and Foreign Relations." Ph.D. diss., University of Oklahoma, 1951.

The Combined Retrospective Index to Journals in History, 1838–1974. 11 vols. Washington, D.C.: Carrolton Press, 1977–1978.

Cortada, James W. *A Bibliographic Guide to Spanish Diplomatic History, 1460–1977.* Westport, CT: Greenwood, 1977.

———. *Spain and the American Civil War: Relations at Mid-Century, 1855–1868.* Transactions of the American Philosophical Society, No. 70, pt. 4. Philadelphia: American Philosophical Society, 1980.

Crawford, Martin. "The Anglo-American Crisis of the Early 1860's: A Framework for Revision." *South Atlantic Quarterly* 82 (4) (1983): 406–423.

———. *The Anglo-American Crisis of the Mid-Nineteenth Century: The Times and America, 1850–1862.* Athens, GA: University of Georgia Press, 1987.

Crook, David Paul. *Diplomacy during the American Civil War.* New York: Wiley, 1975.

———. *The North, the South, and the Powers, 1861–1865.* New York: Wiley, 1974.

Daddysman, James W. (Jim) "British Neutrality and the Matamoros Trade: A Step toward Anglo-American Rapprochement." *Journal of the West Virginia Historical Association* 9 (1) (1985): 1–12.

———. *The Matamoros Trade: Confederate Commerce, Diplomacy, and Intrigue.* Newark, DE: University of Delaware Press; London: Associated Press, 1984.

DeConde, Alexander, ed. *Encyclopedia of American Foreign Policy.* 3 vols. New York: Charles Scribner's Sons, 1978.

Duberman, Martin B. *Charles Francis Adams, 1807–1886.* Boston: Houghton Mifflin, 1961.

Duram, James C. "A Study of Frustration: Britain, the USA, and the African Slave Trade, 1815–1870." *Social Sciences* 40 (4) (1965): 220–225.

Echard, William E., comp. and ed. *Foreign Policy of the French Second Empire: A Bibliography.* Westport, CT: Greenwood Press, 1988.

Egan, Clifford L. "Cuba, Spain, and the American Civil War." *Rocky Mountain Social Science Journal* 5 (2) (1968): 58–63.

Evans, Elliott Arthur Powell. "Napoleon III and the American Civil War." Ph.D. diss., Stanford University, 1941.

Ferrell, Robert H. *American Diplomacy: A History.* 3d ed. New York: W. W. Norton, 1975.

Ferris, Norman B. *Desperate Diplomacy: William H. Seward's Foreign Policy, 1861.* Knoxville, TN: University of Tennessee Press, 1976.

———. "Lincoln and Seward in Civil War Diplomacy: Their Relationship at the Outset Reexamined." *Journal of the Abraham Lincoln Association* 12 (1991): 21–42.

———. "Tempestuous Mission, 1861–1862: The Early Diplomatic Career of Charles Francis Adams." Ph.D. diss., Emory University, 1962.

———, and David M. Pletcher. *The Trent Affair: A Diplomatic Crisis.* Knoxville: University of Tennessee Press, 1977.

Findling, John E. *Dictionary of American Diplomatic History.* New York: Greenwood, 1989.

The First Japanese Embassy to the United States of America. Tokyo: American-Japan Society, 1920.

Fisher, LeRoy H., and B. J. Chandler. "United States–Spanish Relations during the American Civil War." *Lincoln Herald* 75 (4) (1973): 134–147.

Flanders, Stephen A., and Carl N. Flanders. *Dictionary of American Foreign Affairs.* New York: Macmillan, 1993.

Gallas, Stanley. "Lord Lyons and the Civil War, 1859–1864: A British Perspective." Ph.D. diss., University of Illinois, 1982.

Gilbert, Benjamin Franklin. "French Warships on the Mexican West Coast, 1861–1866." *Pacific Historical Review* 24 (February 1955): 25–37.

Goehlert, Robert U., and Elizabeth R. Hoffmeister. *The Department of State and American Diplomacy: A Bibliography.* New York: Garland, 1986.

———, and Fenton S. Martin. *The Presidency: A Research Guide.* Santa Barbara, CA: ABC-CLIO, 1985.

Goldwert, Marvin. "McDougall vs. Maximilian." *Americas* 35 (3) 1981: 36–39.

Graebner, Norman. "European Interventionism and the Crisis of 1862." *Journal of the Illinois State Historical Society* 69 (1) (1976): 35–45.

———. "Northern Diplomacy and European Neutrality." In David Donald, ed., *Why the North Won the Civil War,* pp. 49–75. Baton Rouge, LA: Louisiana State University Press, 1960.

Great Britain. Embassy (U.S.). *Notes from the British Legation in the U.S. to the Department of State, 1791–1906.* 20 microfilm reels. Washington, D.C.: U.S. National Archives and Records Service, 1943.

———. Foreign Office. *British Documents on Foreign Affairs. Reports and Papers from the Foreign Office Confidential Print. Series C: North America: Part I: North America, 1837–1914.* Edited by Kenneth Bourne and D. Cameron Watt. Frederick, MD: University Publications of America, 1986–1987.

Great Britain. Public Records Office. *Never Complain, Never Explain: Records of the Foreign Office and State Paper Office, 1500–c.1960.* Louise Atherton. London: P.R.O. Publications, 1994.

Griffis, William Elliot. *Townsend Harris, the First American Envoy in Japan.* Boston: Houghton Mifflin, 1895.

Haines, Gerald K., and J. Samuel Walker, eds. *American Foreign Relations: A Historiographical Review.* Westport, CT: Greenwood Press, 1981.

Hanna, Alfred Jackson, and Kathryn Abbey Hanna. *Napoleon III and Mexico: American Triumph over Monarchy.* Chapel Hill: University of North Carolina Press, 1971.

Hay, John. *Lincoln and the Civil War in the Diaries and Letters of John Hay.* New York: Dodd, 1939.

Higham, Robin. "The Russian Fleet on the Eastern Seaboard, 1863–1864: A Maritime Chronology." *American Neptune* 20 (1) (January 1960): 49–61.

———. "When the Russians Conquered New York." *Mankind* 3 (8) (1972): 10–17.

Hyman, Harold, ed. *Heard 'Round the World: The Impact Abroad of the Civil War.* New York: Knopf, 1969.

Jenkins, Brian. *Britain and the War for the Union.* 2 vols. Montreal: McGill–Queens University Press, 1974–1980.

Johnson, Andrew. *The Papers of Andrew Johnson.* Edited by LeRoy P. Graf and Ralph W. Haskins. Knoxville: University of Tennessee Press, 1967–.

Jones, Howard. *Union in Peril: The Crisis over British Intervention in the Civil War.* Chapel Hill, NC: University of North Carolina Press, 1992.

Jones, Robert H. "The American Civil War in British Sessional Papers: Catalog and Commentary." *Proceedings of the American Philosophical Society* 107 (5) (October 1963): 415–426.

———. "Anglo-American Relations, 1861–1865: Reconsidered." *Mid-America* 45 (1) (1963): 36–49.

Jordan, Donaldson, and Edwin J. Pratt. *Europe and the American Civil War.* Boston: Houghton Mifflin, 1931.

Keenleyside, Hugh Llewellyn. *Canada and the United States.* New York: Knopf, 1929.

Kennedy, Paul M. *The Rise of the Anglo-German Antagonism, 1860–1914.* London: Allen and Unwin, 1980.

———. "The Tradition of Appeasement in British Foreign Policy, 1865–1939." *British Journal of International Studies* 2 (3) (1976): 195–215.

Lincoln, Abraham. *The Collected Works of Abraham Lincoln.* 9 vols. Edited by Roy P. Basler et al. New Brunswick, NJ: Rutgers University Press, 1953.

Lincove, David A., and Gary R. Treadway, eds. *The Anglo-American Relationship: An Annotated Bibliography of Scholarship, 1945–1985.* Westport, CT: Greenwood, 1988.

Long, David F. *Gold Braid and Foreign Relations: Diplomatic Activities of U.S. Naval Officers, 1798–1883.* Annapolis: Naval Institute Press, 1988.

Macdonald, Helen Grace. *Canadian Public Opinion and the American Civil War.* 1926. Reprint, New York: Octagon Books, 1974.

May, Robert E., ed. *The Union, the Confederacy, and the Atlantic Rim.* West Lafayette, IN: Purdue University Press, 1995.

Merli, Frank J. *Great Britain and the Confederate Navy, 1861–1865.* Bloomington: Indiana University Press, 1970.

Monaghan, Jay. *Diplomat in Carpet Slippers: Abraham Lincoln Deals with Foreign Affairs.* Indianapolis: Charter Books, 1962.

Morse, Benjamin. *The Journal of Benjamin Morse.* 2 vols. Edited by Sarah Agnes Wallace and Frances Elma Gillespie. Chicago: University of Chicago Press, 1948–1949.

Munden, Kenneth W., and Henry P. Beers. *The Union: A Guide to Federal Archives Relating to the Civil War.* Washington, D.C.: National Archives Trust Fund Board, 1986.

Murdock, Eugene C. *The Civil War in the North: A Selective Annotated Bibliography.* New York: Garland, 1987.

Nagengast, William E. "The Visit of the Russian Fleet to the United States: Were Americans Deceived?" *Russian Review* 8 (1949): 560–577.

Nevins, Allan. "Britain, France and the War Issues." In Allan Nevins, ed. *The War for the Union: War Becomes Revolution, 1862–1863,* pp. 242–274. New York: Scribner's, 1960.

———, James I. Robertson, Jr., and Bell I. Wiley, eds. *Civil War Books: A Critical Bibliography.* 2 vols. Baton Rouge, LA: Louisiana State University Press, 1967.

The New York Times Index. (Prior Series.) September 1851–1912. 12 vols. New York: R. R. Bowker, 1966–1976.

Newton, A. P. "Anglo-American Relations during the Civil War, 1860–1865." In Adolphus William Ward and G. P. Gooch, eds. *The Cambridge History of British Foreign Policy, 1783–1919.* Vol. 2: *1815–1866,* pp. 488–521. New York: Macmillan, 1923.

O'Connor, Thomas H. "Lincoln and the Cotton Trade." *Civil War History* 7 (1961): 20–35.

O'Rouke, Mary M. "The Diplomacy of William H. Seward during the Civil War: His Politics as Related to International Law." Ph.D. diss., University of California, 1963.

Orzell, Laurence J. "A Favorable Interval: The Polish Insurrection in Civil War Diplomacy, 1863." *Civil War History* 24 (1978): 332–350.

Owsley, Frank L. "America and the Freedom of the Seas, 1861–1865." In Avery Craven, ed. *Essays in Honor of William E. Dodd,* pp. 194–256. Chicago: University of Chicago Press, 1935.

Palmer, Beverly Wilson, ed. *The Papers of Charles Sumner.* 85 reels. Alexandria, VA: Chadwyck-Healey, 1988.

Palmer, Samuel. *Palmer's Index to the Times Newspaper, 1859–1866.* 7 vols. Vaduz, Liechtenstein: Kraus Reprint, 1965.

Paolino, Ernest N. *The Foundations of the American Empire: William Henry Seward and United States Foreign Policy.* Ithaca, NY: Cornell University Press, 1973.

Pattock, Florence B. "Cassius M. Clay's Mission to Russia, 1861–1862; 1863–1869." *Filson Club Historical Quarterly* 43 (1969): 325–344.

Perkins, Bradford. *The Cambridge History of American Foreign Relations.* Vol. 1: *The Creation of a Republican Empire, 1776–1865.* New York: Cambridge University Press, 1993.

Perkins, Dexter. *The Monroe Doctrine, 1826–1867.* Gloucester, MA: P. Smith, 1965.

Peyton, Thomas J., Jr. "Charles Sumner and United States Foreign Relations during the American Civil War." Ph.D. diss., Georgetown University, 1972.

Plischke, Elmer. *U.S. Foreign Relations: A Guide to Information Sources.* Detroit: Gale Research Co., 1980.

Pomery, Earl S. "The Myth of the Russian Fleet, 1863." *New York History* 31 (1950): 169–176.

Poole, William Frederick, and William Isaac Fletcher. *Poole's Index to Periodical Literature.* 6 vols. Gloucester, MA: Smith, 1893–1908.

Pratt, Julius William, Vincent P. DeSantis, and Joseph M. Siracusa. *A History of United States Foreign Policy.* Englewood Cliffs, NJ: Prentice-Hall, 1980.

Reinhartz, Dennis. "A Convergence of Eagles: Poland and the Cold War Diplomacy of the American Civil War, 1856–1867." *Continuity,* no. 11 (1987): 23–37.

Reuter, Paul H. "United States–French Relations Regarding French Intervention in Mexico: From the Tripartite Treaty to Queretaro." *Southern Quarterly* 6 (4) (1968): 469–489.

Robertson, James R. *A Kentuckian at the Court of the Tsars: The Ministry of Cassius Marcellus Clay to Russia.* Berea, KY: Berea College Press, 1935.

Romero, Matias. *A Mexican View of America in the 1860's: A Foreign Diplomat Describes the Civil War and Reconstruction.* Translated and edited by Thomas D. Schoonover. Rutherford, NJ: Fairleigh Dickinson University Press, 1991.

Saul, Norman E. *Distant Friends: The United States and Russia, 1763–1867.* Lawrence, KS: University Press of Kansas, 1991.

Schell, Ernest. "Our Good Friends, the Russians." *American History Illustrated* 15 (9) (1981): 18–26.

Schick, Frank Leopold. *Records of the Presidency: Presidential Papers and Libraries from Washington to Reagan.* Phoenix, AZ: Oryx Press, 1989.

Schmidt, Karl Michael. *Mexico and the United States, 1821–1973: Conflict and Coexistence.* New York: Wiley, 1974.

Seward, Frederick W. *Reminiscences of a War-Time Statesman and Diplomat, 1830–1915.* New York: G. P. Putnam's Sons, 1916.

Seward, William Henry. *The Papers of William H. Seward.* 198 reels. Woodbridge, CT: Research Publications, 1981.

———. *The Works of William H. Seward.* Vol 5: *The Diplomatic History of the War for the Union.* Edited by George E. Baker. 1884 Reprint, New York: AMS Press, 1972.

Shippee, Lester B. *Canadian-American Relations, 1848–1874.* New Haven, CT: Yale University Press, 1939.

Smith, Walter B. *America's Diplomats and Consuls of 1776–1865: A Geographic and Biographic Directory of the Foreign Service from the Declaration of Independence to the End of the Civil War.* Arlington, VA: Center for the Study of Foreign Service Institute, U.S. Department of State, 1988.

Spencer, Warren F. *The Confederate Navy in Europe.* University, AL: University of Alabama Press, 1983.

Stern, Philip Van Doren. *When the Guns Roared: World Aspects of the American Civil War.* Garden City, NY: Doubleday, 1965.

Stevenson, Charles S. "Abraham Lincoln and the Russian Fleet Myth." *Military Review* 50 (1970): 35–37.

Storey, Moorfield. *Charles Sumner.* Boston: Houghton Mifflin, 1900.

Stouffer, Allen P. "Canadian-American Relations in the Shadow of the Civil War." *Dalhousie Review* 57 (2) (1977): 332–346.

Sumner, Charles. *Memoir and Letters of Charles Sumner.* 2 vols. Boston: Roberts Brothers, 1877–1878.

Taylor, John M. *William Henry Seward.* New York: HarperCollins, 1991.

Teijun, Wada. *American Foreign Policy towards Japan during the Nineteenth Century.* Tokyo: Tokyo Bunko, 1928.

Temple, Henry W. "William H. Seward." In Samuel Flagg Bemis, ed. *The American Secretaries of State and Their Diplomacy,* 7: 3–115. New York: Pageant, 1958.

Thomas, Benjamin P. *Russo-American Relations, 1815–1867.* Baltimore: Johns Hopkins University Press, 1930.

Trask, David F., Michael C. Meyer, and Roger F. Trask. *A Bibliography of United States–Latin American Relations since 1810.* Lincoln, NE: University of Nebraska Press, 1968.

Treat, Payson Jackson. *The Early Relations between the United States and Japan, 1853–1865.* Baltimore: Johns Hopkins University Press, 1917.

Tyrner-Tyrnauer, A. R. *Lincoln and the Emperors.* New York: Harcourt, Brace and World, 1962.

U.S. Department of State. *Correspondence Concerning Claims against Great Britain.* 7 vols. Washington, D.C.: Government Printing Office, 1869–1871.

———. *Despatches from Special Agents of the Department of State.* 11 reels. Washington, D.C.: National Archives, 1955–1965.

———. *Foreign Relations of the United States: Diplomatic Papers, 1861–1866.* 15 vols. Washington, D.C.: Government Printing Office, 1861–1867.

———. *Papers Relating to Foreign Affairs, Accompanying the Annual Message of the President to the Second Session of the Thirty-seventh Congress, 1861.* Washington, D.C.: Government Printing Office, 1861.

———. *Papers Relating to Foreign Affairs, Accompanying the Annual Message of the President to the First Session of the Thirty-eighth Congress.* Washington, D.C.: Government Printing Office, 1864.

———. *Papers Relating to Foreign Affairs Communicated to Congress, December 1, 1862.* Washington, D.C.: Government Printing Office, 1863.

———. *Treaties and Other International Agreements of the United States of America, 1776–1949.* 13 vols. Compiled by Charles I. Bevans. Washington, D.C.: Government Printing Office, 1968–1976.

———. *United States Chiefs of Mission, 1778–1988.* Washington, D.C.: Government Printing Office, 1988.

———. Division of Research and Publication. *Policy of the United States toward Maritime Commerce in War.* Vol. 1: *1776–1914.* Prepared by Carlton Savage. 1934. Reprint, New York: Kraus Reprint Company, 1969.

————. Office of the Historian. *United States Chiefs of Mission, 1778–1988.* Washington, D.C.: Department of State, Bureau of Public Affairs, 1988.

U.S. Library of Congress. Special Materials Cataloging Division. Manuscript Section. *National Union Catalog of Manuscript Collections.* Washington, D.C.: Government Printing Office, 1962–.

U.S. National Archives. *List of Foreign Service Post Records in the National Archives (Record Group 84).* Rev. ed. By Mario Fenyo and John Highbarger. National Archives Publication, no. 67–08. Washington, D.C.: National Archives and Records Service, 1967.

————. *Preliminary Inventory of Records Relating to Civil War Claims: United States and Great Britain (Record Group 76).* Compiled by George S. Ulibarri and Daniel T. Goggin. National Archives Publication, no. 62–6; Preliminary Inventory, no. 135. Washington, D.C.: National Archives, 1962.

————. *Preliminary Inventory of the General Records of the Department of State (Record Group 59).* Compiled by Daniel T. Goggin and H. Stephen Helton. National Archives Publication, no. 64–5; Preliminary Inventory, no. 157. Washington, D.C.: National Archives, 1963.

————. *The Union: A Guide to Federal Archives Relating to the Civil War.* By Kenneth W. Munden and Henry Putney Beers. Washington, D.C.: National Archives and Records Administration, 1986.

U.S. National Historical and Records Commission. *Directory of Archives and Manuscript Repositories in the United States.* Phoenix, AZ: Oryx Press, 1988.

Van Deusen, Glyndon G. *William Henry Seward.* New York: Oxford University Press, 1967.

Ward, Sir Adolphus William, and G. P. Gooch, eds. *The Cambridge History of British Foreign Policy, 1783–1919.* 3 vols. Cambridge: Cambridge University Press, 1922–1923.

Warren, Gordon H. *Fountain of Discontent: The Trent Affair and Freedom of the Seas.* Boston: Northeastern University Press, 1981.

————. "Imperial Dreamer: William Henry Seward and American Diplomacy." In Frank J. Merli and Theodore A Wilson, eds. *Makers of American Diplomacy: From Benjamin Franklin to Henry Kissinger,* pp. 195–221. New York: Charles Scribner's Sons, 1974.

West, Warren Reed. *Contemporary French Opinion on the American Civil War.* Baltimore: Johns Hopkins University Press, 1924.

White, Elizabeth Brett. *American Opinion of France from Lafayette to Poincaré.* New York: Knopf, 1927.

Wieczerzsk, Joseph W. *A Polish Chapter in Civil War America: The Effects of the January Insurrection on American Opinion and Diplomacy.* New York: Twayne, 1967.

Winks, Robin W. *Canada and the United States: The Civil War Years.* Rev. ed. Montreal: Harvest House, 1971.

Woldman, Albert A. *Lincoln and the Russians.* Cleveland: World Publishing, 1952.

Writings on American History. Washington, D.C.: American Historical Association, 1904–.

15

Confederate International Relations

Warren F. Spencer

THE BASIC THEORY OF CONFEDERATE DIPLOMACY

In 1931 Frank Lawrence Owsley published *King Cotton Diplomacy,* a title that captures the essence of the foreign relations of the Confederate States. The South in 1861 had cotton, and the two leading industrialized states of Europe—England and France—needed that cotton to provide employment for their workers and cloth for their general populations. The Confederate policy makers anticipated that the European need for cotton would lead to official diplomatic recognition of the new American state and, they hoped even to military intervention in the American war. The South's first diplomatic act was to place an embargo on the export of cotton, expecting thereby to hasten European intervention in the war. Diplomatic "commissioners" were sent first to Great Britain and to France, the leading industrial countries, and later to other European states, such as Spain, Prussia, and Russia. In addition, agents were sent to the Mexican states adjacent to the Texas-Mexican border.

Confederate diplomatic papers, then, pertain primarily to agents sent to the bordering Mexican states and to the commissioners sent to the various European capitals, particularly to those in London and Paris.

CONFEDERATE COMMISSIONERS ABROAD

John T. Picket was the first emissary sent to a Mexican state; his correspondence with the Confederate government is located in the Picket Papers, Washington, D.C., Archives of the Confederate State Department, Manuscripts Division, Library of Congress.

On February 27, 1861, President Davis, during that odd interlude between secession and war, sent Martin G. Crawford to Washington, D.C., to negotiate "concerning all matters and subjects interesting to both nations." A month later, on March 16, 1861, he sent three "special commissioners"—William L. Yancy, Pierre L. Rost, and A. Dudley Mann—to Great Britain to negotiate with authorized persons of the British government "concerning all matters and subjects interesting to both nations" and to sign a treaty or treaties "on all matters of interest existing between the two governments." The documents pertaining to this diplomatic move are in the U.S. War Department's *Official Records of the Union and Confederate Navies in the War of the Rebellion* (1881–1901) (*ORN*). The proclamations were in effect nullified by the outbreak of war with the firing upon Fort Sumter in April 1861. They do, however, reflect the Confederate government's expectation that it would receive international recognition. The choice of the men to execute President Davis's policy, however, was unfortunate; they failed in their attempts to fulfill their mission.

With the outbreak of war, President Davis sent James M. Mason to London and John Slidell to Paris. They were active first in trying to persuade the European governments to extend official recognition to the Confederate States and, later, in supporting the Confederate navy's ship construction programs in Great Britain and France. Their papers and those of the English and French governments are vital to the understanding of Confederate policy in Europe.

The Mason Papers are located in the Manuscripts Division, Library of Congress. Mason's relations with the British government are also recorded in the Public Records Office, Foreign Office Series, London, as is the correspondence between the British government and Charles Francis Adams, Sr., the U.S. minister to Great Britain. Official correspondence between the British and French governments on their policies toward the Civil War is in the same collection.

John Slidell's efforts in Paris to persuade the French government to grant official recognition to the Confederate government or even to intervene in the Civil War are in the Archives du Ministère des Affaires Etrangères, Paris, as are the counter-efforts of John Bigelow, the U.S. minister to France.

The correspondence between William H. Seward, U.S. secretary of state, and Charles Francis Adams, Sr., in London are in the National Archives, Washington, D.C., Foreign Affairs Division, State Department Correspondence, Great Britain, Despatches, 1861–1865, and Great Britain, Instructions, 1861–1865.

Thus the official correspondence of both North and South with Great Britain and France is available to scholars interested in Confederate diplomacy. Diplomatic and commercial missions were later sent to Spain, the papacy, Russia, and the United States of Mexico. Their instructions were to negotiate for official recognition of the Confederate States; they were to base their presentations on the compact theory of governments.

WARTIME DIPLOMACY

The European powers early on were concerned with the question of recognizing the Confederate States until the news of the outbreak of hostilities reached Europe on April 27. Lord John Russell in London and Edouard Thouvenel in Paris, foreign ministers of their respective countries, were then faced with more pressing issues: those of maritime law and the recognition of Southern belligerency, which would imply the neutrality of the European powers. The foreign ministers each consulted with their experts on international law, then consulted each other. On May 14, 1861, Lord John Russell issued the British proclamation of neutrality; Thouvenel took longer, but on June 10, 1861, he issued a similar French proclamation. These declarations of neutrality raised the Confederate States to an equal position with the United States as an internationally recognized belligerent in the war.

International limitations and rights of both belligerents and neutrals had been established by the Congress of Paris in 1856, at the conclusion of the Crimean War. They provided that a blockade to be recognized by neutrals had to be real—that is, ships had to be stationed at all of the various ports. There still is some question about the effectiveness of the Union blockade of Southern ports.

The European declarations of neutrality raised the Southerners' hopes for official diplomatic recognition. But the two most important states—England and France—had other issues in hand: England was afraid that the United States would attempt to take Canada, and Napoleon III of France had already developed his plan to invade Mexico in order to protect the Latin peoples of the Western Hemisphere from encroachments by the Anglo-Saxons of Europe and North America. Nonetheless, Confederate hopes were raised from time to time by Napoleon III, only to be dashed by a change of imperial policy.

CONFEDERATE SHIPBUILDING IN EUROPE

The South resorted to building cruisers to prey on Northern merchant shipping, and late in the war it began to construct ironclad warships in Great Britain and France. The documents of Confederate navy construction in Europe, Southern blockade running, and the cruises of the various Confederate raiders are in *ORN,* Series I, vols. 1–3; Series II, vols. 1–3, and in the Department of the Navy's *Civil War Navy Chronology: 1861–1865* (1971) and *Register of Officers of the Confederate States Navy: 1861–1865* (1931).

The policy of the United States toward the European powers is revealed in the Seward Manuscripts in the University of Rochester Library as well as in the collections mentioned above.

Until the Battle of Gettysburg in June 1863, naval activities were more closely related to diplomacy than were army battles on land because ships of both belligerents sought neutral ports to reprovision and even make needed repairs. All but one or two of the Confederate cruisers that preyed on Northern merchant shipping were built in England and Scotland. James D. Bulloch, a secret Confederate agent in Great Britain, in 1884 published an account of his various activities in *The Secret Service of the Confederate States in Europe: or How the Confederate Cruisers Were Equipped* (1883). It was largely the result of Bulloch's activities in ship construction and the successes of those ships, especially the CSS *Alabama,* in sinking Northern merchantmen that led the Geneva Convention in 1873 to require Great Britain, in the so-called *Alabama Claims,* to pay $15.5 million in gold to the United States. Adrian Cook in *The Alabama Claims* (1975) analyzes debates and the conclusions reached at the Geneva Convention.

The fine imposed on Great Britain was based on the Geneva decision that a neutral state must impose its neutrality on its subjects through its local law, and if that law is insufficient to prevent unneutral acts by its subjects, the government is nonetheless responsible for any such act committed by its subjects. Indeed, Confederate navy activity in both Great Britain and France raised diplomatic issues that dominated the European powers' actions toward the American war. The most accessible original sources on the Confederate ship construction in Great Britain and France, as well as the cruises of some of the ships built in England, are in *ORN,* Series I, Vol. 2. The Confederate diplomatic agent in France, John Slidell, in 1864 was active in assisting Confederate navy officers in avoiding violation of neutrality laws.

BRITISH AND FRENCH POLICIES TOWARD THE CONFEDERACY

The British government's attitude toward the Confederacy was consistent throughout the war, but the French appeared to change from time to time. The French ministers of foreign affairs were cautious throughout the war, but Napoleon III tended to vacillate from time to time. When he talked to Confederate agents or their British sympathizers, he left the impression of being pro-Southern. In October 1862 he proposed a three-power mediation in the war and at the same time quietly and unofficially initiated the Confederate shipbuilding program in Bordeaux and Nantes.

Neither of his ministers of foreign affairs, Edouard Thouvenel and, after 1862, Edouard Drouyn de Lhuys, approved the emperor's policy. When the French occupied Mexico City and Union forces won the battles of Vicksburg and Gettysburg, Drouyn de Lhuys gained ministerial support to prohibit the delivery of the French-built Confederate ships.

AMERICAN AND EUROPEAN PRIVATE COLLECTIONS

Collections of private papers of several key actors in Civil War diplomacy exist: the John Bigelow Papers, New York Public Library, New York City; William L. Dayton Papers, Princeton University Library, Princeton, New Jersey; Charles Francis Adams Papers, New York Public Library, New York City; Whittle Papers, Kirn Memorial Library, Norfolk, Virginia; and William Conway Whittle Papers, the University of Virginia Library, Manuscripts Department.

For Europeans active in the wartime diplomacy there are the Viscount Henry John Temple Palmerston Letterbooks, British Museum, London, and the Palmerston Papers at the Historical Manuscripts Commission, National Register of Archives, London. The papers of Lord John Russell are in the Public Records Office, London.

On the French side there are two collections of Foreign Minister Edouard Thouvenel's papers: Papiers de Thouvenel, Archives de Ministère des Affaires Etrangères, Paris, and Papiers de la Famille Thouvenel Archives National, Paris. There are no private papers of Edouard Drouyn de Lhuys; his official correspondence is in the Foreign Ministry Archives, Paris.

SECONDARY SOURCES

The only secondary work on French foreign minister Edouard Drouyn de Lhuys is Warren F. Spencer's "Edouard Drouyn de Lhuys and the Foreign Policy of the Second French Empire" (1955). Its emphasis, however, is on European diplomacy, which was the main focus of French diplomatic interests. Lynn M. Case and Warren F. Spencer, *The United States and France: Civil War Diplomacy* (1970), necessarily analyze Confederate activities in France, including Southern shipbuilding and the resulting diplomatic activity. In *The Confederate Navy in Europe* (1983) Spencer details the Southern ship construction in both Great Britain and France and the diplomatic activity created by that construction. These two works, along with Frank Owsley's *King Cotton Diplomacy,* provide the most thorough accounts of both Northern and Southern diplomacy, especially as it relates to the Southern raiders. The most thorough work on Southern shipbuilding remains Confederate agent James Bulloch's *The Secret Service of the Confederate States in Europe* (1883). Because his activities had to be so secret, he minimized his impact on diplomacy.

Semmes aboard the CSS *Alabama* sailed in six of the seven seas, capturing and burning Northern merchant ships and displaying the Confederate flag in various harbors in all of them, creating goodwill for the Confederacy wherever he sailed. He was, perhaps, the best diplomat the South sent abroad. In addition to his own Civil War memoirs, two of his officers published theirs: First Lieutenant John McIntosh Kell, *Recollections of a Naval Life Including the Cruises of the Confederate States Steamers "Sumter" and "Alabama"* (1900), and Lieutenant Arthur Sinclair, *Two Years on the Alabama* (1896). Each of these three authors presents his own slant on the ship and its captain, but they agree on all essentials.

Other British-built Confederate ships played similar roles: the CSS *Florida* sank Union ships in the Gulf of Mexico and the Caribbean Sea and along the coast of South America. Her biographer is Frank L. Owsley, Jr., *The CSS Florida: Her Building and Operations* (1965). Other cruisers Bulloch built in Great

Britain were the CSS *Shenandoah,* which sank a number of ships in icy Alaskan waters long after Appomattox. In addition to cruisers, Bulloch built ironclad ships in England and Scotland. His work is described by Wilbur D. Jones in *The Confederate Rams at Birkenhead* (1961). The Confederate secretary of the navy has his biographer: J. T. Durkin, *Stephen R. Mallory,* (1954), which describes Mallory's steady hand on the till of the Confederate navy.

Indeed, the activities of the Confederate navy in Europe generated the vast majority of Confederate diplomacy with the European governments. David Paul Crook, *The North, the South, and the Powers, 1861–1865* (1974), describes the impact of the Civil War in geopolitical terms that affected all the naval and industrial powers. Through the Confederate navy activities and the resulting diplomacy, the Civil War had a worldwide geopolitical impact. The vehicles of that impact were the European-built ships of the Confederate navy.

Secondary works that contributed to and are derived from Crook's thesis are numerous, some are more important than others. Ephraim Douglas Adams, *Great Britain and the American Civil War* (1925), examined in detail the impact of the war on Great Britain and the necessary diplomatic responses. The activities of the various Confederate commissioners are analyzed in detail. Olive Anderson, *A Liberal State at War* (1967), studied the impact of the Civil War and its necessary diplomacy on the British concept of a liberal government and society. Stuart L. Bernath, *Squall across the Atlantic* (1970), broadens the scope of the impact of the war to include several continental states.

France and the Civil War have been the topic of several studies. John Bigelow, *France and the Confederate Navy, 1862–1868* (1888), was one of the first works to examine the impact of the Confederate navy activities in France. Taking a longer view of U.S.-French relations, Henry Blumenthal in *France and the United States: Their Diplomatic Relations, 1789–1914* (1970) examines the Civil War–era diplomacy, including the Confederate States, within the traditional relations between Washington and Paris. Daniel B. Carroll presents the Civil War diplomacy through the role played by the French minister to Washington in *Henri Mercier and the American Civil War* (1954). Norman B. Ferris analyzed the diplomatic reaction of the United States to the European responses to Southern secession during the first year of the war in his *Desperate Diplomacy: William H. Seward's Foreign Policy, 1861* (1977). The same author analyzed the diplomatic impact of the U.S. forcible removal of two Southern diplomats from the British ship *Trent* on November 8, 1861, in *The Trent Affair: A Diplomatic Crisis* (1977). Brian Jenkins in *Britain and the War for the Union* (1974, 1980), has several good sections on the diplomacy of the war, both Confederate and Union.

The Confederate finances in Europe, a necessary component to Southern diplomacy, is best revealed in Richard I. Lester, *Confederate Finance and Purchasing in Great Britain* (1975). Samuel Bernard Thompson in *Confederate Purchasing Operations Abroad* (1935) details the financial and clandestine activity to which the Southerners had to resort in order to purchase guns, ammunition, and even ships in Europe, particularly in Great Britain.

There is no major treatment of the Confederate diplomats in London and Paris. James Mason, Confederate commissioner to Great Britain, is the subject of Walter M. Case's "James M. Mason, Confederate Diplomat" (1915), available from the Stanford University Library. Virginia Mason, *The Public Life and Diplomatic Correspondence of James M. Mason with Some Personal History by His Daughter,* was published in 1903. It casts very little additional light on Mason's Civil War assignment in London.

John Slidell, on the other hand, has been the subject of two books: Louis M. Sears, *John Slidell* (1925), and Beckles Willson, *John Slidell and the Confederates in Paris, 1862–1865* (1932). These works reveal the close relationship Slidell developed with Napoleon III, partly because of his ability to speak French fluently, as well as his inability to influence the foreign ministers of France, Louis Thouvenel and Edouard Drouyn de Lhuys, both of whom dissuaded the emperor from rash actions toward the American Civil War.

The lack of in-depth studies of the two leading Confederate diplomats in Europe reflects the failed diplomacy of the South. Slidell was more effective in France than was Mason in Great Britain until the 1863 battles of Vicksburg and Gettysburg. Even Napoleon III realized that those battles turned the tide of the war in favor of the United States. Any diplomatic action in behalf of the Confederacy would be not only futile but fatal to French-U.S. relations.

On the policies and attitudes of the two French foreign ministers—Edouard Thouvenel and Edouard Drouyn de Lhuys—see Spencer's "Edouard Drouyn de Lhuys and the Foreign Policy of the Second French Empire" and P.L.E. Pradier-Fodéré, *M. Drouyn de Lhuys* (1881). Lynn M. Case has published several articles on Thouvenel: "La France et l'affaire du 'Trent' " (1961), "La France et la restitution de Mason et Slidell" (1961), "La question de la reconnaissance au début de la Guerre de Sécession" (1963), and "La sécession aux Etats-Unis, probléme diplomatique français" (1963).

Napoleon III was already planning his expedition to Mexico, of which neither of his foreign ministers approved. See Case and Spencer, *The United States and France: Civil War Diplomacy* (1970), for the diplomatic exchanges between Washington and Paris on this subject. John Slidell in Paris, thinking French action in Mexico would antagonize Washington against the French, had encouraged the emperor to proceed with his ill-conceived intervention in Mexico. But because of his Mexican plans, Napoleon III could not afford to antagonize the United States, and Slidell's scheme failed.

The bibliographical material of the Confederate diplomacy is to be found not only in secondary works that are primarily on the subject but also in publications in which Confederate diplomats or the words "Confederate diplomacy" appear. Despite the drudgery of searching through such publications, it is nonetheless a rewarding work, much to be indulged in.

BIBLIOGRAPHY

MANUSCRIPT COLLECTIONS

Archives de Ministère des Affaires Etrangères, Paris
  Papiers de Thouvenel
Archives National, Paris
  Papiers de la Famille Thouvenel
British Museum
  Viscount Henry John Temple Palmerston, Letterbooks
Department of the Navy, Naval History Division
Kirn Memorial Library, Norfolk, Virginia
  Whittle Papers
Library of Congress, Manuscripts Division
  Picket Papers
  Mason Papers
Princeton University Library
  William L. Dayton Papers
Public Records Office, London
  Lord John Russell Papers
National Archives, Foreign Affairs Division
  State Department Correspondence
    Great Britain, Despatches, 1861–1865
    Great Britain, Instructions, 1861–1865
National Register of Archives, London, Manuscripts Commission
  Palmerston Papers
New York Public Library
  Charles Francis Adams Papers
Spencer/Confederate Foreign Relations
  John Bigelow Papers
University of Virginia Library, Manuscripts Division
  William Conway Whittle Papers

PUBLISHED AND SECONDARY SOURCES

Adams, Ephraim Douglas. *Great Britain and the American Civil War.* 2 vols. New York: Russell & Russell, 1925.
Anderson, Olive. *A Liberal State at War.* London: Macmillan, 1967.
Beckles Willson. *John Slidell and the Confederates in Paris, 1862–1865.* New York: Minton, Balch, 1932.
Bernath, Stuart L. *Squall across the Atlantic.* Berkeley: University of California Press, 1970.
Bigelow, John. *France and the Confederate Navy, 1862–1868.* New York: Harper & Brothers, 1888.
Blumenthal, Henry. *France and the United States: Their Diplomatic Relations, 1789–1914.* New York: W. W. Norton, 1970.
Bulloch, James D. *The Secret Service of the Confederate States in Europe: or How the*

Confederate Cruisers Were Equipped. 2 vols. 1883. Reprint, New York and London: Thomas Yoseloff, 1959.

Carroll, Daniel B. *Henri Mercier and the American Civil War.* Princeton: Princeton University Press, 1954.

Case, Lynn M., and Warren F. Spencer. *The United States and France: Civil War Diplomacy.* Philadelphia: University of Pennsylvania Press, 1970.

————. "La France et l'affaire du 'Trent.' " *Revue historique* (July–September 1961).

————. "La France et la restitution de Mason et Slidell." *Bulletin de la Societe d'Histoire moderne* 59 (1961): 57–86.

————. "La question de la reconnaissance au début de la Guerre de Sécession." *Bulletin de la Société d'Histoire moderne* 61 (1963): 3–5.

————. "La sécession aux Etats-Unis, probléme diplomatique français." *Revue d'Histoire Diplomatique* 77 (1963): 290–313.

Case, Walter M. "James Mason, Confederate Diplomat." Master's thesis, Stanford University, 1915.

Cook, Adrian. *The Alabama Claims: American Politics and Anglo-American Relations, 1861–1872.* Ithaca, NY: Cornell University Press, 1975.

Crook, David Paul. *The North, the South, and the Powers, 1861–1865.* New York: Wiley, 1974.

Durkin, J. T. *Stephen R. Mallory: Confederate Navy Chief.* Chapel Hill: University of North Carolina Press, 1954.

Ferris, Norman B. *Desperate Diplomacy: William H. Seward's Foreign Policy, 1861.* Knoxville: University of Tennessee Press, 1977.

————. *The Trent Affair: A Diplomatic Crisis.* Knoxville: University of Tennessee Press, 1977.

Jenkins, Brian. *Britain and the War for the Union.* 2 vols. Montreal: McGill–Queens University Press, 1974, 1980.

Jones, Wilbur D. *The Confederate Rams at Birkenhead: A Chapter in Anglo-American Relations.* Tuscaloosa: Confederate Publishing Co., 1961.

Kell, John McIntosh. *Recollections of a Naval Life Including the Cruises of the Confederate States Steamers "Sumter" and "Alabama."* Washington, D.C.: Neale, 1900.

Lester, Richard I. *Confederate Finance and Purchasing in Great Britain.* Charlottesville: University Press of Virginia, 1975.

Mason, Virginia. *The Public Life and Diplomatic Correspondence of James M. Mason, with Some Personal History by His Daughter.* Roanoke, VA, 1903.

Owsley, Frank Lawrence. *King Cotton Diplomacy.* Chicago: University of Chicago Press, 1959.

————. *The C.S.S. Florida: Her Building and Operations.* Philadelphia: University of Pennsylvania Press, 1965.

Pradier-Fodere, P. L. E. *M. Drouyn de Lhuys.* Paris, 1881.

Sears, Louis M. *John Slidell.* Durham, NC, 1925.

Sinclair, Arthur. *Two Years on the Alabama.* Boston: Lee and Shepard, 1896.

Spencer, Warren F. "Edouard Drouyn de Lhuys and the Foreign Policy of the Second French Empire." Ph.D. diss., University of Pennsylvania, 1955.

————. *The Confederate Navy in Europe.* Tuscaloosa: University of Alabama Press, 1983.

Thompson, Samuel Bernard. *Confederate Purchasing Operations Abroad.* Chapel Hill: University of North Carolina Press, 1935.

————. *The Confederate Navy in Europe.* Tuscaloosa: University of Alabama Press, 1983.

United States. Department of the Navy. *Civil War Navy Chronology: 1861–1865.* Washington, D.C.: Government Printing Office, 1971.

————. Office of Navy. Office of Naval Records and Library. *Register of Officers of the Confederate States Navy: 1861–1865.* Washington, D.C.: Government Printing Office, 1931.

United States. Navy Department. *Official Records of the Union and Confederate Navies in the War of the Rebellion.* 30 volumes and index. Washington, D.C.: Government Printing Office, 1894–1922.

Willson, Beckles. *John Slidell and the Confederates in Paris, 1862–1865.* New York, 1932.

Part VI

Leaders

16

Abraham Lincoln

Mark E. Neely, Jr.

About a hundred years ago, the two dominant traditions of writing on Abraham Lincoln emerged with the publication of landmark works written by people who had known Lincoln personally and well. One tradition comes from John G. Nicolay and John Hay, Lincoln's White House secretaries; the other, from William H. Herndon, his longtime law partner. Neither of these works was critical of Lincoln, and indeed there is no substantial anti-Lincoln tradition. Nicolay and Hay realized as early as 1890 that "the tradition is already complete. The voice of hostile faction is silent, or unheeded; even criticism is gentle and timid." Herndon and the coauthors Nicolay and Hay were all admirers of Lincoln and had all been antislavery Republicans. The assassination of Lincoln in 1865 essentially silenced Lincoln's critics forever. Among the works of serious literature written by professional historians in recent years, only one stands out as sharply critical: *Lincoln, the South, and Slavery: The Political Dimension* (1991), the printed version of a brief series of lectures by Stephen A. Douglas's modern biographer, Robert W. Johannsen.

The two great traditions of writing about Lincoln do not represent romanticism and idealism (Nicolay and Hay), on the one hand, and warts-and-all realism (Herndon), on the other. These unfortunate categories come from Benjamin Thomas's *Portrait for Posterity: Lincoln and the Biographers* (1947), but in fact the two represent the differences between works on policy and public life (Nicolay and Hay) and books on personality and private life (Herndon).

William Herndon, left behind in Springfield when his law partner went to the White House, was nosy. He was curious about Lincoln's bowel movements and his love life. He searched the record for bastardy in Lincoln's lineage and for syphilis in Lincoln's bedroom. After Lincoln boarded the train for Washington in February 1861, Herndon saw him only once, and that briefly. He therefore knew about his old law partner's presidency only what any other reader of newspapers of the day knew. Lincoln the man was Herndon's special field of expertise, and that emphasis has always drawn readers to the book he wrote with Jesse Weik, *Herndon's Lincoln: The True Story of A Great Life* (1889). His book was by his own confession "a limited one—kind of subjective—inner life, with a mere thread of history running along" (p. xi). His avowed object was "to deal with Mr. Lincoln individually and domestically" (p. vii). And the book followed the "hero . . . till he left Springfield in 1861 to be inaugurated President" (p. ix).

By contrast, Nicolay and Hay, the reserved, even stuffy presidential private secretaries, essentially knew only the president. They wanted no scent of bastardy or syphilis in the ten-volume *Abraham Lincoln: A History,* published in 1890. They scorned Herndon's domestic and individual focus on Lincoln; they wished instead "to show his relations to the times in which he moved, the stupendous issues he controlled, the remarkable men by whom he was surrounded" (1:x).

LINCOLN LITERATURE TODAY

A century later, the dominant strain in Lincoln study is a Herndonian emphasis on the domestic individual—on Lincoln's private life, personality, psychology, intimate biography, family history; on Lincoln as son and father, husband and lover; and on Lincoln's wife. Such works have limited uses for Civil War historians, who do not need to know about Ann Rutledge or Lincoln's legal fees to evaluate his policies as president. Only one strand of the Herndon tradition in writing seems immediately relevant to a Civil War bibliography, and that derives less directly from Herndon than indirectly, through the great literary critic Edmund Wilson, who pursued Herndon's interest in Lincoln's psychology into the post-Freudian era. His influential essay, "Abraham Lincoln: The Union as Religious Mysticism," published in the *New Yorker* magazine in 1953 and made famous by inclusion in his pioneering book, *Patriotic Gore: Studies in the Literature of the American Civil War* (1966), spawned several psychological studies of Lincoln, such as Charles Strozier's *Lincoln's Quest for Union: Public and Private Meanings* (1982) and Michael Burlingame's *The Inner World of Abraham Lincoln* (1994), and influenced other works, like Harry V. Jaffa's *Crisis of the House Divided: An Interpretation of the Issues in the Lincoln-Douglas Debates* (1959).

Psychoanalysis was but one of two fascinations Edmund Wilson indulged when he wrote about Lincoln and the Civil War. Wilson, an income tax evader and critic of the income tax, became an extremist on personal liberty. His struggles with the Internal Revenue Service caused him to hate the U.S. government and to compare it readily to fascist or communist regimes. Some who wrote about Lincoln's psyche on inspiration from Wilson imbibed his hidden political agenda too and wrote about Lincoln as though he could be aptly compared to Bismarck or Lenin, as Wilson had done. Among these works are George Forgie's *Patricide in the House Divided: A Psychological Interpretation of Lincoln and His Age* (1979) and, especially, Dwight Anderson, *Abraham Lincoln: The Quest for Immortality* (1982), along with novels by Gore Vidal and William Safire. These writers, who come at Lincoln from both the political left and the political right, find in him the psychological makings of a political tyrant. They guide readers to dark assumptions about the suppression of civil liberties under the wartime Lincoln administration. Among modern authors, only those under Edmund Wilson's spell seem to be able to find this sinister streak in Lincoln's personality. Herndon himself certainly did not think Lincoln a tyrant. Modern students of the Civil War should not follow Edmund Wilson's lead in this regard, as any of the works of constitutional history listed below will show.

Earlier in this century, those who followed Herndon's lead often wrote on genealogy, for Lincoln's genealogy had been a part of Herndon's agenda too. The most notable authors in this direct tradition are Ida M. Tarbell, Louis A. Warren, and William E. Barton. They were often preoccupied with questions of paternity that ultimately stemmed from now-obsolete assumptions about the inheritance of acquired characteristics. All disagreed with Herndon in their conclusions, and Warren even despised him, but Herndon was dictating their research agenda.

Today, Herndon too often still dictates the path of research. A symbol of his modern-day dominance is the surprising amount of serious work that focuses on Ann Rutledge, an obscure associate of Lincoln's youth who has not left one single document in her own hand for historians to study. Herndon could never prove bastardy or syphilis, so Ann Rutledge was his big discovery about Lincoln's past. Virtually singlehandedly he created her historical prominence. The modern works on Lincoln's intimate life share with the genealogists who wrote in the first part of this century not only inspiration by Herndon but also a problematic evidentiary base and, more important, a distant relationship to questions of politics, policy, and presidential administration. They cause us to lose sight of what Nicolay and Hay called "the stupendous issues" Lincoln controlled and "the remarkable men by whom he was surrounded." And the fate of Herndon's modern heirs may turn out the same as that of the students of genealogy: when the vogue of psychoanalysis passes away, their concern with sons and fathers, husbands and wives, lovers and suicide, may seem misplaced.

Whatever the future may hold, works in the Herndon tradition offer little to today's Civil War historian, and the preoccupation with Lincoln's personal life has left his more important public life the victim of neglect in recent years. For example, no subject has suffered more than the political history of the Civil War, as Harvard historian William E. Gienapp pointed out in "Politics Seem to Enter into Everything" (1982). Yet it is crucial to any understanding of the war. Historians would have done well to follow the lead of James A. Rawley in

Turning Points of the Civil War (1966), where he included, along with the commonplace turning points such as the Battle of Gettysburg and the siege of Vicksburg, some less often noted by military historians: the issuance of the emancipation proclamation and the election of 1864.

Emancipation brought about perhaps the only enduring and revolutionary historical result of the Civil War. As social and economic historians point out, the North experienced no significant redistribution of wealth as a result of the war. It saw the creation of no new social classes (despite wartime complaints about a new "shoddy aristocracy" of war profiteers). Nor did the war provide a launching pad for the industrial economy to take off toward the factory system, urbanization, and class consciousness associated with the Gilded Age. Economic historians now tend to think that the war slightly impeded economic growth and, since government contracts were let to a myriad of small firms, did not particularly encourage the factory system.

The war did not bring what political scientists of the critical elections school would call a revolution in the political system, either; the major voter realignment of the mid-century was complete by the 1860 election, when the Republicans attracted enough former Know-Nothing voters to win the presidency. Thereafter, roughly the same ethnic and religious groups and the same economic classes of Americans tended to line up behind the same party in each presidential election until the 1890s. However, Republican victory in the election of 1864, though it was probably not necessary to save the Union, was significant, as it was surely necessary to guarantee freedom to America's black minority.

For now, Civil War historians who want to know about these and other momentous political developments must make do mostly with older books on Lincoln. The standard work on Lincoln's presidency remains James G. Randall's four-volume *Lincoln the President,* published forty years ago (the last volume was posthumously completed by Richard N. Current). It offers careful scholarship and an understanding of history in the rather grand tradition established by Nicolay and Hay. The most recent work in the same tradition, though much shorter, is Phillip S. Paludan's *The Presidency of Abraham Lincoln* (1994).

THE ESSENTIAL LITERATURE

Aside from general works, the literature on Lincoln's presidential years can be divided roughly into four topics: constitutional history, political history, military history, and political history, including, above all, emancipation and Reconstruction but also economic and peripheral questions. Following are essential works in each of these areas.

Constitutional History

Students have to reach back to James G. Randall's *Constitutional Problems under Lincoln* (1926) for an overall survey of the issues. The more recent works offer less complete coverage and more specialized and argumentative focus:

Harold M. Hyman, *A More Perfect Union: The Impact of the Civil War and Reconstruction on the Constitution* (1973) and Mark E. Neely, Jr., *The Fate of Liberty: Abraham Lincoln and Civil Liberties* (1991). In part, constitutional historians have been preoccupied with whether the war shaped the Constitution or the Constitution shaped the war. Of the three works mentioned here, none is completely preoccupied with that question. Randall's answer is ambiguous, for his book was long in the making and felt various influences. He was a man born in the North and named for a Union war hero, who married a Southern woman and studied under a Southern historian (when such sectional factors mattered more, perhaps, than they do now). Hyman argues that the Constitution shaped the war; *The Fate of Liberty* stresses the impact of the war on the Constitution (thus Hyman's subtitle might have been more appropriate for this book than his own).

Political History

James G. Randall's detestation of political parties served political history poorly. As William Gienapp has observed, Randall's treatment of Civil War politics served to deaden interest in what is actually a lively, if not explosive, subject. Equally palsying was the most influential of modern interpretations of Civil War politics, the "two-party system" thesis put forward by Eric McKitrick in 1967 (which will be discussed later).

To Randall, statesmanship was equivalent to transcending party rather than leading it, and he thus misinterpreted many of Lincoln's actions. For example, he called Lincoln's famous letter to Erastus Corning and others defending the suspension of the writ of habeas corpus "one of those dignified, carefully worded statements addressed to a person or occasion, but intended as a kind of state paper" (*Lincoln the President: Midstream,* p. 226). In fact, the June 12, 1863, letter served political purposes from the start. Lincoln himself had numerous copies of it printed and mailed across the country on the frank of his private secretary, John Nicolay (to maintain the president's appearance of staying above politics). The carefully selected political opinion leaders who received the document knew exactly what to do with it. One New York operator reported to the president that 50,000 copies had been printed in pamphlet form by the *New York Tribune* within a week and promised another 500,000 copies later. Politician Roscoe Conkling, also of New York, replied (to the president, not to Nicolay—he knew from whom the document really came), "I received a pamphlet copy under Nicolay's frank, & it makes the best Campaign document we can have in this state."

The publication of a new study of the presidential election of 1864, David E. Long's *The Jewel of Liberty: Abraham Lincoln's Re-election and the End of Slavery* (1994), seems encouraging for a return to the public themes in Lincoln's life. The book, however, is not particularly forward looking in historiography or method. To depict the very Union at stake in the election, Long reaches back in historiography to the idea that the Democratic party contained substantial disloyal elements. He does not take a state-by-state approach to the election, nor does he make much use of voting statistics. William F. Zornow's *Lincoln & the Party Divided* (1954) therefore remains useful. On other political subjects, modern students remain indebted to the older works of Reinhard H. Luthin, who with Harry J. Carman, wrote *Lincoln and the Patronage* (1943) as well as, by himself, *The First Lincoln Campaign* (1944). He also wrote one of the three best one-volume biographies, the information-packed *The Real Abraham Lincoln* (1960).

Abraham Lincoln's murder was a political crime, and a substantial amount of work has been done on the subject in recent years. The most comprehensive and sane is William Hanchett's *The Lincoln Murder Conspiracies* (1983), which supersedes everything that went before on the subject and has not been equaled by anything since.

Military History

Abraham Lincoln's abilities as commander in chief were not widely recognized until European writers began to praise them after World War I. Particularly important was the publication of British general Colin R. Ballard's *Military Genius of Abraham Lincoln: An Essay* (1926). Thereafter respect for Lincoln's military acumen rose to a pinnacle in the work of T. Harry Williams, *Lincoln and His Generals* (1952), and Kenneth Williams, *Lincoln Finds a General: A Military Study of the Civil War* (1949–1959), both of which remain crucial to understanding Lincoln as commander in chief. The former offers more analysis, but the latter offers a detailed narrative of Lincoln's relations with the Union high command.

Policy History

The literature on the most important policy, emancipation, by no means equals its importance in American history. *The Emancipation Proclamation* (1963), written by John Hope Franklin for the document's centennial, was brief and failed to use the Abraham Lincoln Papers at the Library of Congress.

Ironically the modern civil rights revolution hurt the reputation of the proclamation rather than enhancing it. Abraham Lincoln was not a racial egalitarian and could not maintain heroic status as fully in an era that expected of its heroes that they be color-blind. Thus Lerone Bennett's famous article in *Ebony* magazine in 1968, "Was Abe Lincoln a White Supremacist?" marked the death knell of black veneration of Lincoln. It is difficult to imagine a book as respectful of Lincoln as Benjamin Quarles's *Lincoln and the Negro* (1962) being written on the same subject again, though Lincoln has certainly had his defenders, among them, Don E. Fehrenbacher in "Only His Stepchildren: Lincoln and the Negro" (1974).

For the most part, the change in contemporary attitudes on race has led to neglect of the Lincoln administration's record and of the proclamation. Instead, an emphasis on the social history of black society now prevails. The watershed book was Leon F. Litwack's *Been in the Storm So Long: The Aftermath of Slavery* (1979), which, like Harold Hyman's book on the Constitution, was intended at first to form a part of the Impact of the Civil War series. But Professor Litwack felt that his book should test the impact of black people on the Civil War rather than the reverse proposition. He abandoned the series, writing a book on emancipation that has but ten references to the emancipation proclamation in 652 pages, and most of those are incidental and unflattering. Litwack insisted that "the various dimensions of slavery's collapse—the political machinations, the government edicts, the military occupation—should not be permitted to obscure the principal actors in this drama: the four million black men and women for whom enslavement composed their entire memory." From that point of view would emerge the idea of "self-emancipation" (p. xi).

It was an idea whose time had come. More than a hundred years of veneration of the Great Emancipator had failed to show how slaves actually got free from their plantations. To do so during the war required courage and initiative, and the historians' focus on Washington, D.C., and on Lincoln's document slighted the anonymous efforts of the slaves themselves. (To this day there remains no well-informed estimate of the number who gained freedom before the end of the war.) On the other hand, the idea of self-emancipation, carelessly used, can confuse chronology and distort history by suggesting what is not true: that the slaves freed themselves without help and that their anomalous presence in Union lines forced Lincoln to recognize what was already a fait accompli. LaWanda Cox's *Lincoln and Black Freedom: A Study in Presidential Leadership* (1981) reveals in its subtitle a proper emphasis on Lincoln's crucial role.

Closely related to emancipation is the history of wartime reconstruction, also ably dealt with in Cox's book. Well before that, Herman Belz's *Reconstructing the Union: Theory and Policy during the Civil War* (1969) brought clear thinking and fresh insight to the politics of Reconstruction within the Republican party; it remains essential reading.

Among other policies of the Lincoln administration, none has been better described than military technological innovation, the subject of Robert V. Bruce's *Lincoln and the Tools of War* (1956). It is a classic work of Lincolniana but should now be balanced by reading the same author's treatment of Civil War science and technology in *The Launching of Modern American Science* (1987).

With the exceptions mainly of works on race and reconstruction, I have been forced here to rely on books with notably older publication dates than many cited for other areas of Civil War bibliography in this book. More than half of the ones cited in this chapter so far date before 1970. When, less than twenty years after the Civil War centennial, Gabor S. Boritt surveyed what he called "a decade of vigorous Lincoln scholarship from the mid-1970s to the mid-1980s," not even a third of the works reviewed dealt with public, political, and policy questions. None, remarkably, focused on the traditional subject of great interest, the politics of the 1850s and the coming of the Civil War, or on the all-important questions of strategy and war from the presidential years.

One can only speculate, but the reasons for the turn away from public to private meanings might include the growth of psychohistory in the historical profession; the growth of women's history, which puts the focus on family and home life in the nineteenth century; intellectual preoccupations of the "me" decade, as historians turned away from the Vietnam War and Watergate to more personal concerns; and, probably most important, the near death of political history within the profession.

THE SHAPE OF THE FUTURE

The exhaustion of attempts to write about Lincoln's private life will likely occur soon because of the sparseness of documentation. Moreover, the reigning interpretations of the Civil War years appear to me, at least, to be on the verge of breaking down or at least of very considerable revision, and that may well usher in new works with fresh questions about the war president. Together, these developments should revive the Nicolay and Hay tradition.

The two most influential interpretations currently shaping works on Lincoln and the war are the total war thesis and the two-party system thesis. The total war thesis, the regnant interpretation of Union victory as shaped by the Lincoln administration, argues that the North won only when it abandoned the limited war techniques and objectives of the eighteenth century—capturing the enemy's capital, seizing territory, maneuvering and concentrating armies before battle, and respecting civilian lives and property on campaign—and instead applied total war, fighting ceaselessly against the whole of Confederate society, not only its organized armies but its economy and its civilians. The other major interpretation, Eric McKitrick's two-party system thesis, argued that the survival of the two-party politics throughout the war in the North proved a distinct advantage to mobilization and morale, just as the one-party system of the Confederacy caused a failure of political leadership and barrenness in policy formation. Of the two theories, the first has met the most criticism so far—for example, in Eric T. Dean, Jr.'s "Rethinking the Civil War: Beyond 'Revolutions,' 'Reconstructions,' and the 'New Social History' " (1994).

Both theories contradict Lincoln's words. Though he believed the enemy's slaves could be seized for military advantage, Lincoln publicly affirmed his adherence to the other traditional limits on military objectives in 1863: "Civilized belligerents do all in their power to help themselves, or hurt the enemy, except a few things regarded as barbarous or cruel. Among the exceptions are the massacre of vanquished foes, and non-combatants, male and female." And as late as August 1864 he told General Ulysses S. Grant, "The Secretary of War and I concur that you better confer with Gen. Lee and stipulate for a mutual discontinuance of house-burning and other destruction of private property."

Likewise, the celebration of the survival of the two-party system during the Civil War ignores the point of view of the Civil War generation itself. Lincoln, in his only explicit endorsement of the two-party system, in 1852, revealed that he shared the era's uncertainty about the role of political parties. "A free people," Lincoln had said, "in times of peace and quiet—when pressed by no common danger—naturally divide into parties. At such times, the man who is of neither party, is not—cannot be, of any consequence." Lincoln and his age generally accepted the inevitability of parties in peacetime but were by no means certain that parties were natural in times of war.

Moreover, it would have come as news to Lincoln, let alone more partisan Republicans, to learn, as McKitrick maintains, that "Lincoln's leadership of the Union war effort was [not] severely and dangerously hampered by political partisanship." The president told General William T. Sherman quite the opposite in September 1864, when he was trying to persuade the general to furlough Indiana troops to vote in the Indiana state election:

The State election of Indiana occurs on the 11th. of October, and the loss of it to the friends of the Government would go far towards losing the whole Union cause. The bad effect upon the November election, and especially the giving the State Government to those who will oppose the war in every possible way, are too much to risk, if it can possibly be avoided. . . . Any thing you can safely do to let her soldiers, or any part of them, go home and vote at the State election, will be greatly in point.

Fears that the opposition party threatened the very survival of the republic had not been higher in American politics since the Jeffersonian era, and McKitrick's bland celebration of party simply does not accurately reflect the sharp partisan disputes of the Civil War period.

The erosion of these grand but rigidified interpretations will surely bring renewed interest in the explosive political history of the Civil War North and send historians in search of new understandings of Lincoln's performance as commander in chief.

ABRAHAM LINCOLN BEFORE THE WAR

Interest in Lincoln and the Civil War has never been confined to the forty-eight months of warfare from the spring of 1861 to the spring of 1865. In fact, in the older literature the principal interest in the Civil War among professional historians lay outside the war years. In those days, writing on the Civil War for most professional historians was synonymous with writing on the causes of the war. The monument to this outlook is Thomas Pressly's *Americans Interpret Their Civil War* (1954), a historiographical study that has surely disappointed many Civil War historians. There is nothing in the book about the war at all; it concerns only the differing interpretations of the causes of the war. Times have changed, and many historians are interested in the war itself, but it remains true that the events of 1861–1865 cannot be understood without understanding the causes and events leading up to the war. For example, William T. Sherman's soldiers sought political revenge and proved particularly destructive on their march through South Carolina, the state they blamed for causing the war.

Because the historiography of the causes of the war is more complex than that on the war itself, the modern reader should consult the following books essential to a sound interpretive framework: David Potter (with Don E. Fehrenbacher), *The Impending Crisis, 1848–1861* (1976); Eric Foner, *Free Soil, Free Labor, Free Men: The Ideology of the Republican Party before the Civil War* (1970); William E. Gienapp, *The Origins of the Republican Party, 1852–1856* (1987) and " 'Politics Seem to Enter into Everything': Political Culture in the North, 1840–1860" (1982); Michael F. Holt, *The Political Crisis of the 1850s* (1978); and Joel Silbey, *The American Political Nation, 1838–1893* (1991). For a good summary of the great debate over the firing on Fort Sumter, readers should consult Richard N. Current, *Lincoln and the First Shot* (1963).

Sophisticated analysis of Lincoln as a politician began with Albert Beveridge, but modern students owe the biggest debt to David Donald's *Lincoln Reconsidered: Essays on the Civil War Era* (1956), which ranged widely over subjects other than Lincoln. The best work directly on Lincoln has been done by Don E. Fehrenbacher, especially in *Prelude to Greatness: Lincoln in the 1850s* (1962). Tying Lincoln as president to his earliest political career is the special forte of Gabor S. Boritt in *Lincoln and the Economics of the American Dream* (1978). Boritt's and Fehrenbacher's are probably the two most important books written on Abraham Lincoln in the last thirty-five years and are standing the test of time well.

ORIGINAL SOURCES AND REFERENCE WORKS

The most essential books come last: the original sources and reference works necessary to study Abraham Lincoln. *The Collected Works of Abraham Lincoln* (1953–1955 plus supplements, edited by Roy P. Basler, et al.) were among the first of the modern documentary editions of the papers of American historical figures and were thus published before editors decided to include in many such projects, as far as possible, both ends of the correspondence. Therefore the *Collected Works* are not really complete without the Abraham Lincoln Papers at the Library of Congress, available in ninety-seven reels of microfilm. Taken together, the printed *Works,* comprising Lincoln's own letters and speeches with a handful of legal papers, and the microfilm papers, consisting mostly of incoming mail to the White House, add up to some 20,000 documents, the basis of all Lincoln study. Though vast, the collected works have been much studied and are well known, but the Library of Congress collection has never received the attention it deserves. In part, that stemmed from the disappointment of its opening in 1947. Lincoln's son Robert had forbidden use of the papers bequeathed to the Library of Congress until twenty-one years after his death. The pent-up curiosity made the day the collection opened a media event, but there was no treason or bastardy revealed, and the anticlimax somehow kept the papers from figuring as prominently in the research plans of Lincoln historians as they should.

There are special problems involved in authenticating sources for a man who is a cultural patron saint and whose original letters are worth as much as $1,500 *per word.* Readers will gain some appreciation for them in articles by Harold Hyman and Ludwell Johnson about the authenticity of a letter about race Lincoln wrote to General James Wadsworth, as well as in F. Lauriston Bullard's interesting little book, *Abraham Lincoln and the Widow Bixby* (1946). Harold Holzer's new edition of *The Lincoln-Douglas Debates* proves that even an archive as well known as Lincoln's can always be reexamined; it calls into question the text of the great debates (included in the *Collected Works*) that had been accepted by historians for over 130 years.

Don and Virginia Fehrenbacher's *Recollected Words of Abraham Lincoln* (1996) promises to be of great use. For Civil War historians, other standard sources for the Lincoln administration, much consulted in the past, include: Gideon Welles, *Diary* (1911); Tyler Dennett, ed., *Lincoln and the Civil War in the Diaries and Letters of John Hay* (1939); and Salmon P. Chase's diary, newly available in the first volume of *The Salmon P. Chase Papers* (1994). Reference works include Earl Schenck Miers' *Lincoln Day by Day: A Chronology, 1809–1865* (1960) and Mark E. Neely, Jr.'s *The Abraham Lincoln Encyclopedia* (1982). The encyclopedic *Lincoln in American Memory* (1994) by Merrill Peterson is helpful in sorting out the vast accumulation of Lincoln lore. The most useful one-volume biographies, in addition to Reinhard Luthin's mentioned above, are Benjamin Thomas, *Abraham Lincoln: A Biography* (1952) and Stephen Oates, *With Malice Toward None: The Life of Abraham Lincoln* (1977). All are rather dated, and it is good that on the horizon is David Donald's *Lincoln* (1996).

Interpretation of the original sources should begin with the greatest of the secondary works on Lincoln: William Herndon's book, which no one seems to overlook these days, and the much-neglected ten volumes of Nicolay and Hay. Though far from impartial, Nicolay and Hay's treatment remains the most comprehensive, is generally lucid, and can almost always be counted upon to remind the reader of some forgotten aspect of administrative history. Their discussion of the habeas corpus issue, for example, makes the observation about Lincoln's famous Corning letter, mentioned above, that its "language [was] so terse and vigorous that it is difficult to abridge a paragraph without positive mutilation" (7:5), something that might be said for many of Lincoln's letters and papers. Moreover, they mention an important legal case, not to be found in the modern works of Randall or Hyman, on the subject of Lincoln and the Constitution. Thus they provide excellent reminders of matters of day-to-day significance lost sight of in later literature; the little-known decision of the New York Supreme Court in the George W. Jones case brought crucial affirmation of the constitutionality of conscription. And their description of Civil War conscription itself seems admirably simple and accurate: "This was the first law enacted by Congress by which the Government of the United States without the intervention of the authorities of the several States appealed directly to the nation to create large armies" (8:39). With Nicolay and Hay, the serious study of Lincoln's role in the Civil War really began, and their work is not a bad place for anyone to begin the study.

BIBLIOGRAPHY

Anderson, Dwight G. *Abraham Lincoln: The Quest of Immortality.* New York: Knopf, 1982.

Ballard, Colin R. *Military Genius of Abraham Lincoln: An Essay.* London: Oxford University Press, 1926.

Basler, Roy P., ed. *The Collected Works of Abraham Lincoln: Supplement, 1832–1865.* Westport, CT: Greenwood Press, 1974.

Basler, Roy P., et al. *The Collected Works of Abraham Lincoln.* New York: Simon & Schuster, 9 vols. New Brunswick, NJ: Rutgers University Press, 1953–1955.

Basler, Roy P., and Christian O. Basler, eds. *The Collected Works of Abraham Lincoln: Second Supplement, 1848–1865.* New Brunswick, NJ: Rutgers University Press, 1990.

Belz, Herman. *Reconstructing the Union: Theory and Policy during the Civil War.* Ithaca, NY: Cornell University Press, 1969.

Bennet, Lerone, Jr. "Was Abe Lincoln a White Supremacist?" *Ebony* 23 (February 1968): 35–42.

Boritt, Gabor S. *Lincoln and the Economics of the American Dream.* Memphis: Memphis State University Press, 1978.

Bruce, Robert V. *The Launching of Modern American Science, 1846–1876.* New York: Knopf, 1987.

———. *Lincoln and the Tools of War.* Indianapolis: Bobbs-Merrill, 1956.

Bullard, F. Lauriston. *Abraham Lincoln and the Widow Bixby.* New Brunswick, NJ: Rutgers University Press, 1946.

Burlingame, Michael. *The Inner World of Abraham Lincoln.* Champaign: University of Illinois Press, 1994.

Carman, Harry J., and Reinhard H. Luthin. *Lincoln and the Patronage.* New York: Columbia University Press, 1943.

Chase, Salmon. *The Salmon P. Chase Papers.* John Niven, ed. Kent, OH: Kent State University Press, 1994.

Cox, LaWanda. *Lincoln and Black Freedom: A Study in Presidential Leadership.* Columbia: University of South Carolina Press, 1981.

Current, Richard N. *Lincoln and the First Shot.* Philadelphia: Lippincott, 1963.

Dean, Eric T., Jr. "Rethinking the Civil War: Beyond 'Revolutions,' 'Reconstructions,' and the 'New Social History.'" *Southern Historian* 15 (Spring 1994): 28–50.

Dennett, Tyler, ed. *Lincoln and the Civil War in the Diaries and Letters of John Hay.* New York: Dodd, Mead, 1939.

Donald, David H. *Lincoln Reconsidered: Essays on the Civil War Era.* 2d ed. New York: Vintage Books, 1956.

———. *Lincoln.* New York: Simon & Schuster, 1996.

Fehrenbacher, Don E. "Only His Stepchildren: Lincoln and the Negro." *Civil War History* 20 (December 1974): 293–310.

———. *Prelude to Greatness: Lincoln in the 1850s.* Stanford, California: Stanford University Press, 1962.

Fehrenbacher, Don E., and Virginia Fehrenbacher. *Recollected Words of Abraham Lincoln.* San Francisco: Stanford University Press, 1996.

Foner, Eric. *Free Soil, Free Labor, Free Men: The Ideology of the Republican Party Before the Civil War.* New York: Oxford University Press, 1970.

Forgie, George B. *Patricide in the House Divided: A Psychological Interpretation of Lincoln and His Age.* New York: Norton, 1979.

Franklin, John Hope. *The Emancipation Proclamation.* Garden City, NY: Doubleday, 1963.

Fredrickson, George M. "A Man but Not a Brother: Abraham Lincoln and Racial Equality." *Journal of Southern History* 45 (February 1975): 39–58.

Gienapp, William. " 'Politics Seem to Enter into Everything': Political Culture in the North, 1840–1860." In *Essays on American Antebellum Politics, 1840–1860,* pp. 14–69. Edited by Stephen E. Maizlish and John J. Kushma. College Station, TX: Texas A&M University Press, 1982.

———. *The Origins of the Republican Party, 1852–1856.* New York: Oxford University Press, 1987.

Hanchett, William. *The Lincoln Murder Conspiracies.* Urbana: University of Illinois Press, 1983.

Herndon, William H., and Jesse Weik. *Herndon's Life of Lincoln: The History and Personal Recollections of Abraham Lincoln.* Edited by Paul M. Angle. New York: Albert & Charles Boni, 1930.

Holt, Michael F. *The Political Crisis of the 1850s.* New York: Norton, 1978.

Holzer, Harold, ed. *The Lincoln-Douglas Debates: The First Complete Unexpurgated Text.* New York: HarperCollins, 1993.

Hyman, Harold M. *A More Perfect Union: The Impact of Civil War and Reconstruction on the Constitution.* New York: Alfred A. Knopf, 1973.

———. "Lincoln and Equal Rights for Negroes: The Irrelevancy of the 'Wadsworth Letter.' " *Civil War History* 12 (*September* 1966): 66–73.

Jaffa, Harry V. *Crisis of the House Divided: An Interpretation of the Issues of the Lincoln-Douglas Debates.* Garden City, NY: Doubleday, 1959.

Johannsen, Robert W. *Lincoln, the South, and Slavery: The Political Dimension.* Baton Rouge: Louisiana State University Press, 1991.

Johnson, Ludwell H. "Lincoln and Equal Rights: The Authenticity of the Wadsworth Letter." *Journal of Southern History* 32 (February 1966): 83–87.

Litwack, Leon F. *Been in the Storm So Long: The Aftermath of Slavery.* New York: Alfred A. Knopf, 1979.

Long, David E. *The Jewel of Liberty: Abraham Lincoln's Re-election and the End of Slavery.* Mechanicsburg, PA: Stackpole Books, 1994.

Luthin, Reinhard H. *The First Lincoln Campaign.* Cambridge: Harvard University Press, 1944.

———. *The Real Abraham Lincoln.* Englewood Cliffs, NJ: Prentice-Hall, 1960.

Luthin, Reinhard H., and Harry J. Carmen. *Lincoln and the Patronage.* New York: Columbia University Press, 1943.

McKitrick, Eric I. "Party Politics and the Union and Confederate War Efforts." In *The*

American Party Systems: Stages of Political Development, pp. 117–151. Edited by William Nisbet Chambers and Walter Dean Burnham. New York: Oxford University Press, 1967.

Miers, Earl Schenck, ed. *Lincoln Day by Day: A Chronology, 1809–1865.* Washington, D.C.: Lincoln Sesquicentennial Commission, 1960.

Neely, Mark E., Jr. *The Abraham Lincoln Encyclopedia.* New York: McGraw-Hill, 1982.

———. *The Fate of Liberty: Abraham Lincoln and Civil Liberties.* New York: Oxford University Press, 1991.

Nicolay, John G., and John Hay. *Abraham Lincoln: A History.* New York: Century, 1890.

Niven, John, ed. *The Salmon P. Chase Papers.* Vol. 1: *Journals, 1829–1872.* Kent, OH: Kent State University Press, 1993.

Oates, Stephen B. *With Malice toward None: The Life of Abraham Lincoln.* New York: Harper & Row, 1977.

Paludan, Phillip S. *The Presidency of Abraham Lincoln.* Lawrence: Kansas University Press, 1994.

Peterson, Merrill D. *Lincoln in American Memory.* New York: Oxford University Press, 1994.

Potter, David. *The Impending Crisis, 1848–1861.* New York: Harper & Row, 1976.

Pressly, Thomas. *Americans Interpret Their Civil War.* Princeton, NJ: Princton University Press, 1954.

Quarles, Benjamin. *Lincoln and the Negro.* New York: Oxford University Press, 1962.

Randall, James G. *Constitutional Problems under Lincoln.* New York: Appleton, 1926.

———. *Lincoln the President: Springfield to Gettysburg.* 2 vols. New York: Dodd, Mead, 1945.

———. *Lincoln the President: Midstream.* New York: Dodd, Mead, 1953.

———, and Richard N. Current, *Lincoln the President: Last Full Measure.* New York: Dodd, Mead, 1955.

Rawley, James A. *Turning Points of the Civil War.* Lincoln: University of Nebraska Press, 1966.

Silbey, Joel. *The American Political Nation, 1838–1893.* Stanford: Stanford University Press, 1991.

Strozier, Charles B. *Lincoln's Quest for Union: Public and Private Meanings.* New York: Basic Books, 1982.

Thomas, Benjamin P. *Abraham Lincoln: A Biography.* New York: Alfred A. Knopf, 1952.

Thomas, Benjamin P. *Portrait for Posterity: Lincoln and the Biographers.* New Brunswick, NJ: Rutgers University Press, 1947.

Weik, Jesse W., and William H. Herndon. *Herndon's Lincoln: The True Story of A Great Life.* New York: Brentano's, 1889.

Welles, Gideon. *Diary of . . . , Secretary of the Navy under Lincoln and Johnson.* 3 vols. Boston: Houghton Mifflin, 1911.

Williams, Kenneth P. *Lincoln Finds a General: A Military Study of the Civil War.* 5 vols. New York: Macmillan, 1949–1959.

Williams, T. Harry. *Lincoln and His Generals.* New York: Alfred A. Knopf, 1952.

Wilson, Edmund. *Patriotic Gore: Studies in the Literature of the American Civil War.* New York: Oxford University Press, 1966.

Zornow, William Frank. *Lincoln & the Party Divided.* Norman: University of Oklahoma Press, 1954.

17

Jefferson Davis

Michael B. Ballard

Jefferson Davis manuscript material is scattered in repositories from the East to the West Coast. Some of the more important Davis collections are at the University of Alabama Library; Duke University Library; Library of Congress; Museum of the Confederacy; National Archives (Record Group 109, which contains numerous Confederate records); Transylvania University Library; Mississippi Department of Archives and History; Louisiana Historical Association Collection housed at Tulane University; Filson Club collection, Louisville, Kentucky; Miami of Ohio University Library (in the Samuel W. Richey Collection); and Rice University Library. Detailed information on Davis manuscripts can be found in the *National Union Catalog of Manuscripts Collections* (1964–), a multivolume compilation of largely unpublished holdings in libraries and other repositories throughout the United States.

Fortunately for the Davis scholar, the Rice University and the Jefferson Davis Association/Jefferson Davis Papers Project has resulted in the collection, compilation, and publication of most known pertinent Davis material. The first volume of the *Papers of Jefferson Davis* (1971), edited by Haskell M. Monroe, Jr., and James T. McIntosh, covers the years 1808–1840 and includes Davis's autobiography written shortly before his death and a Davis genealogy chart. The first volume also set the pattern for future volumes, featuring a chronology and, most important, solid scholarship. Later volumes include pertinent items not included in the proper time frame of previous volumes. Volume 2 (1974), edited by James McIntosh, includes items from June 1841 to July 1846; volume 3 (1981), edited by McIntosh, for July 1846 to December 1848; volume 4 (1983), edited by Lynda Lasswell Crist, for 1849 to 1852; volume 5 (1985), edited by

Crist and Mary Seaton Dix, for 1853 to 1855; volume 6 (1989), edited by Crist and Dix, for 1856 to 1860; and volume 7 (1992), edited by Crist and Dix, for 1861. Each volume of the series is indexed.

An older, much less inclusive, published set of Davis papers is Dunbar Rowland, ed., *Jefferson Davis, Constitutionalist: His Letters, Papers, and Speeches* (1923), a ten-volume compilation. Volumes 5 through 10 contain documents for that portion of Davis's life not yet covered by the *Papers of Jefferson Davis* project. A comprehensive index is in volume 10.

Another useful published compilation of Davis papers is Hudson Strode, ed., *Jefferson Davis: Private Letters, 1823–1889* (1966). Included are letters that at the time were still in the possession of Davis descendants (most, if not all, have since been deposited in the university libraries of Alabama and Transylvania). Strode, a sympathetic Davis biographer, devotes special attention to the reproduction of letters between Davis and his wife, Varina Howell Davis. Strode did, however, delete portions of the letters without indicating where the deletions occurred.

Davis's Civil War papers are included in *War of the Rebellion: A Compilation of the Official Records of the Union and Confederate Armies* (1880–1901) and the *Official Records of the Union and Confederate Navies in the War of the Rebellion* (1894–1927). Another published collection of Confederate documents that includes Davis papers is James D. Richardson, ed., *The Messages and Papers of Jefferson Davis and the Confederacy, including the Diplomatic Correspondence, 1861–1865* (1966). For other Davis war-related information, see *Journal of the Congress of the Confederate States of America, 1861–1865* (1904–1905), and Charles W. Ramsdell, ed., *Laws and Joint Resolutions of the Last Session of the Confederate Congress (November 7, 1864–March 18, 1865), Together with the Secret Acts of Previous Congresses* (1941).

Among other published primary sources on Davis, there are several significant volumes. Davis wrote his account of his presidency, *The Rise and Fall of the Confederate Government* (1881). Ponderous and argumentative, Davis's volumes defend the theoretical right of secession and the actions of his unpopular friends, Braxton Bragg for example, and attack his enemies like Joseph E. Johnston. Varina Davis's *Jefferson Davis, Ex-President of the Confederate States of America: A Memoir by His Wife* (1890), is more balanced and points out some of Davis's critical shortcomings as president.

Several important memoirs by Confederate government officials provide key insights into the operations of the government and Davis's role as president. Edward Younger, ed., *Inside the Confederate Government: The Diary of Robert Garlick Hill Kean* (1957), is valuable. Kean, chief of the Confederate War Bureau, was an intelligent observer of events in Richmond. J. B. Jones, an opinionated clerk in the War Department, wrote the valuable *A Rebel War Clerk's Diary at the Confederate States Capital* (1935), although some historians believe that Jones may have included material written with the benefit of hindsight. Ordnance Bureau chief Josiah Gorgas's well-written diary has been published under the title, *The Civil War Diary of General Josiah Gorgas,* edited by Frank E. Vandiver (1947). Walter F. McCaleb edited and published Confederate postmaster general John H. Reagan's *Memoirs with Special References to Secession and the Civil War* (1906), which contains significant observations of Davis.

Confederate secretary of the navy Stephen R. Mallory's papers and diaries in the Southern Historical Collection, University of North Carolina at Chapel Hill, are important sources on the Davis presidency. Part of the material was published under the title "Last Days of the Confederate Government," *McClure's Magazine* (1900).

Valuable material on Davis can also be found in the various volumes of *Confederate Veteran Magazine* (1893–1932) and the *Southern Historical Society Papers* (1876–1959). The latter contains session minutes of the Confederate Congress. Indexes are available to both: Louis H. Manarin, ed., *Cumulative Index, the Confederate Veteran Magazine, 1893–1932* (1986), and James I. Robertson, ed., *An Index-Guide to the Southern Historical Society Papers, 1876–1959* (1980).

Biographies of Jefferson Davis have been many, the most recent being the most distinguished, though several of the older works are useful for a variety of reasons. Edward A. Pollard's *Life of Jefferson Davis, with a Secret History of the Southern Confederacy . . .* (1869) was written by the wartime editor of the *Richmond Examiner.* Pollard was a political opponent of Davis and a very vocal critic of administration policies. William E. Dodd's 1907 *Jefferson Davis* was the first scholarly biography of Davis but suffers from the fact that many Davis sources were not yet available. Robert McElroy's two-volume *Jefferson Davis: The Unreal and the Real* (1937) is at times superficial but was probably the most thorough account of Davis's life up to that time. McElroy was eventually surpassed by Hudson Strode's three-volume *Jefferson Davis* (1955–1964). Beautifully written, Strode's volumes are nevertheless marred by a blind partisanship that attempts to transform Davis into an inerrant icon. Clement Eaton's 1977 *Jefferson Davis* is a solid, scholarly effort, but he devotes only a few pages to Davis's postwar years. The most recent Davis biographer, William C. Davis, has produced the most impressive work to date, *Jefferson Davis: The Man and His Hour* (1991). Author Davis offers an interesting interpretation that those aspects of Jefferson Davis's personality that have made him an enigma to most scholars were in fact common personality characteristics that were merely exaggerated in Davis's case. The biography is not definitive because it suffers from the same problem, albeit to a lesser extent, as Eaton's in that Davis's significant postwar years are not examined in depth.

Aside from his biographers, historians have rarely treated Davis's antebellum years. The exceptions are Walter L. Fleming's dated work on Davis's years at the United States Military Academy, *Jefferson Davis at West Point* (1910). Studies of Davis and the Mexican War include Joseph E. Chance, *Jefferson Davis's Mexican War Regiment* (1991), and Lynda J. Lasswell's "The First Regiment of Mississippi Infantry in the Mexican War and Letters of Jefferson Davis Concerning the War'' (1969). Davis's senatorial years are analyzed by Lynda Lass-well Crist in ''A 'Duty Man': Jefferson Davis as Senator'' (1989). On Davis's term as secretary of war, see David Sansing, ''A Happy Interlude: Jefferson Davis and the War Department'' (1989). For the history of Davis's pre–Civil War home see Frank Edgar Everett, Jr., *Brierfield, Plantation Home of Jefferson Davis* (1971).

Davis's Civil War years have been examined much more thoroughly. The debate on Davis's success, or lack thereof, in putting together a Confederate nation persists. Those who find Davis effective and innovative include Emory M. Thomas, *The Confederacy as a Revolutionary Experience* (1971), and Frank E. Vandiver, *Jefferson Davis and the Confederate State,* (1964). Holding the opposite view that Davis failed in his efforts to forge a united Confederacy are Paul D. Escott, *After Secession: Jefferson Davis and the Failure of Confederate Nationalism* (1978), and Douglas B. Ball, *Financial Failure and Confederate Defeat* (1991).

The problems of creating a nation were symbolized in Davis's often troubled and contemptuous relationship with state governors and the Confederate vice president, Alexander H. Stephens. Pertinent studies include two studies of ob-streperous governors, *Joseph E. Brown of Georgia* by Joseph H. Parks (1977), and *The Confederacy and Zeb Vance* by Richard E. Yates (1958). For more insights on the governors and Davis, see W. Buck Yearns, ed., *The Confederate Governors* (1985), and Janet E. Kaufman's ''Sentinels on the Watchtower: The Confederate Governors and the Davis Administration'' (1964). See also the classic *State Rights in the Confederacy,* by Frank Lawrence Owsley (1925).

On the Stephens-Davis feud, see Davis's The *Rise and Fall of the Confederate Government* (1881) and Stephens's *A Constitutional View of the Late War between the States . . .* (1868–1870). For a scholarly treatment, see James Z. Rabun's ''Alexander H. Stephens and Jefferson Davis'' (1953).

Other notable works on Davis and dissension in the Confederacy are Georgia L. Tatum, *Disloyalty in the Confederacy* (1934); Ella Lonn, *Desertion during the Civil War* (1928); William C. Harris, *William Woods Holden: Firebrand of North Carolina Politics* (1987); Horace W. Raper, *William W. Holden: North Carolina's Political Enigma* (1985); and Mark E. Neely, *Confederate Bastille: Jefferson Davis and Civil Liberties* (1993).

There is an abundance of sources on Jefferson Davis and his cabinet, although a new study is needed. General works include Burton J. Hendrick, *Statesmen of the Lost Cause: Jefferson Davis and His Cabinet* (1939), and Rembert Patrick, *Jefferson Davis and His Cabinet* (1944). Other information on the interaction between Davis and his cabinet includes significant works by and on specific cabinet members. There are studies of the four secretaries of war: William C. Harris, *Leroy Pope Walker: Confederate Secretary of War* (1962), William C. Davis, *Breckinridge: Statesman, Soldier, Symbol* (1974), Archer Jones, ''Some Aspects of George W. Randolph's Service as Confederate Secretary'' (1960), and Roy W. Curry, ''James A. Seddon: A Southern Prototype'' (1955). Other significant works are: Joseph T. Durkin, *Stephen R. Mallory: Confederate Navy Chief* (1954); Eli N. Evans's study of Judah P. Benjamin, who served in various posts, as first attorney general and most notably as secretary of state, *Judah P. Benjamin: The Jewish Confederate* (1988); Robert D. Meade, "The Relations between Judah P. Benjamin and Jefferson Davis" (1939); William Y. Thompson's biography of the first Confederate secretary of state, *Robert Toombs of Georgia* (1966); Henry H. Simms's study of another secretary of state, *Life of Robert M. T. Hunter: A Study in Sectionalism and Secession* (1935); and a study of one secretary of the treasury, H. D. Capers, *The Life and Times of C. G. Memminger* (1893). There is a need for a study of the other treasury secretary, George Alfred Trenholm. On Memminger and Davis see also Ball's *Financial Failure and Confederate Defeat.*

Other important studies that reflect on Davis and his bureaucracy are Younger, ed., *Inside the Confederate Government;* Vandiver, ed., *Diary of General Josiah Gorgas;* Jones, *Rebel War Clerk's Diary;* Harrison A. Trexler, "Jefferson Davis and Confederate Patronage" (1929); Paul P. Van Riper and Harry N. Scheiber, "The Confederate Civil Service" (1959); August Dietz, *The Postal Service of the Confederate States of America* (1929); Richard C. Todd, *Confederate Finance* (1954); and Charles W. Ramsdell, *Behind the Lines in the Southern Confederacy* (1944).

Information on Davis as a politician and his relationship with the Confederate Congress can be found in Frank Buckner Mallonee, Jr., "The Political Thought of Jefferson Davis" (1966); Wilfred B. Yearns, *The Confederate Congress* (1960); Thomas B. Alexander and Richard E. Beringer, *The Anatomy of the Confederate Congress: A Study of the Influence of Member Characteristics on Legislative Voting Behavior, 1861–1865* (1972); David M. Potter, "Jefferson Davis and the Political Factors in Confederate Defeat" (1962); and John Brawner Robbins, "Confederate Nationalism: Politics and Government in the Confederate South, 1861–1865" (1964).

On Davis and his foreign policy see D. P. Crook, *The North, the South and the Powers, 1861–1865* (1974); Frank L. Owsley, *King Cotton Diplomacy: Foreign Relations of the Confederate States of America* (1959); Norman B. Ferris, *The Trent Affair: A Diplomatic Crisis* (1977); and Arnold Blumburg, *The Diplomacy of the Mexican Empire, 1863–1867* (1971). On Indian affairs, see Ronald Gibson, ed., *Jefferson Davis and the Confederacy and Treaties Concluded by the Confederate States with Indian Tribes* (1977).

Davis and the Civil War press are treated in J. Cutler Andrews, *The South Reports the Civil War* (1970); Harrison A. Trexler, "The Davis Administration and the Richmond Press, 1861–1865" (1950); Robert Neil Mathis, "Freedom of the Press in the Confederacy: A Reality" (1975); and Michael B. Ballard, "Yankee Editors on Jefferson Davis" (1981).

The literature on Jefferson Davis as a military leader is overwhelming. The serious scholar must consult myriad battle histories, biographies, and technical military studies in order to grasp Davis's status in the military historiography of the Civil War. The following is but a sampling.

On Davis's problems and shortcomings as a military strategist, see Richard E. Beringer et al., *Why the South Lost the Civil War* (1986); Archer Jones, *Confederate Strategy from Shiloh to Vicksburg* (1961); Thomas L. Connelly and Archer Jones, *The Politics of Command: Factions and Ideas in Confederate Strategy* (1973); and Grady McWhiney, "Jefferson Davis and the Art of War" (1975). More lenient toward Davis are Frank E. Vandiver, *Rebel Brass: The Confederate Command System* (1956); Vandiver, "Jefferson Davis and Confederate Strategy" (1959); and William J. Cooper, Jr., "A Reassessment of Jefferson Davis as War Leader: The Case from Atlanta to Nashville" (1970).

On Davis's relationship with his generals, see Steven E. Woodworth, *Jefferson Davis and His Generals: The Failure of Confederate Command in the West* (1990), which challenges long-held tenets about certain generals and challenges the traditional interpretation that Davis was overconfident regarding his military ability. A companion volume, *Davis and Lee at War,* deals with the eastern theater. Emory M. Thomas has recently completed a biography of Robert E. Lee that in part examines Lee's relationship with Davis. There is a great need for a study of Samuel Cooper, adjutant and inspector general of the Confederacy (and its senior general). Joseph E. Johnston's *Narrative of Military Operations, Directed, during the Late War between the States* (1874) gives a one-sided view of that general's long-standing feud with Davis. For a balanced account see Craig Symonds's *Joseph E. Johnston: A Civil War Biography* (1992). Davis's cordial association with Braxton Bragg is analyzed in Woodworth's *Jefferson Davis and His Generals.* See also Grady McWhiney, *Braxton Bragg and Confederate Defeat* (1969), which takes Bragg's career through 1862. Judith Lee Hallock has completed volume 2 of the work (1991) and, like Woodworth, is more sympathetic to Bragg and Davis than McWhiney. For a fresh look at James Longstreet and Jefferson Davis, especially regarding Longstreet's role in the factionalism in the Army of Tennessee, see Woodworth, *Jefferson Davis and His Generals,* and also Jeffry D. Wert, *General James Longstreet, The Confederacy's Most Controversial Soldier: A Biography* (1993). General works on Confederate armies that contain useful information on Davis and his generals include Douglas Southall Freeman's classic, *Lee's Lieutenants: A Study in Command* (1942–1944), and Thomas L. Connelly's equally impressive two-volume study of the Army of Tennessee: *Army of the Heartland: The Army of Tennessee, 1861–1862* (1967), and *Autumn of Glory: The Army of Tennessee, 1862–1865* (1971). See also Connelly and Archer Jones, *The Politics of Command.*

The effect of Davis's ill health on his war performance has long been debated by historians. For an overview of his problems, see Harris D. Riley, Jr., "Jefferson Davis and His Health: June, 1808–December, 1860, Part I," and "Jefferson Davis and His Health: January, 1861–December, 1889, Part II" (1987). Both of Woodworth's books as well as Davis, *Jefferson Davis,* examine Davis's health in detail.

The collapse and retreat of the Confederate government and Davis's role therein has received scattered attention through the years. Burke Davis's *The Long Surrender* (1985) details the retreat and the fate of Davis and the cabinet. Michael B. Ballard in *A Long Shadow: Jefferson Davis and the Final Days of the Confederacy* (1986) focuses on Davis's symbolic role during the retreat and resulting effects on his postwar image. A dated but still useful work is A. J. Hanna, *Flight into Oblivion* (1938). On Davis's capture by Union cavalry see David R. Barbee, "The Capture of Jefferson Davis" (1951); Chester D. Bradley, "Was Jefferson Davis Disguised as a Woman When Captured?" (1954); and Burton N. Harrison (Davis's personal secretary), "The Capture of Jefferson Davis" (1883).

Davis's imprisonment after his capture is detailed in John J. Craven's *Prison Life of Jefferson Davis . . .* (1866). A recent edition of Craven's book, edited by Edward K. Eckert and entitled *"Fiction Distorting Fact": The Prison Life, Annotated by Jefferson Davis* (1987), contains comments written by Davis in the margins of his copy of Craven's book. Eckert also provides background commentary. (There is controversy regarding the authorship of Craven's book; see Eckert and also Ballard, *A Long Shadow*.) Other useful sources include Charles Minor Blackford, *The Trials and Trial of Jefferson Davis* (1901), and James E. Walmsley, ed., "Some Unpublished Letters of Burton N. Harrison" (1904).

There is still much study needed of Davis's postwar years and his emergence as a figure in the Lost Cause movement that swept the South in the latter part of the nineteenth century and remains much in evidence. Aside from sparse coverage in the Davis biographies, a sampling of available literature includes Charles Reagan Wilson, *Baptized in Blood: The Religion of the Lost Cause, 1865–1920* (1980); Ballard, *A Long Shadow*; J. William Jones, *The Davis Memorial Volume; or, Our Dead President, Jefferson Davis, and the World's Tribute to His Memory* (1890); Thomas Connelly and Barbara L. Bellows, *God and General Longstreet: The Lost Cause and the Southern Mind* (1982); Michael B. Ballard, "Cheers for Jefferson Davis" (1981); Rollin G. Osterweis, *The Myth of the Lost Cause, 1865–1900* (1973); and the volume that gave the Lost Cause identity and direction, Edward A. Pollard's *The Lost Cause: A New Southern History of the War of the Confederates* (1866).

BIBLIOGRAPHY

Addey, Markinfield. *Life and Imprisonment of Jefferson Davis, together with the Life and Military Career of Stonewall Jackson.* New York: M. Doolady, 1866.

Alexander, Thomas B., and Richard E. Beringer. *The Anatomy of the Confederate Congress: A Study of the Influence of Member Characteristics on Legislative Voting Behavior, 1861–1865.* Nashville: Vanderbilt University Press, 1972.

Alfriend, Frank H. *Life of Jefferson Davis.* Philadelphia: National Publishing Company, 1868.

Andrews, J. Cutler. *The South Reports the Civil War.* Princeton, NJ: Princeton University Press, 1970.

Ball, Douglas B. *Financial Failure and Confederate Defeat.* Champaign: University of Illinois Press, 1991.

Ballard, Michael B. "Cheers for Jefferson Davis." *American History Illustrated* 16 (May 1981): 8–15.

———. *A Long Shadow: Jefferson Davis and the Final Days of the Confederacy.* Jackson: University Press of Mississippi, 1986.

———. "Yankee Editors on Jefferson Davis." *Journal of Mississippi History* 43 (November 1981): 316–332.

Barbee, David R. "The Capture of Jefferson Davis." *Tyler's Quarterly History and Genealogical Magazine* 32 (April 1951): 282–295.

Beringer, Richard E., et al. *Why the South Lost the Civil War.* Athens: University of Georgia Press, 1986.

Blackford, Charles Minor. *The Trials and Trial of Jefferson Davis.* Lynchburg, VA: J. P. Bell Company, 1901.

Blumburg, Arnold. *The Diplomacy of the Mexican Empire, 1863–1867.* Philadelphia: American Philosophical Society, 1971.

Bradley, Chester D. "Was Jefferson Davis Disguised as a Woman When Captured?" *Journal of Mississippi History* 36 (August 1954): 243–268.

Canfield, Cass. *The Iron Will of Jefferson Davis.* New York: Harcourt Brace Jovanovich, 1978.

Capers, H. D. *The Life and Times of C. G. Memminger.* Richmond, VA: Everett Waddey Company, 1893.

Chance, Joseph E. *Jefferson Davis's Mexican War Regiment.* Jackson: University Press of Mississippi, 1991.

Confederate Veteran Magazine. 1893–1932.

Connelly, Thomas L. *Army of the Heartland: The Army of Tennessee, 1861–1862.* Baton Rouge: LSU Press, 1967.

———. *Autumn of Glory: The Army of Tennessee, 1862–1865.* Baton Rouge: LSU Press, 1971.

Connelly, Thomas L., and Barbara L. Bellows. *God and General Longstreet: The Lost Cause and the Southern Mind.* Baton Rouge: LSU Press, 1982.

Connelly, Thomas L., and Archer Jones. *The Politics of Command: Factions and Ideas in Confederate Strategy.* Baton Rouge: LSU Press, 1973.

Cooper, William J., Jr. "A Reassessment of Jefferson Davis as War Leader: The Case from Atlanta to Nashville." *Journal of Southern History* 36 (May 1970): 189–204.

Craven, John J. *Prison Life of Jefferson Davis . . .* New York: Carleton, 1866.

Crist, Lynda Lasswell. "A 'Duty Man': Jefferson Davis as Senator." *Journal of Mississippi History* 51 (November 1989): 281–196.

———, ed. *Papers of Jefferson Davis. Vol. 4: 1849–1852.* Vol. 4. Baton Rouge: LSU Press, 1983.

Crist, Lynda Lasswell, and Mary Seaton Dix, eds. *Papers of Jefferson Davis. Vol. 5: 1853–1855.* Baton Rouge: LSU Press, 1985.

———, eds. *Papers of Jefferson Davis. Vol. 6: 1856–1860.* Baton Rouge: LSU Press, 1989.

———, eds. *Papers of Jefferson Davis. Vol. 7: 1861.* Baton Rouge: LSU Press, 1992.

Crook, D. P. *The North, the South and the Powers, 1861–1865*. New York: Wiley, 1974.

Curry, Roy W. "James A. Seddon: A Southern Prototype." *Virginia Magazine of History and Biography* 63 (April 1955): 122–150.

Cutting, Elisabeth. *Jefferson Davis: Political Soldier*. New York: Dodd, Mead, 1930.

Davis, Burke. *The Long Surrender*. New York: Random House, 1985.

Davis, Jefferson. Manuscripts.

University of Alabama Library, Tuscaloosa, Alabama

Duke University Library, Durham, North Carolina

Filson Club Collection, Louisville, Kentucky

Library of Congress

Louisiana Historical Association, Tulane University Library, New Orleans, Louisiana

Miami (Ohio) University Library, Oxford, Ohio

Mississippi Department of Archives and History, Jackson

Museum of the Confederacy, Richmond, Virginia

National Archives

Rice University Library, Houston, Texas

Transylvania University Library, Lexington, Kentucky

———. *The Rise and Fall of the Confederate Government*. 2 vols. New York: D. Appleton and Company, 1881.

Davis, Varina. *Jefferson Davis, Ex-President of the Confederate States of America: A Memoir by His Wife*. 2 vols. New York: Belford Company, 1890.

Davis, William C. *Breckinridge: Statesman, Soldier, Symbol*. Baton Rouge: LSU Press, 1974.

———. *Jefferson Davis: The Man and His Hour*. New York: HarperCollins, 1991.

Dietz, August. *The Postal Service of the Confederate States of America*. Richmond, VA: Dietz Press, 1929.

Dodd, William E. *Jefferson Davis*. Philadelphia: G. W. Jacobs and Company, 1907.

Durkin, Joseph T. *Stephen R. Mallory: Confederate Navy Chief*. Chapel Hill: University of North Carolina Press, 1954.

Eaton, Clement. *Jefferson Davis*. New York: Free Press, 1977.

Eckenrode, Hamilton J. *Jefferson Davis: President of the South*. New York: Macmillan, 1923.

Eckert, Edward K., ed. *"Fiction Distorting Fact": The Prison Life, Annotated by Jefferson Davis*. Macon, GA: Mercer University Press, 1987.

Escott, Paul D. *After Secession: Jefferson Davis and the Failure of Confederate Nationalism*. Baton Rouge: LSU Press, 1978.

Evans, Eli N. *Judah P. Benjamin: The Jewish Confederate*. New York: Free Press, 1988.

Everett, Frank Edgar, Jr. *Brierfield, Plantation Home of Jefferson Davis*. Hattiesburg: University and College Press of Mississippi, 1971.

Ferris, Norman B. *The Trent Affair: A Diplomatic Crisis*. Knoxville: University of Tennessee Press, 1977.

Fleming, Walter L. *Jefferson Davis at West Point*. Baton Rouge: LSU Press, 1910.

Freeman, Douglas Southall. *Lee's Lieutenants: A Study in Command*. 3 vols. New York: C. Scribner's Sons, 1942–1944.

Gibson, Ronald, ed. *Jefferson Davis and the Confederacy and Treaties Concluded by the Confederate States with Indian Tribes*. Dobbs Ferry, NY: Oceana Publications, 1977.

Gordon, Armistead C. *Jefferson Davis*. New York: Charles Scribner's Sons, 1918.

Hallock, Judith Lee. *Braxton Bragg and Confederate Defeat.* Vol. 2. Tuscaloosa: University of Alabama Press, 1991.

Hanna, A. J. *Flight into Oblivion.* Richmond: Johnson Publishing Company, 1938.

Harris, William C. *Leroy Pope Walker: Confederate Secretary of War.* Tuscaloosa, AL: Confederate Publishing Company, 1962.

―――. *William Woods Holden: Firebrand of North Carolina Politics.* Baton Rouge: LSU Press, 1987.

Harrison, Burton N. "The Capture of Jefferson Davis." *Century Magazine* 27 (November 1883): 130–145.

Hendrick, Burton J. *Statesmen of the Lost Cause: Jefferson Davis and His Cabinet.* New York: Literary Guild of America, 1939.

Johnston, Joseph E. *Narrative of Military Operations, Directed, during the Late War between the States.* New York: D. Appleton and Company, 1874.

Jones, Archer. *Confederate Strategy from Shiloh to Vicksburg.* Baton Rouge: LSU Press, 1961.

―――. "Some Aspects of George W. Randolph's Service as Confederate Secretary of War." *Journal of Southern History* 26 (August 1960): 299–314.

Jones, J. B. *A Rebel War Clerk's Diary at the Confederate States Capital.* 2 vol. Edited by Howard Swiggett. New York: Old Hickory Bookshop, 1935.

Jones, J. William. *The Davis Memorial Volume; or, Our Dead President, Jefferson Davis, and the World's Tribute to His Memory.* Richmond, VA: B. F. Johnson, 1890.

Journal of the Congress of the Confederate States of America, 1861–1865. 7 vols. Washington, D.C.: Government Printing Office, 1904–1905.

Kaufman, Janet E. "Sentinels on the Watchtower: The Confederate Governors and the Davis Administration." Ph.D. diss., Rice University, 1964.

Langheim, Eric. *Jefferson Davis, Patriot: A Biography.* New York: Vantage Press, 1962.

Lasswell, Lynda J. "The First Regiment of Mississippi Infantry in the Mexican War and Letters of Jefferson Davis Concerning the War." Master's thesis, Rice University, 1969.

Lonn, Ella. *Desertion during the Civil War.* New York, London: Century Company, 1928.

Mallonee, Frank Buckner, Jr. "The Political Thought of Jefferson Davis." Ph.D. diss., Emory University, 1966.

Mallory, Stephen R., "Last Days of the Confederate Government." *McClure's Magazine* 16 (December 1900): 99–107, 239–248.

―――. Papers and Diaries. Southern Historical Collection. University of North Carolina at Chapel Hill Library.

Manarin, Louis H., ed. *Cumulative Index, The Confederate Veteran Magazine, 1893–1932.* 3 vols. Wilmington, NC: Broadfoot Publishing Company, 1986.

Mathis, Robert Neil. "Freedom of the Press in the Confederacy: A Reality." *Historian* 37 (August 1975): 633–648.

McElroy, Robert. *Jefferson Davis: The Unreal and the Real.* 2 vols. New York: Harper and Brothers, 1937.

McIntosh, James T., ed. *Papers of Jefferson Davis. Vol. 2: June 1841–July 1846.* Baton Rouge: LSU Press, 1974.

―――. *Papers of Jefferson Davis. Vol. 3: July 1846–December 1848.* Baton Rouge: LSU Press, 1981.

McWhiney, Grady. *Braxton Bragg and Confederate Defeat*. Vol. 1. New York: Columbia University Press, 1969.

———. "Jefferson Davis and the Art of War." *Civil War History* 21 (June 1975): 101–112.

Meade, Robert D. "The Relations between Judah P. Benjamin and Jefferson Davis." *Journal of Southern History* 5 (November 1939): 468–478.

Monroe, Haskell M., Jr., and James T. McIntosh, eds. *Papers of Jefferson Davis. Vol. 1: 1808–1840*. Baton Rouge: LSU Press, 1971.

National Union Catalog of Manuscript Collections. Washington, D.C.: Library of Congress, 1964–.

Neely, Mark E. *Confederate Bastille: Jefferson Davis and Civil Liberties*. Milwaukee: Marquette University Press, 1993.

Official Records of the Union and Confederate Navies in the War of the Rebellion. 35 vols. Washington, D.C.: Government Printing Office, 1894–1927.

Osterweis, Rollin G. *The Myth of the Lost Cause, 1865–1900*. Hamden, CT: Archon Books, 1973.

Owsley, Frank Lawrence. *King Cotton Diplomacy: Foreign Relations of the Confederate States of America*. Rev. ed. Chicago: University of Chicago Press, 1959.

———. *State Rights in the Confederacy*. Chicago: University of Chicago Press, 1925.

Parks, Joseph H. *Joseph E. Brown of Georgia*. Baton Rouge: LSU Press, 1977.

Patrick, Rembert. *Jefferson Davis and His Cabinet*. Baton Rouge: LSU Press, 1944.

Pollard, Edward A. *Life of Jefferson Davis, with a Secret History of the Southern Confederacy . . .* Philadephia: National Publishing Company, 1869.

———. *The Lost Cause: A New Southern History of the War of the Confederates . . .* New York: E. B. Treat, 1866.

Potter, David M. "Jefferson Davis and the Political Factors in Confederate Defeat." In David Donald, ed. *Why the North Won the Civil War*. Baton Rouge: LSU Press, 1960.

Rabun, James Z. "Alexander H. Stephens and Jefferson Davis." *American Historical Review* 58 (January 1953): 290–321.

Ramsdell, Charles W. *Behind the Lines in the Southern Confederacy*. Baton Rouge: LSU Press, 1944.

———, ed. *Laws and Joint Resolutions of the Last Session of the Confederate Congress (November 7, 1864–March 18, 1865), Together with the Secret Acts of Previous Congresses*. Durham, NC: Duke University Press, 1941.

Raper, Horace W. *William W. Holden: North Carolina's Political Enigma*. Chapel Hill: University of North Carolina Press, 1985.

Reagan, John H., *Memoirs with Special References to Secession and the Civil War*. Edited by Walter F. McCaleb. New York and Washington: Neale Publishing Company, 1906.

Richardson, James D., ed. *The Messages and Papers of Jefferson Davis and the Confederacy, including the Diplomatic Correspondence, 1861–1865*. 2 vols. New York: Chelsea House–R. Hector, 1966.

Riley, Harris D., Jr. "Jefferson Davis and His Health: June, 1808–December, 1860, Part I," and "Jefferson Davis and His Health, January, 1861–December, 1889, Part II." *Journal of Mississippi History* 49 (August, November 1987): 179–202, 261–287.

Robbins, John Brawner. "Confederate Nationalism: Politics and Government in the Confederate South, 1861–1865." Ph.D. diss., Rice University, 1964.

Robertson, James I., ed. *An Index-Guide to the Southern Historical Society Papers, 1876– 1959.* 2 vols. Millwood, NY: Kraus International Publications, 1980.

Rowland, Dunbar, ed. *Jefferson Davis, Constitutionalist: His Letters, Papers and Speeches.* 10 vols. Jackson: Mississippi Department of Archives and History, 1923.

Sansing, David. "A Happy Interlude: Jefferson Davis and the War Department." *Journal of Mississippi History* 51 (November 1989): 297–312.

Schaff, Morris. *Jefferson Davis: His Life and Personality.* Boston: J. W. Luce and Company, 1922.

Simms, Henry H. *Life of Robert M. T. Hunter: A Study in Sectionalism and Secession.* Richmond, VA: William Byrd Press, 1935.

Southern Historical Society Papers, 1876–1959. Millwood, NY: Kraus Reprint Company, 1977.

Stephens, Alexander H. *A Constitutional View of the Late War between the States . . .* 2 vols. Philadelphia: National Publishing Company, 1868–1870.

Strode, Hudson. *Jefferson Davis.* Vol. 1: *American Patriot, 1808–1861.* Vol. 2: *Confederate President.* Vol. 3: *Tragic Hero, the Last Twenty-five Years, 1864–1869.* New York: Harcourt, Brace & World, 1955–1964.

———, ed. *Jefferson Davis: Private Letters, 1823–1889.* New York: Harcourt, Brace & World, 1966.

Symonds, Craig L. *Joseph E. Johnston: A Civil War Biography.* New York: W. W. Norton, 1992.

Tate, Allen. *Jefferson Davis: His Rise and Fall.* New York: Minton, Balch, and Company, 1929.

Tatum, Georgia L. *Disloyalty in the Confederacy.* Chapel Hill: University of North Carolina Press, 1934.

Thomas, Emory M. *The Confederacy as a Revolutionary Experience.* Englewood Cliffs, NJ: Prentice-Hall, 1971.

Thompson, William Y. *Robert Toombs of Georgia.* Baton Rouge: LSU Press, 1966.

Todd, Richard C. *Confederate Finance.* Athens: University of Georgia Press, 1954.

Trexler, Harrison A. "The Davis Administration and the Civil War Press, 1861–1865." *Journal of Southern History* 16 (May 1950): 177–195.

———. "Jefferson Davis and Confederate Patronage." *South Atlantic Quarterly* 27 (January 1929): 45–58.

Vandiver, Frank E. "Jefferson Davis and Confederate Strategy." In Vandiver and Avery O. Craven, eds. *The American Tragedy: The Civil War in Retrospect.* Hampden-Sydney, VA: Hampden-Sydney College Press, 1959.

———. *Jefferson Davis and the Confederate State.* Oxford, Eng.: Clarendon Press, 1964.

———. *Rebel Brass: The Confederate Command System.* Baton Rouge: LSU Press, 1956.

———, ed. *The Civil War Diary of General Josiah Gorgas.* Tuscaloosa: University of Alabama Press, 1947.

Van Riper, Paul P., and Harry N. Scheiber. "The Confederate Civil Service." *Journal of Southern History* 25 (November 1959): 448–470.

Walmsley, James E., ed. "Some Unpublished Letters of Burton N. Harrison." In Franklin

L. Riley, ed. *Publications of the Mississippi Historical Society,* 3:81–85 Oxford, MS: Mississippi Historical Society, 1904.

War of the Rebellion: A Compilation of the Official Records of the Union and Confederate Armies. 128 vols. Washington, D.C.: Government Printing Office, 1880–1901.

Wert, Jeffry D. *General James Longstreet, The Confederacy's Most Controversial Soldier: A Biography.* New York: Simon and Schuster, 1993.

Wilson, Charles Reagan. *Baptized in Blood: The Religion of the Lost Cause, 1865–1920.* Athens: University of Georgia Press, 1980.

Winston, Robert W. *High Stakes and Hair Trigger: The Life of Jefferson Davis.* New York: H. Holt and Company, 1930.

Woodworth, Steven E. *Davis and Lee at War.* Lawrence: University Press of Kansas, 1995.

———. *Jefferson Davis and His Generals: The Failure of Confederate Command in the West.* Lawrence: University Press of Kansas, 1990.

Yates, Richard E. *The Confederacy and Zeb Vance.* Tuscaloosa, AL: Confederate Publishing Company, 1958.

Yearns, Wilfred B. *The Confederate Congress.* Athens: University of Georgia Press, 1960.

———, ed. *The Confederate Governors.* Athens: University of Georgia Press, 1985.

Younger, Edward, ed. *Inside the Confederate Government: The Diary of Robert Garlick Hill Kean.* New York: Oxford University Press, 1957.

18

Union Civilian Leaders

Alan C. Guelzo

The American Civil War was a war of civilians. The fact that 3 million or so of them happened to be in uniform was almost incidental, since the soldiers, sailors, and officers of both the Union and Confederate armies were mostly civilian volunteers who retained close contacts with their civilian social worlds, who brought truculent civilian attitudes into the ranks with them, and who fully expected to return to civilian life as soon as the shooting was over. By the same token, civilian communities in both North and South kept closely in touch with their volunteers all through the war, sustained by peak rates of literacy in both sections and by the military postal services, and nourished by newspapers whose reliance on electrical telegraphy and field correspondents helped erode the customary cognitive distance between soldiers in the field and civilians at home. Above all, the American Civil War was (as Lincoln described it) ''a people's contest'' because it was fought over domestic political issues within a republican political framework, where the consent of the governed (rather than the ambition of an aristocratic or military caste) was understood to be the ultimate arbiter. At almost any point in the war, the military conflict could have been ended by popular civilian decision, since congressional and presidential elections were held in both the North and the South in 1862, 1863, and 1864. If any of those elections had gone that way, there is very little to indicate that either Union or Confederate soldiers would have defied that determination; the only serious moment of military resistance to civilian control, after Lincoln's removal of George McClellan as commander of the Army of the Potomac, fizzled without measurable result. Hardly any other military conflict in the nineteenth century was so much a matter of civilian support, commitment, and willpower.

In the most general sense, Union civilian life has usually been treated as an aspect of the home front, a surprisingly ambiguous term, developed during World War I and suggesting both distance (a separate "front" from military combat) and a subtle claim to a sort of organized mobilization. But nothing stands out more clearly from several of the comprehensive surveys of the Northern war effort than the remarkably perfunctory sense of mobilization that prevailed throughout the war. The most outstanding recent survey of the organization of Northern society during the war, Phillip Shaw Paludan's *A People's Contest: The Union and the Civil War, 1861–1865* (1988), is extraordinarily effective in surveying the dialogue of politics and the channeling of Northern economic resources into the war effort, but nothing emerges from the narrative to suggest that any effort was made during the war to create a Northern wartime mentalité. In fact, what seems striking from Anne Rose's composite cultural portrait of Civil War–era civilians, *Victorian America and the Civil War* (1992), is the unwillingness of Northern elites or Northern bourgeois to come to terms with the war, as though it were a distant aberration that was better ignored than interpreted, while Louise Stevenson's *The Victorian Homefront: American Thought and Culture, 1860–1880* (1991) underscores the absence of any cultural unanimity about the war in the North. Curiously, it has fallen to the social and demographic historians, rather than the cultural and intellectual historians, to begin piecing together answers to the question of a Northern home front. Some of those answers came in Maris Vinovski's outstanding collection of essays, *Toward a Social History of the American Civil War* (1990), which turned the interpretive and analytical tools that historians had honed on early American life in the 1970s and 1980s onto the era of the Civil War. All seven essays in Vinovski's anthology deal with the North, and taken together they suggest a far greater degree of connection and representation between civilian and military life in the North, and in far more concrete terms, than the characters of Rose's or Stevenson's books indicate.

Social historians, however, have rarely found Civil War history, with its weakness for faddism and battle narratives, a very congenial work space. Thus, it has been easier for Civil War historians to divide up Northern civilian life into a series of separate and less comprehensive categories, which, unfortunately, also yield up less comprehensive answers than those that have generated so much debate in Confederate historical circles. None of those categories has bulked larger in the past twenty years, or yielded a richer crop of understanding, than Civil War–era political history and biography. Much of this was certainly a by-product of Eric Foner's classic *Free Soil, Free Labor, Free Men: The Ideology of the Republican Party before the Civil War* (1970), a book whose greatest novelty was the very suggestion that nineteenth-century Americans even possessed a political ideology. And perhaps because Foner's book was the first to resurrect ideology as a driving force in Civil War politics, the Republicans and their Whig predecessors have been the subject of a series of outstanding political histories. Daniel Walker Howe's group portrait of Whig "political culture'' (1979) and Thomas Brown's essays on Whig ''statesmanship'' (1985) have restored the image of the Whigs as a potent ideological force in the politics of antebellum America, while William E. Gienapp (1987), Michael Holt, (1969, 1978), William Dusinberre (1965), Erwin S. Bradley, (1964), Paul Kleppner (1979), James Rawley (1974), and Stephen Maizlish (1983) have forced us to recognize the role of nativism and regionalism in the construction of Republican politics. The Democrats have not been entirely without their remembrancers, and the work of Jean Baker (1979, 1985) and Joel Silbey (1977, 1985) offer highly useful analyses of the ideology of the Democrats in the war years.

Some of the best writing, however, has not been about political ideology but about the Northern politicians themselves. A number of published papers and diaries of Lincoln's staff and cabinet secretaries offer critical glimpses into the operation of wartime politics at the highest levels in the North, beginning with Burton J. Hendrick's survey of *Lincoln's War Cabinet* (1946) and including David Donald's *Inside Lincoln's Cabinet: The Civil War Diaries of Salmon P. Chase* (1954), Howard K. Beale's *The Diary of Gideon Welles* (1960) and *The Diary of Edward Bates* (1933), and Tyler Dennett's selection of excerpts from John Hay's diary and letters, *Lincoln and the Civil War in the Diaries and Letters of John Hay* (1939, 1972). Lincoln's premier civil servant, Secretary of State William Seward, has never enjoyed much of a reputation in Civil War history, despite having attracted a number of surprisingly admiring biographers, beginning in recent times with Glyndon Van Deusen's *William Henry Seward* (1967) and John M. Taylor's *William Henry Seward: Lincoln's Right Hand* (1991). Both Van Deusen and Taylor are unstinting in their praise of Seward as a secretary of state, but Norman Ferris, in *Desperate Diplomacy: William Henry Seward's Foreign Policy, 1861* (1976) and *The Trent Affair: A Diplomatic Crisis* (1977), is substantially less enthusiastic. Gideon Welles, the secretary of the navy, has unaccountably outshone his much more formidable counterpart, Secretary of War Edwin M. Stanton, in terms of simple volume— Beales's edition of Welles's diary, John Niven's *Gideon Welles: Lincoln's Secretary of the Navy* (1973), and Richard S. West, Jr.'s *Gideon Welles: Lincoln's Navy Department* (1953) easily take up more space than the literature on Stanton—but Stanton's great biography by Harold Hyman and Benjamin P. Thomas, *Stanton: The Life and Times of Lincoln's Secretary of War* (1962), makes up for that shortfall by being one of the finest models of Civil War biography ever written. Salmon Chase may actually have done more to carry the war to victory through his oversight of the Treasury than any other member of Lincoln's cabinet, but his forbidding and ambitious personality has been hard for even sympathetic students like Frederick Blue, John Niven, and Louis Gerteis to make likable.

Remembering how important Lincoln's career as a lawyer was to both his image and his conception of his duties as president, relatively little is at hand on the Supreme Court of the war years, apart from Carl Swisher's volume in the O. W. Holmes official history of the Court, *The Taney Period, 1836–1864*

(1974), David Silver's much older study of the Lincoln-era Court, *Lincoln's Supreme Court* (1956), and Willard King's *Lincoln's Manager: David Davis* (1960), a biography of Lincoln's political manager and Supreme Court appointee. Constitutional theory has actually received somewhat better coverage than constitutional jurists, especially in Harold Hyman's *A More Perfect Union: The Impact of the Civil War and Reconstruction on the Constitution* (1973) and Phillip S. Paludan's *A Covenant with Death: The Constitution, Law and Equality in the Civil War Era* (1975). Of all the cases to appear before the Supreme Court during the war years, none may have been more critical than the Prize Cases (which can be seen as Roger Taney's last-ditch attempt to cripple Lincoln's war-making powers) and they have been treated in detail in Stuart Bernath, *Squall across the Atlantic: The American Civil War Prize Cases* (1970) and in Ludwell H. Johnson's "Abraham Lincoln and the Development of Presidential War-making Powers: Prize Cases (1863) Revisited" (1989). But the most invisible parts of the wartime administration were the 195,000 civilian employees who provided so much of the real oil to the war machine and who reaped so much of the political profit of it. Unhappily, patronage and government employment have usually been studied only as a function of political spoils, as in Harry Carman and Reinhard Luthin's *Lincoln and the Patronage* (1943), and even then generally as a footnote to the iron control Lincoln exercised over patronage during the war.

It is not often appreciated how much Congress took leadership of the war into its own hands, in terms of both domestic and war policy. Allan Bogue's *The Congressman's Civil War* (1989) is an excellent brief survey of the operation of the House of Representatives in the Thirty-seventh and Thirty-eighth Congresses, while Leonard Curry's *Blueprint for Modern America: Non-Military Legislation of the First Civil War Congress* (1968) devotes itself to a study of both houses of the Thirty-seventh Congress. But most studies of the Civil War congresses have focused on the parties, with the Republicans again taking the lion's share of the attention. The major questions in this literature have revolved around the identity of Republican factions, and the degree to which the Radical Republicans were Lincoln's allies or critics. In an earlier work, *The Earnest Men: Republicans of the Civil War Senate* (1981), Allan Bogue used a highly sophisticated analysis of roll-call votes to identify a consistent core of Senate Radicals, thus taking sides against Michael Les Benedict's contention in *A Compromise of Principle: Congressional Republicans and Reconstruction, 1863–1869* (1975) that the radicals were united only on civil rights issues. Similarly, Hans L. Trefousse has argued forcibly in *The Radical Republicans: Lincoln's Vanguard for Racial Justice* (1968) that the radicals were Lincoln's secret agents for promoting policies he could not afford to endorse openly, while T. Harry Williams had argued just as forcibly in *Lincoln and the Radicals* (1941) that Lincoln was a moderate who struggled to keep the Radicals from turning the war into a social vendetta against the South. Individual congressional biographies, especially of the Radicals, are fairly numerous: the most famous is David

Donald's two-volume biography of Charles Sumner (1961, 1970), but Henry
Winter Davis, Benjamin Wade, George W. Julian, William Pitt Fessenden,
Henry Wilson, and John P. Hale have all earned major studies of their political
lives. The most contradictory interpretations have swirled around that most contradictory congressman, Thaddeus Stevens, who has been variously interpreted
as an idealist (see Eric Foner's review essay in a special issue of *Pennsylvania
History* in April 1993 devoted to "Thaddeus Stevens and American Democracy"), a disgruntled outsider, as in Fawn Brodie's *Thaddeus Stevens: Scourge
of the South* (1959), and the "enigma" described by Richard N. Current in *Old
Thad Stevens: A Story of Ambition* (1942).

The need to deal with dissent and to give the war some kind of public shape
and meaning called forth the efforts of the North's public intellectuals, and the
best sampling of their literary labors on behalf of the Union can be found in
Frank Freidel's two volumes of *Union Pamphlets of the Civil War* (1967). The
best overall survey of Northern intellectual history in the nineteenth century is
Bruce Kuklick, *Churchmen and Philosophers: From Jonathan Edwards to John
Dewey* (1985), while D. H. Meyer's *The Instructed Conscience: The Shaping
of the American National Ethic* (1972) provides an admirable introduction to
nineteenth-century American ethics and the enthusiasm that public ethics lent to
the antislavery crusade. George M. Frederickson's *The Inner Civil War:
Northern Intellectuals and the Crisis of the Union* (1965) is still the prevailing
interpretation of the involvement of Northern intellectuals in interpreting the
Civil War, but because he focuses so extensively on the secular intellectuals and
the liberal religionists who created the United States Sanitary Commission, the
record that emerges from his book is quite a dismal one, with Northern intellectuals being long on fears for social control and remarkably short on intellectual substance. William Quentin Maxwell, *Lincoln's Fifth Wheel: The Political
History of the United States Sanitary Commission* (1956) is better than Frederickson on the details of the creation of the Sanitary Commission but misses
the elitist pretensions of the commissioners, which Frederickson documents. The
time is thus long overdue for a new intellectual history of the Civil War that
will pay attention to the far more vital areas of American intellectual life than
the fairly resultless meanderings of the New York and Boston literati of the
1860s.

One source for such a new work will be several of the recent biographies of
the standard literary figures of the mid-nineteenth century, including Stanton
Garner's *The Civil War World of Herman Melville* (1993) and Joan Hedrick's
critical biography, *Harriet Beecher Stowe* (1993). But it must also include the
far more culturally potent religious literature of mid-nineteenth Protestantism,
which was then reaching its zenith of public authority. Sidney Ahlstrom's mag-
isterial survey of American religion, *A Religious History of the American People*
(1972), devotes an unusual amount of space to the Civil War, reflecting Ahlstrom's own personal interest in the war, while James Moorhead's *American
Apocalypse: Yankee Protestants and the Civil War, 1860–1869* (1978) ad-

venturously links the allegiance of Northern evangelical Protestants to evangelical hopes that the war might be harbinger of the millennium. Victor B. Howard (1990), Richard Carwardine (1993), and John R. McKivigan (1984) link Protestant evangelicalism more directly to abolition through the takeover of evangelical denominations by antislavery factions who hoped to wed Whiggish Republicanism with public Christianity, including, in the case studied by Martin Borden (1979), to the point of campaigning during the war for a "Christian amendment" to the Constitution. There are a number of highly serviceable biographies of Civil War religious figures, such as William G. McLoughlin's *The Meaning of Henry Ward Beecher: An Essay on the Shifting Values of Mid-Victorian America, 1840–1870* (1970), Keith Hardman's *Charles Grandison Finney, 1792–1875: Revivalist and Reformer* (1987), Barbara Cross's *Horace Bushnell: Minister to a Changing America* (1958), and Richard S. Taylor's "Seeking the Kingdom: A Study in the Life of Jonathan Blanchard, 1811–1892" (1977). But getting access to many Civil War–era religious texts is still problematic, and the only useful anthology of Civil War sermon literature is David B. Chesebrough's *God Ordained This War: Sermons on the Sectional Crisis, 1830–1865* (1991). Another obvious source for developing a new intellectual history of the Civil War era will be the Northern press, whose popular print culture will need to be integrated with the high culture represented by the literati. The Civil War press has generally been treated as a rollicking story of daring journalists, snatching scoops under fire; a good deal less attention has been paid to how the press acted as a forum and a popularizer of political, religious, and intellectual debate.

If the intellectual history of the war has been poorly served so far, the history of Northern women in the war has been almost invisible until very recently. For many years, Mary Elizabeth Massey's *Bonnet Brigades: American Women and the Civil War* (1966) was almost the only women's history of the war era consulted by Civil War historians, and even then Massey concentrated mostly on providing a "contribution" history, dealing only with the contribution women made to what is otherwise described as a predominantly male-gendered event. Three decades after Massey, American women's history has become its own separate department within American studies, and it has now begin to generate its own subdepartment in Civil War studies as well. One mark of the increasing sophistication of gender and family studies of the Civil War era is *Divided Houses: Gender and the Civil War* (1992), a collection of essays on gender and the Civil War edited by Catherine Clinton and Nina Silber, which offers explorations of childhood, spies, nurses, divorce, and even illicit sex. Similarly, Marilyn M. Culpeper's *Trials and Triumphs: Women of the American Civil War* (1991) makes excellent use of a plethora of unpublished women's diaries and letters, although without giving them much interpretive coherence. However, in recovering a women's history of the war, it has been easiest to start at the top, with the North's most elite women. Jean H. Baker's *Mary Todd Lincoln: A Biography* (1987) offers a sympathetic reading of Mary Lincoln's life, but Bak-

er's highly optimistic reading of her has to be balanced against the highly negative testimony of many of her contemporaries, and Mark Neely, Jr., and Gerald
McMurtry returned a serious consideration of Mary Lincoln's mental stability
to front stage with the publication of *The Insanity File: The Case of Mary Todd
Lincoln* (1986). Other prominent Northern women who have received renewed
attention in the past decade include Jessie Benton Frémont, Elizabeth Cady
Stanton, Kate Chase, Abby Kelley, and Clara Barton. The study of elite women
has yielded also to comparative studies of urban and rural women during the
war, and to the publication (in a spectrum of state historical quarterlies) of the
diaries of Northern women across a broad geographical and demographic spectrum. Strangely, we have not yet seen modern critical editions of two of the
most militant Northern women's memoirs from the Civil War era: Mary Ashton
Livermore's *My Story of the War: A Woman's Narrative of Four Years Personal
Experience* (1889) and Sara Emma Edmonds's *Nurse and Spy in the Union
Army: The Adventures and Experiences of a Woman in Hospitals, Camps, and
Battlefields* (1865). The Clinton-Silber anthology, however, points the way toward an important new horizon in Civil War studies, and the way now seems
open for new work on the family, gender, and the ways in which the Civil War
created an ''upside-down'' opportunity in Northern society for women. Beyond
that, these new gender studies will have to address the larger question of the
ambiguity of the war's results for Northern women: how different their world
was from that of the Southern women studied by Drew Faust, George Rable,
and Elizabeth Fox-Genovese, and whether the ''gains'' of Northern women actually translated into anything substantial for the future.

For almost as long as womens' studies had been invisible, so had the study
of Northern African Americans, and what attention Northern blacks had earned
from the historians was almost entirely a matter of the military laurels won by
black soldiers. But the struggle of black soldiers to win freedom and dignity on
the battlefield was matched by a struggle by black Northern civilians to achieve
the same goals on the segregated streetcars and public schools of Northern cities.
Although the Northern states prided themselves on being free, their freedom was
largely a matter of economics—of ''free labor'' rather than social or political
equality. If there was any point at which Northern civilian life really became a
home front of engagement and confrontation, it was precisely over the demand
of Northern blacks after 1861 to win the same civil rights as their fellow Northerners. The story of these battles so closely parallels the civil rights struggles
of the 1950s that it is no surprise that many of the accounts of these efforts
emerged from the ''Second Reconstruction'' of the post–World War II period,
beginning with Benjamin Quarles's *The Negro in the Civil War* (1953) and *The
Black Abolitionists* (1969), and receiving their most comprehensive treatment in
James M. McPherson's *The Struggle for Equality: Abolitionists and the Negro
in the Civil War and Reconstruction* (1964). If these works reflected some of
the optimism of the modern civil rights struggle, the ambiguous results of the
era of Martin Luther King, Jr., were matched by the turn of African-American

Civil War literature toward the equally ambiguous results of the war for Northern blacks. George M. Frederickson in *The Black Image in the White Mind: The Debate on Afro-American Character and Destiny, 1817–1914* (1971), Eric Foner in *Nothing But Freedom: Emancipation and Its Legacy* (1983), and Mary Frances Berry in *Military Necessity and Civil Rights Policy: Black Citizenship and the Constitution, 1861–1868* (1977) have shown that the gains made by blacks on the civilian home front had to be made in the teeth of persistent white resistance, and many of those gains were pragmatic concessions by Northern white society made to accommodate the military necessity of using black soldiers. No other single figure among Northern black civilians was more prominent or has attracted more modern biographical attention than Frederick Douglass. In addition to Philip Foner's edition of *The Life and Writings of Frederick Douglass* (1950), Benjamin Quarles's *Frederick Douglass* (1948), Waldo E. Martin's *The Mind of Frederick Douglass* (1984), D. J. Preston's *The Young Frederick Douglass: The Maryland Years* (1980), and David Blight's *Frederick Douglass' Civil War: Keeping Faith in Jubilee* (1989) have transformed Douglass into one of the most thoroughly examined lives of the American nineteenth century. Northern black women, on the other hand, have just begun to attract attention from biographers, and only for the most prominent abolitionists like Harriet Tubman and Sojourner Truth.

The great danger of using the kinds of categories for the literature on Northern civilians that I have noted thus far is that they presuppose a homogeneous Northern society that felt the differences of race, gender, or politics more than region. That is a highly risky assumption in the still-decentralized world of the American nineteenth century; Jefferson Davis, after all, was so confident of conflict between the North and the West that he fully expected that Minnesota could be persuaded to join the Southern Confederacy, and over 500 Delawareans actually served in the Confederate armies. In just the same way that William Freehling has pointed out that the South was really a composite of at least three "Souths," so the North was a composite of "Norths" with interests and subcultures that could vary wildly based on immigration patterns, economy, demography, and religion. New England states like Vermont enjoy a reputation for being unitedly Republican, antislavery, and Unionist, and Maris Vinovskis (1990) and William Rorabaugh (1986) have found in Massachusetts towns like Newburyport and Concord that support for the war effort resulted in a remarkably even demographic spread of volunteers, so that the war turned out *not* to be a "rich man's war but a poor man's fight." However, Thomas Kemp (1990) and William Marvel (1994) have come to diametrically opposite conclusions about the "rich man's war" problem in nearby New Hampshire, with Kemp finding that Newbury and Conway enlistments showed little demographic distortion and Marvel arguing that the burden of the draft fell disproportionately on Conway's poor. Variations like these require a thorough awareness of the variegated cultural landscape of the North in the Civil War, and fortunately a number of regional studies of the wartime North promote that awareness. The

Civil War centennial observances produced a spate of regional Civil War histories for the Midwest by John Barnhart (1961), Victor Hicken (1966), Morton Rosenberg (1967), and a commissioned series of Ohio essays edited by Kenneth Wheeler (1968). The middle Atlantic states may actually have enjoyed the thickest regional historiography of all, starting with Sidney David Brummer (1967) and Mary P. Hodnett (1971) on the Civil War state politics of New York and including a wide variety of studies of Pennsylvania (Pennsylvania civilians, in fact, may have seen more civilian diaries and letters appear in scholarly print than any other Northern state in the Civil War). But New Jersey, Delaware, West Virginia, and even the Utah Territory, despite their relative smallness of size, have also generated useful Civil War histories by Norman B. Wilkinson (1966), Harold Bell Hancock (1961), Richard Orr Curry (1964), George Ellis Moore (1963), and E. B. Long (1981). Civil War urban history has all too often been swallowed up by New York City and its draft riots or Washington and its politics, but J. Matthew Gallman's *Mastering Wartime: A Social History of Philadelphia during the Civil War* (1990), along with several significant dissertations and new books by Ernest McKay (1990), Theodore J. Karamanski (1993), and Richard H. Abbott (1990), on New York, Chicago, and Boston, respectively, are beginning to open up a new urban history of the Civil War. Unfortunately, apart from the attention grabbed by war-related support agencies like the Sanitary Commission, comparatively little attention has been paid to Northern social and intellectual institutions during the war. A major but often neglected segment of this institutional history is the American college in the Civil War era, which was already on the brink of a major restructuring of collegiate curriculums and missions in the 1860s. Only Oberlin College, which was probably the most famous antislavery college in the North, has received any serious attention as a Civil War–era institution, in Nat Brandt's *The Town That Started the Civil War* (1991) and Robert Samuel Fleming's older *A History of Oberlin College from Its Foundation through the Civil War* (1943).

It is clear that Northern civilian life has not been ignored, but much of this literature lacks a clear interpretive point, and gaining a sense of focus on the Northern home front will emerge only from the way we integrate our understanding to several important issues. First, any new approach to the home front needs to return political ideology to the forefront of attention. Unlike the modern American distaste for ideology, Americans of the prepragmatism era were possessed by extraordinary ideological commitments, and the failure to attend to those commitments lies behind much of the vacuousness of Civil War historiography. That, in turn, should lead to a consideration of the problem of morale. There is, unfortunately, no counterpart in terms of civilian morale to Gerald Linderman's study of "courage" among Civil War soldiers, and in its absence, what we have mostly to contend with is the story of wartime dissent rather than what is obviously more important in the long run, and that is wartime support. If the loss of will that Richard Beringer, Herman Hattaway, Faust, and Rable attribute to various sectors of the Confederate population did so much to deflate the Confederacy, then the apparent staying power of Northern civilians certainly needs a similar degree of appreciation in explaining the triumph of the Union.

Two other areas that demand comprehensive attention for understanding morale are the connection between the war and the rise of mass industrial capitalism, and the war and the decline of public religion. Richard F. Bensel's *Yankee Leviathan: The Origins of Central State Authority in America, 1859–1879* (1990) has taken a number of the old responses to these issues and given them new life, but Bensel's work is really one of political economy rather than a history of the Civil War's impact on the economy, and though he gives the right signals, the path ahead remains to be explored. Similarly, Rose's *Victorian America and the Civil War* is correct to see Northerners use the war to subsume the rising tide of religious doubt in the nineteenth century, but Rose is a cultural historian, and her handling of religious ideology is prone to generalization and fuzziness. Finally, the current explosion in studies of gender needs to move North, so that the sophistication with which Faust, Rable, Fox-Genovese, and others are currently reading the upside-downness of gender in the Southern Civil War roles can yield the same fruits concerning Northern men and women. It will be important, however, to keep such a focus from being too preoccupied with elite northeastern women at the expense of western farmers' wives, and to avoid a similar preoccupation with free black women while missing the even more desperate story of free black men. The questions are provocative, and the resources for answering them are rich. The answers may tell more than we ever could have thought about why the North—the civilian North—won the Civil War.

BIBLIOGRAPHY

Aaron, Daniel. *The Unwritten War: American Writers and the Civil War.* New York: Knopf, 1973.

Abbott, Richard H. *Cotton and Capital: Boston Businessmen and Antislavery Reform, 1854–1868.* Amherst: University of Massachusetts Press, 1991.

Abzug, Robert H. "The Copperheads and Civil War Dissent." *Indiana Magazine of History* 66 (March 1970): 40–55.

Ahlstrom, Sidney E. *A Religious History of the American People.* New Haven: Yale University Press, 1972.

Baker, Jean H. *Affairs of Party: The Political Culture of Northern Democrats in the Mid-Nineteenth Century.* Ithaca; NY: Cornell University Press, 1983.

———. "A Loyal Opposition: Northern Democrats in the Thirty-Seventh Congress." *Civil War History* 25 (June 1979): 139–155.

———. *Mary Todd Lincoln: A Biography.* New York: Norton, 1987.

Banner, Lois W. *Elizabeth Cady Stanton: A Radical for Womens' Rights.* Boston: Little, Brown, 1980.

Barnhart, John D. "The Impact of the Civil War in Indiana." *Indiana Magazine of History* 57 (September 1961): 185–224.

Beale, Howard K., ed. *The Diary of Edward Bates.* Washington: Government Printing Office, 1933.

————. *The Diary of Gideon Welles.* New York: Norton, 1960.

Becker, Carl M. "Newspapers in Battle: The Dayton *Empire* and the Dayton *Journal* during the Civil War." *Ohio History* 99 (Winter–Spring 1990): 29–50.

Belz, Herman. *A New Birth of Freedom: The Republican Party and Freedmens' Rights, 1861–1866.* Westport, CT: Greenwood Press, 1976.

Benedict, Michael Les. *A Compromise of Principle: Congressional Republicans and Reconstruction, 1863–1869.* New York: W. W. Norton, 1975.

Bensel, Richard F. *Yankee Leviathan: The Origins of Central State Authority in America, 1859–1879.* New York: Cambridge University Press, 1990.

Beringer, Richard, Herman Hattaway, Archer Jones, and William N. Still, Jr. *Why the South Lost the Civil War.* Athens: University of Georgia Press, 1986.

Bernath, Stuart. *Squall Across the Atlantic: The American Civil War Prize Cases.* Berkeley: University of California Press, 1970.

Berry, Mary Frances. *Military Necessity and Civil Rights Policy: Black Citizenship and the Constitution, 1861–1868.* Port Washington, NY: Kennikat Press, 1977.

————. *Reconstructing the Union: Theory and Practice during the Civil War.* Ithaca, NY: Cornell University Press, 1969.

Blackett, R.J.M. "William G. Allen: The Forgotten Professor." *Civil War History* 26 (March 1980): 39–52.

Blight, David. *Frederick Douglass' Civil War: Keeping Faith in Jubilee.* Baton Rouge: Louisiana State University Press, 1989.

Bloom, Robert L. "We Never Expected a Battle: The Civilians at Gettysburg, 1863." *Pennsylvania History* 55 (October 1988): 161–200.

Blue, Frederick J. "Friends of Freedom: Lincoln, Chase and Wartime Racial Policy." *Ohio History* 102 (Summer–Autumn 1993): 85–97.

————. *Salmon Chase: A Life in Politics.* Kent, OH: Kent State University Press, 1986.

Bogue, Allan. *The Congressman's Civil War.* New York: Cambridge University Press, 1989.

————. *The Earnest Men: Republicans of the Civil War Senate.* Ithaca: Cornell University Press, 1981.

Borden, Martin. "The Christian Amendment." *Civil War History* 25 (June 1979): 156–167.

Bradley, Erwin S. *The Triumph of Militant Republicanism: A Study of Pennsylvania and Presidential Politics, 1860–1872.* Philadelphia: University of Pennsylvania Press, 1964.

Brandt, Nat. *The Town That Started the Civil War.* New York: Dell, 1991.

Bridges, Robert. "Equality Deferred: Civil Rights for Illinois Blacks, 1865–1885." *Journal of the Illinois State Historical Society* 74 (Summer 1981): 82–108.

Brodie, Fawn. *Thaddeus Stevens: Scourge of the South.* New York: Norton, 1959.

Brown, Thomas. *Politics and Statesmanship: Essays on the American Whig Party.* New York: Columbia University Press, 1985.

Browning, Orville Hickman. *The Diary of Orville Hickman Browning.* Edited by Theodore Pease and J. G. Randall. Springfield: Illinois State Historical Soceity, 1925–1933.

Brummer, Sidney David. *Political History of New York State during the Period of the Civil War.* 1910. Reprint, New York: AMS Press, 1967.

Carman, Harry, and Reinhard Luthin. *Lincoln and the Patronage.* New York: Columbia University Press, 1943.

Carwardine, Richard. *Evangelicals and Politics in Antebellum America.* New Haven: Yale University Press, 1993.

Chase, Salmon P. *Inside Lincoln's Cabinet: The Civil War Diaries of Salmon P. Chase.* Edited by David Donald. New York: Longmans, Green, 1954.

———. *The Salmon Chase Papers.* Vol. 1: *Journals, 1829–1872.* Edited by John Niven, et al. Kent, OH: Kent State University Press, 1993.

———. *The Salmon Chase Papers.* Vol. 2: *Correspondence, 1823–1857.* Edited by John Niven et al. Kent, OH: Kent State University Press, 1995.

Chesebrough, David B. *God Ordained This War: Sermons on the Sectional Crisis, 1830–1865.* Columbia: University of South Carolina Press, 1991.

Clarke, Grace Julian. *George W. Julian.* Indianapolis: Indiana Historical Society, 1923.

Clinton, Catherine, and Nina Silber, eds. *Divided Houses: Gender and the Civil War.* New York: Oxford University Press, 1992.

Coleman, Charles H, and Paul H. Spence. "The Charleston Riot, March 28, 1864." *Journal of the Illinois Historical Society* 33 (March 1940): 7–56.

Cross, Barbara. *Horace Bushnell: Minister to a Changing America.* Chicago: University of Chicago Press, 1958.

Culpeper, Marilyn M. *Trials and Triumphs: Women of the American Civil War.* East Lansing: Michigan State University Press, 1991.

Current, Richard N. *Old Thad Stevens: A Story of Ambition.* Madison: University of Wisconsin Press, 1942.

Curry, Leonard. *Blueprint for Modern America: Non-Military Legislation of the First Civil War Congress.* Nashville: Vanderbilt University Press, 1968.

Curry, Richard Orr. *A House Divided: A Study of Statehood Politics and the Copperhead Movement in West Virginia.* Pittsburgh: University of Pittsburgh Press, 1964.

———. "The Union As It Was: A Critique of Recent Interpretations of the Copperheads." *Civil War History* 13 (March 1967): 25–39.

Cutler, William Parker. "William Parker Cutler's Congressional Diary of 1862–1863." Edited by Allan Bogue. *Civil War History* 33 (December 1987): 315–330.

Dana, Charles A. *Recollections of the Civil War with the Leaders at Washington and in the Field in the Sixties.* New York: Appleton, 1898.

Donald, David. *Charles Sumner and the Coming of the Civil War.* 2 vols. New York: Knopf, 1961.

———. *Charles Sumner and the Rights of Man.* New York: Knopf, 1970.

Dusinberre, William. *Civil War Issues in Philadelphia, 1856–1865.* Philadelphia: University of Pennsylvania Press, 1965.

Edmonds, Sara Emma. *Nurse and Spy in the Union Army: The Adventures and Experiences of a Woman in Hospitals, Camps, and Battlefields.* Hartford, CT: W. S. Williams, 1865.

Einhorn, Robin. "Before the Machine: Municipal Government in Chicago, 1833–1872." Ph.D. diss., University of Chicago, 1988.

Faust, Drew Gilpin. "Altars of Sacrifice: Confederate Women and the Narratives of War." *Journal of American History* 76 (1990): 1200–1228.

Ferris, Norman. *Desperate Diplomacy: William Henry Seward's Foreign Policy, 1861.* Knoxville: University of Tennessee Press, 1976.

———. *The Trent Affair: A Diplomatic Crisis.* Knoxville: University of Tennessee Press, 1977.

Fessenden, Frances. *Life and Public Services of William Pitt Fessenden.* 2 vols. Boston: Houghton, 1907.

Field, Phyllis F. *The Politics of Race in New York: The Struggle for Black Suffrage in the Civil War Era.* Ithaca, NY: Cornell University Press, 1982.

Fite, Emerson. *Social and Industrial Conditions in the North during the Civil War.* New York: Macmillan, 1910, 1963.

Fleming, Robert Samuel. *A History of Oberlin College from Its Foundation through the Civil War.* Oberlin, OH: Oberlin College, 1943.

Foner, Eric. *Free Soil, Free Labor, Free Men: The Ideology of the Republican Party before the Civil War.* New York: Oxford University Press, 1970.

————. *Nothing But Freedom: Emancipation and Its Legacy.* Baton Rouge: Louisiana State University Press, 1983.

Foner, Eric. *Politics and Ideology in the Age of the Civil War.* New York: Oxford University Press, 1980.

Foner, Philip S. *The Life and Writings of Frederick Douglass.* 4 vols. New York: International Publishers, 1950.

Franklin, John Hope. "James T. Ayers, Civil War Recruiter." *Journal of the Illinois State Historical Society* 40 (September 1947): 267–297.

Frederickson, George M. *The Black Image in the White Mind: The Debate on Afro-American Character and Destiny, 1817–1914.* New York: Harper and Row, 1971.

————. *The Inner Civil War: Northern Intellectuals and the Crisis of the Union.* New York: Harper and Row, 1965.

Freehling, William W. *The Road to Disunion.* Vol. 1. *Secessionists at Bay, 1776–1854.* New York: Oxford University Press, 1990.

Freidel, Frank. *Francis Lieber: Nineteenth-Century Liberal.* 1947. Reprint, Gloucester, MA: Peter Smith, 1968.

————. *Union Pamphlets of the Civil War.* 2 vols. Cambridge, MA: Belknap Press of Harvard University Press, 1967.

Gallman, Joseph Matthew. *Mastering Wartime: A Social History of Philadelphia during the Civil War.* New York: Cambridge University Press, 1990.

————. "Preserving the Peace: Order and Disorder in Civil War Philadelphia." *Pennsylvania History* 55 (October 1988): 201–215.

————. *The North Fights the Civil War: The Home Front.* Chicago: Ivan R. Dee, 1994.

Garner, Stanton. *The Civil War World of Herman Melville.* Lawrence: University Press of Kansas, 1993.

Gates, Paul W. *Agriculture and the Civil War.* New York: Knopf, 1965.

George, Joseph, Jr. "Philadelphia's *Catholic Herald:* The Civil War Years." *Pennsylvania Magazine of History and Biography* 103 (April 1979): 196–221.

Gerber, David. *Black Ohio and the Color Line, 1860–1915.* Urbana: University of Illinois Press, 1976.

Gerteis, Louis. "Salmon P. Chase, Radicalism and the Politics of Emancipation." *Journal of American History* 60 (June 1973): 42–62.

Gienapp, William E. *The Origins of the Republican Party, 1852–1856.* New York: Oxford University Press, 1987.

Hancock, Harold Bell. *Delaware during the Civil War: A Political History.* Wilmington: Historical Society of Delaware, 1961.

Hanna, William F. "The Boston Draft Riot." *Civil War History* 36 (September 1990): 262–273.

Hansen, Debra Gold. *Strained Sisterhood: Gender and Class in the Boston Female Anti-Slavery Society.* Amherst: University of Massachusetts Press, 1993.

Harding, Leonard. "The Cincinnati Riots of 1862." *Bulletin of the Cincinnati Historical Society* 25 (October 1967): 229–239.

Hardman, Keith. *Charles Grandison Finney, 1792–1875: Revivalist and Reformer.* Syracuse, NY: Syracuse University Press, 1987.

Harper, Douglas R. *"If Thee Must Fight": A Civil War History of Chester County, Pennsylvania.* West Chester, PA: Chester County Historical Society, 1960.

Hawks, Alice. "The Civil War Home Front: Diary of a Young Girl, 1862–1863." Edited by Virginia Mayberry and Dawn E. Bakken. *Indiana Magazine of History* 87 (March 1991): 24–78.

Hay, John. *Lincoln and the Civil War in the Diaries and Letters of John Hay.* Edited by Tyler Dennett. 1939. New York: Dodd, Mead, 1972.

Hedrick, Joan. *Harriet Beecher Stowe: A Life.* New York: Oxford University Press, 1993.

Hendrick, Burton J. *Lincoln's War Cabinet.* Boston: Little, Brown, 1946.

Henig, Gerald S. *Henry Winter Davis: Antebellum and Civil War Congressman from Maryland.* New York: Twayne, 1973.

Herr, Pamela. *Jessie Benton Frémont.* New York: F. Watts, 1987.

Hesseltine, William. *Lincoln and the War Governors.* New York: Knopf, 1948.

Hicken, Victor. *Illinois in the Civil War.* 1966. Urbana: University of Illinois Press, 1991.

Hodnett, Mary Patricia. "Civil War Issues in New York State Politics." Ph.D. diss., Johns Hopkins University, 1971.

Holt, Michael F. *Forging a Majority: The Formation of the Republican Party in Pittsburgh, 1848–1860.* 1969. Reprint, Pittsburgh, PA: University of Pittsburgh Press, 1990.

———. *The Political Crisis of the 1850s.* New York: Wiley, 1978.

Howard, Victor. *Religion and the Radical Republican Movement, 1860–1870.* Lexington: University of Kentucky Press, 1990.

Howe, Daniel Walker. *The Political Culture of the American Whigs.* Chicago: University of Chicago Press, 1979.

Hunt, H. Draper. *Hannibal Hamlin of Maine: Lincoln's First Vice President.* Syracuse, NY: Syracuse University Press, 1969.

Hyman, Harold. *A More Perfect Union: The Impact of the Civil War and Reconstruction on the Constitution.* New York: Knopf, 1973.

Hyman, Harold, and Benjamin P. Thomas. *Stanton: The Life and Times of Lincoln's Secretary of War.* New York: Knopf, 1962.

Ilisevich, Robert D. *Galusha A. Grow: The People's Candidate.* Pittsburgh: University of Pittsburgh Press, 1988.

Johnson, Ludwell H. "Abraham Lincoln and the Development of Presidential War-making Powers: Prize Cases (1863) Revisited," *Civil War History* 35 (September 1989): 208–224.

———. "The Confederacy: What Was It? A View from the Federal Courts." *Civil War History* 32 (March 1986): 5–22.

Karamanski, Theodore J. *Rally 'Round the Flag: Chicago and the Civil War.* Chicago: Nelson-Hall, 1993.

Keller, Morton. *Affairs of State: Public Life in Late Nineteenth Century America.* Cambridge, MA: Harvard University Press, 1977.

Kemp, Thomas. "Community and War: The Civil War Experience of Two New Hampshire Towns." In *Toward a Social History of the American Civil War*. Edited by Maris A. Vinovskis. New York: Cambridge University Press, 1990.

King, Willard L. *Lincoln's Manager: David Davis*. Cambridge: Harvard University Press, 1960.

Kleppner, Paul. *The Third Electoral System, 1853–1892: Parties, Voters and Political Culture*. Chapel Hill, NC, 1979.

Knupfer, Peter B. *The Union As It Was: Constitutional Unionism and Sectional Compromise, 1787–1861*. Chapel Hill: University of North Carolina Press, 1991

Kuklick, Bruce. *Churchmen and Philosophers: From Jonathan Edwards to John Dewey*. New Haven, CT: Yale University Press, 1985.

Leech, Margaret. *Reveille in Washington, 1860–1865*. New York: Harper & Brothers, 1941.

Lendt, David L. *Demise of Democracy: The Copperhead Press in Iowa, 1856–1870*. Ames: Iowa State University Press, 1973.

Levesque, George A. "Boston's Black Brahmin: Dr. John S. Rock." *Civil War History* 26 (December 1980): 326–346.

Life in the North during the Civil War: A Source History. Edited by George W. Smith and Charles Judah. Albuquerque: University of New Mexico Press, 1966.

Linden, Glenn M. *Politics or Principle: Congressional Voting on the Civil War Amendments and Pro-Negro Measures, 1838–1869*. Seattle: University of Washington Press, 1976.

Linderman, Gerald. *Embattled Courage: The Experience of Combat in the American Civil War*. New York: Free Press, 1987.

Litwack, Leon. *North of Slavery: The Negro in the Free States, 1790–1860*. Chicago: University of Chicago Press, 1961.

Livermore, Mary Ashton Rice. *My Story of the War: A Woman's Narrative of Four Years Personal Experience*. Hartford, CT: A. D. Worthington, 1889.

Long, E. B. *The Saints and the Union: Utah Territory during the Civil War*. Urbana: University of Illinois Press, 1981.

Mabee, Carlton. *Sojourner Truth: Slave, Prophet, Legend*. New York: Oxford University Press, 1993.

Maizlish, Stephen E. *The Triumph of Sectionalism: The Transformation of Ohio Politics, 1844–1856*. Kent, OH: Kent State University Press, 1983.

Marten, James. "For the Good, the True and the Beautiful: Northern Childrens' Magazines and the Civil War." *Civil War History* 41 (March 1995): 57–75.

Martin, Waldo E. *The Mind of Frederick Douglass*. Chapel Hill: University of North Carolina Press, 1984.

Marvel, William. *Andersonville: The Last Depot*. Chapel Hill: University of North Carolina Press, 1994.

Massey, Mary Elizabeth. *Bonnet Brigades: American Women and the Civil War*. New York: Knopf, 1966.

Maxwell, William Quentin. *Lincoln's Fifth Wheel: The Political History of the United States Sanitary Commission*. New York: Longmans, Green, 1956.

McClure, Alexander K. *Lincoln and the Men of War-Times*. Philadelphia: Philadelphia Times Publishing Co., 1892.

———. *Recollections of Half a Century*. Salem, MA: Salem Press Co., 1902.

McCrary, Peyton. "The Party of Revolution: Republican Ideas about Politics and Social Change, 1862–1867." *Civil War History* 30 (December 1984): 330–350.

McKay, Ernest A. *The Civil War and New York City.* Syracuse, NY: Syracuse University Press, 1990.

———. *Henry Wilson: Practical Radical.* Port Washington, NY: Kennikat Press, 1971.

McKivigan, John R. *The War against Pro-Slavery Religion: Abolitionism and the Northern Churches, 1830–1865.* Ithaca, NY: Cornell University Press, 1984.

McLoughlin, William G. *The Meaning of Henry Ward Beecher: An Essay on the Shifting Values of Mid-Victorian America, 1840–1870.* New York: Knopf, 1970.

McPherson, Edward. *Political History of the United States of America during the Great Rebellion.* 1865. Reprint, New York: Negro Universities Press, 1969.

McPherson, James M. *The Struggle for Equality: Abolitionists and the Negro in the Civil War and Reconstruction.* Princeton, NJ: Princeton University Press, 1964.

Meyer, Donald Harvey. *The Instructed Conscience: The Shaping of the American National Ethic.* Philadelphia: University of Pennsylvania Press, 1972.

Mitchell, Reid. *The Vacant Chair: The Northern Soldier Leaves Home.* New York: Oxford University Press, 1993.

Montgomery, David. *Beyond Equality: Labor and the Radical Republicans.* New York: Knopf, 1967.

Moore, George Ellis. *A Banner in the Hills: West Virginia's Statehood.* New York: Appleton-Century-Crofts, 1963.

Moorhead, James H. *American Apocalypse: Yankee Protestants and the Civil War, 1860–1869.* New Haven, CT: Yale University Press, 1978.

Neely, Mark E., Jr., and Gerald McMurtry. *The Insanity File: The Case of Mary Todd Lincoln.* Carbondale: Southern Illinois University Press, 1986.

New Jersey and the Civil War: An Album of Contemporary Accounts. Edited by E. S. Miers. Princeton, NJ: Van Nostrand, 1964.

New York Tribune. Tribune Almanac and Political Register. New York, 1860–1865.

Niven, John. *Gideon Welles: Lincoln's Secretary of the Navy.* New York: Oxford University Press, 1973.

———. *Salmon P. Chase: A Biography.* New York: Oxford University Press, 1995.

Oates, Stephen B. *A Woman of Valor: Clara Barton and the Civil War.* New York: Free Press, 1994.

Oberholtzer, Ellis P. *Jay Cooke: Financier of the Civil War.* 2 vols. New York: Burt Franklin, 1970.

Osterud, Nancy Grey. "Rural Women during the Civil War: New York's Nanticoke Valley, 1861–1865." *New York History* 71 (October 1990): 357–385.

Palladino, Grace. *Another Civil War: Labor, Capital, and the State in the Anthracite Regions of Pennsylvania, 1840–1868.* Urbana: University of Illinois Press, 1990.

Paludan, Phillip Shaw. *A Covenant with Death: The Constitution, Law and Equality in the Civil War Era.* Urbana: University of Illinois Press, 1975.

———. *A People's Contest: The Union and the Civil War, 1861–1865.* New York: Harper and Row, 1988.

Preston, Dickson J. *The Young Frederick Douglass: The Maryland Years.* Baltimore: Johns Hopkins University Press, 1980.

Quarles, Benjamin. *The Black Abolitionists.* New York: Oxford University Press, 1969.

———. *Frederick Douglass.* Washington, DC: Associated Publishers, 1948.

———. *The Negro in the Civil War.* Boston: Little, Brown, 1953.

Rable, George C. *Civil Wars: Women and the Crisis of Southern Nationalism.* Urbana: University of Illinois Press, 1989.

Randall, J. G. *Constitutional Problems under Lincoln*. Urbana: University of Illinois Press, 1951.

Rawley, James. *The Politics of Union: Northern Politics during the Civil War*. 1974. Reprint, Lincoln: University of Nebraska Press, 1980.

Richardson, Elmo, and Alan Farley. *John Palmer Usher: Lincoln's Secretary of the Interior*. Lawrence: University Press of Kansas, 1960.

Riddleberger, Patrick W. *George Washington Julian: Radical Republican*. Indianapolis: Indiana Historical Bureau, 1966.

Roark, James L. "George W. Julian: Radical Land Reformer." *Indiana Magazine of History* 64 (March 1968): 25–38.

Rorabaugh, William. "Who Fought for the North in the Civil War? Concord, Massachusetts, Enlistments." *Journal of American History* 73 (December 1986): 695–701.

Rose, Anne C. *Victorian America and the Civil War*. New York: Cambridge University Press, 1992.

Rosenberg, Morton M. "The People of Iowa on the Eve of the Civil War." *Annals of Iowa* 39 (Fall 1967): 105–133.

Saunders, Judith P. "The People's Party in Massachusetts during the Civil War." Master's, thesis, Boston College, 1970.

Schneider, John C. "Detroit and the Problem of Disorder: The Riot of 1863." *Michigan History* 38 (Spring 1974): 4–24.

Schurz, Carl. *Speeches, Correspondence and Political Papers of Carl Schurz*. Edited by Frederic Bancroft. 2 vols. New York: G. P. Putnam, 1912.

Sewall, Richard. *John P. Hale and the Politics of Abolition*. Cambridge, MA: Harvard University Press, 1965.

Shankman, Arnold M. *The Pennsylvania Anti-War Movement, 1861–1865*. Madison, NJ: Farleigh Dickinson University Press, 1980.

Siegel, Alan A. *For the Glory of the Union: Myth, Reality and the Media in Civil War New Jersey*. Madison, NJ: Farleigh Dickinson University Press, 1984.

Silbey, Joel H. *A Respectable Minority: The Democratic Party in the Civil War Era, 1860–1868*. New York: W. W. Norton, 1977.

———. *The Partisan Imperative: The Dynamics of American Politics before the Civil War*. New York: Oxford University Press, 1985.

Silver, David. *Lincoln's Supreme Court*. Urbana: University of Illinois Press, 1956.

Sokoloff, Alice Hunt. *Kate Chase for the Defense*. New York: Dodd, Mead, 1971.

Stampp, Kenneth M. *Indiana Politics during the Civil War*. Indianapolis: Indiana Historical Bureau, 1949.

Sterling, Dorothy. *Ahead of Her Time: Abby Kelley and the Politics of Anti-Slavery*. New York: W. W. Norton, 1991.

Stevenson, Louise A. *The Victorian Homefront: American Thought and Culture, 1860–1880*. New York: Twayne, 1991.

Strong, George Templeton. *The Diary of George Templeton Strong*. Edited by Allan Nevins and M. H. Thomas. 4 vols. New York: Macmillan, 1952.

Sumner, Charles. *The Selected Letters of Charles Sumner*. Edited by Beverly Wilson Palmer. 2 vols. Boston: Northeastern University Press, 1990.

Swisher, Carl. *The Taney Period, 1836–1864*. New York: Macmillan, 1974.

Taylor, John M. *William Henry Seward: Lincoln's Right Hand*. 1991.

Taylor, Richard S. "Seeking the Kingdom: A Study in the Life of Jonathan Blanchard, 1811–1892." Ph.D. dissertation. De Kalb: Northern Illinois University, 1977.

Thayer, William S. "Politicians in Crisis: The Washington Letters of William S. Thayer, December 1860–March 1861." Edited by Martin Crawford. *Civil War History* 27 (September 1981): 231–247.

Thompson, Harriet Jane. "Civil War Wife: The Letters of Harriet Jane Thompson." *Annals of Iowa* 35 (Winter–Spring 1961): 523–548, 594–615.

Thornbrough, E. L. *Indiana in the Civil War Era.* Indianapolis: Indiana Historical Bureau, 1969.

Thornton, Harrison John. "The State University of Iowa and the Civil War." *Annals of Iowa* 30 (January 1950): 198–209.

Trefousse, Hans L. *Benjamin Franklin Wade: Radical Republican from Ohio.* New York: Twayne, 1963.

———. *The Radical Republicans: Lincoln's Vanguard for Racial Justice.* New York: Knopf, 1968.

[United States Civil War Centennial Commission]. *The United States on the Eve of the Civil War as Described in the 1860 Census.* Washington, DC, 1965.

Van Deusen, Glyndon G. *Horace Greeley: Nineteenth Century Crusader.* Philadelphia, PA: University of Pennsylvania Press, 1953.

———. *William Henry Seward.* New York: Oxford, 1967.

Vinovskis, Maris. *Toward a Social History of the American Civil War.* New York: Cambridge, 1990.

Voegeli, V. Jacques. *Free But Not Equal: The Midwest and the Negro During the Civil War.* Chicago: University of Chicago Press, 1967.

Wainwright, Nicholas B. "The Loyal Opposition in Civil War Philadelphia." *Pennsylvania Magazine of History and Biography* 88 (July 1964): 294–315.

Welter, Rush, *The Mind of America, 1830–1860.* New York: Columbia University Press, 1975.

Wertheim, Lewis J. "The Indianapolis Treason Trials, the Elections of 1864, and the Power of the Partisan Press." *Indiana Magazine of History* 85 (September 1989): 236–260.

West, Richard S., Jr. *Gideon Welles: Lincoln's Navy Department.* Indianapolis: Bobbs-Merrill, 1953.

Wheeler, Kenneth W., ed. *Ohio Leaders in the Civil War.* Columbus: Ohio State University Press, 1968.

Wilkinson, Norman B. *The Brandywine Home Front During the Civil War.* Wilmington, DE: Kaumagraph, 1966.

Williams, T. Harry. *Lincoln and the Radicals.* Madison: University of Wisconsin Press, 1941.

Wilson, Edmund. *Patriotic Gore: Studies in the Literature of the American Civil War.* New York: Oxford University Press, 1962.

Wubben, Hubert T. *Civil War Iowa and the Copperhead Movement.* Ames: Iowa State University Press, 1980.

19

Confederate Civilian Leaders

Robert England

The study of Confederate leaders presents several problems for the student of the Civil War. Most biographies published on the war have been on military men; the emphasis of scholars has been on gallant charges and the many theoretical causes of Confederate defeat in the field. This is compounded by a further issue. Because of the interlocking relationship between military command and political policy, only the most important civilians have received significant attention. Many people served in civilian *and* military capacities during the war.

REFERENCE BOOKS

Over the years, a number of dedicated students of the war assembled competent, useful compendiums that introduce many nonmilitary topics. Colonel Mark Mayo Boatner's *The Civil War Dictionary* (1959) has provided to a generation of scholars a fine one-volume collection of essays on almost every topic that could be of interest to anyone studying the war. Though limited by an inconsistent system of notation, Boatner's *Dictionary* has remained in print and has just been reissued. The late Patricia Faust edited the *Historical Times Illustrated Encyclopedia of the Civil War* (1986). Faust assembled outstanding scholars who wrote detailed articles on battles, leaders, and other aspects of the war. Unfortunately, Faust died before the completion of the volume, and as a result, there are a number of minor, limiting factors such as a complete lack of notation for the articles. With Boatner's volume, *The Encyclopedia of the Civil War* is an essential reference.

Recently, a monumental four-volume reference work on the South during the war was edited by Richard N. Current with the able assistance of Paul D. Escott, Lawrence N. Powell, James I. Robertson, Sr., and Emory M. Thomas. The *Encyclopedia of the Confederacy* (1993) may well set the standard for reference works on the war for years to come. A legion of talented authors contributed detailed articles on a wide variety of Confederate topics, including civilian leaders, with appropriate bibliographic information.

Valuable as a one-volume biographic source is *Who Was Who in the Confederacy* (1988), issued as volume 2 of *Who Was Who in the Civil War*. Written by Stewart Sifkakis, this collection of biographies provides short articles on the majority of Confederate congressmen, cabinet officers, governors, and other officials of the short-lived country. Documentation, however, is scanty. The nonspecialist will find this volume a fine introduction to the many participants on the Confederate side.

BIOGRAPHIES AND OTHER MONOGRAPHS

The Executive Branch

Many scholars have written on Jefferson Davis, president of the Confederacy. Though Davis's life and work are covered in chapter 18 in this book, attention should be drawn to several studies of him. The most comprehensive of the modern biographies is by William C. Davis, *Jefferson Davis: The Man and His Hour* (1991). This balanced account provides a fine introduction to more specialized studies. Of these, two of the most important explain Davis's relations with asepcts of military operations. Archer Jones's *Confederate Strategy from Shiloh to Vicksburg* (1961) introduces Southern attempts to manage systematic planning in the West, along with the complications of departmental organization. The argument between Davis and the so-called Western bloc of military leaders is given a lively twist in Steven E. Woodworth's *Jefferson Davis and His Generals: The Failure of Confederate Command in the West* (1990).

Vice President Alexander H. Stephens proved to be as much of a mystery to his contemporaries as to modern students of the Civil War, as is revealed in the most recent treatment of his life, Thomas E. Schott's *Alexander H. Stephens of Georgia: A Biography* (1988). Stephens's reputation as a brilliant constitutional lawyer and advocate of states' rights is evident in his massive *A Constitutional View of the Late War between the States: Its Causes, Character, Conduct, and Results Presented in a Series of Colloquies at Liberty Hall* (1868–1870). This classic work outlines basic differences between Stephens and President Davis and is probably best known for serving as the origin of the now-popular phrase, ''War Between the States.'' Stephens revealed, without a hint that he understood what he did, the exact nature of the weakness of the Confederate States of America: an absence of political parties meant that opposition thought and action arrived like pellets from a shotgun on the government's doorstep instead of in a distilled, more easily managed form.

Unfortunately, no modern comprehensive study of the Confederate cabinet exists. Rembert Patrick's *Jefferson Davis and His Cabinet* (1944) lacks depth in many areas, particularly in its examination of finance and justice. Much more work should be attempted on relationships between cabinet members and officers of other governmental agencies, as well as issues that crossed jurisdictional lines in an attempt to understand better the mechanics of administering the Confederacy.

Studies of individual departments and excellent biographies, however, provide important and balanced accounts of some officials. The talented Judah P. Benjamin has been examined by several scholars since the Civil War. Simon I. Neiman's *Judah P. Benjamin* (1963) introduced much information on the later life of the man who served as attorney general, secretary of war, and finally as secretary of state. Eli N. Evans's fine study, *Judah P. Benjamin: The Jewish Confederate* (1988), focuses on the relationship between the cabinet officer and Jefferson Davis. Throughout the war, Benjamin did not waver in his loyalty to the chief executive.

A number of studies of the naval service and the exceptional secretary who led the department throughout the war exist. Representative of these are Tom Wells's *The Confederate Navy: A Study in Organization* (1971) and two books by William Still, *Confederate Shipbuilding* (2d, 1986) and *Iron Afloat: The Story of the Confederate Armorclads* (1986). Joseph T. Durkin's *Stephen R. Mallory: Confederate Navy Chief* (1954) is the standard biography.

The delivery of mail in the Confederacy has not excited scholars' efforts to the same extent as foreign affairs, naval service, and operations of the War Department. But the mails ran with regularity until the closing months of the war, largely due to the efforts of the cabinet member charged with this responsibility. The redoubtable Texas scholar Ben Proctor wrote *Not without Honor: The Life of John H. Reagan* (1962), the most complete treatment of the career of the lone postmaster general.

The Confederate Treasury Department has been recently examined by Douglas Ball in *Financial Failure and Confederate Defeat* (1991). Going far beyond a simple study of a cabinet office, Ball's synthesis presents an amazing array of arcane details dredged from endless economic data. He delivers a significant number of new interpretations regarding the effectiveness of a variety of little-known programs while illustrating the ad hoc nature of financial planning that crossed departmental boundaries. Few biographies of the men who served as secretary exist. Henry Dickson Capers, who had the advantage of interviewing many who knew the first secretary, published his biography, *The Life and Times of C. G. Memminger* (1893), just after his subject's death. There is no biography of George Trenholm. Ball sees that the chaos resulting from faulty financial planning rolled over Trenholm's efforts. Patrick's *Jefferson Davis and His Cabinet* provides information on Trenholm.

Like the Navy Department, the War Department has been studied from several perspectives. Archer Jones's *Confederate Strategy from Shiloh to Vicksburg* (1961) examines Secretary of War George W. Randolph's role in the creation and implementation of a Western strategy. George Green Shackleford's recent biography, *George Wythe Randolph and the Confederate Elite* (1988), advances the idea that Confederate defeat should be attributed to poor management of what resources were available. Again, Jones's book is also useful to understand Secretary of War James A Seddon's role in western strategic planning. There has been no biography of Seddon, though sketches of his life and work have been presented in Patrick's *Jefferson Davis and His Cabinet* and in the reprint of J. B. Jones's *A Rebel War Clerk's Diary at the Confederate States Capital* (1993). R.G.H. Kean's diary, edited by Edward Younger and published under the name *Inside the Confederate Government: The Diary of Robert Garlick Hill Kean* (1957), provides an intimate portrait of the day-to-day workings of the war office. The last secretary of war, John C. Breckinridge, served the Confederacy in several capacities in the military and as a civilian. The most useful biography is William C. Davis's *Breckinridge: Statesman, Soldier, Symbol* (1974).

A number of men held the office of attorney general and presided over the Department of Justice. Judah P. Benjamin served early in 1861 but Thomas H. Watts, Wade Keyes, George Davis, and Thomas Bragg have received scant attention from scholars. Only Judah P. Benjamin's life has been studied in any detail with biographies by Simon I. Neiman (1963) and Eli N. Evans (1988). Patrick's *Jefferson Davis and His Cabinet* presents biographical information on these officers and with Emory M. Thomas's *The Confederate Nation: 1861–1865* (1979) raises the issue of the lack of a Confederate supreme court as a major political problem.

The Confederate State Department assumed responsibility for foreign affairs. Neither Robert Toombs, the first secretary, nor his successors, Robert M. T. Hunter and William M. Browne, who served for only eleven days in March 1862, have received much attention from modern students of the war. Judah P. Benjamin, the fourth secretary, has been the subject of several studies. Neiman (1963) and Evans (1988) presented compelling evidence that Benjamin was the most competent of the Confederate cabinet officers once he arrived at his last appointment with the State Department. Patrick's general treatment of the cabinet (1944) provided a general interpretation of the operations of the department. But recently, Confederate foreign affairs—specifically the possibility of European involvement in the war—have been examined by Howard Jones in *Union in Peril: The Crisis over British Intervention in the Civil War* (1992). English military support for the Confederacy was a possibility much later in the war than has been supposed, according to Jones. More study needs to be attempted on Confederate relations with other powers, however, as *Union in Peril* suggests, before historians can be comfortable with what is known of this important aspect of the war.

The Congress

Very few members of the Confederate Congress are well known today. Some, like Generals Roger A. Pryor, T. R. R. Cobb, and Howell Cobb, served ably in politics and war, but most, particularly those who served in the first or provisional congress and returned to private life, are known only to dedicated readers of reference works. Those books cited in the first section of this chapter contain short biographies of even the most obscure politicians who served the Confederacy in the legislature at Montgomery and at Richmond.

Several general histories are worthy of note. Wilfred B. Yearns's *The Confederate Congress* (1960) provides a fine introduction to the rebel legislature. In addition to the references cited earlier, Ezra J. Warner and Yearns compiled *The Biographical Register of the Confederate Congress* (1975). Thomas B. Alexander and Richard Beringer studied the background of individual congressmen in *The Anatomy of the Confederate Congress: A Study of the Influences of Member Characteristics on Legislative Voting Behavior* (1972).

Of all the members of the various Confederate congresses, no one possessed a more distinguished political career than John Tyler. The former president of the United States served in the provisional congress and in the first regular congress until his death in January 1862. The most recent study is by Robert Seager, *And Tyler Too: A Biography of John and Julia Gardiner Tyler* (1963).

The fire-eating leaders of secession and disunion are the best-known Confederate congressmen. Laura Amanda White's *Robert Barnwell Rhett: Father of Secession* (1965) traces his support of states' rights to the nullification crises. More moderate politicians considered him too extreme in his views to be an effective president. Equally ferocious in his insistence on the vindication of the cause of Southern liberties was William Lowndes Yancey of Alabama, a formidable Confederate senator. The best-known biography was written by John Witherspoon Dubose, *The Life and Times of William Lowndes Yancey; A History of Political Parties in the United States from 1834 to 1864; Especially as to the Origins of the Confederate States* (1942). Yancey argued with President Davis over the role of the central government and presidential powers. William Y. Thompson's biography, *Robert Toombs of Georgia* (1966), portrays his subject as only gradually becoming a champion of secession. Toombs served in Congress at the same time he held a commission as a general officer.

The Cobb brothers of Georgia have been the subject of biographies. William B. McCash's *Thomas R. R. Cobb: The Making of a Southern Nationalist* (1983) traces the career of the congressman from his days as a student at the University of Georgia to his death while leading a brigade at Fredericksburg. John Eddins Simpson's fine biography, *Howell Cobb: The Politics of Ambition* (1973), shows Cobb as a reluctant secessionist, favoring disunion only after Lincoln's election. He chaired the convention at Montgomery, Alabama, that organized the provisional government and eventually served as a major general in the army.

Robert S. Holzman's biography, *Adapt or Perish: The Life of General Roger*

A. Pryor, C.S.A. (1976), depicts the varied career of a Confederate patriot. Pryor served as a congressman and general officer, and then his brigade was disbanded. Pryor enlisted as a private and served in the cavalry. Sara Agnes Rice Pryor, the congressman's wife, wrote *Reminiscences of Peace and War* (1904), a credible biography that has proved useful to a variety of scholars over the years.

Another older publication worthy of review is Percy Smith Flippin's *Herschel V. Johnson of Georgia: States' Rights Unionist* (1931) for its balanced treatment of a reluctant rebel who ran for the vice presidency on the Democratic ticket with Stephen A. Douglas in 1860. Johnson served in the Confederate Senate.

Jabez Lamar Monroe Curry served in the Confederate Congress and, after he lost a reelection bid, joined the cavalry. Two biographies provide information on Curry. Edwin Anderson Alderman and Armistead Churchill Gordon's *J. L. M. Curry: A Biography* (1911) provides much information on Curry's postwar career as an educational philanthropist. Jessie Pearl Rice provided a study, *J. L. M. Curry: Southerner, Statesman, and Educator* (1949), which deserves reprinting.

State and Local Leaders

Many studies of state and local leaders appeared soon after the war, and interest remained high in the careers of these men until after the turn of the century. By mid-century, however, it had faded. Perhaps as the centennial of the war approached, military affairs and biographies of national leaders in the congress and executive branch of government attracted the attention of scholars. As a result, few books now in circulation deal exclusively with legislators, governors, and lesser officials.

The most complete directory of state executives may be found in Buck Yearns's *The Confederate Governors* (1985). Yearns maintained that governors generally supported the war effort and President Davis's policies for the first years of the conflict. Some shifting of positions occurred as states' rights within the Confederacy became a central issue.

Joseph H. Parks's biography, *Joseph E. Brown of Georgia* (1977), presents a fine portrait of a governor who did resist the central government. Louise Biles Hill also explored the issues surrounding Brown's dissatisfaction with President Davis in *Joseph E. Brown and the Confederacy* (1972). Brown's insistence on adequate local defense coupled with his hostility to conscription led to the creation of the Georgia State Line, a military formation that grew out of the debate over the constitutionality of the conscript act. It had the mission of guarding bridges on the state railroad and areas on the coast. William Harris Bragg's treatment, *Joe Brown's Army: The Georgia State Line, 1862–1865* (1987), provides a useful introduction to the organization and to sentiment against conscription.

Problems also arose in North Carolina. Glenn Tucker's *Zeb Vance: Champion of Personal Freedom* (1966) is the best biography of the Carolina executive.

John B. Edmonds's biography, *Francis W. Pickens and the Politics of Destruction* (1986), assesses the career of the governor of South Carolina. F. N. Boney wrote *John Letcher of Virginia: The Story of Virginia's Civil War Governor* (1966); Letcher was the coordinator of Virginia's first efforts at self-defense. Both Robert E. Lee and Thomas J. Jackson initially held Virginia commissions.

Malcolm C. McMillan took a different approach to state government during the war. His *The Disintegration of a Confederate State: Three Governors and Alabama's Wartime Home Front, 1861–1865* (1986) examined the wartime administrations of Governors A. B. Morre, John Gill Shorter, and Thomas H. Watts.

Like Governor Letcher of Virginia, Isham Harris, chief executive of Tennessee, played a major role in organizing his state for war. His energy in planning and his enthusiasm for the Southern cause led directly to the formation of the major western Confederate command, the Army of Tennessee. In *Army of the Heartland: The Army of Tennessee, 1861–1862* (1967), Thomas L. Connelly explained Governor Harris's role.

State legislatures in the Confederacy assumed almost impossible tasks. Keeping the roads open, protecting railroads, and working with governors to maintain the militia proved to be formidable assignments in the midst of war. May Spencer Ringold's *The Role of the State Legislature in the Confederacy* (1966) presents a positive portrait of their efforts even as the economy and the military collapsed.

Few significant books on Confederate cities and their leaders have appeared. Charles L. Dufour's *The Night the War Was Lost* (1944) is a fine history of the inadequate defense of New Orleans in early 1862. Arthur W. Bergeron's *Confederate Mobile* (1991) is an assessment of civic life, civilian administration, and military needs. Once again, the interaction between elected officials and the military authorities proved crucial to the continuation of the struggle in the closing days of the war. Despite close cooperation, the loss of the mouth of Mobile Bay ended the city's usefulness to the Confederacy's economy even though the garrison held out until the last days of the war.

BIBLIOGRAPHY

Alderman, Edwin Anderson, and Armistead Churchill Gordon. *J. L. M. Curry: A Biography.* New York: Macmillan, 1911.

Alexander, Thomas B., and Richard E. Beringer. *The Anatomy of the Confederate Congress: A Study of the Influences of Member Characteristics on Legislative Voting Behavior, 1861–1865.* Nashville, TN: Vanderbilt University Press, 1972.

Bakeless, John. *Spies of the Confederacy.* Philadelphia: Lippincott, 1970.

Ball, Douglas B. *Financial Failure and Confederate Defeat.* Urbana: University of Illinois Press, 1991.

Barney, William L. *The Secessionist Impulse: Alabama and Mississippi in 1860.* Princeton: Princeton University Press, 1974.

Bergeron, Arthur W. *Confederate Mobile*. Jackson, MS: University of Mississippi Press, 1991.

Boatner, Mark Mayo. *The Civil War Dictionary*. New York: David McKay Company, 1959.

Boney, F. N. *John Letcher of Virginia: The Story of Virginia's Civil War Governor*. University: University of Alabama Press, 1966.

Bragg, William Harris. *Joe Brown's Army: The Georgia State Line, 1862–1865*. Macon, GA: Mercer University Press, 1987.

Bulloch, James D. *The Secret Service of the Confederate States in Europe or How the Cruisers Were Equipped*. New York: Thomas Yoseloff, 1959.

Capers, Henry Dickson. *The Life and Times of C. G. Memminger*. Richmond: Everett Waddey & Co., 1893.

Confederate States of America. *A Compilation of the Messages and Papers of the Confederacy, Including the Diplomatic Correspondence, 1861–1865*. Nashville: U.S. Publishing Company, 1905.

———. *Journal of the Congress of the Confederate States of America*. 7 vols. Washington, D.C.: Government Printing Office, 1904–1905.

Connelly, Thomas Lawrence. *Army of the Heartland: The Army of Tennessee, 1861–1862*. Baton Rouge: Louisiana State University Press, 1967.

Connelly, Thomas Lawrence and Archer Jones. *The Politics of Command: Factions and Ideas in Confederate Strategy*. Baton Rouge: Louisiana State University Press, 1973.

Coulter, E. Merton. *The Confederate States of America, 1861–1865*. Baton Rouge: Louisiana State University Press, 1950.

Current, Richard N., editor-in-chief. *Encyclopedia of the Confederacy*. New York: Simon & Schuster, 1993.

Curry, J.L.M. *Civil History of the Government of the Confederate States with Some Personal Reminiscences*. Richmond, VA: B. F. Johnson Publishing Co., 1901.

Davis, Jefferson. *The Rise and Fall of the Confederate Government*. New York: Thomas Yoseloff, 1958.

Davis, William C. *Breckinridge: Statesman, Soldier, Symbol*. Baton Rouge: Louisiana State University Press, 1974.

———. *Jefferson Davis: The Man and His Hour*. New York: HarperCollins, 1991.

DeRosa, Marshall L. *The Confederate Constitution of 1861: An Inquiry into American Constitutionalism*. Columbia, MO: University of Missouri Press, 1991.

Dubose, John Witherspoon. *The Life and Times of William Lowndes Yancey: A History of Political Parties in the United States, from 1834 to 1864; Especially as to the Origins of the Confederate States*. New York: Peter Smith, 1942.

Dufour, Charles L. *The Night the War Was Lost*. 1944. Reprint, Lincoln: University of Nebraska Press, 1994.

Durkin, Joseph T. *Stephen R. Mallory: Confederate Navy Chief*. Chapel Hill: University of North Carolina Press, 1954.

Eaton, Clement. *A History of the Southern Confederacy*. New York: Macmillan, 1954.

Edmonds, John B. *Francis W. Pickens and the Politics of Destruction*. Chapel Hill: University of North Carolina Press, 1986.

Escott, Paul. *After Secession: Jefferson Davis and the Failure of Confederate Nationalism*. Baton Rouge: Louisiana State University Press, 1978.

Evans, Eli. *Judah P. Benjamin: The Jewish Confederate*. New York: Free Press, 1988.

Faust, Patricia, ed. *Historical Times Illustrated Encyclopedia of the Civil War.* New York: Harper & Row, 1986.

Fleming, Walter L. *Civil War and Reconstruction in Alabama.* New York: Macmillan, 1905.

Flippin, Percy Smith. *Herschel V. Johnson of Georgia, States' Rights Unionist.* Richmond, VA: Dietz Printing Company, 1931.

Girard, Charles. *A Visit to the Confederate States of America in 1863: A Memoir Addressed to His Majesty Napoleon III.* Translated by William Stanley Hoole. Tuscaloosa, AL: Confederate Publishing Company, 1962.

Harwell, Richard B., ed. *The Confederate Reader.* New York: David McKay Co., 1957.

Hattaway, Herman, and Archer Jones. *How the North Won: A Military History of the Civil War.* Chicago: University of Illinois Press, 1983.

Hill, Louise Biles. *Joseph E. Brown and the Confederacy.* Westport, CT: Greenwood Press, 1972.

Holzman, Robert S. *Adapt or Perish: The Life of General Roger A. Pryor, C.S.A.* Hamden, CT: Archon Books, 1976.

Jones, Archer. *Confederate Strategy from Shiloh to Vicksburg.* Baton Rouge: Louisiana State University Press, 1961.

Jones, Howard. *Union in Peril: The Crises over British Intervention in the Civil War.* Chapel Hill: University of North Carolina Press, 1992.

Jones, John B. *A Rebel War Clerk's Diary at the Confederate States Capital.* Edited by Howard Swiggert. 1935. 2 vols. Baton Rouge: Louisiana State University Press, 1993.

Jones, Wilbur Devereux. *The Confederate Rams at Birkenhead: A Chapter in Anglo-American Relations.* Tuscaloosa, AL: Confederate Publishing Company, 1961.

Kean, Robert Garlick Hill. *Inside the Confederate Government: The Diary of Robert Garlick Hill Kean.* Edward Younger, ed. New York: Oxford University Press, 1957.

McCash, William B. *Thomas R. R. Cobb: The Making of a Southern Nationalist.* Macon, GA: Mercer University Press, 1983.

McMillan, Malcolm C. *The Disintegration of a Confederate State: Three Governors of Alabama's Wartime Home Front, 1861–1865.* Macon, GA: Mercer University Press, 1986.

Neimon, Simon I. *Judah Benjamin.* Indianapolis: Bobbs-Merrill, 1963.

Parks, Joseph H. *Joseph E. Brown of Georgia.* Baton Rouge: Louisiana State University Press, 1977.

Patrick, Rembert W. *Jefferson Davis and His Cabinet.* Baton Rouge: Louisiana State University Press, 1944.

Pollard, E. A. *Southern History of the War.* New York: C. B. Richardson, 1866.

Proctor, Ben. *Not without Honor: The Life of John H. Reagan.* Austin: University of Texas Press, 1962.

Pryor, Sara Agnes Rice. *Reminiscences of Peace and War.* Rev. ed. New York: Macmillan Company, 1908.

Rice, Jesse Pearl. *J. L. M. Curry: Southerner, Statesman & Educator.* New York: King's Crown Press, 1949.

Ringold, May Spencer. *The Role of the State Legislature in the Confederacy.* Athens, GA: University of Georgia Press, 1966.

Schott, Thomas E. *Alexander H. Stephens of Georgia: A Biography.* Baton Rouge: Louisiana State University Press, 1988.

Seager, Robert. *And Tyler Too: A Biography of John and Julia Tyler.* New York: McGraw-Hill, 1963.

Shackleford, George Green. *George Wythe Randolph and the Confederate Elite.* Athens, GA: University of Georgia Press, 1988.

Sifakis, Stewart. *Who Was Who in the Confederacy.* New York: Facts on File, 1988.

Simpson, John Eddins. *Howell Cobb: The Politics of Ambition.* Chicago: Adams Press, 1973.

Sims, Henry Harrison. *Life of Robert M. T. Hunter: A Study in Sectionalism and Secession.* Richmond, Virginia: William Byrd Press, 1935.

Stephens, Alexander H. *A Constitutional View of the Late War between the States: Its Causes, Character, Conduct, and Results Presented in a Series of Colloquies at Liberty Hall,* 2 vols. Philadelphia: National Publishing Company, 1868–1870.

Sterne, Philip Van Doren, ed. *Secret Missions of the Civil War.* Chicago: Rand McNally, 1959.

Still, William. *Confederate Shipbuilding.* Columbia: University of South Carolina Press, 1986.

———. *Iron Afloat: The Story of the Confederate Armorclads.* Columbia: University of South Carolina Press, 1986.

Strode, Hudson. *Jefferson Davis.* 3 vols. New York: Harcourt Brace, 1955–1964.

Thomas, Emory M. *The Confederacy as a Revolutionary Experience.* Columbia: University of South Carolina Press, 1992.

———. *The Confederate Nation, 1861–1865.* New York: Harper & Row, 1979.

Thompson, William Y. *Robert Toombs of Georgia.* Baton Rouge: Louisiana State University Press, 1966.

Tidwell, William A., with James O. Hall and David Winfred Gaddy. *Come Retribution: The Confederate Secret Service and the Assassination of Lincoln.* Jackson: University Press of Mississippi, 1988.

Tucker, Glenn. *Zeb Vance: Champion of Personal Freedom.* Indianapolis: Bobbs-Merrill, 1966.

Wakely, Jon L. *Biographical Dictionary of the Confederacy.* Westport, CT: Greenwood Press, 1977.

Warner, Ezra J., and W. Buck Yearns. *Biographical Register of the Confederate Congress.* Baton Rouge: Louisiana State University Press, 1975.

Wells, Tom Henderson. *The Confederate Navy: A Study in Organization.* University, AL: University of Alabama Press, 1971.

White, Laura Amanda. *Robert Barnwell Rhett: Father of Secession.* Glouster, MA: P. Smith, 1965.

Winters, John D. *The Civil War in Louisiana.* Baton Rouge: Louisiana State University Press, 1963.

Woodworth, Steven. *Jefferson Davis and His Generals: The Failure of Confederate Command in the West.* Lawrence: University of Kansas Press, 1990.

Wooster, Ralph A. *The Secession Conventions of the South.* Princeton, NJ: Princeton University Press, 1962.

Yearns, Wilfred Buck. *The Confederate Congress.* Athens, GA: University of Georgia Press, 1960.

———, ed. *The Confederate Governors.* Athens, GA: University of Georgia Press, 1985.

Part VII

Strategy and Tactics: Operations, Campaigns, and Battles

20

Eastern Theater

Stephen Davis

The "eastern theater" of the Civil War has generally come to mean Virginia, West Virginia, Maryland, and Pennsylvania, at least partly because actions fought in the Carolinas, eastern Georgia, and Florida were either naval in origin or scant in number, until Sherman brought the western theater east late in the war. Civil War historians' study of the eastern theater in the past half-century has brought forth a large number of books devoted to the campaigns and major battles. Adding to this voluminous literature are the countless articles published in both scholarly journals (e.g., *Civil War History, Virginia Magazine of History and Biography*) and popular magazines such as *Civil War Times Illustrated* (begun as *Civil War Times* in 1959) and *Blue and Gray* (1984–). The following review will highlight the most important writing on the war in the East. For these purposes, "eastern theater" will largely mean the Virginia front, except for occasional land battles to the south that are worthy of mention.

When Civil War enthusiasts approach the study of the war in Virginia, they must sooner or later come to terms with Douglas Southall Freeman's *Lee's Lieutenants: A Study in Command* (1942–1944). Indeed, one may say that the modern historiography of battles and campaigns in Virginia begins with *Lee's Lieutenants*. Essentially the story of the Army of Northern Virginia while under Lee's command, Freeman's narrative emphasizes the successes and failures of the army's key generals and how Lee sought to find competent replacements. Half of volume 1 is devoted to the Confederate army in Virginia before Lee took command, June 1, 1862; thence it relates Jackson's Valley campaign and the Seven Days' Battles. Volume 2 carries the story from Cedar Mountain to Chancellorsville, August 1862–May 1863. Freeman's third volume covers the last two years of war, Gettysburg to Appomattox. Although framed in a decidedly Confederate point of view, *Lee's Lieutenants* offers invaluable research, excellent analysis, and refined, often elegant writing; it is indispensable to the study of the eastern battles and campaigns.

As if in response to Freeman's study of the Confederate army in Virginia, Bruce Catton wrote a three-volume history of the Union Army of the Potomac (1951–1953). Omitting consideration of First Manassas through the Seven Days, Catton's *Mr. Lincoln's Army* begins in August 1862; *Glory Road* spans Fredericksburg to Gettysburg; and *A Stillness at Appomattox* covers the war in Virginia, 1864–1865. Like Freeman, Catton was a journalist; his style is just as graceful as that of Lee's chronicler, and maybe even more picturesque. Unlike Freeman's "study in command," however, Catton's trilogy depicts war for the common soldier. As the author wrote in 1962, his was "an attempt to understand the men who fought in the Army of the Potomac." In this light, Freeman's and Catton's two trilogies serve as interesting if unintentional complements to one another.

Beyond these general works, the literature of the eastern theater since 1950 rests mainly on studies of specific campaigns and engagements. The most important writing is here presented in roughly chronological order of event.

MANASSAS TO SECOND MANASSAS

The war began with the Confederate bombardment of Fort Sumter in Charleston harbor, South Carolina, April 12–13, 1861. W. A. Swanberg's *First Blood: The Story of Fort Sumter* (1957) has stood as the comprehensive story of the event, tracing developments in Charleston from the election of Lincoln through the Union garrison's surrender of the fort. Robert Hendrickson's *Sumter: The First Day of the Civil War* (1990) is a more informally written narrative that adds nothing new to Swanberg's account. Useful as a summary is the entire issue of *Civil War Times Illustrated* devoted to the engagement, "Fort Sumter— 1861" (1976), whose text was written by Albert Castel.

The war's first great battle, July 21, 1861, is authoritatively chronicled in William C. Davis's *Battle at Bull Run: A History of the First Major Campaign of the Civil War* (1977). His account begins with the organization of opposing forces in Virginia in the spring of 1861, describing the advance of General Irvin McDowell's Union army, the initial contact at Blackburn's Ford, July 18, and the reinforcement of General G. T. Beauregard's Confederate forces by General Joseph E. Johnston's, brought from the Shenandoah Valley. Davis also wrote *First Blood: Fort Sumter to Bull Run* (1983), tracing the first months of the war in a fast-paced text supplemented by numerous photographs and colorful illustrations. John Hennessy's *The First Battle of Manassas: An End to Innocence July 18–21, 1861* (1989) is a solid account. *Civil War Times Illustrated* (*CWTI*) devoted a special issue in 1973 to the first Manassas campaign, with text by

V. C. Jones. This issue, with selected other articles from *CWTI*, is reprinted as *Battle Chronicles of the Civil War*, edited by James M. McPherson (1989).

The fighting in western Virginia in the latter half of 1861 has been chronicled in magazines and periodicals as well as books. Richard O. Curry, "McClellan's Western Virginia Campaign of 1861" (July 1962), is a respected historian's review of the successful Union campaign that brought General George B. McClellan to President Lincoln's attention. Martin K. Fleming's "The Northwestern Virginia Campaign of 1861" (1993) surveys the actions at Philippi (June 3), Rich Mountain (July 11), Corrick's Ford (July 13), and Cheat Mountain (September 12). A handful of books treat aspects of the fighting in western Virginia early in the war; an example is Jack Zinn, *R. E. Lee's Cheat Mountain Campaign* (1974).

The federal bombardment and capture of Fort Pulaski, near Savannah, Georgia, was an isolated engagement in April 1862 that signified the effectiveness of rifled artillery against old masonry forts. Allen P. Julian relates the story in "Fort Pulaski" (1970). Richard A. Sauers, "Laurels for Burnside: The Invasion of North Carolina January–July 1862" (1988), relates federal successes along the North Carolina coast.

Robert G. Tanner, *Stonewall in the Valley: Thomas J. "Stonewall" Jackson's Shenandoah Valley Campaign Spring 1862* (1976) is the first modern book-length study of Jackson's legendary campaign; its thoroughness of research and perspective render it as the definitive one. Beginning with views of the valley, Jackson's command, his preliminary operations in western Virginia, January 1862, and the opening battle of the Valley campaign (Kernstown, March 23), Tanner's account analyzes the sources of Jackson's success and relates his victories against hapless federal commanders at McDowell (May 8), Winchester (May 25), Cross Keys (June 8), and Port Republic (June 9). James I. Robertson's "Stonewall in the Shenandoah: The Valley Campaign of 1862" fills an entire issue of *CWTI* (1972).

The Peninsula campaign and Seven Days' Battles of May–July 1862 are expertly explained in Stephen W. Sears's fine study, *To the Gates of Richmond: The Peninsula Campaign* (1992). Sears's scope, beginning with the siege of Yorktown, April 15–May 3, includes the fighting at Williamsburg, May 5, and at Hanover Court House, May 27, and also focuses on the campaign's larger actions: Seven Pines (May 31–June 1), Confederate General "Jeb" Stuart's cavalry raid around McClellan's army (June 12–15), and the Seven Days' Battles: Oak Grove, June 25; Mechanicsville, June 26; Gaines' Mill, June 27; Savage's Station, June 29; Glendale, June 30; and Malvern Hill, July 1. Clifford Dowdey's *The Seven Days: The Emergence of Lee* (1964) relates the same train of events. The author's subtitle derives from General Robert E. Lee's assumption of command of the Confederate army in Virginia, June 1, after the wounding of Joseph E. Johnston at Seven Pines. Joseph P. Cullen, one-time historian at the Richmond National Battlefield Park, is author of *The Peninsula Campaign of 1862: McClellan and Lee Struggle for Richmond* (1973), a briefer review than those offered by Sears and Dowdey but still useful. Steven H. Newton's *The Battle of Seven Pines* (1993) is a recent, detailed account of the battle of May 31–June 1. Though written as a survey, Emory Thomas's five-part series, "The Peninsula Campaign," in *CWTI* (1979) stands as a worthwhile monograph. A collection of essays representing recent scholarship is William J. Miller, ed., *The Peninsula Campaign of 1862: Yorktown to the Seven Days* (1993). The work includes Edwin Cole Bearss' " 'Into the very jaws of the enemy . . .': Jeb Stuart's Ride around McClellan," which describes the Confederate exploit of mid-June that helped Lee fix the position of McClellan's army before the Seven Days.

Cedar Mountain, the battle between the forces of "Stonewall" Jackson and Union general John Pope, is usually considered a preliminary to the second Manassas campaign, but it receives detailed study in Robert K. Krick's admirable *Stonewall Jackson at Cedar Mountain* (1990). Krick's account of the engagement, fought August 9, 1862, offers incisive analysis of the leadership of Jackson as independent commander.

Robert E. Lee's victory over Pope at second Manassas, August 29–30, is chronicled in John J. Hennessy's excellent work, *Return to Bull Run: The Campaign and Battle of Second Manassas* (1993). Besides presenting the most thoroughly researched and clearly written account of the battle, Hennessy's book serves as a history of the two-and-a-half-month service of John Pope as commander of his ill-fated Union Army of Virginia. *CWTI* devoted an entire issue to the battle and campaign, with text by Dennis Kelly (1983). Alan D. Gaff's *Brave Men's Tears: The Iron Brigade at Brawner Farm* (1985) is a well-researched account of the fighting on the evening of August 28, which marked the opening of the battle.

THE MARYLAND CAMPAIGN AND BATTLE OF ANTIETAM

Lee's raid into Maryland, September 4–18, 1862, and the great battle fought September 17 along Antietam Creek, have been the subject of several notable books. James V. Murfin's *The Gleam of Bayonets: The Battle of Antietam and the Maryland Campaign of 1862* (1965) and Stephen W. Sears's *Landscape Turned Red: The Battle of Antietam* (1983) are the premier studies. Murfin's description begins with the Confederates' reasons for carrying the war into Maryland and with President Lincoln's misgivings with George McClellan as commander of the Army of the Potomac. Tactically a draw, the battle, as Murfin points out, offered each side a victory of sorts: Lee's success in repulsing the attacks of a heavily superior enemy and McClellan's strategic success in ending Lee's raid. *Landscape Turned Red* combines graceful writing and strong research, particularly in sources not tapped by Murfin, for an excellent account of the campaign. Underpinning the author's perspective is his interest in General McClellan, whose faults Sears sees clearly: his arrogance, capacity for self-deception, and lack of will to fight.

Interesting perspectives by four leading students of the Virginia theater are provided in *Antietam: Essays on the 1862 Maryland Campaign* (1989). Edited by Gary W. Gallagher, the articles are contributed by Gallagher, Dennis E. Frye, Robert K. Krick, and A. Wilson Greene. All are provocative. For example, Krick's essay, "The Army of Northern Virginia in September 1862," argues that Lee's decision to give battle at Sharpsburg, with his campaign plan in enemy hands and his army weakened by straggling, was "probably his worst of the war."

In *Antietam: The Soldier's Battle* (1989), John M. Priest's emphasis is on individual soldiers' experiences rather than interpretation and analysis of the battle as a whole; he thus draws on the writings of junior officers and the rank and file. Priest similarly explains the engagement fought September 14 in *Before Antietam: The Battle for South Mountain* (1992), where Confederates tried to hold back McClellan's advance through Crampton's, Fox's, and Turner's gaps, giving Lee's scattered forces time to gather for battle. Jay Luvaas and Harold W. Nelson collaborated in *The U.S. Army War College Guide to the Battle of Antietam: The Maryland Campaign of 1862* (1987), which weaves the opposing officers' reports with narrative and terrain maps to form a comprehensive tour guide to the Antietam battlefield. Like the army's "staff ride," the aim of Luvaas and Nelson's book is to stimulate an appreciation of battlefields and officers' tactics through study of how the armies fought over the ground. Sites of the Battle of South Mountain and other activity outside the boundaries of Antietam National Battlefield Park are also included.

The popular magazines have given the Maryland campaign its due attention. *Blue and Gray* offered a two-part coverage of the battle, with James V. Murfin contributing the lead article for September 1985 and Stephen W. Sears following in November with "McClellan at Antietam." Sears also wrote "The Battle of South Mountain, September 14, 1862," for *Blue and Gray*'s January 1987 issue. Dennis E. Frye relates Jackson's capture of Harpers Ferry for the same magazine in "Stonewall Attacks! The Siege of Harpers Ferry" (1987). *CWTI* commemorated the centennial of the Maryland Campaign with a special issue in August 1962; Stephen Sears wrote "America's Bloodiest Day: The Battle of Antietam" for *CWTI* in 1987.

CONFEDERATE HIGH TIDE

Robert E. Lee's victory over General Ambrose E. Burnside's Army of the Potomac at Fredericksburg, December 13, 1862, was so straightforward, or so simply defensive tactically, that it has not attracted the modern scholarship of, say, an Antietam or a Gettysburg. Only two "modern" books devoted solely to the battle have appeared. Certainly the better of them is Vorin E. Whan, Jr., *Fiasco at Fredericksburg* (1961), in which the author offers sound explanation of the battle and an unvarnished critique of Burnside's utter failure as Union army commander. Edward J. Stackpole was principal author of *CWTI's* issue dedicated to Fredericksburg in 1965. David E. Roth, editor of *Blue and Gray,* wrote the main text for his magazine's issue devoted to the battle in 1984.

On the Battle of Chancellorsville, Lee's resounding victory over General Joseph Hooker and the Army of the Potomac, May 1–4, 1863, Ernest B. Furgurson's *Chancellorsville 1863: The Souls of the Brave* (1992) is the best book since John Bigelow's *The Campaign of Chancellorsville,* published in 1910. While Bigelow's was largely a study of command, Furgurson's work describes the soldiers' experience as well as the commanding generals' performance. Union general Hooker is credited for an excellent campaign plan and for initially outmaneuvering Lee. Hooker's subsequent loss of nerve and Lee's daring assumption of the offensive, though severely outnumbered, are highlights of Furgurson's text, as are Stonewall Jackson's famous flank attack in the Wilderness and Jackson's tragic wounding late on May 2. Jay Luvaas and Harold Nelson's *The U.S. Army War College Guide to the Battles of Chancellorsville and Fredericksburg* (1988) is on the same model as the author's guide to the Battle of Antietam. Luvaas and Nelson's "staff ride" also offers valuable insights on such matters as the role of intelligence in Lee's success at Chancellorsville. Another view of the battle is provided by Joseph P. Cullen's text for the May 1968 issue of *CWTI.*

Steven A. Cormier, *The Siege of Suffolk: The Forgotten Campaign April 11–May 4, 1863* (1989), reviews the Confederate expedition in the spring of 1863 that prevented Longstreet's corps from participating at Chancellorsville. Cormier's narrative details Longstreet's operations against the Union garrison at Suffolk, Virginia, seventy miles southeast of Richmond, while his troops gathered supplies in the countryside for Lee's army.

Cavalry operations on the Virginia front have received their own study. The first two volumes of Stephen Z. Starr's trilogy, *The Union Cavalry in the Civil War* (1979, 1981), ably record the progress from incompetence to effectiveness of the cavalry arm of the Army of the Potomac. Edward G. Longacre's *Mounted Raids of the Civil War* (1975) recounts twelve equestrian expeditions, five of which occurred in the Virginia theater. The Battle of Brandy Station, June 9, 1863, the biggest cavalry fight of the war, is thoroughly described in Fairfax Downey's *Clash of Cavalry: The Battle of Brandy Station, June 9, 1863* (1959). Gary W. Gallagher's "Brandy Station: The Civil War's Bloodiest Arena of Mounted Combat" (1990), is a good, short account, as is Clark B. Hall's "The Battle of Brandy Station" (1990).

GETTYSBURG

More than any other battle in the East, Gettysburg, July 1–3, 1863, has drawn the attention of Civil War writers. Generally the literature pays attention to several themes: the accidental outbreak of battle, Lee's uncharacteristically mediocre performance, the poor work of all three of his corps commanders, the Federals' combination of good luck and hard fighting that led to their success in repulsing rebel attacks at Little Round Top and Culp's Hill July 2, and the almost mythic Confederate attack against Meade's center on July 3.

Of first-class studies there are several. Edwin B. Coddington, *The Gettysburg Campaign: A Study in Command* (1968), continues to rank as the best single-volume coverage of Lee's raid, the battle, and the Confederate retreat, July 5–12. One of Coddington's key points is the defense of General Meade against critics, especially regarding Meade's decision against a vigorous pursuit of Lee's retreating army after the battle. Another good overview is Glenn Tucker, *High Tide at Gettysburg: The Campaign in Pennsylvania* (1958). In giving generous attention to the Confederates' side of the battle, Tucker seeks to defend I Corps commander General James Longstreet against arguments that he performed badly on the second and third days of the fight. (Tucker advances his pro-Longstreet thesis more pointedly in his *Lee and Longstreet at Gettysburg* [1968].) Jay Luvaas and Harold W. Nelson's *The U.S. Army War College Guide to the Battle of Gettysburg* (1986) presents Confederate and Union officers' reports found in the *Official Records* as parallel reading for a tour of the battlefield, arranged chronologically with the battle. Clifford Dowdey's *Death of a Nation: The Story of Lee and His Men at Gettysburg* (1958) tells the story of the battle from the Confederates' side.

Other scholars have presented distinguished fare, grappling with Gettysburg's scope and complexity by dissecting it into days or phases. Warren W. Hassler, Jr.'s *Crisis at the Crossroads: The First Day at Gettysburg* (1970) traces the convergence of opposing forces, Southerners' assaults on the Union I and XI Corps, and the retreat of the Federals to their positions along Culp's Hill and Cemetery Ridge. Harry W. Pfanz's two recent books are by far the best analysis of the fighting of July 2. Pfanz's *Gettysburg: The Second Day* (1987) details the assault of Longstreet's two divisions on the Union-held Devil's Den, Little Round Top, Wheatfield, and Peach Orchard, closing with the advance of Anderson's division against the Union center. After reviewing the action of July 1, Pfanz's *Gettysburg: Culp's Hill and Cemetery Hill* (1993) takes up the battle of the second day, chronicling the assaults of Ewell's corps against the Union right and right-center. Pfanz also relates the resumption of combat on the morning of July 3 at Culp's Hill.

Supplementing these titles are insightful essays by Alan Nolan, Gary Gallagher, Wilson Greene, Robert Krick, Glenn Robertson and Scott Hartwig, published in Gallagher, ed., *The First Day at Gettyburg: Essays on Confederate and Union Leadership* (1992) and *The Second Day at Gettysburg* (1993). The final volume of this trilogy, *The Third Day at Gettysburg and Beyond* (1994), again edited by Gallagher, features the writings of Gallagher, Krick, and Greene, plus William Garrett Piston, Carol Reardon, and Robert L. Bee.

The centerpiece of Gettysburg's third day is best recounted by George R. Stewart, *Pickett's Charge: A Microhistory of the Final Attack at Gettysburg, July 3, 1863* (1959). Stewart's meticulous, engaging narrative reminds us that Lee's assaulting force numbered some 10,500 muskets (not the legendary

15,000), arrayed in nine brigades from three divisions (not just Pickett's). Kathleen R. Georg and John W. Busey, *Nothing But Glory: Pickett's Division at Gettysburg* (1987), provides fascinating detail on the role of General George E. Pickett's three brigades in Lee's ill-fated assault but does not chronicle the role of the other six Confederate brigades from Heth's and Pender's divisions that also participated in the charge of Pickett, Pettigrew and Trimble.

Other studies of Gettysburg have assumed different focuses. Edward G. Longacre's *The Cavalry at Gettysburg* (1986) is subtitled *A Tactical Study of Mounted Operations during the Civil War's Pivotal Campaign, 9 June–14 July 1863,* and deals ably with the role of Stuart's cavalry during the campaign. Fairfax Downey, *The Guns at Gettysburg* (1958), explains the role of artillery during the battle.

A convenient approach for some writers has been to present the participants' view of the fighting. Earl Schenck Miers and Richard A. Brown, *Gettysburg* (1948), represents the authors' intent to "create the story of Gettysburg in terms of the men and women who lived through the anxiety of the invasion and battle." Union officers' reminiscences, originally given as papers at meetings of the Military Order of the Loyal Legion of the United States (MOLLUS), are presented in two volumes of *The Gettysburg Papers,* compiled by Ken Bandy and Florence Freeland (1978). Richard Rollins has recently edited an admirably varied collection of *Official Records* reports, manuscript letters, and postbellum articles, all related to the Confederate attack of July 3, as *Pickett's Charge! Eyewitness Accounts* (1994).

Blue and Gray magazine has devoted four issues to the battle: November 1987 for July 1, with Marshall D. Krolick as lead author; March 1988 for July 2 (Gary Kross, author); and July 1988 for the third day, with text written principally by Gettysburg Park historian Kathleen Georg Harrison. "Gettysburg Cavalry Operations, June 27–July 3, 1863" is the focus of *Blue and Gray* in October 1988. *CWTI* covers the battle with two special issues. That of July 1963 includes Harry W. Pfanz's article on the development of Gettysburg National Military Park; text for *CWTI*'s summer 1988 issue was written by Jeffry Wert.

Frequently overlooked are the operations of Lee's and Meade's armies in the period from Gettysburg to the Battle of the Wilderness. *The Road to Bristoe Station: Campaigning with Lee and Meade August 1–October 20, 1863,* by William D. Henderson (1987), relates the late summer and early fall campaigns of the two armies in Virginia, including the Battle of Bristoe Station, October 14, 1863, in which Confederates suffered a small but costly repulse. Martin F. Graham and George F. Skoch's *Mine Run: A Campaign of Lost Opportunities October 21, 1863–May 1, 1864* (1987) picks up from Henderson the narrative of events in Virginia. Clark B. Hall's article, "The Winter Encampment of the Army of the Potomac, December 1, 1863–May 1, 1864" (1991) surveys the Union army in Virginia before General Ulysses S. Grant assumed its overall command.

Virgil Carrington Jones's *Eight Hours before Richmond* (1957) tells the story of the notorious Kilpatrick-Dahlgren raid of February 28–March 4, 1864, in which Union cavalrymen aimed for Richmond, allegedly to burn the city and kill or capture President Davis. Meriwether Stuart's article "Colonel Ulric Dahlgren and Richmond's Union Underground" (1964), analyzes contributions of a Unionist fifth column inside the Confederate capital.

GRANT VERSUS LEE

The first great battle in Virginia of 1864, the Wilderness, May 5–6, is well explained by Gordon C. Rhea's *The Battle of the Wilderness, May 5–6, 1864* (1994), in which the author examines Lee's failings in the battle as well as the tension between Meade, commander of the Army of the Potomac, and Grant, general in chief. Before Rhea, Edward Steere's *The Wilderness Campaign* (1960) served as the standard history. Steere explains how the two sides achieved a draw after two days' hard fighting: Grant failed in his objective (destroying Lee's army) just as Lee failed in his (driving Grant back across the Rapidan and Rappahannock rivers). Each side also lost proportionally the same—roughly 14 percent of effective strength. Another treatment of the battle is Robert Garth Scott's *Into the Wilderness with the Army of the Potomac* (1985).

William D. Matter's *If It Takes All Summer: The Battle of Spotsylvania* (1988) is the definitive account of the maneuvers and hard fighting, May 6–21, that followed the Wilderness. Matter expertly assesses the two armies' generalship and graphically records the tough courage of the soldiers in such settings as when exhausted enemies were pitted in trench lines no more than a parapet or musket-length apart. The failure of Lee's corps commanders, Ewell and Hill, with Longstreet wounded and Stuart dead, is one of Matter's most important points, taken up too by Gary W. Gallagher's "The Army of Northern Virginia in May 1864: A Crisis of High Command" (1990), which evaluates the weakness of corps command in Lee's army during the opening of the campaign that forced General Lee's personal involvement on the battlefield.

J. Michael Miller's *The North Anna Campaign: "Even to Hell Itself," May 21–26, 1864* (1989) follows Grant's army from Spotsylvania to the area of Cold Harbor. Miller is the author, too, of the lead article, "Lee and Grant at the North Anna River" (1993), and of "Along the North Anna" (1987). The Battle of Cold Harbor, June 3, 1864, a bloody repulse of Grant's forces, is detailed by Louis J. Baltz III in *The Last Battle of Cold Harbor: May 27–June 13, 1864* (1994).

Following his defeat at Cold Harbor, General Grant called for Meade's army to shift operations south of the James River, against Petersburg, the Confederate capital's railway hub. Brian Holden Reid, "Another Look at Grant's Crossing of the James" (1993), questions the conclusion of some of Grant's admirers (that Grant's plan had all along called for a siege of Petersburg) by deeming Grant's river crossing "an essay in improvisation of a high order." Collaborating for *Blue and Gray*'s issue of April 1994, "Grant and Lee, 1864: From the North Anna to the Crossing of the James," were Robert E. L. Krick, Michael Andrus, and David Ruth, all staff historians at the Richmond National Battlefield Park.

The routes of Grant's and Lee's armies from the Wilderness to the James, including the battles of the Wilderness, Spotsylvania, and Cold Harbor, have come to be called the Overland campaign. The most recent overviews of it are Noah Andre Trudeau's *Bloody Roads South: The Wilderness to Cold Harbor, May–June 1864* (1989), Gregory Jaynes's *The Killing Ground: Wilderness to Cold Harbor* (1986), and R. Wayne Maney's *Marching to Cold Harbor: Victory and Failure, 1864* (1994).

Cavalry actions during the Overland campaign include the Battle of Yellow Tavern, May 11, 1864, which cost Jeb Stuart his life. It is related in William W. Hassler's article, "Yellow Tavern" (1966). W. G. Ryckman, "Clash of Cavalry at Trevilians" (1967), notes that after the death of Stuart on May 12, the attrition of Lee's cavalry force hastened Union victory in Virginia.

As Grant and Meade hammered Lee north of Richmond, part of the Union strategy for the spring of 1864 called for a smaller Federal army under General Benjamin F. Butler to advance toward Richmond from the south of the James River. The story of Confederate general G. T. Beauregard's success in blocking Butler's advance is related in two good studies, William Glenn Robertson's *Back Door to Richmond: The Bermuda Hundred Campaign, April–June 1864* (1987) and Herbert M. Schiller's *The Bermuda Hundred Campaign: Operations on the South Side of the James River—May 1864* (1988).

The Petersburg campaign, June 1864–April 1865, was the war's longest, as Grant pinned Lee's outnumbered forces to static warfare. Petersburg was also the war's decisive campaign, as it led to Union troops eventually cutting off the vital railways south of Petersburg, on which the Confederate capital of Richmond depended. Noah Andre Trudeau's history of the campaign is *The Last Citadel: Petersburg, Virginia, June 1864–April 1865* (1991); William C. Davis's is *Death in the Trenches: Grant at Petersburg* (1986). *Civil War Times Illustrated* devoted its entire August 1970 issue to the siege of Petersburg, with text written by Joseph P. Cullen.

Other books detail specific events or stages of the Petersburg siege operations. William G. Robertson's *The Petersburg Campaign: The Battle of Old Men and Young Boys, June 9, 1864* (1989) describes how home guards of Petersburg repelled Union troops' first effort to take the key city. Thomas J. Howe's *The Petersburg Campaign: Wasted Valor, June 15–18, 1864* (1988) concerns the Federals' unsuccessful assaults on Petersburg, as Lee and Grant shifted their armies south of the James. *The Petersburg Campaign: The Battle of the Crater: "The Horrid Pit," June 25–August 6, 1864* (1989), by Michael A. Cavanaugh and William Marvel, features Grant's dramatic but disastrous effort to break through the Confederate lines after detonating a huge cache of powder under the rebel works, July 30. Events of the Petersburg siege, August 14–25, 1864, are chronicled in John Horn's *The Petersburg Campaign: The Destruction of the Weldon Railroad: Deep Bottom, Globe Tavern, and Reams Station* (1991). Aspects of the siege that the author calls Grant's "fifth offensive," September 29–October 19, are authoritatively explained in Richard J. Sommers' hefty *Richmond Redeemed: The Siege at Petersburg* (1981). The author's theme is that by repelling Grant's initiatives north and south of the James during this three-week period, Lee "redeemed," that is, saved, the capital.

One of the celebrated exploits of Confederate cavalry during the siege was the raid in September 1864 by General Wade Hampton's troopers behind Federal lines to bring out a herd of 3,000 cattle. Edward Boykin's *Beefsteak Raid* (1960) is the book on the subject, supplemented by Richard Lykes, "Hampton's Cattle Raid September 14–17, 1864," *Military Affairs* (Spring 1957).

The Shenandoah Valley's importance as a source of food for Lee's army brought the war with particular intensity to the valley in May 1864. William C. Davis's *The Battle of New Market* (1975) offers an excellent description of the Confederate victory of May 15 over Union general Franz Sigel's invading forces, a battle made famous by the charge of 258 young cadets from the Virginia Military Institute. Marshall Moore Brice's *Conquest of a Valley* (1965) covers the Battle of Piedmont, June 5, fought in the upper (southern) part of the Shenandoah, as Federal forces under General David Hunter (Sigel's successor) subjugated the area.

After Piedmont, Lee was forced to detach General Jubal Early and the II Corps from his lines before Richmond, which enabled Early to drive the Federals from the Shenandoah in late June, then march into Maryland. Early's dramatic sortie is capably related by Frank E. Vandiver's *Jubal's Raid: General Early's Famous Attack on Washington in 1864* (1960), and more recently by Benjamin Franklin Cooling, *Jubal Early's Raid on Washington 1864* (1989). The Battle of Monocacy, Maryland, July 9, as Union forces delayed Early's march on Washington, is the subject of Benjamin Franklin Cooling's feature article, "The Battle That Saved Washington" (1992). John Henry Cramer, *Lincoln under Enemy Fire: The Complete Account of His Experiences during Early's Attack on Washington* (1948), relates the several times when the Northern president came under Confederate fire as he visited Fort Stevens, July 11–12. Finally, the "remarkable feat" of Early and the infantry of Lee's II Corps withdrawing from the lines opposite Grant's army and moving into the valley without the Federals' discovery is the subject of William B. Feis's "A Union Military Intelligence Failure: Jubal Early's Raid, June 12–July 14, 1864" (1990). In retaliation for Union depredations in the valley, Early sent cavalry raiders under General John McCausland to Chambersburg, Pennsylvania, two-thirds of which the Confederates burned on July 30, 1864. Everard D. Smith's "Chambersburg: Anatomy of a Confederate Reprisal" (1991), analyzes how Southerners perceived Chambersburg as "a center of Yankee subversion," to be destroyed. *Southern Revenge! Civil War History of Chambersburg, Pennsylvania* (1989), by Ted

Alexander, Virginia Stake, Jim Neitzel, and William P. Conrad, includes an account of the Confederates' ransoming and burning of the city.

In late July Grant ordered General Philip H. Sheridan and Union troops eventually numbering 50,000 to destroy Early and the Shenandoah's resources. Sheridan's victories at Winchester (September 19), Fisher's Hill (September 22), and Cedar Creek (October 19) are ably related by Jeffry D. Wert in *From Winchester to Cedar Creek: The Shenandoah Campaign of 1864* (1987). Thomas A. Lewis's *The Guns of Cedar Creek* (1988) is a thorough explanation of the key battle that ensured Federal control of the valley. Lewis is also author of *The Shenandoah in Flames: The Valley Campaign of 1864* (1987). Theodore C. Mahr's *Early's Valley Campaign: The Battle of Cedar Creek: Showdown in the Shenandoah, October 1–30, 1864* (1992) is another recent and detailed narration of the battle of October 19. Prominent students of the war in Virginia analyze aspects of the contest between Early and Sheridan in Gary W. Gallagher, ed., *Struggle for the Shenandoah: Essays on the 1864 Valley Campaign* (1991). Gallagher's chapter offers that Sheridan's methodical destruction of the valley's food stores was a logistical disaster for the Confederacy equaled only by the loss of middle Tennessee and Sherman's march through Georgia. Jeff Wert's and Will Greene's essays examine the generalship of Early and Sheridan, while chapters by Bob Krick and Dennis Frye assess the weak role of Confederate cavalry during the campaign.

Warfare along the Confederates' Atlantic coast led to several important engagements in the last year of the war. William H. Nulty, *Confederate Florida: The Road to Olustee* (1990), surveys the war in Florida, 1861–1864, then focuses on the battle of February 20, 1864, in which Confederates blunted a Union expedition into the state. Richard M. McMurry's article, "The President's Tenth and the Battle of Olustee" (1978), frames the battle in terms of Lincoln's hopes to create a Unionist state government if 10 percent of Floridians professed loyalty.

Union efforts in 1863–1864 to capture Charleston, South Carolina, led to bombardment of the city and assaults on Confederate fortifications. E. Milby Burton's *Siege of Charleston 1861–1865* (1970) is a worthwhile volume on Union efforts against Fort Sumter, Battery Wagner, and other Southern positions until the Confederate evacuation of Charleston in February 1865. Stephen R. Wise, *Gate of Hell: Campaign for Charleston Harbor, 1863* (1994), offers excellent scholarship on the fighting of July through September.

Rod Gragg's *Confederate Goliath: The Battle of Fort Fisher* (1991) is an expert accounting of the Union capture of the important bastion guarding Wilmington, North Carolina, whose fall in January 1865 closed the last major Southern port open to blockade runners. Rowena Reed's well-researched *Combined Operations in the Civil War* (1978) includes chapters on the combined army-navy operations at both Charleston and Fort Fisher.

The closing ten days of the war in Virginia began with the Battle of Five Forks, March 31–April 1, 1865, the Union victory by which Grant's forces finally cut Lee's last railway line, the Southside Railroad, leading out of Petersburg. *The Battle of Five Forks* (1985), by Ed Bearss and Chris Calkins, details this important fight. Loss of the railroad and the Federals' breaking of Lee's Petersburg lines on April 2 compelled the Confederate army to abandon its positions, opening Richmond to enemy seizure. Confederate officials' evacuation of the capital and Union occupation, April 2–4, are well explained in Rembert W. Patrick's *The Fall of Richmond* (1960). The same events are the subject of David D. Ryan's *Four Days in 1865: The Fall of Richmond* (1993).

Lee's withdrawal, the dwindling Confederate army's march westward, the Battle of Sayler's Creek on April 6, and final surrender at Appomattox Court House on April 9 are narrated by Burke Davis in *To Appomattox: Nine April Days, 1865* (1959). William C. Davis's "The Campaign to Appomattox" fills an entire issue of *CWTI* (1975). Frank P. Cauble's *The Surrender Proceedings: April 9, 1865—Appomattox Court House* (1987) details the famous meeting of Lee and Grant in the home of Wilmer McLean. James C. Clark's *Last Train South: The Flight of the Confederate Government from Richmond* (1984) and Burke Davis's *The Long Surrender* (1985) describe the exodus of Jefferson Davis and other Confederate leaders from the fallen capital, tracing their route through the Carolinas into Georgia and Florida. Noah Andre Trudeau, *Out of the Storm: The End of the Civil War, April–June 1865* (1994), places the Appomattox campaign and Lee's surrender in context of the total collapse of Confederate resistance and restoration of Federal authority in the South.

PROSPECTS FOR FURTHER STUDY

The war in the eastern theater, with its legendary battles and leaders, will doubtless continue to attract serious study and writing. Given the voluminous literature already at hand, further overview approaches will be of little value. Detailed accounts of major engagements, even those that have been thoroughly explained, will continue to be welcome if they bring to bear new source materials (e.g., Rhea's *The Battle of the Wilderness*) or critically examine issues of leadership (as do the essays on Gettysburg edited by Gallagher) and offer new perspectives.

Nontactical themes should also attract students. The importance of intelligence, for example, is demonstrated by William B. Feis's article, "Neutralizing the Valley: The Role of Military Intelligence in the Defeat of Jubal Early's Army of the Valley, 1864–1865" (1993). The tantalizing speculations of William A. Tidwell, James O. Hall, and David Winfred Gaddy in *Come Retribution: The Confederate Secret Service and the Assassination of Lincoln* (1988) further suggest the interesting work to be done in the intelligence field.

Another relatively new emphasis in eastern theater study is the battlefield. Luvaas and Nelson's "staff rides" remind the otherwise armchair general that the only way to understand a battle is to see its terrain first-hand. Similarly, *Blue and Gray* magazine emphasizes battlefield tour routes and modern site photography for the engagements it chronicles. Given the current national interest in the protection of Civil War battlefields and other historic sites, appreciation of the battlefield will likely be a key emphasis of future Civil War historiography, as well it should be.

BIBLIOGRAPHY

Albright, Harry. *Gettysburg: Crisis of Command.* New York: Hippocrene Books, 1989.

Alexander, Ted, Virginia Stake, Jim Neitzel, and William P. Conrad. *Southern Revenge! Civil War History of Chambersburg, Pennsylvania.* Shippensburg, PA: White Mane Publishing Co., 1989.

Angle, Paul M., and Earl Schenck Miers. *Tragic Years, 1860–1865.* 2 vols. New York: Simon & Schuster, 1960.

Armstrong, Richard L. *The Battle of McDowell, March 11–May 18, 1862.* Lynchburg, VA: H. E. Howard, 1990.

Bailey, Ronald H. *Forward to Richmond: McClellan's Peninsular Campaign.* Alexandria, VA: Time-Life Books, 1983.

————. *The Bloodiest Day: The Battle of Antietam.* Alexandria, VA: Time-Life Books, 1984.

Baltz, Louis J., III. *The Last Battle of Cold Harbor: May 27–June 13, 1864.* Lynchburg, VA: H. E. Howard, 1994.

Bandy, Ken, and Florence Freeland. *The Gettysburg Papers.* 2 vols. Dayton, OH: Press of Morningside Bookshop, 1978.

Battlefields of the Civil War. New York: Arno Press, 1979. (Republication of National Park Service battlefield park pamphlets).

Bearss, Ed, and Chris Calkins. *The Battle of Five Forks.* Lynchburg, VA: H. E. Howard, 1985.

Beatie, R. H., Jr. *Road to Manassas: The Growth of Union Command in the Eastern Theatre from the Fall of Fort Sumter to the First Battle of Bull Run.* New York: Cooper Union Square Publishers, 1961.

Beck, Brandon, and Charles Grunder. *The First Battle of Winchester.* Lynchburg, VA: H. E. Howard, 1992.

Bellah, James Warner. *Soldiers' Battle: Gettysburg.* New York: David McKay Company, 1962.

Boykin, Edward. *Beefsteak Raid.* New York: Funk & Wagnalls Company, 1960.

Brice, Marshall Moore. *Conquest of a Valley.* Charlottesville: University Press of Virginia, 1965.

Brooksher, William R., and David K. Snider. *Glory at a Gallop: Tales of the Confederate Cavalry.* McLean, VA: Brassey's (US), 1993.

Burchard, Peter. *One Gallant Rush: Robert Gould Shaw and His Brave Black Regiment.* New York: St. Martin's Press, 1965.

Burton, E. Milby. *The Siege of Charleston, 1861–1865.* Columbia: University of South Carolina Press, 1970.

Busey, John W., and David G. Martin. *Regimental Strengths at Gettysburg.* Baltimore: Gateway Press, 1982.

————. *These Honored Dead: The Union Casualties at Gettysburg.* Hightstown, NJ: Longstreet House, 1988.

———. *The Last Full Measure: Burials in the Soldiers' National Cemetery at Gettysburg.* Edited by David G. Martin. Highstown, NJ: Longstreet House, 1988.

Calkins, Chris M. *Battles of Appomattox Station and Appomattox Court House, April 8–9, 1865.* Lynchburg, VA: H. E. Howard, 1987.

Cannan, John. *The Antietam Campaign, August–September 1862.* Conshohocken, PA: Combined Books, 1990.

———. *The Wilderness Campaign, May 1864.* Conshohocken, PA: Combined Books, 1993.

———, ed. *War in the East: Chancellorsville to Gettysburg, 1863.* New York: Gallery Books, 1990.

Castel, Albert. "Fort Sumter—1861." *Civil War Times Illustrated* (October 1976).

Catton, Bruce. *Mr. Lincoln's Army.* New York: Doubleday & Company, 1951.

———. *Glory Road: The Bloody Route from Fredericksburg to Gettysburg.* New York: Doubleday & Company, 1952.

———. *A Stillness at Appomattox.* New York: Doubleday & Company, 1953.

———. *Gettysburg: The Final Fury.* Garden City, N.Y.: Doubleday, 1974.

Cauble, Frank P. *The Surrender Proceedings: April 9, 1865—Appomattox Court House.* Lynchburg, VA: H. E. Howard, 1987.

Cavanaugh, Michael A., and William Marvel. *The Petersburg Campaign: The Battle of the Crater: "The Horrid Pit," June 25–August 6, 1864.* Lynchburg, VA: H. E. Howard, 1989.

Christ, Elwood W. *The Struggle for the Bliss Farm at Gettysburg, July 2nd and 3rd, 1863.* Baltimore: Butternut and Blue, 1993.

Clark, Champ. *Decoying the Yanks: Jackson's Valley Campaign.* Alexandria, VA: Time-Life Books, 1984.

———. *Gettysburg: The Confederate High Tide.* Alexandria, VA: Time-Life Books, 1985.

Clark, James C. *Last Train South: The Flight of the Confederate Government from Richmond.* Jefferson, NC: McFarland & Company, 1984.

Coco, Gregory A. *A Vast Sea of Misery: A History and Guide to the Union and Confederate Field Hospitals at Gettysburg, July 1–November 20, 1863.* Gettysburg, PA: Thomas Publications, 1988.

———. *Wasted Valor: The Confederate Dead at Gettysburg.* Gettysburg, PA: Thomas Publications, 1990.

Coddington, Edwin B. *The Gettysburg Campaign: A Study in Command.* New York: Charles Scribner's Sons, 1968.

Cohen, Stan. *The Civil War in West Virginia: A Pictorial History.* Charleston, WV: Pictorial Histories Publishing Company, 1976.

Collins, Darrell L. *Jackson's Valley Campaign: The Battle of Cross Keys and Port Republic, June 8–9, 1862.* Lynchburg, VA: H. E. Howard, 1994.

Commager, Henry Steele, ed. *The Blue and Gray: The Story of the Civil War as Told by Participants.* Indianapolis: Bobbs-Merrill Company, 1950.

Cooling, Benjamin Franklin. *Symbol, Sword, and Shield: Defending Washington during the Civil War.* Hamden, CT: Archon, 1975.

———. *Jubal Early's Raid on Washington 1864.* Baltimore: Nautical & Aviation Publishing Company of America, 1989.

———. "The Battle That Saved Washington." Blue and Gray (December 1992).

Cormier, Steven A. *The Siege of Suffolk: The Forgotten Campaign, April 11–May 4, 1863.* Lynchburg, VA: H. E. Howard, 1989.

Cramer, John Henry. *Lincoln under Enemy Fire: The Complete Account of His Experiences during Early's Attack on Washington.* Baton Rouge: Louisiana State University Press, 1948.

Cullen, Joseph P. *The Peninsula Campaign 1862: McClellan and Lee Struggle for Richmond.* Harrisburg, PA: Stackpole Company, 1973.

———. "The Battle of Chancellorsville." *Civil War Times Illustrated* (May 1968).

———. "The Siege of Petersburg." *Civil War Times Illustrated* (Summer 1988).

Curry, Richard O. "McClellan's Western Virginia Campaign of 1861." *Ohio History* (July 1962).

Davis, Burke. *To Appomattox: Nine April Days, 1865.* New York: Rinehart & Company, 1959.

———. *The Long Surrender.* New York: Random House, 1985.

Davis, William C. *The Battle of New Market.* New York: Doubleday, 1975.

———. *Battle at Bull Run: A History of the First Major Campaign of the Civil War.* New York: Doubleday, 1977.

———. *The Imperiled Union.* 2 vols. New York: Doubleday, 1982, 1983.

———. *First Blood: Fort Sumter to Bull Run.* Alexandria, VA: Time-Life Books, 1983.

———. *Brother against Brother: The War Begins.* Alexandria, VA: Time-Life Books, 1983.

———. *Death in the Trenches: Grant at Petersburg.* Alexandria, VA: Time-Life Books, 1986.

———. "The Campaign to Appomattox." *Civil War Times Illustrated* (April 1975).

Dowdey, Clifford. *Death of a Nation: The Story of Lee and His Men at Gettysburg.* New York: Alfred A. Knopf, 1958.

———. *Lee's Last Campaign: The Story of Lee and His Men against Grant—1864.* Boston: Little, Brown, 1960.

———. *The Seven Days: The Emergence of Lee.* Boston: Little, Brown, 1964.

Downey, Fairfax. *The Guns at Gettysburg.* New York: David McKay Company, 1958.

———. *Clash of Cavalry: The Battle of Brandy Station, June 9, 1863.* New York: David McKay Company, 1959.

Eisenschiml, Otto, and Ralph Newman, eds. *The American Iliad: The Epic Story of the Civil War as Narrated by Eyewitnesses and Contemporaries.* Indianapolis: Bobbs-Merrill, 1947.

Farwell, Byron. *Ball's Bluff: A Small Battle and Its Long Shadow.* McLean, VA: EPM Publications, 1990.

Feis, William B. "A Union Miltary Intelligence Failure: Jubal Early's Raid, June 12–July 14, 1864." *Civil War History* (September 1990).

———. "Neutralizing the Valley: The Role of Military Intelligence in the Defeat of Jubal Early's Army of the Valley, 1864–1865." *Civil War History* (September 1993).

Fleming, Martin K. "The Northwestern Virginia Campaign of 1861." *Blue and Gray* (August 1993).

Foote, Shelby. *The Civil War: A Narrative.* 3 vols. New York: Random House, 1958–1974.

Freeman, Douglas Southall. *Lee's Lieutenants: A Study in Command.* New York: Charles Scribner's Sons, 1942–1944.

Frye, Dennis T. "Stonewall Attacks! The Siege of Harpers Ferry." *Blue and Gray* (September 1987).

Furgurson, Ernest B. *Chancellorsville 1863: The Souls of the Brave.* New York: Alfred A. Knopf, 1992.

Gaff, Alan D. *Brave Men's Tears: The Iron Brigade at Brawner Farm.* Dayton, OH: Morningside Press, 1985.

Gallagher, Gary W., ed. *Antietam: Essays on the 1862 Maryland Campaign.* Kent, OH: Kent State University Press, 1989.

———. "The Army of Northern Virginia in May 1864: A Crisis of High Command." *Civil War History* (June 1990).

———. "Brandy Station: The Civil War's Bloodiest Arena of Mounted Combat." *Blue and Gray* (October 1990).

———, ed. *Struggle for the Shenandoah: Essays on the 1864 Valley Campaign.* Kent, OH: Kent State University Press, 1991.

———, ed. *The First Day at Gettysburg: Essays on Confederate and Union Leadership.* Kent, OH: Kent State University Press, 1992.

———, ed. *The Second Day at Gettysburg: Essays on Confederate and Union Leadership.* Kent, OH: Kent State University Press, 1993.

———, ed. *The Third Day at Gettysburg and Beyond.* Chapel Hill: University of North Carolina Press, 1994.

Georg, Kathleen R., and John W. Busey. *Nothing But Glory: Pickett's Division at Gettysburg.* Hightstown, NJ: Longstreet House, 1987.

Goolrick, William K. *Rebels Resurgent: Fredericksburg to Chancellorsville.* Alexandria, VA: Time-Life Books, 1985.

Gragg, Rod. *Confederate Goliath: The Battle of Fort Fisher.* New York: HarperCollins, 1991.

Graham, Martin F., and George F. Skoch. *Mine Run: A Campaign of Lost Opportunities, October 21, 1863–May 1, 1864.* Lynchburg, VA: H. E. Howard, 1987.

Grunder, Charles, and Brandon Beck. *The Second Battle of Winchester, June 12–15, 1863.* Lynchburg, VA: H. E. Howard, 1989.

Hall, Clark B. "The Battle of Brandy Station." *Civil War Times Illustrated* (June 1990).

———. "The Winter Encampment of the Army of the Potomac, December 1, 1863–May 1, 1864." *Blue and Gray* (April 1991).

Hamblen, Charles P. *Connecticut Yankees at Gettysburg.* Edited by Walter L. Powell. Kent, OH: Kent State University Press, 1993.

Hanson, Joseph Mills. *Bull Run Remembers: The History, Traditions and Landmarks of the Manassas (Bull Run) Campaigns before Washington, 1861–1862.* Manassas, VA: National Capitol Publishers, 1953.

Harrison, Kathleen Georg. "Ridges of Grim War." *Blue and Gray* (July 1988).

Hassler, Warren W., Jr. *Crisis at the Crossroads: The First Day at Gettysburg.* University, AL: University of Alabama Press, 1970.

———. "Yellow Tavern." *Civil War Times Illustrated* (November 1966).

Heleniak, Roman J., and Lawrence L. Hewitt, eds. *The Confederate High Command and Related Topics: The 1988 Deep Delta Civil War Symposium.* Shippensburg, PA: White Mane Publishing Company, 1990 (includes Richard J. Sommers's article on fighting at Petersburg, fall 1864).

Henderson, William D. *The Road to Bristoe Station: Campaigning with Lee and Meade, August 1–October 20, 1863.* Lynchburg, VA: H. E. Howard, 1987.

Hendrickson, Robert. *Sumter: The First Day of the Civil War.* Chelsea, MI: Scarborough House, 1990.

Hennessy, John. *The First Battle of Manassas: An End to Innocence July 18–21, 1861.* Lynchburg, VA: H. E. Howard, 1989.

———. *Return to Bull Run: The Campaign and Battle of Second Manassas.* New York: Simon & Schuster, 1993.

Herdegen, Lance, Jr., and William J. K. Beaudot. *In the Bloody Railroad Cut at Gettysburg.* Dayton, OH: Morningside House, 1990.

Holien, Kim B. *Battle at Ball's Bluff.* Orange, VA: Moss Publications, 1985.

Hollingsworth, Alan M., and James M. Cox. *The Third Day at Gettysburg: Pickett's Charge.* New York: Henry Holt and Company, 1959.

Hoehling, A. A., and Mary Hoehling. *The Day Richmond Died.* 1981. Reprint, *The Last Days of the Confederacy.* New York: Fairfax Press, 1986.

Horn, John. *The Petersburg Campaign: The Destruction of the Weldon Railroad—Deep Bottom, Globe Tavern, and Reams Station, August 14–25, 1864.* Lynchburg, VA: H. E. Howard, 1991.

———. *The Petersburg Campaign: June 1864–April 1865.* Conshohocken, PA: Combined Books, 1993.

Howe, Thomas J. *The Petersburg Campaign: Wasted Valor, June 15–18, 1864.* Lynchburg, VA: H. E. Howard, 1988.

Jaynes, Gregory. *The Killing Ground: Wilderness to Cold Harbor.* Alexandria, VA: Time-Life Books, 1986.

Jones, Virgil Carrington. *Gray Ghosts and Rebel Raiders.* New York: Henry Holt and Company, 1956.

———. *Eight Hours before Richmond.* New York: Henry Holt and Company, 1957.

———. Special issue of *Civil War Times Illustrated.* 1973.

Julian, Allen P. "Fort Pulaski." *Civil War Times Illustrated* (May 1970).

Kelly, Dennis. "Second Manassas: The Battle and Campaign." *Civil War Times Illustrated* (May 1983).

Korn, Jerry. *Pursuit to Appomattox: The Last Battles.* Alexandria, VA: Time-Life Books, 1987.

Krick, Robert E. L., Michael Andrus, and David Ruth. "Grant and Lee, 1864: From the North Anna to the Crossing of the James." *Blue and Gray* (April 1994).

Krick, Robert K. *The Gettysburg Death Roster: The Confederate Dead at Gettysburg.* Rev. ed. Dayton, OH: Press of Morningside Bookshop, 1985.

———. *Stonewall Jackson at Cedar Mountain.* Chapel Hill: University of North Carolina Press, 1990.

Krolick, Marshall D. "The Union Command: Decisions that Shaped a Battle." *Blue and Gray* (November 1987).

Kross, Gary. " 'Rebel Yells' on Both Flanks." *Blue and Gray* (March 1988).

Leckie, Robert. *None Died in Vain: The Saga of the American Civil War.* New York: HarperCollins, 1990.

Lesser, W. Hunter. *Battle at Corricks Ford: Confederate Disaster and Loss of a Leader.* Parsons, WV: McClain Printing Company, 1993.

Lewis, Thomas A. *The Shenandoah in Flames: The Valley Campaign of 1864.* Alexandria, VA: Time-Life Books, 1987.

———. *The Guns of Cedar Creek.* New York: Harper & Row, 1988.

Longacre, Edward G. *Mounted Raids of the Civil War.* New York: A. S. Barnes and Company, 1975.

———. *The Cavalry at Gettysburg: A Tactical Study of Mounted Operations during the Civil War's Pivotal Campaign, 9 June–14 July 1863.* Rutherford, NJ: Fairleigh Dickinson University Press, 1986.

Lowry, Don. *No Turning Back: The Beginning of the End of the Civil War, March–June 1864.* New York: Hippocrene Books, 1991.

———. *Fate of the Country: The Civil War from June to September 1864.* New York: Hippocrene Books, 1992.

———. *Dark and Cruel War: The Decisive Months of the Civil War, September–December 1864.* New York: Hippocrene Books, 1993.

Lowry, Terry. *September Blood: The Battle of Carnifex Ferry.* Charleston, WV: Pictorial Histories Publishing Company, 1985.

Luvaas, Jay, and Harold W. Nelson. *The U.S. Army War College Guide to the Battle of Gettysburg.* Carlisle, PA: South Mountain Press, 1986.

———. *The U.S. Army War College Guide to the Battle of Antietam: The Maryland Campaign of 1862.* Carlisle, PA: South Mountain Press, 1987.

———. *The U.S. Army War College Guide to the Battle of Chancellorsville and Fredericksburg.* Carlisle, PA: South Mountain Press, 1988.

Lykes, Richard. "Hampton's Cattle Raid September 14–17, 1864." *Military Affairs* (Spring 1957).

McKinney, Tim. *The Civil War in Fayette County, West Virginia.* Charleston, WV: Pictorial Histories Publishing Company, 1988.

———. *Robert E. Lee at Sewell Mountain: The West Virginia Campaign.* Charleston, WV: Pictorial Histories Publishing Company, 1990.

McLaughlin, Jack. *Gettysburg: The Long Encampment.* New York: Bonanza Books, 1963.

McLean, James L. *Cutler's Brigade at Gettysburg.* Baltimore: Butternut & Blue Press, 1987.

———, and Judy W. McLean. *Gettysburg Sources.* 3 vols. Baltimore: Butternut & Blue, 1986–1990.

McManus, Howard Rollins. *The Battle of Cloyd's Mountain and the Virginia and Tennessee Railroad Raid, April 29–May 19, 1864.* Lynchburg, VA: H. E. Howard, 1989.

McMurry, Richard M. "The President's Tenth and the Battle of Olustee." *Civil War Times Illustrated* (January 1978).

McPherson, James M. *Battle Cry of Freedom: The Civil War Era.* New York: Oxford University Press, 1988.

———, ed. *Battle Chronicles of the Civil War.* 6 vols. New York: Macmillan, 1989.

———. *Gettysburg: The Paintings of Mort Kunstler.* Atlanta: Turner Publishing, 1993.

Mahr, Theodore C. *Early's Valley Campaign: The Battle of Cedar Creek—Showdown in the Shenandoah, October 1–30, 1864.* Lynchburg, VA: H. E. Howard, 1992.

Maney, R. Wayne. *Marching to Cold Harbor: Victory and Failure, 1864.* Shippensburg, PA: White Mane Publishing Company, 1994.

Martin, David G. *Jackson's Valley Campaign.* Conshohocken, PA: Combined Books, 1988.

———. *The Chancellorsville Campaign, March–May 1863.* Conshohocken, PA: Combined Books, 1991.

————. *The Peninsula Campaign, March–July 1862.* Conshohocken, PA: Combined Books, 1992.

Marvel, William. *Southwest Virginia in the Civil War: The Battles for Saltville.* Lynchburg, VA: H. E. Howard, 1992.

Matter, William D. *If It Takes All Summer: The Battle of Spotsylvania.* Chapel Hill: University of North Carolina Press, 1988.

Meredith, Roy. *Storm over Sumter.* New York: Simon & Schuster, 1957.

Miers, Earl Schenck. *The Last Campaign: Grant Saves the Union.* Philadelphia: J. B. Lippincott Company, 1972.

————, and Richard A. Brown. *Gettysburg.* New Brunswick, NJ: Rutgers University Press, 1948.

Miller, J. Michael. *The North Anna Campaign: "Even To Hell Itself," May 21–26, 1864.* Lynchburg, VA: H. E. Howard, 1989.

————. "Lee and Grant at the North Anna River." *Blue and Gray* (April 1993).

Miller, William J., ed. *The Peninsula Campaign of 1862: Yorktown to the Seven Days.* Campbell, CA: Savas Woodbury Publishers, 1993.

Montgomery, James Stuart. *The Shaping of a Battle.* Philadelphia: Chilton Company, 1959.

Murfin, James V. *The Gleam of Bayonets: The Battle of Antietam and the Maryland Campaign of 1862.* New York: A. S. Barnes and Company, 1965.

————. "Along Antietam Creek September 17, 1862." *Blue and Gray* (September 1985).

Nevins, Allan. *The Ordeal of the Union.* 2 vols. New York: Charles Scribner's Sons, 1947.

————. *The Emergence of Lincoln.* 2 vols. New York: Charles Scribner's Sons, 1950.

————. *The War for the Union.* 4 vols. New York: Charles Scribner's Sons, 1959–1971.

Newton, Steven H. *The Battle of Seven Pines.* Lynchburg, VA: H. E. Howard, 1993.

Nofi, Albert A. *The Gettysburg Campaign, June–July 1863.* Conshohocken, PA: Combined Books, 1993.

————. ed. *The Opening Guns: Fort Sumter to Bull Run, 1861.* New York: Gallery Books, 1988.

Nulty, William H. *Confederate Florida: The Road to Olustee.* Tuscaloosa: University of Alabama Press, 1990.

Nye, Wilbur Sturtevant. *Here Come the Rebels!* Baton Rouge: Louisiana State University Press, 1965.

O'Neill, Robert. *The Cavalry Battles of Aldie, Middleburg and Upperville: Small But Important Riots, June 10–27, 1863.* Lynchburg, VA: H. E. Howard, 1994.

Patrick, Rembert W. *The Fall of Richmond.* Baton Rouge: Louisiana State University Press, 1960.

Persico, Joseph E. *My Enemy, My Brother: Men and Days at Gettysburg.* New York: Macmillan, 1977.

Pfanz, Harry. *Gettysburg: The Second Day.* Chapel Hill: University of North Carolina Press, 1987.

————. *Gettysburg: Culp's Hill and Cemetery Hill.* Chapel Hill: University of North Carolina Press, 1993.

————. "The Development of the Gettysburg National Park." *Civil War Times Illustrated* (July 1963).

Priest, John M. *Antietam: The Soldiers' Battle.* Shippensburg, PA: White Mane Publishing Company, 1989.

———. *Before Antietam: The Battle for South Mountain.* Shippensburg, PA: White Mane Publishing Company, 1992.

Prowell, George R. et al. *Encounter at Hanover: Prelude to Gettysburg.* 1963. Reprint, Shippensburg, PA: White Mane Publishing Company, 1985.

Randall, J. G., and David Donald. *The Divided Union.* Boston: Little, Brown, 1961.

Raus, Edmund J., Jr. *A Generation on the March—The Union Army at Gettysburg.* Lynchburg, VA: H. E. Howard, 1987.

Reed, Rowena. *Combined Operations in the Civil War.* Annapolis, MD: Naval Institute Press, 1978.

Reid, Brian Holden. "Another look at Grant's Crossing of the James." *Civil War History* (December 1993).

Rhea, Gordon C. *The Battle of the Wilderness, May 5–6, 1864.* Baton Rouge: Louisiana State University Press, 1994.

Ripley, Warren. *The Battle of Chapman's Fort.* Green Pond, SC: Privately printed, 1978.

Robertson, James I. *Civil War Sites in Virginia: A Tour Guide.* Charlottesville: University Press of Virginia, 1982.

———. *Civil War Virginia: Battleground for a Nation.* Charlottesville: University Press of Virginia, 1991.

———. "Stonewall in the Shenandoah: The Valley Campaign of 1862." *Civil War Times Illustrated* (May 1972).

Robertson, William Glenn. *Back Door to Richmond: The Bermuda Hundred Campaign, April–June 1864.* Newark, NJ: University of Delaware Press, 1987.

———. *The Petersburg Campaign: The Battle of Old Men and Young Boys. June 9, 1864.* Lynchburg, VA: H. E. Howard, 1989.

Rodick, Burleigh Cushing. *Appomattox: The Last Campaign.* New York: Philosophical Library, 1965.

Rollins, Richard, ed. *Pickett's Charge! Eyewitness Accounts.* Redondo Beach, CA: Rank and File Publications, 1994.

Roth, David E. "The Battle of Fredericksburg, December 13, 1862." *Blue and Gray* (December 1983–January 1984).

Ryan, David D. *Four Days in 1865: The Fate of Richmond.* Richmond: Cadmus Communications Corporation, 1993.

Ryckman, W. G. "Clash of Cavalry at Trevilians." *Virginia Magazine of History and Biography* (1967).

Sauers, Richard Allen. *The Gettysburg Campaign, June 3–August 1, 1863. A Comprehensive, Selectively Annotated Bibliography.* Westport, CT: Greenwood Press, 1982.

———. *A Caspian Sea of Ink: The Meade-Sickles Controversy.* Baltimore: Butternut and Blue, 1989.

———. "Laurels for Burnside: The Invasion of North Carolina January–July 1862." *Blue and Gray* (May 1988).

Schiller, Herbert M. *The Bermuda Hundred Campaign: Operations on the South Side of the James River—May 1864.* Dayton, OH: Press of Morningside Bookshop, 1988.

Scott, Robert Garth. *Into the Wilderness with the Army of the Potomac.* Bloomington: Indiana University Press, 1985.

Sears, Stephen W. *Landscape Turned Red: The Battle of Antietam.* New York: Ticknor & Fields, 1983.

———. "McClellan at Antietam." *Blue and Gray* (November 1985).

———. "The Battle of South Mountain, September 14, 1862." *Blue and Gray* (January 1987).

———. "America's Bloodiest Day: The Battle of Antietam." *Civil War Times Illustrated* (April 1987).

———. *To the Gates of Richmond: The Peninsula Campaign.* New York: Ticknor & Fields, 1992.

Smith, Everard D. "Chambersburg: Anatomy of a Confederate Reprisal." *American Historical Review* (April 1991).

Sommers, Richard J. *Richmond Redeemed: The Siege at Petersburg.* Garden City, NY: Doubleday, 1981.

Stackpole, Edward J. *They Met at Gettysburg.* Harrisburg, PA: Stackpole Company, 1956.

———. *Drama on the Rappahannock: The Fredericksburg Campaign.* Harrisburg, PA: Stackpole Company, 1957.

———. *Chancellorsville: Lee's Greatest Battle.* Harrisburg, PA: Stackpole Company, 1958.

———. *From Cedar Mountain to Antietam, August–September 1862.* Harrisburg, PA: Stackpole Company, 1959.

———. "The Battle of Fredericksburg." *Civil War Times Illustrated* (December 1965).

Starr, Stephen Z. *The Union Cavalry in the Civil War.* Vol. 1: *From Fort Sumter to Gettysburg.* Vol. 2: *The War in the East from Gettysburg to Appomattox.* Baton Rouge: Louisiana State University Press, 1979, 1981.

Stuart, Meriwether. "Colonel Ulric Dahlgren and Richmond's Union Underground." *Virginia Magazine of History and Biography* (1964).

———. *Sheridan in the Shenandoah: Jubal Early's Nemesis.* Harrisburg, PA: Stackpole Company, 1961.

Steere, Edward. *The Wilderness Campaign.* Harrisburg, PA: Stackpole Company, 1960.

Stern, Philip Van Doren. *An End to Valor: The Last Days of the Civil War.* Boston: Houghton Mifflin, 1958.

Stewart, George R. *Pickett's Charge: A Microhistory of the Final Attack at Gettysburg, July 3, 1863.* Boston: Houghton Mifflin, 1959.

Swanberg, W. A. *First Blood: The Story of Fort Sumter.* New York: Charles Scribner's Sons, 1957.

Swank, Walbrook Davis. *Battle of Trevilian Station: The Civil War's Greatest and Bloodiest All Cavalry Battle.* Shippensburg, PA: Burd Street Press, 1994.

Symonds, Craig L. *Gettysburg: A Battlefield Atlas.* Baltimore: Nautical & Aviation Publishing Company of America, 1992.

Tanner, Robert G. *Stonewall in the Valley: Thomas J. "Stonewall" Jackson's Shenandoah Valley Campaign, Spring 1862.* Garden City, NY: Doubleday, 1976.

Teetor, Paul R. *A Matter of Hours: Treason at Harpers Ferry.* Rutherford, NJ: Fairleigh Dickinson University Press, 1982.

Thomas, Emory. "The Peninsula Campaign." *Civil War Times Illustrated* (February–July 1979).

Tidwell, William A., James O. Hall, and David Winfred Gaddy. *Come Retribution: The Confederate Secret Service and the Assassination of Lincoln.* Jackson: University

Press of Mississippi, 1988.

Time-Life Books Editorial Staff. *Lee Takes Command: From Seven Days to Second Bull Run.* Alexandria, VA: Time-Life Books, 1984.

Trudeau, Noah Andre. *Bloody Roads South: The Wilderness to Cold Harbor, May–June 1864.* Boston: Little, Brown, 1989.

———. *The Last Citadel: Petersburg, Virginia, June 1864–April 1865.* Boston: Little, Brown, 1991.

———. *Out of the Storm: The End of the Civil War, April–June 1865.* Boston: Little, Brown, 1994.

Tucker, Glenn. *High Tide at Gettysburg: The Campaign in Pennsylvania.* Indianapolis: Bobbs-Merrill Company, 1958.

———. *Lee and Longstreet at Gettysburg.* Indianapolis: Bobbs-Merrill Company, 1968.

Vandiver, Frank. *Jubal's Raid: General Early's Famous Attack on Washington in 1864.* New York: McGraw-Hill, 1960.

Wert, Jeffry D. *From Winchester to Cedar Creek: The Shenandoah Campaign of 1864.* Carlisle, PA: South Mountain Press, 1987.

———. "Gettysburg." *Civil War Times Illustrated* (Summer 1988).

Whan, Vorin E., Jr. *Fiasco at Fredericksburg.* State College: Pennsylvania State University, 1961.

Wheeler, Richard. *Sword over Richmond: An Eyewitness History of McClellan's Peninsula Campaign.* New York: Harper & Row, 1986.

———. *Witness to Gettysburg.* New York: Harper & Row, 1987.

———. *Witness to Appomattox.* New York: Harper & Row, 1989.

———. *On Fields of Fury: From the Wilderness to the Crater—An Eyewitness History.* New York: Harper & Row, 1991.

———. *Lee's Terrible Swift Sword: From Antietam to Chancellorsville, an Eyewitness History.* New York: HarperCollins, 1992.

———. *A Rising Thunder: From Lincoln's Election to the Battle of Bull Run: An Eyewitness History.* New York: HarperCollins, 1994.

Williams, Kenneth P. *Lincoln Finds a General: A Military Study of the Civil War.* New York: Macmillan, 1949–1959. (First two volumes, 1949, treat eastern theater.)

Wise, Stephen R. *Gate of Hell: Campaign for Charleston Harbor, 1863.* Columbia: University of South Carolina Press, 1994.

Zinn, Jack. *R. E. Lee's Cheat Mountain Campaign.* Parsons, WV: McClain Printing Company, 1974.

21

Western Theater

Mark Grimsley

Until recently the cis-Mississippi west—the sprawling expanse between the Appalachian Mountains and the Mississippi River—was something of a poor relation in Civil War historiography. Despite its obvious importance to the military struggle, the West never attracted the wealth of finely detailed studies lavished upon the campaigns in Virginia. The skewed perspective reflected the unbalanced attention the two theaters received during the war itself. With both national capitals located in the eastern theater, politicians, diplomats, and opinionmakers tended to follow operations in that region most closely. Most of the North's population, and much of the South's, was located east of the Appalachians and that reinforced the focus on the Virginia theater. By contrast, the struggle in the West tended to be perceived in more broadbrush fashion.

In addition to geography, one historian has also blamed "the 'Lee tradition' in historical writing," which "deified" the Virginia army and its generals as the epitome of how Southerners saw themselves: "knightly manners, gentleness, planter society." Southern focus on such Virginians as Robert E. Lee, Stonewall Jackson, and Jeb Stuart helped fix Northern attention on their exploits as well. Even Ulysses S. Grant, the western general par excellence, is known chiefly for his climactic duel with Lee. If the Civil War was an American Iliad, then Virginia has long been its principal Troy.

The past thirty-five years, however, have seen a significant shift in focus. The eastern theater retains its fascination, but historians have been drawn increasingly to the West, believing that the military struggle was decided there. The Union victories at Fort Donelson, Shiloh, and Island Number Ten placed the South at a disadvantage from which it never recovered. The capture of Vicksburg in July 1863 gave the North control of the Mississippi River, and if the purely military significance of that accomplishment is sometimes overdrawn, its powerful psychological impact cannot be gainsaid. The loss of Chattanooga in November 1863 opened the door to the Confederate heartland. Afterward came Atlanta, the march to the sea, and William T. Sherman's final victorious advance through the Carolinas, until the war in the West came to a close, incongruously, less than 150 miles from the Atlantic Ocean.

GENERAL WORKS AND STRATEGIC OVERVIEWS

Despite the general pattern of Northern success, the literature on the western theater is much better for the Confederate side than for the Union. This is due, in no small measure, to two historians, Thomas L. Connelly and Archer Jones. Between them they established the foundation for modern study of the Southern military effort in the West. Since the western Confederate armies suffered a long series of reversals, both men implicitly wondered whether it could have been otherwise. Did the Confederate government manage the defense of the West as well as could be expected, or were there major shortcomings in strategy or generalship? In his earliest work on the subject, *Confederate Strategy from Shiloh to Vicksburg* (1961), Jones offered a basically positive assessment. The decentralized organization created by President Jefferson Davis, which divided the western theater into regional military departments, each responsible for the defense of its own territory and logistical base, seemed "realistic and adapted to conditions." And Davis, despite a few missteps, effectively supplied the necessary interdepartmental coordination.

But although generally impressed by the quality of his research and basic approach to the subject, reviewers tended to reject Jones's conclusions. To them it seemed that Jones's own evidence often pointed the other way—that the geographical orientation of Confederate strategy in the West was inappropriate and led to a dispersion of effort and that Davis's supervision of the theater left much to be desired. The string of Southern defeats in the West argued eloquently that something was amiss.

Thomas L. Connelly's history of the Confederacy's principal field army in the West offered a sustained portrayal of what that "something" might be. In *Army of the Heartland: The Army of Tennessee, 1861–1862* (1967), he described an army seriously handicapped by too much responsibility, too few resources, and too many fractious generals. The Army of Tennessee was obliged to defend an area about ten times the size of Virginia, and because of the Richmond government's failure to appreciate the magnitude of the task, it frequently did so with about half the troops allocated to the Army of Northern Virginia. Logistical support was similarly niggard. And in Connelly's judgment, the principal Southern commanders were inadequate. Albert Sidney Johnston possessed a noble character but poor military judgment; his initial successor, P.G.T. Beauregard, was erratic; and Braxton Bragg, who soon replaced Beauregard, had good strategic and administrative ability but could not get along with his subordinates, some of whom were incompetent. Connelly continued this tale of woe in *Autumn of Glory: The Army of Tennessee, 1862–1865* (1971), which reinforced his assessment of an army soldiering on despite poor leadership and short supplies.

By this time, Connelly had expanded his list of villains to include Robert E. Lee, whom he portrayed as a brilliant but myopic commander obsessed with his native Virginia. Lee, Connelly charged, used his awesome prestige to insist on a mistaken Confederate emphasis on the eastern theater that hamstrung Southern forces in the West. Even before the publication of *Autumn of Glory,* Connelly offered this controversial analysis in "Robert E. Lee and the Western Confederacy: A Criticism of Lee's Strategic Ability" (1969). The article drew a strong response from Albert Castel, himself a noted historian of the trans-Mississippi theater, in "The Historian and the General: Thomas L. Connelly versus Robert E. Lee" (1970). Castel chided Connelly for a variety of "errors and distortions" and concluded that Connelly was "practically blinded by his prejudice against Lee."

Undeterred, Connelly joined forces with Archer Jones to produce *The Politics of Command: Factions and Ideas in Confederate Strategy* (1973), which focused mainly on the western theater. They pointed to five major factors that shaped Confederate strategy: the Napoleonic inheritance, interpreted chiefly by Baron Henri, Antoine de Jomini; the parochial influence of Robert E. Lee; an informal network of Confederate generals and statesmen, collectively dubbed the "western concentration bloc"; a cluster of similar informal networks with other concerns; and the Confederate departmental system. The Napoleonic inheritance suggested a strategy based on the exploitation of interior lines and well-timed Confederate counteroffensives. The Lee influence handicapped this strategy by a mistaken emphasis on Virginia. The "western concentration bloc" stressed the vital importance of the Nashville-Chattanooga-Atlanta corridor and argued, with limited success, for a Confederate counterstroke sufficient to cripple the Union forces threatening that corridor. The remaining informal networks sometimes reinforced and sometimes undermined the proposed western emphasis. The Confederate departmental system functioned effectively in the war's early years but became less flexible over time. In the end it functioned less as a strategic tool and more as the strategy itself.

The Politics of Command deeply influenced two other works on the Confederate experience in the western theater that appeared in the late 1980s: Richard McMurry's *Two Great Rebel Armies: An Essay in Confederate Military History* (1989) and Steven E. Woodworth's *Jefferson Davis and His Generals: The Failure of Confederate Command in the West* (1990). Drawing on the work of Connelly, Jones, and Douglas Southall Freeman, among others, McMurry briefly but tellingly compared the experiences of the Army of Tennessee and its far more successful sister army, the Army of Northern Virginia. Like Connelly and Jones, he underscored the daunting size of the Tennessee army's area of geographical responsibility, its relative poverty of manpower of logistical resources, and its generally lackluster senior commanders. But McMurry rejected the idea, always implicit in the work of Connelly and Jones, that a more substantial Confederate military effort in the West might have yielded decisive results. Instead, he argued, the prospects in the western theater were so poor—and the Army of Tennessee so flawed an instrument—that Robert E. Lee had been essentially correct: the Virginia theater offered the best chance for Southern victory.

Woodworth's study, *Jefferson Davis and His Generals,* disputed Connelly and Jones on some points, buttressed them on others, and extended the dialogue through a sustained focus on the Confederate commander in chief. The emphasis throughout is more on personalities—on Davis's actual relationship with principal commanders—than structural issues. The decision to adopt a departmental system for western defense is treated briefly and approvingly, although Woodworth faults Davis for dispersing too much Confederate manpower around the Southern periphery and, later, for using the Mississippi River as a boundary between departments. Sensibly, Woodworth argues that given the river's obvious potential as a major Union axis of advance, the defense of both banks should have been placed in the hands of a single commander.

But Woodworth is mainly concerned with the generals themselves. Much of his book is implicitly about whether the senior western command was up to the challenge that confronted it. His answer is frequently no, and he chides Davis for too often failing to recognize the fact and to make changes when needed. In particular Davis supported his friend, corps commander Leonidas Polk, long after it should have been obvious that Polk was both incompetent and a troublemaker who actively worked to undermine the authority of Army of Tennessee commander Braxton Bragg. The oft-maligned Bragg, however, is assessed more sympathetically by Woodworth, who argues intelligently, though not always persuasively, that Bragg was more often sinned against than sinning.

The focus on command in Confederate studies of the western theater has resulted in a comparative neglect of the common soldier. Fortunately Larry J. Daniel's *Soldiering in the Army of Tennessee: A Portrait of Life in a Confederate Army* (1991) helps to redress this imbalance. Although in part Daniel follows in the tradition established by Bell Wiley's *The Life of Johnny Reb,* he is alert to features that differentiated soldiers in the western army from their eastern counterparts. With scant tradition of battlefield success and justified skepticism about the quality of their senior leadership, soldiers in the Army of Tennessee had to rely more heavily on a unit cohesion supplied by religious conviction, the threat of punishment, shared suffering, and a kind of survivors' pride in their own resilience.

Given the wealth of scholarship on the Confederacy's war in the West, the dearth of a comparable literature for the Union side is striking. The best extended overview is Kenneth P. Williams's monumental study of the Union senior command, *Lincoln Finds a General* (1949–1959), which was unfortunately still unfinished at the time of Williams's death. Of the five published volumes

(Williams planned at least seven), the first two address the eastern theater; the remaining three deal with the West. The focus of the western volumes is on the general Lincoln eventually "found," Ulysses S. Grant. But the lesser generals whom Lincoln tried and discarded also interested Williams. His design was therefore broad enough, and his treatment extensive enough, to afford detailed coverage to campaigns and battles in which Grant was not involved.

Taken together, the western volumes form a serviceable account of the Union side of the war from the April 1861 through September 1863. Volume 3, subtitled *Grant's First Year in the West* (1952), covers the western war through mid-July 1862 and deals principally with operations along the Tennessee River. The central theme of volume 4, *Iuka to Vicksburg* (1956), is Grant's campaign against the great Confederate river fortress, but Williams also gives extended attention to the Perryville and Stones River campaigns. The last volume, *Prelude to Chattanooga* (1959), focuses initially on mopping-up operations in the wake of the Vicksburg campaign, then turns to the struggle between the Union Army of the Cumberland and Confederate Army of Tennessee for possession of Chattanooga. It concludes with an account of the Battle of Chickamauga.

Williams was a professor of mathematics, not an academically trained historian, and his work has many of the traits associated with gifted amateurs. Its focus is on the personalities of prominent generals, to the near exclusion of the organizational structure within which they operated, and there is little sustained discussion of strategy. Williams is unhesitant and frequently unsparing in his judgment of a general's competence, but his appraisals are uninformed by any explicit model of command. Although *Lincoln Finds a General* offers a good, general narrative of the Union war in the West and contains many astute observations, the work as a whole suffers from a poverty of conceptualization.

Yet little else is available. Bruce Catton's *Grant Moves South* (1960), the second in a classic three-volume military biography of the North's most successful commander, is worth a look, however. Despite its comparative brevity and fairly tight focus on Grant, it yields a level of insight rarely approached in Williams's work, as well an engaging picture of the Union Army of the Tennessee as it lived and fought from Fort Donelson through the Vicksburg campaign. (A portion of the third volume, *Grant Takes Command,* 1969, covers events from the aftermath of Vicksburg through the Chattanooga campaign.) The most satisfactory strategic assessment is Herman Hattaway and Archer Jones, *How the North Won: A Military History of the Civil War* (1983), discussed in chapter 2 of this book.

Bear in mind the old but serviceable Campaigns of the Civil War series, published by Charles Scribner's Sons during the early 1880s. Five volumes cover the western theater: Manning Force, *From Fort Henry to Corinth* (1882); Henry M. Cist, *The Army of the Cumberland* (1885); Francis V. Greene, *The Mississippi* (1882); and *Atlanta* (1882) and *The March to the Sea—Franklin and Nashville* (1883), both by Jacob D. Cox. Although less thoroughly researched than their modern counterparts, these books afford a useful contemporary view of the western campaigns, for each of the authors had also been a participant. The volumes by Greene and Cox are particularly good.

CAMPAIGNS AND BATTLES, 1861–1862

Coverage greatly improves when one turns to works devoted to specific military operations. Every major campaign, and many minor ones, have received book-length attention, and although biographies of Confederate and Union leaders will not be considered here, readers should bear in mind that many contain excellent accounts of the engagements in which their subjects participated.

Chronologically, books focusing on western campaigns and battles begin with Nathaniel C. Hughes's *The Battle of Belmont: Grant Strikes South* (1991). Although technically fought on the Missouri side of the Mississippi River, this November 1861 engagement formed part of the early struggle along the Confederate western line. Created in the autumn of 1861 by General Albert Sidney Johnston, the line ran 300 miles along the southern fringe of Kentucky from Columbus, on the Mississippi River, through the railroad town of Bowling Green, and on to Cumberland Gap in the wilds of Appalachia. Militarily Belmont was not much of a fight, but it gave the war's foremost commander his first exposure to Civil War combat, and Hughes provides a good picture of the strategic context as well as the actual combat. Despite the title, the focus tends to be somewhat less on Grant than on the Confederate generals Gideon J. Pillow and Leonidas Polk.

Strategically, Belmont was meaningless, and in any event the western line remained intact until the late winter of 1862. It snapped first at Mill Springs, where on January 19 a small Union army under General George H. Thomas broke its eastern anchor. The decisive blow occurred a month later, when a combined army-navy force under Grant and flag officer Andrew Foote captured the rebel forts that guarded the Tennessee and Cumberland rivers. Benjamin F. Cooling has written an able study of this campaign, *Forts Henry and Donelson: The Key to the Confederate Heartland* (1987). Like other historians, he stresses the enormous importance of these forts for Confederate prospects in the western theater and faults the Southern high command for its failure to mount an effective defense. But Cooling also performs a needed service by placing the campaign within a larger cultural context, arguing that the North's more vibrant commercial society gave Union leaders a better appreciation for the importance of the western rivers.

The fall of Forts Henry and Donelson forced Sidney Johnston to abandon Nashville and most of western and middle Tennessee. Union gunboats ranged up the Tennessee River as far as Muscle Shoals, Alabama. Grant took his army upstream to Pittsburg Landing; a second Union army under General Don Carlos Buell moved to join him from Nashville. Desperate to repair the disaster, the Confederate government sent reinforcements from all over the South to Johnston's army at Corinth, Mississippi. From there, in early April 1862, Johnston launched a major offensive, hoping to overwhelm Grant's army before Buell could arrive. The resulting battle at Shiloh, far more severe than anything yet seen in North America, defined the fury and carnage that would come to characterize Civil War battlefields.

Two good modern studies of Shiloh exist. Crisp and brief is James Lee McDonough's *Shiloh: In Hell before Night* (1977). Considerably more elaborate is Wiley Sword's *Shiloh: Bloody April* (1974). Both stress the possibility of a complete Confederate victory on the first day had Southern commanders managed to prevent the confusion that drained much of the momentum from the initial attack. Sword tends to place most of the blame on Johnston, especially his inconvenient decision to be mortally wounded at the height of the first day's fighting. McDonough, on the other hand, highlights the failure of Beauregard—Johnston's second in command—to restore control over the battle lines and continue the attack after Johnston's death.

The Union victory at Shiloh set the stage for the capture of the strategic railway junction at Corinth, Mississippi, a few weeks later. But afterward came a prolonged lull in the Union's western offensive as Major General Henry W. Halleck dispersed his large field army to consolidate and garrison the gains of spring. Johnston's eventual successor, General Braxton Bragg, exploited the breather to launch one of the war's most ambitious—and, up to a point, most successful—counterstrokes. In August 1862 he took his army on a long raid into Kentucky, hoping to draw that state into the Confederacy and draw Union forces out of middle Tennessee. The best—and almost the only—modern study of this campaign is James Lee McDonough's *War in Kentucky: From Shiloh to Perryville* (1994).

Stunning in conception and impressive in its early execution, Bragg's invasion culminated in anticlimax. On October 8, most of Bragg's army encountered a portion of Buell's pursuing Union force at Perryville, Kentucky. The resulting battle, documented by Kenneth Hafendorfer in *Perryville: The Battle for Kentucky* (1981), ended tactically in a Confederate victory, but Bragg soon elected to abandon Kentucky and withdraw into Tennessee. The Lincoln administration, relieved by the campaign's outcome but disenchanted with Buell's performance, replaced him with Major General William S. Rosecrans.

Two and a half months later, Rosecrans threw his new command in motion and advanced against Bragg's army encamped near Murfreesboro, Tennessee. Rather than stand on the defensive, Bragg elected to attack, and the Battle of Stones River (December 31, 1862–January 2, 1863) came close to wrecking the larger Union army. Rosecrans, however, managed to stave off defeat, and in the end it was the Army of Tennessee, not the Union Army of the Cumberland, that withdrew. The battle is well covered in two books: James Lee McDonough's *Stones River: Bloody Winter in Tennessee* (1980) and Peter Cozzens's *No Better Place to Die: The Battle of Stones River* (1990).

VICKSBURG AND PORT HUDSON

Shortly before the Stones River campaign, Grant began the first of several attempts to attack the Confederate river fortress at Vicksburg, Mississippi. An earlier waterborne Union offensive against the city, chronicled by Edwin C. Bearss in *Rebel Victory at Vicksburg* (1963), had failed in June 1862. In the meantime the city's defenses had been greatly improved, rendering Vicksburg a formidable nut to crack. Geography complicated matters; it took Grant about six months to find a viable route by which to attack the city. When he did, however, his campaign was a marvel of speed and decisiveness. After a whirlwind offensive in May 1862, Grant succeeded in bottling up a Confederate army of about 35,000 men within Vicksburg's fortifications. The city and its garrison surrendered seven weeks later, on July 4, 1863.

Arguably the most important campaign of the entire Civil War, Vicksburg has been the subject of a number of studies. Samuel Carter III, *The Final Fortress: The Campaign for Vicksburg, 1862–1863* (1980), and Edwin C. Bearss, *Decision in Mississippi: Mississippi's Important Role in the War between the States* (1962), provide overviews of the various struggles for the city, while Peter F. Walker, *Vicksburg: A People at War, 1860–1865* (1960), concentrates on the civilian population, especially during the siege. Also useful, although intended for general readers, is A. A. Hoehling's *Vicksburg: 47 Days of Siege* (1969). For the main 1863 campaign, Earl Schenck Miers offers a readable overview in *The Web of Victory: Grant at Vicksburg* (1955); As its title implies, Miers focuses principally on the Union side. For a Southern perspective, see *Pemberton: Defender of Vicksburg* (1942) by John C. Pemberton, the son and namesake of the Confederate commander. D. Alexander Brown's *Grierson's Raid* (1954) ably chronicles the famous Union cavalry raid that distracted Pemberton at a critical point in the campaign.

Much the most ambitious treatment, however, is Edwin C. Bearss's three-volume *The Vicksburg Campaign* (1985–1986). Volume 1, *Vicksburg Is the Key* (1985), begins with Grant's initial overland advance in November and December 1862, which came to grief when rebel cavalry destroyed his forward supply base at Holly Springs, Mississippi. It also covers William T. Sherman's abortive assault at Chickasaw Bluffs, the capture of Arkansas Post, and Grant's various unsuccessful attempts to get at the Vicksburg fortress during the winter of 1863. Volume 2, *Grant Strikes a Fatal Blow* (1986), describes the Union commander's eventual decision to cross his army south of Vicksburg and isolate the fortress in a swift campaign of maneuver. The final volume, *Unvexed to the Sea* (1986), chronicles the siege that followed.

Despite its length, *The Vicksburg Campaign* is not entirely satisfactory. It tends to wallow in detail for its own sake, without adequate context. It neglects the secondary literature, particularly the highly relevant work of Thomas Connelly and Archer Jones. And although it includes an extensive bibliography, the actual text is too heavily based on the *Official Records*. All in all, Bearss has contributed a useful book of facts concerning the Vicksburg campaign, but a definitive study still awaits its historian.

Even as Grant besieged Vicksburg, a second siege was also in progress at Port Hudson, Louisiana, the Confederacy's other enclave along the lower Mississippi River. Directed by the political general Nathaniel P. Banks, the campaign was hardly a compelling example of military art, and it was in any event clearly subordinate in importance to Vicksburg. Yet surprisingly, while Vicksburg has received less coverage than it deserves, the subsidiary Port Hudson campaign has been the focus of three modern studies. The first, Edward Cunningham's *The Port Hudson Campaign, 1862–1863* (1963), is well written and well researched; its major defect is a pardonable tendency to overplay the campaign's importance. David C. Edmonds's two-volume *The Guns of Port Hudson* (1983–1984) is worth a look, although its writing style is sometimes clumsy, and it occasionally indulges in needless digressions. *Port Hudson: Confederate Bastion on the Mississippi* (1987), by Lawrence Lee Hewitt, rounds out the trio. Despite the title, it deals mainly with the failed Union assault of May 27, an attack memorable chiefly because it was one of the first instances in which African-American troops saw combat during the war.

CHICKAMAUGA, CHATTANOOGA, AND ATLANTA

While Grant and Banks completed the sieges of Vicksburg and Port Hudson, another major Union offensive got under way in middle Tennessee. On June 24, 1863, Rosecrans's Army of the Cumberland left its camps near Murfreesboro and, in a lightning campaign of maneuver, forced Bragg's Army of Tennessee entirely out of its fortified positions around Tullahoma. By early September Rosecrans had ejected the Army of Tennessee from its namesake state and captured Chattanooga, an important railroad town and a gateway into the Southern heartland. At the midpoint of this remarkable campaign, Rosecrans, miffed at a perceived lack of credit, expressed the hope that Lincoln and the War Department would not overlook his achievement because it was not "written in letters of blood." His ghost might address the same complaint to the Civil War community, for this remarkable campaign has never received book-length treatment. Instead, it is invariably subsumed into the introductory chapters of works devoted to the Chickamauga campaign that followed.

Chickamauga remains among the most interesting of all Civil War campaigns. There, for practically the only time on a major battlefield of that conflict, Confederates outnumbered Federals, a rare circumstance made possible by the Southern high command's decision to divert two divisions from Lee's Army of Northern Virginia to enable Bragg to mount a strong counteroffensive. In this instance, if no other, the "western concentration bloc" won the day. As a result, the Army of Tennessee gained the only outright victory of its long career.

The battle has been the subject of two modern studies: Glenn Tucker's *Chickamauga: Bloody Battle in the West* (1961) and Peter Cozzens's *This Terrible*

Sound: The Battle of Chickamauga (1992). Although both works are reliable, Cozzens draws on an array of manuscript as well as published sources, whereas Tucker uses only printed works. Cozzens's book is also thoroughly documented, again in contrast to Tucker's earlier book.

Unique among treatments of western campaigns is Matt Spruill, ed., *Guide to the Battle of Chickamauga* (1993), inspired by three earlier guides to eastern battlefields written by Jay Luvaas and William Nelson. This book, like its predecessors, is deceptively simple. Designed for use on the battlefield itself, it takes readers to various points on the field, where they read excerpted passages from reports and correspondence in the *Official Records*.

After Chickamauga, Rosecrans's battered army withdrew into Chattanooga; the rebels clamped a quasi-siege upon the city, so that Union supplies could come by only a single rutted, winding mountain road. Deeply alarmed, the Northern government sent 37,000 troops, drawn from Mississippi and Virginia, to reinforce the beleaguered Army of the Cumberland. It also sent Ulysses S. Grant to take overall command of the situation. Meanwhile, the senior leaders of the Army of Tennessee squabbled so acrimoniously as to undermine the good order and discipline of the besieging force. As a partial result, when Union forces mounted an offensive to raise the siege in November 1863, they won a surprisingly easy triumph. Hurled from seemingly impregnable Missionary Ridge, the Confederate army withdrew to Dalton, Georgia. Bragg was sacked. Grant, the apparent victor (although George H. Thomas was really more responsible for the Northern success), soon vaulted to command of all the Union armies.

The best overview of the campaign is James Lee McDonough, *Chattanooga: A Death Grip on the Confederacy* (1984). McDonough is especially good at showing how the "impregnable" Confederate position on Missionary Ridge was actually rather vulnerable. Although respectful of the famous, quasi-spontaneous soldiers' charge that carried the Army of the Cumberland to the summit of the ridge, McDonough points out that a number of factors undermined the Confederate defense, among them inadequate numbers, poorly sited positions, and a disastrous decision to create three battle lines—one at the base, one along the lower slope, and one at the crest—which further diluted Confederate strength. For a more detailed examination of operations at divisions and brigade level, see Peter Cozzens, *The Shipwreck of Their Hopes: The Battles for Chattanooga* (1994). Wiley Sword's *Mountains Touched with Fire: Chattanooga Besieged, 1863* (1995) is good, readable study. Much less valuable are Fairfax Downey, *Storming of the Gateway: Chattanooga, 1863* (1960), which also spends considerable space on Chickamauga, and John Bowers, *Chickamauga and Chattanooga: The Battles That Doomed the Confederacy* (1994), which is journalistic and undocumented.

In the weeks prior to the Battle of Chattanooga, a significant subsidiary campaign was also under way in eastern Tennessee. Earlier in the year the Union Army of the Ohio had entered the region in a move roughly coordinated with

Rosecrans's middle Tennessee campaign. After Chickamauga Bragg detached two divisions from his army under James Longstreet with orders to clear the eastern Tennessee valley. The operation culminated with a disastrous Confederate siege of Knoxville and a doomed assault on the Union fortifications. This sharply waged but inconclusive eastern Tennessee campaign has not attracted much study, although Digby Gordon's *Divided Loyalties: Fort Sanders and the Civil War in East Tennessee* (1963) provides a partial introduction.

With Chattanooga firmly in Union hands, the way was now open for a thrust into the Confederate heartland, with Atlanta the obvious target. The five-month struggle for the city began in May 1864, when Union major general William T. Sherman and three Union armies squared off against General Joseph E. Johnston, now in command of the Army of Tennessee. The best study of the Atlanta campaign is also one of the finest books to appear on any Civil War campaign: Albert Castel's *Decision in the West: The Atlanta Campaign of 1864* (1992). The product of many years' research, the book is decidedly unusual in both style (it is written in the present tense) and analysis: it portrays Sherman as a mediocre operational commander as well as a lousy tactician. Although Sherman won the campaign, Castel argues, he did so chiefly through the weight of superior numbers and resources, and he squandered a number of opportunities to gain quicker and more decisive results. In particular, Castel faults Sherman for the failure to bag Johnston's army at Snake Creek Gap and for permitting Hood's army to escape from Atlanta intact and almost unmolested.

The book's greatest strength, however, is not its evaluations of generalship but rather its attention, rare in Civil War campaign books, to the larger context. Better than any previous historian, Castel describes the political significance of the Atlanta campaign for both the Union and the Confederacy. He pays due attention to logistics, communications, and other matters, central to the conduct of a military campaign, that are too often overlooked. His sense of the relationship of the campaign to operations elsewhere is deft and sure. And, refreshingly, he does not simply exploit the fighting for dramatic effect but explains with intelligence and deep understanding the logic and interworkings of the Civil War tactical system. All in all, *Decision in the West* is a model work of its genre.

Castel's book can be supplemented by two others that focus more specifically on the fighting around Atlanta. The first, Samuel Carter III's *The Siege of Atlanta, 1864* (1973), is well written, though marred by a few factual errors. For a treatment focusing on Southern civilians that also deals with the siege, see A. A. Hoehling, *Last Train from Atlanta* (1958).

Finally, Lee Kennett's *Marching through Georgia: The Story of Soldiers and Civilians during Sherman's Campaign* (1995) superbly recreates the feel of the campaign as it was experienced by ordinary people—white and black, in and out of uniform. It covers not only operations against Atlanta but also Sherman's subsequent march to the sea.

THE FINAL CAMPAIGNS

The fall of Atlanta convinced Northerners and Southerners alike that the North was winning the war. More than any other single event, it ensured Lincoln's reelection as president in November 1864. The Davis government consoled itself with the knowledge that Sherman's line of communication with the North was highly vulnerable. It began to consider a major counterstroke that would carry Hood's army into middle Tennessee, disrupt Sherman's supply lines, and, in more delusional moments, perhaps even carry the war to the banks of the Ohio River. Sherman, for his part, was equally aware of the vulnerability of his communications. After a month of fruitless campaigning in northern Georgia, trying to keep Hood away from his railroad, Sherman decided to abandon Atlanta altogether, destroy its war resources, and march 220 miles to Savannah on the Atlantic coast.

November 1864, then, offered the unique spectacle of two rival armies marching determinedly *away* from each other. Sherman left plenty of troops behind to guard Nashville, Tennessee, and keep Hood out of Kentucky; with 60,000 veterans he then embarked on his famous march to the sea. Meanwhile Hood took 45,000 troops on a doomed foray into Tennessee. The best account of this offensive is Wiley Sword's *Embrace an Angry Wind: The Confederacy's Last Hurrah: Spring Hill, Franklin, and Nashville* (1992). Two excellent studies of individual battles are James Lee McDonough and Thomas L. Connelly, *Five Tragic Hours: The Battle of Franklin* (1983), and Stanley Horn, *The Decisive Battle of Nashville* (1956), although Horn does strain a bit hard to demonstrate the decisiveness of his subject engagement.

While Hood's army came to grief at Nashville, Sherman's force completed its march to the sea and occupied Savannah. Five weeks later Sherman renewed his advance, making another nearly unopposed march through the Carolinas. Most treatments of the two operations—officially dubbed the Savannah and Carolinas campaigns—deal with them together. Works such as Burke Davis, *Sherman's March* (1980), Earl Schenck Miers, *The General Who Marched to Hell: William Tecumseh Sherman and His March to Fame and Infamy* (1948), and John M. Gibson, *Those 163 Days: A Southern Account of Sherman's March from Atlanta to Raleigh* (1961), tend to be long on describing the destructiveness of the campaigns and short on rigorously evaluating their significance. More satisfactory in every respect are John G. Barrett's *Sherman's March through the Carolinas* (1961), a thorough, well-documented account; and Joseph T. Glatthaar, *The March to the Sea and Beyond: Sherman's Troops in the Savannah and Carolinas Campaigns* (1985), which uses the march as a lens through which to examine the attitudes and activities of the Union veterans who made it possible.

As many historians have noted, Sherman's campaigns struck an enormous blow to Southern morale. It is less generally recognized that other Union raids in the closing weeks of the war also drove home to white Southerners the helplessness of their position. One of these, James H. Wilson's cavalry foray into the Deep South, is ably described in James Pickett Jones, *Yankee Blitzkrieg: Wilson's Raid through Alabama and Georgia* (1976). Another, George Stoneman's lunge into western North Carolina, receives treatment in *Stoneman's Last Raid* (1961), by Ina Woestemeyer Van Noppen.

DIRECTIONS FOR NEW RESEARCH

Works on Civil War campaigns and battles tend to be much alike. They are usually well researched but just as usually devoid of context. The significance of a battle tends to be assumed rather than argued. They seldom show much engagement with the relevant secondary literature. The focus tends to be on the competence or incompetence of various leaders without, in most cases, providing any explicit model of command. Indeed, sustained attention to the actual business of Civil War command is conspicuously absent, particularly the ways in which leaders at different levels understood their responsibilities. Logistics and communications generally receive short shrift, and close attention to tactics is often lacking. The result, ironically, is that while nonmilitary historians tend to complain about the irrelevance and intellectual sterility of "drums and trumpets" histories, such books provide little aid to the serious military specialist, either.

Instead, the obvious and often explicitly stated purpose of these narratives is to bring their pet battle to life, to convey once again the drama, the valor, the blood-soaked squalor that other writers, on other battles (if not the same one), have already conveyed. The irony is that they generally fail, whereas a more judicious work like Albert Castel's *Decision in the West* creates a far more satisfying drama. Thus in most cases, except for readers interested in a given engagement for its own sake, these books do not compel attention.

That is indeed a pity, for much remains to be done on the war's western theater. For starters, something comparable to *The Politics of Command* is needed for the Union side. The Vicksburg campaign still awaits its historian, as does an account of the struggle for Chattanooga that would encompass the entire Northern effort against that city, including the first abortive try in 1862. Works that systematically address the way in which Civil War armies fought—that participate in the tactical dialogue begun by Grady McWhiney and Perry D. Jamieson and expanded by Paddy Griffith—would also be useful, as would works that pay serious attention to the role of logistics and communications.

Above all, it would be welcome to see campaign histories that give the political dimension of the conflict the prominence it deserves and recognize that the Confederate and Union governments fought, respectively, to maintain and to restore control over Southern civilians. Yet despite general acknowledgment of the North's failure to create a Unionist "reaction" among white Southerners, no one has inquired closely as to whether the North's military strategy may have had something to do with it. Many closet Unionists, after all, remained in the closet because they doubted the ability of Federal troops to protect them against Confederate raids and reprisals. This, in turn, was partly a function of the Northern preference for keeping its field armies as strong as possible, with only limited forces to guard communication lines and strongpoints, and frequently none to maintain effective political control over areas nominally occupied.

Similarly, although writers often stress the importance of a given campaign on civilian morale, we actually know little about this crucial subject, and even less about the weight that battlefield events should be accorded relative to other factors, such as the intrusion of government into private life or the perception—widespread on both sides—that the burdens of war affected rich and poor unequally.

Finally, we still know too little about the way in which Civil War campaigns appeared to private soldiers and junior officers. The letters, diaries, and reminiscences of such men are routinely mined for dramatic anecdotes but seldom examined systematically to produce new insights. Joseph T. Glatthaar's *The March to the Sea and Beyond* and Larry Daniel's *Soldiering in the Army of Tennessee* are worthy beginnings, but much more remains to be done.

BIBLIOGRAPHY

Barrett, John G. *Sherman's March through the Carolinas.* Chapel Hill: University of North Carolina Press, 1956.

Bearss, Edwin C. *Decision in Mississippi: Mississippi's Important Role in the War between the States.* Jackson: Mississippi Commission on the War Between the States, 1962.

———. *Forrest at Brice's Crossroads and in North Mississippi in 1864.* Dayton: Morningside, 1991.

———. *Rebel Victory at Vicksburg.* Vicksburg, MS: Vicksburg Centennial Commemoration Commission, 1963.

———. *The Vicksburg Campaign.* 3 vols. Dayton: Morningside, 1985–1986.

Bearss, Margie Riddle. *Sherman's Forgotten Campaign: The Meridian Expedition.* Baltimore: Gateway Press, 1987.

Bowers, John. *Chickamauga and Chattanooga: The Battles That Doomed the Confederacy.* New York: HarperCollins, 1994.

Brown, D. Alexander. *Grierson's Raid.* Urbana: University of Illinois Press, 1954.

Carter, Samuel III. *The Final Fortress: The Campaign for Vicksburg, 1862–1863.* New York: St. Martin's Press, 1980.

———. *The Siege of Atlanta, 1864.* New York: St. Martin's Press, 1973.

Castel, Albert. *Decision in the West: The Atlanta Campaign of 1864.* Lawrence: University Press of Kansas, 1992.

———. "The Historian and the General: Thomas L. Connelly versus Robert E. Lee." *Civil War History* 16 (1970): 50–63.

Catton, Bruce. *Grant Moves South.* Boston: Little, Brown, 1960.

Cist, Henry M. *The Army of the Cumberland.* New York: Charles Scribner's Sons, 1885.

Connelly, Thomas L. *Army of the Heartland: The Army of Tennessee, 1861–1862.* Baton Rouge: Louisiana State University Press, 1967.

———. *Autumn of Glory: The Army of Tennessee, 1862–1865.* Baton Rouge: Louisiana State University Press, 1971.

———. "Robert E. Lee and the Western Confederacy: A Criticism of Lee's Strategic Ability." *Civil War History* 15 (1969): 116–132.

———. "Vicksburg: Strategic Point or Propaganda Device?" *Military Affairs* 34 (1970): 49–53.

———, and Archer Jones, *The Politics of Command: Factions and Ideas in Confederate Strategy.* Baton Rouge: Louisiana State University Press, 1973.

Cooling, Benjamin F. *Forts Henry and Donelson: The Key to the Confederate Heartland.* Knoxville: University of Tennessee Press, 1987.

Cox, Jacob D. *Atlanta.* New York: Charles Scribner's Sons, 1882.

———. *The Battle of Franklin, Tennessee, November 30, 1864.* New York: Charles Scribner's Sons, 1897.

———. *The March to the Sea—Franklin and Nashville.* New York: Charles Scribner's Sons, 1883.

Cozzens, Peter. *No Better Place to Die: The Battle of Stones River.* Urbana and Chicago: University of Illinois Press, 1990.

———. *The Shipwreck of Their Hopes: The Battles for Chattanooga.* Urbana: University of Illinois Press, 1994.

———. *This Terrible Sound: The Battle of Chickamauga.* Urbana: University of Illinois Press, 1992.

Cunningham, Edward. *The Port Hudson Campaign, 1862–1863.* Baton Rouge: Louisiana State University Press, 1963.

Daniel, Larry J. *Soldiering in the Army of Tennessee: A Portrait of Life in a Confederate Army.* Chapel Hill: University of North Carolina Press, 1991.

Davis Burke. *Sherman's March.* New York: Random House, 1980.

Downey, Fairfax. *Storming of the Gateway: Chattanooga, 1863.* New York: David McKay, 1960.

Edmonds, David C. *The Guns of Port Hudson.* 2 vols. Lafayette, LA: Acadiana Press, 1983–1984.

Force, Manning F. *From Fort Henry to Corinth.* New York: Charles Scribner's Sons, 1882.

Frank, Joseph Allan, and George A. Reeves, *"Seeing the Elephant": Raw Recruits at the Battle of Shiloh.* Contributions in Military History, no. 88. Westport, CT: Greenwood Press, 1989.

Gibson, John M. *Those 163 Days: A Southern Account of Sherman's March from Atlanta to Raleigh.* New York: Coward-McCann, 1961.

Glatthaar, Joseph T. *The March to the Sea and Beyond: Sherman's Troops in the Savannah and Carolinas Campaigns.* New York: New York University, 1985.

Greene, Francis V. *The Mississippi.* New York: Charles Scribner's Sons, 1882.

Hafendorfer, Kenneth A. *Perryville: The Battle for Kentucky.* Owensboro, KY: McDowell, 1981.

Hamilton, James T. *The Battle of Fort Donelson.* New York: Thomas Yoseloff, 1968.

Hattaway, Herman, and Archer Jones. *How the North Won: A Military History of the Civil War.* Urbana: University of Illinois Press, 1983.

Hay, Thomas Robson. *Hood's Tennessee Campaign.* New York: W. Neale, 1929.

Hewitt, Lawrence Lee. *Port Hudson: Confederate Bastion on the Mississippi.* Baton Rouge: Louisiana State University Press, 1987.

Hoehling, A. A. *Last Train from Atlanta.* New York: Thomas Yoseloff, 1958.

———. *Vicksburg: 47 Days of Siege.* Englewood Cliffs, NJ: Prentice-Hall, 1969.

Horn, Stanley F. *The Army of Tennessee.* Norman: University of Oklahoma Press, 1941.

———. *The Decisive Battle of Nashville.* Baton Rouge: Louisiana State University Press, 1956.

Hughes, Nathaniel Cheairs, Jr. *The Battle of Belmont: Grant Strikes South.* Chapel Hill: University of North Carolina Press, 1991.

Jones, Archer. *Confederate Strategy from Shiloh to Vicksburg.* Baton Rouge: Louisiana State University Press, 1961.

Jones, James Pickett. *Yankee Blitzkrieg: Wilson's Raid through Alabama and Georgia.* Athens: University of Georgia Press, 1976.

Keller, Allan. *Morgan's Raid.* Indianapolis: Bobbs-Merrill, 1961.

Kennett, Lee. *Marching through Georgia: The Story of Soldiers and Civilians during Sherman's Campaign.* New York: HarperCollins, 1995.

Lawson, Lewis A. *Wheeler's Last Raid.* Greenwood, FL: Penkevill, 1986.

Lucas, Marion Brunson. *Sherman and the Burning of Columbia.* College Station: Texas A&M University Press, 1976.

Mathews, Duncan K. *The McCook-Stoneman Raid.* Philadelphia: Dorrance, 1976.

McDonough, James Lee. *Chattanooga: A Death Grip on the Confederacy.* Knoxville: University of Tennessee Press, 1984.

———. *Shiloh: In Hell before Night.* Knoxville: University of Tennessee Press, 1977.

———. *Stones River: Bloody Winter in Tennessee.* Knoxville: University of Tennessee Press, 1980.

———. *War in Kentucky: From Shiloh to Perryville.* Knoxville: University of Tennessee Press, 1994.

McDonough, James Lee, and Thomas L. Connelly. *Five Tragic Hours: The Battle of Franklin.* Knoxville: University of Tennessee Press, 1983.

McMurry, Richard M. *Two Great Rebel Armies: An Essay in Confederate Military History.* Chapel Hill: University of North Carolina Press, 1989.

———. "The Atlanta Campaign of 1864: A New Look." *Civil War History* 22 (1976).

McWhiney, Grady. "General Beauregard's 'Complete Victory' at Shiloh: An Interpretation." *Journal of Southern History* 49 (1983): 421–434.

Miers, Earl S. *The General Who Marched to Hell: William Tecumseh Sherman and His March to Fame and Infamy.* New Brunswick, NJ: Rutgers University Press, 1948.

———. *The Web of Victory: Grant at Vicksburg.* New York: Alfred A. Knopf, 1955.

Pemberton, John C. *Pemberton: Defender of Vicksburg.* Chapel Hill: University of North Carolina Press, 1942.

Seymour, Digby Gordon. *Divided Loyalties: Fort Sanders and the Civil War in East Tennessee.* Knoxville: University of Tennessee Press, 1963.

Spruill, Matt, ed. *Guide to the Battle of Chickamauga.* U.S. Army War College Guides to Civil War Battles. Lawrence: University Press of Kansas, 1993.

Starr, Stephen Z. *The Union Cavalry in the Civil War.* Vol. 3: *The War in the West, 1861–1865.* Baton Rouge: Louisiana State University Press, 1985.

Sword, Wiley. *Embrace an Angry Wind: The Confederacy's Last Hurrah: Spring Hill, Franklin, and Nashville.* New York: HarperCollins, 1992. (Also available in paperback as *The Confederacy's Last Hurrah: Spring Hill, Franklin, and Nashville.* Lawrence: University Press of Kansas, 1993.)

————. *Mountains Touched with Fire: Chattanooga Besieged, 1863.* New York: St. Martin's Press, 1995.

————. *Shiloh: Bloody April.* New York: Morrow, 1974.

Tucker, Glenn. *Chickamauga: Bloody Battle in the West.* Indianapolis: Bobbs-Merrill, 1961.

Van Horne, Thomas Budd. *History of the Army of the Cumberland: Its Organization, Campaigns, and Battles . . .* Cincinnati: R. Clark, 1875.

Van Noppen, Ina Woestemeyer. *Stoneman's Last Raid.* Raleigh: North Carolina State College Print Shop, 1961.

Walker, Peter F. *Vicksburg: A People at War, 1860–1865.* Chapel Hill: University of North Carolina Press, 1960.

Williams, Kenneth P. *Lincoln Finds a General: A Military Study of the Civil War.* 5 vols. (Vols. 3–5 treat the western theater). New York: Macmillan, 1949–1959.

Woodworth, Steven E. *Jefferson Davis and His Generals: The Failure of Confederate Command in the West.* Lawrence: University Press of Kansas, 1990.

22

Trans-Mississippi Theater

Anne J. Bailey

The Confederate trans-Mississippi included Texas, Arkansas, Missouri, Indian Territory and the area of Louisiana west of the Mississippi River (thirty-one complete parishes and parts of six others). Although Confederates also laid claim to the Arizona Territory (including part of the modern states of New Mexico and Arizona), after the ill-fated campaign to New Mexico's Rio Grande valley early in the war, the Confederacy abandoned aspirations to expand westward. The fighting west of the Mississippi did not affect the war's outcome, but there were a number of battles and campaigns that influenced events east of the river, and simply by forcing Abraham Lincoln to commit troops to the region, Union authorities acknowledged the area's value. Lincoln recognized the significance of controlling the states west of the river, but President Jefferson Davis did not. Historians writing in the first century after Fort Sumter also failed to see the department's significance. Few works concentrated on military operations in the trans-Mississippi, and historians ignored the impact that fighting there had on other events. Indeed, early writers often rejected the idea that the trans-Mississippi fit into the wider scope of the war. But as an increased interest in the western theater emerged, scholars began to recognize that the river barrier did not necessarily isolate the fighting. Men in trans-Mississippi fought and died just as soldiers did in the grand battles to the east.

Because it was a peripheral theater of operations, neither Confederate nor Union authorities developed an overall military strategy for the region. Those critical locales along the Mississippi River that concerned military strategists— New Orleans, Baton Rouge, and Port Hudson—did not belong to the trans-Mississippi Department. Although strategy and tactics played important roles, the majority of the meetings were small engagements or irregular warfare, the latter a mode of fighting that often involved civilians as well as soldiers. After the first encounters at Wilson's Creek, Missouri, in 1861 and Pea Ridge, Arkansas, in 1862, the armies settled into a pattern that typically involved skirmishes. Although there were some unsuccessful Confederate raids into Missouri, only the Red River campaign in Louisiana and the Arkansas campaign, both in the spring of 1864, ranked as major events. While the fighting along Texas's coast concerned Abraham Lincoln, Jefferson Davis did not see the need to commit significant numbers of troops to the area. It is interesting, however, that one of the Confederacy's finest victories on water, when a small number of Confederates overpowered a superior Union force, occurred at Sabine Pass, Texas, and the war's last clash of arms, one month after Robert E. Lee's surrender, took place along the Rio Grande in May 1865.

Since the war's centennial celebration in the 1960s, numerous works have been published. Although scholars have begun to study the battles of the trans-Mississippi in the context of the larger impact they had on the war, the historical scholarship still lags far behind the two major theaters. The trans-Mississippi has only recently attracted the attention of major publishers, and the number of books specifically relating to military events is meager when compared to the thousands that analyze strategy and tactics in the eastern and western theaters. Therefore, much of the best scholarship is found in journal or magazine articles, and for that reason there are several articles referred to in this chapter that specifically deal with military topics not adequately covered in larger works.

There is still no single study of military events in the trans-Mississippi, and the best overview is a work over two decades old, Robert L. Kerby, *Kirby Smith's Confederacy: The Trans-Mississippi South, 1863–1865* (1972). Although the title indicates that Kerby begins his study halfway through the war, he devotes his opening chapters to the conflict's first years. Kerby has produced an analytical account of the military and domestic affairs of the department and in one volume covers battles, leaders, political events, economics, and social conditions. He points out that the trans-Mississippi was the largest military department in the Confederacy, and that reason alone forced both Union and Confederate military leaders to take the region into consideration when planning campaign strategy. Nonetheless, Kerby has done more than narrate military events; he has shown that it is impossible to separate the military from other factors.

Politics often determined military strategy, and the failure of the Confederate president to consider the trans-Mississippi as a significant component of the nation's political body was a serious error. Steven E. Woodworth, in " 'Dismembering the Confederacy': Jefferson Davis and the Trans-Mississippi West" (1990), concludes that the trans-Mississippi was lost before Vicksburg and Port Hudson surrendered because Davis failed to develop an effective military arrangement that encouraged cooperation between departments bordering on the Mississippi River valley.

Since the bulk of the fighting across the Mississippi was by the cavalry, two other general works of value are Stephen Z. Starr, *The Union Cavalry in the Civil War,* volume 3, *The War in the West 1861–1865* (1985), and Stephen B. Oates, *Confederate Cavalry West of the River* (1961). Oates focuses on the Prairie Grove campaign of December 1862 and the Confederate raids into Missouri in 1863 and 1864, but he also discusses the problems of recruiting and equipping cavalrymen in the trans-Mississippi. He observes that the Confederates had to rely heavily on captured Federal supplies and equipment, while Starr argues that the Union cavalry was not as rich in equipment and supplies as has been supposed. Although Starr covers the fighting for the entire area west of the Alleghenies, he uses the *Official Records* for his foundation and fails to place an equal emphasis on the letters and diaries of participants. Nonetheless, this is a useful tool for the study of Union soldiers fighting in Arkansas, Louisiana, and Missouri.

ARKANSAS AND MISSOURI

The first battle of any significance occurred at Wilson's Creek, Missouri, in August 1861, and the best study of the Union commander is Christopher Phillips, *Damned Yankee: The Life of General Nathaniel Lyon* (1990). This well-researched biography ends with Lyon's attack on the numerically superior Confederate forces at Wilson's Creek (Oak Hills). Unfortunately, Phillips devotes only a few pages to the actual fighting and provides the reader with little analysis of Lyon as a field commander. He does argue, however, that Lyon had a dramatic impact on the problems of irregular warfare that subsequently plagued the state. Still of value, however, is Ed Bearss's older work, *The Battle of Wilson's Creek* (1975). Unlike Phillips, Bearss deals little with analyzing the personalities involved but concentrates on describing the military actions. He relies heavily on the battle reports in the *Official Records.*

An older work that discusses military events along the northern realm of the trans-Mississippi department is Jay Monaghan, *Civil War on the Western Border, 1854–1865* (1955). As the title indicates, this book includes the prewar years and the military actions along the upper boundary of the trans-Mississippi, but it is still useful for some of the significant battles in the department, including Wilson's Creek, Pea Ridge, Prairie Grove, Cabin Creek, Pilot Knob, and Westport.

Military events in Missouri and Arkansas can also be found in Albert Castel, *General Sterling Price and the Civil War in the West* (1968). In this military study, Castel concludes that Price did not possess the qualities (intellect, training, or experience) to be a successful commander. His value was in his ability to inspire men to fight, which would have been useful at divisional level. Even this forte, Castel argues, would have been better employed leading infantry, for Castel judged that Price did not have the skill to command cavalry. Nonetheless, this account of Price's career parallels the story of the war in the trans-

Mississippi West and helps the scholar understand how personalities influenced military events.

One of those clashes where personalities affected overall strategy was the Battle of Pea Ridge, Arkansas, in March 1862. A new study of the battle has become a model for writing military history. Authors William L. Shea and Earl J. Hess, in *Pea Ridge: Civil War Campaign in the West* (1992), have produced an exhaustively researched work that offers the definitive account of the battle. Only part of the book deals with the actual fighting, as the authors devote much of their analysis to the Federal strategy to control northern Arkansas. Shea and Hess persuasively argue that Federal general Samuel Curtis deserves praise, but they do not slight Confederate commander Earl Van Dorn, who had received his assignment in order to mollify the squabbling between Sterling Price and Ben McCulloch. Their evaluations of strategy and tactics provide a model for other writers, as they ably shift from the Federals to the Confederates in order to maintain a balanced account. Not only do they place Pea Ridge into the wider context of the war, they describe small unit tactics and actions. Because Pea Ridge was not a large battle, the authors can discuss nuances of the fighting often ignored in the large clashes: tactics down to the company and battery level, leadership, logistics, medical care, and ethnic and personal conflicts.

Another fine work that deals with the Battle of Pea Ridge is Thomas W. Cutrer's *Ben McCulloch and the Frontier Military Tradition* (1993). This well-researched biography of the Confederate general who lost his life in the fighting allocates five chapters to McCulloch's Civil War career. The reader follows McCulloch from his command of the Army of the West in Indian Territory, to the Battle of Wilson's Creek, his disagreements with Sterling Price over strategy, and finally to his actions and death at the Battle of Pea Ridge.

When the Arkansas Historic Preservation Program became involved in the secretary of the interior's American Battlefield Program in 1990, a goal was to promote interest in Civil War sites within the state. Out of this need to educate came *Rugged and Sublime: The Civil War in Arkansas* (1994), edited by Mark K. Christ. Each chapter covers one year of the war. Since this work focuses on Arkansas battlefields, it is principally a military study. Nonetheless, each author has tried to place events in Arkansas within the larger scope of the war by giving particular attention to the overall planning that affected events in the neighboring regions of Missouri, Indian Territory, and Louisiana. Despite the number of contributors, the book offers a free-flowing narrative and is the best synthesis of work on Arkansas.

A prominent Arkansan whose presence influenced trans-Mississippi military events early in the war was General Thomas Hindman. In *The Lion of the South: General Thomas C. Hindman* (1993) Diane Neal and Thomas W. Kremm chronicle this politician-turned-general's rise through the military ranks and explain how his headstrong, often obdurate, personality led to his downfall. Although this is a biography rather than a military study, the authors adequately describe

Hindman's command of the trans-Mississippi department in 1862 and the defeat of Confederate forces at Prairie Grove in December.

LOUISIANA

Not all of Louisiana belonged to the trans-Mississippi department, and military events that did not have an impact on New Orleans or the Mississippi River valley never really concerned Union authorities. The Mississippi River campaign, including the loss of New Orleans and Port Hudson, does not properly belong in a historiographical essay on military events west of the river, although there were some attempts to relieve Port Hudson and Vicksburg from the Louisiana side of the river. There are numerous articles in state and regional journals that cover various aspects of the fighting in Louisiana, but an overview of those engagements can be found in John D. Winters, *The Civil War in Louisiana* (1963). The author directs most of his attention to the fighting along the Mississippi River, but he does deal with minor engagements, particularly the important ones in the summer and fall of 1863. There is also a section devoted to the Red River campaign of 1864.

Perhaps the most important military action in the trans-Mississippi was the Union offensive in the spring of 1864 when Union general Nathaniel P. Banks marched into central Louisiana, planning to rendezvous at Shreveport with Union general Frederick Steele, whose army moved south out of Little Rock. Still ranking as the finest account of the Red River campaign in Louisiana is Ludwell H. Johnson, *Red River Campaign: Politics and Cotton in the Civil War* (1958). Although the author's thesis is that the campaign was not entirely military but intertwined with political maneuvering and cotton speculating, this remains the best volume on military operations along the Red River. This campaign, more than any other in the trans-Mississippi, affected events to the east, for some of the troops that would have accompanied William T. Sherman to Georgia for the opening of his spring offensive had not rejoined his army.

The Confederate commander during the Red River campaign, General Richard Taylor, is known to scholars for his valuable memoir, *Destruction and Reconstruction: Personal Experiences of the Late War* (1879), reprinted several times in recent years. Building on Taylor's foundation is T. Michael Parrish, who has produced a definitive biography of one of the few non–West Pointers to rise to military heights in *Richard Taylor: Soldier Prince of Dixie* (1992). The Civil War years account for three-fifths of the text, and his discussion of Taylor's service in the trans-Mississippi forms the best part of the book. Parrish offers sound analysis in his outstanding description of the battles at Mansfield and Pleasant Hill, and he focuses on Taylor's leadership and battlefield decisions during the campaign. He also discusses Taylor's problems with General Edmund Kirby Smith and evaluates the actions of General Banks.

While recent works on military actions in Louisiana are scarce, Arthur W. Bergeron, Jr., in *Guide to Louisiana Confederate Military Units, 1861–1865*

(1989), supplies a short history of the state's contribution to the Confederate army. In this reference volume, Bergeron provides a brief historical sketch of Louisiana's artillery, cavalry, and infantry units. Although this publication includes soldiers who fought east of the Mississippi River, it is still a valuable research tool. Bergeron's knowledge of Louisiana is also seen in *The Civil War Reminiscences of Major Silas T. Grisamore* (1993). Grisamore served as a quartermaster in Louisiana from 1863 until the end of the war, and his account of combat in the trans-Mississippi is superbly annotated by Bergeron, making it a worthwhile resource for Civil War Louisiana.

TEXAS

There were no battles in Texas except along the Gulf Coast and in the Rio Grande Valley. Much of Texas military history is found in books dealing with Confederate soldiers, and some of the finest scholarship relating to the state is found in regimental and brigade histories. The first Texas unit to engage in a major battle was the 3d Texas Cavalry, a regiment that participated in the fighting at Wilson's Creek and Pea Ridge. But Douglas Hale, in *The Third Texas Cavalry in the Civil War* (1993), has written more than a traditional military account of the soldiers' exploits. His socioeconomic account follows the trend in military history that focuses on men as well as the battles.

B. P. Gallaway has reconstructed four years in the life of a Confederate cavalryman who served in the trans-Mississippi by weaving a story from the papers, diaries, and letters of David Carey Nance in *The Ragged Rebel: A Common Soldier in W. H. Parsons' Texas Cavalry, 1861–1865* (1988). This book is particularly useful for the fighting in Arkansas in 1862 and the Red River campaign in 1864.

A brief look at Texans in the battles at Blair's Landing and Yellow Bayou is found in Anne J. Bailey, *Texans in the Confederate Cavalry* (1995), while a comprehensive analysis of a Texas unit in Arkansas and Louisiana is provided in *Between the Enemy and Texas: Parsons's Texas Cavalry Brigade in the Civil War* (1989). The latter work begins with Union general Samuel Curtis's White River campaign in 1862 and ends with the skirmishing in Arkansas during the last year of the war. Similar to the sociomilitary studies by Hale and Gallaway, it also looks at the character of the Confederate soldier and how his background and environment influenced the way he fought.

Norman D. Brown has done an impressive job of editing the letters of a Texas Confederate in *Journey to Pleasant Hill: The Civil War Letters of Captain Elijah P. Petty, Walker's Texas Division, C.S.A.* (1982). This monumentally researched and annotated work provides massive information about one of Texas's best-known trans-Mississippi infantry units. Although Petty's letters form the basis for the work, Brown's commentary enhances its value. Also worthy of mention is the 1994 reprint of J. P. Blessington's classic work, *The Campaigns of Walker's Texas Division* (1875), an almost daily account of the unit's military adventures. Another primary account, reprinted in 1987, is the engaging and entertaining description of war in W. W. Heartsill, *Fourteen Hundred and 91 Days in the Confederate Army* (1867). In this unique book on the Civil War, Heartsill describes his career from the trans-Mississippi to the Confederate Army of Tennessee and back to the Army of the trans-Mississippi.

While most Texas soldiers served in the Confederate armies, a small number remained in the state to defend the settlements against Indian raids. David Paul Smith, *Frontier Defense in the Civil War: Texas' Rangers and Rebels* (1992), focuses on the state's western frontier and describes the units that replaced Federal forces and patrolled the western counties from 1861 until 1865. Smith discusses the Indian problems in each military district and traces changes in military policy throughout the war.

An interesting collection of essays is found in *To the Tyrants Never Yield: A Texas Civil War Sampler* (1992) by Kevin R. Young. Although typographical errors mar the text, Young includes useful information about fighting along the Gulf Coast in chapters on the Union attack of Port Lavaca, the Battle of Galveston, the fighting in the Rio Grande Valley, and the Battle of Palmetto Ranch. Young, who hoped to show readers that there was much activity within Texas, particularly along the Mexican border, did not include the Battle at Sabine Pass on the state's eastern boundary.

Nonetheless, the only preserved battlefield in Texas—and it is not an important site in a historic sense—is located at Sabine Pass. This stunning Southern victory was the most significant in Texas during the war, but it has received little attention. Alwyn Barr looks at the encounter in "Sabine Pass, September 1863" (1962) and discusses the wider problem in "Texas Coastal Defense, 1861–1865" (1961).

The Federal blockade could not be enforced against the neutral Mexican port of Bagdad at the mouth of the Rio Grande River, and James A. Irby, *Backdoor at Bagdad: The Civil War on the Rio Grande* (1977), discusses the fighting along the Mexican border that pitted Unionist Texans against Confederate Texans. This short monograph focuses on the military strategy of Confederate commander John S. (Rip) Ford and provides readers with a general understanding of the military and political situation along the international border.

INDIAN TERRITORY

An older but useful overview of military events in the Indian Territory is Lary C. Rampp and Donald L. Rampp, *The Civil War in the Indian Territory* (1975). This work is a comprehensive study of tactical and strategic objectives in the military operations of both Confederate and Union units. The authors emphasize two points: first, that significant military activity occurred in the region and that regimental and brigade activities are as important as corps in understanding the events, and second, that the Cherokee, Creek, Seminole, Choctaw, and Chickasaw tribes played significant roles in the conflict.

The only Indian to become a brigadier general was Stand Watie, and in *Red Fox: Stand Watie and the Confederate Indian Nations during the Civil War Years in Indian Territory* (1988), author Wilfred Knight offers a detailed military account of Watie and his Indian forces. This book must be used with care, however, for numerous errors flaw the narrative, and Knight relies principally on the *Official Records* and secondary sources. As a result, he has produced a new version of an old story but without any fresh interpretations or additional information.

For understanding factions within the Cherokee Nation, and how internal political dissension in the Indian Territory affected the Civil War, see W. Craig Gaines, *The Confederate Cherokees: John Drew's Regiment of Mounted Rifles* (1989). Gaines discusses how the rivalries among the Cherokee, conflicts that had simmered since the tribes' removal from Georgia in the 1830s, divided the Cherokees into pro-Confederate and pro-Union factions. Although Gaines looks at one particular regiment, and only for the first year of the war, he does examine the Indians' role at the Battle of Pea Ridge. Moreover, he includes a general overview of military events in the Indian Territory.

NEW MEXICO

The first campaign of any importance in the trans-Mississippi was a Southern failure. Plans to establish a Confederate empire in the West disintegrated after the rebels lost at Valverde and Glorieta Pass in the New Mexico Territory. Donald S. Frazier, in *Blood and Treasure: Confederate Empire in the Southwest* (1995), offers the most recent interpretation of this venture. Frazier has made use of obscure yet revealing primary sources to argue that the invasion of New Mexico, generally treated as a minor campaign, was the key to Confederate imperialism. He asserts that if Confederate planning had been better and the commanders more competent, the Confederacy could have extended its boundaries all the way to the Pacific.

The Confederate commander responsible for the failure of the New Mexico campaign is treated fairly in a full-scale biography by Jerry D. Thompson, *Henry Hopkins Sibley: Confederate General of the West* (1987). Thompson believes that the small Confederate army could have produced major results, a perspective that differs from previous scholars who have judged that the adventure had little chance of success. This is principally a biography of an unsuccessful field commander, but Thompson does devote three chapters to the New Mexico campaign and one to Sibley's failure in the Louisiana bayous in 1863.

A first-person account of the Sibley expedition is found in Jerry D. Thompson, *Westward the Texans: The Civil War Journal of Private William Randolph Howell* (1990). The diary text consists of only sixty-one pages that are not particularly informative, but Thompson compensates for this lack of substance by using the first fifty-one pages of the book to summarize the campaign and describe a comprehensive range of relevant works, including little-known diaries, letters, memoirs, and newspapers. Unfortunately, many of the resources he mentions are unpublished and accessible only to the most diligent researcher.

Less useful but still of interest is Alvin M. Josephy, Jr., *The Civil War in the American West* (1991). Although Josephy devotes three chapters to the New Mexico campaign, his research is limited to the *Official Records* and secondary sources. The book is also uneven in organization, for it does not follow chronological order. Josephy's tendency to jump from New Mexico to Minnesota, then back to Louisiana for the Red River campaign before returning to Arkansas to discuss the Battle of Pea Ridge (which occurred two years earlier), may disturb some readers. He does, however, give adequate background to events and detailed descriptions of the military actions.

IRREGULAR OPERATIONS

An understanding of the trans-Mississippi is not complete without a look at the irregular operations that plagued the entire department. The best work on guerrilla warfare in the northern regions is Michael Fellman, *Inside War: The Guerrilla Conflict in Missouri during the American Civil War* (1989). Although some scholars fault Fellman for making too great a generalization, his analysis is a worthwhile contribution to understanding the motivations of the men who carried on an irregular war in the West. He does not, however, give enough credit to older works, such as Richard S. Brownlee, *Gray Ghosts of the Confederacy: Guerrilla Warfare in the West, 1861–1865* (1958), which despite its title, focuses primarily on Missouri and Kansas. There is no book that looks at similar problems in Arkansas, but articles that cover the topic are Daniel E. Sutherland, "Guerrillas: The Real War in Arkansas" (1993), and Leo E. Huff, "Guerrillas, Jayhawkers and Bushwhackers in Northern Arkansas during the War" (1965).

Many other fine studies appear in magazines and journals. Of particular interest are journals published in the modern states that formed part of the military department. Some important ones are the *Southwestern Historical Quarterly, East Texas Historical Journal, Panhandle-Plains Historical Review, West Texas Historical Association Year Book, Arkansas Historical Quarterly, Louisiana History* (previously published as *Louisiana Historical Quarterly*), *McNeese Review, North Louisiana Historical Association Journal, the Missouri Historical Review, Chronicles of Oklahoma, New Mexico Historical Review, Rio Grande History, Journal of Arizona History, Arizona History Review, Military History of the West* (previously published as *Texas Military History, Military History of Texas and the Southwest,* and *Military History of the Southwest*).

BIBLIOGRAPHY

Bailey, Anne J. *Between the Enemy and Texas: Parsons's Texas Cavalry in the Civil War.* Forth Worth: Texas Christian University Press, 1989.

———. *Texans in the Confederate Cavalry.* Fort Worth: Ryan Place Publishers, 1995.

Barr, Alwyn Barr. "Sabine Pass, September 1863." *Texas Military History* 2 (1962): 17–22.

———. "Texas Coastal Defense, 1861–1865." *Southwestern Historical Quarterly* 65 (1961): 1–31.

Bearss, Edwin C. *The Battle of Wilson's Creek.* N.p.: George Washington Carver Birthplace District Association, 1975.

Bergeron, Arthur W., Jr. *Guide to Louisiana Confederate Military Units, 1861–1865.* Baton Rouge: Louisiana State University Press, 1989.

———. *The Civil War Reminiscences of Major Silas T. Grisamore, C.S.A.* Baton Rouge: Louisiana State University Press, 1993.

Blessington, Joseph Palmer. *The Campaigns of Walker's Texas Division.* 1875. Reprint, Austin: State House Press, 1994.

Brownlee, Richard S. *Gray Ghosts of the Confederacy: Guerrilla Warfare in the West, 1861–1865.* Baton Rouge: Louisiana State University Press, 1958.

Castel, Albert. *General Sterling Price and the Civil War in the West.* Baton Rouge: Louisiana State University Press, 1968.

Christ, Mark K., ed. *Rugged and Sublime: The Civil War in Arkansas.* Fayetteville: University of Arkansas Press, 1994.

Cutrer, Thomas W. *Ben McCulloch and the Frontier Military Tradition.* Chapel Hill: University of North Carolina Press, 1993.

Fellman, Michael. *Inside War: The Guerrilla Conflict in Missouri during the American Civil War.* New York: Oxford University Press, 1989.

Frazier, Donald S. *Blood and Treasure: Confederate Empire in the Southwest.* College Station: Texas A&M University Press, 1995.

Gaines, W. Craig. *The Confederate Cherokees: John Drew's Regiment of Mounted Rifles.* Baton Rouge: Louisiana State University Press, 1989.

Gallaway, B. P. *The Ragged Rebel: A Common Soldier in W. H. Parsons' Texas Cavalry, 1861–1865.* Austin: University of Texas Press, 1988.

Hale, Douglas. *The Third Texas Cavalry in the Civil War.* Norman: University of Oklahoma Press, 1993.

Heartsill, W. W. *Fourteen Hundred and 91 Days in the Confederate Army.* Edited by Bell Irvin Wiley. 1867. Reprint, Wilmington, NC: Broadfoot Publishing Co., 1987.

Howell, William Randolph. *Westward the Texans: The Civil War Journal of Private William Randolph Howell.* Edited by Jerry D. Thompson. El Paso: Texas Western Press, 1990.

Huff, Leo E. "Guerrillas, Jayhawkers and Bushwhackers in Northern Arkansas during the War." *Arkansas Historical Quarterly* 24 (1965): 127–148.

Irby, James A. *Backdoor at Bagdad: The Civil War on the Rio Grande.* El Paso: Texas Western Press, 1977.

Johnson, Ludwell H. *Red River Campaign: Politics and Cotton in the Civil War.* 1958. Reprint, Kent, Ohio: Kent State University Press, 1993.

Josephy, Alvin M. Jr., *The Civil War in the American West.* New York: Alfred A. Knopf, 1991.

Kerby, Robert L. *Kirby Smith's Confederacy: The Trans-Mississippi South, 1863–1865.* New York: Columbia University Press, 1972.

Knight, Wilfred. *Red Fox: Stand Watie and the Confederate Indian Nations during the Civil War Years in Indian Territory.* Glendale, CA.: Arthur C. Clark Co., 1988.

Monaghan, Jay. *Civil War on the Western Border, 1854–1865.* Boston: Little, Brown, 1955.

Neal, Diane, and Thomas W. Kremm. *The Lion of the South: General Thomas C. Hindman.* Macon: Mercer University Press, 1993.

Oates, Stephen B. *Confederate Cavalry West of the River.* 1961. Reprint, Austin: University of Texas Press, 1992.

Parrish, T. Michael. *Richard Taylor: Soldier Prince of Dixie.* Chapel Hill: University of North Carolina Press, 1992.

Petty, Elijah P. *Journey to Pleasant Hill: The Civil War Letters of Captain Elijah P. Petty, Walker's Texas Division, C.S.A.* Edited by Norman D. Brown. San Antonio: Institute of Texan Cultures, 1982.

Phillips, Christopher. *Damned Yankee: The Life of General Nathaniel Lyon.* Columbia: University of Missouri Press, 1990.

Rampp, Lary C., and Donald L. Rampp. *The Civil War in the Indian Territory.* Austin: Presidial Press, 1975.

Shea, William L., and Earl J. Hess. *Pea Ridge: Civil War Campaign in the West.* Chapel Hill: University of North Carolina Press, 1992.

Smith, David Paul. *Frontier Defense in the Civil War: Texas' Rangers and Rebels.* College Station: Texas A&M University Press, 1992.

Starr, Stephen Z. *The Union Cavalry in the Civil War.* Vol. 3: *The War in the West, 1861–1865.* Baton Rouge: Louisiana State University Press, 1985.

Sutherland, Daniel E. "Guerrillas: The Real War in Arkansas." *Arkansas Historical Quarterly* 52 (1993): 257–285.

Taylor, Richard. *Destruction and Reconstruction: Personal Experiences of the Late War.* London: William Blackwood and Sons, 1879.

Thompson, Jerry. *Henry Hopkins Sibley: Confederate General of the West.* Natchitoches, LA: Northwestern State University Press, 1987.

Winters, John D. *The Civil War in Louisiana.* Baton Rouge: Louisiana State University Press, 1963.

Woodworth, Steven E. " 'Dismembering the Confederacy': Jefferson Davis and the Trans-Mississippi West." *Military History of the Southwest* 20 (1990): 1–22.

Young, Kevin. *To the Tyrants Never Yield: A Texas Civil War Sampler.* Plano, TX: Wordware Publishing, 1992.

23

War on Inland Waters

Benjamin Franklin Cooling

When Francis Miles Finch wrote his poignant 1867 tribute, "The Blue and the Gray," his contemporaries understood that the late Civil War had taken place both ashore and afloat. They related to Finch's first stanza: "By the flow of the inland river, whence the fleets of iron have fled." The Union government in particular had named its principal field armies for those rivers: the Potomac, James, Shenandoah, Ohio, Cumberland, Tennessee, and Mississippi. Residents of heartland America, in particular, could identify with such a river war. Their prewar economic and social fabric had depended in large part upon those streams. They related in ways that future generations, weaned on movie spectaculars like *Gone with the Wind,* and *Gettysburg* or the unceasing rehash of the "100-mile war" for the rival capitals, could appreciate only partially at best.

The Civil War involved more than a bloody minuet over Washington and Richmond. The very moment that Mississippi, Louisiana, Arkansas, and Tennessee seceded from the Union (and Kentucky wavered), the conflict was guaranteed to embrace America's inland waterways. In fact, the war in the trans-Appalachian West was fought on two axes: the great Mississippi River and its tributaries, and the overland and predominantly railroad route from Louisville through Nashville and Chattanooga to Atlanta. Even in the second case, rivers like the Cumberland and Tennessee, as well as the smaller Green, Barren, Harpeth, Duck, Elk, and other streams all figured in the military operations in ways that often elude today's student of the conflict. The geography of the heartland is essential for understanding the Civil War. And the rivers of the heartland were central to both the physical and cultural geography of that era.

A case surely can be made that it was in the West that the Civil War was won and lost—won and lost, in fact, due to the rivers. Before the war, the nascent railroads were little more than feeders of trade to the river commerce. When secession spawned war, it was certainly on those waters that the great army-navy operational teams of the Union moved to ultimate success. Such campaigns featured some of the era's most famous professional as well as citizen soldiers and sailors. Conversely, defense of the western rivers uncovered some of the South's most glaring military and political ineptitude as well as strategic limitations surrounding position defense.

Here lay the great playing fields upon which generals like Grant and Sherman and admirals such as Farragut and Porter trained in modern warfare. Military reputations were won and lost on the inland rivers, with the fate of both Johnstons, Beauregard, Pemberton, Polk, and even Bragg tied in large measure to performance that embraced those features. Of course, a generation of young men in uniform (military and naval, blue and gray) passed into manhood striving to control those geographical features. Civilians too were swept up in this war. Not only cave life in besieged Vicksburg but experiences on river-bottom plantations and in the cities, towns, and smaller farms along their banks tested the mettle of a people all too anxious to resolve the great issues of the day by force of arms. Together, North and South dissipated the flower of their young and the region's treasure in what civilians saw as a struggle to control politically the arteries of commerce and the military viewed as a vehicle for either suppressing rebellion or defending the natural boundaries of a new nation.

The Old Northwest and the younger frontier South knew the rivers as prewar highways of trade and communication. Such indispensable avenues in peace were guaranteed a wartime role. To understand the symbiotic relationship, any study of the war on western waters must begin with classic accounts by Louis Hunter, *Steamboats on the Western Rivers: An Economic and Technological History* (1947), chapter 4 of George Taylor, *The Transportation Revolution, 1815–1860* (1951), and Byrd Douglas *Steamboatin on the Cumberland* (1961). They will ease passage to John Fiske's background *The Mississippi Valley in the Civil War,* (1900), and, hence, to the military application of the rivers to warfare.

Certain generalized assessments are an appropriate introduction to the relationship of the river war to ultimate Union victory and Confederate defeat. See both the often abstruse Herman Hattaway and Archer Jones, *How the North Won* (1983), and a more felicitous Richard Beringer et al., *Why the South Lost* (1986), especially chapter 9. Military application also connotes strategy, with Archer Jones, *Civil War Command and Strategy* (1992), Edward Hagerman, *The American Civil War and the Origins of Modern Warfare* (1988), and Thomas Connelly and Archer Jones, *The Politics of Command* (1973) as appropriate beginnings. Janet Coryell, *Neither Heroine Nor Fool: Anna Ella Carroll of Maryland* (1990), delicately disposes of the myth that the distaff side actually initiated the river war strategy that saved the Union.

None of these studies quite approaches definitive clarification of the riverland relationship as defined by original documents in the army and navy *Official Records.* The wealth of factual detail and nuance in those published documents can be only partially captured in limited narrative syntheses. Nowhere are the joint operational difficulties of river control, logistics, counterguerrilla warfare, and civil-military relations (exemplified in population control) as richly laid out as in the original documents. Some of that detail has been visually conveyed superbly in periodic illustrations first provided in Francis Miller's classic *The Photographic History of the Civil War* (1911), especially volumes 1, 2, 4, and 6, and carried forward by William Davis in the first volume of *Touched by Fire* (1985), as well as the modern update of Miller, *The Image of War* (1981), volumes 1, 2, 4, and 5. Stephen Sears, *The American Heritage Century Collection of Civil War Art* (1974), also builds upon that visual tradition.

Detail is the theme of key reference works for tracking the chronology and topics of the river war, such as E. B. Long's incomparable 1971 work, *The Civil War Day by Day,* Patricia Faust's 1986 *Historical Times Illustrated Encyclopedia of the Civil War,* and statistical accounts by Thomas Livermore (1901) and Frederick Phisterer (1883). None of these works, or even the commendable (if needing revision) study of joint warfare, Reed's *Combined Operations in the Civil War* (1978), does justice to these lesser illumined but possibly pivotal aspects of the river war saga in the West. A recent, almost obscure work by Charles and Kay Gibson, *Assault and Logistics* (1995), by its title alone suggests new and integrative ways to explore joint coastal and river operations.

Of course, waterways imply the preeminence of the naval arm, and both Union and Confederate navies fought two wars, one in coastal waters and upon the high seas, the second on the inland rivers. Each general naval history of the war emphasizes that fact but in varying degrees or proportions. World navies since the late nineteenth century have developed a fetish about identity with the high seas, thanks to the great American naval theorist Alfred Thayer Mahan; hence writers of naval history also have overemphasized that role in the Civil War. Indeed, Mahan reflected that bias in his *The Gulf and Inland Waters* (1883) written for the Scribner's three-volume Navy in the Civil War series. But even Civil War naval officers themselves preferred bluewater assignments to the less glamorous task of what they termed merely army support.

Older naval histories like Charles Boynton, *The History of the Navy during the Rebellion* (1867–1868), and Thomas Scharf, *History of the Confederate States Navy,* (1887), mirrored that approach, and even David Porter, *Naval History of the Civil War* (1886), wistfully hints at the same bias. More modern histories have continued that perspective, if inadvertently, in Bern Anderson, *By Sea and by River* (1962); Ernest Eller and Dudley Knox, *The Civil War at Sea* (1961); William Fowler, *Under Two Flags* (1990); James Merrill, *The Rebel Shore* (1957); Howard Nash, *A Naval History* (1972); Frank Merli, "The Confederate Navy," and Dana Wegner, "The Union Navy," both in Kenneth Hagen, *In Peace and War* (1984); Tom Wells, *The Confederate Navy* (1971); and Richard West, *Mr. Lincoln's Navy* (1957).

But it is clearly a matter of balance, as similar general naval works like Virgil Jones, *The Civil War at Sea* (1960–1962), devotes the second of three volumes to the river war, while the encyclopedic official reference work by the Naval History Division, *Civil War Naval Chronology* (1961–1966), clearly portrays the diversity of roles and missions in balanced fashion. The river war has received more focused attention in several key works. They include the dated but informative Robert Coontz, *From the Mississippi to the Sea* (1930), and Fletcher Pratt, *Civil War on Western Waters* (1956), as well as the more definitive H. Allen Gosnell, *Guns on the Western Waters* (1949), James Merrill, *Battle Flags South* (1970), John Milligan, *Gunboats down the Mississippi* (1965), David Bastian, "Opening of the Mississippi" (1985), and even the focused piece by Maxine Turner, *Navy Gray* (1988).

Together with the general histories of the war afloat, they provide ample, if parochial, treatment of the waterborne side of the river war. But, like Reed, these works suggest the need for a more modern approach, better integrated with army materials for more comprehensive coverage. Regrettably, the military sources remain just as sadly parochial. Of course, works like Bruce Catton, *Grant Moves South* (1960), cannot help but delve into the naval perspective. Similarly, the three volumes in the early Scribner's Campaigns of the Civil War suggest a modicum of integration—but just that. They include Henry Cist, *Army of the Cumberland* (1882), Manning Force, *From Fort Henry to Corinth* (1881), and Francis Greene, *The Mississippi* (1882).

Surprisingly, the focus has only marginally improved over the years, ranging from Thomas Van Horne's venerable *History of the Army of the Cumberland* (1875) to modern historical interpretations of Southern armies like Thomas Connelly, *Army of the Heartland* (1967) and *Autumn of Glory* (1971); Stanley Horn, *Army of Tennessee* (1941); and Richard McMurry's analytical if provocative *Two Great Rebel Armies* (1989). Avowedly, however, any study of western armies as part of the river war must begin with the wealth of data provided in Frank Welcher's second volume of *The Union Army, 1861–1865, Organization and Operations* (1993).

Operational histories of the war in the West naturally feature episodes in the river war. Period authors in the majestic Robert Johnson and Clarence Buel edited classic, *Battles and Leaders of the Civil War* (1887), cover Belmont and Fort Henry battles in volume 1, Fort Donelson, New Madrid, Island Number Ten, Memphis, Shiloh, and New Orleans as well as a brief treatment of the river gunboats themselves in volume 2, and Vicksburg and Port Hudson in volume 3. Even the relationship between river control and the situation at Chattanooga in the fall of 1863 as well as the politically infamous Red River campaign in Arkansas the following year find coverage in volume 4. That the authors were often participants or contemporary to the events lends interest to their essays.

Specific battles and campaigns must be approached through Nathaniel Hughes, *The Battle of Belmont* (1991); Benjamin Cooling (1987) and James Hamilton (1968) on Forts Henry and Donelson; Charles Dufour, *The Night the*

War Was Lost (1960) for New Orleans; Wiley Sword, *Shiloh: Bloody April* (1974); and James McDonough, *Shiloh—In Hell before Night* (1977). Vicksburg may be approached through the dated but useful Samuel Reid, *Vicksburg Campaign and the Battles about Chattanooga* (1882); a more popular Earl Miers, *The Web of Victory* (1955); or single volumes by Edwin Bearss, *Rebel Victory at Vicksburg* (1963), and Samuel Carter, *The Final Fortress* (1980). More definitive, however, is Bearss's three-volume *Campaign for Vicksburg* (1985–1986). Port Hudson finds ample treatment in Edward Cunningham, *The Port Hudson Campaign* (1963), and Lawrence Hewitt, *Port Hudson* (1987). Ludwell Johnson's *Red River Campaign: Politics and Cotton* (1958) still portrays the political-military interrelationships of the river war more adequately than other operational histories. The controversial Confederate attack at Fort Pillow in 1864 has been approached in Richard Fuchs, *An Unerring Fire* (1994). The tragic end-of-war disaster to the troopship *Sultana* illustrates both the frailty of period steamboats and the all-too-typical American rush to demobilize after war, finding coverage in James Elliott, *Transport to Disaster* (1962).

Biography remains one of the most pleasurable ways to approach history. Study of the river war proves no exception. Joseph Glatthaar, *Partners in Command* (1994), T. Harry Williams's classic *Lincoln and His Generals* (1952), K. P. Williams's five-volume *Lincoln Finds a General* (1952–1959), Clarence McCartney, *Mr. Lincoln's Admirals* (1956), together with Steven Woodworth, *Jefferson Davis and His Generals* (1990), and even Frank Vandiver, *Rebel Brass* (1956), paint the background tapestry. Nonetheless, there can be no substitute for individual biographical studies that shed light on the role of the river war.

The river war and top policy makers can be profitably appreciated best through Roy Basler, *Collected Works of Abraham Lincoln* (1953), and the ongoing project of Lynda Crist and Mary Dix, *The Papers of Jefferson Davis* (1994) commencing with volume 7. The Union perspective is provided by Tyler Dennett's use of John Hay's diary and letters in *Lincoln and the Civil War* (1939), by Charles Dana, *Recollections* (1898), and Benjamin Thomas and Harold Hyman, *Stanton* (1962). Richard West, *Gideon Welles, Lincoln's Navy Department* (1943), John Niven, *Gideon Welles* (1973), Welles's three-volume *Diary* as edited by Howard K. Beale (1911), and the Robert Thompson and Richard Wainwright edited version of the *Confidential Correspondence of Gustavus Vasa Fox* (1918–1919) enhance the view for Washington. Such studies often best illumine resolution of the thorny army-navy relational issues that developed at field level in the river war.

Indeed, the field level can often be better understood through the lives of the admirals and generals than conventional narrative histories. James Hoppin, *Life of Andrew Hull Foote* (1874), Farragut biographies including those of James Barnes (1899), Loyall Farragut (1879), J. T. Hadley (1867), Charles Lewis (1941, 1943), Mahan (1892), Christopher Martin (1970), and Noel Gerson (1968), as well as Jim Hill, *Sea Dogs of the Sixties* (1935), are complemented by dated coverage of the navy's "second admiral," David Dixon Porter in

Porter, *Incidents and Anecdotes* (1885), James Soley (1903), and Richard West (1937). River war subordinates are covered in Henry Walke, *Naval Scenes and Reminiscences* (1877), and Charles Davis, *Charles Henry Davis* (1899), as well as Robert Johnson's unsung (1967) biography of John Rodgers, father of the gunboat flotilla.

Biographical coverage of western Union generals showing similar promise for river war study include Grant, *Personal Memoirs* (1885), and more especially John Simon's invaluable multivolume *Papers of Ulysses S. Grant* (1967–1991). Similarly, Sherman's *Memoirs* (1875) must be supplemented by modern biographies like John Marszalek (1993) and Charles Vetter (1992). Charles Royster, *The Destructive War: William Tecumseh Sherman, Stonewall Jackson, and the Americans* (1991), provides provocative analysis of this major practitioner of hard war who developed many of his attitudes and skills combating raiders, guerrillas, and partisans in the river conflict. Harrington's biography of Nathanial Banks offers insight into the inept political general charged with the Red River campaign.

Confederate biographies shedding light on the complexities of the young nation's attempt at position defense may begin with Joseph Durkin, *Stephen R. Mallory: Confederate Navy Chief* (1954). But passage to the role of the generals should be immediate. Charles Roland's portrait, *Albert Sidney Johnston* (1964), is indispensable for a controversial senior general who may well have lost the river war before it began. Similarly, the early river war role of key subordinates should be studied in Alfred Roman, *Military Operations of General Beauregard* (1884), T. Harry Williams, *Beauregard: Napoleon in Gray* (1955), Joseph Parks, *General Leonidas Polk* (1962), and the long-awaited Nathaniel Hughes and Roy Stonesifer, *Life and Wars of Gideon J. Pillow* (1993). Subsequent campaigns on the rivers that reflected less creditably upon the skills of other Confederate generals may be profitably explored in Michael Ballard, *Pemberton: A Biography* (1991), and Craig Symonds, *Joseph E. Johnston* (1992). Much has been made of the incomparable Southern cavalry wizard, Nathan Bedford Forrest, and his occasional forays against the Union war effort on the rivers. Traditional paeans such as those by Thomas Jordon and J. B. Pryor (1868), John Wyeth (1899), Andrew Lytle (1931), Robert Henry (1944), and even Lonnie Maness (1990) are better balanced by Brian Wills (1992) and Jack Hurst (1993).

The river war symbolized the integration of technology and modern war as graphically borne out by the wedding of ironclad and steamboat in the river war and heavy coastal and shipboard ordnance in combat. Commencing with the reference data provided by Mooney (U.S. Naval History Division) in *Dictionary of American Fighting Ships* (1959–), Frank Bennett, *The Steam Navy of the United States* (1896), and James Baxter, *Introduction of the Ironclad Warship* (1933) should yield rapidly to more modern studies, including Robert MacBride, *Civil War Ironclads* (1962), Paul Silverstone's profusely illustrated *Warships of the Civil War Navies* (1989), Charles Dana Gibson and E. Kay Gibson, *Dictionary of Transports and Combatant Vessels, Steam and Sail* (1995), and the more scholarly two volumes by Donald Canney, *The Old Steam Navy* (1990, 1993). Confederate warships can be followed particularly in Maurice Melton, *Confederate Ironclads* (1968), and William Still's *Confederate Shipbuilding* (1969) and *Iron Afloat* (1971). Mine warfare on the rivers finds coverage in Milton Perry, *Infernal Machines* (1965), while Harold Peterson, *Notes on Ordnance* (1959), and Eugene Canfield, *Notes on Naval Ordnance* (1960) and *Civil War Naval Ordnance* (1969) will still provide most readers with the basics of naval ordnance of the period.

Individual ship biographies are not nearly as numerous as unit histories for their army counterparts. In fact, here is a wide-open area for further work. However, Edwin Bearss, *Hardluck Ironclad* (1966), Virgil Jones and Harold Peterson, *U.S.S. Cairo* (1971), and John Wideman, *Sinking of the USS Cairo* (1993), amply document the fascinating story of the gunboat sunk by Confederate mines and raised within modern memory to become a feature attraction at the Vicksburg National Battlefield today. Other interesting ship histories include Edwin Jameson and Sanford Sternlicht, *The Black Devil of the Bayous: The Life and Times of the United States Steam Sloop Hartford* (1970), Tom Parrish, *The Saga of the Confederate Ram Arkansas* (1987), and Myron Smith, *The U.S. Gunboat Carondelet* (1982). The interesting story of the attempted amalgamation of an army-navy unit can be followed best in Warren Crandall, *History of the Ram Fleet and the Mississippi Marine Brigade* (1907).

This chapter cannot cover the plethora of army regimentals, soldier reminiscences, and memoirs that cover the western war in more detail for the overland than the river campaigns perhaps. Comparable coverage of sailors remains remarkably weak and fairly begs for a canvass of repositories around the country to correct the deficiency. James Morgan, *Recollections of a Rebel Reefer* (1917), treats the little-known early war Confederate Mississippi flotilla and Island Number Ten early in the war. James Jones and Edward Keuchel edited the diary of a Civil War marine that tells much about the Red River expedition (1975), while John Milligan similarly compiled letters of two naval participants in *From the Fresh-Water Navy* (1970) to provide a model for what could be done in this genre. Most recently, Peter Josyph, in *The Wounded River* (1993), used letters of a doctor aboard the hospital boat to suggest the sheer boredom that often attended soldier and sailor alike in the river war.

As the study of the Civil War moves into broader upland of study and reflection, even the river war should assume wider integration with the major socioeconomic and political issues of the wider conflict. For example, Ira Berlin and colleagues portray the documentary history of slavery in the region in *Freedom* (1985), Series I, volume I, chapters 4 and 5, as well as *Free at Last* (1992). These documents suggest that Union military and naval activities against Confederate infrastructure (slavery, plantations, war industries, civilian populace) during the river war may have been as important as combat operations. Furthermore, studies of wartime Louisville and Nashville by Robert McDowell (1962) and Walter Durham (1985, 1987) introduce the challenge of studying the changes the war wrought on the urban landscape along the upper south's rivers.

Finally, for both scholars and laypeople, the urge (nay necessity) of visiting Civil War historical sites should prove insatiable. How better to understand that symbiotic relationship between river and war, people and geography? Visual experience complements the published and unpublished words of remembrance and interpretation. Frances Kennedy, *The Civil War Battlefield Guide* (1990), includes essays on National Park Service battlefields of the river war including Fort Donelson, Shiloh, Vicksburg, Chattanooga, and Port Hudson. All of the Park Service sites, and many state-owned ones as well, have interpretive brochures and other material available for visitors. Even more useful as tour guides are Jim Miles, *A River Unvexed: A History and Tour Guide of the Campaign for the Mississippi River* (1994), and Dave Page, *Ship Versus Shore: Civil War Engagements along Southern Shores and Rivers* (1974).

In the end, however, we must remain unfulfilled in our attempt to fathom the war on inland rivers. Once we pass beyond the traditional history of battles and leaders, even the thrill of technology applied to modern war, the story remains murky. We know all too little about the guerrilla actions that dot the pages of *Official Records'* accounts of daily events in the river war. Far more remains to be uncovered about war and society in this conflict. Moreover, even traditional historical accounts have slighted one of the most central themes of the river war story: logistics. As both Erna Risch in her official 1962 study of the army's Quartermaster Corps and James Huston's equally pivotal logistical work, *The Sinews of War* (1966), river transportation was fully as important as the railroads in who won or lost the Civil War in the western theater of operations.

Infamous bean-counting statistical histories will not vie with blood and gore for the attention of Civil War buffs and professional historians perhaps. But who cannot feel just a bit guilty about this glaring weakness of Civil War historiography as it relates to the river war when recalling the comte de Paris's observation that whenever Federal arms were supported by a river, "their progress was certain and their conquests decisive," while the successes obtained by following railroads "were always precarious, new dangers springing up in their rear in proportion as they advanced." A bit more pithy—hence, more American—was William Tecumseh Sherman's memorable quotation:

We are much obliged to the Tennessee which has favored us most opportunely, for I am never easy with a railroad which takes a whole army to guard, each foot of rail being essential to the whole; whereas they can't stop the Tennessee, and each boat can make its own game.

Bluewater sailors would not have liked Uncle Billy Sherman's judgment. But in the end, besides the classic battles at Forts Henry and Donelson, Island Number Ten, New Orleans, Vicksburg, and Port Hudson, army support was what the river war was all about. Along with death from guerrilla snipers, malaria and other diseases in the bottoms, population control during occupation duty, and navigational exploration in support of operations, this combat lacked the glamor of blockade duty for the navy or the clash of titans for the army. These hidden recesses suggest, however, that much remains to be investigated before modern scholarship can consider the story of the Civil War on the inland rivers truly complete.

BIBLIOGRAPHY

Anderson, Bern. *By Sea and by River: The Naval History of the Civil War.* New York: Knopf, 1962.

Ballard, Michael. *Pemberton: A Biography.* Jackson: University Press of Mississippi, 1991.

Barnes, James. *David G. Farragut.* Boston: Small Maynard, 1899.

Basler, Roy P., ed. *The Collected Works of Abraham Lincoln.* 9 vols. New Brunswick: Rutgers University Press, 1953.

Bastian, David F. "Opening of the Mississippi during the Civil War." In Department of History, USNA, ed. *New Aspects of Naval History: Selected Papers from the Fifth Naval History Symposium,* pp. 129–136. Baltimore: Nautical and Aviation Publishing Company, 1985.

Baxter, James Phinney. *The Introduction of the Ironclad Warship.* Cambridge, MA: Harvard University Press, 1933.

Bearss, Edwin C. *Hardluck Ironclad: The Sinking and Salvage of the Cairo.* Baton Rouge: Louisiana State University Press, 1966.

———. *Rebel Victory at Vicksburg.* Vicksburg: Vicksburg Centennial Commemorative Commission, 1963.

———. *The Campaign for Vicksburg.* 3 vols. Dayton: Morningside, 1985, 1986.

Bennett, Frank M. *The Steam Navy of the United States.* 1896. Reprint, Westport, CT: Greenwood, 1972.

Beringer, Richard E., Herman Hattaway, Archer Jones, and William N. Still, Jr. *Why the South Lost the Civil War.* Athens: University of Georgia Press, 1986.

Berlin, Ira, et al. *Free at Last: A Documentary History of Slavery, Freedom, and the Civil War.* New York: Free Press, 1992.

———. *Freedom: A Documentary History of Emancipation, 1861–1867.* Series I, vol. 1: *Destruction of Slavery.* New York: Cambridge University Press, 1985.

Boynton, Charles B. *The History of the Navy during the Rebellion.* 2 vols. New York: Appleton, 1867–1868.

Canfield, Eugene B. *Civil War Naval Ordnance.* Washington, D.C.: Government Printing Office, 1969.

———. *Notes on Naval Ordnance of the American Civil War, 1861–1865.* Washington, D.C.: American Ordnance Association, 1960.

Canney, Donald L. *The Old Steam Navy.* Vol. 1: *Frigates, Sloops and Gunboats, 1815–1885.* Annapolis: Naval Institute Press, 1990.

———. *The Old Steam Navy.* Vol. 2: *The Ironclads, 1842–1885.* Annapolis: Naval Institute Press, 1993.

Carter III, Samuel. *The Final Fortress: The Campaign for Vicksburg, 1862–1863.* New York: St. Martin's, 1980.

Catton, Bruce. *Grant Moves South.* Boston: Little, Brown, 1960.

Cist, Henry M. *The Army of the Cumberland.* Campaigns of the Civil War, vol. 7. New York: Charles Scribner's Sons, 1982.

Connelly, Thomas L. *Army of the Heartland: The Army of Tennessee, 1861–1862.* Baton Rouge: Louisiana State University Press, 1967.

————. *Autumn of Glory: The Army of Tennessee, 1862–1865.* Baton Rouge: Louisiana State University Press, 1971.

————, and Archer Jones. *The Politics of Command: Factions and Ideas in Confederate Strategy.* Baton Rouge: Louisiana State University Press, 1973.

Cooling, Benjamin Franklin. *Forts Henry and Donelson: Key to the Confederate Heartland.* Knoxville: University of Tennessee Press, 1987.

Coontz, Robert E. *From the Mississippi to the Sea.* Philadelphia: Dorrance, 1930.

Coryell, Janet L. *Neither Heroine nor Fool: Anna Ella Carroll of Maryland.* Kent, OH: Kent State University Press, 1990.

Crandall, Warren Daniel. *History of the Ram Fleet and the Mississippi Marine Brigade in the War for the Union on the Mississippi and Its Tributaries.* St. Louis: Burchart Brothers, 1907.

Crist, Lynda Lasswell, and Mary Seaton Dix, eds. *The Papers of Jefferson Davis.* Vol. 3: *1861.* College Station: Texas A&M Press, 1994.

Cunningham, Edward. *The Port Hudson Campaign, 1862–1863.* Baton Rouge: Louisiana State University Press, 1963.

Dana, Charles. *Recollections of the Civil War.* New York: D. Appleton, 1898.

Davis, Charles H. *Life of Charles Henry Davis, Rear Admiral, 1807–1877.* New York: Houghton Mifflin, 1899.

Davis, William C., ed. *Touched by Fire: A Photographic Portrait of the Civil War.* 2 vols. Boston: Little, Brown, 1985.

————. *The Image of the War, 1861–1865.* Garden City, NY: Doubleday, 1981.

Dennett, Tyler. *Lincoln and the Civil War in the Diaries and Letters of John Hay.* New York: Dodd, Mead, 1939.

Douglas, Byrd. *Steamboatin on the Cumberland.* Nashville: Tennessee Book Company, 1961.

Dufour, Charles L. *The Night the War Was Lost.* Garden City, NY: Doubleday, 1960.

Durham, Walter T. *Nashville: The Occupied City; The First Seventeen Months, February 16, 1862, to June 30, 1863.* Nashville: Tennessee Historical Society, 1985.

————. *Reluctant Partners: Nashville and the Union, July 1, 1863, to June 30, 1865.* Nashville: Tennessee Historical Society, 1987.

Durkin, Joseph T. *Stephen R. Mallory: Confederate Navy Chief.* Chapel Hill, NC: University of North Carolina Press, 1954.

Eller, Ernest M., and Dudley W. Knox. *The Civil War at Sea.* Washington, D.C.: Naval Historical Foundation, 1961.

Elliott, James W. *Transport to Disaster.* New York: Holt, Rinehart and Winston, 1962.

Farragut, Loyall. *The Life of David Farragut, First Admiral of the United States Navy; Embodying His Journal and Letters.* New York: Appleton, 1879.

Faust, Patricia, ed. *Historical Times Illustrated Encyclopedia of the Civil War.* New York: Harper & Row, 1986.

Fiske, John. *The Mississippi Valley in the Civil War.* Boston: Houghton Mifflin, 1900.

Force, Manning F. *From Fort Henry to Corinth.* Campaigns of the Civil War, vol. 3. New York: Charles Scribner's Sons, 1881.

Fowler, William M. *Under Two Flags: The American Navy in the Civil War.* New York: Norton, 1990.

Fuchs, Richard L. *An Unerring Fire: The Massacre at Fort Pillow.* Rutherford, NJ: Fairleigh Dickinson University Press, 1994.

Gerson, Noel Bertram. [Paul Lewis, pseud.] *Yankee Admiral: A Biography of David Dixon Porter.* New York: David McKay, 1968.

Gibson, Charles Dana, with E. Kay Gibson. *Assault and Logistics: Union Coastal and River Operations, 1861–1866.* The Army's Navy Series, Volume II. Camden, ME: Ensign Press, 1995.

———. *Dictionary of Transports and Combatant Vessels, Steam and Sail, Employed by the Union Army, 1861–1868.* The Army's Navy Series, Volume I. Camden, ME: Ensign Press, 1995.

Glatthaar, Joseph T. *Partners in Command: The Relationship between Leaders in the Civil War.* New York: Free Press, 1994.

Gosnell, H. Allen. *Guns on the Western Waters: The Story of River Gunboats in the Civil War.* Baton Rouge: Louisiana State University Press, 1949.

Grant, Ulysses S. *Personal Memoirs.* 2 vols. New York: Charles L. Webster, 1885.

Greene, Francis Vinton. *The Mississippi.* Campaigns of the Civil War, vol. 8. New York: Charles Scribner's Sons, 1882.

Hadley, J. T. *Farragut and Our Naval Commanders.* New York: E. B. Treat, 1867.

Hagerman, Edward. *The American Civil War and the Origins of Modern Warfare.* Bloomington, IN: Indiana University Press, 1988.

Hamilton, James. *The Battle of Fort Donelson.* South Brunswick, NJ: Yoseloff, 1968.

Harrington, Fred Harvey. *Fighting Politician: Major General N. P. Banks.* Philadelphia: University of Pennsylvania Press, 1948.

Hattaway, Herman, and Archer Jones. *How the North Won: A Military History of the Civil War.* Urbana, IL: University of Illinois Press, 1983.

Henry, Robert Selph. *"First with the Most" Forrest.* Indianapolis: Bobbs-Merrill, 1944.

Hewitt, Lawrence Lee. *Port Hudson: Confederate Bastion on the Mississippi.* Baton Rouge: Louisiana State University Press, 1987.

Hill, Jim Dan. *Sea Dogs of the Sixties: Farragut and Seven Contemporaries.* Minneapolis: University of Minnesota Press, 1935.

Hoppin, James M. *Life of Andrew Hull Foote, Rear Admiral, United States Navy.* New York: Harper, 1874.

Horn, Stanley F. *The Army of Tennessee.* Indianapolis: Bobbs-Merrill, 1941.

Hughes, Nathaniel Cheairs, Jr. *The Battle of Belmont: Grant Strikes South.* Chapel Hill: University of North Carolina Press, 1991.

———, and Roy P. Stonesifer, Jr. *The Life and Wars of Gideon Pillow.* Chapel Hill: University of North Carolina Press, 1993.

Hunter, Louis. *Steamboats on the Western Rivers: An Economic and Technological History.* Cambridge: Harvard University Press, 1947.

Hurst, Jack. *Nathan Bedford Forrest: A Biography.* New York: Knopf, 1993.

Huston, James A. *The Sinews of War: Army Logistics, 1775–1953.* Army Historical Series. Washington, D.C.: Government Printing Office, 1966.

Jameson, Edwin M., and Sanford Sternlicht. *The Black Devil of the Bayous: The Life and Times of the United States Steam Sloop Hartford, 1858–1957.* Upper Saddle River, NJ: Gregg Press, 1970.

Johnson, Ludwell H. *Red River Campaign: Politics and Cotton in the Civil War.* Baltimore: Johns Hopkins University Press, 1958.

Johnson, Robert Erwin. *Rear Admiral John Rodgers 1812–1882.* Annapolis: United States Naval Institute, 1967.

Johnson, Robert Underwood, and Clarence Clough Buel, eds. *Battles and Leaders of the Civil War.* 4 vols. New York: Century, 1887.

Jones, Archer. *Civil War Command and Strategy: The Process of Victory and Defeat.* New York: Free Press, 1992.

Jones, James P., and Edward F. Keuchel, eds. *Civil War Marine: A Diary of the Red River Expedition 1864.* Washington, D.C.: Marine Corps Historical Division, 1975.

Jones, Virgil Carrington. *The Civil War at Sea.* 3 vols. New York: Holt, Rinehart and Winston, 1960–1962.

————, and Harold L. Peterson. *U.S.S. Cairo: The Story of a Civil War Gunboat.* Washington, D.C.: National Park Service, 1971.

Jordon, Thomas, and J. P. Pryor. *The Campaigns of Lieutenant General N. B. Forrest and of Forrest's Cavalry.* 1868. Reprint, Dayton: Morningside Bookshop, 1977.

Josyph, Peter, ed. *The Wounded River: The Civil War Letters of John Vance Lauderdale, M.D.* East Lansing: Michigan State University Press, 1993.

Kennedy, Frances H., ed. *The Civil War Battlefield Guide.* Boston: Houghton Mifflin, 1990.

Lewis, Charles L. *David Glasgow Farragut.* 2 vols. Annapolis: United States Naval Institute, 1941, 1943.

Livermore, Thomas L. *Numbers and Losses in the Civil War in America, 1861–1865.* 1901. Reprint, Bloomington, IN: Indiana University Press, 1957.

Long, E. B. *The Civil War Day by Day: An Almanac, 1861–1865.* Garden City, NY: Doubleday, 1971.

Lytle, Andrew Nelson. *Bedford Forrest and His Critter Company.* New York: Milton, Balch and Company, 1931.

MacBride, Robert. *Civil War Ironclads: The Dawn of Naval Armor.* Philadelphia: Chilton, 1962.

Mahan, A. T. *Admiral Farragut.* Great Commanders series. New York: Appleton, 1892.

————. *The Gulf and Inland Waters.* The Navy in the Civil War, vol. 3. New York: Charles Scribner's Sons, 1883.

Maness, Lonnie E. *An Untutored Genius: The Military Career of General Nathan Bedford Forrest.* Oxford, MS: Guild Bindery Press, 1990.

Marszalek, John F. *Sherman: A Soldier's Passion for Order.* New York: Free Press, 1993.

Martin, Christopher. *Damn the Torpedoes! The Story of America's First Admiral: David Glasgow Farragut.* New York: Abelard-Shurman, 1970.

McCartney, Clarence E. *Mr. Lincoln's Admirals.* New York: Funk and Wagnalls, 1956.

McDonough, James Lee. *Chattanooga—A Death Grip on the Confederacy.* Knoxville: University of Tennessee Press, 1984.

————. *Shiloh—In Hell before Night.* Knoxville: University of Tennessee Press, 1977.

McDowell, Robert Emmett. *City of Conflict: Louisville in the Civil War.* Louisville: Louisville Civil War Round Table, 1962.

McMurry, Richard M. *Two Great Rebel Armies: An Essay in Confederate Military History.* Chapel Hill: University of North Carolina Press, 1989.

Melton, Maurice. *The Confederate Ironclads*. South Brunswick, NJ: Thomas Yoseloff, 1968.

Merli, Frank J. "The Confederate Navy, 1861–1865." In Kenneth J. Hagen, ed. *In Peace and War: Interpretations of American Naval History, 1775–1984*, pp. 126–144. Westport, CT.: Greenwood, 1984.

Merrill, James M. *Battle Flags South: The Story of the Civil War Navies on Western Waters*. Rutherford, NJ.: Fairleigh Dickinson University Press, 1970.

———. *The Rebel Shore: The Story of Union Sea Power in the Civil War*. Boston: Little, Brown, 1957.

Miers, Earl Schenck. *The Web of Victory: Grant at Vicksburg*. New York: Knopf, 1955.

Miles, Jim. *A River Unvexed: A History and Tour Guide of the Campaign for the Mississippi River*. Nashville: Rutledge Hill, 1994.

Miller, Francis Trevelyan, ed. *The Photographic History of the Civil War*. 10 vols. New York: Review of Books, 1911.

Milligan, John D., compiler. *From the Fresh-Water Navy, 1861–64: The Letters of Acting Master's Mate Henry R. Browne and Acting Ensign Symmes E. Browne*. Annapolis: United States Naval Institute, 1970.

———. *Gunboats down the Mississippi*. Annapolis: United States Naval Institute, 1965.

Morgan, James M. *Recollections of a Rebel Reefer*. Boston: Houghton Mifflin, 1917.

Nash, Howard P., Jr. *A Naval History of the Civil War*. New York: A. S. Barnes, 1972.

Niven, John. *Gideon Welles: Lincoln's Secretary of the Navy*. New York: Oxford University Press, 1973.

Page, Dave. *Ship Versus Shore: Civil War Engagements along Southern Shores and Rivers*. Nashville: Rutledge Hill, 1974.

Parks, Joseph H. *General Leonidas Polk, CSA*. Baton Rouge: Louisiana State University Press, 1962.

Parrish, Tom L. *The Saga of the Confederate Ram Arkansas: The Mississippi Valley Campaign, 1862*. Hillsboro, TX: Hill College Press, 1987.

Perry, Milton F. *Infernal Machines: The Story of Confederate Submarines and Mine Warfare*. Baton Rouge: Louisiana State University Press, 1965.

Peterson, Harold L. *Notes on Ordnance of the Civil War, 1861–1865*. Washington, D.C.: American Ordnance Association, 1959.

Phisterer, Frederick. *Statistical Record of the Armies of the United States*. Campaigns of the Civil War, supplementary volume. New York: Charles Scribner's Sons, 1883.

Porter, David Dixon. *Incidents and Anecdotes of the Civil War*. New York: D. Appleton, 1885.

———. *Naval History of the Civil War*. New York: Sherman Publishing Company, 1886.

Pratt, Fletcher. *Civil War on Western Waters*. New York: Henry Holt, 1956.

Reed, Rowena. *Combined Operations in the Civil War*. Annapolis, MD: Naval Institute Press, 1978.

Reid, Samuel Rockwell. *The Vicksburg Campaign and the Battles about Chattanooga under the Command of General U.S. Grant in 1862–1863: An Historical Review*. Cincinnati: Robert Clarke and Company, 1882.

Risch, Erna. *Quartermaster Support of the Army: A History of the Corps, 1775–1939*. Washington, D.C.: Government Printing Office, 1962.

Roland, Charles P. *Albert Sidney Johnston: Soldier of Three Republics*. Austin: University of Texas Press, 1964.

Roman, Alfred. *The Military Operations of General Beauregard.* 2 vols. New York: Harper and Brothers, 1884.

Royster, Charles. *The Destructive War: William Tecumseh Sherman, Stonewall Jackson, and the Americans.* New York: Knopf, 1991.

Scharf, Thomas. *History of the Confederate States Navy from Its Organization to the Surrender of Its Last Vessel.* 2 vols. New York: Rogers and Sherwood, 1887.

Sears, Stephen W. *The American Heritage Century Collection of Civil War Art.* New York: American Heritage Publishing Company, 1974.

Sherman, William T. *Memoirs.* 2 vols. New York: D. Appleton, 1875.

Silverstone, Paul H. *Warships of the Civil War Navies.* Annapolis: United States Naval Institute, 1989.

Simon, John Y., ed. *The Papers of Ulysses S. Grant.* 18 vols. Carbondale, IL: Southern Illinois University Press, 1967–1991.

Smith, Myron. *The U.S. Gunboat Carondelet, 1861–1865.* Manhattan, KS: AH/MA Publishing Company, 1982.

Soley, James Russell. *Admiral Porter.* Great Commanders series. New York: D. Appleton, 1903.

Still, William N. Jr. *Confederate Shipbuilding.* Athens: University of Georgia Press, 1969.

———. *Iron Afloat: The Story of the Confederate Ironclads.* Nashville: Vanderbilt University Press, 1971.

Sword, Wiley. *Shiloh: Bloody April.* New York: Morrow, 1974.

Symonds, Craig L. *Joseph E. Johnston: A Civil War Biography.* New York: W. W. Norton, 1992.

Taylor, George Rogers. *The Transportation Revolution, 1815–1860.* New York: Rinehart and Company, 1951.

Thomas, Benjamin P., and Harold Hyman. *Stanton: The Life and Times of Lincoln's Secretary of War.* New York: Knopf, 1962.

Thompson, Robert Means, and Richard Wainwright, eds. *Confidential Correspondence of Gustavus Vasa Fox, Assistant Secretary of the Navy, 1861–1865.* 2 vols. New York: Naval Historical Society, 1918.

Turner, Maxine. *Navy Gray: A Story of the Confederate Navy on the Chattahoochee and Appalachicola Rivers.* Tuscaloosa: University of Alabama Press, 1988.

U.S. Navy Department. *Official Records of the Union and Confederate Navies in the War of the Rebellion.* 31 vols. Washington, D.C.: Government Printing Office, 1894–1927.

U.S. Naval History Division. *Civil War Naval Chronology, 1861–1865.* 6 parts. Washington, D.C.: Government Printing Office, 1961–1966, 1971.

———. James L. Mooney et al., eds. *Dictionary of American Fighting Ships.* Washington, D.C.: Government Printing Office, 1959–.

U.S. War Department. *War of the Rebellion: A Compilation of the Official Records of the Union and Confederate Armies.* 128 vols. plus atlas. Washington, D.C.: Government Printing Office, 1880–1901.

Vandiver, Frank. *Rebel Brass: The Confederate Command System.* Baton Rouge: Louisiana State University Press, 1956.

Van Horne, Thomas B. *History of the Army of the Cumberland.* 2 vols. and atlas. Cincinnati: Robert Clarke and Company, 1875.

Vetter, Charles Edmund. *Sherman: Merchant of Terror, Advocate of Peace.* Gretna, LA: Pelican Publishing Company, 1992.

Walke, Henry. *Naval Scenes and Reminiscences of the Civil War in the United States.* New York: F. R. Reed, 1877.

Wegner, Dana M. "The Union Navy, 1861–1865." In Kenneth J. Hagen, ed. *In Peace and War: Interpretations of American Naval History 1775–1984,* pp. 107–125. Westport, CT: Greenwood, 1984.

Welcher, Frank J. *The Union Army, 1861–1865, Organization and Operations. Vol. 2: The Western Theater.* Bloomington, IN: Indiana University Press, 1993.

Welles, Gideon. *Diary.* 3 vols. Edited by Howard K. Beale. Boston: Houghton Mifflin, 1911.

Wells, Tom H. *The Confederate Navy: A Study in Organization.* Tuscaloosa: University of Alabama Press, 1971.

West, Richard S. *Gideon Welles, Lincoln's Navy Department.* Indianapolis: Bobbs-Merrill, 1943.

———. *Mr. Lincoln's Navy.* New York: Longmans, Green, 1957.

———. *The Second Admiral: A Life of David Dixon Porter, 1813–1891.* New York: Coward-McCann, 1937.

Wideman, John C. *The Sinking of the USS Cairo.* Jackson: University Press of Mississippi, 1993.

Williams, Kenneth P. *Lincoln Finds a General: A Military Study of the Civil War.* 5 vols. New York: Macmillan, 1952–1959.

Williams, T. Harry. *Beauregard: Napoleon in Gray.* Baton Rouge: Louisiana State University Press, 1955.

———. *Lincoln and His Generals.* New York: Grosset and Dunlap, 1952.

Wills, Brian Steel. *A Battle from the Start: The Life of Nathan Bedford Forrest.* New York: HarperCollins, 1992.

Woodworth, Steven E. *Jefferson Davis and His Generals: The Failure of Confederate Command in the West.* Lawrence, KS: University Press of Kansas, 1990.

Wyeth, John A. *That Devil Forrest: Life of General Nathan Bedford Forrest.* 1899. Reprint, New York: Harper and Brothers, 1959.

24

War at Sea

Stephen R. Wise, Robert Holcombe, Jr., and Kevin Foster

Unfortunately for maritime scholars, works on Civil War navies have never matched the tremendous outpouring of books and articles on the war's land actions. Nor do the writings contain the historiographical and interpretive counterpoints so prevalent in the works concerning ground forces. Indeed, the general history of the naval war is dominated by the Mahan school of naval writing, wherein the strategic view is stressed, with emphasis on big battles and famous personalities. The existing literature encompasses a wide range of work that varies from popular, almost folklore, accounts to very technical papers on certain aspects of the naval war, such as commerce raiders, blockade running, ordnance, vessel construction, and navigation. What has not yet occurred is a synthesis of the specialized fields with the general literature in order to produce an overall study. The sources for such a work do exist, and when a naval historian combines the primary sources with the secondary works, a nearly complete picture of the navy's role can be produced.

There are some important bibliographies on Civil War navies. For primary sources the best guides are Henry Putney Beers's recently revised *Guide to the Archives of the Government of the Confederate States of America* (1968) and Kenneth W. Munden and Henry Putney Beers's *Guide to Federal Archives Relating to the Civil War* (1962). These works not only list naval records held by the National Archives but also manuscript sources at other institutions. One important set of manuscripts is the Papers of Officers of the Naval Records Library, which contain numerous collections of Civil War officers; once held by the Naval History Division, they are currently housed at the Library of Congress. For a more complete listing of manuscripts outside the National Archives, see the Library of Congress's *National Union Catalogue of Manuscript Collections.*

Bibliographies on naval sources include Myron J. Smith's *American Civil War Navies* (1972), which contains nearly 3,000 listing of books, documents, and articles. *Civil War Books: A Critical Bibliography,* edited by Allan Nevins, James I. Robertson, Jr., and Bell I. Wiley (1967), contains an annotated section on the navies, while Edward W. Sloan's "The Navy in the Nineteenth Century, 1848–1889" (1992), covers entries for the Civil War period. Additional listings can be found in Paolo E. Coletta's *An Annotated Bibliography of U.S. Marine Corps History* (1986) and *A Selected Bibliography of American Naval History* (1988). See also James W. Geary's "Blacks in Northern Blue" (1988). Other bibliographies were printed annually in the journal *Civil War History* through 1987, and bibliographic listings can be found in the *Journal of Southern History.*

An indispensable source for the naval Civil War is *Official Records of the Union and Confederate Navies in the War of the Rebellion* (1894–1922). This is the single most important source for naval records, but it is not as complete as the army's printed official records. Many important naval records were not included in the work and remain in the National Archives. Both the navy and the army official records have been recently reprinted by Broadfoot Press. Another primary source compiled after the war is Robert U. Johnson and Clarence C. Buel, eds., *Battles of the Leaders of the Civil War* (1887–1888), which contains numerous postwar articles written by naval leaders. The set has gone through numerous reprints. Other primary sources can be found in the publications of the Military Order of the Loyal Legion of the United States, which produced volumes of primary accounts in *War Papers,* printed by the organization's various state commanderies. Southern naval accounts can be found in the journals *Confederate Veteran* and the *Southern Historical Society Papers.*

Since the time of the war, the government has produced a number of publications, which include the *Dictionary of American Naval Fighting Ships* (1959–1981), *Civil War Naval Chronology* (1961–1966), and *List of Logbooks of U.S. Navy Ships, Stations and Miscellaneous Units, 1801–1947* (1978). Some general histories of Civil War vessels can be found in Eric Heyl's *Early American Steamers* (1953–1969). The Eric Heyl collection is located at the Great Lakes Research Center at Bowling Green State University, Bowling Green, Ohio. Another useful list is William M. Lytle's *Merchant Steam Vessels of the United States, 1807–1868, "The Lytle List"* (1952). Though the information on blockade runners is incomplete and misleading, Paul H. Silverstone's *Warships of the Civil War Navies* (1989) does provide statistical data on naval vessels used by both the North and the South. Another fine source for the Confederate navy is Frank J. Merli, ed., "Special Commemorative Naval Issue," (1989), which contains articles on the CSS *Alabama,* blockade running, Raphael Semmes, Confederate activities in Liverpool, England, and Confederate ordnance.

GENERAL HISTORIES

General histories are limited; no single work serves as a comprehensive history of the naval war. Bern Anderson's *By Sea and by River* (1962) and James Russell Soley's *The Blockade and the Cruisers* (1883) give fine, broad overviews of the navies, but neither work goes beyond a standard operational description. Both wrongly attribute the defeat of the Confederacy to the blockade and also claim that the main task of the Confederate navy was to break the blockade instead of defending the South's coast, ports, and rivers. Charles Brandon Boykin's *The History of the Navy during the Rebellion* (1867–1868) is a fine, broad study that strongly supports the policies of the Northern secretary of the navy, Gideon Welles. David Dixon Porter's self-serving *The Naval History of the Civil War* (1886) remains the most comprehensive single-volume history, but it is based on the *Official Records,* is highly partisan, and emphasizes large-scale operations, individual commanders, and heroic exploits. Virgil Carrington Jones's *The Civil War at Sea* (1960–1962) is highly entertaining but lacks any single focus and again centers on individuals and major battles.

A welcome newcomer is William M. Fowler's *Under Two Flags* (1990), which carries out a greater analysis of the naval war than most previous works. Besides covering the war's important naval operations, Fowler discusses the importance of combined operations and the use of the blockade as a diplomatic and political weapon that kept the European powers at bay. Fowler also argues that Confederate commerce raiders had no influence on the outcome of the war and probes the effect of the rivalry between Gideon Welles and William Seward on the navy's strategic operations.

A book that goes beyond the standard is Rowena Reed's *Combined Operations in the Civil War* (1978). Reed argues that the army-navy operations in the Civil War were the precursors of the amphibious assaults of World War II. Reed also explores the "what-if" of McClellan's early plans to end the war by the strategic use of combined operations along the South's rivers and coast to establish bases for inland strikes against Southern industrial sites. By Reed's account, McClellan was denied this mode of attack by shortsighted politicians and government officials, thus depriving the North of a method and opportunity to win the war quickly and with much less bloodshed.

Standard works on the Union navy include the well-known James M. Merrill, *The Rebel Shore* (1957), and Richard S. West's *Mr. Lincoln's Navy* (1957). West's book is a broad overview that does not give any comprehensive study of strategy, whereas Merrill's work provides a solid analysis of the North's amphibious operations against the Confederacy. For strong overviews of specific areas of maritime operations, see Alfred Thayer Mahan's *The Gulf and Inland Waters* (1883), Fletcher Pratt's *Civil War on Western Waters* (1956), and James M. Merrill's *Battle Flags South* (1970). These works concentrate on the usual big battle–famous personality aspect. A book that provides a complete regional study is Robert M. Browning, Jr.'s *From Cape Charles to Cape Fear: The North*

Atlantic Blockading Squadron during the Civil War (1993). Browning breaks from the traditional mold and produces a sweeping study that covers all of the operations of the North Atlantic Blockading Squadron from the backwaters of the Carolina rivers to the blockade of Wilmington. He acknowledges that the blockade could not stop basic military supplies from reaching the South but argues that it did deny the Confederacy such goods as heavy equipment and machinery that were needed to maintain the South's infrastructure. What sets Browning's book apart from any other naval work is his emphasis on manpower, logistics, and operations, crucial areas that are rarely studied. Along with Browning's work another study that discusses the day-to-day life of the Northern sailor is William N. Still, Jr.'s ''The Common Sailor: The Civil War's Uncommon Man—Yankee Blue Jackets and Confederate Tars'' (1985), aptly describes the daily routines along with the mundane and boring existence of the Civil War sailor.

An important study that challenges customary interpretation is Benjamin F. Cooling's *Forts Henry and Donelson* (1987). Cooling argues that not only did the combined army-navy attacks against the Confederate works on the Tennessee and Cumberland rivers open up the South's heartland to invasion, but also that the Henry-Donelson campaign was a decisive turning point in the war. Cooling points out that contrary to popular belief, the Confederates at Fort Henry were very close to defeating the Northern ironclads before a series of catastrophes happened in the fort that allowed the Federals to gain a victory. Even so, Cooling believes that a more determined stand by the Southern high command could have defeated Grant and turned back the Union warships.

George E. Buker's *Blockaders, Refugees, and Contrabands: Civil War on Florida's Gulf Coast, 1861–1865* (1993) focuses on the activity of Federal blockaders' operating off the west coast of Florida. Buker points out the Northern blockaders were able to join with pro-Union sympathizers and guerrillas to undermine Confederate commissary operations in Florida while at the same time gain recruits for Northern regiments. Though such actions escape most Civil War books, Buker shows how this minor naval activity cut deeply into the South's ability to feed its armies.

Important technical studies on the Union navy can be found in Donald L. Canney's *The Old Steam Navy* (1990, 1993). In *Frigates, Sloops and Gunboats,* volume 1, Canney traces the modern navy to the pre–Civil War steam navy and emphasizes that a decentralized navy department, both before and during the war, allowed engineers, contractors, and local commanders at individual naval yards to alter designs. Such activity often allowed the completion of a more efficient warship. In volume 2, *The Ironclads,* Canney describes the navy's complete departure from traditional shipbuilding to develop an ironclad fleet that was designed not only to overpower the South but also to awe Europe.

Specific books on the USS *Monitor* include James P. Delgado's *A Symbol of American Ingenuity: Assessing the Significance of the U.S.S. Monitor* (1988), Ernest Peterkin's *Drawings of the U.S.S. Monitor: A Catalog and Technical*

Analysis (1985), and Edward D. Miller's *USS Monitor: The Ship That Launched a Modern Navy* (1987). Peterkin's work includes all 207 surviving drawings of the *Monitor,* while Miller provides a well-documented history of the vessel and discusses a series of modern tests that strongly suggest that the *Monitor* probably sank because the hull plates and rivets suffered structural fatigue during the storm off Cape Hatteras, thus allowing water to enter the hull. Both Peterkin and Miller discuss the archaeological projects centering around the *Monitor* and the possibilities of recovering items from the wreck.

The only comprehensive work done on the ironclad *New Ironsides* can be found in William H. Roberts's "The Neglected Ironclad: A Design and Constructional Analysis of the U.S.S. *New Ironsides*" (1989). Not only is the vessel's history and construction data covered, but Roberts also includes fine comparisons of the *New Ironsides,* the monitors, and European ironclads. In conclusion, Roberts finds the *New Ironsides* to be comparable to European counterparts.

Studies on naval ordnance can be found in Spencer Tucker's *Arming the Fleet: U.S. Ordnance in the Muzzle-Loading Era* (1988) and Robert J. Schneller, Jr.'s "The Last Smoothbore" (1987). Tucker's work is the best compilation for American naval ordnance and is quite complete for USN ordnance but does not delve as thoroughly into Confederate Brooke guns. Schneller's article and book, *A Quest for Glory: John A. Dahlgren, American Naval Ordnance and the Civil War* concentrates on the tribulations of Rear Admiral John Dahlgren while developing the navy's Dahlgren shell gun. Using the entire collection of the Dahlgren papers, Schneller produces a thorough biography and demonstrates that Dahlgren's role as a bureaucratic entrepreneur was just as important as the quality of his gun in getting it approved and used by the navy. He also explains Dahlgren's reluctance to rearm the navy with rifled guns after the war.

CONFEDERATE NAVY

Histories of the Southern navy have always been handicapped by the destruction of the Southern naval archives in Charlotte shortly after the evacuation of Richmond. The standard history of the Southern navy is John T. Scharf's *History of the Confederate Navy* (1887). Scharf's work is organized with individual chapters on each Confederate state, which makes the book disjointed. Nor does it provide a comprehensive view of Confederate naval strategy and programs. However, since Scharf was an officer in the Confederate navy who interviewed and corresponded with his comrades, the book does contain vital information not found in any other work. Though often overlooked because it is a pictorial history, Philip Van Doren Stern's *The Confederate Navy: A Pictorial History* (1962) is a quite satisfactory history, and Stern points out errors in period drawings.

Maxine Turner's *Navy Gray: The Story of the Confederate Navy on the Chattahoochee and Apalachicola Rivers* (1987) is a comprehensive study of the

Confederate navy and its facilities on the lower Chattahoochee River. In this technical study with a human face, Turner describes the little-known and frustrating efforts of the Confederacy to create a naval squadron from nothing.

An important new work is Raimondo Luraghi's *The Southern Navy: The Confederate Navy and the American Civil War* (1995). In this book, previously published in Italy, Luraghi completely revises the commonly accepted view of the naval Civil War. He argues that the Confederate navy, and not the Union navy, was the great innovator and forerunner of modern navies. Because of its lack of an industrial base, the South had to use mines, torpedoes, commando raids, and commerce raiders to fend off the vastly superior Northern navy. At the same time, Luraghi declares that the mission of the Confederate navy was not to break the blockade but to hold the coastline or ''shoulders'' of the nation against attack and to keep the the South's ports open to foreign trade. Luraghi concludes that the Confederate navy was a success and contends that defeat came only when the army failed to support or protect the navy's bases and construction sites.

Milton F. Perry's *Infernal Machines: The Story of Confederate Submarine and Mine Warfare* (1965) serves as the basic work on submarines and torpedoes, though it is not up to date and was not revised when reprinted. A more modern look at infernal machines can be found in Peter Pry and Richard Zetlin's, ''Torpedo Boats: Secret Weapons of the South'' (1984). A recent work on the submarine *Hunley* is R. R. Bowker's *Danger beneath the Waves: History of the Confederate Submarine H. L. Hunley* (1992). Bowker speculates that the *Hunley* survived attack on the *Housatonic* and was lost while returning to its berth near Charleston, South Carolina.

BLOCKADE RUNNING

For many years writings on blockade running have been incomplete. Early accounts often relied on romanticized newspaper stories, inaccurate wartime reports, and faulty memoirs. Many of these erroneous accounts have been repeated in naval histories. The best memoirs are John Wilkinson's *The Narrative of a Blockade Runner* (1877), Augustus C. Hobart-Hampden's *Never Caught* (1867), Thomas E. Taylor's *Running the Blockade* (1897), and Michael P. Usina's *Blockade Running in Confederate Times* (1895). Taylor's memoirs are by far the best for accuracy. Memory lapses flaw John Newland Maffitt's ''Blockade Running'' (1882, 1892).

Three important works that appeared before World War II were Francis B. C. Bradlee's *Blockade Running during the Civil War, and the Effect of Land and Water Transportation on the Confederacy* (1925), James R. Soley's *The Blockade and the Cruisers* (1883), and Frank L. Owsley's *King Cotton Diplomacy: Foreign Relations of the Confederate States of America* (1935). Both Soley and Bradlee correctly point out blockade running's specialized nature and tremendous profits but do not fully discuss its impact on the Confederate war effort and give the impression that the blockade was highly successful in stopping the blockade runners. Owsley, using sources not examined by previous authors, was the first to place blockade running as one of the most important, if not the most important, supplier for the Confederate armies.

Important information and statistics can be found in the six articles written by Marcus Price on blockade running: "Blockade Running as a Business in South Carolina during the War between the States, 1861–1865" (1949), "Four from Bristol" (1957), "Masters and Pilots Who Tested the Blockade of the Confederate Ports, 1861–1865" (1961), "Ships That Tested the Blockade of the Carolina Ports, 1861–1865" (1948), "Ships That Tested the Blockade of the Georgia and East Florida Ports, 1861–1865" (1955), and "Ships That Tested the Blockade of the Gulf Ports, 1861–1865" (1952). Price records the names of vessels, masters, and pilots; however, his listing of violations per vessel for vessels operating along the Southern coastline in 1861 and 1862 is highly inflated and should not be trusted. Another work that includes important statistics and documents is *Confederate Blockade Running through Bermuda, 1861–1865: Letter and Cargo Manifests* edited by Frank Vandiver (1947).

William N. Still, Jr.'s "A Naval Sieve: The Union Blockade in the Civil War" (1983) argues that the Northern blockade was not an important factor in the collapse of the Confederates. The flow of munitions was never checked, and Still contends the South never lost a major engagement because of the lack of essential supplies.

The only comprehensive work on blockade running is Stephen R. Wise's *Lifeline of the Confederacy: Blockade Running during the Civil War* (1988). The book concentrates on the Confederacy's efforts to sustain its war effort through the overseas purchases and importation of military supplies. Wise concludes that blockade running, though tenuous and overly dependent on private enterprise, was a tremendous success and was the most important element of the Confederate supply system. The book also contains comprehensive statistical lists of steam blockade runners and successful runs.

Important recent studies include Kevin Foster's "Phantoms, Will of the Wisps and the Dare, or the Search for Speed under Steam: The Design of Blockade Running Steamships" (1991), which deals with the technical revolution in maritime construction that came out of blockade running. Also, the long-neglected area of the home front and the impact of blockade running and lack of supplies on civilian morale is beginning to be explored in such articles as Robert B. Ekelund, Jr., and Mark Thornton's "The Union Blockade and the Demoralization of the South: Relative Prices in the Confederacy" (1992).

CONFEDERATE IRONCLADS

An area that has always fascinated Civil War readers centers on the Confederate navy's use of armor-plated warships to counter the numerical advantage of the Federal navy. Despite considerable difficulties, the South placed into service nearly two dozen ironclads, and the familiar, sloping, casemated vessels have come to characterize the Confederacy's efforts to defend its home waters. In the past thirty years, the accessibility of primary documents, at both the National Archives and in private and other public collections, has permitted some comprehensive studies. These sources are far from exhausted, and the final word is yet to be written on the construction and operations of Confederate ironclads.

General works that place the Confederate ironclad within the context of the worldwide nineteenth-century revolution in naval technology include James P. Baxter III's *The Introduction of the Ironclad Warship* (1933) and H. W. Wilson's *Ironclads in Action: A Sketch of Naval Warfare from 1855 to 1895, with Some Account of the Development of the Battleship in England* (1896). William N. Still, Jr.'s *Confederate Shipbuilding* (1969) examines the Confederacy's shipbuilding program in general and the effects of labor, material, and facility issues on the South's ability to construct its warships. Articles by Still that focus on specific ironclad construction sites are: "Confederate Shipbuilding in Mississippi" (1968), "The Confederate States Navy at Mobile" (1968), and "Selma and the Confederate States Navy" (1962).

The standard study of Confederate ironclads is William N. Still, Jr.'s *Iron Afloat: The Story of the Confederate Armorclads* (1985). A discussion of the South's strategic use of ironclads is effectively presented in two articles by Still: "Confederate Naval Policy and the Ironclad" (1963) and "Confederate Naval Strategy: The Ironclad" (1961). The only comprehensive study of ironclad design and specifications is A. Robert Holcombe, Jr.'s "The Evolution of Confederate Ironclad Design" (1993). Holcombe's work is based on existing, original plans and other documents containing technical data primary sources. Though dated and in need of revision, descriptive information on Confederate ironclads is available in the U.S. Navy Department's "Confederate Forces Afloat" in *Dictionary of American Naval Fighting Ships* (1973).

With a few exceptions, scholarly studies of specific ironclads are scarce. One notable exception is the *Virginia* (ex-U.S.S. *Merrimac*). An extensive listing of sources on the *Virginia* and its adversary, the U.S.S. *Monitor,* is David R. Smith's *The Monitor and the Merrimac: A Bibliography* (1968). The best general study of the *Virginia* and the Battle of Hampton Roads is *Duel between the Ironclads* (1975) by William C. Davis. Of the many inquiries into the controversy surrounding the origins of the *Virginia*'s design, the following offer important, though divergent, views: John M. Brooke's *"The Virginia* or *Merrimack:* Her Real Projector" (1891) and John W. H. Porter's *A Record of Events in Norfolk County, Virginia, from April 19th, 1861 to May 10th, 1862, with a History of the Soldiers and Sailors of Norfolk County, Norfolk City and Portsmouth Who Served in the Confederate States Army or Navy* (1892).

The *Arkansas* is another ironclad much written about. Two excellent accounts from the perspectives of officers who served aboard are George W. Gift's "The Story of the *Arkansas*" (1884) and Isaac N. Brown's "The Confederate Gunboat

Arkansas" (1887–1888). Two well-researched works on the *Neuse* are William N. Still, Jr.'s "The Career of the Confederate Ironclad *Neuse*," (1966) and *C.S.S. Neuse: A Question of Time and Iron* (1981) by Leslie Bright, William H. Rowland, and James C. Bardon. Turner's *Navy Gray* contains an exhaustively researched history of the ironclad *Jackson (Muscogee)* and the C.S. Naval Iron Works, the largest producer of naval steam machinery in the South. A solid, well-documented history of the *Albemarle* is *Ironclad of the Roanoke: Gilbert Elliott's Albemarle* (1994) by Robert G. Elliott, a descendant of the ironclad's builder. William N. Still, Jr.'s "Confederate Ironclad *Missouri*" (1965) is firmly based on primary sources. Although without citations, his "Confederate Behemoth: The C.S.S. *Louisiana*" (1977) is an important source of information on that vessel.

The Confederate navy's efforts to procure ironclads abroad have been recorded in several worthy volumes. The standard work is *The Secret Service of the Confederate States in Europe, or How the Confederate Cruisers Were Equipped* (1883) by James D. Bulloch, the naval officer charged with securing such weapons. Other important general studies of Confederate navy procurement in Europe include Warren F. Spencer's *The Confederate Navy in Europe* (1983) and Frank J. Merli's *Great Britain and the Confederate Navy, 1861–65* (1970). Merli makes a convincing case that while foreign-built ironclads and commerce raiders were incapable of challenging the Northern supremacy of the sea, they could have sparked a diplomatic incident altering the course of the war. An important monograph focusing on Confederate attempts to get two ironclad rams built in Britain is *The Confederate Rams at Birkenhead: A Chapter in Anglo-American Relations* (1961) by Wilbur Devereux Jones.

CONFEDERATE COMMERCE RAIDERS

An area of study that has received a great deal of attention deals with the Confederate commerce raiders, related overseas Confederate operations, and diplomacy. The Confederates were highly successful in their operations against the Northern merchant marine. Over three hundred Union ships were destroyed, many more were captured, and thousands transferred their registry to other nations. The commerce raiders also caused a great deal of diplomatic tension between Great Britain and the United States, which the Southerners hoped would lead to intervention or mediation.

Only two books have attempted to tell the the entire story of the rebel high seas raiders. The first and most comprehensive is George Walton Dalzell's *The Flight from the Flag: The Continuing Effect of the Civil War upon the American Carrying Trade* (1940). The second work is Chester G. Hearn's *Gray Raiders of the Sea: How Eight Confederate Warships Destroyed the Union's High Sea Commerce* (1992), which concentrates on the most spectacular Confederate raiders.

The only study produced on Southern privateers (privately owned commerce raiders) is William M. Robinson's *The Confederate Privateers* (1928). Robinson's work is meticulous in its detail and listings of individual vessels and their careers. It is unlikely ever to be superseded. Little has been written about individual privateers and their sailors. Mason Philip Smith's *Confederates Down East: Confederate Operations in and around Maine* (1985) is an interesting account of the impact of Southern commerce raiding on the state of Maine. The career of John Clibbon Braine, a sort of commerce raider guerrilla, is presented in John Hay and Joan Hay's *The Last of the Confederate Privateers* (1977).

Confederate purchasing operations in Europe provided the Southern navy with a number of vessels, including blockade runners, commerce raiders, and ironclads. The mastermind of the intricate operation was James Dunwoody Bulloch. His personal account is *The Secret Service of the Confederate States in Europe*. The work of Bulloch and other Confederate agents is analyzed in three scholarly works: Richard I. Lester's *Confederate Finance and Purchasing in Great Britain* (1975), Frank Merli's *Great Britain and the Confederate Navy, 1861–1865* (1970), and Warren F. Spencer's *The Confederate Navy in Europe* (1983).

The story of the most successful commerce raider, the CSS *Alabama,* has been told by several of its officers and dozens of subsequent historians. The indispensable source is by its captain, Admiral Raphael Semmes, in his autobiography, *Memoirs of Service Afloat during the War between the States* (1869). Several of the *Alabama*'s officers wrote autobiographical accounts, such as Semmes's first officer, John McIntosh Kell, who produced *Recollections of a Naval Life; Including the Cruises of the Confederate States Steamers Sumter and Alabama* (1900). Arthur Sinclair, a junior officer, offers his recollections in *Two Years on the Alabama* (1869), while another account can be found in Charles Grayson Summersell, ed., *The Journal of George Townley Fullam, Boarding Officer of the Confederate Sea Raider Alabama* (1973).

Semmes has been the subject of several biographies. The most recent are John M. Taylor's *Confederate Raider, Raphael Semmes of the Alabama* (1994) and Charles M. Robinson III's *Shark of the Confederacy* (1994). Taylor's narrative lacks a bibliography, and Robinson relies heavily on secondary sources. A forthcoming work by Warren F. Spencer, which will be published by the University of Alabama Press, should serve as the main Semmes biography for quite some time. The *Alabama*'s first officer is given thorough coverage in John C. Delaney's *John McIntosh Kell of the Raider Alabama* (1973).

Important studies that cover both the construction and careers of individual ships include Frank L. Owsley, Jr.'s *The C.S.S. Florida: Her Building and Operations* (1965) and Charles Grayson Summersell's *CSS Alabama Builder, Captain and Plans* (1985).

Sailors who wrote about their service onboard other cruisers include James Morris Morgan's *Recollections of a Rebel Reefer* (1918), Douglas French Forrest's *Odyssey in Gray: A Diary of Confederate Service, 1863–1865* (1979), and James I. Waddell's *CSS Shenandoah: The Memoirs of Lieutenant Commanding James I. Waddell, CSN* (1960). A biographical account produced from an officer's journal is William Stanley Hoole's *Four Years in the Confederate Navy: The Career of Captain John Low on the C.S.S. Fingal, Florida, Alabama, Tuscaloosa and Ajax* (1964).

The *Alabama* Claims produced over a hundred volumes of works arguing the various aspects of the case. The most useful works are U.S. Department of State, *The Case of the United States to Be Laid before the Tribunal of Arbitration* (1871) and Thomas Willing Balch's *The Alabama Arbitration* (1900).

MARINE CORPS

Information on either the United States and Confederate States Marine Corps is extremely limited. A brief history with statistical studies and service listings can be found in work by Ralph Donnelly: "Battle Honors and Services of Confederate Marines" (1959), *The History of the Confederate States Marine Corps* (1976), *Service Records of Confederate Enlisted Marines* (1979), and *Biographical Sketches of the Commissioned Officers of the Confederate States Marine Corps* (1973). Revised and updated versions of Donnelly's history of the Confederate Marine Corps and biographical sketches of the commissioned officers have been published in a new, combined work, *Confederate States Marine Corps* (1989).

Other sources on the Confederate Marine Corps include the "Diary of Captain Edward Crenshaw," (1939, 1940); David M. Sullivan's "The Confederate States Marine Corps in South Carolina, 1861–1865" (1985), and "Tennessee Confederate Marines: Memphis Detachment" (19xx).

As yet there is no complete history of the United States Marines Corps in the Civil War, but a number of articles provide both specific studies and overviews. They include Jeffry T. Ryan's "Some Notes on the Civil War–Era Marine Corps" (1992) and "To the Shores of Carolina: Dahlgren's Marine Battalions" (1992); Harry E. Day's "Ellett's Horse Marines" (1939); and Robert D. Heinl Jr.'s "The Cat with More Than Nine Lives" (1954). See also Bernard Nalty's "Blue and Gray" (1960) and *The United States Marines in the Civil War* (1961).

PERSONALITIES

The field of biographies is a long-neglected area of naval Civil War literature. Most existing biographies date to the nineteenth and early twentieth centuries. Such works as James Mason Hoppin's *Life of Andrew Hull Foote, Rear Admiral United States Navy* (1875), Charles H. Davis's *The Life of Charles H. Davis, Rear Admiral, 1807–1877* (1899), Paul H. Kendricken's *Memoirs of Paul H. Kendricken* (1910), Alfred T. Mahan's *Admiral Farragut* (1892); Rebecca Paulding Meade's *Life of Hiram Paulding, Rear Admiral, U.S.N.* (1910), William Barker Cushing's "Outline of the Story of the War Experiences of William Barker Cushing as Told by Himself" (1912), Charles W. Seward's "William Barker Cushing" (1912), William O. Stevens's *David Glasgow Farragut: Our*

First Admiral (1942), Thomas O. Selfridge, *What Finer Tradition: The Memoirs of Rear Admiral Thomas O. Selfridge* (1924), and Richard S. West's *The Second Admiral: A Life of David Dixon Porter, 1813–1891* (1937) remain standard works. However, good, solid, incisive biographies using the full range of available resources are still needed for the war's naval leaders.

Exceptions to the rule are the biographies of the two secretaries of navy. Both Joseph T. Durkin's *Stephen R. Mallory* (1938) and John Niven's *Gideon Welles* (1973) give fine coverage to the politics and operational difficulties experienced by the two secretaries of navy. Neither book serves as a battle study but instead concentrates on the activities in Richmond and Washington and how they related to the politics of command within each department.

Certain commanders have received modern biographies. Dudley Taylor Cornish and Virginia Jeans Laas's *Lincoln's Lee: The Life of Samuel Phillips Lee, United States Navy, 1812–1897* (1987) is a fine study of the pedantic Lee, who struggled to maintain his squadron along the Virginia and North Carolina coasts. Since most of Lee's career centered on the blockade, the authors concentrate on his vital but often thankless task of maintaining his command in the midst of a logistical nightmare.

Two important works on Samuel Francis Du Pont are James M. Merrill's *Du Pont: The Making of an Admiral—A Biography of Samuel Francis Du Pont* (1986) and John D. Hayes, editor, *Samuel Francis Du Pont: A Selection from His Civil War Letters* (1984). Hayes's finely edited book gives excellent insight into the many sides of the brilliant yet self-destructive Du Pont. It also contains the best informative footnotes yet done for a naval Civil War book. West's recent book superbly describes Du Pont's prewar career but does not properly explore the controversies between Du Pont and the Navy Department over the monitors and the failed attack against Charleston that ultimately led to Du Pont's removal from active command.

An important book that stands out in the field of naval biography is Robert Erwin Johnson's *Rear Admiral John Rodgers* (1967). Johnson covers not only Rodgers's long career in the U.S. Navy, but he also discusses Rodgers in the context of the prosecution of the war and advances within naval technology. The book is especially helpful in understanding the North's development and use of monitors.

An area within the field of biographies that needs to be expanded centers on the careers of individual ship captains. Whereas squadron commanders have received some coverage, many important leaders have been neglected. Recent attempts include David P. Werlich's *Admiral of the Amazon: John Randolph Tucker, His Confederate Colleagues and Peru* (1990). Though Werlich concentrates mainly on Tucker's postwar activities mapping the Amazon, the book does contain a good account of Tucker's service in both Virginia and South Carolina waters. Especially helpful is the discussion of the James River Squadron and the Battle of Hampton Roads and Tucker's service with the Charleston Squadron. Royce G. Shingleton in his *John Taylor Wood: Sea Ghost of the*

Confederacy (1979) and *High Seas Confederate: The Life and Times of John Newland Maffitt* (1994), makes a valiant effort to cover the careers of two important Confederate leaders, and though he weaves an intriguing story about two fascinating individuals, he is handicapped by the lack of reliable manuscript material and his reliance on secondary sources. William N. Still, Jr.'s *Ironclad Captains: The Commanding Officers of the USS Monitor* (1988) gives a fine introduction to secondary Northern officers who deserve individual, full-length biographies.

As with the ship commanders, additional studies are needed for the maritime engineers, naval architects, and contractors. At the moment the major works in this area are limited to George M. Brooke's *John M. Brooke: Naval Scientist and Educator* (1980), Gene D. Lewis's *Charles Ellet, Jr.: The Engineer as Individualist, 1810–1862* (1968), and Edward W. Sloan's *Benjamin Franklin Isherwood, Naval Engineer* (1965).

UNDERWATER ARCHAEOLOGY

The only vessels that survive today with a connection to the Civil War are the USS *Constitution* and *Constellation,* but both of these ships are more properly associated with earlier conflicts. As a result, any first-hand contact with ships from the Civil War is obtained only through the work of underwater archaeologists. In the past thirty years, important work has greatly expanded our knowledge of vessels, cargoes, construction methods, and preservation of artifacts. Important studies are Leslie S. Bright, William H. Rowland, and James C. Bardon's *C.S.S. Neuse: A Question of Time and Iron* (1981); Gordon P. Watts's *CSS Chattahoochee: An Investigation of the Remains of a Confederate Gunboat* (1990), Leslie S. Bright's *The Blockade Runner Modern Greece and Her Cargo* (1977), Franklin N. Chance, Paul C. Chance, and David L. Topper's *Tangled Machinery and Charred Relics: The Historical Investigation of the C.S.S. Nashville* (1985), and James Spirek's "The USS *Southfield:* An Archaeological and Historical Investigation of a Civil War Gunboat" (1993). Information on the USS *Cairo* can be found in Roger B. Steakley's "To the Bottom and Back Again" (1985) and Edwin C. Bearss's *Hardluck Ironclad: The Sinking and Salvage of the Cairo* (1966). Civil War wrecks are also covered by George F. Bass, editor, *Ships and Shipwrecks of the Americas: A History Based on Underwater Archaeology* (1988). A new work that combines ship history with underwater archaeology and preservation and also covers laws pertaining to recovering historic artifacts is *The Maple Leaf: An Extraordinary American Civil War Shipwreck,* edited by Keith V. Holland, Lee B. Manley, and W. Towart (1993). Though these sources are not often used by maritime historians, they contain information not found in any other source. They also serve to increase awareness that not all Civil War maritime history comes from books and manuscripts. Vital resources still exist below the waters that must be preserved and studied.

BIBLIOGRAPHY

MANUSCRIPT COLLECTIONS

Eric Heyl Collection, Great Lakes Research Center, Bowling Green State University, Bowling Green, Ohio.

PUBLISHED WORKS

Anderson, Bern. *By Sea and by River.* New York: Knopf, 1962.

Balch, Thomas Willing. *The Alabama Arbitration.* Philadelphia: Allen, Lane and Scott, 1900.

Bass, George F., ed. *Ships and Shipwrecks of the Americas: A History Based on Underwater Archaeology.* London: Thames and Hudson, 1988.

Baxter, James P., III. *The Introduction of the Ironclad Warship.* Cambridge: Harvard University Press, 1933.

Bearss, Edwin C. *Hardluck Ironclad: The Sinking and Salvage of the Cairo.* Baton Rouge: Louisiana State University Press, 1966.

Beers, Henry Putney. *Guide to the Archives of the Government of the Confederate States of America.* Washington, D.C.: Government Printing Office, 1968.

Bowker, R. R. *Danger beneath the Waves: History of the Confederate Submarine H. L. Hunley.* Orangeburg, SC: Sandlapper Publishing Company, 1992.

Boykin, Charles Brandon. *The History of the Navy during the Rebellion.* 2 vols. New York: D. Appleton and Company, 1867–1868.

Bradlee, Francis B. C. *Blockade Running during the Civil War and the Effect of Land and Water Transportation on the Confederacy.* Salem, MA: Essex Institute, 1925.

Bright, Leslie S. *The Blockade Runner Modern Greece and Her Cargo.* Raleigh: Division of Archives and History, 1977.

Bright, Leslie S., William H. Rowland, and James C. Bardon. *C.S.S. Neuse: A Question of Time and Iron.* Raleigh: North Carolina Division of Archives and History, 1981.

Brooke, George M. *John M. Brooke: Naval Scientist and Educator.* Charlottesville: University Press of Virginia, 1980.

Brooke, John M. "The *Virginia* or *Merrimack:* Her Real Projector." *Southern Historical Society Papers* 19 (January 1891): 3–34.

Brown, Isaac N. "The Confederate Gunboat *Arkansas.*" In Robert U. Johnson and Clarence G. Buell, eds. *Battles and Leaders of the Civil War,* 3:579–80. 4 vols. New York: Century, 1887–1888.

Browning, Robert M., Jr. *From Cape Charles to Cape Fear: The North Atlantic Blockading Squadron during the Civil War.* Tuscaloosa: University of Alabama Press, 1993.

Buker, George E. *Blockaders, Refugees, and Contrabands: Civil War on Florida's Gulf Coast, 1861–1865.* Tuscaloosa: University of Alabama Press, 1993.

Bulloch, James D. *The Secret Service of the Confederate States in Europe, or How the Confederate Cruisers Were Equipped.* Reprint, New York: Thomas Yoseloff, 1959.

Canney, Donald L. *The Old Steam Navy.* 2 vols. Annapolis: Naval Institute Press, 1990–1993.

Chance, Franklin N., Paul C. Chance, and David L. Topper. *Tangled Machinery and Charred Relics: The Historical Investigation of the C.S.S. Nashville.* Orangeburg, SC: Sun Printing, 1985.

Coletta, Paolo E. *An Annotated Bibliography of U.S. Marine Corps History.* Lanham, MD: University Press of America, 1986.

———. *A Selected Bibliography of American Naval History.* Lanham, MD: University Press of America, 1988.

Cooling, Benjamin F. *Forts Henry and Donelson.* Knoxville: University of Tennessee Press, 1987.

Cornish, Dudley Taylor, and Virginia Jeans Laas. *Lincoln's Lee: The Life of Samuel Phillips Lee, United States Navy, 1812–1897.* Lawrence: University Press of Kansas, 1987.

Crenshaw, Edward. "Diary of Captain Edward Crenshaw." *Alabama Historical Quarterly* 1 (1939): 261–70, 438–452; 2 (1940): 52–71, 221–238, 365–385, 465–482.

Cushing, William Barker. "Outline of the Story of the War Experiences of William Barker Cushing as Told by Himself," *United States Naval Institute Proceedings* 38 (Aug.–Sept. 1912): 941–91.

Dalzell, George Walton. *The Flight from the Flag: The Continuing Effect of the Civil War upon the American Carrying Trade.* Chapel Hill: University of North Carolina Press, 1940.

Davis, William C. *Duel between the Ironclads.* Garden City, NY: Doubleday, 1975.

Day, Harry E. "Ellett's Horse Marines." *Marine Corps Gazette* 23 (March 1939): 30–33.

Delaney, John C. *John McIntosh Kell of the Raider Alabama.* Tuscaloosa: University of Alabama Press, 1973.

Delgado, James P. *A Symbol of American Ingenuity: Assessing the Significance of the U.S.S. Monitor.* Washington, D.C.: National Park Service, 1988.

Donnelly, Ralph W. "Battle Honors and Services of Confederate Marines." *Military Affairs* 23 (Spring 1959): 37–40.

———. *Biographical Sketches of the Commissioned Officers of the Confederate States Marine Corps.* Washington, NC: Ralph W. Donnelly, 1973.

———. *Confederate States Marine Corps.* Shippensburg, PA: White Mane Press, 1989.

———. *The History of the Confederate States Marine Corps.* Washington, NC: Ralph W. Donnelly, 1976.

———. *Service Records of Confederate Enlisted Marines.* Washington, NC: Ralph W. Donnelly, 1979.

Durkin, Joseph T. *Stephen R. Mallory.* Chapel Hill: University of North Carolina Press, 1938.

Elliott, Robert G. *Ironclad of the Roanoke: Gilbert Elliott's Albemarle.* Shippensburg, PA: White Mane, 1994.

Ekelund, Robert B., Jr., and Mark Thornton. "The Union Blockade and the Demoralization of the South: Relative Prices in the Confederacy." *Social Science Quarterly* 73 (1992): 890–902.

Forrest, Douglas French. *Odyssey in Gray: A Diary of Confederate Service, 1863–1865.* Edited by William N. Still. Richmond: Virginia State Library, 1979.

Foster, Kevin. "Phantoms, Will of the Wisps and the Dare or the Search for Speed under Steam: The Design of Blockade Running Steamships." Master's thesis, East Carolina University, 1991.

Fowler, William M. *Under Two Flags.* New York: W. W. Norton, 1990.

Geary, James W. "Blacks in Northern Blue: A Select Annotated Bibliography of Afro-Americans in the Union Army and Navy during the Civil War." *Bulletin of Bibliography* 45 (September 1988): 183–193.

Gift, George W. "The Story of the *Arkansas.*" *Southern Historical Society Papers* 12 (1884): 48–54, 115–119, 163–170, 205–212.

Hay, John, and Joan Hay. *The Last of the Confederate Privateers.* New York: Crescent Books, 1977.

Hayes, John D. *Samuel Francis Du Pont: A Selection from His Civil War Letters,* 3 vols. Ithaca: Cornell University Press, 1984.

Heath, Chester G. *Gray Raiders of the Sea: How Eight Confederate Warships Destroyed the Union's High Sea Commerce.* Camden, ME: Provincial Press, 1992.

Heinl, Robert D., Jr. "The Cat with More Than Nine Lives." *United States Naval Institute Proceedings* 80 (June 1954): 658–671.

Heyl, Eric. *Early American Steamers.* 6 vols. Private printer, 1953–1969.

Hoppin, James Mason. *Life of Andrew Hull Foote, Real Admiral United States Navy.* New York: Harper Brothers, 1875.

Hobart-Hampden, Augustus C. *Never Caught.* London: John Camden Holton, 1867.

Holcombe, A. Robert, Jr. "The Evolution of Confederate Ironclad Design." Master's thesis, East Carolina University, 1993.

Holland, Keith V., Lee B. Manley, and James W. Towart. *The Maple Leaf: An Extraordinary American Civil War Shipwreck.* Jacksonville: St. Johns Archaeological Expeditions, 1993.

Hoole, William Stanley. *Four Years in the Confederate Navy: The Career of Captain John Low on the C.S.S. Fingal, Florida, Alabama, Tuscaloosa and Ajax.* Athens: University of Georgia Press, 1964.

Johnson, Robert Erwin. *Rear Admiral John Rodgers.* Annapolis: Naval Institute Press, 1967.

Johnson, Robert U., and Clarence C. Buel, eds. *Battles and Leaders of the Civil War.* 4 vols. New York: Century Company, 1887–1888.

Jones, Virgil Carrington. *The Civil War at Sea.* 3 vols. New York: Holt, Rinehart, and Winston, 1960–1962.

Jones, Wilbur Devereux. *The Confederate Rams at Birkenhead: A Chapter in Anglo-American Relations.* Tuscaloosa: Confederate Publishing Co., 1961.

Kell, John McIntosh. *Recollections of a Naval Life: Including the Cruises of the Confederate States Steamers Sumter and Alabama.* Washington, D.C.: Neale, 1900.

Kendricken, Paul H. *Memoirs of Paul H. Kendricken.* Boston: Privately printed, 1910.

Lester, Richard I. *Confederate Finance and Purchasing in Great Britain.* Charlottesville: University of Virginia Press, 1975.

Lewis, Gene D. *Charles Ellet, Jr.: The Engineer as Individualist, 1810–1862.* Urbana: University of Illinois Press, 1968.

Luraghi, Raimondo. *The Southern Navy: The Confederate Navy and the American Civil War.* Annapolis: Naval Institute Press, 1995.

Lytle, William M. *Merchant Steam Vessels of the United States, 1807–1868, "The Lytle List."* Mystic, CT: Steamship Historical Society of America, 1952.

Maffitt, John Newland. "Blockade Running," *United Service* 6 (June 1882): 626–633, 7 (July 1882): 14–22, n.s. 7 (February 1892): 147–173.

Mahan, Alfred Thayer. *Admiral Farragut.* New York: Appleton, 1892.

————. *The Gulf and Inland Waters.* New York: C. Scribner's Sons, 1883.

Meade, Rebecca Paulding. *Life of Hiram Paulding, Rear Admiral, U.S.N.* New York: Baker and Taylor, 1910.

Merli, Frank J. *Great Britain and the Confederate Navy, 1861–65.* Bloomington: Indiana University Press, 1970.

————. ed. Special Commemorative Naval Issue, *Journal of Confederate History* 4 (1989).

Merrill, James M. *Battle Flags South: The Story of the Civil War Navies on Western Waters.* Rutherford, NJ: Farleigh Dickinson University Press, 1970.

————. *Du Pont: The Making of an Admiral—A Biography of Samuel Francis Du Pont.* New York: Dodd, Mead, 1986.

————. *The Rebel Shore.* Boston: Little, Brown, 1957.

Miller, Edward D. *USS Monitor: The Ship That Launched a Modern Navy.* Annapolis: Leeward Publications, 1987.

Morgan, James Morris. *Recollections of a Rebel Reefer.* London: Constable and Co., 1918.

Munden, Kenneth W., and Henry Putney Beers. *Guide to Federal Archives Relating to the Civil War.* Washington, D.C.: Government Printing Office, 1962.

Nalty, Bernard. "Blue and Gray." *Leatherneck Magazine* 53 (November 1960): 54–57.

————. *The United States Marines in the Civil War.* Washington, D.C.: History Branch, U.S. Marine Corps, 1961.

National Archives. *List of Logbooks of U.S. Navy Ships, Stations and Miscellaneous Units, 1801–1947.* Washington, D.C.: National Archives and Records Service, 1978.

Nevins, Allan, James I. Robertson, Jr., and Bell I. Wiley. *Civil War Books: A Critical Bibliography.* Baton Rouge: Louisiana State University Press, 1967.

Niven, John. *Gideon Welles.* New York: Oxford University Press, 1973.

Owsley, Frank L. *The C.S.S. Florida: Her Building and Operations.* Philadelphia: University of Pennsylvania Press, 1965.

————. *King Cotton Diplomacy: Foreign Relations of the Confederate States of America.* Chicago: University of Chicago Press, 1935.

Perry, Milton F. *Infernal Machines: The Story of Confederate Submarine and Mine Warfare.* Baton Rouge: Louisiana State University Press, 1965.

Peterkin, Ernest. *Drawings of the U.S.S. Monitor: A Catalog and Technical Analysis.* Washington, D.C.: U.S. Department of Commerce, 1985.

Porter, David Dixon. *The Naval History of the Civil War.* 1886. Reprint, New York: Castle Books, 1984.

Porter, John W. H. *A Record of Events in Norfolk County, Virginia, from April 19th, 1861, to May 10th, 1862, with a History of the Soldiers and Sailors of Norfolk County, Norfolk City and Portsmouth Who Served in the Confederate States Army or Navy.* Portsmouth: W. A. Fiske, 1892.

Pratt, Fletcher. *Civil War on Western Waters.* New York: Holt, 1956.

Price, Marcus. "Blockade Running as a Business in South Carolina during the War between the States, 1861–1865." *American Neptune* 9 (January 1949): 31–62.

————. "Four from Bristol." *American Neptune* 17 (October 1957): 249–261.

————. "Masters and Pilots Who Tested the Blockade of the Confederate Ports, 1861–1865." *American Neptune* 21 (April 1961): 81–106.

———. "Ships That Tested the Blockade of the Carolina Ports, 1861–1865." *American Neptune* 8 (April 1948): 196–241.

———. "Ships That Tested the Blockade of the Georgia and East Florida Ports, 1861–1865." *American Neptune* 15 (April 1955): 97–132.

———. "Ships That Tested the Blockade of the Gulf Ports, 1861–1865." *American Neptune* 12 (January–July 1952): 52–59, 154–161, 229–238.

Pry, Peter, and Richard Zetlin. "Torpedo Boats: Secret Weapons of the South." *Warship International* 21 (1984): 384–393.

Reed, Rowena. *Combined Operations in the Civil War.* Annapolis: Naval Institute Press, 1978.

Roberts, William H. "The Neglected Ironclad: A Design and Constructional Analysis of the U.S.S. *New Ironsides." Warship International* 26 (1989): 109–134.

Robinson, Charles M., III. *Shark of the Confederacy.* Annapolis: Naval Institute Press, 1994.

Robinson, William M. *The Confederate Privateers.* New Haven: Yale University Press, 1928.

Ryan, Jeffry T. "Some Notes on the Civil War–Era Marine Corps." *Civil War Regiments* 2 (1992): 183–193.

———. "To the Shores of Carolina: Dahlgren's Marine Battalions." *Civil War Regiments* 2 (1992): 194–211.

Scharf, John T. *History of the Confederate Navy.* New York: Robers & Sherwood, 1887.

Schneller, Robert J., Jr. "The Last Smoothbore." *American Society of Arms Collectors Bulletin,* no. 57 (1987): 13–37.

———. *A Quest for Glory: John A. Dahlgren, American Naval Ordnance and the Civil War.* Annapolis: Naval Institute Press, 1995.

Selfridge, Thomas O. *What Finer Tradition: The Memoirs of Rear Admiral Thomas O. Selfridge.* 1924. Reprint, Columbia: University of South Carolina Press, 1987.

Semmes, Raphael. *Memoirs of Service Afloat during the War Between the States.* 1869. Reprint, Edison, NJ: Blue and Grey Press, 1987.

Seward, Charles W. "William Barker Cushing." *United States Naval Institute Proceedings* 38 (Aug.–Sept. 1912): 425–491, 913–39.

Shingleton, Royce G. *High Seas Confederate: The Life and Times of John Newland Maffitt.* Columbia: University of South Carolina Press, 1994.

———. *John Taylor Wood: Sea Ghost of the Confederacy.* Athens: University of Georgia Press, 1979.

Silverstone, Paul H. *Warships of the Civil War Navies.* Annapolis: Naval Institute Press, 1989.

Sinclair, Arthur. *Two Years on the Alabama.* 1896. Reprint, Annapolis: Naval Institute Press, 1989.

Sloan, Edward W. *Benjamin Franklin Isherwood, Naval Engineer.* Annapolis: United States Naval Institute Press, 1965.

———. "The Navy in the Nineteenth Century, 1848–1889." In Robin Higham and Donald Mrozek, eds., *A Guide to the Sources of U.S. Military History: Third Supplement.* Hamden, CT: Archon Publishing, 1992.

Smith, David R. *The Monitor and the Merrimac: A Bibliography.* Los Angeles: University of California Library, 1968.

Smith, Mason Philip. *Confederates Down East: Confederate Operations in and around Maine.* Portland, ME: Provincial Press, 1985.

Smith, Myron J. *American Civil War Navies.* Metuchen, NJ: Scarecrow Press, 1972.

Soley, James Russell. *The Blockade and the Cruisers.* New York: C. Scribner's Sons, 1883.

Spencer, Warren F. *The Confederate Navy in Europe.* Tuscaloosa: University of Alabama Press, 1983.

Spirek, James. "The USS *Southfield:* An Archaeological and Historical Investigation of a Civil War Gunboat." Master's thesis, East Carolina University, 1993.

Steakley, Roger B. "To the Bottom and Back Again." *Civil War Times Illustrated* 24 (1985): 38–43.

Stern, Philip Van Doren. *The Confederate Navy: A Pictorial History.* Garden City, NY: Doubleday, 1962.

Stevens, William O. *David Glasgow Farragut: Our First Admiral.* New York: Dodd, Mead, 1942.

Still, William N., Jr. "The Career of the Confederate Ironclad *Neuse.*" *North Carolina Historical Review* 43 (January 1966): 1–13.

———. "Confederate Behemoth: The C.S.S. *Louisiana.*" *Civil War Times Illustrated* 16 (November 1977): 20–25.

———. "The Common Sailor: The Civil War's Uncommon Man—Yankee Blue Jackets and Confederate Tars." *Civil War Times Illustrated* 23 (1985): 24–39, 24 (1985): 12–19, 36–39.

———. "Confederate Ironclad *Missouri.*" *Louisiana Studies* 4 (Summer 1965): 101–110.

———. "Confederate Naval Policy and the Ironclad." *Civil War History* 9 (June 1963): 145–156.

———. "Confederate Naval Strategy: The Ironclad." *Journal of Southern History* 27 (August 1961): 330–343.

———. *Confederate Shipbuilding.* Athens: University of Georgia Press, 1969.

———. "Confederate Shipbuilding in Mississippi." *Journal of Mississippi History* 30 (November 1968): 291–303.

———. "The Confederate States Navy at Mobile." *Alabama Historical Quarterly* 30 (Fall–Winter 1968): 127–144.

———. *Iron Afloat: The Story of the Confederate Armorclads.* Nashville: Vanderbilt University Press, 1985.

———. *Ironclad Captains: The Commanding Officers of the USS Monitor.* Washington: Government Printing Office, 1988.

———. "A Naval Sieve: The Union Blockade in the Civil War." *Naval War College Review* 36 (1983): 38–45.

———. "Selma and the Confederate States Navy." *Alabama Review* 15 (January 1962): 19–37.

Sullivan, David M. "The Confederate States Marine Corps in South Carolina, 1861–1865." *South Carolina History Magazine* 86 (1985): 113–127.

———. "Tennessee Confederate Marines: Memphis Detachment." *Tennessee Historical Quarterly* 45 (1986): 152–168.

Summersell, Charles Grayson. *CSS Alabama Builder, Captain and Plans.* Tuscaloosa: University of Alabama Press, 1985.

———, ed. *The Journal of George Townley Fullam, Boarding Officer of the Confederate Sea Raider Alabama.* Tuscaloosa: University of Alabama Press, 1973.

Taylor, John M. *Confederate Raider, Raphael Semmes of the Alabama.* Washington, D.C.: Brassey's, 1994.

Taylor, Thomas E. *Running the Blockade.* London: J. Murray, 1897.

Tucker, Spencer. *Arming the Fleet: U.S. Ordnance in the Muzzle-Loading Era.* Annapolis: Naval Institute Press, 1988.

Turner, Maxine. *Navy Gray: The Story of the Confederate Navy on the Chattahoochee and Apalachicola Rivers.* Tuscaloosa: University of Alabama Press, 1987.

U.S. Department of State. *The Case of the United States to Be Laid before the Tribunal of Arbitration.* Washington, D.C.: Government Printing Office, 1871.

U.S. Navy Department. *Civil War Naval Chronology,* 6 vols. Washington, D.C.: Government Printing Office, 1961–1966.

———. *Dictionary of American Naval Fighting Ships.* 8 vols. Washington, D.C.: Government Printing Office, 1959–1981.

———. *Official Records of the Union and Confederate Navies in the War of the Rebellion.* 31 vols. Washington, D.C.: Government Printing Office, 1894–1922.

Usina, Michael, P. *Blockade Running in Confederate Times.* Savannah: George N. Nichols, 1895.

Vandiver, Frank E., ed. *Confederate Blockade Running through Bermuda, 1861–1865: Letter and Cargo Manifests.* Austin: University of Texas Press, 1947.

Waddell, James I. *CSS Shenandoah: The Memoirs of Lieutenant Commanding James I. Waddell, CSN.* Edited by James D. Horan. New York: Crown, 1960.

Watts, Gordon P. *CSS Chattahoochee: An Investigation of the Remains of a Confederate Gunboat.* Greenville, NC: Program in Maritime History and Underwater Research, 1990.

Werlich, David P. *Admiral of the Amazon: John Randolph Tucker, His Confederate Colleagues and Peru.* Charlottesville: University of Virginia Press, 1990.

West, Richard S. *Mr. Lincoln's Navy.* 1957. Reprint, Westport, CT: Greenwood Press, 1976.

———. *The Second Admiral: A Life of David Dixon Porter, 1813–1891.* New York: Coward-McCann, 1937.

Wilkinson, John. *The Narrative of a Blockade Runner.* New York: Sheldon, 1877.

Wilson, H. W. *Ironclads in Action: A Sketch of Naval Warfare from 1855 to 1895, with Some Account of the Development of the Battleship in England.* London: Sampson Low, Marston and Company, 1896.

Wise, Stephen R. *Lifeline of the Confederacy: Blockade Running during the Civil War.* Columbia: University of South Carolina Press, 1988.

Part VIII

Conduct of the War

25

Leadership—Union Army Officers

John F. Marszalek

When the Civil War exploded at Fort Sumter in 1861, the United States Army was a minuscule force, scattered throughout the continental United States and hardly prepared for the awesome conflict that faced it. Under the leadership of its aging commanding general, Winfield Scott, the hero of the War of 1812 and the Mexican War, the army looked back to past glory more than it anticipated future challenges. The 1861 resignations of Southern officers, many of whom Scott had favored in the prewar years, resulted in an immediate leadership crisis.

The search for competent leaders to command the suddenly expanded army became the major problem of the Union military effort far into the Civil War. No soldier in the nation, not even the venerable Winfield Scott himself, had ever led a unit the size of the Civil War armies or fought in a conflict this gigantic.

The literature about the new Union army leaders is extensive. The initial work, memoirs and biographies, was self-serving in tone and content, although there were also some critical writings. Eventually, however, more objective accounts appeared, and most of the major individuals had either a memoir or biography in print. In recent years, the historical profession, responding to the centennial and 125th anniversary celebrations of the war, has produced a spate of excellent biographies, most of which have become the definitive interpretations of their subjects.

SHORT BIOGRAPHICAL SKETCHES

Several books feature short biographical sketches of the leading military fig-ures of the Civil War years. Among older books are Gamaliel Bradford, *Union*

Portraits (1916); T. Harry Williams, *Lincoln and His Generals* (1952); Kenneth P. Williams, *Lincoln Finds a General: A Military Study of the Civil War* (1949–1959); Alfred H. Burne, *Lee, Grant, and Sherman* (1938); Mark M. Boatner, *The Civil War Dictionary* (1959); Ezra J. Warner, *Generals in Blue: Lives of the Union Commanders* (1964); and Warren W. Hassler, *Commanders of the Army of the Potomac* (1962). More recent books containing sketches of Union military leaders are: Patricia L. Faust, ed., *Historical Times Illustrated Encyclopedia of the Civil War* (1986), and Stewart Sifakis, *Who Was Who in the Civil War* (1988). An important new study is Joseph Glatthaar, *Partners in Command: The Relationships between Leaders in the Civil War* (1994).

WINFIELD SCOTT

When the war began in 1861, Winfield Scott briefly headed the Union army. Soon after his retirement, he published a poorly done autobiography, *Memoirs of Lieut.-General Scott, LL.D., Written by Himself* (1864). The best book in a very small field on Scott is Charles W. Elliott, *Winfield Scott: The Soldier and the Man* (1937). Published the same year but not as thorough is Arthur D. Smith, *Old Fuss and Feathers . . .* (1937).

GEORGE B. MCCLELLAN

Scott served as commanding general of the Union army only until November 1861, when an individual of even greater ego, George B. McClellan, replaced him. The charismatic McClellan, beloved by his troops for his superb organizational skills, could not translate his ability and his soldiers' adulation into battlefield success. He constantly hesitated, and President Abraham Lincoln finally saw no recourse except to replace him in 1863.

In *McClellan's Own Story* (1887) he defended his wartime activities and continued to insist he had been right all along. Even more revealing are the letters he wrote to his wife during the war, expressing his messianic complex in bold relief. These are available in Stephen W. Sears, ed., *The Civil War Papers of George B. McClellan: Selected Correspondence, 1860–1865* (1989).

During the 1864 presidential campaign, the well-known Republican Benjamin F. Wade skewered Democratic party presidential candidate McClellan in a pamphlet whose title expresses its thesis: *Facts for the People. Ben Wade on McClellan. And Gens. Hooker & Heintzelman's Testimony. A Crushing Review of Little Napoleon's Military Career* (1864). Not to be outdone, the Democrats published William H. Hurlbert's favorable *The Life and Services of Gen. Geo. B. McClellan* (1864).

In later years, biographers produced books that mildly or vociferously defended McClellan's record and castigated those, like Lincoln, who had questioned his inactivity. Highly supportive of McClellan and critical of Lincoln were Clarence E. Macartney, *Little Mac; The Life of General George B. McClellan* (1940), and Hamilton J. Eckenrode and Bryan Conrad, *George B. Mc-*

Clellan: The Man Who Saved the Union (1941). Still favorable but much more objective was Warren W. Hassler, *General George B. McClellan, Shield of the Union* (1957).

Recognizing that McClellan's personality was central to understanding his activities as a general, several authors have produced character studies. One such early book was William S. Myers, *A Study in Personality, George Brinton Mc-Clellan* (1934). Much less sympathetic and more insightful is the section in T. Harry Williams, *McClellan, Sherman, and Grant* (1962). By far the best personality analysis, a critical one, and the standard biography is Stephen W. Sears, *George B. McClellan: The Young Napoleon* (1988).

POPE, HOOKER, AND BURNSIDE

Following McClellan in command of the Army of the Potomac was an unhappy parade of mediocre generals who were crushingly defeated by the Confederates. Nonetheless, John Pope is sympathetically chronicled in Wallace J. Schutz and Walter N. Trenerry, *Abandoned by Lincoln: A Military Biography of General John Pope* (1990). Joseph ("Fighting Joe") Hooker's only biography is Walter H. Hebert, *Fighting Joe Hooker* (1944). Benjamin Perley Poore, *The Life and Public Service of Ambrose E. Burnside, Soldier, Citizen, Statesman* (1882), and William Marvel, *Burnside* (1991), unsuccessfully attempted to rescue this general's reputation by blaming others for his failures.

MEADE AND HALLECK

George G. Meade oversaw the Union victory at Gettysburg in 1863, but his lack of charisma and the supervisory presence of U. S. Grant during later campaigns have kept him in the background of Civil War historiography. His two-volume *The Life and Letters of George Gordon Meade, Major-General United States Army* (1913) and George R. Agassiz, ed., *Meade's Headquarters, 1863–1865: Letters of Colonel Theodore Lyman from the Wilderness to Appomattox* (1922), are important sources for understanding Meade's role as commander of the Army of the Potomac under Grant's immediate control. The most recent biography is Freeman Cleaves, *Meade of Gettysburg* (1960).

Even more important yet little studied is the individual who served the function of chief of staff for the Union army, Henry W. Halleck. He wrote no memoirs, and the only biography is Stephen E. Ambrose, *Halleck, Lincoln's Chief of Staff* (1962).

ULYSSES S. GRANT

The major Union military leader of the Civil War was, of course, Ulysses S. Grant. This prewar failure became a Civil War success and the postwar two-term president of the United States. Most of the host of books written about him praise his successful leadership of the Union army and either ignore or condemn his activities as president.

Two major sources on Grant are his own two-volume *Personal Memoirs of U.S. Grant* (1885–1886) and John Y. Simon, ed., *The Papers of Ulysses S. Grant* (1967–). His adoring wife's perspective is preserved in John Y. Simon, ed., *The Personal Memoirs of Julia Dent Grant* (1975).

During Grant's lifetime, biographies appeared that were long on praise and short on factual analysis. A laudatory account with detailed information is Adam Badeau, *Military History of Ulysses S., Grant, from April 1861, to April 1865* (1868–1881) and *Grant in Peace: From Appomattox to Mount McGregor* (1887). In more recent times, several books have provided sharper evaluations. British historian J.F.C. Fuller in his *The Generalship of Ulysses S. Grant* (1929) and *Grant and Lee, A Study in Personality and Generalship* (1933) rated Grant above Lee as a general. Lloyd Lewis, *Captain Sam Grant* (1950), presented a favorable account of Grant's life until the outbreak of the Civil War, and Bruce Catton continued the story in *Grant Moves South* (1960) and *Grant Takes Command* (1969). William B. Hesseltine, *Ulysses S. Grant, Politician* (1935), argued that charges of Grant's political ineptitude were largely the result of political partisanship. Bruce Catton, *U.S. Grant and the American Military Tradition* (1954), is a brief synopsis of Grant's entire life.

Most recently, William S. McFeely won the Pulitzer Prize for his *Grant, A Biography* (1981), arguing that Grant was an ordinary man who was able to do only two things: be a general or be president. Brooks D. Simpson, *Let Us Have Peace: Ulysses S. Grant and the Politics of War and Reconstruction, 1861–1868* (1991), argues that Grant was not a political bungler but that his understanding of the political implications of the Civil War helped him succeed as a military leader.

WILLIAM T. SHERMAN

Next to Grant, William Tecumseh Sherman was the leading Union military figure. The pioneer of psychological warfare, he helped revolutionize war by waging one of destruction against the Confederate home front, hoping in that way to prevent further bloodshed. His brand of war was successful in helping bring the conflict to a quicker end, but it also resulted in providing for the later Southern animosity toward him that has continued into modern times.

Sherman's own perceptions of the war can best be seen in his two-volume *Memoirs of General W. T. Sherman* (1875) (reprinted most recently in 1990). These volumes were immediately challenged by reporter Henry V. Boynton, *Sherman's Historical Raid: The Memoirs in Light of the Record* (1875), and quickly defended by Sherman's brother-in-law Charles W. Moulton, *The Review of General Sherman's Memoirs Examined* (1875). Two book-length publications of Sherman correspondence appeared, but their contents are not always accurate when compared to the original manuscripts: Rachel Sherman Thorndike, ed.,

The Sherman Letters: Correspondence between General and Senator Sherman from 1837–1891 (1894), and M. A. DeWolfe Howe, ed., *Home Letters of General Sherman* (1909).

In the post–Civil War years, a number of Sherman biographies appeared, two of particular importance because they were written by individuals who knew Sherman well: S. M. Bowman and R. B. Irwin, *Sherman and His Campaigns: A Military Biography* (1865), and W. Fletcher Johnson and O. O. Howard, *The Life of Gen'l Wm. Tecumseh Sherman* (1891). Bowman was Sherman's lawyer in prewar California, and O. O. Howard was one of his subordinate generals during the conflict.

The early twentieth century saw the publication of two major Sherman biographies: B. H. Liddell-Hart, *Sherman, Soldier, Realist, American* (1929), an emphasis on Sherman's indirect military strategy, and Lloyd Lewis, *Sherman, Fighting Prophet* (1932), a well-written, more complete biography. In recent years, John F. Marszalek analyzed Sherman's stormy press relations in *Sherman's Other War: The General and the Civil War Press* (1981), while Marion B. Lucas, *Sherman and the Burning of Columbia* (1976), convincingly exonerated Sherman of sole blame for that city's terrible fire. Charles Royster, *The Destructive War: William Tecumseh Sherman, Stonewall Jackson, and the Americans* (1991), analyzed the development of the warfare of destruction and Sherman's role in its beginnings, while Albert Castel, *Decision in the West: The Atlanta Campaign of 1864* (1992), is critical of Sherman's generalship in that pivotal campaign. The standard biography, whose thesis is evident in the title, is John F. Marszalek, *Sherman: A Soldier's Passion for Order* (1993).

PHILIP H. SHERIDAN

The third-ranking figure among Union generals was Philip H. Sheridan, most famous for his activities in the Shenandoah Valley. He published the two-volume *Personal Memoirs of Philip Henry Sheridan* (1888), but these reminiscences are not in the same class as those of Grant and Sherman. Richard O'Connor, *Sheridan, the Inevitable* (1953), was the longtime standard account, recently superseded by Roy Morris, *Sheridan: The Life and Wars of General Phil Sheridan* (1992), and Paul A. Hutton, *Phil Sheridan and His Army* (1985).

GEORGE H. THOMAS

George H. Thomas, the "Rock of Chickamauga," never seemed to receive the respect that he, his Army of the Cumberland, and his later biographers believed he deserved. His chroniclers therefore have felt the need to defend him from what they have perceived as unfair detractors. The most important books about him are Richard O'Connor, *Thomas, Rock of Chickamauga* (1948); Freeman Cleaves, *Rock of Chickamauga: The Life of General George H. Thomas* (1949); Francis F. McKinney, *Education in Violence: The Life of George H.*

Thomas and the History of the Army of the Cumberland (1961); and Wilbur Thomas, *General George H. Thomas: The Indominable Warrior* (1964).

THE POLITICAL GENERALS

Playing important roles in the Union war effort were officers who have been derogatorily called the political generals. It was said of them that they were better at politics than they were in battle. Yet they brought with them public support for the war, without which the Union effort could not have survived very long.

Perhaps the most famous of this group of leaders was Benjamin F. Butler, who gained the nickname "Beast" for his occupation activities in New Orleans and was also seen as a military incompetent because of his failures in Virginia. To try to overcome this reputation, he published *Autobiography and Personal Reminiscences of Major General Benjamin F. Butler; Butler's Book* (1892), and his family published Jesse Ames Marshall, ed., *Private and Official Correspondence of Gen. Benjamin F. Butler, during the Period of the Civil War* (1917). Two objective studies are Hans Trefousse, *Ben Butler: The South Called Him Beast!* (1957), and Richard S. West, *Lincoln's Scapegoat General: A Life of Benjamin F. Butler, 1818–1893* (1965).

Equally disdained for his military failure was Nathaniel P. Banks; Fred Harvey Harrington's *Fighting Politician, Major General N. P. Banks* (1948) is the best study of him. John C. Frémont, prewar explorer and politician, never lived up to public expectations and faded out of military view early in the war. He wrote a self-serving reminiscence: *Memoirs of My Life* (1887). A sympathetic biography that emphasizes his non–Civil War experiences is Allan Nevins, *Frémont: The West's Greatest Adventurer* (1928). An intriguing psychological study is Andrew Rolle, *John Charles Frémont: Character as Destiny* (1991).

A much more successful political general was John A. Logan, who, after the death of its commander James B. McPherson, led the Army of the Tennessee to victory at the Battle of Atlanta. Despite this success, Sherman replaced Logan with O. O. Howard, a West Pointer. Logan loyally went back to his corps, but he never forgave Sherman and West Point for this slight and worked against them as a postwar congressman. This animosity can clearly be seen in his *The Volunteer Soldier of America* (1887), which includes his extended military reminiscences. Mrs. John A. Logan was an example of the military wife who continued to defend her husband long after his death. She wrote *A Reminiscence of a Soldier's Wife: An Autobiography* (1913). James P. Jones wrote two modern studies of Logan's life: *"Black Jack": John A. Logan and Southern Illinois in the Civil War* (1967) and *John A. Logan: Stalwart Republican from Illinois* (1982). The military career of Frank Blair, a rival of Logan, is covered well in William E. Smith, *The Francis Preston Blair Family in Politics* (1973).

SCHOFIELD AND HOWARD

John M. Schofield gained his greatest Civil War fame at the Battle of Franklin (1864) and in the late nineteenth century served as commanding general of the army. His memoirs, *Forty-Six Years in the Army* (1897), are disappointing for their lack of introspection. A modern biography is James Lee McDonough, *Schofield: Union General in the Civil War and Reconstruction* (1972).

Better remembered for his work with the Freedman's Bureau and because Howard University is named after him, Oliver Otis Howard nonetheless played an important part in the Civil War in both the eastern theater and as part of Sherman's army in the West. He wrote an important memoir, *Autobiography of Oliver Otis Howard, Major General, U.S. Army* (1907). Two biographical accounts have been published: John A. Carpenter, *Sword and Olive Branch: Oliver Otis Howard* (1964), and William S. McFeely, *Yankee Stepfather: General O. O. Howard and the Freedmen* (1968).

OTHER MILITARY FIGURES

Other books about Union military figures that deserve mention are: Russell F. Weigley, *Quartermaster General of the Union Army: A Biography of M. C. Meigs* (1959); William M. Lamers, *The Edge of Glory: A Biography of General William S. Rosecrans* (1961); Glenn Tucker, *Hancock the Superb* (1960); David M. Jordan, *Winfield Scott Hancock: A Soldier's Life* (1990); Christopher Phillips, *Damned Yankee: The Life of General Nathaniel Lyon* (1990); William H. and Shirley A. Leckie, *Unlikely Warriors: General Benjamin H. Grierson and His Family* (1984); Gregory J. Urwin, *Custer Victorious: The Civil War Battles of General George Armstrong Custer* (1990); Joshua Chamberlain, *The Passing of the Armies* (1915); Alpheus S. Williams, *From the Cannon's Mouth* (1959); William B. Hazen, *A Narrative of Military Service* (1885); John Gibbon, *Personal Recollections of the Civil War* (1928); and Russell Duncan, ed., *Blue-Eyed Child of Fortune: The Civil War Letters of Colonel Robert Gould Shaw* (1992).

BIBLIOGRAPHY

Agassiz, George R. ed. *Meade's Headquarters, 1863–1865: Letters of Colonel Theodore Lyman from the Wilderness to Appomattox.* Boston: Atlantic Monthly Press, 1922.

Ambrose, Stephen E. *Halleck, Lincoln's Chief of Staff.* Baton Rouge: Louisiana University Press, 1962.

Badeau, Adam. *Grant in Peace: From Appomattox to Mount McGregor.* Hartford: S. S. Scranton, 1887.

———. *Military History of Ulysses S. Grant, from April 1861, to April 1865.* 3 vols. New York: D. Appleton, 1868–1881.

Boatner, Mark. *The Civil War Dictionary.* New York: David McKay, 1959.

Bowman, S. M., and R. B. Irwin. *Sherman and His Campaigns: A Military Biography.* New York: C. B. Richardson, 1865.

Boynton, Henry V. *Sherman's Historical Raid: The Memoirs in Light of the Record.* Cincinnati: Wilstach, Baldwin, 1875.

Bradford, Gamaliel. *Union Portraits.* Boston: Houghton Mifflin, 1916.

Burne, Alfred H. *Lee, Grant, and Sherman.* Aldershot: Gale and Polder, 1938.

Butler, Benjamin F. *Autobiography and Personal Reminiscences of Major General Benjamin F. Butler: Butler's Book.* Boston: A. M. Thayer, 1892.

Carpenter, John A. *Sword and Olive Branch: Oliver Otis Howard.* Pittsburgh: University of Pittsburgh Press, 1964.

Castel, Albert. *Decision in the West: The Atlanta Campaign of 1864.* Lawrence: University of Kansas Press, 1992.

Catton, Bruce. *Grant Moves South.* Boston: Little, Brown, 1960.

———. *Grant Takes Command.* Boston: Little Brown, 1969.

———. *U. S. Grant and the American Military Tradition.* Boston: Little, Brown, 1954.

Chamberlain, Joshua. *The Passing of the Armies.* New York: G. P. Putnam's, 1915.

Cleaves, Freeman. *Meade of Gettysburg.* Norman: University of Oklahoma Press, 1960.

———. *Rock of Chickamauga: The Life of General George H. Thomas.* Norman: University of Oklahoma Press, 1949.

Duncan, Russell, ed. *Blue-Eyed Child of Fortune: The Civil War Letters of Colonel Robert Gould Shaw.* Athens: University of Georgia Press, 1992.

Eckenrode, Hamilton J., and Bryan Conrad. *George B. McClellan: The Man Who Saved the Union.* Chapel Hill: University of North Carolina Press, 1941.

Edelstein, Tilden G. *Strange Enthusiasm: A Life of Thomas Wentworth Higginson.* New Haven: Yale University Press, 1968.

Elliott, Charles W. *Winfield Scott: The Soldier and the Man.* New York: Macmillan, 1937.

Faust, Patricia L., ed. *Historical Times Illustrated Encyclopedia of the Civil War.* New York: Harper & Row, 1986.

Frémont, John C. *Memoirs of My Life.* Chicago: Bedford, Clark, 1887.

Fuller, J.F.C. *The Generalship of Ulysses S. Grant.* London: Eyre and Spottiswoode, 1929.

———. *Grant and Lee: A Study in Personality and Generalship.* London: Eyre and Spottiswoode, 1933.

Gibbon, John. *Personal Recollections of the Civil War.* New York: G. P. Putnam's, 1928.

Glatthaar, Joseph. *Partners in Command: The Relationships between Leaders in the Civil War.* New York: Free Press, 1994.

Grant, Ulysses S. *Personal Memoirs of U. S. Grant.* 1885–1886. Reprint, *Memoirs and Selected Letters: Personal Memoirs of U. S. Grant. Selected Letters, 1839–1865.* New York: Library of America, 1990.

Harrington, Fred Harvey. *Fighting Politician, Major General N. P. Banks.* Philadelphia: University of Pennsylvania Press, 1948.

Hassler, Warren W. *Commanders of the Army of the Potomac.* Baton Rouge: Louisiana State University Press, 1962.

———. *General George McClellan: Shield of the Union.* Baton Rouge: Louisiana State University Press, 1957.

Hazen, William B. *A Narrative of Military Service.* Boston: Ticknor, 1885.

Hebert, Walter H. *Fighting Joe Hooker.* Indianapolis: Bobbs-Merrill, 1944.

Hesseltine, William B. *Ulysses S. Grant, Politician.* New York: Dodd, Mead, 1935.

Howard, O. O. *Autobiography of Oliver Otis Howard, Major General, U.S. Army.* New York: Baker and Taylor, 1907.

Howe, M. A. DeWolfe, ed. *Home Letters of General Sherman.* New York: Charles Scribner's Sons, 1909.

Hurlbert, William H. *The Life and Services of Gen. Geo. B. McClellan.* New York: Rand and Avery, 1864.

Hutton, Paul A. *Phil Sheridan and His Army.* Lincoln: University of Nebraska Press, 1985.

Johnson, W. Fletcher, and O. O. Howard. *The Life of Gen'l Wm. Tecumseh Sherman.* Philadelphia: Edgewood, 1891.

Jones, James P. *"Black Jack": John A. Logan and Southern Illinois in the Civil War.* Tallahassee: Florida State University Press, 1967.

———. *John A. Logan: Stalwart Republican from Illinois.* Tallahassee: University Presses of Florida, 1982.

Jordan, David M. *Winfield Scott Hancock: A Soldier's Life.* Bloomington: University of Indiana Press, 1990.

Lamers, William M. *The Edge of Glory: A Biography of General William S. Rosecrans.* New York: Harcourt, Brace, 1961.

Leckie, William H., and Shirley A. Leckie. *Unlikely Warriors: General Benjamin H. Grierson and His Family.* Norman: University of Oklahoma Press, 1984.

Lewis, Lloyd. *Captain Sam Grant.* Boston: Little, Brown, 1950.

———. *Sherman, Fighting Prophet.* New York: Harcourt, Brace, 1932.

Liddell-Hart, B. H. *Sherman, Soldier, Realist, American.* New York: Dodd, Mead, 1929.

Logan, John A. *The Volunteer Soldier in America.* Chicago: R. S. Peale, 1887.

Logan, Mrs. John A. *A Reminiscence of a Soldier's Wife: An Autobiography.* New York: Charles Scribner's Sons, 1913.

Lucas, Marion B. *Sherman and the Burning of Columbia.* College Station: Texas A&M University Press, 1976.

Macartney, Clarence E. *Little Mac: The Life of General George B. McClellan.* Philadelphia: Dorrance, 1940.

McClellan, George B. *McClellan's Own Story.* New York: C. L. Webster, 1887.

McDonough, James Lee. *Schofield: Union General in the Civil War and Reconstruction.* Tallahassee: Florida State University Press, 1972.

McFeely, William S. *Grant: A Biography.* New York: Norton, 1981.

———. *Yankee Stepfather: General O. O. Howard and the Freedmen.* New Haven: Yale University Press, 1968.

McKinney, Francis F. *Education in Violence: The Life of George H. Thomas and the History of the Army of the Cumberland.* Detroit: Wayne State University Press, 1961.

Marshall, Jesse Ames, ed. *Private and Official Correspondence of Gen. Benjamin F. Butler, during the Period of the Civil War.* 5 vols. Norwood, MA: Privately printed, 1917.

Marszalek, John F. *Sherman: A Soldier's Passion for Order.* New York: Free Press, 1993.

———. *Sherman's Other War: The General and the Civil War Press.* Memphis: Memphis State University Press, 1981.

Marvel, William. *Burnside.* Chapel Hill: University of North Carolina Press, 1991.

Meade, George G. *The Life and Letters of George Gordon Meade, Major-General United States Army.* New York: Charles Scribner's Sons, 1913.

Morris, Roy. *Sheridan: The Life and Wars of General Phil Sheridan.* New York: Crown, 1992.

Moulton, Charles W. *The Review of General Sherman's Memoirs Examined.* Cincinnati: R. Clarke, 1875

Myers, William S. *A Study in Personality: George Brinton McClellan.* New York: D. Appleton-Century, 1934

Nevins, Allan. *Frémont: The West's Greatest Adventurer.* 2 vols. New York: Harper, 1928.

O'Connor, Richard. *Sheridan, the Inevitable.* Indianapolis: Bobbs Merrill, 1953.

————. *Thomas, Rock of Chickamauga.* New York: Prentice-Hall, 1948.

Phillips, Christopher. *Damned Yankee: The Life of General Nathaniel Lyon.* Columbia: University of Missouri Press, 1990.

Poore, Benjamin Perley. *The Life and Public Service of Ambrose E. Burnside, Soldier, Citizen, Statesman.* Providence, RI: J. A. and R. A. Reid, 1882.

Rolle, Andrew. *John Charles Frémont: Character as Destiny.* Norman: University of Oklahoma Press, 1991.

Royster, Charles. *The Destructive War: William Tecumseh Sherman, Stonewall Jackson, and the Americans.* New York: Knopf, 1991.

Schofield, John M. *Forty-Six Years in the Army.* New York: Century, 1897.

Schutz, Wallace J., and Walter N. Trenerry. *Abandoned by Lincoln: A Military Biography of General John Pope.* 1990.

Scott, Winfield. *Memoirs of Lieut.-General Scott, LL.D., Written by Himself.* 2 vols. New York: Sheldon, 1964.

Sears, Stephen W., ed. *The Civil War Papers of George B. McClellan: Selected Correspondence, 1860–1865.* New York: Ticknor and Fields, 1989.

————. *George B. McClellan: The Young Napoleon.* New York: Ticknor and Fields, 1988.

Sheridan, Philip H. *Personal Memoirs of Philip Henry Sheridan, General, United States Army.* New York: C. L. Webster, 1888.

Sherman, William T. *Memoirs of General W. T. Sherman.* 1875. Reprint, New York: Library of America, 1990.

Sifakis, Stewart. *Who Was Who in the Civil War.* New York: Facts on File, 1988.

Simon, John Y., ed. *The Papers of Ulysses S. Grant.* 18 vols. Carbondale: Southern Illinois University Press, 1967–1991.

————. *The Personal Memoirs of Julia Dent Grant.* New York: Putnam, 1975.

Simpson, Brooks D. *Let Us Have Peace: Ulysses S. Grant and the Politics of War and Reconstruction, 1861–1868.* Chapel Hill: University of North Carolina Press, 1991.

Smith, Arthur D. *Old Fuss and Feathers . . .* New York: Greystone, 1937.

Smith, William E. *The Francis Preston Blair Family in Politics.* 2 vols. New York: Macmillan, 1973.

Thomas, Wilbur. *General George H. Thomas: The Indominable Warrior.* New York: Exposition, 1964.

Thorndike, Rachel Sherman, ed. *The Sherman Letters: Correspondence between General and Senator Sherman from 1837–1891.* New York: Charles Scribner's Sons, 1894.

Trefousse, Hans. *Ben Butler: The South Called Him Beast!* New York: Twayne, 1957.

Tucker, Glenn. *Hancock the Superb.* Indianapolis: Bobbs-Merrill, 1960.

Urwin, Gregory J. *Custer Victorious: The Civil War Battles of General George Armstrong Custer.* Rutherford: Farleigh Dickinson University Press, 1990.

Wade, Benjamin F. *Facts for the People. Ben Wade on McClellan. And Gens. Hooker and Heintzelman's Testimony. A Crushing Review of Little Napoleon's Military Career.* Cincinnati: C. Clark, 1864.

Warner, Ezra J. *Generals in Blue: Lives of the Union Commanders.* Baton Rouge: Louisiana State University Press, 1964.

Weigley, Russell F. *Quartermaster General of the Union Army: A Biography of M. C. Meigs,* New York: Columbia University Press, 1959.

West, Richard S. *Lincoln's Scapegoat General: A Life of Benjamin F. Butler, 1818–1893.* Boston: Houghton Mifflin, 1965.

Williams, Alpheus S. *From the Cannon's Mouth.* Detroit: Wayne State University Press, 1959.

Williams, Kenneth P. *Lincoln Finds a General: A Military History of the Civil War.* 5 vols. New York: Macmillan, 1949–1959.

Williams, T. Harry. *Lincoln and His Generals.* New York: Knopf, 1952

———. *McClellan, Sherman, and Grant.* New Brunswick, NJ: Rutgers University Press, 1962.

26

Leadership—Confederate Army Officers

Grady McWhiney

Confederate generals—a total of 425—may still outnumber books about Confederate generals, but every year the count gets closer. No Civil War student expects authors to stop producing biographies of Confederate generals; even costly, six-hundred-page monsters sell as well as collections of biographical sketches. Readers often welcome second and even third evaluations of generals. More than fifty biographers have praised, criticized, or tried to explain Robert E. Lee. Every aspect of his life has been examined; investigators have followed him from Texas to heaven and revealed their findings under such intimate titles as *The Face of Lee, The Heart of Lee, The Shadow of Lee,* and even *The Soul of Lee.* One writer called his life of the great rebel *Robert E. Lee, Unionist.*

LEE AND THE EASTERN GENERALS

For a hundred years following the Civil War, study and writing about the conflict conformed to established patterns with little deviation. Measuring potential readers, writers planned books on the Lost Cause more carefully than some Confederate generals planned campaigns. Most successful authors emphasized what had taken place in Virginia and the East; few bothered with actions and commanders between the mountains and the Mississippi, and even fewer devoted pages to either the trans-Mississippi or other less prominent parts of the Confederacy.

One of the first works published after the war exemplified this pattern. In *Southern Generals, Who They Are, and What They Have Done* (1865), reissued in 1867 as *Lee and His Generals,* Captain William P. Snow emphasized Virginia and the East in selecting his eighteen Confederate heroes and apportioning the number of pages devoted to each: R. E. Lee, Stonewall Jackson, P. G. T. Beauregard, Joseph E. Johnston, Samuel Cooper, James Longstreet, Braxton Bragg, Richard S. Ewell, J. E. B. Stuart, A. P. Hill, John B. Hood, Albert S. Johnston, Leonidas Polk, Sterling Price, Edmund Kirby Smith, John H. Morgan, William J. Hardee, and Wade Hampton. Not all of these eighteen, of course, served under Lee, but those who did received special attention. Of the book's 500 pages, 290 recounted the exploits of Lee, his army, and the generals who achieved fame fighting in the East. Lee himself got 160 pages, Jackson 43, and Longstreet 25. Only five of these eighteen generals served solely in the West.

For a hundred years—between the War for Southern Independence and the Civil War centennial—both writers and readers tended to neglect Confederate generals who served outside Virginia and the East. By 1961 twelve of the Confederate generals featured nearly a century before in Snow's book had been the subject of one or more scholarly biographies, but only one of these biographies, Cecil F. Holland's *Morgan and His Raiders* (1942), dealt with someone whose service had been exclusively western.

If in 1961 most books on Confederate generals featured those who fought in the East, for the past thirty years writers and readers have been less neglectful of events and commanders outside Virginia. Today, as the publication dates of various items cited in this chapter indicate, many worthwhile new contributions have ensured not just a more balanced treatment of Confederate generals, wherever they served, but improving standards of biographical scholarship.

The literature on General Lee and the East was impressive even before 1961, and it has continued so. Two classic studies by Douglas Southall Freeman, *R. E. Lee,* (1934) and *Lee's Lieutenants* (1942–1944), remain the most comprehensive and respected works on the Army of Northern Virginia, its commander, and his generals. Professor Francis B. Simkins once jokingly claimed that the biography's thick four-volume size proved Freeman's greatness; only an extraordinary biography, he insisted, could hold the attention of readers through almost 2,500 pages devoted to such "a dull-old-fuddy-duddy as Robert E. Lee, who spent his free time nursing his sick wife, and returned unopened to its giver a fine bottle of whiskey he had carried through the Mexican War."

Other works on Lee include Clifford Dowdey, *Lee* (1965), perhaps still the best single-volume biography; anyone wanting to avoid Douglas Southall Freeman's monumental effort should consult Freeman, *Lee of Virginia* (1958), a tribute, or his *Lee* (1961), an excellent condensation of his four-volume biography edited by Richard Harwell; Burke Davis's *Gray Fox* (1956), lively but at times superficial; Thomas L. Connelly's *The Marble Man* (1977), an analysis of Robert E. Lee's generalship, a psychobiography, and an account of the generally successful effort to canonize Lee after the war; Alan T. Nolan, *Lee Considered* (1991), which claims "there is little truth to the dogmas traditionally set forth about Lee and the war"; Stanley F. Horn, ed., *The Robert E. Lee Reader* (1949), a "portrait" of Lee composed from the writing of other scholars;

Clifford Dowdey and Louis Manarin, eds., *The Wartime Papers of Robert E. Lee* (1961), the most complete collection of Lee's personal, official, and family letters, but containing only a fraction of the letters the general wrote during the war. For additional Lee letters see the U.S. Army, *War of the Rebellion* (1880–1901); *Lee's Dispatches,* edited by Douglas Southall Freeman and Grady McWhiney (1957); and John William Jones, *Personal Reminiscences, Anecdotes, and Letters of Robert Edward Lee* (1906), an affectionate account.

Biographies of Lee's generals are plentiful. Still the best work on Jackson, *Mighty Stonewall* (1957) by Frank E. Vandiver, is outstanding. Lenoir Chambers's *Stonewall Jackson* (1959) is a carefully researched account. George F. R. Henderson's *Stonewall Jackson and the American Civil War* (1898) is an English officer's classic treatment. Robert K. Krick's *Stonewall Jackson at Cedar Mountain* (1990) is a detailed study of a campaign.

Unlike Jackson, whose brief but brilliant career in the Army of Northern Virginia enhanced his fame, James Longstreet lived to hear himself denounced. He rebutted critics in his autobiographical defense, *From Manassas to Appomattox* (1960), edited by James I. Robertson, Jr., who corrects many of Longstreet's errors and gives a balanced evaluation of the Confederacy's senior lieutenant general. In *James Longstreet: Lee's War Horse* (1936), Hamilton J. Eckenrode and Bryan Conrad criticize Longstreet's generalship. Donald B. Sanger and Thomas Robson Hay are more partisan in *James Longstreet* (1952). Recent studies, by William Garrett Piston, *Lee's Tarnished Lieutenant: James Longstreet and His Place in Southern History* (1987), and Jeffry D. Wert, *General James Longstreet: The Confederacy's Most Controversial Soldier* (1993), suggest their themes in subtitles; nevertheless, the reputation of "Old Pete" remains uncertain.

Other Army of Northern Virginia generals have found biographers. The best analysis of the sickly corps commander Hill is the excellent study by James I. Robertson, Jr., *General A. P. Hill* (1987). Emory M. Thomas, *Bold Dragoon* (1986), is the best biography of Lee's chief of cavalry, J.E.B. Stuart. Reading John William Thomason's classic *Jeb Stuart* (1930) stimulated the interests of many Civil War enthusiasts. Burke Davis's *Jeb Stuart* (1957) is fast-paced and sympathetic. Leonard Hal Bridges, *Lee's Maverick General* (1961), the best biography of Daniel Harvey Hill, is scholarly but controversial. Jubal A. Early's *War Memoirs* (1912) is judicious, but as blunt and irascible as the general himself. Clyde N. Wilson, *Carolina Cavalier* (1990), is an able study of Johnston Pettigrew, who commanded a division at Gettysburg. Maury Klein, *Edward Porter Alexander* (1971), is a scholarly account of Longstreet's chief of artillery. See also two works by Alexander, *Military Memoirs of a Confederate* (1907), which offers excellent criticism of operations, and *Fighting for the Confederacy,* edited by Gary W. Gallagher (1989), which is full of "truly personal accounts" and vignettes of senior commanders. Gary W. Gallagher, *Stephen Dodson Ramseur* (1985), effectively described how this North Carolina general fought and died gallantly. Ralph Lowell Eckert, *John Brown Gordon* (1989), recounts the exploits of this fierce Georgian; see also Gordon's *Reminiscences* (1903), perhaps the most entertaining memoir by a general but full of exaggerations. General G. Moxley Sorrel's *Recollections,* edited by Bell I. Wiley (1905), are among the best available, with "touches of humor and swift characterization." General Henry Heth's *Memoirs,* edited by James L. Morrison, Jr. (1974), are full of stories and recollections by a division commander, who knew high-ranking officers on both sides.

THE WESTERN GENERALS

The greatest impact on scholarship in the western Confederacy since the Civil War centennial has been the work of Thomas L. Connelly. He never wrote a biography of a western general, but his two volumes on the Army of Tennessee—*Army of the Heartland* (1967) and *Autumn of Glory* (1971)—influenced what others wrote about Confederate generals and military actions in the West. Connelly did for the western Confederacy and its generals what Freeman had done in the East with *R. E. Lee* and *Lee's Lieutenants* nearly thirty years earlier. Whatever one thought of Connelly's conclusions, which were often controversial, they were not ignored. The Confederacy outside Virginia became either before Connelly or after Connelly; his views influenced the way every author and student viewed Confederate generals in the West.

Western Confederate generals, unlike those in Lee's army, usually served under several different commanders. Biographies have been written on each of the generals who at one time or another commanded the largest Confederate army in the West. Charles P. Roland, *Albert Sidney Johnston* (1964), is the definitive treatment of the Confederate president's favorite general who was killed at Shiloh. T. Harry Williams, *P.G.T. Beauregard* (1955), is still the best biography of the hero of Fort Sumter and First Manassas, who fell from the president's favor and was transferred from Virginia to the West in 1862. See also Alfred Roman's *The Military Operations of General Beauregard* (1884), for all practical purposes Beauregard's personal memoir; by having his former aide's name on the title page, Beauregard could eulogize himself without appearing immodest, and he could also mask his attack on Davis and the Johnstons. Grady McWhiney and Judith Lee Hallock, *Braxton Bragg and Confederate Defeat* (1969, 1991), is critical but understanding of the general who commanded the Army of Tennessee longer than anyone else and later served as the president's military adviser. Gilbert E. Govan and James W. Livingood, *A Different Valor* (1956), is sympathetic toward Joseph E. Johnston; Craig L. Symonds, *Joseph E. Johnston* (1992), is more analytical; Joe Johnston's defense of himself, *Narrative of Military Operations* (1874), is strongly anti-Davis and anti-Hood, but a better book than one might expect. Richard M. McMurry, *John Bell Hood* (1982), is the best biography of the general who destroyed the Army of Tennessee; John P. Dyer, *The Gallant Hood* (1950), is critical and a carefully researched study; Hood's recollections, *Advance and Retreat* (1880), are full of bitterness and errors, but essential to an understanding of Hood and the army he commanded.

Biographies of subordinate commanders in the West have increased from rare to abundant over the years. Nathaniel C. Hughes, *General William J. Hardee* (1965), is a readable and thorough work on the Army of Tennessee's most reliable corps commander. Joseph E. Parks, *General Edmund Kirby Smith* (1954), is a sympathetic study of the undistinguished commander of the Trans-Mississippi Department. Joseph E. Parks, *General Leonidas Polk* (1962), is appreciative but uncritical. Robert G. Hartje, *Van Dorn* (1967), is a thoughtful analysis of General Earl Van Dorn. William C. Davis, *Breckinridge* (1974), is a careful researched and sympathetic treatment of John C. Breckinridge, whose career included presidential candidate, general, and Confederate secretary of war. Herman Hattaway, *General Stephen D. Lee* (1976), is a scholarly treatment of the Confederacy's youngest lieutenant general, who served in both eastern and western armies. *General Sterling Price* (1968) by Albert E. Castel and *Sterling Price* (1971) by Robert E. Shalhope aid in understanding this Missourian. Howell Purdue and Elizabeth Purdue, *Pat Cleburne* (1973), is the only biography of the "Stonewall" of the West. Michael B. Ballard, *Pemberton* (1991), is the most recent and best biography of the defender of Vicksburg. James A. Ramage, *Rebel Raider* (1986), is the most recent study of General John Hunt Morgan. Albert E. Castel, *William Clarke Quantrill* (1962), is an impartial and extensively researched account of a raider. Brian Steel Wills, *A Battle from the Start* (1992), is less than favorable toward General Nathan B. Forrest. Robert S. Henry, *"First with the Most" Forrest* (1944), is moderate in interpretation and soundly researched. Arthur M. Manigault, *A Carolinian Goes to War,* edited by R. Lockwood Tower (1983), is an excellent memoir by an Army of Tennessee brigade commander. T. Michael Parrish, *Richard Taylor* (1992), is a prize-winning study of a previously neglected western commander. See also Richard Taylor, *Destruction and Reconstruction,* edited by Charles P. Roland (1879), which is critical of several Confederates but always temperate, and probably the best-written memoir of the war. Jerry Thompson, *Henry Hopkins Sibley* (1987), features the unsuccessful commander of the New Mexico campaign. William Arceneaux's *Acadian General* (1981) recounts the career of Jean Jacques Alfred Alexander Mouton, a division commander in Louisiana. Wilfred Knight, *Red Fox* (1988), describes the Confederate Indian Nation during the Civil War and General Stand Watie, the only Indian general on either side. St. John R. Liddell, *Liddell's Record,* edited by Nathaniel C. Hughes (1985), is a valuable recollection of an Army of Tennessee brigade commander. Christopher Losson, *Tennessee's Forgotten Warriors* (1990), is a study of General Frank Cheatham, a division commander in the Army of Tennessee. Nathaniel Cheairs Hughes, Jr., and Roy P. Stonesifer, Jr., *The Life and Wars of Gideon J. Pillow* (1993), describes a general, but not a hero, in two wars, who commanded a brigade in the Army of Tennessee. Thomas W. Cutrer, *Ben McCulloch*

(1993), is a vivid account of how the frontier military tradition shaped a Texas general killed in 1862 during the Battle of Pea Ridge.

GENERALS IN GENERAL

All 425 Confederate generals are briefly sketched in Ezra J. Warner's *Generals in Gray* (1959), with photographs, except John Breckinridge Grayson, whose missing portrait reappeared in time for inclusion in William C. Davis, ed., *The Confederate General* (1991), which provides some excellent photographs and more biographical details on each general by named authors. The *Encyclopedia of the Confederacy* (1993), edited by Richard N. Current, also contains fuller biographical sketches plus a bibliography on each Confederate general compiled by named authors but includes photographs of only certain generals. Robert K. Krick's *Lee's Colonels* (1992) contributes biographical sketches, with occasional photographs, of majors, lieutenant colonels, and colonels who served in Lee's army, as well as an appendix listing 3,524 field officers who served in Confederate armies other than Lee's. Charles L. Dufour's collective biography, *Nine Men in Gray* (1963), contains excellent essays with photographs of seven army officers—Generals Richard Taylor, Turner Ashby, Patrick Cleburne, William Mahone, E. P. Alexander, and Colonels William R. J. Pegram and Lucius B. Northrop—Charles W. "Savez" Read, a naval officer, and Henry Hotze, a quasi-diplomat. John C. Waugh's *The Class of 1846* (1994) examines the interrelationships between Southerners and Northerners who were members of that remarkable West Point class. Brief biographies of Confederate generals may be found in Mark Mayo Boatner III, *The Civil War Dictionary* (1959), but unaccompanied by photographs or bibliographies. Francis T. Miller, ed., *The Photographic History of the Civil War* (1911), contains photographs of many Confederate officers. George W. Cullum's *Biographical Register of the Officers and Graduates of the U.S. Military Academy* (1891) lists all West Pointers who joined the Confederacy. Francis B. Heitman's *Historical Register and Dictionary of the United States Army* (1903) includes the service records of all Confederates who served in the "Old Army."

Useful in understanding some of the various military activities of the Confederate government are three books authored or edited by Frank E. Vandiver: *Rebel Brass* (1956), which examines the Confederate command system; *Ploughshares into Swords* (1952), a biography of General Josiah Gorgas, the father of Confederate ordnance; and *The Civil War Diary of General Josiah Gorgas* (1947), valuable as an account of more than just ordnance.

Other useful studies of generals associated with the Confederacy's two major armies, besides the works of Freeman and Connelly previously cited, include Richard M. McMurry's *Two Great Rebel Armies* (1989) and Steven E. Woodworth's *Jefferson Davis and His Generals* (1990), which focuses on the failure of the Confederate command in the West.

The best biography of the Confederacy's commander in chief, who would have rather been a general, is William C. Davis's *Jefferson Davis: The Man and His Hour* (1991), but *The Papers of Jefferson Davis* (1971–), vols. 1–3 (1808–1848), edited by Haskell M. Monroe, Jr., and James T. McIntosh, and vols. 4–8 (1849–1862), edited by Lynda Lasswell Crist and Mary Seaton Dix, are basic to understanding the Confederate president. In his *Rise and Fall of the Confederate Government* (1881), Davis hoped to explain himself and the war he fought but concealed more than he revealed.

BIBLIOGRAPHY

Alexander, Bevin. *Lost Victories: The Military Genius of Stonewall Jackson.* New York: Henry Holt and Company, 1992.

Alexander, Edward Porter. *Fighting for the Confederacy.* Edited by Gary W. Gallagher. Chapel Hill: University of North Carolina Press, 1989.

——. *Military Memoirs of a Confederate.* 1907. Reprint, Bloomington: Indiana University Press, 1962.

Arceneaux, William. *Acadian General: Alfred Mouton and the Civil War.* Lafayette: Center of Louisiana Studies, University of Southwestern Louisiana, 1981.

Ballard, Michael B. *Pemberton: A Biography.* Jackson: University Press of Mississippi, 1991.

Boatner, Mark Mayo, III. *The Civil War Dictionary.* New York: McKay, 1959.

Bowers, John. *Stonewall Jackson: Portrait of a Soldier.* New York: William Morrow and Company, 1989.

Bridges, Leonard Hal. *Lee's Maverick General, Daniel Harvey Hill.* New York: McGraw-Hill, 1961.

Casdorph, Paul D. *Lee and Jackson: Confederate Chieftains.* New York: Paragon House, 1992.

Castel, Albert E. *General Sterling Price and the Civil War in the West.* Baton Rouge: Louisiana State University Press, 1968.

——. *William Clarke Quantrill: His Life and Times.* New York: Fell, 1962.

Chambers, Lenoir. *Stonewall Jackson.* 2 vols. New York: William Morrow and Company, 1959.

Connelly, Thomas L. *Army of the Heartland: The Army of Tennessee, 1861–1862.* Baton Rouge: Louisiana State University Press, 1967.

——. *Autumn of Glory: The Army of Tennessee, 1862–1865.* Baton Rouge: Louisiana State University Press, 1971.

——. *The Marble Man: Robert E. Lee and His Image in American Society.* New York: Alfred A. Knopf, 1977.

Cullum, George W. *Biographical Register of the Officers and Graduates of the U.S. Military Academy.* 3 vols. with supplements. Boston: Houghton Mifflin, 1891.

Cummings, Charles M. *Yankee Quaker Confederate General: The Curious Career of Bushrod Rust Johnson.* Rutherford, NJ: Fairleigh Dickinson University Press, 1971.

Current, Richard N., ed. *The Encyclopedia of the Confederacy.* 4 vols. New York: Simon & Schuster, 1993.

Cutrer, Thomas W. *Ben McCulloch and the Frontier Military Tradition.* Chapel Hill: University of North Carolina Press, 1993.

Davis, Burke. *Gray Fox: Robert E. Lee and the Civil War.* New York: Rinehart & Company, 1956.

———. *Jeb Stuart: The Last Cavalier.* New York: Rinehart & Company, 1957.

Davis, Jefferson. *The Papers of Jefferson Davis.* Edited by Haskell M. Monroe, Jr., James T. McIntosh, Lynda Lasswell Crist, and Mary Seaton Dix. 8 vols. to date, Baton Rouge: Louisiana State University Press, 1971–.

———. *Rise and Fall of the Confederate Government.* 2 vols. 1881. Reprint, New York: Thomas Yoseloff, 1958.

Davis, William C. *Breckinridge: Statesman, Soldier, Symbol.* Baton Rouge: Louisiana State University Press, 1974.

———. *Jefferson Davis: The Man and His Hour.* New York: HarperCollins, 1991.

———, ed. *The Confederate General.* 6 vols. N.p.: National Historical Society, 1991.

Dowdey, Clifford. *Lee.* Boston: Little, Brown, 1965.

Dufour, Charles L. *Nine Men in Gray.* Garden City, NY: Doubleday, 1963.

Dyer, John P. *"Fightin' Joe" Wheeler.* Baton Rouge: Louisiana State University Press, 1941.

———. *The Gallant Hood.* Indianapolis: Bobbs-Merrill, 1950.

Early, Jubal Anderson. *War Memoirs: Autobiographical Sketch and Narrative of the War between the States.* 1912. Reprint, Bloomington: Indiana University Press, 1960.

Eckenrode, Hamilton J., and Bryan Conrad. *James Longstreet: Lee's War Horse.* 1936. Reprint, Chapel Hill: University of North Carolina Press, 1986.

Eckert, Ralph Lowell. *John Brown Gordon: Soldier, Southerner, American.* Baton Rouge: Louisiana State University Press, 1989.

Farwell, Byron. *Stonewall: A Biography of General Thomas J. Jackson.* New York: Norton, 1992.

Freeman, Douglas Southall. *Lee.* Edited by Richard Harwell. New York: Scribner's, 1961.

———. *Lee of Virginia.* New York: Scribner's, 1958.

———. *Lee's Lieutenants: A Study in Command.* 3 vols. New York: Scribner's, 1942–1944.

———. *R. E. Lee: A Biography.* 4 vols. New York: Scribner's, 1934.

French, Samuel G. *Two Wars: An Autobiography.* Nashville: Confederate Veteran, 1901.

Gallagher, Gary W. *Stephen Dodson Ramseur: Lee's Gallant General.* Chapel Hill: University of North Carolina Press, 1985.

Gordon, John Brown. *Reminiscences.* 1903. Reprint, Baton Rouge: Louisiana State University Press, 1993.

Gorgas, Josiah. *The Civil War Diary of General Josiah Gorgas.* Edited by Frank E. Vandiver. University: University of Alabama Press, 1947.

Govan, Gilbert E., and James W. Livingood. *A Different Valor: The Story of General Joseph E. Johnston, C.S.A.* Indianapolis: Bobbs-Merrill, 1956.

Hamlin, Percy Gatlin. *"Old Bald Head" (General R. S. Ewell): The Portrait of a Soldier.* Strasburg, VA: Shenandoah, 1940.

Hartje, Robert G. *Van Dorn: The Life and Times of a Confederate General.* Nashville: Vanderbilt University Press, 1967.

Hassler, William Woods. *A. P. Hill: Lee's Forgotten General.* Richmond: Garrett & Massie, 1957.

Hattaway, Herman. *General Stephen D. Lee.* Jackson: University Press of Mississippi, 1976.

Heitman, Francis B. *Historical Register and Dictionary of the United States Army.* 2 vols. Washington D.C.: Government Printing Office, 1903.

Henderson, George F. R. *Stonewall Jackson and the American Civil War.* 2 vols. London: Longmans, Green, 1898.

Henry, Robert S. *"First with the Most" Forrest.* Indianapolis: Bobbs-Merrill, 1944.

Heth, Henry. *The Memoirs of Henry Heth.* Edited by James L. Morrison, Jr. Westport, CT: Greenwood Press, 1974.

Holland, Cecil F. *Morgan and His Raiders: A Biography of the Confederate General.* New York: Macmillan, 1942.

Hood, John Bell. *Advance and Retreat: Personal Experiences in the United States and Confederate States Armies.* 1880. Reprint, Bloomington: Indiana University Press, 1959.

Horn, Stanley F., ed. *The Robert E. Lee Reader.* Indianapolis: Bobbs-Merrill, 1949.

Hughes, Nathaniel C., Jr. *General William J. Hardee, Old Reliable.* Baton Rouge: Louisiana State University Press, 1965.

———, and Roy P. Stonesifer, Jr. *The Life and Wars of Gideon J. Pillow.* Chapel Hill: University of North Carolina Press, 1993.

Johnston, Joseph E. *Narrative of Military Operations Directed, during the Late War between the States.* 1874. Reprint, Bloomington: Indiana University Press, 1959.

Jones, John William. *Personal Reminiscences, Anecdotes, and Letters of Robert Edward Lee.* New York: D. Appleton, 1906.

Klein, Maury. *Edward Porter Alexander.* Athens: University of Georgia Press, 1971.

Knight, Wilfred. *Red Fox: Stand Watie and the Confederate Indian Nations during the Civil War Years in Indian Territory.* Glendale, CA: Arthur H. Clark Company, 1988.

Krick, Robert K. *Lee's Colonels: A Biographical Register of the Field Officers of the Army of Northern Virginia.* 4th ed. Dayton, OH: Morningside, 1992.

———. *Stonewall Jackson at Cedar Mountain.* Chapel Hill: University of North Carolina Press, 1990.

Lee, Robert E. *Lee's Dispatches: Unpublished Letters of General Robert E. Lee, C.S.A. to Jefferson Davis and the War Department of the Confederate States of America, 1862–65.* Edited by Douglas Southall Freeman and Grady McWhiney. 1957. Reprint, Baton Rouge: Louisiana State University Press, 1994.

———. *The Robert E. Lee Reader.* Edited by Stanley F. Horn. Indianapolis: Bobbs-Merrill, 1949.

———. *The Wartime Papers of Robert E. Lee.* Edited by Clifford Dowdey and Louis H. Manarin. Boston: Little, Brown, 1961.

Liddell, St. John R. *Liddell's Record: St. John Richardson Liddell, Brigadier General, CSA, Staff Officer and Brigade Commander, Army of Tennessee.* Edited by Nathaniel C. Hughes. Dayton, OH: Morningside, 1985.

Longstreet, James. *From Manassas to Appomattox: Memoirs of the Civil War in America.* 1896. New ed., edited by James I. Robertson, Jr., Bloomington: Indiana University Press, 1960.

Losson, Christopher. *Tennessee's Forgotten Warriors: Frank Cheatham and His Confederate Division.* Knoxville: University of Tennessee Press, 1990.

Manigault, Arthur M. *A Carolinian Goes to War: The Civil War Narrative of Arthur Middleton Manigault, Brigadier General, C.S.A..* Edited by Lockwood Tower. Columbia: University of South Carolina Press, 1983.

McMurry, Richard M. *John Bell Hood and the War for Southern Independence*. Lexington: University Press of Kentucky, 1982.

———. *Two Great Rebel Armies: An Essay in Confederate Military History*. Chapel Hill: University of North Carolina Press, 1989.

McWhiney, Grady, and Judith Hallock. *Braxton Bragg and Confederate Defeat*. 2 vols. Tuscaloosa: University of Alabama Press, 1969, 1991.

Miller, Francis T., ed. *The Photographic History of the Civil War*. 10 vols. 1911. Reprint, New York: Thomas Yoseloff, 1957.

Nolan, Alan T. *Lee Considered: General Robert E. Lee and Civil War History*. Chapel Hill: University of North Carolina Press, 1991.

Osborne, Charles C. *Jubal: The Life and Times of General Jubal A. Early, CSA, Defender of the Lost Cause*. Chapel Hill, NC: Algonquin Books of Chapel Hill, 1992.

Parks, Joseph H. *General Edmund Kirby Smith, C.S.A.* Baton Rouge: Louisiana State University Press, 1954.

———. *General Leonidas Polk, C.S.A.: The Fighting Bishop*. Baton Rouge: Louisiana State University Press, 1962.

Parrish, T. Michael. *Richard Taylor: Soldier Prince of Dixie*. Chapel Hill: University of North Carolina Press, 1992.

Paxton, Frank. *The Civil War Letters of General Frank "Bull" Paxton, CSA: A Lieutenant of Lee and Jackson*. Edited by John Gallatin Paxton. Hillsboro, TX: Hill Junior College Press, 1978.

Pender, William Dorsey. *The General to His Lady: The Civil War Letters of William Dorsey Pender to Fanny Pender*. Edited by William W. Hassler. Chapel Hill: University of North Carolina Press, 1965.

Piston, William Garrett. *Lee's Tarnished Lieutenant: James Longstreet and His Place in Southern History*. Athens: University of Georgia Press, 1987.

Purdue, Howell, and Elizabeth Purdue. *Pat Cleburne, Confederate General: A Definitive Biography*. Hillsboro, TX: Hill Jr. College Press, 1973.

Ramage, James A. *Rebel Raider: The Life of General John Hunt Morgan*. Lexington: University of Kentucky Press, 1986.

Robertson, James I., Jr. *General A. P. Hill: The Story of a Confederate Warrior*. New York: Random House, 1987.

Roland, Charles P. *Albert Sidney Johnston: Soldier of Three Republics*. Austin: University of Texas Press, 1964.

Roman, Alfred. *The Military Operations of General Beauregard in the War between the States*. New York: Harper, 1884.

Sanger, Donald B., and Thomas Robson Hay. *James Longstreet: Soldier, Officeholder, and Writer*. Baton Rouge: Louisiana State University Press, 1952.

Shalhope, Robert E. *Sterling Price: Portrait of a Southerner*. Columbia: University of Missouri Press, 1971.

Simpson, Craig M. *A Good Southerner: The Life of Henry A. Wise of Virginia*. Chapel Hill: University of North Carolina Press, 1985.

Snow, William P. *Southern Generals, Who They Are, and What They Have Done*. New York: Richardson, 1865.

———. *Lee and His Generals*. 1867. Reprint, New York: Fairfax Press, 1982.

Sorrel, Gilbert Moxley. *Recollections of a Confederate Staff Officer*. 1905. New ed., edited by Bell I. Wiley, Jackson, TN: McCowat-Mercer, 1958.

Symonds, Craig L. *Joseph E. Johnston: A Civil War Biography.* New York: W. W. Norton, 1992.

Taylor, Richard. *Destruction and Reconstruction: Personal Experiences of the Late War.* 1879. New ed., edited by Charles P. Roland, Waltham, MA: Blaisdell, 1968.

Thomas, Emory. *Bold Dragoon: The Life of J. E. B. Stuart.* New York: Harper & Row, 1986.

Thomason, John William. *Jeb Stuart.* New York: Scribner's, 1930.

Thompson, Jerry. *Henry Hopkins Sibley: Confederate General of the West.* Natchitoches, LA: Northwestern State University Press, 1987.

U.S. Army. *War of the Rebellion: A Compilation of the Official Records of the Union and Confederate Armies.* 128 vols. Washington, D.C.: Government Printing Office, 1880–1901.

Vandiver, Frank E. *Mighty Stonewall.* New York: McGraw-Hill, 1957.

————. *Ploughshares into Swords: Josiah Gorgas and Confederate Ordnance.* Austin: University of Texas Press, 1952.

————. *Rebel Brass: The Confederate Command System.* Baton Rouge: Louisiana State University Press, 1956.

Warner, Ezra J. *Generals in Gray: Lives of Confederate Commanders.* Baton Rouge: Louisiana State University Press, 1959.

Waugh, John C. *The Class of 1846 from West Point to Appomattox: Stonewall Jackson, George McClellan and Their Brothers.* New York: Warner Books, 1994.

Wellman, Manly Wade. *Giant in Gray: A Biography of Wade Hampton of South Carolina.* New York: C. Scribner's Sons, 1949.

Wert, Jeffry D. *General James Longstreet: The Confederacy's Most Controversial Soldier—A Biography.* New York: Simon & Schuster, 1993.

Williams, T. Harry. *P.G.T. Beauregard: Napoleon in Gray.* Baton Rouge: Louisiana State University Press, 1955.

Wills, Brian Steel. *A Battle from the Start: The Life of Nathan Bedford Forrest.* New York: HarperCollins, 1992.

Wilson, Clyde N. *Carolina Cavalier: The Life and Mind of James Johnston Pettigrew.* Athens: University of Georgia Press, 1990.

Woodworth, Steven E. *Davis and Lee at War.* Lawrence: University Press of Kansas, 1995.

Woodworth, Steven E. *Jefferson Davis and His Generals: The Failure of Confederate Command in the West.* Lawrence: University Press of Kansas, 1990.

27

Leadership—Union Naval Officers

Thomas J. Legg

Naval historians continually state that the naval history of the Civil War and the stories of the men who fought it have been sorely neglected. This may indeed be true if the literature of the land war is used as the measuring stick. By most standards, however, a survey of the existing literature, including periodicals, shows that the some 100,000 men who served in the Union navy (about 5 percent of the number in the Union army) are well represented in both the quality and quantity of scholarship.

BIOGRAPHICAL ESSAY COLLECTIONS

The most fruitful place to begin an exploration of the lives and careers of Union naval officers is with the recent, and by far the best, collection of biographical essays on Civil War–era navy officers. Editor James C. Bradford's *Captains of the Old Steam Navy* (1986), one of the Naval Institute Press's Makers of Naval Tradition series, contains thirteen twenty- to thirty-page analytical essays on some of the Civil War's most prominent naval officers, both Union and Confederate. The nine Union officers detailed are John Dahlgren, Samuel DuPont, David Farragut, Andrew Foote, Benjamin Isherwood, David Porter, John Rodgers, Robert Shufeldt, and Charles Wilkes. In addition to placing these men into the broader context of the great changes that navies around the world were undergoing in the mid-nineteenth century, among the many strengths of the volume—which includes appropriate illustrations and maps—are the individual bibliographic essays for each of the subjects, plus a general bibliography pertaining to the nineteenth-century U.S. Navy.

Bradford's volume is just one in a growing list of essay collections about Civil War navy officers. While dated, Joel T. Headley's *Farragut and Our Naval Commanders* (1867) is still useful because it provides information on many relatively unknown officers, including Theodorus Bailey, Stephen Rowan, Henry Bell, Melanchton Smith, and Thomas T. Craven, among its more than thirty biographical entries. Similar other volumes are Jim Dan Hill, *Sea Dogs of the Sixties* (1935), which is strongest on Farragut, and Clarence Macartney, *Mr. Lincoln's Admirals* (1956), which offers one of the longer sketches available on John Worden, the captain of the *Monitor* in March 1862. A comprehensive listing of Civil War navy officers is contained in Lewis R. Hamersly, *The Records of Living Officers of the U.S. Navy and Marine Corps* (1870). Brief biographical sketches of Union officers can be found in Karl Schoun, *U.S. Navy Biographical Dictionary* (1964), and William B. Cogar, *Dictionary of Admirals of the U.S. Navy,* volume 1: 1862–1900 (1989). Another of Bradford's books in the Makers of the American Naval Tradition series, *Admirals of the New Steel Navy* (1990), provides analytical essays for some of the Union navy's junior officers who became prominent after the war, including Stephen B. Luce, who was credited with the creation of the Naval War College; Alfred Mahan, renowned for his influential writings on naval history and theory; and George Dewey, hero of the Battle of Manila Bay. Finally, two related but very different books are the collective biographies of Peter Karsten, *The Naval Aristocracy: The Golden Age of Annapolis and the Emergence of Modern American Navalism* (1972), and Charles Todorich, *The Spirited Years: A History of the Antebellum Naval Academy* (1984), which offer contrasting analytical accounts of the group *mentalité* of the mid-nineteenth century navy.

PROMINENT SQUADRON COMMANDERS

From the outset of the Civil War, the primary role of the Union navy was to blockade the Confederate coast; however, as the members of the Navy Department's ad hoc Blockade Board noted, the navy would also conduct auxiliary operations of "a purely military character." This latter category of operations was where the greatest Civil War naval heroes were made. Foremost was David Glasgow Farragut, and not surprisingly he has received the most interest by historians. The most comprehensive study of Farragut remains Charles L. Lewis's thoroughly researched work, *David Glasgow Farragut* (1941–1943). Volume 1, *Admiral in the Making,* details Farragut's pre–Civil War career; the second volume, *Our First Admiral,* provides an extensive narrative of Farragut's Civil War exploits. While not the first biography of Farragut, Loyall Farragut— the admiral's son—*The Life and Letters of David Glasgow Farragut* (1879), contains a significant amount of primary source material. It also served as the basis for Alfred Thayer Mahan's *Admiral Farragut* (1892). Christopher Martin, *Damn the Torpedoes: The Story of America's First Admiral* (1970), is the most recent book-length study of Farragut. A number of articles provide good supplements. Albert Mordell, "Farragut at the Crossroads" (1931), analyzes Farragut's decision to remain in the U.S. Navy. Richard S. West, Jr., has written two useful articles about Farragut's cooperating with other officers: "Relations between Farragut and Porter" (1935) and "Admiral Farragut and General Butler" (1956).

Second in fame to Farragut, though perhaps not in his own inflated self-opinion, was David Dixon Porter. Selected over scores of senior officers by Secretary of the Navy Gideon Welles to head the Union naval forces on the Mississippi, Porter's Civil War and postwar career seldom lacked for controversy. The best and most even of the Porter biographies in discussing both his strengths and weaknesses is Richard S. West, Jr., *The Second Admiral* (1937). Other biographies include James R. Soley, *Admiral Porter* (1903), and Paul Lewis, *Yankee Admiral* (1968), both of which portray Porter as a one-dimensional hero. A number of other useful works fill out the story on Porter's life and career. David Long's *Nothing Too Daring: A Biography of Commodore David Porter* (1970) gives insights on the younger Porter's early life. Ludwell H. Johnson's insightful *Red River Campaign* (1958) exposes Porter's role in this bungled and ill-conceived campaign, which had little if anything to do with military matters. Lance Buhl, "Mariners and Machines: Resistance to Technological Change in the U.S. Navy, 1865–1869" (1974), and Kenneth J. Hagan, "Admiral David Dixon Porter: Strategist for a Navy in Transition" (1968), offer differing views on Porter's role in the moribund postwar navy. William N. Still, Jr., " 'Porter . . . Is the Best Man': This Was Gideon Welles's View of the Man He Chose to Command the Mississippi Squadron" (1977), details the Navy Department's selection of Porter. Of little use for factual information, Porter's own writings provide further insights into his character, especially *Incidents and Anecdotes of the Civil War* (1885) and *The Naval History of the Civil War* (1886).

Another group of squadron commanders who while perhaps lesser known also served vital roles in the Union navy. Samuel Francis DuPont was probably the navy's most prestigious officer when the Civil War began. DuPont's status soared after capturing Port Royal in 1861. Following this, however, his reluctance to attack Charleston and his ultimate failure to destroy this detested city resulted in his being removed from command in mid-1863. James M. Merrill's *DuPont: The Making of an Admiral* (1986) gives a balanced treatment of DuPont's entire career, including its controversial ending. A family member, Henry A. DuPont, has written the only other book-length biography. His *Rear-Admiral Samuel Francis DuPont* (1926) is a partisan defense of DuPont, especially his failed Charleston campaign and subsequent fight with the Navy Department. John D. Hayes has edited an extremely valuable three-volume edition of DuPont's Civil War correspondence, *Samuel Francis DuPont* (1969). It provides insights not only about DuPont but also many other officers and Washington politicians. Gerald S. Henig's article, "Admiral Samuel F. DuPont, the

Navy Department, and the Attack on Charleston'' (1979), demonstrates that political factors also had an impact on navy policy.

Andrew Hull Foote's career, like DuPont's, did not last the entire war, though for entirely different reasons; he eventually died from wounds he suffered at Fort Donelson. James M. Hoppin's *The Life of Andrew Hull Foote* (1874) remains the only published book-length work on Foote's life, and it contains useful correspondence between Foote and some of his contemporaries not found elsewhere. Gerard A. Forlenza, Jr.'s 1991 Ph.D. dissertation, ''A Navy Life,'' details Foote's pre–Civil War career and analyzes this reform-minded officer's role in the antislavery and temperance movements. H. J. Maihafer's 1967 article, ''The Partnership,'' analyzes Foote's participation in the successful joint operations at Forts Henry and Donelson.

Samuel Phillips Lee, who commanded the North Atlantic Blockading Squadron for a large part of the war, exemplifies the vast majority of officers who did not receive the laurels that accompanied some notable victory, but rather served loyally though unspectacularly on blockade duty. Lee's life has become almost a cottage industry for historian Virginia Jeans Laas. Along with Dudley Taylor Cornish, she coauthored *Lincoln's Lee: The Life of Samuel Phillips Lee* (1986). This well-written biography, and Laas's edited volume of Lee's wife's correspondence, *Wartime Washington: The Civil War Letters of Elizabeth Blair Lee* (1991), detail the politically powerful Lee, who proved steady and non–risk taking. Robert Monroe Browning, Jr., *From Cape Charles to Cape Fear: The North Atlantic Blockading Squadron during the Civil War* (1993), provides a command study.

Charles Wilkes offers an extreme contrast to the cautious Lee. From beginning to end, Wilkes's career was such that he was famous, perhaps even notorious. The only comprehensive biography of Wilkes is Daniel M. Henderson's older, and overly generous, *The Hidden Coasts: A Biography of Admiral Charles Wilkes* (1953). Wilkes's involvement in the *Trent* affair, which almost brought Great Britain to war with the Union, has been the subject of much attention, perhaps most fully described in Norman B. Ferris, *The Trent Affair* (1977). Wilkes's early naval career in which he established himself as an explorer and scientist is best described in William Stanton, *The Great United States Exploring Expedition* (1975). Wilkes was also a prodigious chronicler of his own career. His *Autobiography* (1978) is entertaining reading but clearly one-sided. His five-volume *Narrative of the United States Exploring Expedition* (1844), if carefully mined, is a potential treasure trove.

LESSER-KNOWN SQUADRON COMMANDERS AND OTHER OFFICERS

In addition to their more famous counterparts, a number of other officers also served as squadron commanders, though usually for much shorter periods of time and with much less fanfare. Louis M. Goldsborough led the Atlantic Blockading Squadron—later divided into North and South squadrons—early in the war. His short and stormy tenure, including his severely criticized part in the peninsula campaign which led to his resignation, can be followed in William N. Still, Jr., "Admiral Goldsborough's Feisty Career" (1979). Goldsborough's personal defense is contained in an article edited by Edward Gardiner, "Narrative of Rear Admiral Goldsborough" (1933). Besides relieving Foote on the Mississippi, Charles H. Davis was an important subordinate of DuPont on both the Blockade Board and in the South Atlantic Blockading Squadron, not to mention being chief of the Bureau of Navigation for a large part of the war. His son, Charles H. Davis, Jr., wrote a book extolling his father, *The Life of Charles H. Davis* (1899). Davis's part in Gustavus Fox's controversial pet project of sinking stone-laden vessels in Southern ports is detailed by Arthur Gordon, "The Great Stone Fleet: Calculated Catastrophe" (1968). And while not technically a squadron commander, having only commanded the failed relief expedition to save the Gosport Navy Yard in Norfolk, Hiram Paulding's Civil War career, especially his contributions to the blockade as commandant of the New York Navy Yard, is the subject of Rebecca Paulding Meade's supportive biography, *Life of Hiram Paulding* (1910).

There are a select few other officers for whom there are biographies. John Rodgers, of the famous Rodgers family, is the subject of one of the best naval biographies. Robert E. Johnson, *Rear Admiral John Rodgers, 1812–1882* (1967), gives a fine accounting of Rodgers's life and also provides an outstanding record of the nineteenth-century navy. Another of the Rodgers naval family, C.R.P. Rodgers, who enjoyed a quiet but influential postwar career, is the subject of a commendable article by Stephen Brown, "Christopher Raymond Perry Rodgers: Mentor of the New Navy" (1987). John Winslow, who commanded the *Kearsarge,* is the subject of an older work by John M. Ellicott, *The Life of John Ancrum Winslow* (1902). The exploits of William Cushing have been vividly retold by Ralph J. Roske and Charles Van Doren, *Lincoln's Commando: The Biography of Commander William B. Cushing* (1957). And while perhaps much less dramatic than Cushing, the career of sailor-diplomat Robert Wilson Shufeldt is described by Frederick C. Drake, *The Empire of the Seas* (1984).

Journal articles provide the core for some even lesser-known officers. Two articles—David W. Francis, "The United States Navy and the Johnson's Island Conspiracy: The Case of John C. Carter" (1980), and Bradley A. Rodgers, "The Northern Theater in the Civil War" (1988)—recount the one-vessel Great Lakes fleet commanded by John Carter. Captain John B. Montgomery and his command of the larger Pacific Squadron is described by Mitchell S. Goldberg, "Naval Operations of the United States Pacific Squadron in 1861" (1973). The career of John P. Gillis, who hailed from DuPont's state of Delaware and served under DuPont, is told by Steven Hill, "Commodore John P. Gillis: Delaware's Other Civil War Naval Hero" (1987). Percival Drayton, another DuPont subordinate, tells part of his own story in Ashby Halsey, Jr., ed., "What Its Captain

Thought of the Monitor *Passaic:* 'I Rue the Day I Got into the Ironclad Business' '' (1965).

Finally, about one-half of all of the Union navy's officers were volunteers. The difficulties of one volunteer officer are described by Mark Roman Schultz, "Acting Master Samuel B. Gregory: The Trials of an Unexperienced Captain" (1990). And six chapters of Reuben Elmore Stivers' book, *Privateers and Volunteers: The Men and Women of Our Reserve Naval Forces, 1766 to 1866* (1975), tell the story of this overlooked group of officers, sailors, and nurses.

SCIENTISTS, ENGINEERS, AND INVENTORS

Historians continue to debate whether the Civil War was the first modern war, but without question the technical advances and changes that occurred in the mid-nineteenth century in ordnance, shipbuilding, and ship propulsion had important consequences for the naval war.

John Dahlgren always first and foremost thought of himself as a line officer; however, his reputation stems primarily from his ordnance work, especially his distinctive bottle-shaped smoothbore cannon. While there has been no published biography of Dahlgren, there is a large body of literature relating to his life and career. The usual starting point is Madeleine Vinton Dahlgren, *Memoirs of John A. Dahlgren* (1882). Written by his wife to exonerate her husband and also to secure a pension for herself from Congress, the book was based on Dahlgren's private journals; it must be used with extreme care, as much for what it fails to mention as for what it does. Books on Dahlgren's ordnance research include Spencer Tucker, *Arming the Fleet* (1989), Taylor Peck, *Round-Shot to Rockets* (1949), and Eugene B. Canfield, *Civil War Naval Ordnance* (1969). Dahlgren's relationship as a military adviser to President Lincoln is examined by Robert V. Bruce in *Lincoln and the Tools of War* (1956). Two recent Ph.D. dissertations— Robert John Schneller, Jr., "The Contentious Innovator: A Biography of Rear Admiral John A. Dahlgren" (1991), which emphasizes Dahlgren's work in ordnance, and Thomas J. Legg, "Quest for Glory: The Naval Career of John A. Dahlgren" (1994), which focuses more on Dahlgren's rise to and subsequent command of the South Atlantic Blockading Squadron—provide less glowing assessments of Dahlgren.

Benjamin Franklin Isherwood served as the navy's engineer in chief throughout the Civil War, and he worked diligently to improve the steam power of the navy's fleet. Edward W. Sloan III, *B. F. Isherwood, Naval Engineer* (1965), does a good job placing Isherwood in the larger picture of America's developing industrial economy. Alban Stimers, another navy engineer, is the subject of two essays: John D. Milligan, ed., "An Engineer aboard the Monitor" (1970), and Dana Wegner, "Ericsson's High Priest" (1975).

Neither Charles O. Boutelle nor Charles Ellet, Jr. was a Union navy officer, but both made important contributions to the Union navy. Because of his work with the Coast Survey, Boutelle helped plan a number of expeditions, most of them along the south Atlantic coast. His service is described by Darwin H. Stapleton, "Assistant Charles O. Boutelle of the United States Coast Survey" (1971). Ellet was actually commissioned as a colonel by Secretary of War Edwin Stanton, but he still deserves mention here. A well-known railroad engineer, he fought a long battle to get the navy to build a steam ram. It took the success of the CSS *Virginia* in the Battle of Hampton Roads for him to secure government support, and he eventually designed and commanded a small fleet of rams, which led to the Union's control of the Mississippi, although Ellet himself was wounded and subsequently died. Gene D. Lewis's *Charles Ellet, Jr.: The Engineer as Individualist* (1968) details Ellet's entire life, while John D. Milligan, "Charles Ellet and His Naval Steam Ram" (1963), explains Ellet's efforts to get his rams built.

PUBLISHED PRIMARY SOURCES AND MANUSCRIPT COLLECTIONS

In addition to the many primary sources already cited—John D. Hayes, ed., *Samuel Francis DuPont: A Selection from His Civil War Letters,* most notably—there are a number of invaluable published primary sources. Foremost are the U.S. Navy Department's *Official Records of the Union and Confederate Navies* (1894–1922). Thousands of pertinent documents are also in the U.S. War Department's *The War of the Rebellion: A Compilation of the Official Records of the Union and Confederate Armies* (1880–1901).

Secretary of the Navy Welles began a private diary shortly after the war began, and it contains many interesting statements about various officers. The best edition is edited by Howard K. Beale, *Diary of Gideon Welles* (1960). Robert M. Thompson and Richard Wainwright edited a two-volume collection of Assistant Secretary of the Navy Fox's papers, *Confidential Correspondence of Gustavus Fox* (1918–1919). This private correspondence between Fox and many of the leading officers is only a small portion of the Fox papers at the New-York Historical Society.

The logical place to begin manuscript research is in Washington, D.C. The Library of Congress houses seemingly countless collections of individual officers, not to mention many other collections useful to the study of Civil War navy officers. John R. Sellers, *Civil War Manuscripts* (1986), gives descriptions of more than one thousand Civil War collections at the Library of Congress, many of them part of the large Navy Historical Foundation Collection. The National Archives holds much of the institutional records of the navy. Record Group 45, Naval Records Collection of the Office of Naval Records and Library, and its hundreds of individual entries, is the largest single group of naval documents. Also important are: Record Group 19, Records of the Bureau of Ships; Record Group 23, Records of the Coast and Geodetic Survey; Record Group 59, General Records of the Department of State; Record Group 71, Bureau of Yards and Docks; and Record Group 74, Bureau of Ordnance.

BIBLIOGRAPHY

Barnes, Elinor, and James A. Barnes, eds. *Naval Surgeon.* 2 vols. Bloomington: Indiana University Press, 1963.

Bradford, James C., ed. *Admirals of the New Steel Navy: Makers of the American Naval Tradition, 1880–1930.* Annapolis, MD: Naval Institute Press, 1990.

————. *Captains of the Old Steam Navy: Makers of the American Naval Tradition, 1840–1880.* Annapolis, MD: Naval Institute Press, 1986.

Brown, Stephen D. "Christopher Raymond Perry Rodgers: Mentor of the New Navy." In *Naval History: The Sixth Naval History Symposium, 1983.* Edited by Daniel Masterson. Wilmington, DE: Scholarly Resources, 1987.

Browning, Robert Monroe, Jr. *From Cape Charles to Cape Fear: The North Atlantic Blockading Squadron during the Civil War.* Tuscaloosa: University of Alabama Press, 1993.

Bruce, Robert V. *Lincoln and the Tools of War.* 1956. Reprint, Urbana: University of Illinois Press, 1989.

Buhl, Lance C. "Mariners and Machines: Resistance to Technological Change in the U.S. Navy, 1865–1869." *Journal of American History* 61 (December 1974): 703–727.

Canfield, Eugene. *Civil War Naval Ordnance.* Washington, D.C.: Government Printing Office, 1969.

Chandler, Alfred D., Jr. "DuPont, Dahlgren, and the Civil War Nitre Shortage." *Military Affairs* 13 (Fall 1949): 142–149.

Chandler, Porter R. "How My Grandfather Nearly Lost the Civil War." *American Neptune* 33 (January 1973): 5–15.

Cogar, William B. *Dictionary of Admirals of the U.S. Navy.* Vol. 1: *1862–1900.* Annapolis, MD: Naval Institute Press, 1989.

Cornish, Dudley Taylor, and Virginia Jeans Laas. *Lincoln's Lee: The Life of Samuel Phillips Lee, United States Navy, 1812–1897.* Lawrence: University of Kansas Press, 1986.

Dahlgren, Madeleine Vinton. *Memoirs of John A. Dahlgren, Rear Admiral United States Navy.* Boston: J. R. Osgood, 1882.

Davis, Charles H., Jr. *The Life of Charles H. Davis, Rear Admiral, 1807–1877.* Boston: Houghton Mifflin, 1899.

Drake, Frederick C. *The Empire of the Seas: A Biography of Rear Admiral Robert Wilson Shufeldt, U.S.N.* Honolulu: University of Hawaii Press, 1984.

DuPont, Henry A. *Rear-Admiral Samuel Francis DuPont, United States Navy: A Biography.* New York: National Americana Society, 1926.

Dyson, George. "Benjamin Franklin Isherwood." *U.S. Naval Institute Proceedings* 67 (August 1941): 1139–1146.

Ellicott, John M. *The Life of John Ancum Winslow, Rear Admiral United States Navy.* New York: Putnam, 1902.

Farragut, Loyall. *The Life and Letters of David Glasgow Farragut, First Admiral of the United States Navy.* New York: D. Appleton, 1879.

Ferris, Norman B. *The Trent Affair.* Knoxville: University of Tennessee Press, 1977.

Forlenza, Gerard A., Jr. "A Navy Life: The Pre–Civil War Career of Rear Admiral Andrew Hull Foote." Ph.D. diss., Claremont Graduate School, 1991.

Francis, David W. "The United States Navy and the Johnson Island Conspiracy: The Case of John C. Carter." *Northwest Ohio Quarterly* 52(3) (1980): 229–243.

Gordon, Arthur. "The Great Stone Fleet: Calculated Catastrophe." *U.S. Naval Institute Proceedings* 94 (December 1968): 72–82.

Gardiner, Edward C., ed. "Narrative of Rear Admiral Goldsborough, U.S. Navy." *U.S. Naval Institute Proceedings* 59 (July 1933): 1023–1031.

Goldberg, Mitchell S. "Naval Operations of the United States Pacific Squadron in 1861." *American Neptune* 33 (January 1973): 41–51.

Hagan, Kenneth J. "Admiral David Dixon Porter: Strategist for a Navy in Transition." *U.S. Naval Institute Proceedings* 94 (July 1968): 139–143.

Halsey, Ashby. "What Its Captain Thought of the Monitor *Passaic:* 'I Rue the Day I Got into the Ironclad Business.' " *Civil War Times Illustrated* 4 (April 1965): 28–34.

Hamersly, Lewis R. *The Records of Living Officers of the U.S. Navy and Marine Corps: With a History of Naval Operations during the Rebellion of 1861–1865.* Philadelphia: J. P. Lippincott, 1870.

Hayes, John D., ed. *Samuel Francis DuPont: A Selection from His Civil War Letters.* 3 vols. Ithaca: Cornell University Press, 1969.

Headley, Joel T. *Farragut and Our Naval Commanders.* New York: E. B. Treat, 1867.

Henderson, Daniel M. *The Hidden Coasts: A Biography of Admiral Charles Wilkes.* New York: Sloane, 1953.

Henig, Gerald S. "Admiral Samuel F. DuPont, the Navy Department, and the Attack on Charleston, April 1863." *Naval War College Review* 32(1) (1979): 68–77.

Hill, Jim Dan. "Charles Wilkes—Turbulent Scholar of the Old Navy." *U.S. Naval Institute Proceedings* 57 (July 1931): 867–887.

———. *Sea Dogs of the Sixties: Farragut and Seven Contemporaries.* Minneapolis: University of Minnesota Press, 1935.

Hill, Steven. "Commander John P. Gillis: Delaware's Other Civil War Naval Hero." *Delaware History* 22(3) (1987): 186–203.

Hoppin, James M. *The Life of Andrew Hull Foote, Rear Admiral U.S. Navy.* New York: Harper & Brothers, 1874.

Johnson, Ludwell H., III. *Red River Campaign: Politics and Cotton in the Civil War.* 1958. Reprint, Kent, OH: Kent State University Press, 1993.

Johnson, Robert E. *Rear Admiral John Rodgers, 1812–1882.* Annapolis, MD: Naval Institute Press, 1967.

Karsten, Peter. *The Naval Aristocracy: The Golden Age of Annapolis and the Emergence of Modern American Navalism.* New York: Free Press, 1972.

Laas, Virginia Jeans. " 'On the Qui Vive for the Long Letter': Washington Letters from a Navy Wife, 1861." *Civil War History* 29 (March 1983): 28–52.

———. " 'Sleepless Sentinels': The North Atlantic Blockading Squadron, 1862–1864." *Civil War History* 31 (March 1985): 24–38.

———. "The Courtship and Marriage of Elizabeth Blair and Samuel Phillips Lee: A Problem in Historical Detection." *Midwest Quarterly* 27(1) (1985): 13–29.

———, ed. *Wartime Washington: The Civil War Letters of Elizabeth Blair Lee.* Urbana: University of Illinois Press, 1991.

Legg, Thomas J. "Quest for Glory: The Naval Career of John A. Dahlgren, 1826–1870." Ph.D. diss., College of William and Mary, 1994.

Lewis, Charles L. *David Glasgow Farragut.* 2 vols. Annapolis, MD: Naval Institute Press, 1941–1943.

Lewis, Gene D. *Charles Ellet, Jr.: The Engineer as Individualist, 1810–1862.* Urbana: University of Illinois Press, 1968.

Lewis, Paul. *Yankee Admiral: A Biography of David Dixon Porter.* New York: McKay, 1968.

Long, David. *Nothing Too Daring: A Biography of Commodore David Porter.* Annapolis: Naval Institute Press, 1970.

Long, John S. "Glory Hunting Off Havana: Wilkes and the Trent Affair." *Civil War History* 9 (June 1963): 133–144.

Macartney, Clarence. *Mr. Lincoln's Admirals.* New York: Funk and Wagnalls, 1956.

Mahan, Alfred Thayer. *Admiral Farragut.* New York: D. Appleton, 1892.

Maihafer, H. J. "The Partnership." *U.S. Naval Institute Proceedings* 93 (May 1967): 49–57.

Martin, Christopher. *Damn the Torpedoes: The Story of America's First Admiral, David Glasgow Farragut.* New York: Abelard-Schuman, 1970.

Meade, Rebecca Paulding. *Life of Hiram Paulding, Rear Admiral, U.S.N.* New York: Baker and Taylor Company, 1910.

Merrill, James M. *DuPont: The Making of an Admiral.* New York: Dodd, Mead, 1986.

Milligan, John D. "Charles Ellet and His Naval Steam Ram." *Civil War History* 9 (June 1963): 121–132.

———. "Charles Ellet, Naval Architect: A Study in Nineteenth-Century Professionalism." *American Neptune* 31 (January 1971): 52–72.

———, ed. *From the Fresh Water Navy, 1861–1864: The Letters of Acting Master's Mate Henry R. Browne and Acting Ensign Symmes E. Browne.* Annapolis, MD: Naval Institute Press, 1970.

Mordell, Albert. "Farragut at the Crossroads." *U.S. Naval Institute Proceedings* 57 (February 1931): 151–161.

Peck, Taylor. *Round-Shot to Rockets: A History of the Washington Navy Yard and U.S. Naval Gun Factory.* Annapolis, MD: Naval Institute Press, 1949.

Porter, David Dixon. *Incidents and Anecdotes of the Civil War.* New York: D. Appleton, 1885.

———. *The Naval History of the Civil War.* New York: Shuman Publishing Company, 1886.

Rodgers, Bradley A. "The Northern Theater in the Civil War: The U.S.S. *Michigan* and Confederate Intrigue on the Great Lakes." *American Neptune* 48 (Spring 1988): 96–105.

Roske, Ralph J., and Charles Van Dorn. *Lincoln's Commando: The Biography of Commander William B. Cushing, U.S.N.* New York: Harper & Brothers, 1957.

Schneller, Robert J., Jr. "The Contentious Innovator: A Biography of Rear Admiral John A. Dahlgren, U.S.N. 1809–1870: Generational Conflict, Ordnance Technology, and Command Afloat in the Nineteenth Century Navy." Ph.D. diss., Duke University, 1991.

Schoun, Karl. *U.S. Navy Biographical Dictionary.* New York: Franklin Watts, 1964.

Schultz, Mark Roman. "Acting Master Samuel B. Gregory: The Trials of an Unexperienced Captain on the South Atlantic Blockading Squadron." *American Neptune* 50 (Spring 1990): 89–93.

Sellers, John R. *Civil War Manuscripts: A Guide to Collections in the Manuscript Division of the Library of Congress.* Washington, D.C.: Library of Congress, 1986.

Sloan, Edward W., III. *B. F. Isherwood, Naval Engineer: The Years As Engineer in Chief, 1861–1869.* Annapolis, MD: Naval Institute Press, 1965.

Soley, James R. *Admiral Porter.* New York: D. Appleton, 1903.

Stanton, William. *The Great United States Exploring Expedition of 1838–1842.* Berkeley: University of California Press, 1975.

Stapleton, Darwin H. "Assistant Charles O. Boutelle of the United States Coast Survey with the South Atlantic Blockading Squadron, 1861–1863." *American Neptune* 31 (October 1971): 252–267.

Still, William N., Jr. "Admiral Goldsborough's Feisty Career." *Civil War Times Illustrated* 17(10) (1979): 12–20.

———. " 'Porter . . . Is the Best Man': This Was Gideon Welles's View of the Man He Chose to Command the Mississippi Squadron." *Civil War Times Illustrated* 16(2) (1977): 4–9, 44–47.

Stimers, Alban. "An Engineer aboard the Monitor." Edited by John D. Milligan. *Civil War Times Illustrated* 9 (April 1970): 28–35.

Stivers, Reuben Elmore. *Privateers and Volunteers: The Men and Women of Our Reserve Naval Forces: 1766 to 1866.* Annapolis, MD: Naval Institute Press, 1975.

Thompson, Robert Means, and Richard Wainwright, eds. *Confidential Correspondence of Gustavus Vasa Fox: Assistant Secretary of the Navy, 1861–1865.* 2 vols. 1918–1919. Reprint, New York: Books for Library Press, 1970.

Todorich, Charles. *The Spirited Years: A History of the Antebellum Naval Academy.* Annapolis, MD: Naval Institute Press, 1984.

Tucker, Spencer. *Arming the Fleet: U.S. Navy Ordnance in the Muzzle-Loading Era.* Annapolis, MD: Naval Institute Press, 1989.

United States. Navy Department. *Official Records of the Union and Confederate Navies in the War of the Rebellion.* 31 vols. Washington, D.C.: Government Printing Office, 1894–1922.

United States. War Department. *The War of the Rebellion: A Compilation of the Official Records of the Union and Confederate Armies.* 128 vols. Washington, D.C.: Government Printing Office, 1880–1901.

Wegner, Dana. "Ericsson's High Priest: Alban C. Stimers." *Civil War Times Illustrated* 13 (February 1975): 26–34.

Welles, Gideon. *The Diary of Gideon Welles.* Edited by Howard K. Beale. New York: W. W. Norton, 1960.

West, Richard S., Jr. "Admiral Farragut and General Butler." *U.S. Naval Institute Proceedings* 82 (June 1956): 635–643.

———. "Relations between Farragut and Porter." *U.S. Naval Institute Proceedings* 61 (July 1935): 985–996.

———. *The Second Admiral: A Life of David Dixon Porter, 1813–1891.* New York: Coward-McCann, 1937.

Wilkes, Charles. *Autobiography of Rear Admiral Charles Wilkes, U.S. Navy, 1798–1877.* Edited by William J. Morris et al. Washington, D.C.: Government Printing Office, 1978.

———. *Narrative of the United States Exploring Expedition during the Years 1838, 1839, 1840, 1841, 1842.* 5 vols. Philadelphia: C. Sherman, 1844.

28

Leadership—Confederate Naval Officers

Theodore P. Savas

The men and ships that plied the high seas and inland waterways under the Confederate banner have not enjoyed the widespread attention lavished by historians upon land-based operations. The best place to begin any inquiry in this area remains Thomas Scharf's highly biased century-old *History of the Confederate States Navy* (1887). Scharf, a midshipman in the Southern navy, pieced together this history without the benefit of the scores of manuscript sources now available. Despite its shortcomings, Scharf's work offers good biographical portraits of the Confederate navy's officers. A trio of general studies are Bern Anderson's *By Sea and by River: The Naval History of the Civil War* (1962), Virgil Carrington Jones's three-volume *The Civil War at Sea* (1962), and Fletcher Pratt's more narrowly focused *Civil War on Western Waters* (1956). All offer solid insights and, to a greater or lesser degree, scholarly analysis of the careers of various Confederate officers and of Confederate naval policy in general.

Students desiring a centralized perspective of Richmond's naval policy and its consequences on the war effort will enjoy Joseph T. Durkin's excellent biography of the Confederacy's creative naval secretary, *Stephen R. Mallory: Confederate Navy Chief* (1954). Durkin explores the secretary's relations with his various naval officers and discusses in depth the almost insurmountable difficulties these men faced in constructing and operating the South's motley navy. Tom Wells's award-winning *The Confederate Navy: A Study in Organization* (1969) is especially beneficial and must be consulted. Another excellent policy-related study is William N. Still's "Confederate Naval Strategy: The Ironclad"

(1961). Richmond's naval policy in many cases prescribed the behavior of officers afloat and should be consulted in this regard.

By far the most written-about Southern naval officer is Raphael Semmes, the captain of the magnificent raider CSS *Alabama*. A good place to begin a study of Semmes and his adventures on the high seas is his own recollections, *Memoirs of Service Afloat* (1869). His account chronicles his daring waterborne exploits and includes an interesting but romanticized description of the *Alabama*'s death duel with the USS *Kearsarge* off Cherbourg, France, in 1864. While generally well written, *Service Afloat* is an often caustic and unreliable memoir. It has been reprinted several times under various titles. A relatively recent addition to the Semmes-*Alabama* literature is Charles Grayson Summersell's *CSS* Alabama: *Builder, Captain, and Plans* (1985), a handsome and informative book that includes several suitable-for-framing drawings of the vessel tucked into a rear envelope. Another excellent modern *Alabama* study may be found in "Special Commemorative Naval Issue, CSS *Alabama*, 1864–1989" (1989).

Surprisingly few good biographies of Semmes exist. The latest study, John M. Taylor's 1995 *Confederate Raider: Raphael Semmes of the Alabama*, is a brilliantly written and balanced account of his Confederate service. Taylor's stirring study displaces Edward Boykin's *Ghost Ship of the Confederacy: The Story of the* Alabama *and Her Captain, Raphael Semmes* (1957), an outdated account that focused primarily on Semmes's service with the *Alabama*. A modern article on Semmes's first command is found in Maurice Melton's "Cruise of the Rebel Sea Wolf *Sumter:* Her Career and Triumph" (1982). Another useful article, "The CSS *Alabama:* Roving Terror of the Seas," by Howard P. Nash, Jr. (1963), is a popular account of the *Alabama*'s career. A picturesque account of life on Semmes's ship is found in Arthur Sinclair's *Two Years on the* Alabama (1989). A true collector's piece is the small autobiographical pamphlet *A Short History of Admiral Semmes* (1888), which was tucked inside packages of Duke's cigarettes. Semmes's final weeks of service, with the landlocked fleet of clumsy ironclads on the James River, are chronicled in Stanley Hoole's "Admiral on Horseback: The Diary of Brigadier General Raphael Semmes, February–May, 1865" (1975).

Raphael Semmes's first officer, John M. Kell, was also a man of imposing maritime stature, and not simply because of his better-known captain. Kell, a native Georgian and graduate of Annapolis, spent seventeen years in the U.S. Navy before resigning his commission to serve the Confederacy on the *Sumter, Alabama,* and as captain of the ironclad CSS *Richmond*. His unassuming but solid memoirs, *Recollections of a Naval Life* (1900), is the logical starting point for a study of Kell. His fascinating career, which included service under Semmes on both the *Sumter* and *Alabama,* compelled historian Norman C. Delaney to pen *John McIntosh Kell of the Raider* Alabama (1973), an award-winning biography of the sailor's life. Almost two decades after the *Alabama* came to rest on the bottom of the English Channel, Kell provided an engaging interview on the history and sinking of the ship to Captain Alfred Iverson Barnham, which was published as "The Story of the *Alabama:* Interview with Captain John McIntosh Kell, Executive Officer of the *Alabama*" (1930).

Two other prominent naval officers have enjoyed widely recognized and competent full-length biographies, both penned by the same author. The career of John Taylor Wood, a daring sailor who commanded an aft gun on the CSS *Virginia* during its fight with the USS *Monitor* and who later commanded the CSS *Tallahassee,* is well documented in Royce Shingleton's *John Taylor Wood: Sea Ghost of the Confederacy* (1979). Another less-known (and less reliable) biography of Wood is Arthur Thruston's *Tallahassee Skipper* (1981). A large cache of original material exists on Wood in the form of the John Taylor Wood papers in the Southern Historical Collection, University of North Carolina. This collection includes Wood's own diary. The "Sea Ghost" himself penned three articles after the war. The most widely read of these, "The First Fight of Ironclads," written for *Century Magazine,* deals with the *Virginia-Monitor* engagement and was reprinted in the first volume of Johnson and Buel, eds., *Battles and Leaders of the Civil War* (1956). The remaining articles both appeared in *Century* and include an account of the *Tallahassee* and Woods's escape to Cuba after the collapse of the Confederacy. Several secondary articles on this officer and his daring exploits have graced various periodicals, including Royce Shingleton's "Cruise of the CSS *Tallahassee*" (1976).

Another of Royce Shingleton's biographical subjects is John Newland Maffitt, the first commander of the raider CSS *Florida* and the only Confederate naval officer known to have been born at sea. Shingleton ably chronicles Maffitt's wartime career in his recent *High Seas Confederate: The Life and Times of John Newland Maffitt* (1994). Maffitt is also the subject of an older and now woefully outdated biography, *Sea Devil of the Confederacy: The Story of the* Florida *and Her Captain, John Newland Maffitt* (1959), by Edward C. Boykin. Other Maffitt sources include his widow's romantic tale, *The Life and Services of John Newland Maffitt* (1906), Rose Duncan's *Romantic Career of a Naval Officer, Federal and Confederate: Captain Maffitt of the USS* Crusader *and the CSS* Florida" (1935), and James Sprunt's "Running of the Blockade: A Sketch of Captain Maffitt" (1896).

After Semmes, Kell, Wood, and Maffitt, coverage is more limited. There are a fistful of interesting studies (some modern) on several relatively obscure Confederate officers. One such individual who deserves more attention from historians than he has heretofore received is Charles W. "Savez" Read. After suffering the ignominy of bringing up the rear of his 1860 graduating class of Annapolis, Read experienced active operations on the western inland rivers (which included service on the CSS *Arkansas*), served aboard the CSS *Florida,* and eventually commanded two raiding ships off the northeast coast before being captured. Given his widespread service, it is unfortunate that this daredevil sailor suffered from an aversion to the pen. His brief memoir, "Reminiscences of the Confederate States Navy" (1876), fills a critical gap in the literature, but his exploits deserve a full-length modern treatment. "Cruise of the *Clarence, Tacony-Archer*," by Robert H. Woods, is an informative article on Read's privateering days (1895). A sympathetic but brief account of Read's career can be found in Julia P. Wickham's "Commanders of the Confederate Navy: Charles Read of Mississippi" (1929).

Another interesting officer with a less colorful resumé is William Harwar Parker. The scholastically oriented Parker graduated first in his class at Annapolis in 1848 and served as the captain of the Charleston-based ironclad CSS *Palmetto State* before organizing the Confederate States Naval Academy. He wrote "The Confederate States Navy" (1989) and his own memoirs, *Recollections of a Naval Officer, 1841–1865* (1883). An interesting letter from Parker is "The Merrimac & Monitor" (1883).

Little has been written about the captains and officers of the Confederate ironclads. Exploration down this avenue must begin with a careful reading of William N. Still's *Iron Afloat: The Story of the Confederate Armorclads* (1971), an insightful study rich in well-reasoned analysis and sound conclusions on the construction and operation of the ironclads. *Iron Afloat* accesses the abilities and explores the feats performed by many of the officers who served aboard the ironclads and is a rich mine of naval titles. An earlier Still title, *Confederate Shipbuilding* (1969), is also valuable and should be consulted. Although Maurice Melton's *The Confederate Ironclads* (1968) was substantially superseded by Still's classic, it is worth perusing.

Despite their fearsome appearance and vaunted abilities, the iron behemoths constructed across the South ended the war with a disappointing service record. In most cases they functioned as little more than floating batteries, and service aboard these ships was generally mundane and physically debilitating. Consequently, individual titles examining the careers of the officers of these vessels are scarce. After a long tenure in the U.S. Navy, Duncan Nathaniel Ingraham oversaw the construction of the ironclad CSS *Palmetto State* and participated in a sea raid with the ironclad CSS *Chicora* that failed to lift the blockade of Charleston on January 30, 1863. A brief and favorable account of his life is found in a pamphlet by Francis B. C. Bradlee, *A Forgotten Chapter in Our Naval History: A Sketch of the Career of Duncan Nathaniel Ingraham* (1923). John K. Mitchell, who commanded the James River fleet in the fighting at Trent's Reach in early 1865, is the subject of Wayne D. Lett's "John Kirkwood Mitchell and Confederate Naval Defeat" (1972). Another officer who saw service in Virginia before being put in command of Charleston's naval flotilla was John Randolph Tucker, the subject of James Rochelle's *Life of Rear Admiral John Randolph Tucker* (1903).

First Officer Catesby ap R. Jones, who took command of the CSS *Virginia* when its captain, Franklin "Old Buck" Buchanan, fell wounded in the famous fight with the *Monitor,* left a stirring record of his service and this epic sea battle in "The Iron-Clad *Virginia*" (19xx). Despite Jones's credible performance, he was eventually replaced by Josiah Tattnall, a competent officer whose exploits are chronicled by the prolific Georgian Charles Colcock Jones in the sentimental account, *The Life and Services of Commodore Josiah Tattnall* (1878). The wounded veteran officer replaced by Catesby Jones, Franklin Buchanan, enjoyed a remarkable career with the Confederate navy. In addition to commanding the *Virginia,* he also captained the CSS *Tennessee,* a powerful ironclad that was forced to capitulate after a fierce engagement in Mobile Bay in 1864. Despite his stellar service and opinionated tongue, the only biography of his life is Charles L. Lewis's *Admiral Franklin Buchanan* (1929), an outdated and superficial narrative of little value. A popular overview of Buchanan's exploits may be found in Emory Thomas's "Old Buck—Admiral Franklin Buchanan" (1978).

Other articles written by or dealing with officers serving aboard ironclads include "The Story of the *Arkansas*" (1884), by George W. Gift, who relates his service as a gunnery officer aboard that remarkable vessel during its deadly voyage down the Yazoo and Mississippi rivers to the Confederate bastion of Vicksburg. Harriet Castlen's little-known *Hope Bids Me Onward* (1945) is a useful edited compendium of Gift's letters and musing. Another *Arkansas*-related study, infrequently utilized because it is unpublished, is Cynthia Mosely's "The Naval Career of Henry K. Stevens as Revealed in His Letters" (1951). Mosely's unpublished master's thesis is an assessment of the executive officer (and last captain) of the *Arkansas,* whose candid letters to his wife left a remarkable portrait of the men and ship he served.

Three recent accounts have focused primarily on ironclad operations in specific geographic areas. Robert G. Elliott's long toil has provided readers with a solid full-length study of the fascinating but brief life of the CSS *Albemarle* and the officers that served it in *Ironclad of the Roanoke: Gilbert Elliott's Albemarle* (1994). Gilbert Elliott left his own account of these events in "The Career of the Confederate Ram Albemarle" (1888). Maxine Turner offers an even thinner slice of Southern naval history with her excellent *Navy Gray: A Story of the Confederate Navy on the Chattahoochee and Apalachicola Rivers* (1988). *Navy Gray* is a reworked and expanded edition of her earlier master's thesis, an intelligent discussion of Confederate naval policy that includes valuable information on a number of Southern naval officers. One of the finest accounts to appear in recent years is John M. Coski's microstudy, *The Confederate Navy on the James River* (1995). Coski, a historian with the Museum of the Confederacy, examines in great detail the men and ships that plied the James during the years 1861 through 1865, Confederate naval and river defense policies, shipbuilding, and other matters of waterborne and combined operational interest.

Other articles that directly or indirectly treat lesser-known naval officers and their Confederate careers exist, but not in large numbers. Many are obscure, hard to locate, and difficult to access. Stanley Hoole's rather colorless account, *Four Years in the Confederate Navy: The Career of Captain John Low on the CSS* Fingal, Florida, Alabama, Tuscaloosa, and Ajax (1964), discusses the officers and voyages of those vessels. James I. Waddell, the captain of the CSS

Shenandoah—the bane of the Northern whaling fleet—left his memoirs, *CSS Shenandoah: The Memoirs of Lieutenant Commanding James Waddell* (1960). Another rare *Shenandoah* title, Cornelius E. Hunt's *The* Shenandoah; *or, The Last Confederate Cruiser* (1867) is a valuable memoir by one of that ship's officers. A popular and colorful memoir, *Recollections of a Rebel Reefer* (1971) by James M. Morgan, provides excellent information on several topics and good sketches of a variety of officers, and it includes an observant description of the Confederate naval school. A modern treatment that discusses many of the officers mentioned heretofore, as well as others, may be found in William M. Robinson's *The Confederate Privateers* (1994), an important contribution to naval literature.

Another account of a Confederate officer, not widely read but meriting examination, is Daniel B. Lucas's *Memoir of John Yates Beall: His Life, Trial, Correspondence* (1865), a sympathetic account of the Confederate privateer-spy who was eventually hung for his nefarious activities.

The Confederate submarine service, which launched several underwater and torpedo boats, deserves to be studied more closely. The only successful submarine operated by the Confederates was the CSS *Hunley*, lost off Charleston, South Carolina, in 1864. The best account of the service of these boats and the men who manned them is William A. Alexander's "In the History of the Confederate States Navy: Work of Submarine Boats" (1902).

Reference works that all serious students should consult include the messages, reports, and letters in *War of the Rebellion: Official Records of the Union and Confederate Navies* (1894–1921), the *Register of Officers of the Confederate States Navy, 1861–1865* (1931), and Thomas T. Moebs's privately printed *Confederate Navy Research Guide* (1991).

BIBLIOGRAPHY

Alexander, William A. "In the history of the Confederate States Navy: Work of Submarine Boats." *Southern Historical Society Papers* (1902).

Anderson, Bern. *By Sea and by River: The Naval History of the Civil War.* New York: Knopf, 1962.

Branham, Alfred Iverson. "The Story of the Sinking of *Alabama:* Interview with Captain John McIntosh Kell, Executive Officer of the *Alabama.*" Atlanta: Cornell Press, 1930.

Boykin, Edward C. *Sea Devil of the Confederacy: The Story of the* Florida *and Her Captain, John Newland Maffitt.* New York: Funk & Wagnalls, 1959.

———. *Ghost Ship of the Confederacy: The story of the* Alabama *and Her Captain, Raphael Semmes.* New York: Funk & Wagnalls, 1957.

Bradlee, Francis B. C. *A Forgotten Chapter in Our Naval History: A Sketch of the Career of Duncan Nathaniel Ingraham.* Salem: The Essex Institute, 1923.

Castlen, Harriet G. *Hope Bids Me Onward.* Savannah: Chatham Printing Co., 1945.

Clayton, W. F. *A Narrative of the Confederates States Navy.* Bulletin Pee Dee Historical Association, 1910.

Coker, P. C. *Charleston's Maritime Heritage, 1670–1865.* Charleston, 1987.

"Commissioned and Warrant Officers of the Navy of the Confederate States, January 1, 1864." *Southern Historical Society Papers* 3 (1877): 106–107.

Confederate States of America, Navy Department. *Ordnance Instructions for the Confederate States Navy.* London: Saunders, Otley, 1864.

Coski, John. *The Confederate Navy on the James River.* Campbell, CA: Savas Woodbury, 1995.

Davis, William C. *Duel between the First Ironclads.* Garden City, NY: Doubleday, 1975.

Dawson, Francis W. *Reminiscences of Confederate Service, 1861–1865.* Baton Rouge: Louisiana State University Press, 1980.

Delaney, Norman C. *John McIntosh Kell of the Raider* Alabama. University: University of Alabama Press, 1973.

De Leon, Perry M. *Navies in the War and the Confederate Navy in the War between the States.* Washington, D.C.: Shaw Brothers, 1910.

Donnelly, Ralph W. "Personnel of the Confederate Navy." *Civil War Times Illustrated* (January 1975).

———. *Revenue Marine Service: The Nucleus of the Confederate Navy.* Naval Institute Proceedings.

Doyle, Elizabeth J. "Eleven Letters of Raphael Semmes, 1866–1888." *Alabama Review* 5 (July 1952): 222–232.

Dudley, William S. *Going South: U.S. Navy Officer Resignations and Dismissals on the Eve of the Civil War.* Washington, D.C.: Naval Historical Foundation, 1981.

Duncan, Rose. *Romantic Career of a Naval Officer, Federal and Confederate: Captain Maffitt of the USS* Crusader *and the CSS* Florida. Spray, NC: D. Rose, 1935.

Durkin, Joseph T. *Stephen R. Mallory: Confederate Navy Chief.* Chapel Hill: University of North Carolina Press, 1954.

Dyer, Brainerd. "Confederate Naval and Privateering Activities in the Pacific." *Pacific Historical Review* 3 (1934): 433–443.

Eggleston, John R. "The Navy of the Confederate States." *Confederate Veteran* 15 (1907): 449–453.

Elliott, Gilbert. "The Career of the Confederate Ram Albemarle." *Century Magazine.* 1888.

Elliott, Robert G. *Ironclad of the Roanoke: Gilbert Elliott's* Albemarle. Shippensburg, PA: White Mane, 1994.

Evans, Cerinda W. "A Biographical Sketch of Robert Baker Pegram, 1811–1894, Lieutenant, U.S. Navy, Captain, C.S. Navy." Newport News, VA, n.d.

Folk, Lt. Winston. "The Confederate States Naval Academy." *U.S. Naval Institute Proceedings* 60 (September 1934): 1235–1240.

Gibbons, Tony. *Warships and Naval Battles of the Civil War.* New York: Gallery Books, 1989.

Gift, George W. "The Story of the *Arkansas.*" *Southern Historical Society Papers* (1884).

Gilbert, Benjamin Franklin. "The Confederate Raider *Shenandoah:* The Elusive Destroyer in the Pacific and the Arctic." *Journal of the West* 4, 2 (April 1965).

Hanks, Carlos C. *The Last Confederate Raider.* U.S. Naval Institute Proceedings 67 (1941): 21–24.

———. *A Commerce Raider off New York.* U.S. Naval Institute Proceedings 66 (1940): 1237–1240.

Hearn, Chester G. *Gray Raiders of the Sea: How Eight Confederate Warships Destroyed the Union's High Seas Commerce.* Camden, NJ: International Marine Publishers, 1992.

Heite, Edward F. "Captain Robert B. Pegram: Hero under Four Flags." *Virginia Cavalcade* 14 (Autumn 1965): 38–43.

Herndon, G. Melville. "The Confederate States Naval Academy." *Virginia Magazine of History and Biography* 69 (July 1961): 300–323.

Hoehling, A. A. *Damn the Torpedoes: Naval Incidents of the Civil War.* Winston-Salem, NC: J. F. Blair, 1989.

Holt, Thad, Jr. "The Organization of the Confederate Navy." *Arkansas Historical Quarterly* 7 (1947): 537–541.

Hoole, William Stanley. *Four Years in the Confederate Navy: The Career of Captain John Low on the CSS* Fingal, Florida, Alabama, Tuscaloosa, and Ajax. Athens: University of Georgia Press, 1964.

———. "Admiral on Horseback: The Diary of Brigadier General Raphael Semmes, February–May, 1865." Edited by Stanley Hoole. *Alabama Review* 28 (1975): 129–150.

Hunt, Cornelius E. *The* Shenandoah; *or, The Last Confederate Cruiser.* New York: G. W. Carlton, 1867.

Johnson, Robert U., and Clarence C. Buel, eds. *Battles and Leaders of the Civil War.* 4 vols. New York: Thomas Yoseloff, 1956.

Jones, Catesby ap R. "The Iron-Clad *Virginia.*" *Virginia Magazine of History and Biography.*

Jones, Charles C. *The Life and Services of Commodore Josiah Tattnall.* Savannah: Morning News Steam Printing House, 1878.

Jones, Virgil Carrington. *The Civil War at Sea.* 3 vols. New York: Holt, Rinehart, Winston, 1960–1962.

Kell, John McIntosh. *Recollections of a Naval Life.* Washington, D.C.: The Neale Company, 1900.

Lankford, Nelson D., ed. *An Irishman in Dixie: Thomas Conolly's Diary of the Fall of the Confederacy.* Columbia: University of South Carolina Press, 1988.

Lett, Wayne D. "John Kirkwood Mitchell and Confederate Naval Defeat." Ph.D. dissertation. 1972.

Lewis, Charles L. *Admiral Franklin Buchanan.* Baltimore: The Norman Remington Company, 1929.

Lucas, Daniel B. *Memoir of John Yates Beall: His Life, Trial; Correspondence.* Montreal: J. Lovell, 1865.

Maffitt, Emma Martin. *The Life and Services of John Newland Maffitt.* New York: Neal, 1906.

———. "The Confederate Navy." *Confederate Veteran* 25 (1917): 157–160, 217–221, 264–267, 315–317.

Maffitt, Captain John N. *"Life and Services of Raphael Semmes." South Atlantic* (November–December 1877).

———. *"Reminiscences of the Confederate Navy." United Service* October 1880.

Martin, John L. "Confederate Torpedo Boats." *Confederate Veteran* (1923).

McBlair, Charles H. "Historical Sketch of the Confederate Navy." *United Service* 3 (November 1880): 588–613.

Melton, Maurice. "Cruise of the Rebel Sea Wolf *Sumter:* Her Career and Triumph." *Civil War Time Illustrated* 20 (January 1982): 16–25.

———. *The Confederate Ironclads.* New York: T. Yoseloff, 1968.

———. "First and Last Cruise of the CSS *Atlanta.*" *Civil War Times Illustrated* (November 1971): 4–9, 44–46.

Minor, Hubbard T. "Diary of a Confederate Naval Cadet." *Civil War Times Illustrated* 13 (November 1974): 25–32; (December 1974): 24–28

Mitchell, John K. "Operations of Confederate States Navy." *Southern Historical Society Papers* 2 (1876): 240–244.

Moeb, Thomas T. *Confederate Navy Research Guide.* Williamsburg, VA: Moebs Publishing Co., 1991.

Morgan, James. *Recollections of a Rebel Reefer.* Boston: Houghton, Mifflin, 1917.

Morrison, F. W. "The Confederate Navy." *University of North Carolina Magazine* (November 1911).

Mosely, Cynthia, "The Naval Career of Henry K. Stevens as Revealed in his Letters." Master's thesis, University of North Carolina, 1951.

Moses, Armida. "The Confederate Navy." *Confederate Veteran* (1920).

Nash, Howard P., Jr. "The CSS *Alabama:* Roving Terror of the Seas." *Civil War Times Illustrated* (August 1963).

Officers in the Confederate States Navy, 1861–1865. Washington, D.C.: Government Printing Office, 1898.

Palmyra (Mo.) Confederate Monument Association. "The Confederate States Navy and a Brief History of What Became of It." *Southern Historical Society Papers* 28 (1900): 125–134.

Pappas, James D. "Organization of the Confederate States Navy." *Arkansas Historial Quarterly* 14 (1952): 112–124.

Parker, William Harwar. "The Confederate States Navy." In Clement Evans, ed., *Confederate Military History* 17 (1989): 1–115.

———. *Recollections of a Naval Officer, 1841–1865.* New York: C. Scribner's Sons, 1883.

———. "The *Merrimac & Monitor*" [letter from Captain Parker] *Southern Historical Society Papers* 11 (1883): 34–40.

———. *Elements of Seamanship* [textbook for the midshipmen of the C.S. Navy]. Richmond: McFarlane and Fergusson, 1864.

———. *Instruction for Naval Light Artillery, Afloat and Ashore.* Prepared and arranged by William H. Parker. Newport: J. Atkinson, 1862.

Pratt, Fletcher. *Civil War on Western Waters.* New York, 1956.

Ramsay, H. Aston. "Wonderful Career of the *Merrimac.*" *Confederate Veteran* (1907).

Read, Charles W. "Reminiscences of the Confederate States Navy." *Southern Historical Society Papers* 1 (1876): 331–336.

Roberts, William Paul. "John Dunwoody Bulloch and the Confederate Navy." *North Carolina Historical Review* 24 (July 1947): 315–366.

Robinson, William Morrison. *The Confederate Privateers.* Columbia: University of South Carolina Press, 1994.

Rochelle, James Henry. *Life of Rear Admiral John Randolph Tucker.* Washington, D.C.: Neale, 1903.

Scharf, J. Thomas. *History of the Confederate States Navy.* New York: Roger and Sherwood, 1887.

Selph, Fannie Eoline. "The Confederate Navy." Nashville, 1928.

Semmes, Raphael. *Memoirs of Service Afloat, during the War between the States.* Baltimore: Kelly, Piet, 1869.

———. *A Short History of Admiral Semmes.* New York, 1888.

———. *The Cruise of the* Alabama *and the* Sumter. London: Saunders, Otley, 1864.

Shingleton, Royce G. *John Taylor Wood: Sea Ghost of the Confederacy.* Athens: University of Georgia Press, 1979.

———. *High Seas Confederate: The Life and Times of John Newland Maffitt.* Columbia: University of South Carolina Press, 1994.

———. "Cruise of the CSS Tallahassee." *Civil War Times Illustrated* (May 1976).

Silverstone, Paul H. *Warships of the Civil War Navies.* Annapolis: Naval Institute Press, 1989.

Sinclair, Arthur. *Two Years on the* Alabama. Annapolis: Naval Institute Press, 1989.

Snair, Dale S. "Lt. Thomas P. Bell, C.S.N., and the Action at Trent's Reach." *Blue and Gray Magazine* 3 (February–March 1986): 23–27.

Sprunt, James. "Running of the Blockade: A Sketch of Captain Maffitt." *Southern Historical Society Papers* (1896).

Stern, Philip Van Doren. *The Confederate Navy: A Pictorial History.* Garden City, NY: Doubleday, 1962.

Still, William N., Jr. *Confederate Shipbuilding.* Columbia: University of South Carolina Press, 1969.

———. *Iron Afloat: The Story of the Confederate Armorclads.* Columbia: University of South Carolina Press, 1971.

———. "Confederate Behemoth—the CSS *Louisiana.*" *Civil War Times Illustrated* (November 1977): 20–25.

———. "The Confederate States Navy at Mobile." *American Historical Review* (Fall–Winter 1968): 127–144.

———. "Confederate Naval Policy and the Ironclads." *Civil War History* 9 (June 1963): 145–158.

———. "The Iron Rebel Navy: The Birth of the Armored Confederate Fleet." *Civil War Times Illustrated* (1980): 22–31.

———. "Confederate Naval Strategy: The Ironclad." *Journal of Southern History* 27 (August 1961).

Sulivane, Clement L. "The Arkansas at Vicksburg, 1862." *Confederate Veteran* (1917).

Summersell, Charles Grayson. *CSS* Alabama: *Builder, Captain, and Plans.* University, AL: University of Alabama Press, 1985.

Taylor, John M. *Confederate Raider: Raphael Semmes of the* Alabama. Washington, D.C.: Brassey's, 1995.

Thomas, Emory. "Old Buck: Admiral Franklin Buchanan." *Civil War Times Illustrated* (October 1978): 4–10, 43–46.

Thruston, Arthur. *Tallahassee Skipper: The Biography of John Taylor Wood.* Yarmouth, Nova Scotia: Lescarbot Press, 1981.

Todd, Hubert Henry. "The Building of the Confederate States Navy in Europe." Ph.D. dissertation. Nashville: Vanderbilt University, 1941.

Trexler, Harrison A. "The Confederate Navy Department and the Fall of New Orleans." *Southwestern Review* 19 (1933): 88–102.

Turner, Maxine. *Navy Gray: A Story of the Confederate Navy on the Chattahoochee and Apalachicola Rivers.* University, AL: University of Alabama Press, 1988.

"The *Virginia-Merrimac:* Behind the Scenes in the Confederate Navy Department." *United Services* 13 (May 1895): 493–497.

U.S. War Department. *War of the Rebellion: Official Records of the Union and Confederate Navies.* 29 vols. Washington, D.C., 1894–1921.

Waddell, James I. *CSS* Shenandoah: *The Memoirs of Lieutenant Commanding James I. Waddell.* Edited by James D. Horan. New York: Crown, 1960.

Wells, Tom H. *The Confederate Navy: A Study in Organization.* University, AL: University of Alabama Press, 1969.

Werlich, David P. *Admiral of the Amazon: John Randolph Tucker, His Confederate Colleagues, and Peru.* Charlottesville: University Press of Virginia, 1990.

Wickham, Julia Porter. "Commanders of the Confederate Navy: Charles Read of Mississippi." *Confederate Veteran* 37 (February 1929): 58–61.

Wood, John Taylor. "The First Fight of Iron-clads." In *Battles and Leaders of the Civil War,* 4 vols. New York: Thomas Yoseloff, 1956.

Wilkinson, John. *The Narrative of a Blockade-Runner.* New York: Sheldon, 1877.

Wise, Stephen R. *Lifeline of the Confederacy: Blockade Running during the Civil War* Columbia: University of South Carolina Press, 1990.

Woods, Robert H. "Cruise of the *Clarence, Tacony-Archer.*" *Southern Historical Society Papers* (1895): 274–282.

Woodward, David. "Launching the Confederate Navy." *History Today* 12 (March 1962): 206–212.

29

Modern War/Total War

Mark Grimsley

In the years following World War II, it became common among historians to assert that the American Civil War had foreshadowed the great global struggles of the twentieth century. The war of 1861–1865, after all, had witnessed the early development and use of trench warfare, ironclad warships, rapid-fire weapons, and even airships and crude machine guns. Its soldiers had traveled to the battle front aboard railroad cars and steam-driven transports; its generals had communicated with one another via endless miles of telegraph wire. It was one of the first struggles in which manufacturing and mass politics significantly affected the fighting and the outcome. Perhaps most telling, it was a struggle in which civilians became the focus of deliberate military attack. For all these reasons, historians claimed, the Civil War should properly be seen as the first modern war and the first total war.

Both phrases remain common taglines for the struggle. Yet in recent years their appropriateness has been challenged. Sometimes the objections hinge on misgivings about the utility of such characterizations. Modernity, for example, is an elastic concept. Every war, in a sense, is "modern" when it occurs. The longbowmen of Henry V fought with state-of-the-art weapons, as did the legionnaires of Caesar and the arquebusiers of the duke of Parma. The term "total war" also invites queries: Total in terms of what? The total mobilization of society? The total extermination of an enemy people? Taken literally, such apocalyptic struggles seldom occur. But objections of this sort are mere semantic quibbles. At a more serious level, to assert that the Civil War was the first modern or total war is to make a statement about its proper place in the larger history of warfare.

THE FIRST MODERN WAR?

Proponents of the "first modern war" thesis essentially argue that the Civil War was an important watershed in military history—a demarcation between an older, Napoleonic pattern of warfare and the style of fighting characteristic of the twentieth century. Skeptics, on the other hand, suggest that the breakpoint is misplaced. Perhaps it more usefully belongs with the outbreak of the democratic revolutions of the late eighteenth century, or possibly with the transformation in operations and tactics that occurred during the Napoleonic Wars. Perhaps it is reached only with the outbreak of World War I.

Since few books are devoted specifically to this subject, one must often look to more general works instead, especially to military history textbooks. A standard short survey, *Men in Arms: A History of Warfare and Its Interrelationships with Western Society* (1991), by Richard A. Preston, Alex Roland, and Sydney F. Wise, offers a good, nuanced précis of the first-modern-war interpretation. The authors view the Wars of the French Revolution and the Napoleonic Wars (1792–1815) as a critical break with previous military experience, because they were the first major conflicts to witness mass armies created and held together by the powerful new ideologies of popular sovereignty and nationalism. After Napoleon's defeat at Waterloo, however, this dramatic shift in warfare went into temporary eclipse, replaced by what the authors term "the illusion of limited war" for at least the next forty years. The great exception to this era of limited conflict was the American Civil War. With the struggle between the Union and Confederacy the protean elements of mass armies and nationalism resurfaced. This time, however, they were combined with yet another major force of the modern age—industrialization—"and so [the Civil War] showed the effects of the technological advances in industry and agriculture which were to revolutionize warfare." The technological advances, in turn, contributed to changes in the operational art, as it became both possible and imperative to supply armies across vast distances using railroads and steam vessels. New weapons technologies also contributed to a shift in tactics on the battlefield. The war revealed "the growing importance of fire power and the folly of the traditional close-order charge. . . . It showed that the infantryman was destined to seek shelter in trenches from the devastating power of rifled weapons." Thus one has, in capsule form, the main elements of the first-modern-war thesis: mass armies; ideology as a key factor in both mobilizing and sustaining the armies; industrialization and the new technologies it spawned; and changes in battlefield tactics.

A useful book that accepts the first-modern-war thesis and discusses some of these factors is Edward Hagerman, *The American Civil War and the Origins of Modern Warfare: Ideas, Organization, and Field Command* (1988). Although rather choppily organized (and rather more narrowly focused than its title might suggest), this volume explores a number of salient attributes of the Civil War that give the conflict some of its claim to modernity: the organizational changes that took place as armies tried to address their expanded size and increased logistical needs, the resort to field fortifications, improvements in staff and signals, and modifications in battlefield tactics. Hagerman is best at discussing the problems encountered in supplying Civil War armies across vast but thinly populated distances. He ably shows how logistical difficulties often tyrannized commanders and argues that only a few Civil War generals truly mastered the problems of supplying their armies on active campaign. Such a conclusion suggests that while the Civil War may indeed have been "modern" in the challenges it posed, it did not yet generate a truly modern organizational response.

Also within the first-modern-war interpretation is Grady McWhiney and Perry D. Jamieson, *Attack and Die: Civil War Military Tactics and the Southern Heritage* (1982). Although often criticized for its notorious "Celtic thesis" (the book argues, in part, that Confederate armies attacked so often and so disastrously because of the South's supposedly dominant Celtic heritage), as a study of Civil War tactics *Attack and Die* merits close attention. McWhiney and Jamieson offer the most systematic exploration of the widely held idea that the widespread use of a practical rifled musket widened the danger zone on Civil War battlefields and made frontal attacks in close-order formation not only futile but well-nigh suicidal. Although soldiers in the prewar period recognized that the rifled musket would require changes in battlefield tactics, they saw the rifle as an incremental improvement that required only an incremental tactical response. The prescribed rate of advance for an attacking force was increased, but the shoulder-to-shoulder formation was retained. Thus: modern weapons, antiquated tactics. To this deadly combination goes the blame for years of stalemated warfare and horrible carnage.

Or does it? Paddy Griffith offers an almost point-by-point refutation of this portrayal in *Battle Tactics of the Civil War* (1989). An instructor in war studies at the Royal Military Academy in Great Britain, Griffith brings a European perspective to the study of Civil War battlefields. He argues that the effect of the rifled musket is entirely exaggerated. Much of the case for its allegedly revolutionary impact turns upon the dramatically increased range of such weapons compared with smoothbore muskets (over 400 yards compared with about 150). Griffith, however, asserts that most Civil War battles occurred at smoothbore range or less—partly because of heavily wooded terrain, partly because Civil War commanders often instructed defending troops to hold their fire until the attacking enemy got close. (During Pickett's charge, for example, one colonel actually ordered his men to wait until they saw the whites of the rebels' eyes.) The increased range of the rifled musket therefore cannot be the culprit. Griffith suggests instead that Civil War battles were so often indecisive because attackers did not properly press home their attacks. Instead of advancing right into the enemy line at bayonet point—the classic Napoleonic charge—assaulting Civil War soldiers almost invariably halted between fifty and seventy-five yards from the enemy line and delivered a volley, thereby draining all momentum from their assault and usually creating a sustained firefight at murderously close range. A bold piece of revisionism, *Battle Tactics of the Civil War* is not as well supported with evidence as it might be, but Griffith's argument is both exciting and plausible. One suspects that a more systematic treatment of Civil War battle tactics would vindicate his key contentions.

In Griffith's view, then, the Civil War—at least as it played out on the battlefield—was not a modern war at all but rather a botched Napoleonic conflict. This notion implicitly accepts the idea that Napoleonic warfare was premodern. Robert M. Epstein rejects that characterization. In *Napoleon's Last Victory and the Emergence of Modern War* (1994), he maintains instead that the birth of modern war occurred not in 1861–1865 but rather in 1809, the year of Napoleon's fourth triumph over the Austrian empire. Despite the success, Epstein argues that warfare by that point had increased in scale to a degree that taxed even the genius of Napoleon. Other nations were adopting his way of making war: mass mobilization, the deliberate exploitation of nationalist sentiment, the use of the *corps d'armée* system for greater flexibility of maneuver, and so on. If this is so, the Civil War was merely part of a pattern established half a century before.

TOTAL WAR

Related to the conception of the Civil War as a modern war is that of the conflict as a total war. According to this view, between 1861 and 1864, the conflict evolved from a limited war into what President Abraham Lincoln called a "remorseless, revolutionary struggle." From a policy of deliberate restraint, extending even to the protection of private property and the return of fugitive slaves, Federal armies gradually pursued measures that subjected Southern civilians to the direct pressures of war, by the burning of towns, mills, and factories, the forced evacuation of civilians, and the confiscation of crops and livestock. This destruction involved considerable hardship for Southern civilians, but many Federal generals saw that as an important virtue. Gerald F. Linderman devotes a chapter to this issue in *Embattled Courage: The Experience of Combat in the American Civil War* (1987). "[B]y 1864," he argues, "the Civil War had expanded beyond the battlefield to encompass a warfare of terror directed primarily against the civilian population of the South."

Historical understanding of such "hard-war" operations has gone through two main phases. The first, extending from the close of the Civil War through the 1940s, looked at such episodes as Sherman's march and Sheridan's razing of the Shenandoah Valley chiefly through the lens of morality. Southern writers, like Edward Pollard, usually characterized these operations as atrocities; Northerners, like James Ford Rhodes, attempted to cast them as legitimate military activities conducted within the general framework of Western ethical norms. Not until the end of World War II did a second lens emerge to augment—and eventually replace—the lens of morality. The extensive attacks on populations and economic resources that occurred over 1939–1945, particularly the Allied strategic bombing campaign, offered an obvious new perspective. If World War II formed the supreme example of total war, then surely the war of 1861–1865 exemplified this brand of warfare in its early stages.

The first historian to make this comparison was John Bennett Walters. In "General William T. Sherman and Total War" (1948)—expanded much later into a book, *Merchant of Terror: General Sherman and Total War* (1973)—Walters argued that Sherman "became one of the first of the modern generals to revert to the idea of the use of military force against the civilian population of the enemy." In so doing he demonstrated "the effectiveness of a plan of action which would destroy the enemy's economic system and terrify and demoralize the civilian population. By paralyzing the enemy's economy he destroyed its ability to supply its armies; and by despoiling and scattering the families of soldiers in the opposing army, he undermined the morale of the military forces of the Confederacy." Sherman, in short, had originated the total war conceptions whose matured fury devastated much of the globe in two world wars.

Walters's description of the Civil War as a total war sounded a note that other writers repeated endlessly in the years that followed. In his 1952 study, *Lincoln and His Generals,* for example, T. Harry Williams termed the Civil War "the first of the modern total wars" and argued that the best Northern general, Ulysses S. Grant, eventually grasped the sorts of measures that such a conflict required, while the best Confederate general, Robert E. Lee, never did. Grant realized that "war was becoming total and that the destruction of the enemy's economic resources was as effective and legitimate a form of warfare as the destruction of his armies." Lee, on the other hand, remained mired in the older eighteenth-century conception, which confined the fighting to rival armies. "What was realism to Grant was barbarism to Lee," Williams wrote. "[He] refused to view [war] for what it had become—a struggle between societies."

Walter Millis differed slightly from Williams in conceiving of the Civil War as a "transitional" struggle rather than a truly modern war. In *Arms and Men: A Study of American Military History* (1956), Millis argued that the North and South began by fighting a traditional, battlefield-oriented war. But the industrialization of war altered conditions and made such a victory impossible to achieve. Two of the most important factors were the rifled musket and steam-powered transport. The rifle inflicted horrendous casualties that ordinarily would have crippled armies, but steam transportation made it possible to move troops rapidly and thereby to repair the terrible casualties.

This same industrialization, Millis continued, gave rise to new forms of warfare. "Earlier wars had concentrated upon the capture or destruction of enemy armies in the field. The Civil War was one of the first in which 'strategic warfare,' as the Air Force has taught us to call it, assumed a dominant role." Millis then cited several examples of this new warfare, each aimed, one way or another, at the denial of resources to the Confederacy. These episodes formed "grim examples of what 'strategic' warfare had come to imply, long before the era of airborne 'fire-storms' and 'population bombing.' '' They left a legacy of bitterness, but they also educated Americans to the realities of modern conflict. War, Millis concluded, had changed; the struggle of 1861–1865 had proved it.

Bruce Catton embraced the view of the Civil War as a total war but refined the interpretation in a way that most historians subsequently adopted. In his view, the Civil War began as a limited war but slipped the leash and became total. Others had seen the Civil War as a total war from the outset; Catton, however, gave serious consideration to the idea that the conflict began as a limited war to repress rebellion and might have been won in a limited way. This perspective formed a central theme of *Terrible Swift Sword* (1963), the second volume in his *Centennial History of the Civil War* trilogy.

In Catton's view, the war's transition from limited to total war became ensured the moment Lincoln issued the emancipation proclamation, which he regarded as the war's true turning point. The reason was simple: "A war goal with emotional power as direct and enduring as the Confederacy's own had at last been erected for all men to see." Many historians, of course, had seen the emancipation proclamation in similar terms. Catton, however, was perhaps the first to link this development with the emergence of hard-war attitudes and operations on the part of Union forces.

Russell F. Weigley adopted a similar line of reasoning in *The American Way of War: A History of United States Military Strategy and Policy* (1973). In the war's early stages, Weigley wrote, Northern policymakers sought to defeat the Confederate armies without alienating Southern civilians or damaging the Southern economy. Too much destruction would increase bitterness and reduce the chances for a viable sectional reunion. But the failure to gain an early victory pulled the North toward the destruction not only of Confederate armies but of the Southern economic resources that sustained them. Some Union generals, especially Sherman, came to realize that the destruction of Southern property could also achieve the psychological destruction of Southern morale.

The Civil War's character as a total war, argued both Catton and Weigley, eventually swamped Northern efforts to control its political consequences. "A singular fact about modern war," wrote Catton, "is that it takes charge." Weigley concurred: "Sherman's war against the enemy's mind, like Grant's war for the complete destruction of the enemy armies was a recipe for the achievement of total victory. . . . Considerations of the possibly dangerous effects of military means upon the ultimate ends of postwar sectional understanding had to be sacrificed to the immediate quest for victory, because nothing less than total victory seemed to offer any prospects for reunification at all."

The dynamic assumed to be at work here was the one identified by the Prussian military theorist Carl von Clausewitz. In *On War*, his magnum opus, Clausewitz argued, in part, that the higher the political stakes, the more sweeping the military effort. In the case of the Civil War, the expansion of the political aims, stimulated in part by the escalation of casualties, required a greater totality of effort. Since victory won solely through traditional combat seemed impossible to achieve, Northern commanders ultimately moved—through the nature of war itself—to a strategy in which victory would be won by nontraditional attacks on Southern resources and morale.

Indeed, although *On War* did not appear in English until after the Civil War and Clausewitz was practically unknown among Union and Confederate generals, some historians suggested that the best Union commanders intuitively grasped the central tenets of his thought, which supposedly emphasized war as an act of violence designed to overwhelm the enemy. (The most prominent example of this interpretation was T. Harry Williams's "The Military Leadership of North and South" [1962].) Invidious comparisons were sometimes drawn between Clausewitz, who was supposed to have understood modern war, and the other great military theorist of the age, Antoine Henri de Jomini, allegedly an intellectual throwback to the limited wars of the eighteenth century. In contrast to his Prussian counterpart, however, Jomini was well known to Civil War generals. His ideas were said to have warped the strategic thinking of Federal commanders (like George McClellan and Henry W. Halleck) who embraced them. Fortunately Lincoln and Grant, using their common sense but in fact unconscious disciples of Clausewitz, managed to rescue the Union cause from such backward-looking generals and eventually win the Civil War.

Joseph L. Harsh attacked this view in "Battlesword and Rapier: Clausewitz, Jomini, and the American Civil War" (1974). Historians drew a false dichotomy between the ideas of Jomini and Clausewitz, he argued. They also failed to understand Clausewitzian thought in proper context and, above all, overlooked the Prussian's insistence on the connection between political purposes and military means. It was far from clear, Harsh argued, that the Civil War *had* to degenerate into a remorseless, revolutionary struggle, as Catton, Weigley, and others implied. That outcome could also be seen as "a failure on the part of Northern leadership to apply their resources in policies and strategies in harmony with the aims that carried them into the war." Williams rebutted Harsh in "The Return of Jomini—Some Thoughts on Recent Civil War Writing" (1975).

In recent years a number of Civil War historians have examined the total war thesis more closely. Charles Royster probes the deeper meaning of the struggle's terrible violence in *The Destructive War: William Tecumseh Sherman, Stonewall Jackson, and the Americans* (1991). The author of several distinguished previous studies of war and the American character, Royster argues that from the outset of the Civil War, Americans North and South saw the war in apocalyptic terms as an act of cleansing violence. He examines this theme in many ways: through a sort of parallel biography of Sherman and Jackson, as the subtitle implies; through gripping chapters on the burning of Columbia, South Carolina, and the carnage on Kennesaw Mountain; and through brilliant forays in unexpected directions, as when he investigates how civilians, far removed from the fighting, made sense of the destruction they read about but experienced only vicariously.

"Americans," Royster suggests, "did not invent new methods of drastic war during the Civil War so much as they made real a version of conflict many of them had talked about from the start.'' Such a statement gives too short a shrift to the serious, sustained attempts by both sides to control the level of destructiveness. The Union government in particular pursued a consciously conciliatory policy that enjoyed wide support for the first fifteen months of the war. The policy's purpose, evolution, and eventual demise are traced in Mark Grimsley, ''Conciliation and Its Failure, 1861–1862'' (1993), and Joseph L. Harsh, ''Lincoln's Tarnished Brass: Conservative Strategies and the Attempt to Fight the Early Civil War as a Limited War'' (1988).

Despite the destructiveness of the Civil War, Royster recognizes that it was nevertheless not nearly as destructive as World War II. Property was targeted far more than people, a reality that prompts Mark E. Neely to ask ''Was the Civil War a Total War?'' (1991) and declare that it was not, since Union forces did not wage unrestricted warfare against Southern civilians. Mark Grimsley, in *The Hard Hand of War: Union Military Policy toward Southern Civilians, 1861–1865* (1995), charts the shift from conciliation to hard war and argues that the ultimate policy combined deliberate severity with an equally deliberate attempt at restraint. Grimsley also finds substantial continuities between Sherman's march and similar European episodes during the seventeenth and eighteenth centuries, concluding that Union hard-war operations were neither a departure from past experience nor as destructive as their European counterparts.

DIRECTIONS FOR FUTURE RESEARCH

More work in this area would be welcome. We still know little about the actual extent of the destruction unleashed by the Union and Confederate armies and the effect it may have had on the Southern economy. James L. Sellers's old but still useful article, ''The Economic Incidence of the Civil War in the South'' (1927), suggests that property destruction harmed the postwar Southern economy far less than did the liquidation of so much capital in the form of liberated slaves and worthless Confederate bonds. Using more rigorous methods, Roger L. Ransom and Richard Sutch reach a similar conclusion in *One Kind of Freedom: The Economic Consequences of Emancipation* (1977). (But they also argue, sensibly, that the uncompensated emancipation of the slaves was not a loss to the South but rather a transfer of labor ownership from the masters to the former slaves themselves.) Neither work, however, systematically addresses the scope of the military destruction that did occur. Robert H. McKenzie makes a limited foray toward such a study in ''The Economic Impact of Federal Operations in Alabama during the Civil War'' (1976). One may also consult James F. Doster's ''Were the Southern Railroads Destroyed by the Civil War?'' (1961). Both articles, however, are merely suggestive. It would be helpful to know more about the extent of property destruction—to determine as accurately as possible, for example, the areas affected by Sheridan's razing of the Shenandoah Valley, what property was destroyed, and how much. It would also be useful to know how much property the Confederate army destroyed or stripped from its own population—an amount probably much greater than the losses to Federal troops. Finally, since the Federal hard-war policy is frequently said to have crippled Confederate morale, it would be valuable to see more works like William McNeill's "The Stress of War: The Confederacy and William Tecumseh Sherman during the Last Year of the Civil War" (1973). McNeill examines morale among Georgia soldiers and civilians in 1864–1865 and concludes that the loss of Atlanta, not Sherman's march through the state, contributed most heavily to dampening Southern spirits.

Similarly, much more could be done along the lines of Hagerman's *The American Civil War and the Origins of Modern Warfare* (1988). Many aspects of this subject deserve further attention, among them the exploitation of railroad and riverine transportation, advances in military medicine, the reorganization of field artillery to mass fire more effectively, and the conflict's role as a spur to military professionalism.

The modern war thesis also merits more extended attention. Epstein's *Napoleon's Last Victory and the Emergence of Modern War* (1994) should spark a fruitful debate on where this development belongs in the history of warfare. One hopes that it will also draw greater attention to crucial definitional issues. What does it mean to speak of "modern war"? Armies animated by popular sovereignty and nationalism? A marriage of such armies and industrialization? What threshold of industrialization is required? Great Britain is widely thought to have entered the industrial revolution as early as 1750; the continental powers not until the 1820s and after; the United States not until the 1870s. Clearly, one's assessment of the American Civil War as the first modern war depends on one's assessment of developments in warfare and society that reach far beyond 1861–1865.

BIBLIOGRAPHY

Brinsfield, John W. "The Military Ethics of General William T. Sherman: A Reassessment." *Parameters* 12 (1983): 36–48.

Catton, Bruce. *Terrible Swift Sword.* Garden City, NY: Doubleday, 1963.

Doster, James F. "Were the Southern Railroads Destroyed by the Civil War?" *Civil War History* 7 (1961): 310–320.

Epstein, Robert M. "The Creation and Evolution of Army Corps in the American Civil War." *Journal of Military History* 55 (1991): 21–46.

———. *Napoleon's Last Victory and the Emergence of Modern War.* Lawrence: University Press of Kansas, 1994.

———. "Patterns of Change and Continuity in Nineteenth Century Warfare." *Journal of Military History* 56 (1992): 375–388.

Freidel, Frank. "General Orders 100 and Military Government." *Mississippi Valley Historical Review* 32 (1946): 541–556.

Hartigan, Richard Shelly, ed. *Lieber's Code and the Law of War.* Chicago: Precedent, 1983.

Griffith, Paddy. *Battle Tactics of the Civil War.* New Haven, CT: Yale University Press, 1989.

Grimsley, Mark. "Conciliation and Its Failure, 1861–1862." *Civil War History* 39 (1993): 317–335.

———. *The Hard Hand of War: Union Military Policy toward Southern Civilians, 1861–1865.* New York: Cambridge University Press, 1995.

Hagerman, Edward. *The American Civil War and the Origins of Modern Warfare: Ideas, Organization, and Field Command.* Bloomington: Indiana University Press, 1988.

Harsh, Joseph L. "Battlesword and Rapier: Clausewitz, Jomini, and the American Civil War." *Military Affairs* 38 (December 1974): 133–138.

———. "Lincoln's Tarnished Brass: Conservative Strategies and the Attempt to Fight the Early Civil War as a Limited War." In Roman J. Heleniak and Lawrence L. Hewitt, eds., *The Confederate High Command and Related Topics: Themes in Honor of T. Harry Williams.* Shippensburg, PA: White Mane Publishing, 1988.

Hattaway, Herman, and Archer Jones. *How the North Won: A Military History of the Civil War.* Chicago: University of Illinois Press, 1983.

Janda, Lance. "Shutting the Gates of Mercy: The American Origins of Total War, 1860–1880." *Journal of Military History* 59 (January 1995): 7–26.

Linderman, Gerald E. *Embattled Courage: The Experience of Combat in the American Civil War.* New York: Macmillan, 1987.

Lucie, Patricia M. L. "Confiscation: Constitutional Crossroads." *Civil War History* 23 (1977): 307–321.

McKenzie, Robert H. "The Economic Impact of Federal Operations in Alabama during the Civil War." *Alabama Historical Quarterly* 20 (1976): 51–63.

McNeill, William James. "The Stress of War: The Confederacy and William Tecumseh Sherman during the Last Year of the Civil War." Ph.D. diss., Rice University, 1973.

McWhiney, Grady, and Perry D. Jamieson. *Attack and Die: Civil War Military Tactics and the Southern Heritage.* Tuscaloosa: University of Alabama Press, 1982.

Millis, Walter. *Arms and Men: A Study of American Military History.* New York: Mentor, 1956.

Neely, Mark E., Jr. "Was the Civil War a Total War?" *Civil War History* 37 (1991): 5–28.

Preston, Richard A., Alex Roland, and Sydney F. Wise. *Men in Arms: A History of Warfare and Its Interrelationships with Western Society.* 5th ed. Fort Worth, TX: Holt, Rinehart and Winston, 1991.

Randall, James G. "Captured and Abandoned Property during the Civil War." *American Historical Review* 19 (1913): 65–79.

———. *The Confiscation of Property during the Civil War.* Indianapolis: Mutual Printing and Lithographing, 1913.

Ransom, Roger L., and Richard Sutch. *One Kind of Freedom: The Economic Consequences of Emancipation.* New York: Cambridge University Press, 1977.

Reston, James, Jr. *Sherman's March and Vietnam.* New York: Macmillan, 1984.

Royster, Charles. *The Destructive War: William Tecumseh Sherman, Stonewall Jackson, and the Americans.* New York: Alfred A. Knopf, 1991.

Sellers, James L. "The Economic Incidence of the Civil War in the South." *Mississippi Valley Historical Review* 14 (1927): 179–191.

Shiman, Philip Lewis. "Engineering Sherman's March: Army Engineers and the Management of Modern War." Ph.D diss., Duke University, 1991.

Smith, Everard H. "Chambersburg: Anatomy of a Confederate Reprisal," *American Historical Review* 96 (1991): 432–455.

Sutherland, Daniel E. "Abraham Lincoln, John Pope, and the Origins of Total War." *Journal of Military History* 56 (1992): 567–586.

———. "Introduction to War: The Civilians of Culpeper County, Virginia." *Civil War History* 37 (1991): 120–137.

Walters, John Bennett. "General William T. Sherman and Total War." *Journal of Southern History* 14 (1948): 447–480.

———. *Merchant of Terror: General Sherman and Total War.* Indianapolis: Bobbs-Merrill, 1973.

Weigley, Russell F. *The American Way of War: A History of United States Military Strategy and Policy.* Bloomington: Indiana University Press, 1973.

———. "American Strategy from Its Beginnings through the First World War." In Peter Paret, ed., *Makers of Modern Strategy from Machiavelli to the Nuclear Age.* Princeton, NJ: Princeton University Press, 1986.

Williams, T. Harry. *Lincoln and His Generals.* New York: Alfred A. Knopf, 1952.

———. "The Military Leadership of North and South." In David Donald, ed. *Why the North Won the Civil War.* New York: Collier, 1962.

———. "The Return of Jomini—Some Thoughts on Recent Civil War Writing." 1975.

30

Ordnance

Alan C. Downs

No credible study of the campaigns and battles of the American Civil War could even be contemplated without at least some prior knowledge of the weapons used by the Union and Confederate armies. To understand the strategy and tactics employed by both sides, one must be familiar with the capabilities and limitations of their available weaponry. Yet unlike most other Civil War topics that are the focus of research and scholarship, the academic community has generally avoided the study of ordnance over the past several decades, leaving the field in the hands of nonacademic historians and Civil War enthusiasts.

The limited number of monographs written by professional historians is not indicative of a lack of quality in the extant material. Most of the available books and articles are well researched and well written. It does mean, however, that the quantity of sources may be limited, and researchers may have difficulty obtaining certain monographs (in print or out) published by small presses. In general, the literature cited in this chapter should be available at larger libraries or through interlibrary loan. A few of the classics are more difficult to access.

GENERAL WORKS

Whether or not one considers the Civil War to be the first modern war in American history, it nevertheless is hard to deny that it was a transitional war in terms of the evolution of weaponry. The standardization of rifling, the large-scale introduction of breech-loading and repeating small arms, and the increase in the size and power of artillery are some of the characteristics of this change. Owing to the fact that this evolution occurred while the war was underway, both old and new technology coexisted on the battlefields. Thus, in aggregate, the ordnance employed throughout the four years of conflict necessarily represents an exceptionally wide variety.

The best single-volume overview of Civil War ordnance is Jack Coggins's *Arms and Equipment of the Civil War* (1962). Coggins surveys (among other things) small arms, artillery, naval ordnance, and torpedoes in a richly illustrated book. Especially informative are his cross-sectional drawings of the firing mechanisms for many of the rifles and carbines he describes. Readers may at first be disappointed at the book's lack of photographs, but the high quality of the drawings minimizes the need for greater visual clarity.

A brief, less informative, summary of Civil War ordnance can be found in Harold Peterson's *Notes on Ordnance of the American Civil War, 1861–1865* (1959). This précis is valuable primarily for its tables outlining the principal specifications of commonly used Civil War shoulder weapons, handguns, and artillery.

Francis A. Lord's *Civil War Collector's Encyclopedia* (1963) contains photographs and descriptions of small arms, cannons, mines, torpedoes, rockets, and grenades. A more recent pictorial overview of the weapons employed by each side during the war can be found in Time-Life's *Arms and Equipment of the Union* (1991) and *Arms and Equipment of the Confederacy* (1991), both edited by Henry Woodhead. These two works, however, stress small arms, uniforms, and accoutrements, giving only minimal attention to artillery.

SMALL ARMS

The variety of Civil War weaponry is perhaps best seen in the area of small arms: muskets, rifles, pistols, and swords. The war produced a staggering array of muzzle-loading smoothbore and rifled muskets, breech-loading and repeating rifles and carbines, and handguns—most of which are cataloged in William B. Edwards's *Civil War Guns* (1962). Edwards's comprehensive monograph, although poorly organized and riddled with the author's pontifications, is nevertheless well illustrated and well indexed. Two good works that survey Northern-, Southern-, and foreign-manufactured small arms used by Confederate soldiers and sailors are Claud Fuller and Richard Steuart's *Firearms of the Confederacy* (1944) and William Albaugh and Edward Simmons's *Confederate Arms* (1957).

The primary weapon of the war for both sides was the rifled musket. The wartime history of this weapon and its manufacturers is described in detail in Claud Fuller's *The Rifled Musket* (1958). At the beginning of the conflict, an increasing demand for shoulder arms compelled both Union and Confederate forces to depend on European imports to meet their needs. The Confederacy, in particular, was hard pressed. Wiley Sword's *Firepower from Abroad: The Confederate Enfield and the Le Mat Revolver, 1861–1863* (1986) focuses on the most popular Confederate imported shoulder arm, the British Model 1853 (and 1858) Enfield rifle musket and the more exotic French Le Mat revolver. This monograph includes data on other imported Confederate small arms as well. Jac Weller's "Imported Confederate Shoulder Weapons" (1959) argues that the Enfield, in its several barrel lengths, was at least the equal of any rifle used by the Union infantry during the war.

Although the Union imported Enfields as well, Garry James argues in "The Union's Most Ready Rifle" (1989) that the preferred weapon for Union infantrymen was the Model 1861 Springfield rifle musket. James's conclusions are based primarily upon the strength of the features of the Model 1861 Springfield when compared to those of the Enfield and the Models 1855 and 1863 Springfields. Primary documentation to support his deduction is scant.

In addition to the switch from smoothbore to rifled muskets, the large-scale appearance of breech-loading and repeating small arms confirms the war's significance in the history of American military technology. Not all of the new designs were practical or even safe. A good overview of the varied designs for breech-loading small arms is John McAulay's *Civil War Breech Loading Rifles: A Survey of the Innovative Infantry Arms of the American Civil War* (1987).

Arguably the best design for a single-shot breech-loading shoulder arm was the one developed by Christian Sharps of Philadelphia and patented in 1848. A complete description of the manifestation of this technology in the form of a reliable weapon can be found in Winston Smith's *The Sharps Rifle: Its History, Development and Operation* (1943). Other types of single-shot breech-loading muskets and carbines used during the war are covered collectively in the general works mentioned earlier. The Maynard priming system and the Maynard carbine are also thoroughly described in Wayne Austerman's "Maynard" (1986), and the carbine invented by Ambrose Burnside receives special attention in Edward Hull's *Burnside Breech Loading Carbines, 1853–1866.* (1986).

Especially important among the technological advances in weaponry during the Civil War is the advent of shoulder arms employing a rapid-firing (or repeating) system. Eugene Sloan's "Goodbye to the Single-Shot Musket" (1984) focuses on Christopher Miner Spencer's invention of a magazine-fed repeating rifle. Sloan describes in detail the development and functions of the Spencer repeating rifle and concludes that the weapon was considered by the officers and men of the Union armies to be the best repeating arm available. Confederate cavalrymen came to the same conclusion, and as Wayne Austerman points out in "The Northern Spencer Goes South" (1984), captured Spencer repeating carbines increasingly became the preferred weapon of many Southern troopers. Austerman enumerates the reasons that the weapon was never officially adopted by the Confederate cavalry, including the difficulty the Ordnance Bureau had in procuring the copper required for the production of Spencer cartridges.

Les Jensen briefly describes the development of another popular, but much less widely used, repeating weapon in "Henry's Rifle" (1982). Jensen identifies the expense of the lever-action shoulder arm as the primary impediment to extensive employment of the rifle by the Union armies.

Breech-loading and rapid-fire technology were employed later in the war in long-range shooting, but at the outset, heavy muzzle-loading target rifles with telescopic sights were the standard for Union and Confederate snipers—or sharpshooters. In "Death at a Distance" (1990), Ron Banks discusses the use and demise of the bench-rest rifle and scope, concluding that its cumbersome qualities made it impractical on the battlefield, especially when the enemy was armed with faster loading breechloaders.

In addition to the rifled musket, another popular small arm was the revolver, used predominantly by officers and cavalrymen on both sides. The most extensively used side arms in the Union armies were the .44 caliber army Colt and .44 caliber army Remington pistols. The best overview of these and other handguns is John McAulay's *Civil War Pistols: A Survey of the Handguns of the American Civil War* (1992). Confederate pistol manufacturers (both domestic and foreign) and their products are discussed in depth in William Albaugh, Hugh Benet, and Edward Simmons's *Confederate Handguns* (1963). William Albaugh and Richard D. Steuart's *The Original Confederate Colt* (1953) focuses specifically on handguns produced by Leech, Rigdon and Rigdon, and Ansley and Company and modeled after the 1851 Colt navy revolver.

One of the more popular, albeit imported, Confederate pistols was the French Le Mat revolver with its nine chambers and large additional barrel for grapeshot. Wiley Sword's *Firepower from Abroad* covers the history of the Le Mat, as do Albaugh, Benet, and Simmons in *Confederate Handguns*.

The final category of small arms is edged weapons. Swords and bayonets provided more ornamental flair than combat utility during the Civil War. The variety of Confederate edged weapons and their manufacturers are cataloged in William Albaugh's *Confederate Edged Weapons* (1960) and his *Handbook of Confederate Swords* (1951). Stephen Starr's "Cold Steel: The Saber and the Union Cavalry" (1965) discusses the types and distribution of cavalry sabers, the debate over whether the blade should have a sharp or rounded edge, and the purpose of the saber. Starr emphasizes that the saber had glamour, a quality that set it apart from all other weapons.

ARTILLERY

The Civil War witnessed tremendous advances in the variety and uses of artillery. Two excellent overviews of the artillery used by both sides during the war are volume 5 of Francis Trevelyan Miller's *Photographic History of the Civil War* (1957) and Warren Ripley's *Artillery and Ammunition of the Civil War* (1970). Miller's study is more comprehensive in scope and includes a lengthy discussion of both the Union and Confederate Ordnance Departments, while Ripley's monograph delves into all the details associated with the process of identifying the various models of cannons covered in his book. Attractions of Ripley's book are its inclusion of a chapter on cannon carriages and on the art of the artilleryman, an appendix that includes a glossary, a list of U.S. and Confederate inspectors and manufacturers, a list of British ordnance markings, and a table of specifications for all the types of artillery listed in his book. Many readers will also appreciate Ripley's habit of divulging the current location of the cannons photographed for his book. Three brief, less comprehensive surveys of Civil War artillery are Dean Thomas's *Cannons: An Introduction to Civil War Artillery* (1986), Wayne Austerman's "Case Shot and Canister" (1987), and Albert Manucy's *Artillery through the Ages* (1949).

The standard overview of Civil War field artillery is James C. Hazlett, Edwin Olmstead, and M. Hume Parks's *Field Artillery Weapons of the Civil War* (1983). This well-illustrated, encyclopedic survey of the different types of light artillery used by both sides during the war is similar to Ripley's book although narrower in scope. The authors expound on the development and production of common and less well-known cannons and include specifications and unique features for each.

Of the standard types of field artillery, the model 1857 12-pounder gun-howitzer was the most commonly used smoothbore cannon of the war. Better known as the Napoleon, this weapon had its origins in France, where it was developed as a result of tests initiated in the early 1850s by Napoleon III. In "How the Napoleon Came to America" (1964), Stanley Falk discusses the progression of events that led to the adoption of this weapon by the U.S. Army. Ultimately manufactured in both the North and the South, the Napoleon was omnipresent on the war's battlefields.

James C. Hazlett also has written extensively about the Napoleon, including "The Napoleon Gun: Markings, Bore, Diameters, Weights, and Costs" (1966) and "The Federal Napoleon Gun" (1963). Other common types of Civil War field artillery—both smoothbore and rifled—have received less individual attention. The 3-inch ordnance rifle, also known as the Griffen gun, is covered in Hazlett's "The 3-Inch Ordnance Rifle" (1968). Information about the 10- and 20-pound Parrott rifles must be gleaned from the more general surveys.

Heavy artillery (siege, garrison, and seacoast cannons) is also covered best in the more general works by Coggins, Miller, and Ripley. There are, however, a few articles worthy of special note. Emanuel Lewis attempts to clarify the features that distinguish columbiads from other types of heavy artillery in "The Ambiguous Columbiads" (1964). Lewis's article also contains a discussion of Rodman guns. Walter W. Stephen surveys the less common Brooke gun in "The Brooke Guns from Selma" (1958). Finally, the history of the 8-inch Parrott rifle, better known as the "Swamp Angel," which bombarded Charleston from a range of 8,000 yards until the barrel burst on the thirty-sixth round, can be found in James Goldy's "The Swamp Angel" (1989).

Less accessible (but well worth tracking down) are some contemporary sources on Civil War artillery. Canadian Norman Wiard invented some useful but unpopular designs for light ordnance during the war. He described his ideas to the U.S. government in a pamphlet, *Wiard's System of Field Artillery, As Improved to Meet the Requirements of Modern Service* (1863). Wiard's writings concerning heavy artillery include *Great Guns: The Cause of Their Failure, and the True Method of Constructing Them* (1863) and *Inefficiency of Heavy Ordnance in This Country and Everywhere, and about Parrott and Other Hooped Guns* (1865). Another noteworthy (and available) contemporary source on heavy artillery is Henry Larcom Abbot's *Siege Artillery in the Campaigns against Richmond with Notes on the 15-Inch Gun* (1867).

As was the case with small arms, both Union and Confederate ordnance bureaus initially looked to overseas suppliers to augment their inventory of all types of cannons. The United States was soon able to supply its needs from its own manufacturers, while the Confederacy, by necessity, was forced to continue this practice throughout the war. Jac Weller's "The Confederate Use of British Cannon" (1957) provides a good overview of Confederate artillery manufactured in Britain, as well as a discussion of the three major British firms—Armstrong, Blakely, and Whitworth—that supplied these weapons. Weller concludes that these cannons were the most modern and progressive of all the varieties of Confederate artillery.

NAVAL ORDNANCE

The best overview of naval ordnance for both the Union and Confederate navies is Eugene B. Canfield's *Notes on Naval Ordnance of the American Civil War, 1861–1865* (1960). The first half of this précis surveys naval guns in three basic categories: pivot guns, broadside guns, and boat guns. The other half of Canfield's monograph is devoted to a discussion of Confederate torpedoes. The author includes a table listing the name, date, and location of ships sunk or damaged by torpedoes during the war. Two other general studies worthy of note are Jack Coggins's brief review of naval weaponry, "Civil War Naval Ordnance—Weapons and Equipment" (1964) and the section on naval ordnance in his *Arms and Equipment of the Civil War* (1962).

Most of the published works on naval ordnance focus on U.S. naval armament. Instrumental in the development of new ordnance for the Federal navy during the war was Admiral John A. Dahlgren, who designed a variety of rifled and smoothbore cannons that bore his name. The efficacy of the 9-inch Dahlgren shellgun made it one of the more popular broadside guns in the U.S. Navy, while the 11-inch Dahlgren shellgun served well as a pivot gun. The best survey of the various designs of Dahlgren guns can be found in Ripley's *Artillery and Ammunition of the Civil War*. Also worthy of perusal is Dahlgren's own treatise, *Shells and Shell Guns* (1856).

Two other useful examples of contemporary literature worth searching for are Edward Simpson's *A Treatise on Ordnance and Naval Gunnery* (1862), written to be used as a textbook for the U.S. Naval Academy, and James H. Ward's *Elementary Instruction in Naval Ordnance and Gunnery* (1861). Information on Civil War naval gunnery can be found in Robert W. Neeser's "American Naval Gunnery—Past and Present" (1912).

At the beginning of the war, the inventory of Confederate naval weapons was dominated by items captured from U.S. Navy yards. As the war progressed, however, the Confederacy was able to augment its collection with weapons manufactured within the Confederate States or imported from abroad. A good overview of the assortment of Confederate naval weaponry is Spencer Tucker's "Confederate Naval Ordnance" (1989).

The Brooke gun, manufactured at the Tredegar Foundry in Richmond, Virginia, and at the Confederate Naval Ordnance Works in Selma, Alabama, was the naval rival of the heavy Parrott rifles. As was true for the Dahlgren guns, the development of this weapon receives special treatment in Ripley's overview. Walter Stephen also examines the Brooke gun in "The Brooke Guns from Selma" (1958).

Perhaps the most intriguing aspect of Confederate naval ordnance is the development and use of torpedoes. These essentially defensive weapons were responsible for sinking or damaging at least forty-three U.S. vessels during the war. The best overall study of this technology and its application during the Civil War is Milton Perry's *Infernal Machines: The Story of Confederate Submarine and Mine Warfare* (1965). Perry discusses torpedoes and their inventors, but unfortunately neglects the impact these weapons had on Northern strategic decisions and individual naval operations. A brief sketch of Matthew Fontaine Maury and his aquatic explosives is in Dean Snyder's "Torpedoes for the Confederacy" (1985).

R. O. Crowley's "Making the 'Infernal Machines': A Memoir of the Confederate Torpedo Service" (1973) contains the recollections of an electrician in the "torpedo division" of the Confederate Navy. Crowley discusses torpedo development and operations in such places as James River, Virginia; Wilmington, North Carolina; Charleston Harbor, South Carolina; Savannah, Georgia; Mobile Bay, Alabama; and the Yazoo River in Mississippi. The career of Gabriel J. Rains and a description of some of his designs for torpedoes can be found in Davis Waters's " 'Deception Is the Art of War': Gabriel J. Rains, Torpedo Specialist of the Confederacy" (1989). An added attraction of this article is the inclusion of sketches of Rains's inventions taken from the general's unpublished notebook.

AMMUNITION

The variety of Civil War shoulder arms, handguns, and artillery was paralleled by an equally diverse assortment of ammunition. Much of the material published on this subject was written for an audience composed of Civil War weapons collectors and enthusiasts. Berkeley Lewis's *Notes on Ammunition of the American Civil War, 1861–1865* (1959) is one of the few exceptions to this rule and also happens to be the best general survey of Union and Confederate ammunition. Included in this short monograph are drawings of the common small arms and artillery projectiles used by both sides during the war. Of special value are tables and appendixes, which include information on U.S. powder mills, shoulder arm purchases, types and quantities of cartridges produced, and service test results of rifled projectiles and fuses. Information of this type for the Confederacy is noticeably absent, in part owing to the deficiency of available records.

W. Reid McKee and M. E. Mason's *Civil War Projectiles II: Small Arms and Field Artillery* (1980) contains photographs and drawings of the distinguishing characteristics of a wide range of Union and Confederate projectiles. Small arms projectiles and cartridges are shown in actual size, and several pages of photographs of carved, fired, and unusually shaped bullets provide added interest. The accompanying narrative is poorly written but informative. Stanley Phillips's *Bullets Used in the Civil War, 1861–1865* (1971) is similar in purpose but surveys only small arms projectiles.

Thomas Dickey and Sydney C. Kerksis's *Field Artillery Projectiles of the Civil War, 1861–1865* (1968) and *Heavy Artillery Projectiles of the Civil War, 1861–1865* (1972) use ample photographs to highlight characteristics important in the identification of the more common solid shot and shells for light and heavy artillery. Thomas Dickey and Peter George's *Field Artillery Projectiles of the American Civil War: Including a Selection of Navy Projectiles, Hand Grenades, Rockets, and Land Mines* (1980) is a bit more comprehensive in scope than the preceding two works and includes photographs of some of the rarer projectiles used by both armies. All three works have information (including photographs) on fuses. Good surveys of Civil War artillery ammunition are also included in John D. Bartleson's *A Field Guide for Civil War Explosive Ordnance* (1972) and in Ripley's *Artillery and Ammunition of the Civil War.*

MISCELLANEOUS AND UNUSUAL ORDNANCE

With all the rapid developments in weapons technology during the Civil War, it is not surprising that some of the new designs and devices proved to be impractical or unpopular. In *Lincoln and the Tools of War* (1956), Robert Bruce examines Abraham Lincoln's personal interest in many of the new weapons developed in the North. Bruce outlines the conflict between the president and his first chief of ordnance, Brigadier General James Wolfe Ripley, over the adoption of certain designs, noting that the conservative Ripley usually had his way.

Perhaps the most well-known weapon developed during the war, but not officially adopted, was the Gatling gun. The story of the development of this rapid-fire weapon is included in Paul F. Wahl and Donald R. Toppel's comprehensive *The Gatling Gun* (1965). The authors trace Richard Jordan Gatling's multibarreled invention from the drawing board to its modern use in airborne weapons systems. A brief description of the Gatling gun can be found in Garry James's "The Search for the Ultimate Weapon" (1993). James includes information on other multiple-shot guns such as the Billinghurst-Requa battery, the "Union" gun, the Gorgas gun, the Williams gun, and the Vandenburgh volley gun. The author concludes that while these "machine guns" did not prove their worth on the war's battlefields, they demonstrated the viability of the concept. A more detailed description of the Vandenburgh volley gun is in Chris Calkins's "The Petersburg 'Folly Gun' " (1990).

Another weapon that saw relatively little use during the Civil War was the rocket. Ralph W. Donnelly contends in "Rocket Batteries of the Civil War" (1961) that Congreve- and Hale-type rockets were seen more as specialty weapons rather than all-purpose, primarily because of their poor antipersonnel capabilities. Advances in the range and power of conventional artillery made the use of rockets superfluous for purposes other than the demoralization of the enemy's men and horses. A brief description of Hale rockets can also be found in Frank H. Winter and Mitchell R. Sharp's "Major Lion's Rocketeers: The New York Rocket Battalion" (1973).

Marginally more successful but still seeing only limited use (mainly during siege operations) was the hand grenade. Information on the Adams, Hanes, and Ketchum hand grenades can be found in Francis Lord's *Civil War Collector's Encyclopedia* (1963). Hanes and Ketchum grenades are also briefly described in Coggins's *Arms and Equipment of the Civil War*.

The Civil War had its share of controversial weapons. Before his work on the mining of the James River and his assignment to direct the Confederate army's secretive Torpedo Bureau, Gabriel Rains had already made a name for himself through his invention and deployment of "subterra shells," or land mines. Davis Waters describes the debate over the use of these concealed weapons in his article on Rains. Illustrations of two different types of "subterra shells" are included in the article.

Equally controversial was the use of artillery shells filled with an inflammable agent commonly called "Greek fire." A brief description of this and other incendiary devices can be found in Lord's encyclopedia. The controversy surrounding the use of this weapon is outlined in Arthur Sharp's "Greek Fire, the Spirit of Christian Warfare?" (1984).

Numerous examples of exotic weapons pervade the history of Civil War ordnance. Most of these creations saw limited use, if ever used at all. John Gilleland's invention of a double-barreled cannon is described in Jones Drewry's "The Double-Barrelled Cannon of Athens, Georgia" (1964). Drewry not only discusses the development and rather obvious problems with this design, but he also traces the cannon's history to its present location. In "Grant's Wooden Mortars and Some Incidents of the Siege of Vicksburg" (1940), F. Stansbury Haydon describes the construction and successful use of wooden mortars by Federal troops during the Vicksburg campaign. The mortars were built in part as a response to the Confederate practice of lighting short fuses on barrels filled with powder—"thunder barrels"—and rolling them toward nearby Union entrenchments. Al Gross includes brief mention of Charles Perley's "rocket"— an unmanned balloon designed to carry a "bomb or missile" over to the enemy position—in "Not Quite Flying Machines" (1975). A description and illustration of the Winans steam gun, a steam-driven centrifugal force gun invented by

Charles S. Dickinson, can be found in F. Stansbury Haydon's "Confederate Railroad Battery at Jacksonville, Florida, March, 1863, Not the First Use of Railway Ordnance in the United States" (1938). The design, manufacture, and use of an exploding small arms projectile are outlined in Wayne Austerman's "Abhorrent to Civilization: The Explosive Bullet in the Civil War" (1985). One final, and perhaps more ominous, weapon conceptualized during the war was John W. Doughty's design for a chlorine gas-filled shell that could be used by artillery against the enemy. The description of this concept is in F. Stansbury Haydon's "A Proposed Gas Shell, 1862" (1938).

THE ORGANIZATIONS AND PEOPLE BEHIND THE WEAPONS

Any careful study of Civil War ordnance broadly defined must take into consideration the organizations and individuals that developed, manufactured, and operated the tools of war. One can discover valuable insight about the selection and use of the varieties of ordnance by becoming more familiar with the ideas of contemporaries such as John Gibbon, Henry Hunt, Josiah Gorgas, and E. Porter Alexander, to name but a few. Many of the significant individuals and manufacturers are listed elsewhere in this book. A few monographs, however, are worthy of special note and inclusion in this chapter.

Frank Vandiver provides a look at the administrative side of Confederate ordnance in *The Civil War Diary of General Josiah Gorgas* (1947) and in *Ploughshares into Swords: Josiah Gorgas and Confederate Ordnance* (1952). Both identify the problems Gorgas encountered while serving as the Confederate chief of ordnance. Efforts to overcome shortages of lead, gum arabic, mercury, copper, and oil are outlined in Vandiver's "Makeshifts of Confederate Ordnance" (1951). Comparable studies of James W. Ripley and the U.S. Ordnance Department do not exist.

Also useful in the study of Civil War ordnance are the available handbooks and manuals used by the artillerymen on both sides. John Gibbon's *The Artillerist's Manual* (1860), the U.S. Ordnance Department's *The Ordnance Manual for the Use of the Officers of the United States Army* (1861), and the Confederate States's *The Ordnance Manual for the Use of the Officers of the Confederate States Army* (1863) are noteworthy in that they provide a framework on which to evaluate the performance of individuals operating these weapons during combat and also the tactical utility of the weapons themselves.

The best history of the artillery of the Army of Northern Virginia is Jennings C. Wise's *The Long Arm of Lee* (1915). In a two-volume work, Wise surveys the use of the artillery by this most celebrated of all Confederate armies and examines some of the key personalities behind the guns. Included in volume 1 is a brief history of the Bureau of Ordnance. Larry Daniel's *Cannoneers in Gray: The Field Artillery of the Army of Tennessee, 1861–1865* (1984) assumes a similar mission for the other major Confederate army, the Army of Tennessee.

Daniel argues that the artillery in this western army suffered from a lack of sufficient logistical support and generals, with the exception of Joseph Johnston, who never really understood its proper role on the battlefield.

The Union equivalent of these two studies of Confederate artillery is L. Van Loan Naisawald's *Grape and Canister* (1960). Naisawald traces the history of the artillery in the Army of the Potomac, arguing that Federal cannons were never used to their fullest potential until the Battle of Gettysburg and even after suffered from the disadvantage of restricted fields of fire in the woodlands of Virginia.

The writings highlighted in this chapter represent some of the best material available on the subject of Civil War ordnance. Many of these works can be considered definitive. After all, there is only so much one can say about the specifications of a model 1853 Enfield rifle musket or the advantages and disadvantages of Schenkl versus Parrott shells. Yet there is still plenty of room for continued research and writing on this general topic. Still open to interpretation and revision is the human dimension of ordnance as seen through the selection and employment of these weapons on the battlefield. There is much to be learned as well about the administrative aspects of ordnance, especially in regard to the U.S. Ordnance Department. Our knowledge of domestic and foreign ordnance manufacturing and supply for the United States and the Confederacy also remains incomplete.

BIBLIOGRAPHY

Abbot, Henry Larcom. *Siege Artillery in the Campaigns against Richmond, with Notes on the 15-Inch Gun.* Washington, D.C.: Government Printing Office, 1867.

Albaugh, William Archibald. *Confederate Edged Weapons.* New York: Harper, 1960.

————. *Handbook of Confederate Swords.* Harriman, TN: Pioneer Press, 1951.

Albaugh, William Archibald, Hugh Benet, Jr., and Edward N. Simmons. *Confederate Handguns.* Philadelphia: Riling and Lentz, 1963.

Albaugh, William Archibald, and Edward N. Simmons. *Confederate Arms.* Harrisburg, PA: Stackpole, 1957.

Albaugh, William Archibald, and Richard D. Steuart. *The Original Confederate Colt.* New York: Greenberg, 1953.

Austerman, Wayne. "Abhorrent to Civilization: The Explosive Bullet in the Civil War." *Civil War Times Illustrated* 24 (September 1985): 36–40.

————. "Case Shot and Canister." *Civil War Times Illustrated* 26 (September 1987): 16–29, 43–48.

————. "Maynard." *Civil War Times Illustrated* 25 (April 1986): 42–45.

————. "The Northern Spencer Goes South." *Civil War Times Illustrated* 23 (May 1984): 26–30, 34–35.

Banks, Ron. "Death at a Distance." *Civil War Times Illustrated* 29 (March–April 1990): 48–55.

Bartleson, John D. *A Field Guide for Civil War Explosive Ordnance.* Washington, D.C.: Government Printing Office, 1972.

Bruce, Robert V. *Lincoln and the Tools of War.* Indianapolis: Bobbs-Merrill, 1956.

Calkins, Chris. "The Petersburg 'Folly Gun.' " *Civil War Times Illustrated* 24 (November–December 1990): 18, 82.

Canfield, Eugene B. *Notes on Naval Ordnance of the American Civil War, 1861–1865.* Washington, D.C.: American Ordnance Association, 1960.

Coggins, Jack. *Arms and Equipment of the Civil War.* 1962. Reprint, New York: Fairfax Press 1983.

———. "Civil War Naval Ordnance—Weapons and Equipment." *Civil War Times Illustrated* 4 (November 1964): 16–20.

Confederate States. War Department. *The Ordnance Manual for the Use of the Officers of the Confederate States Army.* Richmond: West and Johnston, 1863.

Crowley, R. O. "Making the 'Infernal Machine': A Memoir of the Confederate Torpedo Service." *Civil War Times Illustrated* 12 (June 1973): 24–35.

Dahlgren, John Adolphus Bernard. *Shells and Shell Guns.* Philadelphia: King & Baird, 1856.

Daniel, Larry J. *Cannoneers in Gray: The Field Artillery of the Army of Tennessee, 1861–1865.* University, AL: University of Alabama Press, 1984.

Davis, Carl L. *Arming the Union: Small Arms in the Civil War.* Port Washington, NY: Kennikat Press, 1973.

Dickey, Thomas S., and Peter C. George. *Field Artillery Projectiles of the American Civil War: Including a Selection of Navy Projectiles, Hand Grenades, Rockets, and Land Mines.* Atlanta: Arsenal Press, 1980.

Dickey, Thomas S., and Sydney C. Kerksis. *Field Artillery Projectiles of the Civil War, 1861–1865.* Atlanta: Phoenix Press, 1968.

———. *Heavy Artillery Projectiles of the Civil War, 1861–1865.* Kennesaw, GA: Phoenix Press, 1972.

Donnelly, Ralph W. "Rocket Batteries of the Civil War." *Military Affairs* 25 (Summer 1961): 69–93.

Drewry, Jones M. "The Double-Barrelled Cannon of Athens, Georgia." *Georgia Historical Quarterly* 48 (December 1964): 442–450.

Edwards, William Bennett. *Civil War Guns: The Complete Story of Federal and Confederate Small Arms: Design, Manufacture, Identification, Procurement, Issue, Employment, Effectiveness, and Postwar Disposal.* Harrisburg, PA: Stackpole, 1962.

Falk, Stanley L. "How the Napoleon Came to America." *Civil War History* 10 (June 1964): 149–154.

Fuller, Claud E. *The Rifled Musket.* Harrisburg, PA: Stackpole, 1958.

Fuller, Claud E., and Richard D. Steuart. *Firearms of the Confederacy.* Huntington, WV: Standard Publications, 1944.

Gibbon, John. *The Artillerist's Manual.* New York: D. Van Nostrand, 1860.

Goldy, James. "The Swamp Angel." *Civil War Times Illustrated* 28 (April 1989): 23–27.

Gross, Al. "Not Quite Flying Machines." *Civil War Times Illustrated* 13 (February 1975): 20–24.

Haydon, F. Stansbury. "Confederate Railroad Battery at Jacksonville, Florida, March,

1863, Not the First Use of Railway Ordnance in the United States." *Journal of the American Military History Foundation* 2 (Winter 1938): 229–234.

――――. "Grant's Wooden Mortars and Some Incidents of the Siege of Vicksburg." *Journal of the American Military Institute* 4 (1940): 30–38.

――――. "A Proposed Gas Shell, 1862." *Journal of the American Military History Foundation* 2 (Spring 1938): 52–54.

Hazlett, James C. "The Federal Napoleon Gun." *Military Collector and Historian* 15 (1963): 103–108.

――――. "The Napoleon Gun: Markings, Bore, Diameters, Weights, and Costs." *Military Collector and Historian* 18 (1966): 109–119.

――――. "The 3-Inch Ordnance Rifle." *Civil War Times Illustrated* 7 (December 1968): 30–36.

Hazlett, James C., Edwin Olmstead, and M. Hume Parks. *Field Artillery Weapons of the Civil War.* Newark, DE: University of Delaware Press, 1983.

Hull, Edward A. *Burnside Breech Loading Carbines, 1853–1866.* Lincoln, RI: A. Mowbray, 1986.

James, Garry. "The Search for the Ultimate Weapon." *Civil War Times Illustrated* 31 (January–February 1993): 48–55.

――――. "The Union's Most Ready Rifle." *Civil War Times Illustrated* 28 (September–October 1989): 10–14.

Jensen, Les. "Henry's Rifle." *Civil War Times Illustrated* 21 (September 1982): 36–37.

Lewis, Berkeley R. *Notes on Ammunition of the American Civil War, 1861–1865.* Washington, DC: American Ordnance Association, 1959.

Lewis, Emanuel Raymond. "The Ambiguous Columbiads." *Military Affairs* 28 (1964): 111–122.

Lord, Francis Alfred. *Civil War Collector's Encyclopedia: Arms, Uniforms, and Equipment of the Union and Confederacy.* 1963. Reprint, Secaucus, NJ: Castle Books, 1982.

McAulay, John D. *Civil War Breech Loading Rifles: A Survey of the Innovative Infantry Arms of the American Civil War.* Lincoln, RI: A. Mowbray, 1987.

――――. *Civil War Pistols: A Survey of the Handguns of the American Civil War.* Lincoln, RI: A. Mowbray, 1992.

McKee, W. Reid, and M. E. Mason, Jr. *Civil War Projectiles II: Small Arms and Field Artillery—with Supplement.* Moss Publications, 1980.

Manucy, Albert. *Artillery Through the Ages.* National Park Service Interpretive Series, no. 3. Washington, D.C.: Government Printing Office, 1949.

Miller, Francis Trevelyan, ed. *The Photographic History of the Civil War.* Vol. 5: *Forts and Artillery.* New York: Thomas Yoseloff, 1957.

Naisawald, Louis Van Loan. *Grape and Canister: The Story of the Field Artillery of the Army of the Potomac, 1861–1865.* New York: Oxford University Press, 1960.

Neeser, Robert W. "American Naval Gunnery—Past and Present." *North American Review* 196 (December 1912): 780–791.

Perry, Milton F. *Infernal Machines: The Story of Confederate Submarine and Mine Warfare.* Baton Rouge: LSU Press, 1965.

Peterson, Harold L. *Notes on Ordnance of the American Civil War.* Washington, D.C.: American Ordnance Association, 1959.

Phillips, Stanley S. *Bullets Used in the Civil War, 1861–1865.* Laurel MD: Wilson's Specialty Company, 1971.

Ripley, Warren. *Artillery and Ammunition of the Civil War*. New York: Van Nostrand Reinhold Company, 1970.

Sharp, Arthur. "Greek Fire, the Spirit of Christian Warfare?" *Civil War Times Illustrated* 23 (November 1984): 32–37.

Simpson, Edward. *A Treatise on Ordnance and Naval Gunnery*. New York: D. Van Nostrand, 1862.

Sloan, W. Eugene. "Goodbye to the Single-Shot Musket." *Civil War Times Illustrated* 23 (May 1984): 31–33.

Smith, Winston O. *The Sharps Rifle: Its History, Development and Operation*. New York: W. Morrow & Company, 1943.

Snyder, Dean. "Torpedoes for the Confederacy." *Civil War Times Illustrated* 24 (March 1985): 40–45.

Starr, Stephen Z. "Cold Steel: The Saber and the Union Cavalry." *Civil War History* 11 (June 1965): 142–159.

Stephen, Walter W. "The Brooke Guns from Selma." *Alabama Historical Quarterly* 20 (Fall 1958): 462–475.

Sword, Wiley. *Firepower from Abroad: The Confederate Enfield and the Le Mat Revolver, 1861–1863: With New Data on a Variety of Confederate Small Arms*. Lincoln, RI: A. Mowbray, 1986.

Thomas, Dean S. *Cannons: An Introduction to Civil War Artillery*. Arendtsville, PA: Thomas Publications, 1986.

Tucker, Spencer. "Confederate Naval Ordnance." *Journal of Confederate History* 2 (1989): 133–152.

United States Ordnance Department. *The Ordnance Manual for the Use of the Officers of the United States Army*. Philadelphia: Lippincott, 1861.

Vandiver, Frank Everson. "Makeshifts of Confederate Ordnance." *Journal of Southern History* 17 (May 1951): 180–193.

———. *Ploughshares into Swords; Josiah Gorgas and Confederate Ordnance*. Austin, TX: University of Texas Press, 1952.

———, ed. *The Civil War Diary of General Josiah Gorgas*. University, AL: University of Alabama Press, 1947.

Wahl, Paul Francis, and Donald R. Toppel. *The Gatling Gun*. New York: Arco Publishing Company, 1965.

Ward, James H. *Elementary Instruction in Naval Ordnance and Gunnery*. New York: D. Van Nostrand, 1861.

Waters, W. Davis. "Deception Is the Art of War." *North Carolina Historical Review* 66 (January 1989): 29–60.

Weller, Jac. "The Confederate Use of British Cannon." *Civil War History* 3 (June 1957): 135–152.

———. "Imported Confederate Shoulder Weapons." *Civil War History* 5 (June 1959): 157–181.

Wiard, Norman. *Great Guns: The Cause of Their Failure, and the True Method of Constructing Them*. New York: Holman, 1863.

———. *Inefficiency of Heavy Ordnance in This Country and Everywhere, and about Parrott and Other Hooped Guns*. Washington, D.C.: H. Polkinhorn & Son, 1865.

———. *Wiard's System of Field Artillery, As Improved to Meet the Requirements of Modern Service*. New York: Holman, 1863.

Winter, Frank H., and Mitchell R. Sharpe. "Major Lion's Rocketeers: The New York Rocket Battalion." *Civil War Times Illustrated* 11 (January 1973): 10–15.

Wise, Jennings Cropper. *The Long Arm of Lee: or, The History of the Artillery of the Army of Northern Virginia; with a Brief Account of the Confederate Bureau of Ordnance.* 2 vols. Lynchburg, VA: J. P. Bell Company, 1915.

Woodhead, Henry, ed. *Arms and Equipment of the Confederacy.* Alexandria, VA: Time-Life Books, 1991.

———. *Arms and Equipment of the Union.* Alexandria, VA: Time-Life Books, 1991.

31

Supplies

Edward Carr Franks

The bulk of the literature on supplying armies in the field during the Civil War is on Southern supply, no doubt because the South experienced the bulk of the supply problems, on an economy-wide basis and at the level of the armies in the field. In contrast, the story for the North is one of great success, save for brief periods of enemy-induced deprivation for certain field armies (Chattanooga being the prime example). It appears that the Northern military success caused historians to focus, quite naturally, on the efficacy of Northern strategy and tactics, whereas students of the Southern military failure were unwilling to attribute that result simply to military incompetence and have therefore sought other explanations.

The reasons for the comparative variation in supply experience between the North and South are reasonably well established. First, the South's ports were blockaded. This caused two important problems: it raised the cost of imports (much more than did the impact of Southern privateers on Northern shipping raise Northern import costs) and forced the South to rely much more heavily on its very limited east-west rail network (the South's river system was so good that much antebellum intra-South commerce occurred port-to-port rather than train depot-to-train depot.) Second, the South lost important production and distribution centers early, mainly Nashville, Memphis, and New Orleans, a critical blow to the South's already limited industrial infrastructure. Third, and perhaps most important, the Southern government by late 1863 was virtually bankrupt and unable to obtain additional credit. As a result, not only could it no longer pay for supplies in Europe, it could not even pay for supplies at home. The resulting de facto price controls and forced impressment of goods and services caused additional, policy-induced shortages. The North suffered virtually none of these problems.

FACTORS AFFECTING MILITARY SUPPLY

The ability to keep an army supplied in the field is dependent on a three-step process: production (both private and public), procurement (by the army in the field and centralized authorities), and distribution. The term "logistics" generally applies only to procurement and distribution and, as such, involves production per se only if a supply bureau decides to create, confiscate, or regulate the production facilities in order to facilitate the procurement of a particular item. For the North, such production was rarely conducted, whereas for the South, such production became the norm as the excess of market prices over government prices grew larger as the war progressed (by war's end, Confederate schedule prices were, on average, only 20 percent of market prices).

Production is a function of various factors including industrial capacity, economic organization (free or regulated markets), manpower shortages due to mobilization, technology, natural resources, transportation infrastructure (from resource location to production centers), and military impediments (enemy destruction of resources, capacity, or output by raiding, or enemy control of same by occupation or naval blockade). The ability to procure supplies once produced generally depends on the efficiency of the military supply departments, the relation of prices paid by those departments to market prices, and the army's rate of locomotion (it is often easier to feed an army in motion, thus reducing the amount of cartage that must be devoted to food and forage). Finally, the distribution capability depends on the army's distance from the supply depot, the form of conveyance available to that location (railroad, water, and/or wagon), the impact of seasonal weather on that conveyance, and the army's size.

The supply duties were generally divided among three organizations within the military: the commissary department (in the South it was called the Subsistence Department, though the chief was still called the commissary general), the Quartermaster's Department, and the Ordnance Bureau. The commissary general's mission was the requisition and distribution of food for the troops. The quartermaster general's mission was to procure and distribute horses, mules, forage, bridles, saddles, horseshoes, wagons, shoes, tents, clothing, and so forth. The Ordnance Bureau's mission was to ensure an adequate supply of weapons and munitions for the artillery, cavalry, and infantry. In the South, the production of much of the quartermaster's needs and virtually all of the ordnance needs was conducted by either government agencies or heavily regulated private firms. In contrast, the Northern supply departments left virtually all production in the hands of unregulated, private firms.

For the North, the quartermaster general was Montgomery C. Meigs, the commissary general was Colonel Joseph P. Taylor (brother of the former president and uncle of Confederate general Richard Taylor), and the ordnance chief was

James W. Ripley until 1863, when he was replaced by Brigadier General Alexander B. Dyer. For the South, the quartermaster general was Abraham C. Myers until August 1863, when he was replaced by Brigadier General Alexander R. Lawton. The commissary general was Colonel Lucius B. Northrop (until replaced on the eve of defeat by Brigadier General Isaac M. St. John in February 1865). Finally, the ordnance chief was Brigadier General Josiah Gorgas.

The general perception of the competence of these various department heads seems to be (not surprisingly) highly correlated with the success or failure of their respective departments in meeting demands. Meigs is hailed by his biographer. Taylor, the commissary general, is generally portrayed as competent and conscientious and his performance credible. Ripley, of the Ordnance Department, though efficient, is portrayed as having been largely responsible for the delay in the adoption of breechloaders. His successor, Dyer, was much younger and apparently more amenable to technical innovation.

For the South, both of the quartermaster generals and the ordnance chief are generally considered to have performed creditably despite enormous odds. In contrast, the commissary general, Northrop, is considered to have been incompetent and the cause of much suffering by the troops, although most nevertheless concede his task was impossible for a variety of reasons. Perhaps the most significant cause of Northrop's failure was that he was forced by his government's explicit policy to impress and transport supplies at prices and fares well below market, which caused suppliers, quite reasonably, to withhold goods or suffer economic ruin at the hands of their own government (no wonder they started invoking states' rights). Even at impressment prices, Northrop's funding was so limited by the government that he and his officers were still forced to issue promissory notes in lieu of payment. St. John, on the other hand, enjoys a good reputation, partly due to his credible performance as the head of the Niter Bureau, a department of the Ordnance Bureau that had an exclusive monopoly on the mining, manufacturing, and distribution of gunpowder. But he also benefited from a fundamental change in government policy that occurred only days after he took over for Northrop: effective March 16, 1865, all impressments were required to be made at fair market prices. This apparently had a spectacular effect on the available supply of procurable goods (though far too late to affect the war's outcome), although St. John was still forced, due to lack of funds, to pay for the goods with promissory notes (this time, though, the promised payments were linked to the gold value of the good impressed).

GENERAL SECONDARY SOURCES

Perhaps the most technically impressive general treatment of military supply issues both North and South can be found in Edward Hagerman, *The American Civil War and the Origins of Modern Warfare* (1988). While the main theme of the book is to investigate the contribution of the Civil War to the "tactical evolution of trench warfare," Hagerman devotes considerable attention to "the development of field transportation and supply to move and maneuver Civil War armies in the field,'' a development necessitated in part, he claims, by the emergence of ''positional trench warfare.'' This book is, however, difficult to read. It is a somewhat disjointed combination of various articles written by the author from 1967 through 1988, coupled with some original material. Much good information is surrounded by text that is filled with dubious assertions and the jargon of political and organizational science. Nevertheless, despite these reservations, the book is important because it provides the first truly comprehensive look at the impact of logistics on the entire course of the war.

The well-known *How the North Won* (1983) by Herman Hattaway and Archer Jones is a remarkably comprehensive, sound, and original, if somewhat disorganized, military history of the Civil War that provides a more limited overview of logistical considerations, most of which is presented in chapters 5, 6, 7, and 10. As in Hagerman's book, the important role of military supply in dictating military strategy is highlighted frequently, as, for example, in Lee's decision to cross the Potomac after Gettysburg (p. 413) and in Buell's difficulties in getting to Chattanooga after Shiloh (p. 215). Some of the chapter endnotes are quite detailed and extensive (one, for example, concerns the seasonal variation in ground moisture and its impact on the marching potential of armies).

These first two books are general military histories of the American Civil War that devote considerable attention to logistics. For a general study of the American Civil War that focuses exclusively on logistics, see a translation by Lieutenant Colonel Henry G. Sharpe and Captain H. F. Kendall of O. Espanet's ''The Art of Supplying Armies in the Field as Exemplified during the Civil War'' (1896).

For a wider survey of logistics that covers more than just the American Civil War or the U.S. Army, see Martin Van Creveld, *Supplying War: Logistics from Wallenstein to Patton* (1977). For a general history of U.S. Army logistics from the American Revolution through the Korean War, see James Huston, *The Sinews of War: Army Logistics, 1775–1953* (1966).

For a narrower focus, and as an example of how complex logistics can get, see John G. Moore, ''Mobility and Strategy in the Civil War'' for a statistical analysis of the functional relationship between wagon needs and the increasing radius of foraging area, the local population, and the size of the army. Moore uses this analysis to support McClellan's contention that a much higher wagon standard was required for the Army of the Potomac than that which had been employed by Napoleon. Moore also considers alternative methods of employing wagon trains, whether in a continuous circuit from the supply depot to the field, or a self-contained supply train that accompanied the army and sent back wagons as they were emptied.

Finally, for a general discussion of transportation during the period of the Civil War, see Forest G. Hill, *Roads, Rails and Waterways: The Army Engineers and Early Transportation* (1957).

THE SOUTH

Secondary Sources

Any discussion of secondary sources on supply in the South must begin with Richard D. Goff's highly acclaimed *Confederate Supply* (1969). This excellent book is limited specifically in scope to the "Confederate government's management of supplies for the armies east of the Mississippi," and then only with respect to the "problem-solving, policy-making, administrative, and organizational aspects of the Confederate supply effort." The technical aspects of manufacturing and farming, railroads management, blockade running, procurement, and distribution in the field have been omitted. In addition, the book does not consider the impact of finance, diplomacy, politics, conscription, private contributions, state supply efforts, and the navy on the military supply problem. The objective of this book is to describe the changes in the Confederate government's supply policy as the war progressed and the reasons for those changes. Goff concludes that supply problems "contributed in large measure to the defeat of the Confederacy" and that these problems were the result of "the accidental accumulation [by the Confederacy] of a number of the characteristics of a centralized state, but without producing the *efficiency* which would have justified it" (emphasis added). The clear implication is that with better central planning, the supply failure could have been averted. This is perhaps not a surprising conclusion to come out of Ph.D. dissertation on a public policy topic written in the early 1960s. (Goff's book was drawn from his dissertation, "Logistics and Supply Problems of the Confederacy" [1963], which, according to Hagerman, has a "sense of process lost in the drastic condensation for publication.")

Regardless, it is clear that one aspect of public policy was fatal to Confederate supply: impressment at "schedule" prices well below market equilibrium prices. Nothing like it was imposed in the North. Such a policy created, in effect, a de facto system of wage and price controls, and no amount of careful planning and implementation could have changed the result: fatal supply shortages due to hoarding. Surprisingly, few studies treat this problem in any detail, and those that do only begin to define the problem; none to date has attempted to measure its full impact. Nevertheless, a complete understanding of Confederate supply problems requires attention to the financial and tax policies that led to inflation (10,800 percent over four years, based on average Richmond market prices of impressable goods, compared to only 132 percent in the North at its worst in December 1864) and, soon after, impressment. Perhaps the best place to start is with Douglas B. Ball's *Financial Failure and Confederate Defeat* (1991); Richard Cecil Todd's *Confederate Finance* (1954); John Christopher Schwab's classic, *The Confederate States of America, 1861–1865: A Financial and Industrial History of the South during the Civil War* (1901); and Ernest Ashton Smith's *The History of the Confederate Treasury* (1901). All four of these books provide a good overview of the development of financial and tax policy, though none devotes more than a handful of pages to impressment—its nature, causes, and effects. Todd's book has the reputation of being the definitive treatment on the subject, though this status may be threatened by Ball's work, which goes much further in providing an extensive counterfactual analysis, even to the point of providing balance sheets for the Confederacy that might have been. Ball falls short, however, in his unconvincing effort to assign blame for the entire fiasco squarely on the shoulders of Memminger, the secretary of the treasury, despite his constant efforts to promote a sound fiscal policy.

For work that focuses mainly on monetary policy and its effects, see James F. Morgan's *Graybacks and Gold: Confederate Monetary Policy* (1985), John Munro Godfrey's *Monetary Expansion in the Confederacy* (1978), and two classic articles by Eugene M. Lerner that played a significant role in raising the credibility of monetarism in the 1950s, "The Monetary and Fiscal Programs of the Confederate Government, 1861–1865" (1954) and "Money, Prices, and Wages in the Confederacy, 1861–1865" (1955).

Finally, for a qualitative assessment of the impact of inflation coupled with impressment on the home front, see Frank Lawrence Owsley's *States Rights in the Confederacy* (1925) and Charles W. Ramsdell's *Behind the Lines in the Southern Confederacy* (1944).

It is generally agreed that railroads played a critical role in the South's effort to supply its armies in the field and that the effort was, in large part, a failure. Goff blames both of the South's quartermaster generals and Jefferson Davis for failing to impose greater controls on the private roads. The definitive exposition on this topic can be found in Robert C. Black's *The Railroads of the Confederacy* (1952). Neither Black nor Goff, however, has much to say about the impact of government-imposed below-market fares on railroad profits and thus efficiency. Most of Goff's observations are derived from Charles W. Ramsdell, "The Confederate Government and the Railroads" (1917). See also Angus J. Johnston's *Virginia Railroads in the Civil War* (1961).

Other studies of interest on the topic of Southern supply in general include June I. Gow, "Theory and Practice in Confederate Military Administration" (1975), Winnifred P. Minter, "Confederate Military Supply" (1959), and Ella Lonn's *Salt as a Factor in the Confederacy* (1933).

For an analysis of procurement and distribution difficulties for a Confederate army in the field, see Frank E. Vandiver, "General Hood as Logistician" (1956), and Charles W. Ramsdell, "General Robert E. Lee's Horse Supply, 1862–1865" (1930).

The only book-length biography of a Confederate supply officer is Frank E. Vandiver's *Ploughshares into Swords: Josiah Gorgas and Confederate Ordnance* (1952). (The only other biography of a Confederate supply officer was an article by Thomas Robson Hay, "Lucius B. Northrop, the Commissary General of the Confederacy" [1963].)

The success of the Ordnance Bureau relative to the other Southern supply departments was due, in part, to the fact that it had far greater control of production than did the other departments. In other words, virtually all lead, copper, and powder production was run by the military. See, for example, the following articles by Ralph W. Donnelly: "Scientists of the Confederate Niter and Mining Bureau" (1956), "Confederate Copper" (1955), and "Confederate Lead Mines of Wythe County, Virginia" (1959). For an article on the extent of Confederate controls of industry in general, see Charles W. Ramsdell, "The Control of Manufacturing by the Confederate Government" (1921).

Since the South, at least early on, lacked sufficient productive capacity, it had to rely far more heavily on imports than did the North to maintain its military. As a result, foreign purchasing operations and blockade running (both to pay for those purchases in the form, usually, of cotton exports, and to import those purchases) played an important role in confederate military supply. For purchasing operations see Samuel B. Thompson, *Confederate Purchasing Operations Abroad* (1935), and William Diamond, "Imports of the Confederate Government from Europe and Mexico" (1940). See also "Imported Confederate Shoulder Weapons" by Jac Weller (1959). For blockade running and the effects of the blockade in general, see Francis B. C. Bradlee, *Blockade Running during the Civil War and the Effect of Land and Water Transportation on the Confederacy* (1925).

To the extent that a free market did exist in the South, see Mary DeCredico's work for an assessment of the ability of entrepreneurs to respond to the needs of a wartime economy despite the myriad Confederate, state, and local government controls and regulations spawned by the war and the extent to which those needs were met (*Patriotism for Profit: Georgia's Urban Entrepreneurs and the Confederate War Effort,* 1990).

Primary Sources

For standards on baggage, subsistence and forage, see *Army Regulations, CSA* (1861, 1862, 1863); *Regulations for the CSA and for the Quartermaster's and Pay Departments* (1861); *Regulations for the CSA for the Quartermaster's Department and Pay Branch Thereof* (1862); and *The Quartermaster's Guide: Being a Compilation of Army Regulations from the Army Regulations and Other Sources* (1862). For the deviation between day-to-day realities of supply and standard of supply, see the papers of Herbert Augustine Clairburne at the Virginia Historical Society.

The Virginia Historical Society also has collections relating to the Confederate Quartermaster General's Office and the Subsistence Department, as well as a manuscript by Fontaine W. Mahood, "History of the Commissary Department of the Confederate States of America." The personal papers of Lucius B. Northrop, the commissary general, are located in the New York Public Library. Additional records of the Confederate subsistence department are found in Record Group 109 at the National Archives. For additional materials on the Quartermaster's Department, see the Alexander R. Lawton papers at the University of North Carolina. For a diary of the quartermaster officer in Lucius Polk's brigade of Cleburne's division, see Jill Garnett's *The Confederate Diary of Robert D. Smith* (1975).

For the Ordnance Department see Frank E. Vandiver's *The Civil War Diary of General Josiah Gorgas* (1947) and Josiah Gorgas, "Notes on the Ordnance Department of the Confederate Government" (1884). For a memoir by an ordnance officer that details one of the rare success stories in Confederate military supply, see *The History of the Confederate Powder Works* (1882) by George Washington Rains. For a memoir on Ordnance Bureau operations in Macon, Georgia, see J. W. Mallet, "Work of the Ordnance Bureau of the War Department of the Confederate States, 1861–1865" (1909).

Finally, an interesting source that relates to a problem unique to Southern supply is the memoir of Caleb Huse, which recounts the tale of obtaining and paying for supplies in Europe for the Confederate army: *The Supplies for the Confederate Army, How They Were Obtained in Europe and How Paid for, Personal Reminiscences and Unpublished History* (1904).

THE NORTH

Secondary Sources

For a general overview of the organization and administration of the U.S. Army during the Civil War, see Fred Albert Shannon's *The Organization and Administration of the Union Army, 1861–1865* (1928). Another general overview of the U.S. Army that contains, according to J. G. Randall, a highly useful study of army control during the Civil War that emphasizes military mistakes and administrative faults is Emory Upton's *The Military Policy of the United States from 1775* (1907).

For a general survey of the U.S. quartermaster and subsistence organization that is partly devoted to the Civil War, see Erna Risch, *Quartermaster Support of the Army: A History of the Corps, 1775–1939* (1962). For a biography of the quartermaster general that devotes considerable detail to the story of the Quartermaster's Department in the Civil War, see Russell F. Weigley, *Quartermaster General of the Union Army: A Biography of M. C. Meigs* (1959). In addition, see Sherrad E. East, "Montgomery C. Meigs and the Quartermaster Department" (1962).

It is perhaps not surprising that what little does exist on Northern army supply is generally devoted to Sherman. The one exception is James A. Huston, "Logistical Support of Federal Armies in the Field" (1961). John G. Barrett's book on Sherman's Carolinas campaign is, according to Hagerman, occasionally and incidentally interested in the organization of field transportation and field supply for Sherman's strategy of total warfare in the Carolinas (*Sherman's March through the Carolinas* [1956]). For Sherman's Atlanta campaign, see Kennedy Duncan and Roger S. Fitch, *Supply of Sherman's Army during the Atlanta Cam-*

paign (1911), and Armin E. Mruck, "The Role of Railroads in the Atlanta Campaign" (1961).

Primary Sources

The records of the Office of the Quartermaster General are located in Record Group 92 at the National Archives. Returns and inspection records are found in Record Group 94. Unfiled and uncataloged trimonthly quartermaster returns of the U.S. Army are found in Record Group 393.

The papers of the commissary general are in the Military History Research Collection at Carlisle Barracks, Pennsylvania.

For standards on baggage, subsistence, and forage, see *Regulations for the Army of the United States* (1857) and Robert Finley Hunter, *Manual for Quartermasters and Commissaries* (1863).

Finally, see N. S. Dodge, *Hints on Army Transportation* (1863) for a tract that Meigs found so compelling that he ordered it circulated throughout the Union armies. Dodge was the quartermaster of the 119th New York volunteers. In this book, according to Hagerman, he claimed his reorganization would so reduce the wagon train as to add six miles daily to an average five-day march. Such enhancements were motivated by the then-prevailing "flying column" wisdom, modeled after the logistical organization in the French army, as described by Alexis Godillot in a circular from Montgomery Meigs dated January 2, 1862 (*The War of the Rebellion: A Compilation of the Official Records of the Union and Confederate Armies,* 1880–1901). But as the wagon and mule supply improved, the foragable supplies diminished, and the need for extreme mobility diminished with the changing strategic conditions in Virginia, the need for a flying column organization diminished; by the time of the Wilderness campaign, it was essentially abandoned by Grant.

CONCLUSION

There are many potentially rewarding areas for further research. For example, much work remains with respect to the explicit linkage of Southern supply problems to campaign results. How many times have we seen the complaint over "lack of transportation"? Bragg cited it after Chickamauga to explain his inability to flank Rosecrans out of Chattanooga. Longstreet cited it as the cause of his delays to Knoxville. Johnston cited it as the reason for the impracticability of the spring 1864 forward movement. Davis cited it to Longstreet in rejecting his plans for a Kentucky invasion. How real was this lack of transportation? How real was the lack of adequate food? Part of Bragg's rationale for recapturing Knoxville may have been to reopen the railroad to Virginia simply to ensure adequate food supplies. He knew by the end of October that he could not rely on the road from Atlanta. By the time of the Battle of Chattanooga, it is well known that his troops, though the besiegers, were suffering terribly from inadequate food and shelter. How serious was the food shortage for Bragg? What was wrong with the Atlanta line, if anything? How serious were equipment shortages? For example, the Army of Tennessee had only 50 percent rifles as of April 30, 1863. What was the ratio at Chickamauga and Chattanooga, and to what extent can the successful Union assault at the latter be attributed to it?

In addition to identifying, measuring, and linking supply problems to campaign results, there is a need to understand what caused these problems—that is, to what extent were these shortages due to immutable factors such as limited natural resources, labor, and productive capacity, and how much was to due to bad public policy such as, for example, impressment at below-market prices and laws against trading through the lines? There is considerable evidence to suggest that many of the supply and transportation problems experienced by the military were in large part attributable to government policy and that, in fact, the Southern economy was relatively prosperous toward the end of the war, despite the near bankruptcy of the Confederate government and the efficacy of the blockade. How prosperous was the South toward the end of the war? How much more prosperous might it have been under some other public policy? Whatever the level of prosperity, was the army doomed to critical shortages by virtue of bad policy? Could some other policy have eliminated critical army shortages even in a depressed economy?

BIBLIOGRAPHY

PRIMARY SOURCES

South

Public Documents

Army Regulations, CSA. Richmond: West and Johnston, 1861.
Army Regulations, CSA. Richmond: J. W. Randolph, 1862.
Army Regulations, CSA. Richmond: J. W. Randolph, 1863.
The Quartermaster's Guide: Being a Compilation of Army Regulations from the Army Regulations and Other Sources. Richmond: West and Johnston, 1862.
Regulations for the CSA and for the Quartermaster's and Pay Departments. New Orleans: Bloomfield and Stell, 1861.
Regulations for the CSA for the Quartermaster's Department and Pay Branch Thereof. Richmond: Ritchie and Dunnavent, 1862.

Personal Papers

Clairburne, Herbert Augustine. Papers. Section 44, Papers Relating to the Subsistence Department, C.S.A. Virginia Historical Society, Richmond, Virginia.
Confederate States of America. Army. Commissary Department; Lucius Bellinger Northrop, Commissary General. New York Public Library.
———. Quartermaster General's Office. Virginia Historical Society, Richmond, Virginia.

————. Subsistence Department, C.S.A. Papers. Virginia Historical Society, Richmond, Virginia.

Lawton Alexander R. Papers. Southern Historical Collection, University of North Carolina.

Mahood, Fontaine W. "History of the Commissary Department of the Confederate States of America." Virginia Historical Society, Richmond, Virginia.

U.S. War Department. Collection of Confederate Records: Record Group 109. Transportation, Subsistence, Special, General, and Field Orders and Circulars for Geographical and Higher Mobile Commands, Confederate States Armies. National Archives of the United States.

Diaries

Garnett, Jill, ed. *Confederate Diary of Robert D. Smith.* Columbia: United Daughters of the Confederacy, 1975.

Vandiver, Frank E., ed. *The Civil War Diary of General Josiah Gorgas.* University: University of Alabama Press, 1947.

Memoirs

Gorgas, Josiah. "Notes on the Ordnance Department of the Confederate Government." *Southern Historical Society Papers* 12 (1884): 66–94.

Huse, Caleb. *The Supplies for the Confederate Army: How They Were Obtained in Europe and How Paid for, Personal Reminiscences and Unpublished History.* Boston: T. R. Marvin and Son, 1904.

Mallet, J. W. "Work of the Ordnance Bureau of the War Department of the Confederate States, 1861–1865." *Southern Historical Society Papers* 37 (1909): 1–20.

Rains, George Washington. *The History of the Confederate Powder Works.* Augusta, GA: Chronicle and Constitutionalist Printers, 1882.

North

Dodge, N. S. *Hints on Army Transportation.* Albany: Charles van Benthuysen, 1863.

Hunter, Robert Finley. *Manual for Quartermasters and Commissaries.* New York: Van Nostrand, 1863.

Meigs, Montgomery. U.S. War Department. *The War of the Rebellion: A Compilation of the Official Records of the Union and Confederate Armies.* 128 vols. Washington, D.C.: Government Printing Office, 1880–1901.

Papers of the Commissary General of the U.S. Army, 1861–1865. Military History Research Collection, Carlisle Barracks, Pennsylvania.

Regulations for the Army of the United States. New York: Harper and Brothers, 1857.

U.S. War Department. Collection of Union Records: Record Group 92, Records of the Office of the Quartermaster General; Record Group 94, Return and Inspection Reports, U.S. Army; Record Group 393, Records of the United States Army Continental Consolidated Commands, 1821–1920; unfiled and uncataloged tri-monthly Quartermaster returns of the Union Army. National Archives of the United States.

SECONDARY SOURCES

General

Espanet, O. "The Art of Supplying Armies in the Field as Exemplified during the Civil War." In "Notes on the Supply of an Army during Active Operations." *Journal of the Military Service Institution of the United States* 18 (1896): 45–95.

Hagerman, Edward. *The American Civil War and the Origins of Modern Warfare.* Bloomington: Indiana University Press, 1988.

Hattaway, Herman, and Archer Jones. *How the North Won.* Urbana: University of Illinois Press, 1983.

Hill, Forest G. *Roads, Rails and Waterways: The Army Engineers and Early Transportation.* Norman: University of Oklahoma, 1957.

Huston, James. *The Sinews of War: Army Logistics, 1775–1953.* Washington, D.C.: Office of the Chief of Military History, United States Army, 1966.

Moore, John G. "Mobility and Strategy in the Civil War." *Military Affairs* 24 (1960): 68–77.

Van Creveld, Martin. *Supplying War: Logistics from Wallenstein to Patton.* Cambridge: Cambridge University Press, 1977.

South

Ball, Douglas B. *Financial Failure and Confederate Defeat.* Urbana: University of Illinois Press, 1991.

Black, Robert C. III *The Railroads of the Confederacy.* Chapel Hill: University of North Carolina Press, 1952.

Bradlee, Francis B. C. *Blockade Running during the Civil War and the Effect of Land and Water Transportation on the Confederacy.* Salem, MA, 1925.

DeCredico, Mary. *Patriotism for Profit: Georgia's Urban Entrepreneurs and the Confederate War Effort.* Chapel Hill: University of North Carolina Press, 1990.

Diamond, William. "Imports of the Confederate Government from Europe and Mexico." *Journal of Southern History* 6 (1940): 470–503.

Donnelly, Ralph W. "Confederate Copper." *Civil War History* 1 (1955): 355–370.

———. "Scientists of the Confederate Niter and Mining Bureau." *Civil War History* 2 (1956).

———. "Confederate Lead Mines of Wythe County, Virginia." *Civil War History* 5 (1959): 402–414.

Godfrey, John Munro. *Monetary Expansion in the Confederacy.* New York: Arno Press, 1978.

Goff, Richard D. "Logistics and Supply Problems in the Confederacy." Ph.D. diss., Duke University, 1963.

———. *Confederate Supply.* Durham: Duke University Press, 1969.

Gow, June I. "Theory and Practice in Confederate Military Administration." *Military Affairs* 21 (1975): 118–123.

Hay, Thomas Robson. "Lucius B. Northrop: Commissary General of the Confederacy." *Civil War History* 9 (1963): 5–23.

Johnston, Angus J. *Virginia Railroads in the Civil War.* Chapel Hill: University of North Carolina Press, 1961.

Lerner, Eugene M. "The Monetary and Fiscal Programs of the Confederate Government, 1861–1865." *Journal of Political Economy* 62(1954): 506–522.

———. "Money, Prices, and Wages in the Confederacy, 1861–1865." *Journal of Political Economy* 63 (1955): 20–40.

Lonn, Ella. *Salt as a Factor in the Confederacy.* New York: W. Neale, 1933.

Minter, Winnifred P. "Confederate Military Supply." *Social Science* 34 (1959): 163–171.

Morgan. James F. *Graybacks and Gold: Confederate Monetary Policy.* Pensacola: Perdido Bay Press, 1985.

Owsley, Frank Lawrence. *States Rights in the Confederacy.* Chicago: University of Chicago, 1925.

Ramsdell, Charles W. "General Robert E. Lee's Horse Supply, 1862–1865." *American Historical Review* 35 (1930): 758–777.

———. *Behind the Lines in the Southern Confederacy.* Baton Rouge: Louisiana State University, 1944.

———. "The Confederate Government and the Railroads." *American Historical Review* 22 (1917): 794–810.

———. "The Control of Manufacturing by the Confederate Government." *Mississippi Valley Historical Review* 8 (1921): 231–249.

Schwab, John Christopher. *The Confederate States of America, 1861–1865: A Financial and Industrial History of the South during the Civil War.* New York: Charles Scribner's Sons, 1901.

Smith, Ernest Ashton. *The History of the Confederate Treasury.* Harrisburg: Harrisburg Publishing Company, 1901.

Thompson, Samuel B. *Confederate Purchasing Operations Abroad.* Chapel Hill: University of North Carolina Press, 1935.

Todd, Richard Cecil. *Confederate Finance.* Athens: University of Georgia, 1954.

Vandiver, Frank E. *Ploughshares into Swords: Josiah Gorgas and Confederate Ordnance.* Austin: University of Texas Press, 1952.

———. "General Hood as Logistician." *Military Affairs* 16 (1956): 1–11.

Weller, Jac. "Imported Confederate Shoulder Weapons." *Civil War History* 5 (1959).

North

Barrett, John G. *Sherman's March through the Carolinas.* Chapel Hill: University of North Carolina Press, 1956.

Duncan, Kennedy, and Roger S. Fitch. *Supply of Sherman's Army during the Atlanta Campaign.* Fort Leavenworth, Kansas, 1911.

East, Sherrad E. "Montgomery C. Meigs and the Quartermaster Department." *Military Affairs* 26 (1962): 183–197.

Huston, James A. "Logistical Support of Federal Armies in the Field." *Civil War History* 7 (1961).

Mruck, Armin, E. "The Role of Railroads in the Atlanta Campaign." *Civil War History* 7 (1961).

Risch, Erna. *Quartermaster Support of the Army: A History of the Corps, 1775–1939.* Washington, D.C.: Quartermaster Historian's Office, Office of the Quartermaster General, 1962.

Shannon, Fred Albert. *The Organization and Administration of the Union Army, 1861–1865.* 2 vols. Cleveland: Arthur H. Clark Co., 1928.

Upton, Emory. *The Military Policy of the United States from 1775.* Washington, D.C., 1907.

Weigley, Russell F. *Quartermaster General of the Union Army: A Biography of M. C. Meigs.* New York: Columbia University Press, 1959.

32

Intelligence Activities

William B. Feis

When used in reference to the American Civil War, the phrase "intelligence activities" calls to mind tales of daring spies and their harrowing adventures. These prevalent images have fostered the mistaken impression that spies and espionage comprised the essence of Civil War intelligence operations. In reality, those engaged in intelligence work, or what contemporaries called secret service, included not only spies but also army scouts, cavalry patrols, government detectives, agents operating abroad, guides, couriers, telegraphers, aerial (balloon) observers, and Signal Corps personnel. To these people, intelligence simply meant information, not, as in the current definition, the end product of information analysis.

Both Federals and Confederates initiated ad hoc secret service operations on many levels and, in some cases, developed organizational structures to support them. However, neither side created a centralized, national-level agency to coordinate wartime diplomatic, political, and military intelligence efforts.

GENERAL WORKS

The literature on Civil War intelligence activities reflects the diverse nature of operations, sources, objectives, and personnel. The best overview remains Edwin C. Fishel's "The Mythology of Civil War Intelligence" (1964) and the revised version, "Myths That Never Die" (1988). Fishel believes that the fascination with mythical cloak-and-dagger adventures has overshadowed the actual contributions of Civil War intelligence, and he challenges the most prevalent myths at the core of what he calls the "magnolia blossom school" of intelligence history.

Spying for America: The Hidden History of U.S. Intelligence (1989) by Nathan Miller provides a good summary of the Civil War experience within the sweep of American intelligence history. G.J.A. O'Toole's *The Encyclopedia of American Intelligence and Espionage: From the Revolutionary War to the Present* (1988) also constitutes a valuable reference for this aspect of the war.

SPIES, ESPIONAGE, AND COVERT OPERATIONS

Although no general monographic treatment of Civil War intelligence exists, spies, espionage, and covert operations have received ample coverage in print. Unfortunately, secondary accounts of Civil War spies typically refurbish tattered and time-worn anecdotes and place them between new covers with little comment on their veracity. Recent examples include Donald E. Markle's *Spies and Spymasters of the Civil War* (1994) and *The War between the Spies: A History of Espionage during the Civil War* (1992) by Alan Axelrod. Although they are informative, the dearth of substantial archival sourcework and critical analysis limits their usefulness. More helpful, at least for the Southern side, is John Bakeless's *Spies of the Confederacy* (1970), which examines the deeds of various Confederate operatives and illuminates military intelligence operations within the gray-clad armies.

Much of what appears with regard to espionage in these secondary works originates from the postwar writings of participants. Reminiscing and ax-grinding in print became a cottage industry after the war, especially among former generals and politicians. Spies also penned their memoirs, sometimes for mercenary or self-inflating purposes. Curtis Carroll Davis discusses these reminiscences in his "Companions of Crisis: The Spy Memoir as a Social Document" (1964). He illuminates the characteristics shared by Civil War spy memoirs as products of the Victorian romanticism common to late-nineteenth-century literature. Unfortunately, these melodramatic, undocumented accounts went unchallenged, and, as a result, many unsubstantiated stories, some with only a nodding acquaintance with the truth, became entrenched as historical fact and reemerged as such in later secondary accounts.

The memoirs of Allan Pinkerton and Lafayette C. Baker illustrate this phenomenon. Pinkerton's *The Spy of the Rebellion* (1888) details, among other things, his efforts to collect military information for General George B. McClellan's Army of the Potomac in 1862, while Baker's *History of the United States Secret Service* (1867) describes his counterintelligence operations and criminal investigations in the Federal capital during his tenure as provost marshal of the War Department. Besides preserving their stories for posterity, the authors had other purposes in mind when they put pen to paper. Pinkerton wrote his apologia to protect his war record and the reputation of his postwar detective dynasty. Likewise, Baker was defending himself against charges that he exceeded his authority and the Constitution in his zealous pursuit of disloyal citizens. Although some historians have accepted them as historical truth, these narratives remain tainted by the ulterior motives, selective memories, and vivid imaginations of their authors.

Their two chief antagonists, and arguably the best-known spies of the war, were Rose O'Neal Greenhow and Belle Boyd. Both women popularized their exploits in print and thereby ensured their immortality in Civil War history. Greenhow's colorful *My Imprisonment and the First Year of Abolition Rule at Washington* (1863), written during her exile in England, describes how she sent crucial information to the Confederates before First Bull Run, although historians now disagree as to the true value of the intelligence she provided. Primarily a work of pro-Confederate propaganda directed at Europe, the memoirs of "Rebel Rose" became a sentimental favorite after her death in 1864 and must be read with a careful eye. Many secondary accounts of Greenhow's activities, including the most recent biography, *Rebel Rose: Life of Rose O'Neal Greenhow, Confederate Spy* (1954) by Ishbel Ross, must also be read with a healthy dose of skepticism since they depend primarily on the spy's suspect reminiscences.

Belle Boyd achieved fame for delivering information to Confederate General Thomas J. "Stonewall" Jackson outside Front Royal, Virginia, in 1862. This deed and the acclaim she reaped as a result earned her the title of "The Civil War's Most Over-Rated Spy" (1965) from Curtis Carroll Davis, who argues that the information she delivered only confirmed what Jackson already knew. Although corroboration constitutes a vital aspect of intelligence work, Davis rejects Boyd's claim that Jackson acted on her information alone.

Davis also critiqued and edited a new edition of her 1865 memoirs, *Belle Boyd in Camp and Prison* (1968), the first attempt of this kind on a Civil War spy memoir. In his introduction, Davis discusses "La Belle Rebelle's" public and private lives and argues that although Boyd created consternation among the Union command, her amateurish behavior limited her effectiveness as a secret agent. However, Davis also believes that, despite some narrative flights of fancy, her memoirs are more truthful than most others of this genre.

Davis's conclusions echo those of Boyd's biographer and former U.S. Army intelligence officer, Louis A. Sigaud, in his *Belle Boyd, Confederate Spy* (1944). Although pro-Boyd in perspective, Sigaud combined professional intelligence expertise and a range of sources to make his treatment the most reliable biography of the famous spy to date.

Unfortunately, the activities of native Southerners who spied for the Union remain little known since the fear of retribution from bitter neighbors in Dixie often silenced their pens after the war. For example, Elizabeth Van Lew, a devout Unionist who directed a spy network from her Richmond home, wrote nothing for fear her memoirs might arouse the wrath of her fellow citizens. If not for Meriwether Stuart, Van Lew's valuable contributions to the Union might have remained lost in the attic of Civil War history. His article, "Colonel Ulric

Dahlgren and Richmond's Union Underground'' (1964), describes one of Van Lew's successful operations and revealed the competency displayed by her operatives, known in official Federal correspondence as ''our friends in Richmond.'' Along with ''Of Spies and Borrowed Names: The Identity of Union Operatives Known as the 'Phillipses' Discovered'' (1981), Stuart's well-researched efforts reveal much about the organization, operations, and effectiveness of one of the Union's most successful spy rings.

Samuel Ruth, superintendent of a major Virginia railroad, headed another group of Union spies in Richmond. Angus J. Johnston II uncovers the linkage between Ruth and Union espionage in his study, ''Disloyalty on Confederate Railroads in Virginia'' (1955). Meriwether Stuart furnishes a more in-depth examination of Ruth's success in hampering Confederate transportation and supply efforts, and his role in providing military information to the Federals, in ''Samuel Ruth and General R. E. Lee: Disloyalty and the Line of Supply to Fredericksburg, 1862–1863'' (1963).

The Richmond spies posed a serious challenge to Confederate counterintelligence and security in the capital. Arch Blakey examines the career of the provost marshal of Richmond and the Confederacy's top spy catcher in *General John H. Winder, C.S.A.* (1990). Although the infamous ''Dictator of Richmond'' arrested hundreds of citizens for espionage and treasonous activity, many important Union agents eluded his grasp.

Despite its counterintelligence problems, the Confederate government enhanced its overall intelligence capability in 1862 when it established the Confederate Signal Corps headed by Major William Norris. From Signal Corps headquarters in Richmond, Norris also ran the Confederacy's secret war against the Union through the War Department's so-called Secret Service Bureau. Until recently, the only history of Norris's ''backroom'' organization was Charles E. Taylor's *The Signal and Secret Service of the Confederate States* (1903). As a former member of the Secret Service Bureau, Taylor provides a rare insider's view of this enigmatic organization. However, not until David Winfred Gaddy's ''William Norris and the Confederate Signal and Secret Service'' (1975) did Norris and Confederate intelligence activities come into focus. Gaddy's research helped save the Secret Service Bureau from obscurity, a fate seemingly sealed by the destruction of most of the bureau's records in the fires that burned Richmond in 1865 and Norris's home in 1890.

In 1988 William A. Tidwell teamed with Gaddy and James O. Hall to author *Come Retribution: The Confederate Secret Service and the Assassination of Lincoln* (1988), which contains an informative chapter, ''The Confederate Intelligence Machinery.'' Tidwell later examined ''Confederate Expenditures for Secret Service'' (1991) and discovered that the Confederate government's secret service bill increased late in the war as it tried to compensate for battlefield reverses with sabotage and political action campaigns against the North. Southern officials devoted considerable attention to an attempt by Confederate operatives in the Northwest and Canada to carve a "Northwest Confederacy" out of the Union with the help of antiwar Northern Democrats.

Both Oscar A. Kinchen's *Confederate Operations in Canada and the North* (1970) and John W. Headley's *Confederate Operations in Canada and New York* (1906) are accounts of the so-called Northwest Conspiracy and of the Confederate agents involved in this and other covert operations in the North. Kinchen's work remains the more scholarly of the two, while Headley, a participant in the botched attempt to firebomb New York City in 1864, furnishes an insider's view of the action. James D. Horan supplies insights into the career of Captain Thomas H. Hines, one of "Morgan's Raiders" and a major figure in the Northwest Conspiracy, in *Confederate Agent: A Discovery in History* (1954). The Northern antiwar groups involved in subversive activities are discussed in Frank L. Klement's *Dark Lanterns: Secret Political Societies, Conspiracies, and Treason Trials in the Civil War* (1984).

The South also endured disloyal behavior and treasonous activity on the home front. Unionists in northern Alabama, eastern Tennessee, and elsewhere throughout the Confederacy prevented loyal Southerners from feeling secure at home. The activities of various pro-Union political and paramilitary organizations in the Confederacy receive excellent coverage in Georgia Lee Tatum's *Disloyalty in the Confederacy* (1934).

INTELLIGENCE ACTIVITY IN EUROPE

Clandestine activities initiated by both sides were not confined to North America. Due to the need for European financial and diplomatic support, Southerners courted foreign governments and established a covert network to acquire arms, ammunition, and naval vessels. A major source regarding this mission is the highly partisan account by James D. Bulloch, *The Secret Service of the Confederate States in Europe* (1884). As chief of Confederate clandestine operations in Europe, Bulloch describes his attempts to acquire a Confederate navy on foreign soil. Frank J. Merli awards Bulloch high marks for his service in *Great Britain and the Confederate Navy* (1970), while Warren F. Spencer examines Bulloch's procurement efforts on the European continent in *The Confederate Navy in Europe* (1983). Although these efforts ultimately failed, it was Bulloch who unleashed the *Florida*, the *Shenandoah*, and the *Alabama* on Northern shipping.

The Federal government recognized the dangers posed by Confederates abroad and instructed Henry S. Sanford, the U.S. minister to Belgium, to watch Bulloch's operatives and squelch his attempts to supply the Confederacy from abroad. The best monographs to date on the Union's foreign operations are *Henry S. Sanford: Diplomacy and Business in Nineteenth-Century America* (1982) by Joseph Fry, and Harriet C. Owsley's "Henry Shelton Sanford and Federal Surveillance Abroad, 1861–1865" (1961). Fry places Sanford's Civil War activities in the context of his diplomatic career; Owsley reconstructs his surveillance network and details its successful operations. For a discussion of the Bulloch-Sanford affair within the context of U.S.-British relations, consult Brian Jenkins's two-volume *Britain and the War for the Union* (1974, 1980).

MILITARY INTELLIGENCE

Intelligence activities from Chicago to Liverpool influenced the war on different levels, but events on the battlefield ultimately decided the war's outcome. The acquisition of information for use during battles and campaigns by Union forces is covered in Bruce Bidwell's *History of the Military Intelligence Division, Department of the Army General Staff, 1775–1941* (1986). He discusses how Federal commanders pursued information on the enemy and places the Civil War experience within the overall development and institutionalization of U.S. Army intelligence organization and capability.

The military maxim that warns leaders to "know your enemy and know yourself" has special relevance in the case of General George B. McClellan and his intelligence officer, Allan Pinkerton. During the 1862 Peninsula campaign, the two consistently overestimated their enemy's size, yet neither man grasped that his own paranoid proclivities had skewed his calculations. Some critics have accused Pinkerton of leading McClellan down the path of procrastination with his tall tales of Confederate strength. Others believe the general forced his own views on his sycophantic intelligence officer. In "Pinkerton and McClellan: Who Deceived Whom?" (1988) Edwin C. Fishel examines how the detective calculated his enemy strength estimates and concludes that Pinkerton's flawed methods produced numbers that he knew supported his commander's paranoid visions of a vastly superior enemy force. This dangerous relationship facilitated McClellan's "slows" and helped lead to defeat on the Peninsula.

Pinkerton departed with McClellan in late 1862, but not until General Joseph Hooker took command in 1863 did the army once again create an organization specifically tasked with gathering and analyzing combat information. Hooker added positive intelligence collection to the functions of the Army of the Potomac's provost marshal general's department and assigned Colonel George H. Sharpe to head the army's new intelligence arm, the Bureau of Military Information. Sharpe's men gathered order-of-battle and other information for the Army of the Potomac's commander and later for Ulysses S. Grant.

Several essays examine these developments within the Army of the Potomac. Wilton P. Moore furnishes a short history, "Union Army Provost Marshals in the Eastern Theater" (1962), while David S. Sparks provides more detail on the activities of Sharpe's bureau in "General Patrick's Progress: Intelligence and Security in the Army of the Potomac" (1964). C. T. Schmidt also examines the evolution of intelligence operations within the army from Pinkerton to Sharpe in "G-2, Army of the Potomac" (1948). Although the designation "G-2" did not emerge in the U.S. Army until 1917, Schmidt describes the vicissitudes of intelligence work within the Union's main eastern army.

Federal intelligence operations in the western theater remain virtually unstudied, although a few works broach the subject. For example, Stanley P. Hirshson's sympathetic biography, *Grenville M. Dodge: Soldier, Politician, Railroad Pioneer* (1967), follows Dodge's wartime career and touches on the intelligence network he operated for Grant in Mississippi. In middle Tennessee, General William S. Rosecrans's intelligence operations, which facilitated his stunning maneuver campaign in 1863 that expelled the Confederates from the region, receive attention in William B. Feis's "The Deception of Braxton Bragg: The Tullahoma Campaign" (1992).

As for Confederate military intelligence in any theater, works of the surface-scratching variety predominate. In the aforementioned *Come Retribution,* Tidwell, Gaddy, and Hall devote only a brief chapter to the collection of tactical information in the Army of Northern Virginia. H. V. Canan supplies the only general examination of combat information in the Southern armies in "Confederate Military Intelligence" (1964), although he adds but a few brush strokes to a much larger canvas.

The best survey of Confederate army security and counterintelligence remains *Rebel Watchdog: The Confederate States Army Provost Guard* (1989) by Kenneth Radley. He details how the Provost Guard, the counterintelligence arm of the Confederate armies, exposed suspected Union spies and subversives through its infamous "passport system." However, the Confederate Provost Guard did not engage in meaningful military intelligence collection, nor did it possess anything comparable to the Union Bureau of Military Information.

MILITARY INTELLIGENCE SOURCES

Whether intelligence duties rested with an organization or an individual, they all faced the task of locating reliable sources and mining them for useful information. Peter Maslowski's excellent essay, "Military Intelligence Sources during the Civil War: A Case Study" (1991), demonstrates that commanders derived information from many diverse sources, including spies, scouts, cavalry patrols, aerial (balloon) reconnaissance, captured enemy documents, and interrogations of prisoners, deserters, refugees, and fugitive slaves. He also discusses information obtained from intercepted enemy telegraph and signal messages. Maslowski's analysis of military intelligence sources, complete with ample bibliographic references, remains a key resource on the topic.

Literature on the specific military intelligence sources is also useful. The most important and consistent military information came from cavalry reconnaissances. Stephen Z. Starr's three-volume *The Union Cavalry in the Civil War* (1979–1985) and Edward G. Longacre's analysis, *The Cavalry at Gettysburg* (1986), provide examples of the vital intelligence role of both the Union and Confederate cavalry in important campaigns.

Whether soldiers or civilian employees of the army, scouts also garnered information from their forays near or into enemy lines and were an additional consistent source. James Peavey's *Confederate Scout: Virginia's Frank String-fellow* (1956) describes the services of General Jeb Stuart's celebrated scout, while Archie P. McDonald's edited *Make Me a Map of the Valley: The Civil War Journal of Stonewall Jackson's Topographer* (1973) follows Jedediah Hotchkiss on scouting missions to obtain topographical intelligence. For the Union, Robert Scott Davis, Jr., describes "The Curious Civil War Career of James George Brown, Spy" (1994). Brown served as a scout for General Nathaniel Banks in Louisiana and later for General George H. Thomas in northern Georgia.

James O. Hall searches for the true identity of perhaps the war's most famous scout in "The Spy Harrison: A Modern Hunt for a Fabled Agent" (1986). He reveals that the scout who warned Lee of the Union army's advance into Pennsylvania prior to Gettysburg was *not,* as many believed, the actor James Harrison but an accomplished army scout named Lieutenant Henry Thomas Harrison. Hall's solution to the mystery illuminates the difficulties and the rewards associated with researching this aspect of the war.

Another source of information was enemy newspapers. Both Union and Confederate commanders read their foe's papers on a regular basis seeking military information. With little systematic censorship, overzealous correspondents sometimes printed military secrets. James G. Pardell discusses this prickly security problem with its constitutional implications in "The Newspaper Problem in Its Bearing upon Military Secrecy during the Civil War" (1918). In addition, J. Cutler Andrews's excellent studies of journalism during the war, *The North Reports the Civil War* (1955) and *The South Reports the Civil War* (1970), also investigate the dilemma war correspondents faced in maintaining the fragile balance between reporting the war and leaking military secrets.

Some commanders recognized the problem and took measures to plug the leaks. The most famous example remains General William T. Sherman's ongoing campaign against Northern war correspondents. Sherman hated newsmen and even threatened to hang a few since they were, in his estimation, worse than spies. John F. Marszalek referees this interesting bout between the general and the journalists in his description of *Sherman's Other War: The General and the Civil War Press* (1981).

Technological advances also affected the collection of military intelligence. The telegraph and a visual signaling system (a wig-wag alphabet transmitted by flag or torch) opened new strategic and tactical communications vistas, allowed for real-time transmission of intelligence, and offered another source of information through the interception of enemy signal traffic, known today as signals intelligence. The most informative work on Civil War telegraphy remains William R. Plum's *The Military Telegraph during the Civil War in the United States* (1882), which details the operations of the civilian United States Military Telegraph (USMT) in various theaters and describes the development of secret codes or "ciphers" to protect signal transmissions from unauthorized ears.

Another useful account is David Homer Bates's *Lincoln in the Telegraph*

Office: Recollections of the United States Military Telegraph Corps during the Civil War (1907). Bates describes how he and fellow War Department telegraphers Charles A. Tinker and Albert B. Chandler, known as the "sacred three," became adept at encoding Union messages (cryptography) and decoding intercepted Confederate signal traffic (cryptanalysis). To place the Civil War experience within the context of the historical development of codes and code breaking, consult David Kahn's *The Codebreakers: The Story of Secret Writing* (1967).

Cipher experts sometimes accompanied commanders into the field to encode and decode tactical transmissions. The services of Ulysses S. Grant's cipher operator are described in John Y. Simon and David L. Wilson's "Samuel H. Beckwith: 'Grant's Shadow' " (1981).

An important source on the U.S. Army Signal Corps is J. Willard Brown's *The Signal Corps, U.S.A. in the War of the Rebellion* (1898). Brown provides historical and organizational background and details signal operations in all departments during the war. David J. Marshall also weighs in with an essay published in Max L. Marshall's edited work *Story of the U.S. Army Signal Corps* (1965), which follows the Signal Corps from the introduction of Major Albert J. Myer's signaling system before the war through its wartime service under his leadership.

More recent works include "Civil War Signals" (1980) by George Raynor Thompson and Paul J. Scheips's "Union Signal Communications: Innovation and Conflict" (1963). Thompson integrates the histories of both Federal and Confederate Signal Corps and telegraphers into his narrative, while Scheips concentrates on the development of Anson Stager's USMT and Myer's Signal Corps and highlights their feud over control of all Union army signal communications.

David W. Gaddy's contributions remain the most informative on the Confederate army Signal Corps. Gaddy's work traces its organizational history, including the adoption of Myer's signal system by his former assistant-turned-Confederate E. P. Alexander and its baptism of fire at First Manassas.

Finally, the appearance of balloons on the battlefield also affected military intelligence collection on a small scale, at least until both sides grounded their airborne "spies" in 1863. Used for aerial reconnaissance, balloons offered commanders an excellent vantage point from which to observe the enemy. The best literature on Civil War balloons includes J. Duane Squires's "Aeronautics in the Civil War" (1937) and F. Stansbury Haydon's *Aeronautics in the Union and Confederate Armies, with a Survey of Military Aeronautics Prior to 1861* (1941). Haydon furnishes a concise history of the Army of the Potomac's civilian balloon corps headed by Professor Thaddeus S. C. Lowe. He also provides an excellent discussion of the balloon's value as an information source since "aeronauts" could observe enemy activity, watch for possible surprise attacks, sketch terrain maps, and even provide fire direction for artillery.

Due to limited resources, Confederate experimentation with balloons never achieved the same organizational or operational sophistication that the Union attained. Joseph Jenkins Cornish III provides a view of aeronauts in gray in *The Air Arm of the Confederacy* (1963), including accounts of the legendary "silk dress" balloons that saw service in Virginia and South Carolina.

INTELLIGENCE AND COMMAND

Resourceful officers sometimes had access to multiple sources of information for use in making command decisions. Quite often, however, the intelligence reports they received were wrong or contradictory, or both. Even with multiple sources, a consistent problem remained: reaping the truth from a whirlwind of rumors, hearsay, and sketchy reports.

Some recent literature examines this process and shows how commanders analyzed and utilized the information at their disposal. Instead of dwelling on collection methods and sources, these works stress the impact of information on command decisions and, by extension, on battles and campaigns. Fishel's 1964 article constitutes the clarion call advocating this approach to Civil War intelligence studies, and his own work attests to the benefits.

Jay Luvaas and William B. Feis examine the impact of intelligence—or lack thereof—on important campaigns. Luvaas discusses "Lee at Gettysburg: A General without Intelligence" (1990) and "The Role of Intelligence in the Chancellorsville Campaign, April–May, 1863" (1990). Feis investigates how faulty intelligence led Ulysses S. Grant astray in "A Union Military Intelligence Failure: Jubal Early's Raid, June 12–July 14, 1864" (1990). The intelligence collaboration between Grant and General Philip H. Sheridan that aided in the Union victory over Confederate forces in the Shenandoah is covered in Feis's "Neutralizing the Valley: The Role of Military Intelligence in the Defeat of Jubal Early's Army of the Valley, 1864–1865" (1993).

Although not an exhaustive list, the literature described in this chapter illustrates the scope of intelligence activities during the war and the diversity of the writings on the topic. A flood of new works on the Civil War inundates the reading public annually, but only a few droplets pertain to intelligence. This aspect of the war cries for more scholarly attention in order to reduce the influence of the myths and the anecdotal accounts that have thus far dominated Civil War intelligence history and to paint a more accurate picture of what Phil Sheridan referred to as a "great essential of success" in warfare: the acquisition and use of information to defeat the enemy.

BIBLIOGRAPHY

Andrews, J. Cutler. *The North Reports the Civil War* Pittsburgh: University of Pittsburgh Press, 1955.
———. *The South Reports the Civil War.* Princeton: Princeton University Press, 1970.

Axelrod, Alan. *The War between the Spies: A History of Espionage during the Civil War.* New York: Atlantic Monthly Press, 1992.

Bakeless, John. *Spies of the Confederacy.* Philadelphia: J. B. Lippincott, 1970.

Baker, Lafayette C. *History of the United States Secret Service.* Philadelphia: L. C. Baker, 1867.

Bates, David Homer. *Lincoln in the Telegraph Office: Recollections of the United States Military Telegraph during the Civil War.* New York: Century Co., 1907.

Bidwell, Bruce W. *History of the Military Intelligence Division, Department of the Army General Staff: 1775–1941.* Frederick, MD: University Publications of America, 1986.

Blakey, Arch. *General John H. Winder, C.S.A.* Gainesville: University of Florida Press, 1990.

Boyd, Belle. *Belle Boyd in Camp and Prison, Written by Herself.* Edited by Curtis C. Davis. New York: Thomas Yoseloff, 1968.

Brown, J. Willard. *The Signal Corps, U.S.A. in the War of the Rebellion.* 1898. Reprint, New York: Arno Press, 1974.

Bulloch, James D. *The Secret Service of the Confederate States in Europe.* 2 vols. 1884. Reprint, New York: Thomas Yoseloff, 1959.

Canan, H. V. "Confederate Military Intelligence." *Maryland Historical Magazine* 59 (March 1964): 34–51.

Cornish, Joseph Jenkins, III. *The Air Arm of the Confederacy.* Richmond, VA: Richmond Civil War Centennial Committee, 1963.

Davis, Curtis Carroll. "Companions of Crisis: The Spy Memoir as a Social Document." *Civil War History* 10 (December 1964): 385–400.

———. "The Civil War's Most Over-Rated Spy." *West Virginia History* 27 (October 1965): 1–9.

———. " 'The Pet of the Confederacy' Still? Fresh Findings about Belle Boyd." *Maryland Historical Magazine* 78 (Spring 1983): 35–53.

Davis, Robert Scott, Jr. "The Curious Civil War Career of James George Brown, Spy." *Prologue* 26 (Spring 1994): 17–31.

Feis, William B. "A Union Military Intelligence Failure: Jubal Early's Raid, June 12–July 14, 1864." *Civil War History* 36 (September 1990): 209–225.

———. "Neutralizing the Valley: The Role of Military Intelligence in the Defeat of Jubal Early's Army of the Valley, 1864–1865." *Civil War History* 39 (September 1993): 199–215.

———. "The Deception of Braxton Bragg: The Tullahoma Campaign." *Blue and Gray Magazine* (October 1992): 10–21, 46–53.

Fishel, Edwin C. "The Mythology of Civil War Intelligence." *Civil War History* 10 (December 1964): 344–367.

———. "Pinkerton and McClellan: Who Deceived Whom?" *Civil War History* 34 (June 1988): 115–142.

———. "Myths That Never Die." *International Journal of Intelligence and Counterintelligence* 2 (Spring 1988): 27–58.

Fry, Joseph. *Henry S. Sanford: Diplomacy and Business in Nineteenth-Century America.* Reno, NV: University of Nevada Press, 1982.

Gaddy, David Winfred. "Gray Cloaks and Daggers." *Civil War Times Illustrated* 14 (July 1975): 20–27.

————. "William Norris and the Confederate Signal and Secret Service." *Maryland Historical Magazine* 70 (Summer 1975): 167–188.

Greenhow, Mrs. [Rose O'Neal]. *My Imprisonment and First Year of Abolition Rule at Washington.* London: Richard Bentley, 1863.

Hall, James O. "The Spy Harrison: A Modern Hunt for a Fabled Agent." *Civil War Times Illustrated* 24 (February 1986): 18–25.

Haydon, F. Stansbury. *Aeronautics in the Union and Confederate Armies, with a Survey of Military Aeronautics prior to 1861.* Baltimore: Johns Hopkins University Press, 1941.

Headley, John W. *Confederate Operations in Canada and New York.* New York: Neale Publishing, 1906.

Hirshson, Stanley P. *Grenville M. Dodge: Soldier, Politician, Railroad Pioneer.* Bloomington: Indiana University Press, 1967.

Horan, James D. *Confederate Agent: A Discovery in History.* New York: Crown Publishers, 1954.

Hotchkiss, Jedediah. *Make Me a Map of the Valley: The Civil War Journal of Stonewall Jackson's Topographer.* Edited by Archie P. McDonald. Dallas: Southern Methodist University, 1973.

Jenkins, Brian. *Britain and the War for the Union.* 2 vols. Montreal: McGill–Queens University Press, 1974, 1980.

Johnston, Angus J., II. "Disloyalty on Confederate Railroads in Virginia." *Virginia Magazine of History and Biography* 68 (October 1955): 410–426.

Kahn, David. *The Codebreakers: The Story of Secret Writing.* New York: Macmillan, 1967.

Kinchen, Oscar A. *Confederate Operations in Canada and the North.* North Quincy, MA: Christopher, 1970.

Klement, Frank L. *Dark Lanterns: Secret Political Societies, Conspiracies, and Treason Trials in the Civil War.* Baton Rouge: Louisiana State University Press, 1984.

Longacre, Edwin. *The Cavalry at Gettysburg: A Tactical Study of Mounted Operations during the Civil War's Pivotal Campaign, 9 June–14 July, 1864.* Rutherford: Farleigh Dickinson University Press, 1986.

Luvaas, Jay. "Lee at Gettysburg: A General without Intelligence." *Intelligence and National Security* 5 (April 1990): 116–135.

————. "The Role of Intelligence in the Chancellorsville Campaign, April–May, 1863." *Intelligence and National Security* 5 (April 1990): 99–115.

Maslowski, Peter. "Military Intelligence Sources during the American Civil War: A Case Study." In Walter T. Hitchcock, ed., *The Intelligence Revolution: A Historical Perspective.* Washington, D.C.: Office of Air Force History, 1991.

Markle, Donald E. *Spies and Spymasters of the Civil War.* New York: Hippocrene Books, 1994.

Marshall, Max L., ed. *Story of the U.S. Army Signal Corps.* New York: Franklin Watts, 1965.

Marszalek, John F. *Sherman's Other War: The General and the Civil War Press.* Memphis: Memphis State University Press, 1981.

Merli, Frank. *Great Britain and the Confederate Navy, 1861–1865.* Bloomington: Indiana University Press, 1970.

Miller, Nathan. *Spying for America: The Hidden History of U.S. Intelligence.* New York: Paragon House, 1989.

Mogelever, Jacob. *Death to Traitors: The Story of General Lafayette C. Baker, Lincoln's Forgotten Secret Service Chief.* Garden City, NY: Doubleday, 1960.

Moore, Wilton P. "Union Army Provost Marshals in the Eastern Theater." *Military Affairs* 26 (1962): 120–126.

O'Toole, G.J.A. *Honorable Treachery: A History of U.S. Intelligence, Espionage, and Covert Action from the American Revolution to the CIA.* New York: Atlantic Monthly Press, 1991.

———. *The Encyclopedia of American Intelligence and Espionage: From the Revolutionary War to the Present.* New York: Facts on File, 1988.

Owsley, Harriet Chappell. "Henry Shelton Sanford and Federal Surveillance Abroad, 1861–1865." *Mississippi Valley Historical Review* 48 (1961): 211–228.

Pardell, James G. "The Newspaper Problem in Its Bearing upon Military Secrecy during the Civil War." *American Historical Review* 23 (January 1918): 303–323.

Peavey, James Dudley. *Confederate Scout: Virginia's Frank Stringfellow.* Onancock, VA: Eastern Shore Publishing, 1956.

Pinkerton, Allan. *The Spy of the Rebellion.* New York: Dillingham, 1888.

Plum, William R. *The Military Telegraph during the Civil War in the United States.* 2 vols. 1882. Reprint, New York: Arno Press, 1974.

Powe, Marc B., and Edward E. Wilson. *The Evolution of American Military Intelligence.* Fort Huachuca, AZ: U.S. Army Intelligence Center and School, 1973.

Radley, Kenneth. *Rebel Watchdog: The Confederate States Army Provost Guard.* Baton Rouge: Louisiana State University Press, 1989.

Ross, Ishbel. *Rebel Rose: Life of Rose O'Neal Greenhow, Confederate Spy.* New York: Harper & Brothers, Publishers, 1954.

Scheips, Paul J. "Union Signal Communications: Innovation and Conflict." *Civil War History* 9 (December 1963): 399–404, 406.

Schmidt, C. T. "G-2, Army of the Potomac." *Military Review* 28 (July 1948): 45–56.

Sigaud, Louis A. *Belle Boyd, Confederate Spy.* Richmond, VA: Dietz Press, 1944.

Simon, John Y., and David L. Wilson, eds. "Samuel H. Beckwith: 'Grant's Shadow.' " In Simon and Wilson, eds. *Ulysses S. Grant: Essays and Documents.* Carbondale: Southern Illinois University Press, 1981.

Sparks, David. "General Patrick's Progress: Intelligence and Security in the Army of the Potomac." *Civil War History* 10 (December 1964): 371–384.

Spencer, Warren F. *The Confederate Navy in Europe.* University: University of Alabama Press, 1983.

Squires, J. Duane. "Aeronautics in the Civil War." *American Historical Review* 42 (July 1937): 635–54.

Starr, Stephen Z. *The Union Cavalry in the Civil War.* 3 vols. Baton Rouge: Louisiana State University Press, 1979–1985.

Stuart, Meriwether. "Colonel Ulric Dahlgren and Richmond's Union Underground, April 1864." *Virginia Magazine of History and Biography* 72 (April 1964): 152–204.

———. "Dr. Lugo: An Austro-Venetian Adventurer in Union Espionage." *Virginia Magazine of History and Biography* 90 (July 1982): 339–358.

———. "Samuel Ruth and General R. E. Lee: Disloyalty and the Line of Supply to Fredericksburg, 1862–1863." *Virginia Magazine of History and Biography* 71 (January 1963): 35–109.

———. "Of Spies and Borrowed Names: The Identity of Union Operatives in Richmond

Known as 'The Phillipses' Discovered." *Virginia Magazine of History and Biography* 89 (July 1981): 308–327.

Tatum, Georgia Lee. *Disloyalty in the Confederacy.* Chapel Hill: University of North Carolina Press, 1934.

Taylor, Charles E. *The Signal and Secret Service of the Confederate States.* 1903. Reprint, Harmans, MD: Toomey Press, 1986.

Thompson, George Raynor. "Civil War Signals." In Paul J. Scheips, ed. *Military Signal Communications.* New York: Arno Press, 1980.

Tidwell, William A., James O. Hall, and David Winfred Gaddy. *Come Retribution: The Confederate Secret Service and the Assassination of Lincoln.* Jackson: University Press of Mississippi, 1988.

———. "Confederate Expenditures for Secret Service." *Civil War History* 37 (September 1991): 219–231.

33

Medical Activities

Harris D. Riley, Jr.

The historian Richard H. Shryock in his article in *American Quarterly* (1962) stated that if the war's medical aspects are omitted, the story is not only incomplete but is unrealistic as a total picture. Paralleling the enormous expansion of literature about the American Civil War has been the growth of attention and writings relating to the medical aspects. Useful guides to the general literature containing specific sections on the medical aspects are Henry P. Beers, *Guide to the Archives of the Confederate States of America* (1968); Robin Higham, *A Guide to the Sources of United States Military History* (1975); Charles E. Dornbusch, *Military Bibliography of the Civil War* (1961–1992); Kenneth W. Munden and Henry P. Beers, *Guide to Federal Archives Relating to the Civil War* (1962); and Allan Nevins, James I. Robertson, Jr., and Bell I. Wiley, *Civil War Books* (1967–1969).

GENERAL STUDIES

The most useful general studies of the medical aspects of the war are George W. Adams's *Doctors in Blue* (1952) describing the Union Medical Department, and Horace H. Cunningham's *Doctors in Gray* (1968) about the Confederate medical effort. Stewart M. Brooks's *Civil War Medicine* (1966) is useful and treats medicine both North and South in a topical rather than chronologic manner. Paul E. Steiner's *Diseases in the Civil War* (1968) and *Physician-Generals in the Civil War* (1966) are very useful. The former is particularly valuable in its discussion of type and incidence of various diseases. Louis C. Duncan's *Medical Department of the United States Army in the Civil War* (n.d.) was originally published as a series of articles in the *Military Surgeon*. It emphasizes the war in the East from the Union standpoint. A publication of the U.S. Surgeon General's office, *The Medical Department of the United States Army from 1775 to 1873* (1873), compiled by Harvey E. Brown, does an immediate postwar review of the Union Medical Department. Mary C. Gillette made a major contribution to Union Civil War medical historiography with the publication of *The Army Medical Department, 1818–1865* (1987). Civil War medicine is covered chronologically from the Union point of view in an excellent manner. Frank R. Freemon has provided students of the Civil War with a valuable reference, *Microbes and Minie Balls: An Annotated Bibliography of Civil War Medicine* (1993). It is divided into primary and secondary sources and does what the title specifies. A booklet, *Two Hundred Years of Military Medicine* (1965), by Rose C. Engleman and Robert U. T. Joy, presents in chronological format important developments in military medicine. Harris D. Riley, Jr., has provided a comprehensive overview of medicine in the Confederate armies in his article that appeared in *Military Medicine* (1956). E. Merton Coulter in his *Travels in the Confederate States: A Bibliography* (1948) includes several citations relating to hospital and medical services. Alvin R. Sunseri has provided a useful series of articles on the organization and operation of the Medical Department of the Confederate Army of Tennessee in the *Journal of the Tennessee Medical Association* (1960). Detailed pictures of medicine during the era of the Civil War are provided by William G. Rothstein in his *American Physicians in the Nineteenth Century* (1972) and by John S. Haller, Jr., in *American Medicine in Transition, 1840–1860* (1981). *Medicine in Virginia in the Nineteenth Century* (1933) by Wyndham B. Blanton contains much of value on the Civil War. *A History of Medicine in South Carolina, 1825–1910* (1967) by Joseph I. Waring contains an excellent chapter on medical activities, both Union and Confederate, in the Civil War. An appendix provides biographical information on many important South Carolina physicians, many of whom were in Confederate service. William D. Sharpe, in his article in *Academy of Medicine Bulletin* (1965), has described Confederate medical services. The late Bell Irvin Wiley's classic *The Life of Johnny Reb* (1943) and *The Life of Billy Yank* (1951) cover the everyday life of the common soldier. Each contains a chapter on medical care and illness. James I. Robertson's excellent history of the common soldier of both sides, *Soldiers Blue and Gray* (1987), contains a chapter on disease, wounds, and health. Larry J. Daniel's *Soldiering in the Army of Tennessee* (1991) tracks the life of the enlisted man and has a chapter on health and medical care. Gerald F. Linderman in his *Embattled Courage* (1987) discusses some of the psychologic and emotional aspects of participation in Civil War combat, especially that of the infantryman. Judith Lee Hallock in the *Journal of Confederate History* (1991) has written about the influence of Southern climate on disease and its effect on the Confederate war effort.

The Civil War was the first American war about which an official medical history was prepared. Prepared by the U.S. Surgeon General's office, *The Med-*

ical and Surgical History of the War of the Rebellion (1875–1885), as the title suggests, describes primarily the Union aspects. It was made possible by the increased emphasis on record keeping growing out of the Crimean War. This mammoth publication, begun by W. A. Hammond and carried to publication by J. K. Barnes, both Union medical officers, consisted of six large books, divided into two volumes of three parts each. It was further designed to preserve all medical experiences for the use of future army medical officers, as Breeden's article (1975) points out. It has recently been reprinted as *The Medical and Surgical History of the Civil War* (1990–1992), with a valuable introduction by James I. Robertson, Jr. (1992) and a helpful index.

In the spring of 1865 the Confederate Surgeon General's Office was burned in the fire that destroyed much of Richmond. Primarily because of this, the official records of the Medical Department of the Confederacy were lost, and there is no comparable study for the South. However, certain Confederate sources of an official character are available. These include Confederate States of America, *Regulations for the Medical Department of the CS Army* (1863). The Confederate States of America, *The Statutes at Large* (1864), contains other official information. Surgeon General Samuel P. Moore of the Confederacy was responsible for the publication of the *Confederate States Medical and Surgical Journal* (1864–1865). Fourteen volumes of this publication appeared in 1864 and 1865. Each issue contains interesting case reports and observations submitted by medical officers throughout the Confederacy, as well as certain official notices. The full series has been reprinted (1959) with an introduction by William D. Sharpe.

Many general works on the Civil War have portions dealing with medical care. Some of these are Nevins's *The Ordeal of the Union* and *The War for the Union* (1947–1971), James M. McPherson's *Battle Cry of Freedom,* and Coulter's *The Confederate States of America, 1861–1865* (1950). *The Civil War* in the Time-Life Book series has an excellent chapter on medical care by James I. Robertson, Jr. (1984).

Cunningham's "Confederate Medical Officer in the Field" (1958) provides a useful account of the medical officer in that location. Freemon's article in *Southern Medical Journal* (1987) describes the administration of the Confederate States Army's medical department. A. J. Bollet has written a multipart series of articles dealing with medical aspects of the war that appeared in *Resident and Staff Physician* (1989, 1990, 1991, 1992). Much of the material is based on analysis of the *Medical and Surgical History of the War of the Rebellion.* Although it emphasizes conditions in Virginia, Breeden has provided a comprehensive view of Confederate medicine in "Confederate Medicine: The View from Virginia" (1991).

The *Official Records* of the Union and Confederate armies by the U.S. War Department (1880–1901) and navies by the U.S. Navy Department (1894–1922) contain certain items of medical interest for both sides of the conflict. A series,

Supplements to the Official Records (Army) (1994–), is in the publication process and contains information of medical interest.

The outbreak of the Civil War found both the North and the South totally unprepared in medical as well as military resources. The situation was particularly desperate on the Southern side because a medical department had to be built from scratch. Ultimately, 3,400 physicians served in the Confederate medical service. Of this number, only 26 had previous military experience. Almost none of the medical officers on either side had had much experience with military medicine. One of the most important steps taken, particularly by the Confederate service, was the publication of military medical manuals. Riley, in "Confederate Medical Manuals" (1988), has reviewed the Civil War manuals.

PERSONAL ACCOUNTS

Personal contemporary accounts are legion. Northern ones of particular value include Charles B. Johnson's *Muskets and Medicine* (1917), John H. Brinton's *Personal Memoirs* (1914), Benjamin F. Stevenson's *Letters from the Army* (1884), and John G. Perry's *Letters from a Surgeon of the Civil War* (1906). Weir Mitchell, a medical officer considerably ahead of his time in the field of neurology, recorded interesting observations concerning his experience as a medical officer in the Civil War (1905, 1914). John D. Billings in his popular *Hardtack and Coffee* (1886) has a chapter dealing with hospitals and ambulances that is pertinent. William Howell Reed, *Hospital Life in the Army of the Potomac* (1886), describes well the transport and treatment of the Union wounded. Joseph J. Woodward, who served with the U.S. Surgeon General's Office, made several valuable observations about various diseases affecting the military in his *Outline of the Chief Camp Diseases* (1863). Thomas T. Ellis was an English physician who volunteered his services to the Union army and left an interesting account, *Leaves from the Diary of an Army Surgeon* (1863). Writings relating to medicine in the United States Navy are sparse. Perhaps the best Union naval memoirs are *Naval Surgeon: The Diary of Samuel P. Boyer* (1963) and those by Charles S. Foltz, *Surgeon of the Seas* (1931), and Charles H. Wheelwright, *Correspondence of Dr. Charles H. Wheelwright* (1958).

Contemporary accounts on the Confederate side are much less common. Some noteworthy ones are: Junius N. Bragg's *Letters of a Confederate Surgeon, 1861–65* (1960), Spencer G. Welch's *A Confederate Surgeon's Letters to His Wife* (1911), and Ferdinand E. Daniel's *Recollections of a Rebel Surgeon* (1899). The last describes some interesting and humorous anecdotes that occurred in the Army of Tennessee. Simon Baruch, the father of the famous Bernard Baruch, recounts interesting experiences as a Confederate surgeon in the eastern theater in his "A Surgeon's Story of Battle and Capture" (1914). *Medical and Surgical Memoirs* by Joseph Jones (1876–1890) is of particular interest and will be discussed later. Samuel H. Stout, medical director of hospitals of the Army of Tennessee, has provided important insight into the Medical Department of the most important army in the West. After the war, Stout published in the *Southern Practitioner* a twenty-three-part series on the activities of the Medical Department of the Army of Tennessee (1900–1903). At the request of Governor James D. Porter, Stout prepared the lengthy *Outline of the Organization and Medical Department of the Confederate Army and Department of Tennessee.* Clark and Riley (1957) have edited it; it provides much of interest about the Army of Tennessee. Edward Warren in his *A Doctor's Experiences in Three Continents* (1885) provides some interesting material about being a Confederate surgeon. He also served as surgeon in chief to the North Carolina navy. LaGrande James Wilson, assistant surgeon of the 42d Mississippi, provides fascinating accounts of the medical activities at the Battle of Gettysburg in *The Confederate Soldier* (1902).

Tom H. Wells in his *The Confederate Navy* (1971) has reviewed the organization of the Confederate Naval Bureau of Medicine and Surgery and its activities. The bureau was under the direction of physician W.A.W. Spotswood and contained approximately eighty-nine medical officers who served on ships and at land installations.

NURSING

The genesis of the nursing profession can be found in the history of the Civil War. Although a few trained Catholic sisters served here and there early in the war, it was generally considered improper for women to work in the hospitals. For lack of anyone else to do the job, women were not only admitted to the wards but actively recruited. Robertson in his "Tenting Tonight" (1984) points out that the U.S. Congress provided for the use of female nurses in August 1861; the Confederacy gave way to such a departure from tradition and followed suit in September 1862. Both sides came to rely heavily on women to care for the sick, and a number of these women left accounts of their experiences, such as those of Julia C. Stinson (1937) and Julia Flikke (1943). *Hands of Mercy* by Norah Smaridge (1900), *Our Army Nurses* by Mary A. Holland (1895), and a more recent article by Ann D. Wood (1972) deal directly with the war. Many of the early nurses recorded and later published their memoirs. Noteworthy Union ones are *My Story of the War* by Mary A. Livermore (1888), Jane S. Woolsey's *Hospital Days* (1868), and Adelaide W. Smith's *Reminiscences of an Army Nurse during the Civil War* (1911). The experiences of a male nurse are described by Walt Whitman in his *Specimen Days in America* (1971) and in *The Wound Dresser* (1949).

Examples from the Confederate side include Fannie A. Beers's *Memories* (1888), Kate Cumming's excellent *Journal of Hospital Life in the Confederate Army of Tennessee* (1866), and Phoebe Y. Pember's *A Southern Woman's Story* (1959). All three provide important insights not only into nursing but also hospital activities and conditions on the home front in the Confederate states. A little-known publication is Susan E. D. Smith's *The Soldier's Friend* (1867), which describes the day-to-day episodes in a hospital in the western theater.

MEDICAL LEADERSHIP

The Civil War has been described as a medical nightmare for combatants, according to James O. Breeden in ''Military and Naval Medicine'' (1975). The medical services provided to soldiers on both sides were adequate at best. That these services were as reasonable as they were is the result of the dedication and efforts of a few individuals. In the Union service Drs. William A. Hammond and Jonathan Letterman were noteworthy. In the Confederate medical service, Surgeon General Samuel P. Moore and Dr. Joseph Jones deserve attention.

William A. Hammond was appointed surgeon general of the Union army in 1864; he was only thirty-four years of age. Although he served only two years, his tenure marked the origin of a new era in the history of the Union Medical Department. He founded the Army Medical Museum and was responsible for initiating the research that led to the publication of *Medical and Surgical History of the War of the Rebellion.* He proposed the establishment of an army medical school and an army general hospital. With the exception of the establishment of the Army Medical Museum, these important accomplishments occurred after Hammond's tenure in office. The Army Medical Museum was founded in 1862 and was the forerunner of the important, present-day Armed Forces Institute of Pathology. Their stories, as well as their contributions to medicine, are described by Robert S. Henry in *The Armed Forces Institute of Pathology* (1964), Saul Jarcho in his article in *Military Medicine* (1963), and Esmond R. Long in ''The Army Medical Museum'' (1973). Dr. Hammond was relieved as surgeon general following a court-martial in 1864. The likely reason was the progressive hostility between Hammond and Secretary of War Edwin M. Stanton and the outcry resulting from Hammond's discontinuation of calomel as a therapeutic staple of the medical department. Freemon's ''Lincoln Finds a Surgeon General'' (1987) provides a narrative of Hammond's Civil War career and analyzes his role in the successes and failures of the Union Medical Department. Hammond's published report (1864) of the court-martial removing him from office is illuminating.

Jonathan Letterman first served as director of the Army of the Potomac, appointed to this position by Hammond. Letterman was the architect for the Union army's system of field hospitals, and he originated the first ambulance unit. Both of these highly important developments are monuments to Letterman's talents. Henry I. Bowditch's *A Brief Plea for an Ambulance System* (1863) was a public plea for the establishment of an ambulance system. Evacuation of casualties by sea is discussed in Olmsted's *Hospital Transports* (1863). Letterman's *Medical Recollections of the Army of the Potomac* (1866) reviews the evolution of the field hospitals and the ambulance service, as does a 1913 article by Louis C. Duncan, ''Evolution of the Ambulance Corps and Field Hospital'' (1913).

Samuel P. Moore, surgeon general of the Confederate States Army, is among the most underrated and least appreciated individuals of the Civil War. In February 1861, Moore resigned from the Union army and subsequently was appointed surgeon general of the Confederate States Army. He faced an almost insurmountable task: establishing a medical department from scratch. He not only developed one but saw that it functioned throughout the war. The Medical Department cared for some 600,000 Confederate soldiers, 270,000 prisoners, and over 3,000,000 wounded or sick persons. Moore's career and activities are reviewed in Riley's article in the *Encyclopedia of Southern Culture* (1989), in articles by Weiss (1930) and Williams (1961), and in an article by Farr (1994). Moore is deserving of a full-scale biography.

Joseph Jones was a versatile medical scientist. In several articles Breeden (1967), Riley (1960, 1984, 1987), and Ikard (1989) have detailed his career. Breeden's *Joseph Jones, M.D.: Scientist of the Old South* (1975) not only provides further details of this remarkable physician-scientist but gives valuable information on medical practice—military and civilian—of that period. Born in 1833, Jones was a Georgian. He graduated from the University of Pennsylvania Medical Department and held academic appointments at several Southern colleges. In 1861 he enlisted as a private in a Georgia military unit and subsequently was commissioned full surgeon in the Confederate States Army. Rather than serving as a combat surgeon, Jones convinced Surgeon General Samuel P. Moore to allow him to conduct investigations in the armies, hospitals, and prisons of the Confederacy. Despite wartime conditions, he was able to contribute information on a variety of diseases, including malaria, tetanus, pneumonia, hospital gangrene, smallpox, typhoid fever, diarrhea, dysentery, and meningitis. An early and devoted user of the microscope, Jones observed the bacilli of gangrene and typhoid fever, but, bound to the contemporary "miasmatic" theory of disease, he failed to recognize their casual relationship to these disorders. Although Jones's writings were discursive and often ill organized, they provide much information on diseases in the military population group studied. His career in Nashville and New Orleans after the Civil War was equally important.

In addition to Jones's important contribution about infectious causes of various diseases, it is well to remind readers of Lister's seminal paper on prevention of infection in wounds by the use of carbolic acid (1867).

ORGANIZATIONS AND PUBLICATIONS

While the demands of the early months of the war almost overwhelmed the medical departments of both sides, many patriotic groups attempted to help in the care and feeding of soldiers. One of the groups responsible for treating the sick and wounded in the North was the United States Sanitary Commission, a less powerful but more persuasive version of a commission that had aided British soldiers during the Crimean War, as pointed out by Breeden in "Military and Naval Medicine" (1975). It also resembled the present-day Red Cross. Charles

J. Stille (1868) provided an early history. The recently published papers of Frederick Law Olmsted (1986) are important in understanding the organization of the commission and the efforts of private individuals to reform the United States Army Medical Bureau. Gillette, in *The Army Medical Department, 1881–1865* (1987), has provided a good overview of the history, organization, and activities of the commission. William Q. Maxwell's *Lincoln's Fifth Wheel* (1956) is a modern history. The work in the western theater is described by Jacob G. Forman (1864).

An important contribution of the United States Sanitary Commission was the publication of medical and surgical articles or essays authored by some of the North's leading physicians. These publications were issued to medical officers in the field and hospital. Surgeon General William Hammond recognized the importance of these essays and in 1864 published seventeen of them in a single volume (1864). After the war, the U.S. Sanitary Commission focused on the medical history of the war and commissioned the two-volume *Surgical Memoirs of the War of the Rebellion* (1870–1871). In 1867 the commission arranged for another two volumes, comprising Austin Flint's *Contributions Relating to the Causation and Prevention of Disease* (1867) and Benjamin A. Gould's *Investigations in the Military and Anthropological Statistics of American Soldiers* (1869). Gould's work was substantially enlarged in 1875 when the U.S. Provost-Marshal-General's Office published its two volumes of medical and anthropological statistics. An 1864 publication of the United States Sanitary Commission, *The Sanitary Commission of the United States Army* (1864), provides a variety of important medical statistics.

Certain other pertinent publications should be mentioned. A number of manuals and other guides for the use of medical manuals appeared on each side. The most popular and extensively used ones in the Northern army were *A Manual of Military Surgery* (1861) by Samuel D. Gross, *A Treatise on Hygiene* (1863) by William A. Hammond, and those by Stephen Smith (1862), John H. Packard (1863), Joseph Woodward (1862), and Charles S. Tripler (1861). Riley (1988) has recently reviewed the manuals used on the Confederate side. The most prominent ones were *A Manual of Military Surgery* (1862) prepared by Julian J. Chisolm, *An Epitome of Practical Surgery* (1863) by Edward Warren, *Resources of the Southern Fields and Forests* (1863) by Frances P. Porcher, and that by a committee established by Surgeon General Moore [Confederate States of America. *A Manual of Military Surgery* (1863)] but largely the work of Dr. Henry F. Campbell. Riley (1988) has pointed out that *The Confederate States Medical and Surgical Journal* (1864–1865) was also helpful during its brief existence. An abridged version of George H. B. Macleod's *Notes on the Surgery of the War in the Crimea* (1862), originally published in 1858, was also used in the South.

CONTRIBUTIONS

The nature and extent of medical contributions from the Civil War vary with different writers. Breeden, in his "Medical and Naval Medicine," acknowledging that the origins of the public health movement and the beginning of the professional nursing service can be traced to the Civil War, states: "It is an incontrovertible fact that little of value for the advancement of American medicine accrued to either side." Blaisdell, in his "Medical Advances during the Civil War" (1988), argues that the medical and surgical accomplishments of the Civil War era have been relatively unappreciated because of comparison to modern standards. Among the accomplishments he includes the publication of the *Medical and Surgical History of the War of the Rebellion,* "the first major academic accomplishment of U.S. medicine"; the development of a system for handling mass casualties that set the pattern for World War I; the pavilion style of hospital construction, copied by civilian hospitals for seventy-five years; the importance of early surgery after major trauma; the new understanding that hygiene and sanitation prevented many diseases; the introduction of female nurses on a large scale; the military standards of army physicians, which became national medical standards; and the United States Sanitary Commission, which set the pattern for the development of the American Red Cross.

Hall (1958) and Farmer (1980) have also analyzed the medical pluses and minuses resulting from the war. Although the American Civil War was not notable for contributions from research, some important scientific research did take place. The investigations and contributions of physician Joseph Jones of the Confederate States Army have been mentioned. His *Medical and Surgical Memoirs* (1876–1890), although lengthy and diffuse, contain important medical information. Breeden (1967) has provided a useful interpretive article on Jones's work. Ochsner has reviewed contributions made by Confederate medical officers in "The Genuine Southern Surgeon" (1992).

Brooks (1966) has recapitulated the contributions made by medical officers on both sides and the contributions emerging from the war. The work on nerve injuries by S. Weir Mitchell (1872), a Union medical officer, deserves emphasis because it was advanced for its time. Its importance is described by Walter (1970) and Salerno (1991). The United States Sanitary Commission (1864) supported an investigation of the treatment of Federal prisoners of war. The Union army's medicine supply has been described by George W. Smith (1962) and that of the Confederacy by the late Norman H. Franke (1953).

MEDICAL AND SURGICAL ASPECTS

Certain military campaigns of the war have good medical histories. These include H. H. Cunningham's *Field Medical Services at the Battles of Manassas* (1968), James O. Breeden's "A Medical History of the Latter Stages of the Atlanta Campaign" (1969), Gordon W. Jones's article on the Battle of Fredericksburg (1963), and Frank R. Freemon's "Medical Care at the Siege of Vicksburg" (1991). Freemon has also discussed the medical challenges of military operations in the Mississippi Valley (1992). Warren Wilkinson's *Mother, May You Never See the Sights I Have Seen* (1990), which concerns the 57th Massachusetts during the 1864–1865 campaign in Virginia, has a chapter on the handling of the casualties after the Battle of the Wilderness.

An article by Dr. Joseph K. Barnes, "The Annual Report of the Surgeon-General" (1867), contains some interesting statistics on the war from the Union side for fiscal year 1866. From 1862 through 1866 the Medical Bureau purchased 3,981 artificial legs and 3,240 arms. During the war, 1,752,377 fluid ounces of quinine and 2,136,600 quinine pills were administered. In the previous year, the Medical Bureau reviewed and classified 210,027 medical discharges based on a surgeon's certificate of disability. The report tells us that 336 Union physicians lost their lives, 29 of them in action.

The publication in 1975 of Breeden's *Joseph Jones: Scientist of the Old South* (1975) represents an important contribution to Civil War medicine. It focuses attention on the Civil War career of this unusual Confederate medical officer. Under orders from Surgeon General Samuel P. Moore to investigate the health problems of the Confederacy, Dr. Jones visited the chief armies of the South, hospitals, and prisoner of war camps. In addition, *Joseph Jones* provides a wealth of valuable information regarding medical conditions in the South in the 1860s and in the Confederate armies. Paul E. Steiner's *Medical History of a Civil War Regiment* (1977) provides a valuable evaluation of the impact of disease on a black Union regiment stationed in Louisiana. Mark A. Quinone's "Drug Abuse during the Civil War" (1975) discusses this problem in rival armies. He maintains that there is insufficient evidence to designate the Civil War as the starting point for the onset of drug addiction in the United States. The article by David Courtwright (1978) evaluating the role of the Civil War in opium addiction of the nineteenth century concludes that the war was but one of several causes that contributed to an increase in opiate addiction in the postwar period.

In the past most of the attention has been on the health of individual soldiers or army units, and it has been focused on them after they began active military duty. Little has been written about the health of state troops before they entered the service of the Union or the Confederacy. John D. Smith's "The Health of Vermont's Civil War Recruits" (1975), does just that. Harris D. Riley, Jr., and Amos Christie located disability and casualty rosters of the Provisional Army of Tennessee. Their article, "Death and Disabilities in the Provisional Army of Tennessee" (1984), analyzed these two rosters in regard to the reasons men were discharged from military service by a surgeon's certificate of disability and the cause of death during 1861. Discharges were due to a wide variety of different disorders, but the most common were diseases of the respiratory and gastrointestinal systems. The leading cause of death in these recruits was typhoid fever, followed by measles and its complications. In addition to the information on the Provisional Army of Tennessee, the paper contains information about health and medical practice in the South and other military units. Smith's "Kentucky Civil War Recruits" (1980) provides a medical profile of recruits in Kentucky.

In 1983 Gordon Dammann's useful *Pictorial Encyclopedia of Civil War Medical Instruments and Equipment* (1983) was published, and a second volume has appeared. *Early Medical Photography in America (1830–1883)* (1983) by Stanley B. Burns contains a valuable chapter on the employment of photography for medical purposes during the Civil War. Many of the photographs are quite rare.

The hazards of camp life are depicted in two recent articles, one for the Union by Kenneth Link, "Potomac Fever: The Hazards of Camp Life" (1983), and one for the Confederacy, Morton R. McInvale's "That Thing of Infamy" (1979).

The hospital at Port Hudson, Louisiana, was an important one. Lawrence L. Hewitt and Arthur W. Bergeron, Jr., have edited *Post Hospital Ledger* (1981). Robert A. Hodge's *A Death Roster of the Confederate General Hospital at Culpeper, Virginia* (1977) provides some useful information on Confederate deaths. Nancy Baird's "There Is No Sunday in the Army" (1979) is the edited diary of Lunsford D. Yandell, an important Confederate medical officer. Phillip D. Jordan in "The Career of Henry M. Farr" (1982) describes the career of a Union surgeon. John R. Brumgardt's edited *Civil War Nurse* (1980) adds to our knowledge of both Union female nurses and medical officers. George P. Cuttino's *Saddle Bag and Spinning Wheel* (1981) describes the war career of a Georgia medical officer, Dr. George W. Peddy. Breeden's "The Forgotten Man of the Civil War" (1979) provides valuable information on the experiences of the combat physician, who has largely been ignored in the past.

An important consideration of any government during wartime is the establishment of procedures for the granting of furloughs and discharges to sick, wounded, and disabled troops. Riley's "Medical Furloughs" (1989) discusses all aspects of medical furloughs in the Confederate States Army.

Jack D. Key's article, "U.S. Army Medical Department and Civil War Medicine" (1968), reviews briefly Union Army medicine with emphasis on its four medical directors: King, Tripler, Letterman, and McFarlin.

Patricia M. LaPointe's "Military Hospitals in Memphis" (1983) provided an excellent review of hospitals in Memphis during the war.

The development of the National Library of Medicine as it evolved from the library of the Surgeon General's Office is described in two publications. Wyndham D. Miles's *A History of the National Library of Medicine* (1982) is a comprehensive history of that library; Dorothy M. Schullian and Frank B. Rogers in "The National Library of Medicine" (1958) provide a briefer overview.

Richard H. Shryock, a renowned medical historian, surveyed Civil War medical history. His "A Medical Perspective on the Civil War" (1962) tells us that the most appalling reason for the high mortality among troops was slow evacuation; many soldiers bled to death or died of exposure. He concludes that the story of the Civil War is incomplete and unrealistic if the medical aspects are omitted. He also believes that if the war could have been postponed for two decades, the respective medical departments would have saved many more lives because of important medical advances.

James Street, in "Under the Influence" (1988), mentions several general officers on each side whose mental state was clouded by opium or alcohol, sometimes taken on the prescription of a physician. His prime example is the performance of General John Bell Hood in the 1864 Tennessee campaign.

Willis G. Diffenbaugh in an article in *Military Medicine* (1965) has offered an overview of surgical treatment in the war. Richard B. Stark and Janet C. Stark in "Surgical Care of the Confederate States Army" (1958) have provided a detailed review of surgical therapy. In "Surgeons and Surgical Care of the Confederate States Army" (1960), two years later, Richard Stark tells about Confederate surgeons and the specific care they rendered. General references dealing with Civil War medicine such as Adams's *Doctors in Blue* (1958) and Cunningham's *Doctors in Gray* (1958) cover surgical aspects, but more detailed coverage is given in various surgical manuals already cited.

Ronald T. Zellem, in "Wounded by Bayonet, Ball and Bacteria" (1985), provides a detailed summary of treatment of combat injuries during the war, with special emphasis on head injuries.

Zone's "Venereal diseases" (1988) discusses sexually transmitted diseases in Nashville and Memphis during the war.

Until recently, little attention has been given to the influence of health on the performance of important figures in the Civil War. Riley in two articles (1978, 1979) has analyzed the health profile of General Robert E. Lee. His study showed that Lee had a number of disabilities and that atherosclerotic heart disease probably began in the spring of 1863 and may have impaired his effectiveness as a leader. Rozear and coworkers (1990) have discussed the final cerebrovascular accident Lee suffered. Gabor S. Boritt and Adam Boritt (1983) challenged the assumption that Abraham Lincoln suffered from Marfan syndrome, a disorder of connective tissue. There is other evidence that he did, however. A British psychologist, W. D. Henry (1979), proposes that Thomas J. "Stonewall" Jackson's opposite personality traits—austere, carefully controlled emotions in day-to-day life and aggressive abandonment on the battlefield— suggest a schizoid personality. Andrew C. Holman, in "Thomas J. Jackson and the Idea of Health" (1992), has recently reviewed Jackson's health, with emphasis on his reliance on hydrotherapy.

Riley, in a two-part article, "Jefferson Davis and His Health" (1987), has presented a detailed analysis of Jefferson Davis's health. It was concluded that Davis almost certainly had a corneal ulceration and keratitis secondary to a herpes simplex virus infection. He suffered a variety of other ailments, which likely contributed to his austereness and difficulty in interpersonal relations. The cause of his death was pneumonia.

Malingering has received renewed attention. Albert Castel in an article in *Civil*

War Times Illustrated (1977) has written on this topic. Donald L. Anderson and Godfrey Anderson's article, "Nostalgia and Malingering in the Military during the Civil War" (1984), examines this problem in detail. Castel in his "On the Duties of the Surgeon in Action" (1978) has edited the reports of Surgeon Richard Vickery about the diseases seen by and the duties of a Civil War medical officer.

SUGGESTED AREAS FOR FUTURE RESEARCH

The entire field of medicine in the Civil War deserves further investigation. More biographical information is needed on several of the medical leaders of both the Confederacy and the Union.

ACKNOWLEDGMENT

Appreciation is expressed to Guin Johnson for typing the manuscript for this chapter.

BIBLIOGRAPHY

Adams, George W. *Doctors in Blue: The Medical History of the Union Army in the Civil War.* New York: H. Schuman, 1952.

Anderson, Donald L., and Godfrey T. Anderson. "Nostalgia and Malingering in the Military during the Civil War." *Perspectives in Biology and Medicine* 28 (1984): 156–166.

Baird, Nancy D. "There Is No Sunday in the Army: Civil War Letters of Lunsford D. Yandell, 1861–1862." *Filson Club Historical Quarterly* 53 (1979): 317–327.

Barnes, Joseph K. "The Annual Report of the Surgeon General." *Medical and Surgical Reporter* 16 (1867): 75–78.

Baruch, Simon. "A Surgeon's Story of Battle and Capture." *Confederate Veteran* 22 (1914): 545–548.

Beers, Fannie A. *Memories: A Record of Personal Experience and Adventure during Four Years of War.* Philadelphia: J. B. Lippincott, 1888.

Beers, Henry P. *Guide to the Archives of the Confederate States of America.* Washington, D.C.: National Archives, General Services Administration, 1968.

Billings, John D. *Hardtack and Coffee, the Unwritten Story of Army Life.* Boston: George M. Smith & Co., 1888.

Blaisdell, F. William. "Medical Advances during the Civil War." *Archives of Surgery* 123 (1988): 1045–1050.

Blanton, Wyndham B. *Medicine in Virginia in the Nineteenth Century.* Richmond: Garrett & Massie, 1933.

Bollet, Alfred J. "To Care for Him That Has Borne the Battle." *Resident and Staff Physician* 35 (1989): 121–129; 36 (1990): 90–100; 37 (1991): 115–122; 38 (1992): 157–163.

Boritt, Gabor S., and Adam Boritt. "Lincoln and the Marfan Syndrome: The Medical Diagnosis of a Historical Figure." *Civil War History* 29 (1983): 212–229.

Bowditch, Henry I. *A Brief Plea for an Ambulance System for the Army of the United States.* Boston: Ticknor and Fields, 1863.

Boyer, Samuel P. *Naval Surgeon: The Diary of Dr. Samuel Pellman Boyer.* 2 vols. Edited by Elinor Barnes and James A. Barnes. Bloomington: Indiana University Press, 1963.

Bragg, Junius N. *Letters of a Confederate Surgeon, 1861–65.* Edited by Mrs. T. J. Gaughan. Camden(?), AR, 1960.

Breeden, James O. "Military and Naval Medicine." In *A Guide to the Sources of United States Military History.* Edited by Robin Higham, Hamden, CT: Anchor Books, 1975.

———. "The Forgotten Man of the Civil War: The Southern Experience." *Bulletin of the New York Academy of Medicine* 55 (1979): 652–669.

———. "Joseph Jones, a Major Source for Nineteenth-Century Southern Medical History." *Tulane University Medical Faculty Bulletin* 26 (1967): 41–48.

———. "A Medical History of the Latter Stages of the Atlanta Campaign." *Journal of Southern History* 35 (1969): 31–59.

———. "Confederate Medicine: The View from Virginia." *Virginia Medical Quarterly* 118 (Fall 1991): 222–231.

———. "Joseph Jones, a Major Source for Nineteenth-Century Southern Medical History." *Tulane University Medical Faculty Bulletin* 26 (1967): 42–48.

———. *Joseph Jones, M.D.: Scientist of the Old South.* Lexington, KY: University Press of Kentucky, 1975.

Brinton, John H. *Personal Memoirs of John H. Brinton, Major and Surgeon U.S.V., 1861–1865.* New York: Neale Publishing Co., 1914.

Brooks, Stewart M. *Civil War Medicine.* Springfield: Charles C. Thomas, 1966.

Brumgardt, John R., ed. *Civil War Nurse: The Diary and Letters of Hannah Ropes.* Knoxville: University of Tennessee Press, 1980.

Burns, Stanley B. *Early Medical Photography in America (1839–1883).* New York: The author, 1983.

Castel, Albert, "On the Duties of the Surgeon in Action: Surgeon Richard Vickery." *Civil War Times Illustrated* 17 (1978): 12–23.

———, ed. "Malingering: 'Many . . . Diseases Are . . . Feigned.' " *Civil War Times Illustrated* 16 (1977): 29–32.

Chisolm, Julian J. *A Manual of Military Surgery, for the Use of Surgeons in the Confederate States Army.* 2d rev. and improved ed. Richmond: West & Johnson, 1862.

Clark, Sam L., and Harris D. Riley, Jr., eds. "Outline of the Organization of the Medical Department of the Confederate Army and Department of Tennessee." *Tennessee Historical Quarterly* 16 (1957): 55–82.

Confederate States of America. Surgeon-General's Office. *A Manual of Military Surgery Prepared for Use of the Confederate Army.* Richmond: Ayres & Wade, 1863.

———. *The Statutes at Large of the Provisional Government of the Confederate States of America, from the Institution of the Government, February 8, 1861 to Its Termination, February 18, 1862.* Edited by James M. Matthews. Richmond: R. M. Smith, 1864.

———. War Department. *Regulations for the Medical Department of the C.S. Army.* Richmond: Ritchie & Dunnavant, 1863.

Confederate States Medical and Surgical Journal. Vol. 1 (12 monthly numbers), 1864; vol. 2 (2 numbers), 1865. Richmond: Ayres & Wade, 1864–1865.

Confederate States Medical and Surgical Journal. Introduction by William D. Sharpe. Metuchen, NJ: Scarecrow Press, 1976.

Coulter, E. Merton. *Travels in the Confederate States: A Bibliography.* Norman: University of Oklahoma Press, 1948.

————. *The Confederate States of America, 1861–1865.* Baton Rouge: Louisiana State University Press, 1950.

Courtwright, David T. "Opiate Addiction as a Consequence of the Civil War." *Civil War History* 24 (1978): 101–111.

Cumming, Kate. *A Journal of Hospital Life in the Confederate Army of Tennessee, from the Battle of Shiloh to the End of the War.* Louisville: J. P. Morgan & Co., 1866.

Cunningham, Horace H. *Doctors in Gray: The Confederate Medical Service.* Baton Rouge: Louisiana State University Press, 1958.

————. *Field Medical Services at the Battles of Manassas (Bull Run).* Athens: University of Georgia Press, 1968.

————. "The Confederate Medical Officer in the Field." *New York Academy of Medicine Bulletin* 34 (1958): 461–488.

Cuttino, George P., ed. *Saddle Bag and Spinning Wheel: Being the Civil War Letters of George W. Peddy, M.D., Surgeon, 56th Georgia Volunteer Regiment, C.S.A., and His Wife, Kate Featherston Peddy.* Macon, GA: Mercer University Press, 1981.

Dammann, Gordon. *A Pictorial Encyclopedia of Civil War Medical Instruments and Equipment.* Missoula, MT: Pictorial Histories Publishing Company, 1983.

Daniel, Ferdinand E. *Recollections of a Rebel Surgeon (and Other Sketches); or, In the Doctors Sappy Says.* Austin TX: Von Boeckmann, Schutze, & Company, 1899.

Daniel, Larry J. *Soldiering in the Army of Tennessee: A Portrait of Life in the Confederate Army.* Chapel Hill: University of North Carolina Press, 1991.

Diffenbaugh, Willis G. "Military Surgery in the Civil War." *Military Medicine* 130 (1965): 429–496.

Dornbusch, Charles E. *Military Bibliography of the Civil War.* 4 vols. New York: New York Public Library, 1961–1992; Dayton: Morningside Press, 1987.

Duncan, Louis C. *The Medical Department of the United States Army in the Civil War.* Washington, D.C., n.d.

————. "Evolution of the Ambulance Corps and Field Hospital." *Military Surgery* 32 (1913): 221–240.

Ellis, Thomas T. *Leaves from the Diary of an Army Surgeon.* New York: J. Bradburn, 1863.

Engleman, Rose C., and Robert U. T. Joy. *Two Hundred Years of Military Medicine.* Fort Detrick, MD: Historical Unit, U.S. Army Medical Department, 1975.

Farmer, H. Frank, Jr. "Contributions of the American Civil War to Medicine." *Journal of the Florida Medical Association* 79 (May 1980): 306–308.

Farr, Warner D. "Confederate Surgeon General Samuel Preston Moore." (1994).

Flikke, Julia. *Nurses in Action.* Philadelphia: J. B. Lippincott, 1943.

Flint, Austin. *Contributions Relating to the Causation and Prevention of Disease, and to Camp Diseases; Together with a Report of the Diseases, etc., among the Prisoners at Andersonville, GA.* New York: Hurd & Houghton, 1867.

Foltz, Charles S. *Surgeon of the Seas: The Adventurous Life of Surgeon General Jonathan M. Foltz in the Days of Wooden Ships.* Indianapolis: Bobbs-Merrill, 1931.

Forman, Jacob G. *The Western Sanitary Commission.* St. Louis: R. P. Studley & Co., 1864.

Franke, Norman H. "Pharmaceutical Conditions and Drug Supply in the Confederacy." *Georgia Historical Quarterly* 37 (1953): 287–329.

Freemon, Frank R. "Administration of the Medical Department of the Confederate States Army, 1861 to 1865." *Southern Medical Journal* 80 (1987): 630–637.

———. "Lincoln Finds a Surgeon General: William A. Hammond and the Transformation of the Union Army Medical Bureau." *Civil War History* 33 (1987): 5–21.

———. *Microbes and Minie Balls: An Annotated Bibliography of Civil War Medicine.* Rutherford, NJ: Fairleigh Dickinson University Press, 1993.

———. "Medical Care at the Siege of Vicksburg." *Bulletin of the New York Academy of Medicine* 67 (1991): 429–438.

———. "The Medical Challenge of Military Operations in the Mississippi Valley during the American Civil War." *Military Medicine* 157 (1992): 494.

Gillette, Mary C. *The Army Medical Department 1818–1865.* Washington, D.C.: Center for Military History, 1987.

Gould, Benjamin A. *Investigations in the Military and Anthropological Statistics of American Soldiers.* New York: Hurd & Houghton, 1869.

Gross, Samuel D. *A Manual of Military Surgery.* Philadelphia: J. B. Lippincott, 1861.

Hall, Courtney R. "The Lessons of the War between the States." *International Record of Medicine* 171 (1958): 408–430.

Haller, John S., Jr. *American Medicine in Transition, 1840–1860.* Urbana: University of Illinois Press, 1981.

Hallock, Judith Lee. " 'Lethal and Debilitating': The Southern Disease Environment as a Factor in Confederate Defeat." *Journal of Confederate History* 7 (1991): 51–61.

Hammond, William A. *Military, Medical and Surgical Essays, Prepared for the United States Sanitary Commission.* Philadelphia: J. B. Lippincott, 1864.

———. *A Treatise on Hygiene, with Special Reference to the Military Service.* Philadelphia: J. B. Lippincott, 1863.

———. *A Statement of the Causes Which Led to the Dismissal of Surgeon-General William A. Hammond from the Army; with a Review of the Evidence Adduced before the Court.* Washington, D.C.: Privately printed, 1864.

Henry, W. D. "Stonewall Jackson—the Soldier Eccentric." *Practitioner* 223 (1979): 580–587.

Henry, Robert S. *The Armed Forces Institute of Pathology, Its First Century, 1862–1962.* Washington, D.C.: Office of the Surgeon General, Department of the Army, 1964.

Hewitt, Lawrence L., and Arthur W. Bergeron, Jr., eds. *Post Hospital Ledger: Port Hudson, Louisiana. 1862–1863.* Baton Rouge: Le Comité des Archives de la Louisiane, 1981.

Higham, Robin. *A Guide to the Sources of United States Military History.* Hamden, CT: Archon Books, 1975.

Hodge, Robert A., comp. *A Death Roster of the Confederate General Hospital at Culpeper, Virginia.* Fredericksburg, VA.: The Author, 1977.

Holland, Mary A. *Our Army Nurses.* Boston: B. Wilkins, 1895.

Holman, Andrew C. "Thomas J. Jackson and the Idea of Health: A New Approach to the Social History of Medicine." *Civil War History* 38 (1992): 131–155.

Ikard, Robert W. "The Short and Stormy Nashville Career of Joseph Jones, Tennessee's First Public Health Officer." *Tennessee Historical Quarterly* 47 (1989): 209–217.

Jarcho, Saul. "The Influence of the Armed Forces Institute of Pathology on Medicine." *Military Medicine* 128 (1963): 473–482.

Johnson, Charles B. *Muskets and Medicine; or, Army Life in the Sixties.* Philadelphia: F. A. Davis, 1917.

Jones, Gordon W. "The Medical History of the Fredericksburg Campaign: Course and Significance." *Journal of the History of Medicine and Allied Sciences,* 18 (1963): 241–256.

Jones, Joseph. *Medical and Surgical Memoirs.* 3 vols. in 4. New Orleans: Clark Hofeline, 1876–1890.

Jordan, Phillip D. "The Career of Henry M. Farr, Civil War Surgeon." *Annals of Iowa* 44 (1982): 191–211.

Key, Jack D. "U.S. Army Medical Department and Civil War Medicine." *Military Medicine* 133 (1968): 181–192.

LaPointe, Patricia M. "Military Hospitals in Memphis." *Tennessee Historical Quarterly* 42 (1983): 325–342.

Letterman, Jonathan. *Medical Recollections of the Army of the Potomac.* New York: D. Appleton, 1866.

Linderman, Gerald F. *Embattled Courage: The Experience of Combat in the American Civil War.* New York: Free Press, 1987.

Link, Kenneth. "Potomac Fever: The Hazards of Camp Life." *Vermont History* 51 (1983): 69–88.

Lister, Joseph. "On a New Method of Treating Compound Fracture, Abscess, etc., with Observations on the Condition of Suppuration." *Lancet* 1 (1867): 357–359.

Livermore, Mary A. *My Story of the War.* Hartford: A. D. Worthington, 1888.

Long, Esmond R. "The Army Medical Museum," *Military Medicine* 128 (1973): 367–377.

Macleod, George H. B. *Notes on Surgery of the War in the Crimea.* Philadelphia: J. B. Lippincott, 1862.

Maxwell, William Q. *Lincoln's Fifth Wheel: The Political History of the United States Sanitary Commission.* New York: Longmans, Green, 1956.

McInvale, Morton R. "That Thing of Infamy: Macon's Camp Oglethorpe during the Civil War." *Georgia Historical Quarterly* 63 (1979): 279–291.

McPherson, James M. *Battle Cry of Freedom: The Civil War Era.* Cambridge: Oxford University Press, 1988.

Miles, Wyndham D. *A History of the National Library of Medicine: The Nation's Treasury of Medical Knowledge.* Washington, D.C.: Government Printing Office, 1982.

Mitchell, Silas Weir. "The Medical Department in the Civil War." *Journal of the American Medical Association* 62 (1914): 1445–1450.

———. "Some Personal Recollections of the Civil War." *Trans. College Physician Phila* 27 (1905): 87–94.

———. *Injuries of Nerves and Their Consequences.* Philadelphia: J. B. Lippincott, 1872.

Munden, Kenneth W., and Henry P. Beers. *Guide to Federal Archives Relating to the Civil War.* Washington, D.C.: National Archives, General Services Administration, 1962.

Nevins, Allan. *The Ordeal of the Union.* 4 vols. New York: Charles Scribner's Sons, 1947–1971.

———. *The War for the Union.* 4 vols. New York: Charles Scribner's Sons, 1947–1971.

Nevins, Allan, James I. Robertson, and Bell I. Wiley, eds. *Civil War Books; A Critical Bibliography.* 2 vols. Baton Rouge: Louisiana State University Press, 1967–1969.

Ochsner, John. "The Genuine Southern Surgeon." *Annals of Surgery* 215 (1992): 397–408.

[Olmsted, Frederick L.] *Hospital Transports. A Memoir of the Embarkation of the Sick and Wounded from the Peninsula of Virginia in the Summer of 1862.* Boston: Ticknor & Fields, 1863.

———. *The Papers of Frederick Law Olmsted.* Vol. 4: *Defending the Union: The Civil War and the U.S. Sanitary Commission, 1861–1863.* Edited by Jane Turner Carson. Baltimore, MD: Johns Hopkins University Press, 1986.

Packard, John H. *A Manual of Minor Surgery.* Philadelphia: J. B. Lippincott, 1863.

Pember, Phoebe Y. *A Southern Woman's Story: Life in Confederate Richmond.* Edited by Bell I. Wiley. Jackson, TN: McCowat-Mercer, 1959.

Perry, John G. *Letters from a Surgeon of the Civil War.* Compiled by Martha D. Perry. Boston: Little, Brown, 1906.

Porcher, Francis P. *Resources of the Southern Fields and Forests: Medical, Economical and Agricultural.* Richmond: West & Johnston, 1863.

Quinone, Mark A. "Drug Abuse during the Civil War (1861–1865)." *International Journal of Addiction* 10 (1975): 1007–1020.

Reed, William H. *Hospital Life in the Army of the Potomac.* Boston: William V. Spencer, 1886.

Riley, Harris D., Jr. "Jefferson Davis and His Health. Part I. June, 1808–December, 1860." *Journal of Mississippi History* 49 (August 1987): 179–202.

———. "Jefferson Davis and His Health. Part II. January, 1861–December, 1889." *Journal of Mississippi History* 49 (November 1987): 261–287.

———. "Robert E. Lee's Battle with Disease." *Civil War Times Illustrated* 18 (December 1979): 12–22.

———. "Joseph Jones, M.D.: An Early Clinical Investigator." *Southern Medical Journal* 80 (May 1987): 623–629.

———. "Doctors Joseph Jones and Stanhope Bayne-Jones: Two Distinguished Louisianians." *Louisiana History* 25 (Spring 1984): 155–180.

———. "Confederate Medical Manuals of the Civil War." *Journal of the Medical Association of Georgia* 77 (1988): 106–108.

———. "Samuel P. Moore." In *Encyclopedia of Southern Culture.* Edited by C. W. Wilson and W. Ferris. Chapel Hill: University of North Carolina Press, 1989.

———. "Medical Furloughs in the Confederate States Army." *Journal of Confederate History* 2 (1989): 115–131.

———. "Joseph Jones: Confederate Surgeon." *Journal of the Tennessee State Medical Association* 53 (November 1960): 493–504.

———. "General Robert E. Lee: His Medical Profile." *Virginia Medical* 105 (July 1978): 495–501.

———. "Medicine in the Confederacy." *Military Medicine* 158 (1956): 53–63, 145–153.

Riley, Harris D., Jr., and Amos Christie. "Deaths and Disabilities in the Provisional

Army of Tennessee." *Tennessee Historical Quarterly* 43 (Summer 1984): 132–154.

Robertson, James I., Jr. Introduction to *The Medical and Surgical History of the Civil War,* 1: iii–ix. Wilmington, NC: Broadfoot Publishing Co., 1990–1992.

———. *Soldiers Blue and Gray.* Columbia: University of South Carolina Press, 1987.

———, et al. "Tenting Tonight. The Soldier's Life." in *The Civil War,* pp. 97–98. Alexandria, VA: Time-Life Books, 1984.

Rothstein, William G. *American Physicians in the Nineteenth Century: From Sects to Service.* Baltimore: Johns Hopkins University Press, 1972.

Rozear, M. P., Massey, E. W., Horner, J., et al. "R.E. Lee's Stroke." *Virginia Magazine of History and Biography* 98 (April 1990): 291–308.

Salerno, S. M. "Advances in Neurology at Turner's Lane Military Hospital." *New Jersey Medicine* 88 (1991): 567–572.

Schullian, Dorothy M., and Frank B. Rogers. "The National Library of Medicine." *Library Quarterly* 78 (1958): 1–17, 95–121.

Sharpe, William D. "Confederate Medical Services during the War between the States." *Academy of Medicine Bulletin* 11 (1965): 32.

Shryock, Richard H. "A Medical Perspective on the Civil War." *American Quarterly* 14 (1962): 161–173.

Smaridge, Norah. *Hands of Mercy: The Story of Sister-Nurses in the Civil War.* New York: Benziger Bros., 1900.

Smith, Adelaide W. *Reminiscences of an Army Nurse during the Civil War.* New York: Greaves, 1911.

Smith, George W. *Medicines for the Union Army: The United States Army Laboratories during the Civil War.* Madison, WI: American Institute of the History of Pharmacy, 1962.

Smith, John D. "The Health of Vermont's Civil War Recruits." *Vermont History* 43 (1975): 185–192.

———. "Kentucky Civil War Recruits: A Medical Profile." *Medical History* 24 (1980): 185–196.

Smith, Stephen. *Hand-Book of Surgical Operations.* New York: Bailliere Bros., 1862.

Smith, Susan E. D. *The Soldier's Friend.* Edited by John Little. Memphis: Bulletin Publishing Co., 1867.

Stark, Richard B., and Janet C. Stark. "Surgical Care of the Confederate States Army." *Bulletin of the New York Academy of Medicine* 34 (1958): 405.

Stark, Richard B. "Surgeons and Surgical Care of the Confederate States Army." *Virginia Medical Monthly* 87 (1960): 230.

Steiner, Paul E. *Medical History of a Civil War Regiment: Disease in the Sixty-fifth United States Colored Infantry.* Clayton, MO: Institute of Civil War Studies, 1977.

———. *Physician-Generals in the Civil War, a Study in Nineteenth Mid-Century American Medicine.* Springfield, IL: Charles C. Thomas, 1966.

———. *Diseases in the Civil War: Natural Biological Warfare in 1861–1865.* Springfield, IL: Charles C. Thomas, 1968.

Stevenson, Benjamin F. *Letters from the Army.* Cincinnati: W. E. Dibble, 1884.

Stinson, Julia C. *History and Manual of the Army Nurse Corps.* Carlisle Barracks Medical Field Service School, 1937.

Stout, Samuel H. "Some Facts of the History of the Organization of the Medical Services of the Confederate Armies and Hospitals." *Southern Practitioner* 22–25 (1900–1903).

Street, James, Jr. "Under the Influence." *Civil War Times Illustrated* 17 (May 1988): 30–35.

Sunseri, Alvin R. "The Organization and Administration of the Medical Department of the Confederate Army of Tennessee." *Journal of the Tennessee Medical Association* 53 (1960): 41–45, 79–82, 166–173, 212–218, 326–331.

Supplement to the Official Records of the Union and Confederate Armies. Part I, Reports, Volume 1. Edited by Janet B. Hewett, Noah A. Trudeau, and Bryce A. Suderow. Wilmington, NC: Broadfoot Publishing Co., 1994–.

Tripler, Charles S. *Hand-Book for the Military Surgeon.* Cincinnati: R. Clarke, 1861.

U.S. Provost-Marshal-General's Bureau. *Statistics, Medical and Anthropological, of the Provost-Marshal-General's Bureau, Derived from Records of the Examination for Military Service in the Armies of the United States during the Late War of the Rebellion.* 2 vols. Compiled by J. H. Baxter. Washington, D.C.: Government Printing Office, 1875.

U.S. Army Medical Department Historical Unit. *Two Hundred Years of Military Medicine.* Edited by Rose C. Engleman and Robert U. T. Joy. Washington, D.C.: Government Printing Office, 1965.

U.S. Navy Department *Official Records of the Union and Confederate Navies in the War of the Rebellion.* 30 vols. Washington, D.C.: Government Printing Office, 1894–1922.

United States Sanitary Commission. *Surgical Memoirs of the War of the Rebellion.* 2 vols. New York: Riverside Press, 1870–1871.

———. *History of the United States Sanitary Commission, Being the General Report of Its Work during the War of the Rebellion.* By Charles J. Stille. New York: Hurd & Houghton, 1868.

———. *The Sanitary Commission of the United States Army: A Short Narrative of Its Words and Purposes.* New York: United States Sanitary Commission, 1864.

———. *Narrative of Privations and Sufferings of United States Officers and Soldiers While Prisoners of War in the Hands of the Rebel Authorities.* Philadelphia: King & Baird, 1864.

U.S. Surgeon-General's Office. *The Medical and Surgical History of the War of the Rebellion, 1861–65.* 3 vols. in 6. Washington, D.C.: Government Printing Office, 1875–1885.

———. *The Medical Department of the United States Army from 1775 to 1873.* Compiled by Harvey E. Brown. Washington, D.C.: Surgeon General's Office, 1873.

U.S. War Department. *The War of the Rebellion: A Compilation of the Official Records of the Union and Confederate Armies.* 70 vols. in 128. Washington, D.C.: Government Printing Office, 1880–1901.

Walter, Richard D. *S. Weir Mitchell, M.D., Neurologist: A Medical Biography.* Springfield, IL: Charles C. Thomas, 1970.

Waring, Joseph I. *A History of Medicine in South Carolina, 1825–1900.* Columbia: South Carolina Medical Association, 1967.

Warren, Edward. *A Doctor's Experiences in Three Continents.* Baltimore: Cushing & Bailey, 1885.

———. *An Epitome of Practical Surgery for Field and Hospital.* Richmond: West & Johnston, 1863.

Weiss, E. R. "Life and Times of Samuel Preston Moore, Surgeon General of the Confederate States of America." *Southern Medical Journal* 23 (October 1930): 916–922.

Welch, Spencer G. *A Confederate Surgeon's Letters to His Wife*. New York: Neale, 1911.

Wells, Thomas H. *The Confederate Navy: Study in Organization*. Tuscaloosa: University of Alabama Press, 1971.

Wheelwright, Charles H. *Correspondence of Dr. Charles H. Wheelwright, Surgeon of the United States Navy*. Edited by Hildegarde B. Forbes. Boston(?), 1958.

Whitman, Walt. *The Wound Dresser; Letters Written to His Mother from the Hospitals in Washington during the Civil War*. Edited by Richard M. Bucke. New York: Bodley, 1949.

————. *Specimen Days*. Boston: Godine, 1971.

Wiley, Bell Irwin. *The Life of Johnny Reb: The Common Soldier of the Confederacy*. Indianapolis: Bobbs-Merrill, 1943.

————. *The Life of Billy Yank: The Common Soldier of the Union*. Indianapolis: Bobbs-Merrill, 1951.

Wilkinson, Warren. *Mother, May You Never See the Sight I Have Seen: The 57th Massachusetts Veteran Volunteers in the Army of the Potomac, 1864–1865*. New York: Harper & Row, 1990.

Williams, Carrington. "Samuel Preston Moore, Surgeon General of the Confederate States Army." *Virginia Medical Monthly* 88 (October 1961): 622–628.

Wilson, LaGrand James. *The Confederate Soldier*. Fayetteville, AR: Privately printed, 1902.

Wood, Ann D. "The War within a War: Women Nurses in the Union Army." *Civil War History* 18 (1972): 197–212.

Woodward, Joseph J. *The Hospital Steward's Manual*. Philadelphia: J. B. Lippincott, 1862.

————. *Outline of the Chief Camp Diseases of the United States Armies as Obtained during the Present War*. Philadelphia: J. B. Lippincott, 1863.

Woolsey, Jane S. *Hospital Days*. New York: D. Van Nostrand, 1868.

Zellem, Ronald T. "Wounded by Bayonet, Ball and Bacteria: Medicine and Neurosurgery in the American Civil War." *Neurosurgery* 17 (1985): 850–860.

Zone, Robert M. "Venereal Diseases: A Historical Perspective." *Journal of the Tennessee Medical Association* 81 (1988): 451–453.

34

Enlisted Soldiers

William Garrett Piston

The common soldier received little attention in Civil War writings until the 1880s, when time had softened animosities between blue and gray and aging veterans looked back on the war as a grand adventure. In an era that embraced social Darwinism, the war took on a new meaning. For white Americans unsettled by rapid urbanization, industrialization, and mechanization, reading about the war did more than satisfy a nostalgia for an allegedly simpler time. Like the joint memorializing of battlefields by Union and Confederate veterans, such readings reflected unity through shared struggle. Emphasis on the suffering and hardships of the common soldiers, rather than the achievements of great generals, allowed reunited Americans to view the war as a great purifying experience that had brought out the best in the Anglo-Saxon "race."

WORKS BY VETERANS

The first major work on the common soldier was written by Carlton McCarthy, a former private in the Richmond Howitzers. His *Detailed Minutiae of Soldier Life in the Army of Northern Virginia* (1882) established, with humor and candor, the topical categories that most subsequent works have followed. Indeed, his descriptions of the way soldiers learned to care for themselves in camp and on the march, their confrontation with the realities of warfare, their resistance to regimentation, and their conflict with officers touch on themes that soldiers of any era would recognize.

Much of what scholars have since written about the common soldier in the Civil War parallels McCarthy. His exploration of soldier life includes "Cooking and Eating'' (rations, food preparation, foraging, sutlers) and ''Comforts, Conveniences, and Consolations'' (alcohol, tobacco, mail, physical shelter, comradeship, preaching, religion). And his description of combat from the common soldiers' perspective reminds us that the ''face of battle'' approach emphasized by historian Michael Keegan (1988) is hardly new. McCarthy writes that a private soldier ''sees very little indeed of the field. What occurs in his own regiment, or probably in his own company, is about all, and is sometimes more than he actually sees or knows'' (p. 94).

John D. Billings, a veteran of the 10th Massachusetts Artillery, apparently never read McCarthy's book, for he describes his *Hardtack and Coffee; or The Unwritten Story of Army Life* (1887) as ''the first attempt to record comprehensively army life in detail; in which both text and illustrations aim to permanently record information which the history of no other war has preserved with equal accuracy and completeness'' (p. vi) Yet the parallels between Billings and McCarthy are numerous. Both describe the transformation of recruits into experienced soldiers, and both cover in great detail those aspects of service that were largely independent of national allegiance: food, clothing, shelter, camp life, marching, discipline, and diversions. In the case of Billings, these are illustrated almost comprehensively by 211 wartime sketches rendered by a fellow artillerist, Charles W. Reed. Additionally, Billings's work is much longer and better organized than McCarthy's, and it is less partisan. It shares McCarthy's honesty by admitting faults as well as virtues among the Union soldiers.

The comprehensive detail found in *Hardtack and Coffee* is astonishing. For example, Billings's eighteen-page chapter on army rations has thirty-seven subheadings, and his study of enlistment, camp life, marching, and foraging is equally thorough. Although McCarthy admits that Southern soldiers were poorly disciplined, Billings describes the punishment of miscreant Northern soldiers in almost encyclopedic detail, covering everything from humiliation to executions. Like McCarthy, Billings's descriptions of camp life include such commonplace activities as roll call, sick call, fatigue duties, drill, and guard duty. But he even includes the musical notation for the bugle calls that accompanied each activity. While Billings tends to emphasize the artillery, he also discusses the signal corps, logistics (including military railroads), the engineers, and medical services. Where but in *Hardtack and Coffee* can one find a description of the items stored in the box beneath an ambulance driver's seat?

COMPREHENSIVE WORKS BY MODERN HISTORIANS

Taken together McCarthy and Billings provide the basic printed sources for the study of the common soldier. A reader of Billings's description of how to cook fritters or McCarthy's account of chewing tobacco might well wonder if any aspects of soldier life remained to be explored. But in the two decades preceding the Civil War centennial, historian Bell Irvin Wiley built upon their foundation to produce his classic companion volumes, *The Life of Johnny Reb:*

The Common Soldier of the Confederacy (1943) and *The Life of Billy Yank: The Common Soldier of the Union* (1952). Wiley's Southern heritage shows clearly in his work, making *Johnny Reb* the better book, but both volumes represent remarkable scholarly achievement. They are based not only on printed sources, such as newspapers, diaries, memoirs, and reminiscences, but also on vast amounts of unpublished archival materials, including 30,000 soldiers' letters.

Johnny Reb resembles the works of McCarthy and Billings in format, beginning with recruits and ending with experienced soldiers, while covering such topics as food, clothing, shelter, camp life, marching, foraging, and battle. But while Wiley's study confirms the accuracy of the two veterans' memories, he goes considerably beyond their works, particularly when investigating the less heroic aspects of soldier life. McCarthy had admitted that all Confederate soldiers were not saints, but compared to *Detailed Minutiae,* Wiley's *Johnny Reb* is downright earthy. He noted that despite the mythology of the Lost Cause, "all the evils usually associated with barrack and camp life flourished in the Confederate Army" (p. 36). Misbehavior—gambling, alcohol abuse, theft of private property, consorting with prostitutes—was a chronic problem involving a huge percentage of the soldiers, not just a few Sunday school dropouts. Like McCarthy, Wiley clearly considers the Southern soldier praiseworthy for unrivaled acts of courage, endurance, and fortitude. But while McCarthy's condemnation of Confederate shirkers and deadbeats is very generalized, Wiley writes in detail of demoralization, panic on the battlefield, and desertion. The last problem, he asserts, reached nightmare proportions, severely damaging the Confederate war effort.

Like the earlier studies of the common soldier, Wiley's is remarkably thorough, covering topics such as weaponry, medicine, music, soldiers' reading habits, the theater, fraternal associations, and debating societies. He pays particular attention to religion, examining military chaplains and discussing religious revivals in the ranks. Wiley also explores the relationship between Johnny Reb and his loved ones, admitting that late in the war, many letters probably contributed to the army's high desertion rate, by describing the misery on the home front and asserting, directly or indirectly, that the soldier had a higher duty to family than to country.

Wiley argues that few Southern soldiers "understood or cared about the Constitutional issues at stake" and were more concerned with white supremacy than defending slavery" (p. 309). Most Confederates believed the average "bluebelly" was an immigrant who enlisted for pay and fought without patriotic motives. Although by late war mutual suffering and contempt for political leaders produced something of a bond between the common soldiers of North and South, this shattered whenever racial issues arose.

Wiley concludes with an important, though somewhat random, social analysis of the Confederate soldier. This includes such topics as occupation, education, literacy, and class. He notes a surprisingly large ethnic element, particularly Irishmen from the urban South. He devotes several pages to Confederate Indians and the role of slaves in sustaining the war effort. Although written from a standpoint of admiration, the author's closing remarks provide a portrait of the average Confederate soldier as above all else human and fallible. "He was far from perfect," Wiley wrote, "but his achievement against great odds in scores of desperate battles through four years of war is an irrefutable evidence of his prowess and an eternal monument to his greatness as a fighting man" (p. 347).

Much of Wiley's *Billy Yank* parallels *Johnny Reb,* emphasizing the tremendous similarities between the Northern and Southern soldiers themselves, as well as their experiences. The list of duplicate topics includes the obvious: recruiting and enlistment, food, shelter, clothing, marching, foraging, camp life, recreation, punishments, religion, morale and desertion, medical affairs, and vice. While demonstrating that the Northern soldier was better equipped and provisioned than his Southern counterpart, Wiley chronicles with sympathy and respect the hardships and sacrifices of the men in blue.

While *Johnny Reb* questions many of the myths associated with the average Confederate, particularly in terms of personal behavior and commitment to the war effort, *Billy Yank* does the same for the sons of the Union. In relation to Northern soldiers' motivation, Wiley concludes that financial inducement was a significant factor in enlistments, particularly among the foreign born. He also credits peer pressure, social ostracism, and a craving for excitement with filling the ranks. "Hence, original impulses of individuals ranged from material considerations and a mere craving for excitement to profound idealism and hatred of traitors. It seems clear, however, that the great bulk of volunteers responded to mixed motives, none of which was deeply felt" (p. 39).

Billy Yank provides a much more detailed account of typical Civil War combat than appears in the earlier volume. Also, since the Northerners were in almost all cases the invading force, Wiley devotes considerable attention to Northern soldiers' reaction to the South and Southerners. Not surprisingly, this ranged from contempt and pity to admiration. He concludes that despite many individual acts of generosity and kindness, in general Northern soldiers gradually turned against slavery without developing much sympathy for the slaves themselves. Black soldiers were welcomed only in the context of achieving victory, as notions of racial equality were as foreign to Billy Yank as to Jeff Davis.

As in the previous volume, Wiley provides a social analysis of the common soldier. "The most striking thing about Union soldiers was their diversity," he writes. "Indeed, there was hardly a type or class of any conceivable kind that was not represented in the Northern ranks" (p. 296). He explores such factors as age, prewar occupation, class, literacy, ethnicity, and race. He notes that the strong rivalries between the eastern and western armies occasionally produced hostilities, and examines state identification and interservice rivalries as well.

Most Union soldiers, the author believes, considered Southerners "a haughty, hot-tempered, overbearing, bloodthirsty people who in utter disregard of Northern concessions had turned their backs on the benefits of Union and thrust the nation into war" (p. 346). But many developed a grudging admiration of their enemies after viewing Confederate courage and tenacity. As a result, there was considerable fraternization.

How then did the two sides differ? Wiley offers a number of conclusions. Because they were better educated, Union soldiers were more reflective, curious, and interested in politics than their counterparts were. Northerners tended to be less religious overall, as well as less emotional in their religious expressions. They were more practical, more money oriented, and less humorous. They did not take to soldiering as readily as Southerners and showed less martial spirit in the ranks, yet they were more efficient and machinelike in their approach to war.

Wiley's work remains crucial to our understanding of the common soldier, but it is deficient in some areas. His research focuses overwhelmingly on the eastern armies, to the expense of the West and the trans-Mississippi. His exploration of the role of African Americans and the complex interaction between women and the military is significant, but by his own admission less than definitive. Such criticisms are mild, of course, in the face of Wiley's achievement.

McCarthy, Billings, and Wiley explore soldier life so thoroughly that all subsequent works can be considered supplements. One of the most significant of these is *Soldiers Blue and Gray* (1988), by James I. Robertson, Jr. Because he does not establish any new categories, the book reads much like an abridgment of *Billy Yank* and *Johnny Reb,* and part of his value lies in presenting an account of soldier life both North and South in one volume. But he does differ significantly from Wiley, implying that Wiley emphasized the negative aspects of soldier life too strongly. "Like soldiers of all ages," Robertson writes, "Civil War troops were human: they rarely spoke in praise of things. They were quick to criticize; and because they were, their writings tend to be more negative and sarcastic than one might expect" (p. ix).

Without denying the shortcomings of Civil War veterans, Robertson argues that the majority earned the adoration that later generations accorded them. "The fortitude these citizen-soldiers displayed was extraordinary on a regular basis," he notes (p. 64). The "overwhelming number of those who wrote letters or kept diaries" disapproved of the drunkenness, gambling, whoring, and other sorts of misbehavior that occurred within the armed forces (p. 81). The average soldiers "were conscientious, devoted men possessed of simple but indelible virtues" (p. 101). Despite the war's seamy side, "the evidence is overwhelming that a majority of soldiers North and South displayed fidelity through words in a letter, longing in the heart, and hopes for the future" (p. 121). Although poorly disciplined, Civil War soldiers were "the best fighters that America has ever produced" (p. 122). "Uncommon valor was a common virtue in most battles of that war" (p. 224).

Robertson clearly believes that Wiley, writing at a time when the less admirable aspects of Civil War service were rarely admitted, emphasizes them too much. In this sense, *Soldiers Blue and Gray* stands as a needful corrective, but

Robertson's admiration for the generation of 1861–1865 is so strong that an aura of moonlight and magnolia, which Wiley studiously avoids, wafts in.

How far a work can vary from those previously discussed and still merit consideration under the topic "common soldiers" is a matter on which judgment will vary. The works discussed below, all published in the past fifteen years, are included either because they break new ground or because they challenge the assumptions and conclusions of earlier studies.

STUDIES OF SUBGROUPS

While scholars have explored the Civil War in terms of the soldiers' ethnicity, race, and religion, African Americans are the only large subgroup who participated in circumstances giving them a significantly different "common soldier" experience than that of other veterans. Some of the printed primary source materials in *Freedom: A Documentary History of Emancipation 1861–1867* (1982), edited by Ira Berlin, relate to recruitment, discipline, military justice and punishments, camp life, health, and other matters relating to African Americans who enlisted. These subjects receive fuller attention in Joseph T. Glatthaar's *Forged in Battle: The Civil War Alliance of Black Soldiers and White Officers* (1990), which provides an excellent overview of trials and tribulations of the average black soldier. As Glatthaar's title indicates, he goes beyond these to discuss government policy, politics, public opinion, and other issues relating to the complex interrelationships of blacks and whites during the war. While African-American soldiers shared most of the experiences of their white comrades in blue, there were differences. For example, "blacks learned faster than whites because they cared more about soldiering. For most whites, military service was a duty; for most blacks, it was an honor and a privilege" (p. 108). Glatthaar also notes that the Union's military justice system punished blacks disproportionately but that those punished seem to have been genuinely guilty.

Historians have also examined military subsets of the whole, testing whether the men in specific forces differed from the profiles sketched by Wiley and company. They are more interested in the men's character, motivations, and performance than in their uniforms and equipment. Glatthaar's *The March to the Sea and Beyond: Sherman's Troops in the Savannah and Carolinas Campaigns* (1985) examines the men who, more than any other group, represented to Southerners the horror of the Civil War. The author explores not only the physical experiences of Sherman's "boys"—duties, hardships, camp life, boredom—but also their attitudes toward "their comrades, blacks, Southern whites, the war, destruction, and reconstruction" (p. xiii). He concludes that the great march succeeded because the men Sherman took with him were experienced veterans whose small unit cohesion allowed them to operate with minimal supervision. The destruction they wrought was terrible, but it was less wanton, and more carefully directed and controlled, than legend has it.

Sherman's force was composed mostly of men who showed their commitment to the Union by voting for Lincoln and by reenlisting when their original terms of service expired. Their views on blacks were complex. Although some advocated political and social equality for the freedmen, most shared the racial prejudice common to American whites. They were united in their belief that the destruction of slavery was a military necessity as well as a fitting punishment for traitors. They held Southern whites responsible for the war, but their bitterness rarely led to mistreatment of them. They enjoyed the physical destruction they caused, partly because revenge was sweet, but also from a belief that making war on civilians would end the conflict in the shortest time possible.

Larry J. Daniel's *Soldiering in the Army of Tennessee: A Portrait of Life in a Confederate Army* (1991) was written to correct a bias in the works of Wiley and Robertson toward the eastern soldiers. But in concentrating on the main Southern army in the West, Daniel also takes up issues raised by historians Thomas L. Connelly and Richard M. McMurry concerning the character of the western army, its commanders, and the degree to which it differed from Robert E. Lee's Army of Northern Virginia.

Exploring the familiar categories of soldier life, Daniel concludes that differences between the main eastern and western armies were more than cosmetic. The westerners had less class distinction, "more rough edges, less self-discipline, and fewer of the gentler refinements" (p. 13). However, he cites statistics of mail delivery to argue that the rate of illiteracy among soldiers of the Army of Tennessee has been overestimated.

Daniel agrees with Connelly that the army's distinct "western spirit" derived from the soldiers' grass-roots élan and self-confidence. But he also believes it was "rooted in the deterrent value of punishments inflicted on deserters, in other words, coercion; a well-timed religious revival that stressed commitment, sacrifice, and the ability to take hardships patiently; an esprit developed through shared suffering of the soldiers; and the troops' often viewing battlefield losses from a different perspective than that of modern historians" (p. 22).

STUDIES OF CHARACTER AND MOTIVATION

A number of recent works attempt to probe the mind, character, and motivations of the Civil War soldier. In general, these eschew descriptions of Sibley tents and shebangs to explore soldiers' attitudes toward combat, the enemy, politics, slavery and race, and other complexities. To a degree, this is familiar ground, but they exceed previous studies by the depth of their exploration, providing new insights not only into the men themselves but the culture and society that shaped them.

Michael Barton's *Goodmen: The Character of Civil War Soldiers* (1981) is "a quantitative sociolinguistic case study in historical psychological anthropology" (p. 4). Using statistical analysis, he studies Civil War letters and diaries to determine how the Victorian character theory, with its emphasis on self-control, was practiced. After a review of the historiographic debate over North-

South regional distinctiveness in terms of character, Barton explores such issues as how moral values were expressed and how styles of character differed. His analysis indicates that Northerners and Southerners shared the same basic set of core values: what one must do and how one must act to be a "goodman." But distinctions existed, with the widest gap being between the Northern enlisted man, who most nearly represented the typical American, and Southern officers. "The book's main theme," Barton notes, "is the importance of emotional control in those times. It tests (and supports) Tocqueville's simple sentence, 'The American South is more given to impulse' " (p. 5).

Gerald Linderman's *Embattled Courage: The Experience of Combat in the American Civil War* (1987) also deals with questions of character and emotional control, as they were part of the complex concept of "courage" that he argues was central to the soldiers' experience of the war. But the contrast between the values soldiers took into war and the realities that confronted them during combat produced in both blue and gray "a harsh disillusionment" (p. 2).

Linderman contends that in Victorian America, courage was at the center of a "constellation of values" (p. 8), which included manliness, godliness, duty, honor, and knightliness, and it saw its fullest expression in "heroic action undertaken without fear" (p. 17). These values constituted the psychological network within which the soldiers operated and were a greater motivator than ideology. Courage was the cement that held the clumsy, ill-disciplined volunteer armies together, in part because Civil War soldiers truly believed that courage could shield them from harm and that the side displaying the most courageous behavior would win. Bullets, however, cared naught for courage. Supplied with long-range rifles, fed by the draft, and supported by the industrial revolution, Civil War armies inflicted ghastly damage upon each other often without producing a decision on the battlefield. Realizing finally that allegiance to society's expectations was suicidal, the soldiers redefined courage in broader terms that emphasized survival and embraced ideas that were previously unthinkable, such as making war on civilians. Disillusionment was finally so profound, Linderman argues, that "those who continued to kill one another in battle often felt less estrangement from their victims than from those in whose behalf they had gone to fight" (p. 239).

Reid Mitchell explores many of these same issues in *Civil War Soldiers: Their Expectations and Their Experiences* (1988) and in *The Vacant Chair: The Northern Soldier Leaves Home* (1993). Although differing in focus and scope, they are united by Mitchell's identification of family and community as central to understanding the war. He links the military and civilian dimensions of the soldiers' experiences, arguing that both reflect the cultural assumptions of Victorian America toward key concepts and relationships: home and family, gender roles, notions of manhood and masculinity, duty and honor, community and government, faith, and paternalism.

In *Civil War Soldiers* Mitchell devotes chapters to recruitment and motivation, the psychology of service, Union soldiers' views of the South, and the Confederate experience. Although it concerns the North only, *The Vacant Chair* is in some ways broader in scope, as much of what Mitchell discovers probably held true for Southerners as well. Beginning with an examination of soldiering, manhood, and the experience of coming of age, Mitchell examines the connections between the soldier and his community. He then explores the relationships between soldiers and their society in terms of family-related issues and concepts, including adolescence, parental authority, home, and gender.

Overall, Mitchell argues that cultural altitudes combined with methods of recruitment and patterns of service to make Civil War soldiers perceive themselves as representatives of their communities. While this helped to sustain them amid the brutalization of war, they eventually transferred their loyalty to their comrades in arms, developing a new identity defined by military units and based on the shared sacrifices of war. This occurred partly because the military provided an authoritarian structure somewhat similar to that of the American family. A soldier's unit could become his family because it made parallel demands in terms of duty, sacrifice, and submission to authority. But the entire experience was filled with tension and stress. In the late war period, a considerable alienation developed between the soldiers and the home front. Soldiers resented profiteering, draft dodging, and any other behavior that suggested less than one hundred percent loyalty to the cause. On the other hand, evidence that loved ones were suffering forced soldiers to choose between duty to country and loyalty to family.

While Barton, Linderman, and Mitchell stress the importance of character in understanding the common soldiers, suggesting that ideology was not a major motivational factor, other historians argue that Civil War soldiers were deeply committed to specific principles. Earl J. Hess's *Liberty, Virtue, and Progress: Northerners and Their War for the Union* (1988) does not study soldiers as a separate group, but many of the quotations he uses to establish Northern opinion come from the common soldiers in blue. Hess does an excellent job of recapturing "a sense of that heady experience when people throughout the North were convinced that the fate of ideals depended upon the success of their war effort" (p. 3). While acknowledging dissent within the North and controversy over emancipation, Hess argues that key cultural values, including self-government, democracy, individualism, egalitarianism, and self-control, gave the Union war effort a strong sense of moral purpose that sustained it to the end. Billy Yank was not the politically indifferent fellow Wiley suggests but instead a committed citizen who "believed that the conflict was a grand struggle to preserve free government in North America, a struggle which had implications for the preservation of political freedom in the world at large" (p. 3).

"Seeing the Elephant": Raw Recruits at the Battle of Shiloh (1989) belongs in one sense to the military subgroups category, but the questions asked by authors Joseph Allan Frank and George A. Reaves place it here. They employ a computer analysis of soldiers' diaries and letters in order to study mobilization,

soldier life, campaigning, combat, and soldiers' attitudes toward battle and their leaders.

Frank and Reaves conclude that the Union and Confederate soldiers at Shiloh were "committed and politically articulate" men who enlisted primarily out of loyalty to country (pp. 30–31). Patriotism was particularly strong among Southerners, who felt the threat of invasion, but slavery was not a significant concern for either side during this early war campaign. A retention of identity with the home community held the new military units together and allowed officers to lead these raw civilians-in-arms into battle.

Frank and Reaves provide a vivid account of the battle from the common soldier's point of view, somewhat in the manner of Keegan's *The Face of Battle*. They go further than Keegan, however, by providing a statistical analysis of soldiers' responses to battle and the way it changed their attitudes. They conclude that less than a third were effective fighters who displayed active courage or leadership. Yet at battle's end, they were acutely conscious of their unit's performance and concerned for their reputations among the folks back home. Most men remained confident in their company and regimental officers but changed their standards of assessment from judging their personality traits to assessing the tactical expertise in combat. The enemy was now personal, and hatred of him intensified to become a prime motivator in continuing the struggle.

Motivation itself is the theme of James M. McPherson's *What They Fought For, 1861–1865* (1994). This brief book is the by-product of a larger project on the common soldier, not yet finished. McPherson concludes that "a large number of those men in blue and gray were intensely aware of the issues at stake and passionately concerned about them" (p. 4). In part, McPherson argues that previous historians have simply missed the evidence, but interpretation is also involved. He believes we should take the Civil War generation at its word and not be blinded by modern cynicism. "What seems like bathos and platitudes to us were real pathos and convictions to them" (p. 13).

McPherson devotes a chapter each to the North and South. His third, and concluding, chapter concerns the impact of the emancipation of soldiers' attitudes toward the war. The great irony of the war is that both Union and Confederate soldiers sincerely considered themselves the heirs of the American Revolution, defending liberty and republicanism. Patriotism and ideological commitment were very strong on both sides, surviving disillusionment and war weariness. In defending their country, Southerners were loyal to their new nation as well as to their culture and social institutions. Feeling no guilt over slavery, they sought self-determination in the face of tyranny and subjugation, and the need to defend hearth and home gave ideological abstractions a concrete form. Later in the war, a bitter hatred of the enemy and desire for revenge were significant motivators for both sides.

McPherson found that Lincoln's writings articulated quite well the sentiments expressed by the common soldiers of the North. They believed they were fighting to preserve the heritage of the American Revolution. Because secession was a threat to representative democracy, the best hope of humanity, the desire to punish treason was strong. Union soldiers were deeply divided over the emancipation proclamation, and war weariness was significant. But just like their Confederate counterparts, they continued to fight not only because of the bonding that mutual suffering had generated but also because the ideological principles remained important to them. Ironically, a shared racism during the postwar period led veterans of both sides to downplay the significance of slavery as a factor during the war.

CURRENT SCHOLARSHIP AND FUTURE DIRECTIONS

Work on the common soldier represents some of the best in Civil War scholarship. It includes as well a wealth of books and articles outside the scope of this chapter, devoted to the minutiae of soldier life. Thanks to the passion of collectors, reenactors, and Civil War buffs generally, astonishingly meticulous studies exist on almost every item Johnny Reb or Billy Yank wore, ate, carried, shot, rode, read, sang, slept in, sat on, or grumbled about. The four volumes of Francis A. Lord's *Civil War Collector's Encyclopedia* (1965–1995) and numerous other works testify to the continued popularity of studying the material culture of Johnny Reb and Billy Yank.

As overviews, the books by McCarthy, Billings, Wiley, and Robertson are not likely to be surpassed. Glatthaar and Daniel, however, remind us of the dangers of generalization, for Sherman's boys had their own character, and the Army of Tennessee was not the Army of Northern Virginia. More analysis of individual armies is in order, and as in so much else, the trans-Mississippi remains the most neglected area.

But additional studies of military subgroups will be truly significant only if they go beyond tin cups and cartridge boxes to explore issues of ideology, character, behavior, morale, and motivation. Objectivity is difficult. For example, historians who downplay ideology and emphasize small unit cohesion as combat motivators may be influenced by post-Vietnam cynicism. They may even be reading back into the past patterns of behavior that were first identified by historians studying veterans of World War II. Conversely, those who argue that Civil War soldiers sacrificed their lives because of deep ideological commitment may be reacting in some fashion to the apparent failure of the civil rights movement of the 1960s and the increasingly shallow, self-centered, and materialistic America of the 1980s and 1990s. Wasn't there, they seem to suggest, a time when people cared? This ongoing debate provides the richest vein for those who wish to sift one more time through the hundreds of thousands of letters, diaries, and reminiscences that constitute our legacy from the common soldier of the Civil War.

BIBLIOGRAPHY

Barton, Michael. *Goodmen: The Character of Civil War Soldiers.* University Park: Pennsylvania State University Press, 1981.

Berlin, Ira, ed. *Freedom: A Documentary History of Emancipation, 1861–1867.* Series II: *The Black Military Experience.* Cambridge: Cambridge University Press, 1982.

Billings, John D. *Hardtack and Coffee; or The Unwritten Story of Army Life.* Boston: Charles W. Reed, 1887.

Daniel, Larry J. *Soldiering in the Army of Tennessee: A Portrait of Life in a Confederate Army.* Chapel Hill: University of North Carolina Press, 1991.

Frank, Joseph Allan, and George A. Reaves. *"Seeing the Elephant": Raw Recruits at the Battle of Shiloh.* Westport, CT: Greenwood Press, 1989.

Glatthaar, Joseph T. *Forged in Battle: The Civil War Alliance of Black Soldiers and White Officers.* New York: Free Press, 1990.

———. *The March to the Sea and Beyond: Sherman's Troops in the Savannah and Carolinas Campaigns.* New York: New York University Press, 1985.

Hess, Earl J. *Liberty, Virtue, and Progress: Northerners and Their War for the Union.* New York: New York University Press, 1988.

Keegan, Michael. *The Face of Battle: A Study of Agincourt, Waterloo, and the Somme.* London: Barrie and Jenkins, 1988.

Linderman, Gerald F. *Embattled Courage: The Experience of Combat in the American Civil War.* New York: Free Press, 1987.

Lord, Francis A. *Civil War Collector's Encyclopedia.* Edison, NJ: Blue and Grey Press, 1965–1995.

McCarthy, Carlton. *Detailed Minutiae of Soldier Life in the Army of Northern Virginia, 1861–1865.* Richmond: Carlton McCarthy and Company, 1882.

McPherson, James M. *What They Fought For.* Baton Rouge: Louisiana State University Press, 1994.

Mitchell, Reid. *Civil War Soldiers: Their Expectations and Their Experiences.* New York: Viking, 1988.

———. *The Vacant Chair: The Northern Soldier Leaves Home.* New York: Oxford University Press, 1993.

Robertson, James I., Jr. *Soldiers Blue and Gray.* New York: Warner Books, 1988.

Wiley, Bell I. *The Life of Billy Yank: The Common Soldier of the Union.* Baton Rouge: Louisiana State University Press, 1952.

———. *The Life of Johnny Reb: The Common Soldier of the Confederacy.* Baton Rouge: Louisiana State University Press, 1943.

35

Prison Camps and Prisoners of War

Michael B. Chesson

Perhaps historians have largely failed to investigate military prisons and prisoners because these subjects have always been the most controversial aspect of the Civil War. Traditionally scholars have focused on battles and leaders, parties and political figures, although some have dealt with the common soldier, the home front, diplomacy, and the economic impact of the war. More recently, a handful of new social historians have taken a belated interest in the war, but their studies deal almost exclusively with the roles of women and African Americans. Prisoners of war continue to be neglected by military historians (having been removed from the battlefield) and by social historians (as being too closely related to military history), just as they were neglected, and sometimes seemingly forgotten, by their respective governments and captors.

PRIMARY SOURCES

As for most other Civil War topics, the *Official Records of the War of the Rebellion* continue to be the indispensable collection of published primary sources. The first eight volumes of the second series (1894–1899) contain 8,750 pages, excluding indexes, arranged chronologically. This material, the first of three major categories of writing on the subject, consists primarily of the correspondence between prison administrators and their military and civilian superiors. The first volume covers surrenders in Texas and Missouri, Union and Confederate "repression" in Maryland and East Tennessee, respectively, and the military treatment of captured and fugitive slaves. Volume 2 deals with suspected and disloyal persons, North and South, most of whom were civilians who became political or diplomatic prisoners, and the suspension of civil liberties. Volumes 3 through 8, from mid-February 1861 to mid-May 1867, contain correspondence, orders, and other documents regarding prisoners of war and political prisoners. Much of the final volume concerns postwar activities, including investigations of Confederate abuse, the trial of Henry Wirz, and the imprisonment of various Southern officials. The last document in this massive collection is an order for the transfer of Jefferson Davis from Fort Monroe to Richmond and his subsequent release. A statistical abstract of the monthly returns (July 1862–November 1865) from the major Federal prisons follows, but detailed reports on Confederate prisons were lacking at the time of compilation, except for some scattered returns from Andersonville.

Miscellaneous references to prison camps and individual prisoners are scattered throughout the *O.R.,* and new material may be included in the fifty-volume update now being published, the *Supplement to the Official Records* (1994–). See also the bibliographies found in most of the works cited in this chapter for primary sources used by the authors. Among them are voluminous manuscript records at the National Archives, now on microfilm, still largely unexamined by scholars. Military prisoners await a treatment comparable to that given political detainees in Mark E. Neely, Jr., *The Fate of Liberty* (1991), which is based on extensive research in similar materials.

GENERAL SUMMARIES

The best summaries continue to be those found in Edward Channing, *A History of the United States* (1925), and James Ford Rhodes, *History of the United States from the Compromise of 1850* (1904). In 1903 General F. C. Ainsworth of the Record and Pension Office gave Rhodes revised prisoner statistics, including the numbers who died on both sides. Rhodes and Channing regarded his figures as authoritative, and most historians ever since have accepted these official estimates as the best we are likely to have. See E. Merton Coulter, *The Confederate States of America* (1950), and J. G. Randall and David Donald, *The Civil War and Reconstruction* (1969).

HESSELTINE: PIONEER IN THE FIELD

The second category of literature, scholarly accounts, is the smallest and most disappointing and consists largely of studies of individual prisons. Among these secondary works there is no satisfactory synthesis. The best general study and introduction to the subject remains William B. Hesseltine's *Civil War Prisons: A Study in War Psychology* (1930), which was completed as a dissertation two years before its publication. Hesseltine's work is comprehensive, straightforward, and remarkably balanced for the 1920s, the era of pro-Southern historians Claude G. Bowers and George F. Milton. In fact, his treatment is more objective than that of some current scholars.

James M. McPherson, *Battle Cry of Freedom* (1988), groups Hesseltine with

"Southern historians" like Shelby Foote. While Hesseltine was born in the Old Dominion and attended both Washington and Lee and the University of Virginia, he took his doctorate at Ohio State University, and spent most, if not all, of his professional career outside the South, teaching at New York University, the University of California, and the University of Wisconsin, where he also served as president of that state's historical society. Hesseltine was perhaps not as biased toward the Confederacy as the Princeton professor, born in North Dakota, is toward the Union. A recent scholar noted that Hesseltine's description of Henry Wirz, for example, is largely negative. And the coverage (and criticism) of Southern prisons is far more extensive than that of Northern ones, continuing an historiographical tradition dating back to the war. The subtitle of Hesseltine's work was apt; he devoted considerable attention to the war psychosis from which both sides suffered. Northerners' belief, exacerbated by the press and politicians, that their prisoners were being deliberately killed by Confederate authorities drove the Union government to adopt a policy of retaliation, which helps to explain why the overall mortality rates on both sides were so close, despite the contrast in resources.

Hesseltine covers the first prisoners of war, in Texas (Union) and Missouri (Confederate); prisoner exchange before adoption of the Dix-Hill cartel of 1862; prisons during the first year of fighting; exchange under the cartel; Libby and Belle Isle in Richmond; Andersonville; other Southern prisons; war psychosis and Northern prisons; exchange under General Benjamin F. Butler during the last year of the war; and the aftermath. His final chapter summarizes the 259 books and articles written between 1862 and 1921, the majority by Northerners. At first they were written out of bitterness and to justify punishment of those responsible, as in what Hesseltine calls the "farcical trial and execution of Henry Wirz." Northern Republicans produced their own highly charged version of events from 1867 hearings, published as House Report No. 85, *Treatment of Prisoners of War by the Rebel Authorities* (1869). *The Trial of Henry Wirz* (1868) is even less reliable.

PRISONER ACCOUNTS: WAVING BLOODY SHIRTS

In the 1880s many Union veterans wrote accounts attempting to win government pensions. Wartime passions could still be found in works that appeared in the early twentieth century. Most of these titles, especially prisoner memoirs, should be used with caution. Many are exaggerated to some degree; some are bogus, the authors never having been prisoners at all. The bibliographies of Hesseltine and the other authors discussed are the best guides to this controversial and often unreliable literature. Hesseltine found 148 personal narratives and prisoner reminiscences of book length, as well as fifty-five articles. He examined "The Propaganda Literature of Confederate Prisons" in a 1935 article.

It was not until 1876, the traditional end of Reconstruction, that the first major

Southern response to Northern charges of deliberate cruelty appeared. J. William Jones compiled "The Treatment of Prisoners during the War between the States," a lengthy rebuttal that appeared in two issues of the *Southern Historical Society Papers* (1876), which he served as secretary. Stung by recent bloody shirt rhetoric in Congress from James G. Blaine and other Republicans, his collection featured letters and testimony from former Confederate officials, including Davis, excerpts from congressional debates, and other material.

A giant in the field and a prolific author, Hesseltine somehow found time to train many fine historians. His final contribution to this subject came a generation later, during the Civil War centennial. He edited an issue of *Civil War History* (1962) with seven articles and contributed a short introduction. The other authors were Ovid L. Futch on Andersonville; Minor H. McLain on Fort Warren, in Boston harbor; T. R. Walker, curator of the museum at the Rock Island Arsenal, on the Illinois prison; James I. Robertson on Elmira, New York; Edward T. Downer on Johnson's Island, in Lake Erie, just north of Sandusky, Ohio; and William M. Armstrong on a Union lieutenant held at various sites. The articles on the Northern prisons remain the best studies available.

HESSELTINE'S DISCIPLE

Since Hesseltine's death in 1963, Frank L. Byrne has been the leading authority. A former student of Hesseltine, he contributed the seventh essay in his collection, a sketch of Union general Neal Dow, a Libby prisoner, based on his earlier biography of the Maine temperance advocate, and excerpts from Dow's diary. Byrne also wrote "Libby Prison: A Study in Emotions" (1958). He compiled the section on "Prisons and Prisoners of War" for *Civil War Books* (1967), an annotated list of 213 titles that remains the best guide to works published before the mid-1960s. Only about one-quarter of the titles deal with Northern prisons or were written by Southern authors. Byrne wrote the text for "Prison Pens of Suffering" in *The Image of War, 1861–1865*, volume 4, *Fighting for Time* (1983). As usual with this series, the photographs are stunning, some not previously published. Those of the disintegrating Andersonville stockade after the war are reminiscent of the photographs of Nazi death camps. More recently, Byrne wrote entries on prisons and prisoners for the *Encyclopedia of the Confederacy* (1993). Each piece has a short bibliography. Both are balanced, comprehensive, and authoritative, though the one on prisons deals only with Confederate sites. Byrne contributed additional entries on individual prisons, North and South, and related topics.

Even more photographs can be found in Francis Trevelyan Miller's *The Photographic History of the Civil War*, volume 7, *Prisons and Hospitals (1911),* long the standard work, but now superseded by Davis. Unfortunately, the pictures were badly reproduced on poor-quality paper in the reprint edition. The older work contains many more photographs, only some of which appear in

Davis, as well as a lengthy text by Holland Thompson, which is moderate and balanced.

BLAKEY'S *WINDER* AND MARVEL'S *ANDERSONVILLE*

The most important monographs to appear since Hesseltine's *Civil War Prisons* are undoubtedly Arch Fredric Blakey's *General John H. Winder, C.S.A.* (1990) and William Marvel's *Andersonville: The Last Depot* (1994). The former is the only scholarly biography of Richmond's provost marshal, Andersonville's commandant, and, belatedly, the first Confederate commissary general of prisons. Blakey's study is compelling and convincing, though his conclusions have provoked controversy. His evidence suggests that rebel prisoners were dying at a faster rate than Yankees until the suspension of the cartel. Blakey handles tough and still bitter topics dispassionately and consistently portrays Winder in a critical but balanced manner. Brief treatments of Winder's lieutenant and successor as commandant are Darrett B. Rutman, "The War Crimes and Trial of Henry Wirz" (1960), and Morgan Peoples, " 'The Scapegoat of Andersonville': Union Execution of Confederate Captain Henry Wirz" (1980).

Marvel's lengthy, wide-ranging, revisionist treatment of Andersonville is a major study that supersedes all previous accounts and is based on extensive new research in a wide variety of primary sources. It is beautifully written, by a nonacademic historian, and even more likely than Blakey's work to provoke controversy. There is considerable discussion of both Winder and Wirz, but Marvel treats virtually all the topics mentioned in this chapter in his remarkably comprehensive work. He must now be considered as the leading authority in the field. In "Johnny Ransom's Imagination" (1955), a brief but scathing indictment of the author of *Andersonville [Diary]*, Marvel completely discredits his famous account, which won critical and popular acclaim and was reprinted as recently as 1986.

OTHER STUDIES OF SOUTHERN PRISONS

There are four slim volumes, all with notes, indexes, and bibliographies, on individual Confederate prisons, including two of the least well known. Ovid L. Futch's *History of Andersonville Prison* (1968) has been superseded by Marvel, who criticizes it for "an unhealthy reliance upon dubious sources" (p. 323). Futch describes the war's most notorious prison, and one of the largest, officially known as Camp Sumter, where at least 12,912 Union prisoners died, at the rate of 100 daily in August 1864. His 150 pages are still helpful for an understanding of what happened there and why. Futch argues that the Confederacy should have released its prisoners if it could not care for them. Given the political pressures and war psychosis of the time, this step was hardly realistic, but would have increased supplies for the South and helped its later image. But Futch is certainly more objective than Union authors from the Civil War into the early twentieth century, such as General N. P. Chipman, *The Tragedy of Andersonville: Trial of Captain Henry Wirz, The Prison Keeper* (1911).

Louis A. Brown's *The Salisbury Prison* (1980) quotes a Union prisoner as calling Libby a "palace" compared to Salisbury. In the western part of the state, Salisbury held perhaps 15,000 prisoners overall, one-third of the total at Andersonville, yet its casualty rate was even higher at its worst (3.5 percent a month versus Andersonville's 3.0 percent). Almost 4,000 died, and Salisbury had the largest number of unidentified graves of any prison, North or South. Brown argues that Salisbury was fairly representative of Southern prisons after the breakdown of the cartel, especially in late 1864 and early 1865. The last six months at Salisbury were the worst, a striking parallel to roughly the same period at Elmira (September 1864–March 1865) and Andersonville (April–September 1864). This work is awkwardly written, repetitive, and poorly proofread; for example, *Sheridan* is misspelled throughout the book. But the volume is a detailed and comprehensive treatment, copiously illustrated, and balanced. It contains an extensive discussion of prisoner rations and caloric needs, along with appendixes and a lengthy bibliography.

F. Lee Lawrence and Robert W. Glover's *Camp Ford C.S.A.* (1964) describes the largest Confederate prison west of the Mississippi River. Though less than one hundred pages, this is a handsome volume with detailed coverage, illustrations, endpapers with a map of the camp, reproductions of the camp "newspaper," *The Old Flag,* a chronology, and a detailed bibliography. The death rate was less than 5 percent among the estimated total of 6,000 prisoners, 286 of whom died. The 234 rebels buried in nearby Tyler, Texas, put the first figure in some perspective. The authors note that "more soldiers died in prisons than were killed in the battles of Shiloh, Chancellorsville, Gettysburg, Sharpsburg, and Chickamauga combined"—in fact, roughly twice as many.

William O. Bryant's *Cahaba Prison and the* Sultana *Disaster* (1990), the facility southwest of Selma, Alabama (also known as Castle Morgan, after General John Hunt Morgan, the Southern raider), was even more crowded than Andersonville. Its inmates' chances of reaching home were lower because of the 1865 Mississippi steamboat explosion that killed over one thousand former prisoners. Jerry O. Potter, *The* Sultana *Tragedy: America's Greatest Maritime Disaster* (1992), is a fine, full-length study of the incident. Total casualties may have exceeded two thousand, or more than from all previous steamboat explosions on the river, and greater than those of the *Titanic.*

LIBBY AND OTHER VIRGINIA PRISONS

Richmond's Libby Prison was easily the best known of all Confederate facilities during the war, from Bull Run onward, and the most photographed building in the South after the war. Its fame derived from the fact that it held mostly officers, including some very prominent ones, such as General Dow, Colonel Michael Corcoran, and Major Paul J. Revere, as well as notable civilians like

Congressman Alfred Ely of New York. After their release, many prisoners wrote sensational accounts that made Libby infamous. The inmates called themselves Libbyans and organized a society with that name. There is no ideal introduction to the genre known as Libbyana, which includes dozens of titles. See Hesseltine's bibliography and Byrne's section in *Civil War Books*.

The Confederate capital had a confusing array of other prisons for soldiers, both Union and Confederate, as well as for political and female prisoners. Some of the buildings were also used at various times as hospitals, and most had been converted from commercial or industrial use. Sandra V. Parker, *Richmond's Civil War Prisons* (1990), is a useful though brief introduction but is marred by factual mistakes as well as dozens of typographical errors, awkward prose, and a disorganized text. Yet there is much detail not only about Libby and Belle Isle (a tented enlisted camp in the James River) but also Castle Thunder, Castle Godwin, the Henrico county jail, and other buildings that were pressed into service. Parker's work has an extensive bibliography, along with notes and an index.

Petersburg and Danville also had prisons. There was another "Castle Thunder" in the former city. James I. Robertson has described the latter's in "Houses of Horror" (1961). Readers comparing this article with his Elmira piece will find that it was possible by the 1960s for the same author, in this case a Virginian, to depict prisons on both sides in a critical way.

There were about 150 prisons North and South, but only 20 were of major importance. Few have been studied. The *Official Records* lists other Confederate facilities at Atlanta, Augusta, Blackshear, Macon, Marietta, Millen, and Savannah, Georgia; Charleston, Columbia, and Florence, South Carolina; Hempstead, Texas; Lynchburg, Virginia; Mobile, Montgomery, and Tuscaloosa, Alabama; and Shreveport, Louisiana.

AFRICAN-AMERICAN PRISONERS

The treatment of captured black Union soldiers is perhaps covered more appropriately as part of the larger subject of African Americans fighting on both sides but has been discussed by Walter L. Williams, "Again in Chains: Black Soldiers Suffering in Captivity" (1981), and Howard C. Westwood, "Captive Black Union Soldiers in Charleston—What to Do?" (1982). Joseph T. Glatthaar, *Forged in Battle: The Civil War Alliance of Black Soldiers and White Officers* (1990) devotes several pages to the matter. The question of whether captured black Union soldiers (and their white officers) would be exchanged on an equivalent basis with white soldiers, sent into slavery, or turned over to state authorities for trial and possible execution as slaves in rebellion is discussed by Hesseltine and other scholars. Authorities agree that Confederate refusal to exchange black soldiers was one reason for the breakdown of the cartel but disagree as to its relative importance compared with the larger issue as put by Grant and Stanton. Exchanging rebel prisoners would send 150,000 men back to Southern armies. Holding them kept them out of the conflict and avoided a war of extermination, though Grant admitted that Union men suffered at Andersonville and elsewhere.

NORTHERN PRISONS

The disparity between published works on Southern and Northern prisons has continued to the present; one looks in vain for recent scholarly monographs on Northern prisons. There is a seeming contradiction between the statements made by Hesseltine and others that the Confederacy's response to the prisoner crisis was improvised and inefficient, as opposed to the superior organization of the Northern juggernaut, but that somehow the defeated nation left more records behind for researchers than the victorious Union.

Clay W. Holmes wrote a lengthy defense of conditions at the facility often described as having the highest death rate of any Union facility, *The Elmira Prison Camp* (1912). Holmes was detailed and comprehensive. There has been no serious treatment of Elmira since, except for the Robertson article cited above, a curious omission by scholars. Holmes included an appendix listing prisoners who died and were buried at the site. He also presented statistics on relative rates of mortality at other prisons, North and South, which make interesting reading. If his figures are correct, the old penitentiary at Alton, Illinois, had a death rate of 31 percent, significantly higher than other Federal prisons, including Elmira, Camp Douglas, Rock Island, and Fort Delaware, and exceeding even Salisbury and Florence. John Kaufhold's "The Elmira Observatory" (1977) is an amusing illustrated account of the towers erected just outside the stockade by competing entrepreneurs who charged townsfolk admission to see the prisoners, as if the rebels were animals in a zoo.

A more balanced and still useful study is Hattie Lou Winslow and Joseph R. H. Moore, *Camp Morton, 1861–1865, Indianapolis Prison Camp* (1940), which has notes but neither an index or bibliography. It first appeared in the proceedings of the Indiana Historical Society. The work includes a statistical abstract of prisoners taken from the *Official Records,* as well as a detailed table of rations distributed in 1864 as recorded by a Confederate sergeant. There is also a list of ration reductions, in retaliation for alleged mistreatment of Union prisoners.

William H. Knauss, *The Story of Camp Chase* (1906), at Columbus, Ohio, is a compilation of letters, articles, and pictures, with four chapters on Johnson's Island. Knauss was a Union veteran wounded at Fredericksburg who worked for sectional reconciliation by preserving the Camp Chase cemetery. Robert Earnest Miller, "War within Walls: Camp Chase and the Search for Administrative Reform" (1987), is an excellent article with analytical strengths lacking in much of the other literature. Contrary to the pattern elsewhere, conditions at Camp Chase improved steadily during the war. A pamphlet that appeared during the Civil War centennial, Philip R. Shriver and Donald J. Breen's *Ohio's Mil-*

itary Prisons in the Civil War (1964), contains "far more data than the standard sources," according to Byrne.

Camp Douglas near Chicago had the distinction of the highest monthly death rate of any other prison camp—10 percent in February 1863—after which a long-needed drainage system was finally installed with prisoner labor. Though Douglas held over 22,000 prisoners during the war, it lacks a study.

Point Lookout, Maryland, with over 52,000 total prisoners according to Byrne, was the largest Union prison, and probably the largest on either side, exceeding the 45,613 held at Andersonville. Over 20,000 were there in April 1865, numbers that do not reflect the resumption of exchanges in February. Edwin W. Beitzell, *Point Lookout Prison Camp for Confederates* (1972), has a brief history of St. Mary's County, Maryland, and Point Lookout, as well as prisoner diaries and drawings, maps and aerial photographs, a list of Confederate dead, and extensive statistical data. The author found a significant number of casualties not reflected in published government sources and concluded that over 4,000 Confederates may have died at Point Lookout. Beitzell's work is more a compilation of a mass of source material than a finished monograph, by a native of the area rather than a professional historian, who tried to fill a gap overlooked by members of the discipline.

POPULAR AND SCHOLARLY ARTICLES

Articles on Civil War prisoners and prisons continue to appear in scholarly and popular journals, many of them in *Civil War Times Illustrated;* a complete listing is beyond the scope of this chapter. One general overview with colored illustrations by prisoners is Bruce Catton, "Prison Camps of the Civil War" (1959). More specialized pieces include George A. Rogers and R. Frank Saunders, Jr., "Camp Lawton Stockade, Millen, Ga., CSA" (1981), and Camilla A. Corlas Quinn's eloquent "Forgotten Soldiers: The Confederate Prisoners at Camp Butler [Springfield, Illinois]" (1988).

Other articles are based on prisoners' letters and diaries, including Paul C. Helmreich, "The Diary of Charles G. Lee in the Andersonville and Florence Prison Camps, 1864" (1976); Gary E. Wilson, "Diary of a Union Prisoner in Texas" (1984); Alvin R. Sunseri, "Transient Prisoner: The Reminiscences of William K. Gilbert" (1981), who spent seventeen months in various prisons; and Warren A. Jennings, "Prisoner of the Confederacy: Diary of a Union Artilleryman" (1975), who was held at Richmond and Danville, and escaped from the latter. George M. Anderson, "A Captured Confederate Officer: Nine Letters from Captain James Anderson to His Family" (1981), has details on life at Point Lookout and Fort Delaware.

Walter L. Williams, "A Confederate View of Prison Life: A Virginian in Fort Delaware, 1863" (1979), states that it held a total of 12,595 prisoners (20 percent died). See also Nancy Travis Keen's excellent "Confederate Prisoners of War at Fort Delaware'' (1968), and W. Emerson Wilson, *Fort Delaware* (1957), an accurate, well-written pamphlet.

DISSERTATIONS

A search for unpublished dissertations found only four titles, a clear sign that research in this field continues to languish. Mary B. Allen, ''Joseph Holt, Judge Advocate General (1862–1875): A Study in the Treatment of Political Prisoners by the United States Government during the Civil War'' (1927), dealt with a major Union figure. Minor H. McLain's ''Prison Conditions in Fort Warren, Boston, during the Civil War'' (1955) was briefly summarized in his 1962 article. E. Marvin Thomas studied ''Prisoner of War Exchange in the Civil War'' (1976). Leslie G. Hunter apparently did not complete a thesis, ''Warden for the Union: General William Hoffman (1807–1884),'' in progress in the late 1960s.

There are no biographies, not only of Hoffman, but of Union figures like Generals John A. Dix, Sullivan A. Meredith, and John Elmer Mulford; or of Confederates such as exchange agent Colonel Robert Ould. The commandants of various major prisons on both sides also lack studies.

CONCLUSION

The treatment of prisoners of war has engendered bitterness and controversy since nations ceased killing their captives and began holding them for exchange. Yet for half a century after Appomattox, Northerners and Southerners accused each other of doing precisely that while insisting that their own hands were clean. The scant attention paid to this subject in the past eighty years is an indictment of the historical profession, particularly those who profess to care about this greatest conflict. The neglect by academic scholars has been remedied in part by William Marvel, who represents a growing trend in Civil War studies. Important books aimed at a broad audience are increasingly being written by nonacademics like William A. Frassanito, Ernest B. Furgurson, Kent Gramm, John J. Hennessy, Alan T. Nolan, Harry W. Pfanz, John Michael Priest, Stephen W. Sears, Noah Andre Trudeau, and Warren Wilkinson, to name only a few. Perhaps we are seeing a return to the days of Bruce Catton, Shelby Foote, Allan Nevins, and Douglas Southall Freeman. Unlike those giants, one can hope that this new generation considers the forgotten men of the Civil War: its prisoners.

BIBLIOGRAPHY

BOOKS

Beitzell, Edwin W. *Point Lookout Prison Camp for Confederates.* Leonardtown, MD: St. Mary's County Historical Society, 1972.
Blakey, Arch Fredric. *General John H. Winder, C.S.A.* Gainesville: University of Florida Press, 1990.

Brown, Louis A. *The Salisbury Prison: A Case Study of Confederate Military Prisons, 1861–1865.* Wendell, NC: Broadfoot, 1980.

Bryant, William O. *Cahaba Prison and the* Sultana *Disaster.* Tuscaloosa: University of Alabama Press, 1990.

Channing, Edward. *A History of the United States.* Vol. 6: *The War for Southern Independence.* New York: Macmillan, 1925.

Chipman, General N[orton] P[arker]. *The Tragedy of Andersonville: Trial of Captain Henry Wirz, the Prison Keeper.* San Francisco: Author, 1911.

Coulter, E. Merton. *The Confederate States of America, 1861–1865.* Vol. 7: *A History of the South.* Baton Rouge: Louisiana State University Press, 1950.

Futch, Ovid L. *History of Andersonville Prison.* Gainesville: University of Florida Press, 1968.

Glatthaar, Joseph T. *Forged in Battle: The Civil War Alliance of Black Soldiers and White Officers.* New York: Free Press, 1990.

Hesseltine, William B. *Civil War Prisons: A Study in War Psychology.* 2d ed. New York: Frederick Ungar, 1930.

Hewett, Janet B., Noah Andrew Trudeau, and Bryce A. Suderow, eds. *The Supplement to the Official Records.* Wilmington, DE: Broadfoot, 1994–.

Holmes, Clay W. *The Elmira Prison Camp: A History of the Military Prison at Elmira, N.Y.* New York: G. P. Putnam's Sons, 1912.

Knauss, William H. *The Story of Camp Chase: A History of Confederate Prisons and Cemeteries.* Nashville and Dallas: Publishing House of the Methodist Episcopal Church South, 1906.

Lawrence, F. Lee, and Robert W. Glover. *Camp Ford C.S.A.* Austin: Texas Civil War Centennial Advisory Committee, 1964.

McPherson, James M. *Battle Cry of Freedom.* New York: Oxford University Press, 1988.

Marvel, William. *Andersonville: The Last Depot.* Chapel Hill: University of North Carolina Press, 1994.

Miller, Francis Trevelyan, ed. *The Photographic History of the Civil War.* Vol. 7: *Prisons and Hospitals.* 2d ed. 1911. Reprint, New York: Thomas Yoseloff, 1957.

Neeley, Mark E., Jr. *The Fate of Liberty: Abraham Lincoln and Civil Liberties.* New York: Oxford, 1991.

Parker, Sandra V. *Richmond's Civil War Prisons.* Lynchburg: H. E. Howard, 1990.

Potter, Jerry O. *The* Sultana *Tragedy: America's Greatest Maritime Disaster.* Gretna, LA: Pelican, 1992.

Randall, J. G., and David Donald. *The Civil War and Reconstruction.* Lexington, MA: D. C. Heath, 1969.

Ransom, John. *Andersonville.* 1881. Reprint, *Andersonville Diary,* Philadelphia: Douglass Brothers, 1883; *John Ransom's Andersonville Diary,* Middlebury, VT: Paul S. Erikkson, 1963, 1986.

Rhodes, James Ford. *History of the United States from the Compromise of 1850.* New York: Macmillan, 1904.

Shriver, Philip R., and Donald J. Breen. *Ohio's Military Prisons in the Civil War.* Columbus: Ohio Historical Society, 1964.

United States. House of Representatives. *The Trial of Henry Wirz.* House Executive Document 23. 40th Cong., 2d sess., 1868.

———. *Report of the Treatment of Prisoners of War, by the Rebel Authorities, during the War of the Rebellion.* House Report 45. 40th Cong. 3d sess., 1869.

United States. Department of War. *The War of the Rebellion: A Compilation of the Official Records of the Union and Confederate Armies.* 2d Ser., 1–8. Washington, D.C.: Government Printing Office, 1894–1899.

Wilson, W. Emerson. *Fort Delaware.* Newark: University of Delaware Press, 1957.

Winslow, Hattie Lou, and Joseph R. H. Moore. *Camp Morton, 1861–1865, Indianapolis Prison Camp.* Indianapolis: Indiana Historical Society, 1940.

ARTICLES

Anderson, George M. ''A Captured Confederate Officer: Nine Letters from Captain James Anderson to His Family.'' *Maryland Historical Magazine* 76 (1981): 62–69.

Armstrong, William M. ''Cahaba to Charleston: The Prison Odyssey of Lt. Edmund E. Ryan.'' *Civil War History* 8 (1962): 218–227.

Byrne, Frank L., ed. ''A General behind Bars: Neal Dow in Libby Prison.'' *Civil War History* 8 (1962): 164–83.

———. ''Libby Prison: A Study in Emotions.'' *Journal of Southern History* 24 (1958): 430–444.

———. ''Prisoners of War.'' In Richard N. Current, ed., *Encyclopedia of the Confederacy,* 3:1256–1264. New York: Simon & Schuster, 1993.

———. ''Prisons.'' In Richard N. Current, *Encyclopedia of the Confederacy,* 3:1265–1269. New York: Simon & Schuster, 1993.

———. ''Prison Pens of Suffering.'' In William C. Davis, ed., *The Image of War, 1861–1865.* Vol. 4: *Fighting for Time.* Garden City, NY: Doubleday, 1983.

———. ''Prisons and Prisoners of War.'' In *Civil War Books,* 1:185–206. Baton Rouge: Louisiana State University Press, 1967.

Catton, Bruce. ''Prison Camps of the Civil War.'' *American Heritage* 10 (1959): 4–13, 96–97.

Downer, Edward T. ''Johnson's Island.'' *Civil War History* 8 (1962): 202–217.

Futch, Ovid. ''Prison Life at Andersonville.'' *Civil War History* 8 (1962): 121–135.

Helmreich, Paul C. ''The Diary of Charles G. Lee in the Andersonville and Florence Prison Camps, 1864.'' *Connecticut Historical Society Bulletin* 41 (1976): 12–28.

Hesseltine, William B. ''Civil War Prisons—Introduction.'' *Civil War History* 8 (1962): 117–120.

———. ''The Propaganda Literature of Confederate Prisons.'' *Journal of Southern History* 1 (1935): 56–66.

Jennings, Warren A., ed. ''Prisoner of the Confederacy: Diary of a Union Artilleryman.'' *West Virginia History* 36 (1975): 309–323.

Jones, J. William, ed. ''The Treatment of Prisoners during the War between the States.'' *Southern Historical Society Papers* 1 (1876): 113–221, 225–327.

Kaufhold, John. ''The Elmira Observatory.'' *Civil War Times Illustrated* 16 (1977): 30–35.

Keen, Nancy Travis. ''Confederate Prisoners of War at Fort Delaware.'' *Delaware History* 13 (1968): 1–27.

McLain, Minor H. ''The Military Prison at Fort Warren.'' *Civil War History* 8 (1962): 136–151.

Marvel, William. ''Johnny Ransom's Imagination.'' *Civil War History* 41 (1995): 181–189.

Miller, Robert Earnest. "War within Walls: Camp Chase and the Search for Administrative Reform." *Ohio History* 96 (1987): 35–56.

Peoples, Morgan. " 'The Scapegoat of Andersonville': Union Execution of Confederate Captain Henry Wirz." *North Louisiana Historical Association Journal* 11 (1980): 3–18.

Quinn, Camilla A. Corlas. "Forgotten Soldiers: The Confederate Prisoners at Camp Butler, 1862–1863." *Illinois Historical Journal* 81 (1988): 35–44.

Robertson, James I., Jr. "Houses of Horror: Danville's Civil War Prisons." *Virginia Magazine of History and Biography* 69 (1961): 329–345.

———. "The Scourge of Elmira." *Civil War History* 8 (1962): 184–201.

Rogers, George A., and R. Frank Saunders, Jr. "Camp Lawton Stockade, Millen, Georgia, C.S.A." *Atlanta History* 25 (1981): 80–94.

Rutman, Darrett B. "The War Crimes and Trial of Henry Wirz." *Civil War History* 6 (1960): 117–133.

Sunseri, Alvin R., ed. "Transient Prisoner: The Reminiscences of William K. Gilbert." *Journal of the Illinois State Historical Society* 74 (1981): 41–50.

Walker, T. R. "Rock Island Prison Barracks." *Civil War History* 8 (1962): 152–163.

Westwood, Harold C. "Captive Black Union Soldiers in Charleston—What to Do?" *Civil War History* 28 (1982): 28–44.

Williams, Walter L. "Again in Chains: Black Soldiers Suffering in Captivity." *Civil War Times Illustrated* 20 (1981): 36–43.

———. "A Confederate View of Prison Life: A Virginian in Fort Delaware, 1863." *Delaware History* 18 (1979): 226–235.

Wilson, Gary E. "Diary of a Union Prisoner in Texas." *Southern Studies* 23 (1984): 103–119.

DISSERTATIONS

Allen, Mary B. "Joseph Holt, Judge Advocate General (1862–1875): A Study in the Treatment of Political Prisoners by the United States Government during the Civil War." Ph.D. diss., University of Chicago, 1925.

Hunter, Leslie G. "Warden for the Union: General William Hoffman (1807–1884)." Ph.D. diss., University of Arizona; in progress 1967–1970; not completed.

McLain, Minor H. "Prison Conditions in Fort Warren, Boston, during the Civil War." Ph.D. diss., Boston University, 1955.

Thomas, E. Marvin, III. "Prisoner of War Exchange in the Civil War." Ph.D. diss., Auburn University, 1976.

Part IX

The Home Front

36

Northern State and
Local Politics

Kyle S. Sinisi

The literature on state and local politics is vast, although no single-volume synthesis exists. Historians have written numerous works on a variety of sub-topics, including parties, dissent, elections, and ethnocultural voting. Most of the literature describes a politics consumed by national war-related matters.

GENERAL WORKS

There are numerous comprehensive treatments of politics in the individual states. For some states, good examinations can be found in histories that also cover military, social, and economic topics. Valuable examples are Arthur C. Cole's *The Era of the Civil War, 1848–1870* (1919), Richard N. Current's *The History of Wisconsin: The Civil War Era, 1848–1873* (1976), E. Merton Coulter's *The Civil War and Readjustment in Kentucky* (1926), William E. Parrish's *Turbulent Partnership: Missouri and the Union, 1861–1865* (1963), and Eugene H. Roseboom's look at Ohio in *The Civil War Era, 1850–1873* (1944).

A number of other histories focus exclusively on wartime politics. Many emphasize the traditional forms of political historiography, primarily conventions and elections. Others focus on the impact of war-related issues, such as emancipation and the draft, at the state level. These works remain very useful for providing the contours of an individual state's wartime political history.

Among the New England states, Jarlath R. Lane's *A Political History of Connecticut during the Civil War* (1941) and Edith E. Ware's *Political Opinion in Massachusetts during the Civil War and Reconstruction* (1916) stand out. Farther south, detailed description of party and factional politics exists in several books, including Sidney Brummer's *Political History of New York State during the Period of the Civil War* (1911), Charles M. Knapp's *New Jersey Politics during the Period of the Civil War and Reconstruction* (1924), and Stanton L. Davis's *Pennsylvania Politics, 1860–1863* (1935). Of these works, Brummer and Davis offer a more broadly conceived picture of state politics. Both analyze the importance of local issues. Brummer's investigation of the larger trends in New York politics should, however, be supplemented by Mary P. Hodnett's "Civil War Issues in New York State Politics" (1970), which concentrates on the impact of emancipation, the suppression of civil liberties, and the draft on the state's politics.

Historians have also developed general studies of the border states. *Delaware during the Civil War: A Political History* (1961) by Harold B. Hancock, *Politics in Maryland during the Civil War* (1952) by Charles B. Clark, *Missouri Politics during the Civil War* (1930) by Sceva B. Laughlin, and *A Frontier State at War: Kansas, 1861–1865* (1958) by Albert Castel all provide comprehensive coverage. Castel, in particular, paints a vivid portrait of factional politics in a state dominated by the Republican party.

Some of the more interesting studies of border state politics have focused on West Virginia. Most of this historiographical interest stems from the unique circumstances of West Virginia's creation. George E. Moore casts a favorable pro-Union judgment on statehood's legitimacy in *A Banner in the Hills: West Virginia's Statehood* (1963), while James C. McGregor dissents capably in *The Disruption of Virginia* (1922). Perhaps the best treatment is Richard O. Curry's *A House Divided: A Study of Statehood Politics and the Copperhead Movement* (1964). Curry concentrates little on the constitutional legitimacy of statehood, preferring instead to determine the level of Union sentiment in the state. He ultimately concludes that in 1861 a majority of the people in northwestern Virginia were pro-Union.

In the states of the Old Northwest, George Porter's *Ohio Politics during the Civil War Period* (1911) and Frank L. Klement's *Wisconsin and the Civil War* (1963) remain important. Both reinforce traditional themes. Where Porter emphasizes the impact of the great issues on state affairs, Klement details party competition and elections. Somewhat different, and broader in scope, is Kenneth M. Stampp's *Indiana Politics during the Civil War* (1949). Stampp focuses on the interplay of economic concerns and politics, while also providing a thoughtful analysis of the wartime Democratic opposition.

The western states have yet to receive complete investigation. Gerald Stanley's "Civil War Politics in California" (1982) is the most recent interpretation of that state, but it does not attempt comprehensive coverage. Stanley argues that eastern war-related issues, such as slavery and the emancipation proclamation, dominated California's wartime politics. Although he devotes little analysis to other political matters, Stanley undercuts his main argument by noting that California's congressmen were far more interested in local railroad matters.

Similar to California, Nevada lacks a quality monograph. Leslie B. Gray's recent *The Source and the Vision: Nevada's Role in the Civil War* (1990) is a weak analysis of both the statehood movement and Nevada's subsequent politics. Russell R. Elliot's *Servant of Power: A Political Biography of Senator William M. Stewart* (1983) and Jud Samon's "Sagebrush Falstaff: A Biographical Sketch of James Warren Nye" (1979) fill in much of the state's political history through the eyes of two early leaders.

FEDERALISM AND GOVERNORS

While much of the literature has focused on general treatments of state politics, historians have written a variety of more sharply defined studies. Some of the better works examine federal relations. William B. Hesseltine's *Lincoln and the War Governors* (1948) continues to be the standard introduction. Hesseltine underscores the primacy of war issues within the states and argues convincingly that the power and influence of the governors, relative to that of the presidency, dwindled throughout the war. Although Hesseltine reduces wartime federalism to a simple component of the quality of the relationship between Lincoln and any given governor, his work provides an excellent view of wartime high politics.

The biographies of the governors provide a similar lens through which to study wartime federalism. They can also present a good overview of an individual state's politics. Unfortunately, the war governors have received mixed scholarly treatment. Most biographies are outdated and suffer from a high degree of bias. Some, nevertheless, offer good information on wartime politics. George T. Clark's *Leland Stanford* (1931), though uncritical of his subject, has five helpful chapters on the administration of one of California's chief executives. Don Wilson's *Governor Charles Robinson of Kansas* (1975) describes in detail the battles for political supremacy waged between Robinson and rival James H. Lane. Mitchell Stewart's *Horatio Seymour of New York* (1938) remains the standard analysis of this controversial Democrat. It is particularly valuable for Seymour's role in the 1863 draft controversy, but it should be supplemented by Eugene C. Murdock's highly critical "Horatio Seymour and the 1863 Draft" (1965). Rebecca G. Albright's extended article, "The Civil War Career of Andrew Gregg Curtin, Governor of Pennsylvania" (1964, 1965), illuminates Pennsylvania's factional politics and Curtin's often stormy relationship with the Lincoln administration. "Oliver P. Morton and Hoosier Politics during the Civil War" (1968) by Lorna L. Sylvester offers a balanced portrayal of the Indiana governor that faults national policies for many of Morton's state political problems. Sylvester's biography replaces the influential, and very favorable, work by William D. Foulke, *Life of Oliver P. Morton, Including His Important Speeches* (1899). Martin D. Lewis illuminates Michigan's last war governor in *Lumberman from Flint: The Michigan Career of Henry D. Crapo, 1855–1869* (1958). Perhaps even more important, Lewis has valuable material on Crapo's career as a legislator and those few issues that impinged on a state's wartime political agenda.

PARTIES AND ELECTIONS

No less important to understanding state politics have been a number of studies dealing with party structure during the entire period of sectional conflict and Reconstruction. In *The Triumph of Militant Republicanism: A Study of Pennsylvania and Presidential Politics, 1860–1872* (1964), Erwin S. Bradley studies Pennsylvania's Republican party through the factional feud between Governor Andrew Curtin and Lincoln's one-time secretary of war, Simon Cameron. Bradley covers wartime politics too briefly, but he demonstrates the national importance of the Pennsylvania Grand Old Party.

Two other examinations of party structure emphasize historical continuity during the middle period. Jean H. Baker, in *The Politics of Continuity: Maryland Political Parties from 1858 to 1870* (1973), provides a convincing rebuttal to political scientists and historians who have seen the Civil War as reworking the structure and ideology of the parties. Balancing traditional methods of scholarship with quantitative analysis, she finds that both Democrats and Republicans had experienced their ideological and structural transformations before the war. Jerome Mushkat places Democratic restructuring later than Baker, but he too emphasizes ideological continuity in *The Reconstruction of the New York Democracy, 1861–1874* (1981). According to Mushkat, although the state Democratic party experienced wartime difficulties, it had clearly reconstructed itself with traditional beliefs by the end of 1864.

Among the more interesting examinations of parties have been those of the so-called ethnocultural historians, who have emphasized the centrality of religion and ethnicity in determining grass-roots party loyalty. For the Civil War era, the most complete of the ethnocultural studies is Paul Kleppner's *The Third Electoral System, 1853–1892: Parties, Voters, and Political Culture* (1979). Some historians, however, have modified the ethnocultural thesis. Dale Baum has revealed a more economically motivated basis for party affiliation in his concise and important *The Civil War Party System: The Case of Massachusetts, 1848–1876* (1984). Walter D. Kamphoefner presents another dissenting voice in "German-Americans and Civil War Politics: A Reconsideration of the Ethnocultural Thesis" (1991). Though Kamphoefner does not argue for Baum's economic determinism, he concludes that local factors such as nativism mitigated ethnocultural factors.

Two important recent studies of the wartime parties avoid the ethnocultural framework. Lex Renda has investigated party cohesion in his perceptive "Credit and Culpability: New Hampshire State Politics during the Civil War" (1993). Using modern statistical methods, Renda finds little party cohesion on state and local issues in the roll-call votes of legislators. He therefore helps substantiate the traditional historical assumption that local issues rarely influenced the strength of partisan activity during the war.

Martin Hershock's "Copperheads and Radicals: Michigan Partisan Politics during the Civil War Era, 1860–1865" (1992) complements Renda. Hershock, searching for the meaning of partisanship in Michigan's electoral campaigns, ultimately concludes that each party saw itself as the sole nonpartisan defender of republicanism. Within such a construct, each party perceived the other one as partisan and, hence, an enemy of republicanism.

Despite numerous attempts to harness partisanship and fuse Democrats and Republicans into a Union party during the war, Democratic opposition flourished. Historians have long studied this political opposition, though they have often struggled with its legitimacy. Consequently, much of the literature on state Democratic parties has conflated party history with investigations into treason and secret political conspiracies against the Union. While earlier historians, such as Mayo Fesler in "Secret Political Societies in the North during the Civil War" (1918) and Wood Gray in *The Hidden Civil War* (1942), have described a conspiratorial and inept Democratic opposition, a flood of more recent studies has resurrected its legitimacy.

Frank L. Klement has written numerous works puncturing the idea that large-scale wartime conspiracies and secret societies existed. His *Dark Lanterns: Secret Political Societies, Conspiracies, and Treason Trials in the Civil War* (1984) is an excellent summary. Klement also disputes charges of Democratic disloyalty in *The Copperheads in the Middle West* (1960). To Klement, Copperheads, or midwestern peace Democrats, fit perfectly within a traditional pattern of agrarian dissent and fear of eastern dominance. In response, Ronald P. Formisano and William G. Shade have challenged Klement's emphasis on the agrarian tradition. Nevertheless, their work on the Illinois constitutional convention of 1862, "The Concept of Agrarian Radicalism" (1970), reinforces an emerging portrait of the Democracy as a reasonable wartime opposition.

Other historians have looked at the Democrats in the individual states. One example is Hubert H. Wubben's *Civil War Iowa and the Copperhead Movement* (1980). After digging in a wide variety of primary sources, Wubben reveals a fragmented Democratic opposition containing few disloyal or outright traitorous elements. Although concerned primarily with the state's political opposition, Wubben's book also stands as the single best treatment of Iowa's wartime politics. Joanna D. Cowden's studies of Connecticut are of equal value. Her "Civil War and Reconstruction Politics in Connecticut, 1863–1868" (1975) and "The Politics of Dissent: Civil War Democrats in Connecticut" (1983) both minimize the importance and radicalism of the peace element. Arnold Shankman describes the Democracy in similar terms in *The Anti-War Movement in Pennsylvania, 1861–1865* (1980). Still more emphatic in its defense of Democratic motives and actions is G. R. Tredway's *Democratic Opposition to the Lincoln Administration in Indiana* (1973). Tredway faults Lincoln for provoking a legitimate

Democratic concern of despotism, but he sees little connection between the peace movement and direct support for the South.

Democratic opposition to the Republican party led to sharply contested elections. Both parties galvanized their members and campaigned hard for their candidates. General studies of the states contain excellent coverage of the electoral campaigns, but reports of specific elections also exist. Numerous articles focus on the national election of 1864 and the role of a particular state or community in that election. One example is Daniel W. Crofts' "Re-electing Lincoln: The Struggle in Newark" (1984). A heavily annotated collection of letters, this article details the organizational and electoral activities of a Union League council. It is a fascinating illustration of local political culture and the methods of voter mobilization. Other investigations include Winfred A. Harbison's "Indiana Republicans and the Re-election of President Lincoln" (1937) and Ivor D. Spencer's "Chicago Helps to Re-elect Lincoln" (1970). Harbison emphasizes the importance of the collapse of the Republican boom for John C. Frémont, the Democratic nomination of George B. McClellan, and the fall of Atlanta in gaining Indiana's vote for Lincoln. In contrast, Spencer looks more closely at the electoral impact on Chicago of the discovery of an alleged Copperhead attempt to free Confederate prisoners at nearby Camp Douglas.

While historians have concentrated heavily on the election of 1864, they have not totally ignored others. However, coverage of particular state and local elections has usually centered on the impact of war-related issues. Charles Wagandt furnishes a good example of the importance of emancipation in "Election by Sword and Ballot: The Emancipation Victory of 1863" (1964). Wagandt describes Unionist irregularity at the polls in 1863 and argues persuasively that Republican emancipationists stole the seats of five congressmen and almost every member of the state legislature. Similarly, historians have looked at a number of state elections in 1862 as vehicles for the repudiation of the Lincoln administration. "The Election of 1862 as a Vote of Want of Confidence in President Lincoln" (1930) by Winfred A. Harbison and "The Repudiation of Lincoln's War Policy in 1862—Stuart-Swett Congressional Campaign" (1931) by Harry E. Pratt are but two examples.

Another significant factor in wartime elections was the military vote. Absentee voting for military personnel helped soften the electoral difficulty that the Republicans experienced beginning with the elections of 1862. While the absentee votes of soldiers decided few state elections, a number of states established a precedent of military participation. The standard introduction remains Josiah Benton's *Voting in the Field: A Forgotten Chapter of the Civil War* (1915). A better guide to the state-by-state handling of soldier voting can be found in Oscar Winther's "The Soldier Vote in the Election of 1864" (1944). Although marred by faulty data and an absence of modern statistical methods, all of Winther's conclusions still appear valid. Most important, he offers evidence that although soldiers tended to vote more for Lincoln, they did not decide the election of 1864.

There are a variety of studies of soldier voting in the individual states. Most address the specific systems established by the states and corrupt practices. "The Soldier Vote and Minnesota Politics, 1862–1865" (1945) by Lynwood G. Downs is a positive account of Minnesota's handling of absentee balloting and the relative uniqueness of a system run by bipartisan commissioners. Less kind, and more analytical, is Frank L. Klement in his "The Soldier Vote in Wisconsin during the Civil War" (1944). Klement describes an absentee system dominated by Republican regimental officers who manipulated the vote. Ohio's election revealed a similar situation. Arnold Shankman, in "Soldier Votes and Clement L. Vallandigham in the 1863 Ohio Gubernatorial Election" (1973), unveils a system that was highly susceptible to Republican abuse. Though Shankman does not attempt to disclose the extent of that abuse, his data suggest that Ohio's troops were firmly Republican, and manipulation of returns was not necessary to guarantee Vallandigham's defeat.

Samuel T. McSeveney has authored two excellent articles that differ in focus from Shankman's and Klement's writing. In "Winning the Vote for Connecticut Soldiers in the Field, 1862–1864: A Research Note and Historiographical Comment" (1985), he traces the political movement for adoption of absentee voting and the important role of the Republican party in the effort. A later piece, "Reelecting Lincoln: The Union Party Campaign and the Military Vote in Connecticut" (1986), details how the state Union party coordinated its efforts with the Republican National Committee and the government to secure victory in 1864. It is an excellent study that illustrates the extent of fund raising and the mechanics of getting out the vote.

RACE AND POLITICS

While voter mobilization depended largely on party organization, the electorate needed issues to energize it. In recent years, few other such issues have received as much scholarly notice as race. V. Jacque Voegeli has written a good introduction in *Free But Not Equal: The Midwest and the Negro during the Civil War* (1967). Voegeli emphasizes the primacy of racism in the Midwest, and he shows clearly that the Democratic party did not hold a monopoly on it. Throughout the war, midwestern Republicans tried to dissociate themselves from the perceived racial radicalism of eastern Republicans. The strong midwestern desire to free the slaves, Voegeli argues, did not mean that midwesterners wanted blacks living among them. Edward Noyes uses a similar, though less substantiated, argument in his "White Opposition to Black Migration into Civil War Wisconsin" (1971).

A good example of the intersection of race and politics during the war concerned the emancipation proclamation. Historians have given particular attention to the reaction of the individual states to emancipation. Three examples are Bill R. Lee's "Missouri's Fight over Emancipation in 1863" (1951), Larry A. Greene's "The Emancipation Proclamation in New Jersey and the Paranoid

Style" (1973), and Sherman W. Jackson's "Emancipation, Negrophobia, and Civil War Politics in Ohio, 1863–1865" (1980). Both Jackson and Greene offer interesting analyses. Jackson argues convincingly that local Republican and Democratic resistance to emancipation and equality allowed Negrophobia to become a major postwar political tool. Less persuasive is Greene's article. While in search of the basis for New Jersey's negative reaction to emancipation, he overstates his case. Greene too readily rejects the intellectual and constitutional basis of Democratic thought in his rush to condemn Democratic actions as a paranoid fear of black freedom and empowerment.

A more general study of race and its political ramifications is Phyllis F. Field's *The Politics of Race in New York: The Struggle for Black Suffrage in the Civil War Era* (1982). She investigates the evolution of Republican attitudes toward black suffrage between 1821 and 1870. Field delineates three distinct phases in which the idea of black suffrage grew increasingly popular but concludes that the issue lurked only on the political periphery. New York rejected a referendum on suffrage in 1869 just as debate on the Fifteenth Amendment began. Hubert H. Wubben attempts a comparable investigation in his "The Uncertain Trumpet: Iowa Republicans and Black Suffrage, 1860–1868" (1984). Though the evidence is inconclusive, Wubben believes that the Republicans came to support suffrage primarily as a means of retaining political prestige and highlighting differences with the Democrats.

COMMUNITY POLITICS

Just as race and other war-related issues influenced state politics, so too did they affect local levels of political activity. Not surprisingly, historians have given considerable notice to larger cities, bypassing smaller communities. New York, in particular, has benefited from this pattern of investigation. *The Civil War and New York City* (1990) by Ernest A. McKay is a good introduction. Essentially a chronology of reactions to the political crises of the war, this book concentrates on the city's gradual acceptance of emancipation. Other relevant explorations of New York City have examined its machine politics. Samuel A. Pleasants's *Fernando Wood of New York* (1948) is a helpful introduction to those politics and the life of New York City's Copperhead mayor. New York's most powerful machine, Tammany Hall, has been the subject of numerous monographs. Although notably thin on the war years, they offer differing perspectives. See, for example, Alexander B. Callow's critical *The House that Tweed Built* (1965), Jerome Mushkat's dispassionate *Tammany: The Evolution of a Political Machine, 1789–1865* (1971), and Leo Hershkowitz's sympathetic *Tweed's New York: Another Look* (1977).

Historians have lavished an equal amount of comment on Philadelphia. William Dusinberre's *Civil War Issues in Philadelphia, 1856–1865* (1965) is an important work. It concentrates on politics, emphasizing Democratic responses to Republican activities. Nicholas B. Wainright probes Democratic elites and the Irish for evidence of Southern sympathy in ''The Loyal Opposition in Civil War Philadelphia'' (1964). Just as important for political culture is Maxwell Whiteman's *Gentlemen in Crisis: The First Century of the Union League of Philadelphia, 1862–1962* (1975). A solid institutional history, this work not only describes the local origins and activities of the creation of the league but also its nationwide pamphleteering and propagandizing for the Republican party. Though not explicitly political, *Mastering Wartime: A Social History of Philadelphia during the Civil War* (1990) by Matthew Gallman is valuable for its analysis of the coordination between public and private sectors in administering the city's war effort.

Inquiry into the politics of Washington, D.C., has been much more limited. Two books have been written—Constance M. Green's *Washington: Village and Capital, 1800–1878* (1962) and Margaret Leech's Pulitzer Prize–winning *Reveille in Washington, 1860–1865* (1941)—but a total picture is missing. Green has only two brief chapters on the war, and Leech focuses little on local politics and municipal government.

The Union's other prominent cities have received scattered attention. Among the available studies, John H. Holliday's *Indianapolis and the Civil War* (1911) stands as a good account of how one city met wartime crises. Another capable treatment is George S. May's ''Politics of Ann Arbor during the Civil War'' (1953), although May provides little analysis in his descriptions of Ann Arbor's conventions and elections. More tightly focused on specific events are Matthew Ellenberger's ''Whigs in the Streets? Baltimore Republicanism in the Spring of 1861'' (1991) and David B. Dick's ''Resurgence of the Chicago Democracy, April–November 1861'' (1963). Ellenberger's interpretation of the Baltimore riots has broad ramifications as it details the still vibrant republicanism of one major border city. Dick, however, looks at the efforts of Stephen A. Douglas to provide a vision for a battered Democratic party in Chicago. Dick concludes that Douglas gave city Democrats a much needed platform emphasizing preservation of the Union and the Constitution.

Secondary work on smaller communities is much harder to find. It is but one gap in the literature on state and local politics. This bibliography provides only a sampling of books, articles, and dissertations, but it does hint at areas demanding further exploration. State and local politics merit a single-volume synthesis. State Union parties need even the most basic of studies. Many of the war governors require fresh biographical investigation. Wartime federalism needs examination beyond the activities of Lincoln and the governors. Legislatures warrant further roll-call analyses. And finally, the recent larger historiographical emphasis on social history has yet to be fully integrated into Civil War politics. Despite the existence of an almost overwhelming body of literature, the study of Northern state and local politics remains a fertile field for future research.

BIBLIOGRAPHY

Albright, Rebecca G. "The Civil War Career of Andrew Gregg Curtin, Governor of Pennsylvania." *Western Pennsylvania Magazine of History* 47 (1964): 321–341; 48 (1965): 19–42, 151–173.

Baker, Jean H. *The Politics of Continuity: Maryland Political Parties from 1858 to 1870.* Baltimore, MD: Johns Hopkins University Press, 1973.

Baum, Dale. *The Civil War Party System: The Case of Massachusetts, 1848–1876.* Chapel Hill, NC: University of North Carolina Press, 1984.

Benton, Josiah H. *Voting in the Field: A Forgotten Chapter of the Civil War.* Boston: Plimpton Press, 1915.

Bradley, Erwin S. *The Triumph of Militant Republicanism: A Study of Pennsylvania and Presidential Politics, 1860–1872.* Philadelphia: University of Pennsylvania Press, 1964.

Brummer, Sidney D. *Political History of New York State during the Period of the Civil War.* New York: Columbia University Press, 1911.

Callow, Alexander B. *The House that Tweed Built.* New York: American Heritage, 1965.

Castel, Albert. *A Frontier State at War.* Ithaca, NY: Cornell University Press, 1958.

Clark, Charles B. *Politics in Maryland during the Civil War.* Chestertown, MD: N.p., 1952.

Clark, George T. *Leland Stanford.* Stanford, CA: Stanford University Press, 1931.

Cole, Arthur C. *The Era of the Civil War, 1848–1870.* Springfield, IL: Illinois Centennial Commission, 1919.

Coulter, E. Merton. *The Civil War and Readjustment in Kentucky.* Chapel Hill, NC: University of North Carolina Press, 1926.

Cowden, Joanna D. "Civil War and Reconstruction Politics in Connecticut, 1863–1868." Ph.D. diss., University of Connecticut, 1975.

———. "The Politics of Dissent: Civil War Democrats in Connecticut." *New England Quarterly* 56 (1983): 538–554.

Crofts, Daniel W. "Re-electing Lincoln: The Struggle in Newark." *Civil War History* 30 (1984): 54–79.

Current, Richard N. *The History of Wisconsin: The Civil War Era, 1848–1873.* Madison, WI: State Historical Society of Wisconsin, 1976.

Curry, Richard O. *A House Divided: A Study of Statehood Politics and the Copperhead Movement in West Virginia.* Pittsburgh: University of Pittsburgh Press, 1964.

Davis, Stanton L. *Pennsylvania Politics, 1860–1863.* Cleveland, OH: The Bookstore, Western Reserve University, 1935.

Dick, David B. "Resurgence of the Chicago Democracy, April–November 1861." *Journal of the Illinois State Historical Society* 56 (1963): 139–149.

Downs, Lynwood G. "The Soldier Vote and Minnesota Politics, 1862–1865." *Publications of the Minnesota Historical Society* 26 (1945): 187–210.

Dusinberre, William. *Civil War Issues in Philadelphia, 1856–1865.* Philadelphia: University of Pennsylvania Press, 1965.

Ellenberger, Matthew. "Whigs in the Streets? Baltimore Republicanism in the Spring of 1861." *Maryland Historical Magazine* 86 (1991): 23–38.

Elliot, Russell R. *Servant of Power: A Political Biography of Senator William M. Stewart.* Reno, NV: University of Nevada Press, 1983.

Fesler, Mayo. "Secret Political Societies in the North during the Civil War." *Indiana Magazine of History* 14 (1918): 183–286.

Field, Phyllis F. *The Politics of Race in New York: The Struggle for Black Suffrage in the Civil War Era.* Ithaca, NY: Cornell University Press, 1982.

Formisano, Ronald P., and William G. Shade, "The Concept of Agrarian Radicalism." *Mid-America* 52 (1970): 3–30.

Foulke, William D. *Life of Oliver P. Morton, Including his Important Speeches.* 2 vols. Indianapolis, IN: Bowen-Merrill, 1899.

Gallman, J. Matthew. *Mastering Wartime: A Social History of Philadelphia during the Civil War.* Cambridge: Cambridge University Press, 1990.

Gray, Leslie B. *The Source and the Vision: Nevada's Role in the Civil War.* Sparks, NV: Gray Trust, 1990.

Gray, Wood. *The Hidden Civil War.* New York: Viking Press, 1942.

Green, Constance M. *Washington: Village and Capital, 1800–1878.* Princeton, NJ: Princeton University Press, 1962.

Greene, Larry A. "The Emancipation Proclamation in New Jersey and the Paranoid Style." *New Jersey History* 91 (1973): 108–124.

Hancock, Harold. *Delaware during the Civil War.* Wilmington, DE: Historical Society of Delaware, 1961.

Harbison, Winfred A. "The Election of 1862 as a Vote of Want of Confidence in President Lincoln." *Michigan Academy of Sciences, Arts, and Letters Papers* (1930): 499–513.

———. "Indiana Republicans and the Reelection of President Lincoln." *Indiana Magazine of History* 33 (1937): 277–303.

Hershock, Martin J. "Copperheads and Radicals: Michigan Partisan Politics during the Civil War Era, 1860–1865." *Michigan Historical Review* 18 (1992): 28–69.

Hesseltine, William B. *Lincoln and the War Governors.* New York: Knopf, 1948.

Hodnett, Mary P. "Civil War Issues in New York State Politics." Ph.D. diss., St. John's University, 1970.

Holliday, John H. *Indianapolis and the Civil War.* Indianapolis, IN: E. J. Hecker, 1911.

Hershkowitz, Leo. *Tweed's New York: Another Look.* New York: Doubleday, 1977.

Jackson, W. Sherman. "Emancipation, Negrophobia, and Civil War Politics in Ohio, 1863–1865." *Journal of Negro History* 65 (1980): 250–260.

Kamphoefner, Walter D. "German-Americans and Civil War Politics: A Reconsideration of the Ethnocultural Thesis." *Civil War History* 37 (1991): 232–246.

Klement, Frank L. *The Copperheads in the Middle West.* Chicago: University of Chicago Press, 1960.

———. *Dark Lanterns: Secret Political Societies, Conspiracies, and Treason Trials in the Civil War.* Baton Rouge, LA: Louisiana State University Press, 1984.

———. "The Soldier Vote in Wisconsin during the Civil War." *Wisconsin Magazine of History* 28 (1944): 37–47.

———. *Wisconsin and the Civil War.* Madison: State Historical Society of Wisconsin, 1963.

Kleppner, Paul. *The Third Electoral System, 1853–1892: Parties, Voters, and Political Culture.* Chapel Hill, NC: University of North Carolina Press, 1979.

Knapp, Charles M. *New Jersey Politics during the Period of the Civil War and Reconstruction.* Geneva, NY: W. F. Humphrey, 1924.

Lane, Jarlath R. *A Political History of Connecticut during the Civil War*. Washington, D.C.: Catholic University Press, 1941.

Laughlin, Sceva. *Missouri Politics during the Civil War*. Salem, OR: N.p., 1930.

Lee, Bill R. "Missouri's Fight over Emancipation in 1863." *Missouri Historical Review* 45 (1951): 256–274.

Leech, Margaret. *Reveille in Washington, 1860–1865*. New York: Harper, 1941.

Lewis, Martin D. *Lumberman from Flint: The Michigan Career of Henry D. Crapo, 1855–1869*. Detroit, MI: Wayne State University Press, 1958.

May, George S. "Politics in Ann Arbor during the Civil War." *Michigan History* 37 (1953): 53–73.

McGregor, James C. *The Disruption of Virginia*. New York: Macmillan, 1922.

McKay, Ernest A. *The Civil War and New York City*. Syracuse, NY: Syracuse University Press, 1990.

McSeveney, Samuel T. "Re-electing Lincoln: The Union Party Campaign and the Military Vote in Connecticut." *Civil War History* 32 (1986): 139–158.

———. "Winning the Vote for Connecticut Soldiers in the Field, 1862–1864: A Research Note and Historiographical Comment." *Connecticut History* 26 (1985): 115–124.

Mitchell, Stewart. *Horatio Seymour of New York*. Cambridge, MA: Harvard University Press, 1938.

Moore, George E. *A Banner in the Hills: West Virginia's Statehood*. New York: Appleton-Century-Crofts, 1963.

Murdock, Eugene C. "Horatio Seymour and the 1863 Draft." *Civil War History* 11 (1965): 117–141.

Mushkat, Jerome. *The Reconstruction of the New York Democracy, 1861–1874*. Rutherford, NJ: Farleigh Dickinson University Press, 1981.

———. *Tammany: The Evolution of a Political Machine, 1789–1865*. Syracuse, NY: Syracuse University Press, 1971.

Noyes, Edward. "White Opposition to Black Migration into Civil-War Wisconsin." *Lincoln Herald* 73 (1971): 181–191.

Parrish, William E. *Turbulent Partnership: Missouri and the Union, 1861–1865*. Columbia, MO: University of Missouri Press, 1963.

Pleasants, Samuel A. *Fernando Wood of New York*. New York: Columbia University Press, 1948.

Porter, George H. *Ohio Politics during the Civil War Period*. New York: Longmans Green and Co., 1911.

Pratt, Harry E. "The Repudiation of Lincoln's War Policy in 1862—Stuart-Swett Congressional Campaign." *Journal of the Illinois State Historical Society* 24 (1931): 129–140.

Renda, Lex. "Credit and Culpability: New Hampshire State Politics during the Civil War." *Historical New Hampshire* 48 (1993): 2–84.

Roseboom, Eugene H. *The Civil War Era, 1850–1873*. Columbus, OH: Ohio State Archaeological and Historical Society, 1944.

Samon, Jud. "Sagebrush Falstaff: A Biographical Sketch of James Warren Nye." 2 vols. Ph.D. diss., University of Maryland, 1979.

Shankman, Arnold. "Soldier Votes and Clement L. Vallandigham in the 1863 Ohio Gubernatorial Election." *Ohio History* 82 (1973): 88–104.

————. *The Anti-War Movement in Pennsylvania, 1861–1865.* Rutherford, NJ: Fairleigh Dickinson Press, 1980.

Spencer, Ivor D. "Chicago Helps to Reelect Lincoln." *Journal of the Illinois State Historical Society* 63 (1970): 167–179.

Stampp, Kenneth M. *Indiana Politics during the Civil War.* Indianapolis, IN: Indiana Historical Bureau, 1949.

Stanley, Gerald. "Civil War Politics in California." *Southern California Quarterly* 64 (1982): 115–132.

Stewart, Mitchell. *Horatio Seymour of New York.* Cambridge: Harvard University Press, 1938.

Sylvester, Lorna L. "Oliver P. Morton and Hoosier Politics during the War." Ph.D. diss., Indiana University, 1968.

Tredway, G. R. *Democratic Opposition to the Lincoln Administration in Indiana.* Indianapolis, IN: Indiana Historical Bureau, 1973.

Trenerry, Walter N. "Votes for Minnesota's Civil War Soldiers." *Publications of the Minnesota Historical Society* 36 (1959): 167–172.

Voegeli, V. Jacque. *Free But Not Equal: The Midwest and the Negro during the Civil War.* Chicago: University of Chicago Press, 1967.

Wagandt, Charles. "Election by Sword and Ballot: The Emancipation Victory of 1863." *Maryland Historical Magazine* 59 (1964): 143–164.

Wainwright, Nicholas B. "The Loyal Opposition in Civil War Philadelphia." *Pennsylvania Magazine of History and Biography* 88 (1964): 294–315.

Ware, Edith E. *Political Opinion in Massachusetts during the Civil War and Reconstruction.* Columbia University Studies in History, Economics and Public Law, vol. 74, no. 2. New York: Columbia University, 1916.

Whiteman, Maxwell. *Gentlemen in Crisis: The First Century of the Union League of Philadelphia, 1862–1910.* Philadelphia: Union League of Philadelphia, 1975.

Wilson, Don. *Governor Charles Robinson of Kansas.* Lawrence, KS: University Press of Kansas, 1975.

Winther, Oscar O. "The Soldier Vote in the Election of 1864." *New York History* 15 (1944): 440–458.

Wubben, Hubert H. *Civil War Iowa and the Copperhead Movement.* Ames, IA: Iowa State University Press, 1980.

————. "The Uncertain Trumpet: Iowa Republicans and Black Suffrage: 1860–1868." *Annals of Iowa* 47 (1984): 409–429.

37

Southern State and Local Politics

Bradley G. Bond

Juxtaposed to the corpus of works written about antebellum and Reconstruction-era Southern politics, the number of Southern Civil War political studies is curiously small. Likewise, the volume and sophistication of literature about Southern state and local politics during the Civil War era pale in comparison to those of works about Northern states. Historians of states that remained loyal to the Union have embraced the latest methodologies and placed their studies within the context of broad historiographic concerns, while political historians of the South during the Civil War remain mired in discussions of familiar themes: the competition between advocates of federalism and states' rights, individual and collective acts of dissent, and the expansion of state authority.

STATE POLITICS IN GENERAL STUDIES

When Frank Lawrence Owsley described the Confederacy as having been hamstrung by the philosophy of states' rights, which he believed undergirded its formation, he introduced into the historiography of the Civil War a perennial theme. Owsley's *State Rights in the Confederacy* (1925) provided historians their first working model of the irony of Southern history. Owsley portrays the fledgling nation as incapable of reconciling its idealized notion of the authority of states with the competing concept of a permanent and strong federal government. In an essay published in the edited volume *Why the North Won the Civil War* (1960), David Donald expands on Owsley's argument that states' rights philosophy crippled the South politically and asserts that the Confederacy died of the related factor—democracy.

Testifying to the sway that Owsley's argument possesses, Drew Gilpin Faust reiterates and refines his primary contention in *The Creation of Confederate Nationalism* (1988). Faust's theoretically informed work traces the ideological origins of Civil War state-federal controversies to antebellum assumptions about the nature of society. She portrays that society as paternalistic and religious, bound by the concept of mutual and voluntary sacrifice. The wartime necessity of creating a Confederate nationalism, as well as the influence of poor whites and blacks, forced the nascent nation to alter social and political relations, which in turn provided Confederate nationalism its chief strength and weakness: it demanded unanimity and could not control dissent.

Authors of general studies, too, have emphasized the detrimental influence of Southern political ideology (and the resulting dissent) on the Confederate war effort, including: E. Merton Coulter, *The Confederate States of America, 1861–1865* (1950), Eric L. McKitrick, "Party Politics and the Union and Confederate War Efforts" (1967), Emory M. Thomas, *The Confederacy as a Revolutionary Experience* (1971), and Paul D. Escott, *After Secession* (1978). William M. Robinson, Jr., in his *Justice in Grey* (1941), studies the impact of ideology on the structure of Southern courts, discussing in the process the issue of states' rights and local politicians. A collective biography of Southern governors edited by Wilfred Buck Yearns, *The Confederate Governors* (1985), treats local politicians and their relationship with the Federal government too.

Two older works—Albert Burton Moore's *Conscription and Conflict in the Confederacy* (1924) and Georgia L. Tatum's *Disloyalty in the Confederacy* (1934)—examine the themes of dissent and political ideology; and Bell I. Wiley's *The Plain People of the Confederacy* (1943) identifies a class consciousness among political dissenters, as does Stephen E. Ambrose in "Yeoman Discontent in the Confederacy" (1962).

Three additional studies provide challenging perspectives on Southern wartime politics. Historians interested in state and local politics should not neglect Kenneth C. Martis's *The Historical Atlas of the Congresses of the Confederate States of America* (1994). A geographer by training, Martis introduces Civil War political historians to a unique and helpful way of studying their subject. Although the work focuses on politics at the Federal level, Martis discusses local electoral processes and significant legislation. Charts and multicolored maps depict Confederate congressional election results.

Neither should scholars overlook *Federalism in the Southern Confederacy* (1966) by Curtis Arthur Amlund. While historians of Southern politics during the Civil War argue that the ideology of states' rights proved injurious to the Confederate war effort, Amlund, a political scientist, concludes that political discord signified the health of the Federal system. Such contention, he says, typifies mature political systems.

George C. Rable's *The Confederate Republic* (1994), the most recent study of wartime political affairs and in many ways the most impressive, examines the interplay and tensions engendered by Southern political ideology and practical politics. Whereas most historians view Civil War–era politics as moribund, Rable argues that dynamic political struggles characterized state and local elections, just as they had during the antebellum period. In the same way that Owsley's work served two generations as a paradigm for the study of politics, so too will Rable's study for future generations.

Despite the prevalence of the view that southern state governments jealously protected the supremacy of their authority, historians have also recognized that the states expanded their authority over the economy and society. May Spencer Ringold's *The Role of the State Legislatures in the Confederacy* (1966) outlines the way in which states augmented their power, as does Charles W. Ramsdell in his older monograph, *Behind the Lines in the Southern Confederacy* (1944). Difficulties in expanding state power, particularly the states' ability to provide for the welfare of all, are treated in Paul D. Escott's " 'The Cry of the Sufferers' " (1977). Efforts by the states to obtain an important commodity are discussed in Ella Lonn's *Salt as a Factor in the Confederacy* (1933); her *Desertion during the Civil War* (1928) in part treats desertion as a political act carried out in defiance of expanded state and Confederate policies. The role of states in promoting transportation is covered by Robert C. Black in *The Railroads of the Confederacy* (1952).

STATE AND LOCAL STUDIES

In studies devoted solely to state and local politics, the themes of state-federal controversies, the enlargement of state power, and dissent are prevalent. North Carolina and Georgia, home to noteworthy and contentious political fracases during the Civil War, have received more attention from historians than most other states.

Scholars of North Carolina concentrate on the struggle between rival politicians and between states' rights factions, even peace advocates, and the Confederate government. Several studies touch on aspects of the political climate in wartime North Carolina, providing a frame of reference for works more focused on Civil War politics. Paul D. Escott's *Many Excellent People* (1985) places politics in the context of societal and economic developments, and Marc W. Kruman's *Parties and Politics in North Carolina* (1983) follows the course of Jacksonian-era politics through the close of hostilities. Class tensions in low-country North Carolina society and the disintegration of politics into guerrilla war are two subjects treated by Wayne K. Durrill in *War of Another Kind* (1990), while James Lawrence Lancaster, in his dissertation, "The Scalawags of North Carolina" (1974), concentrates on the wartime political opposition of tarheel politicians who later affiliated with the Republican party.

Opposition to secession and the prosecutors of war also receives coverage in Mary Shannon Smith's *Union Sentiment in North Carolina during the Civil War* (1915) and in William T. Auman's study of central North Carolina, "Neighbor against Neighbor" (1984). Auman, who explores Randolph County and its environs, argues that persisting unionism and class tensions prompted yeoman whites to oppose Confederate policy. Yeomen living in counties farther west likewise resented Confederate policy and voted against politicians friendly to Richmond policy makers, according to Robin E. Baker in "Class Conflict and Political Upheaval" (1992). Memory F. Mitchell makes a similar argument in *Legal Aspects of Conscription and Exemption in North Carolina* (1965). All of these authors agree that the economic, political, and social inferiority of plain whites accounted for their inability to alter the course of politics. Marc W. Kruman pursues a more structural line of argument to account for political opposition and its failure. In "Dissent in the Confederacy" (1981), he contends that the absence of a political party system in wartime North Carolina hindered the development of effectual dissent.

Governor Zebulon Vance and opposition leader William W. Holden, North Carolina's most prominent politicians, have been the focus of numerous works. North Carolina political battles and the roles of Vance and Holden are chronicled in *North Carolina Civil War Documentary* (1980) by W. Buck Yearns and John G. Barrett.

Biographers of Vance, including Glenn Tucker, *Zeb Vance* (1965), Richard S. Yates, *The Confederacy and Zeb Vance* (1958), and Clement Dowd, *Life of Zebulon Vance* (1897), portray him as a states' rights advocate and opponent of Confederate policies. In a now-dated article, "Governor Vance and the Peace Movement" (1940), Yates suggests that political posturing and a desire to provide effective political leadership informed the governor's long-running feud with Jefferson Davis. David D. Scarboro in "North Carolina and the Confederacy" (1979) rewrites the revolutionary role typically assigned to Vance, arguing that although Vance complained vociferously about the Confederacy's intrusions into his domain, he realized the futility of defiance.

William Holden's biographers include Horace W. Raper (*William W. Holden* [1985]) and William C. Harris (*William Woods Holden* [1987]), both of whom ably account for Holden's unionist background, leadership of the peace movement in North Carolina, and eventual elevation to governor. A political crony of Holden has also garnered Norman D. Brown's attention in *Edward Stanly* (1974).

Georgia's political history during the Civil War contains many of the same elements as North Carolina's. Adequate overviews of the period are provided in Isaac W. Avery's *The History of the State of Georgia from 1850 to 1881* (1881) and in T. Conn Bryan's *Confederate Georgia* (1953). Kenneth Coleman's *Confederate Athens, 1861–1865* (1967) should also be consulted. Two articles by James Horace Bass, "The Attack upon the Confederate Administration" (1934) and "The Georgia Gubernatorial Elections of 1861 and 1863" (1935), briefly summarize the complexity of state politics and the maneuvering of political figures to create alliances.

Serious students of the Civil War politics in Georgia must consider Steven Hahn's *The Roots of Southern Populism* (1983), which traces the origins of New

South political dissent in hill country Georgia to opposition to Confederate and state policies. When the Georgia government refused to address the concerns of plain folk, yeoman farmers began to characterize the conflagration as a rich man's war and a poor man's fight.

Georgia's wartime governor, Joseph E. Brown, has been the subject of two biographies. Louise Biles Hill, in her *Joseph E. Brown and the Confederacy* (1939), depicts Brown as a political chameleon who altered his politics to suit any situation, and Joseph H. Parks, in his *Joseph E. Brown of Georgia* (1977), does much the same in a massive and more readable work. "State Rights in a Crisis" (1966) by Parks, examines Brown's difficulties with Jefferson Davis and the Confederate government at Richmond, and John E. Talmadge's essay, "Peace-Movement Activities in Civil War Georgia" (1953), properly credits Brown and Alexander Stephens with initiating the movement in Georgia.

Stephens, the vice president of the Confederacy, has also received scholarly attention. Thomas E. Schott, in *Alexander H. Stephens of Georgia* (1988), offers the most modern assessment, one that outlines his role in Georgia politics. William Y. Thompson, in *Robert Toombs of Georgia* (1966), affirms that Toombs belonged to the triumvirate, along with Brown and Stephens, that opposed Jefferson Davis. Lesser-known pro-Davis politicians, like Benjamin H. Hill, have their biographers too. Hill, a moderate on the question of secession, a member of the Confederate Senate, and a pro-Richmond politician from a generally hostile Georgia, is the subject of Haywood J. Pearce, Jr.'s *Benjamin H. Hill* (1928). William B. McCash has written an admirable study, *Thomas R. R. Cobb* (1983), about the involvement of a Confederate congressman in state politics, and Percy S. Flippin's *Herschel V. Johnson of Georgia* (1931), though hagiographic in tone and dated, assigns the Confederate senator a prominent place as a defender of states' rights.

Virginia politics and government policies are outlined in F. N. Boney's *John Letcher of Virginia* (1966), and the political debate about expanding the military rolls is discussed in Thomas M. Preisser's "The Virginia Decision to Use Negro Soldiers in the Civil War" (1975). Dissent, especially in the rural districts of Virginia, has been a theme of Virginia political history. In a seminal article about disloyalty in Appalachia, Henry T. Shanks (1944) argues that disaffection came only after battlefield defeats and government policies forced mountain dwellers to rise against political leaders. Kenneth W. Noe (1992) agrees that distaste for the Confederate government of Virginia arose late in the war but contends that rebellious acts were rare. Political affairs in Richmond are chronicled in Emory M. Thomas's *The Confederate State of Richmond* (1971), while William J. Kimball's "The Bread Riot in Richmond" (1961) examines the political motivations behind one famous episode of political defiance.

Historians have bestowed scant attention on South Carolina and Florida. Charles Edward Cauthen has written a survey of the Palmetto State in wartime, *South Carolina Goes to War* (1950); Lillian A. Kibler's *Benjamin F. Perry, South Carolina Unionist* (1946) examines the role of an antebellum unionist turned state legislator; and John B. Edmunds, Jr., has published a biography of the Calhounite governor of Confederate South Carolina, *Francis W. Pickens and the Politics of Destruction* (1986). For Florida, the best coverage of political affairs remains John Edwin Johns's *Florida during the Civil War* (1963), though Jerrell H. Shofner's *Nor Is It Over Yet* (1974) should also be consulted.

Works on Alabama, Mississippi, and Louisiana are slightly more numerous. *Civil War and Reconstruction in Alabama* (1905) by Walter L. Fleming is a dated but widely available examination of politics and political rivalries in the state. Political dissent and factionalism in hill country Alabama have been the focus of three books: *Winston: An Antebellum and Civil War History of a Hill County of North Alabama* (1972) by Don Dodd; *The Disintegration of a Confederate State* (1986) by Malcolm C. McMillan; and *The Scalawag in Alabama Politics, 1865–1881* (1977) by Sarah Woolfolk Wiggins.

John K. Bettersworth's *Confederate Mississippi* (1943) covers military affairs and political infighting in the Magnolia State, and Bradley G. Bond's *Political Culture in the Nineteenth-Century South* (1995) devotes one chapter to the development of class tensions and the expansion of state authority during the war. Biographers of three leading political figures in Mississippi should also be consulted. *John Jones Pettus, Mississippi Fire-Eater* (1975) by Robert W. Dubay is a brief and sympathetic biography of a Confederate governor that recounts the familiar story of state-federal rivalries and difficulties of implementing wartime policies. Of lesser value to Civil War historians are *Albert Gallatin Brown, Radical Southern Nationalist* (1937) by James B. Ranck and *James Lusk Alcorn* (1966) by Lillian A. Pereyra.

Louisiana, like other Southern states, also has a general text that covers the years 1861 to 1865. Jefferson D. Bragg's *Louisiana in the Confederacy* (1941) examines state politics, relations with the government at Richmond, and finances. Roger W. Shugg, in his *Origins of the Class Struggle in Louisiana* (1939), develops the theme of class conflict during the Civil War, and Vincent H. Cassidy and Amos E. Simpson offer a solid biography of a Louisiana governor in their *Henry Watkins Allen of Louisiana* (1964). The contour of political affairs is discussed, too, in Willie Malvin Caskey's *Secession and Restoration of Louisiana* (1938).

Tennessee, the site of significant Civil War battles, has interested political historians less than military ones. James Welch Patton's *Unionism and Reconstruction in Tennessee, 1860–1867* (1934) surveys wartime political developments, and E. Merton Coulter's biography of William Brownlow, *William G. Brownlow, Fighting Parson of the Southern Highlands* (1937), devotes a single chapter to political dissent.

Michael B. Dougan's *Confederate Arkansas* (1976) supplants David Y. Thomas's *Arkansas in War and Reconstruction* (1926) as the basic text about wartime Arkansas. Both books discuss political affairs, including the emergence of dissent and antipathy toward Confederate policies. Wartime politics and loyalists are the focus of separate chapters in Carl H. Moneyhon's *The Impact of the Civil War and Reconstruction on Arkansas* (1994), and John I. Smith has written a sympathetic biography of Arkansas governor Isaac Murphy, *The Courage of a Southern Unionist* (1979).

James Marten discusses the persistence of wartime unionism in Texas and offers an introduction to state politics in his *Texas Divided* (1990). Two dissertations—"A Political Labyrinth" by Nancy Head Bowen and "The Texas Governorship, 1861–1865" by Fredericka Ann Meiners—treat political alignments, state-federal relations, military affairs, and financial matters.

Despite the broad coverage of Civil War–era politics, literature about the Southern states is limited in scope and sophistication. Scholars interested in the topic have a wide-open field in which to develop new studies that will take the discussion of politics in the period 1861 to 1865 beyond familiar debates about federal-state rivalry, dissent, and the expansion of government authority. Updated surveys of state government and politics in the various states are needed, as are general works on the Democratic and opposition parties. Significant Confederate cities—New Orleans, Charleston, Mobile, Nashville—deserve attention, and our understanding of the politics of common people—urban and rural, white and black—suffers from a lack of study.

BIBLIOGRAPHY

Ambrose, Stephen E. "Yeoman Discontent in the Confederacy." *Civil War History* 8 (1962): 259–268.

Amlund, Curtis Arthur. *Federalism in the Southern Confederacy.* Washington, D.C.: Public Affairs Press, 1966.

Auman, William T. "Neighbor against Neighbor: The Inner Civil War in the Randolph County Area of Confederate North Carolina." *North Carolina Historical Review* 61 (1984): 59–92.

Avery, Isaac W. *The History of the State of Georgia from 1850 to 1881.* New York: Brown and Derby, 1881.

Baker, Robin E. "Class Conflict and Political Upheaval: The Transformation of North Carolina Politics during the Civil War." *North Carolina Historical Review* 69 (1992): 148–178.

Bass, James Horace. "The Attack upon the Confederate Administration in Georgia in the Spring of 1864." *Georgia Historical Quarterly* 18 (1934): 228–247.

———. "The Georgia Gubernatorial Elections of 1861 and 1863." *Georgia Historical Quarterly* 17 (1935): 167–188.

Bettersworth, John K. *Confederate Mississippi: The People and Policies of a Cotton State.* Baton Rouge, LA: Louisiana State University Press, 1943.

Black, Robert C. III. *The Railroads of the Confederacy.* Chapel Hill, NC: University of North Carolina Press, 1952.

Bond, Bradley G. *Political Culture in the Nineteenth-Century South.* Baton Rouge: Louisiana State University Press, 1995.

Boney, F. N. *John Letcher of Virginia: The Story of Virginia's Civil War Governor.* University, AL: University of Alabama Press, 1966.

Bowen, Nancy Head. "A Political Labyrinth: Texas in the Civil War—Questions in Continuity." Ph.D. diss., Rice University, 1974.

Bragg, Jefferson D. *Louisiana in the Confederacy*. Baton Rouge, LA: Louisiana State University Press, 1941.

Brown, Norman D. *Edward Stanly: Whiggery's Tarheel "Conqueror."* University, AL: University of Alabama Press, 1974.

Bryan, T. Conn. *Confederate Georgia*. Athens, GA: University of Georgia Press, 1953.

Caskey, Willie Malvin. *Secession and Restoration of Louisiana*. Baton Rouge, LA: Louisiana State University Press, 1938.

Cassidy, Vincent H., and Amos E. Simpson. *Henry Watkins Allen of Louisiana*. Baton Rouge, LA: Louisiana State University Press, 1964.

Cauthen, Charles Edward. *South Carolina Goes to War, 1860–1865*. Chapel Hill, NC: University of North Carolina Press, 1950.

Coleman, Kenneth. *Confederate Athens, 1861–1865*. Athens, GA: University of Georgia Press, 1967.

Coulter, E. Merton. *The Confederate States of America, 1861–1865*. Baton Rouge, LA: Louisiana State University Press, 1950.

———. *William G. Brownlow, Fighting Parson of the Southern Highlands*. Chapel Hill, NC: University of North Carolina Press, 1937.

Dodd, Don. *Winston: An Antebellum Civil War History of a Hill County of North Alabama*. Jasper, AL: C. Elliott, 1972.

Donald, David H. "Died of Democracy." In *Why the North Won the Civil War*. Edited by David H. Donald. Baton Rouge, LA: Louisiana State University Press, 1960.

Dougan, Michael B. *Confederate Arkansas: The People and Policies of a Frontier State in Wartime*. University, AL: University of Alabama Press, 1976.

Dowd, Clement. *Life of Zebulon B. Vance*. Charlotte, NC: Observer Printing, 1897.

Dubay, Robert W. *John Jones Pettus, Mississippi Fire-Eater: His Life and Times, 1813–1867*. Oxford, MS: University Press of Mississippi, 1975.

Durrill, Wayne K. *War of Another Kind*. New York: Oxford University Press, 1990.

Edmunds, John B., Jr. *Francis W. Pickens and the Politics of Destruction*. Chapel Hill, NC: University of North Carolina Press, 1986.

Escott, Paul D. *After Secession: Jefferson Davis and the Failure of Confederate Nationalism*. Baton Rouge, LA: Louisiana State University Press, 1978.

———. *Many Excellent People: Power and Privilege in North Carolina, 1850–1900*. Chapel Hill, NC: University of North Carolina Press, 1985.

———. " 'The Cry of the Sufferers': The Problem of Welfare in the Confederacy." *Civil War History* 23 (1977): 228–240.

Faust, Drew Gilpin. *The Creation of Confederate Nationalism: Ideology and Identity in the Civil War South*. Baton Rouge, LA: Louisiana State University Press, 1988.

Fleming, Walter L. *Civil War and Reconstruction in Alabama*. New York: Columbia University Press, 1905.

Flippin, Percy S. *Hershel V. Johnson of Georgia: State Rights Unionist*. Richmond, VA: Dietz Printing Co., 1931.

Hahn, Steven. *The Roots of Southern Populism: Yeoman Farmers and the Transformation of the Georgia Upcountry, 1850–1890*. New York: Oxford University Press, 1983.

Harris, William C. *William Woods Holden: Firebrand of North Carolina Politics*. Baton Rouge, LA: Louisiana State University Press, 1987.

Hill, Louise Biles. *Joseph E. Brown and the Confederacy.* Chapel Hill, NC: University of North Carolina, 1939.

Johns, John Edwin. *Florida during the Civil War.* Gainesville, FL: University of Florida Press, 1963.

Kibler, Lillian A. *Benjamin F. Perry, South Carolina Unionist.* Durham, NC: Duke University Press, 1946.

Kimball, William J. "The Bread Riot in Richmond, 1863." *Civil War History* 7 (1961): 149–154.

Kruman, Marc W. "Dissent in the Confederacy: The North Carolina Experience." *Civil War History* 27 (1981): 293–313.

———. *Parties and Politics in North Carolina, 1836–1865.* Baton Rouge, LA: Louisiana State University Press, 1983.

Lancaster, James Lawrence. "The Scalawags of North Carolina, 1850–1868." Ph.D. diss., Princeton University, 1974.

Lonn, Ella. *Desertion during the Civil War.* New York: Century, 1928.

———. *Salt as a Factor in the Confederacy.* New York: Neale, 1933.

Marten, James. *Texas Divided: Loyalty and Dissent in the Lone Star State.* Lexington, KY: University Press of Kentucky, 1990.

Martis, Kenneth C. *The Historical Atlas of the Congresses of the Confederate States of America, 1861–1865.* New York: Simon & Schuster, 1994.

McCash, William B. *Thomas R. R. Cobb, 1823–1862: The Making of a Southern Nationalist.* Macon, GA: Mercer University Press, 1983.

McKitrick, Eric L. "Party Politics and the Union and Confederate War Efforts." In *The American Party Systems.* Edited by William Nisbet Chambers and Walter Dean Burnham. New York: Oxford University Press, 1967.

McMillan, Malcolm C. *The Disintegration of a Confederate State: Three Governors and Alabama's Wartime Home Front, 1861–1865.* Macon, GA: Mercer University Press, 1986.

Meiners, Fredericka Ann. "The Texas Governorship, 1861–1865: A Biography of an Office." Ph.D. diss., Rice University, 1974.

Mitchell, Memory F. *Legal Aspects of Conscription and Exemption in North Carolina, 1861–1865.* Chapel Hill, NC: University of North Carolina Press, 1965.

Moneyhon, Carl H. *The Impact of the Civil War and Reconstruction on Arkansas: Persistence in the Midst of Ruin.* Baton Rouge, LA: Louisiana State University Press, 1994.

Montgomery, Horace. *Howell Cobb's Confederate Career.* Tuscaloosa, AL: Confederate Publishing Co., 1959.

Moore, Albert Burton. *Conscription and Conflict in the Confederacy.* New York: Macmillan, 1924.

Noe, Kenneth W. "Red String Scare: Civil War Southwest Virginia and the Heroes of America." *North Carolina Historical Review* 69 (1992): 301–322.

Owsley, Frank Lawrence. *State Rights in the Confederacy.* Chicago: University of Chicago Press, 1925.

Parks, Joseph H. *Joseph E. Brown of Georgia.* Baton Rouge, LA: Louisiana State University Press, 1977.

———. "State Rights in a Crisis: Governor Joseph E. Brown versus President Jefferson Davis." *Journal of Southern History* 32 (1966): 3–24.

Patton, James Welch. *Unionism and Reconstruction in Tennessee, 1860–1867*. Chapel Hill, NC: University of North Carolina Press, 1934.

Pearce, Haywood, J., Jr. *Benjamin H. Hill: Secession and Reconstruction*. Chicago: University of Chicago Press, 1928.

Pereyra, Lillian A. *James Lusk Alcorn: Persistent Whig*. Baton Rouge, LA: Louisiana State University Press, 1966.

Preisser, Thomas M. "The Virginia Decision to Use Negro Soldiers in the Civil War, 1864–65." *Virginia Magazine of History and Biography* 83 (1975): 98–113.

Rable, George C. *The Confederate Republic: A Revolution against Politics*. Chapel Hill, NC: University of North Carolina Press, 1994.

Ramsdell, Charles W. *Behind the Lines in the Southern Confederacy*. Edited by Wendell H. Stephenson. Baton Rouge, LA: Louisiana State University Press, 1944.

Ranck, James B. *Albert Gallatin Brown, Radical Southern Nationalist*. New York: D. Appleton-Century Co., 1937.

Raper, Horace W. *William W. Holden: North Carolina's Political Enigma*. Chapel Hill, NC: University of North Carolina Press, 1985.

Ringold, May Spencer. *The Role of the State Legislature in the Confederacy*. Athens, GA: University of Georgia Press, 1966.

Robinson, William M., Jr. *Justice in Grey: A History of the Judicial System of the Confederate States of America*. Cambridge, MA: Harvard University Press, 1941.

Scarboro, David D. "North Carolina and the Confederacy: The Weakness of States' Rights during the Civil War." *North Carolina Historical Review* 56 (1979): 133–149.

Schott, Thomas E. *Alexander H. Stephens of Georgia: A Biography*. Baton Rouge, LA: Louisiana State University Press, 1988.

Shanks, Henry T. "Disloyalty to the Confederacy in Southwestern Virginia, 1861–1865." *North Carolina Historical Review* 21 (1944): 118–135.

Shofner, Jerrell H. *Nor Is It Over Yet: Florida in the Era of Reconstruction, 1863–1877*. Gainsville: University Press of Florida, 1974.

Shugg, Roger W. *Origins of the Class Struggle in Louisiana: A Social History of White Farmers and Laborers during Slavery and After, 1840–1875*. Baton Rouge: Louisiana State University Press, 1939.

Smith, John I. *The Courage of a Southern Unionist: A Biography of Isaac Murphy, Governor of Arkansas, 1864–1868*. Little Rock, AR: Rose Publishing Co., 1979.

Smith, Mary Shannon. *Union Sentiment in North Carolina during the Civil War*. Raleigh: Meredith College, 1915.

Talmadge, John E. "Peace-Movement Activities in Civil War Georgia." *Georgia Review* 7 (1953): 190–203.

Tatum, Georgia L. *Disloyalty in the Confederacy*. Chapel Hill, NC: University of North Carolina Press, 1934.

Thomas, David Y. *Arkansas in War and Reconstruction*. Little Rock, AR: Arkansas Division, United Daughters of the Confederacy, 1926.

Thomas, Emory M. *The Confederacy as a Revolutionary Experience*. Englewood Cliffs, NJ: Prentice-Hall, 1971.

———. *The Confederate State of Richmond*. Austin, TX: University of Texas Press, 1971.

Thompson, William Y. *Robert Toombs of Georgia*. Baton Rouge, LA: Louisiana State University Press, 1966.

Tucker, Glenn. *Zeb Vance: Champion of Personal Freedom.* Indianapolis, IN: Bobbs-Merrill, 1965.

Wiggins, Sarah Woolfolk. *The Scalawag in Alabama Politics, 1865–1881.* Tuscaloosa, AL: University of Alabama Press, 1977.

Wiley, Bell I. *The Plain People of the Confederacy.* Baton Rouge, LA: Louisiana State University Press, 1943.

Yates, Richard E. "Governor Vance and the Peace Movement." *North Carolina Historical Review* 17 (1940): 1–25, 89–113.

———. *The Confederacy and Zeb Vance.* Tuscaloosa, AL: Confederate Publishing Co., 1958.

Yearns, Wilfred Buck, ed. *The Confederate Governors.* Athens, GA: University of Georgia Press, 1985.

Yearns, W. Buck, and John G. Barrett. *North Carolina Civil War Documentary.* Chapel Hill, NC: University of North Carolina Press, 1980.

38

Industry, Agriculture, and the Economy

Lee A. Craig

The traditional view of the economics of the Civil War saw the conflict as an inevitable struggle between competing forms of economic organization: Northern industrialism and Southern agrarianism. Charles and Mary Beard's *The Rise of American Civilization* (1927) represents the seminal treatise on this theme, and the notion remains strongly, if often implicitly, imbedded in subsequent volumes on the subject. At the root of this conflict supposedly lay slavery, which was considered a fundamental characteristic of Southern life, and the tariff, which favored manufacturers at the expense of planters. In fact, numerous studies by economic historians over the past several decades reveal that economic conflict was not an inherent condition of North-South relations during the antebellum era and did not cause the Civil War.

Although certain groups, such as western farmers, justifiably feared the potential competition from slave agriculture, slavery neither threatened nor contended with other features of the Northern economy, and it actually complemented the economic interests of many Northerners. For example, in *The Political Economy of the Cotton South* (1978) Gavin Wright explains how slavery allowed Southern cotton growers to transcend the labor supply constraint faced by family farms. Breaking this constraint led to a greater supply (and thus a lower price) of raw cotton, which was used in Northern textile mills; furthermore, slavery kept blacks from competing with Northern urban workers for industrial jobs. Although the tariff did redistribute income from Southern cotton growers to Northern capitalists and workers, the average tariff rate, as measured by the ratio of duties paid to the value of free and dutiable imports, approached its lowest level of the nineteenth century (between 15 and 20 percent) on the eve of the war.

Rather than any inherent economic conflict, it was the threat posed by abolitionism to the future of Southern property rights in slaves that led to secession. This and other issues relating to the causes of the war are reviewed in Roger L. Ransom's *Conflict and Compromise: The Political Economy of Slavery, Emancipation, and the American Civil War* (1989), perhaps the best single volume on the economic causes and consequences of the war. In particular Ransom focuses on the political economy of the dispute between free farmers and slave owners over the expansion of slavery into the territories. In *Without Consent of Contract* (1989) Robert W. Fogel explains how abolitionists used this dispute to forge a political coalition, which slaveholders perceived as a threat to the perpetuation of their property rights in slaves. This conflict led to secession and war, which had dramatic effects on each sector of the economy—agriculture, industry, and finance—in both regions.

AGRICULTURE

The Civil War is often portrayed as a stimulus to overall economic growth in general and agricultural progress (at least in the North) in particular. Such arguments can be found in a number of classic volumes and articles on the history of American agriculture, which often emphasize the role of mechanization in this process. Wayne Rasmussen's "The Civil War: A Catalyst of Agricultural Revolution" (1965) offers an example of such a view. In "Agricultural Productivity Growth during the Decade of the Civil War" (1993) Lee A. Craig and Thomas Weiss show that during the Civil War decade, agricultural output per worker grew at a faster rate (1.35 percent per year) than any other decade in the nineteenth century. Although this observation is consistent with traditional characterizations of the war's effect on Northern agriculture, Craig and Weiss argue that in the North, much of this increase resulted from an increase in the time at work, not mechanization; thus the increase in agricultural productivity during and after the war should not necessarily be equated with economic progress.

In the South, evidence of the war's effect on agriculture is less ambiguous. In *Southern Agriculture during the Civil War Era, 1860–1880* (1994) John Otto reports that on the eve of the war, the future Confederate States produced 25 percent more corn, 100 percent more hogs, and 60 percent more cattle (all per capita) than the states remaining in the Union. Despite its superior position in pork production, the South was still a net importer of pork due to its enormous consumption. While (U.S.) per capita production of pork was roughly 140 (net) pounds a year, Southern consumption was nearly 10 percent greater than this figure, and the official daily ration of the Confederate army called for 0.75 pound per soldier, or 275 pounds annually. Despite the Confederacy's superior per capita stocks of hogs, Otto calculates that achieving self-sufficiency in pork production would have required 20 percent more hogs than Southern farmers possessed at the outset of the war; thus, even with its relatively greater stocks of hogs, the Confederate States remained net importers of pork, and they proved unable to generate enough pork to maintain prewar consumption levels.

Of course, the South possessed a comparative advantage in cotton production. By embargoing cotton early in the war, the Confederacy hoped to use its market power in the staple to persuade European consumers to support and their governments to recognize the Confederacy. Unfortunately for the Confederate cause, the 1860 crop had been enormous (5.2 million bales), thus ameliorating the short-run effects of the embargo. In addition, as a net importer of foodstuffs and manufactured goods, the South either had to trade cotton for those goods or convert its economy to their production. In *Agriculture and the Civil War* (1965) Paul Gates reports that cotton production fell steadily throughout the war—4.5 million bales in 1861, 1.6 million in 1862, 0.4 million in 1863, and 0.3 million in 1864—and millions of acres were converted from cotton to corn and other provisions such as peas, beans, and peanuts.

The role of cotton in financing the war continues to be debated. In *The Political Economy of the Cotton South* (1978) Gavin Wright argues that "in 1860 the textiles industry stood on the crest of a major crisis of overproduction" (p. 96), resulting in a declining demand for Southern cotton; thus, even in the absence of the war, the South stood to suffer economically from changes in the world demand for cotton. In "Cotton's Potential as Economic Weapon: The Antebellum and Wartime Markets for Cotton Textiles" (1994) David G. Surdam challenges Wright's thesis, arguing that the world demand for cotton remained strong during the war and that the South could have used its market power in cotton to shift the cost of the war to cotton consumers, which would have freed manpower for the Confederate military. The South's ability to exchange cotton for food and munitions hinged on the effectiveness of the North's blockade of Southern ports. Cotton smuggling was reportedly an extremely profitable enterprise, but in "Through the Blockade: The Profitability and Extent of Cotton Smuggling, 1861–1865" (1981) Stanley Lebergott concludes that after adjusting for risk, blockade running probably did not yield greater returns than equivalent activities. Furthermore, by the end of 1862, only two deepwater ports—Wilmington, North Carolina, and Charleston, South Carolina—remained in Confederate hands.

In the North the war resulted in an increase in both agricultural output and productivity, and neither the Northern population nor the Union army suffered from a dearth of food. Such was not the case in the Confederacy. In *Southern Agriculture during the Civil War Era*, Otto attributes the failure of the Confederacy to supply its troops (and civilians) adequately with food to the "uninspired" (p. 23) leadership of Confederate Commissary-General Lucius Northrop, who became "the most cussed and vilified man in the Confederacy." Otto notes that by 1864, "the Confederate soldier possessed first-class ordnance but had second-class accouterments and ate third-class rations" (p. 28)—when he ate, that is.

MANUFACTURING

Just as the positive effects of the war on Northern agriculture were overstated by an earlier generation of scholars, so too have the war's effects on manufacturing been inflated. In the North the largess of the Federal government proved valuable to some industries, but others were untouched, and some were harmed by the war. Due to the increased scarcity of cotton, the woolens industry expanded, and army contracts led to the rise of the meatpacking industry, which had a lasting effect on the processed food industry and made Chicago the Midwest's most important urban area, but these two industries were exceptions. In spite of the Union army's demands, Matthew Gallman notes in *The North Fights the Civil War: The Home Front* (1994) that the overall production of textiles, shoes, and munitions did not expand during the war. The technology of war yielded little in the way of either sophisticated or heavy machinery, and despite the railroads' demands for replacement rails, pig iron production grew at its slowest rate in decades. Indeed, after small arms, horseshoes represented the second greatest use of iron.

It is generally believed that industrial workers were among the noncombatants hit hard by the economic effects of the war. For example, the real wages of Northern workers fell by roughly 20 percent during the war. Wage increases did not keep up with inflation and the cost of living in either region, but because of the greater degree of industrialization in the North, this wage lag affected a greater number of Northern workers. In "Inflation and the Wage Lag during the American Civil War" (1977) Stephen DeCanio and Joel Mokyr attribute the majority of the decline in real wages, and thus living standards, to the unanticipated inflation that resulted from an overly expansionary monetary policy. Reuben Kessel and Armen Alchian, however, argue in "Real Wages in the North During the Civil War: Mitchell's Data Reinterpreted" (1959) that the decline in real incomes resulted primarily from the deterioration of American terms of trade with the rest of world, which itself resulted from the disruption in the export of antebellum America's most important export: raw cotton. In either case, the effect on the living standards of workers and their families was substantial.

With prices rising and wages lagging behind, the war had the potential to increase the profits of Northern business to some extent. Because the North possessed a more developed manufacturing and financial network, the Union authorities relied more heavily than their Confederate counterparts did on private contractors for the procurement of military supplies. This reliance had the paradoxical effect of providing an efficient means of securing stores, at least relative to Confederate efforts, while simultaneously leaving contractors vulnerable to charges of profiteering. In the Confederacy, such charges were less frequent, but the trade-off was the inefficiency that results when such endeavors are under-taken by governments.

Unlike the North, which contained a well-developed (by contemporary stan-dards) manufacturing sector, the Confederate States suffered from a paucity of manufacturing capacity. At the outbreak of the war, the only establishment in the Confederacy capable of producing iron rails and heavy artillery was the Tredegar Iron Works in Richmond. These issues are well summarized and crit-ically evaluated using a great deal of empirical evidence by Fred Bateman and Thomas Weiss in *A Deplorable Scarcity: The Failure of Industrialization in the Slave Economy* (1981). Bateman and Weiss conclude that the relative profita-bility of slave agriculture retarded Southern industrialization, and this left the South ill prepared for the economic demands of a protracted war. In ''The Industrial Retardation of Southern Cities, 1860–1880'' (1988) David R. Meyer analyzes the development of Southern manufacturing during and after the war, and he concludes that rather than alleviating the antebellum gap in North-South industrial development, the war widened it.

FINANCE

The U.S. government directly spent $1.8 billion on the Civil War, and the Confederate government spent $1.0 billion. These funds could be raised in three ways: taxing, borrowing, or inflating—that is, printing money. In *The North Fights the Civil War*, Gallman reports that the U.S. government derived the majority of its war finances from bond sales (66 percent) as opposed to taxation (21 percent) and inflation (13 percent) whereas the Confederate government turned to inflation (60 percent) as the primary source of funds, with borrowing (35 percent) and taxation making up the rest (5 percent). The difference between the two governments' choices in the ratio of borrowing to inflation says much about the condition of both public and private finance in each region.

Initially the U.S. Treasury Department under Salmon P. Chase hoped to rely on higher tariffs, excise taxes, and an income tax to finance the war, but by the end of 1861 the poor showing of the Union army and its drain on resources led to a crisis in confidence in the Northern financial system that resulted in the hoarding of specie. The result was the suspension of specie payments (December 30, 1861) and the Legal Tender Act of (February) 1862. The latter of these two acts provided for the issuance of $150 million in greenbacks, and subsequent legislation increased the total issue to $450 million. The suspension of specie payments and the circulation of greenbacks led to inflation and the depreciation of the currency. After Grant's setback at Cold Harbor and the congressional prohibition of gold futures contracts (both in June 1864), the premium of gold over greenbacks peaked, with $2.85 to $2.88 in greenbacks required to purchase $1.00 in gold. Overall, between 1860 and 1865 the cost of living rose roughly 70 percent.

Despite its inflationary policy, the U.S. government relied on bonds as the primary means of financing the war. Of course, the bonds had to be sold. In 1862 Philadelphia securities broker Jay Cooke organized a nationwide campaign to sell bonds to individual citizens. While Cooke's efforts helped, Congress determined that a nationwide financial system would provide a more efficient means of placing the bonds. At the outset of the war, there was no national banking system in the United States. Banking and bank regulation were solely the domain of the states. As Richard Sylla explains in the chapter on the United States in Rondo Cameron's *Banking and Economic Development* (1972), to assist the financing of the war effort, Congress passed the National Banking Act of 1863 and amended it in each of the following two years. The acts granted the right to issue national bank notes to banks that purchased U.S. Treasury bonds, thus providing a market for the bonds. The conversion of charters did not occur as rapidly as Congress would have liked, so subsequent revisions taxed the notes of state banks—2 percent in 1864 and 10 percent in 1865. While the long-run effect of this tax was substantial, it was established too late to be of much use to the Union war effort.

Whereas the United States relied primarily on borrowing to finance the war, the Confederate government relied on inflation. Confederate inflation resulted partly from inept monetary policy and partly from the declining fortunes of the Confederate army. With respect to the former, in *Financial Failure and Confederate Defeat* (1991) Douglas Ball argues that much of the Confederacy's financial failures can be blamed on the incompetence of Treasury Secretary Christopher G. Memminger. Among Memminger's most glaring errors was the failure to monopolize the Confederate note issue or at the very least attempt to control the note-issuing practices of the states, banks, and other private firms. Unlike the United States, the Confederate government did not make its notes legal tender, it did not prevent the states from issuing their own notes, and it did not develop a national system of banking. What it did do was print more money than the economy could absorb at par and which was unbacked by specie or, ultimately, faith in the government that issued it. The result was that in early 1865, the Confederate notes had fallen to less than two cents on the dollar in gold, and by the end of the war the price level in the Confederacy was more than ninety times its prewar level.

Ironically, Confederate interest rates remained relatively stable, as Eugene Lerner notes in "The Monetary and Fiscal Programs of the Confederate Government, 1861–1865" (1954). Lerner suggests patriotism may have played a role in the willingness of Southerners to accept Confederate securities. George K. Davis and Gary M. Pecquet explore the stability of Confederate interest rates and Lerner's explanation of them in "Interest Rates in the Civil War South" (1990). Davis and Pecquet explain the "Lerner paradox" by exploring the peculiar characteristics of Confederate securities. The Confederate treasury issued non–interest bearing notes, treasury notes, and fixed-rate call certificates redeemable at par. Any upward pressure on the yield of treasury notes would result in a call, which would halt the rise in nominal interest rates but also increase the money supply and prices; thus when converted into gold, Confederate interest rates followed the South's fortunes on the battlefield. Similarly, Richard C. K. Burdekin and Farrokh K. Langdana show in "War Finance in the Southern Confederacy, 1861–1865" (1993) that Confederate inflation was ultimately driven by the success or failure of the Confederate army, and as the army's fortunes turned down after the summer of 1863, so did Confederate finances.

CONSEQUENCES

The traditional treatment of the Civil War's effects on the postbellum economy can be found in the Beards' *The Rise of American Civilization* (1927) and Louis Hacker's *The Triumph of American Capitalism* (1940) in which the authors return to the argument that the war represented the triumph of Northern industrialists over Southern agrarians and paved the way for subsequent economic growth. In its broadest interpretation, this view was dealt a fatal blow by Stanley Engerman, who showed in "The Economic Impact of the Civil War" (1966) that the war represented a pause rather than a stimulus to subsequent growth. In "Commodity Output, 1839–99" (1960) Robert Gallman provides evidence supporting Engerman's claim. Specifically, commodity output in the entire United States grew at a 4.6 percent annual rate in the two decades before the war and at a 4.4 percent rate in the two decades following 1870, but during the Civil War decade, output grew at less than half (2.0 percent) those rates.

Overall, then, it is hard to make a case that the war stimulated economic growth, though the war substantially *altered* the economy, and some of those changes may have affected the path of economic growth. For example, while the Confederate states were out of the Union, Congress passed a number of acts that had been considered before the war but were blocked at least partly by Southern economic interests. These included the Land-Grant College Act (1862), the Homestead Act (1862), and the Pacific Railway Act (1862). Individually and collectively these acts had the effect of promoting western expansion, which had been the perceived threat to Southern property rights that drove the South to secession.

In addition, the war ushered in the political dominance of Northern Republicans who raised tariffs, and by the end of the war the tariff rate had more than doubled from its prewar level. In "Watersheds and Turning Points: Conjectures on the Long-Term Impact of Civil War Financing" (1974) Jeffrey Williamson argues that the Civil War tariffs drove up the price of consumer goods relative to capital goods, thus spurring capital formation and economic growth. Similarly, other war-induced policies and innovations had indirect effects on the economy. For example the experience acquired in handling the shear volume of government debt during the war—the national debt soared from $65 million in 1860 to $2.7 billion in 1865—proved valuable in marketing private securities, and although the national banks did not play the large role intended for them during the war, they increased in importance as financial intermediaries in later decades.

In the final analysis, however, the rare instances of the war's positive contributions must be weighed against the destruction of human and physical capital. In "The Economic Cost of the American Civil War: Estimates and Implications" Claudia D. Goldin and Frank D. Lewis estimate that direct costs of the war were $3.4 billion in the Northern states and $3.3 billion in the South. In other words, the war cost about $200 per capita in 1860 dollars. To put these figures into perspective, consider that in "The Economics of Emancipation" (1973) Goldin estimates that the cost of purchasing the freedom of the entire slave stock in 1860 would have been $2.7 billion, or about 40 percent of the war's actual cost. Financed by the issue of thirty-year bonds at 6 percent interest, this option would have cost the Northern population $9.66 in taxes per person per year. Of course, such mean calculations distort the fact that the fundamental economic condition of war is not its average cost or benefit but rather its distributional effect. The economic benefits of the Civil War were bestowed upon those who were able to take advantage of the changes it generated, while its costs were most heavily borne by those who suffered and died on its fields of glory.

BIBLIOGRAPHY

Ball, Douglas B. *Financial Failure and Confederate Defeat.* Urbana, IL: University of Illinois Press, 1991.

Bateman, Fred, and Thomas Weiss. *A Deplorable Scarcity: The Failure of Industrialization in the Slave Economy.* Chapel Hill, NC: University of North Carolina Press, 1981.

Beard, Charles, and Mary Beard. *The Rise of American Civilization.* New York: Macmillan, 1927.

Burdekin, Richard C. K., and Farrokh K. Langdana. "War Finance in the Southern Confederacy, 1861–1865." *Explorations in Economic History* 30 (1993): 352–376.

Craig, Lee A., and Thomas Weiss. "Agricultural Productivity Growth during the Decade of the Civil War." *Journal of Economic History* 53 (1993): 527–548.

Davis, George K., and Gary M. Pecquet. "Interest Rates in the Civil War South." *Journal of Economic History* 50 (1990): 133–148.

DeCanio, Stephen, and Joel Mokyr. "Inflation and the Wage Lag during the American Civil War." *Explorations in Economic History* 14 (1977): 311–336.

Engerman, Stanley. "The Economic Impact of the Civil War." *Explorations in Economic History* 3 (1966): 176–199.

Fogel, Robert W. *Without Consent or Contract: The Rise and Fall of American Slavery.* New York: W. W. Norton and Company, 1989.

Gallman, J. Matthew. *The North Fights the Civil War: The Home Front.* Chicago: Ivan R. Dee, 1994.

Gallman, Robert. "Commodity Output, 1839–99." In William Parker, ed. *Trends in the American Economy in the Nineteenth Century.* Princeton, NJ: Princeton University Press, 1960.

Gates, Paul W. *Agriculture and the Civil War*. New York: Alfred Knopf, 1965.

Goldin, Claudia D. "The Economics of Emancipation." *Journal of Economic History* 33 (1973): 66–85.

Goldin, Claudia D., and Frank D. Lewis. "The Economic Cost of the American Civil War: Estimates and Implications." *Journal of Economic History* 35 (1975): 299–326.

Gunderson, Gerald. "The Origin of the American Civil War." *Journal of Economic History* 34 (1974): 915–950.

Hacker, Louis. *The Triumph of American Capitalism*. New York: Columbia University Press, 1940.

James, John A. "The Optimal Tariff in the Antebellum United States." *American Economic Review* 71 (1981): 726–734.

Kessel, Reuben, and Armen Alchian. "Real Wages in the North during the Civil War: Mitchell's Data Reinterpreted." *Journal of Law and Economics* 2 (1959): 95–113.

Lebergott, Stanley. "Through the Blockade: The Profitability and Extent of Cotton Smuggling, 1861–1865." *Journal of Economic History* 41 (1981): 867–888.

Lerner, Eugene. "The Monetary and Fiscal Programs of the Confederate Government, 1861–1865." *Journal of Political Economy* 62 (1954): 506–522.

———. "Money, Prices, and Wages in the Confederacy, 1861–1865." *Journal of Political Economy* 63 (1955): 20–40.

Meyer, David R. "The Industrial Retardation of Southern Cities, 1860–1880." *Explorations in Economic History* 25 (1988): 366–386.

Olmstead, Alan. "The Civil War as a Catalyst of Technological Change in Agriculture." *Business and Economic History* 5 (1976): 36–50.

Otto, John Solomon. *Southern Agriculture during the Civil War Era, 1860–1880*. Westport, CT: Greenwood, 1994.

Paludan, Phillip S. *A People's Contest: The Union and Civil War, 1861–1865*. New York: Harper & Row, 1988.

Pecquet, Gary M. "Money in the Trans-Mississippi Confederacy and the Confederate Currency Reform Act of 1864." *Explorations in Economic History* 24 (1987): 218–243.

Ransom, Roger L. *Conflict and Compromise: The Political Economy of Slavery, Emancipation, and the American Civil War*. New York: Cambridge University Press, 1989.

Rasmussen, Wayne. "The Civil War: A Catalyst of Agricultural Revolution." *Agricultural History* 39 (1965): 187–195.

Roll, Richard. "Interest Rates and Price Expectations during the Civil War." *Journal of Economic History* 32 (1972): 476–498.

Surdam, David G. "Cotton's Potential as Economic Weapon: The Antebellum and Wartime Markets for Cotton Textiles." *Agricultural History* 68 (1994): 122–145.

Sylla, Richard. "The United States, 1863–1913." In Rondo Cameron, ed. *Banking and Economic Development: Some Lessons from History*. New York: Oxford University Press, 1972.

Temin, Peter. "The Post-Bellum Recovery of the South and the Cost of the Civil War." *Journal of Economic History* 36 (1976): 898–907.

Todd, R. C. *Confederate Finance*. Athens, GA: University of Georgia Press, 1954.

Williamson, Jeffrey G. "Watersheds and Turning Points: Conjectures on the Long-Term

Impact of Civil War Financing.'' *Journal of Economic History* 34 (1974): 636–661.

Wright, Gavin. *The Political Economy of the Cotton South.* New York: W. W. Norton and Company, 1978.

39

Northern Social Conditions

J. Matthew Gallman

Until fairly recently, histories of the American Civil War paid scant attention to social conditions on the Northern home front. The more comprehensive texts devoted a few paragraphs to New York City's draft riots and perhaps to the voluntary efforts of the United States Sanitary Commission, but then they quickly returned to the more familiar political events and economic conditions. Nineteenth-century social and urban historians traditionally gave the Civil War equally shabby treatment. Case studies spanning the 1860s often made only the barest nod toward the four years of carnage before turning to broader patterns of development. Those scholars who did focus on Northern home front topics did not seem engaged in the debates that framed broader historical discourse. Thus, works on women during the war did not necessarily speak to the emerging literature in women's history; wartime urban studies were cast in traditional city biography fashion. In 1989 Maris Vinovskis surveyed this terrain and asked a *Journal of American History* audience, "Have Social Historians Lost the Civil War?"

In truth, Vinovskis's essay was less a call to arms than a rallying cry. For a decade or more, graduate students trained in various facets of social history had begun turning their attention to the Civil War. Others, with broader chronological fish to fry, were asking how the Civil War affected their areas of interest. In 1990 Vinovskis brought some of this early work together in an edited collection, *Toward a Social History of the American Civil War: Exploratory Essays*. More recently, these new findings have helped shape not only Civil War histories but other topical texts. The fourth edition of Howard P. Chudacoff and Judith E. Smith's fine *The Evolution of American Urban Society* (1994) includes the section "Cities and the Civil War," which did not exist in the 1988 edition. Consequently, the social historian of the Civil War must cast an increasingly wide bibliographic net. Glenna Matthews's *The Rise of Public Woman: Woman's Power and Woman's Place in the United States, 1630–1970* (1992) will not turn up in even the most craftily designed Civil War computer search, but it includes a superb chapter, "Northern Women and the Crisis of the Union."

This chapter summarizes the central books and articles on Northern social conditions, but students should also take care to consider broader topical studies that span the war years.

GENERAL HISTORIES AND BIBLIOGRAPHIES

Social historians should not neglect the information and arguments in the leading general histories of the Civil War. Both James M. McPherson's monumental narrative history, *Battle Cry of Freedom: The Civil War Era* (1988), and his excellent text, *Ordeal by Fire: The Civil War and Reconstruction* (1992), address the central social issues in the context of broader military and political concerns. For a useful chronology of the war, with some attention to home front events, see Eugene B. Long, *The Civil War Day by Day: An Almanac, 1861–1865* (1971).

A more detailed exploration should begin with Emerson David Fite, *Social and Industrial Conditions in the North during the Civil War* (1910). Fite was particularly interested in economic issues, and some of his findings are now dated, but anyone venturing into this classic book will be rewarded with valuable insights and useful pearls. Nevertheless, Fite's book has been largely superseded by Phillip Shaw Paludan's *"A People's Contest": The Union and Civil War, 1861–1865* (1989). Paludan's book, part of the New American Nation series, is particularly interested in exploring the interactions between the Civil War and the industrial revolution in shaping American development. Whereas *"A People's Contest"* sees the sectional conflict as a crucial step in the process of modernization, J. Matthew Gallman's *The North Fights the Civil War: The Home Front* (1994) finds broad continuities beneath many of the war-related changes.

For a useful collection of primary sources, with occasional commentary, see Charles Winston Smith and Charles Judah, editors, *Life in the North during the Civil War: A Source History* (1966). And for a sampling of the recent scholarship see Vinovskis's *Toward a Social History of the American Civil War*. Vinovskis's "Have Social Historians Lost the Civil War?" which is reprinted in this collection, includes a superb discussion of the demographic impact of the war on the North. On the war's impact on organized labor see David Montgomery's *Beyond Equality: Labor and the Radical Republicans* (1967). Although he is most concerned with economic and political issues, Richard F. Bensel's provocative *Yankee Leviathan: The Origins of Central State Authority in America, 1859–1879* (1990)—offering a political scientist's perspective on the Civil War era—includes interesting challenges for the social historian.

The books by McPherson, Paludan, and Gallman include extensive bibliographic essays, but for more bibliographic information, see Eugene C. Murdock, *The Civil War in the North: A Selective Annotated Bibliography* (1987). Garold L. Cole, *Civil War Eyewitnesses: An Annotated Bibliography of Books and Articles, 1955–1986* (1988), is a comprehensive, well-indexed list of published accounts by soldiers and civilians, including many that speak to social conditions on the home front.

LOCAL STUDIES

Students seeking the wartime history of a particular town or city will very likely discover at least one study tracing the movements of local regiments and documenting the actions of political leaders, benevolent organizations, and the like. Some of these books and articles appear in Murdock's bibliography. But although such studies are an excellent entrée into the history of a particular place, as well as a useful source for personal narratives, they tend to be anecdotal rather than analytic and thus are of less value to social historians in search of broader patterns of experience. There are also several—largely political—studies of particular Northern states: Arthur C. Cole, *The Era of the Civil War, 1848–1870* (1919); Eugene H. Rosenboom, *The Civil War Era, 1850–1873* (1944) (on Ohio); John Niven, *Connecticut for the Union* (1965); Emma Lou Thornbrough, *Indiana in the Civil War, 1850–1880* (1965); and Richard N. Current, *The History of Wisconsin: The Civil War Era, 1848–1873* (1976).

Of the older local studies, the most useful is Margaret Leech's Pulitzer Prize–winning *Reveille in Washington, 1860–1865* (1941), which was reprinted in 1991 with a new introduction by James M. McPherson. On the nation's capital, see also Constance McLaughlin Green, *Washington: Village and Capital, 1800–1878* (1962). Most of the path-breaking community studies of the 1960s and 1970s ignored the Civil War, sometimes by relying on decadal data from the U.S. census. Among the noteworthy exceptions are Michael Frisch, *Town into City: Springfield, Massachusetts, and the Meaning of Community, 1840–1880* (1972), which examines the dramatic effect that the war had on the site of a major Union arsenal; and Don Harrison Doyle, *The Social Order of a Frontier Community: Jacksonville, Illinois, 1825–1870* (1978), a study of a small midwestern town that suffered through crippling divisions during the Civil War. Alan Dawley's *Class and Community: The Industrial Revolution in Lynn* (1976) includes some discussion of the ways in which the issues and ideals of the Civil War undercut the creation of class consciousness.

Several more recent studies have examined the wartime histories of Northern cities. J. Matthew Gallman, *Mastering Wartime: A Social History of Philadelphia during the Civil War* (1990), considers how that city adjusted to the war's challenges in a series of topical discussions including recruiting, separation, benevolence, civic ritual, and disorder. For an examination of political conflicts in the City of Brotherly Love, see William Dusinberre, *Civil War Issues in Philadelphia, 1856–1865* (1965). Despite its title, Iver Bernstein's *The New York City Draft Riots: Their Significance for American Society and Politics in the Age of the Civil War* (1990) is less a detailed analysis of the July 1863 riots than it is a fascinating reconstruction of the interaction of class, race, and ethnicity in midcentury New York. For a more comprehensive but much less analytic account of wartime New York City, see Ernest A. McKay, *The Civil War and New York City* (1990). Theodore Karamanski's *Rally 'Round the Flag: Chicago and the Civil War* (1993), like McKay's study, surveys the city's contribution to wartime events without attempting to place the story in a broader interpretive context. Robin Einhorn examines the war's impact on Chicago politics in "The Civil War and Municipal Government in Chicago," in Vinovskis's *Toward a Social History of the American Civil War*. For a study of the wartime labor conflicts in the Pennsylvania coal fields, written largely from the workers' perspective, see Grace Palladino, *Another Civil War: Labor, Capital, and the State in the Anthracite Regions of Pennsylvania, 1840–68* (1990).

Two important articles have treated the war's effect on smaller New England communities. For an account of one Massachusetts town, see Emily J. Harris, "Sons and Soldiers: Deerfield, Massachusetts, and the Civil War" (1984). Thomas R. Kemp's "Community and War: The Civil War Experience in Two New Hampshire Towns" (in the Vinovskis collection) compares the wartime experiences of the pro-Republican Claremont, New Hampshire, and the Democratic Newport.

SOLDIERS AND COMMUNITIES

The task of filling the ranks presented the Union with crucial political and logistical challenges while testing the resolve of individual communities charged with meeting enlistment quotas. For studies of the draft and its implications for Northern society, see James W. Geary, *We Need Men: The Union Draft in the Civil War* (1991), and Eugene C. Murdock, *One Million Men: The Civil War Draft in the North* (1971). Geary's book surveys the extensive article literature on conscription, but see also his "Civil War Conscription in the North: A Historiographical Review" (1986).

One of the perennial problems for Civil War historians concerns the makeup of the Union army. To what extent did the legislation allowing for substitutes and commutation fees create a "Rich Man's war and a Poor Man's fight"? Both Geary and Murdock address the issue, as do McPherson and Gallman, but see also Eugene C. Murdock, "Was It a Poor Man's Fight?" (1964); Hugh Earnhart, "Commutation: Democratic or Undemocratic?" (1966); and Peter Levine, "Draft Evasion in the North during the Civil War, 1863–1865" (1981). Murdock's study of portions of New York State and Earnhart's analysis of Ohio data agree that the controversial commutation fee actually aided the working classes by maintaining a ceiling on the cost of avoiding service. Levine takes a broader view, examining those draft districts that had the highest numbers of conscripts who failed to report once called. In "Who Fought for the North in the Civil War?" (1986), William Rorabaugh considers the variables that led Concord, Massachusetts, men to serve in the Union army. For a more sophisticated analysis of the effects of age, ethnicity, occupation, wealth, and education on enlistments in Newburyport, Massachusetts, see Vinovskis, "Have Social Historians Lost the Civil War?"

In addition to the extensive scholarship on recruiting and the draft, there has been a rising interest in the connections between soldiers and the home front. Gerald Linderman's *Embattled Courage: The Experience of Combat in the American Civil War* (1987) traces the soldier's evolving view of courage over four years of bloody conflict. One of Linderman's crucial observations is that as men in the field underwent a painful transition from enthusiasm to disillusionment, they found less and less common ground with the home front patriots they left behind. In *Civil War Soldiers: Their Expectations and Their Experiences* (1988) Reid Mitchell discusses reasons for enlistment and touches on relationships between soldiers and civilians. Mitchell takes the latter issues much further in his prize-winning *The Vacant Chair: The Northern Soldier Leaves Home* (1993), which established the myriad of powerful emotional and symbolic links between the military camps and the home front. For an interesting analysis of another side of the community-soldier relationship, see Judith Hallock, "The Role of the Community in Civil War Desertion" (1983). Linderman includes a useful discussion about the soldier's postwar experience, but see also Stuart McConnell, *Glorious Contentment: The Grand Army of the Republic, 1865–1900* (1992).

VOLUNTARISM AND BENEVOLENCE

There is still much work to be done on Civil War voluntarism. For an excellent broad survey see Robert H. Bremner, *The Public Good: Philanthropy and Welfare in the Civil War Era* (1980). Bremner places wartime philanthropy in a broader context in his *American Philanthropy* (1988). For a useful institutional history of the United States Sanitary Commission, see William Q. Maxwell, *Lincoln's Fifth Wheel: The Political History of the United States Sanitary Commission* (1956). J. Matthew Gallman's "Voluntarism in Wartime: Philadelphia's Great Central Fair," in Vinovskis's *Toward a Social History of the American Civil War,* considers the structural and gender implications of a major Sanitary Commission fund raiser.

One particular issue that deserves further scrutiny is the importance of wartime voluntarism in molding postwar experiences. George Frederickson's *The Inner Civil War: Northern Intellectuals and the Crisis of the Union* (1965) argues that the Sanitary Commission's central (male) leadership used the war as an opportunity to inculcate the virtues of efficiency and order. Gallman's

Mastering Wartime finds evidence that benevolent Philadelphians followed traditional, decentralized practices despite the national rhetoric. Karamanski's *Rally 'Round the Flag* notes the importance of female leadership—most notably Mary Livermore and Jane C. Hoge—in directing the efforts of the Sanitary Commission's midwestern branch. For much more material on the role of women in wartime benevolence, see the next section.

WOMEN AND WARTIME

In the years after the Civil War, various books chronicled the contributions of women from both the North and the South. Two widely distributed books were Frank Moore, *Women of the War: Their Heroism and Self-Sacrifice* (1866), and Linus Pierpont Brockett and Mary C. Vaughan, *Women at War: A Record of Their Patriotic Contributions, Heroism, Toils and Sacrifice during the Civil War* (1867). As their subtitles suggest, both volumes celebrated women who volunteered at home and on the battlefield. For more recent surveys, see Agatha Young, *Women and the Crisis: Women of the North in the Civil War* (1959), and Mary Elizabeth Massey, *Bonnet Brigades* (1966), which also discusses the South. Together these books provided a good overview of the contributions of individual women to the war effort, but as interpretative histories of women's wartime experiences, they left much room for further scholarship. Although the last several years have witnessed the publication of numerous studies addressing the experience of Northern women, we still lack a comprehensive history on the order of George C. Rable's *Civil Wars: Women and the Crisis of Southern Nationalism* (1989).

For a good, if uneven, sampling of the recent literature on gender in both the North and the South, see Catherine Clinton and Nina Silber, eds., *Divided Houses: Gender and the Civil War* (1992). Marilyn Mayer Culpepper's *Trials and Triumphs: The Women of the American Civil War* (1991) is an interesting combination of forms, blending quotations from a wide range of primary sources with short analytic passages into a topical history of white women during wartime. On the experiences of African-American women, see Dorothy Sterling, ed., *We Are Your Sisters: Black Women in the Nineteenth Century* (1984).

Three recent books spanning the war years discuss important aspects of women's public activism. Mary Ryan's fascinating *Women in Public: Between Banners and Ballots, 1825–1880* (1990) uncovers the public experiences of women in New Orleans, New York, and San Francisco. For a sophisticated reading of the effect of benevolent work on a cohort of young Northern women, see Lori Ginsberg, *Women and the Work of Benevolence: Morality, Politics, and Class in the Nineteenth-Century United States* (1992). Building on George Fredrickson's analysis of male Northern intellectuals, Ginsberg finds that these young female activists developed a powerful "passion for efficiency," which stayed with them into the postwar years. And for an analysis of leading wartime women in the abolitionist movement and their connections to national politics, see

Wendy Hamand Venet, *Neither Ballots nor Bullets: Women Abolitionists and the Civil War* (1991). For an excellent brief survey of the public roles of wartime women in the context of American history, see Matthews, *The Rise of Public Woman*. Two recent books have revisited the contributions of specific Northern women. In *Yankee Women: Gender Battles in the Civil War* (1994), Elizabeth D. Leonard traces the lives of Sophronia Bucklin, Annie Wittenmyer, and Mary Walker, arguing that each of these middle-class women had to work within a world of rigid antebellum gender roles. For a biography of one of the North's great benevolent figures, see Stephen Oates, *A Woman of Valor: Clara Barton and the Civil War* (1994). In her article "Race, Gender, and Bureaucracy: Civil War Army Nurses and the Pension Bureau" (1994) Jane E. Schultz mines the Federal pension records for evidence of the wartime and postwar experiences of female nurses and hospital workers, with particular attention to the importance of racial discrimination.

AFRICAN AMERICANS ON THE HOME FRONT

The historiographies of emancipation and black military service are discussed elsewhere in this book. Although there are several fine collections of primary documents, we still do not have a complete history of Northern African Americans during the Civil War. For an older general history of the black wartime experience see Benjamin Quarles, *The Negro in the Civil War* (1953). For an excellent history of abolitionism and the pursuit of racial equality—by both black and white abolitionists—see James M. McPherson, *The Struggle for Equality: Abolitionists and the Negro in the Civil War and Reconstruction* (1964). McPherson also assembled a wide assortment of primary sources, interspersed with analytic commentary, in *The Negro's Civil War* (1991). For documentary evidence on African-American women see Sterling's *We Are Your Sisters*. A superb collection of primary sources on all aspects of the Civil War experience of African Americans is assembled in Ira Berlin et al., eds., *Freedom: A Documentary History of Emancipation* (1982–). Several of the books and essays discussed below consider antiblack violence during the war years.

OPPOSITION TO THE WAR

Northerners questioned the Union's war measures at various levels of public life, from organized party politics to violent street protests. Politics in the North is discussed elsewhere in this book, but for a good summary of the political context of organized dissent, see James A. Rawley, *The Politics of Union: Northern Politics during the Civil War* (1974), and Joel Silbey, *A Respectable Minority: The Democratic Party in the Civil War Era* (1977). And for debates within Congress, see Allan G. Bogue's *The Earnest Men: Republicans of the Civil War Senate* (1981) and *The Congressman's Civil War* (1989).

Some of the most energetic debate—then and now—centered on the constitutional issues raised by the Lincoln administration. Mark E. Neely, Jr., *The*

Fate of Liberty: Abraham Lincoln and Civil Liberties (1991), is an exhaustive study of civil liberties in the North, including valuable estimates of political arrests and intriguing analysis of the ebbs and flows in the fate of Northern liberty. For a more top-down analysis of the intersection of constitutional and political issues, James G. Randall's classic *Constitutional Problems under Lincoln* (1951) is still useful, but see also Harold Hyman, *"A More Perfect Union": The Impact of the Civil War and Reconstruction on the Constitution* (1973); Phillip Shaw Paludan, *A Covenant with Death: The Constitution, Law and Equality in the Civil War Era* (1975); and Harold Hyman and William Wiecek, *Equal Justice under Law: Constitutional Development* (1982). For a vigorous defense of Abraham Lincoln's commitment to the Constitution, see Paludan, *The Presidency of Abraham Lincoln* (1994), which includes an extensive bibliographic essay touching on constitutional and political issues. Many of the leading pamphlets of the day are assembled in Frank Freidel, ed., *Union Pamphlets of the Civil War, 1861–1865* (1967).

Frank Klement has examined the public and secret actions of the North's most extreme political dissenters in *The Limits of Dissent: Clement Vallandigham and the Civil War* (1970) and *Dark Lanterns: Secret Political Societies, Conspiracies, and Treason Trials in the Civil War* (1984). For a discussion of dissent and political arrests in Philadelphia and Pennsylvania, see Dusinberre, *Civil War Issues in Philadelphia,* and Arnold Shankman, *The Pennsylvania Antiwar Movement, 1861–1865* (1980).

Although we lack a comprehensive history of home front violence, several community and regional studies have connected rioting to particular local issues. On the April 1861 riots in Baltimore, see Charles B. Clark, "Baltimore and the Attack on the Sixth Massachusetts Regiment, April 19, 1861" (1961). For the mayor's version of events, see William Brown, *Baltimore and the Nineteenth of April, 1861* (Baltimore, 1887). Bernstein's *The New York City Draft Riots* has the July 1863 bloodshed at its center, but for a more comprehensive treatment, see Adrian Cook, *The Armies of the Streets: The New York City Draft Riots of 1863* (1974). Grace Palladino's *Another Civil War* examines violence in the Pennsylvania coal fields, finding crucial links between labor unrest and tensions over conscription. J. Matthew Gallman asks how Philadelphia managed to avoid wartime rioting in "Preserving the Peace: Order and Disorder in Civil War Philadelphia" (1988). Gallman's article also surveys the article literature on wartime riots in other Northern cities and towns. For an excellent account of guerrilla warfare in an occupied border state, see Michael Fellman, *Inside War: The Guerrilla Conflict in Missouri during the American Civil War* (1989).

The issue of Civil War crime has attracted periodic scholarly interest. For the classic formulation of the issues see Edith Abbott, "The Civil War and the Crime Wave of 1865–1870" (1927). Eric Monkkonen tackled the issue in *Police in Urban America, 1860–1920* (1981), but see also Gallman, *Mastering Wartime.*

LITERARY AND INTELLECTUAL HISTORIES

The Civil War has always posed particularly intriguing questions for intellectual historians of all stripes. Such unprecedented carnage *must* have left an enormous mark on the nation's psyche; exactly what shape did that mark take? Although we lack a comprehensive history, various scholars have examined particular strata of Northern intellectual life.

For a discussion of wartime literature, encompassing diaries and pamphlets as well as fiction and poetry, see Edmund Wilson, *Patriotic Gore: Studies in the Literature of the American Civil War* (1962). Whereas Wilson's sprawling history remains a valuable resource, readers should also see literary critic Daniel Aaron's *The Unwritten War: American Writers and the Civil War* (1973). Both Aaron and Wilson are disappointed that the nation's great conflict never produced a literary epic worthy of its terrible cost. As Aaron points out, although many of the era's great writers were touched by the war, most studiously avoided full immersion in its butchery. For a good introduction to the works of one possible exception, see Walter Lowenfels, ed., *Walt Whitman's Civil War* (1960). Louis P. Masur has collected diaries, letters and occasional essays from Whitman and thirteen other authors—primarily Northerners—in *". . . the real war will never get in the books": Selections from Writers during the Civil War* (1993). For an application of literary-critical theory to two aspects of Civil War "reporting," see Timothy Sweet, *Traces of War: Poetry, Photography, and the Crisis of the Union* (1990). There is still much to learn about the war's impact on popular literature. Kathleen Diffley, *Where My Heart Is Turning Ever: Civil War Stories and Constitutional Reform, 1861–1876* (1992), considers several hundred stories published in popular magazines. For a valuable catalog of Civil War fiction written both during and after the war, see Albert J. Menendez, *Civil War Novels: An Annotated Bibliography* (1986).

George Frederickson's *The Inner Civil War* is still the best analysis of the war's impact on Northern intellectuals and of their impact on the war and its aftermath. For a wide-ranging analysis of Lincoln as orator and of his most famous speech, see Garry Wills, *Lincoln at Gettysburg: The Words That Remade America* (1992). Several scholars have asked how the events surrounding the war affected popular thought. For antebellum context see Lewis Saum, *The Popular Mood of Pre-Civil War America* (1980). In *Liberty, Virtue, and Progress: Northerners and Their War for the Union* (1988), Earl Hess examines Northerners' private and public writings, concluding that the core values that they took into the conflict survived the war largely unscathed. Randall C. Jimerson's *The Private Civil War: Popular Thought during the Sectional Conflict* (1988) takes a similar approach but uses a broader range of sources from both the Union and the Confederacy to consider a smaller range of topics. The popular response to Lincoln's assassination is the focus of Thomas Reed Turner, *Beware the People Weeping: Public Opinion and the Assassination of Abraham Lincoln* (1982). Anne C. Rose, *Victorian America and the Civil War* (1992), mines the memoirs of seventy-five middle-class men and women to place the war in a broader intellectual context, concluding that the Civil War—and its memory—was shaped by the central tenets of Victorian culture. For a short history of mid-nineteenth century American culture spanning the war years, see Louise A. Stevenson, *The Victorian Homefront: American Thought and Culture, 1860–1880* (1991).

Information from the battlefield arrived home with unfamiliar speed during the Civil War. Several older studies survey the history of wartime newspaper reporting. See J. Cutler Andrews, *The North Reports the Civil War* (1955); Louis M. Starr, *Bohemian Brigade: Civil War Newsmen in Action* (1953); and Bernard A. Weisberger, *Reporters for the Union* (1953). But it was not the reported words, but the pictures, that made this war a new and alarming experience for civilians at home. William A. Frassanito has painstakenly reconstructed the photographic history of the East's two greatest battles in *Antietam: The Photographic Legacy of America's Bloodiest Day* (1978) and *Gettysburg: A Journey in Time* (1975).

Phillip Paludan's *"A People's Contest,"* which considers various aspects of the Civil War's intellectual history, is particularly strong in grappling with the conflict's religious implications. For the Civil War's impact on Protestantism, see James Moorhead, *American Apocalypse: Yankee Protestants and the Civil War, 1860–1869* (1978). For the wartime experience of American Jews see Bernard Korn, *American Jewry and the Civil War* (1951). Edward Needles Wright's *Conscientious Objectors and the Civil War* (1931) includes important information, but it should be supplemented with the more recent manpower studies.

BIBLIOGRAPHY

Aaron, Daniel. *The Unwritten War: American Writers and the Civil War.* New York: Knopf, 1973; rev. ed., Madison, WI: University of Wisconsin Press, 1987.

Abbott, Edith. "The Civil War and the Crime Wave of 1865–1870." *Social Science Review* 1 (June 1927): 212–234.

Andrews, J. Cutler. *The North Reports the Civil War.* 1955. Reprint, Pittsburgh: University of Pittsburgh Press, 1985.

Bensel, Richard F. *Yankee Leviathan: The Origins of Central State Authority in America, 1859–1879.* New York: Cambridge University Press, 1990.

Berlin, Ira, et al., eds. *Freedom: A Documentary History of Emancipation, 1861–1867.* New York: Cambridge University Press, 1982–.

Bernstein, Iver. *The New York City Draft Riots: Their Significance for American Society and Politics in the Age of the Civil War.* New York: Oxford University Press, 1990.

Bogue, Allan G. *The Congressman's Civil War.* New York: Cambridge University Press, 1989.

———. *The Earnest Men: Republicans of the Civil War Senate.* Ithaca: Cornell University Press, 1981.

Bremner, Robert H. *American Philanthropy*. 2d ed. Chicago: University of Chicago Press, 1988.

———. *The Public Good: Philanthropy and Welfare in the Civil War Era*. New York: Knopf, 1980.

Brockett, Linus Pierpont, and Mary C. Vaughan. *Women at War: A Record of Their Patriotic Contributions, Heroism, Toils and Sacrifice during the Civil War*. 1867. Reprint, New York: Longmeadow, 1993.

Brown, William. *Baltimore and the Nineteenth of April, 1861*. Baltimore, 1887.

Chudacoff, Howard P., and Judith E. Smith. *The Evolution of American Urban Society*. Englewood Cliffs, NJ: Prentice Hall, 1994.

Clark, Charles B. "Baltimore and the Attack on the Sixth Massachusetts Regiment, April 19, 1861." *Maryland Historical Magazine* 56 (March 1961): 39–71.

Clinton, Catherine, and Nina Silber, eds. *Divided Houses: Gender and the Civil War*. New York: Hill and Wang, 1992.

Cole, Arthur C. *The Era of the Civil War, 1848–1870*. 1919. Reprint, Urbana: University of Illinois Press, 1987.

Cole, Garold L. *Civil War Eyewitnesses: An Annotated Bibliography of Books and Articles, 1955–1986*. Columbia: University of South Carolina Press, 1988.

Cook, Adrian. *The Armies of the Streets: The New York City Draft Riots of 1863*. Lexington, KY: University of Kentucky Press, 1974.

Culpepper, Marilyn Mayer, ed. *Trials and Triumphs: The Women of the American Civil War*. East Lansing: Michigan State University Press, 1991.

Current, Richard. *The History of Wisconsin: The Civil War Era, 1848–1873*. 1976. Reprint, State Historical Society of Wisconsin, 1987.

Dawley, Alan. *Class and Community: The Industrial Revolution in Lynn*. Cambridge, MA: Harvard University Press, 1976.

Diffley, Kathleen. *Where My Heart Is Turning Ever: Civil War Stories and Constitutional Reform, 1861–1876*. Athens: University of Georgia Press, 1992.

Doyle, Don Harrison. *The Social Order of a Frontier Community: Jacksonville, Illinois, 1825–1870*. Urbana: University of Illinois Press, 1978.

Dusinberre, William. *Civil War Issues in Philadelphia, 1856–1865*. Philadelphia: University of Pennsylvania Press, 1965.

Earnhart, Hugh. "Commutation: Democratic or Undemocratic?" *Civil War History* 12 (June 1966): 132–142.

Fellman, Michael. *Inside War: The Guerrilla Conflict in Missouri during the American Civil War*. New York: Oxford University Press, 1989.

Fite, Emerson David. *Social and Industrial Conditions in the North during the Civil War*. 1910. Reprint, New York: Ungar, 1963.

Frassanito, William A. *Antietam: The Photographic Legacy of America's Bloodiest Day*. New York: Charles Scribner's Sons, 1978.

———. *Gettysburg: A Journey in Time*. New York: Charles Scribner's Sons, 1975.

Frederickson, George. *The Inner Civil War: Northern Intellectuals and the Crisis of the Union*. New York: Harper & Row, 1965.

Freidel, Frank, ed. *Union Pamphlets of the Civil War, 1861–1865*. 2 vols. Cambridge, MA: Harvard University Press, 1967.

Frisch, Michael. *Town into City: Springfield, Massachusetts, and the Meaning of Community, 1840–1880*. Cambridge, MA: Harvard University Press, 1972.

Gallman, J. Matthew. *Mastering Wartime: A Social History of Philadelphia during the Civil War*. New York: Cambridge University Press, 1990.

———. *The North Fights the Civil War: The Home Front*. Chicago: Ivan Dee, 1994.

———. "Preserving the Peace: Order and Disorder in Civil War Philadelphia." *Pennsylvania History* 55 (October 1988): 201–215.

Geary, James W. *We Need Men: The Union Draft in the Civil War*. DeKalb: Northern Illinois University Press, 1991.

———. "Civil War Conscription in the North: A Historiographical Review." *Civil War History* 32 (September 1986): 208–228.

Ginsberg, Lori. *Women and the Work of Benevolence: Morality, Politics, and Class in the Nineteenth-Century United States*. New Haven: Yale University Press, 1992.

Green, Constance McLaughlin. *Washington: Village and Capital, 1800–1878*. Princeton: Princeton University Press, 1962.

Hallock, Judith. "The Role of the Community in Civil War Desertion." *Civil War History* 29 (June 1983): 123–134.

Harris, Emily J. "Sons and Soldiers: Deerfield, Massachusetts, and the Civil War." *Civil War History* 30 (June 1984): 157–171.

Hess, Earl. *Liberty, Virtue, and Progress: Northerners and Their War for the Union*. New York: New York University Press, 1988.

Hyman, Harold. *"A More Perfect Union": The Impact of the Civil War and Reconstruction on the Constitution*. New York: Knopf, 1973.

Hyman, Harold, and William Wiecek. *Equal Justice under Law: Constitutional Development*. New York: Harper & Row, 1982.

Jimerson, Randall C. *The Private Civil War: Popular Thought during the Sectional Conflict*. Baton Rouge: Louisiana State University Press, 1988.

Karamanski, Theodore J. *Rally 'Round the Flag: Chicago and the Civil War*. Chicago: Nelson Hall, 1993.

Klement, Frank. *Dark Lanterns: Secret Political Societies, Conspiracies, and Treason Trials in the Civil War*. Baton Rouge: Louisiana State University Press, 1984.

———. *The Limits of Dissent: Clement Vallandigham and the Civil War*. Lexington: University of Kentucky Press, 1970.

Korn, Bertram. *American Jewry and the Civil War*. 1951. Reprint, New York: Atheneum, 1970.

Leech, Margaret. *Reveille in Washington, 1860–1865*. 1941. Reprint, New York: Carroll and Graf Publishers, 1991.

Leonard, Elizabeth D. *Yankee Women: Gender Battles in the Civil War*. New York: Norton, 1994.

Levine, Peter. "Draft Evasion in the North during the Civil War, 1863–1865." *Journal of American History* 67 (March 1981): 816–134.

Linderman, Gerald. *Embattled Courage: The Experience of Combat in the American Civil War*. New York: Free Press, 1987.

Long, Eugene B. *The Civil War Day by Day: An Almanac, 1861–1865*. Garden City, NY: Doubleday, 1971.

Lowenfels, Walter, ed. *Walt Whitman's Civil War*. New York: Da Capo Press, 1960.

McConnell, Stuart. *Glorious Contentment: The Grand Army of the Republic, 1865–1900*. Chapel Hill: University of North Carolina Press, 1992.

McKay, Ernest A. *The Civil War and New York City*. Syracuse: Syracuse University Press, 1990.

McPherson, James M. *Battle Cry of Freedom: The Civil War Era.* (New York: Oxford University Press, 1988.

———. *The Negro's Civil War: How American Blacks Felt and Acted during the War for the Union.* 1965. 3d ed., New York: Ballantine, 1991.

———. *Ordeal by Fire: The Civil War and Reconstruction.* 2d ed. New York: Alfred A. Knopf, 1992.

McPherson, James M. *The Struggle for Equality: Abolitionists and the Negro in the Civil War and Reconstruction.* Princeton: Princeton University Press, 1964.

Massey, Mary Elizabeth. *Bonnet Brigades.* 1966. Reissued, Lincoln: University of Nebraska Press, 1994.

Masur, Louis P., ed. *". . . the real war will never get in the books": Selections from Writers during the Civil War.* New York: Oxford University Press, 1993.

Matthews, Glenna. *The Rise of Public Woman: Woman's Power and Woman's Place in the United States, 1630–1970.* New York: Oxford University Press, 1992.

Maxwell, William Q. *Lincoln's Fifth Wheel: The Political History of the United States Sanitary Commission.* New York: Longmans, 1956.

Mitchell, Reid. *Civil War Soldiers: Their Expectations and Their Experiences.* New York: Touchstone, 1988.

Menendez, Albert J. *Civil War Novels: An Annotated Bibliography.* New York: Garland Publishers, 1986.

Mitchell, Reid. *The Vacant Chair: The Northern Soldier Leaves Home.* New York: Oxford University Press, 1993.

Monkkonnen, Eric. *Police in Urban America, 1860–1920.* New York: Cambridge University Press, 1981.

Montgomery, David. *Beyond Equality: Labor and the Radical Republicans.* New York: Vintage, 1967.

Moore, Frank. *Women of the War: Their Heroism and Self-Sacrifice.* Hartford, CT: S. S. Scranton, 1866.

Moorhead, James. *American Apocalypse: Yankee Protestants and the Civil War, 1860–1869.* New Haven: Yale University Press, 1978.

Murdock, Eugene C. *The Civil War in the North: A Selective Annotated Bibliography.* New York: Garland, 1987.

———. *One Million Men: The Civil War Draft in the North.* 1971. Reprint, Wesport, CT: Greenwood Press, 1980.

———. "Was It a Poor Man's Fight?" *Civil War History* 10 (September 1964): 241–245.

Neely, Mark E., Jr. *The Fate of Liberty: Abraham Lincoln and Civil Liberties.* New York: Oxford University Press, 1991.

Niven, John. *Connecticut for the Union: The Role of the State in the Civil War.* New Haven: Yale University Press, 1965.

Oates, Stephen. *A Woman of Valor: Clara Barton and the Civil War.* New York: Free Press, 1994.

Palladino, Grace. *Another Civil War: Labor, Capital, and the State in the Anthracite Regions of Pennsylvania, 1840–68.* Urbana: University of Illinois, 1990.

Paludan, Phillip Shaw. *"A People's Contest": The Union and Civil War, 1861–1865.* New York: Harper & Row, 1989.

———. *A Covenant with Death: The Constitution, Law and Equality in the Civil War Era.* Urbana: University of Illinois Press, 1975.

———. *The Presidency of Abraham Lincoln.* Lawrence: University of Kansas Press, 1994.

Quarles, Benjamin. *The Negro in the Civil War.* 1953. Reprint, New York: Da Capo, 1989.

Rable, George C. *Civil Wars: Women and the Crisis of Southern Nationalism.* Urbana: University of Illinois Press, 1989.

Randall, James G. *Constitutional Problems under Lincoln.* Urbana: University of Illinois Press, 1951.

Rawley, James A. *The Politics of Union: Northern Politics during the Civil War.* Lincoln: University of Nebraska Press, 1974.

Rorabaugh, William. "Who Fought for the North in the Civil War? Concord, Massachusetts, Enlistments." *Journal of American History* 73 (December 1986): 695–701.

Rose, Anne C. *Victorian America and the Civil War.* New York: Cambridge University Press, 1992.

Rosenboom, Eugene H. *The Civil War Era, 1850–1873.* Columbus: Ohio State Archaeological and Historical Society, 1944.

Ryan, Mary. *Women in Public: Between Banners and Ballots, 1825–1880.* Baltimore: Johns Hopkins University Press, 1990.

Saum, Lewis. *The Popular Mood of Pre–Civil War America.* Westport, CT: Greenwood Press, 1980.

Schultz, Jane E. "Race, Gender, and Bureaucracy: Civil War Army Nurses and the Pension Bureau." *Journal of Women's History* 6 (Summer 1994): 45–69.

Shankman, Arnold. *The Pennsylvania Antiwar Movement, 1861–1865.* Cranbury, NJ: Fairleigh Dickinson University Press, 1980.

Silbey, Joel. *A Respectable Minority: The Democratic Party in the Civil War Era.* New York: Norton, 1977.

Smith, Charles Winston, and Charles Judah, eds. *Life in the North during the Civil War: A Source History.* Albuquerque: University of New Mexico Press, 1966.

Starr, Louis M. *Bohemian Brigade: Civil War Newsmen in Action.* 1953. Reprint, Madison, WI: University of Wisconsin Press, 1987.

Sterling, Dorothy, ed. *We Are Your Sisters: Black Women in the Nineteenth Century.* New York: Norton, 1984.

Stevenson, Louise A. *The Victorian Homefront: American Thought and Culture, 1860–1880.* New York: Twayne, 1991.

Sweet, Timothy. *Traces of War: Poetry, Photography, and the Crisis of the Union.* Baltimore: Johns Hopkins University Press, 1990.

Thornbrough, Emma Lou. *Indiana in the Civil War, 1850–1880.* 1965. Reprint, Indianapolis: Indiana University Press, 1992.

Turner, Thomas Reed. *Beware the People Weeping: Public Opinion and the Assassination of Abraham Lincoln.* Baton Rouge: Louisiana State University Press, 1982.

Venet, Wendy Hamand. *Neither Ballots nor Bullets: Women Abolitionists and the Civil War.* Charlottesville: University of Virginia Press, 1991.

Vinovskis, Maris. *Toward a Social History of the American Civil War: Exploratory Essays.* New York: Cambridge University Press, 1990.

———. "Have Social Historians Lost the Civil War? Some Preliminary Demographic Speculations." *Journal of American History* 76 (June 1989): 34–58.

Weisberger, Bernard A. *Reporters for the Union.* Boston: Little, Brown, 1953.

Wills, Garry. *Lincoln at Gettysburg: The Words That Remade America.* New York: Simon & Schuster, 1992.

Wilson, Edmund. *Patriotic Gore: Studies in the Literature of the American Civil War.* 1962. Reprint, Boston: Northeastern University Press, 1984.

Wright, Edward Needles. *Conscientious Objectors and the Civil War.* Philadelphia: University of Pennsylvania Press, 1931.

Young, Agatha. *Women and the Crisis: Women of the North in the Civil War.* New York: McDowell, Obolensky, 1959.

40

Southern Social Conditions

Bill Cecil-Fronsman

The study of the Confederate home front has undergone a dramatic transformation over the past several decades. The subject has been examined with a great deal of care by some of the region's best historians, but students who compare older studies with newer ones will be struck by changes in tone and emphasis. Many of the earlier studies of the Confederate home front were written by scholars who were themselves Southerners and were generally sympathetic with Southern society. More recent studies have taken a critical look at the South and in many instances have been written by Yankees (such as this author). This chapter will emphasize the more recent studies, though students would do well to consult both kinds. A good bibliographic guide to the earlier studies is Mary Elizabeth Massey, "The Confederate States of America: The Homefront" (1965).

GENERAL STUDIES

Most research topics are covered to some extent in a variety of general studies of the Confederacy. The most thorough account of the Confederate experience is E. Merton Coulter, *The Confederate States of America, 1861–1865* (1950). The book, part of a multivolume history of the South, is the product of a tremendous amount of research in primary and secondary sources. It is abounding with insight into numerous questions, but it also reflects an age when Southern social history could be written without paying adequate regard to women and African Americans, and its author's Confederate sympathies are apparent. A more modern treatment is Emory M. Thomas, *The Confederate Nation, 1861–*

1865 (1979). Also part of a larger series, the book emphasizes economics and government and is not as thorough as the older treatment. Nevertheless, it will introduce the student to many critical issues in the area of social developments. Other older though useful general accounts include Clement Eaton, *A History of the Southern Confederacy* (1954), and Charles P. Roland, *The Confederacy* (1960).

Two other older works address a wide range of issues on the general subject of the Confederate home front: Bell I. Wiley, *The Plain People of the Confederacy* (1944), and Charles W. Ramsdell, *Behind the Lines in the Southern Confederacy* (1944). Although less comprehensive than the other general accounts, they are highly readable volumes that offer considerable insight and detail and will help students get started. These works do tend to celebrate Southern society and do not take African Americans seriously. A more recent essay addresses social concerns from a different angle. Drew Gilpin Faust, *The Creation of Confederate Nationalism* (1988), explores the impact of the war (and ultimate defeat) on Confederates' ideology and identity.

State studies typically discuss military, political, and economic affairs, subjects that are beyond the scope of this chapter, but they also typically include a good deal of material on how the war affected ordinary people's lives. More to the point, they help establish the context in which social changes occurred. Some of the older state studies with material on social history are: Walter Lynwood Flemming, *Civil War and Reconstruction in Alabama* (1903); Jefferson Davis Bragg, *Louisiana in the Confederacy* (1941); John K. Bettersworth, *Confederate Mississippi* (1943); Charles E. Cauthen, *South Carolina Goes to War, 1861–1865* (1950); T. Conn Bryan, *Confederate Georgia* (1953); John G. Barnett; *The Civil War in North Carolina* (1963); and John E. Johns; *Florida during the Civil War* (1963).

More recent state treatments tend to be more focused on politics than on social history. Nevertheless, they contain material that will help students understand the tremendous ways that the war transformed social life. The most up-to-date treatment is in Archie P. McDonald, ed., *A Nation of Sovereign States: Secession and War in the Confederacy* (1994), a collection of essays on the individual Southern states by experts on each of them. For students interested in the impact of the war on an individual state, this is the place to begin.

For more recent book-length studies, see Malcolm C. McMillan, *The Disintegration of a Confederate State* (1986), for an account of Alabama. For a state whose role in the Old South and Confederacy has rarely been examined, see William H. Nulty, *Confederate Florida* (1990). Another recent account focuses on Florida's Gulf Coast: George E. Buker, *Blockaders, Refugees, and Contrabands* (1993). The most recent examination of a Confederate state is Carl Moneyhon, *The Impact of the Civil War and Reconstruction on Arkansas, 1850–1874* (1994). But also see Michael B. Dougan, *The People and Policies of a Frontier State in Wartime* (1976).

Though technically not a part of the Confederacy, the border slave states experienced many of the same patterns as their Confederate neighbors. Jean H. Baker, *The Politics of Continuity* (1973), is the best look at Maryland's home front. E. Merton Coulter wrote the classic account of Kentucky: *The Civil War and Readjustment in Kentucky* (1926), though more recent accounts supersede much of its treatment. See especially Lowell Harrison, *The Civil War in Kentucky* (1975). William E. Parrish, *Turbulent Partnership: Missouri and the Union, 1861–1865* (1963), rounds out the field. For a recent look at Oklahoma, see Mary Jane Warde, "Now the Wolf Has Come: The Civilian Civil War in the Indian Territory" (1993).

COMMUNITY STUDIES

Although state and regional studies help us to understand the Confederate home front, they necessarily obscure the day-to-day experiences of many Southerners. By looking at a community or group of communities, students get a greater sense of the tremendous diversity of Civil War experiences. They enable the student of social history to look at patterns under a microscope. Community studies have tended to point to a number of issues. They frequently highlight the suffering of ordinary people wrought by the war. As men went off to war, the women and remaining males had to survive with what was left. The war effort commanded a tremendous volume of resources, leading to serious shortages. Community studies also do an excellent job of highlighting the very real patterns of dissent that existed in the Confederacy.

Several accounts focus on the capital of the Confederacy. Alfred H. Bill, *The Beleaguered City* (1946), was among the first, though students should compare it with Emory M. Thomas, *The Confederate State of Richmond* (1971). An excellent study of a city that found itself in the middle of the war is Peter F. Walker, *Vicksburg: A People at War* (1960). For a follow-up of what happened after the Union occupied it, see James T. Currie, *Enclave: Vicksburg and Her Plantations, 1863–1870* (1980). Other book-length studies of Confederate cities are: Gerald M. Capers, *Occupied City: New Orleans under the Federals, 1862–1865* (1965); Kenneth Coleman, *Confederate Athens, 1861–1865* (1968); E. Milby Burton, *The Siege of Charleston, 1861–1865* (1970); Arthur W. Bergeron, *Confederate Mobile* (1991); and Peter Maslowski's account of wartime Nashville, *Treason Must Be Made Odious* (1978).

A number of articles look at the home front in Southern cities: Edward L. White III, "Key West during the Civil War: An Island of Discontent?" (1988); Ludwell H. Johnson III, "Blockade or Trade Monopoly: John A. Dix and the Union Occupation of Norfolk" (1985); Gary Mills, "Alexandria, Louisiana: A 'Confederate' City at War with Itself" (1980); Fedora Small Frank, "Nashville during the Civil War" (1980); David C. Humphrey, "A 'Very Muddy and Conflicting' View: The Civil War as Seen from Austin, Texas" (1991); Dora Alford, "A Decade of Change: Austin County, Texas, 1860–1870" (1994); and Dale A. Somers, "War and Play: The Civil War in New Orleans" (1973).

Studies of cities distort the picture of the typical Confederate because so few people lived in them. To appreciate the war's social impact, one needs to examine life in rural communities. Several recent books do excellent jobs of looking at the dynamics of rural Southern society during the war. Wayne K. Durrill, *War of Another Kind* (1990), is an in-depth analysis of Washington County, North Carolina, an eastern plantation county that fell into Union hands early on. Stephen V. Ash, *Middle Tennessee Transformed, 1860–1870* (1988), focuses on a group of counties that also came under Union occupation. Walter T. Durham, *Rebellion Revisited: A History of Sumner County, Tennessee, from 1861 to 1870* (1982), contains excellent Civil War material.

Several scholarly studies of local areas contain valuable material on social patterns during the war. Randolph B. Campbell, *A Southern Community in Crisis* (1983), examines power and class relations in Harrison County, Texas, and concludes that the war did not substantially alter these relationships. Robert C. Kenzer, *Kinship and Neighborhood in a Southern Community* (1987), examines the impact of the war on family and community life in Orange County, North Carolina. Another excellent study with substantial Civil War material is Daniel W. Crofts, *Old Southampton: Politics and Society in a Virginia County* (1992). For a review of other Virginia material see Gary W. Gallagher, "Home Front and Battlefield: Some Recent Literature Relating to Virginia and the Confederacy" (1990).

DISSENT

Several decades ago, historians discarded the notion that the Civil War saw a unified North battling a unified South. The first comprehensive look at the problem was Georgia L. Tatum, *Disloyalty in the Confederacy* (1934). A standard work by a leading historian of the South puts dissenters in a broader context: Carl N. Degler, *The Other South* (1974).

Although a variety of factors help explain the level of dissent, the tendency of recent studies has been to point to class divisions. In the prewar South, around three out of four whites lived in families that did not own slaves. Most of those whites who did own slaves owned only a handful. Fewer than 5 percent of all white families owned as many as twenty slaves, yet this minority commanded a disproportionately large share of the region's wealth, power, and prestige. The result was that class tensions existed during the prewar period, tensions that exploded into conflict once the Civil War broke out. Throughout the South, nonslaveholders (also known as yeomanry or common whites) resisted the Confederacy's attempts to force them to support the war effort. An older but still useful look at their role is Stephen E. Ambrose, "Yeoman Discontent in the Confederacy" (1962). Paul D. Escott has devoted much of his scholarly attention to this question. His "Southern Yeomen and the Confederacy" (1978) surveys the field, while his *Many Excellent People* (1985) addresses the broader issues of class in North Carolina during the second half of the nineteenth century.

The upper South, especially North Carolina, was the site of considerable wartime resistance, in large part because there were more nonslaveholders there than in the lower South. A good overview for the state is Marc Kruman, "Dissent in the Confederacy: The North Carolina Experience" (1981). I have examined the difficulty of securing the support for these "common whites" in *Common Whites: Class and Culture in Antebellum North Carolina* (1992), difficulties that greatly increased once the war broke out. Escott's *Many Excellent People* also emphasizes class conflict. Phillip Shaw Paludan, *Victims: A True Story of the Civil War* (1981), examines the massacre of thirteen unarmed dissenters in the North Carolina mountains. William T. Auman has studied the conflict in the North Carolina Piedmont: "Neighbor against Neighbor: The Inner Civil War in the Randolph County Area of Confederate North Carolina" (1984). Auman and David Scarboro report on North Carolinians' involvement in a Unionist organization: "The Heroes of America in Civil War North Carolina" (1981). Victoria E. Bynum, *Unruly Women* (1992), analyzes women's activities during the conflict in the Piedmont. Durrill's *War of Another Kind* examines the conflict in the northeastern part of the state. William W. Holden ran for governor in 1864 on a peace platform and has been the subject of two recent biographies: Horace C. Raper, *William W. Holden: North Carolina's Political Enigma* (1985), and William C. Harris, *William Woods Holden: Firebrand of North Carolina Politics* (1987).

Arkansas is another state with an extensive history of internal conflict. Moneyhon's *The Impact of the Civil War and Reconstruction on Arkansas* is the place to start. Ted R. Worley, "The Arkansas Peace Society of 1861" (1958) is an older but helpful look. A series of recent studies examines the guerrilla war in Arkansas: Carl H. Moneyhon, "Disloyalty and Class Consciousness in Southwestern Arkansas, 1852–1865" (1993); Daniel E. Sutherland, "Guerrillas: The Real War in Arkansas" (1993); and Kenneth C. Barnes, "The Williams Clan: Mountain Farmers and Union Fighters in North Central Arkansas" (1993).

Tennessee also had extensive Unionist movements. Fred Arthur Bailey, *Class and Tennessee's Confederate Generation* (1987), examines the comments of 1,250 former Confederates who responded to a questionnaire about their lives and prewar experiences and concludes that class relations shaped their lives. East Tennessee, like western North Carolina, was the scene of much anti-Confederate activity. J. Reuben Sheeler, "The Development of Unionism in East Tennessee" (1944), is an older look at the subject. A more recent study is Richard P. Gildrie, "Guerrilla Warfare in the Lower Cumberland River Valley, 1862–1865" (1990). William G. "Parson" Brownlow led East Tennessee opponents of the Confederacy. E. Merton Coulter, *William G. Brownlow: Fighting Parson of the Southern Highlands* (1937), is a good older account. See also

James W. Patton, *Unionism and Reconstruction in Tennessee, 1860–1867* (1934).

Much of the dissent in Virginia was in the western counties, which seceded in 1861 and joined the Union as the state of West Virginia in 1863. For an overview of that process, see Richard O. Curry, *A House Divided: A Study of Statehood Politics and the Copperhead Movement in West Virginia* (1964). But within the area that remained in the state, opposition to the Confederacy existed. Henry T. Shanks, "Disloyalty to the Confederacy in Southwestern Virginia, 1861–1865" (1944), and Kenneth W. Noe, "Red String Scare: Civil War Southwest Virginia and the Heroes of America" (1992), discuss the conflict in the southwestern part of the state. Although it never joined the Confederacy, Missouri was the scene of the most intense guerrilla conflict—with pro-Confederate and pro-Union forces. Michael Fellman, *Inside War* (1989), examines this bloody episode.

Although the lower South seems to have been more unified, conflicts did occur within the region. Two recent studies of common whites in Georgia examine their role in the Civil War and explain their support (or lack thereof) for the Confederacy: Stephen Hahn, *The Roots of Southern Populism* (1983), and J. William Harris, *Plain Folk and Gentry in a Slave Society* (1985). A recent analysis of Georgia's guerrilla war is Jonathan D. Sarris, "Anatomy of an Atrocity: The Madden Branch Massacre and Guerrilla Warfare in North Georgia" (1993).

Opposition to the Confederacy in Texas may have been of a different character than in the other states. An older look at Unionist sentiment in the Lone Star State is Claude Elliott, "Union Sentiment in Texas, 1861–1865" (1947). A more recent work, which focuses more on cultural differences among Anglos, Germans, blacks, and Hispanics rather than on class divisions, is James Marten, *Texas Divided* (1990). David P. Smith, "Conscription and Conflict on the Texas Frontier" (1990), looks at one area of resistance. Richard B. McCaslin, *Tainted Breeze* (1994), is an in-depth analysis of the execution of more than forty alleged Texas Unionists in 1862.

The remaining Confederate states appear to have had less opposition. On Alabama see two articles by Hugh C. Bailey: "Disloyalty in Early Confederate Alabama" (1957) and "Disaffection in the Alabama Hill Country, 1861" (1958). Durward Long, "Unanimity and Disloyalty in Secessionist Alabama" (1965), looks at the range of responses. An older but still useful look at class conflict in Louisiana throughout the nineteenth century is Roger W. Shugg, *Origins of Class Struggle in Louisiana* (1939). Other examinations of dissent include Ethel Taylor, "Discontent in Confederate Louisiana" (1961), and Barnes F. Lathrop, "Disaffection in Confederate Louisiana: The Case of William Hyman" (1958). Relatively little work has been done on dissenters in Mississippi. Rumors of a strong indigenous Unionist movement in Mississippi were put to rest in Rudy H. Leverett, *Legend of the Free State of Jones* (1984).

WOMEN

One of the great changes in the way historians have looked at the past is the growing emphasis on women's history. As contemporary women's rights advocates have called for a reassessment of women's place in society, historians have reassessed women's places in past societies. The movement to study women occurred concurrently with efforts to study ordinary people (rather than elites). Consequently, there have been many new works on women's history, and these newer studies look very different from those written before the feminist revolution.

The subject of women in the Confederacy attracted interest from a variety of traditional historians, who tended to emphasize elite women and pointed to their heroism and sacrifice. Francis B. Simkins and James W. Patton, *The Women of the Confederacy* (1936), was among the earliest scholarly versions of this genre. Other prefeminist histories of Confederate women include Mary Elizabeth Massey, *Bonnet Brigades* (1966), still in many ways the standard text; Katherine Jones, *When Sherman Came: Southern Women and the "Great War"* (1964); and Bell Irwin Wiley, *Confederate Women* (1975), which, although written after the feminist revolution had begun, nevertheless reflects the concerns of an older generation.

The first scholarly examination of Southern women to be influenced by feminism is Anne Firor Scott, *The Southern Lady* (1970), which covers women in the South from 1830 to 1930, including the Civil War. A good survey of women's lives in the nineteenth century, written by a scholar of Southern women's history, is Catherine Clinton, *The Other Civil War* (1984).

The most comprehensive modern account of Confederate women is George C. Rable, *Civil Wars: Women and the Crisis of Southern Nationalism* (1989), which examines how women's commitments to the Confederate cause held fast during the struggle. For women who were not committed to the cause, see Victoria Bynum's *Unruly Women*. Indispensable for students of women and the Confederacy is Catherine Clinton and Nina Silber, eds., *Divided Houses: Gender and the Civil War* (1992), a collection of essays that brings together much of the recent scholarship on gender and contains several important articles on Confederate women. Surprisingly, little has been done on Confederate women's experiences in specific regions. H. E. Sterkx, *Partners in Rebellion* (1970), is an older look at women in Alabama. John C. Inscoe, "Coping in Confederate Appalachia: Portrait of a Mountain Woman and Her Community at War" (1992), and Gordon McKinney, "Women's Role in Civil War Western North Carolina" (1992), discuss how women outside the plantation belt dealt with the crisis.

Diaries constitute one of the best sources of women's history. Every year far more Southern women's diaries are published than can be reviewed here. The most famous Civil War diary is that of Mary Chesnut, published most recently in a version edited by C. Vann Woodward: *Mary Chesnut's Civil War* (1981).

See also C. Vann Woodward, and Elisabeth Muhlenfield, *The Private Mary Chesnut: The Unpublished Civil War Diaries* (1984). For an essay that sheds tremendous light on how to interpret these diaries, see Drew Gilpin Faust, "Altars of Sacrifice: Confederate Women and the Narratives of War" (1990).

Students of women in the Confederacy should not neglect that in the states that seceded, 40 percent of the women were black. The Civil War experiences of African Americans will be examined in chapter 43 in this volume. But students of women's history should not neglect Jacqueline Jones, *Labor of Love, Labor of Sorrow* (1985), the definitive history of African-American women.

BIBLIOGRAPHY

Alford, Dora. "A Decade of Change: Austin County, Texas, 1860–1870." *South Texas Studies* 5 (1994): 131–163.

Ambrose, Stephen E. "Yeoman Discontent in the Confederacy." *Civil War History* 8 (1962): 259–268.

Ash, Steven V. "A Community War: Montgomery County, 1861–65." *Tennessee Historical Quarterly* 36 (1977): 30–43.

——. *Middle Tennessee Transformed, 1860–1870.* Baton Rouge: Louisiana State University Press, 1988.

——. "Poor Whites in the Occupied South, 1861–1865." *Journal of Southern History* 57 (1991): 39–62.

——. "White Virginians under Federal Occupation, 1861–1865." *Virginia Magazine of History and Biography* 98 (1990): 169–192.

Auman, William T. "Neighbor against Neighbor: The Inner Civil War in the Randolph County Area of Confederate North Carolina." *North Carolina Historical Review* 52 (1984): 59–92.

Auman, William T., and David Scarboro. "The Heroes of America in Civil War North Carolina." *North Carolina Historical Review* 58 (1981): 327–363.

Bailey, Fred Arthur. *Class and Tennessee's Confederate Generation.* Chapel Hill: University of North Carolina Press, 1987.

Bailey, Hugh C. "Disaffection in the Alabama Hill Country, 1861." *Civil War History* 4 (1958): 183–194.

——. "Disloyalty in Early Confederate Alabama." *Journal of Southern History* 23 (1957): 522–528.

Baker, Jean H. *The Politics of Continuity: Maryland Political Parties from 1858 to 1870.* Baltimore: Johns Hopkins University Press, 1973.

Barnes, Kenneth C. "The Williams Clan: Mountain Farmers and Union Fighters in North Central Arkansas." *Arkansas Historical Quarterly* 52 (1993): 286–317.

Barnett, James. "Munfordville in the Civil War." *Register of the Kentucky Historical Society* 79 (September 1971): 339–361.

——. *The Civil War in North Carolina.* Chapel Hill: University of North Carolina Press, 1963.

Bergeron, Arthur W. *Confederate Mobile.* Jackson: University Press of Mississippi, 1991.

Bettersworth, John K. *Confederate Mississippi: The People and Policies of a Confederate State.* Baton Rouge: Louisiana State University Press, 1943.

————. ed. "Mississippi Unionism: The Case of the Reverend James A. Lyon." *Journal of Mississippi History* 1 (1939): 37–52.

Bill, Alfred H. *The Beleaguered City: Richmond, 1861–1865.* New York: Alfred A. Knopf, 1946.

Bragg, Jefferson Davis. *Louisiana in the Confederacy.* Baton Rouge: Louisiana State University Press, 1941.

Brown, Norman D. "A Union Election in Civil War North Carolina." *North Carolina Historical Review* 43 (1966): 381–400.

Buker, George E. *Blockaders, Refugees, and Contrabands: Civil War on Florida's Gulf Coast.* Tuscaloosa: University of Alabama Press, 1993.

Burton, E. Milby. *The Siege of Charleston, 1861–1865.* Columbia: University of South Carolina Press, 1970

Burton, Orville Vernon. *In My Father's House Are Many Mansions: Family and Community in Edgefield, South Carolina.* Chapel Hill: University of North Carolina Press, 1985.

Bryan, Charles F., Jr. " 'Tories' amidst Rebels: Confederate Occupation of East Tennessee." *East Tennessee Historical Society Publications* 60 (1988): 3–22.

Bryan, T. Conn. *Confederate Georgia.* Athens: University of Georgia Press, 1953.

Bynum, Victoria E. *Unruly Women: The Politics of Social and Sexual Control in the Old South.* Chapel Hill: University of North Carolina Press, 1992.

Campbell, Randolph B. *A Southern Community in Crisis: Harrison County, Texas, 1850–1880.* Austin: Texas State Historical Association, 1983.

Capers, Gerald M. *Occupied City: New Orleans under the Federals, 1862–1865.* Lexington: University Press of Kentucky, 1965.

Cauthen, Charles E. *South Carolina Goes to War, 1861–1865.* Chapel Hill: University of North Carolina Press, 1950.

Cecil-Fronsman, Bill. *Common Whites: Class and Culture in Antebellum North Carolina.* Lexington: University Press of Kentucky, 1992.

Chesebrough, David B. "Dissenting Clergy in Confederate Mississippi." *Journal of Mississippi History* 55 (May 1993): 115–131.

Clinton, Catherine. *The Other Civil War: American Women in the Nineteenth Century.* New York: Hill and Wang, 1984.

Clinton, Catherine, and Nina Silber, eds. *Divided Houses: Gender and the Civil War.* New York: Oxford University Press, 1992.

Coleman, Kenneth. *Confederate Athens, 1861–1865.* Athens: University of Georgia Press, 1968

Coulter, E. Merton. *The Civil War and Readjustment in Kentucky.* Chapel Hill: University of North Carolina Press, 1926.

————. *The Confederate States of America, 1861–1865.* Baton Rouge: Louisiana State University Press, 1950).

————. *William G. Brownlow: Fighting Parson of the Southern Highlands.* Chapel Hill: University of North Carolina Press, 1937.

Coulter, Nate. "The Impact of the Civil War upon Pulaski County, Arkansas." *Arkansas Historical Quarterly* 41 (1982): 67–82.

Crawford, Martin. "Confederate Volunteering and Enlistment in Ashe County, North Carolina." *North Carolina Historical Review* 37 (1991): 29–50.

Crofts, Daniel W. *Old Southampton: Politics and Society in a Virginia County.* Charlottesville: University Press of Virginia, 1992.

Currie, James T. *Enclave: Vicksburg and Her Plantations, 1863–1870.* Jackson: University Press of Mississippi, 1980.

Curry, Richard O. *A House Divided: A Study of Statehood Politics and the Copperhead Movement in West Virginia.* Pittsburgh: University of Pittsburgh Press, 1964.

Degler, Carl N. *The Other South: Southern Dissenters in the Nineteenth Century.* New York: Harper & Row, 1974.

DeLozier, Mary Jean. "The Civil War and Its Aftermath in Putnam County." *Tennessee Historical Quarterly* 38 (1979): 436–461.

Dew, Aloma William. " 'Between the Hawk and the Buzzard': Owensboro during the Civil War." *Register of the Kentucky Historical Society* 77 (1979): 1–14.

Dimick, Howard T. "Peace Overtures of July, 1864." *Louisiana Historical Quarterly* 29 (1946): 1241–1258.

Dougan, Michael B. "Life in Confederate Arkansas." *Arkansas Historical Quarterly* 31 (1972): 15–35.

———. *The People and Policies of a Frontier State in Wartime.* University, AL: University of Alabama Press, 1976.

Durham, Walter T. *Rebellion Revisited: A History of Sumner County, Tennessee, from 1861 to 1870.* Gallatin: Sumner County Museum Association, 1982.

Durrill, Wayne K. *War of Another Kind: A Southern Community in the Great Rebellion.* New York: Oxford University Press, 1990.

Eaton, Clement. *A History of the Southern Confederacy.* New York: Macmillan, 1954.

Elliott, Claude. "Union Sentiment in Texas, 1861–1865." *Southwestern Historical Quarterly* 50 (1947): 449–477.

Endres, Kathleen L. "The Women's Press in the Civil War: A Portrait of Patriotism, Propaganda, and Prodding." *Civil War History* 30 (1984): 31–53.

Escott, Paul D. *After Secession: Jefferson Davis and the Failure of Confederate Nationalism.* Baton Rouge: Louisiana State University Press, 1978.

———. *Many Excellent People: Power and Privilege in North Carolina, 1850–1900.* Chapel Hill: University of North Carolina Press, 1985.

———. "Southern Yeomen and the Confederacy." *South Atlantic Quarterly* 77 (1978): 146–158.

Escott, Paul D., and Jeffrey J. Crow. "The Social Order and Violent Disorder: An Analysis of North Carolina in the Revolution and the Civil War." *Journal of Southern History* 52 (1986): 373–402.

Faust, Drew Gilpin. "Altars of Sacrifice: Confederate Women and the Narratives of War." *Journal of American History* 76 (1990): 1200–1228.

———. "Christian Soldiers: The Meaning of Revivalism in the Confederate Army." *Journal of Southern History* 53 (1987): 63–90.

———. *The Creation of Confederate Nationalism: Ideology and Identity in the Civil War South.* Baton Rouge: Louisiana State University Press, 1988.

Fellman, Michael. *Inside War: The Guerrilla Conflict in Missouri during the American Civil War.* New York: Oxford University Press, 1989.

Flemming, Walter Lynwood. *Civil War and Reconstruction in Alabama.* New York: Columbia University Press, 1903.

———. "The Peace Movement in Alabama during the Civil War." *South Atlantic Quarterly* 2 (1903): 114–124, 246–260.

Frank, Fedora Small. "Nashville during the Civil War." *Tennessee Historical Quarterly* 39 (1980): 310–322.

Gallagher, Gary W. "Home Front and Battlefield: Some Recent Literature Relating to Virginia and the Confederacy." *Virginia Magazine of History and Biography* 98 (1990): 135–168.

Gaston, Kay Baker. "A World Overturned: The Civil War Experiences of Dr. William A. Cheatham." *Tennessee Historical Quarterly* 50 (1991): 3–16.

Gildrie, Richard P. "Guerrilla Warfare in the Lower Cumberland River Valley, 1862–1865." *Tennessee Historical Quarterly* 49 (1990): 161–176.

Hahn, Steven. *The Roots of Southern Populism: Yeoman Farmers and the Transformation of the Georgia Upcountry.* New York: Oxford University Press, 1983.

Harris, J. William. *Plain Folk and Gentry in a Slave Society: White Liberty and Black Slavery in Augusta's Hinterlands.* Middletown, CT: Wesleyan University Press, 1985.

Harris, William C. "East Tennessee's Civil War Refugees and the Impact of the War on Civilians." *Journal of East Tennessee History* 64 (1992): 3–19.

———. *William Woods Holden: Firebrand of North Carolina Politics.* Baton Rouge: Louisiana State University Press, 1987.

Harrison, Lowell. *The Civil War in Kentucky.* Lexington: University Press of Kentucky, 1975.

Howe, Barbara J. "The Civil War at Bulltown." *West Virginia History* 44 (1982): 1–40.

Humphrey, David C. "A 'Very Muddy and Conflicting' View: The Civil War as Seen from Austin, Texas." *Southwestern Historical Quarterly* 94 (1991): 368–414.

Hyman, Harold M. "Deceit in Dixie." *Civil War History* 3 (1957): 65–82.

Inscoe, John C. "Coping in Confederate Appalachia: Portrait of a Mountain Woman and Her Community at War." *North Carolina Historical Review* 69 (1992): 388–413.

Jimerson, Randall C. *The Private Civil War: Popular Thought during the Sectional Conflict.* Baton Rouge: Louisiana State University Press, 1988.

Johns, John E. *Florida during the Civil War.* Gainesville: University of Florida Press, 1963.

Johnson, Ludwell H., III. "Blockade or Trade Monopoly: John A. Dix and the Union Occupation of Norfolk." *Virginia Magazine of History and Biography* 93 (1985): 54–78.

———. "Contraband Trade during the Last Year of the Civil War." *Mississippi Valley Historical Review* 49 (1963): 635–653.

Johnston, Angus J. "Disloyalty on Confederate Railroads in Virginia." *Virginia Magazine of History and Biography* 63 (1955): 410–426.

Jones, Jacqueline. *Labor of Love, Labor of Sorrow: Black Women, Work, and the Family from Slavery to the Present.* New York: Basic Books, 1985.

Jones, Katherine. *When Sherman Came: Southern Women and the "Great War."* Indianapolis: Bobbs-Merrill, 1964.

Kenzer, Robert C. *Kinship and Neighborhood in a Southern Community: Orange County, North Carolina, 1849–1881.* Knoxville: University of Tennessee Press, 1987.

Klingberg, Frank W. "The Case of the Minors: A Unionist Family within the Confederacy." *Journal of Southern History* 13 (1947): 27–45.

———. *The Southern Claims Commission.* Berkeley: University of California Press, 1955.

Kruman, Marc. "Dissent in the Confederacy: The North Carolina Experience." *Civil War History* 27 (1981): 293–313.

Lady, Claudia Lynn. "Five Tri-State Women during the Civil War: Day-to-Day Life." *West Virginia History* 44 (1982): 189–226

———. "Five Tri-State Women during the Civil War: Views on the War." *West Virginia History* 44 (1982): 302–321.

Lathrop, Barnes F. "Disaffection in Confederate Louisiana: The Case of William Hyman." *Journal of Southern History* 24 (1958): 308–338.

Leverett, Rudy H. *Legend of the Free State of Jones.* Jackson: University Press of Mississippi, 1984.

Long, Durward. "Unanimity and Disloyalty in Secessionist Alabama." *Civil War History* 11 (1965): 257–274.

McCaslin, Richard B. *Tainted Breeze: The Great Hanging at Gainesville, Texas, 1862.* Baton Rouge: Louisiana State University Press, 1994.

McDonald, Archie, ed. "A Nation of Sovereign States: Secession and War in the Confederacy." *Journal of Confederate History* 10 (1994).

McKenzie, Robert Tracy. "Civil War and Socioeconomic Change in the Upper South: The Survival of Local Agricultural Elites in Tennessee, 1850–1870." *Tennessee Historical Quarterly* 52 (1993): 170–184.

McKinney, Gordon. "Women's Role in Civil War Western North Carolina." *North Carolina Historical Review* 69 (1992): 37–56.

McMillan, Malcolm C. *The Disintegration of a Confederate State: Three Governors and Alabama's Wartime Homefront.* Macon, GA: Mercer University Press, 1986.

Maddenn, David. "Unionist Resistance to Confederate Occupation: The Bridge-Burners of East Tennessee." *East Tennessee Historical Society Publications* 52 (1980–1981): 22–39.

Marten, James. *Texas Divided: Loyalty and Dissent in the Lone Star State, 1856–1874.* Lexington: University Press of Kentucky, 1990.

Massey, Mary Elizabeth. *Bonnet Brigades: American Women and the Civil War.* New York: Alfred A. Knopf, 1966.

———. "The Confederate States of America: The Home Front." In *Writing Southern History: Essays in Historiography in Honor of Fletcher M. Green,* 249–272. Edited by Arthur S. Link and Rembert W. Patrick. Baton Rouge: Louisiana State University Press, 1965.

———. *Ersatz in the Confederacy.* Columbia: University of South Carolina Press, 1952.

———. *Refugee Life in the Confederacy.* Baton Rouge: Louisiana State University Press, 1964.

Maslowski, Peter. *Treason Must Be Made Odious: Military Occupation and Wartime Reconstruction in Nashville, Tennessee, 1862–65.* Millwood, NY: KTO Press, 1978.

Mills, Gary. "Alexandria, Louisiana: A 'Confederate' City at War with Itself." *Red River Valley Historical Review* 5 (1980): 23–36.

Moneyhon, Carl H. "Disloyalty and Class Consciousness in Southwestern Arkansas, 1852–1865." *Arkansas Historical Quarterly* 52 (1993): 223–243.

———. *The Impact of the Civil War and Reconstruction on Arkansas, 1850–1874: Persistence in the Midst of Ruin.* Baton Rouge: Louisiana State University Press, 1994.

Murdock, Eugene C. "Was It a 'Poor Man's Fight'?" *Civil War History* 10 (1965): 241–245.

Noe, Kenneth W. "Red String Scare: Civil War Southwest Virginia and the Heroes of America." *North Carolina Historical Review* 69 (1992): 301–322.

Nulty, William H. *Confederate Florida: The Road to Olustee.* Tuscaloosa: University of Alabama Press, 1990.

Owens, Harry P., and James J. Cooke. *The Old South and the Crucible of War.* Jackson: University Press of Mississippi, 1983.

Paludan, Phillip Shaw. *Victims: A True Story of the Civil War.* Knoxville: University of Tennessee Press, 1981.

Parrish, William. *Turbulent Partnership: Missouri and the Union, 1861–1865.* Columbia: University of Missouri Press, 1963.

Patton, James W. *Unionism and Reconstruction in Tennessee, 1860–1867.* Chapel Hill: University of North Carolina Press, 1934.

Rable, George C. *Civil Wars: Women and the Crisis of Southern Nationalism.* Urbana: University of Illinois Press, 1989.

Ramsdell, Charles. *Behind the Lines in the Southern Confederacy.* Baton Rouge: Louisiana State University Press, 1944.

Raper, Horace W. "William W. Holden and the Peace Movement in North Carolina." *North Carolina Historical Review* 31 (1954): 493–516.

————. *William W. Holden: North Carolina's Political Enigma.* Chapel Hill: University of North Carolina Press, 1985.

Roark, James L. *Masters without Slaves: Southern Planters in the Civil War and Reconstruction.* New York: W. W. Norton, 1977.

Roberts, A. Sellew. "The Peace Movement in North Carolina." *Mississippi Valley Historical Review* 11 (1924): 190–199.

Roland, Charles P. *The Confederacy.* Chicago: University of Chicago Press, 1960.

Sarris, Jonathan D. "Anatomy of an Atrocity: The Madden Branch Massacre and Guerrilla Warfare in North Georgia." *Georgia Historical Quarterly* 77 (Winter 1993): 679–710.

Scott, Anne Firor. *The Southern Lady: From Pedestal to Politics, 1830–1930.* Chicago: University of Chicago Press, 1970.

Shaffer, John W. "Loyalties in Conflict: Union and Confederate Sentiment in Barbour County." *West Virginia History* 50 (1991): 109–128.

Shanks, Henry T. "Disloyalty to the Confederacy in Southwestern Virginia, 1861–1865." *North Carolina Historical Review* 21 (1944): 118–135.

Sheeler, J. Reuben. "The Development of Unionism in East Tennessee." *Journal of Negro History* 29 (1944): 166–203.

Shugg, Roger W. *Origins of Class Struggle in Louisiana.* Baton Rouge: Louisiana State University Press, 1939.

Silber, Nina. " 'A Woman's War': Gender and Civil War Studies." *Magazine of History* 8 (1993): 11–13.

Simkins, Francis Butler, and James Welch Patton. *The Women of the Confederacy.* Richmond, VA: Garrett and Massie, 1936.

Smith, David P. "Conscription and Conflict on the Texas Frontier." *Civil War History* 36 (1990): 250–261.

Somers, Dale A. "War and Play: The Civil War in New Orleans." *Mississippi Quarterly* 26 (1973): 3–28.

Sterkx, H. E. *Partners in Rebellion: Alabama Women in the Civil War.* Rutherford, NJ: Fairleigh Dickinson University Press, 1970.

Stolz, Jack. "Kaufman County in the Civil War" *East Texas Historical Journal* 28 (1990): 37–44.

Stuart, Meriwether. "Samuel Ruth and General R. E. Lee: Disloyalty and the Line of Supply to Fredricksburg, 1862–1863." *Virginia Magazine of History and Biography* 71 (1963): 35–109.

Sutherland, Daniel E. "Getting the 'Real War' into the History Books." *Virginia Magazine of History and Biography* 98 (1990): 193–222.

———. "Guerrillas: The Real War in Arkansas." *Arkansas Historical Quarterly* 52 (Autumn 1993): 257–285.

———. "Introduction to War: The Civilians of Culpeper County, Virginia." *Civil War History* 37 (1991): 120–137.

Tatum, Georgia L. *Disloyalty in the Confederacy.* Chapel Hill: University of North Carolina Press, 1934.

Taylor, Ethel. "Discontent in Confederate Louisiana." *Louisiana History* 2 (1961): 410–428.

Tenkotte, Paul Allen. "A Note on Regional Allegiances during the Civil War: Kenton County, Kentucky as a Test Case." *Register of the Kentucky Historical Society* 79 (1981): 211–218.

Thomas, Emory M. *The Confederate Nation, 1861–1865.* New York: Harper & Row, 1979.

———. *The Confederate State of Richmond: A Biography of the Capital.* Austin: University of Texas Press, 1971.

Walker, Peter F. *Vicksburg: A People at War, 1860–1865.* Chapel Hill: University of North Carolina Press, 1960.

Wallenstein, Peter. "Rich Man's War, Rich Man's Fight: Civil War and the Transformation of Public Finance in Georgia." *Journal of Southern History:* 50 (1984): 15–43.

Warde, Mary Jane. "Now the Wolf Has Come: The Civilian Civil War in the Indian Territory." *Chronicles of Oklahoma* 71 (Spring 1993): 64–87.

White, Edward, L., III. "Key West during the Civil War: An Island of Discontent?" *Southern Historian* 9 (1988): 38–50.

———. "A Question of Security: The Confederacy's Policy in East Tennessee, 1861–1863." *Southern Historian* 11 (1988): 1–23.

Whites, LeeAnn. "The Charitable and the Poor: The Emergence of Domestic Politics in Augusta, Georgia, 1860–1880." *Journal of Social History* 17 (1984): 601–615.

Wiley, Bell Irwin. *Confederate Women.* Westport, CT: Greenwood Press, 1975.

———. *The Plain People of the Confederacy.* Baton Rouge: Louisiana State University Press, 1944.

Woodward, C. Vann, ed. *Mary Chesnut's Civil War.* New Haven: Yale University Press, 1981.

Woodward, C. Vann, and Elisabeth Muhlenfield. *The Private Mary Chesnut: The Unpublished Civil War Diaries.* New York: Oxford University Press, 1984.

Wooster, Ralph A., and Robert Wooster. "A People at War: East Texas during the Civil War." *East Texas Historical Journal* 28 (1990): 3–16.

Worley, Ted R. "The Arkansas Peace Society of 1861: A Study in Mountain Unionism." *Journal of Southern History* 24 (1958): 445–456.

Part X

Reconstruction and Beyond

41

Southern Occupation

Richard M. Zuczek

In "The American Experience with Military Government," published in 1944, Ralph Gabriel, professor of history at Yale, devoted a single paragraph to the army's role in the Southern states following the Civil War. Yet in that paragraph lay a sentence laden with unexplored potential: "The rule of the generals in the South was one of the longer American experiences with military government." Although the accuracy of the statement is questionable—the generals never exercised complete power, nor did their "rule" last very long—Gabriel's comment focused attention on a glaring gap in the Civil War literature. Soon a new breed of scholars, reared in the era of World War II and Korea, began to examine postwar developments and military occupation. The civil rights movement served as another catalyst; questions of blacks' place in American society, and the Federal government's role in creating and protecting that place, were once again pressing issues. As America embarked on its second Reconstruction, it seemed only natural to reach back for lessons and leftovers from the first.

This is not to say that recent years have seen a flood of books on the military during Reconstruction. Only one scholarly overview of the army's role in the postwar South has been published: James Sefton's *The United States Army and Reconstruction, 1865–1877* (1968). As one might imagine with a study covering the entire South in the Reconstruction period, there are gaps in coverage. The focus is on the military's role in enforcing civil policy from 1865 to 1868; Sefton bypasses wartime Reconstruction, which he believed was "fundamentally different" from the postwar, and treats postreadmission years only briefly. Even with these limitations, Sefton can provide only anecdotal examples as he scans across years and states. Still, *The United States Army and Reconstruction* does a fine job of balancing affairs in Washington with the action in the South, providing the reader with a solid, if general, understanding of the tremendous and varied tasks facing the army. John Kirkland's "Federal Troops in the South Atlantic States during Reconstruction, 1865–1877" (1968) is another overview of the army's performance but lacks any real analysis (1968). At times tedious, it is largely a list of duties punctuated by sweeping hypotheses that are introduced abruptly and passed over without development.

These studies leave unexamined many important contributions by the military. Any attempt at understanding the army's role in Reconstruction must begin before Appomattox, and several useful works help clarify the military's role as an occupation force before the war's end. Two recent studies (unavailable for review at the time of this chapter) should create an intellectual stir in the historical community. Mark Grimsley's *The Hard Hand of War: Union Military Policy toward Southern Civilians* (1995) and Stephen V. Ash's *When the Yankees Came: Conflict and Chaos in the Occupied South* (1995) promise to shed new insights, and encourage new investigation, into the controversial and complicated relationship between the Union army and Southern civilians during the war. In a more limited way, Kenneth St. Clair, "Military Justice in North Carolina, 1865: A Microcosm of Reconstruction" (1965), examines the confusion and inconsistency inherent in the military justice system at work in occupied North Carolina. The administration of justice was complex and difficult, as officers had neither experience nor doctrine to guide them; controversies over jurisdiction, not only between civil and military courts but among military ones, brought little peace out of the chaos. In a more general way, Joseph Parks, "Memphis under Military Rule, 1862–1865" (1942), has drawn similar conclusions, demonstrating that the Union occupation of Memphis, 1862–1865, served little purpose and resulted in a substantial decline in the quality of life in the city. The same remorseful, cynical vibrations rumble through Peter Maslowski's dissertation, published a decade after its completion under the cumbersome title, *Treason Must Be Made Odious: Military Occupation and Wartime Reconstruction in Nashville, Tennessee, 1862–1865* (1978). Maslowski presents a local case study of wartime reconstruction and the factors involved in its failure. Federal authorities in Nashville faced the same obstacles as elsewhere: the lack of informed direction from above, poor cooperation and communication between Federal military and civilian authorities, and a local population that was more loyal to the Confederacy than Northerners wanted to believe.

Some of the more noted older monographs come to the same conclusions concerning wartime attempts at laying a foundation for the postwar Union. In *Rehearsal for Reconstruction: The Port Royal Experiment* (1964), Willie Lee Rose chronicled the heroic efforts of both the freedmen and the military and how those efforts came to naught before a shortsighted, conservative government. This shortsightedness also surfaced in Louis Gerteis's *From Contraband to Freedmen: Federal Policy toward Southern Blacks, 1861–1865* (1973). Although during the war the Federal government sought to mobilize blacks in the

South, it had no intention of overturning basic components of Southern society, including black dependence and submission. The army was again the agent of ambivalent Northern policy, offering liberation to blacks as a war necessity but restricting that freedom as a requirement for postwar peace.

Not all historians see the army's role in such a negative light, and some have drawn more positive conclusions about wartime occupation. Gilbert Govan and James Livingood, "Chattanooga under Military Occupation, 1863–1865" (1951), saw Federal rule in Chattanooga in a positive light, with the army participating in the social life of the city at the same time it attended to relief functions. As with many of the other authors here, Robert J. Futrell found a lack of direction at the highest levels but saw it compensated for by innovative, determined field commanders. His "Federal Military Government in the South, 1861–1865" (1951) makes an interesting statement about Union commanders and their understanding of civil-military relations. Futrell showed that while military authorities dominated civil functionaries in wartime, commanders consistently pushed for a speedy return to civil control with the restoration of peace.

Even the notorious Benjamin Butler had some redeeming qualities, argued Howard Johnson, who credited Butler with suppressing crime, improving sanitation, and stabilizing a chaotic economy ("New Orleans under General Butler" [1941]). Despite the title, Hans Trefousse's biography of Butler, *Ben Butler: The South Called Him Beast!* (1957), has only a short discussion of his New Orleans duties. The best examination of Butler in context is Gerald M. Capers's *Occupied City: New Orleans under the Federals, 1862–1865* (1965), which provides a more thorough examination of the occupation. Capers analyzes the succession of commanding officers, their differing approaches to the problems of occupation duty, and their influence on local politics and society. Perhaps the most interesting work on the impact of military commanders on local politics is William Alderson's "The Influence of Military Rule and the Freedmen's Bureau on Reconstruction in Virginia, 1865–1870" (1952). Alderson concludes that the policies and actions of Alfred Terry and later John Schofield led directly to the formation of a conservative and moderate Republican alliance, accounting for Virginia's avoidance of Radical Republican rule. More such studies are needed to explore the extent and impact of the military's presence beyond the functions of peacekeeper and ration provider.

In fact, many of the more recent studies of the army and occupation do explore new directions. Stuart C. McGehee has argued in "Military Origins of the New South" (1988) that the nature of Chattanooga in the postwar era was directly related to its experience under Federal control; physical and economic segregation, the influx of new trades and industry, and the failure of racial reconciliation can all be traced to the Army of the Cumberland. The impact of war on local society is also the subject of one of the most active "occupation" scholars, Stephen V. Ash, whose *Middle Tennessee Society Transformed, 1860–1870: War and Peace in the Upper South* (1988) deals with the social and cultural impact of war and occupation. Ash has stepped off the beaten political path to analyze the sociological impact of the Union wartime presence and how it resulted in the dissolution of the institutions, hierarchies, and ideological foundations of a community. In "Poor Whites in the Occupied South, 1861–1865" (1991) Ash applied his sociological approach to the relationship of poor whites, planters, and Union soldiers, delivering a refreshing discussion of the effect that expectations and perceptions can have on behavior in war (see also Ash's "White Virginians under Federal Occupation, 1861–1865" [1990]).

One cannot discuss occupation and wartime Reconstruction without discussing local resistance. Oddly enough, the literature on guerrilla warfare during the Civil War is minimal. The past few years, however, have produced attempts to explain the nature, course, and results of irregular conflict. In 1989 Michael Fellman published *Inside War: The Guerrilla Conflict in Missouri during the American Civil War,* a sociological study that leaned dangerously to psychohistory and told readers more about the guerrilla in general than about the Missouri episode. Nonetheless, Fellman's book will stand as a pathbreaking work on the Missouri struggle, for it covers, albeit briefly, a wide range of issues, from the operations of soldiers to the policies of the opposing governments and their impact on civilians.

Several recent works explore guerrilla warfare in other regions. Despite the improbable title, Carl Beamer's "Gray Ghostbusters: Eastern Theater Union Counterguerrilla Operations in the Civil War, 1861–1865" (1988) is an interesting indictment of Union counterguerrilla policy. In fact, Beamer argues there was no policy, with operations left largely in the hands of local commanders who concentrated on defense rather than offense; when the military did turn to aggressive techniques, the results were counterproductive. Noel Fisher's award-winning dissertation, " 'War at Every Man's Door': The Struggle for East Tennessee, 1860–1869" (1993), goes even further, brilliantly merging the violence of guerrilla warfare and military occupation with the internal local struggle for control of East Tennessee. Fisher has succeeded in analyzing two intersecting wars—one between Union and Confederate forces (regular and otherwise) and the other pitting Unionists against secessionists. Due to be published soon, Fisher's study will complement superbly Wayne Durrill's *War of Another Kind: A Southern Community in the Great Rebellion* (1990). Durrill was the first to analyze how the military's presence opened a pandora's box that wreaked havoc with the social and political status quo between white classes. Limited in scope—the book covers a single county in North Carolina—it may prompt similar examinations of other regions and perhaps some generalizations about the interaction between Unionists and Federal forces across the South.

Exciting as counterguerrilla operations and government building may have been, these represented neither the most pressing of occupation duties nor the longest in duration. From the waning days of the war through readmission, the primary responsibility of the army was the relief and protection of the freed slaves. Even more so than with its other undertakings, the army had neither the experience nor the training to serve as protector, provider, and referee in the

South. The task was the most difficult yet; the military became caught between conflicting governmental branches, between varying economic systems, and between opposing classes and races in the South.

Unlike other aspects of military occupation, the literature on the army's duties concerning the freed people is voluminous. Readers are reminded that the Bureau of Refugees, Freedmen, and Abandoned Lands was an agency of the War Department, with a majority of its agents and all of its commissioners military officers. Several general works serve as excellent introductions to the problems facing the military and the freedmen. Although brief and dated, George Bentley's *A History of the Freedmen's Bureau* (1955) is still a useful overview of the War Department agency; many of the questions he raised, such as the bureau's role in the politicization of blacks, remain unexamined to this day. William S. McFeely's *Yankee Stepfather: General O. O. Howard and the Freedmen* (1968) also utilizes a top-down approach, although with a greater focus on the bureau's commissioner. Often criticized for its condemnation of Howard, *Yankee Stepfather* is nonetheless an informative account of Washington policy making that supplements every study of the bureau in the Southern states.

Other historians have focused on a particular function or issue relating to freed people and the military. For example, Claude Oubre's *Forty Acres and a Mule: The Freedmen's Bureau and Black Land Ownership* (1978) was the first work to deal specifically with the question of black landownership after the Civil War. Oubre reviewed the efforts of military commanders to provide land (William T. Sherman is the supreme example), the options facing lawmakers, Freedmen's Bureau agents, and blacks during Reconstruction, and finally the reasons behind the failure to create an independent black yeomanry. Published at about the same time, *To Set the Law in Motion: The Freedmen's Bureau and the Legal Rights of Blacks, 1865–1868* (1979) sought to explain the reasons for the failure in providing legal and civil rights for former slaves. Donald G. Nieman has done a superb job documenting the functions and problems of bureau agents in the former Confederacy. His coverage of martial law, military justice and law enforcement, and civil-military relations is excellent. In addition, Nieman touches on the jurisdictional struggles between the bureau's assistant commissioners and the regular army's military commanders; it is a subject not often covered, yet one that demonstrates the confusion and complexity of administration in the postwar South.

Even education, once seen as one of the brighter spots in the bureau's tenure, has come under fire for failure to improve the situation of blacks. Unfortunately, historians have yet to provide a comprehensive, objective analysis of the bureau's educational program. For example, *Northern Schools, Southern Blacks, and Reconstruction: Freedmen's Education, 1862–1875* (1980) by Ronald E. Butchart is an indictment of the bureau for its role in allegedly reinforcing white values of black submission. While Butchart does have a case, he provides little support; he does not explore the options available at the time, place the educational system in context, or evaluate the educational program's clear successes.

The best overview is Robert Morris's *Reading, 'Riting, and Reconstruction: The Education of the Freedmen in the South, 1861–1870* (1982). Morris's research is more substantial and relevant than Butchart's, but his emphasis on educators and only brief treatment of policy goals, resources, and opposition does not reveal a complete picture of the school systems' contributions.

As for the military's contribution, most of the best works on the military focus on a particular state. Far from providing an exhaustive list, I will mention only works particularly useful for understanding the army's role in Reconstruction. Moreover, treatment is uneven; while some states are suffering from neglect, others must endure a browbeating at the hands of historians. One scholar, William Richter, is single-handedly dissecting the army's role in Texas during Reconstruction. In addition to thirteen articles, Richter has also published two books on the subject. *The Army in Texas during Reconstruction, 1865–1870* (1987) is a well-written and ably researched overview of military operations in Texas during Reconstruction. Richter covers the Freedmen's Bureau, the regular army, and the interplay between the military and the civilian state government. While providing glimpses into the wide range of duties facing the troops, Richter's emphasis is on the political role and influence of the military and results in a less-than-objective indictment of army activity. In *Overreached on All Sides: The Freedmen's Bureau Administrators in Texas, 1865–1868* (1991), Richter concentrates his efforts more narrowly, delivering a blow-by-blow account of the individual experiences of the bureau's military officers. More narrative than analytical, the study is useful for examining bureau operations at the local level, as is the extensive bibliography.

Along the same lines, Barry Crouch's *The Freedmen's Bureau and Black Texans* (1992) also denies being a history of the Freedmen's Bureau in the state and instead follows a case study approach that explains the course of bureau operations in one subdistrict. Where Richter saw exploitation and interference, however, Crouch found cooperation and success. By comparison, the literature on Louisiana might be more balanced and informative. Howard White's *The Freedmen's Bureau in Louisiana* (1970), although dated, provides a brief narrative introduction to the military agency's relief, administrative, and protection duties in the state. When used in conjunction with Joe Gray Taylor's *Louisiana Reconstructed, 1863–1877* (1974) and Ted Tunnell's *Crucible of Reconstruction: War, Radicalism, and Race in Louisiana, 1862–1877* (1984), a scholar can come away with a fairly complete understanding of the impact—both beneficial and damaging—that the military and the Freedmen's Bureau had on Louisiana during Reconstruction. To this list can be added *Army Generals and Reconstruction: Louisiana, 1862–1877* (1982) by Joseph G. Dawson, which directly targets army commanders and their interaction with state officials and the freedmen. As his critics have suggested, the high marks Dawson bestows on military officials might not be justified; still, the book stands as the best examination of the middle level of the army during Reconstruction, an interesting and informative discussion of those responsible for interpreting, directing, and executing

Reconstruction policy. These authors do not concur on all points: Dawson and Tunnell, for example, diverge over the effectiveness and overall success of the bureau. Taken together, they deliver the most comprehensive account of the responsibilities, successes, and failures of military officers in any Southern state.

Not all states have had the luxury—or the misfortune—of undergoing such scrutiny with respect to Federal military presence. However, any good state history of Reconstruction should include a survey of army and Freedmen's Bureau activities. A case in point is Jerrell H. Shofner's *Nor Is It Over Yet: Florida in the Era of Reconstruction* (1974). Shofner has written a model study of state politics during Reconstruction but ventures far afield to capture the social, economic, and legal consequences of defeat and readjustment in an oft-forgotten state. Shofner successfully integrates the military into his overall discussion without exaggerating the importance of the army's activities. The reader comes to understand how martial law, the Freedmen's Bureau, voting registration, and law enforcement influenced the outcome of Reconstruction in Florida.

Because of their difficulty, state syntheses will remain rare, with more narrowly focused bureau studies dominating the field. Despite their limited scope, such works can answer questions—or raise them—about the military and Reconstruction, as well as help draw generalizations about the army's role across the South.

The first book-length study of the bureau at the state level, Martin Abbott's *The Freedmen's Bureau in South Carolina, 1865–1872* (1968), suffers from brevity and lack of detail but does deal with issues affecting the entire South, such as officers' attitudes, white opposition, and Federal commitment to supporting black readjustment. Abbott's argument that officials were genuinely concerned about black rights and quality of life, and that their failure was largely due to local opposition and a shortsighted government, is reiterated in Randy Finley's "The Freedmen's Bureau in Arkansas" (1992). Gail Snowden Hasson conveys the same message in "The Medical Activities of the Freedmen's Bureau in Reconstruction Alabama, 1865–1868" (1982). Paul Cimbala, author of several articles on Reconstruction, examines the various approaches of bureau commanders in his 1983 dissertation, "The Terms of Freedom: The Freedmen's Bureau and Reconstruction in Georgia, 1865–1870." Cimbala also sees failure in the face of insurmountable odds but presents an interesting comparison of how several bureau officials faced the crisis, each adopting different strategies and emphasizing different goals to reach their elusive end.

A "built-in" dual strategy existed in the bureau's educational program, according to Michael Goldhaber. In "A Mission Unfulfilled: Freedmen's Education in North Carolina, 1865–1870" (1992), Goldhaber identified two solutions that bureau schooling was intended to cultivate. The Federal government's temporary system could create an independent black community capable of providing for itself, or it could cajole the state governments into assuming the responsibility. A law student at Yale, Goldhaber reminds historians that analyzing policies, intentions, and goals is as important as narration; otherwise, scholars working at the local level may be maneuvering puzzle pieces without having seen the complete picture.

As scholars continue to concentrate on the local study, they must make plain to readers the context and significance of their work. A case in point is the dissertation of noted Civil War historian Harry W. Pfanz, "Soldiering in the South during the Reconstruction Period, 1865–1877" (1958). A thorough description of the lives of ordinary soldiers in the South—Pfanz covers everything from clothing to discipline—the dissertation more closely resembles a reference work than a monograph. As a source on the conditions of service after Appomattox, "Soldiering in the South" has no equal, but since it does not answer crucial questions, provide significant interpretations, or offer interesting episodes, there is little chance that this mundane, information-packed volume will ever be published. On the other hand, limited as it is, James Marten's "For the Army, the People, and Abraham Lincoln: A Yankee Newspaper in Occupied Texas" (1993) is an object lesson in the supralocal study. Not really a work on occupation policy or practice, the article examines army life during Reconstruction through a detailed investigation of the newspapers published by and for soldiers. While sweeping generalizations are still a distance away, Marten is able to make interesting observations about the cares and concerns of the ordinary soldier serving in the South.

Marten selected Brownsville as his subject because the region was at peace, allowing a glimpse into the more ordinary and personal interests of the soldiers. As we have seen, this was not usually the case prior to Appomattox, and even after the South's collapse, the protection of life and property remained a central function of the Freedmen's Bureau and regular army. With the readmission of states to the Union, the coming of black suffrage, and the curtailing of the bureau's presence, white opposition to the postwar order became more organized and more violent. The most notorious manifestation of this sentiment was the Ku Klux Klan.

There are a few interesting (though not informative or necessarily accurate) accounts of the Reconstruction Klan, including James Melville Beard, *K.K.K. Sketches: Humorous and Didactic, Treating the More Important Events of the Ku-Klux-Klan Movement in the South* (1877), and J. C. Lester and D. L. Wilson, *Ku Klux Klan: Its Origins, Growth, and Disbandment* (1884), this being the only known work attributed to one of the original founders of the Klan. In fact, there even exists a bibliography for scholars, compiled by Lenwood G. Davis and Janet Sims-Wood, *The Ku Klux Klan: A Bibliography* (1984), which favors the later generations of Klans but does include material on the Reconstruction episode.

As the existence of a bibliography makes clear, historians have not neglected the Klan. Several of the studies referred to cover the entire Reconstruction period and deal with the army as an assistant in enforcing civil law. One study stands above the rest: Allen W. Trelease's *White Terror: The Ku Klux Klan Conspiracy and Southern Reconstruction* (1971), which remains the best work on the Reconstruction Klan, as well as the finest description of the efforts of the army and state governments to squash the movement. Everette Swinney's *Suppressing the Ku Klux Klan: The Enforcement of the Reconstruction Amendments, 1870–1877* (1987) is more limited, but it covers better than Trelease the legal and constitutional battles after the decline of the Klan. Unfortunately George Rable's *But There Was No Peace: The Role of Violence in the Politics of Reconstruction* (1984) is weak in terms of explaining white violence and the attempts to quash it. Rable presents snapshots of various outbreaks, and although the book describes white violence beyond the Klan, it does not adequately explain why whites acted as they did or how state and Federal governments reacted.

Rable's monocausational conclusion of racial dominance is fundamentally accurate but perhaps overly simplistic. Some recent works have attempted to draw sharper distinctions and explanations for white opposition. With quantitative analysis, Gregg Cantrell ties white violence directly to political changes in "Racial Violence and Reconstruction Politics in Texas, 1867–1868" (1990). Cantrell shows a correlation between the implementation of law and a rise in violence, arguing that whites—believing legal options had slipped beyond their control—resorted to illegal options instead. For Paul David Phillips, it is the challenge to white control in general that is the catalyst for violence. In "White Reaction to the Freedmen's Bureau in Tennessee" (1966), Phillips postulates that the bureau was innately antagonistic, as it was an outside force meddling in the most sacred of relationships: that of whites and blacks in the South. A recent addition to the school of racial dominance and local control is Richard Zuczek's *State of Rebellion: Reconstruction South Carolina, 1865–1877* (1996), which approaches the period as part of the Civil War, with war waged after 1865 by other means. Zuczek argues that Reconstruction was a continuation of the struggle by conservative whites for control of their region and a continuation of the Federal government's attempts to enforce Federal law.

Worth mentioning here are two books that provide interesting comparative views on Federal law enforcement. Wilbur R. Miller's *Revenuers and Moonshiners: Enforcing Federal Liquor Law in the Mountain South, 1865–1900* (1991) describes a successful effort by the Federal government to enforce revenue and liquor laws in the Appalachians. Miller confronts directly the government's attempt to enforce unpopular laws and suggests reasons that the army and Justice Department succeeded in Appalachia but failed in the Reconstruction South. Less cohesive but still informative is Stephen Cresswell's *Mormons and Cowboys, Moonshiners and Klansmen: Federal Law Enforcement in the South and West, 1870–1893* (1991). Cresswell's four case studies add little to the standard accounts, but his rather sweeping hypothesis—that these various undertakings were attempts by the Federal government to stamp out oddities and create a "uniform nation"—requires far more research and may attract far more attention. If so, historians will need to grapple with the role of the military in this standardizing of late-nineteenth-century America.

Many other noteworthy studies of the military in the South exist, but the dictates of space are inflexible. As this chapter comes to a close, a mention of the army's so-called withdrawal from the South is appropriate. The best summation of the Compromise of 1877 and the removal controversy is Vincent DeSantis, "Rutherford B. Hayes and the Removal of the Troops and the End of Reconstruction" (1982), which provides an excellent bibliographic-historiographic examination of army activity during the waning months of Reconstruction (in *Region, Race and Reconstruction: Essays in Honor of C. Vann Woodward*, 1982, 417–450). Also deserving of mention are several published primary works that are invaluable for their contemporary views on the military and Reconstruction. Among the most useful are John Williams DeForest, *A Union Officer in the Reconstruction* (1948), Sidney Andrews, *The South since the War* (1866), Edward King, *The Great South* (1875), Whitelaw Reid, *After the War: A Tour of the Southern States, 1865–1866* (1866), and James T. Trowbridge, *The South: A Tour of Its Battlefields and Ruined Cities* (1866).

Unfortunately, these primary works cannot fill the gaps that scholars have left untended. The political role of the military in the South merits further investigation, as do the civil-military dilemmas faced by the army after Southern readmission. Even in areas where much work has been done, questions persist. Was the army composed of altruistic heroes or racist oppressors, for example? But I am optimistic, for the past few years have shown a marked increase in scholarly interest concerning the military during Reconstruction. More research, analysis, and imagination will better explain the military's significance during Reconstruction and eventually allow the army to move out from behind the shadow of its earlier achievements and accept credit for another task well done.

BIBLIOGRAPHY

Abbott, Martin. *The Freedmen's Bureau in South Carolina, 1865–1872.* Chapel Hill: University of North Carolina Press, 1968.

Alderson, William. "The Influence of Military Rule and the Freedmen's Bureau on Reconstruction in Virginia, 1865–1870." Ph.D. diss., Vanderbilt University, 1952.

Alexander, Roberta Sue. *North Carolina Faces the Freedmen: Race Relations during Presidential Reconstruction.* Durham, NC: Duke University Press, 1985.

Anderson, Eric, and Alfred A. Moss, eds. *The Facts of Reconstruction: Essays in Honor of John Hope Franklin.* Baton Rouge: Louisiana State University Press, 1991.

Andrews, Sidney. *The South since the War.* 1866. Reprint New York: Arno Press and New York Times, 1969.

Ash, Stephen V. *When the Yankees Came: Conflict and Chaos in the Occupied South, 1861–1865.* Chapel Hill: University of North Carolina Press, 1995.

———. *Middle Tennessee Society Transformed, 1860–1870: War and Peace in the Upper South.* Baton Rouge: Louisiana State University Press, 1988.

———. "Poor Whites in the Occupied South, 1861–1865." *Journal of Southern History* 55 (February 1991): 39–62.

————. "White Virginians under Federal Occupation, 1861–1865." *Virginia Magazine of History and Biography* 98 (April 1990): 169–192.

Aston, B. W. "Federal Military Occupation of the Southwest." *Texas Military History* 8 (1970): 123–134.

Beamer, Carl. "Gray Ghostbusters: Eastern Theater Union Counterguerrilla Operations in the Civil War, 1861–1865." Ph.D. diss., Ohio State University, 1988.

Beard, James Melville. *K.K.K. Sketches: Humorous and Didactic, Treating the More Important Events of the Ku-Klux-Klan Movement in the South.* Philadelphia: Claxton, Remsen, and Haffelfinger, 1877.

Bentley, George. *A History of the Freedmen's Bureau.* Philadelphia: University of Pennsylvania Press, 1955.

Berlin, Ira, Joseph P. Reidy, and Leslie S. Rowland, eds. *Freedom: A Documentary History of Emancipation Series II: The Black Military Experience.* New York: Cambridge University Press, 1982.

Breihan, Carl W. *Quantrill and His Civil War Guerrillas.* Denver: Sage Books, 1959.

Brownlee, Richard S. *Gray Ghosts of the Confederacy: Guerrilla Warfare in the West, 1861–1865.* Baton Rouge: Louisiana State University Press, 1958.

Butchart, Ronald E. *Northern Schools, Southern Blacks, and Reconstruction: Freedmen's Education, 1862–1875.* Westport, CT: Greenwood Press, 1980.

Cantrell, Gregg. "Racial Violence and Reconstruction Politics in Texas, 1867–1868." *Southwestern Historical Quarterly* 93 (January 1990): 333–356.

Capers, Gerald M. *Occupied City: New Orleans under the Federals, 1862–1865.* Louisville: University of Kentucky Press, 1965.

Carpenter, A. H. "Military Government of the Southern Territory, 1861–1865." In *Annual Report of the American Historical Association for the Year 1900,* 1: 467–498. Washington, D.C., 1901.

Carter, Dan T. *When the War Was Over: The Failure of Self-Reconstruction in the South, 1865–1867.* Baton Rouge: Louisiana State University Press, 1985.

Castel, Albert. *A Frontier State at War: Kansas 1861–1865.* Ithaca, NY: Cornell University Press, 1958.

————. *William Clarke Quantrill: His Life and Times.* New York: Frederick Fell, Publishers, 1962.

————. *General Sterling Price and the Civil War in the West.* Baton Rouge: Louisiana State University Press, 1968.

————. "Orders No. 11 and the Civil War on the Border." *Missouri Historical Review* 52 (July 1963): 357–368.

Cimbala, Paul. "The Freedmen's Bureau, the Freedmen, and Sherman's Grant in Georgia, 1865–1867." *Journal of Southern History* 55 (November 1989): 597–632.

————. "The Terms of Freedom: The Freedmen's Bureau and Reconstruction in Georgia, 1865–1870." Ph.D. diss., Emory University, 1983.

Cresswell, Stephen. *Mormons and Cowboys, Moonshiners and Klansmen: Federal Law Enforcement in the South and West, 1870–1893.* Tuscaloosa: University of Alabama Press, 1991.

Crouch, Barry A. *The Freedmen's Bureau and Black Texans.* Austin: University of Texas Press, 1992.

Davis, Lenwood G., and Janet Sims-Wood, eds. *The Ku Klux Klan: A Bibliography.* Westport, CT: Greenwood Press, 1984.

Dawson, Joseph G. *Army Generals and Reconstruction: Louisiana, 1862–1877.* Baton Rouge: Louisiana State University Press, 1982.

DeForest, John Williams. *A Union Officer in the Reconstruction.* Edited by James H. Croushore and David M. Potter. New Haven, CT: Yale University Press, 1948.

Durham, Walter T. *Nashville: The Occupied City.* Nashville: Tennessee Historical Society, 1985.

———. *Reluctant Partners: Nashville and the Union, 1863–1865.* Nashville: Tennessee Historical Society, 1987.

Durrill, Wayne K. *War of Another Kind: A Southern Community in the Great Rebellion.* New York: Oxford University Press, 1990.

Fellman, Michael. *Inside War: The Guerrilla Conflict in Missouri during the American Civil War.* New York: Oxford University Press, 1989.

Finley, Randy. "The Freedmen's Bureau in Arkansas." Ph.D. diss., University of Arkansas, 1992.

Fisher, Noel. " 'War at Every Man's Door': The Struggle for East Tennessee, 1860–1869." Ph.D. diss., Ohio State University, 1993.

Freidel, Frank B. "General Orders 100 and Military Government." *Mississippi Valley Historical Review* 32 (March 1946): 541–556.

Futrell, Robert J. "Federal Military Government in the South, 1861–1865." *Military Affairs* 15 (Winter 1951): 181–191.

Gabriel, Ralph H. "The American Experience with Military Government." *American Historical Review* 49 (July 1944): 630–643.

Gerteis, Louis S. *From Contraband to Freedmen: Federal Policy toward Southern Blacks, 1861–1865.* Westport, CT: Greenwood Press, 1973.

Gildrie, Richard P. "Guerrilla Warfare in the Lower Cumberland Valley, 1862–1865." *Tennessee Historical Quarterly* 49 (Fall 1990): 161–176.

Gillette, William. *Retreat from Reconstruction, 1869–1879.* Baton Rouge: Louisiana State University Press, 1980.

Goldhaber, Michael. "A Mission Unfulfilled: Freedmen's Education in North Carolina, 1865–1870." *Journal of Negro History* 77 (Fall 1992): 199–210.

Goodrich, Thomas. *Bloody Dawn: The Story of the Lawrence Massacre.* Kent, OH: Kent State University Press, 1991.

Govan, Gilbert E., and James W. Livingood. "Chattanooga under Military Occupation, 1863–1865." *Journal of Southern History* 17 (February 1951): 23–47.

Greenough, Mark K. "Aftermath at Appomattox: Federal Military Occupation of Appomattox County, May–November 1865. *Civil War History* 31 (March 1985): 5–23.

Grimsley, Mark. *The Hard Hand of War: Union Military Policy toward Southern Civilians, 1861–1865.* New York: Cambridge: Cambridge University Press, 1995.

Hasson, Gail Snowden. "The Medical Activities of the Freedmen's Bureau in Reconstruction Alabama, 1865–1868." Ph.D. diss., University of Alabama, 1982.

Johnson, Howard Palmer. "New Orleans under General Butler." *Louisiana Historical Quarterly* 24 (April 1941): 434–536.

King, Edward. *The Great South.* 1875. Reprint, New York: Arno Press and New York Times, 1969.

Kirkland, John R. "Federal Troops in the South Atlantic States during Reconstruction, 1865–1877." Ph.D. diss., University of North Carolina, 1968.

Kousser, Morgan, and James M. McPherson, eds. *Region, Race and Reconstruction:*

Essays in Honor of C. Vann Woodward. New York: Oxford University Press, 1982.

Lester, J. C., and D. L. Wilson. *Ku Klux Klan: Its Origins, Growth, and Disbandment.* 1884. Reprint, New York: Da Capo Press, 1973.

Lieber, Francis. "Instructions for the Government of the Armies of the United States in the Field (General Orders No. 100)." In *The War of the Rebellion: A Compilation of the Official Records of the Union and Confederate Armies,* ser. III, 3: 148–164. Washington, D.C.: Government Printing Office, 1880–1901.

McFeely, William S. *Yankee Stepfather: General O. O. Howard and the Freedmen.* New Haven: Yale University Press, 1968.

McGehee, Stuart C. "Military Origins of the New South: The Army of the Cumberland and Chattanooga's Freedmen." *Civil War History* 34 (1988): 323–343.

Majeske, Penelope K. "Johnson, Stanton, and Grant: A Reconsideration of the Events Leading to the First Reconstruction Act." *Southern Studies* 22 (1983): 340–350.

———. "Virginia after Appomattox: The United States Army and the Formation of Presidential Reconstruction Policy." *West Virginia History* 43 (1982): 95–117.

Mantell, Martin E. *Johnson, Grant, and the Politics of Reconstruction.* New York: Columbia University Press, 1973.

Marten, James, "For the Army, the People, and Abraham Lincoln: A Yankee Newspaper in Occupied Texas." *Civil War History* 39 (June 1993): 126–147.

Maslowski, Peter. *Treason Must Be Made Odious: Military Occupation and Wartime Reconstruction in Nashville, Tennessee, 1862–1865.* Millwood, NY: KTO Press, 1978.

Miller, Wilbur R. *Revenuers and Moonshiners: Enforcing Federal Liquor Law in the Mountain South, 1865–1900.* Chapel Hill: University of North Carolina Press, 1991.

Mink, Charles R. "General Orders No. 11, the Forced Evacuation of Civilians during the Civil War." *Military Affairs* 34 (1970): 132–136.

Monaghan, Jay. *Civil War on the Western Border, 1854–1865.* New York: Bonanza Books, 1955.

Morris, Robert C. *Reading, 'Riting, and Reconstruction: The Education of the Freedmen in the South, 1861–1870.* Chicago: University of Chicago Press, 1982.

Nieman, Donald G. *To Set the Law in Motion: The Freedmen's Bureau and the Legal Rights of Blacks, 1865–1868.* Millwood, NY: KTO Press, 1979.

Olsen, Otto ed. *Reconstruction and Redemption in the South.* Baton Rouge: Louisiana State University Press, 1980.

Oubre, Claude F. *Forty Acres and a Mule: The Freedmen's Bureau and Black Land Ownership.* Baton Rouge: Louisiana State University Press, 1978.

Parks, Joseph H. "Memphis under Military Rule, 1862–1865." *East Tennessee Historical Society Publications* 14 (1942): 31–58.

Pfanz, Harry W. "Soldiering in the South during the Reconstruction Period, 1865–1877." Ph.D. diss., Ohio State University, 1958.

Phillips, Paul David. "White Reaction to the Freedmen's Bureau in Tennessee." *Tennessee Historical Quarterly* 25 (Spring 1966): 50–62.

Pierce, Paul Skeels. *The Freedmen's Bureau: A Chapter in the History of Reconstruction.* 1904. Reprint, New York: Haskell House Publishers, 1971.

Rable, George C. *But There Was No Peace: The Role of Violence in the Politics of Reconstruction.* Athens: University of Georgia Press, 1984.

Reid, Whitelaw. *After the War: A Tour of the Southern States, 1865–1866.* 1866. Reprint, New York: Harper & Row, 1965.

Richter, William L. *The Army in Texas during Reconstruction, 1865–1870.* College Station, TX: Texas A&M University Press, 1987.

———. *Overreached on All Sides: The Freedmen's Bureau Administrators in Texas, 1865–1868.* College Station, TX: Texas A&M University Press, 1991.

———. "The Revolver Rules the Day! Colonel DeWitt C. Brown and the Freedmen's Bureau in Paris, Texas, 1867–1868." *Southwestern Historical Quarterly* 93 (January 1990): 303–332.

Ripley, C. Peter. *Slaves and Freedmen in Civil War Louisiana.* Baton Rouge: Louisiana State University Press, 1976.

Rose, Wille Lee. *Rehearsal for Reconstruction: The Port Royal Experiment.* Indianapolis: Bobbs-Merrill, 1964.

St. Clair, Kenneth E. "Military Justice in North Carolina, 1865: A Microcosm of Reconstruction." *Civil War History* 11 (December 1965): 341–350.

Sefton, James E. *The United States Army and Reconstruction, 1865–1877.* Baton Rouge: Louisiana State University Press, 1968.

Shofner, Jerrell H. *Nor Is It Over Yet: Florida in the Era of Reconstruction.* Gainesville: University Presses of Florida, 1974.

Simpson, Brooks D. *Let Us Have Peace: Ulysses S. Grant and the Politics of War and Reconstruction.* Chapel Hill: University of North Carolina Press, 1991.

Smallwood, James. "When the Klan Rode: White Terror in Reconstruction Texas." *Journal of the West* 25 (October 1986): 4–13.

Swinney, Everette. *Suppressing the Ku Klux Klan: The Enforcement of the Reconstruction Amendments, 1870–1877.* New York: Garland Publishing, 1987.

Taylor, Joe Gray. *Louisiana Reconstructed, 1863–1877.* Baton Rouge: Louisiana State University Press, 1974.

Trefousse, Hans Louis. *Ben Butler: The South Called Him Beast!* New York: Twayne Publishers, 1957.

Trelease, Allen W. *White Terror: The Ku Klux Klan Conspiracy and Southern Reconstruction.* New York: Harper & Row, 1971.

Trowbridge, James T. *The South: A Tour of Its Battlefields and Ruined Cities.* 1866. Reprint, New York: Arno Press and New York Times, 1969.

Tunnell, Ted. *Crucible of Reconstruction: War, Radicalism, and Race in Louisiana, 1862–1877.* Baton Rouge: Louisiana State University Press, 1984.

Wade, Wyn Craig. *The Fiery Cross.* New York: Simon & Schuster, 1987.

White, Howard A. *The Freedmen's Bureau in Louisiana.* Baton Rouge: Louisiana State University Press, 1970.

Williams, James Levon, Jr. "Civil War and Reconstruction in the Yazoo Mississippi Delta, 1863–1875." Ph.D. diss., University of Arizona, 1992.

Zuczek, Richard. *State of Rebellion: Reconstruction South Carolina, 1865–1877.* Columbia: University of South Carolina Press, forthcoming.

42

Economics

Howard Bodenhorn

Economic scholarship on the Reconstruction era has generated a voluminous literature. Almost since the inception of Reconstruction in 1865, economists and historians have dealt with such issues as the economic ramifications of emancipation, the commercialization of agriculture, the agrarian protests, the rise of the modern industrial enterprise, urban growth, the trusts, the railroads, and finance and money. Each of these is dealt with in turn in this chapter. The careful reader will quickly notice, however, that relatively little of the extant work is integrative—that is, painting sweeping landscapes with broad brushes. This is partly explained by the size of the subject and partly by the inclination of historians and economists. The American experience, even during the relatively compact span of 1865 to 1914, was too varied and too expansive to lend itself to broad-brush interpretation. Readable economic history requires unifying themes and narrowness of focus. Without it, all that can be achieved is description without interpretation, a fruitless enterprise indeed. The books and articles discussed within demonstrate this narrowness, and it is left to critical and thoughtful readers to paint their own sweeping intellectual landscape.

Common to most of the cited works is their following the tradition of the new economic history. Since the early 1960s, economic history has experienced a revolution of sorts—a cliometric revolution, some have labeled it. This new approach's most significant contribution to the study of history has been its wholehearted acceptance of John Clapham's (1930) dictum: every economic historian should "have acquired what might be called the statistical sense, the habit of asking in relation to any institution, group or movement the questions: how large? how long? how often? how representative?" Armed with mathematical economic theory and electronic computers, new economic historians repeatedly attempt to answer Clapham's questions and have become, as Donald McCloskey (1992) wrote, the careful carpenters of history—measuring twice, cutting once. Cliometric history is therefore characterized by two elements: the application of explicit economic theory to the study of historical events and the use of modern data-gathering and statistical techniques. Most of the books and articles discussed follow in this tradition, but every attempt was made to highlight works accessible to nonspecialists. For those interested in the development and early achievements of cliometrics, Donald McCloskey's *Econometric History* (1987) provides a concise introduction.

Before one dives headlong into detailed economic studies of the Reconstruction era, it would benefit the casual reader and serious student alike to familiarize themselves with the economic approach to history. There are several well-written textbooks that discuss in considerable detail the post–Civil War period. Gary Walton and Hugh Rockoff's *History of the American Economy* (1994), Jonathan Hughes's *American Economic History* (1990), and Jeremy Atack and Peter Passell's *A New Economic View of American History* (1994) are all quite readable and serve as useful introductions. *The Americans: An Economic Record,* by Stanley Lebergott (1984), will appeal to those looking for something with less resemblance to a textbook. Lebergott's style is lively, his book is well documented, and both traditional and modern interpretations are served up with generous portions of his opinions. For those more accustomed to the style of historians, Stuart Bruchey's *Enterprise: The Dynamic Economy of a Free People* (1990) will make them feel right at home. Although its discussion of some issues is dated, Robert Higgs's *Transformation of the American Economy* (1971) is a good starting point for those who would appreciate both a short refresher course in economics and a general outline of the economics of Reconstruction.

EMANCIPATION AND THE SOUTHERN EXPERIENCE

Any discussion of Reconstruction begins (and generally ends) with the economic ramifications of emancipation. The issues are manifold, but they have sorted themselves out into two broad categories: the economic implications of emancipation and racism on the freedmen themselves, and their effects on the general development of the South as a distinct regional economy. *Black Reconstruction in America* by W. E. B. Du Bois (1935) has acquired the status of a classic. It is a remarkable study of the role freedmen played in Reconstruction, but its chapters on economic issues per se are written from a decidedly Marxian viewpoint that have an anachronistic ring to modern ears. DuBois's treatment of Reconstruction as a class struggle, however, set the tone for the subsequent debate. Other useful introductions to the Southern experience—though from the point of view of the pure historian—are George Tindall's *The Pursuit of Southern History* (1964) and *South Carolina Negroes, 1877–1900* (1952).

The concurrent, yet independent, publication of *One Kind of Freedom* (1977) by Roger Ransom and Richard Sutch and *Competition and Coercion* (1977) by Robert Higgs opened the modern cliometric debate and set the boundaries for subsequent research. Ransom and Sutch provide a readable historical narrative "describing and interpreting the economic changes that swept through the South following emancipation." Since whites, especially poor whites, viewed economic competition with blacks as a zero-sum game, they developed institutions and rules (the notorious Jim Crow laws, for example) that effectively proscribed black advancement. Given that approximately one-half the Southern population was in near peonage, the relatively slow growth of the Southern economy as a whole becomes easily understandable. In *Competition and Coercion,* Higgs comes to nearly opposite conclusions. He argues that while the political sphere was one of coercion, the economic sphere was one of competition. Higgs musters considerable evidence to support his hypothesis and argues that although racism kept freedmen from achieving their full potential, it did not disallow all progress. *Market Institutions and Economic Progress in the New South, 1865–1900* (1981), edited by Gary Walton and James Shepherd, is a collection of essays by various prominent economic historians and represents a significant contribution for several reasons. Each essay critically analyzes one of Ransom and Sutch's major conclusions. Some find considerable support; others do not. In addition, Ransom and Sutch contribute two chapters responding directly to their critics and providing a glimpse of academic debate at its best. In *Old South, New South,* (1986) Gavin Wright succeeds in integrating the debate. He argues that the unique Southern economy reflects the legacy of slavery. Southern labor markets were isolated from the national market and, when combined with the lack of an indigenous technological community and the late start compared to the North, the relative backwardness of Southern industry becomes immediately explicable.

CROPPERS, TENANTS, AND PROTEST: AGRICULTURE, NORTH AND SOUTH

While economist historians have painted a picture of the Southern economy with relatively broad brushes, none has attempted to do so for the Northern economy. While the old Confederacy is often viewed as a unique and unified economic and political entity, the North is less rigidly defined and represented by quite disparate histories. Obviously, the experiences of the manufacturing Northeast do not well reflect the experiences of the agricultural Midwest, so defining the archetypal Northern experience has eluded economic historians. The history of the North therefore has been written as the history of both specific industrial sectors and specific regions.

More volumes have been devoted to agriculture than any other subject of the postbellum era, and sorting through them represents a daunting task. The topography of the literature varies in emphasis and point of view but typically deals with the westward push into the prairies, the increased commercialization and mechanization of Northern agriculture, the alleged overspecialization in cotton and the relative stagnation of Southern agriculture, farm tenancy, and, of course, the rising and ebbing tide of agrarian protest movements from the 1870s through the 1890s. *Readings in the Economic History of American Agriculture* (1925), edited by Louis Schmidt and Earle Ross, provides a dated but useful introduction to the issues. *Agriculture and National Development* (1990), edited by Lou Ferleger, brings together several essays by prominent agricultural and economic historians that address many of the same issues. The difference, of course, is the incorporation of the methods of the new economic history and sixty-five years of additional research. The essays are of consistently high quality and provide an excellent introduction.

   The Farmer's Last Frontier (1945) by Fred Shannon provides a comprehensive survey of the history of agriculture in the postbellum era but gives relatively little space to the problems inherent in Southern agriculture. Shannon is generally sympathetic to the claims by agrarian protestors of an eastern cabal of money lenders, bankers, railroad men, manufacturers, and politicians, all seemingly bent on destroying western agriculture. Allan Bogue's *From Prairie to Corn Belt* (1963), while sympathetic to the plight of western farmers, is reluctant to blame eastern monopolists. Bogue, like Shannon, provides a comprehensive survey but is considerably more objective in viewpoint. His book is a masterpiece of economic history, mixing primary and secondary source materials into an engaging and eminently readable story that overturns some traditional interpretations, validates others, and questions all with a critical eye. There would be no better book than Bogue's if one were to read but a single volume on early prairie agriculture.

   Dominating the histories of Northern and western agricultural are interpretations of the tide of agrarian protest in the late nineteenth century. John Hicks's *The Populist Revolt* (1961) provides a useful introduction to the issues, events, and politics of the Alliance movement. Paul Gates, *Landlords and Tenants on the Prairie Frontier* (1973), attributes agrarian discontent to the relative impoverishment of western farmers. To Gates the growing number of farm tenants relative to owner-operators was a sign of hard times and systemic institutional failure. Land was abundant in the West, and the inability of farmers to own it represented nothing less than the power of land monopolists, railroads, speculators, and bankers to extort and evict hapless farmers. Donald Winters, *Farmers without Farms* (1978), on the other hand, argues that tenancy was a rational economic response. Tenancy represented a rung on the agricultural ladder whereby young men worked as farm labor to learn the trade. They later graduated to tenancy or renter status, and, once enough experience had been gained and capital saved, they moved up to full owner-operator status. Jeremy Atack, "Tenants and Yeomen in the Nineteenth Century" (1988), also shows that increased farm tenancy in the later nineteenth century was an evolutionary, not a revolutionary, process.

   Increased tenancy coincided with the increased commercialization of agriculture. With increased capital requirements and a growing reliance on the market, some amount of agrarian discontent was to be expected. Douglass North, *Growth and Welfare in the American Past* (1966), argues, however, that this provided little basis for complaint. Railroad rates fell during the postbellum era, and the agriculture terms of trade improved. Anne Mayhew, "A Reappraisal of the Causes of Farm Protest in the United States, 1870–1900" (1972), argues that discontent grew more from the increased commercialization than from movements in relative prices. Before the Civil War, success as a subsistence farmer required some experience and much hard work. After the war, success depended as much on business savvy as on farming skills. Robert McGuire, "Economic Causes of Late Nineteenth Century Agrarian Unrest" (1981), largely supports Mayhew's thesis but argues that the root cause of discontent arose from varying yields and prices of farm output—a problem of lesser consequence if farming is less commercialized. James Stock, "Real Estate Mortgages, Foreclosures, and Midwestern Agrarian Unrest, 1865–1920" (1984), too finds support for the Mayhew thesis but places more emphasis on the need for mortgage financing in the new agricultural order. Although the annual number of foreclosures remained small throughout the postbellum era, most farm owners were mortgaged and had witnessed a relative, friend, or neighbor foreclosed on. This situation created an atmosphere of fear and distrust of eastern money lenders. Peter and JoAnne Argersinger add a new dimension to the discussion in "The Machine Breakers" (1984). Farmworkers (as opposed to tenants and owners) have previously received scant attention. These authors point out that increased mechanization of agriculture displaced farm laborers who, in hard times, went on rampages of machine breaking, barn burning, and other forms of vandalism.

Dominant themes in Southern agriculture revolve around tenancy, sharecropping, rural credit, and the alleged overproduction of cotton. Ransom and Sutch's *One Kind of Freedom* remains the best introduction to the modern debate, with several chapters given over to Southern agricultural problems. The "labor problem" following emancipation ultimately resolved itself in sharecropping whereby freedmen worked the former plantations for a share of the crops. Since they were never given their promised forty acres and a mule, sharecropping made the best of an undesirable situation. The traditional interpretation of sharecropping was that it was imposed by whites who doubted the abilities of former slaves to apply themselves diligently and make sensible production decisions. Joseph Reid's "Sharecropping as an Understandable Market Response" (1973) argues that sharecropping lowered transaction costs between landlords and laborers and created incentives for each to renegotiate in the face of extraordinary events. Donald Winters, "Postbellum Reorganization of Southern Agriculture" (1988), believes that sharecropping arose because it provided a basis for credit for a majority of citizens who owned no real and very little personal property. Southern courts ruled that crops grown under share agreements constituted assignable property that could be transferred in return for much-needed credit.

That credit created, many believed, an oppressive system of debt peonage.

Sharecroppers assigned their crops to country merchants in exchange for essentials or to landlords for necessary supplies who then doctored the books keeping their croppers in perpetual debt and thus tied to the land. Ransom and Sutch largely accept this interpretation, but several papers (e.g., Winters 1988) have argued that it was not nearly as pervasive as once believed. Peter Temin, "Freedom and Coercion: Notes on the Analysis of Debt Peonage in *One Kind of Freedom*" (1979), argues that such a system would have been profitable for neither debtors nor creditors. And Price Fishback, "Debt Peonage in Postbellum Georgia" (1989), shows that average indebtedness was falling throughout the 1880s.

Several recent papers have also challenged the conventional wisdom that a majority of freedmen made their way as sharecroppers. Richard Fuke, "Planters, Apprenticeship, and Forced Labor" (1988), argues that many freedmen aspired to sharecropping status because it held the potential for eventual landownership, but most labored as fixed-wage employees. James Irwin, "Farmers and Laborers" (1990), also shows that outside the Cotton South, most blacks were laborers rather than renters or sharecroppers.

Two issues that have received surprisingly scant attention are the effect of increasing commercialization of agriculture and the late adoption of mechanized practices on Southern farms. Ann Patton Malone, "Piney Woods Farmers of South Georgia, 1850–1900" (1986), offers some early results from a larger project aimed at a study of commercialization; her findings are disheartening. Lumber and turpentine industries entered the region in the 1880s, and, by the late 1890s, society and economy had been radically altered, not necessarily to the betterment of the original inhabitants. Warren Whatley, "Southern Agrarian Labor Contracts as Impediments to Cotton Mechanization" (1987), deals with the early twentieth century, but his findings can be generalized to the earlier era. Sharecropping, he believes, inhibited the search for and eventual adoption of new agricultural techniques.

THE IRON HORSE: INDUSTRY AND ENTERPRISE

In industry it was the rise of the modern, multiplant, industrial enterprise that has captured the attention of economic historians. Glenn Porter's *The Rise of Big Business, 1860–1910* (1973) is a quick and useful introduction. Edward Kirkland's *Industry Comes of Age: Business, Labor and Public Policy, 1860–1897* (1961) is more comprehensive but is dated in many places. The unquestioned magnum opus of the literature remains Alfred Chandler's *The Visible Hand* (1977). Chandler argues that the large-scale industrial firm arose as it became more cost-effective for managerial structures, rather than markets, to direct resource flows into and out of the business enterprise. Vertically integrated firms developed to ensure a relatively stable flow of inputs into production processes and to organize appropriate marketing structures for their finished products. *The Great Merger Movement in American Business, 1895–1904*

(1985) by Naomi Lamoreaux investigates an alternative route: the horizontal combination. These enterprises arose for very different reasons: avoiding competition, particularly in industries where fixed costs were high relative to operating costs. That the merger movement appeared when it did was not an accident; it resulted from pressures created by the depression of the mid-1890s.

Although there have been studies of almost all major (and several minor) American industries, the two that have attracted the greatest attention have been steel and the railroads. Among the best investigating the former are Peter Temin, *Iron and Steel in Nineteenth-Century America* (1964), and Harold Livesay, *Andrew Carnegie and the Rise of Big Business* (1975). The study of railroads, however, has created a great rift within the literature.

Despite historians' continued insistence that railroads were indispensable to the development of the modern economy, business and economic historians have long questioned the validity of this view and have applied their quantitative methods to the subject. In *The Railroads* Alfred Chandler (1965) sets out a persuasive case for the pathbreaking role of railroads, arguing that their real importance lay in their solving many of the organizational problems that would confront later industrial concerns. In *Railroads and American Economic Growth* (1964), Robert Fogel denies that the railroad was indispensable to economic growth and proposes that an equally effective alternative—the canal—already existed. Jeffrey Williamson, "The Railroads and Midwestern Development 1870–90" (1975), disputes some of Fogel's findings but shows that the developing transportation network inhibited midwestern industrialization and only marginally affected westward migration. Despite the questioning of long-held assumptions by economic historians, many pure historians continue to heap reams of superlatives upon the iron horse. Albro Martin, *Railroads Triumphant* (1992), for example, still says: "There has never been any sustained attack on the idea that the steam railroad was the most significant invention . . . in the rise of industrial society." After the dust cleared, it is difficult to determine who prevailed, but both Chandler's and Fogel's arguments remain persuasive (a Nobel laureate's [Fogel] studies should be ignored only at one's intellectual peril).

GIVE US YOUR TIRED AND POOR: POPULATION, IMMIGRATION, AND LABOR

Population and labor is currently a growth industry in economic history, but several studies already exist. *Manpower in Economic Growth* (1964) by Stanley Lebergott remains the most carefully documented study of labor in the American economy from 1800 through 1960. Thomas Weiss, "The Industrial Distribution of the Urban and Rural Workforce" (1972), updates some of Lebergott's findings. Michael Haines and Barbara Anderson, "New Demographic History of the Late nineteenth-Century United States" (1988), provide a survey and critical interpretation of modern findings. Recent work has focused on the position of women and minorities in the labor force. Among the more Interesting dealing with black labor history are Gerald Jaynes's *Branches without Roots* (1986); a volume edited by W.E.B. Du Bois, *The Negro in Business* (1899); Robert Higgs, "Participation of Blacks and Immigrants in the American Merchant Class, 1890–1910" (1976); and Paul Worthman, "Black Workers and Labor Unions in Birmingham, Alabama, 1897–1904" (1969). Two articles by Claudia Goldin, "Female Labor Force Participation" (1977) and "The Work and Wages of Single Women, 1870 to 1920" (1980), are good introductions to the problems faced by female workers.

The literature on immigration and how immigrants fared is growing, though no consensus has been reached or seems likely. Brinley Thomas's *Migration and Economic Growth* (1954) traces the cyclical waves of immigration, linking them to developments in both Europe and the United States. Larry Neal and Paul Uselding, "Immigration, a Neglected Source of American Economic Growth" (1972), show that immigration provided a social savings to the American economy, promoting development rather than slowing it, as contemporaries claimed. Paul McGouldrick and Michael Tannen, "Did American Manufacturers Discriminate against Immigrants before 1914?" (1977), find that employers discriminated against recent immigrants. Robert Higgs, "Race, Skill, and Earnings" (1971), however, finds little evidence of effective discrimination.

GREENBACKS AND BANKS: MONEY, CAPITAL, AND FINANCE

The post–Civil War experience with money, finance, and capital has spawned a large and still growing literature. To finance the war, the Federal government issued large volumes of fiat legal tender (greenbacks) and largely abandoned the gold standard. Wesley Clair Mitchell's pioneering work, *History of the Greenbacks* (1903), remains one of the best studies relating greenback issues, the gold premium, and wholesale prices, all within an international context. In *The Money Question during Reconstruction* (1967), Walter T. K. Nugent provides a useful introduction to the generally rancorous politics of money between 1865 and 1900. At times, however, his characterization of the classical school's defense of a gold standard is oversimplified, to the point of making it grotesque and comical. His analysis of the international context of the American debate, on the other hand, provides a balanced and informative portrait. In addition he argues that the "Crime of '73" (the demonetization of silver) was no crime but rather an attempt to preserve the public credit by abandoning bimetallism in the face of falling silver prices.

Any serious student of the monetary history of the period must ultimately turn to Milton Friedman and Anna Jacobson Schwartz's *Monetary History of the United States, 1867–1960* (1963). In one of the most cited, most influential works in economics of the twentieth century, Friedman and Schwartz provide a thoroughly documented history of monetary movements in the United States, showing that general economic instability could usually be traced to monetary instability. The first four chapters flesh out the period from the Civil War through Reconstruction and provide a monetarist interpretation of both the course of events and political discussions of the day.

Two recent studies have linked the money question back to agrarian unrest and show that there may have been some legitimate basis for complaint. Milton Friedman, in "The Crime of 1873" (1990), challenges Nugent's view of the Crime of '73. He argues that had the United States retained bimetallism, the gold-silver exchange rate would have remained relatively stable and the United States would have experienced a modest inflation rather than the severe deflation that actually developed. Demonetization of silver was a mistake, generating adverse consequences for both the American and world economies. In "The 'Wizard of Oz' as Monetary Allegory" (1990), Hugh Rockoff relates Frank Baum's classic children's story to the political debate over money in the 1890s. Rockoff convincingly demonstrates that such things as Dorothy's silver slippers (changed to ruby for visual effect in the film), the yellow brick road, and Oz are all monetary allusions.

Banking and capital markets have also attracted considerable attention. In *The Molding of American Banking: Men and Ideas* (1968), Fritz Redlich sketches the broad outlines of the history of banking from both theoretical (what they were supposed to do) and practical (what they actually did) viewpoints. If there is any single shortcoming in the monetary history of the Reconstruction era, however, it is the lack of a definitive study of postbellum banking comparable to Bray Hammond's classic antebellum study, *Banks and Politics from the Revolution to the Civil War* (1957). The overriding concern among financial historians has been the inability of postbellum markets to allocate capital efficiently. Lance Davis opens the modern debate with "The Investment Market, 1870–1914" (1965) showing that financial institutions and markets did not allocate capital very well. Interest rates remained relatively low in the capital-rich East, relatively high in the capital-poor South and West, and few funds flowed in between. Davis's original article spawned a voluminous literature. Two of the best subsequent efforts are *The American Capital Market, 1846–1914* (1975) by Richard Sylla and *Money and Capital Markets in Postbellum America* (1978) by John James.

Barry Eichengreen provides a missing piece overlooked by most previous writers in "Mortgage Interest Rates in the Populist Era" (1984). He links agrarian complaints about high western interest rates to the much-discussed regional differentials. Instead of finding a legitimate basis for the farmers' complaints in a "money monopoly," however, Eichengreen argues that mortgage interest rates were higher in the West because of the inherently greater risks of farming on or near the frontier. Allan G. Bogue's *Money at Interest* (1955) is necessary reading for any student of postbellum finance. Bogue traces the history of three mortgage companies that raised funds in the East to lend in the West. Predating Eichengreen's more rigorous statistical evidence, Bogue also demonstrates that farmers had little basis for complaint. Although mortgage rates in the West exceeded those in the East, the differences were attributable more to risk than a "monied aristocracy."

CONCLUSION

It is obvious that the economic literature on the Reconstruction era has been divergent, in terms of both topics and approaches, but it has also been and remains an area of lively intellectual debate. The rise of the new economic history in the past thirty years has added much and will undoubtedly continue to do so. Its most significant contribution has certainly been its nearly wholesale adoption of John Clapham's counsel of "measure it, then measure it again." Economic assertions once vaguely justified upon slim empirical and much anecdotal evidence and strong intellectual priors—the exploitation of sharecroppers or the importance of the railroad, for example—have been put under the modern economist's microscope. Some have stood up to their rampant revisionism; many have not. Others are not (and may never be) definitively decided upon.

Despite all this rampant revisionism of long-standing issues, the one constant is the continued liveliness of the debate, the search for new ways to answer old questions, and the raising of new ones. Recent scholarship has begun to look into the historical record for answers to questions of contemporary interest. Work dealing with the economic consequences of health, morbidity, and the roles of women is beginning to appear. Other pathbreaking methodologies are also finding their way into the debate. A significant problem confronting the economic historian who wishes to address the standard of living in times past is the lack of reasonable measures of living standards. Modern economists can turn to measures of gross domestic product, personal disposable income, and the like. Economic historians are forced to look elsewhere. One exciting recent development is the use of anthropometric data to gauge standards of living in earlier eras. A person's attained adult height, for example, depends critically upon his or her intake of protein and other necessary nutrients during childhood. Preliminary findings have been published for other places and other times—for example, Fogel's "Nutrition and the Decline in Mortality since 1700" (1986) and Komlos's. "Toward an Anthropometric History of African-Americans" (1992). When studies are completed for the Reconstruction era, we may gain some new insights into the standard of living of manufacturing workers, Southern sharecroppers, and midwestern farmers. If the old adage that the only thing that remains constant is change is true, it is certainly so for the field of economic history. Economic historians are always bumping up against the limits imposed by conventional data and are forced to look to new sources, which often yield previously unthought-of interpretations of our past. Whatever the results may be of the new research and wherever they lead us, they will certainly spark new rounds of debate.

BIBLIOGRAPHY

Argersinger, Peter H., and JoAnne E. Argersinger. "The Machine Breakers: Farmworkers and Social Change in the Rural Midwest of the 1870s." *Agricultural History* 58 (1984): 393–410.

Atack, Jeremy. "Tenants and Yeomen in the Nineteenth Century." *Agricultural History* 63 (1988): 6–32.

Atack, Jeremy, and Peter Passell. *A New Economic View of American History.* 2d ed. New York: W. W. Norton & Company, 1994.

Bodenhorn, Howard. "Capital Mobility and Financial Integration in Antebellum America." *Journal of Economic History* 52 (1992): 585–610.

Bodenhorn, Howard, and Hugh Rockoff. "Regional Interest Rates in Antebellum America." In *Strategic Factors in Nineteenth Century American Economic History: A Volume to Honor Robert W. Fogel,* 159–87. Edited by Claudia Goldin and Hugh Rockoff. Chicago: University of Chicago Press, 1992.

Bogue, Allan G. *Money at Interest: The Farm Mortgage on the Middle Border.* Ithaca: Cornell University Press, 1955.

———. *From Prairie to Corn Belt: Farming on the Illinois and Iowa Prairies in the Nineteenth Century.* Chicago: University of Chicago Press, 1963.

Bruchey, Stuart. *Enterprise: The Dynamic Economy of a Free People.* Cambridge: Harvard University Press, 1990.

Chandler, Alfred D., Jr. *The Railroads: The Nation's First Big Business.* New York: Harcourt, Brace & World, 1965.

———. *The Visible Hand: The Managerial Revolution in American Business.* Cambridge: Harvard University Press, 1977.

Clapham, John. "Economic History as a Discipline." In *Enterprise and Secular Change.* Edited by F. C. Lane and J. C. Riemersma. Homewood: Irwin, 1953.

Davis, Lance. "The Investment Market, 1870–1914: The Evolution of a National Market." *Journal of Economic History* 25 (1965): 355–399.

Doyle, Don H. *New Men, New Cities, New South: Atlanta, Nashville, Charleston, Mobile, 1860–1910.* Chapel Hill: University of North Carolina Press, 1990.

Du Bois, W. E. B., ed. *The Negro in Business.* Atlanta: Atlanta University Press, 1899.

———. *Black Reconstruction in America.* 1935. Reprint, New York: Atheneum, 1992.

Eichengreen, Barry. "Mortgage Interest Rates in the Populist Era." *American Economic Review* 74 (1984): 995–1015.

Ferleger, Lou, ed. *Agriculture and National Development Views on the Nineteenth Century.* Ames: Iowa State University Press, 1990.

Field, Alexander J. "Modern Business Enterprise as a Capital-Saving Innovation." *Journal of Economic History* 47 (1987): 473–485.

Fishback, Price. "Debt Peonage in Postbellum Georgia." *Explorations in Economic History* 26 (1989): 219–236.

Fogel, Robert W. *Railroads and American Economic Growth: Essays in Econometric History.* Baltimore: Johns Hopkins Press, 1964.

———. "Nutrition and the Decline in Mortality since 1700: Some Preliminary Findings." In *Long-Term Factors in American Economic Growth.* Edited by Stanley Engerman and Robert Gallman. Chicago: University of Chicago Press, 1986.

Friedman, Milton. "The Crime of 1873." *Journal of Political Economy* 98 (1990): 1159–1194.

Friedman, Milton, and Anna Jacobson Schwartz. *A Monetary History of the United States, 1867–1960.* Princeton: Princeton University Press, 1963.

Fuke, Richard Paul. "Planters, Apprenticeship, and Forced Labor: The Black Family under Pressure in Post-Emancipation Maryland." *Agricultural History* 62 (1988): 57–74.

Gates, Paul W. *Landlords and Tenants on the Prairie Frontier: Studies in American Land Policy.* Ithaca: Cornell University Press, 1973.

Goldin, Claudia. "Female Labor Force Participation: The Origin of Black and White Differences, 1870 and 1880." *Journal of Economic History* 37 (1977): 87–108.

———. "The Work and Wages of Single Women, 1870 to 1920." *Journal of Economic History* 40 (1980): 81–88.

Grob, Gerald N. "Organized Labor and the Negro Worker, 1865–1900." *Labor History* 1 (Spring 1960): 164–176.

Haines, Michael R., and Barbara A. Anderson. "New Demographic History of the Late Nineteenth-Century United States." *Explorations in Economic History* 25 (1988): 341–365.

Hammond, Bray. *Banks and Politics in America from the Revolution to the Civil War.* Princeton: Princeton University Press, 1957.

Harbeson, Robert. "Railroads and Regulation, 1877–1916: Conspiracy or Public Interest." *Journal of Economic History* 27 (1967): 230–242.

Harley, C. Knick. "Western Settlement and the Price of Wheat, 1872–1913." *Journal of Economic History* 38 (1978): 865–878.

Hicks, John D. *The Populist Revolt: A History of the Farmers' Alliance and the People's Party.* Lincoln: University of Nebraska Press, 1961.

Higgs, Robert. "The Growth of Cities in a Midwestern Region, 1870–1900." *Journal of Regional Science* 9 (1969): 369–375.

———. *The Transformation of the American Economy, 1865–1914: An Essay in Interpretation.* New York: John Wiley & Sons, 1971.

———. "Race, Skill, and Earnings: American Immigrants in 1909." *Journal of Economic History* 31 (1971): 420–428.

———. "Participation of Blacks and Immigrants in the American Merchant Class, 1890–1910: Some Demographic Relations." *Explorations in Economic History* 13 (1976): 153–164.

———. *Competition and Coercion: Blacks in the American Economy, 1865–1914.* Cambridge: Cambridge University Press, 1977.

Hughes, Jonathan. *American Economic History.* 3d ed. Glenview IL: Scott, Foresman, 1990.

Irwin, James R. "Farmers and Laborers: A Note on Black Occupations in the Postbellum South." *Agricultural History* 64 (1990): 53–60.

James, John A. *Money and Capital Markets in Postbellum America.* Princeton: Princeton University Press, 1978.

Jaynes, Gerald David. *Branches without Roots: Genesis of the Black Working Class in the American South, 1862–1882.* New York: Oxford University Press, 1986.

Kirkland, Edward C. *Industry Comes of Age: Business, Labor, and Public Policy, 1860–1897.* New York: Holt, Rinehart and Winston, 1961.

Kolko, Gabriel. *Railroads and Regulation, 1877–1916.* Princeton: Princeton University Press, 1965.

Komlos, John. "Toward an Anthropometric History of African-Americans: The Case of Free Blacks in Antebellum Maryland." In *Strategic Factors in Nineteenth Century American Economic History: A Volume to Honor Robert W. Fogel.* Edited by Claudia Goldin and Hugh Rockoff. Chicago: University of Chicago Press, 1992.

Lamoreaux, Naomi R. *The Great Merger Movement in American Business, 1895–1904.* Cambridge: Cambridge University Press, 1985.

Lebergott, Stanley. *Manpower in Economic Growth: The American Record since 1800.* New York: McGraw-Hill, 1964.

———. *The Americans: An Economic Record.* New York: W. W. Norton & Company, 1984.

Lewis, Frank D. "Explaining the Shift of Labor from Agriculture to Industry in the United States: 1869 to 1899." *Journal of Economic History* 39 (1979): 681–698.

Livesay, Harold C. *Andrew Carnegie and the Rise of Big Business.* Boston: Little, Brown, 1975.

Malone, Ann Patton. "Piney Woods Farmers of South Georgia, 1850–1900: Jeffersonian Yeomen in an Age of Expanding Commercialism." *Agricultural History* 60 (1986): 51–84.

Martin, Albro. *Railroads Triumphant.* New York: Oxford University Press, 1992.

Mayhew, Anne. "A Reappraisal of the Causes of Farm Protest in the United States, 1870–1900." *Journal of Economic History* 32 (1972): 464–475.

McCloskey, Donald N. *Econometric History.* Houndmills: Macmillan Education, 1987.

———. "Robert William Fogel: An Appreciation by an Adopted Student." In *Strategic Factors in Nineteenth Century American Economic History: A Volume to Honor Robert W. Fogel.* Edited by Claudia Goldin and Hugh Rockoff. Chicago: University of Chicago Press, 1992.

McGouldrick, Paul F., and Michael B. Tannen. "Did American Manufacturers Discriminate against Immigrants before 1914?" *Journal of Economic History* 37 (1977): 723–746.

McGuire, Robert A. "Economic Causes of Late Nineteenth Century Agrarian Unrest." *Journal of Economic History* 41 (1981): 835–849.

Mitchell, Wesley Clair. *A History of the Greenbacks.* Chicago: University of Chicago Press, 1903.

Neal, Larry and Paul Uselding. "Immigration, a Neglected Source of American Economic Growth: 1790 to 1912." *Oxford Economic Papers* 24 (1972): 68–88.

North, Douglass C. *Growth and Welfare in the American Past: A New Economic History.* Englewood Cliffs, NJ: Prentice-Hall, 1966.

Nugent, Walter T. K. *The Money Question during Reconstruction.* New York: W. W. Norton & Company, 1967.

Porter, Glenn. *The Rise of Big Business, 1860–1910.* New York: Thomas Y. Crowell Company, 1973.

Pred, Allan R. *The Spatial Dynamics of U.S. Urban-Industrial Growth, 1800–1914.* Cambridge: MIT Press, 1966.

Ransom, Roger L., and Richard Sutch. "Debt Peonage in the Cotton South after the Civil War." *Journal of Economic History* 32 (1972): 641–669.

————. "The Ex-Slave in the Postbellum South: A Study of the Impact of Racism in a Market Environment." *Journal of Economic History* 33 (1973): 131–148.

————. "The Impact of the Civil War and of Emancipation on Southern Agriculture." *Explorations in Economic History* 12 (1975): 1–28.

————. *One Kind of Freedom: The Economic Consequences of Emancipation.* Cambridge: Cambridge University Press, 1977.

————. "The Labor of Older Americans: Retirement of Men on and off the Job, 1870–1937." *Journal of Economic History* 46 (1986): 1–30.

Redlich, Fritz. *The Molding of American Banking: Men and Ideas.* New York: Johnson Reprint Company, 1968.

Reid, Joseph D., Jr. "Sharecropping as an Understandable Market Response: The Postbellum South." *Journal of Economic History* 33 (1973): 106–130.

Rockoff, Hugh. "The 'Wizard of Oz' as Monetary Allegory." *Journal of Political Economy* 98 (1990): 739–760.

Schlomowitz, Ralph. "Bond or Free? Black Labor in Cotton and Sugarcane Farming, 1865–1880." *Journal of Southern History* 50 (1984): 569–596.

Schmidt, Louis Bernard, and Earle Dudley Ross, eds. *Readings in the Economic History of American Agriculture.* New York: Macmillan, 1925.

Shannon, Fred A. *The Farmer's Last Frontier: Agriculture, 1860–1897.* New York: Farrar & Rinehart, 1945.

Stock, James H. "Real Estate Mortgages, Foreclosures, and Midwestern Agrarian Unrest, 1865–1920." *Journal of Economic History* 44 (1984): 89–105.

Sylla, Richard. "Federal Policy, Banking Market Structure and Capital Mobilization in the United States, 1863–1913." *Journal of Economic History* 29 (1969): 657–686.

————. *The American Capital Market, 1846–1914: A Study of the Effects of Public Policy on Economic Development.* New York: Arno Press, 1975.

Temin, Peter. *Iron and Steel in Nineteenth-Century America: An Economic Inquiry.* Cambridge: MIT Press, 1964.

————. "Freedom and Coercion: Notes on the Analysis of Debt Peonage in *One Kind of Freedom.*" *Explorations in Economic History* 16 (1979): 56–63.

Thomas, Brinley. *Migration and Economic Growth.* Cambridge: Cambridge University Press, 1954.

Tindall, George Brown. *South Carolina Negroes, 1877–1900.* Columbia: University of South Carolina Press, 1952.

————. *The Pursuit of Southern History.* Baton Rouge: Louisiana State University Press, 1964.

Walton, Gary M., and James F. Shepherd, eds. *Market Institutions and Economic Progress in the New South, 1865–1900.* New York: Academic Press, 1981.

Walton, Gary M., and Hugh Rockoff. *History of the American Economy.* 7th ed. Fort Worth: Dryden Press, 1994.

Weiher, Kenneth. "The Cotton Industry and Southern Urbanization, 1880–1930." *Explorations in Economic History* 14 (1977): 120–140.

Weiss, Thomas. "The Industrial Distribution of the Urban and Rural Workforce: Estimates for the United States, 1870–1910." *Journal of Economic History* 32 (1972): 919–937.

Whatley, Warren C. "Southern Agrarian Labor Contracts as Impediments to Cotton Mechanization." *Journal of Economic History* 47 (1987): 45–70.

Williamson, Jeffrey G. "The Railroads and Midwestern Development 1870–90: A General Equilibrium History." In *Essays in Nineteenth Century Economic History: The Old Northwest*, 269–352. Edited by David C. Klingaman and Richard K. Vedder. Athens: Ohio University Press, 1975.

Winters, Donald L. *Farmers without Farms: Agricultural Tenancy in Nineteenth-Century Iowa*. Westport, CT: Greenwood Press, 1978.

———. "Postbellum Reorganization of Southern Agriculture: The Economics of Sharecropping in Tennessee." *Agricultural History* 62 (1988): 1–19.

Worthman, Paul B. "Black Workers and Labor Unions in Birmingham, Alabama, 1897–1904." *Labor History* 10 (1969): 375–407.

Wright, Gavin. *Old South, New South: Revolutions in the Southern Economy since the Civil War*. New York: Basic Books, 1986.

43

Emancipation, Freedmen, and the Freedmen's Bureau

James Alex Bagget

This is a chapter about emancipation in the American South and of the national policy that initiated it. Its content extends from the freeing of the first Virginia "contrabands" in 1861 to the granting of citizenship and the vote to the freedmen. It broadly outlines those works describing wartime emancipation and black employment in Union-held areas along the Atlantic coast, the Mississippi Valley, and the Gulf coast. While doing so it suggests how historians have related what was happening to blacks in the occupied areas to the Union's needs for manpower and soldiers and to the establishment of policy in Washington. This chapter bridges the gap between wartime emancipation and the Freedmen's Bureau and related agencies. Finally, it summarizes some exceptional collections of essays on emancipation. Overall, my purpose is to introduce some significant books and writers who have best come to grips with the issue of emancipation. For the most part the works discussed here were published during or after the peak of the civil rights movement of the 1960s.

WARTIME EMANCIPATION

For an overview of Federal policy toward the blacks of the Civil War South, see Bell Irvin Wiley's old but good, *Southern Negroes, 1861–1865* (1938). Wiley traces the status of slaves within Union army lines from the invasion of the Virginia Tidewater in spring 1861. After General Benjamin F. Butler found that slaves had been used by Confederates to construct fortifications, he declared them to be "contraband of war." Soon after, Congress broadened the policy to include all slaves of Confederates. Then when Butler occupied the South Carolina Sea Islands in the fall of 1861, he found that policy was needed for 10,000 slaves abandoned by fleeing disloyal planters. Meanwhile in the upper mid-South many runaway slaves entered Union lines. Because officials in Washington often were noncommittal about such circumstances, Union army officers pursued a variety of policies. In Kentucky and Missouri, their decisions ran all the way from returning all slaves to their owners, to excluding all, to admitting some, to admitting all. Negroes flocked to Federal army camps in West Tennessee in the fall of 1862, and as General Ulysses S. Grant moved south, the number multiplied. To stop slaves from becoming government charges, plans were made for their employment by loyal civilians. General Butler, now in Louisiana, faced a similar situation as the slaves of loyal and disloyal owners entered his lines. When Lincoln acted on matters related to blacks, he proved more conservative than his party in Congress and many of his generals. Still, by the summer of 1862, he believed that emancipation was necessary to win the war. On January 1, 1863, he issued his proclamation. In addition to officially freeing the slaves behind Confederate lines, it sanctioned the use of Negro troops by the Union army. Soon after his party pushed for a constitutional amendment abolishing slavery everywhere. Covering much of the same story as Wiley and perhaps with greater emotion (but without notes of documentation) is Benjamin Quarles in *The Negro in the Civil War* (1953). To a greater degree than Wiley, he sees "the Negro . . . as an instigator of action, as an agent acting on his own volition."

For a work with greater interpretation of policy than either that of Wiley's or Quarles's, see Louis S. Gerteis, *From Contraband to Freedmen: Federal Policy toward Southern Blacks, 1861–1865* (1973). Gerteis shows how conditions at the front, especially the need for black laborers and soldiers, shaped policy. He also demonstrates how ideology and experience predetermined postwar policy. He divides his work into three parts: Virginia and the Carolinas, Louisiana, and the Mississippi Valley. Despite geographical differences, he sees overall policy agreement aimed at "the mobilization" of blacks and the "prevention of violent change." Because of this, he finds that the lives of most blacks within Union lines unfortunately were "untouched by the government's labor systems." His picture of wartime emancipation is perhaps too dismal given the humanitarian efforts exhibited and the primary purpose of the war, saving the Union.

For an optimistic version of wartime emancipation, see Herman Belz, *A New Birth of Freedom: The Republican Party and the Freedmen's Rights, 1861–1866* (1976), followed by his *Emancipation and Equal Rights: Politics and Constitutionalism in the Civil War Era* (1978). In both he traces, with a different emphasis, national decision making concerning Southern blacks from the Confiscation Act of 1862 to the emancipation proclamation, to the creation of the Freedmen's Bureau and the Civil Rights Act of 1866. And in *Emancipation and Equal Rights* he extends his coverage to 1883. If seen from a nineteenth-century setting, he argues, emancipation in the American South was revolutionary. Given the nation's constitutionalism and capitalism, it was natural that events and policy turned out the way they did. "Not only was it common sense to employ freed slaves as did the administration," Belz contends, "but the blacks had their homes in the South and naturally wished to stay there." He pummels those who would interpret the Civil War era in terms of the post–World War II civil rights era. He contends that emancipation meant that blacks were indeed free in spite of racism and poverty.

Although John Hope Franklin, in *The Emancipation Proclamation* (1963), sees emancipation as "a war measure, conceived and promulgated to put down the rebellion and save the Union," he finds it contributed significantly to the way the nation viewed the war. The document allowed freedmen to defend their freedom by joining the Federal army. And it omitted any reference to the colonization of blacks, previously recommended by Lincoln. Although it did not apply to the border states, according to Franklin, "slavery, in or out of the Confederacy, could not possibly have survived the Emancipation Proclamation." Even more strongly than Franklin, Mary Frances Berry, in *Military Necessity and Civil Rights Policy: Black Citizenship and the Constitution, 1861–1868* (1977), insists that Federal policy followed necessity, that the key to the policy of the North was the need for black soldiers, and that by 1863 Lincoln "believed that using black troops extensively was absolutely essential for defeating the Confederacy."

Other works describe wartime emancipation in specific states or areas. Emancipation on the Sea Islands is brilliantly described by Willie Lee Rose in her award-winning *Rehearsal for Reconstruction: The Port Royal Experiment* (1964). When Federals occupied the Sea Islands in the fall of 1861, whites (comprising fewer than one-fifth of the population) had fled to the mainland, leaving behind 10,000 slaves long accustomed to organizing their own labor after completing daily tasks. Following the occupation, these blacks resisted growing the "slave crop," cotton, but caught between bureaucrats, idealists, and entrepreneurs, they could not chart their own course. In 1863, Treasury officials started auctioning off land seized for nonpayment of Federal taxes. Only a few blacks could pool their resources to buy land. But living standards and social circumstances for most blacks improved.

More typical of emancipation elsewhere, then and later, was that in Louisiana. C. Peter Ripley, writer of *Slaves and Freedmen in Civil War Louisiana* (1976), much like Gerteis, feels that Federals could have created greater opportunities for blacks but failed. Ripley shows that during 1862, because of efforts to cultivate white loyalty, Federals sought to save slavery. But later freedmen received not only wages but book learning, their day in court, and an opportunity to serve as soldiers. Yet sadly, Ripley argues, Louisiana blacks never really "moved much beyond the terms set by the wartime experiment."

John Cimprich in *Slavery's End in Tennessee, 1861–65* (1985), describes another area of wartime emancipation. Cimprich writes that the question of what to do with large numbers of contraband occurred quickly in West Tennessee and that army commanders had limited guidance. For a short time in 1863, a network of authorized contraband camps extended across the state's Third Grand Division under Grant's appointee, Colonel John Eaton. Various post commanders in Middle Tennessee established some unauthorized contraband camps, but most slaves, even those within Union lines, never left the plantation. Cimprich finds "paternalism, pragmatism, isolation, or affection kept some slaves loyal to their masters." Other slaves feared the Federals and/or resented their impressment of slaves. On the other hand, some slaves ran away from their owners or were abandoned by them as the Union army approached. Generally Federals created greater opportunities for slaves to make choices, much of what freedom was all about.

On a much larger scale, Leon F. Litwack also finds a wide variation of reaction by blacks to emancipation in his Pulitzer Prize–winning *Been in the Storm So Long: The Aftermath of Slavery* (1979). Litwack looks at "the countless ways in which freedom was perceived and experienced" by former slaves, as well as "how they acted . . . to help shape their condition and future." He finds that on the whole, slaves championed neither revolution nor the status quo. They expressed a wide range of emotions toward emancipation, including hope, fear, and joy. Their feelings grew out of their perception of whites, including the Yankees, of freedom itself, and of a multitude of personal matters. Litwack leaves little doubt that given the choice, blacks preferred freedom to slavery. In addition to Litwack's study, there are several excellent works on the reactions to emancipation in individual states. Model state studies include Joel Williamson's *After Slavery: The Negro in South Carolina during Reconstruction, 1861–1877* (1965) and Peter Kolchin's *First Freedom: The Responses of Alabama's Blacks to Emancipation and Reconstruction* (1972).

Responses of blacks to emancipation and to military service in the Union army appear in several printed collections and books. By far the most significant work is that of the multivolume *Freedom: A Documentary History of Emancipation, 1861–1867, Selected from the Holdings of the National Archives of the United States* (1982–), edited by Ira Berlin, Joseph P. Reidy, and Leslie Rowland. The documents are taken from twenty-three record groups, including those of the American Freedmen's Inquiry Commission, the Bureau of Colored Troops, and those of the Bureau of Refugees, Freedmen, and Abandoned Lands. Each volume contains a lengthy essay introducing the subject of the volume as well as shorter pieces introducing the book's subsections. If there is any one central theme to the response to emancipation, it is that there was no stereotypical reaction by blacks to freedom.

Still the most complete story of black soldiers is *The Sable Arm: Negro Troops in the Union Army, 1861–1865* (1956) by Dudley T. Cornish, parts of which had been told with fewer details by Wiley and Quarles. The purpose of Cornish's work is to "describe . . . the movement to arm the Negro; to follow that movement through the . . . obstacles that had to be overcome, circumvented, or ignored before the Negro was permitted to do more for the freedom of his race than drive . . . cook . . . or labor . . . ; and, finally, to show the gradual emergence of the Negro soldier . . . and to assess his contribution to that army and to the outcome of the war.'' While there were reports of black enlistment in Kansas and Missouri earlier, the first large-scale effort to arm Negroes was that of General David Hunter on the Sea Islands in the spring of 1862. Still Lincoln did not officially allow the use of black troops until his emancipation proclamation of January 1, 1863. By the spring of 1863, the War Department urged the recruitment of black soldiers, and eventually more than 200,000 blacks entered the Union army. They served, however, under several disadvantages: the enemy refused to recognize them as soldiers of war, their own government refused them equal pay, and they were denied officers of their own race.

Important reading for bridging the gap between wartime reconstruction and postwar reconstruction is Eric Foner's massive *Reconstruction: America's Unfinished Revolution, 1863–1877* (1988). Foner highlights the fact that his book begins with the emancipation proclamation. He argues that blacks forced emancipation upon America. Rather than being simply passive victims, they became, by their behavior, shapers of Federal policy. Although ultimately denied ''forty acres and a mule'' by the nation, blacks established as much independence as possible, consolidated their families and communities, and claimed equal citizenship with whites. Three of the early chapters in Foner's work deal almost entirely with emancipation: ''Rehearsals for Reconstruction,'' describing the areas of wartime emancipation; ''The Meaning of Freedom,'' explaining how blacks responded to freedom and Federal policy; and ''Ambiguities of Free Labor,'' the response of postwar America to the ''Negro Question.'' Another chapter, ''The Making of Radical Reconstruction,'' traces the origins of federal postwar legislation related to blacks. For a work that addresses the issue at the presidential level, see LaWanda Cox's *Lincoln and Black Freedom: A Study in Presidential Leadership* (1981). According to Cox, while Lincoln wanted to ''expand freedom for blacks; Johnson was content to have their freedom contained.'' Moreover, unlike Johnson's scruples, ''Lincoln's constitutional scruples . . . did not preclude the expansion of federal authority,'' an essential ingredient for resolving the problems of the freedmen.

FREEDOM AND THE FREEDMEN'S BUREAU

After March 1865, much of the former slave's story was related to the War Department's Bureau of Refugees, Freedmen, and Abandoned Lands. The creation of the Freedmen's Bureau was largely based on the army's experience in dealing with black refugees in the wartime South. George R. Bentley, in *A History of the Freedmen's Bureau* (1955), sees the bureau's primary benefit as providing the freedmen food, education, and protection. Anything beyond that intervened into the internal matters of Southerners, who knew the Negro best. He sees the bureau as an ally of Radicals within the Republican party rather than as an army agency subject to more than the typical political pressures. While Bentley's work is a sort of summation of earlier, shorter accounts that the bureau exceeded its limits and became too political, later works see the bureau as too conservative, institutionally and philosophically. William S. McFeely, in *Yankee Stepfather: General O. O. Howard and the Freedmen* (1968), describes how before 1866, rather than stopping freedmen from falling into the hands of the planters and their friends, the Freedmen's Bureau became President Johnson's tool to achieve exactly that. Nonetheless, by insisting that it was their agency, even as events proved otherwise, blacks made the bureau deal with them and helped to change Federal policy. Seeing General Howard as the key to understanding the bureau's work, McFeely concentrates on him. "Although the bureau men had been subjected to intense pressures," he writes, "this alone does not account for the results." The failure was one of leadership and lack of dedication to the cause for which the bureau existed, the freedmen.

A somewhat more favorable view is presented in Donald G. Nieman's *To Set the Law in Motion: The Freedmen's Bureau and the Legal Rights of Blacks, 1865–1868* (1979). Blacks faced the fact that the governments created by Lincoln and Johnson wanted to apply to the freedmen the severe antebellum black code initially intended for prewar free blacks. Bureau agents were hampered by institutional and political realities in their effort to guard freedmen from discriminatory judicial decisions and law. Also, the congressional Republicans who created the bureau failed to provide adequate bureau personnel to exercise effective judicial authority for blacks. Moreover, President Johnson directed the bureau to turn over jurisdiction in cases involving freedmen to state courts as soon as laws prohibiting blacks from testifying against whites were set aside. Consequently, during late 1865 and thereafter, bureau judicial authority began to shrink.

William L. Richter's *Overreached on All Sides: The Freedmen's Bureau Administrators in Texas, 1865–1868* (1991) presents a thorough view of one state's bureau by looking at its four assistant commissioners, each of whom served about a year, and at the state's district agents. During 1865 and 1866, the Texas Bureau secured freedom itself for blacks; their rights to contract, to sue, and to be sued; the consolidation of marriage and family; the opportunity for education; and, in 1867, the vote. Although hindered by national political differences, the Texas assistant commissioners contributed to the failure of the bureau in the Lone Star State because, on the whole, they lacked a dedication to the task at hand. Although the subassistant commissioners did not neglect their bureau duties, they were too restricted to their headquarters, unable to move about the countryside freely, powerless to enforce their edicts, and inundated by a sea of red tape. As a group, they ranged from good to indifferent to corrupt. Barry Crouch in *The Freedmen's Bureau and Black Texans* (1992) deals with the state's bureau from the bottom up. Crouch's book contains less cynicism about the bureau's aims and more sympathy toward bureau personnel. He argues that Texas agents "enhanced the opportunities for blacks to experience the full realities of freedom." His work is selective and his focus is local, using a case study approach to generalize about the larger scene (perhaps too much so).

Claude F. Oubre, in *Forty Acres and a Mule: The Freedmen's Bureau and Black Land Ownership* (1978), shows that although Congress provided land through its confiscation legislation and the Southern Homestead Act, freedmen experienced considerable difficulty in acquiring it. The responsibility, he feels, must be shared by Congress, the president, the military, the Federal land offices, Southern whites, and the freedmen themselves. Initially any plan had to be self-supporting since it was secondary to the war effort. Although necessary, the bureau's contract labor system proved detrimental to initial homesteading efforts. Congress ignored the inferior quality of the land included in the Southern Homestead Act and failed to recognize that any plan to homestead the freedmen could succeed only with additional assistance. Also, most of the local Federal land offices were not reopened until several years after the war.

Robert C. Morris, in *Reading, 'Riting, and Reconstruction: The Education of Freedmen in the South, 1861–1870* (1981), writes that educators believed that the future of freedmen depended on their literacy, industry, and amity toward whites. To this end, workhorses of Northern aid societies and the Freedmen's Bureau stressed book learning, self-help, and forbearance. During the war, a government-private bureaucracy arose from efforts to relieve suffering, reduce ignorance, and promote order. From 1865 to late 1870, an assistant superintendent in each state provided needed transportation, school buildings, and rations. Morris's composite picture is of bureaucrats and teachers wary of offending whites and equally eager to teach freedmen responsibility. Virtually the same views are expressed by Ronald E. Butchart in his *Northern Schools, Southern Blacks, and Reconstruction: Freedmen's Education, 1862–1875* (1980). Butchart argues that education failed to produce black liberation, which could be gained only "by a revolutionary reordering of national and regional priorities," and that Northern educators were paternalistic at best and outright racist at worst. A more optimistic view appears in Joe M. Richardson's *Christian Reconstruction: The American Missionary Association and Southern Blacks, 1861–1890* (1986), a solid addition to historical scholarship on the work of Yankee missionaries among the freedmen. Richardson argues that the AMA struggled to prepare the liberated slaves for civil and political equality by freeing them of the shackles of ignorance, superstition, and sin. These contributions, however, he writes, were mainly at the collegiate and secondary level and among the black leadership.

ESSAYS ON EMANCIPATION

Several significant collections of essays on emancipation have appeared since the 1960s, including *What Was Freedom's Price?* (1978), five essays originally presented at the 1976 Chancellor's Symposium on Southern History at the University of Mississippi. Editor David G. Sansing poses these questions: What was freedom actually like for blacks in the South? Did emancipation produce social revolution? Were there alternatives to a segregated society? Was sharecropping a mechanism for social control or a means for organizing labor? How was emancipation treated in other slave societies? Willie Lee Rose writes that Federal land policy was basically incorrect but that a redistribution of land would not have resulted in a permanent change in the landowning system. Joel Williamson argues that blacks were caught between opposing poles of whiteness and blackness, with pressures in American life pushing them in both directions. Richard Sutch and Roger Ransom conclude that sharecropping grew almost entirely because of the desire of black workers to have a labor system in which they would have the maximum degree of freedom at their work. George M. Frederickson and C. Vann Woodward compare emancipation in different societies with that in the United States. Frederickson sees major differences in the way domination was reestablished. Woodward sees emancipation in the American South as unique because it involved by far the largest number of freed slaves and it attempted to establish political equality for the freed population.

In *Essays on the Postbellum Southern Economy* (1985), edited by Thavolia Glymph and John J. Kaskma, each essay develops the central theme of the "revolutionary impact of emancipation." Armstead L. Robinson points out that "freedom came to mean different things to different groups of freed people— depending on their personal situation, their location, and the timing of formal emancipation." Glymph demonstrates that freedmen attempted to use the share-wage system to demand a voice in management of land and time. Barbara Jeanne Fields, placing emancipation in global perspective, concludes that had mixed-farming peasant agriculture developed in the postbellum South, better race relations could have developed. And Harold D. Woodman concludes that emancipation alone was not sufficient to guarantee the success of the new capitalist order from the North in the South.

One final group of essays certainly worth reading is Frank McGlynn and Seymour Dreschar, eds., *The Meaning of Freedom: Economics, Politics, and Culture after Slavery* (1992). Several of its eleven essays deal with emancipation in the American South. Some describe what they consider to be the largely predetermined economic circumstances following emancipation in the South; others dwell on what might have been if America had not been a racist society. The most optimistic one concerning Federal policy during the Civil War and Reconstruction is Peter Kolchin's "The Tragic Era? Interpreting Southern Reconstruction in Comparative Perspective." According to Kolchin, despite dramatic changes in Reconstruction historiography, the Tragic Era concept remains a persistent theme of all schools of thought. But he disagrees with the idea. The birth of freedom was troubled everywhere, he argues—in Russia and in the Americas elsewhere. Comparison suggests that conditions for freedmen were better in the Southern United States than elsewhere. Segregated schools, for example, were far preferable to no schools at all. Compared to their previous status, he writes, the changed position of the freedmen was miraculous. Who could have predicted in the 1850s that within the next decade not only would slavery be abolished, but former slaves would be attending school, voting, and serving on juries.

The works mentioned in this piece represent the latest findings of scholars while raising almost all the questions that have been asked about emancipation during the last one hundred years. Hardly any suggest that all would have been well for the freedmen if the South had been left alone. But they do point to a growing impression: that while much more could have been done by the national government for the freedmen—economically, educationally, and legally—there were no cure-alls available. Freedmen were provided with limited welfare, opportunities for education, and citizenship and the vote, but their problems were far more complex than could be resolved within a generation. Almost everyone agrees that race was significant. But even if the freedmen had been white, as they were in Russia during this time, there still would have been monumental problems. Indeed the degree of economic and social progress among poor white Southern farmers during that era was very limited. Comparative studies indicate that Southern freedmen were in fact better off than those of other freedmen elsewhere. Of course, they were worse off when compared with other Americans. When compared with white Southerners of the same economic class, however, the difference narrows substantially, because both lived in an economically depressed area. Many recent works face the question of what was really possible for the freedmen given the total circumstances. Some, such as Peter Kolchin and Herman Belz, have gone so far as to suggest that despite almost universal agreement to the contrary among other scholars, for the freedmen emancipation and its aftermath was not a "Tragic Era." Despite drawbacks, largely caused by the nature of the nation, and to a degree of the Western world, emancipation in the American South, on the whole, was revolutionary because it brought both rapid legal and social benefits for blacks to establish their identity and their institutions.

BIBLIOGRAPHY

Belz, Herman. *A New Birth of Freedom: The Republican Party and the Freedmen's Rights, 1861–1866.* Westport, CT: Greenwood Press, 1976.
———. *Emancipation and Equal Rights: Politics and Constitutionalism in the Civil War Era.* New York: Norton, 1978.
Bentley, George R. *A History of the Freedmen's Bureau.* Philadelphia: University of Pennsylvania Press, 1955.
Berlin, Ira, Joseph P. Reidy, and Leslie Rowland, eds. *Freedom: A Documentary History of Emancipation, 1861–1867, Selected from the Holdings of the National Archives of the United States.* Cambridge: Cambridge University Press, 1982–.
Berry, Mary Frances. *Military Necessity and Civil Rights Policy: Black Citizenship and the Constitution, 1861–1868.* Port Washington, NY: Kennikat, 1977.
Butchart, Ronald E. *Northern Schools, Southern Blacks, and Reconstruction: Freedmen's Education: 1862–1875.* Westport, CT: Greenwood Press, 1980.

Cimprich, John. *Slavery's End in Tennessee, 1861–65*. University: University of Alabama Press, 1985.

Cornish, Dudley T. *The Sable Arm: Negro Troops in the Union Army, 1861–1865*. New York: Longmans, 1956.

Cox, LaWanda. *Lincoln and Black Freedom: A Study in Presidential Leadership*. Columbia: University of South Carolina Press, 1981.

Crouch, Barry. *The Freedmen's Bureau and Black Texans*. Austin: University of Texas Press, 1992.

Foner, Eric. *Reconstruction: America's Unfinished Revolution, 1863–1877*. New York: Harper, 1988.

Franklin, John Hope. *The Emancipation Proclamation*. New York: Doubleday, 1963.

Gerteis, Louis S. *From Contraband to Freedmen: Federal Policy toward Southern Blacks, 1861–1865*. Westport, CT: Greenwood Press, 1973.

Glymph, Thavolia, and John J. Kaskma, eds. *Essays on the Postbellum Southern Economy*. College Station: Texas A&M University Press, 1985.

Kolchin, Peter. *First Freedom: The Responses of Alabama's Blacks to Emancipation and Reconstruction*. Westport, CT: Greenwood Press, 1972.

Litwack, Leon F. *Been in the Storm So Long: The Aftermath of Slavery*. New York: Knopf, 1979.

McFeely, William S. *Yankee Stepfather: General O. O. Howard and the Freedmen*. New Haven: Yale University Press, 1968.

McGlynn, Frank, and Seymour Dreschar, eds. *The Meaning of Freedom: Economics, Politics, and Culture after Slavery*. Pittsburgh: University of Pittsburgh Press, 1992.

Morris, Robert C. *Reading, 'Riting, and Reconstruction: The Education of Freedmen in the South, 1861–1870*. Chicago: University of Chicago Press, 1981.

Nieman, Donald G. *To Set the Law in Motion: The Freedmen's Bureau and the Legal Rights of Blacks 1865–1868*. Millwood, NY: KTO Press, 1979.

Oubre, Claude F. *Forty Acres and a Mule: The Freedmen's Bureau and Black Land Ownership*. Baton Rouge: Louisiana State University Press, 1978.

Quarles, Benjamin. *The Negro in the Civil War*. Boston: Little, Brown, 1953.

Richardson, Joe M. *Christian Reconstruction: The American Missionary Association and Southern Blacks, 1861–1890*. Athens: University of Georgia Press, 1986.

Richter, William L. *Overreached on All Sides: The Freedmen's Bureau Administrators in Texas, 1865–1868*. College Station: Texas A&M Press, 1991.

Ripley, C. Peter. *Slaves and Freedmen in Civil War Louisiana*. Baton Rouge: Louisiana State University Press, 1976.

Rose, Willie Lee. *Rehearsal for Reconstruction: The Port Royal Experiment*. Indianapolis: Bobbs-Merrill, 1964.

Sansing, David G., ed. *What Was Freedom's Price?* Jackson: University Press of Mississippi, 1978.

Wiley, Bell Irvin. *Southern Negroes, 1861–1865*. New Haven: Yale University Press, 1938.

Williamson, Joel. *After Slavery: The Negro in South Carolina during Reconstruction, 1861–1877*. Chapel Hill: University of North Carolina Press, 1965.

44

Veterans' Organizations and Memories of the War

Gaines M. Foster

When Johnny came marching home from the Civil War, the bands played, people shouted, and the ladies all turned out. Many historians, too, have cheered the soldiers' sacrifice and exploits in battle. But they have paid far less attention to what the veterans did once the parades were over. Social historian Maris A. Vinovskis had a point when, in 1990, he complained that "almost nothing has been written about the postwar experience of Civil War veterans" (p. 21). Historians do lack systematic, perhaps inevitably quantitative, examinations of what happened to the veterans—their health, social mobility, and other aspects of their lives. Yet Vinovskis clearly exaggerated. Many studies, although few of them focus specifically on veterans, provide information on the soldiers' lives after the Civil War. They examine the associations Union and Confederate veterans formed and the role these organizations played in providing for the veterans' care, in shaping society's view of the past, and in promoting reunion.

THE VETERANS' EXPERIENCES

Two books focus specifically on veterans, not just those of the Civil War but of other American wars as well. Toward the end of World War II, Dixon Wecter published *When Johnny Comes Marching Home* (1944), a subtle discussion of veterans of the American Revolution, the Civil War, and World War I. In a long section on the Civil War, Wecter addresses the problems the returning soldiers faced during the first months and years after the war: the psychological shock of combat, the loss of girlfriends, the search for employment. But he also tells of their successes: their return to school, economic advancement, and important role in sectional reconciliation and postwar politics. Wecter mentions veterans' organizations and argues that through the efforts of one of them, the Grand Army of the Republic, Federal pensions for Union veterans became generous—too generous, in his opinion. Wecter believes that this largesse turned patriots into mercenaries. Forty-five years after Wecter's book appeared, in 1989, Richard Severo and Lewis Milford published *The Wages of War: When America's Soldiers Came Home—From Valley Forge to Vietnam*, which offers a far less complex interpretation of the veterans' experiences. Outraged by the treatment of Vietnam veterans, Severo and Milford seek to show that similar mistreatment followed earlier American wars. Their chapters on the Civil War criticize discrimination against Union veterans and the public's tendency to blame them for problems with drugs and crime. In contrast to Wecter, Severo and Milford judge Civil War pensions modest and stress that many Southerners and some Northerners opposed the system.

Beyond these broad surveys, much of the scholarship on the lives of Civil War veterans looks at Southern rather than Northern soldiers. In his 1949 Fleming lectures, published as *Confederate Leaders in the New South,* William B. Hesseltine examines the postwar careers of a sample of military and civilian leaders. He finds that some preached defiance while others practiced reconciliation, but concludes that more of them, especially among those in business, sought compromise with the North. In *The Confederate Veteran* (1962), William W. White discusses all veterans, not just their leaders. He offers brief, impressionistic observations about their postwar employment and involvement in politics, as well as an overview of veterans' organizations and pensions. White concludes that Confederate veterans exercised restraint, played a positive role in Southern society, and helped foster loyalty to a reunited nation.

Several other studies explore the attitudes or behavior of former Confederate soldiers, although they look not just at veterans but at all white Southerners, and offer a less sanguine view of the former Confederates' adjustment than White does. Several books and articles tell the story of a Confederate exodus to Mexico, Brazil, and other Latin American countries in the first few years after the war. *The Confederados: Old South Immigrants in Brazil* (1995), edited by Cyrus and James Dawsey, discusses the most successful of these colonies. Most of its essays focus on life in Brazil rather than on why the Confederates left the South. The majority of historians who have examined the reasons for this postwar emigration interpret it as an attempt to escape defeat or life in a world of free blacks. Daniel E. Sutherland, in "Exiles, Emigrants, and Sojourners: The Post–Civil War Confederate Exodus in Perspective" (1985)—the best overview of this movement, which provides citations to earlier studies—differs in portraying foreign emigration as a search for economic opportunity. Other ex-Confederates, he adds, chose to move North after the war; Sutherland tells their story in *The Confederate Carpetbaggers* (1988). It describes the lives of these Southern emigrés, analyzes their contribution to sectional reconciliation, chronicles their efforts in behalf of the South, and explores their persistent Southern identity.

Other studies offer insights into the lives of Confederates who chose to stay in the South. Three accounts of the Lost Cause, the postwar celebration of the Confederacy and its soldiers, stress the cultural and psychological adjustments soldiers and other Southerners faced: Susan Speare Durant, "The Gently Furled Banner: The Development of the Myth of the Lost Cause, 1865–1900" (1972), Thomas L. Connelly and Barbara L. Bellows, *God and General Longstreet: The Lost Cause and the Southern Mind* (1982), and Gaines M. Foster, *Ghosts of the Confederacy: Defeat, the Lost Cause, and the Emergence of the New South, 1865–1913* (1987).

Not just Southern but also Northern veterans experienced difficulties in adjusting to peace. A few former officers seemed to go in search of new wars. William B. Hesseltine and Hazel C. Wolf tell the story of leaders of both sides who hired out to the Egyptian army, and David P. Werlich recounts the career of a handful of Confederate leaders who went to war for Peru. Thomas C. Leonard, in *Above the Battle: War-Making in America from Appomattox to Versailles* (1978), argues that many Civil War veterans sought—and found—a new, worthy enemy during the Indian campaigns. Other veterans also seemed unable to put the war behind them; some, for instance, became tramps after the war. Perhaps inevitably, historians have begun to draw comparisons with the problems Vietnam veterans encountered. In a recent article, " 'We Will All Be Lost and Destroyed' " (1992), Eric T. Dean, Jr., provides preliminary evidence of posttraumatic stress disorder among Union veterans.[1]

Most historians, though, have minimized the continuing hold of the war's violence. These scholars conclude that both Northerners and Southerners, civilians and soldiers, created a romanticized version of the war that sentimentalized its violence and ignored its horrors. Leonard makes such a case, and Gerald F. Linderman presents a forceful exposition of this interpretation in *Embattled Courage: The Experience of Combat in the American Civil War* (1987). Primarily a discussion of the soldiers' wartime experience, Linderman's book argues that recruits enlisted with romantic notions of battle, but the grim, savage reality of combat led to a deep, personal disillusionment with war. After Appomattox, Linderman continues, the veterans went into "hibernation" for a time and suppressed their memories. In the 1880s and 1890s, interest in the war revived, but by then the veterans, their suppression complete, once again embraced the civilians' romantic militarism.[2]

The most sustained and sophisticated corrective to the idea that the veterans and their society sentimentalized Civil War violence is Charles Royster's *The Destructive War* (1991). Few if any historians have done more to reveal the horror of the Civil War. Royster not only evokes its physical and human costs but exposes the enthusiasm with which Americans of both sides participated in its violence, either directly or vicariously, and explores the way in which the war destroyed so many of their illusions about democracy, the state, and ultimately themselves. Faced with this destructiveness and their shame in their embrace of it, Americans North and South did not wholly sentimentalize the violence but also acknowledged its ferocity and horror. For their own well-being, however, they had to interpret it in such a way as to deflect the shame, defend their actions, and render intelligible the savagery and destruction. Often they blamed the war on the other section, Royster concludes, even as they attributed "transcendent results" to it, a permanent nation of power and progress. Although not primarily an account of the veterans, Royster's is nevertheless the best book with which to begin a study of veterans and their memory of the war.

VETERANS' ORGANIZATIONS

The need to make the Civil War intelligible as well as to justify the continuing sense of horror and fascination it evoked helps explain why Civil War solders formed a host of veterans' organizations in the years after Appomattox. Their associations, however, were not unique. Many other patriotic societies as well as benevolent and fraternal groups thrived in the late nineteenth century. Hence, the veterans' activities may well have reflected not only the continuing hold of the war but the demands of the new society. Wallace E. Davies, in *Patriotism on Parade: The Story of Veterans' and Hereditary Organizations in America, 1783–1900* (1955), offers some of the context into which to place Civil War veterans' organizations, as well as a good introduction to specific groups, North and South. In each region, numerous veterans' organizations formed, but one group came to dominate; the pattern of development in the two regions differed, however. In the North, the dominant group, the Grand Army of the Republic, formed in 1867, after a decade or so declined, only to revive in the 1880s. In the South, a number of local or unit associations organized shortly after the war, but only in 1889 did a regional group, the United Confederate Veterans, form.

Little if any work has been done on unit or local veterans' groups in the North, but a substantial body of scholarship exists on the Grand Army of the Republic (GAR). Frank H. Heck, George J. Lankevich, and Elmer E. Noyes have written state studies. More useful are two first-rate and complementary accounts of the GAR as a whole. The first, Mary R. Dearing's *Veterans in Politics: The Story of the G.A.R.* (1952) traces the GAR's close ties with Radical Republicanism during Reconstruction, its continuing alliance with the GOP despite growing political diversity within its ranks in the 1880s, and finally its increasing conservatism in the 1890s, when it stood firmly for traditional economic views and against labor strikes. Dearing also discusses the GAR's efforts to secure bountiful pensions for its members. With its success in that cause and factional disputes sapping its strength, she concludes, the GAR entered a permanent decline in the 1890s. The second study, published in 1992, leaves politics to its predecessor and provides a social history of the GAR. Stuart McConnell's *Glorious Contentment: The Grand Army of the Republic, 1865–1900* (1992) furnishes a quantitative social analysis of the GAR's membership, finding it overwhelmingly middle class and native born, and an intriguing interpretation of its rituals and activities, pointing out how they resembled those of other fraternal groups of the era. More important, McConnell sketches the social vision of the GAR, showing how its members fought for their interpretation of the war, supported the growing national patriotism of the late nineteenth century, and clung to an older vision of the republic despite dramatic social changes.

One important aspect of the GAR remains relatively unexplored: the participation of African-American veterans. Dearing ignores them; McConnell points out that a few posts had a small number of black members, but for the most part the GAR practiced a variation on the idea of "separate but equal." Wallace Davies, in "The Problem of Race Segregation in the Grand Army of the Republic" (1947), recounts the fights that led to this policy. He shows that all-black GAR posts existed, especially in the South, but historians as yet know little about them.[3]

No book discusses the United Confederate Veterans (UCV) or other Confederate organizations in the way Dearing and McConnell do the GAR. Nevertheless, a few articles on the veterans' groups and several books exploring larger themes provide considerable, probably sufficient, information on Confederate veterans' organizations. White's *The Confederate Veteran* provides an introduction to the early, independent societies. Of these groups, the Association of the Army of Northern Virginia and its allied Southern Historical Society (technically not a veterans' organization) have received the most attention. In the 1870s, these two groups fell under the control of former Confederate general Jubal A. Early and other Virginians, who then expended enormous amounts of energy, and venom, celebrating Robert E. Lee and Confederate history. Thomas L. Connelly's *The Marble Man* (1977) and William G. Piston's *Lee's Tarnished Lieutenant* (1987) make a convincing case that these groups transformed Lee into an unblemished hero, in large measure by blaming Longstreet for Confederate failure at Gettysburg. Their version of history offered Southerners, especially veterans, a way to explain away their failures and ease doubts about their role in the war. Foster's *Ghosts of the Confederacy* tells more about the operation of the two groups than does Connelly or Piston but adds little to their story of Lee and Longstreet. It interprets their celebration of Lee as part of a general defense of the Confederacy, indeed an attempt to revitalize it, but concludes that few Southerners took these efforts very seriously.

The UCV, on the other hand, organized camps throughout the South and became very influential. Several scholars offer information about its operation. Howard Dorgan (1971) analyzes ceremonial addresses by its leaders, Herman Hattaway provides an account of its Louisiana division (1975), and White (1962) gives a solid description of the UCV's structure and activities. In *Ghosts of the Confederacy* Foster furnishes data on membership, finding that the UCV drew from a broad spectrum of Southern society. He also analyzes how its rituals and reunions, during the years between 1890 and 1912, eased the veterans' painful memories of defeat and dishonor, as well as facilitated the South's transition into a new society.

Despite differences in the way veterans' organizations North and South developed, as well as in the nature of the scholarship about them, four topics dominate scholarly discussions of veterans' activities: the veterans' role in politics, the pensions and other aid they received, veterans' attempts to shape the public memory of the war, and the veterans' role in reconciliation between the sections.

POLITICS AND PENSIONS

Since the GAR actively participated in Republican party politics and "bloody shirt" rhetoric long remained a staple of Republican campaigns, much has been written about Union veterans in politics. Dearing (1952) provides the most extensive account. In a similar fashion, most historians of the South contend that Confederate veterans dominated postwar Southern politics and evoked the memory of the Lost Cause in behalf of the Democratic party. The UCV and most other Confederate groups, however, disclaimed any partisan affiliation. *Ghosts of the Confederacy* argues that the UCV did a surprisingly thorough—though never complete—job of keeping overt partisanship out of its meetings but stresses that its activities and its interpretation of the war supported a vision of a deferential social order of white, male supremacy. Its celebration of the Confederacy therefore helped make the South a conservative, ordered society as well as, indirectly, helped ensure that the Democratic party dominated the region. Others have made similar though more sweeping arguments. David Herbert Donald in "A Generation of Defeat" (1981) explains the emergence of segregation and disfranchisement as an attempt by Confederate veterans to teach the succeeding generation how to control blacks. Fred A. Bailey (1991, 1995) contends that the UCV and other groups promulgated a version of the past that supported aristocratic control of the region.

The GAR played a more active and direct role in politics than did the UCV, in part because the rewards were more concrete. The GAR, particularly in the 1880s, became one of the nation's first successful political pressure groups, seeking to expand and increase the benefits of the Federal pension system. Before the war ended, Congress had established a veterans' preference in hiring and a system of pensions for widows and those soldiers who could document war-related disabilities. The pension system later underwent two expansions; the first, in 1879, allowed retroactive claims, the second, in 1890, redefined disability so broadly that old age itself qualified most veterans for pensions. The best account of the expansion of the pension system remains one of the first: William H. Glasson's *Federal Military Pensions in the United States* (1918). More recent studies, which still rely heavily on Glasson, address additional aspects of the system, such as Amy E. Holmes's study (1980) of a small sample of widows who held pensions. The most comprehensive and important of these new studies is found in *Protecting Soldiers and Mothers: The Political Origins of Social Policy in the United States* (1992), by sociologist Theda Skocpol. Skocpol offers a good overview of the pension system and goes on to argue that critics of its largesse, though unable to curtail it, still ensured that "Civil War benefits would become an obstacle rather than an entering wedge for more general old-age pensions and working-men's insurance in the United States" (p. 532). Pensions were not the only benefits offered to the Union veterans. Both the Federal government and, often at the instigation of the GAR, individual Northern states operated soldiers' homes. Judith G. Cetina (1977) surveys the development of both systems, as well as discusses life within them. Patrick J. Kelly (1992) examines the network of homes in the National Home for Disabled Volunteer Soldiers, and Larry M. Logue (1992) also analyzes the population of and discipline within some of these institutions.

Southern states never proved as generous toward their veterans as the Federal government was, but most offered small pensions and established retirement homes. Glasson, White, James R. Young, and Thomas L. Miller discuss grants and pensions to Confederate veterans. Although useful, these studies are not as full as those for the North. A better study of Southern than Northern veterans' homes exists, though. In *Living Monuments: Confederate Soldiers' Homes in the New South* (1993), R. B. Rosenburg traces the creation of these institutions, provides a statistical analysis of the veterans who lived in them, and describes life for those residents.

THE MEMORY OF THE WAR

Even with the recent scholarly interest in the benefits veterans received, far more attention has been devoted to the ways veterans and others (these studies rarely center only on veterans) tried to preserve the memory of the war. One way to do so was to preserve its battlefields, a movement that originated with Northern veterans. Ronald F. Lee's *The Origin and Evolution of the National Military Park Idea* (1973) traces the development of these parks. Edward T. Linenthal, in *Sacred Ground: Americans and Their Battlefields* (1993), offers a more theoretical perspective, arguing that battlefield parks become "sacred patriotic space where memories of the transformative power of war and the sacrificial heroism of the warrior are preserved" (p. 3) but also places where, later, people fought over competing visions of the past. The only Civil War battlefield Linenthal discusses is that at Gettysburg, about which several other scholars have written as well. The most comprehensive of these studies, an account of both the development of the site and the meaning of the battlefield for Americans, is Amy J. Kinsel's " 'From These Honored Dead': Gettysburg in American Culture, 1863–1938" (1992). James W. Livingood, in "Chickamauga and Chattanooga National Military Park" (1964), recounts the campaign to create that park. In "Lest We Forget" Michael W. Panhorst furnishes an introduction to, as its subtitle says, "Monuments and Memorial Sculpture in National Military Parks on Civil War Battlefields, 1861–1917" (1988).

Veterans' and other groups, most often associations of female descendants, put up monuments in towns as well as on battlefields. Two books reproduce pictures of these statues: Mildred C. Baruch and Ellen J. Beckman, *Civil War Union Monuments: A List of Union Monuments, Markers, and Memorials of the Civil War, 1861–1865* (1978), and Ralph W. Widener, Jr., *Confederate Monuments: Enduring Symbols of the South and the War between the States* (1982). No substantial study of such statues in the North exists. Confederate monuments, on the other hand, have drawn considerable attention. Stephen Davis (1982) offers an informed discussion of their design and inscriptions; John L. Winberry (1983) provides the most extensive and fully documented discussion of their placement and design.

Even more than battlefield parks and monuments, schools could teach the next generation about the war and the soldiers who fought it. Both the GAR and the UCV sought to ensure that only "proper" history was taught in them, primarily by influencing the selection of textbooks but also by attacking any book or individual that they thought deviated from accepted "truth." Dearing and, more extensively, McConnell discuss these efforts in the North. Herman Hattaway (1971) and Fred A. Bailey (1991, 1992, 1995) do so for the South. Hattaway concludes that the UCV's promotion of history proved beneficial, but Bailey takes a more critical view, in one article labeling it an attempt at "mind control."

As a final means to preserve a public memory of the war, the GAR and the UCV encouraged the formation of descendants' groups for both males and females. Other than an overview in Davies's *Patriotism on Parade* (1955), little has been written on Northern descendants' societies. Foster (1987) sketches the early history of both the United Daughters of the Confederacy and the Sons of Confederate Veterans, suggesting that in the first decades of the twentieth century, since it fulfilled many needs unique to women, the former succeeded while the latter struggled. Not much else has been done on the Sons. Angie Parrott (1991) writes of the UDC in Richmond; Patricia F. Climer (1973) describes its Tennessee division.[4]

Preserving battlefields, erecting monuments, censoring textbooks, encouraging the organization of descendants' associations: all contributed to the veterans' organizations' attempt to shape a public memory of the war that justified their participation and honored their contribution. Several books, each with a distinctive perspective, help elucidate the structure and function of this memory. Merrill D. Peterson (1994) examines the nature and use of the image of the war's ultimate hero, Abraham Lincoln. Thomas J. Pressly's *Americans Interpret Their Civil War* (1962) provides an able overview of published histories. Jim Cullen, in *The Civil War in Popular Culture* (1995), discusses the treatment of the war in movies, rock 'n' roll, and other popular forms. Robert Penn Warren, in *The Legacy of the Civil War: Meditations on the Centennial* (1961), develops a personal vision of the tragic nature of the conflict but also explores what he calls the North's "Treasury of Virtue"—its belief that having freed the slaves justified almost anything it did after the war, and the South's "Great Alibi," its proclivity to excuse any and all failings by blaming them on the war and Reconstruction. Nevertheless, Royster's *The Destructive War* is the best introduction to what Americans told themselves about the war.

Specific accounts of Northern veterans' views of the war remain few in number. McConnell's *Glorious Contentment* (1992), the most helpful discussion, finds that the GAR rested veterans' claims for virtue and honor not on ending slavery—indeed the GAR talked little of emancipation—but in preserving the Union. More work has been done on the UCV's interpretation of the war. Dorgan, Hattaway, and Bailey offer accounts, and Foster's *Ghosts of the Confederacy* not only summarizes the UCV's view but argues that in the decades before and after 1900, it shaped that of Southern society.

The South's memory of the Civil War, what most have called the cult or myth of the Lost Cause, has not suffered from scholarly neglect. Several books and dissertations have examined it: Richard M. Weaver, *The Southern Tradition at Bay: A History of Postbellum Thought* (1968), Rollin G. Osterweis, *The Myth of the Lost Cause, 1865–1900* (1973), Durant, "The Gently Furled Banner" (1972), Lloyd C. Hunter, "The Sacred South: Postwar Confederates and the Sacralization of Southern Culture" (1978), Charles Reagan Wilson, *Baptized in Blood: The Religion of the Lost Cause, 1865–1920* (1980), and Connelly and Bellows, *God and General Longstreet*. Most of these studies agree that the South and its veterans believed their cause just, interpreted defeat as God's will but not God's judgment, and came to celebrate the veterans' role in the war and proclaimed them the equals or superiors of their foes in heroism and honor. Beyond that, these works differ in how they interpret the implications of the Lost Cause. Weaver treats it as a sustained counterattack on the modern world. Wilson and Hunter stress not only its religious characteristics but its role in preserving a special sense of Southern identity. Similarly, Connelly and Bellows argue that a Lost Cause way of thinking survived in modern country music. Foster, on the other hand, concludes that by 1913 the memory of the Confederacy had become poorly defined; Confederate symbolism bore little direct relation to the original cause and could be invoked in behalf of a multitude of diverse causes. Royster, in *The Destructive War,* reaches much the same conclusion.

SECTIONAL RECONCILIATION

A malleable Confederate heritage could easily be reconciled with renewed nationalism. The persistence of a special Southern identity, on the other hand, might hamper reunion. Southern opposition to sectional reconciliation is therefore implicit in many accounts of the Lost Cause. In a chapter on the Civil War in his *Mystic Chords of Memory* (1991), Michael Kammen picks up on this theme and concludes that the South never fully embraced reconciliation. Dearing, McConnell, and Nina Silber find that many GAR members continued to express hostility toward the former rebels and challenged any celebration of the South or its view of the war.

Most scholars, though, conclude that veterans played an important role in reuniting the nation. The best introduction to the topic of sectional reconciliation remains Paul H. Buck, *The Road to Reunion, 1865–1900,* which won the Pulitzer Prize for history when published in 1937. Buck stresses the importance of economic integration and the role of Southern writers in fostering reunion, which he concludes culminated in the Spanish-American War. But Buck also argues that veterans were among the first to embrace reconciliation. In an important article, Bruce Stark (1975) offers an explanation. Veterans of both sections romanticized the war's violence, skirted its issues, and could therefore establish a common bond based on their mutual experience of combat and camp. More recently, Nina Silber has published *The Romance of Reunion* (1993), which draws heavily on an analysis of gender images. Silber ties reconciliation to social changes and tensions during the late-nineteenth century and contends that the marriage of a Northern man to a Southern woman became the primary metaphor for reconciliation. Reunion was finally achieved, however, through a "spirit of masculine, virile patriotism" (p. 196) that developed during the Spanish-American War.[5]

Reconciliation also rested, Silber and other scholars show, on growing racism in the North and on the Federal government's abandonment of intervention in Southern race relations. The emerging peace between whites therefore came at the expense of blacks, as Frederick Douglass pointed out at the time. It also rested, in part, on an interpretation of the war that reduced, if not, eliminated the role of blacks. African Americans, however, developed a dissenting historical tradition that celebrated black troops and placed slavery at the center of the conflict. Emancipation Day became an important holiday in many black communities. Historians have done little to examine these celebrations or explicate the African-American view of the war. In two pioneering and important articles, however, David W. Blight has developed these themes and begun to rectify the failing.[6]

Despite such gaps in the literature as the dearth of discussion of the African-American memory of the war and the absence of extensive, systematic studies of the veterans' postwar careers, historians have nevertheless done much to tell the veterans' story. They have begun to explore not only the problems the veterans faced but the way in which the war horrified as well as fascinated them. The stories that veterans told themselves and their society to make sense of these paradoxical emotions and to justify their sacrifice and brutality helped create the public memory of the war. The soldiers' stories after the war therefore become central to the history of the war, especially to an understanding of its importance and implications. The participants' version of the Civil War shaped that of future generations, even as the war no doubt shaped the veterans' lives.

NOTES

1. William B. Hesseltine and Hazel C. Wolf, *Blue and Gray on the Nile* (Chicago: University of Chicago Press, 1961); David P. Werlich, *Admiral of the Amazon: John Randolph Tucker, His Confederate Colleagues, and Peru* (Charlottesville: University Press of Virginia, 1990). For a discussion of and references to veterans as tramps, see Royster, *Destructive War,* pp. 400, 513, n. 400. Gaines M. Foster, "Coming to Terms with Defeat: Post Vietnam America and the Post Civil War South," *Virginia Quarterly Review* 66 (1990): 17–35, suggests some comparisons between the veterans' experiences in these two wars.

2. Royster, *Destructive War,* points out a substantial literature interpreting only one aspect of this issue, Oliver Wendell Holmes, Jr.'s speech "A Soldier's Faith." See pp. 283–284, 487–488, n. 283.

3. Donald E. Shaffer is writing a dissertation on African-American veterans.

4. There is, however, considerable work being done on the UDC.

5. Cecilia O'Leary is completing another study of sectional reconciliation. For her preliminary findings, see her article cited in the Bibliography.

6. William H. Wiggins, Jr., *O Freedom! Afro-American Emancipation Celebrations* (Knoxville: University of Tennessee Press 1987), discusses contemporary celebrations but provides little historical background.

BIBLIOGRAPHY

Bailey, Fred A. "The Textbooks of the 'Lost Cause': Censorship and the Creation of Southern State Histories." *Georgia Historical Quarterly* 75 (1991): 507–533.

———. "Free Speech and the Lost Cause in the Old Dominion." *Virginia Magazine of History and Biography* 103 (1995): 237–266.

———. "Free Speech at the University of Florida: The Enoch Marvin Banks Case." *Florida Historical Quarterly* 71 (1992): 1–17.

Baruch, Mildred C., and Ellen J. Beckman. *Civil War Union Monuments: A List of Union Monuments, Markers, and Memorials of the Civil War, 1861–1865.* Washington, D.C.: Daughters of Union Veterans of the Civil War, 1978.

Blight, David W. "For Something beyond the Battlefield: Frederick Douglass and the Struggle for the Memory of the Civil War." *Journal of American History* 75 (1989): 1156–1178.

———. " 'What Will Peace among the Whites Bring?' Reunion and Race in the Struggle over the Memory of the Civil War in American Culture." *Massachusetts Review* 33 (1993): 393–409.

Buck, Paul H. *The Road to Reunion, 1865–1900.* Boston: Little, Brown, 1937.

Cetina, Judith G. "A History of Veterans' Homes in the United States, 1811–1930." Ph.D. diss., Case Western Reserve University, 1977.

Climer, Patricia F. "Protectors of the Past: The United Daughters of the Confederacy, Tennessee Division, and the Lost Cause." Master's thesis, Vanderbilt University, 1973.

Connelly, Thomas L. *The Marble Man: Robert E. Lee and His Image in American Society.* New York: Alfred A. Knopf, 1977.

———, and Barbara L. Bellows. *God and General Longstreet: The Lost Cause and the Southern Mind.* Baton Rouge: Louisiana State University Press, 1982.

Cullen, Jim. *The Civil War in Popular Culture: A Reusable Past.* Washington, D.C.: Smithsonian Institution Press, 1995.

Davies, Wallace E. *Patriotism on Parade: The Story of Veterans' and Hereditary Organizations in America, 1783–1900.* Cambridge: Harvard University Press, 1955.

———. "The Problem of Race Segregation in the Grand Army of the Republic." *Journal of Southern History* 13 (1947): 354–372.

Davis, Stephen. "Empty Eyes, Marble Hand: The Confederate Monument and the South." *Journal of Popular Culture* 16 (1982): 2–21.

Dawsey, Cyrus B., and James M. Dawsey. *The Confederados: Old South Immigrants in Brazil.* Tuscaloosa: University of Alabama Press, 1995.

Dean, Eric T., Jr. " 'We Will All Be Lost and Destroyed': Post-Traumatic Stress Disorder and the Civil War." *Civil War History* 37 (1992): 138–153.

Dearing, Mary R. *Veterans in Politics: The Story of the G.A.R.* Baton Rouge: Louisiana State University Press, 1952.

Donald, David Herbert. "A Generation of Defeat." In *From the Old South to the New: Essays on the Transitional South,* 3–20. Edited by Walter J. Fraser, Jr., and Winfred B. Moore, Jr. Westport, CT: Greenwood Press, 1981.

Dorgan, Howard. "The Doctrine of Victorious Defeat in the Rhetoric of Confederate Veterans." *Southern Speech Communication Journal* 38 (1972): 119–130.

———. "Rhetoric of the United Confederate Veterans: A Lost Cause Mythology in the Making." In *Oratory in the New South,* 143–173. Edited by Waldo W. Braden. Baton Rouge: Louisiana State University Press, 1979.

———. "Southern Apologetic Themes, as Expressed in Selected Ceremonial Speaking of Confederate Veterans, 1889–1900." Ph.D. diss., Louisiana State University, 1971.

Dorris, Jonathan T. *Pardon and Amnesty under Lincoln and Johnson: The Restoration of the Confederates to Their Rights and Privileges, 1861–1898.* Chapel Hill: University of North Carolina Press, 1953.

Durant, Susan Speare. "The Gently Furled Banner: The Development of the Myth of the Lost Cause, 1865–1900." Ph.D. diss., University of North Carolina, 1972.

Ellingsworth, Hubert W. "Southern Reconciliation Orators in the North, 1869–1899." Ph.D. diss., Florida State University, 1955.

Foster, Gaines M. *Ghosts of the Confederacy: Defeat, the Lost Cause, and the Emergence of the New South, 1865–1913.* New York: Oxford University Press, 1987.

Glasson, William H. *Federal Military Pensions in the United States.* New York: Oxford University Press, 1918.

———. "The South's Care for Her Confederate Veterans." *Review of Reviews* 36 (July 1907): 40–47.

———. "The South's Pension and Relief Provisions for the Soldiers of the Confederacy." In *Proceedings of the Eighteenth Annual Session of the State Literary and Historical Association of North Carolina.* Publications of the North Carolina Historical Commission, Bulletin 23. Raleigh: Edwards & Broughton, 1918.

Gulley, Harold E. "Southern Nationalism on the Landscape: County Names in Former Confederate States." *Names* 38 (1990): 231–242.

———. "Women and the Lost Cause: Preserving a Confederate Identity in the American Deep South." *Journal of Historical Geography* 19 (1993): 125–141.

Hattaway, Herman. "Clio's Southern Soldiers: The United Confederate Veterans and History." *Louisiana History* 12 (1971): 213–242.

———. "The United Confederate Veterans in Louisiana." *Louisiana History* 16 (1975): 5–37.

Heck, Frank H. *The Civil War Veteran in Minnesota Life and Politics.* Oxford, OH: Mississippi Valley Press, 1941.

Hesseltine, William B. *Confederate Leaders in the New South.* 1950. Reprint, Westport, CT: Greenwood Press, 1970.

Holmes, Amy E. " 'Such Is the Price We Pay': American Widows and the Civil War Pension System." In *Toward a Social History of the American Civil War: Exploratory Essays,* 171–195. Edited by Maris A. Vinovskis. Cambridge: Cambridge University Press, 1990.

Hunter, Lloyd A. "The Sacred South: Postwar Confederates and the Sacralization of Southern Culture." Ph.D. diss., St. Louis University, 1978.

Kammen, Michael. *Mystic Chords of Memory: The Transformation of Tradition in American Culture.* New York: Alfred A. Knopf, 1991.

Kelly, Patrick J. "Creating a National Home: The Postwar Care of Disabled Union Soldiers and the Beginning of the Modern State in America." Ph.D. diss., New York University, 1992.

Kinsel, Amy J. " 'From These Honored Dead': Gettysburg in American Culture, 1863–1938." Ph.D. diss., Cornell University, 1992.

Lankevich, George J. "The Grand Army of the Republic in New York State, 1865–1898." Ph.D. diss., Columbia University, 1967.

Lee, Ronald F. *The Origin and Evolution of the National Military Park Idea.* Washington, D.C.: U.S. National Park Service, Office of Park Historic Preservation, 1973.

Leonard, Thomas C. *Above the Battle: War-Making in America from Appomattox to Versailles.* New York: Oxford University Press, 1978.

Linenthal, Edward T. *Sacred Ground: Americans and Their Battlefields.* 2d ed. Urbana: University of Illinois Press, 1993.

Linderman, Gerald F. *Embattled Courage: The Experience of Combat in the American Civil War.* New York: Free Press, 1987.

Livingood, James W. "Chickamauga and Chattanooga National Military Park." *Tennessee Historical Quarterly* 23 (1964): 3–23.

Logue, Larry M. "Union Veterans and Their Government: The Effects of Public Policies on Private Lives." *Journal of Interdisciplinary History* 22 (1992): 411–434.

McConnell, Stuart. *Glorious Contentment: The Grand Army of the Republic, 1865–1900.* Chapel Hill: University of North Carolina Press, 1992.

Miller, Thomas L. "Texas Land Grants to Confederate Veterans and Widows." *Southwestern Historical Quarterly* 69 (1965): 59–65.

Noyes, Elmer E. "A History of the Grand Army of the Republic in Ohio from 1866 to 1900." Ph.D. diss., Ohio State University, 1945.

O'Leary, Cecilia. " 'Americans All': Reforging a National Brotherhood, 1876–1917." *History Today* 44 (1994): 20–27.

Osterweis, Rollin G. *The Myth of the Lost Cause, 1865–1900.* Hamden, CT: Archon Books, 1973.

Panhorst, Michael W. "Lest We Forget: Monuments and Memorial Sculpture in National Military Parks on Civil War Battlefields, 1861–1917." Ph.D. diss., University of Delaware, 1988.

Parrott, Angie. " 'Love Makes Memory Eternal': The United Daughters of the Confederacy in Richmond, Virginia, 1897–1920." In *The Edge of the South: Life in*

Nineteenth-Century Virginia, 219–238. Edited by Edward L. Ayers and John C. Willis. Charlottesville: University Press of Virginia, 1991.

Peterson, Merrill D. *Lincoln in American Memory.* New York: Oxford University Press, 1994.

Piston, William G. *Lee's Tarnished Lieutenant: James Longstreet and His Place in Southern History.* Athens: University of Georgia Press, 1987.

Pressly, Thomas J. *Americans Interpret Their Civil War.* New York: Free Press, 1962.

Rosenburg, R. B. *Living Monuments: Confederate Soldiers' Homes in the New South.* Chapel Hill: University of North Carolina Press, 1993.

Royster, Charles. *The Destructive War: William Tecumseh Sherman, Stonewall Jackson, and the Americans.* New York: Alfred A. Knopf, 1991.

Sanders, Heywood T. "Paying for the 'Bloody Shirt': The Politics of Civil War Pensions." In *Political Benefits: Empirical Studies of American Public Programs,* 137–159. Edited by Barry S. Rundquist. Lexington, MA: D. C. Heath and Company, 1980.

Schultz, Jane E. "Race, Gender, and Bureaucracy: Civil War Army Nurses and the Pension Commission." *Journal of Women's History* 6 (1994): 45–69.

Severo, Richard, and Lewis Milford. *The Wages of War: When America's Soldiers Came Home—From Valley Forge to Vietnam.* New York: Simon & Schuster, 1989.

Silber, Nina. *The Romance of Reunion: Northerners and the South, 1865–1900.* Chapel Hill: University of North Carolina Press, 1993.

Skarstedt, Vance R. "The Confederate Veteran Movement and National Reunification." Ph.D. diss., Florida State University, 1993.

Skocpol, Theda. *Protecting Soldiers and Mothers: The Political Origins of Social Policy in the United States.* Cambridge: Belknap Press of Harvard University Press, 1992.

Stark, Cruce. "Brothers at/in War: One Phase of Post–Civil War Reconciliation." *Canadian Review of American Studies* 6 (1975): 174–181.

Sutherland, Daniel E. *The Confederate Carpetbaggers.* Baton Rouge: Louisiana State University Press, 1988.

———. "Exiles, Emigrants, and Sojourners: The Post–Civil War Confederate Exodus in Perspective." *Civil War History* 31 (1985): 237–256.

Towns, W. Stuart. "Ceremonial Orators and National Reconciliation." In *Oratory in the New South,* 119–142. Edited by Waldo W. Braden. Baton Rouge: Louisiana State University Press, 1979.

Vinovskis, Maris A. "Have Social Historians Lost the Civil War? Some Preliminary Demographic Speculations." In *Toward a Social History of the American Civil War: Exploratory Essays,* 1–30. Edited by Maris A. Vinovskis. Cambridge: Cambridge University Press, 1990.

Warren, Robert Penn. *The Legacy of the Civil War: Meditations on the Centennial.* New York: Alfred A. Knopf, 1961.

Weaver, Richard M. *The Southern Tradition at Bay: A History of Postbellum Thought.* Edited by George Core and M. E. Bradford. New Rochelle, NY: Arlington House, 1968.

Wecter, Dixon, *When Johnny Comes Marching Home.* Cambridge, MA: Houghton Mifflin, 1944.

White, William W. *The Confederate Veteran.* Confederate Centennial Studies, 22. Tuscaloosa: Confederate Publishing Co., 1962.

Widener, Ralph W., Jr. *Confederate Monuments: Enduring Symbols of the South and the War between the States.* Washington, D.C.: Andromeda, 1982.

Wilson, Charles R. *Baptized in Blood: The Religion of the Lost Cause, 1865–1920.* Athens: University of Georgia Press, 1980.

Winberry, John L. " 'Lest We Forget': The Confederate Monument and the Southern Townscape." *Southeastern Geographer* 23 (1983): 107–121.

Young, James R. "Confederate Pensions in Georgia, 1886–1929." *Georgia Historical Quarterly* 66 (1982): 47–52.

Part XI

Popular Media

45

Novels and Other Fictional Accounts

Sharon L. Gravett

In an essay published in 1961, Robert Penn Warren asserts that the "Civil War is, for the American imagination, the great single event of our history. Without too much wrenching, it may, in fact, be said to *be* American history" (p. 270). This war had such an imaginative impact, he says, because it was "the prototype of all war, for in the persons of fellow citizens who happen to be the enemy, we meet again, with the old ambivalence of love and hate and with all the old quilts, the blood brothers of our childhood" (pp. 300–301). A conflict between the past and the future, between Southern agrarianism and Northern industrialism, between states' rights and unionism, between principles of equality and slavery, the Civil War raised issues that continue to reverberate into the present, thus providing an exceptionally rich and varied canvas for literature. This literature challenges contemporary readers both to comprehend the war in its own time and to realize its continuing impact. Warren suggests that readers need to transport themselves "into the documented, re-created moment of the past and, in a double vision, see the problems and values of that moment and those of our own, set against each other in mutual criticism and clarification" (p. 306).

This task of examining the literature of the American Civil War is a complex one, not only because of the difficulties inherent in the works themselves, but also because of the sheer volume of literature available. Literally thousands of works of fiction have been written about the Civil War and its aftermath. Albert J. Menendez's *Civil War Novels: An Annotated Bibliography* (1986) lists 1,028 entries. Authors as diverse as Richard Adams (*Traveller,* 1988), Horatio Alger (*Frank's Campaign,* 1864), Louis Auchincloss (*Watchfires,* 1982), James M. Cain (*Mignon,* 1962, and *Past All Dishonor,* 1946), Willa Cather (*Sapphira and the Slave Girl,* 1940), William Dean Howells (*A Fearful Responsibility,* 1881), Sidney Lanier (*Tiger Lilies,* 1867), and Gore Vidal (*Lincoln,* 1984) have all written Civil War fiction. No survey can claim to offer a complete picture of all the fictional works produced about the war. It might be helpful, however, to discuss briefly some of the many different kinds of literature this war has evoked, for the fictions produced are as various as the individual experiences of the war and its aftermath. The multifaceted nature of the conflict is revealed by stories of soldiers on the battlefield, of women in the hospitals, of slaves on the plantation, and of families before, during, and after the war.

SOLDIERS' STORIES

Tales from the battlefield abound in the works of fiction about the Civil War. A number blend fact and fiction in intriguing ways as real-life battles form the backdrop of many novels and short stories. Shelby Foote's *Shiloh* (1952) recounts that battle through the eyes of a number of participants from both sides, while Michael Shaara's Pulitzer Prize–winning *The Killer Angels* (1974) and MacKinlay Kantor's *Long Remember* (1934) do the same for the Battle of Gettysburg. Perry Lentz's *The Falling Hills* (1967) dramatizes the Fort Pillow Massacre in Tennessee. Other authors sweep more widely over the conflict, using a number of battles in their fiction. Mary Johnston, the daughter of a Confederate artillery officer and a relative of Confederate general Joseph E. Johnston, produced two acclaimed war novels: *The Long Roll* (1911), which covers events up to the Battle of Chancellorsville, and *Cease Firing* (1912), which follows through to the end of the war. John Esten Cooke records his own experiences as an officer of horse artillery in *Surry of Eagle's Nest* (1866). Other novels in this vein include Douglas C. Jones's *Elkhorn Tavern* (1980) and Tom Wicker's *Unto This Hour* (1984).

Of course, a soldier's life consists of more than battle, and a number of novels show the men's lives at home as well as at the front. Thomas Keneally's *Confederates* (1982) and Joseph Kirkland's *The Captain of Company K* (1891) follow events of a group of Southern soldiers both at home and on the field. Caroline Gordon's *None Shall Look Back* (1937) chronicles the war in the West through the lives of the Allard family. Andrew Lytle's *The Long Night* (1936) depicts the McIvor family's quest for vengeance against the backdrop of the war, particularly the Battle of Shiloh.

Soldiers also appear in places other than at home or in battle. MacKinlay Kantor's *Andersonville* (1955), which won a Pulitzer Prize, describes life in the notorious Southern prisoner-of-war camp. Louisa May Alcott takes a slightly different approach to battle in her *Hospital Sketches* (1869). This work, which presents, in fictional form, Alcott's own experiences as a nurse in Washington, D.C., points out that women served on the front lines in their own ways.

Perhaps the best-known soldier's story is Stephen Crane's *The Red Badge of Courage* (1895). Ironically, this novel was written by a young man who was born six years after the war was over, and, in many ways, it could be about any conflict. More than the story of a particular battle, *Red Badge* depicts the frightening initiation of one young man into the realities of war. Henry Fleming's dreams of glory and honor collapse violently when reality diverges significantly from his preconceived notions.

This growing sense of disillusionment plays a prominent role in many of the works of fiction about soldiers. For example, Mark Twain's short story "The Private History of a Campaign That Failed" recounts the adventures of "one who started out to do something in it, but didn't" (p. 119). From the beginning, the protagonist obviously is not deeply committed to either side of the conflict; even when he eventually joins a military company with a group of his friends, their soldierly endeavors consist mostly of romping around the countryside, living off the bounty of the neighboring farmers, and quarreling among themselves. However, their shenanigans take on a serious tone when they kill an approaching stranger. The sight of his dead body brings home war's sober truths. The narrator realizes:

And it seemed an epitome of war, that all war must be just that, the killing of strangers against whom you feel no animosity, strangers whom in other circumstances you would help if you found them in trouble, and who would help you if you needed it. (139)

Twain's darkly humorous look at this abortive company draws an ironic contrast between the lure of military life and its harsh reality.

The ironies of a soldier's life are also at the center of the short stories of Ambrose Bierce. Young men—men who could be friends, neighbors, sons, or brothers—turn into totally different entities when they become soldiers. For example, Private Jerome Searing in "One of the Missing" shows that a soldier's aims differ from those of ordinary men. Sent on a scouting mission, Private Searing successfully completes his task and should report back immediately, but, tempted by the sight of the retreating Confederates, he decides to go ahead and take a shot: "That would probably not affect the duration and result of the war, but it is the business of a soldier to kill" (p. 6). This pause, to carry out an essentially useless function, costs Searing his life. While he is taking his aim, a shot from one of the rebel soldiers brings down the house where he is standing.

Not only does a soldier, often to his detriment, become a trained killer, but he becomes a machine as well. In Bierce's stories, the soldier often turns into an unthinking automaton who blindly obeys whatever orders he is given. In "One Kind of Officer," General Cameron tells one of his officers, "Captain Ransome, it is not permitted to you to know *anything*. It is sufficient that you obey my order" (p. 29). Captain Ransome takes the general at his word and follows his orders to the letter, even when it becomes apparent that he has been killing his own men.

The most common irony in the Civil War is the possibility of killing a member of one's own family. Bierce fully exploits this situation in a number of his tales. In "A Horseman in the Sky," Carter Druse, a Virginian serving in the Federal army, had split with his father over his decision to serve North rather than South. His father's parting words to his son were: "Well, go, sir, and whatever may occur do what you conceive to be your duty" (p. 99). These words come back to haunt the younger Druse when he is on sentry duty and spots a rebel soldier. After an internal struggle, he does his duty and kills his enemy, who turns out to be his father. In "The Mocking-Bird," Private William Grayrock hears a noise while on sentry duty and immediately fires. The next day, as he searches for his victim, he discovers that he has killed his twin brother, John Grayrock, a Confederate soldier. He then kills himself. Bierce continually demonstrates that the profession of soldiership transforms men and makes them perform actions they would typically reprehend.

The war is, in fact, so disturbing that it even disrupts time itself. In perhaps his best-known story, "An Occurrence at Owl Creek Bridge," Bierce manipulates chronology in both his story and the life of his protagonist, Peyton Farquhar, who momentarily escapes the hangman's noose as the last moments of his life seem to expand almost indefinitely.

STORIES FROM THE HOME FRONT

Soldiers are not the only participants in war; those left at home are affected as well, and the literature reflects this situation. A number of works look at the life of women during the war. One is John DeForest's *Miss Ravenal's Conversion from Secession to Loyalty* (1867), which, although it does feature some battlefield scenes, largely concerns Lillie Ravenal's move, not only from pro-Southern to pro-Northern sympathies but from her immature infatuation with the dashing but irresponsible Colonel Carter to her more mature love for Edward Colburne. Henry James also wrote several stories detailing the relationships between soldiers and the women at home: "The Story of a Year" (1865), "Poor Richard" (1865), and "A Most Extraordinary Case" (1868). In *Clarence* (1896) by Bret Harte, the war exacerbates the conflict in the marriage between a Union general and his Southern-sympathizing wife.

Some women did not stay at home but went to battle themselves. Rita Mae Brown's *High Hearts* (1986) tells the story of a woman who disguises herself as a man in order to join her husband at the front. The adventures of yet another set of women are recounted in F. Scott Fitzgerald's short story "The Night before Chancellorsville" (1935), in which a group of prostitutes unexpectedly find themselves in the midst of a battle. They join other fictional women whose lives are unalterably affected by the conflict. For example, Amantha Starr, in Robert Penn Warren's *Band of Angels* (1955), finds herself entangled in the reasons behind the conflict when she learns, upon her plantation-owning father's death, that she is a slave and must be sold. A similar fate awaits the title character in Frances Ellen Watkins Harper's *Iola Leroy* (1892). In Margaret Walker's

Jubilee (1967), Vyry, the daughter of a white plantation owner and his black mistress, triumphs through the war and its aftermath.

These women learn to persevere despite the difficult circumstances in which they find themselves. Strong women are featured prominently in novels such as William Faulkner's *The Unvanquished* (1938). Grandmother Rosa Millard keeps the Sartoris family together during the war and even loses her life as the result of her activities; Cousin Drusilla Hawk ends up fighting disguised as a man and then, after the war, marries John Sartoris and continues to battle to preserve the Southern way of life. Influenced by these strong women is Bayard Sartoris. Twelve years of age when the novel begins, young Bayard experiences the hardships and sacrifices of war. Yet his real test occurs once the fighting is supposedly over, when he is summoned home from college to avenge his father's murder. His decision not to participate in the cycle of violence earns him Drusilla's wrath but marks his passage to true manhood. This family drama of the war and its aftermath should not be unusual coming from William Faulkner. After all, his grandfather, Colonel William C. Falkner [*sic*], penned *The White Rose of Memphis* (1881), a novel covering much of the same territory.

Another family story is told in Allen Tate's *The Fathers* (1938), where Lacy Buchan, fifteen years old when the novel begins, faces not only the war but the struggles of growing up in a traditional Southern family. In fact, problems within the family mirror the issues involved in the external conflict. The Buchan family, steeped in notions of honor, suffers in its relationship by marriage to the Poe-like Posey clan, whose mulatto son, Yellow Jim, brings tragedy to both families. Divisions in both the family and the community are also shown in Harold Frederic's *The Copperhead* (1892) in which a man's pro-Southern sympathies damage his relationships in his family and in his community. Other novels featuring family, as well as regional, conflicts are Ellen Glasgow's *The Battle-Ground* (1902), Stark Young's *So Red the Rose* (1934), and John Jakes's *North and South* (1982).

Furthermore, places, like the fictional Mordington in Virginia, are also affected by the war as in the collection of short stories, *Many Thousands Gone* (1931) by John Peale Bishop. Similarly, Charleston society is at odds with the protagonist in DuBose Heyward's *Peter Ashley* (1932), in which an artist who cannot accept the prevailing attitudes of his community is then slowly swept into them.

STORIES OF RECONSTRUCTION

Although the war years constitute the bulk of much fiction, the period after the war proves to be as tumultuous as the conflict itself, and in a number of works, Reconstruction is prominently featured. Often these works demonstrate the failure of plans to rehabilitate the South.

Joel Chandler Harris's *Gabriel Tolliver* (1902) shows blacks adjusting to their new lives while whites seek refuge in the Ku Klux Klan. Southern resistance is also shown in *Red Rock* (1898) by Thomas Nelson Page. Thomas Dixon, the author of a number of novels, including *The Clansman* (1905), glorified the KKK and painted a grim picture of life in the postwar South. Dixon's novel was later made into the film *Birth of a Nation*. A more balanced, but no less despairing, novel about Reconstruction is Albion Tourgée's *A Fool's Errand* (1879), which tells the tumultuous story of a former Union officer, Comfort Servosse, who settles in the South after the war in an attempt to heal old wounds. His new neighbors, however, distrust his motives; governmental policies do not help matters. The Fool finds himself embroiled in a conflict every bit as tense and threatening as his war experiences. Charles Chesnutt's *The Colonel's Dream* (1905) also presents the problems inherent in trying to rebuild the Southern economy.

From a different perspective, Howard Fast's *Freedom Road* (1944) attacks Southern whites during Reconstruction, using an illiterate black man as its protagonist, while Harper's *Iola Leroy* (1892) tells the story of a group of recently freed slaves and charts their attempts to provide an uplifting standard for the rest of their race.

A WAR OF MEMORY

Even as the War between the States receded further into the past, it remained a vital part of the literary imagination in both North and South as fiction began to explore the impact of the war on subsequent generations. These works examined the devastating after-effects of the conflict, not only on the generation who lived through the war but on those who followed them. In these novels, the war is history, yet this past event continues to exert its influence into the present.

Among the novels that blend past and present, the war and its aftermath, are Allan Gurganus's *Oldest Living Confederate Widow Tells All* (1989) and Joseph Stanley Pennell's *The History of Rome Hanks and Kindred Matters* (1944). One short story that uses the site of a Civil War battle as the backdrop for a contemporary story of marital disintegration is Bobbie Ann Mason's ''Shiloh'' (1982).

Perhaps no other novel expresses this continual presence of the past more compellingly than William Faulkner's *Absalom, Absalom!* (1936). In this novel, the war itself appears only in backward glances, with the present action taking place in 1909; however, the past becomes the motivating obsession for characters. For example, Quentin Compson finds the presence of the past so overwhelming that his very personality begins to splinter. The past's haunting presence is even more pronounced in Toni Morrison's Pulitzer Prize–winning *Beloved* (1987), set in the year 1873; in this novel, a vengeful ghost refuses to let prior events be forgotten.

Thus the past plays a crucial role in both novels and is linked to a central event that remains shrouded through much of each narrative. In *Absalom*, Quentin is obsessed by the story of Thomas Sutpen and his family. Sutpen had been the wealthiest landowner in his region, a self-made man who struggled to make his fortune, only to see it all destroyed. The pivotal event in the novel is the murder of Charles Bon, a suitor to Sutpen's daughter, Judith, who is killed by Sutpen's son, Henry, at the gates of the family's home. This act serves as the central mystery that continues to enthrall members of the town years after it occurs.

Absalom thus features the gradual unraveling of the reasons behind Charles Bon's murder. The first explanation, that Bon's mistress and child were offensive to Henry, is quickly discarded. The second, that Judith would be committing incest because Bon was Thomas Sutpen's first child from a previous marriage, is also dismissed. Instead, the belief that Bon's mother was black seems to be the major objection; miscegenation, not incest, was the sin that precipitated his murder. This revelation of the injustice and hypocrisy at the heart of Southern society dramatically affects Quentin, who finds he cannot escape it, even during a cold winter at Harvard. At the end of the novel, he exclaims about the South, *"I don't hate it. . . . I dont. I dont! I dont hate it! I dont hate it!"* (p. 303).

In *Beloved,* readers struggle to discover why a spiteful baby haunts the house. Although they know that the baby's throat was cut, the reason remains mysterious. It is gradually revealed that the baby's mother, Sethe, had escaped from slavery, crossed over the Ohio, and made it into a free state, where she apparently was safe. Yet this condition did not last long—only twenty-eight days— and Sethe has since been rejected by her community. Only midway through the novel do readers finally learn that Sethe's owner had pursued her across the river, and rather than let herself or her children be recaptured, she attempted to kill them, succeeding only in killing her little girl.

In the rest of the novel, Sethe must come to terms with the legacy of her past—not only her murdered child but her degraded condition as a slave. These memories become harder and harder to repress, particularly when a mysterious young woman appears, whom Sethe comes to believe is her daughter, known only as Beloved, the name on her tombstone. Beloved becomes the physical embodiment of the past, and her presence nearly destroys Sethe. Oddly, she is rescued by the same coalition of neighborhood women who had deserted her before: "Whatever Sethe had done, [they] didn't like the idea of past errors taking possession of the present" (p. 256).

Like *Absalom, Absalom! Beloved* is a novel about memory and dealing with the horrors of the past. Both novels stand as monuments to people whom history threatens to forget—the discarded and murdered Charles Bon, the murdered Beloved: two children whose heritage as blacks in Southern slave society cuts them out of the world. For Morrison, Beloved comes to represent the thousands of black women who perished anonymously in the chains of slavery. In the final chapter, the narrator writes, "Everybody knew what she was called, but nobody knew her name. Disremembered and unaccounted for, she cannot be lost because no one is looking for her, and even if they were, how can they call her if they don't know her name?" (p. 274).

THE EPICS

Many Civil War novels are ambitious, but a few stand out because of their scope. These novels defy easy categorization in one of the previously mentioned groups; they can fit, with ease, into a number of them. Among the most technically innovative of the Civil War novels is Evelyn Scott's *The Wave* (1929). Using a panoramic technique, Scott relates a number of individual incidents that together form the history of the war like an overwhelming wave. Another novel that features an ambitious sweep of time, if not place, is Ross Lockridge, Jr.'s *Raintree County* (1948). Set on one day—July 4, 1892—in the life of John Wickliff Shawnessy, the novel moves back and forth through time as Johnny remembers key events from his life before, during, and after the war in Raintree County, Indiana. His life reveals both the idealism and optimism of the antebellum America, the savage disillusionment of the war years, and his struggle to find a new and satisfying life in the corrupt years following the conflict. Another novel of sweeping scope, and tremendous popularity, is Margaret Mitchell's *Gone with the Wind* (1936). Although best known for its romance between Scarlett O'Hara and Rhett Butler, the novel offers a complex portrait of Southern society before, during, and after the war.

CONCLUSION

Even in the twentieth century, the Civil War remains central to the American literary imagination. The conflict of over a century ago with its legacy of slavery, secession, regionalism, and sectional war remains a vital part of not only our heritage but of our contemporary life.

Perhaps the Civil War retains its grasp because many of the issues and events of the war are equally relevant today. The past is never far from us; it lives with us still.

BIBLIOGRAPHY

Adams, Richard. *Traveller.* New York: Knopf, 1988.

Alcott, Louisa May. *Hospital Sketches.* 1869. Reprint, Chester, CT: Applewood Books, n.d.

Auchincloss, Louis. *Watchfires.* Boston: Houghton Mifflin, 1982.

Bierce, Ambrose. *The Civil War Short Stories of Ambrose Bierce.* Lincoln: University of Nebraska Press, 1970.

Bishop, John Peale. *Many Thousands Gone.* New York: Scribner's Sons, 1931.

Brown, Rita Mae. *High Hearts.* Toronto: Bantam Books, 1986.

Cain, James M. *Mignon.* New York: Dial Press, 1962.

———. *Past All Dishonor.* New York: A. A. Knopf, 1946.

Cather, Willa. *Sapphira and the Slave Girl.* New York: A. A. Knopf, 1940.

Chesnutt, Charles. *The Colonel's Dream.* 1905. Reprint, Upper Saddle River, NJ: Gregg Press, 1968.

Cooke, John Esten. *Surry of Eagle's Nest.* Chicago: M. A. Donohue & Co., 1894.

Crane, Stephen. *The Red Badge of Courage.* 1895. Reprint, New York: Avon Books, 1982.

DeForest, John William. *Miss Ravenal's Conversion from Secession to Loyalty.* 1867. Reprint, New York: Holt, Rinehart and Winston, 1964.

Dixon, Thomas. *The Clansman.* 1905. Reprint, New York: Grosset & Dunlap, 1915.

Falkner, William C. *The White Rose of Memphis.* 1881. Reprint, New York: Coley Taylor, 1953.

Fast, Howard. *Freedom Road.* New York: Book Find Club, 1944.

Faulkner, William. *Absalom, Absalom!* 1936. Reprint, New York: Vintage International, 1990.

———. *The Unvanquished.* 1938. Reprint, New York: Vintage International, 1990.

Foote, Shelby. *Chickamauga and Other Civil War Stories.* New York: Delta, 1993.

———. *Shiloh.* 1952. Reprint, New York: Vintage Books, 1991.

Frederic, Harold. *The Copperhead.* 1892. Reprint, New York: Garrett Press, 1969.

Glasgow, Ellen. *The Battle-Ground.* New York: Doubleday, Page & Co., 1902.

Gordon, Caroline. *None Shall Look Back.* 1937. Reprint, Nashville: J. S. Sanders & Company, 1992.

Gurganus, Allan. *Oldest Living Confederate Widow Tells All.* New York: Ivy Books, 1989.

Harper, Frances Ellen Watkins. *Iola Leroy, or Shadows Uplifted.* Boston: James H. Earle, 1892.

Harris, Joel Chandler. *Gabriel Tolliver.* 1902. Reprint, Ridgewood, NJ: Gregg Press, 1967.

Harte, Bret. *Clarence.* Boston: Houghton Mifflin, 1896.

Heyward, DuBose. *Peter Ashley.* New York: Farrar & Rinehart, 1932.

Howells, William Dean. *A Fearful Responsibility and Other Stories.* Boston: J. R. Osgood and Company, 1881.

Jakes, John. *North and South.* New York: Harcourt, Brace, Jovanovich, 1982.

Johnston, Mary. *Cease Firing.* Boston: Houghton Mifflin, 1912.

———. *The Long Roll.* Boston: Houghton Mifflin, 1911.

Jones, Douglas. *Elkhorn Tavern.* New York: Holt, Rinehart and Winston, 1980.

Kantor, MacKinley. *Andersonville.* 1955. Reprint, New York: Plume, 1993.

———. *Long Remember.* New York: Literary Guild, 1934.

Keneally, Thomas. *Confederates.* 1982. Reprint, New York: HarperPerennial, 1994.

Kirkland, Joseph. *The Captain of Company K.* 1891. Reprint, Ridgewood, NJ: Gregg Press, 1968.

Lanier, Sidney. *Tiger-Lilies.* Chapel Hill: University of North Carolina Press, 1969.

Lentz, Perry. *The Falling Hills: A Novel of the Civil War.* 1967. Reprint, Columbia: University of South Carolina Press, 1994.

Lockridge, Ross, Jr. *Raintree County.* 1948. Reprint, New York: Penguin Books, 1994.

Lytle, Andrew. *The Long Night.* 1936. Reprint, Tuscaloosa: University of Alabama Press, 1988.

Mason, Bobbie Ann. *Shiloh and Other Stories.* New York: Harper & Row, 1982.

Menendez, Albert J. *Civil War Novels: An Annotated Bibliography.* New York: Garland Publishing, 1986.

Mitchell, Margaret. *Gone with the Wind.* 1936. Reprint, New York: Macmillan, 1977.

Morrison, Toni. *Beloved.* New York: Plume, 1987.

Page, Thomas Nelson. *Red Rock.* 1898. Reprint, New York: Charles Scribner's Sons, 1927.

Pennell, Joseph Stanley. *The History of Rome Hanks and Kindred Matters.* New York: Scribner, 1944.

Scott, Evelyn. *The Wave.* New York: J. Cape and H. Smith, 1929.

Shaara, Michael. *The Killer Angels.* 1974. Reprint, New York: Ballantine Books, 1990.

Tate, Allen. *The Fathers and Other Fiction.* 1938. Reprint, Baton Rouge: Louisiana State University Press, 1977.

Tourgée, Albion. *A Fool's Errand: A Novel of the South during Reconstruction.* 1879. Reprint, Prospect Heights, IL: Waveland Press, 1991.

Twain, Mark. "The Private History of a Campaign That Failed." In *The Portable Mark Twain,* 119–142. New York: Viking Press, 1946.

Vidal, Gore. *Lincoln: A Novel.* New York: Random House, 1984.

Walker, Margaret. *Jubilee.* New York: Bantam Books, 1967.

Warren, Robert Penn. *Band of Angels.* 1955. Reprint, Baton Rouge: Louisiana State University Press, 1994.

———. "The Legacy of the Civil War: Meditations on the Centennial." In *A Robert Penn Warren Reader,* 270–310. New York: Vintage Books, 1988.

———. *Wilderness: A Tale of the Civil War.* New York: Random House, 1961.

Wicker, Tom. *Unto This Hour.* New York: Viking Press, 1984.

Young, Stark. *So Red the Rose.* 1934. Reprint, Nashville, TN: J. S. Sanders, 1992.

46

Films and Television

Brian Steel Wills

Capturing the imagination of viewers from the silent film era to the present, the American Civil War has provided a rich mosaic of personalities and events. The images are powerful, and they transcend time to rest in the collective consciousness of a nation: the quiet dignity of Robert E. Lee, who gambles for victory yet accepts responsibility for defeat; the homespun wisdom of Abraham Lincoln as he guides the nation through its greatest test; a dashing Confederate cavalier on horseback whose defense of hearth and home is as valiant as it is futile; the former slave, freed from bondage but unwilling to remain outside the fight that will free others; a southern belle who experiences the harshest realities of war yet vows to endure. The fundamental nature of the conflict allows the war to lend itself easily to both the sweeping panorama of cinema's big screen and the intimacy of television's smaller screen.

The earliest films to feature Civil War themes borrowed many of their conventions and storylines from those established by literary and theatrical productions. Building on this familiar foundation offered viewers a relatively safe and acceptable transition from the detachment of the written word or the stage to the realism of cinema. Until World War I, directors like D. W. Griffith frequently used the Civil War as a central element of their work. Beginning with *The Guerrilla* (1908) and *In Old Kentucky* (1909) Griffith perfected his craft, enabling him to produce the silent film classic *The Birth of a Nation* in 1915. Adapted from Thomas Dixon's novel *The Clansman,* this landmark film captured the battlefield in a way that no stage ever could. Evelyn Ehrlich's brief essay in *The South and Film* (1981), edited by Warren French, has provided a useful examination of the Civil War film's origins, while Everett Carter looked specifically at *The Birth of a Nation* in *Hollywood as Historian* (1983).

Another silent era film used the war in a different way. Based loosely on the 1862 raid of Union spy James J. Andrews, *The General* (1927) portrayed the war in comedic terms. Buster Keaton's slapstick antics made the film a classic as he first pursued the Federal raiders who stole his train and his girl and then helped to stave off a Union attack. Similarly, the Three Stooges treated the Civil War with their usual irreverence and slapstick humor. But a later film, *Advance to the Rear* (1964), starring Glenn Ford, failed to bring the Civil War comedy to a new generation of movie-goers.

Films that targeted younger audiences were also successful at presenting the war without its attendant horrors. Shirley Temple starred in *The Littlest Rebel* (1935) as a child who used both charm and dance to help her Confederate father. *Johnny Shiloh* (1963), with Brian Keith as the veteran watching over Union drummer boy Kevin Corcoran, and *The Million Dollar Dixie Deliverance* (1978), with Brock Peters rescuing kidnapped children, represented two of Disney's war-related projects.

Of course, not all films concerning the war were humorous or aimed exclusively at younger audiences. One of the most compelling and enduring symbols of Civil War cinema has been the embattled and divided family. Hollywood has attempted to tap into this important human element with such films as *Friendly Persuasion* (1956) and *Shenandoah* (1965). In *Friendly Persuasion* Quakers Gary Cooper and Anthony Perkins confronted war and the dilemma of avoiding conflict while defending their home. *Shenandoah* (1965) offered James Stewart as the powerful patriarch who struggled to hold his family together but found war a more powerful force at tearing it apart.

The image of the cavalryman has also been powerful. The West provided both an appropriate setting for cavalry and a suitable common foe—the Indian— to bring Northern and Southern soldiers together again. Thus, in the mutual quest of survival, the two sides could set aside their differences and be reconciled.

The 1940s and 1950s featured numerous films that carried this reconciliation theme. Errol Flynn teamed up with his would-be opponents in *Virginia City* (1940) to defeat a band of Mexican bandits and in *Rocky Mountain* (1950) to ward off Indians. In *Two Flags West* (1950) a unit of "galvanized Confederates" under Joseph Cotten served under an embittered Union commander (Jeff Chandler) who harbored suspicions concerning their loyalty. Grudgingly, the Southerners demonstrated their sincerity, and together the former enemies joined forces to fend off the Indians. Similarly, *The Last Outpost* (1951) put a Southern Ronald Reagan against his Northern brother before they too set aside their hostility to fight the Indians.

Hollywood's efforts to create dramatic tension have led to some rather dubious settings. *Escape from Fort Bravo* (1953) placed Confederate prisoners of war in a camp in Arizona, despite the questionable historical grounds for having them so disposed. Nevertheless, the opposing sides forged an alliance as they confronted the ever-present Indian threat. *Revolt at Fort Laramie* (1957) again placed the two sides in a western fort as an officer (John Dehner) struggled between his duty and his loyalty to the South. And Sam Peckinpah's ambitious *Major Dundee* (1965) united Union commander Charlton Heston and Confederate prisoner Richard Harris in pursuit of a band of ruthless Apaches.

Occasionally the West served as little more than background or as an extension of the war. The characters in the 1966 film *The Good, the Bad, and the Ugly* were far more interested in finding buried gold than in serving in the war. *A Time for Killing* (1967) pitted George Hamilton and Glenn Ford against each other, more for the sake of revenge than anything else. And *A Reason to Live, a Reason to Die* (1974), retitled more provocatively *Massacre at Fort Holman,* had little to do with the war except to use it as an excuse for the bloody elimination of a sadistic Confederate (Telly Savalas) and his garrison.

One of the more popular movie conventions has been to present a dramatization of a battle, raid, or other historical event. The 1864 St. Albans (Vermont) raid served as the basis for the 1954 film *The Raid,* with Confederates infiltrating a small New England town, robbing it, and fleeing into Canada. *The Great Locomotive Chase* (1956) depicted the same raid that inspired Buster Keaton's *The General,* with Fess Parker as Andrews and Jeffrey Hunter as his chief adversary. John Ford's *The Horse Soldiers* (1959) placed John Wayne in the role of Union general Benjamin Grierson in Hollywood's dramatization of the 1863 cavalry raid. The 1966 film *Alvarez Kelly* depicted a fictionalized version of Confederate general Wade Hampton's 1864 "beefsteak" raid, with entrepreneur William Holden and Confederate officer Richard Widmark as unwilling allies.

More recently, *Ironclads* (1991) and *Gettysburg* (1993) have depicted significant events from the war. The 1991 made-for-cable movie portrayed the dramatic confrontation between the CSS *Virginia* and the USS *Monitor,* amid an unnecessary and distracting love story. *Gettysburg* featured elements of one of the war's most important battles faithfully based on Michael Shaara's Pulitzer Prize–winning novel *The Killer Angels.* The film used the services of thousands of historical reenactors, thereby allowing it to achieve the sense and scope of an epic. Although first appearing in movie theaters, the producers also billed *Gettysburg* as a television event.

The trials and dilemmas of the common soldier have been frequent subjects of Civil War cinema as well. Often such stories were predictable and universal civil war themes: brother versus brother, friend versus friend, or father versus son. This was the case with the 1951 film *Drums in the Deep South,* where James Craig and Guy Madison portrayed two friends on opposite sides. The Confederate officer (Craig) had the difficult task of halting Federal supply shipments by placing artillery on a mountain overlooking a railroad. The threat forced Union officer Madison to drive the Southerners off the ridge.

In addition to the theme of person versus person, Civil War films have dealt with the attempts of various individuals to come to terms with themselves. The fundamental issue of survival made for compelling drama on the screen, as in the film adaptations of Stephen Crane's novel, *The Red Badge of Courage*. Two versions explored the moment of truth when the young soldier confronted and fled from mortality on the battlefield and the effect this had on him as he sought to redeem himself. The powerful coming-of-age story first appeared in 1951 under the direction of John Huston and starred western and action film star Audie Murphy. A later version appeared in 1974 and featured television star Richard Thomas.

Journey to Shiloh (1968) told the story of a group of Texan youths who went East to join the war and found it, as well as a great deal of hardship, along the way. The film culminated with the Battle of Shiloh, where the last member of the group (James Caan) escaped with the generous assistance of a typically inflexible Braxton Bragg. Designed to expose the horrors and futility of war, the film has remained interesting more for its young stars (Caan, Jan-Michael Vincent, and Harrison Ford).

Another film that suggested the harsh realities of war was *The Beguiled* (1971). Starring Clint Eastwood as a badly wounded Union soldier who found refuge in a Southern girls' school, the story evolved into a war of wits. Accepted until he violated their trust and their friendship, the Eastwood character's unsavory nature ultimately was his undoing. In dealing with the lustful and emotional Union soldier, the previously sheltered girls had to confront the harsh lessons imposed on them by the war.

In more recent years, the contribution of African Americans in the war has found a place on the movie screen. Yet while this has represented a welcome development, even the 1989 film *Glory* presented the story of the 54th Massachusetts, a black regiment, through the eyes of its white commander, Colonel Robert Gould Shaw (Matthew Broderick). Still, actors Denzel Washington and Morgan Freeman received professional recognition with an Academy Award and an Oscar nomination, respectively.

Glory generated both popular and academic reactions. The CBS program *Forty Eight Hours* produced a segment on the making of the film (1989) and a documentary, *The True Story of Glory Continues* (1991), carried the story of the 54th Massachusetts through the war to its disbandment. Historians William S. McFeely and Michael C. C. Adams assessed the film in essays for academic journals. These scholars agreed that the movie suffered from a lack of historical accuracy but nevertheless suggested that it had much to offer audiences.

Perhaps the best-known and most widely copied type of Civil War film is *Gone with the Wind* (1939). For many, this celluloid version of Margaret Mitchell's novel has remained the most popular cinematic construction of the Old South and the Civil War. MGM sought to recreate the success of *Gone with the Wind* with *Raintree County* (1957) starring Elizabeth Taylor and Montgomery Clift. Generally considered long and meandering, the film failed to generate much enthusiasm. Like other attempts to repeat the successful formula of the

1939 classic, *Raintree County,* and subsequent films, such as *Love's Savage Fury* (1979), with Jennifer O'Neill, and *Beulah Land* (1980), with Lesley Ann Warren, fell glaringly short. The concluding chapter of the *Gone with the Wind* saga came with the 1994 television miniseries *Scarlett* starring Joanne-Whalley Kilmer and Timothy Dalton, in the roles of Scarlett O'Hara and Rhett Butler, respectively. Once again, the only element that the sequel and its original shared was their aim to achieve romance rather than history.

The Civil War has served as the backdrop or prologue for a number of films. In these productions, the war provided the violent beginning, usually represented by a climactic battle scene, from which the lead character settled old scores or attempted to start a new life. In *The Outlaw Josey Wales* (1976) Clint Eastwood portrayed a man caught up in the particularly brutal internecine warfare in Missouri. When, near the beginning of the film, his compatriots tried to surrender, they were gunned down, compelling Josey Wales to continue his particular brand of resistance and retribution.

Two films featuring John Wayne opened with Civil War scenes that required either revenge or rescue as their stories progressed. In *Rio Lobo* (1970) a Union officer (Wayne) avenged the robbery of a train and the death of a close friend made possible by information given by a traitor. *The Undefeated* (1969) began with a scarred battleflag and a battle scene that was interrupted with the news of Robert E. Lee's surrender in Virginia. Despite subsequently being mustered out of the service, Wayne's men had to help a band of ex-Confederates when they got trapped in the civil war in Mexico. At the end of the film, the members of the two groups returned to start over in their common homeland as friends.

Several other films have dealt with individuals returning from the war. In *Three Violent People* (1956) Charlton Heston came back to a Texas to find his life complicated by a deceptive wife and a jealous brother. *The Shadow Riders* (1982) featured two returning brothers, one Union (Tom Selleck) and one Confederate (Sam Elliott). Richard Gere returned to take the place of a dead man in *Sommersby* (1993), an American version of *The Return of Martin Guerre* (1982). Ironically, in *Dances with Wolves* (1990) Kevin Costner's character left the war in the "civilized" East to learn about himself among the Indians.

Television has sought to achieve the grandeur and scope of cinema with its miniseries. Two of these have focused on the Civil War in particular: *The Blue and the Gray* (1982) and *North and South Book II* (1986), both aimed at placing television audiences in the company of important persons and historical events. *The Blue and the Gray* offered Gregory Peck as Abraham Lincoln and followed the war through the eyes of a young newspaper artist and his family. *North and South* carried two families, representing the two sections, through the crucible of war. Presented in the romantic mold of *Gone with the Wind,* the program lost few opportunities to employ dramatic license. Despite their historical limitations, such productions have attracted large audiences.

Television miniseries have also provided examinations of President Lincoln. Although he had been the subject of earlier cinematic studies, the television versions focused on the war years. These productions included a series that first appeared in 1974 and featured Hal Holbrook, entitled *Carl Sandberg's Lincoln.* Gore Vidal's fictionalized account of the sixteenth president's term in office served as the basis for a later miniseries, *Gore Vidal's Lincoln* (1988).

Other televised programs have dealt with Civil War subjects as well. *The Andersonville Trial* (1970) was the dramatization of the trial of Confederate prison commandant Henry Wirz (Richard Basehart), which resulted in his conviction and execution as a war criminal. Popular CBS News anchorman Walter Cronkite hosted the innovative series *You Are There,* which featured various episodes devoted to Civil War themes. Attempting to place the viewer on the scene of great historical events, the series incorporated interviews with significant personalities and other evening news features. In a similar vein, David L. Wolper produced a docudrama, *Surrender at Appomattox,* that drew heavily on Bruce Catton's Pulitzer Prize–winning study, *A Stillness at Appomattox,* as part of his series, *Appointment with Destiny.*

In more recent years, the Civil War has figured prominently in nonfiction television productions. These documentaries have presented the war through the use of professional historians, voice-overs, and period images. One of the best of these was Peter Batty's *The Divided Union* (1987). *The Civil War* (1990), produced by Ken Burns, Ric Burns, and Geoffrey C. Ward, was PBS's award-winning and precedent-setting documentary of the war. The montage of images and music of the period were among the program's best features. The format of fast-paced chapters conformed well to television.

Civil War Journal (1994–1995), narrated and hosted by veteran film star Danny Glover, has featured a weekly series of one-hour programs devoted to various aspects of the war. These shows have focused on specific topics and deftly blended elements from earlier documentaries to generate a professionally packaged television production. The Smithsonian Institute has developed a seven-part, nine-hour series, *Great Battles of the Civil War,* that feature voice-overs by actors (such as Charlton Heston as Abraham Lincoln) and footage of Civil War reenactors, to present a more militarily oriented documentary.

Academics have increasingly recognized the significance of the screen image in providing a general audience with a sense of history. William McFeely (1990) noted the importance of films like *Glory* in conveying visual images of the past to a broader viewership than would read the written works of historians. The 1994 meeting of the Southern Historical Association featured a session entitled, "Writing about the Civil War in the Age of Ken Burns and Beyond," with Pulitzer Prize–winning historian James M. McPherson presiding.

Popular historical magazines have begun devoting more space to Civil War–related motion pictures and television productions. For example, *Civil War Times Illustrated* gave coverage to the film *Gettysburg* in a section of its November–December 1993 issue, and *Blue and Gray Magazine* offered a review of the movie *The Horse Soldiers* in its June 1993 issue featuring the raid of Union general Grierson.

Box office sales and television ratings reflect the continuing popular appeal of the Civil War. Interestingly, both a recent television series (*I'll Fly Away*) and a motion picture (*Forrest Gump*) featured characters named for Confederate cavalry general Nathan Bedford Forrest. Whether such references are accidental or deliberate, something about this war touches us and ensures that it will remain a part of our common cultural heritage.

BIBLIOGRAPHY

Adams, Michael C. C. "Seeking Glory: Our Continuing Involvement with the 54th Massachusetts." *Studies in Popular Culture* 14 (1992): 11–19.

Biggs, Gregg. Review of the film *The Horse Soldiers*. *Blue and Gray Magazine* (June 1993): 46.

Campbell, Jr., Edward D. C. *The Celluloid South: Hollywood and the Southern Myth.* Knoxville: University of Tennessee Press, 1981. Campbell's and Kirby's works are the best narrative treatments of the South and cinema. Kirby takes a broader approach by including other media as well.

Carter, Everett. "Cultural History Written with Lightning: The Significance of *The Birth of a Nation* (1915)." In *Hollywood as Historian: American Film in a Cultural Context.* Edited by Peter C. Rollins. Lexington: University Press of Kentucky, 1983.

Cassidy, John M. *Civil War Cinema: A Pictorial History of Hollywood and the War between the States.* Missoula, MT: Pictorial Histories Publishing Company, 1986. The best study to examine the Civil War in film; contains a chapter on television as well.

French, Warren, ed. *The South and Film.* Jackson: University Press of Mississippi, 1981.

Jorgensen, C. Peter. "Gettysburg: How a Prize-Winning Novel Became a Motion Picture." *Civil War Times Illustrated* 32 (November–December 1993): 40–49, 92–93, 113.

Kirby, Jack Temple. *Media-Made Dixie: The South in the American Imagination.* Baton Rouge: Louisiana State University Press, 1978.

McFeely, William S. "Notes on Seeing History: The Civil War Made Visible." *Georgia Historical Quarterly* 76 (Winter 1990): 666–671.

Sklar, Robert. *Movie-made America: A Cultural History of American Movies.* New York: Vintage Books, 1975.

Spehr, Paul C. *The Civil War in Motion Pictures: A Bibliography of Films Produced in the United States since 1897.* Washington, D.C.: Government Printing Office, 1961. A useful reference source for earlier Civil War films.

Zebrowski, Carl. "Remote History." *Civil War Times Illustrated* 33 (March–April 1994): 44–47.

47

Musical and Narrative Recordings

Susan Hamburger

THE SONGS

The Civil War spawned a wealth of books, articles, motion pictures, photographs, and music. Nowhere else is the war brought home so poignantly as in the music played and sung by the Northern and Southern soldiers. Rallying, stirring, maudlin, religious, humorous, banal—songs expressed the emotions felt by the men at war and their loved ones back home.

The music of the Civil War falls into several categories: vocal, instrumental band, contemporary, patriotic, martial, sentimental, and standards, variations, and parodies. The song of the 1860s was a simple vocal ballad, not a dance tune or piano solo. Soldiers sang songs they grew up with, new songs written specifically about the war by professional songwriters and amateurs, and parodies or adaptations of songs identified with the other side.

Both Northern and Southern publishers printed small songbooks (pocket-sized songsters) and broadsides for the soldiers to carry off to war and sheet music for the folks at home to sing from in their parlors (*War Songs of the American Union; Songs and Ballads of Freedom; The Bugle-Call; Soldiers' and Sailors' Patriotic Songs; The Southern Soldier's Prize Songster*). Various military units had instrumental bands that performed traditional and original marching tunes.

Civil War songs exist in published songbooks (Crawford, *The Civil War Songbook* [1977]; Silber, *Songs of the Civil War*), printed sheet music and broadsides (especially the Lester S. Levy Collection of Sheet Music at Johns Hopkins University), and manuscript collections in libraries and archives throughout the

United States (for example, State Historical Society of Wisconsin, and Duke and Brown universities). From these sources, and from other performers in the oral tradition, contemporary performers glean the lyrics and music to record interpretations of the songs. Some use authentic arrangements and period instruments (26th North Carolina Band, 1st Brigade Band, Americus Brass Band); others update the songs with modern sounds (*The Civil War Music Collector's Edition*); some perform with acoustic instruments for a folk or country sound (Jay Ungar and Molly Mason, *Live at Gettysburg College*); others add full orchestration (Richard Bales, *The Union* and *The Confederacy*); while still others compose new songs evocative of the period (Margaret Buechner, *The American Civil War Symphonic Trilogy; White Mansions; Gettysburg: Music from the Original Motion Picture Soundtrack*).

The core body of songs identified with the Civil War includes "Dixie," "John Brown's Body/The Battle Hymn of the Republic," "Marching through Georgia," "Battle Cry of Freedom," "Just before the Battle, Mother," "Tenting on the Old Camp Ground," "Tramp, Tramp, Tramp," "The Bonnie Blue Flag," "Maryland, My Maryland," and "Goober Peas." The premier songwriters of the day were George Frederick Root, Charles Carroll Sawyer, and Henry Clay Work in the North and Armand Edward Blackmar, John Hill Hewitt, Harry Macarthy, and Herman L. Schreiner in the South.

Often songs contain new lyrics written for tunes with which people were familiar. For example, Harry Macarthy set "Bonnie Blue Flag" to the tune of an 1850s song, "The Irish Jaunting Car," and James Ryder Randall derived the tune for his "Maryland, My Maryland" from the old German carol "O Tannenbaum." Using familiar tunes made it easy for lyricists to put their songs before the public quickly. A printer could reproduce the words on a cheap broadside with a note, "Air" or "To the tune of . . . ," and avoid the more expensive printing of musical scores.

The prevalent themes in Civil War songs reflect the concern with freedom and individual rights ("The Southron's Chaunt of Defiance"), the belief that God was on their side, no matter which side they fought for ("Marching through Georgia"), the determination to fight for home and mother ("Marching Along"), and the demonstration of flag patriotism ("Bonnie Blue Flag," "The Star-Spangled Banner"). The lyricists frequently used symbolism common to their audience to express their feelings ("Do They Think of Me at Home," "When This Cruel War Is Over") rather than blatant, bloody descriptions of battles, although songs about specific battles exist ("The Battle of Shiloh's Hill", " 'Twas at the Siege of Vicksburg"). Naval songs are rare ("The *Alabama*"). The songs also offer a different perspective toward the homeland than in songs from past wars, considering the common origins of the men from both sides. Humor, so necessary to lighten a somber mood, appeared in songs as well ("Goober Peas," "Here's Your Mule," "Hard Crackers Come Again No More," "The Invalid Corps"). Richard Crawford in *The Civil War Songbook* (1977) found antiwar songs scarce, if nonexistent.

Antislavery songs did not have widespread appeal, even among Northerners. This theme did not pervade the popular music. Slaves and freedmen sang spirituals and songs by white composers, as well as songs based on their African heritage ("No More Auction Block for Me"). Many of the songs about slaves were written in dialect by white composers for minstrel performances on stage ("Kingdom Coming").

Composers also wrote songs extolling the virtues of Confederate leaders ("General Lee's Grand March," "Stonewall Jackson's Way," "Stonewall's Requiem," "John Hunt Morgan's Song"), Union leaders ("Sherman Will March to the Sea"), and presidents Abraham Lincoln ("Old Abe Lies Sick," "Old Abe's Lament," "We'll Fight for Uncle Abe," "We Are Coming, Father Abraham") and Jefferson Davis ("Jefferson Davis Grand March").

Those songs that continue to be performed and recorded do not specifically describe battles but rather speak to the universality of the human condition that transcends time and place.

THE RECORDINGS

Music

Albums, cassettes, compact discs, and videocassettes offer original Civil War songs, recent music evocative of the period, and a mixture of both. A number of recordings contain some of the same songs but in different musical settings, with individual interpretations, or offering different verses. *Who Shall Rule This American Nation?* presents classical singers, chorus, and a pianist performing a selection of Henry Clay Work's songs. The Dear Friends, a resident performing ensemble at the Stephen Foster Memorial, University of Pittsburgh, exemplifies the contemporary interpreter of Foster's and Civil War–era music, using historical arrangements and wearing period costumes in concert (*The Blues and the Grays*). The Southern Horizon members (*The Girl I Left Behind Me*), an acoustical band from Virginia, consider themselves historical music interpreters who research the musical archives for their song selections and dress in mid-nineteenth century dresses and Confederate uniforms for live performances.

Individual performers, whether solo, duo, or group, have their own recordings, while compilation collections present various performers' versions of Civil War songs (*The Civil War Music Collector's Edition*). Ken Burns's *Civil War* series spawned *Songs of the Civil War,* a video of live performances of period songs by well-known singers plus Jay Ungar's 1982 haunting melody, "Ashokan Farewell." Ungar and his musical partner, Molly Mason, recorded their performance for the 1993 Civil War Institute at Gettysburg College in which they introduce each song (*Live at Gettysburg College*), as do Keith and Rusty McNeil on *Civil War Songs with Historical Narration*. Individual performer Bobby Horton to date has recorded a series of five cassettes of Confederate (*Homespun Songs of the CSA*) and three of Union songs (*Homespun Songs of the Union Army*), while

Wayne Erbsen has recorded three cassettes of Southern Civil War songs. Cathy Barton (*Johnny Whistletrigger*) has recorded twenty-two little-known songs from the western border not recorded by anyone else, except for "I Goes to Fight Mit Sigel." *The Civil War: Its Music and Sounds* uses the manuscript part books of the 26th North Carolina Regiment, as well as other sources, to record regimental band music on authentic instruments, as it would have been played during the war.

Books

Books on tape have become popular, providing an easy and enjoyable way to listen first to novels and more frequently to nonfiction books. Civil War books, enjoying a resurgence in popularity since Ken Burns's PBS *Civil War* series, focused the layperson's attention on the war, increasingly find their way onto cassettes.

The narrative cassettes reproduce unabridged and abridged books of fiction (*Civil War Stories* by Stephen Crane, Ambrose Bierce, Mark Twain, and Hamlin Garland; Michael Shaara's *The Killer Angels;* Stephen Crane's *The Red Badge of Courage;* Shelby Foote's *Shiloh; Allan Gurganus Reads from Oldest Living Confederate Widow Tells All, and Talks about the Civil War, North Carolina, and Narrative Voice*), poetry (Walt Whitman's *Eyewitness to the Civil War*), and satire (*Dear Abe Linkhorn, the Satire of the Civil War*).

Nonfiction includes autobiographies and memoirs (*The Personal Memoirs of U.S. Grant; The Memoirs of William T. Sherman: Autobiography;* John L. Ransom's *The Andersonville Diary, a True Account*), biographies (William S. McFeely's *Grant, a Biography;* Burke Davis's *Gray Fox: Robert E. Lee and the Civil War;* Carl Sandburg's *Abraham Lincoln: The Prairie Years* and *The War Years;* Gene Smith's *Lee and Grant*), and diaries (Elijah Hunt Rhodes's *All for the Union*).

Scholarly works are represented also by lectures (*The Black Man in the Civil War;* Edgar Toppin's *The Civil War and Slavery: A Lecture on the Causes and Interpretations of the Civil War:* Charles R. Branham's *Black Troops in the Civil War: The Contributions of Blacks to the Union's Victory;* Frank E. Vandiver's *Strategy and Tactics of the Confederate Army*), and monographs (Bruce Catton's *The Centennial History of the Civil War;* Jeffrey D. Wert's *Mosby's Rangers;* and Frank E. Vandiver's *Voices of Valor, Words of the Civil War*). The National Park Service offers narrative cassettes of the Gettysburg and Richmond battlefields tours, among others. *The Union Restored* combines readings of Civil War documents and letters with period music.

SOURCES

Some of the music recordings are available in libraries and music stores; others are local or regional productions available at Civil War battlefield sites.

The books on tape can be obtained in libraries or bookstores, or from producers or distributors.

SELECTED DISCOGRAPHY

INSTRUMENTAL

Americus Brass Band. *Music of the Civil War, Original Instruments.* Compact disc. Summit Records, Box 26850, Tempe, AZ 85282. DCD 126. 1991. An authentic recreation of the regimental brass band music of the Civil War, played on original instruments. Program notes and list of performers are inserted in container. Recorded March 1991 at Little Bridges Auditorium, Pomona College of Claremont, California.

When the Cruel War Is Over and Hoist Up the Flag Quick Step

Americus Quick Step

Fireman's Polka

Tenting on the Old Camp Ground

Dixie's Land Medley Quick Step

Battle Cry of Freedom and Kingdom Coming Quick Step

Excerpt from *William Tell*

Sumter Light Guard March

Bonnie Eloise Quick Step

Amazing Grace

Glory Hallelujah Grand March

Scenes That Are Brightest and in Happy Moments Quick Step

Kazoodie Ko Whirl Overture

Woodman, Spare That Tree

Fireman's Quick Step

When Johnny Comes Marching Home

Medley: Oh, Suzanna/Bonnie Blue Flag/Jordan Am a Hard Road/Garry Owen/The Girl I Left Behind Me

Coronation March from *The Prophet*

Buechner, Margaret. *The American Civil War Symphonic Trilogy.* Performed by the Royal Scottish National Orchestra, conducted by John Varineau. 60:28 minutes. Compact disc. Nord-Disc 2028. 1992. Program notes by Byron Henderson and words for the melodies of the songs, as arranged for orchestra, are inserted in the compact disc container.

Slaves Working in the Fields

Go Down, Moses

Many Thousand Gone

Oh Freedom

Recruitment of the Soldiers and Their Farewells

Hard Times Come Again No More

The Vacant Chair

The Rebel Soldier and the Southern Soldier Boy

Beautiful River and Somebody's Darling

Six Hundred Thousand Dead

Schubert—Das Wirtshaus (Field of the Dead)

Desolation and Rebuilding of the Country

The Blue and the Gray

Peace—The United Country and Coda

In Memoriam

Camp Chase Fifes and Drums (featured in the movie *Gettysburg*). The American Civil War, Period Pieces. Cassette. Vol. 1.

Side A

Newport Quick Step

Cadence #8/Owl Creek/New Tatter Jack

Double Doodle

The Yellow Rose of Texas/Stonewall Jackson's Way/Dixie

Duke of York's Favorite Troop

Three Camps/Slow Scotch

Roast Beef

Hell on the Wabash

Old 1812/Welcome Here Again

Peas on a Trencher

Granny Will Your Dog Bite?

The Minstrel Boy

Side B

Downfall of Paris

Cadence #4/Campbells Are Coming

Three Cheers/Slow ¾ Retreat/Three Cheers

Sole Leather/Drums and Guns (Fifes Tacit)/Sole Leather

The Girl I Left Behind Me/Empty Pockets

Muffled Drum/Rakes of Mallow

Frog in the Well/Old Zip Coon

Hanover/Montezuma

Cadence #3/Road to Boston/Recruiting Sergeant/Road to Boston/Army ¾ Cadence

Slow Scotch Air (Drums Tacit)

Civil War Favorites: The Best of the 8th Regiment Band. Compact disc. 1990. P.O. Box 2593, Rome, GA 30164 (404/232-4567). Authentic brass band music of the Civil War. Directed by John Carruth, chief musician; Frederick Fennell, guest conductor, ''Washington Grays.'' The disc contains:

Dixie and The Bonnie Blue Flag

The Star-Spangled Banner

God Save the South

Battle Hymn Quick Step

Aura Lee

Washington Grays

Rachel Waltzes

Col. Meeker's Quick Step

Come Dearest, the Daylight Is Gone

Cruel War and Hoist Up the Flag

Tenting Tonight

Lulu Is Gone

Webster's Funeral March

Easter Galop

Garry Owen

Home Again

Fireman's Polka

Waltz

Red, White and Blue

Maryland, My Maryland

Battle Cry and Kingdom Coming Quick Step

When the Swallows Homeward Fly

Kitty Dear and Do They Miss Me Quick Step

The Girl I Left Behind Me

Sweet Home

Dixie Medley Quick Step

Marseillaise

The Civil War: Its Music and Its Sounds. 153:47 minutes. 2 compact discs. Mercury, New York. 1990. Band music, bugle calls, songs, and battle sounds. Contains a fifty-two page illustrated insert of notes by Frederick Fennell, Harold T. Peterson, and Charles L. Dufour. Performed by the Eastman Wind Ensemble, conducted by Frederick Fennell; the reactivated Civil War unit Battery B, 2d New Jersey Light Artillery; and narrated by Martin Gabel. The music was recorded in the

Eastman Theatre, Rochester, New York, December 1960 and May 1962. Battle sounds and other special effects were recorded in Gettysburg, Pennsylvania, in October 1960 and at West Point, New York, in December 1960.

Disc 1: Fort Sumter to Gettysburg

Band music of the Union troops

Band music of the Confederate troops

Field music of Union and Confederate troops (camp, garrison, and field calls for fifes and drums; cavalry bugle signals)

Sounds of conflict: Fort Sumter to Gettysburg

Disc 2: Gettysburg to Appomattox

Band music of the Union troops

Band music of the Confederate troops

Field music of the Union and Confederate troops (bugle signals for the service of the skirmishers; drum calls; camp and field duty calls for the fifes and drums; the Appomattox bugle)

Songs of the Union and Confederate soldiers

Firearms of the Civil War

The sounds of conflict: Gettysburg to Appomattox

Civil War. Original soundtrack recording. Compact disc. Elektra Nonesuch, Beverly Hills, Ca. 1990. Traditional American songs and instrumental music featured in the film by Ken Burns performed by various musicians. Recorded at Soundesign, Brattleboro, Vermont, and Soundtrack, 39th Street Music, and BMG Studios, New York.

Drums of War

Oliver Wendell Holmes quote

Ashokan Farewell

Battle Cry of Freedom

We Are Climbing Jacob's Ladder

Dixie

Bonnie Blue Flag

Cheer Boys Cheer

Angel Band

Johnny Has Gone for a Soldier

Lorena

Parade

Hail Columbia

Dixie

Kingdom Coming

Battle Hymn of the Republic

All Quiet on the Potomac

Flag of Columbia

Weeping Sad and Lonely

Yankee Doodle

Palmyra Schottische

When Johnny Comes Marching Home

Shenandoah

When Johnny Comes Marching Home

Marching through Georgia

Marching through Georgia (lament)

Battle Cry of Freedom

Battle Hymn of the Republic

Ashokan Farewell

Sullivan Ballou letter

11th North Carolina Regiment Band. Vol. 1. Cassette. REG-0386.

Side 1 The National Anthem

The Old North State

God Save the South

Carry Me Back to Old Virginny's Shore

Aura Lea

Kingdom Coming

Somebody's Darling

Home Sweet Home

The Marseillaise

Home Again

Kitty Dear and Do They Miss Me at Home Quickstep

Grand March from "Norma"

Slumber Polka

Listen to the Mockingbird

The Yellow Rose of Texas

Side 2

Come, Dearest, the Daylight Is Gone

Col. Kirkland's March

Cheer, Boys, Cheer

My Maryland

When the Swallows Homeward Fly

Lulu Is Gone Quickstep

Yankee Doodle

Call Me Not Back from the Echoless Shore

Bonnie Eloise Quickstep

Gen. Joseph E. Johnston Manassas Quickstep

Lorena

Dixie and the Bonnie Blue Flag

Auld Lang Syne

1st Brigade Band. *Band Music of the Confederacy.* Making History Live, vol. 4. Stereo LP. Heritage Military Music Foundation, P.O. Box 1864, Milwaukee, WI 53201. 1981.

Side 1

Dixie's Land

Call Me Not Back from the Echoless Shore

Mocking Bird Quick Step

Come Dearest the Daylight Is Gone

The Girl I Left Behind

My Old Kentucky Home

Garry Owen

Side 2

My Maryland

Carry Me Back to Old Virginny's Shore

Juanita

Annie May Quick Step

Sweet Home

Massa's in the Cold Ground

Auld Lang Syne

1st Brigade Band. *Cheer Boys Cheer.* Stereo LP. Making History Live, vol. 6. Nicholas Contorno, Bandmaster. 1978.

Side 1

Cheer Boys Cheer

Colonel White's Quickstep

Though the Sinner Bloom Again

Old Abe the Battle Eagle

Tenting Tonight on the Old Camp Ground

Red House Polka

Tramp, Tramp, Tramp

Kingdom Coming

Side 2

Irish Medley

Vacant Chair

Cavalry Polka

Abide with Me

Goober Peas

Just before the Battle Mother

Bonnie Blue Flag

Garry Owen

Marching through Georgia

1st Brigade Bands. *Civil War Military Band Music: Original Music on Original Instruments.* Stereo LP. Making History Live, vol. 2. David Ridgely, Bandmaster. 1972.

Side 1

The Star Spangled Banner, 1854

Cape May Polka

Robin Adair

Twinkling Stars Quick Step

Nightingale Waltzes

La Marseillaise

Andante and Waltz Number 31

Side 2

Hurrah Storm Galop

Palmyra Schottische

Un Ballo in Maschera Quick Step

Come Where My Love Lies Dreaming

Port Royal Galop

Parade March Number 13

Street Parade Sequence, Garry Owen

Marching through Georgia

1st Brigade Band. *Dixie's Land.* Stereo LP. Making History Live, vol. 7. Nicholas Contorno, Bandmaster. 1981.

Side 1

Introduction Dixy

General Lee's Grand March

My Maryland and North State

Ellen Bayne

Come Where My Love Lies Dreaming

Yellow Rose of Texas

Hurrah Storm Galop

Side 2

Bonnie Eloise

All Quiet along the Potomac Tonight

Kitty Dear

Call Me Not Back from the Echoless Shore

When the Swallows Homeward Fly

Dixy Quick Step

1st Brigade Band. *The Grand Review.* Stereo LP. Making History Live, vol. 9. Dan Woolpert, Bandmaster. 1985.

Side 1

When This Cruel War Is Over

America

Hail Columbia

St. Louis Quickstep

Home Sweet Home

I Set My Heart on a Flower

Mocking Bird Quickstep

Side 2

Reville

National Quickstep

Andante Funeral March No. 1

Tattoo

Captain Shepherd's Quickstep

When Sherman Marched down to the Sea

When This Cruel War Is Over and Hoist Up the Flag

Side 3

Etappen Quickstep

Three Hymns: Come Ye Disconsolate/Playels Hymn/Notting Hill

Battle Cry of Freedom and Kingdom Coming

The Dearest Spot on Earth to Me Is Home

Star Spangled Banner

Home Again Serenade

Leona Quickstep

Side 4

Reel Set: Dixie/Reel No. 1/Reel No. 3/Reel No. 2

Sophia Waltz

Sophia Polka

Stanley Schottisch

Lima Waltz

Mountain Echo Polka

1st Brigade Band. *Music for the President.* Stereo LP. Making History Live, vol. 3. Nicholas Contorno, Bandmaster. 1975.

Side 1

Hail to the Chief

Union March

Grafulla's 7th Regiment. Drum Corps Quick Step

The Star-Spangled Banner

1st Massachusetts Regiment. Quick Step

7th Massachusetts Regiment. Quick Step

The Doxology

Side 2

Home Quick Step

Oft in the Stilly Night

Mrs. Sprague's Bridal Polka and Waltz

Medley of Patriotic Airs

America

Dixie's Land

Yankee Doodle

1st Brigade Band. *Rally 'Round the Flag.* Stereo LP. Making History Live, vol. 5. Nicholas Contorno, Bandmaster. 1976.

Side 1

Old Dog Tray

Light of Other Days

Ever of Thee

Hail Columbia

When Johnny Comes Marching Home

Battle Hymn Quick Step

Side 2

Dixie/Bonnie Blue Flag

Wilderness Quickstep

Lorena

Morning Star Quickstep

Wildwood Schottische

Washington Grays

Gettysburg: Music from the Original Motion Picture Soundtrack. Music by Randy Edelman. Cassette. Milan Entertainment, distributed by BMG Music. 1993. ISBN 3138-35654-4.

Side 1

Main Title

Men of Honor

Battle of Little Round Top

Fife and Gun

General Lee at Twilight

The First Battle

Dawn

From History to Legend

Over the Fence

We Are the Flank

Side 2

Charging Up the Hill

Dixie

General Lee's Solitude

Battle at Devil's Den

Killer Angel

March to Mortality (Pickett's Charge)

Kathleen Mavourneen

Reunion and Finale

Honor to Our Soldiers: Music of the Civil War. Compact disc. Musical Heritage Society, Ocean, NJ. 1991. Performed on period instruments, from the books of the Band of the 26th North Carolina Regiment, C.S.A., by Classical Brass: Woodrow English, Dennis Edelbrock, trumpets; Lynden Mitchell, horn; Scott Shelsta, trombone; Jack Tilbury, tuba. Recorded at St. Paul United Methodist Church, Woodbridge, Va. Program notes by Jack Tilbury on insert.

The Star-Spangled Banner

Dixie and the Bonnie Blue Flag

Honor to Our Soldiers

Salutation to America Grand Polka

Lustspiel Overture

My Heart's with My Nora

Meridian Waltz

O Ye Tears

Holiday Polka

Polonaise

Wrecker's Daughter Quickstep

Selections from *Rigoletto*

Polka Mazurka

Maud Schottisch

Vida Galop

Wood Up Quickstep

Vergistmeineiht [Vergistmeinnicht]

Ninetta Polka

Sextet and Cavating from *Lucia di Lammermoor*

Juanita

Martha Quickstep

Home Again

Louisa Polka

Light Cavalry Overture

2d South Carolina String Band. *We're Tenting Tonight; Favorite Campfire Songs of the Civil War, North and South.* Vol. 1. Cassette. Palmetto Productions, P.O. Box 6186, Holliston, MA 01746. 1991.

Side 1

Tenting on the Old Campground

Battle Cry of Freedom

Cavalier's Waltz

When Johnny Comes Marching Home

Cindy

Oh, Susanna

Invalid Corps

Side 2

Southern Soldier

Buffalo Gals

Old Dan Tucker

Kingdom Coming

Yellow Rose of Texas

Dixie

26th North Carolina Band. *Dusty Roads and Camps.* Cassette. Making History Live, vol. 10. Heritage Military Music Foundation, Inc., P.O. Box 1864, Milwaukee, WI 53201. Dan Woolpert, Bandmaster. 1987.

7th Regimental Drum Corp Quickstep

Mother Kissed Me in My Dreams

Tramp, Tramp, Tramp

Rock beside the Sea

Wearing of the Green

Prayer for Victory, Fort Donaldson Waltzes 44 and 34

Jine the Cavalry

The Girl I Left behind Me

The Yellow Rose of Texas

Our First President's Quickstep

Lorena

Old Dan Tucker

Somebody's Darling

Cap'n Finch's Quickstep and Polka

Aura Lee

Old Abe, the Battle Eagle

Marching Through Georgia

26th North Carolina Band. *1st Brigade Band Plays General Lee's Favorites.* Cassette. Making History Live, vol. 8. Dan Woolpert, Bandmaster. 1986.

Side 1

Come Dearest, the Daylight Is Gone

Slumber Polka

Listen to the Mockingbird

Dixie/Bonnie Blue Flag

Waltz

Luto Quickstep

Last Rose of Summer

Col. Kirkland's March

Side 2

Cheer Boys Cheer

Lulu Is Gone Quickstep

Home Again Serenade

La Marseillaise

Juanita

Martha Quickstep

Louisa Polka

Carry Me Back to Old Virginny's Shore March

VOCAL

Bales, Richard. *The Confederacy.* Sony Music Special Products. Cassette AT 41723
  compact disc AK 41723. Originally released in 1953 as a mono LP, it includes
  a fifty-two-page book of historic photographs, drawings, letters, essays by Bruce
  Catton and Clifford Dowdey, and lyrics. It features the National Gallery Orchestra, conducted by Richard Bales; with Cantata Choir, Lutheran Church of the
  Reformation, with Florence Kopleff, mezzo-soprano, and Thomas Pyle, baritone;
  narrated by Edmund Jennings Lee.

General Lee's Grand March

All Quiet along the Potomac Tonight

The Bonnie Blue Flag

Lorena

The Yellow Rose of Texas

Somebody's Darling

We All Went Down to New Orleans for Bales

General Robert E. Lee's farewell orders to the Army of Northern Virginia, Appomattox
  Courthouse, Virginia, April 10, 1865

The Conquered Banner

Dixie's Land/Quickstep/Interlude: Year of Jubilo

————. *The Union; A Cantata on Music in the North During the Years 1861–1865.*
  Sony Music Special Products. Cassette AT 41724; compact disc AK 41724. Orig-
  inally released in 1958 as mono LP, it includes a ninety-six-page book of historic
  photographs, drawings, letters, essays by Bruce Catton, Clifford Dowdey, and
  Allan Nevins, biographical notes by Morris Hastings, and lyrics. It features the
  National Gallery Orchestra, conducted by Richard Bales; Cantata Choir, Lutheran
  Church of the Reformation, with Peggy Zabawa, soprano, and Jule Zabawa, bar-
  itone; narrated by Raymond Massey.

The American Army

Tenting on the Old Camp Ground

The Battle Cry of Freedom

Aura Lea

The Invalid Corps

Just before the Battle, Mother

The Field at Gettysburg/The Gettysburg Address/The President's Hymn

The Vacant Chair

Abraham Lincoln's Funeral March/Taps/The President's Grave

The Grand Review of the Union Armies

  Assembly of Guard Detail

  Dress Parade and Dress Guard Mounting

  The Signal Cannon

When Johnny Comes Marching Home

The Battle Hymn of the Republic

Tramp! Tramp! Tramp!

Hold On, Abraham

Marching through Georgia

Raw Recruits

Kingdom Coming

The Girl I Left behind Me

Flourish for Review

Barton, Cathy. *Johnny Whistletrigger: Civil War Songs from the Western Border.* Compact disc. 70 minutes. Big Canoe Records, Boonville, MO. 1993. It includes a twenty-nine-page booklet. Performed by: Cathy Barton: vocals, banjo, dulcimer; Dave Para: vocals, guitars; Bob Dyer: vocals, guitar; with various additional musicians and vocalists.

Marmaduke's Hornpipe

Abolitionist Hymn

Marais des Cygne

Song of the Kansas Emigrants and Call to Kansas

The Invasion of Camp Jackson

General Sigel's Grand March

I Goes to Fight Mit Sigel

Johnny Whistletrigger

Lyon's Funeral March

Honest Pat Murphy

Price's Proclamation

Pea Ridge

Muddy Road to Moberly

Quantrill Side

Nature of the Guerrilla

Guerrilla Man

Prairie Grove

Quantrill

Kate's Song

Shelby's Mule

The Last Great Rebel Raid

Knot of Blue and Gray

The Blues and the Grays. Cassette. Thomas Studios, Pittsburgh, Pennsylvania. 1987. Performed by the Dear Friends, resident performing ensemble at Stephen Foster

Memorial, University of Pittsburgh. Music by the Commonwealth Ancients Band of Musick, Hyde's Fidley Division, Fifes and Drums. Side 1 recorded at Frick Auditorium, University of Pittsburgh, for a record album commemorating the university's bicentennial. Side 2 recorded live at a performance in Foster Auditorium, April 13, 1986.

Side 1:

Yankee Doodle

Get Off the Track

Battle Cry of Freedom

Just before the Battle, Mother

Variations on "I Wish I Was in Dixie's Land"

The Bonnie Blue Flag

Homespun Dress

Lorena

Goober Peas

Army Beans

Kingdom Coming

Side 2

John Brown's Body

Lincoln and Liberty

Song of the Southern Volunteer

The Girl I Left behind Me

Annie Laurie

Was My Brother in the Battle?

Sanitary Fair Grand March

Tenting Tonight

When This Cruel War Is Over

Tramp, Tramp, Tramp (Prisoner's Song)

The Civil War Music Collector's Edition. Compact discs. Time-Life Music. R103-12. 1991. Performed by Nancy Blake, Norman Blake, Polly Brecht, Will Brecht, Susan Brockman, James Bryan, Bob Carlin, Ed Dye, Pat Enright, 1st Brigade Band, Doug Green, John Hartford, Mark Howard, Hutchinson Family Singers, Morning Sun Singers, Bruce Nemerov, Alan O'Bryant, Jerry Perkins, Princely Players, Paul Ritscher, Doug Seroff, James Stickley, Jr., Teressia Ward, Paul F. Wells.

Disc A

Hard Times Come Again No More

Jenny Lind Polka

Arkansas Traveler

Jordan Is a Hard Road to Travel

Get Off the Track!

Annie Laurie

Mockingbird Quick Step/In Happy Moments

I Wish I Was in Dixie's Land

Hymn Medley: Come Ye Disconsolate/Pleyel's Hymn/Notting Hill

The First Gun Is Fired! May God Protect the Right!

The Song of the Contrabands: O, Let My People Go

Quick Step and Battle Hymn of the Republic

Grafted into the Army

The Southrons' Chaunt of Defiance

The Bonnie Blue Flag

Bonnie Blue Schottische

Just before the Battle, Mother

Dixie Quick Step

Disc B

Reveille

Glory! Glory! Hallelujah! (John Brown's Body)

Hard Crackers Come Again No More

The Rogue's March

The Battle Cry of Freedom/Kingdom Coming

Aura Lea

Opera Reel

There Is a Fountain Filled with Blood

Home, Sweet Home

Richmond Is a Hard Road to Travel

The Yellow Rose of Texas

Stonewall Jackson's Way

For Bales

Natchez under the Hill

Goober Peas

Children of the Heavenly King

Lorena

Tattoo

Disc C

Weeping, Sad and Lonely, or, When This Cruel War Is Over

When Johnny Comes Marching Home

Go in the Wilderness

Marching through Georgia

The Vacant Chair, or, We Shall Meet But We Shall Miss Him

The Southern Girl, or, The Homespun Dress

Stonewall Jackson's Prayer

General Lee's Grand March

Home, Sweet Home

Booth Killed Lincoln

Camp Chase

Roll, Jordan, Roll

Beautiful Dreamer

O, I'm a Good Old Rebel

Old Dan Tucker

Spanish Fandango

Amazing Grace

Erbsen, Wayne. *Ballads and Songs of the Civil War: A Stirring Collection of Civil War Music Played on Historical Instruments.* Cassette. 50 minutes. Native Ground NG 004. 1994. ISBN 3-883206-05-7.

Side 1

I Can Whip the Scoundrel

Bonnie Blue Flag

Just before the Battle, Mother

John Brown's Dream

Cumberland Gap

Here's Your Mule

Battle Cry of Freedom

Side 2

The Southern Soldier

Lorena

Tramp, Tramp, Tramp

Dixie's Land

There Was an Old Soldier

The Cumberland and the Merrimac

The Southern Wagon

Erbsen, Wayne. *The Home Front: Seventeen Authentic Tunes of the Civil War.* Cassette. 45 minutes. Native Ground, 006. ISBN 0-9629327-8-7. 1992. Song lyrics are included on the insert.

Side 1

Kingdom Come

Yellow Rose of Texas

Cumberland Gap

Camptown Races

When Johnny Comes Marching Home

Run Johnny Run

My Old Kentucky Home

The Minstrel Boy

Side 2

Buffalo Gals/Alabama Gals

The Rebel Soldier

Wild Horses at Stoney Point

Darling Nelly Gray

Old Dan Tucker

Johnny Is Gone for a Soldier

Leather Britches

Cotton-Eyed Joe

When I Saw Sweet Nelly Home

Erbsen, Wayne. *Southern Soldier Boy: Sixteen Authentic Tunes of the Civil War.* Cassette. 45 minutes. Native Ground, 005. ISBN 0-9629327-7-9. 1992. Song lyrics are included on the insert.

Side 1

Richmond Is a Hard Road to Travel

Turkey in the Straw

Southern Soldier Boy

Johnson Boys

Pattyroller

Home Sweet Home!

Soldier's Joy

Goober Peas

Side 2

Boatman

The Battle of Shiloh's Hill

The Girl I Left Behind

Oh I'm a Good Old Rebel

Battle Cry of Freedom

Rabble Soldier

Listen to the Mockingbird

Dixie's Land

Ford, Tennessee Ernie. *Tennessee Ernie Ford Sings Songs of the Civil War.* Compact disc. Capitol Records, Hollywood, Calif., CDP 7 95705 2. 1991. Program notes are inserted in the container.

Civil War Songs of the North

The Army of the Free

Virginia's Bloody Soil

Marching Song (of the First Arkansas Negro Regiment)

The Why and the Wherefore

The Vacant Chair

The Fall of Charleston

The New York Volunteer

The Faded Coat of Blue

Marching through Georgia

Just Before the Battle, Mother

The Girl I Left behind Me

Union Dixie

Civil War Songs of the South

Stonewall Jackson's Way

Lorena

Riding a Raid

Maryland, My Maryland

Goober Peas

I Can Whip the Scoundrel

The Bonnie Blue Flag

The Valiant Conscript

The Rebel Soldier

The Southern Wagon

Flight of the Doodles

Dixie

Gone for a Soldier: Homefront Airs of the Civil War Period. Cassette. Titchner, Ridgway, PA. 1993. Performed by Three Cheers and a Tiger.

Somebody's Darling

Johnny Is Gone for a Soldier

Was My Brother in the Battle?

Weeping, Sad and Lonely

Brother Green

Grafted into the Army

Take Your Gun and Go, Soldier

Soldier Won't You Marry Me?

Johnny Is My Darling

The Southern Soldier Boy

Gentle Annie

Johnny Is Gone for a Soldier (reprise)

The Rebel Soldier

The Battle Hymn of the Republic

Horton, Bobby. *Homespun Songs of the CSA*. Cassette. 3430 Sagebrook Lane, Birmingham, AL 35243. 1985.

Side A

Everybody's Dixie

God Save the South

Maryland, My Maryland

Rose of Alabama

All Quiet along the Potomac

Stonewall Jackson's Way

Homespun Dress

Battle Cry of Freedom

Yellow Rose of Texas

The Rebel Soldier

Side B

Bonnie Blue Flag

Ridin' a Raid

Lorena

'Twas at the Siege of Vicksburg

Home Sweet Home

Oh I'm a Good Old Rebel

Long Ago

Dixie

Horton, Bobby. *Homespun Songs of the CSA*. Cassette. Vol. 2. HM002. 1986.

Side 1

Wait for the Wagon

Virginia Marseillaise

Jine the Cavalry

Willie Boy

Evelina

For Bales

Stonewall's Requiem

Old Abe Lies Sick

Side 2

Cumberland Gap

The Young Volunteer

John Hunt Morgan's Song

On the Plains of Manassas

The Upidee Song

Rock of Ages/On Jordan's Stormy Banks

Kennesaw Line

Dixie

Horton, Bobby. *Homespun Songs of the CSA*. Cassette. Vol. 3. HM003. 1987.

Side 1

Old Abner's Shoes

Cheer Boys Cheer

God Save the Southern Land

Root Hog or Die

Somebody's Darling

The Reluctant Conscript

The Southern Soldier Boy

Goober Peas

Just before the Battle Mother (parody)

The Captain with His Whiskers

Side 2

Boys Keep Your Powder Dry

Mister Here's Your Mule

The Drummer Boy of Shiloh

Gay and Happy

Katy Wells

A Life on a Vicksburg Bluff

A Soldier's Grave

Wearing of the Gray

Dixie

Horton, Bobby. *Homespun Songs of the CSA*. Cassette. Vol. 4. HM004-C. 1988.

Side 1

Dixie, the Land of King Cotton

March of the Southern Men

We Conquer or Die

The Soldier with a Wooden Leg

The Battle of Shiloh Hill

The Southern Soldier

Think of Your Head

Johnny Is Gone for a Soldier

Soldier's Joy

Side 2

Strike for the South

Melt the Bells

Richmond Is a Hard Road to Travel

Pray, Maiden, Pray

The Brass Mounted Army

When upon the Field of Glory

Short Rations (to the "Corn-fed" Army of Tennessee)

Roll Alabama Roll

Bonnie Blue Flag

Horton, Bobby. *Homespun Songs of the CSA*. Cassette. Vol. 5. HM005-C. ISBN 1-882604-24-5. 1993.

Side A

Ye Cavaliers of Dixie

The Soldier's Farewell

The Cross of the South

Old Abe's Lament

The North Carolina War Song

The Cavalier's Glee

The Bowld Sojer Boy

Do They Miss Me at Home?

The Kentucky Battle Song

Side B

The Infantry

John Harrolson

The Soldier's Suit of Grey

The South Shall Rise Up Free

General Butler

The Mother of the Soldier Boy

General Forrest, a Confederate

Hood's Old Brigade

The Conquered Banner

Horton, Bobby. *Homespun Songs of the Union Army*. Cassette. Vol. 1. HM00U1. 1987.

Side 1

Battle Cry of Freedom

The Army of the Free

New York Volunteer

May God Save the Union

We'll Fight for Uncle Abe

Pat Murphy of the Irish Brigade

Marching Along

The Vacant Chair

The Why and Wherefore

Side 2

We Are Coming Father Abraham

Grafted into the Army

Weeping Sad and Lonely

Kingdom Coming

Take Your Gun and Go John

Tenting on the Old Camp Ground

Good-bye, Old Glory

Battle Hymn of the Republic

Horton, Bobby. *Homespun Songs of the Union Army*. Cassette. Vol. 2. HM00U2. 1990.

Side A

The Battle Hymn of the Republic

The Girl I Left behind Me

Johnny Is My Darling

Aura Lea

Clear the Tracks

Lincoln and Liberty

The Army Bean

Brother Green

The Invalid Corps

Side B

The Flag of Columbia

What's the Matter

Gary Owen

Just before the Battle Mother

Corporal Schnapps

We Are Marching on to Richmond

Virginia's Bloody Soil

When Johnny Comes Marching Home

Horton, Bobby. *Homespun Songs of the Union Army.* Cassette. Vol. 3. HM00U3. 1991.

Side 1

Stand Up for Uncle Sam

God Save the Nation

To Canaan

Billy Barlow

Who Will Care for Mother Now

De Day Ob Liberty

God Bless My Boy Tonight

Skedaddle

Vicksburg Is Taken

Side 2

Hard Times in Dixie

Faded Coat of Blue

Union Dixie

Tramp, Tramp, Tramp

Come in Out of the Draft

When This Dreadful War Is Ended

Hard Crackers

The Fall of Charleston

The Songs We Sang upon the Old Camp Ground

McNeil, Keith and Rusty, *Civil War Songs with Historical Narration.* 2 cassettes. WEM Records, 16230 Van Buren Blvd., Riverside, CA 92504 (909) 780-2322. WEM 507C, 508C. 1989. Rusty McNeil: narration, vocals, guitar. Keith McNeil: narration, vocals, guitar, twelve-string guitar, tenor banjo, five-string banjo, clarinet, harmonica, mandolin, Highland bagpipes. Darrin Schuck: piano, guitar. Choruses: Keith, Rusty, David, Jennifer, and Sarah McNeil, Darrin Schuck, Ed Wilbourne, Jr., Cinthea Hartig, Ed and Vilma Pallette, Clabe Hangan, and Robin Bartunek. Lead vocals on "The Homespun Dress": Jennifer, Sarah, and Rusty McNeil. Lead vocal on "Slavery Chain Done Broke at Last" and "Free at Last": Clabe Hangan

Side 1: The War Begins

All Quiet along the Potomac Tonight

Lincoln and Liberty

The Southern Wagon

God Save the South

Maryland, My Maryland

The Bonnie Blue Flag

Dixie's Land

Dixie Parodies

The Yellow Rose of Texas

Virginia Marseillaise

What's the Matter?

Treasury Rats

Yankee Doodle

Abraham's Daughter

Ellsworth Avengers

Side 2: The Realities of War

Just before the Battle, Mother

Riding a Raid

Stonewall Jackson's Way

Battle Hymn of the Republic

The Battle of Shiloh Hill

The Battle Cry of Freedom

Southern Battle Cry of Freedom

Goober Peas

Hard Crackers Come Again No More

Army Grub/The Army Bean/Army Bugs

The Homespun Dress

We Are Coming, Father Abraham

Come In out of the Draft

We Are Coming, Father Abraham, $300 More

For Bales

Side 3: The Changing War

Kingdom Coming

No More Auction Block for Me

Slavery Chain Done Broke at Last

Oh Freedom

Go Down Moses

Free at Last

John Brown's Body

Marching Song of the First Arkansas Regiment

The *Cumberland* and the *Merrimac*

The Alabama

Kentucky, Oh Kentucky

How Are You John Morgan?

Tramp, Tramp, Tramp

The Bonnie White Flag

When Johnny Comes Marching Home

Side 4: The Union Forever

The Last Fierce Charge

Lorena

Aura Lea

The Children of the Battlefield

'Twas at the Siege of Vicksburg

I Go to Fight Mit Sigel

Old Abe Lincoln Came Out of the Wilderness

We Are the Boys of Potomac's Ranks

Marching through Georgia

We Are Marching on to Richmond

Tenting on the Old Camp Ground

Songs of the Civil War. VHS video. 60 minutes. Sony Music Video, New York; American
   Documentaries, Inc. and Ginger Group Productions, Inc. 1991. A musical companion to the award-winning PBS series *The Civil War,* it presents songs drawn
   entirely from the Civil War era (except ''Ashokan Farewell''). It uses still photographs and spoken passages along with newly filmed live performances, by
   various musicians, to evoke emotion and link the songs to the history of the war.
   Also available as a Columbia Records (CT48607) cassette.

Run, Mourner, Run—Sweet Honey in the Rock

Give Us a Flag—Richie Havens

Shiloh—John Hartford

The Secesh—John Hartford

Somebody's Darling—Kathy Mattea

Taps—United States Military Academy Band

The Vacant Chair—Kathy Mattea

Better Times Are Coming—Kate and Anna McGarrigle

Lorena—John Hartford

Marching through Georgia—Jay Ungar and Molly Mason with Fiddle Fever

Hard Times Come Again No More—Kate and Anna McGarrigle

Old Unreconstructed—Waylon Jennings

When Johnny Comes Marching Home—Ronnie Gilbert

Ashokan Farewell (reprise)—Jay Ungar and Molly Mason with Fiddle Fever

Ashokan Farewell—Jay Ungar and Molly Mason with Fiddle Fever

No More Auction Block for Me—Sweet Honey in the Rock

Lincoln and Liberty (The Liberty Ball)—Ronnie Gilbert

Dixie's Land—United States Military Academy Band

The Southern Soldier Boy—Kathy Mattea

Aura Lee—John Hartford

The Rebel Soldier—Waylon Jennings

Follow the Drinking Gourd—Richie Havens

Battle Hymn of the Republic (John Brown's Body)—Judy Collins

When Johnny Comes Marching Home—United States Military Academy Band

The Yellow Rose of Texas—Hoyt Axton

Southern Horizon. *The Girl I Left behind Me.* Cassette. Live Productions, P.O. Box 448, Hanover, VA 23069. LP-73. Robert A. "Robbie" Watts: guitar, vocals. John Robison: banjo, guitar, autoharp, harmonica, pennywhistle, vocals. Su Tarr: violin, vocals. Carrington Wise: vocals.

Side 1 Flowers of Edinborough

Redwing

Battle Cry of Freedom

Drink Your Tea Love

Just before the Battle Mother

Dixie

The Homespun Dress

The Girl I Left behind Me

Side 2 Golden Slippers

Lovely Nancy

Lorena

The Greenwood Tree

Yellow Rose of Texas

Cupid's Waltz

Ten Penney Bit

Goober Peas

Ungar, Jay, and Molly Mason. *Live at Gettysburg College.* Cassette. Fiddle & Dance Records, RD 1 Box 489, West Hurley, NY 12491. (914) 338-2996. FDCS 102. 1994. A concert sponsored by the Civil War Institute at Gettysburg College, November 20, 1993. Jay Ungar: vocals, fiddle, viola, harmonica, banjo. Molly Mason: vocals, guitar, banjo, piano.

Side A

The Girl I Left behind Me/Waiting for the Federals

Lorena

Cumberland Gap

Hard Times Come Again No More

The Yellow Rose of Texas

Tenting on the Old Camp Ground

Hard Crackers

Marching through Georgia

Side B

Hits of the 60s: Kingdom Coming/Battle Cry of Freedom/Dixie/Battle Hymn of the
    Republic

The Faded Coat of Blue

President Lincoln's Hornpipe/Devil's Dream

Fisher's Hornpipe/Leather Britches/Bill Cheatham

Ashokan Farewell

The Union Restored. The Sounds of History: A Supplement to the Life History of the
    United States, record 6: 1861–1876. Mono LP. Time, New York, NY. 1963.
    Program notes are on the container and in the accompanying text, with an eight-
    page bibliography laid in the container. Fredric March and Florence Eldridge,
    narrators; original music composed and conducted by Hershy Kay; vocal and
    choral direction by Lehman Engel; connective passages read by Charles Colling-
    wood; music edited by Virgil Thomson.

Side 1: Documents

The Aftermath of Bull Run

U.S. Grant's Letter

Clara Barton's Letter

William Thompson Lusk's Letters

Abraham Lincoln's Letter to General George B. McClellan, October 13, 1862

Writing the "Battle Hymn of the Republic"

Pickett's Charge

Lee after Gettysburg

Charles Blackford's Letter

William T. Sherman's Letter

Lee's Surrender

Lee's Farewell to His Troops

Eliza Andrews Describes Defeat

Lincoln's Gettysburg Address

Side 2: Music of the Civil War

Bugles and Drums

Marching through Georgia

Aura Lee

Oh, I'm a Good Old Rebel

Fifes and Drums

Battle of Shiloh

Grafted into the Army

Lorena

Bugle Ensemble

Mother Kissed Me in My Dream

Goober Peas

The Centennial Meditation of Columbia

White Mansions: A Tale from the American Civil War, 1861–1865. Stereo LP. A&M
    Records, Beverly Hills, Calif., SP-6004. 1978.

Story to Tell—Jessie Colter

Dixie, Hold On—Waylon Jennings

Join around the Flag—John Dillon

White Trash—Steve Cash

The Last Dance/The Kentucky Racehorse—John Dillon and Jessie Colter

Southern Boys—Steve Cash

The Union Mare/The Confederate Grey—Waylon Jennings and Jessie Colter

No One Would Believe a Summer Could Be So Cold—John Dillon

The Southland's Bleeding—Waylon Jennings

Bring Up the Twelve Pounders—John Dillon

They Laid Waste to Our Land—Steve Cash, John Dillon, and Waylon Jennings

Praise the Lord—The Voices of Deliverance

The King Has Called Me Home—Steve Cash

Bad Man—John Dillon

Dixie, Now You're Done—Waylon Jennings

Who Shall Rule This American Nation? Songs of the Civil War Era. Stereo LP. Nonesuch.
    1975. Selections of songs written by Henry Clay Work. Performed by Joan Mor-
    ris, mezzo-soprano; Clifford Jackson, baritone; William Bolcom, piano; and the
    Camerata Chorus of Washington. Recorded April 1975 in the Grand Salon of the
    Renwick Gallery, Smithsonian Institution, Washington, D.C. Durations, program
    notes by J. Newsom, and words (four pages) are bound in the container.

Who Shall Rule This American Nation?

Grafted into the Army

Poor Kitty Popcorn; or The Soldier's Pet

When the "Evening Star" Went Down

The Buckskin Bag of Gold

Come Home, Father

Uncle Joe's "Hail Columbia!"

Grandfather's Clock

Kingdom Coming

The Picture on the Wall

Now, Moses!

Take Them Away, They'll Drive Me Crazy

Agnes by the River

Crossing the Grand Sierras

The Silver Horn

NARRATIVE: FICTION

Civil War Stories. Mono LP. Vanguard. 1962. Program notes are on the slipcase. Nelson Olmstead reads fiction.

Stephen Crane, *A Mystery of Heroism*

Ambrose Bierce, *Chickamauga* and *A Son of the Gods*

Mark Twain, *The Private History of a Campaign That Failed*

Hamlin Garland, *The Return of a Private*

Crane, Stephen. *The Red Badge of Courage.* 4 cassettes. Blackstone Audio Books, Ashland, OR. 1994. Read by Pat Bottino; Brilliance Corporation, Grand Haven, MI. 6 cassettes (5 hours). 1993. Read by Roger Dressler. In this fiction set during the 1863 Battle of Chancellorsville, Virginia, Henry Fleming joins the Union troops fighting the Civil War to prove his patriotism and courage; overcome with blind fear he runs away. To redeem himself during battle, he seizes the regiment's colors in a daring charge that proves him truly courageous.

Foote, Shelby. *Shiloh.* 4 cassettes. Recorded Books, Prince Frederick, MD. 1992. Various narrators read this unabridged version of the fictionalized account of the 1862 Battle of Shiloh.

Gurganus, Allan. *Allan Gurganus Reads from* Oldest Living Confederate Widow Tells All, *and Talks about the Civil War, North Carolina, and Narrative Voice.* Cassette. 30 minutes. Moveable Feast, New York, NY. 1990. Tom Vitale interviews Allan Gurganus about his novel.

Selected Stories from Mark Nesbitt's Ghosts of Gettysburg. Narrated by Lally Cadeau and Patrick Colgan; music composed and performed by Meg Neiderer. Cassette. 30 minutes. Visionary Music, VM 9301. 1993.

Side 1

Introduction

The Homecoming

Forever a Soldier

The Horseman

The Woman in White

Side 2

Seeking a Childhood

Old Dorm

The Bottom Floor

The Sartorial Spirit

The Blue Boy

Shaara, Michael. *The Killer Angels.* 9 cassettes. Books on Tape, Newport Beach, CA. 1985. Read by Ken Ohst; Recorded Books, Prince Frederick, MD. 10 cassettes (14 hours, 15 minutes). 1991. Narrated by George Guidall; Blackstone Audio Books, Ashland, OR. 9 cassettes. 1992. Read by Christopher Hurt. This fictionalized account describes the Battle of Gettysburg through the eyes of Lee, Longstreet, and others who fought there. The basis for Turner Network Television's *Gettysburg.*

Whitman, Walt. *Eyewitness to the Civil War.* 2 mono LPs. Caedmon, New York, NY. 1969. Program notes by Frederic Shriver Klein on the container. Ed Begley reads selected poems from *Leaves of Grass* that pertain to the Civil War.

NARRATIVE: NONFICTION

The Black Man in the Civil War: The Political and Military Importance of Blacks in the Civil War. Cassette. 27 minutes. Center for Cassette Studies, North Hollywood, CA. 1974. Edgar Toppin and Benjamin Quarles discuss the impact of emancipation, the black desire to fight against slavery, and the influence of Frederick Douglass in assisting black participation in the war. Notes are inserted in the container.

Branham, Charles R. *Black Troops in the Civil War: The Contributions of Blacks to the Union's Victory.* Cassette. 25 minutes. Center for Cassette Studies, North Hollywood, CA. 1974. Branham discusses the role of the black soldier during the Civil War in the United States.

Catton, Bruce. *The Centennial History of the Civil War.* 40 cassettes. 60 hours. Books on Tape, Newport Beach, CA. 1980. An unabridged narration of Catton's 1965 book examines the American Civil War from December 1862 to the end of the conflict at Appomattox. Michael Prichard reads volume 1, *The Coming Fury;* volume 2, *The Terrible Swift Sword;* and volume 3, *Never Call Retreat.*

The Civil War. Excerpts from the book by Geoffrey C. Ward with Ric Burns and Ken Burns; read by Ken Burns. 2 cassettes. 3 hours. Sound editions from Random House. ISBN 0–679–40373–6. 1990.

Civil War, Afro-Americans and Abraham Lincoln. 3 cassettes. 90 minutes. Southern California Library of Social Studies and Research, Los Angeles, CA. ca. 1969–1981. Soundtrack of the television series *Black Heritage: A History of the Afro-American,* first shown in 1969.

Tape 1: Road to Emancipation, 1861–63, by Edgar Toppin

Tape 2: Fighting for Freedom, 1863–65, by Edgar Toppin

Tape 3: Abraham Lincoln, Afro-Americans and the American Dream, by Lerone Bennett

The Civil War and Slavery: Lecture on the Causes and Interpretations of the Civil War. Cassette. 28 minutes. Center for Cassette Studies. 1974. Lecture by Edgar Allan Toppin.

Davis, Burke. *Gray Fox: Robert E. Lee and the Civil War.* 9 cassettes. Blackstone Audio Books, Ashland, OR. 1990. Christopher Hurt reads this unabridged biography of Lee, written in 1956, which covers just the war years.

Dear Abe Linkhorn: The Satire of the Civil War: A Selection from the Contemporary Satirical Writing of Artemus Ward, Petroleum V. Nasby, Bill Arp, and "A Disbanded Volunteer." Mono LP. Folkways Records, New York, NY. 1962. Program notes and texts (eight pages) are inserted in the container. Selected, recorded, and with a critical introduction by Samuel Charters; read by David Cort.

"A disbanded volunteer" and Honest Abe

Nasby on the Fall of Savannah

Artemus Ward in Richmond

Nasby Encourages Secession

Artemus Ward Visits A. Lincoln

Bill Arp Writes Mr. Linkhorn

Nasby and the Draft

Genovese, Eugene D., and Eric Foner. *The Coming of the Civil War.* Cassette. Educational Productions Ltd., Wakefield, England. 1975. A booklet contains notes on the discussion, bibliography, and study questions (five pages) is laid in container.

Gettysburg National Military Park: Complete Tour of Battlefield. Cassette. 90 minutes. CCInc., Auto Tape Tours Division, Scarsdale, NY. 1990. Contains a one-page fact sheet. Presents a guided tour of Gettysburg National Military Park, Pennsylvania, describing the Civil War battle that was fought there July 1–3, 1863. Includes music and sound effects.

Grant, Ulysses S. *The Personal Memoirs of U.S. Grant.* 17 cassettes. 24 hours. Recorded Books, Charlotte Hall, MD. 1987–1988. Peter Johnson reads from Grant's unabridged autobiography.

Kunhardt, Philip B., Peter W. Kunhardt, and Philip B. Kunhardt III. *Lincoln.* 2 cassettes. 180 minutes. Random House Audio, New York, NY. 1992. Frank Langella reads this companion piece to the four-hour television miniseries about Abraham Lincoln.

McFeely, William S. *Grant: A Biography.* 21 cassettes. Books on Tape, Newport Beach, CA. 1989. Dick Estell reads this unabridged version of the biography of Ulysses S. Grant.

Ransom, John L. *The Andersonville Diary: A True Account.* 5 cassettes. Recorded Books, Charlotte Hall, MD. 1988. Unabridged narration by Adrian Cornauer of this eyewitness account of the Confederate prison in Georgia.

Rhodes, Elijah Hunt. *All for the Union.* 8 cassettes. Edited by Robert Hunt Rhodes. 11 hours, 30 minutes. Recorded Books, Prince Frederick, MD. 1991. Norman Dietz narrates this unabridged recording of the book of letters and diaries of the Rhode Island infantryman.

Richmond National Battlefield Driving Tape Tour. Cassette. National Park Series, CT-11. 87 minutes. Eastern National Park and Monument Association, 3215 E. Broad Street, Richmond, VA 23223. 1987. Covers the Seven Days' battles around Richmond in 1862; includes cassette, official map, and guide booklet.

Sandburg, Carl. *Abraham Lincoln: The Prairie Years* and *The War Years.* Cassettes. 4 volumes, unabridged. Books on Tape, Newport Beach, CA. 1994. To portray this complex man as he struggled with politics and the war, Sandburg quoted from diaries and letters, lending a human touch to the crises. Narrated by Dick Estell.

Sherman, William T. *The Memoirs of William T. Sherman: Autobiography.* 3 cassettes. 270 minutes. Recorded Books, Charlotte Hall, MD. 1989. Nelson Runger narrates from the memoirs of General W. T. Sherman, *Atlanta and the March to the Sea.*

Smith, Gene. *Lee and Grant.* 8 cassettes. 12 hours. Recorded Books, Clinton, MD. 1984. Peter Johnson narrates the readable, popular biography of Robert E. Lee and Ulysses S. Grant based on Smith's 1984 psychological study of the two generals.

Vandiver, Frank E. *Strategy and Tactics of the Confederate Army.* Cassette. Voices of History M-7. 51 minutes. M. Glazier, 1210A King Street, Wilmington, DE 19801. In this lecture, Vandiver reviews the offensive and defensive military strategies of the Confederate Army. Includes a ten-page guide.

Vandiver, Frank E. *Voices of Valor: Words of the Civil War.* Cassette, compact disc. Texas A&M University Press, College Station, TX 77843-4354. Contains commentary by Vandiver and readings of letters and memoirs from soldiers in the field, speeches from great orators, period music, and historic documents.

Part 1

Lincoln's editorial on union, *New York Tribune,* 1862

Davis's farewell to the U.S. Senate, 1861

"Go Down, Moses"

John Brown's trial

John Brown's Body, by Stephen Vincent Benét

South Carolina's Declaration of Causes, 1860

Davis's inaugural address, 1861

Lincoln's first inaugural address, 1861

Henry Ward Beecher on fighting at Fort Sumter

Henry A. Wise's call to arms

Sam Houston's call to arms

"Dixie"

Sullivan Ballou to his wife, Sarah, 1861

Louisiana private's letters on army life

First draft law, Confederate Congress, 1862

Haskell on Gettysburg

Part 2

Frederick Douglass on the great opportunity for the nation, 1861

Douglass on conscription, 1863

General Nathaniel P. Banks on his black troops, 1863

Emancipation Proclamation

McClellan addressing the Northern army

Sherman on the value of railroads, 1864

Lincoln's letter appointing Hooker to Potomac Command, 1863

Lee's request to be replaced, 1863

Letter from a rebel to his mother, Spotsylvania Court House, 1864

"Battle Hymn of the Republic"

Lincoln's Gettysburg Address

Sherman's reply to the citizens of Atlanta, 1864

"Sherman's Buzzin' Along to de Sea"

Lincoln on Reconstruction, 1865

Resolutions of McGowan's South Carolina Brigade, 1865

Davis's last message to the Confederate people, 1865

Lee's farewell to his army, 1865

Grant's final report on the war, 1865

Lincoln's second inaugural address, 1865

Wert, Jeffrey D. *Mosby's Rangers.* 9 cassettes. 13.5 hours. Books on Tape, Newport Beach, CA. 1992. Dick Estell reads the 1990 study of the 43d Battalion of Virginia cavalry, the partisan raiders led by John Singleton Mosby.

BIBLIOGRAPHY

Crawford, Richard. *The Civil War Songbook; Complete Original Sheet Music for 37 Songs.* New York: Dover, 1977.

Harwell, Richard Barksdale. "Confederate Carrousel: Southern Songs of the Sixties." *Emory University Quarterly* 6 (June 1950): 84–100.

————. *Confederate Music.* Chapel Hill: University of North Carolina Press, 1950.

Heaps, Willard A., and Porter W. Heaps. *The Singing Sixties: The Spirit of Civil War Days Drawn from the Music of the Times.* Norman: University of Oklahoma Press, 1960.

Hoogerwerf, Frank W. *Confederate Sheet-Music Imprints.* ISAM Monographs, number 21. Brooklyn, NY: Institute for Studies in American Music, Conservatory of Music, Brooklyn College, 1984.

Root, George F., ed. *The Bugle-Call.* Chicago: Root & Cady, 1863.

Scheurer, Timothy E. " 'Who Shall Rule This American Nation?' The Civil War Era." In *Born in the U.S.A.: The Myth of America in Popular Music from Colonial Times to the Present.* Jackson: University Press of Mississippi, 1991.

Soldiers' and Sailors' Patriotic Songs. New York: Loyal Publication Society, 1864.

Silber, Irwin. *Songs of the Civil War.* New York: Columbia University Press, 1960.

Songs and Ballads of Freedom: A Choice Collection Inspired by the Incidents and Scenes of the Present War. New York: J. F. Feeks, 1864.

The Southern Soldier's Prize Songster, Containing Martial and Patriotic Pieces Applicable to the Present War. Mobile, Ala.: W. F. Wisely, 1864.

War Songs of the American Union. Boston: William V. Spencer, 1861.

Appendix: Publishers and Dealers of Civil War Literature

T. Michael Parrish

This list is extensive but by no means comprehensive. Literally thousands of dealers and publishers handle books and other graphic materials about the Civil War. Perhaps the best method to identify them in any given locale is to consult the telephone directory's Yellow Pages, looking under the headings "Book Dealers—Retail," "Book Dealers—Used and Rare," and "Publishers—Book." A growing number are involved in dual operations as dealers and publishers. In this list, dealers and/or publishers are identified as such in brackets, unless the fact is obvious by the business name. Bookstores located at Civil War battlefields and other historical sites are emphasized by the word "Bookstore" in parentheses. One of the best means of staying current on a national basis is to consult the advertisements and book reviews published monthly in *Civil War News* (see below).

The Internet also offers an increasing abundance of information about booksellers and publishers. See the following World Wide Web URL addresses:

> http://www.yahoo.com/Entertainment/Books
>
> http://www.dsu.edu/~janke/civilwar.html#Biblio

Abbey Book Shop, P.O. Box 64384, Los Angeles, CA 90064.

Abraham Lincoln Birthplace National Historic Site (Bookstore), 2995 Lincoln Park Rd., Hodgenville, KY 42748. Tel.: 502-358-3137. FAX: 502-358-3874.

Abraham Lincoln Bookshop (Daniel Weinberg), 357 West Chicago Ave., Chicago IL 60610. Tel.: 312-944-3085. FAX: 312-944-5549.

Abraham Lincoln Boyhood National Monument (Bookstore), Lincoln City, IN 47552. Tel.: 812-937-4541.

Abraham Lincoln Home National Historic Site (Bookstore), 425 South Seventh St., Springfield, IL 62705. Tel.: 217-523-3421.

Abshire Books [dealer], 198 Foundry St., P.O. Box 1020, Morgantown, WV 26505.

Acadiana Press, P.O. Box 42290, Lafayette, LA 70504-2290.

Acorn Books (Jennifer L. Miller) [dealer], 521 Park Ave., Winter Park, FL 32789. Tel.: 407-647-2755. FAX: 407-647-3855.

Alexander Autographs, 34 East Putnam Ave., Suite 121, Greenwich, CT 06830. P.O. Box 101, Cos Cob, CT 06807. Tel.: 203-622-8444. FAX: 203-622-8765.

Algonquin Books of Chapel Hill [publisher], P.O. Box 2225, Chapel Hill, NC 27515-2225.

R. R. Allen, Books [dealer], 5300 Bluefield Rd., Knoxville, TN 37921. Tel.: 615-584-4487.

Karl Altau [dealer], 800 Warwick Circle, Waynesboro, VA 22980. Tel.: 703-949-8867.

Always Books (Jim and Barbara McMillan) [dealer], 707 South 18th St., Quincy, IL 63201. Tel.: 217-223-7963.

American Political Biography (Jeffrey R. Speirs) [dealer and publisher], 39 Boggs Hill, Newtown, CT 06470. Tel.: 203-270-9777.

Americana Historical Books (Robert H. Kerlin) [dealer], P.O. Box 1272, Fayetteville, GA 30214. Tel.: 404-460-0984.

Andersonville National Historic Site (Bookstore), Highway 49, Andersonville, GA 31711. Tel.: 912-924-0343. FAX: 912-928-9640.

Andover Square Books (Jo and Allan Yeomans) [dealer], 805 Noragate Rd., Knoxville, TN 37919. Tel.: 615-693-8984.

Antebellum Covers [dealer], P.O. Box 8006, Gaithersburg, MD 20885. Tel.: 301-869-2623.

Ray Anthony Autographs [dealer], 505 South Beverly Hills Dr., Suite 1265, Beverly Hills, CA 90212. Tel.: 800-626-3393 or 310-471-7498. FAX: 310-471-7799.

Antietam National Battlefield (Bookstore), P.O. Box 158, Sharpsburg, MD 21782. Tel.: 301-432-5124.

Antiquarian Book Mart (Frank Kellel) [dealer], 3127 Broadway, San Antonio, TX 78209. Tel.: 512-828-7433 or 512-828-4885.

Antiquarian Bookworm (Billie Weetall), 1329 Templeton Place, Rockville, MD 20852. Tel.: 301-309-8888.

Antiquarian Map and Book Den (James Hess), 217 East New St., Lititz, PA 17543. Tel.: 800-432-8183 or 717-626-5002. FAX: 717-626-5002.

Antiques Americana (K. C. Owings, Jr.) [dealer], P.O. Box 19-R, North Abington, MA 02351.

Antiquities Ltd. [dealer], P.O. Box 18659, Atlanta, GA 30326. Tel.: 404-451-2897.

Appomattox Courthouse National Historic Site (Bookstore), Rt. 24, Box 218, Appomattox, VA 24522. Tel.: 804-352-2136. FAX: 804-352-8330.

Arabesque Books (John Schulz) [dealer], P.O. Box 12312, Atlanta, GA 30355. Tel.: 404-264-9649. FAX: 404-264-9649.

Argosy Book Store, 116 East 59th St., New York, NY 10022. Tel.: 212-753-4455. FAX: 212-593-4784.

Arkansas Post National Monument (Bookstore), Rt. 1, P.O. Box 16, Gillett, AR 72055. Tel.: 501-548-2207.

Aspen Book Shop, 5986 Memorial Dr., Stone Mountain, GA 30083. Tel.: 404-296-5933.

Associated University Presses, 440 Forsgate Dr., Cranbury, NJ 08512.

Atlanta Cyclorama (Bookstore), P.O. Box 89191, Atlanta, GA 30312. Tel.: 404-622-6264. FAX: 404-658-7045.

Atlanta Vintage Books, 3666 Clairmont Rd., Atlanta, GA 30341.

Atlantic Books [dealer], 310 King St., Charleston, SC 29401.

Atlantic Trading Company (John and Juanita Hammer) [dealer], 3464 Vivian St., Norfolk, VA 23513. Tel.: 804-853-1013.

BE Books [dealer], 3712 Walnut Ave., Altoona, PA 16601-1342.

BPC Publishers, P.O. Box 436, Mahomet, IL 61853.

Balcony Books [dealer], 214 South Broad St., Holly, MI 48442.

Baltimore Book Co. [auction house], 2112 North Charles St., Baltimore, MD 21218. Tel.: 410-659-0550.

Catherine Barnes [dealer], 2031 Walnut St., Philadelphia, PA 19103. Tel.: 215-854-0175. FAX: 215-854-0831.

Barrister, Inc. (Sheldon and Rosalind Kurland) [dealer], 4400 Southwest 95th Ave., Fort Lauderdale, FL 33328. Tel.: 305-475-1856.

Bob and Pat Bartosz [dealer], 226 Wenonah, Wenonah, NJ 08090.

Robert F. Batchelder, Bookseller, 1 West Butler Ave., Ambler, PA 19002. Tel.: 215-643-1430. FAX: 215-643-6613.

The Battlefield [dealer], 1600-B West Lake St., Minneapolis, MN 55408. Tel.: 612-823-3711.

Beck's Antiques and Books, 708 Caroline St., Fredericksburg, VA 22401.

Bell, Book & Candle (Patricia Ewald) [dealer], 106 Robinson St., Ashland, VA 23005. Tel.: 804-798-9047.

Belle Grove Publishing Co., P.O. Box 483, Kearny, NJ 07032. Tel.: 800-861-1861.

Walter R. Benjamin, Autographs, P.O. Box 255, Hunter, NY 12442. Tel.: 518-263-4133 or 518-263-4134. FAX: 518-263-4134.

Between Books [dealer], 2703 Philadelphia Pike, Claymount, DE 19703. Tel.: 302-798-3378.

R.O. Billingsly [dealer], 115 Lang Ave., Clarksburg, WV 26301.

Black Swan Books (J. Michael Courtney) [dealer], 505 East Maxwell St., Lexington, KY 40502. Tel.: 602-252-7255.

John F. Blair, Publisher, 1406 Plaza Dr., Winston-Salem, NC 27103.

Blackhorse Books (Jim Synnott), 4703 Charade, Houston, TX 77066. Tel.: 713-597-1568.

Roy Bleiweiss, Fine Books and Autographs, 92 Northgate Ave., Berkeley, CA 94708. Tel.: 510-548-1624.

Blue Acorn Press, 5589 Shawnee Dr., P.O. Box 2684, Huntington, WV 25726. Tel.: 304-733-3917.

Blue and Grey Press, 110 Enterprise Ave., Secaucus, NJ 07094.

Blue Mountain Books & Manuscripts (Ric Zank) [dealer], P.O. Box 363, Catskill, NY 12414. Tel.: 518-943-4771. FAX: 518-943-2949.

Bohemian Brigade Bookshop and Publishers (Ed Archer), 7347 Middlebrook Pike, Knoxville, TN 37909. Tel.: 615-694-8227. FAX: 615-531-1846.

Bohling Book Co. (Curt and Lynn Bohling), P.O. Box 204, Decatur, MI 49045. Tel.: 616-423-8786.

Bolerium Books [dealer], 2141 Mission St., Suite 300, San Francisco, CA 94110. Tel.: 415-863-6353. FAX: 415-255-6499.

Edward M. Bomsey [dealer], 7317 Farr St., Annandale, VA 22003. Tel.: 703-642-2040.

Book and Specialty Shop [dealer], 107 South St., P.O. Box 646, Cashiers, NC 29717.

Book Barn [dealer], U.S. Route 1, P.O. Box 557, Wells, ME 04090.

Book Broker (Vesta Lee Gordon) [dealer], 310 East Market St., Charlottesville, VA 22902. Tel.: 804-296-2194.

A Book Buyers Shop (Chester Doby), 1305 South Shepherd, Houston, TX 77019. Tel.: 713-529-1059.

Book Collector (James Taylor) [dealer], 2347 University Blvd., Houston, TX 77005. Tel.: 713-661-BOOK.

Book Dispensary [dealer], 1600 Broad River Rd., Columbia, SC 29210.

Book Finders of Fairfax (Jerome Elswit) [dealer], P.O. Box 3173, Warrenton, VA 22186. Tel.: 703-349-3281.

Book Harbor (Frederica and George Spurgeon) [dealer], 32 West College Ave., Westerville, OH 43081. Tel.: 614-895-3788.

Book House (Edward Hughes) [dealer], 805 North Emerson St., Arlington, VA 22205. Tel.: 703-527-7797.

Book-in-Hand (Helen and Bill Crawshaw) [dealer], 103 Condon Rd., Stillwater, NY 12170. Tel.: 518-587-0040. FAX: 518-587-0040.

Book Shelf (William Snell) [dealer], 3765 Hillsdale Dr., N.E., Cleveland, TN 37312-5133. Tel.: 615-472-8408.

Book Trader (Carolyn Floyd), 304 South Main St., P.O. Box 603, Fairmont, NC 28340. Tel.: 919-628-0945.

Bookery (Gary and Jeanette Braggs) [dealer], 107 West Nelson St., Lexington, VA 24450. Tel.: 703-464-3377.

Bookquest (Mike and Diane Bailey) [dealer], 19 Otis St., Greenville, SC 29605.

Bookroom (Kenneth Parrish) [dealer], 733 West Johnson St., Suite 104, Raleigh, NC 27603. P.O. Box 5131, Raleigh, NC 27650. Tel.: 919-755-0701.

Books and Things Gallery, 60 North Main St., St. Albans, VT 05478. Tel.: 800-762-1658.

Books! By George (Frank George) [dealer], 2424 Seventh Ave. South, Birmingham, AL 35233. Tel.: 205-323-6036.

Bookshop (Jim Croom) [dealer], P.O. Box 1011, Fredericksburg, TX 78624. Tel.: 210-997-9781.

Bookshop (Bill Loeser) [dealer], 400 West Franklin St., Chapel Hill, NC 27516. Tel.: 919-942-5178.

Bookstack (Judy and Charlie Brothers) [dealer], 112 West Lexington Ave., Elkhart, IN 46516. Tel.: 219-293-3815.

Bookstore [dealer], 104 South Jefferson, Lewisburg, WV 24901.

Bookworm and Silverfish (Jim Presgraves) [dealer], P.O. Box 639, Wytheville, VA 24382. Tel.: 703-686-5813.

Mike Brackin, Bookseller, P.O. Box 23, Manchester, CT 06045. Tel.: 860-647-8620.

Brandy Station Bookshelf (Budd Parrish) [dealer and publisher], P.O. Box 1863, Harrah, OK 73045-1863. Tel.: 405-964-5730.

Brattle Book Shop (Ken Gloss), 9 West St., Boston, MA 02111. Tel.: 800-447-9595 or 617-542-0210.

Breedlove Enterprises [dealer], 110 Water St., Bolivar, OH 44612. Tel.: 800-221-1863 or 216-874-2828. FAX: 216-874-3773.

Brighton Books (Jeffrey Wood), 321 Twelfth Ave., New Brighton, PA 15066. Tel.: 412-847-2211.

Broadfoot's Bookmark and Broadfoot Publishing Co. (Tom Broadfoot), 1907 Buena

Vista Circle, Wilmington, NC 28405. Tel.: 800-537-5243 or 910-686-4816. FAX: 910-686-4379.

Budd Press [publisher], 71-16 66th St., Glendale, NY 11385.

William J. B. Burger [dealer], P.O. Box 832, Pine Grove, CA 95665. Tel.: 209-296-7970.

Burke's Books (Harriette Beeson) [dealer], 1719 Poplar Ave., Memphis, TN 38104. Tel.: 901-388-3677.

Burkwood Books (Robert Hodges) [dealer], P.O. Box 172, Urbana, IL 61801. Tel.: 217-344-1419.

Stanley Butcher, Autographs, 4 Washington Ave., Andover, MA 01810. Tel.: 508-475-0146.

Butternut and Blue (Jim and Judy McLean) [dealer and publisher], 3411 Northwind Rd., Baltimore, MD 21234. Tel.: 410-256-9220.

C. W. Historicals Publishing (Blake Magner), 901 Lakeshore Dr., Westmont, NJ 08108.

C. Craig Caba Antiques [publisher], 206 York St., Gettysburg, PA 17325.

Andrew Cahan, Bookseller, 3000 Blueberry Lane, Chapel Hill, NC 27516. Tel.: 919-968-0538. FAX: 919-968-0538.

Cambridge University Press, 40 West 20th St., New York, NY 10011-4211. Tel.: 800-872-7423.

Camp Chase Gazette [magazine], P.O. Box 707N, Marietta, OH 45750. Tel.: 800-204-2407 or 614-373-1865.

Camp Pope Bookshop (Clark Kenyon) [dealer and publisher], 117 East Davenport, Iowa City, IA 52245, P.O. Box 2232, Iowa City, IA 52244-2232. Tel.: 319-351-2407.

Caravan Book Store, 550 South Grand Ave., Los Angeles, CA 90071. Tel.: 213-626-9944.

Tom Cardineau [dealer], P.O. Box 1255, Sound Beach, NY 11789.

Carolina Bookshop (Gordon Briscoe, Jr.), 2440 Park Rd., Charlotte, NC 28203-9527. Tel.: 704-375-7305.

Carolina Trader [dealer], P.O. Box 769, Monroe, NC 28111. Tel.: 704-289-1604.

J. W. Carson Co. [publisher], 130 Myrtle St., Le Roy, NY 14482.

Carter House (Bookstore), 1140 Columbia Ave., P.O. Box 555, Franklin, TN 37064. Tel.: 615-791-1861.

Barry Cassidy, Rare Books, 2005 "T" St., Sacramento, CA 95814. Tel.: 916-456-6307.

Cather and Brown Books (James Pat Cather) [dealer and publisher], P.O. Box 313, Birmingham, AL 35201. Tel.: 205-591-7284. FAX: 205-252-3718.

Center for Louisiana Studies, University of Southwestern Louisiana [publisher], P.O. Box 40831, Lafayette, LA 70504.

Chamberlain Press (Nancy Heverly), 355 Kingsbury Way #33, Westminster, MD 21157.

Chapel Hill Rare Books (Doug O'Dell), P.O. Box 456, Carrboro, NC 27510. Tel.: 919-929-8351. FAX: 919-967-2532.

Chickamauga and Chattanooga National Military Park (Bookstore), P.O. Box 2128, Fort Oglethorpe, GA 30742. Tel.: 706-866-9241.

Choctaw Books (Fred and Frank Smith), 926 North St., Jackson, MS 39202. Tel.: 601-352-7281.

Christie's [auction house], 502 Park Ave., New York, NY 10022. Tel.: 212-546-1000. FAX: 212-980-8163.

Christine's Books (Christine Pegram) [dealer], 1502 Main St., Sarasota, FL 34236. Tel.: 813-365-0586.

Robert Cianci [dealer], 50 Heron Rd., East Hartford, CT 06118. Tel.: 860-568-2945.

Civil War Lady Magazine, 622 Third Ave., S.W., Pipestone, MN 56164. Tel. or FAX: 507-825-3182.

Civil War News [magazine], Monarch Hill Rd., Rt. 1, Box 36, Tunbridge, VT 05077. Tel.: 800-222-1861 or 802-889-3500.

Civil War Store [dealer], 212 Chartres St., New Orleans, LA 70130. Tel.: 504-522-3328.

Stan Clark Military Books [dealer and publisher], 915 Fairview Dr., Gettysburg, PA 17325. Tel.: 717-337-1728.

Cohasco, Inc. [dealer], Postal 821, Yonkers, NY 10702. Tel.: 914-476-8500.

Collector's Books [dealer], 730 West Coronado Rd., Phoenix, AZ 85007. Tel.: 602-253-8331.

Collectors' Old Book Shop (Mary Clark Roane), 15 South Fifth St., Richmond, VA 23219. Tel.: 804-355-2437.

Colophon Bookshop (Robert and Christine Liska), 117 Water St., Exeter, NH 03833. Tel.: 603-772-8443.

Columbia Athenaeum (Ronald Bridwell and Carol Waldron) [dealer], 1215 Hampton St., P.O. Box 7875, Columbia, SC 29202. Tel.: 803-779-4048.

Columbia Books (Annette Kolling-Weaver) [dealer], 13 North 9th St., P.O. Box 27, Columbia, MO 65201. Tel.: 314-449-7417.

Combined Books, Inc. [publisher], East 10th Ave., Conshohocken, PA 19428.

Confederate Calendar Works (Larry Jones) [dealer], P.O. Box 2084, Austin, TX 78768.

The Conflict (Pauline Peterson)[dealer], 213 Steinwehr Ave., Gettysburg, PA 17325. Tel.: 800-847-0911 or 717-334-8003.

Connecticut Book Galleries (Y. J. Skutel) [dealer], 251 Carroll Rd., Fairfield, CT 06430. Tel.: 203-259-1997.

Country Lane Books (Ed Myers), P.O. Box 47, Collinsville, CT 06022. Tel.: 860-489-8852.

Countryman Press, P.O. Box 175, Woodstock, VT 05091. Tel.: 800-245-4151. FAX: 802-457-3250.

Cover to Cover (Mark Shuman) [dealer], P.O. Box 687, Chapel Hill, NC 27514. Tel.: 919-967-1032.

Crescent City Sutler [publisher], 17810 Hwy. 57, Evansville, IN 47711. Tel.: 812-983-4217.

Culpin's Antiquarian Bookshop (Alan Culpin), 3827 West 32d Ave., Denver, CO 80211. Tel.: 800-545-2665 or 303-455-0317. FAX: 303-433-8040.

Russ Cummings [dealer], 1009 Condor Dr., Greensboro, NC 27410. Tel.: 919-855-1929.

Q. M. Dabney and Co. (Michael Schnitter) [dealer], P.O. Box 42026, Washington, DC 20015. Tel.: 301-881-1470. FAX: 301-881-0843.

Da Capo Press, Inc., 233 Spring St., New York, 10013. Tel.: 212-620-8000. FAX: 212-463-0742.

Dad's Old Bookstore (Ed Penny), Green Hills Court, 4004 Nashville Rd., Nashville, TN 37215. Tel.: 615-298-5880. FAX: 615-298-2822.

Danville Books (James and Eleanor Sherriff) [dealer], 404 Hartz Ave., Danville, CA 94526. Tel. 510-837-4200.

Herman Darvick, Autographs Auctions, P.O. Box 467, Rockville Centre, NY 11571.

George S. Deed, Book Finder [dealer], 226 Sixteenth St. #1, Seal Beach, CA 90740-6515.

Henry Deeks [dealer], 468 Main St., Acton, MA 01720. Tel.: 508-263-1861.

C. Dickens (Tom Hamm) [dealer], 3393 Peachtree Rd. N.E., Atlanta, GA 30326. Tel.: 404-231-3825. FAX: 404-364-0713.

Dr. K. Dietrich, Civil War Memorabilia, P.O. Box 994, Stockbridge, MA 01262. Tel.: 413-298-5279.

David E. Doremus [dealer], 100 Hillside Ave., Arlington, MA 02174. Tel.: 617-646-0892.

Doubleday Publishers, 666 Fifth Ave., New York, NY 10103. Orders: 501 Franklin Ave., Garden City, NY 11530. Tel.: 800-223-6834 or 212-765-6500. FAX: 212-492-9862.

Downs Books (Katherine Downs) [dealer], 351 Washington Ave. N.E., 774 Mary Ann Dr., Marietta, GA 30068. Tel.: 404-971-1103.

Drumbeat Americana Books [dealer], 124 West Monroe, Kirkwood, MO 63122.

Drummer Boy American Militaria (Tom O'Dea) [dealer and publisher], R.R. 4, Box 7198, Christian Hill Rd., Milford, PA 18337.

Cora Duncan, Book [dealer], 1737 Gratiot Ave., Saginaw, MI 48602.

V&J Duncan, Antique Maps, Prints, and Books (Virginia and John Duncan), 12 East Taylor St., Savannah, GA 31401. Tel.: 912-232-0338.

EPM Publications, 1003 Turkey Run Rd., McLean, VA 22101. Tel.: 800-289-2339 or 703-442-0599. FAX: 703-442-0599.

Eakin Publications, P.O. Box 90159, Austin, TX 78709-0159. Tel.: 512-288-1771.

William B. Earley [dealer], 165 East Washington St., Chambersburg, PA 17201.

Early American Numismatic Auctions, Inc., P.O. Box 3341, La Jolla, CA 92038. Tel.: 619-459-4159 or 1-800-473-5686. FAX: 619-459-4373. Internet: http://www.cts.com/browse/ean

East Coast Books (Merv Slotnick) [dealer], P.O. Box 849, Wells, ME 04090. Tel.: 207-646-3584.

Edmonston Publishing, Inc., 30 Maple Ave., Hamilton, NY 13346. Tel.: 315-824-1965.

Elder's Bookstore [dealer], 2115 Elliston Pl., Nashville, TN 37203.

Elliott and Clark Publishing Company, P.O. Box 21365, Washington, DC 20009.

Elliott's Book Shop (Charles Elliott) [dealer], Village Square, 3020 College Dr., Baton Rouge, LA 70808. Tel.: 504-924-1060.

Facts on File, Inc. [publisher], 460 Park Ave. South, New York, NY 10016. Tel.: 800-322-8755 or 212-683-2244.

Fair Oaks Sutler [publisher], 9905 Kershaw Ct., Spotsylvania, VA 22553. Tel.: 703-972-7744.

Farnsworth Military Gallery, 401 Baltimore St., Gettysburg, PA 17325. Tel.: 717-334-8838.

Fields of Glory [dealer], 55 York St., Gettysburg, PA 17325. Tel.: 800-517-3382 or 717-337-2837.

First Corps Books [dealer and publisher], 42 Eastgrove Ct., Columbia, SC 29212-2404. Tel.: 803-781-2709.

Five Cedars Press, 841 Wardensville Grade, VA 22602.

Norman Flayderman and Co. [dealer], R.D. 2, New Milford, CT 06776. Tel.: 860-354-5567.

Fordham University Press, 1444 U.S. Rt. 42, R.D. 1, P.O. Box 2039, Mansfield, OH 44903. Tel.: 212-579-2319. FAX: 212-579-2708.

Fort Donelson National Battlefield (Bookstore), Box 434, Highway 79, VC, Dover, TN 37058. Tel.: 615-232-5706. FAX: 615-232-6331.

Fort Pulaski National Monument (Bookstore), Highway 80 East, P.O. Box 30757, Savannah, GA 31410. Tel.: 912-786-5787.

Fort Sumter National Monument (Bookstore), 1214 Middle St., Sullivan's Island, SC 29382. Tel.: 803-883-3123.

Gary A. Foster, Bookseller, P.O. Box 366, Cross River, NY 10518. Tel.: 914-232-9201.

Richard C. Frajola, Inc. [dealer], 125 West Park Ave.; P.O. Box 608, Empire, CO 80438.

Frazier Americana, 10509 Water Point Way, Mitchelville, MD 20721.

Fredericksburg National Military Park (Bookstore), 1013 Lafayette Blvd., Fredericksburg, VA 22401. Tel.: 703-373-6122. FAX: 703-371-1907.

Free Press, 1230 Avenue of the Americas, New York, NY 10022. Tel.: 800-323-7445.

Frontier America Corp. (Fred White, Jr.) [dealer], P.O. Box 9193, Albuquerque, NM 87119-9193. Tel.: 505-266-2923.

Gallery 30 [dealer], 30 York St., Gettysburg, PA 17325. Tel.: 717-334-0335.

Garret Gallery (Richard Astle) [dealer], 33 Seneca Turnpike, Clinton, NY 13323. Tel.: 315-853-8145.

Garrett Productions [publisher], 185-B Newberry Commons, Etters, PA 17319.

Gauley Mount Press, 313 Lounsbury Court N.E., Leesburg, VA 22075.

Geen's Books [dealer], King of Prussia Plaza, King of Prussia, PA 19406. Tel.: 215-265-6210.

Genealogical Publishing Co., 1001 North Calvert St., Baltimore, MD 21202. Tel.: 800-296-6687.

Peter C. George [publisher], P.O. Box 74, Mechanicsville, VA 23111.

Gettysburg National Military Park (Bookstore), Visitor Center, 95 Terrytown Rd., P.O. Box 1080, Gettysburg, PA 17325. Tel.: 717-334-1124.

Paul and Linda Gibson [dealer], P.O. Box 962, Blountville, TN 37617. Tel.: 615-323-2427.

Michael Ginsberg—Books, P.O. Box 402, Sharon, MA 02067. Tel.: 617-784-8181 or 617-784-6929. FAX: 617-784-1826.

Glover's Bookery (John Glover) [dealer], 826 South Broadway, Rt. 68, Lexington, KY 40504. Tel.: 606-253-0614.

Golden Bough Bookstore (Lilly Brannon), 348 Second St., Macon, GA 31201. Tel.: 912-744-2446.

Goodspeed's Book Shop, Inc., 7 Beacon St., Boston, MA 02108. Tel.: 617-523-5970.

Brian and Maria Green Autographs [dealer], P.O. Box 1816, Kernersville, NC 27285-1816. Tel.: 910-993-5100.

Greenwood Publishing Group, 88 Post Rd. West, P.O. Box 5007, Westport, CT 06881-9990. Tel.: 800-225-5800 (ext. 700) or 203-226-3571. FAX: 203-222-1502.

David Grossblatt [dealer], P.O. Box 25042, Dallas, TX 75225-1042.

Frank Guarino [dealer], P.O. Box 89, DeBary, FL 32713. Tel.: 305-663-5973.

Guidon Books (Aaron and Ruth Cohen) [dealer], 7117 Main St., Scottsdale, AZ 85251. Tel.: 602-945-8811.

Hamilton's Book Store (Jack Hamilton), 1784 Jamestown Rd., Williamsburg, VA 23185. Tel.: 804-220-3000.

J&J Hanrahan—Antiques and Books (Jack and Joyce Hanrahan), 320 White Oak Ridge Rd., Short Hills, NJ 07078. Tel.: 201-912-8907. FAX: 201-912-0116.

Harper & Row, Publishers. See HarperCollins.

HarperCollins, Publishers, 10 East 53d St., New York, NY 10022-5299. Tel.: 800-242-7737 (in Pennsylvania: 800-982-4377) or 212-207-7000. FAX: 212-207-7222.

Harpers Ferry National Historical Park (Bookstore), P.O. Box 65, Harpers Ferry, WV 25425. Tel.: 304-535-6223.

Chris Hartmann, Bookseller, 219 W. A. Harris Rd., Morgantown, NC 28655-9014.

Harvard University Press, 79 Garden St., Cambridge, MA 02138. Tel.: 800-448-2242. FAX: 1-800-962-4983.

Hawthorne Blvd. Books [dealer], 3129 Southeast Hawthorne Blvd., Portland, OR 97214.

Hawthorne Village [dealer], 3032 North Decatur Rd., Scottdale, GA 30079.

Jim Hayes [dealer], P.O. Box 12560, James Island, SC 29422. Tel.: 803-795-0732.

Robert G. Hayman, Antiquarian Books, P.O. Box 188, Carey, OH 43316. Tel.: 419-396-6933.

S. A. Hearn, Bookseller, P.O. Box 67, Potts Grove, PA 17865.

Heartwood Books (Paul Collinge), 5 Elliewood Ave., Charlottesville, VA 22903. Tel.: 804-295-7083. FAX: 804-295-7083.

Michael D. Heaston, Rare Books and Manuscripts, P.O. Box 91147, Austin, TX 78709-1147. Tel.: 512-261-8045.

Gary Hendershott [dealer], P.O. Box 22520, Little Rock, AR 72221. Tel.: 501-224-7555.

B. William Henry—Bookseller, P.O. Box 775493, St. Louis, MO 63177. Tel.: 314-772-1072.

George Herget—Books [dealer], 3109 Magazine St., New Orleans, LA 70115. Tel.: 504-891-5595.

Heritage Books [publisher], 1540-E Pointer Ridge Pl., Bowie, MD 20716. Tel.: 800-398-7709.

Heritage Collectors' Society (Thomas A. Lingenfelter) [dealer], 161 Peddlers Village, Lahaska, PA 18931. Tel.: 215-794-0901. FAX: 215-794-7035.

Heritage Partnership [publisher], 202 Meadowdale Lane, Frederick, MD 21702. Tel.: 301-663-3736.

High Ridge Books (Fred Baron) [dealer], P.O. Box 286, Rye, NY 10580. Tel.: 914-967-3332. FAX: 914-967-6056.

Hill's Books (F. M. Hill) [dealer], P.O. Box 1037, Kingsport, TN 37662.

Historical Collections (John and Shirley Herbert) [dealer], P.O. Box 31623, Houston, TX 77231-1623. Tel.: 713-723-0296.

History Book Club [publisher], P.O. Box 8813, Camp Hill, PA 17012-0001.

Virginia Hobson—Books [dealer], P.O. Box 1182, Sea Island, GA 31561-1182. Tel.: 912-638-6700. FAX: 912-638-6700.

Leonard Hoffnung, Books [dealer], Route 1, Box 148, Martinton, IL 60951.

Holmes Book Co. [dealer], 274 Fourteenth St., Oakland, CA 94612. Tel.: 510-893-6860.

Hooked on History [dealer], 15 North Elmhurst Ave., Mt. Prospect, IL 60056-3400.

Horse Soldier (Chet Small) [dealer], 777 Baltimore St., Gettysburg, PA 17325; P.O. Box 184, Cashtown, PA 17310.

Houghton Mifflin Co., 1 Beacon St., Boston, MA 02108. Tel.: 800-225-3362 or 617-725-5000. FAX: 617-227-5409.

H. E. Howard, Inc. [publisher], P.O. Box 4161, Lynchburg, VA 24502. Tel.: 804-846-1146.

Murray A. Hudson, Antiquarian Books and Maps, 109 South Church, Box 163, Halls, TN 38040. Tel.: 800-748-9946 or 901-836-9057. FAX: 901-836-9057.

Hughes Books (Bill Grady) [dealer and publisher], P.O. Box 840237, New Orleans, LA 70184. Tel.: 504-948-2427. FAX: 504-944-9603.

Timothy Hughes, Rare and Early Newspapers, P.O. Box 3636, Williamsport, PA 17701. Tel.: 717-326-1045. FAX: 717-326-7606.

Hungry Gargoyle Bookshop (Colleen and Ken Preston), 1 Green St., Medfield, MA 02052. Tel.: 508-359-9890.

Paul Hunt [dealer], P.O. Box 10907, Burbank, CA 91510.

Indiana University Press, 10th and Morton Sts., Bloomington, IN 47405. Tel.: 800-842-6796 or 812-855-6804. FAX: 812-855-7931.

Gwyn L. Irwin [dealer], 400 Maple Ave., Marysville, PA 17053.

JFF Company, Inc. [dealer], P.O. Box 86337, Madeira Beach, FL 33738. Tel.: 813-397-4992. FAX: 813-584-7542.

JJM Books (Joan and John Marchaterre) [dealer], 1209 Atlas Lane, Naperville, IL 60540. Tel.: 708-398-7767.

Jack Noel Jacobson, Jr., Collectors Antiquities, Inc., 60 Manor Rd., Room 300, Staten Island, NY 10310. Tel.: 718-981-0973.

Peter L. Jackson Military Books [dealer], 23 Castle Green Crescent, Weston, Ontario, Canada M9R 1N5. Tel.: 416-249-4796.

James River Publications (dealer & publisher), 102 Maple Lane, Williamsburg, VA 23185-8106. Tel.: 804-220-4912.

C & D Jarnagin Company [dealer], P.O. Box 1860, Corinth, MS 38834. Tel.: 601-287-4977. FAX: 601-287-6033.

Jefferson Rarities, 2400 Jefferson Hwy., Sixth Floor, Jefferson, LA 70121. Tel.: 800-877-8847.

Kaller Historical Documents, P.O. Box 173, Allenhurst, NJ 07711. Tel.: 908-774-0222. FAX: 908-774-9401.

Kane Antiquarian Auction, 1525 Shenkel Rd., Pottstown, PA 19464.

Kenneth Karmiole, Bookseller, 509 Wilshire Blvd., Santa Monica, CA 90401; P.O. Box 464, Santa Monica, CA 90406. Tel.: 310-451-4342. FAX: 310-458-5930.

Brian Katherenes [dealer], 124 Pickford Ave., Trenton, NJ 08618. Tel.: 609-530-1350.

W. M. Kennan Publications, 2016 Fidler Ave., Long Beach, CA 90815.

Kennesaw Mountain National Battlefield Park (Bookstore), P.O. Box 1167, Marietta, GA 30061.

Kennesaw Mountain Press, 1810 Old Hwy. 41, Kennesaw, GA 30144. Tel.: 404-424-5225.

Kenston Rare Books (Ken Huddleston), P.O. Box 6824, San Antonio, TX 78209. Tel.: 210-828-0182. FAX: 210-824-4668.

Kent State University Press, 101 Franklin Hall, Kent, OH 44242. Tel.: 800-247-6553 or 419-281-1802. FAX: 419-281-6883.

John K. King Books [dealer], 901 West Lafayette Blvd., Detroit, MI 48226. Tel.: 313-961-0622.

Sergeant Kirkland's Museum (Ronald Seagrave) [dealer and publisher], 912 Lafayette Blvd., P.O. Box 7171, Fredericksburg, VA 22404. Tel.: 703-899-5565.

William Klette [dealer], 201 W. King St., Carson City, NV 89703. Tel.: 702-882-4447.

Alfred A. Knopf, Inc. [publisher], 201 East 50th St., New York, NY 10022. Tel.: 800-638-6460 or 212-751-2600. FAX: 212-272-2593.

Sidney Kramer Books [dealer], 11910-U Parklawn Dr., Rockville, MD 20852. Tel.: 800-423-2665.

Kraus Reprints and Periodicals, Rt. 100, Millwood, NY 10546. Tel.: 800-223-8323 or 914-762-2200.

Marshall Krolick, Civil War Enterprises [dealer], 225 West Washington St., Suite 1700, Chicago, IL 60606.

Alfred Kronfeld, Bookseller, 1621 Golden Gate Ave., Los Angeles, CA 90026-1013.

Robert A. Lacovara [publisher], 2089 Rt. 9, Cape May Court House, NJ 08210.

Philip B. Lamb [dealer], P.O. Box 15850, New Orleans, LA 70175. Tel.: 504-899-4710.

O. G. Lansford's Books [dealer], 300 Railroad St., Powersville, GA 31008.

Richard La Posta [dealer], 154 Robindale Dr., Kensington, CT 06037. Tel.: 860-828-0921.

Kenneth R. Laurence Galleries [dealer], 1007 Kane Concourse, Bay Harbor Islands, FL 33154. Tel.: 800-345-5595 or 305-866-3600. FAX: 305-866-8040.

Legacy Books (Larry Dean) [dealer], 3019 Kaye Lawn Dr., Louisville, KY 40220. Tel.: 502-499-9563.

David M. Lesser [dealer], P.O. Box 1729, New Haven, CT 06507. Tel.: 203-787-5910. FAX: 203-787-2847.

W. Hunter Lesser [publisher], Rt. 2, Box 191-A, Elkins, WV 26241.

Lexington Historical Shop (Bob Lurate) [dealer], P.O. Box 1428, Lexington, VA 24450. Tel.: 703-463-2615.

Leland N. Lien—Books [dealer], 57 South 9th St., Minneapolis, MN 55402. Tel.: 612-332-7081.

Light of Parnell Bookshop, 3362 Mercersburg Rd., Mercersburg, PA 17236.

Lighthouse Books (Michael Slicker) [dealer], 1735 First Ave. North, St. Petersburg, FL 33713. Tel.: 813-822-3278.

Little, Brown & Co., Inc. [publisher], 34 Beacon St., Boston MA 02108. Tel.: 800-343-9204 or 617-227-0730.

Longstreet House [publisher], P.O. Box 730, Hightstown, NJ 08520.

Louisiana State University Press, P.O. Box 25053, Baton Rouge, LA 70894-5053. Tel.: 504-388-8271. FAX: 504-388-6461.

James Lowe Autographs, 30 East 60th St., Suite 907, New York, NY 10022. Tel.: 212-759-0775.

Robert F. Lucas [dealer], Rte. 23, Box 63, Blandford, MA 01008. Tel.: 413-848-2061.

M&M Books (Marvin and Miriam Feinstein) [dealer], 21 Perth Pl., East Northport, NY 11731. Tel.: 516-368-4858.

M&S Rare Books (Dan Siegel), 245 Waterman St., Suite 303, P.O. Box 2594, East Side Station, Providence, RI 02906. Tel.: 401-421-1050. FAX: 401-272-0381.

Mac Donald's Military [publisher], Coburn Gore, Eustis, ME 04936. Tel.: 207-297-2751.

McElfresh Map Co. [publisher], P.O. Box 565, Olean, NY 14760. Tel.: 716-372-8801.

McGinty Publications, Department of History, Louisiana Tech University, P.O. Box 3038, T. S., Ruston, LA 71272.

McGowan Book Co. (Doug Sanders) [dealer], 125 Kingston Dr., Suite 206, Chapel Hill, NC 27514, P.O. Box 16325, Chapel Hill, NC 27516. Tel.: 919-968-1121.

McGowan Book Co., 39 Kimberly Drive, Durham, NC 27707. Tel.: 919-403-1503. FAX: 919-403-1706.

McIntire Rare Collectibles (Robert and Peggy McIntire), P.O. Box 546, Jacksonville, AR 72078. Tel.: 501-985-1663.

George S. MacManus Co. (Clarence Wolf) [dealer], 1317 Irving St., Philadelphia, PA 19107. Tel.: 215-735-4456. FAX: 215-735-3635.

Mail Call [newsletter], P.O. Box 5031, South Hackensack, NJ 07606.

Main Street Fine Books and Manuscripts (William and Yolanda Butts) [dealer], 301 South Main St., Galena, IL 61036. Tel.: 815-777-3749.

Man at Arms Bookshelf [dealer], P.O. Box 460, Lincoln, RI 02865. Tel.: 800-999-4697.

Manassas National Battlefield (Bookstore), 6511 Sudley Rd., Manassas, VA 22110. Tel.: 703-361-1339. FAX: 703-754-1107.

Tony Marion, Books (dealer), P.O. Box 504, Blountstown, TN 37617. Tel.: 615-323-8559.

Bill Mason Books [dealer], 104 North Seventh St., Morehead City, NC 28557. Tel.: 919-247-6161 or 919-247-5923.

Mason's Rare and Used Books (Jon and Susan Mason), 115 South Main St., Chambersburg, PA 17201. Tel.: 717-261-0541.

Mast Landing Books [dealer], 4 Flying Point Rd., Freeport, ME 04032.

Meherrin River Press, 301 East Broad St., Murfreesboro, NC 27885. Tel.: 919-398-3554.

Meinig's Memorabilia [dealer], 517 Manor, Peotone, IL 60468. Tel.: 708-258-9487.

Melvin Marcher, Bookseller, 6204 North Vermont, Oklahoma City, OK 73112-1312. Tel.: 405-946-6270.

Memorial Hall (Bookstore), Louisiana Historical Association, 929 Camp St., New Orleans, LA 70130. Tel.: 504-523-4522.

Menig's Memorabilia [dealer], 517 Manor, Peotone, IL 60468. Tel.: 708-258-9487.

Mercer University Press, Macon, GA 31207. Tel.: 800-637-2378 or 912-752-2880.

Daniel Metts Books (Evelyn Metts) [dealer], P.O. Box 7353, Macon, GA 31209. Tel.: 912-474-8269.

Michigan State University Press, 1405 South Harrison Rd., Suite 25, East Lansing, MI 48823-5202. Tel.: 517-355-9543. FAX: 1-800-678-2120.

Military Bookman [dealer], 29 East 93d St., New York, NY 10128. Tel.: 212-348-1280.

Military Books (Richard Williams) [dealer], 3226 Woodley Rd. NW, Washington, DC 20008. Tel.: 202-333-7308.

Military Heritage Appraisals, P.O. Box 30244, Raleigh, NC 27622. Tel.: 919-787-0206. FAX: 919-782-1718.

Military History Shop, 110 West State St., Kennett Square, PA 19348. Tel.: 215-444-2883.

Military Images [magazine], Route 1, Box 99-A, Henryville, PA 18332.

Minerva Center on Women and the Military [publisher], 20 Granada Rd., Pasadena, MD 22112. Tel.: 410-437-5379.

Kenneth Mink [publisher], 980 Highland Ave., Gettysburg, PA 17325.

Missouri River Press, 1664 Highridge Circle, Columbia, MO 65203. Tel.: 314-446-3764.

Monetary Ltd. of Dallas [dealer], P.O. Box 12584, Dallas, TX 75225. Tel.: 214-691-7005.

Monroe Books (John M. Pertz) [dealer], 359 East Shaw Ave., No. 102, Fresno, CA 93710. Tel.: 209-224-7000.

Morningside Bookshop [dealer] and Morningside House, Inc. [publisher] (Bob Younger), P.O. Box 1087, Dayton, OH 45401; 260 Oak St., Dayton, OH 45410. Tel.: 800-648-9710. FAX: 513-461-4260.

W. M. Morrison Books (Richard Morrison) [dealer and publisher], 15801 La Hacienda, Austin, TX 78734. Tel.: 512-266-3381.

William Morrow & Co. [publisher], 105 Madison Ave., New York, NY 10016. Tel.: 800-843-9389. FAX: 212-689-9139.

Donald S. Mull [dealer], 1706 Girard Dr., Louisville, KY 40222.

Mt. Sterling Rebel (Terry Murphy) [dealer], P.O. Box 481, Mt. Sterling, KY 40353. Tel.: 606-498-5821.

Jim Mundie, Books [dealer], 12122 Westmere Dr., Houston, TX 77077. Tel.: 713-531-8639.

Tom Munnerlyn, Books [dealer], P.O. Drawer 15247, Northeast Station, Austin, TX 78761. Tel.: 512-835-1648.

Museum Books and Prints [dealer], P.O. Box 7832, Reading, PA 19603.

Nate's Autographs, 1015 Gayley Ave. #1168, Los Angeles, CA 90024. Tel.: 310-575-3851. FAX: 310-575-4051.

National Archives and Records Administration, Publications Division, 8th and Pennsylvania Ave., N.W., Washington, DC 20408. Tel.: 202-724-0086. FAX: 202-501-5239.

National Historical Society [publisher], P.O. Box 975, Hicksville, NY 11802-9731, or c/o Haddon Craftsmen, Winfield Warehouse, 600 Sanders St., Scranton, PA 18505.

Naval Institute Press, Annapolis, MD 21402. Tel.: 800-233-USNI or 301-268-6110. FAX: 301-269-7940.

New Hampshire Book Auctions, 92 Woodbury Rd., P.O. Box 460, Weare, NH 03281. Tel.: 603-529-7432.

Lowell S. Newman and Co. [dealer], 1500 Harbor Blvd., Weehawken, NJ 07087. Tel.: 201-223-0100. FAX: 201-223-1202.

Ralph Geoffrey Newman [dealer], 175 East Delaware Pl., Chicago, IL 60611. Tel.: 312-787-1860.

F. Don Nidiffer [dealer], P.O. Box 8184, Charlottesville, VA 22906. Tel.: 804-296-2067.

North Carolina Division of Archives and History, Historical Publications Section, 109 East Jones St., Raleigh, NC 27601-2807. Tel.: 919-733-7442. FAX: 919-733-1439.

North Shore Manuscript Co., P.O. Box 458, Roslyn Heights, NY 11577. Tel.: 516-484-6826. FAX: 516-625-3327.

North South Trader's Civil War [magazine], P.O. Drawer 631-N, Orange, VA 22960. Tel.: 703-67-CIVIL.

North State Books (Richard Jones) [dealer], 107 West Court Square, Lincoln, NC 28092. Tel.: 704-732-8562.

W. W. Norton & Co., Inc. [publisher], 500 Fifth Ave., New York, NY 10110. Tel.: 800-233-4830 or 212-354-5500.

Not Forgotten Books (Russ Cummings) [dealer], 1009 Condor Dr., Greensboro, NC 27410. Tel.: 919-855-1929.

O'Brisky Books [dealer], P.O. Box 585, Micanopy, FL 32667.

Ohio Book Store, Inc., 726 Main St., Cincinnati, OH 45202. Tel.: 513-621-5142.

Oinonen Book Auctions, P.O. Box 476, Sunderland, MA 01375. Tel.: 413-665-3253. FAX: 413-665-8790.

Old Army Press, P.O. Box 2243, Fort Collins, CO 80522. Tel.: 800-627-0079 or 303-484-5535.

Old Book Corner (Andrew McLean) [dealer], 312 Sixth St., Racine, WI 53403. Tel.: 414-632-0215.

Old Colony Shop (Gary D. Eyler) [dealer], 222-B South Washington, Alexandria, VA 22314. Tel.: 703-548-8008.

Old Erie Bookstore (Mark Robert Stueve), 2128 East 9th St., Cleveland, OH 44115. Tel.: 216-575-0743.

Old Favorites Bookshop (Gary O'Neal), 610 North Sheppard St., Richmond, VA 23221. Tel.: 804-355-2437.

Old Paperphiles [dealer], P.O. Box 135, Tiverton, RI 02878. Tel.: 401-624-9420. FAX: 401-624-4204.

Olde Book Shop (Barbara Clover) [dealer], 1551 Parham Rd., Richmond, VA 23229-4604. Tel.: 804-282-6990.

Olde Soldier Books (Dave Zullo) [dealer and publisher], 18779-B North Frederick Rd., Gaithersburg, MD 20879. Tel.: 301-963-2929. FAX: 301-963-9556.

William R. Orbelo [dealer], 912 Garraty, San Antonio, TX 78209. Tel.: 210-828-1873.

Owens Civil War Books (Michael Owens) [dealer], and Owens Publishing Company, 2728 Tinsley Dr., Richmond, VA 23235. Tel.: 804-272-8888.

Oxford Too Books [dealer], 2395 Peachtree Rd., Atlanta, GA 30305. Tel.: 404-262-3411.

Oxford University Press, 200 Madison Ave., New York, NY 10016. Orders: 2001 Evans Rd., Cary, NC 27513. Tel.: 1-800-451-7556 or 919-677-0977.

Page One, Inc. [publisher], 2211 West Grace St., Richmond, VA 23220.

Palmetto Books (David Cupka) [dealer], 1811 Kempton Ave., Charleston, SC 29412. Tel.: 803-795-1996.

Palmetto Bookworks [publisher], P.O. Box 11551, Columbia, SC 29211.

Palmetto Historical Works [publisher], 120 Branch Hill Dr., Elgin, SC 29045.

Paper Americana [dealer], 1314 Third Ave., Duncansville, PA 16635.

Paper Antiquities [dealer], P.O. Box 408, Coventry, RI 02816. Tel.: 401-823-8440.

T. Michael Parrish, Rare Americana [dealer], 6322 Bon Terra Dr., Austin, TX 78731. Tel.: 512-453-1861 or 512-450-1955. FAX: 512-453-1861.

Patrex Press, 16205 White Creek Cove, Austin, TX 78717.

Pea Ridge National Military Park (Bookstore), Highway 62 East, Pea Ridge, AR 72751. Tel.: 501-451-8122.

Pelican Publishing Company, P.O. Box 3110, Gretna, LA 70053.

Barb and John Pengelly [dealer], 502 Madison Ave., Fort Washington, PA 19034. Tel.: 215-643-5646.

Pennsylvania State University Press, Barbara Bldg. I, Suite C, University Park, PA 16802. Tel.: 1-800-326-9180. FAX: 814-863-1408.

Petersburg National Battlefield (Bookstore), Box 549, Petersburg, VA 23804. Tel.: 804-732-3531. FAX: 804-732-5149.

Pictorial Histories Publishing Co., 4103 Virginia Ave. S.E., Charleston, WV 25304.

Ponder Books [publisher], P.O. Box 573, Doniphan, MO 63935.

Poverty Press, 103 Corrine Dr., Pennington, NJ 08534.

Prairie Archives (John Paul) [dealer], 522 East Adams, Springfield, IL 62701-1510. Tel.: 217-522-9742.

Wallace D. Pratt [dealer], 1801 Gough St. #204, San Francisco, CA 94109.

Prescott Hill Books (Shirley Jarvella) [dealer], R.R. 1, Box 707, Prescott Hill Rd., Belfast, ME 04915. Tel.: 207-338-6346.

Presidio Press, 505-B San Marin Dr., Suite 300, Novato, CA 94945. Orders: P.O. Box 1764, Novato, CA 94948. Tel.: 415-898-1081. FAX: 415-898-0383.

Princeton University Press, 41 William St., Princeton, NJ 08540. Tel.: 800-777-4726 or 609-896-1344. FAX: 609-895-1081.

Profiles in History (Joseph Maddalena) [dealer], 9440 Santa Monica Blvd., Beverly Hills, CA 90210. Tel.: 1-800-942-8856.

Peter Pun Books [dealer], 835 Bowie Rd., Rockville, MD 20852.

R&R Enterprises [dealer], P.O. Box 2000-A, Amherst, NH 03031. Tel.: 800-937-3880. FAX: 603-886-1224.

Peter S. Raab [dealer], 2033 Walnut St., Philadelphia, PA 19103. Tel.: 215-446-6193.

Random House, Inc. [publisher], 201 East 50th St., New York, NY 10022. 800-726-0600 or 212-751-2600. FAX: 212-872-8026.

Rank and File Publications, 1926 S. PCH #228, Redondo Beach, CA 90277.

Morris Raphael [publisher], 1040 Bayou Side Dr., New Iberia, LA 70560.

Reading Room Books [dealer], 264 South Wabash St., Wabash, IN 46992.

Recollections [dealer], Box 10, West Long Branch, NJ 07764. Tel.: 908-747-3858. FAX: 908-758-9730.

William Reese Co. [dealer], 409 Temple St., New Haven, CT 06511. Tel.: 203-789-8081. FAX: 203-865-7653.

Remember When Antiquities [dealer], P.O. Box 629, Acton, ME 04001.

Diana J. Rendell, Inc. [dealer], 177 Collins Rd., Waban, MA 02168. Tel.: 617-969-1774.

Kenneth W. Rendell, Inc., [dealer], P.O. Box 9001, Wellesley, MA 02181. Tel.: 617-431-1776 or 703-938-2237. FAX: 703-938-9057.

Reprint Company, Publishers, P.O. Box 5401, Spartanburg, SC 29304. Tel.: 803-582-0732.

L&T Respess Books (Lin and Tucker Respess) [dealer], P.O. Box 1604, Charlottesville, VA 22902. Tel.: 804-293-3553.

Reston's Used Book Shop, 1623 Washington Plaza, Reston, VA 22090.

Riba Auctions, Inc., 894 Main St., P.O. Box 53, South Glastonbury, CT 06073. Tel.: 860-663-3076.

Richmond Book Store [dealer], 6423-R Richmond Ave., Houston, TX 77057.

Richmond National Battlefield Park (Bookstore), 3215 East Broad St., Richmond, VA 23223. Tel.: 804-226-1981. FAX: 804-771-8522.

River City Books [dealer], 3374 Government St., Baton Rouge, LA 70806.

Robbins's Rarities (LeRoy Robbins) [dealer], 2038-C Laurens Rd., Greenville, SC 29607. Tel.: 860-297-7948.

Cedric L. Robinson, Booksellers, 597 Palisado Ave., Windsor, CT 06095. Tel.: 860-688-2582.

Wallace A. Robinson, Books [dealer], R.D. 6, Box 574, Meadville, PA 16335.

Rock Creek Bookshop, 1214 Wisconsin Ave., Washington, D.C. 20007.

Rockbridge Publishing Company, P.O. Box 351, Berryville, VA 22611.

Len Rosa [dealer], P.O. Box 3965, Gettysburg, PA 17325. Tel.: 717-337-2853. FAX: 717-337-1963.

Irving Roth, Old Books, 89 Whittlessey Ave., Norwalk, OH 44857.

Stephen M. Rowe, Book Dealer, P.O. Box 19671, Raleigh, NC 27619. Tel.: 919-787-8336.

Royal Oak Bookshop, 207 South Royal Ave., Front Royal, VA 22630.

Joseph Rubinfine [dealer], 505 South Flagler, Suite 1301, West Palm Beach, FL 33401. Tel.: 407-659-7077.

Robert Ruland [dealer], 317 Thoroughman Ave., Ferguson, MO 63135.

Rutledge Hill Press, 211 Seventh Ave. North, Nashville, TN 37219. Tel.: 800-234-4234 or 615-244-2700. FAX: 615-244-2978.

John Rybski, Bookseller, 2319 West 47th Pl., Chicago, IL 60609. Tel.: 312-847-5082.

Michael Saks [dealer], 2 Catalpa, Providence, RI 02906. Tel.: 401-272-6318.

Sandlin's Books and Bindery [dealer], 70 Lincolnway, Valparaiso, IN 46383-5522.

John M. Santarelli, Civil War Books [dealer], 226 Paxson Ave., Glenside, PA 19038-4612. Tel.: 215-576-5358.

Savas Woodbury Publishers (Theodore Savas and David Woodbury), 1475 South Bascom Ave., Suite 204, Campbell, CA 95008.

Scanrom Publications, P.O. Box 72, Cedarhurst, NY 11516. Tel.: 800-269-2237.

Scholar's Bookshelf [dealer], 110 Melrich Rd., Cranbury, NJ 08512.

Seaport Autographs (Norman Boas) [dealer], 6 Brandon Lane, Mystic, CT 06355. Tel.: 860-572-8441. FAX: 860-572-8441.

Second/II Corps Civil War Books (Merlin Sumner) [dealer], 209 High St., Petersburg, VA 23803. Tel.: 804-861-1863.

Second Story Books (Allan Stypeck) [dealer], 4836 Bethesda Ave. Row, Bethesda, MD 20814. Tel.: 301-770-0477. FAX: 301-770-9544.

Servant and Company [dealer], 230 Steinwehr Ave., Gettysburg, PA 17325. Tel.: 717-334-9712.

Shiloh National Military Park (Bookstore), P.O. Box 67, Shiloh, TN 38376. Tel.: 901-689-5275. FAX: 901-689-5450.

Jerry N. Showalter, Bookseller, P.O. Box 84, Ivy, VA 22945. Tel.: 804-295-6413.

Robert A. Siegel, Auction Galleries, Park Ave. Tower, 17th Floor, 65 East 55th St., New York, NY 10022. Tel.: 212-753-6421. FAX: 212-753-6429.

Silver Shovel Antiques and Books [dealer], 110 W. Locust St., Bloomington, IL 61701. Tel.: 309-829-2908.

Simon & Schuster [publisher], 1230 Avenue of the Americas, New York, NY 10020. Tel.: 800-223-2336 or 212-698-7000.

B. L. Sims [dealer], 4 Ault Court, Wilmington, DE 19808.

James Smalldon Americana (dealer), 1 Main St., Jackson, CA 95642. Tel.: 209-223-4023.

R. M. Smith Auctions, 26 Broadway, New York, NY 10004. Tel.: 800-622-1880 or 212-943-1880. FAX: 212-908-4047.

Sotheby's [auction house], 1334 York Ave., New York, NY 10021. Tel.: 212-606-7385. FAX: 212-606-7041.

Southeast Antique Books (Rolland Sayers), P.O. Box 629, Brevard, NC 28712. Tel.: 704-883-9562 or 704-696-8202.

Southern Heritage Magazine, P.O. Box 3181, Merrifield, VA 22116.

Southern Heritage Press, P.O. Box 1615, Murfreesboro, TN 37133.

Southern Illinois University Press, P.O. Box 3697, Carbondale, IL 62902-3697. Tel.: 800-444-8525 ext. 950 or 618-453-2281.

Spanish Trail Books [dealer], 1006 Thorn Ave., Ocean Springs, MS 39564.

Richard W. Spellman, Old and Rare Historical Newspapers, 610 Monticello Dr., Bricktown, NJ 08723. Tel.: 908-477-2413.

Stackpole Books [publisher], 5067 Ritter Rd., Mechanicsburg, PA 17055. Tel.: 800-732-3669 or 717-796-0411. FAX: 717-796-0412.

Staley's Sundries [dealer], 710 Caroline St., Fredericksburg, VA 22401. Tel.: 703-899-6464. FAX: 703-373-2469.

Rex Stark [dealer], 49 Wethersfield Rd., Bellingham, MA 02019.

State House Press (Tom Munnerlyn), P.O. Drawer 15247, Northeast Station, Austin, TX 78761. Tel.: 800-421-3378.

Stephens's Books (John and Gloria Stephens) [dealer], P.O. Box 111184, Memphis, TN 38111-1184. Tel.: 901-685-6341.

Sterling Publishing Co., 387 Park Ave., New York, NY 10016.

Henry Stevens, Son and Stiles (Thomas P. MacDonnell) [dealer], P.O. Box 1299, Williamsburg, VA 23187. Tel.: 804-220-0825 or 804-229-1809. FAX: 804-229-1809.

Christophe Stickel [dealer], 167 Central Ave., Pacific Grove, CA 93950.

Stone Mountain Relics (John Sexton), 968 Main Street, Stone Mountain, GA 30083. Tel.: 404-469-1425. FAX: 404-413-7922.

Stone of Scone Antiques, Books, and Firearms (Tom and Jan Stratton), 19 Water St., Canterbury, CT 06331. Tel.: 860-546-9917.

Stones River National Battlefield (Bookstore), 3501 Old Nashville Hwy., Murfreesboro, TN 37129. Tel.: 615-893-9501. FAX: 615-893-9508.

Strand Book Store (Fred Bass), 828 Broadway at 12th St., New York, NY 10003. Tel.: 212-473-1452. FAX: 212-473-2591.

Sulgrave Press, 2005 Longest Ave., Louisville, KY 40204.

Superior Auction Galleries, 9478 West Olympic Blvd., Beverly Hills, CA 90212. Tel.: 800-421-0754 or 310-203-9855. FAX: 310-203-0496.

Sutlers Wagon [dealer], P.O. Box 5, Cambridge, MA 02139. Tel.: 617-864-1628.

Swann Galleries [auction house], 104 East 25th St., New York, NY 10010. Tel.: 212-254-4710. FAX: 212-979-1017.

Tom Swinford, Bookseller, 7136 Main St., Scottsdale, AZ 85251. Tel.: 602-946-0222 or 602-596-1437.

Sword and Saber (John Pannick) [dealer], 2159 Baltimore Pike, P.O. Box 4417, Gettysburg, PA 17325. Tel.: 717-334-0205.

T&S Books [dealer], P.O. Box 14077, Covington, KY 41014.

Tauscher Bookstore at Brist Mall [dealer], 403 Commonwealth Ave., Bristol, VA 24201.

Tenderfoot Books and Antiques (Clay and Edna Garrison) [dealer], 1674 Kessler Canyon Dr., Dallas, TX 75208-2645. Tel.: 214-942-0909.

Tennessee Books & Autographs (George Webb, Jr.), 109 South Church St., P.O. Box 637, Rogersville, TN 37857-0637. Tel.: 615-921-9017. FAX: 615-921-9017.

Territorial Bookman (Robert Norris) [dealer], 8437 South Toledo Ave., Tulsa, OK 74137. Tel.: 918-481-0436.

Texas A&M University Press, Drawer C, College Station, TX 77843. Tel.: 800-826-8911 or 409-845-1436. FAX: 409-847-8752.

Texas State Historical Association [publisher], 2306 Sid Richardson Hall, University Station, Austin, TX 78712. Tel.: 512-471-1525. FAX: 512-471-1551.

Theme Prints, Ltd. (Jack Donahue) [dealer], 488 Grand Ave., P.O. Box 123, Bayside, NY 11361. Tel.: 718-225-4067.

Thomas Publications, P.O. Box 3031, Gettysburg, PA 17325. Tel.: 800-840-6782. FAX: 717-334-8440.

C. Clayton Thompson [dealer], 20 Jay Dr., Gulfport, MS 39503.

Time and Again Old Book Shop (Doris Welch Reid), 3201 West 6th Ave., Amarillo, TX 79106. Tel.: 806-371-0271.

Time-Life Books, Inc. [publisher], 777 Duke St., Alexandria, VA 22314. Tel.: 800-621-7026 or 703-838-7000. FAX: 703-684-5224.

Toomey's Bookshop [dealer and publisher], Shipley-Linthicum Shopping Center, Linthicum, MD 21090.

Gordon Totty [dealer], 347 West Shady Lake Pkwy., Baton Rouge, LA 70810.

Trans-Allegheny Books [dealer], 725 Green St., Parkersburg, WV 26101.

Traveller Books (John Keck), P.O. Box 2323, Laredo, TX 78040. Tel.: 210-727-8505.

Twice-Sold Tales (Jeanette Kirkland) [dealer], 309 Ascauga Lake Rd., Graniteville, SC 29829. Tel.: 803-663-3498.

Unicorn Bookshop, Route 50, P.O. Box 154, Trappe, MD 21673. Tel.: 301-476-3838.

Union Publishing Co., R.R. 2, Box 7355, Union, ME 04862.

Union Times [magazine], 7214 Laurel Hill Rd., Orlando, FL 32818. Tel.: 407-295-7510.

University Archives (John Reznikoff) [dealer], 600 Summer St., Stamford, CT 06901. Tel.: 1-800-237-5692. FAX: 203-348-3560.

University Microfilms International [publisher of dissertations and theses], 300 North Zeeb Rd., Ann Arbor, MI 48106. 800-521-0600 or 313-761-4700.

University of Alabama Press, P.O. Box 870380, Tuscaloosa, AL 35487-0380. Tel.: 205-348-5182. FAX: 205-348-9201.

University of Arkansas Press, 201 Ozark, Fayetteville, AR 72701. Tel.: 800-525-1823 or 501-575-3246. FAX: 501-575-6044.

University of Georgia Press, Athens, GA 30602-1743. Tel.: 404-542-2830. FAX: 404-542-0601.

University of Illinois Press, 1325 South Oak St., Champaign, IL 61820. Tel.: 217-244-0626. FAX: 217-244-8082.

University of Massachusetts Press, P.O. Box 429, Amherst, MA 01004. Tel.: 413-545-2217.

University of Missouri Press, 2910 LeMone Blvd., Columbia, MO 65201. Tel.: 800-828-1894 or 314-882-3000. FAX: 314-884-4498.

University of Nebraska Press, 901 North 17th St., Lincoln, NE 68588. Tel.: 800-755-1105 or 402-472-3584. FAX: 1-800-526-2617 or 402-472-6214.

University of North Carolina Press, P.O. Box 2288, Chapel Hill, NC 27515-2288. Tel.: 800-848-6224 or 919-966-3561. FAX: 1-800-272-6817 or 919-966-3829.

University of Oklahoma Press, 1005 Asp Ave., Norman, OK 73109. Orders: P.O. Box 787, Norman, OK 73070-0787. Tel.: 800-6277-7377. FAX: 405-325-4000.

University of Pittsburgh Press, 127 North Bellefield Ave., Pittsburgh, PA 15260. Orders: CUP Services, P.O. Box 6525, Ithaca, NY 14851. Tel.: 800-666-2211.

University of South Carolina Press, 1716 College St., Columbia, SC 29208. Tel.: 803-777-5243. FAX: 803-777-0160.

University of Tennessee Press, 293 Communications Bldg., Knoxville, TN 37996-0325. Orders: c/o Cornell University Press, P.O. Box 6525, Ithaca, NY 14850. Tel.: 800-666-2211. FAX: 615-974-6435.

University of Texas Press, P.O. Box 7819, Austin, TX 78713-7819. Tel.: 512-471-7233. FAX: 512-320-0668.

University Press of Florida, 15 Northwest 15th St., Gainesville, FL 32603. Tel.: 1-800-226-3822 or 904-392-1351. FAX: 904-392-7302.

University Press of Kansas, 2501 West 15th St., Lawrence, KS 66045. Tel.: 913-864-4155. FAX: 913-864-4586.

University Press of Kentucky, 663 South Limestone St., Lexington, KY 40508-4008. Orders: P.O. Box 6525, Ithaca, NY 14851 or 663 South Limestone St., Lexington, KY 40508-4008. Tel.: 800-666-2211 or 607-277-2211. FAX: 800-688-2877.

University Press of Mississippi, 3825 Ridgewood Rd., Jackson, MS 39211. Tel.: 601-928-6205. FAX: 601-982-6610.

University Press of Virginia, P.O. Box 3608, University Station, Charlottesville, VA 22903. Tel.: 804-924-3469 or 804-924-3468. FAX: 804-982-2655.

Vicksburg National Military Park (Bookstore), 3201 Clay St., Vicksburg, MS 39180. Tel.: 601-634-6286. FAX: 601-636-9497.

Michael Vinson, Rare Books and Americana, P.O. Box 142147, Austin, TX 78714. Tel.: 512-454-6464 or 512-451-5035.

Vintage Cover Story [dealer], 975, Burlington, NC, 27215. Tel.: 910-570-2810. FAX: 910-570-2748.

Virginiana Rare Books (John Offley), 6600 Richmond Rd., Williamsburg, VA 23090. Tel.: 804-565-1754. FAX: 804-565-1803.

Ray S. Walton, Rare Books, 11109 Henge Dr., Austin, TX 78759. Tel.: 512-250-5416.

Wantagh Rare Books (C. E. Van Norman), P.O. Box 605, Neversink, NY 12765. Tel.: 914-985-7482. FAX: 914-985-7482.

Warbirds and Warriors Military [dealer], P.O. Box 266, Leicester, NY 14481.

Warner Books, Inc. [publisher], 666 Fifth Ave., New York, NY 10103. Tel.: 212-484-2900. FAX: 212-484-2713.

Waverly Auctions, 7649 Old Georgetown Rd., Bethesda, MA 20814.

Wentworth and Leggett Rare Books, 905 W. Main St., Brightleaf Square, Durham, NC 27701. Tel.: 919-688-5311. FAX: 919-941-1938.

Whistlestop Bookshop, 104 Carlisle St., Gettysburg, PA 17325. Tel.: 717-334-0319.

Whistlestop Bookshop, 152 West High St., Carlisle, PA 17013. Tel.: 717-243-4744.

White Mane Publishing Co., 63 West Burd St., P.O. Box 152, Shippensburg, PA 17257. Tel.: 717-532-2237. FAX: 717-532-7704.

Letty Wilder [dealer], 212 South Highland Way, Myrtle Beach, SC 29572.

Wildman's Civil War Surplus [dealer], 28798 Main St. N.W., Kennesaw, GA 30144.

Courtney B. Wilson and Associates, American Military Antiques [dealer], 8398 Court Ave., Ellicott City, MD 21043. Tel.: 410-465-6827.

Wilson's Creek National Battlefield (Bookstore), Rt. 2, Box 75, Republic, MO 65738. Tel.: 65738. Tel.: 417-732-2662.

Richard Wolffers Auctions, Inc., 133 Kearny St., Suite 400, San Francisco, CA 94108. Tel.: 415-781-5127. FAX: 415-956-0483.

Wolf's Head Books [dealer], 48 San Marco Ave., P.O. Box 3705, St. Augustine, FL 32085. Tel.: 904-824-9357.

Leon Wood [dealer], P.O. Box 67, Darden, TN 38328-0067.

Workman Publishing Co., 708 Broadway, New York, NY 10003.

Wright Collection (Hugh and Linda Wright) [dealer], 333 Harbin St., Waxahachie, TX 75165. Tel.: 214-937-6502.

Yale University Press, 302 Temple St., New Haven, CT 06511. Tel.: 203-432-0960. FAX: 203-432-0948.

Yankee Peddler Bookshop (John Westerberg), 4299 Lake Rd, Box 118, Lake, Pultneyville, NY 14538. Tel.: 315-589-2063.

Yankees and Rebels Bookshop (David and Sue Bowers), P.O. Box 244, Elsberry, MO 63343. Tel.: 1-800-834-1861 or 314-898-3255.

Yesterday's News, USA (K. Weingarden) [dealer], P.O. Box 385204, Bloomington, MN 55438. Tel.: 612-829-9116.

Yesteryear Book Shop (Frank Walsh and Polly Fraser), 3201 Maple Dr. N.E., Atlanta, GA 30305. Tel.: 404-237-0163.

Yesteryear Books (Robert and Patsy Weimer) [dealer], 420 Lincoln Ave., Lincoln, IL 62656. Tel.: 217-732-6474.

Zellner's Book Search [dealer], 2839 Norton Ave., Easton, PA 18042. Tel.: 215-258-3882.

Zubal Auction Company, 2969 West 25th St., Cleveland, OH 44113. Tel.: 216-241-7640.

Index

ABOUT THE CONTRIBUTORS

Alan C. Aimone is Chief of Special Collections at the United States Military Academy Library, West Point, New York.

James Alex Bagget is Dean of the College of Arts and Sciences at Union University, Jackson, Tennessee.

Anne J. Bailey is associate professor of history at the University of Arkansas.

Michael B. Ballard is a librarian at Mississippi State University.

Daniel K. Blewett is history bibliographer at Cudahy Library, Loyola University of Chicago.

Frederick J. Blue is professor of history at Youngstown State University, Youngstown, Ohio.

Howard Bodenhorn is professor of economics at Lafayette College, Easton, Pennsylvania.

Bradley G. Bond is assistant professor of history at the University of Southern Mississippi.

David Bosse is a librarian at Memorial Library, Deerfield, Massachusetts.

Bill Cecil-Fronsman is professor of history at Washburn University of Topeka.

Michael B. Chesson is associate professor of history at the University of Massachusetts–Boston.

Benjamin Franklin Cooling lives and works in Chevy Chase, Maryland.

Lee A. Craig is associate professor of economics at North Carolina State University.

Stephen Davis lives and writes in Atlanta, Georgia.

Alan C. Downs is assistant professor of history at Georgia Southern University.

Robert England is assistant professor of history at Shoals Community College, Muscle Shoals, Alabama.

William B. Feis is assistant professor of history at Buena Vista University, Storm Lake, Iowa.

Steven Fisher is a special collections librarian at the Penrose Library of the University of Denver.

Gaines M. Foster is professor of history at Louisiana State University.

Kevin Foster is Chief of the National Maritime Initiative of the National Park Service.

Edward Carr Franks is a professional economist in Los Angeles, California.

J. Matthew Gallman is associate professor of history at Loyola University, Baltimore, Maryland.

Sharon L. Gravett is associate professor of English at Valdosta State University, Valdosta, Georgia.

Mark Grimsley is a Lincoln-Prize-winning historian and assistant professor of history at Ohio State University.

Alan C. Guelzo is professor of history at Eastern College, St. Davids, Pennsylvania.

Judith Lee Hallock is a retired public school teacher and lives on Long Island.

Susan Hamburger is a special collections librarian at Pattee Library, Penn State University.

Robert Holcombe, Jr., is curator of the Confederate Naval Museum, Columbus, Georgia.

Gary Dillard Joiner lives and writes in Louisiana.

Thomas J. Legg is assistant professor of history at California State University–Northridge.

John F. Marszalek is professor of history at Mississippi State University.

James M. McPherson is a Pulitzer-Prize-winning historian and George Henry Davis '86 Professor of American History at Princeton University.

Grady McWhiney is distinguished scholar-in-residence at the University of Southern Mississippi.

Mark E. Neely, Jr., is a Pulitzer-Prize-winning historian and assistant professor of history at St. Louis University.

T. Michael Parrish lives and writes in Austin, Texas.

William Garrett Piston is associate professor of history at Southwest Missouri State University, Springfield, Missouri.

Michael L. Renshawe is a librarian at McLennan Library, McGill University, Montreal, Canada.

Harris D. Riley, Jr., is a pediatrician at the Children's Hospital of Vanderbilt University Medical Center.

James M. Russell is associate professor of history at the University of Tennessee–Chattanooga.

Theodore P. Savas, director and founder of Savas Woodbury Publishing, lives and works in Campbell, California.

Kyle S. Sinisi is assistant professor of history at The Citadel, Charleston, South Carolina.

Warren F. Spencer is emeritus professor of history at the University of Georgia.

Daniel E. Sutherland is associate professor of history at the University of Arkansas.

The late **Charles Edmund Vetter** was professor of sociology at Centenary College, Shreveport, Louisiana.

Eric H. Walther is assistant professor of history at the University of Houston.

Brian Steel Wills is assistant professor of history at Clinch Valley College, Wise, Virginia.

Stephen R. Wise is curator of the United States Marine Corps Museum, Paris Island, South Carolina.

Steven E. Woodworth is associate professor of history at Toccoa Falls College.

Richard M. Zuczek works in the Andrew Johnson project at the University of Tennessee.

ISBN 0-313-29019-9

9 780313 290190

HARDCOVER BAR CODE